THE OXFORD HANDBOOK OF
PSYCHOLINGUISTICS

THE OXFORD HANDBOOK OF

PSYCHOLINGUISTICS

SECOND EDITION

Edited by
SHIRLEY-ANN RUESCHEMEYER
and
M. GARETH GASKELL

Great Clarendon Street, Oxford, OX2 6DP,
United Kingdom

Oxford University Press is a department of the University of Oxford.
It furthers the University's objective of excellence in research, scholarship,
and education by publishing worldwide. Oxford is a registered trade mark of
Oxford University Press in the UK and in certain other countries

© Oxford University Press 2018

Chapter 40 epigraph: Reprinted from *Electroencephalography and Clinical Neurophysiology,* 1 (1),
V. J. Walter and W. Grey Walter, The central effects of rhythmic sensory stimulation, pp. 57–86,
Copyright © 1949, Elsevier Ireland Ltd. with permission from Elsevier

The moral rights of the authors have been asserted
First Edition published in 2007
Second Edition published in 2018
Impression: 1

All rights reserved. No part of this publication may be reproduced, stored in
a retrieval system, or transmitted, in any form or by any means, without the
prior permission in writing of Oxford University Press, or as expressly permitted
by law, by licence or under terms agreed with the appropriate reprographics
rights organization. Enquiries concerning reproduction outside the scope of the
above should be sent to the Rights Department, Oxford University Press, at the
address above

You must not circulate this work in any other form
and you must impose this same condition on any acquirer

Published in the United States of America by Oxford University Press
198 Madison Avenue, New York, NY 10016, United States of America

British Library Cataloguing in Publication Data
Data available

Library of Congress Control Number: 2017961742

ISBN 978–0–19–878682–5

Printed and bound by
CPI Group (UK) Ltd, Croydon, CR0 4YY

Oxford University Press makes no representation, express or implied, that the
drug dosages in this book are correct. Readers must therefore always check
the product information and clinical procedures with the most up-to-date
published product information and data sheets provided by the manufacturers
and the most recent codes of conduct and safety regulations. The authors and
the publishers do not accept responsibility or legal liability for any errors in the
text or for the misuse or misapplication of material in this work. Except where
otherwise stated, drug dosages and recommendations are for the non-pregnant
adult who is not breast-feeding

Links to third party websites are provided by Oxford in good faith and
for information only. Oxford disclaims any responsibility for the materials
contained in any third party website referenced in this work.

Preface

The past decades have been an exciting time to work both in cognitive psychology and in psycholinguistics. In the 10 years since the publication of the first edition of this book, we've seen incredibly rapid changes in our field. Some of these changes have been driven by advances in experimental methods; others have been driven by the growing desire of cognitive scientists in all areas of research to understand their own field in relation to other cognitive domains. As psycholinguists, we remain fundamentally interested in how language works, but we recognize that the answers to our questions cannot be answered without considering how attention, memory, visual processing, social cognition, and so on, work as well. In addition, a growing number of researchers are interested in moving away from understanding language as a system of symbols to understanding how we achieve communication through language. In the current edition of this *Handbook*, we've tried to capture these exciting areas of growth; while many chapters cover traditional areas of psycholinguistics, wherever possible the authors explore new insights that novel experimental techniques and connections with other research domains have contributed to their own field.

The current edition is organized in five sections. In the first two sections (Language comprehension, Language production) an overview of traditional psycholinguistic domains is provided. Here, the reader can find excellent overviews of language research ranging from sublexical acoustic processing, through word comprehension and production, to the processing of complex sentences. In addition, links between language comprehension and production are explored. Section III looks at how we use language as a communicative tool in social interactions. This is a new section for the *Handbook*, and reflects the growing movement we see in our field to understand language in the social context. The fourth section looks at language development from both an ontogenetic and a phylogenetic perspective. This enhances focus on the evolution of language in comparison with the first edition, which reflects movement in the field to explore language in the context of other relevant domains. The final section explicitly outlines some of the novel techniques that have been used to investigate language over the past decade: authors present work ranging from new twists on older methods (e.g., statistical advances in language research) to completely novel methods (e.g., intracranial electrophysiology in the study of language). In sum, the *Handbook* aims to provide readers with an excellent overview of established research, but also to ignite interest in thinking about how language can be studied in novel ways and in relation to other cognitive domains.

The *Handbook* was only possible to pull together because so many amazing researchers were willing to offer their time and expertise so generously. Over 70 authors contributed to the chapters in this edition: we would like to extend our very warm thanks to all of them. We would also like to say thank you to Lois Perry, who helped us enormously with proofreading and keeping us organized, to the team at Oxford University Press, and to our families: Lou, Stan, and Frank Gaskell for unceasing inspiration, and Georg, Sophia, and Isabel Rueschemeyer for their patience and their energy.

Table of Contents

List of Contributors … xiii
List of Abbreviations … xvii

PART I LANGUAGE COMPREHENSION

Section I: Sublexical and Lexical Level

1. Segmentation of speech … 5
   LAURENCE WHITE

2. Spoken word recognition … 31
   MICHAEL S. VITEVITCH, CYNTHIA S. Q. SIEW, AND NICHOL CASTRO

3. Visual word recognition … 48
   KATHLEEN RASTLE

4. Lexico-semantics … 71
   LOTTE METEYARD AND GABRIELLA VIGLIOCCO

5. Lexical ambiguity … 96
   JENNIFER RODD

6. Visual word recognition in multilinguals … 118
   TON DIJKSTRA AND WALTER J. B. VAN HEUVEN

7. Varieties of semantic deficit: Single-word comprehension … 144
   ELIZABETH JEFFERIES AND HANNAH THOMPSON

Section II: Sentence and discourse level

8. Sentence comprehension … 171
   MARYELLEN C. MACDONALD AND YALING HSIAO

9. Text comprehension … 197
   EVELYN C. FERSTL

10. Bilingual sentence processing 217
    Arturo E. Hernández, Eva M. Fernández,
    and Noemí Aznar-Besé

11. Sentence level aphasia 239
    David Caplan

12. Language in deaf populations: Signed language and orthographic processing 259
    David P. Corina and Laurel A. Lawyer

PART II LANGUAGE PRODUCTION

Section I: Sublexical level

13. Speech production: Integrating psycholinguistic, neuroscience, and motor control perspectives 291
    Grant Walker and Gregory Hickok

14. Links between perception and production: Examining the roles of motor and premotor cortices in understanding speech 306
    Carolyn McGettigan and Pascale Tremblay

Section II: Lexical level

15. Spoken word production: Representation, retrieval, and integration 335
    Linda R. Wheeldon and Agnieszka E. Konopka

16. Connectionist principles in theories of speech production 372
    Laurel Brehm and Matthew Goldrick

17. From thought to action: Producing written language 398
    Brenda Rapp and Markus F. Damian

18. Grammatical encoding 432
    Victor S. Ferreira, Adam Morgan, and L. Robert Slevc

Section III: Sentence and discourse level

19. Cross-linguistic/bilingual language production 461
    Francesca M. Branzi, Marco Calabria, and Albert Costa

20. The relationship between syntactic production and comprehension ... 482
   PETER INDEFREY

21. Word production and related processes: Evidence from aphasia ... 506
   MYRNA F. SCHWARTZ

22. Attention and structural choice in sentence production ... 527
   ANDRIY MYACHYKOV, MIKHAIL POKHODAY, AND RUSSELL TOMLIN

PART III INTERACTION AND COMMUNICATION

23. Perspective-taking during conversation ... 549
   SARAH BROWN-SCHMIDT AND DAPHNA HELLER

24. Alignment during interaction ... 573
   SIMON GARROD, ALESSIA TOSI, AND MARTIN J. PICKERING

25. Role of gesture in language processing: Toward a unified account for production and comprehension ... 592
   ASLI ÖZYÜREK

26. Pragmatics and inference ... 608
   ALAN GARNHAM

27. Experimental pragmatics ... 623
   IRA NOVECK

28. Language comprehension, emotion, and sociality: Aren't we missing something? ... 644
   JOS J. A. VAN BERKUM

PART IV LANGUAGE DEVELOPMENT AND EVOLUTION

Section I: Ontogenetic development

29. The development of prosodic phonology ... 675
   KATHERINE DEMUTH

30. How well does statistical learning address the challenges of real-world language learning? 690
Lucia Sweeney and Rebecca L. Gómez

31. First word learning 714
Marilyn May Vihman

32. Language and conceptual development 736
Susan A. Gelman and Steven O. Roberts

33. Artificial grammar learning and its neurobiology in relation to language processing and development 755
Julia Uddén and Claudia Männel

34. Developmental dyslexia 784
Marianna E. Hayiou-Thomas, Julia M. Carroll, and Margaret J. Snowling

35. Developmental language disorder 814
Cristina McKean, James Law, Angela Morgan, and Sheena Reilly

Section II: Phylogenetic development

36. Evolution of speech 841
Bart de Boer and Tessa Verhoef

37. The genetics of language: From complex genes to complex communication 865
Paolo Devanna, Dan Dediu, and Sonja C. Vernes

38. Models of language evolution 899
Cathleen O'Grady and Kenny Smith

PART V METHODOLOGICAL ADVANCES IN PSYCHOLINGUISTIC RESEARCH

39. Generalizing over encounters: Statistical and theoretical considerations 917
Dale J. Barr

40. Cognitive electrophysiology of language 930
    THOMAS P. URBACH AND MARTA KUTAS

41. Source estimation, connectivity, and pattern analysis
    of EEG/MEG data in psycholinguistics 955
    OLAF HAUK

42. New fMRI methods for the study of language 975
    ROEL M. WILLEMS AND MARCEL A. J. VAN GERVEN

43. Intracranial electrophysiology in language research 992
    ADEEN FLINKER, VITÓRIA PIAI, AND ROBERT T. KNIGHT

Name Index 1011
Subject Index 1021

List of Contributors

Noemí Aznar-Besé, University of Houston, USA

Dale J. Barr, University of Glasgow, UK

Francesca M. Branzi, University of Manchester, UK

Laurel Brehm, Max Planck Institute for Psycholinguistics, the Netherlands

Sarah Brown-Schmidt, Vanderbilt University, USA

Marco Calabria, Universitat Pompeu Fabra, Spain

David Caplan, Massachusetts General Hospital/Harvard University, USA

Julia M. Carroll, Coventry University, UK

Nichol Castro, University of Kansas, USA

David P. Corina, University of California, Davis, USA

Albert Costa, ICREA, Universitat Pompeu Fabra, Spain

Markus F. Damian, University of Bristol, UK

Bart de Boer, Vrije Universiteit Brussels, Belgium

Dan Dediu, Max Planck Institute for Psycholinguistics, the Netherlands

Katherine Demuth, Macquarie University, Australia

Paolo Devanna, Max Planck Institute for Psycholinguistics, the Netherlands

Ton Dijkstra, Donders Institute for Brain, Cognition and Behaviour, Centre for Cognition, the Netherlands

Eva M. Fernández, City University of New York, USA

Victor S. Ferreira, University of California, San Diego, USA

Evelyn C. Ferstl, University of Freiburg, Germany

Adeen Flinker, New York University, School of Medicine, USA

Alan Garnham, University of Sussex, UK

Simon Garrod, University of Glasgow, UK

Susan A. Gelman, University of Michigan, USA

Matthew Goldrick, Northwestern University, USA

Rebecca L. Gómez, University of Arizona, USA

Olaf Hauk, University of Cambridge, UK

Marianna E. Hayiou-Thomas, University of York, UK

Daphna Heller, University of Toronto, Canada

Arturo E. Hernández, University of Houston, USA

Gregory Hickok, University of California, Irvine, USA

Yaling Hsiao, Oxford University, UK

Peter Indefrey, Heinrich Heine University Düsseldorf, Germany

Elizabeth Jefferies, University of York, UK

Robert T. Knight, University of California, Berkeley, USA

Agnieszka E. Konopka, University of Aberdeen, UK

Marta Kutas, University of California, San Diego, USA

James Law, Newcastle University, UK

Laurel A. Lawyer, University of Essex, UK

Maryellen C. MacDonald, University of Wisconsin, USA

Claudia Männel, Max Planck Institute for Human Cognitive and Brain Sciences, Germany

Carolyn McGettigan, Royal Holloway, University of London, UK

Cristina McKean, Murdoch Children's Research Institute, Australia

Lotte Meteyard, University of Reading, UK

Adam Morgan, University of California, San Diego, USA

Angela Morgan, Murdoch Children's Research Institute, Australia

Andriy Myachykov, Northumbria University Newcastle, UK and National Research University Higher School of Economics, Moscow, Russia

Ira Noveck, Institut des Sciences Cognitives—Marc Jeannerod, France

Cathleen O'Grady, University of Edinburgh, UK

Asli Özyürek, Radboud University Nijmegen and Max Planck Institute for Psycholinguistics, the Netherlands

Vitória Piai, Radboud University, Donders Centre for Cognition, Radboud University Medical Center, Department of Medical Psychology, the Netherlands

Martin J. Pickering, University of Edinburgh, UK

Mikhail Pokhoday, Higher School of Economics, Russia

Brenda Rapp, Johns Hopkins University, USA

Kathleen Rastle, Royal Holloway, University of London, UK

Sheena Reilly, Menzies Institute Queensland, Griffith University, Australia

Steven O. Roberts, University of Michigan, USA

Jennifer Rodd, University College London, UK

Myrna F. Schwartz, Mass Rehabilitation Research Institute, USA

Cynthia S. Q. Siew, University of Kansas, USA

L. Robert Slevc, University of Maryland, USA

Kenny Smith, University of Edinburgh, UK

Margaret J. Snowling, University of Oxford, UK

Lucia Sweeney, University of Arizona, USA

Hannah Thompson, University of Surrey, UK

Russell Tomlin, University of Oregon, USA

Alessia Tosi, University of Edinburgh, UK

Pascale Tremblay, Université Laval, Canada

Julia Uddén, Max Planck Institute for Psycholinguistics, the Netherlands; Stockholm University, Sweden

Thomas P. Urbach, University of California, San Diego, USA

Jos J. A. van Berkum, University of Utrecht, the Netherlands

Marcel A. J. van Gerven, Radboud University, the Netherlands

Walter J. B. van Heuven, University of Nottingham, UK

Tessa Verhoef, Leiden Institute of Advanced Computer Science, Leiden University, the Netherlands

Sonja C. Vernes, Max Planck Institute for Psycholinguistics, the Netherlands

Gabriella Vigliocco, University College London, UK

Marilyn May Vihman, University of York, UK

Michael S. Vitevitch, University of Kansas, USA

Grant Walker, University of California, Irvine, USA

Linda R. Wheeldon, University of Agder, Norway

Laurence White, Newcastle University, UK

Roel M. Willems, Radboud University, the Netherlands

List of Abbreviations

AAVE	African-American vernacular English
ABR	auditory brain stem response
ACC	anterior cingulate cortex
ACE	action-compatibility effect
ACS	associative chunk strength
ADC	apparent diffusion coefficient
ADHD	attention deficit/hyperactivity disorder
ADS	adult-directed speech
AEP	auditory evoked potential
AFP	anterior forebrain pathway
AG	angular gyrus
AGL	artificial grammar learning
ALC	Affective Language Comprehension
ALE	activation likelihood estimation
ANN	artificial neural networks
ANOVA	analysis of variance
AoA	age-of-acquisition
AQ	autism quotient
ART	auditory repetition task
ASD	autism spectrum disorder
ASL	American Sign Language
ATL	anterior temporal lobe
BIA	Bilingual Interactive Activation
BOLD	blood-oxygen-level-dependent
CAT	Communicative Accommodation Theory
CMA	cingulate motor area
CMLP	cross-modal lexical priming
CNP	conjoined noun phrase
CSF	cerebrospinal fluid
CSI	cumulative semantic interference
CV	consonant-vowel
CVC	consonant-vowel-consonant
DIVA	Directions into Velocities of Articulators
ECoG	electrocorticography
ECS	Emotionally Competent Stimulus
EEG	electroencephalography
ELN	Extended Language Network

ERP	event-related potential
ERSP	event-related spectral perturbations
ESM	electrical stimulation mapping
fMRI	functional magnetic resonance imaging
GSA	gesture as simulated action
GSC	gradient symbolic computation
HFB	high frequency band
HSFC	hierarchical state feedback control
iEEG	intracranial electroencephalography
ICM	inhibitory control model
IDS	infant-directed speech
IFG	inferior frontal gyrus
IFS	inferior frontal sulcus
IP	intonational phrase
ITG	inferior temporal gyrus
ITI	intertrial interval
LA	lexical-auditory
LAN	left anterior negativity
LFP	local field potential
LI	language impairment
LIFG	left inferior frontal gyrus
LLD	language learning delay
LM	lexical-motor
LMEM	linear mixed-effects model
LPC	late positive component
LSA	latent semantic analysis
LSM	language style matching
LTM	long-term memory
MEG	magnetoencephalography
MEP	motor-evoked potentials
MFG	middle frontal gyrus
MMN	mismatch negativity
MNI	Montreal Neurological Institute
MPFC	medial prefrontal cortex
MTG	middle temporal gyrus
MTSP	Motor Theory of Speech Perception
MVPA	multivoxel pattern analysis
NP	noun phrase
O-LTM	orthographic long-term memory
O-WM	orthographic working memory
OCC	occipital cortex
PA	phonological awareness
PAM	population-average models
PET	positron emission tomography
PGC	phoneme-grapheme conversion
PND	phonological neighborhood density

PNT	Philadelphia Naming Test
PP	phonological phrase
pSTG	posterior superior temporal gyrus
PT	planum temporale
PW	Prosodic Word
PWC	Possible Word Constraint
PWD	pure word deafness
PWI	perfusion weighted imaging
RAN	rapid automatized naming
RAP	rapid auditory processing
RDM	representational dissimilarity matrix
RHM	Revised Hierarchical Model
RIF	retrieval-induced forgetting
RMSE	root mean square error
ROC	receiver operating characteristic
RSA	representational similarity analysis
RSVP	rapid serial visual presentation
RT	reaction time
sEEG	stereotactic electroencephalography
SA	semantic aphasia
SD	semantic dementia
SFC	state feedback control
SFG	superior frontal gyrus
SL	statistical learning
SLAM	semantic-lexical-auditory-motor model
SLI	specific language impairment
SMA	supplementary motor area
SMG	supramarginal gyrus
SNR	signal-to-noise ratio
SOA	stimulus-onset asynchrony
SOSH	Syllable Onset Segmentation Heuristic
SOV	subject-verb-object
SP	Semantic-Phonological
SPM	Standard Pragmatic Model
SRN	simple recurrent network
STG	superior temporal gyrus
STM	short-term memory
STRF	spectro-temporal receptive field
STS	superior temporal sulcus
SVO	subject-verb-object
TF	transcription factor
TFA	Time Frequency Analysis
TMS	transcranial magnetic stimulation
TP	transitional probabilities
TPJ	temporoparietal junction
UB	utterance boundaries

UG	universal grammar
UMLL	Unified Model of Language Learning
VLSM	Voxel-based Lesion Symptom Mapping
VMS	vocal motor schemes
VP	verb phrase
VVS	visual ventral stream
VWFA	Visual Word Form Area
WA	Wernicke's aphasia
WES	whole exome sequencing
WGS	whole genome sequencing

PART I

LANGUAGE COMPREHENSION

SECTION I
Sublexical and Lexical Level

CHAPTER 1

SEGMENTATION OF SPEECH

LAURENCE WHITE

1.1 INTRODUCTION

THE power of words may have been overstated in communication research. A useful, reductivist schema for spoken interaction is a linear information chain: concepts in the speaker's mind are encoded into a stream of physical sounds, picked up by the ears of listeners and appropriately decoded in their minds. This is closely analogous to Morse code telegraphy: an active, encoding transmitter and a passive, decoding receiver. Although Morse code is now dustily antiquated as a communication system, the information transmission model has been implicit in much—highly productive—psycholinguistic research.

Morse code is famously a binary digital system, but the sequence of dots and dashes that represent letters—*dot dot dot dash dash dash dot dot dot* for "SOS"—are delimited by silent intervals, short between letters, and longer between words. Morse signals would not be interpretable without this explicit segmentation. These aspects of electrical telegraphy have informed assumptions about speech comprehension: firstly, that identification—decoding—of the individual words of a message is the primary goal of spoken interaction; secondly, that locating boundaries between words is a prerequisite to lexical decoding.

Spoken communication entails much more than physical encoding and perceptual decoding of word sequences, of course. Speech is typically produced in an interactive, reciprocal and negotiated context, with speaker and listener roles shifting in a dynamic process only partially mediated by sentential meaning. Prosody—particularly modulation of pitch and timing—conveys information about not only linguistic meaning but also turn-taking, attitudes, and physical and emotional states. Critical information also flows through channels physically distinct from the acoustic stream, notably visual, but potentially also haptic and proprioceptive.

Words, therefore, are not all there is to speech. And yet words themselves are not illusory. Early infant forays into language production demonstrate that words are true building blocks of communication, and a full account of speech processing must make reference to how we extract words and associate them with meaning. The first stage of this process, speech segmentation, is often characterized by reference to the absence of consistent boundaries between spoken words, by contrast with the white spaces between words on a page or screen of text. Furthermore, speech sounds themselves are contextually variable. In sections 1.2 and 1.3, we review how research on the problems of continuity and variation has reframed concepts of speech representation and informed the search for universal segmentation mechanisms against a background of linguistic diversity.

The continuity problem and the information transmission model imply that explicitly locating word boundaries is a prerequisite for speech understanding. Given clear, unambiguous input, however, lexical knowledge can provide segmentation implicitly, as discussed in section 1.4. In the face of ambiguity or signal degradation, listeners exploit a range of "non-lexical" (segmental and prosodic) segmentation cues, reviewed in section 1.5. Interactions between implicit, lexically driven segmentation and explicit use of non-lexical cues are discussed in section 1.6. We note that much of the experimental work reviewed here pertains to languages of European origin, a reflection of the extant literature in English: while specific non-lexical cues may have more relevance for some languages than others—lexical stress or vowel harmony, for example—the primary aim is to show the language-general mechanisms whereby different sources of segmentation information are weighted and integrated by listeners.

The requirement for controlled speech stimuli in laboratory perception studies neglects the dynamic nature of speaker-listener interactions, but in section 1.7 we consider the active role of infant-directed speech in facilitating young learners' extract of words from the speech stream, and briefly examine the parallels and contrasts between first language and second language segmentation.

1.2 Problems in speech segmentation: Continuity and variation

We experience the continuity of speech when overhearing fluent conversation in an unfamiliar language. While intonation and gesture offer clues to the nature of the interaction—particularly its social and emotional significance—individual words are rarely obvious, except when highlighted by rhetorical devices such as repetition or exaggerated pausing. The momentary recognition arising from sudden code-switching into a familiar language (e.g., "*Je vais parler aux builders ce soir*") strikingly emphasizes the power of lexical knowledge to impose discrete structure on continuity.

Even in familiar languages, however, lexical access cannot simply be a matter of mapping sound sequences to stored representations (Norris & Cutler, 1985). The scarcity of unambiguous boundary markers means that new lexical candidates could potentially be activated with every new segment, causing a combinatorial explosion in word hypotheses. The variable realization of speech sounds also introduces uncertainty: indeed, unless we can generalize from phonetic variability, connecting two repetitions of a word with their common underlying representation would be highly problematic.

An abstract level of representation, intervening between acoustic processing and the search for lexical matches, therefore, has intuitive appeal. Norris and Cutler (1985) draw a theoretical contrast between "classification" and "segmentation." Classification entails dividing speech into a series of labeled units, of a particular type, to produce a phonological specification (e.g., a string of phonemes or syllables). Classification must be exhaustive—no parts of an utterance should be left unclassified—and there should be some systematic mapping from phonological units to words themselves. One theoretical attraction of an intervening, sublexical level of representation is its power to constrain the search space: any spoken language could encode tens of thousands of words, but a few dozen phonemes and a few hundred different syllables. Indeed, segmenting continuous speech into discrete words is potentially boosted by sublexical classification, particularly into a sequence of syllables. Syllable boundaries represent points of look-up for new lexical candidates, but that process need not be initiated within syllables. As discussed next, however, claims about the power and ubiquity of the syllable as a perceptual unit have been empirically challenged.

1.3 Problems in speech segmentation: The syllable in prelexical classification

Much early experimental psycholinguistics focused on parsing of the speech stream into units of perception, "building blocks of prelexical processing . . . [generating] a transcript of the signal as a sequence of units (e.g., phonemes, demi-syllables, syllables)" (Mattys & Melhorn, 2005, p. 224). In a key study, Mehler, Dommergues, Frauenfelder and Segui (1981) used word-monitoring latencies to assess French listeners' sensitivity to syllable structure. After visual presentation of the target *pa*, for example, participants were quicker to detect it in *palace* than in *palmier*, but quicker to detect *pal* in *palmier* than in *palace*. This crossover interaction was interpreted as facilitation of detection when the target (*pa* vs. *pal*) exactly corresponded to a syllable, based on French syllabification *pa.lace* vs. *pal.mier*. Mehler et al. thus proposed that the syllable constitutes a perceptual unit of processing; furthermore, that syllabification is prior to, and necessary for, lexical access.

The "syllable effect" interpretation was challenged by similar studies with English listeners. English has a larger range of syllable structures than French, with multiple consonants allowed in onset and coda clusters, and appears less straightforward to syllabify. For example, the medial consonant in strong-weak words like *balance* is typically regarded as ambisyllabic (see Table 1.1 for definitions of phonetic terms), evidenced by native English speakers' variable intuitions about *ba.lance* or *bal.ance* as the appropriate syllabification (Anderson & Jones, 1974; Cutler, Mehler, Norris, & Segui, 1986). Indeed, English listeners did not demonstrate the syllable effect, but showed—for both open and closed targets, for example *ba* and *bal*, respectively—quicker detection in words with ambisyllabic medial consonants (e.g., *ba[l]ance*) than unambiguous syllable structures (e.g., *bal.cony*) (Cutler et al., 1986).

Interpreting different French and English responses to equivalent materials, Cutler et al. (1986, p. 397) argued that "language-specific components [of a psycholinguistic theory] are highly undesirable; if language specificity at this level is possible, why not dialect specificity or even speaker specificity? [. . .] For this reason we feel compelled to suggest a language-universal framework [. . .]." Specifically, they proposed that listeners may have both phonemic and syllabic segmentation strategies available, mediated by experience and task demands. Thus, their English results suggest that simple CVCV structures may

Table 1.1 Glossary of some phonetic terms used in this review: these are intended as heuristics for understanding rather than theoretical definitions

ambisyllabic	Ambisyllabic consonants are regarded as belonging to both the preceding and following syllable, as the /l/ in English *balance*.
full vowel / reduced vowel	Full vowels are produced with a non-centralized articulation and are typically of significantly longer duration than reduced/centralized vowels. In English, full vowels include monophthongs (e.g., the vowels in *seat, set, sat*) and diphthongs (e.g., the vowels in *boat, bait, bout*). Reduced vowels include schwa, as in the first syllable of *commend*, and [I] in unstressed syllables like the second syllable of *captain*.
hyperarticulation / hypoarticulation	Hyperarticulation is the exaggeration of phonetic gestures so as to produce speech sounds that are maximally distinctive, as in clear speech styles. Hypoarticulation is the reduction, assimilation, or elimination of sounds, as in casual speech styles, through which some phonemic distinctions may be lost.
lexical stress	In phonetic terms, lexical stress is prominence of a particular syllable within a word, conveyed through lengthening, loudness, and pitch.
phrasal accent	In phonetic terms, phrasal accent is prominence of a particular syllable or word within a phrase, conveyed through pitch, lengthening, and loudness.
strong syllable / weak syllable	In English, a strong syllable contains a full vowel, as in the first syllable of *captain* or the second syllable of *commend*; a weak syllable contains a reduced vowel or no vowel, as in the first syllable of *commend* or the second syllables of *captain* and *bottle*. Most strong syllables in English are lexically stressed, but some are unstressed (e.g., the second syllable in *insight*).

boost prelexical phonemic classification, but this is overridden when unambiguous native language syllabification experience biases listeners' decisions, as in Mehler et al. (1981) for French.

Cutler et al. (1986) ruled out a role for lexical stress in biasing English listeners' responses, because they showed the same bias—quicker for both *ba* and *bal* in *balance* than *balcon*—in French words with consistent final accent (contrary to predominant English stress, section 1.4). Stress came to the fore subsequently, however. Cutler and Norris (1988) found that English listeners' detection of, for example, *mint* in strong–weak (SW) *mintef* was faster than in strong–strong (SS) *mintayf*, but *thin* was no more quickly detected in *thintef* than *thintayf*. They concluded that strong syllables—specifically, full vowels—trigger a search for new lexical items beginning with a matching syllable (see Table 1.1 for working definitions of phonetic terms). Because medial /t/ in SS contexts syllabifies as a syllable onset (*-tavye*), it activates compatible lexical representations and interferes with activation of *mint*, for which the same /t/ is required. Weak syllables would not initiate lexical access: thus the representation of the /t/ as word-final in *mint* is not blocked by *mintef*.

When the target is wholly contained within the first syllable—*thin* in both *thintayf* and *thintef*—initiation of lexical access by the following syllable becomes irrelevant (Cutler & Norris, 1988). The precise matching of the target with a complete syllable—the first syllable in the context being *thin* or *thint*—does not matter without a competing attempt at lexical access. This represents a theoretical shift from Mehler et al. (1981). Cutler and Norris see no need to predicate lexical access on exhaustive classification into sublexical units: rather, certain events within utterances trigger the initiation of hypothesis-testing about words (Cutler, McQueen, Norris, & Somejuan, 2001) and languages differ in their provision of such triggering events. The *universal* requirement is that word boundaries are located; the language-specific variation is not in the units of sublexical processing, but rather the strategies available for triggering boundary hypotheses.

Content, Meunier, Kearns, and Frauenfelder (2001) presented a further challenge to the syllable effect, noting that Sebastián-Gallés, Dupoux, Segui, and Mehler (1992) only found the effect for Catalan speakers with unstressed syllables, and found no effect at all for Spanish speakers unless response times were slowed with a parallel semantic task. In non-slowed trials, Spanish speakers showed an overall faster response for CV targets over CVC targets (also found for Italian listeners, Tabossi, Collina, Mazzetti, & Zoppello, 2000). Content, Meunier, et al. themselves found a syllable effect in French only where the pivotal consonant was a liquid (e.g., *ba[l]ance, ba[l]con*)—as in Mehler et al. (1981)—but even for such stimuli the effect relied on specific test-trial blocking and relative response slowness. Like Cutler and Norris (1988), they rejected a mandatory prelexical syllabification stage, interpreting results in terms of phoneme-level matching, informed by allophonic and coarticulatory information (Content, Meunier, et al.). Significantly, they propose that incoming speech information is used for lexical access as it becomes available.

Content, Kearns, and Frauenfelder (2001) broke altogether with the conception of segmentation as a process of identifying boundaries between adjacent constituents. Rather, they emphasized that identification of potential lexical onsets is prior to, and distinct from, judgments about offsets. Theoretically, the hierarchical, recursive nature of linguistic structure means that a constituent can begin before another constituent of the same type has ended. Empirically, Content, Kearns, et al. cited metalinguistic syllabification tasks, where French participants' judgments about syllable codas, but not syllable onsets, were influenced by stimulus characteristics and task demands.

Regarding segmentation, the primary proposal of Content, Kearns, and Frauenfelder (2001) was that the onset of any strong (full vowel) syllable may be taken to be a possible word onset. (The strong syllable qualification accounts for differences between French and English studies, given that French does not manifest widespread vowel reduction.) This proposal presupposes that listeners are sensitive to syllabic structure, but does not require an exhaustive classification into contiguous, non-overlapping syllables. Accordingly, Dumay, Frauenfelder, and Content (2002) found that misalignment of target syllable onsets in nonsense carrier strings was more problematic for word-spotting than misalignment of syllable codas; for example, participants were slower to spot *lac* in misaligned /zy.glak/ than /zyn.lak/, but no difference between /lak.tyf/ and misaligned /la.klyf/. Similar asymmetries between onset and coda misalignment were demonstrated for Dutch (McQueen, 1998; Vroomen & de Gelder, 1997).

The Syllable Onset Segmentation Heuristic (SOSH) captures a theoretical shift: the critical information for lexical access is the location of possible word onsets (Content, Kearns, & Frauenfelder, 2001). Which syllable onsets activate possible words is proposed to be mediated by language-specific factors such as metrical structure. Dumay et al. (2002, p. 14) further observed that "syllable-based segmentation strategies such as SOSH [. . .] are not deterministic rules but heuristics, so that their effect could be modulated or compensated by other cues, such as lexical information." As discussed in section 1.6, where lexical information about structure is adequately informative, it may render non-lexical heuristics superfluous.

1.4 Segmentation strategies: Word recognition and implicit segmentation

1.4.1 Models of word recognition

Models of word recognition are typically based on simultaneous activation of multiple lexical candidates and competition between those candidates; for example, TRACE (McClelland & Elman, 1986); Shortlist (Norris, 1994; Norris & McQueen, 2008). Models often have multi-level connectionist architecture, with discrete nodes at one or more levels of sublexical representation (e.g., features and/or phonemes) together with nodes corresponding to individual words. Phonetic input activates sublexical representations which then excite compatible lexical nodes, while incompatible lexical nodes are inhibited. Levels of activation are determined both by bottom-up goodness of fit and competition—via inhibitory connections—at the word level (models such as TRACE also allow top-down excitation, McClelland & Elman, 1986). Eventually, competition results in recognition of the most strongly activated candidate word. Given the temporal nature of speech, the whole process is continuous and overlapping, with further word candidates being activated as new phonetic input is received.

Segmentation emerges naturally from the outcome of lexical competition. For example, the phrase "*silver doorbell*" provides phoneme-level evidence to temporarily activate the boundary-straddling *adore*. As the activation of the optimally matching sequence ultimately prevails, the boundary (" . . . ver#door . . . ") is respected, but this veridical segmentation is achieved without explicit reference to boundary-specific features of the signal.

Models differ, however, in whether segmentation cues explicitly inform lexical hypotheses. TRACE identifies words purely through activation between levels and inhibition within levels (McClelland & Elman, 1986). By contrast, Shortlist allows certain boundary-relevant constraints to influence activation: in particular, the Possible Word Constraint (PWC) requires that lexical solutions do not leave stray segments—specifically vowel-free syllables—that could not be viable words (Norris, McQueen, Cutler, & Butterfield, 1997). Thus, in "*red frock*," activation of the sequence "*red rock*" is disfavored because this strands a lone /f/, not a possible English word. Metrical information also constrains activation in some instantiations of Shortlist: Norris, McQueen, and Cutler (1995) proposed a segmentation boost to all (English) lexical candidates with onsets aligned to strong syllables (excepting that all post-silence syllables must be word-initial). Subsequently, Norris et al. (1997) integrated this metrical constraint with the PWC, penalizing lexical candidates that leave impossible words (i.e., stray consonants) between hypothesized word edges and boundaries in the signal (silences and strong syllable onsets): thus, *apple* is harder to detect in *fapple* than in *vuffapple*.

Whether, and how much, explicit segmentation information is utilized in word recognition is debatable. The time-course of lexical activation indicates that candidates disfavored by non-lexical cues (timing, allophony, phonotactics, and so on) are still considered. Embedded words (e.g., subset *bone* in superset *trombone*) are activated (Shillcock, 1990), with activation modulated by degree of subset-superset overlap (Bowers, Davis, Mattys, Damian, & Hanley, 2009). Boundary-straddling words are also activated: for example, Italian *visite* ("*visits*") in response to *visi tediati* ("*bored faces*"), even when strong distributional cues disfavor the overlapping word (Tabossi et al., 2000; see also Gow & Gordon, 1995). While overlapping words are relatively rare, embedded words abound: McQueen, Cutler, Briscoe, and Norris (1995) reported that 84% of English polysyllables contain at least one shorter word, most often with coincident onsets (e.g., *mace* in *masonry*), although—as in *bone/trombone*—later embedded words are also activated.

Thus, non-lexical segmentation cues do not serve to rule out alternative parses of the input signal at an early stage, but lexical competition has a strong effect. Target words embedded in contexts with no competitor words are recognized more quickly; for example, *sack* is detected more quickly in /sækrək/, with no competitors, than /sækrəf/, potentially completed as *sacrifice* (McQueen, Norris, & Cutler, 1994). Moreover, graded effects of the number of competitors are also found: specifically, detection of targets is impeded with increasing cohort size of alternative parses (Vroomen & de Gelder, 1995, see section 1.5.2).

By contrast, non-lexical cues to segmentation are strengthened by the cumulative weight of lexical evidence, the theoretical power of English metrical segmentation being just one example (Cutler & Carter, 1987). Non-lexical segmentation cues should be more reliable given greater numbers of words with equivalent features, in contrast to the negative effects of neighborhood on word recognition. Explicit segmentation and word recognition thus appear distinct, influenced by contrasting statistical contingencies: "Information on what is a word in the language appears to behave quite differently from information on what is likely to be a word in the language" (Newman, Sawusch, & Wunnenberg, 2011, p. 474).

1.4.2 Evidence for the role of lexicality, syntax, and semantics in segmentation

There is abundant support for the power of lexical knowledge to impose structure on speech. For example, listeners' ability to extract new words from artificial language streams is enhanced when the stream includes already familiarized non-words (Cunillera, Càmara, Laine, & Rodríguez-Fornells, 2010; Dahan & Brent, 1999). This "segmentation-by-lexical-subtraction" strategy accords with evidence from cross-modal fragment priming (Mattys, White, & Melhorn, 2005): in this paradigm, a lexical decision (respond "word" or "non-word") to a visually presented trisyllabic target (e.g., "*corridor*") is preceded by a five-syllable auditory stream containing a trisyllabic context and the first two syllables of the target (e.g., *anythingcorri*). Mattys et al. found that where the auditory context was a word (e.g., *anything[corri]* versus non-word *imoshing[corri]*), there was faster lexical decision to the target, indicating more effective segmentation of the auditory prime *corri*. Thus, the lexical status of a context word promotes the extraction of the subsequent—contiguous, non-overlapping—word, in accordance with the concept of implicit segmentation through word recognition. Using the same paradigm, Mattys et al. further found that, where lexicality provided a segmentation solution, a range of non-lexical cues—stress, phonotactics, decoarticulation—were neglected by listeners (section 1.6).

Despite the power of segmentation-by-lexical subtraction, Vroomen and de Gelder (1995) found no effect of the *wordlikeness* of non-words that were contiguous with, but did not overlap, the target; for example, target BEL in *belkem* vs. *belkeum* vs. *belkaam* (in increasing order of cohort size of the second syllable, k_m). Likewise, Newman et al. (2011) found no effect of lexical neighborhood of the preceding non-word syllable in a word-spotting task. Identifying a word in an utterance creates edges in the speech stream, but the cohort effects that are a feature of recognition—specifically, the plausibility of non-words—do not influence boundary perception where non-words do not overlap with lexical candidates.

Cunillera, Laine, and Rodríguez-Fornells (2016) demonstrated a neurophysiological correlate of the power of lexical knowledge: using artificial language learning, they found that familiarized words in the language stream elicited greater stimulus-preceding negativity (SPN), a frontal event-related potential (ERP) associated with expectation for relevant upcoming information. Cunillera et al. inferred that this activity is an index of orientation to the subsequent novel word in the stream, also finding that SRN magnitude decreases with better recognition of the novel words: thus, upcoming segmental material elicits lower activity as the language becomes more familiar.

Listeners' interpretations are, of course, influenced by syntactic structure, semantics, pragmatics and contextual factors beyond the signal (Cole, Jakimik, & Cooper, 1980). Although the acoustic evidence may permit ambiguity, on hearing "*Time and tide wait for . . .*", we are unlikely to conjure the mysterious character "Gnome Ann" from the subsequent segments. Likewise, "*four candles*" is a pragmatically more plausible hardware shop request than "*fork [h]andles.*" Reviewing the evidence, however, McQueen (2005) suggested that foregoing context does not influence what lexical representations are initially activated, but rather the outcome of lexical competition. This secondary role for context accords with Mattys, Melhorn, and White (2007), who modulated acoustic and syntactic evidence for the parsing of ambiguous phrases such as *takes pins* vs. *take spins*. The latter interpretation, when given a foregoing plural subject (e.g., *Those women take spins*), was strongly favored whatever the acoustics, showing a clear role for context. The singular context (e.g., *That woman takes pins*) was much less constraining, however, and acoustics dominated the parse. Critically, in the plural case, the lexical affiliation of the ambiguous /s/ was late and so context could influence activation, but where /s/ was affiliated to the preboundary verb, the acoustics were already adjudicating on the ambiguity.

Some investigations of the role of speakers in actively modulating explicit cues to segmentation actually reinforce the power of syntactic and segmental context over acoustics. Kim et al. (2012) found that speakers provided minimal acoustic cues to the segmentation of ambiguous schwa-initial sequences (e.g., *a door* vs. *adore*), and those cues that were available did not guide listeners to discriminate the alternatives. Prior syntactic and semantic context favoring one or other reading (e.g., *The hallway leads to . . .*) were highly biasing, however.

Kim et al. (2012) used an offline metalinguistic judgment task (e.g., "Did you hear one word or two?"), which could have biased listeners to favor context over acoustics. The power of higher-level information was, however, reinforced in a cross-modal identity-priming study (White, Mattys, & Wiget, 2012b), examining how acoustic segmentation cues were modulated by speech style: specifically, spontaneous map task speech versus read versions of the same utterances. In two-word phrases with no juncture ambiguity, but contrasting semantic predictability (e.g., high predictability—*oil tanker*; low predictability—*seal tanker*), there was relative hypoarticulation of acoustic cues in the map descriptions compared to read speech. However, despite the contrasting acoustic cue strength, there was no effect of speech style on the cross-modal priming these phrases elicited, while semantic relatedness boosted priming (White et al., 2012b). As in Kim et al.'s study, available lexical and semantic cues dominated acoustics (see also Mattys et al., 2005, Experiment 5).

1.5 Segmentation strategies: The role of non-lexical cues

Speech production studies demonstrate that the signal provides diverse potential segmentation cues. Many cues are language-specific, including allophony conditioned by word and phrase boundaries, and distributional patterns, notably consonant phonotactics and vowel harmony. Such patterns must be inferred from linguistic experience and some degree of phonological generalization: vowel harmony-based segmentation in Finnish, for example, requires listeners to categorically distinguish front and back vowels (Suomi, McQueen, & Cutler, 1997). Prosodic cues require broader abstraction: to apply metrical segmentation, learners must categorize syllables as strong or weak, and learn their distributional regularities. Whether there are segmentation cues so general as to apply universally, regardless of language-specific experience, remains an open question. Phonetic and perceptual evidence suggests, however, that—apart from between-word pauses—prosodic edge cues, reviewed next, are the strongest candidates for universality.

Potential cues to word boundaries are not deterministic. Even silent pauses can occur within words in disfluent speech. To exploit non-lexical segmentation cues, therefore, listeners must not only generalize about the phonological categories to which they apply, but also infer heuristics about cue reliability. For example, most English content words begin with strong syllables, but strict metrical segmentation would cause frequent misparsing (Harrington, Watson, & Cooper, 1989). Furthermore, the strength of acoustic-phonetic or prosodic cues varies according to speaking context, speech rate, and speaker awareness of ambiguity and listeners' needs (Lindblom, 1990). And, despite the potential of audience design considerations to account for variation, speakers do not always provide disambiguating information (Kim et al., 2012), nor do listeners necessarily exploit all available cues (White et al., 2012b).

Production and perception studies of non-lexical segmentation cues are reviewed next, focusing first on those that may pertain regardless of listeners' native language(s).

1.5.1 Language-general cues

1.5.1.1 *Pauses*

It is a commonplace that boundaries between words in fluent speech are rarely associated with pauses, although we perceive familiar languages as discrete words. One function of infant-directed speech may be to break up utterances into short or even single-word prosodic phrases to promote segmentation (section 1.7.1). Adult-directed speech is also characterized by shorter, pause-delimited phrases in hyperarticulated clear speech style, with concomitant intelligibility benefits (Smiljanić & Bradlow, 2008), although speakers vary in clear speech strategies and how far they assist the listener (Smiljanić & Bradlow, 2009).

Where available, even subliminally short between-word pauses promote learning in artificial languages (Peña, Bonatti, Nespor, & Mehler, 2002), and longer, perceptible pauses are associated with ERP signatures of word learning (Mueller, Bahlmann, & Friederici, 2008). Thus, as expected, pauses promote segmentation in novel linguistic conditions (also Finn & Hudson Kam, 2008), and clear speech styles associated with difficult listening conditions manifest greater pause frequency. However, constraints on communicative efficiency, the power of implicit segmentation through lexical recognition and the availability of other non-lexical cues all serve to limit pause frequency in typical conversational contexts.

1.5.1.2 *Cross-boundary decoarticulation*

The speech continuity problem arises not only because words are contiguous, but because sounds are coarticulated: the phonetic realization of phonemes depends upon preceding and following segmental material (Öhman, 1966). Articulatory gestures are, however, strengthened immediately before and after word boundaries, entailing less gestural overlap, and this decoarticulation increases with prosodic boundary strength (Fougeron & Keating, 1997). Such articulatory strengthening is also associated with lengthening: for word-initial consonants, both are widely observed across languages (Keating, Cho, Fougeron, & Hsu, 2004).

Decoarticulation is interpreted as a boundary cue in artificial language learning, carrying more weight in clear speech than syllable transition probabilities (Fernandes, Ventura, & Kolinsky, 2007); in noisy speech, however, transition probabilities dominate, presumably because subtle acoustic variations associated with decoarticulated boundaries were masked. In a cross-modal fragment priming paradigm, Mattys (2004) showed the power of boundary decoarticulation over lexical stress cues in English, again with the pattern reversed in noise.

1.5.1.3 *Prosodic lengthening*

Edges of words and higher-level prosodic domains are associated with segmental lengthening. Onset consonants are longer word-initially than medially (e.g., Oller, 1973) and greater lengthening is observed phrase-initially (Fougeron & Keating, 1997; although utterance-initial consonants are often acoustically short, see White, 2014, for a functional interpretation). Preboundary lengthening of vowels and coda consonants is widely observed across languages (e.g., Berkovits, 1991; Wightman, Shattuck-Hufnagel, Ostendorf, & Price, 1992). Whether word-final lengthening is observed phrase-medially is debatable: certainly, any preboundary lengthening is attenuated in the absence of a phrase boundary (White & Turk, 2010). With regard to the heads of prosodic domains: in addition to lengthening of lexically stressed syllables, both stressed and unstressed syllables are lengthened within phrasally accented words (Turk & White, 1999). Accentual lengthening of the primary stressed syllable is attenuated in longer words, giving rise to observations of so-called "polysyllabic shortening" (e.g., *cap* longest as a monosyllable, shorter in *captain*, shorter still in *captaincy*), an effect which is minimal in the absence of phrase-level lengthening effects (White & Turk, 2010).

Preboundary lengthening, particularly of vowels, clearly promotes boundary detection (e.g., Price, Ostendorf, Shattuck-Hufnagel, & Fong, 1991; Saffran, Newport, & Aslin,

1996); indeed, this is claimed to be a universal cue (Tyler & Cutler, 2009; but see Ordin, Polyanskaya, Laka, & Nespor, 2017). Lengthening of word-initial consonants boosts English listeners' segmentation of artificial languages (White, Mattys, Stefansdottir, & Jones, 2015; see Shatzman & McQueen, 2006, regarding initial consonant lengthening and Dutch segmentation). Moreover, the locus of lengthening is important: where the vowel in the initial syllable is lengthened rather than the consonant, segmentation is not boosted (White et al., 2015). Shortening of stressed syllables in longer words (due to attenuation of prosodic lengthening, White & Turk, 2010) helps rule out lexical embedding (e.g., *ham* vs. *hamster*; Davis, Marslen-Wilson, & Gaskell, 2002; Salverda, Dahan, & McQueen, 2003). Finally, faster foregoing speech rate increases the power of boundary lengthening cues, suggesting that listeners dynamically adjust predictions about the timing of speech events (Reinisch, Jesse, & McQueen, 2011).

1.5.1.4 *Cross-boundary glottalization*

When words lack vocalic onsets, the parallel of initial lengthening/strengthening is initial-vowel glottalization (also known as creaky voice/laryngealization/vocal fry), realized as irregular glottal pulses, often with amplitude reduction (Dilley, Shattuck-Hufnagel, & Ostendorf, 1996). Many languages manifest glottalization at vowel-to-vowel word boundaries; furthermore, the incidence of pre and postboundary glottalization increases with boundary strength (Dilley et al., 1996; Pompino-Marschall & Żygis, 2010). Listeners duly interpreted vowel glottalization as a cue to preceding boundaries (Nakatani & O'Connor-Dukes, 1980; Newman et al., 2011). In contrast with some other boundary-related allophonic variations, the qualitative nature of initial-vowel glottalization may make it particularly salient.

1.5.1.5 *Intonational boundaries*

Intonational patterns are highly variable cross-linguistically, but association of the heads and edges of prosodic structure with accents and boundary tones is very widely observed (Ladd, 2008). Thus, while intonational marking of phrase boundaries is language and context specific, the power of pitch events to cue phrasal segmentation is plausibly universal (e.g., Spinelli, Grimault, Meunier, & Welby, 2010, for French). Furthermore, certain intonational features (e.g., initial rise, falling pitch toward the final boundary) may be universally interpretable (Bolinger, 1964). Indeed, Shukla, Nespor, and Mehler (2007) demonstrated that intonational boundary cues, combined with timing effects, could either reinforce or override statistical cues in artificial language learning, even when the intonational contours were non-native (Italian speakers listening to Japanese intonation).

1.5.2 Language-specific cues

1.5.2.1 *Phonotactics*

Languages are diversely restricted in how they construct syllables. Certain consonant sequences are permissible within syllable onsets and codas (e.g., English /st/, /sp/), while others are restricted to one syllable position; for example, English onsets, but not codas, allow /tr/ or /fr/; codas but not onsets allow /nd/ and /mp/. Languages differ in phonotactic constraints: thus, /zm/ and /zb/ are well-formed onsets in Italian but not English.

Listeners are sensitive to native language phonotactics. Functional near-infrared spectroscopy showed more strongly left-lateralized fronto-temporal responses to German phonotactically legal non-words (e.g., *brop*) than illegal non-words (e.g., *bzop*); furthermore, ERP data indicated a stronger N400 to legal non-words, suggesting that illegal words are discarded prelexically (Rossi et al., 2011).

Phonotactics constraints restrict possible syllabifications; for example, the syllable boundary in *dovecote* must be between /v/ and /k/, as the sequence /vk/ cannot be an onset or coda. Using word-spotting, McQueen (1998) showed that phonotactics constraints influenced Dutch listeners' ease of detecting monosyllables: for example, *pil* detected more quickly in *pil.vrem* than *pilm.rem* (periods indicating phonotactically legal syllabifications). The phonotactic effect was stronger for word-final targets: *rok* was spotted more quickly in *fiemrok* than *fiedrok*, as in Dutch /mr/ is not a legal onset or coda, while /dr/ must be an onset because /d/ does not occur as a coda. This asymmetry reinforces the importance of onsets for lexical access (Content, Kearns, & Frauenfelder, 2001).

Newman et al. (2011) found that English constraints on word-final vowels did not influence segmentation: legal tense-vowel-final syllables and illegal lax-vowel-final syllables were equivalent in allowing following consonants to be realigned as codas (lax: *vuhf-apple*; tense: *veef-apple*). Skoruppa, Nevins, Gillard, and Rosen (2015) reported, however, that the lax vowel constraint was used by English listeners segmenting nonsense words.

Knowledge of what sequences may occur within and between words suggests useful segmentation heuristics. However, converging lines of evidence indicate that listeners do not systemically exploit phonotactic knowledge where more direct sources of segmentation information are available. Harrington et al. (1989) showed that a segmentation algorithm based on trigram occurrence within versus between English words successfully detected only 37% of boundaries in a transcribed corpus.

Furthermore, as observed by Mattys and Bortfeld (2015), phonemically based distributional generalizations neglect the impact of connected speech processes, such as contextual allophony, assimilations, deletions, and insertions.

Using cross-modal identity priming, White et al. (2012b) found that differences in distributional regularities of consonant diphones had no impact on segmentation. Two-word phrases—for example, *cream rickshaw* vs. *drab rickshaw*—contrasted in within-word and between-word frequencies of cross-boundary diphones: thus, /mr/ is vanishingly rare within English words, but not uncommon across boundaries; /br/ is frequent within words, but rare across boundaries. Even these strong contrasts in sequential frequencies had no impact on segmentation as indexed by cross-modal priming from the second word. White et al. proposed that phonotactic segmentation effects only appear in the absence of full lexical solutions. Similarly, Mattys et al. (2005) pitted lexicality and semantic dependencies against phonotactic frequencies and found phonotactic effects emerged only when stimulus truncation delexicalized the materials.

The Possible Word Constraint was proposed as a language-universal mechanism (Norris et al., 1997). In particular, single consonants may not be left stranded in word recognition; for example, the embedded word *right* is disfavored in *shining bright* because the residual /b/

lacks another syllabic attachment. What is a minimal legal syllable varies between languages, however: Hanulíková, McQueen, and Mitterer (2010) found no word-spotting penalty for stranding isolated consonants that are allowable words in Slovak.

1.5.2.2 *Vowel harmony*

Vowel harmony is a widespread phenomenon, notably in agglutinating languages. For example, the front/back feature of the first vowel in a Finnish word determines the allowable vowels throughout the word, which (unless one of two neutral vowels) must share the first vowel's frontness/backness. Finnish listeners can use vowel harmony for segmentation: for example, the word target *hymy* was detected more quickly in the disharmonious context *puhymy* than in the harmonious context *pyhymy* (Suomi et al., 1997). Exploitation of vowel harmony depends on linguistic experience: thus, Finnish, but not French or Dutch, listeners benefited from vowel harmony for learning an artificial language (Vroomen, Tuomainen, & de Gelder, 1998).

1.5.2.3 *Allophony*

While domain-edge lengthening and initial-vowel glottalization are widespread in the world's languages, other forms of positional allophony are language or dialect-specific. Newman et al. (2011) found that English consonant allophonic differences between word-initial and word-final position modulated segmentation behavior according to consonant class: being pronounced as initial or final influenced segmentation more for voiceless stops and /l/ than for fricatives, which have weaker position-specific allophony. Positional timing effects (consonants longer initially than finally) tended to apply across consonant classes.

1.5.2.4 *Lexical stress*

Features of English stress converge to suggest a metrical segmentation strategy (Norris & Cutler, 1985). Firstly, consonants between strong and weak syllables may be ambisyllabic (e.g., *ho[ll]ow, fo[c]us*...), thus strong syllable onsets are more reliable boundary locations. Secondly, stressed syllables are more salient, and the segments therein more recognizable and informative about lexical identity (Cutler & Foss, 1977; Huttenlocher & Zue, 1983). Thirdly, strong syllables tend to begin words in English. Cutler and Carter (1987) analyzed the distribution of strong and weak syllables in the London-Lund corpus of English conversational speech. Cutler and Carter found that 90% of lexical (open-class) words were either monosyllables or polysyllables beginning with a strong syllable (i.e., containing a full vowel, the primary cue to English lexical stress, Fear, Cutler, & Butterfield, 1995). Furthermore, 74% of strong syllables were the initial or only syllables of lexical words, 11% were function (closed-class) word-initial, and 15% were non-initial in lexical or function words. Only 5% of weak syllables were lexical-word-initial. Accordingly, Cutler and Butterfield's (1992) analysis of juncture misperceptions found that English listeners were more likely to insert a spurious word boundary before a strong syllable than a weak syllable and—conversely—to delete a boundary before a weak syllable (hence errors such as "*Sheila Fishley*" for "*She'll officially*" and "*How bigoted?*" for "*How big is it?*").

In Dutch, like English, most content words begin with stressed syllables, thus a metrical segmentation heuristic is similarly plausible. Vroomen and de Gelder (1995) used cross-modal priming to investigate how stress and lexical competition affected segmentation. The materials were broadly analogous to the *mintef/mintayf* sets used by Cutler and Norris (1988), where activation of the target *mint* was blocked by the competing activation of the strong second syllable *tayf*, while weak second syllables do not trigger lexical access (section 1.3). For example, Dutch listeners made lexical decisions to visual targets (e.g., *melk*) seen at the offset of auditory contexts: in the critical trials, strong-weak (SW) *melkem*, SS *melkeum*, SS *melkaam*. Second-syllable cohort size was manipulated, with many more Dutch words beginning *kaa-* than *keu-* and cohort size negligible for the weak syllable in *melkem*. Cohort size was inversely related to the magnitude of priming effects, suggesting that lexical competition from the overlapping second syllable, rather than its stress status, is the critical factor.

Another series of cross-modal priming experiments (Mattys, 2004; Mattys et al., 2005), pitted metrical segmentation pairwise against other cues: decoarticulation, phonotactics, the lexical status of a context word preceding the target. In clear listening conditions, stress was ignored in favor of the other cues; however, against a background of noise, stress became effective, suggesting that stress is a fallback cue when more reliable sources of information are compromised. Indeed, native-language-congruent stress patterns—as cued by pitch accent—boost artificial language learning: Dutch and English, but not French, listeners benefited from word-initial pitch cues (Tyler & Cutler, 2009), as did Dutch and Finnish, but not French listeners (Vroomen et al., 1998).

As we have already noted, vowel harmony was also available to segment the artificial languages of Vroomen et al. (1998): when words had initial stress, however, the impact of vowel harmony disappeared. This is contrary to findings for English—where stress is only relied on when other cues are diminished (Mattys et al., 2005)—and suggests that in fixed-initial-stress language like Finnish, metrical segmentation may be weighted more highly. Cue weighting apparently correlates with consistency.

1.6 Segmentation strategies: Cues in combination

The accumulated evidence indicates the dominance of implicit segmentation through lexical recognition, suggesting that activation and competition provide a complete lexical solution wherever possible. Non-lexical segmentation cues are stochastic in nature: for example, the use of metrical segmentation in English would incur a significant error rate (Harrington et al., 1989). However, when required, listeners can exploit a range of non-lexical cues derived from prosodic and acoustic-segmental regularities with respect to boundaries. Thus, segmentation proceeds through dynamic, strategic exploitation of available information, with parsimonious processing of the potentially redundant encoding of boundaries in the signal: the cues that speakers provide are not necessarily what listeners use.

Mattys et al. (2005) proposed a hierarchical framework for segmentation, based on English data, identifying three tiers of information—from highest to lowest weighted—lexical, segmental, and prosodic (i.e., metrical). Thus, word recognition in a familiar language can proceed wholly via the lexical tier and without reference to non-lexical segmentation cues at all. Non-lexical cues may be invoked due to ambiguity at the lexical level (as in cases of homophony: *gray tanker* vs. *great anchor*) or, more generally, where words in an utterance are not yet represented in the listener's mental lexicon, as in first or second language acquisition. Alternatively, signal degradation and ambiguity due to articulatory imprecision or environmental noise may make adjudication between alternative lexical solutions impossible without recourse to explicit strategies. For English, Mattys et al. suggested that metrical segmentation is a last resort for native adult speakers, presumably because of its relative lack of reliability (Harrington et al., 1989).

Newman et al. (2011) suggested a refinement of the segmentation hierarchy, weighting cues within the segmental tier according to relative salience. Thus, they proposed that strong acoustic cues—word-initial-vowel glottalization, word-initial consonant aspiration—carry more weight than distributional cues, such as syllable-final vowel phonotactics. This accords with suggestions that phonotactic patterns are rarely exploited where other cues are available (White et al., 2012b). Newman et al. (2011) also suggested that exploitation of segmental cues may be modulated by the strength of speakers' production. The dynamic interaction between listener needs and speaker behavior is explored next with respect to infant-directed speech.

1.7 Segmentation in first and second language acquisition

Although implicit segmentation often arises via word recognition for adults listening to their native language, infant first language (L1) and adult second language (L2) learners need other strategies through which to extract words and build vocabulary. For infants, this requirement has generated the hypothesis that acoustic events associated with word boundaries—in particular, the marking of the heads and edges of prosodic constituents—are critical in "bootstrapping" language acquisition (Fernald & McRoberts, 1996; Morgan & Demuth, 1996). Furthermore, the infant learner typically experiences an interactional style rather different from adult conversation. Evidence suggests that features of infant-directed speech (IDS) promote explicit segmentation and thus facilitate early word learning, with infants moving to implicit segmentation as vocabulary grows. The latter observation is also true of adult L2 learning, but there appears to be an interaction, for the mature learner, between non-lexical cues relevant to L1 and L2 segmentation.

1.7.1 The role of infant-directed speech

Dialogs between caregivers and infants demonstrate as clearly as any discourse context how speakers adjust their articulation to take account of perceived listener needs, in accordance with Lindblom's (1990) H&H hypothesis (hyperarticulation/hypoarticulation). Compared to typical adult speech, infants prefer infant-directed speech—slower rate; longer, more frequent pauses; substantial lengthening before prosodic boundaries; higher pitch; higher pitch range—particularly when these IDS features are exaggerated (Dunst, Gorman, & Hamby, 2012). Beyond simply engaging the infant's attention, IDS enhances segmental distinctiveness by expanding the vowel space, and highlights focused words through structure and prosody (e.g., Cristia, 2013). In addition, helping the child to extract individual words may be a critical function of IDS (Thiessen, Hill, & Saffran, 2005).

IDS exposes infants to a greater number of isolated words than adult-directed speech (ADS), with learning of those words consequently enhanced (Brent & Siskind, 2001). Furthermore, IDS utterances are often realized as sequences of short phrases, providing at least one reliable edge for many words, with exaggerated final lengthening and boundary tones complementing or replacing silent pauses (e.g., Cristia, 2013). Indeed, infants distinguish aligned and misaligned syntactic and prosodic phrasing in IDS, but not ADS (Nelson, Hirsh-Pasek, Jusczyk, & Cassidy, 1989), indicating sensitivity to boundary cues. Furthermore, suprasegmental cues to both boundaries and stress are exaggerated in IDS (Albin & Echols, 1996, for English; Fernald et al., 1989, for a range of languages). The relative weighting of suprasegmental cues varies cross-linguistically: in American English directed to 14-month-olds, Fisher and Tokura (1996) found utterance-internal phrase boundaries were associated with lengthening, while the primary phrasing cue in comparable speech of Japanese mothers was pitch variation.

Thus, infant-directed speech serves to boost young children's ability to extract words from speech, building their vocabulary and gradually facilitating a shift from predominantly explicit to adult-style, predominantly implicit, lexicon-driven segmentation.

1.7.2 Infant sensitivity to segmentation cues

Segmentation must precede word recognition in acquisition, but language-specific knowledge rapidly accumulates in typical development, and known words allow infants to infer the edges of flanking words (Brent, 1997). Bortfeld et al. (2005) demonstrated the importance of limited lexical knowledge for identifying boundaries in six-month-olds, who recognized less familiar words when preceded by familiar words in infant-directed speech (e.g., *feet* in *Mommy's feet*).

For infants, however, lexically driven segmentation must be complemented by non-lexical cues. In accordance with the metrical segmentation hypothesis, English-learning infants are sensitive to the distribution of stressed syllables: thus, 7.5-month-olds extracted trochaic words (e.g., *kingdom, hamlet*) from utterances, but with iambic words (e.g., *guitar*) tended to recognize strong–weak boundary-straddling sequences (e.g., *taris,* from "*Your guitar is in the studio*"; Jusczyk, Houston, & Newsome, 1999). English-speaking eight-month-olds also segmented trochaic words from Italian utterances (Pelucchi, Hay, & Saffran, 2009): thus, despite prosodic differences, infants can apply metrical segmentation to extract phonotactically legal, but phonetically non-native words. This argues against the utility of the concept of "rhythm class" in determining segmentation strategies (Nespor, Shukla, & Mehler, 2011), as Italian and English have been proposed to belong to distinct classes (see White, Mattys, & Wiget, 2012a, for a review). Italian and English have contrastive lexical stress and predominant trochaic structure in common, however, and a series of studies of eight-month-old monolingual Canadians indicated the importance of familiarity with native metrical structure (Polka & Sundara, 2012). Canadian French-learners extracted iambic words (e.g., *beret, guitar*) from French, and Canadian English-learners extracted trochaic words (e.g., *hamlet, candle*) from English; however, both groups failed to segment words from their non-native language. Here the importance of rhythm in early segmentation is to allow infants to induce the predominant metrical structure of their native words (iambic vs. trochaic).

Although Canadian French eight-month-olds could extract disyllables from Canadian and European French utterances (Polka & Sundara, 2012), European French infants were not found to achieve this, even in their native dialect, until 16 months (Nazzi, Iakimova, Bertoncini, Frédonie, & Alcantara, 2006). Speech style may be a critical difference between studies: the European French stimuli (Nazzi et al.) "were less infant-directed [...] produced with a faster speech rate, lower pitch, and smaller pitch excursions" (Nazzi, Mersad, Sundara, Iakimova, & Polka, 2014). The importance of IDS style for segmentation was highlighted by Floccia et al. (2016): reporting 13 studies of British English infants, from 8 to 10.5 months, they failed to replicate American English findings in all but one study. The positive segmentation effect was found with 10.5-month-old infants listening to speech in an "exaggerated IDS" style, which Floccia et al. suggested was closer to natural American English IDS.

Segmentation differences between (both French- and English-learning) North American and European infants thus may relate to contrasts in the typical style of IDS to which they are regularly exposed, rather than merely arising from between-study methodological differences. Consequently, Floccia et al. suggested that exaggerated North American IDS may contribute to higher vocabulary scores for American compared to British children between one and two years (Hamilton, Plunkett, & Schafer, 2000). This would accord with behavioral and electrophysiological studies showing a link between performance on segmentation tasks in the first year and language proficiency later in childhood (Junge & Cutler, 2014; Junge, Cutler, & Hagoort, 2012; Kooijman, Junge, Johnson, Hagoort, & Cutler, 2013; Newman, Ratner, Jusczyk, Jusczyk, & Dow, 2006). Furthermore, the relationship between pre-12-months segmentation outcomes and language proficiency is specific: early performance on language discrimination tasks is not predictive of vocabulary in two-year-olds, and early segmentation performance predicts language scores, but not general cognitive abilities, between four and six years of age (Newman, Ratner, Jusczyk, Jusczyk, & Dow, 2006).

In addition to metrical segmentation, there have been demonstrations of infant sensitivity to a range of non-lexical cues exploited by adults in some listening contexts. Infants as young as 10 months can use prosodic edge cues, in particular lengthening before and after phrase boundaries, to determine the location of word boundaries (Gout, Christophe, & Morgan, 2004): both 10- and 13-month old children showed a familiarity response to words such as *paper* over phonologically parallel sequences separated by a phrase boundary (e.g., *pay performs*). Decoarticulation, other allophonic cues, and phonotactics are all utilized by eight-month-olds (Johnson & Jusczyk, 2001; Mattys & Jusczyk, 2001a, 2001b), who also have a preference for words with onset consonants rather than word-initial vowels (Mattys & Jusczyk, 2001a).

An influential line of research considers infants' ability to extract statistical regularities from speech and use them to infer the location of word boundaries. Saffran et al. (1996) familiarized eight-month-olds to artificial languages composed of four non-words (*pabiku, golatu, tibudo, daropi*), finding that they subsequently listened longer to the part-words *tudaro* and *pigola* rather than the words themselves. Although the part-words occurred in the language stream, across the boundaries of the words themselves (e.g., *daropigolatu*), the infants showed sensitivity to the frequencies of co-occurrence of successive syllables, preferring the relatively infrequent sequences. Subsequent studies demonstrated not merely sensitivity to overall sequential frequencies, but to their transitional probabilities (i.e., frequency of syllable B following syllable A/frequency of syllable A).

The use of such statistical regularities is often contrasted with exploitation of other non-lexical cues, such as lexical stress (Johnson & Jusczyk, 2001). Given that non-lexical cues are essentially stochastic rather than deterministic in nature, however, the development of segmentation heuristics, whether framed as *statistical* or not, presumably relies on extraction of regularities from the signal. Thus, rather than using categorically distinct segmentation strategies, infants can be seen as extracting regularities from speech at different levels of abstraction. To exploit native stress patterns, English infants must classify syllables into strong and weak, and generalize that most words begin with a strong syllable. Phonotactic segmentation requires a generalization at the phonemic level. Allophonic cues such as decoarticulation require recognition of subphonemic patterns (i.e., the same phoneme realized differently in boundary and word-internal contexts). Most specifically, infants can utilize knowledge of individual words.

Thus, infants' exploitation of segmentation cues typically progresses from the more general to the more specific, while—at any particular stage of development—making use of whatever knowledge of contingent regularities they have thus far extracted.

1.7.3 Non-native segmentation

Visiting another country and hearing an unfamiliar language, who has not had the impression that native speakers are talking unusually quickly? Cutler (2012) calls this—often illusory—impression the "gabbling foreigner" effect, and it arises from our inability to process the unfamiliar stream of sounds into discrete words, in contrast with our native language.

First and second language acquisition appear similar with respect to implicit segmentation through word recognition, but somewhat distinct regarding explicit strategies. As for infants (Bortfeld et al., 2005), word knowledge appears to be exploited for L2 segmentation as soon as acquired. Thus, Hungarian native speakers, even at low levels of English L2 proficiency, used segmentation-by-lexical-subtraction when listening to English (White, Melhorn, & Mattys, 2010). Lexical segmentation effects, similar to native speakers, have been observed for Japanese and Spanish speakers of L2 English (Sanders, 2003); however, an electrophysiological signature of segmentation in native speakers, the word-onset-associated N100, was found to be absent even for competent Japanese speakers of L2 English.

Cutler and Otake (1994) reflected that fluent bilinguals may operate effectively in two languages while manifesting segmentation biases specific to one or other language. Thus, implicit segmentation may sometimes mask differences in explicit strategies. Weber and Cutler (2006) found that proficient German speakers of L2 English could use English phonotactics for segmentation, while showing some persistence of German-derived regularities. Similarly, competent Japanese and Spanish speakers of L2 English used stress for segmentation purposes where lexical information was not available, but their specific application of stress depended on native language characteristics (Sanders, Neville, & Woldorff, 2002). Similarly, Tremblay and Spinelli (2014) found that competent English speakers of L2 French exploited distributional information like native French speakers for distinguishing word-initial and liaison consonants, but also showed sensitivity to L1-relevant durational cues.

Thus, the use of non-lexical segmentation cues—stress, phonotactics, timing, allophony—all show influences of both L1 and L2 experience.

1.8 Summary and outlook

First and second language learners' segmentation behavior demonstrates the power of lexical knowledge, as described earlier for adult listeners. Where segmentation can be achieved implicitly through word recognition, there may be minimal use of non-lexical cues. However, explicit segmentation strategies, drawing on a range of generalizations about native language sound patterns, are critical in many speech contexts. Adult listeners faced with suboptimal listening conditions, from noise and degraded input to ambiguity and imperfect lexical knowledge, must call upon segmental and prosodic segmentation cues relevant to their native or non-native languages. Likewise, infants will exploit whatever regularities they can infer from their linguistic experience, starting with the most general, to facilitate identification of word edges and expand their vocabulary, thus gradually moving to an implicit mode of segmentation.

Neuroscientific methods offer the prospect of new perspectives on some long-running debates in psycholinguistics in general, and speech segmentation in particular. A fully developed theory of segmentation should specify the units of representation—phonemes, syllables, words, and so on—that are required to extract structure from the signal and should account for the integration and relative influence of signal-derived and knowledge-derived cues to that structure. Cognitive neuroscience has shown potential for insights, complementary to the well-established results of behavioral psycholinguistics, on both key questions. Firstly, electroencephalography (EEG) studies have measured ERPs in listeners which correspond to structure in auditory linguistic input, notably—with regard to word segmentation—the N100 (Sanders, Newport, & Neville, 2002). Secondly, many recent studies have demonstrated the entrainment of endogenous neural oscillations to the speech signal (see Peelle & Davis, 2012, for a review), an acoustically driven effect that is neither special to speech nor to humans (Steinschneider, Nourski, & Fishman, 2013), but nonetheless has generated much theoretical interest regarding speech perception. In particular, phase-resetting of theta oscillations (in the 4–8 Hz range) tracks the structure of the speech amplitude envelope, which has been taken as a rough proxy for syllable-level organization (but see Cummins, 2012, regarding the limitations of this parallel). Furthermore, some studies have shown an enhancement of theta-range phase-locking for intelligible compared to unintelligible speech (e.g., Peelle, Gross, & Davis, 2013), while Ding, Chatterjee, and Simon (2014) found entrainment in the delta range to be predictive of listeners' comprehension of the signal. Such interactions between acoustic and linguistic processing suggest the potential for neuroscience methods to further illuminate how knowledge-based prediction is integrated with the range of acoustic and sublexical segmentation cues described here.

More generally, segmentation research has yet to establish which cues apply regardless of specific linguistic background, information that may enhance understanding of language evolution and change. The role of broader cognitive processes in language processing will be informed by studies of individual differences in segmentation tasks. Finally, edging out of the laboratory to explore the dynamic negotiation of support for segmentation in natural conversation is a challenge yet to be fully confronted.

References

Albin, D. D., & Echols, C. H. (1996). Stressed and word-final syllables in infant-directed speech. *Infant Behavior and Development*, 19(4), 401–18.

Anderson, J., & Jones, C. (1974). Three theses concerning phonological representations. *Journal of Linguistics*, 10(1), 1.

Berkovits, R. (1991). The effect of speaking rate on evidence for utterance-final lengthening. *Phonetica*, 48(1), 57–66.

Bolinger, D. (1964). Intonation as a universal. In: *Proceedings of the 5th Congress of Phonetics, Cambridge 1962* (pp. 833–848).

Bortfeld, H., Morgan, J. L., Golinkoff, R. M., & Rathbun, K. (2005). Mommy and me: Familiar names help launch babies into speech-stream segmentation. *Psychological Science*, 16(4), 298–304.

Bowers, J. S., Davis, C. J., Mattys, S. L., Damian, M. F., & Hanley, D. (2009). The activation of embedded words in spoken word identification is robust but constrained: Evidence from the picture-word interference paradigm. *Journal of Experimental Psychology: Human Perception and Performance*, 35(5), 1585.

Brent, M. R. (1997). Toward a unified model of lexical acquisition and lexical access. *Journal of Psycholinguistic Research*, 26(3), 363–75.

Brent, M. R., & Siskind, J. M. (2001). The role of exposure to isolated words in early vocabulary development. *Cognition*, 81(2), B33–B44.

Cole, R. A., Jakimik, J., & Cooper, W. E. (1980). Segmenting speech into words. *The Journal of the Acoustical Society of America*, 67(4), 1323–32.

Content, A., Kearns, R. K., & Frauenfelder, U. H. (2001). Boundaries versus onsets in syllabic segmentation. *Journal of Memory and Language*, 45(2), 177–99.

Content, A., Meunier, C., Kearns, R. K., & Frauenfelder, U. H. (2001). Sequence detection in pseudowords in French: Where is the syllable effect? *Language and Cognitive Processes*, 16(5–6), 609–36.

Cristia, A. (2013). Input to language: The phonetics and perception of infant-directed speech. *Language and Linguistics Compass*, 7(3), 157–70.

Cummins, F. (2012). Oscillators and syllables: a cautionary note. *Frontiers in Psychology*, 3, 364.

Cunillera, T., Càmara, E., Laine, M., & Rodríguez-Fornells, A. (2010). Words as anchors: Known words facilitate statistical learning. *Experimental Psychology*, 57(2), 134–41.

Cunillera, T., Laine, M., & Rodríguez-Fornells, A. (2016). Headstart for speech segmentation: a neural signature for the anchor word effect. *Neuropsychologia*, 82, 189–99.

Cutler, A. (2012). *Native Listening: Language Experience and the Recognition of Spoken Words*. MIT Press, Cambridge, MA.

Cutler, A., & Butterfield, S. (1992). Rhythmic cues to speech segmentation: Evidence from juncture misperception. *Journal of Memory and Language*, 31(2), 218–36.

Cutler, A., & Carter, D. M. (1987). The predominance of strong initial syllables in the English vocabulary. *Computer Speech & Language*, 2(3), 133–42.

Cutler, A., & Foss, D. J. (1977). On the role of sentence stress in sentence processing. *Language and Speech*, 20(1), 1–10.

Cutler, A., McQueen, J. M., Norris, D., & Somejuan, A. (2001). The roll of the silly ball. In: Dupoux, E. (Ed.), *Language, Brain and Cognitive Development: Essays in honor of Jacques Mehler* (pp. 181–94). MIT Press, Cambridge, MA.

Cutler, A., Mehler, J., Norris, D., & Segui, J. (1986). The syllable's differing role in the segmentation of French and English. *Journal of Memory and Language, 25*(4), 385–400.

Cutler, A., & Norris, D. (1988). The role of strong syllables in segmentation for lexical access. *Journal of Experimental Psychology: Human Perception and Performance, 14*(1), 113.

Cutler, A., & Otake, T. (1994). Mora or phoneme? Further evidence for language-specific listening. *Journal of Memory and Language, 33*(6), 824.

Dahan, D., & Brent, M. R. (1999). On the discovery of novel wordlike units from utterances: an artificial-language study with implications for native-language acquisition. *Journal of Experimental Psychology: General, 128*(2), 165–85.

Davis, M. H., Marslen-Wilson, W. D., & Gaskell, M. G. (2002). Leading up the lexical garden path: Segmentation and ambiguity in spoken word recognition. *Journal of Experimental Psychology: Human Perception and Performance, 28*(1), 218–44.

Dilley, L., Shattuck-Hufnagel, S., & Ostendorf, M. (1996). Glottalization of word-initial vowels as a function of prosodic structure. *Journal of Phonetics, 24*(4), 423–44.

Ding, N., Chatterjee, M., & Simon, J. Z. (2014). Robust cortical entrainment to the speech envelope relies on the spectro-temporal fine structure. *NeuroImage, 88*, 41–6.

Dumay, N., Frauenfelder, U. H., & Content, A. (2002). The role of the syllable in lexical segmentation in French: word-spotting data. *Brain and Language, 81*(1–3), 144–61.

Dunst, C., Gorman, E., & Hamby, D. (2012). Preference for infant-directed speech in preverbal young children. *Center for Early Literacy Learning, 5*(1), 1–13.

Fear, B. D., Cutler, A., & Butterfield, S. (1995). The strong/weak syllable distinction in English. *The Journal of the Acoustical Society of America, 97*(3), 1893–904.

Fernald, A., & McRoberts, G. (1996). Prosodic bootstrapping: A critical analysis of the argument and the evidence. In: Morgan, J. L., & Demuth, K., *Signal to Syntax: Bootstrapping from Speech to Grammar in Early Acquisition*, (365–88). Psychology Press, Hove.

Fernald, A., Taeschner, T., Dunn, J., Papousek, M., de Boysson-Bardies, B., & Fukui, I. (1989). A cross-language study of prosodic modifications in mothers' and fathers' speech to preverbal infants. *Journal of Child Language, 16*(03), 477–501.

Fernandes, T., Ventura, P., & Kolinsky, R. (2007). Statistical information and coarticulation as cues to word boundaries: A matter of signal quality. *Perception & Psychophysics, 69*(6), 856–64.

Finn, A. S., & Hudson Kam, C. L. (2008). The curse of knowledge: First language knowledge impairs adult learners' use of novel statistics for word segmentation. *Cognition, 108*(2), 477–99.

Fisher, C., & Tokura, H. (1996). Acoustic cues to grammatical structure in infant-directed speech: cross-linguistic evidence. *Child Development, 67*(6), 3192–218.

Floccia, C., Keren-Portnoy, T., DePaolis, R., Duffy, H., Delle Luche, C., Durrant, S., ... Vihman, M. (2016). British English infants segment words only with exaggerated infant-directed speech stimuli. *Cognition, 148*, 1–9.

Fougeron, C., & Keating, P. A. (1997). Articulatory strengthening at edges of prosodic domains. *The Journal of the Acoustical Society of America, 101*(6), 3728–40.

Gout, A., Christophe, A., & Morgan, J. L. (2004). Phonological phrase boundaries constrain lexical access II. Infant data. *Journal of Memory and Language, 51*(4), 548–67.

Gow, D. W., & Gordon, P. C. (1995). Lexical and prelexical influences on word segmentation: Evidence from priming. *Journal of Experimental Psychology: Human Perception and Performance*, 21(2), 344–59.

Hamilton, A., Plunkett, K., & Schafer, G. (2000). Infant vocabulary development assessed with a British communicative development inventory. *Journal of Child Language*, 27(03), 689–705.

Hanulíková, A., McQueen, J. M., & Mitterer, H. (2010). Possible words and fixed stress in the segmentation of Slovak speech. *The Quarterly Journal of Experimental Psychology*, 63(3), 555–79.

Harrington, J., Watson, G., & Cooper, M. (1989). Word boundary detection in broad class and phoneme strings. *Computer Speech & Language*, 3(4), 367–82.

Huttenlocher, D. P., & Zue, V. W. (1983). Phonotactic and lexical constraints in speech recognition. In: *Proceedings of the Third AAAI Conference on Artificial Intelligence* (pp. 172–76). AAAI Press, Palo Alto, CA.

Johnson, E. K., & Jusczyk, P. W. (2001). Word segmentation by 8-month-olds: When speech cues count more than statistics. *Journal of Memory and Language*, 44(4), 548–67.

Junge, C., & Cutler, A. (2014). Early word recognition and later language skills. *Brain Sciences*, 4(4), 532–59.

Junge, C., Cutler, A., & Hagoort, P. (2012). Electrophysiological evidence of early word learning. *Neuropsychologia*, 50(14), 3702–12.

Jusczyk, P. W., Houston, D. M., & Newsome, M. (1999). The beginnings of word segmentation in English-learning infants. *Cognitive Psychology*, 39(3), 159–207.

Keating, P., Cho, T., Fougeron, C., & Hsu, C.-S. (2004). Domain-initial articulatory strengthening in four languages. In: Local, J., Ogden, R., & Temple, R. (Eds.), *Phonetic Interpretation: Papers in Laboratory Phonology VI* (pp. 143–61). Cambridge University Press, Cambridge.

Kim, D., Stephens, J. D., & Pitt, M. A. (2012). How does context play a part in splitting words apart? Production and perception of word boundaries in casual speech. *Journal of Memory and Language*, 66(4), 509–29.

Kooijman, V., Junge, C., Johnson, E. K., Hagoort, P., & Cutler, A. (2013). Predictive brain signals of linguistic development. *Frontiers in Psychology*, 4, 25.

Ladd, D. R. (2008). *Intonational Phonology*. Cambridge University Press, Cambridge.

Lindblom, B. (1990). Explaining phonetic variation: A sketch of the H&H theory. In: Hardcastle, W. J., & Marchal, A. (Eds.), *Speech Production and Speech Modelling* (pp. 403–39). Springer, Dordrecht.

Mattys, S. L. (2004). Stress versus coarticulation: Toward an integrated approach to explicit speech segmentation. *Journal of Experimental Psychology: Human Perception and Performance*, 30(2), 397.

Mattys, S. L., & Bortfeld, H. (2015). Speech segmentation. In: Gaskell, M. G., & Mirkovic, J. (Eds.), *Speech Perception and Spoken Word Recognition*. Taylor and Francis, Oxford.

Mattys, S. L., & Jusczyk, P. W. (2001a). Do infants segment words or recurring contiguous patterns? *Journal of Experimental Psychology: Human Perception and Performance*, 27(3), 644–55.

Mattys, S. L., & Jusczyk, P. W. (2001b). Phonotactic cues for segmentation of fluent speech by infants. *Cognition*, 78(2), 91–121.

Mattys, S. L., & Melhorn, J. F. (2005). How do syllables contribute to the perception of spoken English? Insight from the migration paradigm. *Language and Speech*, 48(2), 223–52.

Mattys, S. L., Melhorn, J. F., & White, L. (2007). Effects of syntactic expectations on speech segmentation. *Journal of Experimental Psychology: Human Perception and Performance*, 33(4), 960–77.

Mattys, S. L., White, L., & Melhorn, J. F. (2005). Integration of multiple speech segmentation cues: A hierarchical framework. *Journal of Experimental Psychology: General*, 134(4), 477–500.

McClelland, J. L., & Elman, J. L. (1986). The TRACE model of speech perception. *Cognitive Psychology*, 18(1), 1–86.

McQueen, J. M. (1998). Segmentation of continuous speech using phonotactics. *Journal of Memory and Language*, 39(1), 21–46.

McQueen, J. M. (2005). Speech perception. In: Lamberts, K., & Goldstone, R. (Eds.), *The Handbook of Cognition* (pp. 255–75). Sage Publications, London.

McQueen, J. M., Cutler, A., Briscoe, T., & Norris, D. (1995). Models of continuous speech recognition and the contents of the vocabulary. *Language and Cognitive Processes*, 10(3–4), 309–31.

McQueen, J. M., Norris, D., & Cutler, A. (1994). Competition in spoken word recognition: Spotting words in other words. *Journal of Experimental Psychology: Learning, Memory, and Cognition*, 20(3), 621.

Mehler, J., Dommergues, J. Y., Frauenfelder, U., & Segui, J. (1981). The syllable's role in speech segmentation. *Journal of Verbal Learning and Verbal Behavior*, 20(3), 298–305.

Morgan, J. L., & Demuth, K. (1996). *Signal to syntax: Bootstrapping from speech to grammar in early acquisition*. Psychology Press, Hove.

Mueller, J. L., Bahlmann, J., & Friederici, A. D. (2008). The role of pause cues in language learning: The emergence of event-related potentials related to sequence processing. *Journal of Cognitive Neuroscience*, 20(5), 892–905.

Nakatani, L. H., & O'Connor-Dukes, K. (1980). *Phonetic Parsing Cues for Word Perception* [unpublished manuscript]. Bell Laboratories, Murray Hill, NJ.

Nazzi, T., Iakimova, G., Bertoncini, J., Frédonie, S., & Alcantara, C. (2006). Early segmentation of fluent speech by infants acquiring French: Emerging evidence for crosslinguistic differences. *Journal of Memory and Language*, 54(3), 283–99.

Nazzi, T., Mersad, K., Sundara, M., Iakimova, G., & Polka, L. (2014). Early word segmentation in infants acquiring Parisian French: Task-dependent and dialect-specific aspects. *Journal of Child Language*, 41(03), 600–33.

Nelson, D. G. K., Hirsh-Pasek, K., Jusczyk, P. W., & Cassidy, K. W. (1989). How the prosodic cues in motherese might assist language learning. *Journal of Child Language*, 16(01), 55–68.

Nespor, M., Shukla, M., & Mehler, J. (2011). Stress-timed vs. syllable-timed languages. *The Blackwell Companion to Phonology*, 2, 1147–59.

Newman, R. S., Ratner, N. B., Jusczyk, A. M., Jusczyk, P. W., & Dow, K. A. (2006). Infants' early ability to segment the conversational speech signal predicts later language development: A retrospective analysis. *Developmental Psychology*, 42(4), 643.

Newman, R. S., Sawusch, J. R., & Wunnenberg, T. (2011). Cues and cue interactions in segmenting words in fluent speech. *Journal of Memory and Language*, 64(4), 460–76.

Norris, D. (1994). Shortlist: A connectionist model of continuous speech recognition. *Cognition*, 52(3), 189–234.

Norris, D., & Cutler, A. (1985). Juncture detection. *Linguistics*, 23(5), 689–706.

Norris, D., & McQueen, J. M. (2008). Shortlist B: A Bayesian model of continuous speech recognition. *Psychological Review*, 115(2), 357.

Norris, D., McQueen, J. M., & Cutler, A. (1995). Competition and segmentation in spoken-word recognition. *Journal of Experimental Psychology: Learning, Memory, and Cognition*, 21(5), 1209.

Norris, D., McQueen, J. M., Cutler, A., & Butterfield, S. (1997). The possible-word constraint in the segmentation of continuous speech. *Cognitive Psychology*, 34(3), 191–243.

Öhman, S. E. (1966). Coarticulation in VCV utterances: Spectrographic measurements. *The Journal of the Acoustical Society of America*, 39(1), 151–68.

Oller, D. K. (1973). The effect of position in utterance on speech segment duration in English. *The Journal of the Acoustical Society of America*, 54(5), 1235–47.

Ordin, M., Polyanskaya, L., Laka, I., & Nespor, M. (2017). Cross-linguistic differences in the use of durational cues for the segmentation of a novel language. *Memory & Cognition*, 45(5), 863–76.

Peelle, J. E., & Davis, M. H. (2012). Neural oscillations carry speech rhythm through to comprehension. *Frontiers in Psychology*, 3. https://doi.org/10.3389/fpsyg.2012.00320

Peelle, J. E., Gross, J., & Davis, M. H. (2013). Phase-locked responses to speech in human auditory cortex are enhanced during comprehension. *Cerebral Cortex*, 23(6), 1378–87.

Pelucchi, B., Hay, J. F., & Saffran, J. R. (2009). Statistical learning in a natural language by 8-month-old infants. *Child Development*, 80(3), 674–85.

Peña, M., Bonatti, L. L., Nespor, M., & Mehler, J. (2002). Signal-driven computations in speech processing. *Science*, 298(5593), 604–7.

Polka, L., & Sundara, M. (2012). Word segmentation in monolingual infants acquiring Canadian English and Canadian French: Native language, cross-dialect, and cross-language comparisons. *Infancy*, 17(2), 198–232.

Pompino-Marschall, B., & Żygis, M. (2010). Glottal marking of vowel-initial words in German. *ZAS Papers in Linguistics*, 52, 1–17.

Price, P. J., Ostendorf, M., Shattuck-Hufnagel, S., & Fong, C. (1991). The use of prosody in syntactic disambiguation. *The Journal of the Acoustical Society of America*, 90(6), 2956–70.

Reinisch, E., Jesse, A., & McQueen, J. M. (2011). Speaking rate affects the perception of duration as a suprasegmental lexical-stress cue. *Language and Speech*, 54(2), 147–65.

Rossi, S., Jürgenson, I. B., Hanulíková, A., Telkemeyer, S., Wartenburger, I., & Obrig, H. (2011). Implicit processing of phonotactic cues: Evidence from electrophysiological and vascular responses. *Journal of Cognitive Neuroscience*, 23(7), 1752–64.

Saffran, J. R., Newport, E. L., & Aslin, R. N. (1996). Word segmentation: The role of distributional cues. *Journal of Memory and Language*, 35(4), 606–21.

Salverda, A. P., Dahan, D., & McQueen, J. M. (2003). The role of prosodic boundaries in the resolution of lexical embedding in speech comprehension. *Cognition*, 90(1), 51–89.

Sanders, L. D. (2003). An ERP study of continuous speech processing: II. Segmentation, semantics, and syntax in non-native speakers. *Cognitive Brain Research*, 15(3), 214–27.

Sanders, L. D., Neville, H. J., & Woldorff, M. G. (2002). Speech segmentation by native and non-native speakers: The use of lexical, syntactic, and stress-pattern cues. *Journal of Speech, Language, and Hearing Research*, 45(3), 519–30.

Sanders, L. D., Newport, E. L., & Neville, H. J. (2002). Segmenting nonsense: an event-related potential index of perceived onsets in continuous speech. *Nature Neuroscience*, 5(7), 700–3.

Sebastián-Gallés, N., Dupoux, E., Segui, J., & Mehler, J. (1992). Contrasting syllabic effects in Catalan and Spanish. *Journal of Memory and Language*, 31(1), 18–32.

Shatzman, K. B., & McQueen, J. M. (2006). Segment duration as a cue to word boundaries in spoken-word recognition. *Perception & Psychophysics*, 68(1), 1–16.

Shillcock, R. C. (1990). Lexical hypotheses in continuous speech. In: Altmann, G. T. M. (Ed.), *Cognitive Models of Speech Processing: Psycholinguistic and Computational Perspectives* (pp. 24–49). MIT Press, Cambridge, MA.

Shukla, M., Nespor, M., & Mehler, J. (2007). An interaction between prosody and statistics in the segmentation of fluent speech. *Cognitive Psychology*, 54(1), 1–32.

Skoruppa, K., Nevins, A., Gillard, A., & Rosen, S. (2015). The role of vowel phonotactics in native speech segmentation. *Journal of Phonetics*, 49, 67–76.

Smiljanić, R., & Bradlow, A. R. (2008). Temporal organization of English clear and conversational speech. *The Journal of the Acoustical Society of America*, 124(5), 3171.

Smiljanić, R., & Bradlow, A. R. (2009). Speaking and hearing clearly: talker and listener factors in speaking style changes. *Language and Linguistics Compass*, 3(1), 236–64.

Spinelli, E., Grimault, N., Meunier, F., & Welby, P. (2010). An intonational cue to word segmentation in phonemically identical sequences. *Attention, Perception, & Psychophysics*, 72(3), 775–87.

Steinschneider, M., Nourski, K. V., & Fishman, Y. I. (2013). Representation of speech in human auditory cortex: Is it special? *Hearing Research*, 305, 57–73.

Suomi, K., McQueen, J. M., & Cutler, A. (1997). Vowel harmony and speech segmentation in Finnish. *Journal of Memory and Language*, 36(3), 422–44.

Tabossi, P., Collina, S., Mazzetti, M., & Zoppello, M. (2000). Syllables in the processing of spoken Italian. *Journal of Experimental Psychology: Human Perception and Performance*, 26(2), 758.

Thiessen, E. D., Hill, E. A., & Saffran, J. R. (2005). Infant-directed speech facilitates word segmentation. *Infancy*, 7(1), 53–71.

Tremblay, A., & Spinelli, E. (2014). English listeners' use of distributional and acoustic-phonetic cues to liaison in French: Evidence from eye movements. *Language and Speech*, 57(3), 310–37.

Turk, A. E., & White, L. (1999). Structural influences on accentual lengthening in English. *Journal of Phonetics*, 27(2), 171–206.

Tyler, M. D., & Cutler, A. (2009). Cross-language differences in cue use for speech segmentation. *The Journal of the Acoustical Society of America*, 126(1), 367–76.

Vroomen, J., & de Gelder, B. (1995). Metrical segmentation and lexical inhibition in spoken word recognition. *Journal of Experimental Psychology: Human Perception and Performance*, 21(1), 98–108.

Vroomen, J., & de Gelder, B. (1997). Activation of embedded words in spoken word recognition. *Journal of Experimental Psychology: Human Perception and Performance*, 23(3), 710.

Vroomen, J., Tuomainen, J., & de Gelder, B. (1998). The roles of word stress and vowel harmony in speech segmentation. *Journal of Memory and Language*, 38(2), 133–49.

Weber, A., & Cutler, A. (2006). First-language phonotactics in second-language listening. *The Journal of the Acoustical Society of America*, 119(1), 597–607.

White, L. (2014). Communicative function and prosodic form in speech timing. *Speech Communication*, 63–64, 38–54.

White, L., Mattys, S. L., Stefansdottir, L., & Jones, V. (2015). Beating the bounds: Localized timing cues to word segmentation. *The Journal of the Acoustical Society of America*, 138(2), 1214–220.

White, L., Mattys, S. L., & Wiget, L. (2012a). Language categorization by adults is based on sensitivity to durational cues, not rhythm class. *Journal of Memory and Language*, 66(4), 665–79.

White, L., Mattys, S. L., & Wiget, L. (2012b). Segmentation cues in conversational speech: robust semantics and fragile phonotactics. *Frontiers in Psychology*, 3, 375.

White, L., Melhorn, J. F., & Mattys, S. L. (2010). Segmentation by lexical subtraction in Hungarian speakers of second-language English. *The Quarterly Journal of Experimental Psychology*, 63(3), 544–54.

White, L., & Turk, A. E. (2010). English words on the Procrustean bed: Polysyllabic shortening reconsidered. *Journal of Phonetics*, 38(3), 459–71.

Wightman, C. W., Shattuck-Hufnagel, S., Ostendorf, M., & Price, P. J. (1992). Segmental durations in the vicinity of prosodic phrase boundaries. *The Journal of the Acoustical Society of America*, 91(3), 1707–17.

CHAPTER 2

SPOKEN WORD RECOGNITION

MICHAEL S. VITEVITCH, CYNTHIA S. Q. SIEW, AND NICHOL CASTRO

2.1 Searching the lexicon

COGNITIVE psychology is the branch of psychology that studies mental *representations* and the *processes* involved in the acquisition, long-term storage, retrieval, and other manipulations of those representations. With regards to human language, a fundamental representation is the word. The many words that one knows in a given language are stored in that part of long-term memory called the *mental lexicon*. To comprehend speech the listener must retrieve a word from the mental lexicon, a process known as spoken word recognition.

There is a long list of factors that are known to influence the speed and accuracy with which a spoken word is recognized. Over 35 years ago Cutler (1981) provided a list of several important factors that were known at the time to influence spoken word recognition including the frequency with which the word occurs in the language, the length of the word, the grammatical part of speech of the word, age of acquisition, concreteness, number of meanings, imagery, orthographic regularity, emotionality, isolation point, and so on. For a more recent description of several additional factors that affect spoken word recognition, see Vitevitch and Luce (2016). Rather than recapitulate these lists of factors that affect spoken word recognition in the present chapter—a list that would quickly become obsolete with every new publication—we will instead focus on a number of theoretical developments that have shaped research on spoken word recognition over the past few decades (in the remainder of section 2.1, as well as in sections 2.2 and 2.3), highlight a few emerging approaches that are guiding current research in spoken word recognition (in section 2.4), and point to a few challenges that researchers may wish to consider in the future (in section 2.5).

Just as cognitive psychologists used the digital computer as a metaphor to describe and model the representations and processes (e.g., inputs, outputs, stored representations, symbols being manipulated) that humans used in problem solving, thinking, and various aspects of memory, psycholinguists also used contemporary technologies to describe and model how words were organized in and retrieved from the mental lexicon. An early metaphor used to describe the mental lexicon likened a search through the mental lexicon to the way one searched for a book in a library with the card catalog system used at the time (Forster, 1978; for other metaphors of the mental lexicon, see Turvey & Moreno, 2006).

To find a book in a library using the card catalog system, a person would search through one of three sets of alphabetically ordered cards based on the subject, title, or author of the book. Once the card representing the desired book was found, the "address" indicating the location of the book in the library was given in the form of the Dewey Decimal Classification number (or some other classification system such as the Universal Decimal Classification system), enabling an individual to retrieve the desired book from the library.

To find a word in the mental lexicon, Forster (1978) suggested that one searched though one of three access files based on the orthographic, phonological, or semantic/syntactic characteristics of the word. Rather than being alphabetically ordered, each access file was ordered based on the frequency of occurrence of the words. More common words were stored at the top of the bins, thereby facilitating more rapid access compared to the less common words stored near the bottom of the bin. Once an individual found the access code representing the word that was read (i.e., via search through the orthographic bin), heard (i.e., via search through the phonological bin), or desired for production (i.e., via search through the semantic/syntactic bin), a "pointer"—akin to the library classification number—indicated the location of that word in the master lexicon, enabling an individual to retrieve the desired word from long-term memory.

What is interesting about the Forster (1978) model of the mental lexicon—aside from the historic artifact of the library card catalog—is that it marks a point in time when models of the mental lexicon attempted to account for more than one language-related process in a single model: speech production, speech perception, reading, and so on (see also MacKay, 1987). Shortly after this point in time researchers and the models they developed became increasingly specialized, tending to focus only on a single aspect of language.

On the one hand, findings showing that how a word is spelled can influence spoken word recognition (Ziegler & Ferrand, 1998) and that certain aspects of how a word is pronounced influences visual word recognition (Jared, 1997) seem to justify having a single model to account for both visual and spoken word recognition. On the other hand, the many differences that exist in the two input signals seems to justify the specialization found in models of visual word recognition (i.e., reading) and spoken word recognition. For example, in written language the words on a page can be reaccessed simply by moving one's eyes back to the word that might have been initially overlooked. However, in the case of speech the sound waves that carry spoken words to our ears quickly fade over time, making the spoken input much more transient than its written counterpart. That is, one cannot move one's ears back through time to rehear something that has already been said.

Another significant difference between written and spoken language is that blank spaces are used to neatly separate words from each other in written language. The equivalent of a blank space in spoken language might be silence. However, moments of silence often occur within spoken words rather than between words making silence or pauses a less reliable marker of where a spoken word begins or ends. This means that the process of recognizing a spoken word is tightly tied to the process of segmenting words from fluent speech.

Finally, letters in written words are the same—with the exception of capital letters in the first word of a sentence—regardless of where they appear in a word (another exception can be found in handwriting, a topic that is woefully understudied and, with the increased use of keyboard and speech recognition interfaces, may be a skill that is on the decline; e.g., Kiefer et al., 2015). However, phonemes, the basic sounds found in a given language, can be altered by the context in which they are found. That is, /t/ at the beginning of a word is slightly different than /t/ in the middle or at the end of a word. Early speech researchers initially assumed that a theory of phoneme perception would be sufficient to recognize spoken words (see Luce & Pisoni, 1987). However, this line of reasoning was turned on its head by the work of Marslen-Wilson and Welsh (1978) and the development of cohort theory (Marslen-Wilson, 1987), which suggested that speech input did not need to be mapped onto phonemes first, but could instead be directly mapped onto words.

2.2 Activation of multiple word forms

In addition to suggesting that acoustic-phonetic input mapped directly onto words rather than phonemes then words, the work of Marslen-Wilson and others highlighted a characteristic of spoken word recognition that continued to appear in subsequent models of the process, namely that multiple similar sounding words are activated in memory (see also Morton, 1969). In a series of shadowing studies in which participants repeated spoken stimuli as quickly as possible, Marslen-Wilson and Welsh (1978) demonstrated that phoneme perception was not sufficient for spoken word recognition. Rather, the acoustic-phonetic information at the beginning of a word activated all similar sounding words in the mental lexicon that were consistent with the input; one did not need to first perceive a string of phonemes, then assemble them into words. As additional input in the word is processed, that set of initially activated words, known as the *cohort*, dwindles as words that are inconsistent with the subsequent input drop out. For example, hearing the /k/ sound might activate words like *cake, café, cape, canary, carbohydrate*, and so on. With additional input, such as /kae/, words like *cake, canary,* and *carbohydrate* that are no longer consistent with the input will drop out of the cohort. Recognition of a word occurs when sufficient acoustic-phonetic information has whittled down the cohort to a single word.

In the original cohort theory, the number of similar sounding words initially activated in the cohort did not affect processing time or accuracy. That is, there was no cost in cognitive resources or consequences on outcome for the activation and processing of all of the words in the cohort. Rather, processing time was believed to depend solely on the point at which a word diverged from all other words in the lexicon. Words with "uniqueness points" that occurred later in the word—that is, much of the word must be heard before it could be uniquely distinguished from all other words in the lexicon—would be responded to more slowly than words with uniqueness points that occurred earlier in the word (allowing them to be readily distinguished from other words in the lexicon).

However, several pieces of evidence proved problematic for some of the claims of the early cohort theory. For example, Connine, Blasko, and Titone (1993) found in several experiments using cross-modal priming that non-words that deviated from a word by one linguistic feature still produced priming effects in the base word. That is, a non-word like *goronet*, which differs from the real word *coronet* by one phonetic feature in the onset of the word still produced priming effects for *coronet*, calling into question the earlier claims in cohort theory that the initial part of a word was important for activating words in the cohort.

The early claim in cohort theory that the uniqueness point of the word was the primary determinant of how quickly a spoken word was recognized was called into question by a computational analysis of the uniqueness points of words. Luce (1986) found that a high percentage of words, especially short words, have uniqueness points that occur after the end of the word. That is, there are many short words that completely overlap with the initial portions of longer words (e.g., *car* in *carbohydrate*), indicating that most short words do not, in fact, possess uniqueness points, and therefore cannot be distinguished from the longer words in which they are embedded. Given that short words tend to be the most frequently occurring words in the language, this analysis called into question the claim that the uniqueness point was the primary determinant of the speed with which spoken words are recognized. It is important to note, however, that more recent instantiations of the cohort theory have accounted for some of the issues that were problematic for earlier versions of the model (Gaskell & Marslen-Wilson, 1997).

Research on similarity neighborhoods further undermined the cost-free processing claims (i.e., the number of words in the cohort did not affect processing) of earlier versions of cohort theory and led to the development of the neighborhood activation model (Luce & Pisoni, 1998). As in cohort theory, the neighborhood activation model proposed that acoustic-phonetic input activated multiple similar sounding word forms in memory. However, the set of activated word forms in the *neighborhood* was not constrained by the sounds in the initial portion of the word as they were in the *cohort*. Furthermore, the words in the neighborhood would then compete among each other to be recognized. The competition would be determined in part by: (1) the frequency with which the target word occurs in the language, (2) the number of words in the neighborhood (referred to as *neighborhood density*), and (3) the mean of the frequency of occurrence of the neighbors (referred to as *neighborhood frequency*). These determinants could also be described in an adaptation of R. D. Luce's (1961) choice rule:

$$p(\text{target identification}) = \frac{p(\text{target word}) \times \text{frequency}}{\Sigma\left(p(\text{neighbor}_i) \times \text{frequency}\right)}$$

In a perceptual identification task (in which listeners must identify a word mixed with noise), a lexical decision task (in which listeners must indicate as quickly and as accurately as possible if they heard a real English word or a made-up nonsense word) and an auditory naming task (in which listeners must repeat as quickly and as accurately as possible the word that they heard presented without noise) Luce and Pisoni (1998) found that the neighborhood probability rule predicted the results they observed in their three experiments. That is, (1) words that occur frequently in the language were responded to more quickly and accurately than words that occur less frequently in the language, (2) words with few phonological neighbors were responded to more quickly and accurately than words with many phonological neighbors, and (3) words with less frequent neighbors were responded to more quickly and accurately than words with more frequent neighbors.

It is often erroneously assumed that the neighborhood activation model only makes predictions for short, monosyllabic words, and cannot account for longer words in English. This is not so. While it is true that many longer words do not have many (if any) phonological neighbors, empirical evidence demonstrates that longer words are responded to in the same way that short, monosyllabic words are responded to in English (Vitevitch, Stamer, & Sereno, 2008); words with few phonological neighbors are responded to more quickly and accurately than words with many phonological neighbors.

Furthermore, the influence of word frequency and the number of phonological neighbors on spoken word recognition is not limited to laboratory-based tasks used by psycholinguists. Influences of word frequency and the number of phonological neighbors have also been observed in the speech perception errors known as *slips of the ear* (Vitevitch, 2002). In a slip of the ear the speaker correctly produces an utterance, but the listener does not correctly perceive it (Bond, 1999). Slips of the ear differ from the speech production errors known as *slips of the tongue*, where the speaker does not correctly produce an utterance (see Vitevitch, 1997, and Vitevitch et al., 2015).

2.3 Connectionist approaches

The work examining the claims of cohort theory and the neighborhood activation model shifted the focus of spoken language researchers from a search process, as exemplified in the Forster (1978) model, to the activation of multiple word forms and competition among those forms as the processes that underlie spoken word recognition. Concurrently in other areas of cognitive psychology, a type of artificial neural network known as interactive-activation—sometimes called *connectionist*—models were (re-)emerging as a useful approach to capture various phenomena of interest to cognitive scientists; for a brief history of connectionism, see Medler (1998; also see relevant chapters in the present handbook). Whereas cognitive psychology has classically been defined as the study of mental *representations* and *processes*, connectionists were attempting to redefine the field by arguing that representations and processes were one and the same, with representations *emerging from* continual processing.

In the interactive-activation approach many simple processing units are connected via excitatory and inhibitory connections. Units that closely match the input are activated to a greater extent than units that do not match the input as much. Those strongly activated units will excite other units that they are connected to if they are consistent with the input but will inhibit those units that are inconsistent with the input. For example, if a /k/ is heard, the /k/ unit will be strongly activated. Units that are similar to /k/ will be less strongly activated, and units that are not similar to /k/ at all will be inhibited. Once a sufficient level of activation has crossed a certain threshold, the activated unit will influence other units it is connected to. Thus, various words that contain the /k/ sound will be strongly activated, words containing phonemes that are similar to /k/ will be less strongly activated, and those words without a /k/ will be inhibited. As more input is received these excitatory and inhibitory connections update their states again based on goodness of fit to the input. The continual updating of activations over time allows interactive-activation systems to entertain multiple hypotheses about the identity of the stimulus.

In an attempt to explore the computational and psychological adequacy of the interactive-activation approach to spoken language processing, McClelland and Elman (1986) introduced the TRACE model. *Computational adequacy* refers to the idea of a model that has been engineered to recognize speech. That is, a computer or other machine can successfully recognize human speech, but the means by which it does so may not necessarily resemble the means by which humans recognize speech. To help illustrate this point compare the jet propulsion methods engineered by humans to fly to the wing-flapping methods used by birds and insects to fly; humans, birds, and insects all fly, but do so via very different means. *Psychological adequacy* refers to the idea that a model accounts for certain aspects of psychological data. That is, the description of the process of speech perception is consistent with the present data that indicates how humans perceive speech. To continue with the flight analogy to illustrate psychological adequacy, one would build an ornithopter to better understand the principles involved in flight by living creatures.

The TRACE model consisted of many processing units organized into three layers: (1) units representing acoustic-phonetic-like features, (2) units representing phonemes, and (3) units representing words. The units in each layer would be excited or inhibited based on how well they continued to match the mock-speech input that unfolded over time. To capture the temporal nature of speech, McClelland and Elman (1986) divided time into discrete "slices," and the layers of processing units were replicated at each time slice in order to process the updated input. The pattern of activation that spanned the three processing layers over "time" was referred to as "the Trace," thereby providing the moniker for the model.

Because McClelland and Elman (1986) were exploring both the computational and psychological adequacy of interactive-activation principles as instantiated in the TRACE model, some of the engineering decisions they made to make the model actually work became easy targets for language researchers who were more concerned with the psychological adequacy of the model. This occurred despite McClelland and Elman (1986) acknowledging that they made several simplifying assumptions to examine how interactive-activation principles might process speech:

> *Obviously, then, TRACE II sidesteps many fundamental issues about speech. But it makes it much easier to see how the mechanism can account for a number of aspects of phoneme and word recognition. A number of further simplifying assumptions were made to facilitate examination of basic properties of the interactive activation processes taking place within the model.* (McClelland & Elman, 1986; p. 14)

One of the obvious characteristics of TRACE targeted by researchers more interested in the psychological adequacy of the model was the reduplication of processing units over time; from the psychological perspective this was computationally expensive and not physiologically supported either. Another common criticism raised against TRACE was that it did not account for one of the most widely studied phenomena in language processing, namely, the word frequency effect (e.g., Catlin, 1969). The *word frequency effect* refers to a finding observed in a variety of tasks in which words that occur often in the language are typically responded to more quickly and accurately than words that occur less often in the language. Subsequent experimental research and computer simulations examined three different means by which to modify TRACE in order to implement a mechanism to enable the model to account for the word frequency effect (Dahan, Magnuson, & Tanenhaus, 2001).

The characteristic of TRACE that perhaps sparked the most controversy was the highly interactive nature of the model. That is, processing at the phoneme layer could influence processing in the feature layer and in the word layer; processing at the word layer could feed back to the phoneme layer to revise processing in that layer; and so on. In response to the highly interactive model—a characteristic that some viewed as being so powerful that the model could do anything—Norris (1994) proposed the Shortlist model.

Like TRACE, Shortlist was also based on the principles of interactive-activation, would entertain in parallel multiple lexical hypotheses, and had prelexical and lexical processing units. The crucial difference was that Shortlist had a strictly feed-forward architecture that did not allow online feedback like TRACE did. Numerous simulations demonstrated that the strictly feed-forward architecture of Shortlist could account for many of the same phenomena as TRACE. Given the more simple assumptions in Shortlist (i.e., no feedback), the criterion of theoretical parsimony was invoked by some to favor Shortlist, igniting a long series of behavioral experiments by a number of researchers attempting to definitively identify whether processing was interactive or strictly feed-forward (see Norris, McQueen, & Cutler, 2000); this debate has still not been resolved unequivocally.

Recall that McClelland and Elman (1986) were simply exploring the principles and limits of the interactive-activation approach in a domain that has traditionally been thought of as too difficult for computers to master: spoken language processing. They did not set out to propose a psychologically adequate model of spoken word recognition like those proposed by Marslen-Wilson and others. Despite not being a "true" model of spoken word recognition, the TRACE model had a big impact on the field. Indeed, according to a Google Scholar search (February 24, 2017) the 1986 paper by McClelland and Elman has been cited well over 2,500 times—over 30 years after it was first published.

One of the important influences that the TRACE model had on the field of psycholinguistics was increasing interest in and highlighting the benefits of computational simulations to examine psycholinguistic phenomena (Lewandowsky, 1993). Indeed, several language scientists developed connectionist instantiations of their verbal models to better examine the principles and assumptions of those theories—consider the distributed model based on the principles of cohort theory (Gaskell & Marslen-Wilson, 1997) as well as the connectionist model, PARSYN, based in part on the principles of the neighborhood activation model (Auer & Luce, 2008). An easier to use version of TRACE has been made available to further encourage researchers to use computational simulations in addition to laboratory-based experiments to test their research questions (Strauss, Harris, & Magnuson, 2007).

2.4 Innovative Approaches to Spoken Word Recognition

Although current research on spoken word recognition continues to situate their findings in comparison to TRACE, Shortlist, cohort theory, and the neighborhood activation model, the field of spoken word recognition is also moving forward in a number of interesting directions. In the sections that follow we describe three avenues that language researchers are pursing. The work in each of these areas is still on-going and not as mature as the other models described to this point. Nevertheless, these approaches are intriguing, and force researchers to consider alternative explanations for their findings.

2.4.1 Bayesian models

Interest in Bayesian models of cognitive processes has increased across various domains of the cognitive sciences (Griffiths, Kemp, & Tenenbaum, 2008). The Bayesian approach as applied to spoken word recognition is exemplified in Shortlist B (Norris & McQueen, 2008), which retains many of the key theoretical assumptions of the original Shortlist model (Norris, 1994), but uses a Bayesian framework instead of an interactive-activation approach to implement those assumptions. Rather than model the process of spoken word recognition as a pattern of activations over time as in the original Shortlist model (dubbed Shortlist A—for Activation—by Norris & McQueen, 2008), Shortlist B works like other Bayesian classifiers. That is, the model assumes that human listeners employ an optimal decision-making process using likelihood and probability in the form of posterior probabilities to indicate which word will be recognized. This assumption is captured in equation (2) from Norris and McQueen (2008):

$$P(Word_i|Evidence) = \frac{P(Word_i|Evidence) \times P(Word_i)}{\sum_{j=1}^{j=n} P(Word_j|Evidence) \times P(Word_j)}$$

where n is the number of words in the lexicon. The adaptation of Bayes' theorem to word recognition provides the conditional probability of each word, given the available evidence for that word. Using Shortlist B, Norris & McQueen (2008) simulated several key findings involving the segmentation of words from fluent speech, the word frequency effect (which was missing from the original TRACE and Shortlist A models), and the effect of mispronunciations on lexical access.

2.4.2 Network science

Concurrent with the expansion of the Bayesian approach into various areas of cognition is the growth of network science, with network analyses being applied to various areas of the cognitive sciences (e.g., Bullmore & Sporns, 2009; Steyvers & Tenenbaum, 2005). *Network science* is an interdisciplinary field using principles from Mathematics, Sociology, Physics, Computer Science and a number of other fields to examine the structure of complex systems found in various domains (Barabási, 2009; Watts, 2004). The networks examined in the network science approach should not be confused with other types of networks that cognitive scientists have used in the past, such as artificial neural networks (Rosenblatt, 1958), networks of semantic memory (Quillian, 1967), or network-like models of language (e.g., *linguistic nections*: Lamb, 1970; *Node Structure Theory*: MacKay, 1987). In the network science approach, a complex system is modeled as a web-like structure called a *network*, which is comprised of *nodes* (also known as *vertices* in the network science literature) representing entities in the system, and connections between nodes called *links* (also known as *edges* in the network science literature) representing a relationship between entities.

Network analyses are often used to examine social groups, with nodes representing people in the group and links connecting people who are friends with each other (e.g., Lewis et al.,

2008). However, network analyses have also been applied fruitfully to a wide range of domains including language where nodes represent words in the mental lexicon and links are placed between words if the words are related phonologically (Vitevitch, 2008), orthographically (Kello & Beltz, 2009), or semantically (Hills et al., 2009; Solé, Corominas-Murtra, Valverde, & Steels; 2010; Steyvers & Tenenbaum, 2005).

One of the central tenets of network science is that the structure of a network can influence the processes that operate on that network (Strogatz, 2001). To illustrate this point, consider that two networks can have the same number of nodes and the same number of links, but the way in which the links connect the nodes in the two networks may differ. In one of those networks a search algorithm may perform with near optimal efficiency. However, in the other network with the same number of nodes and links, but with a slightly different structure, the same search algorithm may now perform quite inefficiently (Kleinberg, 2000). The emphasis in network science on the structure of the network (and how that structure can influence processing) contrasts with much of the research on spoken word recognition to this point where the emphasis has been on discovering the processes used to retrieve words from the lexicon with little attention paid to the way that words in the lexicon are organized and how that structure may influence lexical retrieval.

A number of studies have examined how the structure of a network at the micro-level, the meso-level, and the macro-level influence spoken word recognition (for reviews, see Vitevitch & Castro, 2015, and Vitevitch, Goldstein, Siew, & Castro, 2014). For example, at the micro-level (examining the characteristics of a word and its immediate neighbors) Chan and Vitevitch (2009) found that the phonological similarity *among* the neighbors of a word also influenced processing. That is, for words with the same number of phonological neighbors, words with neighbors that tend to be similar to each other (such as *cot, cut, coat, kit*, and *kite* in Fig. 2.1) are responded to more slowly than words with the same number of neighbors, but the neighbors tend to not be similar to each other. Importantly, computer simulations using jTRACE (Strauss et al., 2007) have demonstrated that earlier models of spoken word recognition cannot account for several findings regarding the influence of the lexical structure on processing (Chan & Vitevitch, 2009).

At the macro-level (looking at characteristics of the whole network) Siew and Vitevitch (2016) found that words in the giant component (the largest group of words connected to each other in some way in the lexical network) were responded to more slowly and less accurately than words with the same number of immediate neighbors but were located in smaller groups of interconnected words (so-called *lexical islands*). This result further suggests that the structure of the network may have important influences on processing, and that previous models of spoken word recognition that do not consider how words in the lexicon are organized may not be able to fully account for spoken word recognition.

To examine the meso-level of analysis (looking at characteristics of a network that measure more than the individual node and immediately surrounding nodes, but less than the entire network) Siew (2013) performed a community detection analysis of the phonological network. Communities are collections of nodes that tend to be more connected to other nodes in that community than to nodes in other communities or other parts of the network. When Siew examined the words that populated each community of tightly connected words, she found that the words in each community tended to contain certain sequences of phonological segments. For example, in the community that was home to words like *brink, drink*, and *wrinkle*, the phoneme sequences of /ŋk/, /Iŋ/, and/rI/ were found in many other words in

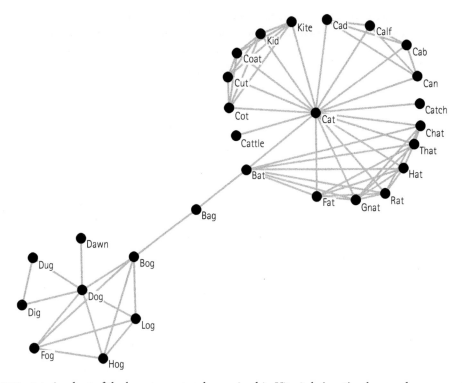

FIG. 2.1 A subset of the language network examined in Vitevitch (2008), where nodes represent words in the mental lexicon and links are placed between words if they are phonologically related. Two words were "phonologically related" if one word could be turned into the other word via the addition, substitution, or deletion of a single phoneme.

that community. Rather than relying on separate representations of phonological segments and sequences of segments that are distinct from lexical representations as has been proposed in certain models of spoken word recognition (e.g., Shortlist; Norris, 1994), Siew suggested that knowledge of phonotactic information (Vitevitch & Luce, 2016) may emerge solely from interconnected groups of lexical representations. The results of these and other studies examining the lexical network suggest that lexical processing may be influenced not only by the characteristics of individual words that language scientists typically examine—word frequency, word length, neighborhood density, phonotactic probability—but also by the structure that emerges from the similarity relations among words in the lexical network.

2.4.3 Discriminative learning

Recall that in the original cohort model, and in the neighborhood activation model as well, acoustic-phonetic input mapped directly on to words. In subsequent models of spoken word recognition, such as TRACE and Shortlist A, input mapped on to prelexical (e.g., features, phonemes, and so on) and then lexical representations. In the emerging Bayesian approach, exemplified in Shortlist B, prelexical and lexical representations still play a prominent role. Similarly, in research following the network approach (e.g., Vitevitch & Goldstein, 2014) words are still considered the fundamental representation of the mental lexicon. (See the community analysis in Siew (2013) for a way in which sublexical representations might be an emergent property of a lexical network.)

In a radical departure from previous approaches, Baayen, Shaoul, Willits, and Ramscar (2016) have proposed a model of spoken language comprehension that eschews representations for features, phonemes, and even words. This approach, relying on the principles of discriminative learning as captured in the Rescorla-Wagner equation (Rescorla & Wagner, 1972), takes as input triphones obtained from a window that moves across utterance-length stimuli. The use of triphones, which span multiple phonemes, enables the model to capture the changes that context imposes on phonemes via coarticulatory influences.

Triphones in the input layer map onto an output layer of *lexomes*, which Baayen et al. define as theoretical constructs that can be thought of as major lexical categories that are constantly being updated by continued experience and exposure to the world. They give the example of the lexome, WALK, which in the utterance *I'll walk home* refers to a method of moving from point A to point B, but in the utterance *I'll walk the dog* refers to the routine related to the bodily functions of a domesticated animal. The connections between triphones and lexomes are weighted and continually updated via the error-driven learning algorithm of Rescorla and Wagner (1972) rather than alternative learning algorithms commonly seen in connectionist networks, such as backpropagation.

One characteristic that distinguishes this approach from previous models of spoken word recognition is that representations for words do not exist. Rejecting the assumption that words are stored in memory means that the separate processes of word-learning and word-segmentation may not be required, nor does one need to quibble about the definition of what constitutes a word or build words into the model a priori. Rather, speakers acquire a *lexical system* in which the meaning of a lexome is "defined" in contrast to other lexomes, and by a richly structured world. The meaning of a lexome is further refined by continued exposure, capturing the gradual acquisition of meaning that is often missing from other models where the word is either known (and represented) or not known (and not represented) in the system. Instead of creating an internal symbolic system representing the world as many previous models have, this approach suggests that the language system simply decodes the information contained in the signal.

This approach also differs from previous models of spoken word recognition in that learning is an inherent part of the model, not simply assumed to have happened, or relegated to a separate learning module or process. This continual learning may enable this model to adapt to speakers with various accents, as well as handle mispronunciations and other forms of variability that characterize human speech but prove to be challenging to other models of spoken word recognition. With its questioning of several fundamental assumptions of word recognition this approach warrants further attention to determine its limits.

2.5 Challenges we still face

The innovative approaches to spoken word recognition described in section 2.4 are still emerging and in their infancy. Much work remains to thoroughly test each of these approaches to find their limits, and to clarify what advantages each approach has over the other approaches and over earlier approaches to modeling spoken word recognition. There are many well-studied factors that influence how quickly and accurately a spoken word is recognized that any model of spoken word recognition will need to account for. Cutler (1981) provided an extensive list of factors that were known to affect the retrieval of a word, and this list has only grown since then (e.g., Vitevitch & Luce, 2016). In addition to accounting for those well-known influences on spoken word recognition, a model will need to be able to address several additional challenges that have emerged over the years.

In reading the scientific literature on spoken word recognition one might be struck by the overwhelming number of studies in which the language being examined is English. One could argue that English can be viewed as a model language, akin to a model organism in biology (Vitevitch, Chan, & Goldstein, 2014). That is, resources characterizing various aspects of English as well as speakers of English to use in laboratory-based experiments are numerous and readily available. Unfortunately, there are several characteristics of English that may limit how broadly studies using this language can generalize to the other 6,000 or so languages spoken on the planet.

One obvious difference between English and many languages spoken on the planet is that English does not use tones to distinguish among words, as do languages like Mandarin, Cantonese, and Vietnamese. It is unclear how current and emerging models of spoken word recognition might address how lexical tone is processed, although some proposals for modification have been made (Ye & Connine, 1999).

Another obvious difference between English and other languages spoken on the planet is its limited use of morphology. Other languages make much more use of morphology to form words. Furthermore, in languages like Arabic a very different morphological procedure operates to form words. Attention to such languages is increasing (e.g., Aljasser & Vitevitch, 2018; Boudelaa & Marslen-Wilson, 2015), but much more work is required before we have a clear understanding of how spoken words are recognized in more morphologically rich languages.

Even languages not so different from English are posing interesting challenges to our current understanding of the process of spoken word recognition. For example, some evidence suggests that an increasing number of phonologically similar words produces increased competition among word forms in English (Luce & Pisoni, 1998), but in the case of Spanish an increasing number of phonologically similar words appears to facilitate processing (Vitevitch & Rodríguez, 2005). Such findings raise interesting questions about how a bilingual speaker who knows both English and Spanish might recognize spoken words (for an example of a bilingual model of language processing, see van Heuven & Dijkstra, 2010).

One does not even need to consider other languages to find challenges that need to be addressed in models of spoken word recognition. Within a given language there is significant variability among speakers due to differences in gender, regional dialect, foreign accent, speech disorder, level of fatigue, and so on. Most of the models described here consisted of abstract prelexical and lexical representations. It is unclear how such models can accommodate the variability that naturally exists among speakers. However, Norris and McQueen (2008) provide evidence that the Bayesian approach might be able to accommodate some forms of variability in the speech signal. Similarly, models based purely on exemplars rather than abstract representations might also accommodate such variability (Goldinger, 1998);

see McLennan and Luce (2005) for another framework that might accommodate certain forms of variability in spoken word recognition.

Another challenge to models of spoken word recognition is integrating them with other language-related cognitive processes. For example, there is evidence indicating that how a word is spelled can influence spoken word recognition (Ziegler & Ferrand, 1998) and that certain aspects of how a word is pronounced influences visual word recognition (Jared, Ashby, Agauas, & Levy, 2016), which suggests that visual word recognition may not be as distinct from spoken word recognition as the models of each process might imply. Similarly, the process of speech production may also be influenced by spoken word recognition, and vice versa as suggested by Roelofs, Özdemir, & Levelt (2007).

In order to gain new insights about the processes involved in spoken word recognition, language researchers may need to consider what auditory illusions like the speech-to-song illusion (Deutsch, Henthorn, & Lapidis, 2011) and other language-related phenomena might reveal about language processing. Language researchers may also need to venture out of the laboratory to mine new sources of naturally occurring data, such as collections of speech recognition errors known as slips of the ear (Vitevitch et al., 2015; see also Marxer, Barker, Cooke, & Garcia Lecumberri, 2016). Another fruitful direction for those interested in how humans recognize speech might be increased interaction with those who develop computer-based systems to recognize speech (Scharenborg, Norris, ten Bosch, & McQueen, 2005).

Perhaps the biggest challenge facing not just models of spoken word recognition, but all models of cognitive processing and representation is the integration of cognitive models with models of language processing based on electrophysiological and neuroimaging data (e.g., Stowe, Haverkort, & Zwarts, 2005). Said another way, how does one best map the mind onto the brain? One strategy is to find a "common language" that can be used for both cognitive and neural models of language processing. Poeppel and Embick (2005) suggested that a computational framework might be used to bridge the mind and the brain. Another alternative for a "common language" might be network science given the use of this approach to understand language processing (Vitevitch, Chan, & Roodenrys, 2012) and the structure and function of the brain (Bassett & Siebenhuhner, 2013). The current state of the field indicates that our knowledge about how humans recognize spoken words has grown considerably. However, there remains much more to be learned.

References

Aljasser, F. & Vitevitch, M. S. (2018). A web-based interface to calculate phonotactic probability for words and nonwords in Modern Standard Arabic. *Behavior Research Methods*, 50(1), 313–22. doi: 10.3758/s13428-017-0872-z.

Auer, E. T., Jr., & Luce, P. A. (2008). Probabilistic phonotactics in spoken word recognition. In: Pisoni, D. B., Remez, R. E. (Eds.), *The Handbook of Speech Perception* (pp. 610–30). Blackwell Publishing, Malden.

Baayen, R. H., Shaoul, C., Willits, J., & Ramscar, M. (2016). Comprehension without segmentation: A proof of concept with naïve discriminative learning. *Language, Cognition, and Neuroscience*, 31(1), 106–28.

Barabási, A. L. (2009). Scale-free networks: A decade and beyond. *Science*, 325, 412–13.

Bassett, D. S., & Siebenhuhner, F. (2013). Multiscale network organization in the human brain. In: Pesenson, M. M., & Schuster, H. G. (Eds.), *Multiscale Analysis and Nonlinear Dynamics: From Genes to the Brain* (pp. 179–204). Wiley, Berlin.

Bond, Z. S. (1999). *Slips of the Ear: Errors in the Perception of Casual Conversation*. Academic Press, New York.

Boudelaa, S., & Marslen-Wilson, W. D. (2015). Structure, form, and meaning in the mental lexicon: Evidence from Arabic. *Language, Cognition, and Neuroscience*, 30(8), 955–92.

Bullmore, E., & Sporns, O. (2009). Complex brain networks: Graph theoretical analysis of structural and functional systems. *Nature Reviews Neuroscience*, 10, 186–98.

Catlin, J. (1969). On the word frequency effect. *Psychological Review*, 76, 504–6.

Chan, K. Y. & Vitevitch, M. S. (2009). The influence of the phonological neighborhood clustering-coefficient on spoken word recognition. *Journal of Experimental Psychology: Human Perception and Performance*, 35, 1934–49.

Connine, C. M., Blasko, D. G., & Titone, D. (1993). Do the beginnings of spoken words have a special status in auditory word recognition? *Journal of Memory and Language*, 32, 193–210.

Cutler, A. (1981). Making up materials is a confounded nuisance, or: Will we be able to run any psycholinguistic experiments at all in 1990? *Cognition*, 10, 65–70.

Dahan, D., Magnuson, J. S., & Tanenhaus, M. K. (2001). Time course of frequency effects in spoken-word recognition: Evidence from eye movements. *Cognitive Psychology*, 42, 317–367.

Deutsch, D., Henthorn, T., & Lapidis, R. (2011). Illusory transformation from speech to song. *Journal of the Acoustical Society of America*, 129, 2245–52.

Forster, K. I. (1978). Accessing the mental lexicon. In: Walker, E. (Ed.), *Explorations in the Biology of Language*. Bradford, Montgomery, VT.

Gaskell, M. G., & Marslen-Wilson, W. D. (1997). Integrating form and meaning: A distributed model of speech perception. *Language and Cognitive Processes*, 12, 613–56.

Goldinger, S. D. (1998). Echoes of echoes? An episodic theory of lexical access. *Psychological Review*, 105, 251–79.

Griffiths, T. L., Kemp, C., & Tenenbaum, J. B. (2008). Bayesian models of cognition. In: Sun, R. (Ed.), *The Cambridge Handbook of Computational Psychology* (pp. 59–100). Cambridge University Press, Cambridge.

Hills, T. T., Maouene, M., Maouene, J., Sheya, A., & Smith, L. (2009). Longitudinal analysis of early semantic networks: Preferential attachment or preferential acquisition? *Psychological Science*, 20, 729–39.

Jared, D. (1997). Spelling-sound consistency affects the naming of high-frequency words. *Journal of Memory and Language*, 36(4), 505–29.

Jared, D., Ashby, J., Agauas, S. J., & Levy, B. A. (2016). Phonological activation of word meanings in Grade 5 readers. *Journal of Experimental Psychology: Learning, Memory, and Cognition*, 42, 524–41.

Kello, C. T. & Beltz, B. C. (2009). Scale-free networks in phonological and orthographic wordform lexicons. In: Chitoran, I., Coupé, C., Marsico, E., & Pellegrino, F. (Eds.), *Approaches to Phonological Complexity* (pp. 171–92). Mouton de Gruyter, Berlin.

Kiefer, M., Schuler, S., Mayer, C., Trumpp, N. M., Hille, K. & Sachse, S. (2015). Handwriting or typewriting? the influence of pen- or keyboard-based writing training on reading and writing performance in preschool children. *Advances in Cognitive Psychology*, 11, 136–46.

Kleinberg, J. M. (2000). Navigation in a small world. *Nature*, 406, 845.

Lamb, S. (1970). Linguistic and cognitive networks. In: Garvin, P. (Ed.), *Cognition: A Multiple View* (pp. 195–222). Spartan Books, New York, NY.

Lewandowsky, S. (1993). The rewards and hazards of computer simulations. *Psychological Science, 4*, 236–43.

Lewis, K., Kaufman, J., Gonzalez, M., Wimmer, A., & Christakis, N. (2008). Tastes, ties, and time: A new social network dataset using Facebook.com. *Social Networks, 30*, 330–42.

Luce, P. A. (1986). A computational analysis of uniqueness points in auditory word recognition. *Perception & Psychophysics, 39*(3), 155–8.

Luce, P. A., & Pisoni, D. B. (1987). Speech perception: New directions in research, theory, and applications. In: Winitz, H. (Ed.), *Human Communication and Its Disorders, A Review, Vol. 1* (pp. 1–87). Ablex, Westport, CT.

Luce, P. A., & Pisoni, D. B. (1998). Recognizing spoken words: The neighborhood activation model. *Ear & Hearing, 19*, 1–36.

Luce, R. D. (1961). A choice theory analysis of similarity judgments. *Psychometrika, 26*, 151–63.

MacKay, D. G. (1987). *The Organization of Perception and Action: A Theory for Language and Other Cognitive Skills*. Springer-Verlag, New York, NY.

Marslen-Wilson, W. D. (1987). Functional parallelism in spoken word-recognition. *Cognition, 25*(1), 71–102.

Marslen-Wilson, W. D., & Welsh, A. (1978). Processing interactions and lexical access during word recognition in continuous speech. *Cognitive Psychology, 10*(1), 26–63.

Marxer, R., Barker, J., Cooke, M., & Garcia Lecumberri, M. L. (2016) A corpus of noise-induced word mispronunciations for English. *Journal of the Acoustical Society of America, 150*, EL458.

McClelland, J. L., & Elman, J. L. (1986). The TRACE model of speech perception. *Cognitive Psychology, 18*(1), 1–86.

McLennan, C. T., & Luce, P. A. (2005). Examining the time course of indexical specificity effects in spoken word recognition. *Journal of Experimental Psychology: Learning, Memory, and Cognition, 31*, 306–21.

Medler, D. A. (1998). A brief history of connectionism. *Neural Computing Surveys, 1*(2), 18–72.

Morton, J. (1969). Interaction of information in word recognition. *Psychological Review, 76*, 165–78.

Norris, D. (1994). Shortlist: A Connectionist model of continuous speech recognition. *Cognition, 52*, 189–234.

Norris, D., & McQueen, J. M. (2008). Shortlist B: A Bayesian model of continuous speech recognition. *Psychological Review, 115*, 357–95.

Norris, D., McQueen, J. M., & Cutler, A. (2000). Merging information in speech recognition: Feedback is never necessary. *Behavioural and Brain Sciences, 23*, 299–370.

Poeppel, D., & Embick, D. (2005). Defining the relation between linguistics and neuroscience. In: Cutler, A. (Ed.), *Twenty-first Century Psycholinguistics: Four Cornerstones*. Lawrence Erlbaum, Mahwah, NJ.

Quillian, R. (1967). Word concepts: A theory and simulation of some basic semantic capabilities. *Behavioral Science, 12*, 410–30.

Rescorla, R. A., & Wagner, A. R. (1972). A theory of pavlovian conditioning: Variations in the effectiveness of reinforcement and nonreinforcement. In: Black, A. H., & Prokasy, W. F. (Eds.), *Classical Conditioning II: Current Research and Theory* (pp. 64–99). Appleton Century Crofts, New York, NY.

Roelofs, A., Özdemir, R., & Levelt, W. J. M. (2007). Influences of spoken word planning on speech recognition. *Journal of Experimental Psychology: Learning, Memory, and Cognition, 33*, 900–13.

Rosenblatt, F. (1958). The perceptron: A probabilistic model for information storage and organization in the brain. *Psychological Review*, 65, 386–408.

Scharenborg, O., Norris, D., ten Bosch, L., & McQueen, J. M. (2005). How should a speech recognizer work? *Cognitive Science*, 29, 867–918.

Siew, C. S. Q. (2013). Community structure in the phonological network. *Frontiers in Psychology*, 4, 00553.

Siew, C. S. Q., & Vitevitch, M. S. (2016). Spoken word recognition and serial recall of words from components in the phonological network. *Journal of Experimental Psychology: Learning, Memory, and Cognition*, 42, 394–410.

Solé, R. V., Corominas-Murtra, B., Valverde, S., & Steels, L. (2010). Language networks: Their structure, function, and evolution. *Complexity*, 15, 20–26.

Steyvers, M., & Tenenbaum, J. B. (2005). The large-scale structure of semantic networks: Statistical analyses and a model of semantic growth. *Cognitive Science*, 29, 41–78.

Stowe, L. A., Haverkort, M., & Zwarts, F. (2005). Rethinking the neurological basis of language. *Lingua*, 115, 997–1042.

Strauss, T. J., Harris, H. D., & Magnuson, J. S. (2007). jTRACE: A reimplementation and extension of the TRACE model of speech perception and spoken word recognition. *Behavior Research Methods*, 39, 19–30.

Strogatz, S. H. (2001). Exploring complex networks. *Nature*, 410, 268–76.

Turvey, M. T., & Moreno, M. (2006). Physical metaphors for the mental lexicon. *The Mental Lexicon*, 1, 7–33.

van Heuven, W. J. B., & Dijkstra, T. (2010). Language comprehension in the bilingual brain: fMRI and ERP support for psycholinguistic models. *Brain Research Reviews*, 64, 104–22.

Vitevitch, M. S. (1997). The neighborhood characteristics of malapropisms. *Language and Speech*, 40, 211–28.

Vitevitch, M. S. (2002). Naturalistic and experimental analyses of word frequency and neighborhood density effects in slips of the ear. *Language and Speech*, 45, 407–34.

Vitevitch, M. S. (2008). What can graph theory tell us about word learning and lexical retrieval? *Journal of Speech, Language and Hearing Research*, 51, 408–22.

Vitevitch, M. S. & Castro, N. (2015). Using network science in the language sciences and clinic. *International Journal of Speech-Language Pathology*, 17, 13–25.

Vitevitch, M. S., Chan, K. Y., & Goldstein, R (2014). Using English as a "model language" to understand language processing. In: Miller, N., & Lowit, A. (Eds.), *Motor Speech Disorders: A Cross-Language Perspective* (pp. 58–73). Multilingual Matters, Bristol.

Vitevitch, M. S., Chan, K. Y., & Roodenrys, S. (2012). Complex network structure influences processing in long-term and short-term memory. *Journal of Memory and Language*, 67, 30–44.

Vitevitch, M. S., & Goldstein, R. (2014). Keywords in the mental lexicon. *Journal of Memory and Language*, 73, 131–47.

Vitevitch, M. S., Goldstein, R., Siew, C. S. Q., & Castro, N. (2014). Using complex networks to understand the mental lexicon. *Yearbook of the Poznań Linguistic Meeting*, 1, 119–38.

Vitevitch, M. S., & Luce, P. A. (2016). Phonological neighborhood effects in spoken word perception and production. *Annual Review of Linguistics*, 2, 75–94.

Vitevitch, M. S., & Rodríguez, E. (2005). Neighborhood density effects in spoken word recognition in Spanish. *Journal of Multilingual Communication Disorders*, 3, 64–73.

Vitevitch, M. S., Siew, C. S. Q., Castro, N., Goldstein, R., Gharst, J. A., Kumar, J. J., & Boos, E. B. (2015). Speech error and tip of the tongue diary for mobile devices. *Frontiers in Psychology*, 6, 1190.

Vitevitch, M. S., Stamer, M. K., & Sereno, J. A. (2008). Word length and lexical competition: Longer is the same as shorter. *Language & Speech*, 51, 361–83.

Watts, D. J. (2004). The" new" science of networks. *Annual Review of Sociology*, 30, 243–70.

Ye, Y., & Connine, C. M. (1999). Processing spoken Chinese: The role of tone information. *Language and Cognitive Processes*, 14, 609–30.

Ziegler, J., & Ferrand, L. (1998). Orthography shapes the perception of speech: The consistency effect in auditory word recognition. *Psychonomic Bulletin & Review*, 5(4), 683–9.

CHAPTER 3

VISUAL WORD RECOGNITION

KATHLEEN RASTLE

3.1 INTRODUCTION

Because the emissary, his mouth (being) heavy, was not able to repeat (it), The lord of Kulaba patted clay and wrote the message like (on a present-day) tablet—Formerly, the writing of messages on clay was not established—Now, with Utu's bringing forth the day, verily this was so.—from Enmerkar and the Lord of Arrata, cited in Schmandt-Besserat, 1996, p. 2

THIS Sumerian epic provides the oldest known account of the development of a system for written language (Schmandt-Besserat, 1996). It tells the story of an emissary sent by Enmerkar, lord of Kulaba, to negotiate the purchase of timber, metals, and precious stones from the lord of a distant land. Following many rounds of difficult negotiations, a day came that the emissary was unable to commit Enmerkar's full instructions to memory. Enmerkar dealt remarkably effectively with this problem: He invented a system for writing language, which he used to inscribe his instructions onto a clay tablet. On that day, Enmerkar perhaps unwittingly also provided the foundation for what was to become a cognitive skill central to life in modern society: reading.

Though the contribution of Enmerkar himself is dubious, the Sumerians of Mesopotamia are generally credited with the invention of writing, and by implication reading, at the end of the fourth millennium BC. Thus, unlike our inborn capacity to use spoken language, reading constitutes a cultural invention and an astonishing form of expertise. Understanding the mechanisms underlying skilled reading is at the center of modern psycholinguistics and has been a topic of considerable interest since the beginnings of psychology as a scientific discipline (e.g., Cattell, 1886; Huey, 1908). This chapter considers the foundation of the skilled reading process—how we recognize visually presented single words and compute their meanings.

3.2 ORTHOGRAPHIC REPRESENTATIONS

Our discussion begins with a term used in early psycholinguistic theories to denote a mental dictionary thought to package together all of the orthographic (spelling), semantic (meaning), and phonological (pronunciation) information about known words: the mental lexicon. This term still surfaces in the literature on the recognition of printed words, and it is not particularly out of the ordinary to see references to "lexical access" or "access to the mental lexicon" from the visual stimulus. However, there is now wide agreement that information about the orthographic forms of words is stored separately from information about their spoken realizations and meanings (see e.g., Allport & Funnell, 1981; Borowsky & Besner, 2006; Coltheart, 2004; Coltheart et al., 2001; Dehaene & Cohen, 2011; Fischer-Baum et al., 2017; Forster & Davis, 1984; Grainger & Jacobs, 1996; Morton, 1979; Morton & Patterson, 1980). Implemented models of skilled reading such as the DRC model (Coltheart et al., 2001), the CDP+ model (Perry et al., 2007, 2010), the SOLAR model (Davis, 1999, 2010), the MROM model (Grainger & Jacobs, 1996), and the distributed-connectionist models (Harm & Seidenberg, 2004; Plaut, McClelland, Seidenberg, & Patterson, 1996) thus postulate bodies of orthographic knowledge, which are distinct from bodies of semantic knowledge and bodies of phonological knowledge. The process of visual word recognition requires access to these orthographic representations.

3.2.1 Orthographic input coding: Letters and letter positions

The earliest theories of visual word recognition (Cattell, 1886) posited that words are recognized not in terms of their component letters but as whole units on the basis of their shapes. Though this hypothesis continues to engender fascination (e.g., Pelli, Farell, & Moore, 2003; Perea & Rosa, 2002; Saenger, 1997), modern theories suggest that word recognition is based on the analysis of letters. There is a broad consensus, based on evidence from behavioral (see e.g., Bowers, 2000), neuroscientific (Dehaene & Cohen, 2011; Rothlein & Rapp, 2014) and neuropsychological (Coltheart, 1981; see also Rapp, Folk, & Tainturier, 2001) studies, that these representations are *abstract letter identities*. They are abstract in the sense that they are independent of surface properties such as case, position, font, color, retinal location, or size. Thus, for example, the stimuli in Figure 3.1 all map onto the same abstract letter identity. Mapping the visual stimulus onto abstract letter representations enables skilled readers to recognize words rapidly, even though they may appear in surface contexts (e.g., handwriting, typeface) with which the reader has no experience.

Representations of orthographic form need to encode more than abstract letter identities, however. They also need to encode information about the position of the letters in the stimulus. Otherwise, readers would not be able to detect the difference between anagram stimuli like TOP, POT, and OPT, which share all of the same letters. Implemented models solve this problem through the use of slot-based coding. In this scheme, there are slots for each letter position in a stimulus, and each of these slots is filled with a separate set of letter units (one unit for each letter of the alphabet; e.g., Coltheart et al., 2001). For example, the word CLAM would be represented by selecting C in the first slot, L in the second slot, A in the third slot, and M in the fourth slot ($C_1L_2A_3M_4$). Sometimes the slots are further structured into onset

FIG. 3.1 An example of visual stimuli thought to map onto a single abstract letter identity.

and rime units in which vowels are aligned in each syllable (e.g., Harm & Seidenberg, 2004; Perry et al., 2007, 2010).

The past decade has seen substantial evidence of the inadequacy of these schemes, but also intense debate over the true nature of letter position coding. The general problem is that research on a range of Indo-European languages now clearly shows that stimuli that are perceptually very similar may be represented by very different slot-based codes (Davis, 1999, 2010). Consider the text presented next, which was taken from an email message circulated globally that purported to address the mechanisms underlying letter position coding.

> Aoccdrnig to rseearch at Cmabrigde Uinervtisy, it deosn't mttaer in waht oredr the ltteers in a wrod are, the olny iprmoetnt tihng is taht the frist and lsat ltteer be at the rghit pclae.

The reason why we can read this passage so easily is that stimuli with letter transpositions (e.g., OLNY) are perceived as being similar to their base words. Empirical evidence for this claim arises from experiments demonstrating that the recognition of a target stimulus (e.g., SERVICE) is faster when it is preceded by a masked transposed-letter prime (e.g., sevrice) than when it is preceded by a masked substitution prime (e.g., sedlice; Schoonbaert & Grainger, 2004; see Adelman et al., 2014 for large-scale study of these effects). This result is important because according to slot-based coding, these two types of prime should have equivalent perceptual overlap with the target. More recent results suggest that transposed letter effects extend to even more extreme modifications; for example, the recognition of SANDWICH is speeded by the prior masked presentation of prime *snawdcih* relative to the prime *skuvgpah* (Guerrera & Forster, 2008).

These results have led to new theoretical accounts of letter position coding that postulate a degree of sloppiness or uncertainty, such as the spatial coding model (Davis, 2010), the overlap model (Gomez et al., 2008), and the open bigram model (Whitney, 2001; see Grainger et al., 2016 for review). However, recent research has also highlighted that effects of position uncertainty are not universal; for example, primes with transposed letters do not facilitate recognition of their base words in Hebrew (Velan & Frost, 2009). Further research is required to understand why position uncertainty appears more prevalent in some writing systems than others. One strong possibility is that there is pressure to develop very precise orthographic representations when writing systems are orthographically dense (i.e., have many anagrams), as is the case in Hebrew (Frost, 2012; Lerner et al., 2014). This account fundamentally disagrees with extant models of orthographic coding which view position uncertainty as a consequence of basic visual (Grainger et al., 2016) or neural (Dehaene et al., 2005) processes. Instead, Frost (2012; also Frost et al., 2013) views the acquisition of literacy as a statistical learning problem, of developing representations that reflect relationships between form and meaning in the particular writing system being learned. Thus, letter coding may be sloppy when the writing system is structured in such a way that sloppy codes do not compromise access to meaning, but may be very precise in crowded writing systems with many anagrams. Testing this hypothesis that the linguistic environment shapes front-end processes and representations in the reading system should be an important research priority in the coming years.

3.2.2 Frequency, cumulative frequency, and age of acquisition

It has long been argued that the most powerful determinant of the time taken to recognize a word is the frequency with which it occurs (see e.g., Monsell, 1991; New et al., 2007). Effects of word frequency have been reported in lexical decision (e.g., Balota, Cortese, Sergent-Marshall, Spieler, & Yap, 2004; Forster & Chambers, 1973) along with every other task thought to contact the orthographic representations involved in visual word recognition. These include, for example, perceptual identification (e.g., Broadbent, 1967), reading aloud (e.g., Balota & Chumbley, 1984), and eye fixation times in reading (e.g., Inhoff & Rayner, 1986; Schilling, Rayner, & Chumbley, 1998). Provided frequency estimates are derived from a suitably large corpus of text (about half of the frequency effect occurs for words between 0 and 1 occurrences per million; van Heuven et al., 2014), word frequency estimates can explain over 40% of the variance in lexical decision time (Brysbaert & New, 2009). Such data have been used to argue that lexical experience is somehow encoded in orthographic representations, and influences the ease with which these representations are accessed.

The history of research on the frequency effect in visual word recognition has seemed at times rather unsatisfying because it has appeared to focus on empirical questions such as the size of the frequency effect across tasks (Balota & Chumbley, 1984), whether frequency is better described by other (poorly defined) variables such as word familiarity (Gernsbacher, 1984), or whether some corpora are better than others for estimating frequency (van Heuven et al., 2014). However, more recent research has begun to articulate much more clearly how the nature of the frequency effect can inform our understanding of the acquisition of literacy. For example, Adelman and Brown (2008; also Adelman et al., 2006) have argued that the effect of frequency may actually be an effect of contextual diversity—that is, the number of contexts in which a word has been experienced. Similarly, Brysbaert et al. (2016) have argued that word prevalence—the extent to which particular words are known across the population—may be a superior predictor of recognition than frequency. Both of these hypotheses raise important questions about the process of reading acquisition (i.e., how we build up experience with printed words), and specifically why some words may be easier to learn than others of similar frequencies.

One very important debate in this literature has asked whether the age at which we acquire a word may be an important determinant of our experience with words (e.g., Gerhand & Barry, 1999; Morrison & Ellis, 1995). Might this factor also shape the representation of orthographic form? Substantial empirical work has sought to determine whether the frequency effect is actually an age-of-acquisition effect (e.g., Gerhand & Barry, 1999; Morrison & Ellis, 1995; Stadthagen-Gonzales et al., 2004), but methodological limitations have made it difficult to draw firm conclusions from this literature. For one, there are substantial limitations in the estimation of both frequency and age of acquisition; age of acquisition is often based on subjective recollection of when certain words were acquired (Gilhooly & Logie, 1980), and while frequency is an objective measure, the quality of the measure is influenced by the size of the corpus and the source (van Heuven et al., 2014). Further, it is well known that printed word frequency and age of acquisition are highly correlated (high frequency words are those most likely to be learned early; $r = -.68$, Carroll & White, 1973), making it difficult to design informative experiments. Finally, it has been argued quite persuasively that age of acquisition and frequency are actually two dimensions of a single variable—cumulative frequency (i.e., the frequency with which an individual is exposed to a particular word over their lifetime; e.g., Lewis, Gerhand, & Ellis, 2001; Zevin & Seidenberg, 2002).

The most recent consensus in this literature suggests that the age at which a word is acquired is an important determinant of word recognition, and that this probably reflects some fundamental characteristic of reading acquisition. Indeed, work using connectionist models has shown that age-of-acquisition effects may be a key property of models that learn incrementally over time (Monaghan & Ellis, 2010). This computational work has also suggested that age-of-acquisition effects may be more prevalent when input-to-output mappings are less systematic. The reason for this is that the solution space for early-acquired items will be less helpful for later-acquired items when the mapping is more arbitrary (Monaghan & Ellis, 2010). This observation is consistent with the empirical literature which finds particularly robust effects of age-of-acquisition in tasks that require semantic involvement such as object naming (e.g., Ghyselinck et al., 2004a), translation judgment (Izura & Ellis, 2004), and living versus non-living decisions (e.g., Ghyselinck et al., 2004b). Further computational research in which models learn incrementally and in an interleaved manner (as opposed to massed exposure to the whole training set, e.g., Harm & Seidenberg, 2004; Plaut et al., 1996) will be important in revealing how our experience with words shapes the development of orthographic representations over time.

3.2.3 Morphology

The vast majority of words in English and across the world's languages are built by combining multiple morphemes (e.g., darkness, repainting). Thus, it is unsurprising that learned representations of orthographic form should reflect morphological relationships. Two main sources of evidence have led to this conclusion. The first is the finding that the frequency of a stem within a morphologically complex word (e.g., the "dark" in darkness) influences the time taken to recognize the word (e.g., Ford et al., 2010; Taft & Ardasinski, 2006). This result appears to indicate that participants access the stems of words during recognition, or alternatively, that the orthographic representations of words like "darkness" are strengthened during acquisition by experience with their stems (see Tamminen et al., 2015 for a related finding and learning-based account). The second key finding is that the recognition of a stem target (e.g., dark) is facilitated by the prior masked presentation of a morphologically related prime (e.g., darkness; Rastle et al., 2000, 2004). This facilitation appears to arise at the level of orthographic representations, as it is equally powerful when primes have only the *appearance* of morphological structure (e.g., corner priming corn). Critically, these priming effects cannot be ascribed to pure letter overlap, as they are not observed when primes and targets share letters but no apparent morphological structure (e.g., brothel priming broth; -el is not a suffix in English; see Rastle & Davis, 2008 for review). Once again, these findings appear to suggest that orthographic representations are structured morphologically, such that readers activate the stems of morphologically structured words during recognition, or that the representations of morphologically structured words overlap those of their stems in a special manner.

3.3 Processing dynamics and mechanisms for selection

Thus far, our discussion has converged on a theory of visual word recognition that consists of multiple layers of orthographic representation. The visual stimulus is analyzed in terms of its features; these features map onto a level of representation that codes abstract letter identity as well as letter position; and these representations then activate representations of known words that are structured morphologically and shaped through experience. However, this theory, so far, consists only of the architecture. How is information transmitted through these levels of representation? Further, what is the mechanism by which a single local word unit corresponding to the target is selected? These are the questions that are considered in this section.

3.3.1 The interactive-activation model

Two empirical findings, the word superiority effect (Reicher, 1969; Wheeler, 1970) and the pseudoword superiority effect (Carr, Davidson, & Hawkins, 1978; McClelland & Johnston, 1977), were crucially important in constraining early accounts of visual word recognition. In the Reicher-Wheeler experiments, a word (e.g., WORK) or a non-word (e.g., OWRK) was flashed very briefly and then replaced by a pattern mask. Participants then decided which of two letters (e.g., D or K), presented adjacent to the position of the previous target letter, was in the stimulus. Results showed that letter identification was more accurate when letters had been presented within word stimuli than within non-word stimuli. Further experiments (Carr et al., 1978; McClelland & Johnston, 1977) demonstrated that the letter-identification benefit seen with words extends to pronounceable non-words (e.g., K is identified with greater accuracy in TARK than in ATRK). These findings provided benchmark phenomena for the development of the interactive-activation model (McClelland & Rumelhart, 1981; Rumelhart & McClelland, 1982), which many still consider to be the cornerstone of our understanding of processing and selection in visual word recognition (see e.g., Coltheart et al., 2001; Davis, 2003; Grainger & Jacobs, 1996; but see Forster, 2005; Murray & Forster, 2004 for important criticisms). The model is depicted in Figure 3.2.

In the model, information from the visual stimulus flows through feature, letter, and word levels of representation. Each of these levels of representation consists of individual units called nodes. The connections between these adjacent levels of representation are both excitatory and inhibitory. Nodes at every level excite nodes at adjacent levels with which they are consistent and inhibit nodes at adjacent levels with which they are inconsistent. For example, the initial letter T in a stimulus will activate word nodes for TAKE, TALL, and TREE while inhibiting word nodes for CAKE, MALL, and FREE. Information flows continuously (i.e., in "cascade"; McClelland, 1979) through these levels of representation. Unlike the logogen models that preceded it (e.g., Morton, 1969; Morton, 1979), information at one level of representation does not have to reach a threshold before being passed on to another level of representation (see Coltheart et al., 2001 for a discussion).

Information flows between adjacent layers of the model in a bidirectional manner (e.g., information travels from letters to words and also from words to letters). It is through these bidirectional connections that the model explains how knowledge of a higher-level unit (e.g., a word) can influence the processing of a lower-level unit (e.g., a letter). Letters embedded in words are particularly easy to recognize (i.e., the word superiority effect) because they enjoy top-down support from nodes activated by the stimulus at the word level. Letters embedded in pronounceable pseudowords (i.e., the pseudoword superiority effect) may also enjoy top-down support through these bidirectional connections. Even though pseudowords are

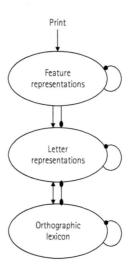

FIG. 3.2 The interactive-activation model of visual word recognition (McClelland & Rumelhart, 1981; Rumelhart & McClelland, 1982).

not represented by nodes at the word level, they too can activate (and derive support from) nodes at this level that represent visually similar words (e.g., TARK activates and derives support from nodes for PARK, DARK, TURK, and so on).

The discussion so far has indicated that printed letter strings (whether words or non-words) can activate multiple nodes at the word level. For example, the stimulus CAKE activates the node for CAKE at the word level, but also activates nodes for visually similar alternatives like CARE, FAKE, CAPE, RAKE, and COKE. When the printed stimulus corresponds to a word, nodes for alternative candidates will be activated more weakly than the node for the target, but will be activated nonetheless. How, then, does the recognition system select the node corresponding to the target from these multiple candidates? One possible mechanism is search. Both the search model (Forster, 1976; Murray & Forster, 2004) and the activation-verification model (Paap et al., 1982; Paap & Johansen, 1994) posit that target selection is achieved through a frequency-ordered serial search or verification process that seeks to establish which candidate provides the best fit to the stimulus. The interactive-activation model solves this target selection problem in a different manner, however: through competition. In the model, inhibitory connections between word nodes enable the most active node (typically that of the target) to drive down the activation of multiple alternative candidates. Of course, the presence of many competing candidates will also make it difficult for the target to reach a critical recognition threshold, since inhibition emanating from those competing candidates will act to drive down activation of the target (see e.g., Davis, 2003; Davis & Lupker, 2006, for a discussion of competitive mechanisms in target selection).

3.3.2 Neighborhood (N) effects

One way in which this prediction has been tested is by looking at the impact of lexical similarity on visual word recognition. If a letter string is similar to many words (and thus activates multiple candidates), then it should be more difficult to recognize than a letter string that is similar to few words (and thus does not activate multiple candidates). However, the phrase "similar to many words" raises a key point that takes us back to section 3.2.1. That is, what counts as similar depends on the nature of the scheme adopted for coding letter position. Two stimuli that have large overlap according to one scheme may have much less overlap according to another scheme. This principle is illustrated by considering deletion neighbors such as CHARM and HARM. On a left-aligned slot-based coding scheme, these items share no orthographic overlap at all. However, on a coding scheme based on relative position such as spatial coding (Davis, 2010), the overlap between these items is much greater. This issue is critically important in considering previous research on lexical similarity effects (Davis & Taft, 2005), as the vast majority of this work has used an overly restrictive (and almost certainly incorrect) conceptualization of lexical similarity known as Coltheart's N (Coltheart, Davelaar, Jonasson, & Besner, 1977).

Coltheart et al. (1977) defined the neighborhood size of a stimulus (N) as the number of words of the same length that can be created by changing one letter of that stimulus. Using this metric of lexical similarity, the word CAKE, for example, has a very large neighborhood (e.g., BAKE, LAKE, CARE, COKE, CAVE, and so on). Coltheart et al. (1977) reported that high-N non-words (e.g., PAKE) were rejected more slowly in lexical decision than low-N non-words (e.g., PLUB), an effect now replicated by a number of investigators (e.g., Davis & Taft, 2005; Forster & Shen, 1996; McCann, Besner, & Davelaar, 1988). It is not hard to see why high-N non-words should be difficult to reject in lexical decision. Such non-words activate many nodes at the word level (i.e., they look like many actual words), and this total activation makes it difficult to decide that the stimulus is not a word. However, Coltheart et al. (1977) also reported no effect of N on the YES response in lexical decision: High-N and low-N words were recognized with similar latencies. This result is interesting, since it is inconsistent with both of the mechanisms for target selection described here (i.e., search and competition). These mechanisms would seem to predict that a large N should be detrimental to the recognition of words, since a large N implies the activation of many competing candidates.

This issue surfaced again ten years later, when Andrews (1989) observed that high-N words are *easier* to recognize in lexical decision than low-N words, especially when these words are of a low printed frequency. Simultaneously, however, Grainger et al. (1989) reported inhibitory effects of neighborhood frequency on lexical decision. They found that words with at least one higher-frequency neighbor are recognized more slowly than words with no higher-frequency neighbors, an effect seemingly in line with the predictions of competitive network models like the interactive-activation model. These findings would appear to be contradictory, since words with many neighbors usually have at least one higher-frequency neighbor—presumably all that it takes to delay lexical decision (Sears, Hino, & Lupker, 1995). Thus, the first three examinations of the effect of N on the recognition of words produced the three logically possible results: no effect (Coltheart et al., 1977); facilitation (Andrews, 1989); and inhibition (Grainger et al., 1989). Empirical findings over the next years did not especially clarify the matter (see Andrews, 1997 for a review). Several investigators continued to report facilitatory effects of N on the YES response in lexical decision (Andrews, 1992; Balota et al., 2004; Forster & Shen, 1996; Sears et al., 1995) while several others continued to report inhibitory effects of neighborhood frequency (Carreiras et al., 1997; Grainger, 1990; Grainger et al., 1992; Grainger & Jacobs, 1996; Grainger & Segui, 1990; Huntsman & Lima, 1996; Perea & Pollatsek, 1998).

This puzzling pattern of results seems to indicate that effects of lexical similarity on visual word recognition reflect a balance of facilitation and inhibition. Several hypotheses have been put forward to try to understand the nature of that balance. Some authors have focused on cross-linguistic differences (e.g., Andrews, 1997; Ziegler & Perry, 1998), and in particular, the possibility that facilitation may be the more typical pattern in English because of reliance on larger units (e.g., rimes; Ziegler & Goswami, 2005). Other authors have proposed that task-based considerations may impact when facilitation and inhibition are observed. Specifically, it may be the case that inhibition is observed when the task emphasizes processing of a specific lexical item (which is subject to competition from other lexical items), whereas facilitation is observed when the task enables participants to make decisions based on global word-likeness (de Moor et al., 2005; Grainger & Jacobs, 1996). Still other authors have focused on the rigidity of Coltheart's N as a metric of lexical similarity (Davis & Taft, 2005; Yarkoni et al., 2008). Yarkoni et al. (2008) introduced Orthographic Levenshtein Distance 20 (OLD20), a measure of the distance (in terms of single letter deletions, additions, or substitutions) between a word and its 20 nearest neighbors. Using analyses of large-scale studies (e.g., Balota et al., 2007), they demonstrated that OLD20 exerts facilitation on visual word recognition, but that the frequency of OLD20 neighbors exerts inhibition. However, all of these avenues seem to have been false trails in trying to account for the complex pattern of neighborhood effects. Using simulations from a simple interactive-activation model implementing competitive processing, Chen and Mirman (2012) demonstrated that the full pattern of facilitation and inhibition is captured by a simple computational principle. Specifically, neighbors activated in visual word recognition yield net inhibition when they are strongly activated but yield net facilitation when they are weakly activated.

3.3.3 Masked form priming effects

Masked form priming effects are another important source of evidence concerning selection mechanisms in visual word recognition. Masked form priming is a technique in which a briefly presented lower-case prime (e.g., 50 ms) is sandwiched between a forward pattern mask and an upper-case target presented for some type of lexical processing task (including lexical decision, reading aloud, semantic categorization, perceptual identification; e.g., Evett & Humphreys, 1981; Forster & Davis, 1984; Forster & Davis, 1991; Forster et al., 1987). Because participants in these experiments do not have conscious experience of the prime (they typically report seeing a flash or nothing at all prior to the target), it is argued that masked priming provides a highly desirable situation in which neither strategic nor episodic factors can be invoked to explain the priming effects observed (but see Bodner & Masson, 2001). Researchers using this technique over the past 20 years have normally sought to determine how the recognition of a target word is influenced by the prior presentation of a visually similar word or non-word prime.

Priming in the interactive-activation model is conceptualized as a balance between facilitation and inhibition (Davis, 2003; Ziegler, Ferrand, Jacobs, Rey, & Grainger, 2000). Primes activate visually similar targets, thus producing savings in the time it takes for those targets to reach a critical recognition threshold of activation. However, primes can also activate word nodes that compete with targets for recognition. Davis (2003) therefore suggested that prime lexicality (i.e., the word/non-word status of a prime) should be a particularly influential factor in determining the magnitude of form priming effects. Non-word primes (e.g., azle–AXLE) should typically produce robust facilitation, because these primes activate nodes for their corresponding targets without also activating any strongly competitive nodes. In contrast, word primes (e.g., able-AXLE) activate nodes for their corresponding targets but also activate their own nodes, which compete with the target nodes for recognition. The interactive-activation model therefore predicts that word primes should facilitate target recognition to a much lesser degree than non-word primes (Davis, 2003). Search models (e.g., Forster et al., 1987; Forster & Veres, 1998), on the other hand, predict facilitation of visually similar masked primes on target recognition because these models propose that visually similar primes (whether words or non-words) constrain the area of the orthographic lexicon that is searched.

Broadly speaking, data from masked form priming seem to show support for the interactive-activation model. First of all, masked non-word primes facilitate lexical decisions to target words (e.g., bontrast-CONTRAST). This result was first obtained by Forster and Davis (1984), and has since been replicated numerous times (e.g., Adelman et al., 2014; Andrews & Lo, 2012; Davis & Lupker, 2006; Forster et al., 1987; Forster, Mohan, & Hector, 2003; Forster & Veres, 1998; Perea & Lupker, 2003). In contrast, most of the experiments that have examined the effects of masked word primes on target recognition have revealed inhibitory effects or null effects (e.g., Andrews & Lo, 2012; Davis & Lupker, 2006; de Moor & Brysbaert, 2000; Drews & Zwitserlood, 1995; Forster & Veres, 1998; Grainger, Colé, & Segui, 1991; Grainger & Ferrand, 1994; Segui & Grainger, 1990). Further research investigating individual differences in masked form priming suggests that these inhibitory effects are particularly robust in good spellers, suggesting that well-specified orthographic representations are particularly effective competitors (Andrews & Hersch, 2010).

One interesting exception to the effect of lexical status on masked form priming arises in the case of masked word primes comprising a morphological structure (e.g., darkness, corner). Such primes *always* facilitate recognition of their embedded stems (e.g., Lavric et al., 2007; McCormick et al., 2008; Rastle et al., 2004; Rastle & Davis, 2008), with no effect of the lexical status of the prime on the magnitude of priming (Longtin & Meunier, 2005; McCormick, Brysbaert, & Rastle, 2009; but see Andrews & Lo, 2013 for important qualifications based on individual differences analyses). One explanation for this set of results is that morphological surface structure enables a rapid perceptual segmentation of a prime, which disables that prime's ability to activate a word node that would normally compete against the target for recognition. For example, the prime *brother* may be rapidly segmented into {broth} + {er}, thus enabling activation of the word node for the target (broth) without activating the competing word node for the prime (brother). Primes such as *brothel* cannot be segmented because they do not comprise a morphological structure (i.e., -el never functions as an English suffix), and thus end up competing with the target for recognition. Research using ERPs as a dependent measure has revealed that this form of analysis arises within 200 ms of stimulus onset, and prior to the activation of semantic information (Lavric, Clapp, & Rastle, 2007; Rastle et al., 2015).

3.4 WORD RECOGNITION AND THE READING SYSTEM

This chapter has put forward an understanding of visual word recognition based on a hierarchical analysis of visual features, letters, morphemes, and ultimately orthographic representations of known words. However, while visual word recognition is typically conceived as a process based on the analysis of orthography, it is also embedded in a reading system comprising processes to compute sounds and meanings from print. Further, while there is evidence to suggest that visual word recognition is possible in the presence of severe semantic and/or phonological impairment (Coltheart, 2004), it is indisputable that semantic and phonological information can contribute to this process.

There is wide agreement that meaning from the visual form can be computed via two pathways—one specializing in whole-word processes linking orthography to meaning, and one specializing in componential processes mapping orthography to meaning via phonology (Coltheart et al., 2001; Harm & Seidenberg, 2004; Perry et al., 2007; see also Taylor et al., 2013 for a meta-analysis of neural evidence of this dual-pathway structure). Critically, these models assert that visual word recognition can be influenced by semantic and phonological knowledge, either via bidirectional information flow between these bodies of knowledge (e.g., Coltheart et al., 2001) or as a result of learning processes whereby orthographic representations are shaped by phonological and semantic knowledge (e.g., Harm & Seidenberg, 2004; Plaut & Gonnerman, 2000). These mechanisms provide a basis for understanding phonological and semantic effects on visual word recognition.

3.4.1 Phonological influences on recognition

There is substantial evidence to indicate that phonological representations impact on the recognition of printed words. Rubenstein, Lewis, and Rubenstein (1971) presented homophonic words (e.g., MAID, SALE), non-homophonic words (e.g., PAID, RAIL), pseudohomophones (e.g., BURD, KOAT), and non-pseudohomophonic non-words (e.g., GURD, WOAT) to participants for lexical decision. They observed that YES responses were slower for homophones than they were for non-homophonic words, and that NO responses were slower for pseudohomophones than they were for non-pseudohomophonic non-words. Both of these effects on lexical decision—the homophone effect and the pseudohomophone effect—have been replicated repeatedly (homophone effect: Ferrand & Grainger, 2003; Pexman, Lupker, & Jared, 2001; pseudohomophone effect: Besner & Davelaar, 1983; Coltheart et al., 1977; McCann, Besner, & Davelaar, 1988; McQuade, 1981; Vanhoy & Van Orden, 2001; Ziegler, Jacobs, & Klüppel, 2001).

Priming studies also reveal an influence of phonology on the recognition of printed words. Numerous studies have now revealed that target recognition is speeded by the prior brief presentation of a masked pseudohomophone prime (e.g., koat-COAT) relative to an orthographic control (e.g., poat-COAT). This benefit from phonology is observed in lexical decision (e.g., Drieghe & Brysbaert, 2002; Ferrand & Grainger, 1992; Lukatela, Frost, & Turvey, 1998) as well as a multitude of other tasks that tap recognition components of the reading system (e.g., Perfetti, Bell, & Delaney, 1988; Perfetti & Bell, 1991; see Rastle & Brysbaert, 2006, for a review). These findings indicate not only that phonology influences the recognition of printed words, but that phonological influences become apparent very early in processing, a conclusion supported by electrophysiological data (Grainger et al., 2006). This evidence for "fast" phonology led a number of researchers (e.g., Drieghe & Brysbaert, 2002; Frost, 1998; Lukatela & Turvey, 1994; Xu & Perfetti, 1999) to suggest that phonological recoding of a printed stimulus plays a leading or even obligatory role in its recognition. While this *strong phonological theory* of visual word recognition (Frost, 1998) has fallen out of favor in more recent years, the evidence is unequivocal that sound-based representations are computed rapidly as a matter of routine during reading (see Rastle & Brysbaert, 2006 for review). This state of affairs is perhaps unsurprising given broad consensus around the importance of sound-based codes in reading acquisition (e.g., Melby-Lervag et al, 2012; see Rayner et al., 2001 for review).

3.4.2 Semantic influences on recognition

It is increasingly recognized that aspects of word meaning have a powerful impact on visual word recognition (see Taylor et al., 2015 for review). There is good evidence that words with particularly rich semantic representations are recognized more quickly than words with more impoverished semantic representations, although without a precise theory of the nature of semantic representations, it is not yet known exactly how semantic richness is best conceptualized. Potential candidates include imageability (Balota et al., 2004; Cortese & Schock, 2013; Yap et al., 2012), sensory experience (Juhasz et al., 2011), number of semantic features (Pexman, Lupker, & Hino, 2002), semantic neighborhood density (Locker, Simpson, & Yates, 2003; Mirman & Magnuson, 2008), number of (related) meanings (Azuma & Van Orden, 1997; Hino & Lupker, 1996), and number of related senses (Rodd, Gaskell, & Marslen-Wilson, 2002). Rodd et al. (2002) qualified this conclusion by demonstrating that those words with multiple *unrelated* meanings (e.g., bark) impair visual word recognition.

It is also well known that the recognition of words (e.g., DOCTOR) can be primed by the prior presentation of semantically related words (e.g., NURSE; Meyer & Schvaneveldt, 1971; see also reviews by Hutchison, 2003; Lucas, 2000; Neely, 1991). The dominant metaphor for explaining semantic priming is spreading activation (Collins & Loftus, 1975; Neely, 1977). The idea is that the orthographic representation of the prime activates a semantic node, which then sends positive activation to related nodes (including the target) at the semantic level of representation. This preactivation of the target by the prime facilitates its later recognition. However, in contrast to effects of orthographic and phonological similarity, masked semantic priming effects have been difficult to find. Lavric et al. (2007) argued that when they have been reported, they have usually involved associates rather than category coordinates, classification of primes in visible form prior to subliminal presentation, severely restricted prime sets, or prime durations at the boundary of visibility. Similarly, previous reports of masked semantic priming on the N400 component in ERP research (e.g., Kiefer, 2002) have typically used prime durations at the boundary of visibility and may be explained by conscious perception of primes on some of the trials (Holcomb et al., 2005; see also Grainger & Holcomb, 2009). These observations suggest that the activation of semantic information in visual word recognition takes more time than the activation of orthographic, phonological, or morphological information.

3.5 CONCLUSIONS AND FURTHER DIRECTIONS

The printed word presents the skilled reader with a challenging problem. Readers are faced with considerable variability in the forms of the symbols presented to them, and the density of the orthographic space renders words highly confusable. Information about the spellings, sounds, and meanings of these words must be stored; and one form of information must be accessed rapidly from the other. Further, these challenges present themselves to an organism that is not endowed with special hardware for reading. The skilled reader solves all of these problems remarkably well. Skilled reading is not only highly accurate but also effortless; and we have seen evidence in this chapter that decoding a printed stimulus begins even before we are aware of its existence.

Over the next decade, our understanding of visual word recognition will almost certainly be enhanced through new advances in neuroscience. Electrophysiological approaches have been part of the reading researcher's toolbox for some years and have been instrumental in providing a temporal characterization of the analysis of orthographic, phonological, morphological, and semantic information (e.g., Grainger & Holcomb, 2009; Lavric et al., 2012). However, while we now have a good grasp of the brain regions that underpin the recognition of printed words (e.g., Taylor et al., 2013, for meta-analysis), this has not yet translated to major developments in our understanding of the nature of orthographic representations, or the way in which semantic and phonological representations contribute to the recognition process.

One avenue to push further involves the assessment of neural priming effects (e.g., Henson & Rugg, 2003). Unlike behavioral priming paradigms, in which the analysis is typically focused on the extent to which a prime facilitates target recognition in speed or accuracy, neural priming paradigms permit this analysis in a *region-specific manner*. Because we increasingly understand how different brain regions underpin the reading process, we are able to draw conclusions about the nature of the priming effect that might not be possible using behavioral measures alone. For example, if we observed that behavioral morphological priming effects were of the same magnitude as semantic and/or orthographic priming effects, we might conclude that they were driven by those forms of similarity. However, this conclusion would require refinement if it were demonstrated that the neural priming effects for these forms of similarity were observed in separate brain regions (see e.g., Devlin et al., 2004; Gold & Rastle, 2007 for relevant empirical work).

Recent advances in multivariate pattern analysis also provide new possibilities for using neuroscientific methods to interrogate the nature of representations used in reading. In particular, representational similarity analysis (RSA; Kriegeskorte et al., 2008) permits the researcher to assess the extent to which voxels in the brain treat different stimuli as similar, and to compare these similarity scores to those generated from quantitative theories of cognition. These methods have allowed researchers to determine which areas of the brain represent different forms of similarity present in letters (e.g., Rothlein & Rapp, 2014) and words (e.g., Fischer-Baum et al., 2017). It should now be increasingly possible to use these methods to adjudicate between cognitive theories of orthographic representation. For example, do the brain regions concerned with orthographic processing treat words with shared open bigrams as similar; or is similarity based on spatial coding a better predictor of brain responses in these regions? Similar questions could be asked of phonological, morphological, or semantic representations.

In addition to opportunities from neuroscience, our understanding of visual word recognition will be enhanced by increasingly close connections between research on skilled reading and research on reading acquisition. On the one hand, research on skilled reading provides a picture of the "end state" of the reading acquisition process, and thus poses important questions about how aspects of skilled reading develop that need to be investigated.

For example, there is broad agreement that orthographic representations in Indo-European languages are specified loosely for position, but whether this coding becomes more flexible (Ziegler et al., 2013) or more precise (Kezilas et al., 2017) as reading acquisition progresses is unknown. Similarly, while there is strong evidence for rapid morphological analysis in skilled readers (Rastle et al., 2004), this form of analysis has yet to be observed in developing readers (Beyersmann et al., 2012). On the other hand, insights from reading acquisition have much to offer to our understanding of skilled reading. We have already seen how an acquisition perspective (Monaghan & Ellis, 2010) has assisted our understanding of why age-of-acquisition effects in skilled readers emerge most strongly in particular tasks. Similarly, the insight that experiencing words in multiple contexts may be a critical part of orthographic learning (Nation, 2017) should inform any attempts to model contextual diversity effects in skilled word recognition (e.g., Adelman & Brown, 2008). More generally, this work will be supported by advances in the computational modeling of the reading acquisition process.

In summary, research over the past 40 years on the functional mechanisms that underpin visual word processing has been a great success story. This research provides a sound basis for which to discover how the brain supports the mind in respect of this remarkable human achievement, and how children can best be taught to develop the reading skill.

3.6 Acknowledgments

The author would like to acknowledge funding from the Economic and Social Research Council (ES/L002264/1) and the Leverhulme Trust (RPG-2013-04), and research assistance from Clare Lally and Rebecca Crowley.

References

Adelman, J. S., & Brown, G. D. A. (2008). Modelling lexical decision: The form of frequency and diversity effects. *Psychological Review, 115*, 214–27.

Adelman, J. S., Brown, G. D. A., & Quesada, J. F. (2006). Contextual diversity, not word frequency, determines word-naming and lexical decision times. *Psychological Science, 17*, 814–23.

Adelman, J. S., Johnson, R. L., McCormick, S. F., McKague, M., Kinoshita, S., Bowers, J. S., ... & Yap, M. J. (2014). A behavioural database for masked form priming. *Behavior Research Methods, 46*, 1052–67.

Allport, D. A., & Funnell, E. (1981). Components of the mental lexicon. *Philosophical Transactions of the Royal Society of London, B295*, 397–410.

Andrews, S. (1989). Frequency and neighborhood effects on lexical access: Activation or search? *Journal of Experimental Psychology: Learning, Memory, and Cognition, 15*, 802–14.

Andrews, S. (1992). Frequency and neighbourhood effects on lexical access: Lexical similarity or orthographic redundancy. *Journal of Experimental Psychology: Learning, Memory, and Cognition, 18*, 234–54.

Andrews, S. (1997). The effect of orthographic similarity on lexical retrieval: Resolving neighbourhood conflicts. *Psychonomic Bulletin & Review, 4*, 439–61.

Andrews, S., & Hersch, J. (2010). Lexical precision in skilled readers: Individual differences in masked neighbour priming. *Journal of Experimental Psychology, 139,* 299–318.

Andrews, S., & Lo, S. (2012). Not all skilled readers have cracked the code: Individual differences in masked form priming. *Journal of Experimental Psychology: Learning, Memory, and Cognition, 38,* 152–163.

Andrews, S., & Lo, S. (2013). Is morphological priming stronger for transparent than opaque words? It depends on individual differences in spelling and vocabulary. *Journal of Memory and Language, 68,* 279–96.

Azuma, T., & Van Orden, G. (1997). Why safe is better than fast: The relatedness of a word's meaning affects lexical decision times. *Journal of Memory and Language, 36,* 484–504.

Balota, D. A., & Chumbley, J. I. (1984). Are lexical decisions a good measure of lexical access? The role of word frequency in the neglected decision stage. *Journal of Experimental Psychology: Human Perception and Performance, 10,* 340–57.

Balota, D. A., Cortese, M. J., Sergent-Marshall, S. D., Spieler, D. H., & Yap, M. J. (2004). Visual word recognition of single-syllable words. *Journal of Experimental Psychology: General, 133,* 283–316.

Balota, D. A., Yap, M. J., Cortese, M. J., Hutchison, K. A., Kessler, B., Loftis, B., ... & Treiman, R. (2007). The English Lexicon Project. *Behavior Research Methods, 39,* 445–59.

Besner, D., & Davelaar, E. (1983). Suedohomofoan effects in visual word recognition: Evidence for phonological processing. *Canadian Journal of Psychology, 37,* 300–5.

Beyersmann, E., Castles, A., & Coltheart, M. (2012). Morphological processing during visual word recognition in developing readers: Evidence from masked priming. *Quarterly Journal of Experimental Psychology, 65,* 1306–26.

Bodner, G. E., & Masson, M. J. (2001). Prime validity affects masked repetition priming: Evidence for an episodic resource account of priming. *Journal of Memory and Language, 45,* 616–47.

Borowsky, R., & Besner, D. (2006). Parallel distributed processing and lexical-semantic effects in visual word recognition: Are a few stages necessary? *Psychological Review, 113,* 181–95.

Bowers, J. S. (2000). In defence of abstractionist theories of repetition priming and word identification. *Psychonomic Bulletin & Review, 7,* 83–99.

Broadbent, D. E. (1967). Word-frequency effects and response bias. *Psychological Review, 74,* 1–15.

Brysbaert, M., & New, B. (2009). Moving beyond Kučera and Francis: A critical evaluation of current word frequency norms and the introduction of a new and improved word frequency measure for American English. *Behaviour Research Methods, 41,* 977–90.

Brysbaert, M., Stevens, M, Mandera, P., & Keuleers, E. (2016). The impact of word prevalence on lexical decision times: Evidence from the Dutch Lexicon Project 2. *Journal of Experimental Psychology: Human Perception and Performance, 42,* 441–58.

Carr, T. H., Davidson, B. J., & Hawkins, H. L. (1978). Perceptual flexibility in word recognition: Strategies affect orthographic computation but not lexical access. *Journal of Experimental Psychology: Human Perception and Performance, 4,* 674–90.

Carreiras, M., Perea, M., & Grainger, J. (1997). Effects of the orthographic neighborhood in visual word recognition: Cross-task comparisons. *Journal of Experimental Psychology: Learning, Memory, and Cognition, 23,* 857–71.

Carroll, J. B., & White, M. N. (1973). Word frequency and age of acquisition as determiners of picture naming latencies. *Quarterly Journal of Experimental Psychology, 25,* 85–95.

Cattell, J. (1886). The time it takes to see and name objects. *Mind, 11,* 63–5.

Chen, Q., & Mirman, D. (2012). Competition and cooperation among similar representations: Toward a unified account of facilitative and inhibitory effects of lexical neighbors. *Psychological Review, 119*, 417–30.

Collins, A. M., & Loftus, E. F. (1975). A spreading-activation theory of semantic processing. *Psychological Review, 82*, 407–28.

Coltheart, M. (1981). Disorders of reading and their implications for models of normal reading. *Visible Language, 15*, 245–86.

Coltheart, M. (2004). Are there lexicons? *Quarterly Journal of Experimental Psychology, 57A*, 1153–71.

Coltheart, M., Davelaar, E., Jonasson, J. T., & Besner, D. (1977). Access to the internal lexicon. In: Dornic, S. (Ed.), *Attention and Performance, VI* (pp. 535–555). Erlbaum, Hillsdale, NJ.

Coltheart. M., Rastle, K., Perry, C., Langdon, R., & Ziegler, J. (2001). DRC: A dual route cascaded model of visual word recognition and reading aloud. *Psychological Review, 108*, 204–56.

Cortese, M. J., & Schock, J., (2013). Imageability and age of acquisition effects in disyllabic word recognition. *Quarterly Journal of Experimental Psychology, 66*, 946–72.

Davis, C. J. (1999). *The Self-Organising Lexical Acquisition and Recognition (SOLAR) Model of Visual Word Recognition* [unpublished doctoral dissertation].

Davis, C. J. (2003). Factors underlying masked priming effects in competitive network models of visual word recognition. In: Kinoshita, S., & Lupker, S. J. (Eds.), *Masked Priming: The State of the Art* (pp. 121–70). Psychology Press, Hove.

Davis, C. (2010). The spatial coding model of visual word identification. *Psychological Review, 117*(3), 713–58.

Davis, C. J., & Lupker, S. J. (2006). Masked inhibitory priming in English: Evidence for lexical inhibition. *Journal of Experimental Psychology: Human Perception and Performance, 32*, 668–87.

Davis, C., & Taft, M. (2005). More words in the neighborhood: Interference in lexical decision due to deletion neighbors. *Psychonomic Bulletin & Review, 12*, 904–10.

de Moor, W., & Brysbaert, M. (2000). Neighborhood frequency effects when primes and targets are of different lengths. *Psychological Research, 63*, 159–62.

de Moor, W., Verguts, T., & Brysbaert, M. (2005). Testing the "multiple" in the multiple read-out model of visual word recognition. *Journal of Experimental Psychology: Learning, Memory, and Cognition, 31*, 1502–8.

Dehaene, S., & Cohen, L. (2011). The unique role of the visual word form area in reading. *Trends in Cognitive Sciences, 15*, 254–62.

Dehaene, S., Cohen, L, Sigman, M., & Vinckier, F. (2005). The neural code for written words: A proposal. *Trends in Cognitive Sciences, 9*, 335–41.

Devlin, J. T., Jamison, H. L., Matthews, P. M., Gonnerman, L. M. (2004). Morphology and the internal structure of words. *Proceedings of the National Academy of Sciences, 101*, 14984–8.

Drews, E., & Zwitserlood, P. (1995). Morphological and orthographic similarity in visual word recognition. *Journal of Experimental Psychology: Human Perception and Performance, 21*, 1098–116.

Drieghe, D., & Brysbaert, M. (2002). Strategic effects in associative priming with words, homophones, and pseudohomophones. *Journal of Experimental Psychology: Learning, Memory, and Cognition, 28*, 951–61.

Evett, L. J., & Humphreys, G. W. (1981). The use of abstract graphemic information in lexical access. *Quarterly Journal of Experimental Psychology, 33A*, 325–50.

Ferrand, L., & Grainger, J. (1992). Phonology and orthography in visual word recognition: Evidence from masked non-word priming. *Quarterly Journal of Experimental Psychology, 45A*, 353–72.

Ferrand, L., & Grainger, J. (2003). Homophonic interference effects in visual word recognition. *Quarterly Journal of Experimental Psychology, 56A*, 403–19.

Fischer-Baum, S., Bruggemann, D., Gallego, I. F., Li, D. S. P., & Tamez, E. R (2017). Decoding levels of representation in reading: A representational similarity approach. *Cortex, 90*, 88–102.

Ford, M. A., Davis, M. H., & Marslen-Wilson, W. D. (2010). Derivational morphology and base morpheme frequency. *Journal of Memory and Language, 63*, 117–30.

Forster, K. I. (1976). Accessing the mental lexicon. In: Wales, R. J., & Walker, E. C. T. (Eds.), *New Approaches to Language Mechanisms* (pp. 257–87). North Holland, Amsterdam.

Forster, K. I. (2005). Five challenges for activation models. In: Andrews, S. (Ed.), *From Inkmarks to Ideas: Challenges and Controversies About Word Recognition and Reading*. Psychology Press, Hove.

Forster, K. I., & Chambers, S. (1973). Lexical access and naming time. *Journal of Verbal Learning and Verbal Behaviour, 12*, 627–35.

Forster, K. I., & Davis, C. (1984). Repetition priming and frequency attenuation in lexical access. *Journal of Experimental Psychology: Learning, Memory, and Cognition, 10*, 680–9.

Forster, K. I., & Davis, C. (1991). The density constraint on form-priming in the naming task: Interference effects from a masked prime. *Journal of Memory and Language, 30*, 1–25.

Forster, K. I., Davis, C., Schoknecht, C., & Carter, R. (1987). Masked priming with graphemically related forms: Repetition or parallel activation? *Quarterly Journal of Experimental Psychology: Human Experimental Psychology, 39A*, 211–51.

Forster, K. I., & Shen, D. (1996). No enemies in the neighborhood: Absence of inhibitory neighborhood effects in lexical decision and semantic categorization. *Journal of Experimental Psychology: Learning, Memory, and Cognition, 22*, 696–713.

Forster, K. I., Mohan, K., & Hector, J. (2003). The mechanics of masked priming. In: Kinoshita, S., & Lupker, S. J. (Eds.), *Masked Priming: The State of the Art* (pp. 3–37). Psychology Press, Hove.

Forster, K. I., & Veres, C. (1998). The prime lexicality effect: Form priming and a function of prime awareness, lexical status, and discrimination difficulty. *Journal of Experimental Psychology: Learning, Memory, and Cognition, 24*, 498–514.

Frost, R. (1998). Toward a strong phonological theory of visual word recognition: True issues and false trails. *Psychological Bulletin, 123*, 71–99.

Frost, R. (2012). Towards a universal model of reading. *Behavioural and Brain Sciences, 35*, 263–329.

Frost, R, Velan, H., & Deutsch, A. (2013). The flexibility of letter-position flexibility: Evidence from eye movements in reading Hebrew. *Journal of Experimental Psychology: Human Perception and Performance, 39*, 1143–52.

Gerhand, S., & Barry, C. (1999). Age of acquisition, word frequency, and the role of phonology in the lexical decision task. *Memory & Cognition, 27*, 592–602.

Gernsbacher, M. A. (1984). Resolving 20 years of inconsistent interactions between lexical familiarity and orthography, concreteness, and polysemy. *Journal of Experimental Psychology: General, 113*, 256–81.

Ghyselinck, M., Lewis, M. B., & Brysbaert, M. (2004a). Age of acquisition and the cumulative-frequency hypothesis: A review of the literature and a new multi-task investigation. *Acta Psychologica*, 115, 43–67.

Ghyselinck, M., Custers, R., & Brysbaert, M. (2004b). The effect of age of acquisition in visual word processing: Further evidence for the semantic hypothesis. *Journal of Experimental Psychology*, 30, 550–4.

Gilhooly, K. J., & Logie, R. H. (1980). Age-of-acquisition, imagery, concreteness, familiarity, and ambiguity measures for 1,944 words. *Behavior Research Methods, Instruments, & Computers*, 12, 395–427.

Gold, B., & Rastle, K. (2007). Neural correlates of morphological decomposition during visual word recognition. *Journal of Cognitive Neuroscience*, 19, 1983–93.

Gomez, P., Ratcliff, R., & Perea, M. (2008). The overlap model: A model of letter position coding. *Psychological Review*, 115, 577–600.

Grainger, J. (1990). Word frequency and neighbourhood frequency effects in lexical decision and naming. *Journal of Memory and Language*, 29, 228–44.

Grainger, J., Colé, P., & Segui, J. (1991). Masked morphological priming in visual word recognition. *Journal of Memory and Language*, 30, 370–84.

Grainger, J., Dufau, S., & Ziegler, J. C. (2016). A vision of reading. *Trends in Cognitive Sciences*, 20, 171–9.

Grainger, J., & Ferrand, L. (1994). Phonology and orthography in visual word recognition: Effects of masked homophone primes. *Journal of Memory and Language*, 33, 218–33.

Grainger, J., & Holcomb, P. J. (2009). Watching the word go by: On the time-course of component processes in visual word recognition. *Language and Linguistic Compass*, 3, 128–56.

Grainger, J., & Jacobs, A. M. (1996). Orthographic processing in visual word recognition: A multiple read-out model. *Psychological Review*, 103, 518–65.

Grainger, J., Kiyonaga, K., & Holcomb, P. J. (2006). The time course of orthographic and phonological code activation. *Psychological Science*, 17, 1021–6.

Grainger, J., O'Regan, J. K., Jacobs, A. M., & Segui, J. (1989). On the role of competing word units in visual word recognition: The neighbourhood frequency effect. *Perception & Psychophysics*, 45, 189–95.

Grainger, J., O'Regan, J. K., Jacobs, A. M., & Segui, J. (1992). Neighborhood frequency effects and letter visibility in visual word recognition. *Perception & Psychophysics*, 51, 49–56.

Grainger, J., & Segui, J. (1990). Neighborhood frequency effects in visual word recognition: A comparison of lexical decision and masked identification latencies. *Perception & Psychophysics*, 47, 191–8.

Guerrera, C., & Forster, K. (2008). Masked form priming with extreme transposition. *Language and Cognitive Processes*, 23, 117–42.

Harm, M., & Seidenberg, M. S. (2004). Computing the meanings of words in reading: Cooperative division of labor between visual and phonological processes. *Psychological Review* 111, 662–720.

Henson, R. N. A., & Rugg, M. D. (2003). Neural response suppression, haemodynamic repetition effects, and behavioural priming. *Neuropsychologia*, 41, 263–70.

Hino, Y., & Lupker, S. J. (1996). Effects of polysemy in lexical decision and naming: An alternative to lexical access accounts. *Journal of Experimental Psychology: Human Perception and Performance*, 22, 1331–56.

Holcomb, P. J., Reder, L., Misra, M., & Grainger, J., (2005). The effects of prime visibility on ERP measures of masked priming. *Cognitive Brain Research*, 24, 155–72.

Huey, E. B. (1908). *The Psychology and Pedagogy of Reading*. Repr. 1968. MIT Press, Cambridge, MA.

Huntsman, L. A., & Lima, S. D. (1996). Orthographic neighborhood structure and lexical access. *Journal of Psycholinguistic Research*, 25, 417–29.

Hutchison, K. A. (2003). Is semantic priming due to association strength or feature overlap? A micro-analytic review. *Psychonomic Bulletin & Review*, 10, 785–813.

Inhoff, A. W., & Rayner, K. (1986). Parafoveal word processing during eye fixations in reading: Effects of word frequency. *Perception & Psychophysics*, 40, 431–9.

Izura C., & Ellis, A. W. (2004). Age of acquisition effects in translation judgment tasks. *Journal of Memory and Language*, 50, 165–81.

Juhasz, B. J., Yap, M. J., Dicke, J., Taylor, S. C., & Gullick, M. M. (2011). Tangible words are recognized faster: The grounding of meaning in sensory and perceptual systems. *Quarterly Journal of Experimental Psychology*, 64, 1683–91.

Kezilas, Y., McKague, M., Kohnen, S., Badcock, N. A., & Castles, A. (2017). Disentangling the developmental trajectories of letter position and letter identity coding using masked priming. *Journal of Experimental Psychology: Learning, Memory, and Cognition*, 43, 250–8.

Kiefer, M. (2002). The N400 is modulated by unconsciously perceived masked words: Further evidence for an automatic spreading activation account of N400 priming effects. *Cognitive Brain Research*, 13, 27–39.

Kriegeskorte, N., Mur, M., & Bandettini, P. (2008). Representational similarity analysis—connecting the branches of systems neuroscience. *Frontiers in Systems Neuroscience*, 2, 4.

Lavric, A., Clapp, A., & Rastle, K. (2007). ERP evidence of morphological analysis from orthography: A masked priming study. *Journal of Cognitive Neuroscience*, 19, 866–77.

Lavric, A., Elchlepp, H., & Rastle, K. (2012). Tracking hierarchical processing in morphological decomposition with brain potentials. *Journal of Experimental Psychology: Human Perception and Performance*, 38, 811–16.

Lerner, I., Armstrong, B. C., Frost, R. (2014). What can we learn from learning models about sensitivity to letter-order in visual word recognition? *Journal of Memory and Language*, 77, 40–58.

Lewis, M. B., Gerhand, S., & Ellis, H. D. (2001). Re-evaluating age-of-acquisition effects: Are they simply cumulative frequency effects? *Cognition*, 72, 189–205.

Locker, L., Simpson, G. B., & Yates, M. (2003). Semantic neighbourhood effects on the recognition of ambiguous words. *Memory & Cognition*, 31, 505–15.

Longtin, C. M., & Meunier, F. (2005). Morphological decomposition in early visual word processing. *Journal of Memory and Language*, 53, 26–41.

Lucas, M. (2000). Semantic priming without association: A meta-analytic review. *Psychonomic Bulletin & Review*, 7, 618–30.

Lukatela, G., Frost, S. J., & Turvey, M. T. (1998). Phonological priming by masked nonword primes in the lexical decision task. *Journal of Memory and Language*, 39, 666–83.

Lukatela, G., & Turvey, M. T. (1994). Visual lexical access is initially phonological: Evidence from associative priming by words, homophones, and pseudohomophones. *Journal of Experimental Psychology: General*, 123, 107–28.

McCann, R. S., Besner, D., & Davelaar, E. (1988). Word recognition and identification. Do word-frequency effects reflect lexical access? *Journal of Experimental Psychology: Human Perception and Performance*, 14, 693–706.

McClelland, J. L. (1979). On the time relations of mental processes: A framework for analyzing processes in cascade. *Psychological Review, 86*, 287–330.

McClelland, J. L., & Johnston, J. C. (1977). The role of familiar units in perception of words and nonwords. *Perception & Psychophysics, 22*, 249–61.

McClelland, J. L., & Rumelhart, D. E. (1981). An interactive activation model of context effects in letter perception: Part 1. An account of basic findings. *Psychological Review, 88*, 375–407.

McCormick, S., Brysbaert, M., & Rastle, K. (2009). Is morphological decomposition limited to low-frequency words? *The Quarterly Journal of Experimental Psychology, 62*, 1706–15.

McCormick, S., Rastle, K., & Davis, M. H. (2008). Is there a "fete" in "fetish"? Effects of orthographic opacity on morpho-orthographic segmentation in visual word recognition. *Journal of Memory and Language, 58*, 307–26.

McQuade, D. V. (1981). Variable reliance on phonological information in visual word recognition. *Language and Speech, 24*, 99–109.

Melby-Lervag, M., Lyster, S. A., & Hulme, C. (2012). Phonological skills and their role in learning to read: A meta-analytic review. *Psychological Bulletin, 138*, 322–52.

Meyer, D. E., & Schvaneveldt, R. W. (1971). Facilitation in recognizing pairs of words: Evidence of a dependence between retrieval operations. *Journal of Experimental Psychology, 90*, 227–34.

Mirman, D., & Magnuson, J. S. (2008). Attractor dynamics and semantic neighbourhood density: Processing is slowed by near neighbors and speeded by distant neighbors. *Journal of Experimental Psychology: Learning, Memory, and Cognition, 34*, 65–79.

Monaghan, P., & Ellis, A. W. (2010). Modelling reading development: Cumulative, incremental learning in a computational model of word naming. *Journal of Memory and Language, 63*, 506–25.

Monsell, S. (1991). The nature and locus of word frequency effects in reading. In: Besner, D. & Humphreys, G. W. (Eds.), *Basic Processes in Reading: Visual Word Recognition*. Erlbaum, Hillsdale, NJ.

Morrison, C. M., & Ellis, A. W. (1995). Roles of word frequency and age of acquisition in word naming and lexical decision. *Journal of Experimental Psychology: Learning, Memory, and Cognition, 21*, 116–33.

Morton, J. (1969). Interaction of information in word recognition. *Psychological Review, 76*, 165–78.

Morton, J. (1979). Facilitation in word recognition: Experiments causing change in the logogen model. In: Kolers, P. A., Wrolstad, M. E., & Bouma, H. (Eds.), *Processing of Visible Language* (Vol. 1). Plenum Press, New York, NY.

Morton, J., & Patterson, K. (1980). A new attempt at an interpretation, or, an attempt at a new interpretation. In: Coltheart, M., Patterson, K., & Marshall, J. C. (Eds.), *Deep Dyslexia*. Routledge & Kegan Paul, London.

Murray, W. S., & Forster, K. I. (2004). Serial mechanisms in lexical access: The rank hypothesis. *Psychological Review, 111*, 721–56.

Nation, K. (2017). Nurturing a lexical legacy: Reading experience is critical for the development of word reading skill. *NPJ Science of Learning, 2*. doi:10.1038/s41539-017-0004-7

Neely, J. H. (1977). Semantic priming and retrieval from lexical memory: Roles of inhibitionless spreading activation and limited-capacity attention. *Journal of Experimental Psychology: General, 106*, 226–54.

Neely, J. H. (1991). Semantic priming effects in visual word recognition: A selective review of current findings and theories. In: Besner, D., & Humphreys, G. W. (Eds.), *Basic Processes in Reading: Visual Word Recognition* (pp. 264–336). Erlbaum, Hillsdale, NJ.

New, B., Brysbaert, M., Veronis, J., & Pallier, C. (2007). The use of film subtitles to estimate word frequencies. *Applied Psycholinguistics, 28*, 661–77.

Paap, K. R., & Johansen, L. S. (1994). The case of the vanishing frequency effect: A retest of the verification model. *Journal of Experimental Psychology: Human Perception and Performance, 20*, 1129–57.

Paap, K. R., Newsome, S. L., McDonald, J. E., & Schvaneveldt, R. W. (1982). An activation-verification model for letter and word recognition: The word-superiority effect. *Psychological Review, 89*, 573–94.

Pelli, D. G., Farell, B., & Moore, D. C. (2003). The remarkable inefficiency of word recognition. *Nature, 423*, 752–6.

Perea, M., & Lupker, S. J. (2003). Does jugde activate COURT? Transposed-letter similarity effects in masked associative priming. *Memory & Cognition, 31*, 829–41.

Perea, M., & Pollatsek, A. (1998). The effects of neighborhood frequency in reading and lexical decision. *Journal of Experimental Psychology: Human Perception and Performance, 24*, 767–79.

Perea, M., & Rosa, E. (2002). Does "whole word shape" play a role in visual word recognition? *Perception & Psychophysics, 64*, 785–94.

Perfetti, C. A., & Bell, L. C. (1991). Phonemic activation during the first 40ms of word identification: Evidence from backward masking and priming. *Journal of Memory and Language, 30*, 473–85.

Perfetti, C. A., Bell, L. C., & Delaney, S. M. (1988). Automatic (prelexical) phonetic activation in silent word reading: Evidence from backward masking. *Journal of Memory and Language, 27*, 59–70.

Perry, C., Ziegler, J. C., & Zorzi, M. (2007). Nested modeling and strong inference testing in the development of computational theories: The CDP + model of reading aloud. *Psychological Review, 27*, 301–33.

Perry, C., Ziegler, J. C., & Zorzi, M. (2010). Beyond single syllables: Large-scale modelling of reading aloud with the Connectionist Dual Process (CDP ++) model. *Cognitive Psychology, 61*, 106–51.

Pexman, P. M., Lupker, S. J., Hino, Y. (2002). The impact of feedback semantics in visual word recognition: Number of features effects in lexical decision and naming tasks. *Psychonomic Bulletin & Review, 9*, 542–9.

Pexman, P. M., Lupker, S. J., & Jared, D. (2001). Homophone effects in lexical decision. *Journal of Experimental Psychology: Learning, Memory, and Cognition, 22*, 139–56.

Plaut, D. C., & Gonnerman, L. M. (2000). Are non-semantic morphological effects incompatible with a distributed connectionist approach to lexical processing? *Language and Cognitive Processes, 15*, 445–85.

Plaut, D. C., McClelland, J. L., Seidenberg, M. S., & Patterson, K. (1996). Understanding normal and impaired word reading: Computational principles in quasi-regular domains. *Psychological Review, 103*, 56–115.

Rapp, B., Folk, J. R., & Tainturier, M. (2001). Word reading. In: Rapp, B. (Ed.), *The Handbook of Cognitive Neuropsychology: What Deficits Reveal about the Human Mind* (pp. 183–210). Psychology Press, New York, NY.

Rastle, K., & Brysbaert, M. (2006). Masked phonological priming effects in English: A critical review and two decisive experiments. *Cognitive Psychology, 53*, 97–145.

Rastle, K., Davis, M., & New, B. (2004). The broth in my brother's brothel: Morpho-orthographic segmentation in visual word recognition. *Psychonomic Bulletin & Review, 11*, 1090–8.

Rastle, K., & Davis, M. H. (2008). Morphological decomposition based on the analysis of orthography. *Language and Cognitive Processes, 23*, 942–71.

Rastle, K., Davis, M. H., Marslen-Wilson, W. D., & Tyler, L. K. (2000). Morphological and semantic effects in visual word recognition: A time-course study. *Language and Cognitive Processes, 15*, 507–37.

Rastle, K., Lavric, A., Elchlepp, H., & Crepaldi, D. (2015). Processing differences across regular and irregular inflections revealed through ERPs. *Journal of Experimental Psychology: Human Perception and Performance, 41*, 747–60.

Rayner, K., Foorman, B. R., Pesetsky, D., & Seidenberg, M. S. (2001). How psychological science informs the teaching of reading. *Psychological Science in the Public Interest, 2*, 31–74.

Reicher, G. M. (1969). Perceptual recognition as a function of meaningfulness of stimulus material. *Journal of Experimental Psychology, 81*, 275–80.

Rodd, J., Gaskell, M. G., & Marslen-Wilson, W. (2002). Making sense of semantic ambiguity: Semantic competition in lexical access. *Journal of Memory and Language, 46*, 245–66.

Rothlein, D, & Rapp, B. (2014). The similarity structure of distributed neural responses reveals the multiple representations of letters. *NeuroImage, 89*, 331–44.

Rubenstein, H., Lewis, S. S., & Rubenstein, M. A. (1971). Evidence for phonemic recoding in visual word recognition. *Journal of Verbal Learning and Verbal Behavior, 10*, 645–57.

Rumelhart, D. E., & McClelland, J. L. (1982). An interactive activation model of context effects in letter perception: Part 2. The contextual enhancement effect and some tests and extensions of the model. *Psychological Review, 89*, 60–94.

Saenger, P. H. (1997). *Space Between Words: The Origins of Silent Reading.* Stanford University Press, Stanford, CA.

Schilling, H. E. H., Rayner, K., & Chumbley, J. I. (1998). Comparing naming, lexical decision, and eye fixation times: Word frequency effects and individual differences. *Memory & Cognition, 26*, 1270–81.

Schmandt-Besserat, D., (1996). *How Writing Came About.* University of Texas Press, Austin, TX.

Schoonbaert, S., & Grainger, J. (2004). Letter position coding in printed word perception: Effects of repeated and transposed letters. *Language and Cognitive Processes, 19*, 333–67.

Sears, C. R., Hino, Y., & Lupker, S. J., (1995). Neighborhood size and neighborhood frequency effects in word recognition. *Journal of Experimental Psychology: Human Perception and Performance, 21*, 876–900.

Segui, J., & Grainger, J. (1990). Priming word recognition with orthographic neighbors: Effects of relative prime-target frequency. *Journal of Experimental Psychology: Human Perception and Performance, 16*, 65–76.

Stadthagen-Gonzales, H., Bowers, J. S., & Damian, M. F. (2004). Age-of-acquisition effects in visual word recognition: Evidence from expert vocabularies. *Cognition, 93*, B11–B26.

Taft, M., & Ardasinski, S. (2006). Obligatory decomposition in reading prefixed words. *The Mental Lexicon, 1*, 183–99.

Tamminen, J., Davis, M. H., & Rastle, K. (2015). From specific example to general knowledge in language learning. *Cognitive Psychology, 79*, 1–39.

Taylor, J. S. H., Rastle, K., & Davis, M. H. (2013). Can cognitive models explain brain activation during word and pseudo-word reading? A meta-analysis of 36 neuroimaging studies. *Psychological Bulletin, 134*, 766–91.

Taylor, J. S. H., Duff, F., Woollams, A., Monaghan, P., & Ricketts, J. (2015). How word meaning influences word reading. *Current Directions in Psychological Science, 24*, 322–8.

van Heuven, W. J. B., Mandera, P., Keuleers, E., & Brysbaert, M. (2014). SUBTLEX-UK: A new and improved word frequency database for British English. *The Quarterly Journal of Experimental Psychology, 67*, 1176–90.

Vanhoy, M., & Van Orden, G. C. (2001). Pseudohomophones and word recognition. *Memory & Cognition, 29*, 522–9.

Velan, H., & Frost, R. (2009). Letter transposition effects are not universal: The impact of transposing letters in Hebrew. *Journal of Memory and Language, 61*, 285–302.

Wheeler, D. D. (1970). Processes in visual word recognition. *Cognitive Psychology, 1*, 59–85.

Whitney, C. (2001). How the brain encodes the order of letters in a printed word: The SERIOL model and selective literature review. *Psychonomic Bulletin & Review, 8*, 221–43.

Xu, B., & Perfetti, C. A. (1999). Nonstrategic subjective thresholds in phonemic masking. *Memory & Cognition, 27*, 26–36.

Yap, M. J., Pexman, P. M., Wellsby, M., Hargreaves, I. S., & Huff, M. J. (2012). An abundance of riches: Cross-task comparisons of semantic richness effects in visual word recognition. *Frontiers in Human Neuroscience, 6*, 1–10.

Yarkoni, T., Balota, D., & Yap, M., (2008). Moving beyond Coltheart's N: A new measure of orthographic similarity. *Psychonomic Bulletin & Review, 15*, 971–9.

Zevin, J. D., & Seidenberg, M. S. (2002). Age of acquisition effects in word reading and other tasks. *Journal of Memory and Language, 47*, 1–29.

Ziegler, J. C., Bertrand, D., Lété, B., & Grainger, J. (2013). Orthographic and phonological contributions to reading development: Tracking developmental trajectories using masked priming. *Developmental Psychology, 50*, 1026–36.

Ziegler, J. C., Ferrand, L., Jacobs, A. M., Rey, A., & Grainger, J. (2000). Visual and phonological codes in letter and word recognition: Evidence from incremental priming. *Quarterly Journal of Experimental Psychology, 53A*, 671–92.

Ziegler, J. C., & Goswami, U. C. (2005). Reading acquisition, developmental dyslexia and skilled reading across languages: A psycholinguistic grain size theory. *Psychological Bulletin, 131*, 3–29.

Ziegler, J. C., Jacobs, A. M., & Klüppel, D. (2001). Pseudohomophone effects in lexical decisions: Still a challenge for current word recognition models. *Journal of Experimental Psychology: Human Perception and Performance, 27*, 547–59.

Ziegler, J. C., & Perry, C. (1998). No more problems in Coltheart's neighbourhood: Resolving neighbourhood conflicts in the lexical decision task. *Cognition, 68*, B53–B62.

CHAPTER 4

LEXICO-SEMANTICS

LOTTE METEYARD AND GABRIELLA VIGLIOCCO

4.1 INTRODUCTION

THIS chapter presents a theoretical review of how humans represent and process word meaning (lexico-semantics). We start with a review of current theoretical approaches. The review is necessarily brief and incomplete but attempts to provide a cross-disciplinary perspective on word meaning informed by cognitive and developmental psychology, cognitive neuroscience, linguistics, and computational sciences. We then move to a discussion of what we believe are core theoretical issues that ought to be addressed by any theory of *lexical* semantics. These key issues are: (1) whether and how we should distinguish between concepts and word meanings; (2) the format of lexico-semantic representations; and (3) whether lexico-semantics should be considered as fundamentally context-independent or as context-dependent. We focus in particular on the issue of context-invariance vs. context-dependency as we see this as a core contemporary challenge that needs to be comprehensively addressed in order for the field to move forward. We define context as the conditions under which meaning is learnt and processed. At a minimum this includes the cognitive context (e.g., the prior knowledge of the individual, the learning history), the task context (e.g., language encountered before and after the word itself, what the individual is doing with the linguistic stimuli), and the physical context (e.g., co-occurring non-linguistic information such as perceived faces, gestures, environmental stimuli, and so on).

While there is a long-standing tradition that considers word meaning as dynamic, influenced by both linguistic and non-linguistic context and a large body of evidence showing context-effects on processing word meanings, very few attempts have been made at providing a systematic overview of what, when, and how context matters in lexico-semantic processing.

4.2 Current theoretical approaches to the study of word meaning

Theories of lexico-semantics are concerned with how a word can *mean* something. Current theories can be divided into those that consider meaning as derivable from constituent features or attributes (which we will refer to as "attributional" theories), those that consider meaning as derivable from language use (which we will refer to as "distributional" theories), and those that consider both sources of information (see Andrews et al., 2009; Speed et al., 2015).

4.2.1 Attributional theories

Attributional theories place emphasis on attributes of meaning as building blocks (e.g., Collins & Loftus, 1975; McRae, de Sa, & Seidenberg, 1997). Sets of features are bound together to form a lexical representation of a word's meaning. For example, the meaning of *chair* could be defined by features including <has legs>, <made of wood>, and <is sat on>. Featural properties have been modeled to explain category-specific deficits in different forms of brain damage and to shed light on the organization of the semantic system (e.g., Devlin, Gonnerman, Andersen, & Seidenberg, 1998; Farah & McClelland, 1991; Plaut & Shallice, 1993). These theories describe semantic similarity between words in terms of types of features that are the most common for a particular concept (e.g., visual, motor, and so on; Farah & McClelland, 1991; Vigliocco et al., 2004), feature correlations and overlap across different concepts (e.g., Cree & McRae, 2003; Tyler & Moss, 2001), and feature weights (McRae & Boisvert, 1998; Smith, Shoben, & Rips, 1974). These properties have been shown to account for behavioral effects such as reaction times during semantic priming (e.g., Cree & McRae 2003; Vigliocco et al., 2004) and patterns of category-specific deficits in patient groups (e.g., Cree & McRae, 2003; Garrard, Lambon Ralph, Hodges, & Patterson, 2001; Tyler & Moss, 2001).

Attributional theories can be easily extended to encompass more recent theories from embodiment. The basic idea is that sensory, motor, and affective information from our experience constitute semantics. For example, the attributes for "mouse" are made up of our visual experiences of seeing mice, auditory and haptic experiences of hearing and touching mice, and emotional reactions we have had to mice (Meteyard, Cuadrado, Bahrami, & Vigliocco, 2012). Simulation or selective reactivation of experiences are a means for modality specific information to constitute the building blocks for semantic representations (e.g., Wilson, 2002; Zwaan, 2014). As such, featural attributes can be linked to specific sensory and motor information. For example, the feature <squeak> for *mouse* would be linked to auditory experiences and perceptual traces from hearing mice and rodents squeaking.

Challenges for embodied and attributional theories that are grounded in experiential traces include the problem of integration. If lexico-semantics is composed of distributed attributes, how do these form a coherent representation that has emergent properties not reducible to any particular component? (Reilly et al., 2016). Such properties are, for example, the way that a word can mean *the same thing* across different situations and sit within hierarchical categorical relationships (e.g., British short hair—cat—mammal). Amodal and localist theories propose that there must be some core, abstracted information that stands as *the* coherent lexico-semantic representation (Mahon & Hickok, 2016; Patterson, Nestor, & Rogers, 2007; Reilly et al., 2016). Abstract words and concepts such as *truth, beauty,* and *liberty* do not have straightforward experiential referents (Dove, 2011; Shallice & Cooper, 2013), posing another challenge for simple attributional/embodied approaches. One way of explaining abstract concepts within the attributional approaches is to include emotion, in the form of affective features. Thus, whereas the meaning of concrete words would be made primarily of sensory-motor properties, the meaning of abstract words would be grounded primarily in our internal affective states (Kousta et al., 2011).

4.2.2 Distributional theories

Distributional theories have a long tradition in Computational Linguistics (Andrews, Vigliocco, & Vinson, 2009; Griffiths, Steyvers, & Tenenbaum, 2007; Mitchell & Lapata, 2010). Through the use of a large corpora of text, word meaning is formalized through the relationships that words have to each other. For example, the words *mouse* and *rat* are related as small, furry animals that can be pests, but the words *mouse* and *cheese* are related as one eats the other. These words are used together in diverse ways (i.e., in different contexts, and in the company of different words) so it is possible to reconstruct the semantic relationship between them by compiling distributional information from text corpora. This can be captured by plotting word-to-word relationships as networks (linking one word to another, e.g., Collins & Loftus, 1975), associations or distributions (how often words appear with other words: Burgess, 1998; Landauer & Dumais, 1997; Lund & Burgess, 1996; Shaoul & Westbury, 2006, 2010). Since these models typically use only text corpora as input (i.e., essentially lists of words, sentences, or passages), they compute meaning from usage statistics for a set of symbols (the words, passages, or whatever unit of analysis) rather than linking to a word's referent in the embodied world (Landauer & Dumais, 1997). That is, these models formalize what a word means by how often and in what typical patterns it occurs with other words. In this way, distributional models capture the linguistic context in which words are encountered. An advantage of these approaches is that word meaning can be quantified by measuring the modeled distance between words (Mitchell & Lapata, 2010). One of the first examples is latent semantic analysis (LSA; Landauer & Dumais, 1997) in which a large corpus of text is analyzed with each word marked for the passage or document that it appears within. This creates a large matrix of words and where they appear. The matrix is simplified to produce vectors for each word. Words with similar vectors (and therefore similar meanings) tend to appear in the same kinds of passages and documents.

Distributional models have been shown to predict human performance across different tasks. For example, semantic priming (Lund & Burgess, 1996) and ratings of how easy it is to imagine or picture a word's meaning (Westbury et al., 2013). They have been extended to extract topics rather than vectors (e.g., Griffiths, Steyvers, & Tenenbaum, 2007). Topics are probability distributions, constituted by a set of words with high probabilities (e.g., *test, studying, homework, class, try, teacher, need, try*). Griffiths et al. (2007) showed that topics naturally capture the different senses of a word, as these senses are articulated when words appear across more than one topic (e.g., *test, method, hypothesis, evidence, scientific*). It was also shown that topic models are better at predicting word associates than LSA, and were comparably good in correctly selecting synonyms for a given word. As larger and larger corpora become available and as new, more powerful algorithms are developed new distributional models show improved performance in accounting for lexical and semantic decisions as well as ratings of concreteness and imageability (see, e.g., Rotaru et al., 2016). Importantly, it should be noted that these models do not consider serial (or hierarchical) relationships between words, such that important semantic information is lost (e.g., "the dog bites the man" and "the man bites the dog" are treated as providing the same information). For this reason, they are usually referred to as "bags of words" models. There are some attempts to go beyond bags of words that suggest the importance of the serial order information (Andrews & Vigliocco, 2010). Another extension has been the development of models that can account for "higher" units of meaning such as phrases or sentences (Mitchell & Lapata, 2010).

4.2.3 Hybrid, multilevel, and combined models

As is typical in scientific research, opposing theories each with supporting evidence can be reconciled by an inclusive approach. It is sensible to hypothesize that lexico-semantics calls upon our full range of experiences; that is, a combination of attributional and distributional information (Andrews, Frank, & Vigliocco, 2014). Andrews et al. (2009) show that combining attributional and distributional information is critical for developing the rich semantic system typical of adults. As the number of concepts we can learn via direct experience is necessarily limited, statistical distributions of words in language provide another crucial way in which we learn concepts and words. It has been shown that models that combine both types of data perform better in simulating semantic effects than either alone (Andrews, Vigliocco, & Vinson, 2009). Moreover, and crucially, models that embed both sensory-motor and linguistic information allow for making inferences. Andrews et al. (2009) and Johns and Jones (2012) showed how sensori-motor properties for word meanings acquired only via distributional information can be inferred, when a model includes both types of information for several other concepts/words. For example, if I had only ever read or talked about *mice* I would still be able to infer that *mice* have sensori-motor properties like other animals (audible squeaks, soft fur, gray, or brown coloring). Thus, distributional information can be grounded when it is combined with a sensori-motor system. However, sometimes the model inferences may be incorrect (e.g., inferring "soft" for rat). It remains an open question whether children learning unfamiliar words and concepts (such as "rat") may make similar errors (Andrews et al., 2009).

There are now several models that combine distributional information from texts with visual information derived from computer vision or images (Anderson et al., 2015; Bruni, Tran, & Baroni, 2014; Cassani & Lopopolo, 2015; Kiela, Hill, Korhonen, & Clark, 2014). Bruni, Tran, and Baroni (2014) combined a linguistic distributional model with a "bag of visual words" extracted from images (i.e., images analyzed to identify salient and information rich regions which can then be collated and compared). Combined models showed modest improvements when compared to distributional models alone, for example, supplementing performance particularly for concrete concepts (see also Kiela, Hill, Korhonen, & Clark, 2014). There is evidence that combined models map onto activity in expected brain regions.

Anderson et al. (2015) asked participants to read a list of object words while undergoing brain scanning (e.g., *bed, hammer, dress, window*). They found that brain activity in visual processing regions (e.g., ventral temporal cortex, medial occipital gyrus) correlated with an image based model of the same objects, while brain activity in language areas (e.g., left inferior frontal gyrus and middle temporal gyrus) correlated with a linguistic distributional model of the object names. This supports the idea that lexico-semantic representations are constituted by different sources of information, in this case linguistic distributions and visual images.

This theme continues in arguments that the conceptual system has a dual or manifold nature with modal and amodal content that is responsible for different aspects of meaning (Dove, 2009, 2011). Amodal elements may form a stable core of semantic information with sensory and motor attributes activated as supplementary content (Dove, 2009, 2011; Lebois et al., 2015; Mahon & Hickok, 2016; Patterson, Nestor, & Rogers, 2007; Reilly et al., 2016). Alternatively, linguistic representations may be activated first and then a later situated simulation involves sensory-motor systems (Barsalou, Santos, Simmons, & Wilson, 2008). Under this description, linguistic information includes word frequency and associations and embodied information is perceptual, motor, and introspective content (Barsalou, 1982; Barsalou, Santos, Simmons, & Wilson, 2008; Louwerse, 2011). In support of such a combined view, effect sizes for embodied, perceptual variables are larger for "deeper" conceptual tasks (judging whether word pairs appeared in their canonical vertical relation, e.g., *attic* above *basement*) than in a "shallow" task with the same items (judging whether two words are related) (Louwerse & Jeuniaux, 2010; Meyer & Schvaneveldt, 1971; see also Solomon & Barsalou, 2004). Embodied variables predict performance more strongly for picture stimuli than word stimuli, and effect sizes for experiments demonstrating embodiment are smaller when single words are used—presumably because less experiential information is available for simulation (Louwerse, Hutchinson, Tillman, & Recchia, 2015).

In sum, it is highly likely that lexico-semantic representations are constituted by multiple sources of information. Distributed, attributional, and hybrid theories propose that these multiple sources of information *are* the lexico-semantic representation. This sets them apart from amodal and localist theories which propose that these multiple sources of information become redundant or unnecessary for "true" semantic processing once an abstract representation is formed.

4.3 KEY ISSUES IN SEMANTIC REPRESENTATION

There are at least three main issues that any theory of lexico-semantics needs to address. The first concerns the clarity of the domain under consideration: is the theory a theory of word meaning, of conceptual representation, or both? The second concerns the format of representation and the third concerns the role of context. These three issues are not independent from one another, for example, choices of format of representation influence the presumed relationship between lexical and conceptual knowledge, as well as whether these are shaped by context. Next we address each in turn, focusing especially on the issue of context.

4.3.1 Concepts and word meanings

When discussing word meaning, we are immediately presented with the thorny issue of whether and how to separate our knowledge of what words mean from our mental representations for objects, events, qualities, and so on—namely, from our conceptual knowledge. As discussed in Vigliocco and Vinson (2007), word meanings need to map into our mental representations of the world so that we can use it to share experiences, needs, thoughts, desires, and so on. In addition, children come to the language learning task already equipped with knowledge about the world (based on innate biases and concrete experience) (e.g., Bloom, 2000; Smith & Gasser, 2005). Thus, word meanings (or semantics) must be grounded in conceptual knowledge (mental representations of objects, events, and so on that are non-linguistic). But are they the same thing? A key problem for theories that do not distinguish between concepts and word meanings is that the mapping is not one word to one concept, and the relationship is inherently flexible (e.g., Lakoff, 1990). For example, languages lexicalize concepts in separate ways. English and Dutch have two words for *leg* and *foot*, whereas Japanese has only one: *ashi*. Moreover, it is very likely the case that neither conceptual nor lexico-semantic representations are holistic and localistic (although see Levelt, 1999). Current evidence suggests that the process of extracting meaning from language is highly distributed across the brain (Huth, Nishimoto, Vu, & Gallant, 2012; Huth et al., 2016). As language is a powerful tool for categorization (Lupyan, Rakison, & McClelland, 2007) a reasonable assumption is that lexico-semantic representations bind conceptual information (McRae, de Sa, & Seidenberg, 1997; Vigliocco et al., 2004), bringing distributed representations or patterns of activation into unified experiences.

One way in which this can be conceptualized is in terms of convergence zones (Damasio, 1989; Damasio & Damasio, 1994; Martin, 2016; Simmons & Barsalou, 2003). These are collections of processing units in the cortex that receive input and encode activity from multiple coactivated inputs (McNorgan, Reid, & McRae, 2011; see also Vigliocco, Tranel, & Druks, 2012). Such integration is essential for lexical processing in order to map between conceptual properties and phonological/orthographic information about words. By assuming that binding within convergence zones is dynamic, we do not abide to "simple nativism" (Levinson, 2003), according to which "linguistic categories are a direct projection of universal concepts that are native to the species" (p. 28). Dynamic binding of information allows for language specific properties to impact our representations of word meaning (see discussion in Vigliocco et al., 2004). Crucially, it also allows for context (during learning and processing) to impact on word meanings, as we will further discuss. Variations on convergence zones may also provide a means for embodied or attributional theories to meet the challenges posed by amodal, localist theories. If convergence zones can capture higher-order multimodal associations, they can also capture more abstract properties and relationships (Martin, 2016). As such, convergence zones are the basis for a number of neuroscientific and neuropsychological theories of meaning (see Chen, Lambon Ralph, & Rogers, 2017; Martin, 2016; Pulvermüller, 2013; Simmons & Barsalou, 2003). As noted previously here, a challenge for theories of lexico-semantics is binding (i.e., bringing together different aspects of meaning to form a coherent representation). Convergence zones provide a neurologically motivated means for this process.

4.3.2 The format and content of representations: embodied or amodal?

A second key issue for word meaning is the cognitive format of semantic representations. In other words, what is the content of word meanings? One assumption is that word meaning is abstract and amodal (Levelt, 1999; Patterson, Nestor, & Rogers, 2007), separated from experience and stored as symbols in the brain, in much the same way that a computer represents various kinds of information as abstract binary code. In contrast, embodied theories of semantics have proposed that word meaning is grounded in everyday perception, action, and internal states, and constituted of sensory, motor, and affective traces from our experiences (Clark, 1998; see Meteyard et al., 2012, for a review). Symbolic theories tend to be associated with localist representations that are stored in hubs or a constrained set of brain regions (McNorgan, Reid, & McRae, 2011; Patterson, Nestor, & Rogers, 2007; Reilly et al., 2016). Embodied theories tend to be associated with multimodal and distributed representations, encompassing sensory, motor and affective brain regions as well as convergence zones that can abstract and unify across modalities (e.g., Martin, 2016; Simmons & Barsalou, 2003).

There is a large body of evidence that points toward some level of embodiment in word meaning, for example demonstrating the activation of sensory and motor brain regions during language comprehension, or interactions between language and perception, or language and action (see review of the evidence in Meteyard et al., 2012). For example, Meteyard, Bahrami, and Vigliocco (2007) showed that visual discrimination of moving dots is hindered when listening to direction verbs (e.g., "dive," "rise") of the same direction. Similarly, processing words that denote manipulable objects that typically evoke actions toward or away from the body (e.g., "key," "cup") is facilitated when an action was planned in the same direction as the object's typical movement (Rueschemeyer, Pfeiffer, & Bekkering, 2010).

Numerous imaging studies have also provided support for embodied language processing, showing that areas of the brain involved in perception and action are engaged when processing words with similar content. For example, listening to action verbs has been shown to activate the motor cortex somatotopically using verbs related to leg, face, or arm action such as "kick," "lick," and "pick" (Hauk, Johnsrude, & Pulvermüller, 2004; but also see Tomasino & Rumiati, 2013, and Kemmerer, 2015 for critical reviews). Neuropsychological studies have focused primarily on patients with impairments in planning and executing actions, for example patients with lesions to areas of the brain involved in motor production (e.g., Neininger & Pulvermüller, 2003), patients with motor neuron disease (e.g., Bak et al., 2001), and patients with Parkinson's disease (e.g., Boulenger et al., 2008). Bak et al. (2001) looked at language comprehension and production in patients with motor neuron disease, which predominantly affects motor functions. Comprehension and production of verbs was found to be significantly more impaired than nouns for motor neuron disease patients but not for healthy controls or patients with Alzheimer's disease who have both semantic and syntactic language impairments. This selective deficit in the patients with motor neuron disease suggests that the processes underlying verb representation are closely linked to those of the motor systems (Kemmerer, 2015; see Vigliocco et al., 2011, for a review). It is important to note, however, that effects in all these studies (especially behavioral and patient studies) are small and variable (Kemmerer, 2015; Tomasino & Rumiati, 2013), leaving open the possibility that perceptual and motor engagement is epiphenomenal and occurs via spreading activation from a "true" core of amodal content (Mahon & Hickok, 2016). However, an alternative plausible explanation for the variable effects, as we discuss next, is that the specific context of processing matters (Zwaan, 2014). The challenge then is how to constrain a theory of context-dependent processing to avoid the risk of circularity (i.e., variable effects mean context dependence, context dependence means variable effects, Mahon & Hickok, 2016). It must specify which contextual variations will produce a variation in word meaning and which will not, giving both null and alternative hypotheses.

For embodied theories, it remains a challenge to account for the representation of abstract words and language that does not refer to concrete sensory or motor experiences (Meteyard et al., 2012; Reilly et al., 2016). As already mentioned, Kousta et al. (2011) have put forward the proposal that abstract meanings may be grounded in our emotional experience. Such a claim is based on the observation that most abstract concepts have emotional connotations, while this is not the case for concrete concepts. Further, valenced abstract words are among the first abstract words being learnt by children (Ponari et al., 2017b) and the emotion network in the brain is activated in processing abstract words (Vigliocco et al., 2014).

It is however the case that emotion grounding may not provide a full account for the acquisition and processing of the rich repertoire of abstract concepts and words typical of adult speakers. Hybrid and combined models, like those outlined already (see section 4.2.3), have also been discussed as a way in which we can move beyond the simple argument of "symbolic" vs. "embodied." In their simplest formulation, the idea is that abstract words would be more reliant on linguistic information for their acquisition and representation. For example, measures of lexical richness (such as number of neighbors) predict concreteness and imageability ratings (Rotaru, Frank, & Vigliocco, 2016). Recchia and Jones (2012) found that lexical decision times for abstract words were predicted by their number of semantic neighbors (a measure of their lexical richness) whereas reaction times for concrete words were predicted by the number of features generated for them (a measure of their physical or experiential richness). If linguistic information plays a greater role for abstract words, we would expect in development that children who have specific language impairment (SLI) would be especially impaired in learning abstract words and concepts as they would not be able to take advantage of the statistical information about meaning provided in the linguistic input. This is not, however, the case. In recent work, Ponari, Norbury, and Vigliocco (2017a) have specifically assessed the knowledge of concrete and abstract vocabulary of SLI children and their typically developing (TD) peers and found that whereas SLI children had poorer vocabularies than their TD peers, the difference between the groups was quantitative, not qualitative. In other words, there was not a disproportionate impairment for abstract words for the SLI children. Thus, while it is likely the case that emotion and linguistic distributional information are important in grounding abstract knowledge, neither of them is sufficient to account for their acquisition and processing. Understanding how these concepts and words are learnt and processed continues to be a challenge for future research.

Coming back to the key issue of representational format, the convergence zone framework again offers a plausible manner in which embodied and amodal theories can be reconciled. It is proposed that convergence zones capture associations between modality specific, sensory-motor experiences (see Mann, Kaplan, Damasio, & Meyer, 2012). Higher-order structure emerges from this process, with increasingly complex associations (and dissociations) emerging as we move away from modality specific regions (e.g., auditory and visual cortex) toward anterior convergence zones (e.g., anterior temporal lobes) (e.g., Martin,

2016). For example, a lower-order association may be to pair the gray color of a mouse's fur and the squeak it makes, or between the yellow of cheese and a crumbly texture. A higher-order association may be to pair these pairings, and then link those to the word forms *mouse* and *cheese* and their distributional profiles (i.e., other words associated with them). To remain consistent with this framework, amodal theories would propose that there is some "final" point of higher-order association that constitutes an abstract, semantic representation. This is context invariant, stable, and symbolic. Examples of this can be seen in theories that propose a semantic "hub" that captures these higher-order associations (see Chen, Lambon Ralph, & Rogers, 2017; Patterson, Nestor, & Rogers, 2007; Rogers et al., 2004). We agree that there are higher-order associations (this is uncontroversial), but there may not be a final symbolic, invariant state that can be labeled *a* or *the* lexico-semantic representation.

4.3.3 The role of context: Context-invariance vs. context-dependency?

Theories of word meaning are concerned with identifying a core of information that gives a word its meaning. Despite cogent arguments that lexico-semantic representations are dynamic (e.g., Kutas & Federmeier, 2011), the empirical strategy favored by most is to assume that there is a core of word meaning that does not vary across contexts. For example, task independent effects are taken as an index that lexico-semantic or conceptual processing has actually taken place (Hoenig et al., 2008; Yee & Thompson-Schill, 2016). Under this description, context is extraneous stuff that happens when a word is used and this has to be *integrated* with packets of word meaning (e.g., Hagoort et al., 2009). If a word's meaning does vary, the word is considered to have multiple meanings (polysemy) and this brings ambiguity into the comprehension process. Ambiguity must be resolved, and this requires cognitive resources to select the appropriate meaning to integrate with the context (e.g., Rodd, Johnsrude, & Davis, 2012). Context-invariance has been argued to be essential for a healthy, functioning semantic system (Lambon Ralph, 2014; Patterson, Nestor, & Rogers, 2007; Woollams, 2012). For example, it allows me to identify, name, or draw a picture of a *spoon* at home, at the office, or in a different country no matter what the unique properties of the particular spoon (e.g., teaspoon, soup spoon, ice-cream spoon). The human ability to deploy semantic information *across any context* is seen as prima-facie evidence that this information must be context invariant, that is: (a) abstracted away from experience and (b) not dependent on a particular modality of input or output (Patterson, Nestor, & Rogers, 2007). It is argued that typicality matters so much precisely because semantic representations are abstract and amodal/transmodal (Lambon Ralph, 2014; Patterson, 2007). An apple is a typical fruit because it shares many features with other fruit (sweet, has seeds, juicy) whereas an avocado is atypical (savory, stone, oily) (Woollams, 2012; McRae, de Sa, & Seidenberg, 1997). The semantic system has extracted and *abstracted* typical features (e.g., for fruits), so it is then easier to process something that is a typical exemplar of a fruit than something that is atypical (Patterson, 2007; Rogers et al., 2004).

It has long been known, however, that this cannot be the whole story. Context appears to have pervasive effects across tasks and is argued by some to be an essential factor in understanding conceptual and lexico-semantic processing (e.g., Hoenig et al., 2008; Kutas &

Federmeier, 2011; Skipper, 2015; Yee & Thompson-Schill, 2016). Thus, a central question, addressed next, is whether context-dependent variation of word meaning should be seen as the norm.

4.4 WORD MEANING IN CONTEXT

An important implication of the hybrid theories discussed here is that different sources of information may vary in importance, not only for different word types but also in the context in which a particular word is used. Take the example of task context. If I am asked to decide whether *mouse* and *cheese* are related, I can call upon the distributional information that tells me if these words appear together often. If I am asked to describe what a *mouse* looks like I can call upon sensory and motor attributes (Barsalou, 1982; Louwerse, 2011; Simmons et al., 2008; Solomon & Barsalou, 2004). Notably, there is a confound here: words reflect the world, so information from attributional and distributional sources will be correlated (Louwerse, 2011). Evidence that the lexico-semantic system does call upon sensory-motor information in a task specific manner was found by Hsu and colleagues (2012). They found that when a lexico-semantic task (i.e., decide which is lighter *lemon* or *basketball*) and a perceptual task (i.e., decide whether color patches are ordered lightest to darkest) were highly similar both tasks engaged overlapping regions in posterior visual cortex. This was taken as an indicator of perceptual processing occurring in both tasks (Hsu, Frankland, & Thompson-Schill, 2012). Activation of sensory-motor regions does not occur when the lexico-semantic task is simply more difficult or demanding (Hsu, Frankland, & Thompson-Schill, 2012; Martin, 2016).

4.4.1 What is "context"?

By definition, context is everything, making sensible discussions difficult. In empirical research we like to separate out different elements in order to make predictions, so our attempt here is to sketch-out three parts of contextual variation. These move from the internal state of the individual (cognitive context) to the current internally and externally determined task (goal-driven short-term context) to the external environment (physical context). We discuss them separately here in an attempt to operationalize context (see Yee & Thompson-Schill, 2016, for a review of the same issue for conceptual representation). As we will see, these various aspects of context (internal, goal-related, and external) are intimately and dynamically related since the individual experiences them simultaneously.

4.4.1.1 *The individual (the role of experience and current cognitive context)*

The "internal" state of the individual includes their current psycho-physiological state (e.g., affect, fatigue, hunger, motivation), prior knowledge and learning (long-term memory and experience). For affective states, there is a large body of literature on lexico-semantic processing (e.g., the stroop effect) in clinical populations and in healthy adults with a positive or negative induced mood, framed in terms of cognitive or attentional biases toward mood and concern congruent stimuli. In the emotional stroop task, participants name the ink color of emotion words. Williams, Mathews, and MacLeod (1996) reviewed emotional stroop studies across a range of clinical populations (anxiety, phobias, panic, depression), finding that individuals with emotional disturbances show large interference effects for negative stimuli (compared to positive or neutral stimuli). This has been replicated with healthy adults who had a positive or negative induced mood, and showed longer color naming latencies for emotion words congruent with their induced mood (Gilboa-Schechtman, Revelle, & Gotlib, 2000). State based congruence effects should be ubiquitous. That is, aspects of meaning congruent with a given state will be more salient, aspects of meaning incongruent with a given state will be less salient and aspects of meaning neutral as regards the state will show no difference in processing. One possibility is that this change in salience is because the semantic representation of the word itself has changed.

Yee and Thompson-Schill (2016) review evidence that increased exposure or expertise with objects in particular modalities is associated with increased brain activations for those modalities. For example, increased motor experience with objects through pantomiming use or playing sports is linked to greater activity in motor regions of the brain when these objects are encountered (both as pictures, and also as words or sentences). The implication is that for those individuals with more motor experience or expertise, the conceptual and lexico-semantic representations for these items are qualitatively different and contain more motor content than for individuals who do not have this level of experience. Rodd et al. (2016) found that individuals who belonged to rowing clubs produced more word associates that had rowing related meanings when presented with ambiguous words (e.g., *crab*, dominant meaning: crustacean, subordinate rowing meaning: when the blade of the oar gets caught in the water); however, this effect was reduced with age. This is an interesting example of how two contextual factors shape lexico-semantic representations. On the one hand experience with rowing makes particular meanings more salient, but overall experience with the language tends to reassert the dominant meaning.

Brief training or learning experiences can also change effects of lexico-semantic activation. Collina, Tabossi, and De Simone (2013) used a picture-word interference paradigm in which pictures are presented for naming along with a distracter word. The canonical finding is that pictures take longer to name when the distracter word is semantically related to the target (e.g., *dog* presented with *fox*). This is accounted for in terms of competition for production between the two. When participants were familiarized with the picture stimuli before testing, related distracters produced the standard interference effect. However, when a separate group of participants were not familiarized with the pictures, surprisingly, a related distracter produced facilitation. In a follow-up experiment, participants learnt to retrieve a target name to an unrelated picture (e.g., name *frog* as *arrow*). Here, related distracters produced interference. The authors argued that familiarization builds an association between the semantic features of a pictured item and a target name, such that related distracters interfere with the retrieval of that target at test. Without familiarization, participants must first identify the picture name, and the distracter word aids this by activating similar concepts for naming. In sum, subtle variations in the task produce markedly different effects of lexico-semantic processing, explainable by the influence of task goals and prior learning. Effects of embodied metaphorical extension (i.e., understanding abstract word meanings by grounding them with a concrete interpretation) also change after brief training. English speakers would normally use horizontal spatial metaphors for time, with the past = behind and the future = in front. A group were trained to use a vertical metaphor instead (the past = above and the future = below, e.g., "Monday is above Tuesday"). At test, individuals were presented with spatial primes (pictured objects arranged horizontally or vertically) and then questions about time ("March comes before April"). Trained English speakers were facilitated by congruent vertical spatial primes, whereas a separate group of untrained English speakers were facilitated by congruent horizontal spatial primes (Boroditsky, 2001).

Another important dimension related to experience is age, considered here as a proxy for amount of experience. It has been shown that older adults find it more difficult to learn new associations between pairs of semantically non-associated words (e.g., jury-eagle) than associated words (e.g., up-down), and they also find it more difficult to correctly recall people's names. While this has been attributed to cognitive decline, an alternative account is that it may be a direct product of a lifetime of experiences with existing associations (and lack of associations for semantically unrelated items) and a lifetime of encountering an ever-increasing corpus of forenames and surnames (Ramscar et al., 2014). That is, the greater the individual's prior knowledge of word associations and proper names, the harder it may become to reassociate and retrieve specific instances. Further support for this comes from Rodd et al. (2016), who completed an elegant experiment in which individuals were asked to generate word associations to ambiguous words (e.g., *court, match*) after listening to short stories on a national radio program (e.g., a story about tennis). Participants were more likely to generate associates to primed meanings (i.e., tennis related) at short delays (e.g., 1 vs. 10 hours after listening), but this priming effect was reduced by age. Older individuals showed less priming, supporting the idea that the more experience we have with language (i.e., over a lifetime) the harder it is to reassociate or modulate those meanings.

In a similar vein, word priming is greater for low than high frequency words (Neely, 1991) and the impact of priming particular meanings for ambiguous words is greater for subordinate meanings than for dominant meanings (e.g., *pen*, subordinate meaning: animal enclosure, dominant meaning: writing utensil, Rodd et al., 2013, 2016). Low frequency words and subordinate meanings are by definition ones that we do not encounter often, so they will get a greater benefit if the immediate context has made them easier to anticipate. However, in real-world language use (e.g., conversation) there is typically a rich set of information that can be used to prime and predict the upcoming linguistic input, therefore one hypothesis is that differences between low and high frequency words or dominant and subordinate meanings should be reduced or even absent during naturalistic processing tasks. Some evidence compatible with this prediction comes from eye-tracking studies, where looks to cohort competitors (e.g., looking at *cloud* when you hear *clown*) were shown to be equally likely as looks to unrelated words during a language game in which participants conversed in order to arrange items into identical patterns. Critically, looks to cohort competitors were higher than to unrelated words when item names were heard individually, i.e., outside conversation (Brown-Schmidt, Campana, & Tanenhaus, 2005; Tanenhaus & Brown-Schmidt, 2008).

4.4.1.2 *The task (the role of goal-driven, short-term context)*

Task is defined here in broad terms to encompass both tasks completed in daily life (e.g., informal conversation, public speaking, instruction, and so on) and linguistic tasks completed in experimental settings. In laboratory settings we have many clear examples of the effects of task context. We have already seen how slight differences in task structure affect picture-word interference (Collina, Tabossi, & De Simone, 2013). In single-word priming with longer durations between prime and target, priming is only found for words that participants are expecting to see (e.g., following task instructions; Neely, 1991). Becker (1980) found that facilitation or interference in lexical decision depended on stimulus sets. When semantic relationships in an item set were specific and predictable, priming for related pairs was substantial. When semantic relationships were more general and variable, priming for related pairs was small and interference arose for unrelated pairs. In a prescient discussion, Becker (1980) concluded that individuals were using the item context to generate predictions about upcoming stimuli such that processing was speeded up for stimuli that match the predicted salient context (priming) and slowed down when specific predictions are not easily generated (interference). This is clearly in line with many current accounts that argue for predictions to drive cognitive processing.

Whether the task draws attention to one modality or another also matters. Connell and Lynott (2014) found that words referring to objects that are highly visual (e.g., cloudy) are responded to with shorter reaction times during visual lexical decision, whereas words that are highly auditory (e.g., noisy) are produced more quickly during reading aloud. The authors argue that the tasks draw attention to specific modalities of processing (visual—lexical decision, auditory—reading aloud) which facilitates the processing of corresponding semantic information. Pecher, Zeelenberg, and Raaijmakers (1998) found that semantic priming for visual form (e.g., "pizza" priming "coin") was only present when visual form was made salient by a preceding task in which all items were judged for their shape (oblong object or not?). van Dam, Rueschemeyer, Lindemann, and Bekkering (2010) found that reaction times for lexical decision were faster for words congruent with the direction of hand movement participants made to respond (e.g., necklace—toward the body, vase—away from the body). However, this was only the case when the target word was preceded by a context that made the functional/motor aspects of the target word salient (e.g., thirst—cup). Lebois et al. (2015) found that congruency effects for judging vertically paired object words (e.g., attic and basement) only occurred when verticality was made salient, either through task instruction or a previous semantic judgment. These findings show that embodied aspects of meaning are activated in a context-dependent manner.

Embodied theories predict that sensory and motor words should *consistently* activate sensory and motor brain areas (Meteyard et al., 2012). For example, words referring to motor actions (e.g., kick, pinch, kiss) should activate areas directly involved in movement (e.g., motor regions involved in kicking, pinching, and kissing). Tomasino and Rumiati (2013) discuss the consistency of motor activations for mental rotation and action/motor verbs in linguistic tasks. There are studies that do and do not show activation of primary motor cortex in highly similar tasks (e.g., when action verbs are passively heard or read, generated, or categorized). Tomasino and Rumiati (2013) conclude that sensory-motor activations are not automatically triggered, bottom-up, when stimuli such as action verbs are encountered. Rather, these activations are a product of task demands and strategy use. In a similar vein, Kemmerer (2015) concludes that motor features underpinning the meaning of action verbs are not always automatically activated, nor necessary to complete all tasks with these verbs. This does not imply that motor features are not part of the long-term semantic representation for action verbs. Rather, such sensory-motor features are recruited in flexible fashion by a semantic system that adapts to different tasks (Kemmerer, 2015).

Recent neuroimaging studies show considerable flexibility and variability in lexico-semantic processing. Hoenig et al. (2008) had participants judge the meaningful fit between attributes and objects. Pairings were manipulated by crossing action-salient or visual-salient attributes (e.g., to cut vs. elongated) with action-salient or visual-salient objects (e.g., knife vs. banana). Therefore, attributes could match or mismatch the salient sensory dimensions of the object. Data showed cross-over interactions in a number of brain areas, with higher BOLD activity when the non-dominant attribute was probed (i.e., to cut—banana). Notably, these interactions were demonstrated in modality specific regions that process action, visual, and motion information (inferior frontal gyrus, inferior temporal gyrus, inferior/middle temporal gyrus). ERP data showed that these interactions appeared early on in processing (<200 ms after stimulus onset). The authors argue that flexibility, rather than wholly embodied or amodal content, is the only sufficient explanation for the data. van Dam, van Dijk, Bekkering, and Rueschemeyer (2012) asked participants to make a color or action judgment on auditory words. Words were either abstract (e.g., justice), objects associated to a specific color (e.g., tennis ball), objects associated to a specific action (e.g., doorbell), or objects associated with both a specific action and color (e.g., boxing glove). For action-color words, brain regions associated with action and motion (the inferior parietal lobule, intraparietal sulcus, and middle temporal gyrus) were more active when an action decision was being made, not when a color decision was being made. Interactions were not observed for the fusiform gyrus (associated with object color and visual form), with the authors arguing that color properties do not vary with context in the same way as action properties.

These studies demonstrate that different aspects of meaning become available, salient, or accessed depending on the demands of the task. It could be argued that all of these variations take place for non-essential parts of meaning, but this begs the questions of what, then, is necessary or essential? This is an old question, most famously answered by Wittgenstein (1958)—the meanings of words come from the way they are used. Trying to provide absolute definitions, find semantic components ("simple constituents"), or comprehensively detail how words are related is impossible. One implication from the aforementioned studies is that variation in lexico-semantic representations will be pronounced in (a) tasks where there is rich preceding and concurrent information with which to identify the word's meaning and (b) tasks which make only one aspect of the word's meaning salient or useful for task completion. Interestingly, functional brain imaging data will continue to be vitally important here. An extreme prediction is that, with a strong manipulation of context, it may be possible to find non-overlapping cortical representations for the same word (i.e., not homonyms) across different contexts.

4.4.1.3 *The environment (the role of physical context)*

The physical context is the environment in which a particular task takes place. This includes stimuli present in the physical environment (objects, sounds, smells, and so on) as well as the communicative environment (face, body, gestures), that complement verbal or written stimuli (i.e., linguistic stimuli; Perniss & Vigliocco, 2014).

The use of information from the environment has been argued to reduce dependence on long-term memory (i.e., cognitive representations) (Zwaan, 2014). Theories of embodied cognition have long argued that the brain uses the environment and the body to operate efficiently in real-time, rather than spend unnecessary energy "modeling" the world with cognitive representations (Clark, 1998; Wilson, 2002). In cases where there is little environmental context but much detail in the language (such as reading a novel) there is likely to be heavy reliance on internal processes (simulation and representation, Meteyard et al., 2012; Zwaan, 2014). Wherever possible, cognition will reduce the need for representation by offloading onto available environmental and external support. For example, when communication is face-to-face, gesture and other consistent cues between linguistic form and meaning will be used to reduce the burden on simulation and representation. Iconic properties of word forms (i.e., consistent mappings between form and meaning, such as onomatopoeia) facilitate language processing (Imai, Kita, Nagumo, & Okada, 2008; Meteyard et al., 2015) and are more common across languages than previously thought (Perniss, Thompson, & Vigliocco, 2010; Perniss & Vigliocco, 2014). Cortical areas involved in mapping phonological to semantic information (e.g., superior temporal cortex, supramarginal gyrus) respond to meaningful gestures that accompany speech, but not to non-meaningful co-speech gestures such as adjusting one's glasses (Skipper et al., 2009). There is also a rich literature from tracking eye movements to pictures and objects during sentence comprehension—also known as situated language processing. These studies demonstrate how objects in the environment (the "referential domain" being talked about in a sentence) are used to decide what a sentence means (Spivey et al., 2002; Tanenhaus & Brown-Schmidt, 2008; see next).

Zwaan (2014) proposes that the degree to which we rely on any mental representation during communication will be driven by how embedded language use is, in a given physical situation or context. The critical factors are what the communication is about (the reference) and whether this can be derived from the immediate physical environment (where the communication takes place) or whether it must rely on mental representations from long-term memory (individual knowledge). For example, in a demonstration there will be minimal reliance on any mental representations as reference is made to the environment (e.g., deictic expressions like "I put this one here"). Compare this to instruction, where the goal is to change the current environment in some way (e.g., "Can you fill the kettle?"). This requires embodied representations, so an individual can recognize and operate on the environment (e.g., kettle, tap, water, action of filling). In contrast, abstractions will refer to mostly abstract concepts (e.g., this article you are reading) relying on symbolic representations except when grounding can aid comprehension (e.g., the examples we have been using). For Zwaan, we can only understand the importance of these factors by considering naturalistic communication, not "by analyzing decontextualized snippets of language" (2014, p. 231).

Studies in situated language processing have long argued for the use of naturalistic tasks with real-time, online measures. In a typical experiment, participants will take part in a natural language task (such as following instructions to manipulate objects, narrative comprehension, or conversation) while having their eye movements tracked as they watch the presented visual stimuli (the visual world) (Tanenhaus & Brown-Schmidt, 2008). Experiments have demonstrated that individuals use the physical world to aid comprehension online and at speed. These experiments typically use temporally ambiguous sentences such as "*put the apple on the towel into the box.*" Before the arrival of the "*into the box*" phrase, the sentence could refer to putting the apple on a towel, or moving the apple from a towel into a box. These experiments show that ambiguity is removed when the visual scene does not support multiple interpretations. For example, a visual display with two apples (one on a towel and one on a tray) disambiguates the sentence to mean moving the apple from the towel. Under these conditions, participants show significantly fewer looks to competitor locations (i.e., looking at a towel rather than a box) (Spivey, Tanenhaus, Eberhard, & Sedivy, 2002). The goal of the task, actions being performed, and knowledge of the world reduce uncertainty and thus aid comprehension (Tanenhaus & Brown-Schmidt, 2008, p. 1119). Another way to frame this is to say that multiple sources of information are used to predict upcoming linguistic stimuli; these multiple sources of information make up the individual's internal representation of the context of the utterance being comprehended (Kuperberg & Jaeger, 2016).

4.4.2 Theories of context-dependent lexico-semantics

Theories of the lexico-semantics described here assume a "core" lexico-semantic information. In 1982, Barsalou defined as "traditional" theories proposing that all word meaning is context-independent and the same across all instances of word use. This view has persisted to the present day. However, what appears to be a "core" of information, could also represent aspects of meaning that are ubiquitous across many different tasks and internal/external contexts. Aspects of meaning that are salient or relevant for a given task will increase in importance at a given time and appear context-dependent (Barsalou, 1982; Lebois et al., 2015). An early theory of context-dependent meaning is the context availability hypothesis (Schwanenflugel & Shoben, 1983), which states that individuals need context for successful comprehension. In this proposal, context could be internal (their own world knowledge) or external (the immediate environment). When contextual information is not available or degraded, comprehension is more difficult. Context availability ratings reflect how easy it is to think of a real-world circumstance for a word; for example, "the world cup" or "my local park on a Saturday" for the word *football*. Schwanenflugel, Harnishfeger, and Stowe (1988) demonstrated that such ratings were a better explanation of reaction times in lexical decision than whether a word was concrete (e.g., football) or abstract (e.g., inversion), and a stronger predictor of reaction times than imageability or familiarity. A recent extension of this work has defined context availability as the range of different contexts in which a word occurs (semantic diversity), measured from distributional co-occurence statistics (Hoffman, Rogers, & Lambon Ralph, 2011). Words that appear across a wide range of different contexts (typically abstract words) will have greater variation in meaning, and will benefit more from contextual support (e.g., a preceding sentence). This is because it is harder to retrieve a coherent context and/or meaning for them in isolation. In psycholinguistic research, frequency, length, typicality, concreteness, familiarity, and other lexical variables are held to be critically important. However, the vast majority of tasks we use put words in isolation (lexical decision, reading aloud, picture naming, semantic decision, and so on; see also Skipper, 2015). Lexical variables may take on importance precisely because it is *more difficult* to process words in isolation than in a contextually supported situation. Processing in isolation has to rely on whatever information is available, which would usually be restricted to participant knowledge and task parameters. That is, what I am being asked to do (e.g., decide if this is a real word), how many times I have seen that word (frequency), how similar it is to other words I know (typicality, familiarity), and what other words appear (task stimulus sets).

Rather than viewing word meanings as a set or list of information stored in long-term memory, Elman (2004) proposed that word meanings can be viewed as sets of stimuli that affect our internal states (i.e., our cognitive/brain state). Word meanings create reliable and bounded patterns of activation, but the precise way in which that pattern is created will depend on the context of processing. For example, specific instances of a particular word will each have their own unique pattern (e.g., "the *mouse* ate the cheese," "the *mouse* ran away from the cat," "she squeaked like a *mouse*") but in each instance the patterns of activation are similar enough that we know they are all instances of *mouse*. The meaning of the word is understood as the effect it has on internal states: the cues that it provides to meaning. Much of the support for this work has come from studies in online sentence comprehension, which have demonstrated the way in which individuals use multiple sources of information (e.g., lexico-semantic, pragmatic, physical environment) to predict upcoming words and parse sentences during reading or listening (for a review, see Elman, 2009). This view of comprehension as prediction is now ubiquitous in current theories of language.

For example, there is consistent evidence from electroencephalography (EEG) that meaning is constructed on the fly (i.e., it is dynamic) and that we need to use dynamic methods with fine temporal resolution to fully understand semantic processing (Hauk 2016; Yee & Thompson-Schill, 2016). There are critical junctures where incoming stimuli (e.g., words that are read or heard) are recognized and mapped onto the ongoing multimodal landscape of the semantic system (Kutas & Federmeier, 2011). The processing of meaning is "in constant flux in response to both external and internal events and states ... dynamically created and highly context dependent" (Kutas & Federmeier, 2011, p. 640–1). Skipper (2015) proposed a model of language comprehension in which the whole brain is used to predict incoming language (phonology, morphology, lexical items, sentence structure, and so on). Contextual information of all kinds (internal and external to the listener) is composed in dynamic cortical networks that constrain the interpretation of incoming signals, allowing rapid and robust comprehension.

In support of dynamic and distributed processes, there is increasing evidence that all "levels" of linguistic processing are available and interact (Kuperberg & Jaeger, 2016; Spivey, 2016) directly challenging classical box-and-arrow cognitive psychology which partitions modules for different sources of information (e.g., phonology, morphology, syntax, lexicon, and so on; Martin, 2016; Spivey & Dale, 2004). Highly interactive theories place an emphasis on real-time processes, moving away from the idea that fixed representations (e.g., a packet of word meaning) are retrieved from long-term memory (Elman, 2004; Spivey & Dale, 2004). Instead, meaning is established from cognitive states that change rapidly over time. When the pattern of activity matches a probable distribution, and can be interpreted at a given point within the context of processing, that is sufficient for meaning (Elman, 2004). For example, in the sentence "the dog chases the cat" the meaning for cat would have a distribution that reflects being chased, legs, speed, and running. Alternatively, in the sentence "the woman feeds her cat" the distribution for cat would reflect being a pet and eating. Recent studies have demonstrated how dispersed semantic processing is across the cortex. Huth et al. (2012) annotated movies to mark the location of 1,364 different objects and actions, coded as nouns and verbs (e.g., woman, car, talking, building). A whole brain analysis for five participants established which objects and actions enhanced or suppressed the BOLD response in a given voxel, while they watched the movies. Broad areas of cortex selectively responded to a coherent group of objects and events. Principal components analysis extracted groupings such as human vs. non-human, mobile vs. immobile, and place vs. non-place. A second study conducted a similar analysis from seven participants listening to two hours of autobiographical stories (Huth et al., 2016). The authors used word co-occurrence statistics (distributional information) to construct a semantic space that could model each word heard by participants. As in the first study, much of brain was classified as responding selectively to coherent semantic groups (e.g., human/social vs. perceptual/location). Both studies used naturalistic stimuli (movies, narratives) that provide a coherent context for comprehension, and under these conditions we do not see only "language" or "category" areas being active. This argues against a special role for particular brain regions in semantic representation, and by extension, the idea that semantic processing calls upon fixed packets of information from these special regions.

4.5 CONCLUSION

In this chapter we have presented current theories of lexico-semantics. We have traced the move from semantic information as a collection of attributes or measures of association and correlation, to theories that propose ways to combine different information sources. This is situated in a broader theoretical shift from cognitive representations as fixed, retrieved packets of information, toward dynamic constructions that are highly interactive and multimodal. Much of the argument about lexico-semantics has focused on what is the "true" or necessary meaningful information that allows us to complete semantic processing (e.g., is it embodied, is it amodal, is it distributional). We have also seen that lexico-semantic representations can be conceptualized as statistical regularities, collections of features or embodied attributes, markers of co-occurence, associations, and probabilistic relationships between words. All of these are potentially valid sources of information if we think of word meaning as a phenomenon that is dynamic, multimodal, and built on the fly (Hauk, 2016; Kuperberg & Jaeger, 2016; Kutas & Federmeier, 2011; Skipper, 2015).

A unifying framework for understanding this shift is to focus on the *context* of language use (see also Tanenhaus & Brown-Schmidt, 2008). We have made the argument that evidence for context-invariance can be viewed as a product of experiments that present words outside their typically rich cognitive and physical contexts. As a result, the importance of task context and its related variables (e.g., typicality, frequency, constructed relations in stimulus sets) has been exaggerated theoretically. We attempted to separate contextual variation into three broad components which can be subject to empirical study. The internal state of the individual can be manipulated to make certain stimuli more salient or to change the experience of those stimuli through training and exposure. We have argued that more naturalistic, richer tasks will potentially allow more striking variations in word meaning to be demonstrated. It should be relatively straightforward to manipulate the meaning of a word through training and increased exposure under specific conditions. This should be especially the case for low frequency words (i.e., those for which we have less experience already), subordinate meanings for ambiguous words, or for more abstract words (i.e., less tied to specific objects, already appearing across multiple contexts, already more dependent on context for their meaning). There is already intriguing evidence that different timescales of experience will interact, with age tending to assert the dominant and highly frequent patterns in a language. For task context, there is already ample evidence that goals, actions, and the preceding linguistic stimuli influence lexico-semantic processing, with research in sentence processing, EEG, visual world paradigms, and interest in prediction during language comprehension paving the way experimentally. For physical context, the multimodal nature of language use needs to be embraced. Non-verbal cues and environmental stimuli are used in real-time to support lexico-semantic representation and processing, constraining ambiguity, and the construction of meaning on the fly. The ideal demonstration of variation in lexico-semantic representation will be to show that the same word can have different, non-overlapping meanings depending on the context in which it is used. The manipulation should demonstrate this variation online (i.e., it is not a case of ambiguity, homonymy, polysemy, or extensive training). When individual, task, and physical contexts are explored more fully we predict that variation in lexico-semantic representations will be shown to be the norm.

REFERENCES

Anderson, A. J., Bruni, E., Lopopolo, A., Poesio, M., & Baroni, M. (2015). Reading visually embodied meaning from the brain: Visually grounded computational models decode visual-object mental imagery induced by written text. *NeuroImage*, *120*, 309–22.

Andrews, M., Frank, S., & Vigliocco, G. (2014). Reconciling embodied and distributional accounts of meaning in language. *Topics in Cognitive Science*, *6*(3), 359–70.

Andrews, M., & Vigliocco, G. (2010). The hidden Markov topic model: A probabilistic model of semantic representation. *Topics in Cognitive Science*, *2*(1), 101–13.

Andrews, M., Vigliocco, G., & Vinson, D. (2009). Integrating experiential and distributional data to learn semantic representations. *Psychological Review*, *116*(3), 463.

Bak, T. H., O'Donovan, D. G., Xuereb, J. H., Boniface, S., & Hodges, J. R. (2001). Selective impairment of verb processing associated with pathological changes in Brodmann areas 44 and 45 in the motor neurone disease–dementia–aphasia syndrome. *Brain*, *124*(1), 103–20.

Barsalou, L. W. (1982). Context-independent and context-dependent information about concepts. *Memory & Cognition*, *10*, 82–93.

Barsalou, L. W., Santos, A., Simmons, W. K., & Wilson, C. D. (2008). Language and simulation in conceptual processing. In: de Vega, M., Glenberg, A. M., & Gaesser, A. C. (Eds.), *Symbols, Embodiment, and Meaning* (pp. 245–83). Oxford University Press, Oxford.

Becker, C. A. (1980). Semantic context effects in visual word recognition: An analysis of semantic strategies. *Memory & Cognition*, *8*(6), 493–512.

Bloom, P. (2000). *How Children Learn the Meanings of Words*. MIT Press, Cambridge, MA.

Boulenger, V., Mechtouff, L., Thobois, S., Broussolle, E., Jeannerod, M., & Nazir, T. A. (2008). Word processing in Parkinson's disease is impaired for action verbs but not for concrete nouns. *Neuropsychologia*, *46*(2), 743–56.

Boroditsky, L. (2001). Does language shape thought? Mandarin and English speakers' conceptions of time. *Cognitive Psychology*, *43*(1), 1–22.

Brown-Schmidt, S., Campana, E., & Tanenhaus, M. K. (2005). Real-time reference resolution in a referential communication task. In: Trueswell, J. C., & Tanenhaus, M. K. (Eds.), *Processing World-situated Language: Bridging the Language-as-action and Language-as-product Traditions* (pp. 153–71). MIT Press, Cambridge, MA.

Bruni, E., Tran, N. K., & Baroni, M. (2014). Multimodal distributional semantics. *Journal of Artificial Intelligence Research (JAIR)*, 49, 1–47.

Burgess, C. (1998). From simple associations to the building blocks of language: Modeling meaning in memory with the HAL model. *Behavior Research Methods, Instruments, & Computers*, 30, 188–98.

Cassani, G., & Lopopolo, A. (2015). Multimodal distributional semantic models and conceptual representations in sensory deprived subjects. Poster presented at Computational Linguistics in the Netherlands (CLIN26), December 18, 2015. doi: 10.13140/RG.2.1.3394.3924

Chen, L., Lambon Ralph, M. A., & Rogers, T. T. (2017). A unified model of human semantic knowledge and its disorders. *Nature Human Behaviour*, 1, 0039.

Clark, A. (1998). *Being There: Putting Brain, Body, and World Together Again*. MIT Press, Cambridge, MA.

Collina, S., Tabossi, P., & De Simone, F. (2013). Word production and the picture-word interference paradigm: The role of learning. *Journal of Psycholinguistic Research*, 42(5), 461–73.

Collins, A. M., & Loftus, E. F. (1975). A spreading-activation theory of semantic processing. *Psychological Review*, 82(6), 407.

Connell, L., & Lynott, D. (2014). I see/hear what you mean: Semantic activation in visual word recognition depends on perceptual attention. *Journal of Experimental Psychology: General*, 143(2), 527.

Cree, G. S., & McRae, K. (2003). Analyzing the factors underlying the structure and computation of the meaning of chipmunk, cherry, chisel, cheese, and cello (and many other such concrete nouns). *Journal of Experimental Psychology: General*, 132(2), 163.

Damasio, A. R. (1989). The brain binds entities and events by multiregional activation from convergence zones. *Neural Computation*, 1, 123e132.

Damasio, A. R., & Damasio, H. (1994). Cortical systems for retrieval of concrete knowledge: The convergence zone framework. In: Koch, C., & Davis, J. L. (Eds.), *Large-scale Neuronal Theories of the Brain* (Chapter 4). MIT Press, London.

Devlin, J. T., Gonnerman, L. M., Andersen, E. S., & Seidenberg, M. S. (1998). Category-specific semantic deficits in focal and widespread brain damage: A computational account. *Journal of Cognitive Neuroscience*, 10(1), 77–94.

Dove, G. (2009). Beyond perceptual symbols: A call for representational pluralism. *Cognition*, 110, 412–31.

Dove, G. (2011). On the need for embodied and dis-embodied cognition. *Frontiers in Psychology*, 1, article 242. doi: 10.3389/fpsyg.2010.00242

Elman, J. L. (2004). An alternative view of the mental lexicon. *Trends in Cognitive Sciences*, 8(7), 301–6.

Elman, J. L. (2009). On the meaning of words and dinosaur bones: Lexical knowledge without a lexicon. *Cognitive Science*, 33(4), 547–82.

Farah, M. J., & McClelland, J. L. (1991). A computational model of semantic memory impairment: modality specificity and emergent category specificity. *Journal of Experimental Psychology: General*, 120(4), 339.

Garrard, P., Lambon Ralph, M. A., Hodges, J. R., & Patterson, K. (2001). Prototypicality, distinctiveness, and intercorrelation: Analyses of the semantic attributes of living and nonliving concepts. *Cognitive Neuropsychology*, 18(2), 125–74.

Gilboa-Schechtman, E., Revelle, W., & Gotlib, I. H. (2000). Stroop interference following mood induction: Emotionality, mood congruence, and concern relevance. *Cognitive Therapy and Research*, 24(5), 491–502.

Griffiths, T. L., Steyvers, M., & Tenenbaum, J. B. (2007). Topics in semantic representation. *Psychological Review*, *114*, 211–44.

Hagoort, P., Baggio, G., & Willems, R. M. (2009). Semantic unification. In: Gazzaniga, M. S. (Ed.), *The Cognitive Neurosciences*, 4th Edition (pp. 819–36). MIT Press, Boston, MA.

Hauk, O. (2016). Only time will tell—why temporal information is essential for our neuroscientific understanding of semantics. *Psychonomic Bulletin & Review*, *23*(4), 1072–9.

Hauk, O., Johnsrude, I., & Pulvermüller, F. (2004). Somatotopic representation of action words in human motor and premotor cortex. *Neuron*, *41*(2), 301–7.

Hoenig, K., Sim, E. J., Bochev, V., Herrnberger, B., & Kiefer, M. (2008). Conceptual flexibility in the human brain: dynamic recruitment of semantic maps from visual, motor, and motion-related areas. *Journal of Cognitive Neuroscience*, *20*, 1799–814.

Hoffman, P., Rogers, T. T., & Lambon Ralph, M. A. (2011). Semantic diversity accounts for the "missing" word frequency effect in stroke aphasia: Insights using a novel method to quantify contextual variability in meaning. *Journal of Cognitive Neuroscience*, *23*(9), 2432–46.

Hsu, N. S., Frankland, S. M., & Thompson-Schill, S. L. (2012). Chromaticity of color perception and object color knowledge. *Neuropsychologia*, *50*, 327–33.

Huth, A. G., de Heer, W. A., Griffiths, T. L., Theunissen, F. E., & Gallant, J. L. (2016). Natural speech reveals the semantic maps that tile human cerebral cortex. *Nature*, *532*(7600), 453–8.

Huth, A. G., Nishimoto, S., Vu, A. T., & Gallant, J. L. (2012). A continuous semantic space describes the representation of thousands of object and action categories across the human brain. *Neuron*, *76*(6), 1210–24.

Imai, M., Kita, S., Nagumo, M., & Okada, H. (2008). Sound symbolism facilitates early verb learning. *Cognition*, *109* (1), 54–65.

Johns, B. T., & Jones, M. N. (2012). Perceptual inference through global lexical similarity. *Topics in Cognitive Science*, *4*(1), 103–20.

Kemmerer, D. (2015). Are the motor features of verb meanings represented in the precentral motor cortices? Yes, but within the context of a flexible, multilevel architecture for conceptual knowledge. *Psychonomic Bulletin & Review*, *22*(4), 1068–75.

Kiela, D., Hill, F., Korhonen, A., & Clark, S. (2014). Improving multi-modal representations using image dispersion: Why less is sometimes more. *InACL*, (2), 835–41.

Kousta, S. T., Vigliocco, G., Vinson, D. P., Andrews, M., & Del Campo, E. (2011). The representation of abstract words: Why emotion matters. *Journal of Experimental Psychology: General*, *140*(1), 14.

Kuperberg, G. R., & Jaeger, T. F. (2016). What do we mean by prediction in language comprehension? *Language, Cognition and Neuroscience*, *31*(1), 32–59.

Kutas, M., & Federmeier, K. D. (2011). Thirty years and counting: Finding meaning in the N400 component of the event related brain potential (ERP). *Annual Review of Psychology*, *62*, 621.

Lakoff, G. (1990). *Women, Fire, and Dangerous Things: What Categories Reveal About the Mind* (pp. 1987–1987). University of Chicago Press, Chicago, IL.

Lambon Ralph, M. A. (2014). Neurocognitive insights on conceptual knowledge and its breakdown. *Philosophical Transactions of the Royal Society of London B: Biological Sciences*, *369*(1634), 20120392.

Landauer, T. K., & Dumais, S. T. (1997). A solution to Plato's problem: The latent semantic analysis theory of acquisition, induction, and representation of knowledge. *Psychological Review*, *104*(2), 211.

Lebois, L. A., Wilson-Mendenhall, C. D., & Barsalou, L. W. (2015). Are automatic conceptual cores the gold standard of semantic processing? The context-dependence of spatial meaning in grounded congruency effects. *Cognitive Science*, 39(8), 1764–801.

Levelt, W. J. (1999). Models of word production. *Trends in Cognitive Sciences*, 3(6), 223–32.

Levinson, S. C. (2003). *Space in Language and Cognition: Explorations in Cognitive Diversity (Vol. 5)*. Cambridge University Press, Cambridge.

Louwerse, M. M. (2011). Symbol interdependency in symbolic and embodied cognition. *Topics in Cognitive Science*, 3(2), 273–302.

Louwerse, M. M., & Jeuniaux, P. (2010). The linguistic and embodied nature of conceptual processing. *Cognition*, 114(1), 96–104.

Louwerse, M. M., Hutchinson, S., Tillman, R., & Recchia, G. (2015). Effect size matters: The role of language statistics and perceptual simulation in conceptual processing. *Language, Cognition and Neuroscience*, 30(4), 430–47.

Lund, K., & Burgess, C. (1996). Producing high-dimensional semantic spaces from lexical co-occurrence. *Behavior Research Methods, Instruments, & Computers*, 28(2), 203–8.

Lupyan, G., Rakison, D. H., & McClelland, J. L. (2007). Language is not just for talking: redundant labels facilitate learning of novel categories. *Psychological Science*, 18(12), 1077–83.

Mahon, B. Z., & Hickok, G. (2016). Arguments about the nature of concepts: Symbols, embodiment, and beyond. *Psychonomic Bulletin & Review*, 23, 941–58.

Mann, K., Kaplan, J. T., Damasio, A., & Meyer, K. (2012). Sight and sound converge to form modality-invariant representations in temporoparietal cortex. *Journal of Neuroscience*, 32(47), 16629–36.

McRae, K., & Boisvert, S. (1998). Automatic semantic similarity priming. *Journal of Experimental Psychology: Learning, Memory, and Cognition*, 24(3), 558.

McRae, K., de Sa, V. R., & Seidenberg, M. S. (1997). On the nature and scope of featural representations of word meaning. *Journal of Experimental Psychology: General*, 126(2), 99.

Martin, A. (2016). GRAPES—Grounding representations in action, perception, and emotion systems: How object properties and categories are represented in the human brain. *Psychonomic Bulletin & Review*, 23, 979–90.

Meyer, D. E., & Schvaneveldt, R. W. (1971). Facilitation in recognizing pairs of words: evidence of a dependence between retrieval operations. *Journal of Experimental Psychology*, 90(2), 227.

McNorgan, C., Reid, J., & McRae, K. (2011). Integrating conceptual knowledge within and across representational modalities. *Cognition*, 118(2), 211–33.

Meteyard, L., Bahrami, B., & Vigliocco, G. (2007). Motion detection and motion verbs language affects low-level visual perception. *Psychological Science*, 18(11), 1007–13.

Meteyard, L., Cuadrado, S. R., Bahrami, B., & Vigliocco, G. (2012). Coming of age: A review of embodiment and the neuroscience of semantics. *Cortex*, 48(7), 788–804.

Meteyard, L., Stoppard, E., Snudden, D., Cappa, S. F., & Vigliocco, G. (2015). When semantics aids phonology: A processing advantage for iconic word forms in aphasia. *Neuropsychologia*, 76, 264–75.

Mitchell, J., & Lapata, M. (2010). Composition in distributional models of semantics. *Cognitive Science*, 34(8), 1388–429.

Neely, J. H. (1991). Semantic priming effects in visual word recognition: A selective review of current findings and theories. In: Besner, D., & Humphreys, G. W. (Eds.), *Basic Processes in Reading: Visual Word Recognition* (pp. 264–336). Lawrence Erlbaum Associates, Inc., Hillsdale, NJ.

Neininger, B., & Pulvermüller, F. (2003). Word-category specific deficits after lesions in the right hemisphere. *Neuropsychologia*, 41(1), 53–70.

Patterson, K. (2007). The reign of typicality in semantic memory. *Philosophical Transactions of the Royal Society of London B: Biological Sciences*, 362(1481), 813–21.

Patterson, K., Nestor, P. J., & Rogers, T. T. (2007). Where do you know what you know? The representation of semantic knowledge in the human brain. *Nature Reviews Neuroscience*, 8(12), 976–87.

Pecher, D., Zeelenberg, R., & Raaijmakers, J. G. (1998). Does pizza prime coin? Perceptual priming in lexical decision and pronunciation. *Journal of Memory and Language*, 38(4), 401–18.

Perniss, P., Thompson, R. L., & Vigliocco, G. (2010). Iconicity as a general property of language: Evidence from spoken and signed languages. *Frontiers in Psychology*, 1, 227.

Perniss, P., & Vigliocco, G. (2014). The bridge of iconicity: From a world of experience to the experience of language. *Philosophical Transactions of the Royal Society B*, 369(1651), 20130300.

Plaut, D. C., & Shallice, T. (1993). Deep dyslexia: A case study of connectionist neuropsychology. *Cognitive Neuropsychology*, 10(5), 377–500.

Ponari, M., Norbury, C., & Vigliocco, G. (2017a). Acquisition of abstract concepts is not only based on language: Evidence from Specific Language Impairment. Available at: https://mindmodeling.org/cogsci2017/papers/0648/paper0648.pdf

Ponari, M., Norbury, C., & Vigliocco, G. (2017b). How do children process abstract concepts? Evidence from a lexical decision task. *Developmental Science*. doi 10.1111/desc.12549

Pulvermüller, F. (2013). How neurons make meaning: Brain mechanisms for embodied and abstract-symbolic semantics. *Trends in Cognitive Sciences*, 17(9), 458–70.

Ramscar, M., Hendrix, P., Shaoul, C., Milin, P., & Baayen, H. (2014). The myth of cognitive decline: Non-linear dynamics of lifelong learning. *Topics in Cognitive Science*, 6(1), 5–42.

Recchia, G., & Jones, M. (2012). The semantic richness of abstract concepts. *Frontiers in Human Neuroscience*, 6, 315.

Reilly, J., Peelle, J. E., Garcia, A., & Crutch, S. J. (2016). Linking somatic and symbolic representation in semantic memory: the dynamic multilevel reactivation framework. *Psychonomic Bulletin & Review*, 23(4), 1002–14.

Rodd, J. M., Cai, Z. G., Betts, H. N., Hanby, B., Hutchinson, C., & Adler, A. (2016). The impact of recent and long-term experience on access to word meanings: Evidence from large-scale internet-based experiments. *Journal of Memory and Language*, 87, 16–37.

Rodd, J. M., Johnsrude, I. S., & Davis, M. H. (2012). Dissociating frontotemporal contributions to semantic ambiguity resolution in spoken sentences. *Cerebral Cortex*, 22(8), 1761–73.

Rodd, J. M., Lopez Cutrin, B., Kirsch, H., Millar, A., & Davis, M. H. (2013). Long-term priming of the meanings of ambiguous words. *Journal of Memory and Language*, 68, 180–98.

Rogers, T. T., Lambon Ralph, M. A., Garrard, P., Bozeat, S., McClelland, J. L., Hodges, J. R., & Patterson, K. (2004). Structure and deterioration of semantic memory: a neuropsychological and computational investigation. *Psychological Review*, 111(1), 205.

Rotaru A., Frank, S., & Vigliocco, G. (2016). From words to behavior via semantic nets. *Proceedings of the 38th Conference of the Cognitive Science Society*. Available at: https://www.researchgate.net/publication/303174471_From_words_to_behaviour_via_semantic_networks

Rueschemeyer, S. A., Pfeiffer, C., & Bekkering, H. (2010). Body schematics: On the role of the body schema in embodied lexical–semantic representations. *Neuropsychologia*, 48(3), 774–81.

Shallice, T., & Cooper, R. P. (2013). Is there a semantic system for abstract words? *Frontiers in Human Neuroscience*, 7, 175.

Schwanenflugel, P. J., & Shoben, E. J. (1983). Differential context effects in the comprehension of abstract and concrete verbal materials. *Journal of Experimental Psychology: Learning, Memory, and Cognition*, 9, 82–102.

Schwanenflugel, P. J., Harnishfeger, K. K., & Stowe, R. W. (1988). Context availability and lexical decisions for abstract and concrete words. *Journal of Memory and Language*, 27, 499–520.

Shaoul, C., & Westbury, C. (2006). Word frequency effects in high-dimensional co-occurrence models: A new approach. *Behavior Research Methods*, 38(2), 190–5.

Shaoul, C., & Westbury, C. (2010). Exploring lexical co-occurrence space using HiDEx. *Behavior Research Methods*, 42(2), 393–413.

Simmons, K. W., & Barsalou, L. W. (2003). The similarity-in-topography principle: Reconciling theories of conceptual deficits. *Cognitive Neuropsychology*, 20(3/4/5/6), 451e486.

Simmons, W. K., Hamann, S. B., Harenski, C. L., Hu, X. P., & Barsalou, L. W. (2008). fMRI evidence for word association and situated simulation in conceptual processing. *Journal of Physiology - Paris*, 102(1), 106–19.

Skipper, J. I. (2015). The NOLB model: A model of the natural organization of language and the brain. In: Willems, R. M. (Ed.), *Cognitive Neuroscience of Natural Language Use*. Cambridge University Press, Cambridge.

Skipper, J. I., Goldin-Meadow, S., Nusbaum, H. C., & Small, S. L. (2009). Gestures orchestrate brain networks for language understanding. *Current Biology*, 19(8), 661–7.

Smith, E. E., Shoben, E. J., & Rips, L. J. (1974). Structure and process in semantic memory: A featural model for semantic decisions. *Psychological Review*, 81(3), 214.

Smith, L., & Gasser, M. (2005). The development of embodied cognition: Six lessons from babies. *Artificial Life*, 11(1–2), 13–29.

Solomon, K. O., & Barsalou, L. W. (2004). Perceptual simulation in property verification. *Memory & Cognition*, 32(2), 244–59.

Speed, L. J., Vinson, D. P., & Vigliocco, G. (2015). Representing meaning. In: Dabrowska, E., & Divjak, D. (Eds.), *Handbook of Cognitive Linguistics* (pp. 190–211). De Gruyter Mouton, London.

Spivey, M. J. (2016). Semantics influences speech perception: Commentary on Gow and Olson (2015). *Language, Cognition and Neuroscience*, 31, 869–75.

Spivey, M. J., & Dale, R. (2004). On the continuity of mind: Toward a dynamical account of cognition. *Psychology of Learning and Motivation*, 45, 87–142.

Spivey, M. J., Tanenhaus, M. K., Eberhard, K. M., & Sedivy, J. C. (2002). Eye movements and spoken language comprehension: Effects of visual context on syntactic ambiguity resolution. *Cognitive Psychology*, 45(4), 447–81.

Tanenhaus, M. K., & Brown-Schmidt, S. (2008). Language processing in the natural world. *Philosophical Transactions of the Royal Society of London B: Biological Sciences*, 363(1493), 1105–22.

Tomasino, B., & Rumiati, R. I. (2013). At the mercy of strategies: The role of motor representations in language understanding. *Frontiers in Psychology*, 4, 27.

Tyler, L. K., & Moss, H. E. (2001). Towards a distributed account of conceptual knowledge. *Trends in Cognitive Sciences*, 5(6), 244–52.

van Dam, W. O., Rueschemeyer, S. A., Lindemann, O., & Bekkering, H. (2010). Context effects in embodied lexical-semantic processing. *Frontiers in Psychology*, 1, 150.

van Dam, W. O., van Dijk M., Bekkering, H., & Rueschemeyer, S. A. (2012). Flexibility in embodied lexical-semantic representations. *Human Brain Mapping*, *33*, 2322–33.

Vigliocco, G., Kousta, S. T., Della Rosa, P. A., Vinson, D. P., Tettamanti, M., Devlin, J. T., & Cappa, S. F. (2014). The neural representation of abstract words: the role of emotion. *Cerebral Cortex*, *24*(7), 1767–77.

Vigliocco, G., Tranel, D., & Druks, J. (2012). Language production. In: Spivey, M. J., McRae, K., & Joanisee, M. F. (Eds.), *The Cambridge Handbook of Psycholinguistics* (Chapter 22). Cambridge University Press, Cambridge.

Vigliocco, G., & Vinson, D. P. (2007). Semantic representation. In: Gaskell, M. G. (Ed.), *Oxford Handbook of Psycholinguistics*. Oxford University Press, Oxford.

Vigliocco, G., Vinson, D. P., Druks, J., Barber, H., & Cappa, S. F. (2011). Nouns and verbs in the brain: A review of behavioural, electrophysiological, neuropsychological and imaging studies. *Neuroscience & Biobehavioral Reviews*, *35*(3), 407–26.

Vigliocco, G., Vinson, D. P., Lewis, W., & Garrett, M. F. (2004). Representing the meanings of object and action words: The featural and unitary semantic space hypothesis. *Cognitive Psychology*, *48*(4), 422–88.

Westbury, C. F., Shaoul, C., Hollis, G., Smithson, L., Briesemeister, B. B., Hofmann, M. J., & Jacobs, A. M. (2013). Now you see it, now you don't: On emotion, context, and the algorithmic prediction of human imageability judgments. *Frontiers of Psychology*, *4*(991), 10–3389.

Williams, J. M. G., Mathews, A., & MacLeod, C. (1996). The emotional Stroop task and psychopathology. *Psychological Bulletin*, *120*, 3–24.

Wilson, M. (2002). Six views of embodied cognition. *Psychonomic Bulletin & Review*, *9*(4), 625–36.

Wittgenstein, L. (1958). *Philosophical Investigations* (3rd Edition), Basil Blackwell Ltd., Oxford, UK.

Woollams, A. M. (2012). Apples are not the only fruit: The effects of concept typicality on semantic representation in the anterior temporal lobe. *Frontiers of Human Neuroscience*, *6*, 85.

Yee, E., & Thompson-Schill, S. L. (2016). Putting concepts into context. *Psychonomic Bulletin & Review*, 1–13.

Zwaan, R. A. (2014). Embodiment and language comprehension: Reframing the discussion. *Trends in Cognitive Sciences*, *18*(5), 229–34.

CHAPTER 5

LEXICAL AMBIGUITY

JENNIFER RODD

5.1 INTRODUCTION

MOST words are ambiguous: a single word form can refer to more than one different concept. For example, the word form "bark" can refer either to the noise made by a dog, or to the outer covering of a tree. This form of ambiguity is often referred to as "lexical ambiguity." Some researchers prefer the term "semantic ambiguity" as this makes it clear that it is the *meaning* of the word that is ambiguous and not its form or grammatical properties (Vitello & Rodd, 2015), but these terms are largely interchangeable. This chapter uses the term "lexical ambiguity" due to its more widespread use.

Lexical ambiguity is ubiquitous. In English over 80% of common words have more than one dictionary entry (Rodd, Gaskell, & Marslen-Wilson, 2002), with some words having very many different definitions. Take for example, the first sentence in a recent reading comprehension test given to 10–11-year-old children in England (Key Stage 2 English Reading Booklet, 2016): "Dawn was casting spun-gold threads across a rosy sky over Sawubona game reserve." If we look up each of these words in a typical dictionary (Parks, Ray, & Bland, 1998) they have, on average, 8.8 definitions per word. To correctly understand the meaning intended by the author, the reader must select a single, contextually appropriate meaning for each word. For example, they must work out that "Dawn" does not refer to a girl's name and that "game" does not refer to a form of competitive sport. And yet, despite the proliferation of ambiguity throughout this sentence, readers are usually unaware of the alternative possible meanings for such words.

One situation in which people do become explicitly aware of lexical ambiguity is when understanding puns that are deliberately constructed to make reference to both meanings of a lexically ambiguous word. For example, in the joke "What did the fish say when he swam into a wall? Dam.," both meanings of the ambiguous word form "dam/damn" (i.e., wall of a reservoir vs. expression of anger) are partially consistent with the sentence context and in order to understand the humor of the pun, both meanings must be accessed. But puns are the exception that illustrate the rule—in most circumstances listeners/readers are only aware of the contextually appropriate meaning that was intended by the speaker/author.

In summary, the language comprehension system is highly skilled at dealing with the high level of lexical ambiguity in natural language. Readers and listeners are (usually) able to find a single meaningful interpretation for each sentence that they encounter without being overtly distracted by the myriad of other possible meanings for the constituent words. This chapter will introduce the different forms that lexical ambiguity can take and explore what is known about how these words are learned, represented, and processed, such that they can be rapidly and accurately understood.

5.2 Different Forms of Lexical Ambiguity

Words can be ambiguous in different ways. Sometimes, as for the word "bark," the different alternative meanings are not semantically related to each other and do not share a common origin within the history of the language. For these words, it is a historical accident that the language has evolved over time such that a single word form corresponds to two separate, unrelated meanings. Unrelated meanings like these are usually given separate entries in dictionaries and these words are usually referred to by linguists as *homonyms*. However, a word like "bark" can also be referred to as a *homograph*, which indicates more specifically that the two meanings share their spelling. English also contains homographs where the two different meanings share only their spelling and not their pronunciation (e.g., "sow," "lead," and "close"; Fig. 5.1). In contrast, the term *homophone* refers specifically to words that share their pronunciation and so includes both words like "bark" as well as words that have different spellings (e.g., "meet/meat," "buy/by," "there/their/they're"), and which are therefore ambiguous in spoken, but not written, language. True homonyms like "bark" are relatively rare: a dictionary count of these words revealed that only about 7% of common English words should be classified as homonyms (Rodd et al., 2002).

A second, and more common, form of lexical ambiguity is the ambiguity between semantically related word senses, usually referred to as polysemy. For example, the word "run" is a polysemous word with many related dictionary definitions (e.g., "the athlete runs down the

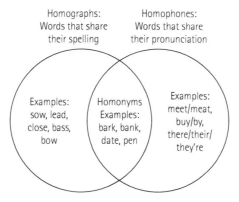

FIG. 5.1 Terminology used to describe words with multiple different meanings.

track," "the mayor runs for election," "the film runs at the cinema"). These different ways in which the word "run" can be used overlap somewhat in their meanings, but to fully understand any sentence that contains the word "run" the reader/listener must figure out exactly which definition was intended by the writer/speaker. Rodd et al. (2002) estimated that at least 80% of common words have multiple related dictionary senses. In addition, the list of word senses that we might find for a particular word in any given dictionary probably only captures a small subset of the range of ways in which that word is used in natural conversation. In contrast to homonyms, which can be viewed as a troublesome form of ambiguity that makes comprehension more difficult without any clear benefit, polysemy is of huge benefit in terms of the communicative richness of language. That words can be used in a highly flexible way to capture numerous subtly different shades of meaning is a key property of language—if we were restricted to one tightly specified meaning per word then the range of possible meanings that we could convey would be greatly reduced (see Piantadosi, Tily, & Gibson, 2012, for further discussion).

This distinction between the ambiguity that exists between unrelated word meanings (homonymy) and related word senses (polysemy) is well established within the linguistic literature (e.g., Cruse, 1986), and is respected by the lexicographers who have created all standard dictionaries. As will be discussed in the following sections, this distinction has also been shown to have important consequences for how words are represented and processed by readers/listeners (Klein & Murphy, 2001; Rodd et al., 2002).

Thus far, we have only considered the forms of ambiguity that exist for a monolingual speaker of English or other languages. But it is important to consider the extent to which for bilingual speakers, who know words from more than one language, the level of ambiguity is even higher. The impact of such cross-language ambiguity is limited by several factors that make individual languages different to each other. First, individual languages differ in the inventories of sounds from which their words are built. In addition, languages tend to differ in terms of the ways in which these individual sounds are combined together. For example, Japanese has strict rules on how consonants can be combined, such that many English words with complex consonant clusters could not exist in Japanese. Taken together, these factors mean that many words that occur in an individual's first language could not also occur in their second language (see Marian, Bartolotti, Chabal, & Shook, 2012; Vitevitch, 2012 for discussion of the extent to which various European languages contain words with similar phonology/orthography).

However, despite these clear differences between languages, cross-language ambiguity can occur, especially for the written forms of languages that are descended from a common ancestral language. Take for example the Dutch word "room," which translates to "cream" but shares its form with an English word with a very different meaning. These words, which are relatively rare, are known as "false friends" or "interlingual homographs." Interestingly, despite the very strong contextual cues that are present during reading as to which language, and therefore which meaning, was intended this form of ambiguity can cause additional disruption for bilingual speakers (e.g., Dijkstra, Grainger, & Van Heuven, 1999; Poort, Warren, & Rodd, 2016). In addition, Dutch-English bilinguals will also encounter cognates: words like "film" that have similar meanings in their two languages. These cognates can be relatively common in closely related languages. For example, using an automated approach that compared the spellings of word pairs that were classified as "translation equivalents" from a database used by professional translators, Schepens, Dijkstra, and Grootjen (2012) found relatively high numbers of cognates for closely related languages (e.g., Dutch and German: 3,785 cognates) and lower numbers for more distantly related pairs (e.g., Spanish and German: 869 cognates). (Note that many more cognates were identified that had similar, but not identical spellings, e.g., "idea"—"idee"). The presence of such cognates is usually viewed as helpful for readers as the two lexical items will share a common meaning and therefore if both are (partially) activated in parallel this would help rather than hinder the readers.

Finally, it is important to note that lexical ambiguity is not a static phenomenon. Any individual speaker of a language will continue to gain new meanings/senses for the words that they already know throughout their lifetime. Both children and adults continue to learn meanings/senses that they did not previously know, for example because they have taken up a new hobby, career, or academic subject (e.g., the sailing related meaning of "boom" or the statistical meaning of "normal"). In addition, individuals will also need to learn new meanings/senses that are added to the language over time due, for example, to technological developments such as the social media senses of "tweet," "post," and "friend" (Blank, 1999; Rodd et al., 2002).

In summary, lexical ambiguity is a ubiquitous phenomenon: most of the words that we use can refer to more than one possible concept. Although levels of lexical ambiguity can differ across languages (Bates, Devescovi, & Wulfeck, 2001), lexical ambiguity is the norm and not the exception. Therefore, any general account of how word meanings are represented and accessed must incorporate an explanation of meaning representation and access for ambiguous words.

5.3 How are ambiguous words represented?

Over the past 50 years, psycholinguists have debated how ambiguous words are represented within the "mental lexicon," the memory store that contains information about all the words that an individual person knows. An early experimental finding that was highly influential in framing this discussion was the "ambiguity advantage" in the visual lexical decision task. This task, which is a staple of psycholinguistic research, requires participants to decide, as quickly and accurately as possible, whether each string of letters that they see is a real word in their language (e.g., "hat") or a made-up non-word (e.g., "wug"). A relatively large set of studies reported faster visual lexical decisions for ambiguous words compared with unambiguous words (Azuma & Van Orden, 1997; Borowsky & Masson, 1996; Hino & Lupker, 1996; Kellas, Ferraro, & Simpson, 1988; Jastrzembski, 1981; Millis & Button, 1989; Pexman & Lupker, 1999; Rubenstein, Garfield, & Millikan, 1970).

Early explanations for this "ambiguity advantage" were framed within a view of the mental lexicon that can broadly be characterized as the "localist" approach. Models of this type assume that each word that we know is represented by a single entry in our mental lexicon. Within the connectionist framework these entries correspond to individual "nodes" or "units." (See the Interactive Activation and Competition Model (McClelland & Rumelhart, 1981) and TRACE (McClelland & Elman, 1986) for influential models of written and spoken word recognition that include such localist representations.) Within this framework, these localist word units are seen as the gateway to information about a word's meaning: as soon as one of these units has been sufficiently activated in response to the incoming visual/auditory input the reader/listener can then retrieve all the information about that word's meaning (and its grammatical properties). Researchers using lexical decision tasks commonly assumed that participants were able to make a "yes" response as soon as one of these localist word units reached some threshold level of activation. Within this framework a common interpretation of this ambiguity advantage, was that ambiguous words benefit from having multiple entries within the mental lexicon (Fig. 5.2A). For example, Jastrzembski (1981) suggested that ambiguity advantage arises because of the noise that is present in the system and that can produce random fluctuations in the degree to which individual units are activated during word recognition: because ambiguous words have more than one "competitor" in the race for recognition, on average by any given point in time, one of the two competitors is more likely to have reached the threshold for recognition compared with an unambiguous word with only one competitor. Thus, the ambiguity advantage was taken as evidence for the

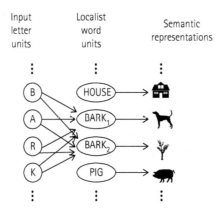

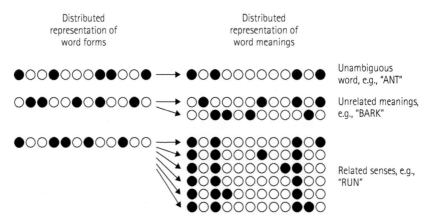

FIG. 5.2 Localist (A) and distributed (B) views on how ambiguous words are represented in the mental lexicon.

claim that words are represented as localist word units, and that ambiguous words have multiple separate representations—one for each meaning.

However subsequent research suggested that this early view was too simplistic. First, it became clear that the "one unit per meaning" approach could not fully explain the different types of ambiguity that exist. While this approach is plausible for words with completely distinct, unrelated meanings (e.g., "bark"), it was far from clear how words with large clusters of highly related word senses (e.g., "run") should be represented within such a scheme, or how the system would distinguish between these two forms of ambiguity—many words have meanings that are intermediate in relatedness between these two extremes. In contrast, some authors argued that this variability in the relatedness of word meanings can be captured more naturally by an alternative, and conceptually very different, view of word recognition, often referred to as the "distributed" approach (Rodd, Gaskell, & Marslen-Wilson, 2004). This approach abandons the idea that words are represented by single "localist" entries in the mental lexicon and instead assumes that each word that we know is represented as a unique pattern of activation across sets of units that collectively represent its form (i.e., spelling/orthography or sound/phonology) and its meaning (Fig. 5.2b). These units can be thought of as representing different features of the words' form/meaning. Words with similar spelling (or sound) will activate similar sets of orthographic (or phonological) input units, while words with similar meanings will activate similar sets of semantic units (see Gaskell & Marslen-Wilson, 1997; Hinton & Shallice, 1991; Joordens & Besner, 1994; Plaut, 1997; Plaut & Shallice, 1993 for models of this type). Within this distributed framework, the single orthographic (or phonological) input pattern for an ambiguous word must map onto multiple different semantic patterns that correspond to its different meanings or senses. For example, a word like "bark" would map onto two completely uncorrelated patterns of semantic activation, whereas a word like "run" will correspond to many highly correlated semantic patterns (Fig. 5.2B).

Although this "distributed" view of the mental lexicon seemed highly plausible in terms of its capacity to represent the wide variety of ambiguous words that exist in natural language, the finding of a benefit in lexical decision for ambiguous words seemed hard to explain within this framework. When the orthographic (or phonological) pattern is presented to the network, the model will attempt to simultaneously instantiate both of the word's meanings across the same set of semantic units. These competing semantic representations are likely therefore to interfere with each other, and this interference effect means that models of this type generally predict *slower* recognition of words that are lexically ambiguous. (Although see Borowsky & Masson, 1996; Joordens & Besner, 1994; Kawamoto, Farrar, & Kello, 1994 for attempts to explain how an ambiguity advantage might arise; see Rodd et al., 2004 for detailed discussion.)

This apparent discrepancy between the prediction that the meanings of ambiguous words should interfere with each other during recognition, and the reported "ambiguity advantage" in visual lexical decision tasks was addressed by Rodd, Gaskell, and Marslen-Wilson (2002), who argued that the previous studies did not adequately take account of the distinction discussed above between homonyms like "bark" that have two semantically unrelated meanings, and polysemous words like "run" that have a collection of semantically related word senses. They argued that the lexical-semantic representations of these different types of words will be very different and that the two types of ambiguity could potentially have different effects on how easily a word's meaning is accessed. In a set of visual and auditory lexical decision experiments, Rodd, Gaskell, and Marslen-Wilson (2002) only replicated the classic ambiguity advantage for words that have many highly related word senses (e.g., "run"). In contrast, for words with multiple unrelated meanings (e.g., bark), they found the reverse effect: an ambiguity *disadvantage*. They suggested that the prevalence of an advantage for ambiguity in the earlier experiments reflected the fact that ambiguity between related word senses is very much more frequent than ambiguity between unrelated word meanings, and that previous studies tended to select more of the former word types within their category of lexically ambiguous words (see Beretta, Fiorentino, & Poeppel, 2005; Klepousniotou & Baum, 2007 for replications of this finding; see Rodd et al., 2012 for an analogous effect for newly learned word senses/meanings; see Rodd, 2004 for a sense benefit in word naming for words with inconsistent spelling).

The observed disadvantage for words with multiple unrelated meanings can easily be accommodated by distributed connectionist models. As described above, these models assume that the unrelated, uncorrelated meanings of these words will interfere with each other during meaning access and this interference delays the point in time at which the participant has retrieved a sufficiently stable representation to be able to confidently press the "yes" button during the lexical decision task. Rodd, Gaskell, Marslen-Wilson (2004) implemented a connectionist model of this type and confirmed that this form of competition to access a single coherent word meaning does indeed produce slower retrieval for the meanings of ambiguous words. This model was also able to provide an account of the benefit for words with multiple senses (i.e., polysemous words). In their implementation of the model, the authors assumed that these words, which have partially overlapping meanings, are represented by a range of different, but highly correlated, patterns of activation across the semantic units such that only a subset of the word's possible semantic features are present for any specific word sense. This variability in the precise semantic representation of these polysemous words resulted in the formation of highly robust representations as the network learned these words. Importantly, they argued that this benefit for words with multiple senses should only be seen on tasks such as lexical decision in which it is not necessary to retrieve a very specific sense, but rather where it is sufficient to retrieve a very general "blend" of its different meanings.

However, it is important to note that while this model adequately explains the patterns of behavior seen in lexical decision tasks by assuming that these reflect important differences in the speed of access to different types of word meanings, there has subsequently been some disagreement about whether these differences arise because of competition at the level of decision making (Hino, Pexman, & Lupker, 2006) or at the level of lexical-semantic processing (Armstrong & Plaut, 2016). Future work is still needed to clarify the extent to which these effects are being driven by lexical-semantic or decision-level effects.

5.4 How are ambiguous meanings learned?

The studies described above focus on how words that have multiple meanings are represented within the mental lexicon of adults for whom both meanings are already highly familiar. This naturally leads to the question of how these meanings are learned in the first place, by both children and adults. Most studies on this topic have focused on the situation where one meaning is already highly familiar, and within the course of the experiment the participants are required to learn an additional (often fictitious) meaning for these familiar words. This is akin to the situation that is frequently faced by adult learners when they encounter a new meaning that has recently entered the language, or the specialist vocabulary of a new academic subject or hobby (e.g., a rower learning that "feather" refers to a position of their oar; Rodd et al., 2016).

Several studies using this approach have shown that children (aged 3–10) find it relatively difficult to assign new meanings for words that they already know (Casenhiser, 2005; Doherty, 2004; Mazzocco, 1997). For example, they find it more difficult to learn that the familiar word such as "spade" refers to an unfamiliar novel object compared with assigning an entirely unfamiliar word form to this novel meaning. These studies are consistent with the view that children find it easiest to learn the mapping from form to meaning when this mapping is "one-to-one" (i.e., each form maps on to only one meaning), and that "one-to-many" mappings are intrinsically more difficult to learn due to interference or competition from the alternative meaning (see Dautriche & Chemla, 2016 for further discussion of why this difficulty arises; see Rodd et al., 2004 for details of how this effect is explained within a connectionist modeling framework). In contrast, data from Storkel and colleagues (Storkel & Maekawa, 2005; Storkel, Maekawa, & Aschenbrenner, 2013) suggests that children find it *easier* to learn new meanings for familiar words (compared to completely novel form-meaning pairs) because in the latter situation the child has the additional demand of having to learn a new word form.

Recent studies with adults have pointed toward one explanation for these apparently contradictory findings; Fang, Perfetti, and Stafura (2016) suggest that two different factors play an important role in determining whether it is easier to learn a new meaning for a familiar or unfamiliar word. First, they suggest that for familiar words, learners benefit from a relatively short-lived boost in learning that is due to their existing familiarity with the word form, which is already in their mental lexicon and does not need to be newly learned. This benefit ceases to be present once learners have become sufficiently familiar with the new word forms. But, crucially, learning of new meanings for familiar words is also made more challenging due to interference from the alternative, familiar meaning. Fang, Perfetti, and Stafura suggest that although this lexical-semantic interference is present throughout learning, it only becomes evident once the benefit from familiarity has diminished. Thus, the pattern of results that are observed in any given experiment will depend on how well the meanings are learned when the individual is tested.

Studies of word-meaning learning with adult learners have also revealed that not all ambiguous words are equally difficult to learn. In particular, adults find it easier to learn new meanings for existing words, when the new meaning is semantically related to the existing meaning (e.g., that "ant" refers to a very small, mobile listening device) compared with a completely unrelated meaning (Rodd et al., 2012). This finding suggests that partial overlap between the old and new meanings can facilitate learning. Given the finding that ambiguity between multiple related word senses is far more common than ambiguity between unrelated word meanings (Rodd et al., 2002), this finding helps to explain how word meanings such as the social media meanings of "tweet" and "troll" appear to enter the language relatively easily: acquisition of such word meanings is facilitated by their semantic relationship with the existing familiar meaning.

In addition to the studies described above that require participants to learn just one novel meaning for a familiar word, a smaller set of studies have explored the situation in which the learner is simultaneously exposed to two different meanings for a novel word form. This situation is more akin to the challenge facing a young child in the early stages of language acquisition where they hear, for example, the word "bark" being used to refer to two very different concepts in the world, and where they are still relatively uncertain about both meanings. These studies show that despite the additional challenges associated with learning ambiguous words, it is clear that children (and adults) can (and frequently do) learn that words can have multiple meanings. For example, when children are exposed to two new meanings for a novel word form that are semantically distinct (e.g., the word form "blicket" is used to refer to both snakes and monkeys), they tend to assume that the word form is ambiguous between these two relatively specific meanings, and do not usually assume that it corresponds to some very general superordinate meaning that also encompasses all other animals (Dautriche & Chemla, 2016; Dautriche, Chemla, & Christophe, 2016).

There is also evidence that children as young as four can benefit from a relatively sophisticated understanding of how some forms of ambiguity can be highly systematic. For example, Srinivasan and Snedeker (2011) showed that when four-year-old children were taught that a novel word form (e.g., "blicket") refers to the physical object of a book, they readily understood this word form can also be used to refer to the contents of the book (e.g., "the shiny blicket" vs. "the interesting blicket"). In contrast, they showed no such extension between the two meanings of a homograph, such as "bat": if they were taught that "blicket" referred to the flying mammal meaning of "bat" they did not readily assume that it also meant a "baseball bat." Studies have also shown that adult participants are highly skilled at working out the meanings of novel word senses (e.g., using the name of a famous person to refer to a book they have written; Clark & Gerrig, 1983; Frisson & Pickering, 2007). There is also evidence that children systematically overestimate the range of possible senses that a familiar word can have, for example considering that the word "movie" can refer to the disk on which it is stored, a meaning that adults would usually consider unlicensed (Rabagliati, Marcus, & Pylkkänen, 2010).

Taken together, these results show that although lexical ambiguity can make word learning significantly more difficult, both children and adults are able to learn the meanings of ambiguous words by being highly sensitive to the precise contexts in which words are used. However, it remains a challenge for models of word learning to explain the precise mechanism(s) by which ambiguous words are learned. Many influential models of word meaning learning focus primarily on how unambiguous words are learned and do not make explicit claims about how word learners deal with lexical ambiguity (see Dautriche et al., 2016 for extensive discussion).

5.5 Understanding Ambiguous Words in Sentences

While tasks using single words presented in isolation (e.g., Rodd et al., 2002) provide important insights into how lexically ambiguous words might be represented, to understand how these words are processed in natural language requires experiments in which they are presented within sentence contexts. Understanding the mechanisms by which only the contextually appropriate meaning is selected for each word from the range of possible word meanings is a necessary component of any model of language comprehension. Such a model must explain how, for example, the word "bark" can be interpreted differently in sentences like "the girl saw the bark" compared with "the girl heard the bark." Without such a disambiguation mechanism, virtually any sentence in natural language would be impossible to understand accurately.

Although there is some disagreement on the details of how disambiguation proceeds, the literature has converged on the view that whenever a listener (or reader) encounters an ambiguous word (e.g., "bark") they rapidly and automatically retrieve in parallel, at least to some extent, all the meanings that they know for this word (e.g., "dog noise," "tree covering"), and then, within a few hundred milliseconds, select the single meaning that is most likely to be correct (Duffy, Morris, & Rayner, 1988; Rodd, Johnsrude, & Davis, 2010; Simpson & Kang, 1994; Twilley & Dixon, 2000). This view is somewhat at odds with most people's introspection—most people feel that they can directly access the correct meaning of each word that they encounter, and do not have any conscious experience of retrieving and then having to reject inappropriate meanings. But the experimental literature indicates that there is indeed transient, albeit largely unconscious, access of multiple meanings for ambiguous words during sentence comprehension.

This view that we retrieve multiple meanings and then select just one of them, is often referred to as the "exhaustive access" model, because the listener/reader "exhaustively" retrieves all possible meanings. Initial support for this claim came from experiments using the cross-modal semantic priming paradigm. In this paradigm, participants first hear an ambiguous word (e.g., "bug") in a sentence context, and then make lexical decision responses to visual probe words that are related to one of other of its meanings (e.g., "spy" vs. "ant"). If people are faster at making lexical decisions to these probe words compared with an unrelated word (e.g., "sew") then this is taken as evidence that they have accessed the relevant meanings of the initial prime word (i.e., "bug"). Researchers using this paradigm found that even when the ambiguous word (e.g., "bug") is heard within a sentence that was only consistent with one of the meanings (e.g., "The man was not surprised when he found several spiders, roaches, and other *bugs*"), if the visual probe appears immediately after the ambiguous word, then responses were faster for probes that were semantically related to either the contextually appropriate meaning (e.g., "ANT") or to the inappropriate word meaning (e.g., "SPY") (Onifer & Swinney, 1981; Swinney, 1979). This finding indicates that both these meanings had been automatically activated even though the preceding words provided enough information to rule out one of these meanings. In contrast, if the visual probe appears a short while after the ambiguous word (e.g., 3 syllables in Swinney, 1979), then faster responses are only seen for the contextually appropriate meaning (i.e., "ANT" but not "SPY"). This latter finding indicates that listeners are able to select the more appropriate meaning relatively quickly, such that any other meanings are no longer active.

Following on from these early cross-modal priming experiments, other researchers have shown that, for sentences in which the words that come before the ambiguous words are very strongly constrained toward the dominant (more frequent) meaning (e.g., "the violent hurricane did not damage the ships which were in the PORT"), then only the contextually appropriate meaning appears to be active (Tabossi, 1988; Tabossi & Zardon, 1993). Together with convergent evidence from experiments that monitor how readers' eye-movement changes when they encounter an ambiguous word, this evidence supports the view that when readers/listeners encounter an ambiguous word, its multiple meanings are usually activated in parallel but that the level of this activation is influenced by two key factors, sentence context and meaning frequency, such that meanings that are highly frequent or very strongly supported by the preceding context are more readily available (MacDonald, Pearlmutter, & Seidenberg, 1994; Simpson & Kang, 1994; Twilley, Dixon, Taylor, & Clark, 1994). This view is exemplified in the highly influential "reordered access" model of ambiguity resolution (Duffy et al., 1988).

So far, we have just considered the case where the preceding sentence context provides a strong cue as to which word meaning is correct, but cross-modal priming experiments have also provided insights into what occurs when the preceding context is consistent with multiple meanings (e.g., "the woman noticed the bark"). There are, logically, two possible strategies when faced with such a sentence. Either the listener/reader maintains the multiple possible interpretations in parallel until the point where there is enough information to rule out one of the options, or they make a "best guess" about which meaning is more likely to be correct, and then if necessary reinterpret the sentence if this guess turns out to be incorrect. The results from early cross-modal priming studies are more consistent with the latter view. These studies found that listeners do not maintain multiple meanings for long but instead make a rapid selection within a few hundred milliseconds of encountering an ambiguous word (e.g., Seidenberg, Tanenhaus, Leiman, & Bienkowski, 1982; Swinney, 1979). Seidenberg et al. (1982) proposed that this strategy is used because limits on processing capacity make it difficult to maintain multiple interpretations of sentences in parallel (but see Mason & Just, 2007; Miyake, Just, & Carpenter, 1994). In the absence of strong sentence context that could indicate which meaning is most likely to be correct, research indicates that the primary cue used by readers/listeners to make their "best guess" is meaning dominance, that is, the relative frequencies of the different meanings (Armstrong, Tokowicz, & Plaut, 2012; Twilley et al., 1994). All other things being equal the most frequent meaning will be selected (e.g., the "writing implement" meaning of "pen," not the "animal enclosure" meaning).

More recent studies have additionally highlighted the contribution of recent experience, demonstrating that we are biased to select recently-encountered meanings. For example, when we encounter an ambiguous word like "pen" without any sentence context, we are more likely to retrieve the lower frequency (subordinate) meaning if we had already encountered this meaning 20 minutes earlier (Rodd et al., 2013). This finding, known as word-meaning priming, has been shown both in laboratory studies and in more naturalistic settings where individuals encounter the target ambiguous words in subordinate meaning contexts either as part of a radio program or while participating in their usual hobby (Betts et al., 2018; Gilbert et al., in press; Rodd et al., 2013; Rodd et al., 2016). This finding that access to word meanings can by modulated by recent experience has even been shown across languages—earlier experience with the Dutch meaning of "room" can make it harder to then access the unrelated English meaning of this word form (compared to a word like "film" that has a similar meaning in both languages; Poort et al., 2016). Finally, Cai et al., (2017) have shown that listeners are able to learn about how speakers of different dialects use words, and are able to use this knowledge to modulate word-meaning access. The critical words in their experiments had possible meanings that were more typical for Americans (such as the hat meaning of bonnet) as well as alternative meanings that were more typical in the United Kingdom (such as the car hood meaning of bonnet). British listeners were more likely to interpret these words as having the American meaning when they were spoken in an American accent. Taken together these findings suggest that adults continue to update their representations of ambiguous words throughout their lifespan based on their changing language experience to help to make appropriate word meanings more easily accessible.

One consequence of this "early selection" strategy, whereby a "best guess" is made on the basis of meaning frequency, recent experience, or other knowledge about how word meanings are typically used is that inevitably sometimes the wrong meaning will be selected. This situation is perhaps most common when the lexically ambiguous word is preceded by a neutral context and is later followed by context that does not support the expected, "best guess" meaning. For example, if a listener was to hear the sentence "he mentioned that he'd been to the bank of the river" they would be likely to initially select the more common but incorrect, financial institution, meaning of "bank." This initial, incorrect, selection will then cause problems when the listener gets to the word "river," as this word is incompatible with the meaning of "bank" that they have selected. Thus, the listener will have to revisit their initial interpretation of the sentence in order to find a word meaning that is compatible with this later information. Experiments using a wide range of methods have shown that this reinterpretation process can be very cognitively demanding. In the case of printed sentences, studies have shown that reading times are particularly long for such sentences, with readers being very likely to refixate on earlier parts of the sentences as they try to find an appropriate interpretation (Duffy et al., 1988; Kambe, Rayner, & Duffy, 2001). For spoken sentences, the additional processing load has been revealed by dual-task paradigms in which participants listen to sentences while performing an unrelated concurrent task (e.g., detecting whether a word on a screen is in upper or lower case). Performance on this unrelated task has been shown to decline when the sentence is likely to require reinterpretation, compared with a relatively unambiguous sentence, presumably because of the additional resources being used to reinterpret the sentence (Rodd et al., 2010). In addition, numerous functional magnetic resonance imaging (fMRI) studies have shown an increase in blood flow to left frontal and temporal brain regions that occurs when a sentence requiring reinterpretation is encountered either in the written (Mason & Just, 2007; Zempleni, Renken, Hoeks, Hoogduin, & Stowe, 2007) or spoken modality (Rodd, Johnsrude, & Davis, 2012; Vitello, Warren, Devlin, & Rodd, 2014).

In summary, research using both spoken and written sentences and using a range of different experimental methods has converged on the view that whenever an ambiguous word is encountered, multiple meanings are initially activated and a "best guess" is then rapidly made about which meaning is most likely to be correct. This "best guess" is driven primarily by the immediate sentence context, but is also influenced by the overall frequency (dominance) of the word's different meanings, and by the listener/reader's recent experience with the ambiguous word. In contrast to this general agreement about how ambiguity resolution proceeds, there is, as yet, no agreement about the exact fate of any non-selected meanings. It is unclear whether the non-selected meanings are completely suppressed in order to prevent them interfering with subsequent processing (MacDonald et al., 1994), or whether they retain a low level of activation such that they can be more easily reactivated if the initial interpretation proves to be incorrect (McRae, Spivey-Knowlton, & Tanenhaus, 1998).

As well as the wealth of studies exploring how skilled adult comprehenders process words with multiple meanings, there is a smaller, but important, set of studies looking at how the ability to process ambiguous words develops during childhood, and on how this ability relates to individual differences in comprehension skill. Broadly speaking, the literature has converged on the view that young children use a similar approach to adults when processing ambiguous words: they make relatively rapid guesses about how best to interpret each ambiguous word based on all the evidence that is currently available to them, and do not hold off on interpreting ambiguities until the end of the sentence (see Rabagliati, Pylkkänen, & Marcus, 2013 for review). For example, Rabagliati et al., (2013) have shown that children as young as four can perform relatively well on a task that requires them to understand phrases like "Snoopy chased/swung the BAT" in which a single word indicates which meaning of the target ambiguous word is correct. In addition, they showed that children do not rely solely on strong lexical associations between the individual words in the sentences to decide which meaning to select, but they can also make use of a more global assessment of which meaning is most plausible in the sentence context. However, it is worth noting that these young children did make many more errors than adults in understanding these ambiguous words, suggesting that the ability to disambiguate ambiguous words rapidly and accurately can be relatively challenging for young children.

Several studies have shown that children who perform relatively poorly on general tests of comprehension skill also perform poorly on tasks that specifically involve resolving lexical ambiguities, compared to more skilled comprehenders. These studies have shown that difficulties faced by poor comprehenders when processing lexical ambiguities is likely to be caused, at least in part, by children's relatively weak lexical-semantic representations, especially for the lower frequency meanings (Henderson, Snowling, & Clarke, 2013). In addition, difficulties in understanding low-frequency meanings of ambiguous words can also reflect weaknesses in the executive control processes that are needed to suppress/inhibit the more frequent meaning of an ambiguous word. This link between ambiguity resolution and executive function has been shown for non-clinical samples of both children (Khanna & Boland, 2010) and adults (Gernsbacher & Faust, 1991; Gernsbacher, Varner, & Faust, 1990). In addition, van der Schoot et al. showed that poor comprehenders (aged 10–12) found ambiguous words particularly challenging when the disambiguating information occurred *after* the ambiguity (van der Schoot et al., 2009), suggesting that less skilled comprehenders monitor their comprehension less effectively than more skilled comprehenders. Finally, Norbury (2005) has shown that children (aged 9–17) with diagnosed language impairments are not able to use context as efficiently as control participants. Thus, it seems that difficulties in understanding sentences with ambiguous words is likely to be a key factor that can limit an individual's ability to rapidly and fluently comprehend language. Further research is needed to better understand the complex causes of these difficulties and how these skills might best be improved.

5.6 THE BRAIN MECHANISMS OF AMBIGUITY RESOLUTION

Over the past 20 years, researchers have increasingly made use of brain imaging methods to study sentence comprehension (Hagoort & Indefrey, 2014; Rodd, Vitello, Woollams, & Adank, 2015). These studies have given key insights, not only into which brain regions are involved in understanding lexically ambiguous words, but also into questions about the nature of the cognitive mechanisms involved, and in particular, how these disambiguation processes relate to other aspects of comprehension.

The results from the set of published studies that have used fMRI to study how lexically ambiguous words are processed have been remarkably consistent, and have highlighted three, spatially distinct brain regions that show an increased hemodynamic response (i.e., increased blood flow) for high-ambiguity sentences compared with closely matched low-ambiguity sentences: the left inferior frontal gyrus (pars opercularis; pars triangularis) and the left posterior temporal cortex (especially the left inferior temporal gyrus and middle temporal gyrus), and (to a lesser extent) the right inferior frontal gyrus (Fig. 5.3; Bekinschtein, Davis, Rodd, & Owen, 2011; Davis et al., 2007; Mason & Just, 2007; Rodd, Davis, & Johnsrude, 2005; Rodd et al., 2012; Rodd, Longe, Randall, & Tyler, 2010; Tahmasebi et al., 2012; Zempleni et al., 2007: see Vitello & Rodd (2015) for recent review and Rodd et al. (2015) for formal meta-analyses that includes these studies).

Of the three brain regions associated with the processing of sentences containing lexical ambiguities, the most well-studied and best understood is the left inferior frontal gyrus (LIFG), more specifically the posterior and middle subdivisions of the LIFG (pars triangularis; pars opercularis). This region of the posterior frontal lobe is sometimes referred to as "Broca's Area" due its association with Paul Broca who reported language impairments in individuals with damage to this region. Not only has this area been very consistently activated in *all* studies that have used sentences containing lexical ambiguities (see Vitello & Rodd, 2015 for a recent review), but a recent study has also confirmed that recruitment of

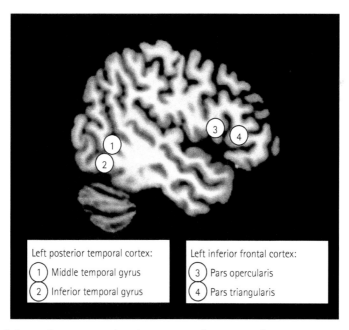

FIG. 5.3 Left hemisphere regions that show increased activation for sentences containing lexical ambiguities (shown on structural scan from single participant; Rorden & Brett, 2000).

Figure created using MRIcro software package, as described in *Behavioural Neurology*, 12 (4), Chris Rorden and Matthew Brett, Stereotaxic display of brain lesions, pp. 191–200 © 2000, IOS Press, with permission from IOS Press.

this region is highly consistent across individuals: 95% of participants showed an ambiguity-related response in close proximity to the group LIFG peak (Vitello et al., 2014).

Rodd et al. (2012) provided evidence that this region supports multiple aspects of disambiguation, including both the initial selection between alternative interpretations when an ambiguous word is first encountered, as well as any subsequent reinterpretation if the wrong meaning was initially chosen. Rodd et al. (2012) found activation in this region for spoken sentences in which the disambiguating information came before the ambiguous word (e.g., "the *hunter* thought that the *hare/hair* in the field was actually a rabbit"). Because these sentences used the lower frequency meaning of all the ambiguous words, it was relatively difficult for listeners to select the correct meaning for the ambiguous word when they first encountered it, but because of the strongly constraining context that preceded the ambiguity, it is highly likely that the correct meaning would be selected, and that no later reinterpretation would be required. Thus, the greater LIFG activation that was seen for these sentences, compared with low-ambiguity controls, is most likely to reflect the involvement of this region in the initial selection of the ambiguous word's meaning. LIFG activation was also seen for sentences in which the critical disambiguating information occurred a few words *after* the ambiguous word (e.g., "the scientist thought that the *film* on the *water* was from the pollution"). An analysis of the time-course of activation for sentences that varied in the position of the disambiguating words confirmed that this activation was driven primarily by the disambiguating information and not by the ambiguity itself, providing strong evidence for the involvement of this region in sentence reinterpretation. (See also Mason & Just, 2007; Zempleni et al., 2007; Vitello et al., 2014 for evidence of LIFG involvement in reinterpretation.)

Importantly, although the LIFG is clearly important for processing lexical ambiguities, it does *not* seem to be specialized for this form of linguistic processing. First, within the field of sentence comprehension Rodd et al. (2010) found that the same posterior LIFG region (peak in pars opercularis) was activated for both lexical ambiguities and for *syntactically* ambiguous sentences (e.g., "visiting relatives is/are . . . "). This indicates that this region provides a relatively general processing resource for resolving linguistic ambiguities, regardless of the specific linguistic nature of the ambiguity. In addition, activation in this region has been reported in numerous studies using a very diverse range of sentence types and experimental manipulations that require additional sentence-level processing, such as semantic/syntactic anomalies or complex grammatical structures (see Rodd et al., 2015 for detailed review and formal meta-analysis). Perhaps most importantly, activation in the posterior LIFG has been seen in numerous studies using non-sentence stimuli, such as single words or pictures (e.g., Bedny, McGill, & Thompson-Schill, 2008; Kan & Thompson-Schill, 2004; Thompson-Schill, D'Esposito, Aguirre, & Farah, 1997; Whitney et al., 2011), emphasizing that its role is not confined to sentence processing.

In response to this heterogeneity in the types of studies that produce activation in the LIFG, several important theoretical accounts of its function have been proposed. A neurobiological model of language put forward by Hagoort and colleagues (Hagoort, 2005; Hagoort & Indefrey, 2014) subdivides language processing into three components: memory, unification, and control. Within this theory, the LIFG constitutes a unification space which allows basic units of linguistic information to be combined together to form more complex representations of individual sentences and of longer pieces of discourse. Under this view, it is the increased combinatorial demands of high-ambiguity sentences that drives greater

LIFG activation for these sentences, as well as for sentences that contain anomalies or that use complex grammatical structures.

In contrast to this "unification" account of LIFG function, which focuses primarily on sentence comprehension, an alternative neurocognitive account of LIFG function, known as the "conflict resolution account" (Novick, Kan, Trueswell, & Thompson-Schill, 2009; Novick, Trueswell, & Thompson-Schill, 2005; Thompson-Schill et al., 1997), takes a broader view and argues that the key function of the LIFG is to resolve competition between activated representations for both sentence and non-sentential stimuli. Specifically, Novick et al. (2009) suggested that the LIFG supports conflict resolution either when there is a prepotent but irrelevant response, or when multiple representations are available, but no dominant response exists. Although this account can easily accommodate the findings from the lexical ambiguity literature—activation increases when the word's strongly dominant (i.e., prepotent) meaning is not consistent with the sentence context (e.g., "the sheep was in the *pen*") or when two equally likely meanings are both consistent with a relatively neutral context (e.g., "he mentioned the organ").

In summary, different theories of LIFG function can explain the involvement of this region in ambiguity resolution in terms of a relatively general role in either combinatorial processing or conflict resolution. These are both cognitive functions that are *not* specifically restricted to the processing of lexical ambiguities and both accounts emphasize the involvement of relatively generic forms of cognitive processing in resolving these ambiguities. This emphasis in the neurocognitive models is in contrast to the psycholinguistic models reviewed above, which focus more on specifying the specific processes used within processing of lexical ambiguities.

Finally, as previously noted, it important to recall that lexical ambiguities also produce consistent activation in the posterior portion of the left temporal lobe (Davis et al., 2007; Rodd et al., 2005; Rodd et al., 2012; Tahmasebi et al., 2012; Zempleni et al., 2007), and (less consistently) in the *right* IFG (Mason & Just, 2007; Rodd et al., 2012; Zempleni et al., 2007). Unfortunately, in stark contrast with the literature on LIFG function, the precise locations of these activations are highly variable, and the field has made relatively little progress in specifying the precise contributions of these regions and how they relate to the literature beyond lexical ambiguity. Thus, at the current time, although it seems clear that both of these regions make an important contribution to the processing of lexical ambiguities, future research is needed to specify the cognitive nature of this contribution (see Vitello et al., 2014 for a more extensive review).

5.7 Conclusions

Resolving lexical ambiguities is a key component of skilled language comprehension. Without the ability to access the contextually appropriate, intended meaning for each word we encounter, accurate communication between individuals would be impossible. Evidence from behavioral experiments has indicated that retrieval of word meanings can be modeled within a distributed connectionist framework in which words compete to produce coherent patterns of activation across an array of semantic "units." Ambiguity between multiple meanings can interfere with this process, making it more challenging to retrieve the meanings of these words compared to unambiguous words. However, once a sentence context is provided that strongly supports just one of a word's possible meanings, then readers and listeners are able to make use of executive function control processes to select the most likely meanings, and if necessary reinterpret the sentence in the light of subsequent information.

Acknowledgments

Thanks to Becky Gilbert for providing the terrible pun about the fish. And more importantly for her insightful comments on a draft version of this chapter.

References

Armstrong, B. C., & Plaut, D. C. (2016). Disparate semantic ambiguity effects from semantic processing dynamics rather than qualitative task differences. *Language, Cognition and Neuroscience, 31,* 940–66.

Armstrong, B. C., Tokowicz, N., & Plaut, D. C. (2012). eDom: Norming software and relative meaning frequencies for 544 English homonyms. *Behavior Research Methods, 44,* 1015–27.

Azuma, T., & Van Orden, G. C. (1997). Why SAFE is better than FAST: The relatedness of a word's meanings affects lexical decision times. *Journal of Memory and Language, 36,* 484–504.

Bates, E., Devescovi, A., & Wulfeck, B. (2001). Psycholinguistics: A cross-language perspective. *Annual Review of Psychology, 52,* 369–96.

Bedny, M., McGill, M., & Thompson-Schill, S. L. (2008). Semantic adaptation and competition during word comprehension. *Cerebral Cortex, 18,* 2574–85.

Bekinschtein, T. A., Davis, M. H., Rodd, J. M., & Owen, A. M. (2011). Why clowns taste funny: The relationship between humor and semantic ambiguity. *Journal of Neuroscience, 31,* 9665–71.

Beretta, A., Fiorentino, R., & Poeppel, D. (2005). The effects of homonymy and polysemy on lexical access: An MEG study. *Cognitive Brain Research, 24,* 57–65.

Betts, H. N., Gilbert, R. A., Cai, Z. G., Okedara, Z. B., & Rodd, J. M. (2018). Retuning of lexical-semantic representations: Repetition and spacing effects in word-meaning priming. *Journal of Experimental Psychology: Learning, Memory, and Cognition,* doi: 10.1037/xlm0000507

Blank, A. (1999). Why do new meanings occur? A cognitive typology of the motivations for lexical semantic change. In: Blank, A., & Koch, P. (Eds.), *Historical Semantics and Cognition* (pp. 61–90). Mouton de Gruyter, Berlin/New York.

Borowsky, R., & Masson, M. E. J. (1996). Semantic ambiguity effects in word identification. *Journal of Experimental Psychology: Learning, Memory and Cognition, 22,* 63–85.

Cai, Z. G., Gilbert, R. A., Davis, M. H., Gaskell, M. G., Farrar, L., Adler, S., & Rodd, J. M. (2017). Accent modulates access to word meaning: Evidence for a speaker-model account of spoken word recognition. *Cognitive Psychology, 98,* 73–101.

Casenhiser, D. M. (2005). Children's resistance to homonymy: An experimental study of pseudohomonyms. *Journal of Child Language, 32,* 319–43.

Clark, H. H., & Gerrig, R. J. (1983). Understanding old words with new meanings. *Journal of Verbal Learning and Verbal Behavior, 22,* 591–608.

Cruse, A. D. (1986). *Lexical Semantics.* Cambridge University Press, Cambridge, UK.

Dautriche, I., & Chemla, E. (2016). What homophones say about words. *PLoS One*, 11, e0162176.

Dautriche, I., Chemla, E., & Christophe, A. (2016). Word learning: Homophony and the distribution of learning exemplars. *Language Learning and Development*, 12, 231–51.

Davis, M. H., Coleman, M. R., Absalom, A. R., Rodd, J. M., Johnsrude, I. S., Matta, B. F., . . . Menon, D. K. (2007). Dissociating speech perception and comprehension at reduced levels of awareness. *Procedings of the National Academy of Sciences U.S.A*, 104, 16032–7.

Dijkstra, T., Grainger, J., & Van Heuven, W. J. B. (1999). Recognition of cognates and interlingual homographs: The neglected role of phonology. *Journal of Memory and Language*, 41(4), 496–518.

Doherty, M. J. (2004). Children's difficulty in learning homonyms. *Journal of Child Language*, 31, 203–14.

Duffy, S. A., Morris, R. K., & Rayner, K. (1988). Lexical ambiguity and fixation times in reading. *Journal of Memory and Language*, 27, 429–46.

Fang, X., Perfetti, C., & Stafura, J. (2016). Learning new meanings for known words: Biphasic effects of prior knowledge. *Language, Cognition and Neuroscience*, 32(5), 637–49.

Frisson, S., & Pickering, M. (2007). The processing of familiar and novel senses of a word: Why reading Dickens is easy but reading Needham can be hard. *Language and Cognitive Processes*, 22, 595–613.

Gaskell, M. G., & Marslen-Wilson, W. D. (1997). Integrating form and meaning: A distributed model of speech perception. *Language and Cognitive Processes*, 12(5–6), 613–56.

Gernsbacher, M. A., & Faust, M. E. (1991). The mechanism of suppression: A component of general comprehension skill. *Journal of Experimental Psychology: Learning, Memory and Cognition*, 17, 245–62.

Gernsbacher, M. A., Varner, K. R., & Faust, M. E. (1990). Investigating differences in general comprehension skill. *Journal of Experimental Psychology: Learning, Memory and Cognition*, 16, 430–45.

Gilbert, R. A., Davis, M. H., Gaskell, M. G., & Rodd, J. M. (2018). Listeners and readers generalize their experience with word meanings across modalities. *Journal of Experimental Psychology: Learning, Memory, and Cognition*, doi: 10.1037/xlm0000432

Hagoort, P. (2005). Unification in language and the brain. In: Cutler, A. (Ed.), *Twenty-First Century Psycholinguistics: Four Cornerstones* (pp. 157–72). Lawrence Erlbaum Associates, Mahwah, NJ.

Hagoort, P., & Indefrey, P. (2014). The neurobiology of language beyond single words. *Annual Review of Neuroscience*, 37, 347–62.

Henderson, L., Snowling, M., & Clarke, P. (2013). Accessing, integrating, and inhibiting word meaning in poor comprehenders. *Scientific Studies of Reading*, 17, 177–98.

Hino, Y., & Lupker, S. J. (1996). Effects of polysemy in lexical decision and naming—an alternative to lexical access accounts. *Journal of Experimental Psychology: Human Perception and Performance*, 22, 1331–56.

Hino, Y., Pexman, P. M., & Lupker, S. J. (2006). Ambiguity and relatedness effects in semantic tasks: Are they due to semantic coding? *Journal of Memory and Language*, 55, 247–73.

Hinton, G. E., & Shallice, T. (1991). Lesioning an attractor network: Investigations of acquired dyslexia. *Psychological Review*, 98(1), 74–95.

Jastrzembski, J. E. (1981). Multiple meanings, number of related meanings, frequency of occurrence, and the lexicon. *Cognitive Psychology*, 13, 278–305.

Joordens, S., & Besner, D. (1994). When banking on meaning is not (yet) money in the bank—explorations in connectionist modeling. *Journal of Experimental Psychology: Learning, Memory and Cognition*, 20, 1051–62.

Kambe, G., Rayner, K., & Duffy, S. A. (2001). Global context effects on processing lexically ambiguous words: Evidence from eye fixations. *Memory & Cognition, 29,* 363–72.

Kan, I. P., & Thompson-Schill, S. L. (2004). Effect of name agreement on prefrontal activity during overt and covert picture naming. *Cognitive, Affective & Behavioral Neuroscience, 4,* 43–57.

Kawamoto, A. H., Farrar, W. T., & Kello, C. T. (1994). When two meanings are better than one: Modeling the ambiguity advantage using a recurrent distributed network. *Journal of Experimental Psychology: Human Perception and Performance, 20,* 1233–47.

Kellas, G., Ferraro, F. R., & Simpson, G. B. (1988). Lexical ambiguity and the timecourse of attentional allocation in word recognition. *Journal of Experimental Psychology: Human Perception and Performance, 14,* 601–9.

Key Stage 2 English Reading Booklet (2016). Key Stage 2 English Reading Booklet [Electronic version]. Available at: https://www.gov.uk/government/publications/key-stage-2-tests-2016-english-reading-test-materials

Khanna, M. M., & Boland, J. E. (2010). Children's use of language context in lexical ambiguity resolution. *Quarterly Journal of Experimental Psychology, 63,* 160–93.

Klein, D. E., & Murphy, G. L. (2001). The representation of polysemous words. *Journal of Memory and Language, 45,* 259–82.

Klepousniotou, E., & Baum, S. R. (2007). Disambiguating the ambiguity advantage effect in word recognition: An advantage for polysemous but not homonymous words. *Journal of Neurolinguistics, 20,* 1–24.

MacDonald, M. C., Pearlmutter, N. J., & Seidenberg, M. S. (1994). The lexical nature of syntactic ambiguity resolution. *Psychological Review, 101,* 676–703.

Marian, V., Bartolotti, J., Chabal, S., & Shook, A. (2012). Clearpond: Cross-linguistic easy-access resource for phonological and orthographic neighborhood densities. *PLoS One, 7,* e43230.

Mason, R. A., & Just, M. A. (2007). Lexical ambiguity in sentence comprehension. *Brain Research, 1146,* 115–127.

Mazzocco, M. M. M. (1997). Children's interpretations of homonyms: A developmental study. *Journal of Child Language, 24,* 441–67.

McClelland, J. L., & Elman, J. L. (1986). The TRACE model of speech perception. *Cognitive Psychology, 18,* 1–86.

McClelland, J. L., & Rumelhart, D. E. (1981). An interactive activation model of context effects in letter perception: Part 1. An account of basic findings. *Psychological Review, 88,* 375–407.

McRae, K., Spivey-Knowlton, M. J., & Tanenhaus, M. K. (1998). Modeling the influence of thematic fit (and other constraints) in on-line sentence comprehension. *Journal of Memory and Language, 38,* 283–312.

Millis, M. L., & Button, S. B. (1989). The effect of polysemy on lexical decision time: Now you see it, now you don't. *Memory & Cognition, 17,* 141–147.

Miyake, A., Just, M. A., & Carpenter, P. A. (1994). Working memory constraints on the resolution of lexical ambiguity: Maintaining multiple interpretations in neutral contexts. *Journal of Memory and Language, 33,* 175–202.

Norbury, C. F. (2005). Barking up the wrong tree? Lexical ambiguity resolution in children with language impairments and autistic spectrum disorders. *Journal of Experimental Child Psychology, 90,* 142–71.

Novick, J. M., Kan, I. P., Trueswell, J. C., & Thompson-Schill, S. L. (2009). A case for conflict across multiple domains: Memory and language impairments following damage to ventrolateral prefrontal cortex. *Cognitive Neuropsychology, 26*, 527–67.

Novick, J. M., Trueswell, J. C., & Thompson-Schill, S. L. (2005). Cognitive control and parsing: Reexamining the role of Broca's area in sentence comprehension. *Cognitive, Affective & Behavioral Neuroscience, 5*, 263–81.

Onifer, W., & Swinney, D. A. (1981). Accessing lexical ambiguities during sentence comprehension—effects of frequency of meaning and contextual bias. *Memory & Cognition, 9*, 1–39.

Parks, R., Ray, J., & Bland, S. (1998). Wordsmyth English Dictionary-Thesaurus [Electronic version]. University of Chicago, Chicago, IL. Available at: http://www.wordsmyth.net/

Pexman, P. M., & Lupker, S. J. (1999). Ambiguity and visual word recognition: Can feedback explain both homophone and polysemy effects? *Canadian Journal of Experimental Psychology, 53*, 323–34.

Piantadosi, S. T., Tily, H., & Gibson, E. (2012). The communicative function of ambiguity in language. *Cognition, 122*, 280–91.

Plaut, D. C. (1997). Structure and function in the lexical system: insights from distributed models of word reading and lexical decision. *Language and Cognitive Processes, 12*(5–6), 765–805.

Plaut, D. C., & Shallice, T. (1993). Deep dyslexia: A case study of connectionist neuropsychology. *Cognitive Neuropsychology, 10*(5), 377–500.

Poort, E. D., Warren, J. E., & Rodd, J. M. (2016). Recent experience with cognates and interlingual homographs in one language affects subsequent processing in another language. *Bilingualism, 19*, 206–12.

Rabagliati, H., Marcus, G. F., & Pylkkänen, L. (2010). Shifting senses in lexical semantic development. *Cognition, 117*, 17–37.

Rabagliati, H., Pylkkänen, L., & Marcus, G. F. (2013). Top-down influence in young children's linguistic ambiguity resolution. *Developmental Psychology, 49*, 1076–89.

Rodd, J. M. (2004). The effect of semantic ambiguity on reading aloud: A twist in the tale. *Psychonomic Bulletin & Review, 11*, 440–5.

Rodd, J. M., Berriman, R., Landau, M., Lee, T., Ho, C., Gaskell, M. G., & Davis, M. H. (2012). Learning new meanings for old words: Effects of semantic relatedness. *Memory & Cognition, 40*, 1095–108.

Rodd, J. M., Cai, Z. G., Betts, H. N., Hanby, B., Hutchinson, C., & Adler, A. (2016). The impact of recent and long-term experience on access to word meanings: Evidence from large-scale internet-based experiments. *Journal of Memory and Language, 87*, 16–37.

Rodd, J. M., Davis, M. H., & Johnsrude, I. S. (2005). The neural mechanisms of speech comprehension: fMRI studies of semantic ambiguity. *Cerebral Cortex, 15*, 1261–9.

Rodd, J. M., Gaskell, M. G., & Marslen-Wilson, W. D. (2002). Making sense of semantic ambiguity: Semantic competition in lexical access. *Journal of Memory and Language, 46*, 245–66.

Rodd, J. M., Gaskell, M. G., & Marslen-Wilson, W. D. (2004). Modelling the effects of semantic ambiguity in word recognition. *Cognitive Science, 28*, 89–104.

Rodd, J. M., Johnsrude, I. S., & Davis, M. H. (2010). The role of domain-general frontal systems in language comprehension: Evidence from dual-task interference and semantic ambiguity. *Brain and Language, 115*, 182–8.

Rodd, J. M., Johnsrude, I. S., & Davis, M. H. (2012). Dissociating frontotemporal contributions to semantic ambiguity resolution in spoken sentences. *Cerebral Cortex, 22*, 1761–73.

Rodd, J. M., Longe, O. A., Randall, B., & Tyler, L. K. (2010). The functional organisation of the fronto-temporal language system: Evidence from syntactic and semantic ambiguity. *Neuropsychologia, 48*, 1324–35.

Rodd, J. M., Lopez Cutrin, B., Kirsch, H., Millar, A., & Davis, M. H. (2013). Long-term priming of the meanings of ambiguous words. *Journal of Memory and Language, 68*, 180–98.

Rodd, J. M., Vitello, S., Woollams, A. M., & Adank, P. (2015). Localising semantic and syntactic processing in spoken and written language comprehension: An activation likelihood estimation meta-analysis. *Brain and Language, 141*, 89–102.

Rorden, C., & Brett, M. (2000). Stereotaxic display of brain lesions. *Behavioural Neurology, 12*, 191–200.

Rubenstein, H., Garfield, L., & Millikan, J. A. (1970). Homographic entries in the internal lexicon. *Journal of Verbal Learning and Verbal Behavior, 9*, 487–94.

Schepens, J., Dijkstra, T., & Grootjen, F. (2012). Distributions of cognates in Europe as based on Levenshtein distance. *Bilingualism, 15*, 157–66.

Seidenberg, M. S., Tanenhaus, M. K., Leiman, J. M., & Bienkowski, M. (1982). Automatic access of the meanings of ambiguous words in context—Some limitations of knowledge-based processing. *Cognitive Psychology, 14*, 489–537.

Simpson, G. B., & Kang, H. (1994). Inhibitory processes in the recognition of homograph meanings. In: Dagenbach, D., & Carr, T. (Eds.), *Inhibitory Processes in Attention, Memory, and Language* (pp. 359–81). Academic Press, New York, NY.

Srinivasan, M., & Snedeker, J. (2011). Judging a book by its cover and its contents: The representation of polysemous and homophonous meanings in four-year-old children. *Cognitive Psychology, 62*, 245–72.

Storkel, H. L., & Maekawa, J. (2005). A comparison of homonym and novel word learning: The role of phonotactic probability and word frequency. *Journal of Child Language, 32*, 827–53.

Storkel, H. L., Maekawa, J., & Aschenbrenner, A. J. (2013). The effect of homonymy on learning correctly articulated versus misarticulated words. *Journal of Speech, Language, and Hearing Research, 56*, 694–707.

Swinney, D. A. (1979). Lexical access during sentence comprehension: (Re)consideration of context effects. *Journal of Verbal Learning and Verbal Behavior, 18*, 645–59.

Tabossi, P. (1988). Accessing lexical ambiguity in different types of sentential contexts. *Journal of Memory and Language, 27*, 324–40.

Tabossi, P., & Zardon, F. (1993). Processing ambiguous words in context. *Journal of Memory and Language, 32*, 359–72.

Tahmasebi, A. M., Davis, M. H., Wild, C. J., Rodd, J. M., Hakyemez, H., Abolmaesumi, P., & Johnsrude, I. S. (2012). Is the link between anatomical structure and function equally strong at all cognitive levels of processing? *Cerebral Cortex, 22*, 1593–603.

Thompson-Schill, S. L., D'Esposito, M., Aguirre, G. K., & Farah, M. J. (1997). Role of left inferior prefrontal cortex in retrieval of semantic knowledge: A reevaluation. *Proceedings of the National Academy of Sciences of the United States of America, 94*, 14792–7.

Twilley, L. C., & Dixon, P. (2000). Meaning resolution processes for words: A parallel independent model. *Psychonomic Bulletin & Review, 7*, 49–82.

Twilley, L. C., Dixon, P., Taylor, D., & Clark, K. (1994). University of Alberta norms of relative meaning frequency for 566 homographs. *Memory & Cognition, 22*, 111–26.

van der Schoot, M., Vasbinder, A. L., Horsley, T. M., Reijntjes, A., & van Lieshout, E. C. D. M. (2009). Lexical ambiguity resolution in good and poor comprehenders: An eye fixation and self-paced reading study in primary school children. *Journal of Educational Psychology*, *101*, 21–36.

Vitello, S., & Rodd, J. M. (2015). Resolving semantic ambiguities in sentences: cognitive processes and brain mechanisms. *Linguistics and Language Compass*, *9*, 391–405.

Vitello, S., Warren, J. E., Devlin, J. T., & Rodd, J. M. (2014). Roles of frontal and temporal regions in reinterpreting semantically ambiguous sentences. *Frontiers in Human Neuroscience*, *8*, 530.

Vitevitch, M. S. (2012). What do foreign neighbors say about the mental lexicon? *Bilingualism*, *15*, 167–72.

Whitney, C., Kirk, M., O'Sullivan, J., Lambon Ralph, M. A., & Jefferies, E. (2011). The neural organization of semantic control: TMS evidence for a distributed network in left inferior frontal and posterior middle temporal gyrus. *Cerebral Cortex*, *21*, 1066–75.

Zempleni, M. Z., Renken, R., Hoeks, J. C., Hoogduin, J. M., & Stowe, L. A. (2007). Semantic ambiguity processing in sentence context: Evidence from event-related fMRI. *NeuroImage*, *34*, 1270–9.

CHAPTER 6

VISUAL WORD RECOGNITION IN MULTILINGUALS

TON DIJKSTRA AND WALTER J. B. VAN HEUVEN

6.1 INTRODUCTION

As contacts between nations increase due to economical, political, and technological developments, so does the importance of being able to speak and understand a different language from one's own. One part of the world where this is strongly felt is the European Union. In 2012, 54% of all civilians indicated that they could speak a foreign language well enough to converse in it, whereas this was the case for 74% of young people between 15–24 years of age (Eurobarometer, 2012). Countries in which over 90% of the inhabitants speak at least one language (L2) in addition to their mother tongue (L1) are Luxembourg, Latvia, the Netherlands, Malta, Slovenia, Lithuania, and Sweden. For about 38% of the inhabitants of the Union, this second language is English. About a quarter of the Europeans should be called *multilingual* rather than *bilingual*, because they speak at least three languages. In the last decades, foreign language use by Europeans has received a boost via the internet, international computer games, movies and television series, and social media. Although precise numbers are lacking, in the world at large there may be more multilinguals than monolinguals when we define "multilingualism" as the regular use of two or more languages.

This prominence of multilingualism in the world not only has its consequences for educational systems (e.g., with respect to foreign language teaching), but also for psycholinguistic research, because the language processing system might be differently organized in monolinguals and bilinguals. In fact, research might miss out on important characteristics or limitations of the language processing system when the workings of only one language (often English) are investigated.

In this chapter, we focus on the basic "building block" of languages, the word, and how it is processed by multilingual language users during reading. The study of multilingual word recognition raises several unique and fundamental questions. First, there is a *structure-oriented* question: Are the words of the different languages that a multilingual knows stored in one *integrated lexicon* or in *separate lexicons*? The latter option would, for instance, entail that a polyglot would possess several, even up to 20, different lexical databases. This question has been investigated both by means of behavioral studies (RTs) and neuroimaging studies (e.g., event-related potentials (ERPs) and fMRI).

There is a second question that is closely related and hard to disentangle (van Heuven et al., 1998). This *process-oriented* question is: Can the retrieval of a word in one language be affected by (word candidates in) another language? According to the *language non-specific lexical access* hypothesis, the word identification system cannot initially know if an input word is from one language or another; to be "on the safe side," all words in any language that are similar to the input are activated in parallel. In contrast, according to the *language-specific lexical access* hypothesis, the word identification system always uses contextual information pro-actively to restrict the word selection process to only one language. For instance, a target language may be indicated by the preceding words in a sentence or conversation, or because the utterance to be understood is produced by a monolingual speaker.

According to the language-specific access hypothesis, the effect of the (language) context is so strong that it can restrict word retrieval to one lexicon from the very beginning. This brings up a third question: To what extent is multilingual word identification dependent on the circumstances in which it takes place? According to a *context-sensitive lexical access* hypothesis, lexical access is initially language non-specific, but context can quickly kick in (reactively) to speed up the selection of the actually presented word. For instance, for any target word in a sentence (or even after a single word), a language non-specific set of word candidates might initially be activated, followed by a candidate elimination process making use of contextual information. This issue about context effects on multilingual word retrieval is crucial, because in daily life we usually read words as parts of sentences. Furthermore, the context of language processing also includes the task that the participants perform and the composition of the stimulus lists that they work through. The analysis of the contribution of all these factors is facilitated by the arrival of new, more "naturalistic" measurement techniques that allow precise temporal measurements, such as those involving ERPs and eye-tracking.

The first three questions are directly related to a fourth one, namely about the general role of a word's *language membership* in processing. Knowing to what language a word belongs might be used to facilitate lexical processing for both isolated words and words presented in (sentence) context. In recent years, researchers have become aware that under particular conditions this word characteristic can facilitate word selection.

In the last decades, the issues of storage, processing, context, and language membership have been investigated in many studies on multilingualism. They are accounted for in different ways by current models of multilingual word recognition. We will discuss the most prominent models of visual word recognition by adult multilinguals. Special attention will be paid to computational models, including a recent model on word translation.

Space limitations unfortunately make it impossible for us to address a number of recent other developments and extensions in the field. Not only will we leave aside bilingual auditory word recognition and spoken word production, but also will we be silent about second language acquisition research, which extends the findings for late multilinguals to learners and early multilinguals. This area is quickly gaining interest from psychologists, after having been studied for decades by linguists, teachers, and others (for reviews, see Kootstra, Dijkstra, & Starren, 2015; Meade & Dijkstra, in press).

To sum up, in the following we will consider a number of prominent issues with respect to the multilingual lexicon:

- What kind of "special" words can we use to study the multilingual lexicon? (section 6.2)
- How are such "special" and other words stored in the multilingual lexicon? (section 6.3)
- How does a multilingual read words in isolation? (section 6.4)
- What is the effect of sentence context on multilingual processing? (section 6.5)
- What role does language membership play in multilingual processing? (section 6.6)
- What models have been proposed to account for the available data? (section 6.7)

In each of these issues, three word types figure prominently: neighbors, false friends (including interlingual homographs and interlingual homophones), and cognates. Before we consider the storage of words in the multilingual lexicon, these "special" item types are defined in the next section.

6.2 Prominent word types in multilingual studies

It is estimated that monolinguals possess a mental lexicon of 50,000 words or more, from which they can retrieve a word within a third of a second in comprehension and production (see Aitchison, 2003, pp. 5–7). Multilinguals who are reasonably fluent in other languages as well, must therefore have stored tens of thousands of additional words for their second language, and the number of extra words from yet other languages is often considerable. And yet, the cost associated to the ability of processing more than one language in terms of processing time and error rate seems to be mild. In their comparison of bilingual and monolingual performance in different tasks, Ransdell and Fischler (1987, p. 400) concluded that "Becoming fluent in a second language appears to have only slight impact on the ability to process the first." They observed, for instance, that bilinguals made English lexical decisions on words that were only about 125 ms slower than those of monolinguals (given RTs of 700–900 ms), but just as accurate. Furthermore, in a recent more natural reading study (Cop, Drieghe, & Duyck, 2015; Cop, Keuleers, Drieghe, & Duyck, 2015; Cop et al., 2016), Dutch-English bilinguals and English monolinguals read a novel by Agatha Christie in English or Dutch. The readers' eye movements revealed no statistical differences in the single fixation durations for non-cognate content words between bilinguals and monolinguals reading the novel in their L1 (Dutch or English, respectively). Apparently, the bilinguals' reading did not suffer from any lowered bilingual exposure to their native language (if there was any of that). On average, the bilinguals fixated longer in L2 (English) than in L1 (Dutch) reading, but the difference was not large, in the order of 15–25 ms for single fixation durations. How can multilinguals retrieve the right words from their mental lexicon so quickly, both in their L1 and their L2?

The mental lexicon stores a language user's knowledge with respect to words. All words must be represented with respect to spelling (orthography), sound (phonology), meaning (concepts/semantics), and several other characteristics, among which the language to which a word belongs (language membership information), morphology, and pragmatics.

The mental lexicon is usually considered as a storage space set up along these multiple dimensions, or as a multidimensional network connecting all different properties of a word. During reading, the entry dimension and first activated code is orthographic in nature; during listening, it is phonological; and during speaking it is some kind of conceptual or semantic message specification. On the basis of the first activated code, all other codes in the lexicon can be reached by spreading activation (see Thierry & Wu, 2007). Evidence that activation can spread between lexicons comes from studies using various types of stimuli, such as neighbors, false friends, and cognates. These stimulus types are discussed now.

6.2.1 Neighbors

Each word can be specified with respect to dimensions like spelling, sound, or meaning, and has its own unique position in multidimensional space. Similar words are stored in similar regions of this space. The orthographic similarity of words can be assessed by applying a *similarity metric*, like that of the *neighborhood* (Coltheart, Davelaar, Jonasson, & Besner, 1977). To the neighborhood of a target word belong all *competitor* words or *neighbors* that differ in only one letter position (i.e., substitution neighbors). For instance, BIN has neighbors like GIN, BUN, and BIG. According to the language non-specific access hypothesis, a Dutch-English bilingual reading the English word BIN will not only activate (known) neighbors from both English (L2), but also from Dutch (L1), like BON, VIN, and BIL.

Following the strict definition of a neighbor as just described, BIND would not be a neighbor of BIN and would not be activated. However, so-called addition neighbors (BIND) and deletion neighbors (IN) also affect target processing (e.g., Davis & Taft, 2005; Davis, Perea, & Acha, 2009). To account for the different types of neighbors a slightly different metric can be used. The *Levenshtein distance* defines the spelling difference between two words as the number of operations that need to be performed in order to change one into the other (Levenshtein, 1966). For instance, in order to transform BUN into BIND, one letter must be replaced (U into I) and one must be added (D). When two words are different in length, the Levenshtein distance can be normalized by dividing by the maximum length of the two words (as suggested by Schepens, Dijkstra, & Grootjen, 2012; Schepens, Dijkstra, Grootjen, & van Heuven, 2013). In case of BUN and BIND, this results in a normalized value of 2/4 =.50.

Because the orthographic similarity of words from within a language is on average larger than that between languages, the number of words that are similar to a target word increases relatively slowly when a new language is added to the first one (Dijkstra, 2003, p. 18). Factors that increase the distance between (words of different) languages include differences in script, morphology, diacritical markers, bigram frequencies, phonological repertoire, and phonotactics.

6.2.2 False friends

Although many words have an orthographic form that is unique, there are exceptions. Within English, for instance, the orthographic word form BANK refers to a financial institution or the edge of a river, and word forms like COLONEL and KERNEL are to considerable extent ambiguous in terms of their phonology. The two item types are referred to as, respectively, intralingual homographs and intralingual homophones. There is an analogous case of ambiguity across languages. Here *interlingual homographs* exist, words that share their orthographic word form across languages, but may be different in meaning and phonology. A Dutch-English example is a letter string like BOND, meaning "fellowship, union" in Dutch; a French–English example is COIN, meaning "corner" in French. In contrast, *interlingual homophones* are very similar in terms of their phonological representation. An example is an English word like AID relative to Dutch EED, meaning "oath." Note that the members of such pairs may differ in their frequency of usage in the two languages. Interlingual homographs and homophones are referred to by the general term *false friends*.

6.2.3 Cognates

Another special type of words is translation equivalents with word forms that are similar or identical across languages. Such items, like HOTEL, ECHO, and DEMOCRACY (with the same meaning across languages) are called *cognates*. In contrast to linguists, psycholinguists use this term irrespective of etymological relationship. For example, Dutch VIJF and French CINQ are historically related, but psychologists would not refer to these as cognates, because the form relationship is not transparent to the average language user.

For closely related language pairs like Dutch and English, the number of cognates and false friends is considerable. Van Hell (1998, p. 14) found that about half of the 200 most frequent English words were closely similar in sound or spelling to their Dutch translation equivalents. Schepens, Dijkstra, and Grootjen (2012) defined cognates as word translations of three to eight letters with a high degree of cross-linguistic orthographic similarity (i.e., a normalized Levenshtein distance score of 0.5 and higher). Following their definition, about 20% or more of the word translations between Dutch and five other European languages (English, French, German, Italian, and Spanish) were cognates. Lemhöfer et al. (2008) and Friel and Kennison (2001) reported similar percentages of about 20% for Dutch-English and German-English. Of course, for language combinations with different scripts, all orthographic forms are language specific, but even for combinations like English with Japanese or Chinese there are interlingual (near-) homophones. An example is the set of the numbers 1 through 4 in Japanese that are (more or less) pronounced as the English words "itchy," "knee," "son," and "she." In the case of interlingual homographs and homophones, their form similarity across languages is more or less coincidental and goes unaccompanied by translation equivalence or historically common origin; as a consequence, there are considerably fewer of these items than cognates.

6.3 The Storage of Words in the Multilingual Lexicon

Although interlingual homographs, interlingual homophones, and cognates are well-suited to investigate the *processing* issue mentioned in the Introduction, they are not suitable to investigate the issue of lexicon *structure*. Differences in response time to such "special" items and matched words that exist in only one language, do not necessarily constitute evidence in favor of an integrated lexicon. For instance, when a letter string like T-R-O-L-L is presented, it is no surprise if both the English and the Dutch reading of the cognate TROLL would be activated, because it has an orthographically identical form in the two languages. Furthermore, an orthographically identical cognate like TROLL might have a separate rather than a shared orthographic representation in each language of the multilingual. In fact, this would be reasonable, because the word's frequency, gender, and plural may differ across languages (cf. plural TROLLS in English to TROLLEN in Dutch).

Coactivation of languages is harder to explain in terms of a separate lexicons view in case of non-identical cognates, such as TOMATO (English) and TOMAAT (Dutch). However, the most convincing evidence in favor of an integrated lexicon has been obtained in studies involving target words with neighbors and morphologically related words in another language. For these item types, an input word has been shown to activate words in the non-target language that are not actually present. Studies involving cross-linguistic neighbors (e.g., LION and PION, Dutch for "PAWN") will be discussed in the next section (Grossi, Savill, Thomas, & Thierry, 2012; Midgley, Holcomb, van Heuven, & Grainger, 2008; van Heuven, Dijkstra, & Grainger, 1998). The most convincing evidence in favor of an integrated lexicon has been obtained in studies on cross-linguistic *morphological family size* effects. A morphological family of a target word is the set of words that are morphologically related. For instance, an English word like WORK has family members like the compounds SERVICE WORK and WORK HORSE. Similarly, the Dutch word WERK (cognate with WORK) has family members like WERKBAAR and HUISWERK. Behavioral and ERP studies have shown that responses to interlingual homographs and cognates (both identical and non-identical) are affected by the number of morphological family members in both the first and the second language (see Dijkstra, 2005, for interlingual homographs; Mulder, Schreuder, & Dijkstra, 2013; Mulder, Dijkstra, Schreuder, & Baayen, 2014; Mulder, Dijkstra, & Baayen, 2015, for cognates). This indicates that the recognition of a target word is affected by general properties of the other-language lexicon, which cannot be explained if separate lexicons are assumed (but see Kroll, van Hell, Tokowicz, & Green, 2010, for a different view).

6.4 The Process of Visual Word Recognition in Multilinguals

6.4.1 Neighbors

Research on monolingual word recognition indicates that upon the presentation of a letter string, representations of all words in the mental lexicon that are similar to the input letter string become activated (for reviews see, Andrews, 1997; Perea & Rosa, 2000). If in bilinguals, neighbors from both languages are activated upon the presentation of a word that belongs uniquely to one language, that would be in line with language-non-specific access to the mental lexicon (*process issue*). Furthermore, if neighbors from both languages interact in their effect on target word identification latencies, this is evidence that the multilingual lexicon is integrated across languages (*structure issue*). Van Heuven et al. (1998) showed that word candidates from both languages are indeed activated in parallel and that they mutually affect target word recognition. They manipulated the number of orthographic neighbors of the target words in the same and the other language of the bilinguals in a series of progressive demasking and lexical decision experiments involving Dutch-English bilinguals. Increasing the number of Dutch orthographic neighbors systematically slowed responses to English target words. Within the target language itself, an increase in neighbors consistently produced inhibitory effects for Dutch target words and facilitatory effects for English target words. Monolingual English readers also showed facilitation due to English neighbors, but no effects of Dutch neighbors. Highly correlated and very similar result patterns were obtained for several one-language (pure) and two-languages (mixed) experiments.

Dirix, Cop, Drieghe, and Duyck (2017) conducted a generalized Dutch-English lexical decision experiment and a large-scale eye-tracking study in which Dutch-English participants read the Dutch (L1) or English (L2) version of a novel by Agatha Christie. The generalized lexical decision experiment was comparable in several respects to van Heuven et al. (1998, Experiment 3). In line with the earlier study, Dirix et al. reported an inhibitory effect of Dutch (L1) neighborhood density on English (L2) words with low bigram frequency, and a higher error rate for L2 words with more cross-linguistic neighbors in a mixed-effect model analysis. In the natural English reading study, the presence of cross-language neighborhood effects in an L2 context was confirmed, but the effects were largely facilitatory (rather than inhibitory) in nature.

Consistent with the findings of both studies, Midgley et al. (2008) observed effects of cross-language neighbors in an EEG experiment. French–English bilinguals read pure-language lists of words that varied in number of orthographic neighbors in the non-target language and contained filler words referring to body parts. Participants were asked to press a button whenever they saw a word referring to a body part (go/no-go semantic categorization). The brain waves of proficient bilinguals were affected by the between-language neighborhood density of words in both their L1 (French) and their L2 (English). A more negative N400 was obtained for words with many rather than few between-language neighbors. The effect arose earlier in time and was more widely distributed across the scalp for English (L2) targets. English monolingual participants did not show the same pattern of ERPs to these stimuli. Early influences of the L1 (French) orthographic neighbors on L2 (English) processing were found, emerging as early as 200 ms after target onset.

In an ERP study with English-Welsh bilinguals, Grossi et al. (2012) partially replicated these results. Early and late bilinguals performed a semantic categorization task on English and Welsh words. In late bilinguals, words with many cross-language neighbors elicited more negative ERPs than words with few of them between 175 to 500 ms after word onset. This effect interacted with language (English or Welsh) in the 300–500 ms window. Early bilinguals showed a more complex pattern of early effects and no N400 effects. The authors suggest that activation of cross-language orthographic neighbors is sensitive to how bilinguals learn and use their languages. Just like morphological family size effects discussed earlier, cross-language neighborhood effects indicate that the orthographic lexicon of bilinguals is integrated and accessed language non-selectively.

6.4.2 False friends

Target words in cross-linguistic neighborhood studies exist in one language only. This is different for *false friends*, which have either an orthographic form (interlingual homographs) or a phonological form (interlingual homophones) that exists as a word in more than one language. False friends have two important characteristics: their relative frequency in the two languages, and their cross-linguistic overlap in terms of orthography and/or phonology. Each of these two factors has an impact on visual word recognition.

In a series of closely related lexical decision experiments, Dijkstra, van Jaarsveld, and Ten Brinke (1998) manipulated the *relative frequency* of the two members of *interlingual homograph* pairs. In a first experiment, Dutch-English participants performed an English lexical decision task including interlingual homographs and cognates, as well as exclusively English control words. Participants responded about equally fast to interlingual homographs and exclusively English matched controls (and faster to cognates). In a second experiment, purely Dutch words were added to the stimulus list (requiring a "no"-response). Responses now became much slower for interlingual homographs than for the matched controls, especially when the homographs were low-frequency in English and high-frequency in Dutch (e.g., for RAMP, meaning "disaster" in Dutch). The inhibition effects were attributed to a frequency-dependent competition between the two readings of the homographs, where the non-target language reading of the interlingual homograph could not be ignored by the participants. Finally, in a third experiment, participants were instructed to "say yes to English and/or Dutch words" (generalized lexical decision), implying they could in principle respond as soon as either of the two readings of a homograph became available. Here a facilitation effect was found, the size of which depended on the frequency of both the English and the Dutch readings of the homograph. The largest benefit to the RTs was observed for the homographs with low-frequency English and high-frequency Dutch readings. Participants were apparently able to respond to either reading of an interlingual homograph. The study demonstrates that stimulus list composition and task demands affect performance in a systematic but complex way, resulting in null-effects, inhibition effects, or facilitation effects depending on the exact empirical circumstances (see de Groot, Delmaar, & Lupker, 2000, for supporting results and conclusions; and Dijkstra, Timmermans, & Schriefers, 2000, for evidence from other tasks). Thus, the bilingual word recognition process can be understood properly only if one takes into account item characteristics, stimulus list composition, and task demands.

Van Heuven, Schriefers, Dijkstra, and Hagoort (2008) considered the competition effect between the two readings of interlingual homographs in a combined RT/fMRI study (cf. Hsieh et al., 2017). Dutch-English bilinguals performed an English lexical decision task or a Dutch-English generalized lexical decision task. English monolinguals performed the English lexical decision task as a control group. Slower RTs to interlingual homographs relative to English control words were obtained only for the bilinguals performing the English lexical decision task. This inhibition reflects the lexical competition between the two readings of the interlingual homographs (e.g., ROOM can be mapped on either the "yes" or the "no" response, depending on whether it is considered as an English or a Dutch word). The fMRI data also reflected this lexical conflict, because greater activation for homographs than for control words was found in the left inferior/middle frontal gyrus, which is associated with phonological and semantic processing. Importantly, the fMRI data of the English lexical decision task revealed activations in the pre-SMA and dorsal anterior cingulate cortex (dACC) for the contrast between homographs and English control words. However, no activations in these regions were observed in the generalized lexical decision task. This suggests that the pre-SMA/dACC was only involved when language conflict occurred at response level.

Recently, the time course of inhibition during the recognition of interlingual homographs has become a topic of investigation. Using a behavioral semantic relatedness paradigm, Martín, Macizo, and Bajo (2010) observed inhibition effects for the English reading of Spanish-English interlingual homographs when these were presented together with words related to the Spanish reading of the homograph. When the English translation of this Spanish meaning was presented 500 ms after responding to a homograph, the responses slowed down (cf. Dijkstra et al., 2000), but not when this happened after 750 ms. In a similar paradigm, Durlik, Szewczyk, Muszyński, and Wodniecka (2016) also observed strong interference effects for Polish-English interlingual homographs in a pure L2 context; their effects further suggested that the homograph's irrelevant meaning suppresses a whole semantic category rather than a single item.

Several combined RT/EEG studies have also considered the coactivation of both readings of interlingual homographs using a priming paradigm with interlingual homographs. Kerkhofs et al. (2006) found that the response to interlingual homographs was facilitated when they were preceded by semantically related primes relative to unrelated primes. Responses of Dutch-English bilinguals were faster when the homographs' English word frequency was high or their Dutch word frequency was low. In the related condition, N400 effects were found that were modulated by word frequency in both L1 and L2. Hoshino and Thierry (2012) also found smaller N400 effects in related conditions in a study with English-Spanish bilinguals, both for the L1 and the L2 (non-target language) reading of the interlingual homograph. There was also an effect in the late positive component (LPC; 500–650 ms after target onset) for the related conditions, but not for the Spanish meaning of the homograph. The LPC has been associated with stimulus re-evaluation and is also prominent in language switching (e.g., Martin, Thierry, & Démonet, 2010; see also Müller, Duñabeitia, & Carreiras, 2010). They concluded that the non-target meaning of the interlingual homograph is suppressed after 400 ms.

Apart from lexical (frequency) effects on interlingual homographs, an important issue is the extent to which orthographic and phonological cross-linguistic similarity contribute to these effects. Lemhöfer and Dijkstra (2004) compared the RTs to control words and Dutch-English false friends with overlap in both orthography and phonology (OP: SPOT, Dutch meaning "irony"), only orthography (O: GLAD, Dutch meaning "slippery"), or only phonology (P: COW—KOU, Dutch meaning "cold"). Dutch-English bilinguals processed these items in an English lexical decision task or a generalized lexical decision task. The Dutch-English bilinguals were found to respond to the first available lexical code, which is orthography in word reading. Relative to control words, the coactivation of the Dutch and English homograph readings in English lexical decision led to comparably faster RTs for O and OP items, but P items without O overlap were responded to just as slowly as controls. In the generalized lexical decision task, faster responses were obtained for the English but not the Dutch reading of interlingual homographs, indicating that the participants relied on the quickly available Dutch (L1) reading. The results imply that homographs have two O representations, one for each language (cf. Dijkstra et al., 1998).

6.4.3 Cognates

Many studies have investigated the processing of orthographically non-identical and identical cognates. Most of these have shown a *cognate facilitation effect* in the L2, i.e., cognates are processed more quickly and with fewer errors during reading, listening, and speaking than matched one-language words (e.g., van Hell & Tanner, 2012). Brain waves to cognates and matched control words are different (e.g., in terms of the N400 component; Comesaña et al., 2012; Dijkstra, van Hell, & Brenders, 2015; Midgley, Holcomb, & Grainger, 2011; Peeters, Dijkstra, & Grainger, 2013). Faster RTs to cognates in various tasks have also been observed in different script bilinguals (e.g., Chinese-English: Dong & Lin, 2013; Hebrew-English: Gollan, Forster, & Frost, 1997; Greek-French: Voga & Grainger, 2007; Japanese-English: Allen & Conklin, 2013; Hoshino & Kroll, 2008; Nakayama, Sears, Hino, & Lupker, 2012; Korean-English: Kim & Davis, 2003).

The cognate facilitation effect is usually larger in a second language than in a first language (Brenders, van Hell, & Dijkstra, 2011; Cop et al., 2016), although it also occurs in the mother tongue if the bilingual is sufficiently proficient in the foreign language (Cop et al., 2016; Titone et al., 2011; van Assche, Duyck, Hartsuiker, & Diependaele, 2009; van Hell & Dijkstra, 2002). Van Hell and Dijkstra (2002) had trilinguals with Dutch as their L1, English as their L2, and French as their L3, perform a word association task or a lexical decision task in their native language. Shorter association and lexical decision times were observed for Dutch-English non-identical cognates than for non-cognates. For trilinguals with a higher proficiency in French, lexical decision responses were faster for both Dutch-English and Dutch-French cognates. Thus, even when their orthographic and phonological overlap across languages is incomplete, cognates may still be recognized faster than non-cognates in the *native* language. Stronger facilitation effects can arise if the cognates in question exist in three languages rather than in two, like the word ECHO that exists in English, German, and Dutch (Lemhöfer, Dijkstra, & Michel, 2004; Lijewska & Chmiel, 2015; Szubko-Sitarek, 2011).

The cognate facilitation effect depends on code overlap in terms of meaning (semantics), spelling (orthography), and/or pronunciation (phonology) across languages. Dijkstra, Grainger, and van Heuven (1999) examined the effects of different types of *code overlap* in cognate and interlingual homograph processing. Dutch-English bilinguals performed an English lexical decision task with English words varying in their degree of semantic (S), orthographic (O), and phonological (P) overlap with Dutch words. Three groups of cognates (+ S) and three groups of false friends (-S) were selected that varied in the degree of orthographic and phonological overlap. Items were, for instance, SPORT (overlap in S, O, and P codes), CHAOS (SO), WHEEL (SP; Dutch item: WIEL), PINK (OP), GLAD (O), and CORE (P; Dutch item: KOOR). Lexical decisions were facilitated by cross-linguistic orthographic and semantic overlap relative to control words that belonged only to English. In contrast, phonological overlap produced inhibitory effects. Effects of cross-language phonological overlap have also been found with homophones, although the effect was facilitatory and depended on stimulus composition and L2 proficiency (Haigh & Jared, 2007).

The cognate effect does not only depend on stimulus list composition (e.g., Brenders, van Hell, & Dijkstra, 2011; Comesaña, Ferré, Romero, Guasch, Soares, & García-Chico, 2015), but also on the task at hand. It can even turn into an interference effect, for instance, in a language decision task in which participants determine if a word belongs to one language or another (Dijkstra et al., 2010; Lavaur & Font, 1998). In other words, form overlap helps if one does not have to distinguish the two readings of the cognate, but it hinders if one must discern them.

In recent years, evidence has accrued that there may be structural, processing, and decision level differences between identical cognates and non-identical cognates. For example, qualitative differences between identical and non-identical cognates have been observed by Dijkstra et al. (2010). In an English lexical decision task performed by Dutch-English bilinguals, the cognate effect increased gradually when the cross-lingual form overlap of the non-identical cognates became larger (with constant meaning overlap), for instance from COLOR (Dutch: KLEUR) to WHEEL (Dutch: WIEL); it then increased even more strongly to identical cognates like ALARM (Dutch: ALARM). There were facilitation effects of 40 ms for form-identical cognates relative to English controls (e.g., ALARM-ALARM), decreasing to 25 ms for cognates that are one letter different between languages (*neighbor cognates*, like BAKER and BAKKER), and to even less for cognates different in more letters. Van Assche, Drieghe, Duyck, Welvaert, and Hartsuiker (2011, p. 95) also observed a linear effect of orthographic overlap but did not replicate the non-linear effect between non-identical and identical cognates. However, their study included a smaller number of items.

To summarize, the large majority of empirical studies on multilingual reading support the view of language non-selective lexical access to a mental lexicon that is integrated across languages. Observed cross-linguistic orthographic and phonological effects depend on the similarity or identity of lexical representations rather than on the language to which they belong. Thus, it appears that lexical dimensions like orthography, phonology, and semantics are primary determinants of the organization of the multilingual lexicon, whereas language membership is secondary. Nevertheless, language information must be stored somewhere in the multilingual lexicon, because it is directly relevant for language processing: The correct selection of a target word may depend on its language membership. Before we consider the role of language membership in bilingual word recognition in more detail, we will first discuss the effects of the (language of the) preceding sentence.

6.5 Context effects on multilingual word recognition

Studies considering the recognition of words in isolation have generally found effects that are not restricted to one language. This finding of language non-specific lexical access suggests that the multilingual word retrieval system as a pattern recognition system on its own results in coactivation of input-similar lexical representations as a sort of default; at the very least, the architecture *allows* language non-selective access. The question is if lexical access is *always* language non-selective, or if a more language-specific item retrieval process might be induced on the basis of task- and context-dependent decision criteria. Said differently, does word retrieval proceed in a language selective or non-selective way depending on the situation?

This issue has been investigated by considering the recognition of words in a particular language when they are embedded in stories or sentences of the same or another language. Some studies have investigated whether both readings of interlingual homographs are still activated in restraining sentence context; many other studies have included both cognates and interlingual homographs. Because the basic research question is the same in both types of study, the next section provides an overview combining both types of materials.

6.5.1 False friends and cognates

Elston-Güttler, Gunter, and Kotz (2005) were the first to study how the activation of the two readings of interlingual homographs was affected by global discourse context and local sentence context. Global language context was manipulated by first playing a 20-min silent movie to German-English bilinguals, accompanied by a narrative in either L1 (German) or L2 (English). In the experiment following this movie, German-English bilinguals made lexical decisions on English target words that were presented following English sentences ending on German-English homographs. For example, the German-English interlingual homograph "tag" (which means "day" in English) or a control word (e.g., label) followed the sentence "*Joan used scissors to remove the.*" Next, a target word (e.g., "day") was presented on which an English lexical decision was made. Semantic priming effects arose in the behavioral and ERP data, but only in the first part of the experiment, directly after the German movie. The preceding global context apparently affected the priming effect, reflected in a modulation of the N200 and N400 component and in the RTs for the first part of the first block following the German movie. Furthermore, in the local English sentence context the non-target reading of the homograph (e.g., "tag") was apparently suppressed or not even activated. The authors argued that bilinguals who saw the German movie had to zoom in to their L2 (English) by gradually raising decision criteria in order to diminish non-target language effects of L1 (German) on the target language L2 (English). In all, the results are in line with the more general view that sentence context can affect the activation of representations in the multilingual word identification system. The role of global language context remains to be considered, because a later study by Paulmann, Elston-Güttler, Gunter, and Kotz (2006) did not obtain an effect of global language context when the stimulus words were presented as isolated prime-target pairs in the same task.

Using a rapid serial visual presentation (RSVP) paradigm, involving word-by-word sentence presentation, Schwartz and Kroll (2006) asked Spanish-English bilinguals to name cognates, interlingual homographs, and control words in semantically more or less constraining English sentences. An example of a high-constraint sentence is "*Before playing, the composer first wiped the keys of the* piano *at the beginning of the concert.*" The word *piano* appeared in red and had to be named as quickly and accurately as possible. In low-constraint sentence context, cross-linguistic cognate effects persisted. In high-constraint sentences, they arose for low proficiency but not for high proficiency bilinguals. No cross-linguistic effects were observed for interlingual homographs.

Duyck, van Assche, Drieghe, and Hartsuiker (2007) also applied an RSVP technique in their study of cognates in sentences. Dutch-English bilinguals processed low-constraint English sentences with form-identical and non-identical cognates, control words, and non-words at the end. They then made an English lexical decision on these items. Responses to both form-identical and non-identical cognates were facilitated relative to controls. The facilitation effects were at least as large as for the same items processed in isolation. In an eye-tracking experiment, the sentences with their cognates and a continuation phrase were next represented as wholes on a computer screen. Here the cognate effects for identical cognates were replicated, but not those for non-identical cognates. The observed effects emerged already during the first fixation on the cognate targets. The authors concluded that bilingual lexical access may be language non-selective both when words are recognized in isolation and in sentences. Lexical properties of the words to be recognized, such as cross-linguistic overlap, may interact with sentence context and influence cross-lingual activation spreading. In a follow-up study, van Assche et al. (2011) again obtained cognate facilitation effects for both early and late eye movement measures in both low- and high-constraint sentences. The authors concluded that their study was in line "with a limited role for top-down influences of semantic constraints on lexical access in both early and later stages of bilingual word recognition" (p. 88). However, other studies indicate that this conclusion is too strong: Semantic sentence constraints do play a role in restricting lexical access (e.g., Dijkstra, van Hell, & Brenders, 2015; Hoversten & Traxler, 2016; Jouravlev & Jared, 2014; Libben & Titone, 2009; Titone, Libben, Mercier, Whitford, & Pivneva, 2011; van Hell & de Groot, 2008).

Several of the conclusions obtained in laboratory circumstances have been extended to normal reading in daily life. As already mentioned, the study by Cop et al. (2016) registered the eye movements of Dutch-English bilinguals reading a novel in Dutch and English and analyzed them for identical and non-identical noun cognates. In English (L2), cross-linguistic orthographic overlap resulted in cognate facilitation. Identical cognates were facilitated extra in later eye movement measures. In Dutch (L1), for the first fixation duration of longer nouns, facilitation arose for non-identical cognates, while identical high-frequency cognates were facilitated with respect to total reading time.

In an important recent meta-analytic review, Lauro and Schwartz (2017) analyzed the effect sizes of 26 studies on cognate processing in sentence context and the influence of moderator variables (concerning task and language). They arrived at several conclusions. First, lexical access appears to be fundamentally language non-selective and sentence context alone is not strong enough to result in selective lexical access in bilinguals. Second, the language membership of preceding words in combination with semantically biasing information does exert an attenuating influence on cross-linguistic effects. Third, cognate facilitation in both low-constraint and high-constraint sentences is modulated by the language of the sentence. Smaller effects arise in L1 experiments than in L2 experiments. Fourth, in L2 cognate facilitation effects are found in both high- and low-constraint sentences, while in L1 only low-constraint sentences yield significant cognate effects. Fifth, cognate effects depend on task type. Tasks like picture naming and translation, with considerable top-down information flow, result in the largest effects, followed by tasks like naming and lexical decision that rely more on bottom-up processing, and, finally, eye-tracking tasks that result in small effects that are not significant in high-constraint sentences.

6.6 Language membership

If one asks bilinguals to which language a word belongs, they can usually do so without much effort. How is this language membership information represented for each word and when in processing is it accessed and used? Are all word forms of a language linked up to one and the same language membership representation? Is language membership a sort of category or set label, or rather a semantic or lemma representation?

It seems unavoidable that language membership information codetermines word retrieval in multilingual word *production*, given that a language-independent meaning (thought) must be conveyed in terms of a language-specific phonological word form (de Bot, 2004;

Poulisse & Bongaerts, 1994). The language membership of an item might already be present in the speaker's intention; at the very least it functions as a selection criterion for words to be uttered.

After several years of research, it is now recognized that language membership also plays a more general role in multilingual word *recognition*. In fact, it appears to play a role at lexical, sublexical, and sentence levels (Dijkstra & Snoeren, 2004; van Kesteren, Dijkstra, & de Smedt, 2012). In the next section, we review the evidence for each of these.

6.6.1 Language membership at the lexical level

One particular task used in bilingual word recognition studies is *language decision*. In this two-choice forced response task, participants press one button if a presented word belongs to one language (e.g., English) and another when it belongs to a second language (e.g., Dutch). It is obvious that this task cannot be performed without retrieving the language membership (node) of a word. There is some evidence that the degree of activation of each language node is affected by the neighborhood in the two languages activated by an input word (van Heuven et al., 1998). Furthermore, the process of parallel activation of the language nodes by word candidates from the two languages might be followed by a more sequential read-out of node activation (Dijkstra et al., 2010), perhaps to avoid errors on weaker-language targets.

Language membership also plays a role in less obvious circumstances, for instance in language-specific lexical decision involving mixed language lists. The bilinguals in Experiment 2 from Dijkstra et al. (1998), mentioned here, performed an English lexical decision task, in which English and Dutch words were included, as well as non-words. In this situation, Dutch items had to be rejected, because they did not belong to the target language (English). To reject them, participants had to retrieve information about the language to which the words belonged. Because the RTs to control words in this experiment were about as fast as when no Dutch words were included, this suggests that participants can retrieve language information rather quickly, before they arrive at the meaning of an word. At the same time, however, they apparently could not use such information in time to ignore the non-target readings of interlingual homographs, which were processed slower when Dutch words were present. In all, the data suggest that language membership information often becomes available directly following word identification.

In a review of the role of language membership in bilingual word recognition, Dijkstra and Snoeren (2004) compared latencies in lexical decision and language decision tasks and concluded that language information may be available as quickly as 50 ms after lexical identification. According to Casaponsa, Carreiras, and Duñabeitia (2015), ERP studies involving masked priming indicate that bilingual readers identify the language of the words within approximately 200 ms. On the basis of a go/no-go ERP study, Hoversten, Brothers, Swaab, and Traxler (2015) also argued that language membership information can become available quickly, before semantics. They suggest (p. 2115) that "It may be possible that the accumulation of language membership information begins earlier than 300 msec poststimulus onset." If language membership information is available that quickly, it might then be used in a top-down way to modulate processing in each of the bilinguals' languages. Alternatively, a task/decision system might combine the accumulating language membership information (partly based on sublexical input information) and lexical input information to speed up word selection.

6.6.2 Language membership at the sublexical level

The orthotactic and phonotactic properties of a word may hint at the language to which it belongs. For instance, the "wh-" onset of an English word like "whiskey" does not standardly occur in Dutch (although the word itself was borrowed). In a French–English language decision study by Vaid and Frenck-Mestre (2002), English (L2) words that were orthographically marked in terms of language-specific bigrams received faster responses than undermarked words, and the English L2 marked words were responded to faster than French (L1) marked words. The authors concluded that using a sublexical strategy for marked words and a lexical strategy for unmarked words was useful, because the items were always marked for the language they belonged to.

Van Kesteren et al. (2012) showed that bilinguals used sublexical language membership information to speed up their word recognition process depending on the task situation. Norwegian-English bilinguals performed a Norwegian-English language decision task, a mixed English lexical decision task, or a mixed Norwegian lexical decision task. The mixed lexical decision experiments included words from the non-target language that required a "no" response. The language specificity of the Bokmål (a Norwegian written norm) and English (non)words was varied by including language-specific letters ("smør," "hawk") or bigrams ("dusj," "veal"). Bilinguals were found to use both types of sublexical markedness to facilitate their decisions, language-specific letters leading to larger effects than language-specific bigrams. The use of sublexical language information was strategically dependent on the task at hand, for instance, it was used differently when both words and non-words were marked. Importantly, decisions were directly based on sublexical (bigram) stimulus characteristics rather than on lexical representations.

Casaponsa et al. (2015) obtained corroborating evidence by testing Spanish-Basque bilinguals and Spanish monolinguals (as a control group) in a masked priming study combined with ERPs. Spanish target words were preceded by short unrelated Spanish or Basque prime words. Unrelated Basque words could contain bigrams that were plausible or implausible in Spanish. A language switch effect arose in the N250 and N400 for marked Basque primes in both participant groups. However, for unmarked Basque primes, a language switch effect arose only in bilinguals. This is evidence that sublexical statistical orthographic regularities affect language identification.

The activation of sublexical language membership information is also evident from the way multilinguals process non-words, for instance, in lexical decision. Several studies have shown that the time it takes to reject a non-word depends on its similarity to items in target and non-target language (Lemhöfer & Radach, 2009; van Heuven et al., 1998).

6.6.3 Language membership at the sentence level

In section 6.5, we saw that language membership plays a role in bilingual sentence processing studies where the language of the target may switch. A consideration of the available studies reveals a complex pattern of interactions between the properties of the sentence, the target word, and their interaction. Lauro and Schwartz (2017) concluded that, in combination with semantically biasing information, the language membership of preceding words in a sentence (L1/L2) may modulate cross-linguistic effects, for instance, for cognates in both low-constraint and high-constraint sentences. The effects of language switching have been the focus of several recent studies (see Bultena, Dijkstra, & van Hell, 2014, for a review).

6.7 Models of multilingual word processing

Having reviewed the behavioral and neuroscientific evidence on between-language neighbors, false friends, cognates, and language membership, the question is how to integrate these empirical findings in a model of bilingual lexical processing.

Theoretical model development began over 25 years ago, when the available empirical evidence was still rather scarce. One of the earliest and most prominent models in the field was the Revised Hierarchical Model (RHM; Kroll & Stewart, 1994). The account of this verbal model focuses on word production and translation in relation to L2 acquisition. In its original form, the model held that the lexical representations of two languages are independent at the lexical level but shared at the conceptual level. Due to the overwhelming evidence in favor of language non-specific processing discussed already here, it is now assumed that word representations of multiple languages can be activated in parallel (Kroll, Michael, Tokowicz, & Dufour, 2002). However, the assumption of separate lexical representations for each language is still adhered to, so L1 and L2 words are found in different databases. Links between lexical forms and conceptual links are active, but the strength of such links differs as a function of L2 fluency. Relatively strong *lexical form* links map L2 words onto L1 words during the early stages of second language acquisition (e.g., *horse* to *Pferd*), whereas the form links from L1 to L2 are relatively weak. This leads to a processing asymmetry in studies investigating the translation from L1 into L2 and vice versa (Kroll et al., 2002; Kroll & Stewart, 1994; Sholl, Sankaranarayanan, & Kroll, 1995). Early in L2 acquisition, the *conceptual* links between L1 words and concepts are already in place, but those between L2 items and concepts must be developed and are strengthened as bilinguals become more fluent in their L2. Thus, both lexical and conceptual links are bidirectional, but they differ in strength in the two directions.

The assumption of coactivated word forms on the basis of the input, in principle allows RHM to account for effects of overlap between target items and distractors, as well as neighborhood effects within and between languages. However, the processing of "special" items like cognates and false friends is difficult to pinpoint within the RHM framework, because no distinction has been made at the form level between orthographic and phonological representations. This makes it impossible to decide on the temporal availability and interaction of these codes during lexical processing and word translation. Furthermore, although some predictions of the RHM were initially supported by empirical data (see Kroll & De Groot, 1997, for a review), more recent evidence indicates that early semantic effects can arise in L2 learning (e.g., Altarriba & Mathis, 1997; Comesaña, Perea, Piñeiro, & Fraga, 2009; Finkbeiner & Nicol, 2003). Another problem for the RHM is that stronger L2-to-L1 than L1-to-L2 lexical form links would lead to a larger priming effect from L2 to

L1 than from L1 to L2 in masked translation priming (Schoonbaert, Duyck, Brysbaert, & Hartsuiker, 2009). The experimental evidence overwhelmingly shows the opposite pattern (for a review, see Wen & van Heuven, 2017). Perhaps most problematic for the RHM is the lack of implementation, preventing it to make quantitative predictions (Brysbaert & Duyck, 2010).

Two implemented models that can account for the effects of between-language neighborhood and to some extent false friends, are the localist connectionist models called Bilingual Interactive Activation (BIA) and its successor BIA + (Dijkstra, van Heuven, & Grainger, 1998; Dijkstra & van Heuven, 2002). The models, derived from the Interactive Activation model (McClelland & Rumelhart, 1981), assume parallel activation of representations. BIA is an orthographic model that contains four layers of representations: visual features, letters, words, and language nodes. Key connections between these layers are inhibitory and excitatory links from features to letters and from letters to words. They ensure that representations consistent with the input are activated and representations inconsistent with the input are suppressed. Furthermore, there are excitatory connections back from words to letters, so activated words reinforce the letters they contain. In the BIA model, words are connected to language nodes that can suppress words from another language. The successor of this model, BIA +, includes phonological and semantic representations. A major difference with BIA is that language nodes do usually not suppress lexical representations during the presentation of isolated words, because their feedback does not arrive in time. This is in line with most empirical findings (e.g., Dijkstra et al., 1998; Dijkstra & van Heuven, 2002; Martin, Dering, Thomas, & Thierry, 2009; but see Hoversten et al., 2015). However, according to BIA + the language nodes are able to exert top-down effects when target words are processed in sentence context (see Dijkstra, van Hell, & Brenders, 2015). Both BIA and BIA + have a language non-selective mechanism of lexical access and propose a functional distinction between a word identification system and a task/decision system. The models have successfully simulated many empirical studies on bilingual word recognition (see Dijkstra & van Heuven, 2002). The models have recently been applied to L2 acquisition (BIA-d; see Grainger, Midgley, & Holcomb, 2010; and BIA with discrete stages, see Dijkstra, Haga, Bijsterveld, & Sprinkhuizen-Kuyper, 2012). A review of neuroimaging studies showed that the BIA + model maps relatively well on the available neuroscientific evidence (van Heuven & Dijkstra, 2010). Ongoing research focuses on building a computational version of the BIA + model (for an implementation with orthographic and phonological representations, see van Heuven, 2005, and for an orthographic implementation only, see van Heuven, 2016).

Due to the absence of semantic representations, BIA and BIA + cannot adequately simulate cognate processing. This problem has been resolved in a recent computational model called Multilink (Dijkstra & Rekké, 2010). The model has similarities to both RHM and BIA/BIA +, but is different from these in several respects (e.g., it does not implement a sublexical level of representation). Due to a fully implemented orthographic, semantic, and phonological network, Multilink can account for visual word recognition, semantic processing, and word translation. On the comprehension side, it accounts for neighborhood effects, frequency effects, and cognate effects. A presented input word activates a set of word candidates that are orthographically like the input in terms of Levenshtein distance. This implies that words of different length can also become active. For instance, ABLE will also activate TABLE. As in BIA/BIA +, words have a resting level activation, which in Multilink is directly based on the word's frequency of usage. To simulate word recognition studies, a threshold on semantic activation determines the word's recognition time. Correlations between monolingual and bilingual empirical data (e.g., in databases like the British Lexicon Project (Keuleers, Lacey, Rastle, & Brysbaert, 2012) and the Dutch Lexicon Project (Keuleers, Diependaele, & Brysbaert, 2010)) and Multilink are found to be higher than with BIA/BIA +. Multilink can also simulate orthographic and semantic priming effects, but, most importantly, it simulates word translation data for non-cognates and cognates of different length. For instance, it can translate orthographic English BIKE into phonological Dutch /fiets/. It also resolves certain problems in translation production (e.g., ANT being translated into /tante/, meaning /aunt/, instead of the correct /mier/).

Other implemented models for bilingual visual word recognition include distributed models (for a review see Thomas & van Heuven, 2005). Li and colleagues developed a series of distributed connectionist models based on self-organizing maps (e.g., Li & Farkas, 2002; Zhao & Li, 2007, 2010, 2013). For example, the SOMBIP model (Self-Organizing Model of Bilingual Processing) by Li and Farkas (2002) applies unsupervised learning to simulate bilingual lexical access. SOMBIP incorporates two interconnected self-organizing neural networks, coupled to a recurrent network that extracts lexical co-occurrences. First, in a Hebbian learning phase, transcribed recordings of bilingual conversations were presented to the model. After learning, the model was then able to distinguish words of different languages (Chinese-English in this case), had acquired meaningful lexical-semantic categories, and accounted for a variety of priming effects in bilinguals differing in proficiency and working memory capacity. The dynamic model was able to separate languages without assuming language membership nodes (cf. French, 1998). A more recent model making use of three self-organizing maps was developed by Zhao and Li (2010, 2013). This model is based on an unsupervised network model of first language acquisition, DevLex-II (Li, Zhao, & MacWhinney, 2007). Simulations with the bilingual Chinese-English model reveal that it can capture several findings of translation and cross-language priming studies (e.g., translation priming asymmetry).

Finally, the verbal Inhibitory Control model by Green (1998) focused on cognitive control in both bilingual lexical production and comprehension. It was applied to language switching and word translation data. More recently, Green and Abutalebi have reformulated their ideas on cognitive control in terms of brain activity (e.g., Green & Abutalebi, 2008). In their neurocognitive model, a shared neural network represents various dimensions of L1 and L2, while a network of cortical and subcortical regions (prefrontal cortex, anterior cingulate cortex, basal ganglia, and the inferior parietal lobule) is involved in the inhibitory control of language and lexical selection.

Although current models account for a wide range of empirical findings, only a few implemented ones allow simulations to be conducted. The implemented models all have their limitations. For example, the purely orthographic BIA model's letter position coding is position specific, so that the model cannot capture the influence of neighbors that are longer or shorter. Furthermore, due to the nature of its representations, the model can only handle alphabetic languages. The models based on self-organizing maps (Li & Farkas, 2002; Zhao & Li, 2010, 2013) are limited to phonological input and output within a particular format. Finally, current computational models are limited to simulating bilingual word recognition in isolation.

6.8 Conclusions, limitations, and future research

In the present chapter, we considered how words are stored in the multilingual lexicon, how multilinguals read words in isolation and in sentence context, how language membership impacts multilingual processing, and how models of multilingual word processing handle all these aspects.

Visual word identification in multilinguals appears to be based on a language-independent pattern recognition procedure that coactivates lexical-orthographic representations in all stored languages to the extent that they are similar to the input letter string. Orthographically, phonologically, and morphologically related words from multiple languages are activated as lexical competitors during the recognition of (non-) identical cognates. The reviewed evidence on neighbors, false friends, and cognates indicates that words from different languages are integrated in one big lexical database. Words are selected from that database via a language non-specific activation process. However, this lexical selection can be facilitated by using language-specific sublexical information in the stimulus word (e.g., language-specific bigrams and letters). When words are processed in a bilingual sentence context, properties of the sentence and target item interact in a complex way. Apart from semantic, syntactic, and lexical aspects, which also play a role in monolingual processing, language membership is important. For instance, language switching results in a slowing down of lexical processing.

A huge amount of behavioral, neuroscientific, and modeling research has been conducted in the last decades to study the multilingual word recognition system. A topic of behavioral investigation that is gradually attracting more and more attention is the relationship between multilingual language processing and other cognitive domains, like those of emotion and action. For instance, relative to monolinguals, taboo words, and other emotion-laden words result in different arousal states, which induce changes to language and decision processes in multilinguals (for a review, see Chen, Lin, Chen, Lu, & Guo, 2015). This new research signals the gradual replacement of a modular view on language by a non-modular and intermodal perspective. Furthermore, the potential impact of multilingualism on domain-general executive control skills has attracted a huge amount of interest (see Bialystok, Craik, Green, & Gollan, 2009; Hervais-Adelman, Moser-Mercer, & Golestani, 2011; Paap, Johnson, & Sawi, 2015; Valian, 2015). This discussion underlines the importance of adequately describing and profiling the multilingual who participates in our experiments. For instance, appropriate and detailed objective measures to define L2 proficiency are crucial for investigating, for example, the impact of L2 proficiency in meta-analyses (Lauro & Schwartz, 2017; Wen & van Heuven, 2017).

These new topics are now almost standardly also investigated by means of neurophysiological and neuroimaging techniques, which are becoming more and more sophisticated (e.g., time-frequency analysis in EEG). Because of the high sensitivity of these innovative measurement techniques, effects may arise in ERPs or in fMRI without associated findings in their behavioral counterpart. As a consequence, we learn more and more about how the techniques themselves affect measurement in various stages of processing. Finally, the combination of available techniques makes it possible to study precisely where, when, and how multilingual processing takes place in the human brain.

References

Aitchison, J. (2003). *Words in the Mind: An Introduction to the Mental Lexicon*. Blackwell Publishing, Oxford.

Allen, D. B., & Conklin, K. (2013). Cross-linguistic similarity and task demands in Japanese-English bilingual processing. *PLoS One*, 8(8), e72631.

Altarriba, J., & Mathis, K. M. (1997). Conceptual and lexical development in second language acquisition. *Journal of Memory and Language*, 36(4), 550–68.

Andrews, S. (1997). The effect of orthographic similarity on lexical retrieval: Resolving neighborhood conflicts. *Psychonomic Bulletin & Review*, 4(4), 439–61.

Bialystok, E., Craik, F. I., Green, D. W., & Gollan, T. H. (2009). Bilingual Minds. *Psychological Science in the Public Interest*, 10(3), 89–129.

Brenders, P., van Hell, J. G., & Dijkstra, T. (2011). Word recognition in child second language learners: Evidence from cognates and false friends. *Journal of Experimental Child Psychology*, 109(4), 383–96.

Brysbaert, M., & Duyck, W. (2010). Is it time to leave behind the Revised Hierarchical Model of bilingual language processing after fifteen years of service? *Bilingualism: Language and Cognition*, 13(03), 359–71.

Bultena, S., Dijkstra, T., & van Hell, J. G. (2014). Cognate effects in sentence context depend on word class, L2 proficiency, and task. *The Quarterly Journal of Experimental Psychology*, 67(6), 1214–41.

Casaponsa, A., Carreiras, M., & Duñabeitia, J. A. (2015). How do bilinguals identify the language of the words they read? *Brain Research*, 1624, 153–66.

Chen, P., Lin, J., Chen, B., Lu, C., & Guo, T. (2015). Processing emotional words in two languages with one brain: ERP and fMRI evidence from Chinese–English bilinguals. *Cortex*, 71, 34–48.

Coltheart, M., Davelaar, E., Jonasson, J. T., & Besner, D. (1977). Access to the internal lexicon. In: Long, J., & Baddeley, A. (Eds.), *Attention and Performance VI* (pp. 535–55). Academic Press, New York, NY.

Comesaña, M., Ferré, P., Romero, J., Guasch, M., Soares, A. P., & García-Chico, T. (2015). Facilitative effect of cognate words vanishes when reducing the orthographic overlap: The role of stimuli list composition. *Journal of Experimental Psychology: Learning, Memory, and Cognition*, 41(3), 614–35.

Comesaña, M., Perea, M., Piñeiro, A., & Fraga, I. (2009). Vocabulary teaching strategies and conceptual representations of words in L2 in children: evidence with novice learners. *Journal of Experimental Child Psychology*, 104(1), 22–33.

Comesaña, M., Sánchez-Casas, R., Soares, A. P., Pinheiro, A. P., Rauber, A., ... Fraga, I. (2012). The interplay of phonology and orthography in visual cognate word recognition: An ERP study. *Neuroscience Letters*, 529(1), 75–9.

Cop, U., Dirix, N., van Assche, E., Drieghe, D., & Duyck, W. (2016). Reading a book in one or two languages? An eye movement study of cognate facilitation in L1 and L2 reading. *Bilingualism: Language and Cognition*, 20(4), 1–23.

Cop, U., Drieghe, D., & Duyck, W. (2015). Eye movement patterns in natural reading: A comparison of monolingual and bilingual reading of a novel. *PLoS One*, *10*(8), e0134008.

Cop, U., Keuleers, E., Drieghe, D., & Duyck, W. (2015). Frequency effects in monolingual and bilingual natural reading. *Psychonomic Bulletin & Review*, *22*(5), 1216–34.

Davis, C. J., Perea, M., & Acha, J. (2009). Re (de) fining the orthographic neighborhood: the role of addition and deletion neighbors in lexical decision and reading. *Journal of Experimental Psychology: Human Perception and Performance*, *35*(5), 1550–70.

Davis, C. J., & Taft, M. (2005). More words in the neighborhood: Interference in lexical decision due to deletion neighbors. *Psychonomic Bulletin & Review*, *12*(5), 904–10.

de Bot, K. (2004). The multilingual lexicon: Modelling selection and control. *International Journal of Bilingualism*, *1*, 17–32.

de Groot, A. M. B., Delmaar, P., & Lupker, S. J. (2000). The processing of interlexical homographs in translation recognition and lexical decision: Support for non-selective access to bilingual memory. *The Quarterly Journal of Experimental Psychology A*, *53*(2), 397–428.

Dijkstra, T. (2003). Lexical processing in bilinguals and multilinguals: The word selection problem. In: Cenoz, J., Hufeisen, B., & Jessner, U. (Eds.), *The Multilingual Lexicon* (pp. 11–26). Kluwer Academic Publishers, Dordrecht.

Dijkstra, T. (2005). Bilingual visual word recognition and lexical access. In: Kroll, J., & de Groot, A. (Eds.), *Handbook of Bilingualism: Psycholinguistic Approaches* (pp. 179–201). Oxford University Press, Oxford.

Dijkstra, T., Grainger, J., & van Heuven, W. J. B. (1999). Recognition of cognates and interlingual homographs: The neglected role of phonology. *Journal of Memory and Language*, *41*(4), 496–518.

Dijkstra, T., Haga, F., Bijsterveld, A., & Sprinkhuizen-Kuyper, I. (2012). Lexical competition in localist and distributed connectionist models of L2 acquisition. In: Altarriba, J., & Isurin, L. (Eds.), *Memory, Language, and Bilingualism: Theoretical and Applied Approaches* (pp. 48–73). Cambridge University Press, Cambridge.

Dijkstra, T., Miwa, K., Brummelhuis, B., Sappelli, M., & Baayen, H. (2010). How cross-language similarity and task demands affect cognate recognition. *Journal of Memory and Language*, *62*(3), 284–301.

Dijkstra, T., & Rekké, S. (2010). Towards a localist-connectionist model of word translation. *The Mental Lexicon*, *5*(3), 401–20.

Dijkstra, T., & Snoeren, N. D. (2004). Appartenance linguistique dans la reconnaissance et la production des mots chez les bilingues. In: Ferrand, L., & Grainger, J. (Eds.), *Psycholinguistique Cognitive: Essais en l'honneur de Juan Seguí* (pp. 377–99). De Boeck Supérieur, Bruxelles.

Dijkstra, T., Timmermans, M., & Schriefers, H. (2000). On being blinded by your other language: Effects of task demands on interlingual homograph recognition. *Journal of Memory and Language*, *42*(4), 445–64.

Dijkstra, T., van Hell, J. G., & Brenders, P. (2015). Sentence context effects in bilingual word recognition: Cognate status, sentence language, and semantic constraint. *Bilingualism: Language and Cognition*, *18*(04), 597–613.

Dijkstra, T., & van Heuven, W. J. B. (2002). The architecture of the bilingual word recognition system: From identification to decision. *Bilingualism: Language and Cognition*, *5*(3), 175–97.

Dijkstra, T., van Heuven, W. J. B., & Grainger, J. (1998). Simulating cross-language competition with the bilingual interactive activation model. *Psychologica Belgica*, *38*(3–4), 177–96.

Dijkstra, T., Van Jaarsveld, H., & Ten Brinke, S. (1998). Interlingual homograph recognition: Effects of task demands and language intermixing. *Bilingualism: Language and Cognition*, 1(01), 51–66.

Dirix, N., Cop, U., Drieghe, D., & Duyck, W. (2017). Cross-lingual neighborhood effects in generalized lexical decision and natural reading. *Journal of Experimental Psychology: Human Perception and Performance*, 43, 887–915.

Dong, Y., & Lin, J. (2013). Parallel processing of the target language during source language comprehension in interpreting. *Bilingualism: Language and Cognition*, 16(03), 682–92.

Durlik, J., Szewczyk, J., Muszyński, M., & Wodniecka, Z. (2016). Interference and inhibition in bilingual language comprehension: evidence from Polish-English interlingual homographs. *PLoS One*, 11(3), e0151430.

Duyck, W., van Assche, E. V., Drieghe, D., & Hartsuiker, R. J. (2007). Visual word recognition by bilinguals in a sentence context: evidence for nonselective lexical access. *Journal of Experimental Psychology: Learning, Memory, and Cognition*, 33(4), 663–79.

Elston-Güttler, K. E., Gunter, T. C., & Kotz, S. A. (2005). Zooming into L2: global language context and adjustment affect processing of interlingual homographs in sentences. *Cognitive Brain Research*, 25(1), 57–70.

Finkbeiner, M., & Nicol, J. (2003). Semantic category effects in second language word learning. *Applied Psycholinguistics*, 24, 369–83.

French, R. M. (1998). *A Simple Recurrent Network model of bilingual memory*. In: *Proceedings of the Twentieth Annual Cognitive Science Society Conference* (pp. 368–73). Erlbaum, Mahwah, NJ.

Friel, B. M., & Kennison, S. M. (2001). Identifying German–English cognates, false cognates, and non-cognates: Methodological issues and descriptive norms. *Bilingualism: Language and Cognition*, 4(3), 249–74.

Gollan, T. H., Forster, K. I., & Frost, R. (1997). Translation priming with different scripts: Masked priming with cognates and noncognates in Hebrew–English bilinguals. *Journal of Experimental Psychology: Learning, Memory, and Cognition*, 23(5), 1122.

Grainger, J., Midgley, K., & Holcomb, P. J. (2010). Re-thinking the bilingual interactive-activation model from a developmental perspective (BIA-d). In: Kail, M., & Hickmann, M. (Eds.), *Language Acquisition Across Linguistic and Cognitive Systems* (pp. 267–83). John Benjamins Publishing Company, Amsterdam.

Green, D. W. (1998). Mental control of the bilingual lexico-semantic system. *Bilingualism: Language and Cognition*, 1(02), 67–81.

Green, D. W., & Abutalebi, J. (2008). Understanding the link between bilingual aphasia and language control. *Journal of Neurolinguistics*, 21(6), 558–76.

Grossi, G., Savill, N., Thomas, E., & Thierry, G. (2012). Electrophysiological cross-language neighborhood density effects in late and early English-Welsh bilinguals. *Frontiers in Psychology*, 3, 408.

Haigh, C. A., & Jared, D. (2007). The activation of phonological representations by bilinguals while reading silently: Evidence from interlingual homophones. *Journal of Experimental Psychology: Learning, Memory, and Cognition*, 33(4), 623–44.

Hervais-Adelman, A.G., Moser-Mercer, B., & Golestani, N. (2011). Executive control of language in the bilingual brain: Integrating the evidence from neuroimaging into neuropsychology. *Frontiers in Psychology*, 2, 234.

Hoshino, N., & Kroll, J. F. (2008). Cognate effects in picture naming: Does cross-language activation survive a change of script? *Cognition*, 106(1), 501–11.

Hoshino, N., & Thierry, G. (2012). Do Spanish-English bilinguals have their fingers in two pies—or is it their toes? An electrophysiological investigation of semantic access in bilinguals. *Frontiers in Psychology*, 3, 9.

Hoversten, L. J., Brothers, T., Swaab, T. Y., & Traxler, M. J. (2015). Language membership identification precedes semantic access: Suppression during bilingual word recognition. *Journal of Cognitive Neuroscience*, 27(11), 2108-116.

Hoversten, L. J., & Traxler, M. J. (2016). A time course analysis of interlingual homograph processing: Evidence from eye movements. *Bilingualism: Language and Cognition*, 19(02), 347-60.

Hsieh, M.-C., Jeong, H., Hitomi Dos Santos Kawata, K., Sasaki, Y., Lee, H.-C., Yokoyama, S., . . . & Kawashima, R. (2017). Neural correlates of bilingual language control during interlingual homograph processing in a logogram writing system. *Brain and Language*, 174, 72-85.

Jouravlev, O., & Jared, D. (2014). Reading Russian-English homographs in sentence contexts: Evidence from ERPs. *Bilingualism: Language and Cognition*, 17(1), 153-68.

Kerkhofs, R., Dijkstra, T., Chwilla, D. J., & de Bruijn, E. R. (2006). Testing a model for bilingual semantic priming with interlingual homographs: RT and N400 effects. *Brain Research*, 1068(1), 170-83.

Keuleers, E., Diependaele, K., & Brysbaert, M. (2010). Practice effects in large-scale visual word recognition studies: A lexical decision study on 14,000 Dutch mono-and disyllabic words and nonwords. *Frontiers in Psychology*, 1, 174.

Keuleers, E., Lacey, P., Rastle, K., & Brysbaert, M. (2012). The British Lexicon Project: lexical decision data for 28,730 monosyllabic and disyllabic English words. *Behavior Research Methods*, 44(1), 287-304.

Kim, J., & Davis, C. (2003). Task effects in masked cross-script translation and phonological priming. *Journal of Memory and Language*, 49(4), 484-99.

Kootstra, G. J., Dijkstra, T., & Starren, M. (2015). Second language acquisition. In: Wright, J. D. (Ed.), *International Encyclopedia of the Social & Behavioral Sciences*, 2nd Edition (pp. 349-59). Elsevier, Cambridge, MA.

Kroll, J. F., & De Groot, A. (1997). Lexical and conceptual memory in the bilingual: Mapping form to meaning in two languages. In: de Groot, A. M. B., & Kroll, J. F. (Eds.), *Tutorials in Bilingualism: Psycholinguistic Perspectives* (pp. 169-99). Lawrence Erlbaum Associates, Mahwah, NJ.

Kroll, J. F., Michael, E., Tokowicz, N., & Dufour, R. (2002). The development of lexical fluency in a second language. *Second Language Research*, 18(2), 137-71.

Kroll, J. F., & Stewart, E. (1994). Category interference in translation and picture naming: Evidence for asymmetric connections between bilingual memory representations. *Journal of Memory and Language*, 33(2), 149-74.

Kroll, J. F., van Hell, J. G., Tokowicz, N., & Green, D. W. (2010). The revised hierarchical model: A critical review and assessment. *Bilingualism: Language and Cognition*, 13(3), 373-81.

Lauro, J., & Schwartz, A. I. (2017). Bilingual non-selective lexical access in sentence contexts: A meta-analytic review. *Journal of Memory and Language*, 92, 217-33.

Lavaur, J. M., & Font, N. (1998). Représentation des mots cognats et non cognats en mémoire chez les bilingues français-espagnol. *Psychologie française*, 43(4), 329-38.

Lemhöfer, K., & Dijkstra, T. (2004). Recognizing cognates and interlingual homographs: effects of code similarity in language-specific and generalized lexical decision. *Memory & Cognition*, 32(4), 533-50.

Lemhöfer, K., Dijkstra, T., & Michel, M. (2004). Three languages, one ECHO: Cognate effects in trilingual word recognition. *Language and Cognitive Processes, 19*(5), 585–611.

Lemhöfer, K., Dijkstra, T., Schriefers, H., Baayen, R. H., Grainger, J., & Zwitserlood, P. (2008). Native language influences on word recognition in a second language: A megastudy. *Journal of Experimental Psychology: Learning, Memory, and Cognition, 34*(1), 12–31.

Lemhöfer, K., & Radach, R. (2009). Task context effects in bilingual nonword processing. *Experimental Psychology, 56*(1), 41–7.

Levenshtein, V. I. (1966). Binary codes capable of correcting deletions, insertions and reversals. *Soviet Physics Doklady, 10*(8), 707–10.

Li, P., & Farkas, I. (2002). A self-organizing connectionist model of bilingual processing. In: Heredia, R. & Altarriba, J. (Eds.), *Advances in Psychology: Vol. 134. Bilingual Sentence Processing* (pp. 59–85). Elsevier Science Publisher, North Holland.

Li, P., Zhao, X., & MacWhinney, B. (2007). Dynamic self-organization and children's word learning. *Cognitive Science, 31*, 581–612.

Libben, M. R., & Titone, D. A. (2009). Bilingual lexical access in context: Evidence from eye movements during reading. *Journal of Experimental Psychology: Learning, Memory, and Cognition, 35*(2), 381–90.

Lijewska, A., & Chmiel, A. (2015). Cognate facilitation in sentence context–translation production by interpreting trainees and non-interpreting trilinguals. *International Journal of Multilingualism, 12*(3), 358–75.

Martin, C. D., Dering, B., Thomas, E. M., & Thierry, G. (2009). Brain potentials reveal semantic priming in both the "active" and the "non-attended" language of early bilinguals. *NeuroImage, 47*(1), 326–33.

Martin, C. D., Thierry, G., & Démonet, J. F. (2010). ERP characterization of sustained attention effects in visual lexical categorization. *PLoS One, 5*(3), e9892.

Martín, M. C., Macizo, P., & Bajo, T. (2010). Time course of inhibitory processes in bilingual language processing. *British Journal of Psychology, 101*(Pt 4), 679–93.

McClelland, J. L., & Rumelhart, D. E. (1981). An interactive activation model of context effects in letter perception: I. An account of basic findings. *Psychological Review, 88*(5), 375.

Meade, A., & Dijkstra, T. (2017). Mechanisms underlying word learning in second language acquisition. In: Libben, M., Goral, M., & Libben, G. (eds.), *Bilingualism: A Framework for Understanding the Mental Lexicon* (pp. 49–72). John Benjamins, Amsterdam.

Midgley, K. J., Holcomb, P. J., van Heuven, W. J. B., & Grainger, J. (2008). An electrophysiological investigation of cross-language effects of orthographic neighborhood. *Brain Research, 1246*, 123–35.

Midgley, K. J., Holcomb, P. J., & Grainger, J. (2011). Effects of cognate status on word comprehension in second language learners: An ERP investigation. *Journal of Cognitive Neuroscience, 23*(7), 1634–47.

Mulder, K., Dijkstra, T., & Baayen, R. H. (2015). Cross-language activation of morphological relatives in cognates: The role of orthographic overlap and task-related processing. *Frontiers in Human Neuroscience, 9*, 16.

Mulder, K., Dijkstra, T., Schreuder, R., & Baayen, H. R. (2014). Effects of primary and secondary morphological family size in monolingual and bilingual word processing. *Journal of Memory and Language, 72*, 59–84.

Mulder, K., Schreuder, R., & Dijkstra, T. (2013). Morphological family size effects in L1 and L2 processing: An electrophysiological study. *Language and Cognitive Processes, 28*(7), 1004–35.

Müller, O., Duñabeitia, J. A., & Carreiras, M. (2010). Orthographic and associative neighborhood density effects: What is shared, what is different? *Psychophysiology, 47*(3), 455–66.

Nakayama, M., Sears, C. R., Hino, Y., & Lupker, S. J. (2012). Cross-script phonological priming for Japanese-English bilinguals: Evidence for integrated phonological representations. *Language and Cognitive Processes, 27*(10), 1563–83.

Paap, K. R., Johnson, H. A., & Sawi, O. (2015). Bilingual advantages in executive functioning either do not exist or are restricted to very specific and undetermined circumstances. *Cortex, 69*, 265–78.

Paulmann, S., Elston-Güttler, K. E., Gunter, T. C., & Kotz, S. A. (2006). Is bilingual lexical access influenced by language context? *NeuroReport, 17*(7), 727–31.

Peeters, D., Dijkstra, T., & Grainger, J. (2013). The representation and processing of identical cognates by late bilinguals: RT and ERP effects. *Journal of Memory and Language, 68*(4), 315–32.

Perea, M., & Rosa, E. (2000). The effects of orthographic neighborhood in reading and laboratory word identification tasks: A review. *Psicológica: Revista de metodología y psicología experimental, 21*(3), 327–40.

Poulisse, N., & Bongaerts, T. (1994). First language use in second language production. *Applied Linguistics, 15*(1), 36–57.

Ransdell, S. E., & Fischler, I. (1987). Memory in a monolingual mode: When are bilinguals at a disadvantage? *Journal of Memory and Language, 26*(4), 392–405.

Schepens, J., Dijkstra, T., & Grootjen, F. (2012). Distributions of cognates in Europe as based on Levenshtein distance. *Bilingualism: Language and Cognition, 15*(01), 157–66.

Schepens, J., Dijkstra, T., Grootjen, F., & van Heuven, W. J. B. (2013). Cross-language distributions of high frequency and phonetically similar cognates. *PLoS One, 8*(5), e63006.

Schoonbaert, S., Duyck, W., Brysbaert, M., & Hartsuiker, R. J. (2009). Semantic and translation priming from a first language to a second and back: Making sense of the findings. *Memory & Cognition, 37*(5), 569–86.

Schwartz, A. I., & Kroll, J. F. (2006). Bilingual lexical activation in sentence context. *Journal of Memory and Language, 55*(2), 197–212.

Sholl, A., Sankaranarayanan, A., & Kroll, J. F. (1995). Transfer between picture naming and translation: A test of asymmetries in bilingual memory. *Psychological Science, 6*(1), 45–9.

Special Eurobarometer 386 (2012). Europeans and their languages. European Commission: Wave EB77.1. Available at: http://ec.europa.eu/commfrontoffice/publicopinion/archives/ebs/ebs_386_en.pdf

Szubko-Sitarek, W. (2011). Cognate facilitation effects in trilingual word recognition. *Studies in Second Language Learning and Teaching, 1*(2), 189–208.

Thierry, G., & Wu, Y. J. (2007). Brain potentials reveal unconscious translation during foreign-language comprehension. *Proceedings of the National Academy of Sciences of the United States of America, USA, 104*(30), 12530–5.

Thomas, M. S. C., & van Heuven, W. J. B. (2005). Computational models of bilingual comprehension. In: Kroll, J. F. & de Groot, A. M. B. (Eds.), *Handbook of Bilingualism: Psycholinguistic Approaches* (pp. 202–25). Oxford University Press, Oxford.

Titone, D., Libben, M., Mercier, J., Whitford, V., & Pivneva, I. (2011). Bilingual lexical access during L1 sentence reading: The effects of L2 knowledge, semantic constraint, and L1-L2 intermixing. *Journal of Experimental Psychology: Learning, Memory, and Cognition, 37*(6), 1412–31.

Vaid, J., & Frenck-Mestre, C. (2002). Do orthographic cues aid language recognition? A laterality study with French-English bilinguals. *Brain and Language*, 82(1), 47–53.

Valian, V. (2015). Bilingualism and cognition. *Bilingualism: Language and Cognition*, 18(1), 3–24.

van Assche, E., Drieghe, D., Duyck, W., Welvaert, M., & Hartsuiker, R. J. (2011). The influence of semantic constraints on bilingual word recognition during sentence reading. *Journal of Memory and Language*, 64(1), 88–107.

van Assche, E., Duyck, W., Hartsuiker, R. J., & Diependaele, K. (2009). Does bilingualism change native-language reading? Cognate effects in a sentence context. *Psychological Science*, 20(8), 923–7.

van Hell, J. G. (1998). *Cross-language processing and bilingual memory organization* [Unpublished Doctoral thesis]. University of Amsterdam, the Netherlands.

van Hell, J. G., & de Groot, A. M. (2008). Sentence context modulates visual word recognition and translation in bilinguals. *Acta Psychologica*, 128(3), 431–51.

van Hell, J. G., & Dijkstra, T. (2002). Foreign language knowledge can influence native language performance in exclusively native contexts. *Psychonomic Bulletin & Review*, 9(4), 780–9.

van Hell, J. G., & Tanner, D. (2012). Second language proficiency and cross-language lexical activation. *Language Learning*, 62(s2), 148–71.

van Heuven, W. J. B. (2005). Bilingual interactive activation models of word recognition in a second language. In: Cook, V., & Bassetti, B. (Eds.), *Second Language Writing Systems* (pp. 260–88). Multilingual Matters, Bristol.

van Heuven, W. J. B. (2016). jIAM: Interactive Activation Models in JavaScript. Available at: http://www.psychology.nottingham.ac.uk/staff/wvh/jiam/

van Heuven, W. J. B., & Dijkstra, T. (2010). Language comprehension in the bilingual brain: fMRI and ERP support for psycholinguistic models. *Brain Research Reviews*, 64(1), 104–22.

van Heuven, W. J. B., Dijkstra, T., & Grainger, J. (1998). Orthographic neighborhood effects in bilingual word recognition. *Journal of Memory and Language*, 39(3), 458–83.

van Heuven, W. J. B., Schriefers, H., Dijkstra, T., & Hagoort, P. (2008). Language conflict in the bilingual brain. *Cerebral Cortex*, 18(11), 2706–16.

van Kesteren, R., Dijkstra, T., & de Smedt, K. (2012). Markedness effects in Norwegian-English bilinguals: Task-dependent use of language-specific letters and bigrams. *The Quarterly Journal of Experimental Psychology*, 65(11), 2129–54.

Voga, M., & Grainger, J. (2007). Cognate status and cross-script translation priming. *Memory & Cognition*, 35(5), 938–52.

Wen, Y., & van Heuven, W. J. B. (2017). Non-cognate translation priming in masked priming lexical decision experiments: A meta-analysis. *Psychonomic Bulletin & Review*, 24(3), 879–86.

Zhao, X., & Li, P. (2007). Bilingual Lexical Representation in a Self-Organizing Neural Network Model. In: *Proceedings of the 29th Annual Cognitive Science Society*, Nashville, TN.

Zhao, X., & Li, P. (2010). Bilingual lexical interactions in an unsupervised neural network model. *International Journal of Bilingual Education and Bilingualism*, 13(5), 505–24.

Zhao, X., & Li, P. (2013). Simulating cross-language priming with a dynamic computational model of the lexicon. *Bilingualism: Language and Cognition*, 16(02), 288–303.

CHAPTER 7

VARIETIES OF SEMANTIC DEFICIT
Single-word comprehension

ELIZABETH JEFFERIES AND HANNAH THOMPSON

7.1 INTRODUCTION

SEMANTIC cognition is a fundamental component of mind and behavior: it brings meaning to our ongoing experiences and memories and allows us to use this knowledge to drive context- and time-appropriate behavior (Lambon Ralph, Jefferies, Patterson, & Rogers, 2017). It is at the core of language and communication as well as non-verbal, everyday skilled behaviors (e.g., using objects and sequencing actions to achieve a goal). Consequently, patients who have semantic comprehension impairments are greatly affected in all aspects of life.

This chapter will review neuropsychological literature on comprehension impairments. Evidence from patients suggests that semantic cognition can be impaired multiple ways, giving rise to different patterns of behavioral deficits. Firstly, individuals can show progressive degradation of central conceptual representations, as in semantic dementia (SD; Hodges, Patterson, Oxbury, & Funnell, 1992; Snowden, Goulding, & Neary, 1989; Warrington, 1975). This erosion of semantic knowledge gives rise to poor comprehension across all input and output modalities (Bozeat, Lambon Ralph, Patterson, Garrard, & Hodges, 2000; Patterson, Nestor, & Rogers, 2007). Secondly, patients might show deficits in "accessing" information, and this might occur for two reasons. Firstly, patients may be unable to recognize an object in a specific modality because they are unable to map the sensory input into the conceptual store (Catani & Ffytche, 2005). For example, patients with Wernicke's aphasia (WA) have particular difficulty in accessing concepts from auditory inputs (Eggert, 1977). A second "access" disorder is semantic aphasia (SA; Jefferies & Lambon Ralph, 2006). Here, patients are unable to access information in a *controlled*, task-appropriate way. Although in some circumstances, it may be sufficient for efficient task performance to access dominant aspects of meaning relatively automatically, in many other situations, we need to access distant semantic associations or weakly activated features in a more controlled way, while inhibiting task-irrelevant knowledge. We also need to configure the components of the semantic network in line with our current goals or expectations and to monitor our semantic retrieval so that control processes can be adjusted if necessary. It is these processes which appear to be impaired in SA. In this chapter, we will discuss the nature of each type of comprehension disorder in turn.

7.2 Semantic dementia: Degradation of conceptual knowledge across modalities

Contemporary perspectives on conceptual representation propose that stored knowledge of the meanings of words and objects draws on both sensory and motor regions that represent particular aspects of experience—such as shape, color, praxis, visual motion, action, smell, and taste—and also areas which integrate across sensory and motor domains (Damasio, 1989; Mahon & Caramazza, 2008; Patterson et al., 2007; Pulvermüller, 2013). The "hub-and-spokes" model (Patterson et al., 2007) proposes that sensory and motor "spokes" are integrated within a "hub" in the anterior temporal lobes (ATL), which maps between different inputs and outputs to form coherent concepts. Our semantic knowledge is heteromodal: we are able to determine the meanings of items encountered via any of our senses. Thus, the ATL hub may be crucial for (1) extracting task- and context-independent conceptual representations, so that we can recognize and categorize objects from pre-existing knowledge, even when there are many dissimilarities to related items in specific modalities—such as knowing a SPHYNX is a type of CAT despite its lack of fur and whiskers (Lambon Ralph, Sage, Jones, & Mayberry, 2010; Mayberry, Sage, Ehsan, & Lambon Ralph, 2011); (2) activating whole concepts from a single modality, so that we can visualize a DOG from the sound of its bark (Bozeat et al., 2000). The "hub-and-spokes" model makes the prediction that damage to the ATL "hub" will give rise to semantic impairment across the full range of modalities and tasks, while damage to modality-specific regions ("spokes") will elicit semantic deficits that disproportionately affect certain classes of knowledge and tasks.

Semantic dementia (SD), the temporal lobe variant of frontotemporal dementia, is associated with bilateral atrophy in the ATL, and progressive deterioration of semantic knowledge across modalities and tasks (Bozeat et al., 2000, 2003; Bozeat, Lambon Ralph, Patterson, & Hodges, 2002; Coccia, Bartolini, Luzzi, Provinciali, & Lambon Ralph, 2004; Garrard & Carroll, 2006; Hodges et al., 1992; Lambon Ralph, Graham, Patterson, & Hodges, 1999; McClelland & Rogers, 2003; Patterson et al., 2007; Snowden et al., 1989). SD patients exhibit a systematic decline in their knowledge, which affects less familiar, atypical, and specific-level concepts more severely and at an earlier stage of the disease (Bozeat et al., 2003; Hodges, Graham, & Patterson, 1995; Patterson et al., 2007; Rogers, Lambon Ralph, Hodges, & Patterson, 2004; Rogers, Patterson, Jefferies, & Lambon Ralph, 2015; Woollams, Cooper-Pye, Hodges, & Patterson, 2008). Other aspects of cognition are relatively well-preserved in these cases, including non-verbal reasoning, day-to-day memory, and speech fluency (Patterson et al., 2007; Snowden et al., 1989; Warrington, 1975). The impairment in SD is thought to reflect degradation of heteromodal knowledge in the "hub" in the ATL, giving rise to the progressive dissolution of conceptual knowledge (Lambon Ralph, 2014; Lambon

Ralph & Patterson, 2008). General information that is shared across many semantically related concepts (e.g., ANIMALS HAVE FOUR LEGS) is better preserved than specific information that is not shared (e.g., GIRAFFES HAVE LONG NECKS) (Bozeat et al., 2003; Lambon Ralph & Patterson, 2008). For example, in object decision tasks, patients are likely to accept pictures in which a relatively unique feature has been replaced by an incorrect shared feature (GIRAFFE WITH A SHORT NECK) but can readily reject pictures in which a shared feature has been replaced by a unique one (ELEPHANT WITH A LONG NECK) (Rogers, Lambon Ralph, Hodges, et al., 2004). In addition, when the same concepts are probed using different input/output modalities or different types of semantic task, SD patients are highly consistent in the concepts they can demonstrate knowledge of and the concepts that are impaired, even when frequency/familiarity is taken into account (Bozeat et al., 2000; Jefferies & Lambon Ralph, 2006; Rogers et al., 2015). This supports the view that SD produces degradation of a central store of semantic knowledge: the degree of damage to a particular concept in an individual patient therefore predicts performance on any given semantic task probing that concept.

SD patients have damage bilaterally, and patients with unilateral lesions of the ATL (e.g., with temporal lobectomies for intractable epilepsy) show subtle and much less dramatic semantic impairments (Lambon Ralph, Cipolotti, Manes, & Patterson, 2010; Lambon Ralph, Ehsan, Baker, & Rogers, 2012), with deficits in comprehension only on the most demanding tasks (Lambon Ralph & Patterson, 2008). If semantic representations are bilateral, drawing on both the left and right ATL, bilateral damage may be needed for catastrophic loss of knowledge. In addition, in TLE patients, the insidious onset may allow for a degree of reorganization, which reduces the impact of surgery.

7.3 CONVERGENT EVIDENCE FOR A HETEROMODAL SEMANTIC HUB IN THE ANTERIOR TEMPORAL LOBES

The proposal that ATL provides a store of heteromodal conceptual representations proved initially controversial, for at least two reasons: (i) Much of the key evidence was provided by studies of patients with SD, which is a relatively rare condition. Semantic deficits are seen more commonly in the context of stroke aphasia, following lesions in temporoparietal and/or frontal regions, suggesting alternative regions are crucial for comprehension (see next). Moreover, SD patients have progressive neurodegeneration which spreads from ATL to posterior temporal and inferior prefrontal regions (Hoffman, Jones, & Lambon Ralph, 2012; Mummery et al., 2000). It is therefore hard to establish the extent to which damage to these additional regions contributes to the conceptual deficit in SD: however, the strongest correlation between heteromodal semantic deficits and atrophy is found in ventral ATL, suggesting that this region plays a critical role (Binney, Embleton, Jefferies, Parker, & Lambon Ralph, 2010; Mion et al., 2010). (ii) Neuroimaging studies employing functional MRI have often failed to observe ATL activation during semantic tasks, compared with studies using positron emission tomography (PET; Visser, Jefferies, & Lambon Ralph, 2010). Standard echo-planar imaging fMRI sequences are affected by magnetic susceptibility artifacts that produce signal loss and distortion in ventral parts of ATL (Embleton et al., 2010)—that is, regions that are the most strongly implicated in semantic processing in SD patients.

As a consequence, some influential reviews of the neural basis of semantic cognition have proposed that semantic knowledge is represented in alternative regions, such as posterior temporal or inferior parietal cortex, instead of, or as well as, ATL (Binder, Desai, Graves, & Conant, 2009; Martin, 2007; Pulvermüller, 2013). Additionally, there is a large "embodied cognition" literature, which argues that components of knowledge are grounded in sensorimotor systems (Kemmerer, Castillo, Talavage, Patterson, & Wiley, 2008; Martin, 2016). While some "embodied" accounts argue against amalgamation of these features in a central conceptual hub (Pulvermüller, 2005), many argue some coordination between sensory-specific regions—for example different language skills converging as lexical semantics (Hillis, Kane, et al., 2001; Hillis, Wityk, et al., 2001). There has been a growing consensus that modality convergence allows conceptual representation to be abstracted away from individual aspects of experience (Dove, 2016; Mazon, 2015; Meteyard, Cuadrado, Bahrami, & Vigliocco, 2012; Pulvermüller, 2013; Reilly, Peelle, Garcia, & Crutch, 2016; Zwaan, 2014). The hub-and-spokes model proposes, in line with "embodied" accounts, that modality-specific "spokes" make a necessary contribution to conceptual representations (Pobric, Jefferies, & Lambon Ralph, 2010b), although these spokes are also integrated to form heteromodal conceptual representations in the ATL. Several similar accounts propose heteromodal hubs, or convergence zones, that support the representation of aspects of knowledge (Binder & Desai, 2011; Damasio, Tranel, Grabowski, Adolphs, & Damasio, 2004; Gainotti, 2011).

Given the potential difficulties in drawing strong conclusions about the localization of function from patients with neurodegenerative disease, converging evidence from different neuroscientific techniques is particularly important in delineating the contribution of ATL in heteromodal conceptual processing (Binney et al., 2010; Chen et al., 2016; Hoffman, Jefferies, & Lambon Ralph, 2010; Lambon Ralph, 2014). Acquisition and analysis methods can be optimized in fMRI studies to maximize signal from ATL, and studies employing ATL-sensitive fMRI methods frequently show bilateral activation in this region for heteromodal semantic processing (Murphy et al., 2017; Peelen & Caramazza, 2012; Tyler et al., 2004; Visser, Embleton, Jefferies, Parker, & Lambon Ralph, 2010; Visser, Jefferies, Embleton, & Lambon Ralph, 2012; Visser, Jefferies, et al., 2010). These findings converge with reports of bilateral ATL activation in studies employing PET (Bright, Moss, & Tyler, 2004; Noppeney & Price, 2002; Price, Devlin, Moore, Morton, & Laird, 2005; Rogers et al., 2006; Sharp, Scott, & Wise, 2004; Spitsyna, Warren, Scott, Turkheimer, & Wise, 2006; Vandenberghe et al., 1996), TMS (Pobric, Jefferies, & Lambon Ralph, 2010a), plus MEG and EEG (Clarke, Taylor, & Tyler, 2011; Halgren et al., 2006; Marinkovic et al., 2003; Mollo, Cornelissen, Millman, Ellis, & Jefferies, 2017). This converging evidence across multiple methods has led to increased recognition of the role of the ATL in semantic representation across categories and modalities (Lambon Ralph et al., 2017; Rice, Lambon Ralph, & Hoffman, 2015; Visser, Jefferies, et al., 2010).

7.4 A GRADED HUB?

Recent research has identified graded connectivity to different input and output systems in the ATL (Bajada et al., 2017; Binney, Hoffman, & Lambon Ralph, 2016; Jackson, Bajada, Rice, Cloutman, & Lambon Ralph, 2017; Lambon Ralph et al., 2017), such as vision, language, and emotion. This has given rise to the proposal that ATL is a "graded hub"; that is, there are functional gradients within ATL, which reflect these patterns of connectivity, and the most heteromodal "hub" region lies equidistant from all the inputs and outputs. Using fMRI methods designed to be sensitive to signals in ATL, Visser et al. (2012) examined the way that pictorial and language information converge by quantifying the response to words and pictures in different anatomical subregions of the anterior and posterior temporal lobes. Posterior superior temporal gyrus (STG) and posterior inferior temporal gyrus (ITG)/fusiform showed a preference for words and pictures respectively, with a heteromodal response in posterior middle temporal gyrus (the role of pMTG is discussed further later under the heading *Convergent evidence for a distributed semantic control network*). In anterior regions of the temporal lobes, STG and fusiform continued to show a clear modality preference, for words and pictures, respectively. Anterior ITG, however, changed its response from predominately visual to equivalent across modalities. This suggests that word and picture information may converge in inferior anterior parts of the ATL (see also Chen, Lambon Ralph, & Rogers, 2017; Murphy et al., 2017).

In addition to functional subdivisions within each ATL, there may be subtle functional distinctions between left and right ATL, which are also explained by differential connectivity (Rice, Lambon Ralph, et al., 2015). In SD, damage is bilateral but can also be asymmetric, with more atrophy on one side of the brain than the other (Mummery et al., 2000). Patients with left > right ATL atrophy show greater impairment in speech production and tasks involving written words (Lambon Ralph et al., 2001; Mion et al., 2010; Rice, Lambon Ralph, et al., 2015; Snowden, Thompson, & Neary, 2004), which may be explained by stronger connections between left ATL and other language regions of the left hemisphere. In contrast, SD cases with right > left ATL atrophy can show greater deficits with pictures or faces (Mion et al., 2010; Snowden et al., 2004). The right ATL has also been associated with understanding social behavior (Fournier et al., 2008; Perry et al., 2001; Pulvermüller, 2013; Zahn et al., 2009), and the right superior ATL is implicated in the representation of social concepts (Binney, Hoffman, & Lambon Ralph, 2016; Skipper, Ross, & Olson, 2011; Zahn et al., 2007). This hypothesis received recent support from a TMS study in healthy participants (Pobric, Lambon Ralph, & Zahn, 2016). The contribution of ATL to understanding social situations is seen across modalities and tasks, including the naming of people (Semenza, 2006), famous and familiar faces (Bai et al., 2011; Leveroni et al., 2000; Ross & Olson, 2012; Sergent, Ohta, & Macdonald, 1992; Sugiura, Mano, Sasaki, & Sadato, 2011), social vs. non-social gestures (Straube, Green, Jansen, Chatterjee, & Kircher, 2010) and sounds evoking a social scene such as footsteps (Saarela & Hari, 2008). The uncinate fasciculus connects the ATL to orbital and medial frontal cortex (Bajada et al., 2017; de Schotten, Dell'Acqua, Valabregue, & Catani, 2012) and this pathway may be crucial for nuanced social behavior. These findings are compatible with a graded version of the hub-and-spokes hypothesis, with relatively subtle hemispheric differences emerging from differential patterns of connectivity from left and right ATL to modality-specific sensory, motor, and limbic cortices (Bajada et al., 2017; Rice, Lambon Ralph, et al., 2015; Visser, Embleton, & Lambon Ralph, 2012).

7.5 ROLE OF THE SPOKES: CATEGORY-SPECIFIC DEFICITS

The "hub-and-spokes" model (Patterson et al., 2007) proposes that modality- or feature-specific sensory and motor "spokes" make a crucial contribution to the representation of meaning, alongside the heteromodal hub in ATL. Information is coded across the cortex and amalgamated in ATL, and this combination of domain-specific and domain-general processing gives rise to comprehension. This framework can potentially account for category-specific semantic disorders, since particular categories of knowledge are thought to rely especially strongly on visual or motor representations: consequently, damage to a particular "spoke," or to a region of the graded hub that disproportionately receives input from a specific modality, can elicit category-specific semantic deficits.

When properties critical for defining or distinguishing a category are damaged, category-specific effects are thought to follow (Shallice, 1993; Tyler, Moss, Durrant-Peatfield, & Levy, 2000; Warrington & McCarthy, 1987; Warrington & Shallice, 1984). For example, disorders affecting the motor system in patients with ideational apraxia following stroke are associated with selective impaired processing of action-related words and sentences (Buxbaum & Saffran, 2002; Fernandino et al., 2013a, 2013b; Grossman et al., 2008). In contrast, SD patients with atrophy focused on the ventral ATL rarely show category-specific semantic disorders when frequency- or familiarity-matched materials are used, except in the case of expertise within a particular domain, which has a protective effect (Jefferies, Rogers, & Lambon Ralph, 2011). This pattern of category-general impairment following disruption to ATL versus category-specific impairment for manipulable objects following disruption of hand praxis regions in the inferior parietal cortex has also been demonstrated using TMS (Pobric et al., 2010b).

Damage to anterior medial temporal lobe regions, such as fusiform and entorhinal cortex, is associated with category-specific semantic impairment for animals (Noppeney et al., 2007), for example in patients with herpes simplex encephalitis (Blundo, Ricci, & Miller, 2006; Lambon Ralph, Lowe, & Rogers, 2007; Warrington & Shallice, 1984). Medial anterior temporal regions are thought to be important in the interaction between vision and meaning (Clarke, 2015; Clarke & Tyler, 2015; Tyler et al., 2004; Wright, Randall, Clarke, & Tyler, 2015); a view that fits well with the "graded hub" hypothesis since visual inputs to ATL are via the fusiform (Chen et al., 2017). Animals require particularly fine-grained visual discrimination, since their visual features are often highly correlated and yet subtle visual distinctions may play a critical role in separating one type of animal from another (e.g., it is only stripes that strongly distinguish a ZEBRA from a HORSE) (Warrington & Shallice, 1984).

7.6 Access to the ATL: Input processing deficits

Disorders of semantic processing do not only arise from a loss of conceptual knowledge (i.e., from damage to heteromodal conceptual representations or modality-specific "spokes"); they can also follow from difficulties in accessing this knowledge. Semantic deficits in stroke aphasia are typically thought to reflect difficulties in semantic access and not the degradation of conceptual knowledge itself as in SD, since stroke rarely affects the ventral ATL for several reasons. Firstly, this brain region has a blood supply from two arteries: (i) the anterior temporal cortical artery, which branches off the middle cerebral artery, and (ii) the anterior temporal branch of the distal posterior cerebral artery. Stroke rarely disrupts both of these blood supplies simultaneously (Conn, 2003). Thus, although the superior parts of the ATL are more vulnerable to stroke, ventral regions associated with the representation of conceptual knowledge across modalities are watershed regions (Phan, Donnan, Wright, & Reutens, 2005; Phan, Fong, Donnan, & Reutens, 2007). Secondly, the artery branch supplying the anterior temporal lobe subdivides below the main trifurcation of the artery: this might make it less vulnerable to emboli, which can pass beyond this point (Borden, 2006). Thirdly, the ATL stores semantic knowledge bilaterally, and it is unusual to have a bilateral stroke (Visser, Jefferies, et al., 2010). Thus, stroke patients with comprehension deficits are likely to have an intact store of semantic knowledge in the ventral ATL.

Impairments of "access" can occur in at least two ways: patients can have difficulties accessing conceptual knowledge from specific sensory inputs, and they can show deficits in constraining retrieval and selection such that semantic access is appropriate to the current task or context. Disorders of auditory speech perception are an example of the first kind of access impairment and affect comprehension of spoken words in patients with pure word deafness (PWD) and Wernicke's aphasia (Hart & Gordon, 1990), although WA patients have additional cognitive deficits (see next). Word deafness in its purest form is very rare (Denes & Semenza, 1975); however, both PWD and WA patients show poor understanding of spoken language reflecting impaired discrimination of phonemes (Ackermann & Mathiak, 1999; Robson, Grube, Lambon Ralph, Griffiths, & Sage, 2013; Robson, Keidel, Lambon Ralph, & Sage, 2012), in the context of more intact comprehension in other modalities. In PWD, poor speech comprehension can occur alongside good reading, writing, and spoken word production (Poeppel, 2001; Saffran, Marin, & Yeni-Komshian, 1976). Strikingly, some cases even show intact comprehension of non-speech auditory information, with difficulties restricted to understanding spoken language, though most cases also have some impairment of non-speech sound processing (Poeppel, 2001; Polster & Rose, 1998).

Patients with PWD have damage to auditory cortex (Griffith, Flees, & Green, 1999; Tanaka, Yamadori, & Mori, 1987), while WA patients often have damage extending to temporoparietal, middle temporal, and/or inferior frontal cortex (Robson, Sage, & Lambon Ralph, 2012; Thompson, Robson, Lambon Ralph, & Jefferies, 2015). In addition to poor auditory comprehension, WA patients have fluent speech characterized by phonological paraphasias and neologisms (Goldblum & Albert, 1972; Harris, 1970; Goodglass, Kaplan, & Barresi, 2001; Luria, 1970), and they commonly show milder non-verbal comprehension deficits (Cohen, Kelter, & Woll, 1980; de Renzi, Faglioni, Scotti, & Spinnler, 1972; Gainotti, Silveri, Villa, & Caltagirone, 1983; Ogar et al., 2011; Robson, Sage, et al., 2012; Thompson et al., 2015). These deficits do not appear to reflect degraded conceptual knowledge, since performance is inconsistent across tests employing the same items with varied task demands (Robson, Sage, et al., 2012; Thompson et al., 2015). A recent hypothesis suggests a dual deficit to explain this pattern: WA patients may have poor auditory input processing combined with (mild) semantic control impairments (see next) that affect performance across modalities (Robson, Sage, et al., 2012; Thompson et al., 2015).

7.7 Access deficits: Controlled retrieval and selection impairments

We have knowledge of a vast number of features and associations for any given concept and typically only a subset of our knowledge is required for a task: other aspects of knowledge may actually be inappropriate and unhelpful. For example, thinking about COINS and LOANS is probably not helpful when trying to understand the sentence "The bank was slippery" (since in this context, the word BANK is likely to refer to a river). Similarly, playing the piano requires information about fine movements of the fingers to be retrieved, yet if your task is to move a piano across the room, it is necessary to retrieve very different actions associated with piano (Saffran, 2000). Control processes therefore play an essential role in shaping the activation within the semantic system, such that context- and task-relevant aspects of meaning are accessed (Badre, Poldrack, Paré-Blagoev, Insler, & Wagner, 2005; Badre & Wagner, 2007; Jefferies & Lambon Ralph, 2006; Thompson-Schill, D'Esposito, Aguirre, & Farah, 1997).

Patients with SA appear to retain their conceptual knowledge but have difficulty controlling retrieval such that it is appropriate to the task and context (Jefferies & Lambon Ralph, 2006; Thompson et al., 2015). The term semantic aphasia (SA) has been used for nearly a century (Gainotti, 2014; Head, 1926; Luria, 1976), and early descriptions typically referred to a "high-level" deficit in understanding, involving conceptual combinations, a failure to perceive complex relationships, and difficulties beyond language in grasping critical aspects of meaning—with limited description of single-item deficits (see also Ardila, Concha, & Rosselli, 2000; Hier, Mogil, Rubin, & Komros, 1980). In more recent studies, we used this term to refer to patients with comprehension deficits beyond language, affecting both verbal and non-verbal tasks, who have difficulty shaping retrieval so that it focuses on relevant aspects of knowledge (Corbett, Jefferies, Ehsan, & Lambon Ralph, 2009; Gardner et al., 2012; Jefferies & Lambon Ralph, 2006; Noonan, Jefferies, Corbett, & Lambon Ralph, 2010; Thompson et al., 2015). These patients' deficits include complex high-level processes such as action sequencing (Corbett, Jefferies, & Lambon Ralph, 2009), as well as simpler single-item tasks, such as word, sound, and picture-to-picture matching, with deficits across modalities (Gardner et al., 2012; Jefferies & Lambon Ralph, 2006; Thompson et al., 2015). The term semantic aphasia transcends standard Boston classifications; patients may be classified as showing transcortical sensory aphasia (if the deficit is largely restricted to comprehension), or mixed transcortical or global aphasia (if there are additional problems with nonfluent speech and/or receptive language processing). This is because studies have selected SA patients to have comprehension impairments for both words and pictures, and irrespective of additional language deficits. Heteromodal semantic impairment in SA is associated with damage to left inferior frontal and/or posterior temporal regions (Berthier, 2001; Chertkow, Bub, Deaudon, & Whitehead, 1997; Dronkers, Wilkins, van Valin, Redfern, & Jaeger, 2004; Hart & Gordon, 1990). Although SA patients show impairment on the same range of verbal and non-verbal semantic tasks as patients with SD, they show qualitative differences, consistent with the view that semantic representations are gradually degrading in SD, while patients with SA have deficits controlling their access to largely intact conceptual knowledge. The differences between SD and SA patients are listed next:

(1) SD patients show strong *correlations and trial-by-trial consistency* between diverse semantic tasks that probe the same concepts, which are thought to reflect the degree of degradation of the underlying knowledge (Bozeat et al., 2000). In contrast, SA patients only show correlations and consistency between tasks with equivalent control demands (Jefferies & Lambon Ralph, 2006).
(2) SA patients have been shown to be highly sensitive to semantic control manipulations. (i) SA patients are vulnerable to strong distracters in synonym matching tasks (e.g., matching HAPPY with CHEERFUL, with the strong distractor SAD). This is because

when two concepts are strongly related, their relationship becomes hard to ignore even when this is irrelevant to the task (Samson, Connolly, & Humphreys, 2007). (ii) Patients find it difficult to process less dominant meanings of ambiguous words, such as PEN to mean an enclosure on a farm. In this case, participants have to inhibit their dominant meaning and select a distantly related alternative (Noonan et al., 2010). (iii) SA cases are affected by how close in semantic space two items from the same category are, with worse performance for distant compared to close relations (e.g., a close relation such as HAT and CAP, and a distant relation such as HAT and STOCKING). When probes and targets are closely related, they share a large amount of semantic structure/features, but when they are more distant, they require additional semantic control to work out the relevant semantic link (Noonan et al., 2010).

(3) SA patients are highly susceptible to being aided by *cues* and misled by miscues that are semantically related to the target or distracters (Corbett, Jefferies, & Lambon Ralph, 2011; Noonan et al., 2010; Soni et al., 2009; Soni, Lambon Ralph, & Woollams, 2011); in contrast, SD patients show smaller yet significant effects of cueing (Jefferies, Patterson, & Lambon Ralph, 2008). Cues boost activation of the target word relative to semantically related competitors, to narrow the field of competing responses dramatically (Dell & O'Seaghdha, 1992; Dell, Schwartz, Martin, Saffran, & Gagnon, 1997; Schwartz, Dell, Martin, Gahl, & Sobel, 2006). This suggests that these patients have intact semantic representations which are not utilized in a task-appropriate way. Soni et al. argued that if semantic activation of a group of category nodes was activated, then cueing a semantically related competitor (e.g., providing /l/ for TIGER) should boost activation of the competitor LION and reduce the patients' ability to produce the correct label (Soni et al., 2009). They found that miscueing SA patients led to lower accuracy and more semantic errors than with no cue (Noonan et al., 2010; Soni et al., 2011). Cueing also aids performance on non-verbal semantic tasks. For example, Corbett et al. (2011) found that SA patients were better able to mime an action for an object when shown a picture cue of the recipient of the action (e.g., NAIL for HAMMER).

(4) SD patients show relative preservation of concepts that are commonly encountered, while those with SA show a weaker effect of frequency (or in some cases even a reversal of the normal high > low frequency effect) (Almaghyuli, Thompson, Lambon Ralph, & Jefferies, 2012; Hoffman, Rogers, & Lambon Ralph, 2011; Jefferies & Lambon Ralph, 2006; Jefferies, Patterson, Jones, & Lambon Ralph, 2009; Warrington & Cipolotti, 1996). Frequently occurring items develop more robust semantic representations (Hoffman et al., 2011); thus poorer performance on low frequency items in patients with SD is associated with degradation of conceptual knowledge itself (Rogers, Lambon Ralph, Garrard, et al., 2004). The surprising lack of a frequency effect in SA patients has been linked to the control deficits in this group. Hoffman and colleagues (2011) argued that high-frequency items have higher semantic control demands, because they have higher "contextual diversity" leading to the automatic activation of a high number of lexical associates, contexts, and meanings. For example, a high-frequency word such as "dog" can be used to mean a number of different things, such as "HE'S REALLY GONE TO THE DOGS," and "THE DETECTIVE WILL DOG YOUR FOOTSTEPS," and so on (Adelman, Brown, & Quesada, 2006; Hoffman et al., 2011).

(5) In picture naming, SA patients produce more associative errors (e.g., SQUIRREL—NUT), while SD patients produce more superordinate errors (e.g., SQUIRREL—ANIMAL) (Jefferies & Lambon Ralph, 2006; Jefferies et al., 2008). This suggests that SA patients have difficulty directing activation toward the target name and away from irrelevant prepotent associations. This notable difference in picture naming errors between patients with lesions in ATL and temporoparietal cortex was the main motivation for Schwartz et al.'s (2011) proposal of multiple "hubs" supporting the representation of taxonomic knowledge (in ATL) and thematic knowledge (in angular gyrus, or posterior middle temporal gyrus). However, an alternative interpretation is that patients with left prefrontal and/or temporoparietal lesions have deficits of semantic control, and as a result, they retrieve task-irrelevant but strong associations (i.e., thematic errors). In contrast, patients with ATL lesions have degraded semantic representations; consequently, they are unlikely to make thematic errors (which require the retention of associations, Soni et al., 2011), and instead produce high-frequency category coordinates and superordinate labels.

(6) SA patients resemble the "access" cases described by Warrington and colleagues (1983) in that they show progressive deterioration of comprehension on cyclical word-picture matching tasks when sets of semantically related concepts are probed repeatedly (Jefferies, Baker, Doran, & Lambon Ralph, 2007; Warrington & Cipolotti, 1996; Warrington & Crutch, 2004; Warrington & McCarthy, 1983). In contrast, SD patients resemble "storage" patients in that they show stable performance across cycles. One explanation of this pattern is that when targets become distracters (and vice versa), demands on post-retrieval selection mechanisms increase, reflecting strong competition from previously selected items that are now distracters (Gardner et al., 2012; Jefferies et al., 2007; Schnur, Schwartz, Brecher, & Hodgson, 2006; Schnur et al., 2009; Thompson et al., 2015). SA patients appear to show this pattern for both verbal tasks (word-picture matching) and non-verbal tasks (picture-picture matching) (Forde & Humphreys, 1997; Gardner et al., 2012; Thompson et al., 2015), although there has been some debate about whether this is the case for access patients more generally (Crutch & Warrington, 2008, 2011; Warrington & Crutch, 2004). In a recent study, Thompson et al. (2015) found deterioration with repetition in both SA and WA patients following damage to the left prefrontal cortex, potentially reflecting these patients' difficulty in controlling competition. WA patients showed an additional modality effect, with greater impairment for spoken words, in line with the "dual deficit" hypothesis for WA patients just outlined.

(7) SA patients show *executive control impairments* beyond the semantic domain, which correlate with the degree of impairment on semantic tasks (Jefferies & Lambon Ralph, 2006). In contrast, SD patients have good performance on other cognitive tasks: their deficits are largely restricted to semantic processing (McCarthy & Warrington, 2015). This suggests that at least part of the explanation for deficient semantic control in SA follows from damage to domain-general executive functions. Areas implicated in semantic control overlap with brain regions implicated in executive control more generally (Duncan, 2006, 2010; Duncan & Owen, 2000; Humphreys & Lambon Ralph, 2015; Noonan, Jefferies, Visser, & Lambon Ralph, 2013). However, the large lesions of SA patients may mask potential dissociations between domain-general executive control and processes that shape memory retrieval more specifically.

7.8 Semantic control across modalities

Patients with SA have difficulty controlling semantic access across modalities, suggesting that a heteromodal store of knowledge interacts with modality-general control mechanisms (Corbett, Jefferies, Ehsan, et al., 2009; Corbett, Jefferies, & Lambon Ralph, 2009; Corbett et al., 2011). SA patients perform poorly on picture association tests and on complex mechanical puzzles (Corbett, Jefferies, Ehsan, et al., 2009). They also show strong sensitivity to manipulations of semantic control in object use: they have difficulty using their knowledge of specific semantic features to flexibly support the non-canonical uses of objects (e.g., using a newspaper as a fly swat), they show poor inhibition of semantically related distracters in this context, and their object use is improved with the provision of verbal and pictorial cues designed to constrain the task (Corbett et al., 2011).

A recent comparison of left and right hemisphere stroke has found deficits across modalities in both patient groups (Thompson, Henshall, & Jefferies, 2016). This is supported by a meta-analysis of fMRI data showing left inferior frontal gyrus (IFG) and right IFG respond across multiple semantic tasks requiring control (Noonan et al., 2013). However, there is a possibility of subtle hemispheric differences in semantic control, with the left mid-IFG showing an equivalent response to words and pictures while right mid-IFG is more responsive to pictures (Krieger-Redwood et al., 2015). This possibility remains to be further explored.

7.8.1 Convergent evidence for a distributed semantic control network

SA patients have damage to left prefrontal and/or temporoparietal areas. Damage to either prefrontal or temporoparietal regions appears to produce similar neuropsychological profiles, although most studies have put these two subgroups together in statistical analyses, and lesion comparisons have included relatively few patients to date (Corbett, Jefferies, Ehsan, et al., 2009; Corbett et al., 2011; Gardner et al., 2012; Jefferies & Lambon Ralph, 2006; Jefferies et al., 2008; Noonan et al., 2010; Thompson et al., 2015). Patients with transcortical sensory aphasia (similar to those with SA) can similarly have anterior or posterior lesions, resulting in similar comprehension impairments (Berthier, 2001). This suggests that anterior and posterior brain regions form a large-scale distributed cortical network underpinning semantic control. Nevertheless, patients with large and variable lesions are not ideally suited to producing a detailed neural model of semantic control: SA patients' deficits could conceivably follow damage to white matter tracts and/or their cortical damage could span several functionally separable regions (Butler, Lambon Ralph, & Woollams, 2014). Consequently, convergent evidence from other neuroscientific methods is important to evaluate the proposal that semantic control draws on both prefrontal and posterior regions.

In fMRI, left IFG responds most strongly to semantic control demands, but other areas show a similar response, suggesting a distributed network underpinning semantic control (Davey et al., 2016; Hallam, Whitney, Hymers, Gouws, & Jefferies, 2016; Noonan et al., 2013). Sites in posterior temporal cortex (pMTG and pITG) and dorsal angular gyrus/ inferior parietal sulcus (dAG/IPS) also show activation modulated by semantic control demands (Badre et al., 2005; Nagel, Schumacher, Goebel, & D'Esposito, 2008; Noonan et al., 2013; Thompson-Schill et al., 1997). Moreover, these areas are functionally dissociable from ATL and mid-AG, which are part of the default mode network and respond more strongly to relatively automatic forms of semantic retrieval (Davey, Cornelissen, et al., 2015; Davey et al., 2016; Humphreys, Hoffman, Visser, Binney, & Lambon Ralph, 2015). The distributed semantic control system, including left and right IFG, pMTG, and dAG, responds strongly to experimental manipulations of semantic control demands, including a stronger response to (i) ambiguous words (with multiple meanings) than unambiguous words (Bedny, McGill, & Thompson-Schill, 2008; Rodd, Davis, & Johnsrude, 2005; Whitney, Grossman, & Kircher, 2009), (ii) associations based on specific semantic features (i.e., color, shape) as opposed to associations based on global semantic relatedness (Whitney, Kirk, O'Sullivan, Lambon Ralph, & Jefferies, 2012), (iii) decisions involving many versus few response options (Badre & Wagner, 2007), and (iv) matching word-pairs when associative strength is low versus high (Badre et al., 2005; Thompson-Schill et al., 1997; Wagner, Maril, Bjork, & Schacter, 2001). Thus, the network appears to provide the foundation for semantic control across a broad range of tasks and domains (Noonan et al., 2013). Inhibitory TMS delivered to either LIFG or pMTG elicits behavioral disruption of comparable magnitude, supporting the conclusion that both components play a necessary role in controlled semantic retrieval (Whitney et al., 2011). Moreover, TMS to LIFG increases the response within pMTG during the retrieval of weak associations, suggesting functional compensation (Hallam et al., 2016).

Regions implicated in semantic control overlap with domain-general executive regions (Humphreys & Lambon Ralph, 2015; Noonan et al., 2013; Thompson et al., in press). There are, however, subtle differences (Davey et al., 2016; Devlin, Matthews, & Rushworth, 2003; Gough, Nobre, & Devlin, 2005; Nagel et al., 2008), with semantic control recruiting regions such as anterior IFG and pMTG which are not part of the multiple demand network (Duncan, 2006, 2010; Duncan & Owen, 2000). Anterior IFG and pMTG are likely to be involved in particular aspects of control unique to semantics, such as providing a semantic context to link distant or weakly related concepts (such as linking SALT with ICY) (Lerner, Honey, Silbert, & Hasson, 2011; Turken & Dronkers, 2011; Whitney, Jefferies, & Kircher, 2011). Other components of control, such as inhibiting dominant distractors or selecting knowledge in a goal-driven way, may draw on domain-general resources (Davey, Cornelissen, et al., 2015; Davey et al., 2016; Whitney et al., 2012). The nature of the relationship between semantic control and domain-general executive control is currently being explored.

7.9 CONCLUSION

Semantic knowledge is critical for all our experiences and memories, and in this chapter we have reviewed the major single-word comprehension disorders. As we learn more about the nature of the disorders, we can inform future therapies (Hoffman, 2014; Hoffman, Clarke, Jones, & Noonan, 2015; Jefferies et al., 2008).

Converging evidence supports the view that semantic knowledge is stored throughout the cortex and brought together in a hub in the ATL. The hub-and-spoke model can account for the degradation of semantic knowledge across modalities and tasks in semantic dementia, following focal atrophy of ATL (Binney et al., 2010; Mummery et al., 2000; Patterson et al., 2007). Category-specific semantic disorders, on the other hand, may be explicable in terms of damage to sensory-motor "spokes" and/or within a "graded hub" account, in which specific inputs are combined within the ATL in a graded fashion. For example, damage focused on the medial aspects of ATL in HSVE produces disproportionate deficits for animals, potentially reflecting their reliance on fine-grained visual discrimination (Lambon Ralph et al., 2007; Moss, Tyler, & Jennings, 1997; Warrington & Shallice, 1984). Additionally, patients can have difficulty accessing conceptual information from a specific modality, such as patients with pure word deafness or Wernicke's aphasia who have auditory comprehension deficits.

We also need to retrieve *relevant* conceptual information for the task in hand, or the context we are in. SA patients have heteromodal semantic impairments which reflect difficulty *controlling* retrieval in a flexible way, such that it is appropriate to the task demands, following left prefrontal and/or temporoparietal stroke (Jefferies & Lambon Ralph, 2006; Noonan et al., 2010). Since disruption occurs in the *controlled access* rather than the *storage* of knowledge, SA patients can be aided by cues and misled by miscues (Corbett et al., 2011; Jefferies et al., 2008; Noonan et al., 2010; Soni et al., 2009; Soni et al., 2011).

Although much progress has been made in the understanding of the nature of single-item comprehension deficits and their implications for normal comprehension, there are still unanswered questions that remain. In terms of the storage of knowledge, researchers are now asking not *whether* the ATLs are involved, but *how* the hub interacts with the spokes and *how* knowledge is represented in a graded fashion across the two hemispheres (Chen et al., 2017; Hoffman et al., 2012; Jackson, Lambon Ralph, & Pobric, 2015; Pobric et al., 2010b; Rice, Hoffman, & Lambon Ralph, 2015). Researchers are also exploring the role of the ATL within the default mode network, and the contribution of the angular gyrus (Davey, Cornelissen, et al., 2015; Davey et al., 2016; Humphreys & Lambon Ralph, 2015; Jackson, Hoffman, Pobric, & Lambon Ralph, 2016)—ATL may be able to flexibly change its connectivity to support visual object recognition, automatic semantic retrieval, and more goal-driven or controlled semantic retrieval states.

In terms of "controlled access," the specific contribution of the distributed areas within the semantic control network remains unclear (Davey et al., 2016; Gardner et al., 2012; Humphreys & Lambon Ralph, 2015; Krieger-Redwood et al., 2015; Thompson et al., 2016). A related question concerns whether an identical network supports semantic control for verbal and non-verbal tasks: research has almost exclusively relied on verbal tasks, so the existence of separate linguistic control areas is currently hard to rule out (Noonan et al., 2013). We still know relatively little about how semantic control interacts with the store of knowledge, such that processing is focused on task-relevant features, and how these task-relevant elements are integrated (Davey, Cornelissen, et al., 2015; Davey, Rueschemeyer, et al., 2015; Davey et al., 2016). We also know relatively little about the relative contribution of domain-general executive and semantic control processes to different tasks (Davey et al., 2016; Humphreys & Lambon Ralph, 2015).

Finally, while the research reviewed in this chapter has made an important contribution to our understanding of the variety of semantic deficits, the implications for rehabilitation and speech and language therapy requires further work. For SA patients, recovery may be facilitated by the use of training tasks that focus on strengthening semantic control processes, as opposed to attempts to retrain "lost" semantic knowledge.

References

Ackermann, H., & Mathiak, K. (1999). Symptomatologie, pathologischanatomische Grundlaqen und Pathomechanismen zentraler Hörstörungen (reine Worttaubheit, auditive Agnosie, Rindentaubheit). [Symptomatology, Neuroanatomical Correlates and Pathomechanisms of Central Hearing Disorders (Pure Word Deafness, Verbal/Nonverbal Auditory Agnosia, Cortical Deafness)]. *Fortschritte der Neurologie-Psychiatrie, 67*(11), 509–23.

Adelman, J. S., Brown, G. D. A., & Quesada, J. F. (2006). Contextual diversity, not word frequency, determines word-naming and lexical decision times. *Psychological Science, 17*, 814–23.

Almaghyuli, A., Thompson, H. E., Lambon Ralph, M. A., & Jefferies, E. (2012). Deficits of semantic control produce absent or reverse frequency effects in comprehension: Evidence from neuropsychology and dual task methodology. *Neuropsychologia, 50*(8), 1968–79.

Ardila, A., Concha, M., & Rosselli, M. (2000). Angular gyrus syndrome revisited: Acalculia, finger agnosia, right-left disorientation and semantic aphasia. *Aphasiology, 14*(7), 743–54.

Badre, D., Poldrack, R. A., Paré-Blagoev, E. J., Insler, R. Z., & Wagner, A. D. (2005). Dissociable controlled retrieval and generalized selection mechanisms in ventrolateral prefrontal cortex. *Neuron, 47*(6), 907–18.

Badre, D., & Wagner, A. D. (2007). Left ventrolateral prefrontal cortex and the cognitive control of memory. *Neuropsychologia, 45*(13), 2883–901.

Bai, H. M., Wang, W. M., Li, T. D., Liu, Y., & Lu, Y. C. (2011). Functional MRI mapping of category-specific sites associated with naming of famous faces, animals and man-made objects. *Neuroscience Bulletin, 27*(5), 307–18.

Bajada, C. J., Jackson, R. L., Haroon, H. A., Azadbakht, H., Parker, G. J. M., Lambon Ralph, M. A., & Cloutman, L. L. (2017). A graded tractographic parcellation of the temporal lobe. *NeuroImage, 155*, 503–12.

Bedny, M., McGill, M., & Thompson-Schill, S. L. (2008). Semantic adaptation and competition during word comprehension. *Cerebral Cortex, 5*(11), 2574–2585.

Berthier, M. L. (2001). Unexpected brain-language relationships in aphasia: Evidence from transcortical sensory aphasia associated with frontal lobe lesions. *Aphasiology, 15*(2), 99–130.

Binder, J. R., & Desai, R. H. (2011). The neurobiology of semantic memory. *Trends in Cognitive Sciences, 15*(11), 527–536.

Binder, J. R., Desai, R. H., Graves, W. W., & Conant, L. L. (2009). Where is the semantic system? A critical review and meta-analysis of 120 functional neuroimaging studies. *Cerebral Cortex, 19*(12), 2767–96.

Binney, R. J., Embleton, K. V., Jefferies, E., Parker, G. J. M., & Lambon Ralph, M. A. (2010). The ventral and inferolateral aspects of the anterior temporal lobe are crucial in semantic memory: Evidence from a novel direct comparison of distortion-corrected fMRI, rTMS, and semantic dementia. *Cerebral Cortex, 20*(11), 2728–38.

Binney, R. J., Hoffman, P., & Lambon Ralph, M. (2016). Mapping the multiple graded contributions of the anterior temporal lobe representational hub to abstract and social concepts: Evidence from distortion-corrected fMRI. *Cerebral Cortex, 26*(11), 4227–41.

Blundo, C., Ricci, M., & Miller, L. (2006). Category-specific knowledge deficit for animals in a patient with herpes simplex encephalitis. *Cognitive Neuropsychology, 23*(8), 1248–68.

Borden, N. M. (2006). *3D Angiographic Atlas of Neurovascular Anatomy and Pathology*. Cambridge University Press, Cambridge.

Bozeat, S., Lambon Ralph, M. A., Graham, K. S., Patterson, K., Wilkin, H., Rowland, J., ... Hodges, J. R. (2003). A duck with four legs: Investigating the structure of conceptual knowledge using picture drawing in semantic dementia. *Cognitive Neuropsychology, 20*(1), 27–47.

Bozeat, S., Lambon Ralph, M. A., Patterson, K., Garrard, P., & Hodges, J. R. (2000). Non-verbal semantic impairment in semantic dementia. *Neuropsychologia, 38*(9), 1207–15.

Bozeat, S., Lambon Ralph, M. A., Patterson, K., & Hodges, J. R. (2002). When objects lose their meaning: What happens to their use? *Cognitive, Affective, & Behavioral Neuroscience, 2*(3), 236–51.

Bright, P., Moss, H., & Tyler, L. K. (2004). Unitary vs multiple semantics: PET studies of word and picture processing. *Brain and Language, 89*(3), 417–32.

Butler, R. A., Lambon Ralph, M. A., & Woollams, A. M. (2014). Capturing multidimensionality in stroke aphasia: Mapping principal behavioural components to neural structures. *Brain, 137*(12), 3248–66.

Buxbaum, L. J., & Saffran, E. M. (2002). Knowledge of object manipulation and object function: Dissociations in apraxic and nonapraxic subjects. *Brain and Language, 82*, 179–99.

Catani, M., & Ffytche, D. H. (2005). The rises and falls of disconnection syndromes. *Brain, 128*(10), 2224–39.

Chen, L., Lambon Ralph, M. A., & Rogers, T. T. (2017). A unified model of human semantic knowledge and its disorders. *Nature Human Behaviour, 1*(3), pii: 0039. doi: 10.1038/s41562-016-0039

Chen, Y., Shimotake, A., Matsumoto, R., Kunieda, T., Kikuchi, T., Miyamoto, S., ... Lambon Ralph, M. A. (2016). The "when" and "where" of semantic coding in the anterior temporal lobe: Temporal representational similarity analysis of electrocorticogram data. *Cortex, 79*, 1–13.

Chertkow, H., Bub, D., Deaudon, C., & Whitehead, V. (1997). On the status of object concepts in aphasia. *Brain and Language, 58*(2), 203–32.

Clarke, A. (2015). Dynamic information processing states revealed through neurocognitive models of object semantics. *Language, Cognition and Neuroscience, 30*(4), 409–19.

Clarke, A., Taylor, K. I., & Tyler, L. K. (2011). The evolution of meaning: Spatio-temporal dynamics of visual object recognition. *Journal of Cognitive Neuroscience, 23*(8), 1887–99.

Clarke, A., & Tyler, L. K. (2015). Understanding what we see: How we derive meaning from vision. *Trends in Cognitive Science, 19*(11), 677–87.

Coccia, M., Bartolini, M., Luzzi, S., Provinciali, L., & Lambon Ralph, M. A. (2004). Semantic memory is an amodal, dynamic system: Evidence from the interaction of naming and object use in semantic dementia. *Cognitive Neuropsychology, 21*(5), 513–27.

Cohen, R., Kelter, S., & Woll, G. (1980). Analytical competence and language impairment in aphasia. *Brain and Language, 58*, 203–32.

Conn, P. M. (2003). *Neuroscience in Medicine* (2nd Edition). Humana Press, New York, NY.

Corbett, F., Jefferies, E., Ehsan, S., & Lambon Ralph, M. A. (2009). Different impairments of semantic cognition in semantic dementia and semantic aphasia: Evidence from the non-verbal domain. *Brain, 132*(9), 2593–608.

Corbett, F., Jefferies, E., & Lambon Ralph, M. A. (2009). Exploring multimodal semantic control impairments in semantic aphasia: Evidence from naturalistic object use. *Neuropsychologia, 47*(13), 2721–31.

Corbett, F., Jefferies, E., & Lambon Ralph, M. A. (2011). Deregulated semantic cognition follows prefrontal and temporoparietal damage: Evidence from the impact of task constraint on non-verbal object use. *Journal of Cognitive Neuroscience, 23*(5), 1125–35.

Crutch, S. J., & Warrington, E. K. (2008). The influence of refractoriness upon comprehension of non-verbal auditory stimuli. *Neurocase, 14*(6), 494–507.

Crutch, S. J., & Warrington, E. K. (2011). Different patterns of spoken and written word comprehension deficit in aphasic stroke patients. *Cognitive Neuropsychology, 28*(6), 414–34.

Damasio, A. R. (1989). The brain binds entities and events by multiregional activation from convergence zones. *Neural Computation, 1*, 123–32.

Damasio, H., Tranel, D., Grabowski, T., Adolphs, R., & Damasio, A. (2004). Neural systems behind word and concept retrieval. *Cognition, 92*(1–2), 179–229.

Davey, J., Cornelissen, P. L., Thompson, H. E., Sonkusare, S., Hallam, G., Smallwood, J., & Jefferies, E. (2015). Automatic and controlled semantic retrieval: TMS reveals distinct contributions of posterior middle temporal gyrus and angular gyrus. *Journal of Neuroscience, 35*(46), 15230–9.

Davey, J., Rueschemeyer, S. A., Costigan, A., Murphy, N., Krieger-Redwood, K., Hallam, G., & Jefferies, E. (2015). Shared neural processes support semantic control and action understanding. *Brain and Language, 142*, 24–35.

Davey, J., Thompson, H. E., Hallam, G., Karapanagiotidis, T., Murphy, C., De Caso, I., ... Jefferies, E. (2016). Exploring the role of the posterior middle temporal gyrus in semantic cognition: Integration of anterior temporal lobe with executive processes. *NeuroImage, 137*, 165–177.

de Renzi, E., Faglioni, P., Scotti, G., & Spinnler, H. (1972). Impairment in associating colour to form concomitant with aphasia. *Brain, 95*(2), 293–304.

de Schotten, M. T., Dell'Acqua, F., Valabregue, R., & Catani, M. (2012). Monkey to human comparative anatomy of the frontal lobe association tracts. *Cortex, 48*(1), 82–96.

Dell, G. S., & O'Seaghdha, P. G. (1992). Stages of lexical access in language production. *Cognition, 42*, 287–314.

Dell, G. S., Schwartz, M. F., Martin, N., Saffran, E. M., & Gagnon, D. A. (1997). Lexical access in aphasic and nonaphasic speakers. *Psychological Review, 104*, 801–38.

Denes, G., & Semenza, C. (1975). Auditory modality-specific anomia: Evidence from a case of pure word deafness. *Cortex, 11*(4), 401–11.

Devlin, J. T., Matthews, P. M., & Rushworth, M. F. S. (2003). Semantic processing in the left inferior prefrontal cortex: A combined functional magnetic resonance imaging and transcranial magnetic stimulation study. *Journal of Cognitive Neuroscience, 15*(1), 71–84.

Dove, G. (2016). Three symbol ungrounding problems: Abstract concepts and the future of embodied cognition. *Psychonomic Bulletin & Review, 23*(4), 1109–21.

Dronkers, N. F., Wilkins, D. P., van Valin, R. D., Redfern, B. B., & Jaeger, J. J. (2004). Lesion analysis of the brain areas involved in language comprehension. *Cognition, 92*(1–2), 145–77.

Duncan, J. (2006). EPS Mid-Career Award 2004: Brain mechanisms of attention. *The Quarterly Journal of Experimental Psychology, 59*(1), 2–27.

Duncan, J. (2010). The multiple-demand (MD) system of the primate brain: Mental programs for intelligent behaviour. *Trends in Cognitive Sciences, 14*(4), 172–9.

Duncan, J., & Owen, A. M. (2000). Common regions of the human frontal lobe recruited by diverse cognitive demands. *Trends in Neurosciences, 23*(10), 475–83.

Eggert, G. H. (1977). *Wernicke's Work on Aphasia: A Sourcebook and Review*. Mouton Publishers, The Hague.

Embleton, K. V., Haroon, H. A., Morris, D. M., Lambon Ralph, M. A., & Parker, G. J. M. (2010). Distortion correction for diffusion-weighted MRI tractography and fMRI in the temporal lobes. *Human Brain Mapping, 31*(10), 1570–87.

Fernandino, L., Conant, L. L., Binder, J. R., Blindauer, K., Hiner, B., Spangler, K., & Desai, R. H. (2013a). Parkinson's disease disrupts both automatic and controlled processing of action verbs. *Brain and Language, 127*, 65–74.

Fernandino, L., Conant, L. L., Binder, J. R., Blindauer, K., Hiner, B., Spangler, K., & Desai, R. H. (2013b). Where is the action? Action sentence processing in Parkinson's disease. *Neuropsychologia, 51*, 1510–17.

Forde, E. M. E., & Humphreys, G. W. (1997). A semantic locus for refractory behaviour: Implications for access storage distinctions and the nature of semantic memory. *Cognitive Neuropsychology, 14*(3), 367–402.

Fournier, N. M., Calverley, K. L., Wagner, J. P., Poock, J. L., & Crossley, M. (2008). Impaired social cognition 30 years after hemispherectomy for intractable epilepsy: The importance of the right hemisphere in complex social functioning. *Epilepsy & Behavior, 12*(3), 460–71.

Gainotti, G. (2011). The organization of semantic-conceptual knowledge: Is the "amodal hub" the only plausible model? *Brain and Cognition, 75*, 299–309.

Gainotti, G. (2014). Old and recent approaches to the problem of non-verbal conceptual disorders in aphasic patients. *Cortex, 53*, 78–89.

Gainotti, G., Silveri, M. C., Villa, G., & Caltagirone, C. (1983). Drawing objects from memory in aphasia. *Brain, 106*, 613–22.

Gardner, H. E., Lambon Ralph, M. A., Dodds, N., Jones, T., Eshan, S., & Jefferies, E. (2012). The differential contributions of pFC and temporoparietal cortices to multimodal semantic control: Exploring refractory effects in semantic aphasia. *Journal of Cognitive Neuroscience, 24*(4), 778–93.

Garrard, P., & Carroll, E. (2006). Lost in semantic space: A multi-modal, non-verbal assessment of feature knowledge in semantic dementia. *Brain, 129*(5), 1152–63.

Goldblum, M. C., & Albert, M. L. (1972). Phonemic discrimination in sensory aphasia. *International Journal of Mental Health, 1*, 25–9.

Goodglass, H., Kaplan, E., & Barresi, B. (2001). *The Assessment of Aphasia and Related Disorders* (3rd Edition). Lippincott Williams & Wilkins, Baltimore, MD.

Gough, P. M., Nobre, A. C., & Devlin, J. T. (2005). Dissociating linguistic processes in the left inferior frontal cortex with transcranial magnetic stimulation. *Journal of Neuroscience, 25*(35), 8010–16.

Griffith, T. D., Flees, A., & Green, G. G. R. (1999). Disorders of human complex sound processing. *Neurocase, 5*(5), 365–78.

Grossman, M., Anderson, C., Khan, A., Avants, B., Elman, L., & McCluskey, L. (2008). Impaired action knowledge in amyotrophic lateral sclerosis. *Neurology, 71*, 1396–401.

Halgren, E., Wang, C. M., Schomer, D. L., Knake, S., Marinkovic, K., Wu, J. L., & Ulbert, I. (2006). Processing stages underlying word recognition in the anteroventral temporal lobe. *NeuroImage, 30*(4), 1401–13.

Hallam, G. P., Whitney, C., Hymers, M., Gouws, A. D., & Jefferies, E. (2016). Charting the effects of TMS with fMRI: Modulation of cortical recruitment within the distributed network supporting semantic control. *Neuropsychologia, 93*, 40–52.

Harris, C. M. (1970). *Phonemic Errors Made by Aphasic Subjects in the Identification of Monosyllable Words* [Unpublished doctoral dissertation]. University of Minnesota, Minneapolis, MN.

Hart, J., & Gordon, B. (1990). Delineation of single-word semantic comprehension deficits in aphasia, with anatomical correlation. *Annals of Neurology, 27*(3), 226–31.

Head, H. (1926). *Aphasia and Kindred Disorders of Speech*. Cambridge University Press, London.

Hier, D. B., Mogil, S. I., Rubin, N. P., & Komros, G. R. (1980). Semantic aphasia: A neglect entity. *Brain and Language*, 10, 120–31.

Hillis, A. E., Kane, A., Tuffiash, E., Ulatowski, J. A., Barker, P. B., Beauchamp, N. J., & Wityk, R. J. (2001). Reperfusion of specific brain regions by raising blood pressure restores selective language functions in subacute stroke. *Brain and Language*, 79(3), 495–510.

Hillis, A. E., Wityk, R. J., Tuffiash, E., Beauchamp, N. J., Jacobs, M. A., Barker, P. B., & Selnes, O. A. (2001). Hypoperfusion of Wernicke's area predicts severity of semantic deficit in acute stroke. *Annals of Neurology*, 50, 561–6.

Hodges, J. R., Graham, N., & Patterson, K. (1995). Charting the progression in semantic dementia: Implications for the organisation of semantic memory. *Memory*, 3(3), 463–95.

Hodges, J. R., Patterson, K., Oxbury, S., & Funnell, E. (1992). Semantic Dementia—progressive fluent aphasia with temporal-lobe atrophy. *Brain*, 115(6), 1783–806.

Hoffman, P. (2014). Assessment and therapy for language and communication difficulties in dementia and other progressive diseases. *Neuropsychological Rehabilitation*, 24(2), 302–3.

Hoffman, P., Clarke, N., Jones, R. W., & Noonan, K. A. (2015). Vocabulary relearning in semantic dementia: Positive and negative consequences of increasing variability in the learning experience. *Neuropsychologia*, 76, 240–53.

Hoffman, P., Jefferies, E., & Lambon Ralph, M. A. (2010). Ventrolateral prefrontal cortex plays an executive regulation role in comprehension of abstract words: Convergent neuropsychological and repetitive TMS evidence. *The Journal of Neuroscience*, 30(46), 15450–6.

Hoffman, P., Jones, R. W., & Lambon Ralph, M. A. (2012). The degraded concept representation system in semantic dementia: Damage to pan-modal hub, then visual spoke. *Brain*, 135, 3770–80.

Hoffman, P., Rogers, T. T., & Lambon Ralph, M. A. (2011). Semantic diversity accounts for the "missing" word frequency effect in stroke aphasia: Insights using a novel method to quantify contextual variability in meaning. *Journal of Cognitive Neuroscience*, 23, 2432–46.

Humphreys, G. F., Hoffman, P., Visser, M., Binney, R. J., & Lambon Ralph, M. (2015). Establishing task-and modality-dependent dissociations between the semantic and default mode networks. *Proceedings of the National Academy of Sciences*, 112(25), 7857–62.

Humphreys, G. F., & Lambon Ralph, M. A. (2015). Fusion and fission of cognitive functions in the human parietal cortex. *Cerebral Cortex*, 25(10), 3547–60.

Jackson, R. L., Bajada, C. J., Rice, G. E., Cloutman, L. L., & Lambon Ralph, M. A. (2017). An emergent functional parcellation of the temporal cortex. *NeuroImage*. 2017 Apr 15. pii: S1053-8119(17)30316-6. doi: 10.1016/j.neuroimage.2017.04.024.

Jackson, R. L., Hoffman, P., Pobric, G., & Lambon Ralph, M. A. (2016). The semantic network at work and rest: Differential connectivity of anterior temporal lobe subregions. *Journal of Neuroscience*, 36(5), 1490–501.

Jackson, R. L., Lambon Ralph, M., & Pobric, G. (2015). The timing of anterior temporal lobe involvement in semantic processing. *Journal of Cognitive Neuroscience*, 27(7), 1388–96.

Jefferies, E., Baker, S. S., Doran, M., & Lambon Ralph, M. A. (2007). Refractory effects in stroke aphasia: A consequence of poor semantic control. *Neuropsychologia*, 45(5), 1065–79.

Jefferies, E., & Lambon Ralph, M. A. (2006). Semantic impairment in stroke aphasia versus semantic dementia: A case-series comparison. *Brain*, 129(8), 2132–47.

Jefferies, E., Patterson, K., Jones, R. W., & Lambon Ralph, M. A. (2009). Comprehension of concrete and abstract words in semantic dementia. *Neuropsychology*, 23(4), 492–9.

Jefferies, E., Patterson, K., & Lambon Ralph, M. A. (2008). Deficits of knowledge versus executive control in semantic cognition: Insights from cued naming. *Neuropsychologia, 46*(2), 649–58.

Jefferies, E., Rogers, T. T., & Lambon Ralph, M. A. (2011). Premorbid expertise produces category-specific impairment in a domain-general semantic disorder. *Neuropsychologia, 49*, 3213–23.

Kemmerer, D., Castillo, J. G., Talavage, T., Patterson, S., & Wiley, C. (2008). Neuroanatomical distribution of five semantic components of verbs: Evidence from fMRI. *Brain and Language, 107*(1), 16–43.

Krieger-Redwood, K., Teige, C., Davey, J., Hymers, M., & Jefferies, E. (2015). Conceptual control across modalities: Graded specialisation for pictures and words in inferior frontal and posterior temporal cortex. *Neuropsychologia, 76*, 92–107.

Lambon Ralph, M. A. (2014). Neurocognitive insights on conceptual knowledge and its breakdown. *Philosophical Transactions of the Royal Society B: Biological Sciences, 369*(1634), 20120392.

Lambon Ralph, M. A., Cipolotti, L., Manes, F., & Patterson, K. (2010). Taking both sides: Do unilateral anterior temporal lobe lesions disrupt semantic memory? *Brain, 133*, 3243–55.

Lambon Ralph, M. A., Ehsan, S., Baker, G. A., & Rogers, T. T. (2012). Semantic memory is impaired in patients with unilateral anterior temporal lobe resection for temporal lobe epilepsy. *Brain, 135*, 242–58.

Lambon Ralph, M. A., Graham, K. S., Patterson, K., & Hodges, J. R. (1999). Is a picture worth a thousand words? Evidence from concept definitions by patients with semantic dementia. *Brain and Language, 70*(3), 309–35.

Lambon Ralph, M., Jefferies, E., Patterson, K., & Rogers, T. T. (2017). The neural and computational bases of semantic cognition. *Nature Reviews Neuroscience, 18*, 42–55.

Lambon Ralph, M. A., Lowe, C., & Rogers, T. T. (2007). Neural basis of category-specific semantic deficits for living things: Evidence from semantic dementia, HSVE and a neural network model. *Brain, 130*, 1127–37.

Lambon Ralph, M. A., McClelland, J. L., Patterson, K., Galton, C. J., & Hodges, J. R. (2001). No right to speak? The relationship between object naming and semantic impairment: Neuropsychological evidence and a computational model. *Journal of Cognitive Neuroscience, 13*(3), 341–56.

Lambon Ralph, M. A., & Patterson, K. (2008). Generalization and differentiation in semantic memory: Insights from semantic dementia. *Annals of the New York Academy of Science, 1124*, 61–76.

Lambon Ralph, M. A., Sage, K., Jones, R. W., & Mayberry, E. J. (2010). Coherent concepts are computed in the anterior temporal lobes. *Proceedings of the National Academy of Sciences, 107*(6), 2717–22.

Lerner, Y., Honey, C. J., Silbert, L. J., & Hasson, U. (2011). Topographic mapping of a hierachy of temporal receptive windows using a narrated story. *The Journal of Neuroscience, 31*, 2906–15.

Leveroni, C. L., Seidenberg, M. S., Mayer, A. R., Mead, L. A., Binder, J. R., & Rao, S. M. (2000). Neural systems underlying the recognition of familiar and newly learned faces. *Journal of Neuroscience, 20*, 878–86.

Luria, A. R. (1970). *Traumatic Aphasia*. Mouton & Co., The Hague.

Luria, A. R. (1976). *Disturbances of Understanding of Verbal Communication in Patients with Sensory Aphasia*. Mouton & Co., The Hague.

Mahon, B. Z., & Caramazza, A. (2008). A critical look at the embodied cognition hypothesis and a new proposal for grounding conceptual content. *Journal of Physiology – Paris*, 102, 59–70.

Marinkovic, K., Dhond, R. P., Dale, A. M., Glessner, M., Carr, V., & Halgren, E. (2003). Spatiotemporal dynamics of modality-specific and supramodal word processing. *Neuron*, 38(3), 487–97.

Martin, A. (2007). The representation of object concepts in the brain. *Annual Review of Psychology*, 58(1), 25–45.

Martin, A. (2016). GRAPES—Grounding representations in action, perception, and emotion systems: How object properties and categories are represented in the human brain. *Psychonomic Bulletin & Review*, 23(4), 979–90.

Mayberry, E. J., Sage, K., Ehsan, S., & Lambon Ralph, M. A. (2011). Relearning in semantic dementia reflects contributions from both medial temporal lobe episodic and degraded neocortical semantic systems: Evidence in support of the complementary learning systems theory. *Neuropsychologia*, 49, 3591–8.

Mazon, B. Z. (2015). What is embodied about cognition? *Language, Cognition and Neuroscience*, 30(4), 420–9.

McCarthy, R. A., & Warrington, E. K. (2015). Past, present and prospects: Reflections 40 years on from the selective impairment of semantic memory. *The Quarterly Journal of Experimental Psychology*, 6, 1–28.

McClelland, J. L., & Rogers, T. T. (2003). The parallel distributed processing approach to semantic cognition. *Nature Reviews Neuroscience*, 4(4), 310–22.

Meteyard, L., Cuadrado, S. R., Bahrami, B., & Vigliocco, G. (2012). Coming of age: A review of embodiment and the neuroscience of semantics. *Cortex*, 48(7), 788–804.

Mion, M., Patterson, K., Acosta-Cabronero, J., Pengas, G., Izquierdo-Garcia, D., Hong, Y. T., . . . Nestor, P. J. (2010). What the left and right anterior fusiform gyri tell us about semantic memory. *Brain*, 133(11), 3256–68.

Mollo, G., Cornelissen, P. L., Millman, R. E., Ellis, A. W., & Jefferies, E. (2017). Oscillatory dynamics supporting semantic cognition: MEG Evidence for the contribution of the anterior temporal lobe hub and modality-specific spokes. *PloS One*, 12(1), 1–25.

Moss, H. E., Tyler, L. K., & Jennings, F. (1997). When leopards lose their spots: Knowledge of visual properties in category-specific deficits for living things. *Cognitive Neuropsychology*, 14(6), 901–50.

Mummery, C. J., Patterson, K., Price, C. J., Ashburner, J., Frackowiak, R. S. J., & Hodges, J. R. (2000). A voxel-based morphometry study of semantic dementia: Relationship between temporal lobe atrophy and semantic memory. *Annals of Neurology*, 47(1), 36–45.

Murphy, C., Rueschemeyer, S. A., Watson, D., Karapanagiotidis, T., Smallwood, J., & Jefferies, E. (2017). Fractionating the anterior temporal lobe: MVPA reveals differential responses to input and conceptual modality. *NeuroImage*, 147, 19–31.

Nagel, I. E., Schumacher, E. H., Goebel, R., & D'Esposito, M. (2008). Functional MRI investigation of verbal selection mechanisms in lateral prefrontal cortex. *NeuroImage*, 43(4), 801–7.

Noonan, K. A., Jefferies, E., Corbett, F., & Lambon Ralph, M. A. (2010). Elucidating the nature of deregulated semantic cognition in semantic aphasia: Evidence for the roles of prefrontal and temporo-parietal cortices. *Journal of Cognitive Neuroscience*, 22(7), 1597–613.

Noonan, K. A., Jefferies, E., Visser, M. E. J., & Lambon Ralph, M. A. (2013). Going beyond inferior prefrontal involvement in semantic control: Evidence for the additional contribution of parietal and posterior middle temporal cortex. *Journal of Cognitive Neuroscience, 25*(11), 1824–50.

Noppeney, U. T. A., Patterson, K., Tyler, L. K., Moss, H., Stamatakis, E. A., Bright, P., ... Price, C. J. (2007). Temporal lobe lesions and semantic impairment: A comparison of herpes simplex virus encephalitis and semantic dementia. *Brain, 130*, 1138–47.

Noppeney, U. T. A., & Price, C. J. (2002). Retrieval of visual, auditory, and abstract semantics. *NeuroImage, 15*, 917–26.

Ogar, J. M., Baldo, J. V., Wilson, S. M., Brambati, S. M., Miller, B. L., Dronkers, N. F., & Gomo-Tempini, M. L. (2011). Semantic dementia and persisting Wernicke's aphasia: Linguistic and anatomical profiles. *Brain and Language, 117*(1), 28–33.

Patterson, K., Nestor, P. J., & Rogers, T. T. (2007). Where do you know what you know? The representation of semantic knowledge in the human brain. *Nature Reviews Neuroscience, 8*(12), 976–87.

Peelen, M. V., & Caramazza, A. (2012). Conceptual object representations in human anterior temporal cortex. *Journal of Neuroscience, 32*(45), 15728–36.

Perry, R., Rosen, H. J., Kramer, J., Beer, J., Levenson, R., & Miller, B. L. (2001). Hemispheric dominance for emotions, empathy and social behavior: Evidence from right and left handers with frontotemporal dementia. *Neurocase, 7*, 145–60.

Phan, T. G., Donnan, G. A., Wright, P. M., & Reutens, D. C. (2005). A digital map of middle cerebral artery infarcts associated with middle cerebral artery trunk and branch occlusion. *Stroke, 36*(5), 986–91.

Phan, T. G., Fong, A. C., Donnan, G. A., & Reutens, D. C. (2007). Digital map of posterior cerebral artery infarcts associated with posterior cerebral artery trunk and branch occlusion. *Stroke, 38*(6), 1805–11.

Pobric, G., Jefferies, E., & Lambon Ralph, M. A. (2010a). Amodal semantic representations depend on both anterior temporal lobes: Evidence from repetitive transcranial magnetic stimulation. *Neuropsychologia, 48*(5), 1336–42.

Pobric, G., Jefferies, E., & Lambon Ralph, M. A. (2010b). Category-specific versus category-general semantic impairment induced by transcranial magnetic stimulation. *Current Biology, 20*(10), 964–8.

Pobric, G., Lambon Ralph, M., & Zahn, R. (2016). Hemispheric specialization within the superior anterior temporal cortex for social and nonsocial concepts. *Journal of Cognitive Neuroscience, 28*(3), 351–60.

Poeppel, D. (2001). Pure word deafness and the bilateral processing of the speech code. *Cognitive Science, 25*, 679–93.

Polster, M. R., & Rose, S. B. (1998). Disorders of auditory processing: Evidence for modularity in audition. *Cortex, 34*, 47–65.

Price, C. J., Devlin, J. T., Moore, C. J., Morton, C., & Laird, A. R. (2005). Meta-analyses of object naming: Effect of baseline. *Human Brain Mapping, 25*(1), 70–82.

Pulvermüller, F. (2005). Brain mechanisms linking language and action. *Nature Reviews Neuroscience, 6*, 576–82.

Pulvermüller, F. (2013). How neurons make meaning: Brain mechanisms for embodied and abstract-symbolic semantics. *Trends in Cognitive Sciences, 17*(9), 458–70.

Reilly, J., Peelle, J. E., Garcia, A., & Crutch, S. J. (2016). Linking somatic and symbolic representation in semantic memory: The dynamic multilevel reactivation framework. *Psychonomic Bulletin & Review, 23*(4), 1002–14.

Rice, G. E., Hoffman, P., & Lambon Ralph, M. (2015). Graded specialisation within and between the anterior temporal lobes. *Annals of the New York Academy of Sciences, 1359*, 84–97.

Rice, G. E., Lambon Ralph, M. A., & Hoffman, P. (2015). The roles of left versus right anterior temporal lobes in conceptual knowledge: An ALE meta-analysis of 97 functional neuroimaging studies. *Cerebral Cortex, 25*(11), 4374–91.

Robson, H., Grube, M., Lambon Ralph, M. A., Griffiths, T. D., & Sage, K. (2013). Fundamental deficits of auditory perception in Wernicke's aphasia. *Cortex, 49*(7), 1808–22.

Robson, H., Keidel, J. L., Lambon Ralph, M. A., & Sage, K. (2012). Revealing and quantifying the impaired phonological analysis underpinning impaired comprehension in Wernicke's aphasia. *Neuropsychologia, 50*, 276–88.

Robson, H., Sage, K., & Lambon Ralph, M. A. (2012). Wernicke's aphasia reflects a combination of acoustic-phonological and semantic control deficits: A case-series comparison of Wernicke's aphasia, semantic dementia and semantia aphasia. *Neuropsychologia, 50*, 266–75.

Rodd, J. M., Davis, M. H., & Johnsrude, I. S. (2005). The neural mechanisms of speech comprehension: fMRI studies of semantic ambiguity. *Cerebral Cortex, 15*(8), 1261–9.

Rogers, T. T., Hocking, J., Noppeney, U. T. A., Mechelli, A., Gorno-Tempini, M. L., Patterson, K., & Price, C. J. (2006). Anterior temporal cortex and semantic memory: Reconciling findings from neuropsychology and functional imaging. *Cognitive, Affective, & Behavioral Neuroscience, 6*(3), 201–13.

Rogers, T. T., Lambon Ralph, M. A., Garrard, P., Bozeat, S., McClelland, J. L., Hodges, J. R., & Patterson, K. (2004). Structure and deterioration of semantic memory: A neuropsychological and computational investigation. *Psychological Review, 111*, 205–35.

Rogers, T. T., Lambon Ralph, M. A., Hodges, J. R., & Patterson, K. (2004). Natural selection: The impact of semantic impairment on lexical and object decision. *Cognitive Neuropsychology, 21*(2), 331–52.

Rogers, T. T., Patterson, K., Jefferies, E., & Lambon Ralph, M. A. (2015). Disorders of representation and control in semantic cognition: Effects of familiarity, typicality, and specificity. *Neuropsychologia, 76*, 220–39.

Ross, L. A., & Olson, I. R. (2012). What's unique about unique entities? An fMRI investigation of the semantics of famous faces and landmarks. *Cerebral Cortex, 22*, 2005–15.

Saarela, M. V., & Hari, R. (2008). Listening to humans walking together activates the social brain circuitry. *Social Neuroscience, 3*(3–4), 401–9.

Saffran, E., Marin, O., & Yeni-Komshian, G. (1976). An analysis of speech perception in word deafness. *Brain and Language, 3*, 209–28.

Saffran, E. M. (2000). The organization of semantic memory: In support of a distributed model. *Brain and Language, 71*(1), 204–12.

Samson, D., Connolly, C., & Humphreys, G. W. (2007). When "happy" means "sad": Neuropsychological evidence for the right prefrontal cortex contribution to executive semantic processing. *Neuropsychologia, 45*, 896–904.

Schnur, T. T., Schwartz, M. F., Brecher, A., & Hodgson, C. (2006). Semantic interference during blocked-cyclic naming: Evidence from aphasia. *Journal of Memory and Language, 54*(2), 199–227.

Schnur, T. T., Schwartz, M. F., Kimberg, D. Y., Hirshorn, E., Coslett, H. B., & Thompson-Schill, S. L. (2009). Localizing interference during naming: Convergent neuroimaging and neuropsychological evidence for the function of Broca's area. *Proceedings of the National Academy of Sciences, 106*(1), 322–7.

Schwartz, M. F., Dell, G. S., Martin, N., Gahl, S., & Sobel, P. (2006). A case-series test of the interactive two-step model of lexical access: Evidence from picture naming. *Journal of Memory and Language*, 54, 228–64.

Schwartz, M. F., Kimberg, D. Y., Walker, G. M., Brecher, A., Faseyitan, O. K., Dell, G. S., ... Coslett, H. B. (2011). Neuroanatomical dissociation for taxonomic and thematic knowledge in the human brain. *Proceedings of the National Academy of Sciences*, 108(20), 8520–4.

Semenza, C. (2006). Retrieval pathways for common and proper names. *Cortex*, 42(6), 884–91.

Sergent, J., Ohta, S., & Macdonald, B. (1992). Functional neuroanatomy of face and object processing: A positron emission tomography study. *Brain*, 115(1), 15–36.

Shallice, T. (1993). Multiple semantics: Whose confusions? *Cognitive Neuropsychology*, 10, 251–61.

Sharp, D. J., Scott, S. K., & Wise, R. (2004). Retrieving meaning after temporal lobe infarction: The role of the basal language area. *Annals of Neurology*, 56, 836–46.

Skipper, L. M., Ross, L. A., & Olson, I. R. (2011). Sensory and semantic category subdivisions within the anterior temporal lobes. *Neuropsychologia*, 49(12), 3419–29.

Snowden, J. S., Goulding, P. J., & Neary, D. (1989). Semantic dementia: A form of circumscribed cerebral atrophy. *Behavioural Neurology*, 2, 167–82.

Snowden, J. S., Thompson, J. C., & Neary, D. (2004). Knowledge of famous faces and names in semantic dementia. *Brain*, 127, 860–72.

Soni, M., Lambon Ralph, M. A., Noonan, K. A., Ehsan, S., Hodgson, C., & Woollams, A. M. (2009). "L" is for tiger: Effects of phonological (mis)cueing on picture naming in semantic aphasia. *Journal of Neurolinguistics*, 22(6), 538–47.

Soni, M., Lambon Ralph, M. A., & Woollams, A. M. (2011). "W" is for bath: Can associative errors be cued? *Journal of Neurolinguistics*, 24(4), 445–65.

Spitsyna, G., Warren, J. E., Scott, S. K., Turkheimer, F. E., & Wise, R. (2006). Converging language streams in the human temporal lobe. *Journal of Neuroscience*, 26, 7328–36.

Straube, B., Green, A. J., Jansen, A., Chatterjee, A., & Kircher, T. (2010). Social cues, mentalizing and the neural processing of speech accompanied by gestures. *Neuropsychologia*, 48(2), 382–93.

Sugiura, M., Mano, Y., Sasaki, A., & Sadato, N. (2011). Beyond the memory mechanism: Person selective and nonselective processes in recognition of personally familiar faces. *Journal of Cognitive Neuroscience*, 23, 699–715.

Tanaka, Y., Yamadori, A., & Mori, E. (1987). Pure word deafness following bilateral lesions: A psychophysical analysis. *Brain*, 110, 381–403.

Thompson-Schill, S. L., D'Esposito, M., Aguirre, G. K., & Farah, M. J. (1997). Role of left inferior prefrontal cortex in retrieval of semantic knowledge: A reevaluation. *Proceedings of the National Academy of Sciences of the United States of America*, 94(26), 14792–7.

Thompson, H. E., Almaghyuli, A., Noonan, K. A., Barak, O., Lambon Ralph, M. A., & Jefferies, E. (in press). The contribution of executive control to semantic cognition: Convergent evidence from semantic aphasia and executive dysfunction. *Journal of Neuropsychology*, doi: 10.1111/jnp.12142

Thompson, H. E., Henshall, L., & Jefferies, E. (2016). The role of the right hemisphere in semantic control: A case-series comparison of right and left hemisphere stroke. *Neuropsychologia*, 85, 44–61.

Thompson, H. E., Robson, H., Lambon Ralph, M. A., & Jefferies, E. (2015). Varieties of semantic "access" deficit in Wernicke's aphasia and semantic aphasia. *Brain*, 138(12), 3776–92.

Turken, A. U., & Dronkers, N. F. (2011). The neural architecture of the language comprehension network: Converging evidence from lesion and connectivity analysis. *Frontiers in Systems Neuroscience*, 5(1), 1–20.

Tyler, L. K., Moss, H., Durrant-Peatfield, M. R., & Levy, J. P. (2000). Conceptual structure and the structure of concepts: A distributed account of category-specific deficits. *Brain and Language*, 75, 195–231.

Tyler, L. K., Stamatakis, E. A., Bright, P., Acres, K., Abdallah, S., Rodd, J. M., & Moss, H. (2004). Processing objects at different levels of specificity. *Journal of Cognitive Neuroscience*, 16, 351–62.

Vandenberghe, R., Price, C. J., Wise, R., Josephs, O., & Frackowiak, R. S. J. (1996). Functional anatomy of a common semantic system for words and pictures. *Nature*, 383(6597), 254–6.

Visser, M. E. J., Embleton, K. V., Jefferies, E., Parker, G. J. M., & Lambon Ralph, M. A. (2010). The inferior, anterior temporal lobes and semantic memory clarified: Novel evidence from distortion-corrected fMRI. *Neuropsychologia*, 48(6), 1689–96.

Visser, M. E. J., Embleton, K. V., & Lambon Ralph, M. A. (2012). Evidence for a caudo-rostral gradient of information convergence in the temporal lobes: An fMRI study of verbal and non-verbal semantic processing. *Journal of Cognitive Neuroscience*, 24(8), 1766–78.

Visser, M. E. J., Jefferies, E., Embleton, K. V., & Lambon Ralph, M. A. (2012). Both the middle temporal gyrus and the ventral anterior temporal area are crucial for multimodal semantic processing: Distortion-corrected fMRI evidence for a double gradient of information convergence in the temporal lobes. *Journal of Cognitive Neuroscience*, 24(8), 1766–78.

Visser, M. E. J., Jefferies, E., & Lambon Ralph, M. A. (2010). Semantic processing in the anterior temporal lobes: A meta-analysis of the functional neuroimaging literature. *Journal of Cognitive Neuroscience*, 22(6), 1083–94.

Wagner, A. D., Maril, A., Bjork, R. A., & Schacter, D. L. (2001). Prefrontal contributions to executive control: fMRI evidence for functional distinctions within lateral prefrontal cortex. *NeuroImage*, 14(6), 1337–47.

Warrington, E. K. (1975). Selective impairment of semantic memory. *Quarterly Journal of Experimental Psychology*, 27(4), 635–57.

Warrington, E. K., & Cipolotti, L. (1996). Word comprehension—The distinction between refractory and storage impairments. *Brain*, 119(2), 611–25.

Warrington, E. K., & Crutch, S. J. (2004). A circumscribed refractory access disorder: A verbal semantic impairment sparing visual semantics. *Cognitive Neuropsychology*, 21(2–4), 299–315.

Warrington, E. K., & McCarthy, R. A. (1983). Category specific access dysphasia. *Brain*, 106(4), 859–78.

Warrington, E. K., & McCarthy, R. A. (1987). Categories of knowledge—further fractionations and an attempted integration. *Brain*, 110(5), 1273–96.

Warrington, E. K., & Shallice, T. (1984). Category specific semantic impairments. *Brain*, 107, 829–54.

Whitney, C., Grossman, M., & Kircher, T. T. J. (2009). The influence of multiple primes on bottom-up and top-down regulation during meaning retrieval: Evidence for two distinct neural networks. *Cerebral Cortex*, 19(11), 2548–60.

Whitney, C., Jefferies, E., & Kircher, T. T. J. (2011). Heterogeneity of the left temporal lobe in semantic representation and control: Priming multiple vs. single meanings of ambiguous words. *Cerebral Cortex*, 21, 831–44.

Whitney, C., Kirk, M., O'Sullivan, J., Lambon Ralph, M. A., & Jefferies, E. (2012). Executive semantic processing is underpinned by a large-scale neural network: Revealing the contribution of left prefrontal, posterior temporal, and parietal cortex to controlled retrieval and selection using TMS. *Journal of Cognitive Neuroscience, 24*(1), 133–47.

Woollams, A. M., Cooper-Pye, E., Hodges, J. R., & Patterson, K. (2008). Anomia: A doubly typical signature of semantic dementia. *Neuropsychologia, 46*(10), 2503–14.

Wright, P., Randall, B., Clarke, A., & Tyler, L. K. (2015). The perirhinal cortex and conceptual processing: Effects of feature-based statistics following damage to the anterior temporal lobes. *Neuropsychologia, 76*, 192–207.

Zahn, R., Moll, J., Iyengar, V., Huey, E. D., Tierney, M., Krueger, F., & Grafman, J. (2009). Social conceptual impairments in frontotemporal lobar degeneration with right anterior temporal hypometabolism. *Brain, 132*, 604–16.

Zahn, R., Moll, J., Krueger, F., Huey, E. D., Garrido, G., & Grafman, J. (2007). Social concepts are represented in the superior anterior temporal cortex. *Proceedings of the National Academy of Sciences, 104*(15), 6430–5.

Zwaan, R. A. (2014). Embodiment and language comprehension: Reframing the discussion. *Trends in Cognitive Sciences, 18*(5), 229–34.

SECTION II
Sentence and discourse level

CHAPTER 8

SENTENCE COMPREHENSION

MARYELLEN C. MACDONALD AND YALING HSIAO

8.1 INTRODUCTION

FLUENT users of English who encounter the words *dogs, chase,* and *squirrels* in this order will rapidly understand that *dogs* is the agent of the chasing action and the squirrels are chased. The process of converting a linguistic signal into an understanding of a sentence's thematic roles (who did what to whom) is the part of language comprehension that is typically called *sentence processing*. Defined in this way, sentence processing clearly overlaps with many other language comprehension processes, including word recognition, interpretation of prosody, interpretation of pronouns, pragmatics, discourse processes, and many others. Nonetheless, as the existence of this chapter attests, researchers have actively pursued research that is focused on sentence interpretation while at least partially setting aside these related processes, and while recognizing that deriving a thematic interpretation (who did what to whom) is both important and also a waystation on the path to a broader discourse interpretation.

Historically, sentence processing was a distinct field in part because researchers assumed that sentence meaning is recovered from a linear string of words only via generating an explicit syntactic structure or *parse* for the input (Frazier, 1987; Frazier & Clifton, 1996; Frazier & Fodor, 1978; see Vosse & Kempen, 2000, for some parsing history and an alternative lexico-syntactic parsing model). For example, to interpret *Dogs chase squirrels*, Frazier hypothesized that a modular syntactic processor generated a syntactic structure from the grammatical categories of the input (noun, verb, noun), initially without access to word meaning or other context. As with all cognitive processes, the building of syntactic structures can be assumed to be effortful and demanding of memory, which naturally leads to research questions such as whether more complex syntactic structures require more memory. Similarly, researchers can ask how the system confronts the computational burdens of syntactic ambiguity, in which the input is compatible with more than one syntactic structure: are multiple structures built or is one chosen by some metric?

More recently, the notion of obligatory syntactic structure building during sentence processing has come under scrutiny, including by researchers who suggest that sensitivity to words' serial order may supplant at least some hierarchical representations (Christiansen

& Chater, 2001; Frank & Bod, 2011; MacDonald & Christiansen, 2002, cf. Fossum & Levy, 2012), and researchers within several different theoretical frameworks who argue that there is variability across situations (and potentially, across individuals) in the extent to which sentence interpretation is underpinned by construction of a syntactic structure of the input (Ferreira, Bailey, & Ferraro, 2002; Gibson, Bergen, & Piantadosi, 2013; Kuperberg, 2007; Sanford & Sturt, 2002). Despite these reassessments of the necessity of explicit syntactic structure building in interpretation, sentence comprehension remains an active field because the central questions—how perceivers turn a stream of input into an understanding of who did what to whom—have not gone away.

8.2 Measuring sentence processing

Questions concerning the nature of sentence processing are often operationalized as questions about the *difficulty* of sentence comprehension. It is a striking fact that comprehension usually seems effortless, but careful measurements can reveal that some sentences are harder for perceivers to understand than others. An account of these patterns of comprehension ease and difficulty is likely to lead to insight about the underlying comprehension processes. A central tenet of sentence processing research has been that "online" measures of sentence interpretation, collected as a sentence is being perceived, can provide information about comprehension processes that "offline" measures, such as sentence final comprehension questions or judgments of sentence plausibility, cannot (Marslen-Wilson & Tyler, 1975; Tyler & Marslen-Wilson, 1977). Psycholinguists therefore seek tightly time-locked measures of difficulty that can be collected continuously as a sentence is being perceived. These take a number of forms. The most common measures are measures of reading—either eye-tracking (Radach & Kennedy, 2013) or self-paced "moving window" reading in which participants press a key to read each new word of a sentence (Just, Carpenter, & Woolley, 1982). Eye-tracking also offers a behavioral measure of spoken sentence comprehension in "visual world" studies in which comprehenders hear speech while viewing and interacting with a scene (Henderson & Ferreira, 2004; Tanenhaus, Spivey-Knowlton, Eberhard, & Sedivy, 1995; Trueswell & Tanenhaus, 2005). Speed-accuracy tradeoff measures (Foraker & McElree, 2011; McElree, Foraker, & Dyer, 2003) are not quite so continuous but do measure processing at many points in a sentence. Physiological measures of difficulty are continuous and need not require an overt behavioral response during comprehension. These measures include event-related potentials (ERPs) to spoken or written sentences (Kaan, 2007; Kutas & Federmeier, 2011) and magnetoencephalography (MEG) (Dikker, Rabagliati, Farmer, & Pylkkänen, 2010). Other brain-imaging techniques provide information about localization of brain areas involved in language processing, but their timing parameters make them less useful for studies of the time course of comprehension processes (for review, see Osterhout, Kim, & Kuperberg, 2012).

Online assessments of comprehension in the lab are often augmented by one or more other measures. The advent of large speech and text corpora, including ones that are tagged for part of speech and in some cases parsed, allow researchers to examine the relative frequency of alternative words, syntactic structures, lexico-syntax combinations, and other measures that provide estimates of comprehenders' linguistic experiences (Roland, Dick, & Elman,

2007). Another method to estimate the probability of alternative sentence interpretations is to ask participants to rate or complete sentence fragments (McRae, Spivey-Knowlton, & Tanenhaus, 1998; Taraban & McClelland, 1988) and use these offline data to predict online measures such as reading times, thereby providing an estimate of how the probability of alternative interpretations influences comprehension difficulty. The power of large corpora is also harnessed in combinations of these methods—there are now corpora of eye movement data from newspaper reading (Kennedy, Hill, & Pynte, 2003) as well as large-scale normative data about verb-argument usage (for discussion, see Gahl, Jurafsky, & Roland, 2004; Roland & Jurafsky, 2002).

Computational models of sentence processing provide another route to understanding the nature of comprehension processes, via simulating human comprehension performance. Some of these models contain a component that builds an explicit syntactic structure (Vosse & Kempen, 2000, 2009), but most assume that hierarchical-like representations can be learned from more local relationships, provided that the model has an architecture (such as a recurrent network) that can "remember" longer stretches of linguistic input (see Frank & Bod, 2011, for discussion of several architectures). Some of these models are focused on semantic interpretation and thematic role assignment (St. John & McClelland, 1990), but the most common and best known computational models of sentence processing are simple recurrent networks (SRNs), originally developed by Elman (1990).

All of these measures provide insight into sentence comprehension only via a theory's "linking hypothesis" between the empirical data and hypothesized internal processes or computations. As we will see, important developments in the field in recent years have come about via reconsidering linking hypotheses between data and underlying processes. For example, long reading times in certain regions of ambiguous sentences have been variously viewed as reflecting syntactic reanalysis (Frazier & Rayner, 1982), competition or difficulty settling into an interpretation (MacDonald, Pearlmutter, & Seidenberg, 1994), or violation of prediction (Hale, 2001). Similarly, in ERP studies, some researchers have interpreted certain patterns of brain potentials as evidence for syntactic-semantic distinctions (Friederici, 2002), while others see evidence of much more shared processing (Kuperberg, 2007). Michael Tanenhaus has strongly advocated the need for making linking hypotheses more explicit in sentence processing (e.g., Tanenhaus, Magnuson, Dahan, & Chambers, 2000). Following Tanenhaus's advice, we use researchers' linking hypotheses as an organizing principle in discussing alternative models of sentence processing in the next section.

8.3 Sentence Processing Models

Most research in sentence processing is directed at answering one of two central questions: How do people cope with rampant ambiguity, especially syntactic ambiguity, as the linguistic signal unfolds over time? And how is sentence interpretation affected by variations in syntactic complexity? The hypothesized answers to these questions tend to gather in two broad theoretical approaches: those that emphasize innate processing mechanisms to cope with ambiguity and/or complexity, and those that emphasize the role of prior linguistic experience in sentence interpretation. Many of the theories discussed next appear in Figure 8.1, which arrays the various theoretical approaches on two dimensions. On the

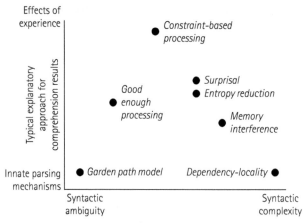

FIG. 8.1 Sentence processing models discussed in this chapter, arranged on two axes indicating the models' general emphasis in explanations for comprehension data and the type of materials most typically studied by proponents of the approach. The axes are meant only to express relative *emphases*, not absolute positions.

x-axis, we show the ambiguity-complexity dimension, indicating the degree to which a given theoretical approach has tended to study comprehension difficulty as a function of ambiguity in the sentence or as a function of syntactic complexity; placement in the middle of this axis reflects an approach that has investigated these two language domains roughly equally. The y-axis shows the general emphasis in explanation for comprehension difficulty. Such emphases are only relative: A theory that emphasizes the role of experience will still assume some innate components and vice versa. The figure is meant to provide a cast of characters for the following discussion and is not meant to capture all ways in which these theories differ, and of course it cannot capture changes in theoretical approaches over time.

One of the striking features in reviewing these models is the proliferation of approaches to the question of what causes comprehension difficulty. In the late twentieth century, the central debate was between modular approaches in which a syntactic parser was initially autonomous from knowledge of word meanings and discourse (Frazier's 1987 Garden Path model) and "constraint-based" accounts (MacDonald, Pearlmutter, & Seidenberg, 1994; Tanenhaus & Trueswell, 1995) and their precursors (Bever, 1970; Marslen-Wilson, 1975), in which syntactic and non-syntactic information richly combine to arrive at an interpretation (for additional sentence processing history, see Sanz, Laka, & Tanenhaus, 2013). Difficulty in the Garden Path model comes not from building an initial syntactic structure but from having to revise it if the initial analysis (which was developed without any access to word meaning or plausibility of alternative interpretations) turns out to be incorrect (Rayner, Carlson, & Frazier, 1983). The constraint-based models have no distinct stages of parsing, semantic interpretation, and reanalysis, and instead emphasize the rapid application of many sources of probabilistic information (Tanenhaus et al., 1995). Difficulty here arises when the probabilistic information conflicts, so that the system cannot "settle" on a single interpretation (MacDonald & Seidenberg, 2006).

Following those debates about modular vs. constraint-based accounts, many more approaches have bloomed. The proliferation of models reflects a typical and healthy progression in science (Preston, 2005), in which new data promote model development. Relatedly, variability in models has emerged in part as a reaction to researchers studying different languages or phenomena that seem to demand different sorts of approaches. For example, Ferreira and colleagues' Good Enough approach to sentence processing (Ferreira et al., 2002; Ferreira & Lowder, 2016; Slattery, Sturt, Christianson, Yoshida, & Ferreira, 2013; Sturt, Sanford, Stewart, & Dawydiak, 2004) focuses less on difficulty of interpretation and emphasizes evidence that incorrect interpretations of ambiguous or complex sentences appear to linger even after a complete syntactic analysis should have ruled them out (see also Christianson, Hollingworth, Halliwell, & Ferreira, 2001).

8.3.1 Innate mechanism vs. experience-driven accounts of ambiguity resolution

Hockett (1954, 1961) discussed how syntactic ambiguities, such as *old men and women*, where it is ambiguous whether this string has a syntactic structure [old [men and women]] in which *old* is modifying both *men* and *women* or the structure [[old men] and [women]] in which *old* modifies only *men* could pose difficulties for comprehenders. He coined the term *garden path* to mean an ambiguous sentence with a very unexpected resolution that gives rise to a conscious feeling of having been led astray. The most famous example in English, owing to Bever (1970), is *The horse raced past the barn fell*, in which it seems initially that the horse is racing, but in fact the meaning is equivalent to *The horse that was raced past the barn fell*. Bever pointed to the importance of lexical information in explaining why this ambiguity led to a garden path, but that claim remained controversial for decades (see discussion in Frazier, 1987; MacDonald et al., 1994; Rayner et al., 1983; Sanz et al., 2013; Trueswell, Tanenhaus, & Garnsey, 1994).

Another example of the contrast between innate and experience-based accounts of comprehension difficulty can be found in a different set of ambiguities (listed 1–3, next). These sentences have a final phrase that could potentially modify, or in syntactic terms, attach to, one of two earlier phrases. A fully ambiguous sentence is given in the (a) versions, and disambiguated versions are in (b–c), with some simplified bracket notation to convey the modification relationships. In the (b) versions, the final phrase modifies a nearby noun or verb, and so is called *local modification* or *low attachment* (because this modified phrase is low in the syntactic structure that the parser generates). The (c) examples show distant modification/high attachment.

1. a. Adverb modification ambiguity: Maria said that her cousins left yesterday.
   b. Local modification: Maria said [that her cousins will leave tomorrow].
   c. Distant modification: Maria will say [that her cousins left] tomorrow.
2. a. Prepositional phrase modification ambiguity: The cat on the rug with black stripes.
   b. Local modification: The cat [on the rug with black tassels].
   c. Distant modification: The cat [on the rug] with black whiskers.

3. a. Relative clause modification ambiguity: The servant of the actress who was on the balcony.
   b. Local modification: The servants [of the actress who was on the balcony].
   c. Distant modification: The servants [of the actress] who were on the balcony.

Although these three kinds of ambiguities have typically been studied separately, they have similar outcomes, at least in English, where comprehenders take longer to read the distant modification (c) sentences compared to the local modification (b) versions (Altmann, van Nice, Garnham, & Henstra, 1998; Cuetos & Mitchell, 1988; MacDonald & Thornton, 2009). Some researchers have explained these patterns with an innate sentence parsing mechanism that causes comprehenders to first attempt to build a syntactic structure in which the ambiguous phrase attaches to the most recent constituent, consistent with the local modification. Several variants of this hypothesis have been developed, the best known of which is the Late Closure principle (Frazier, 1987; for other formulations, see Gibson, Pearlmutter, Canseco-Gonzalez, & Hickok, 1996; Kimball, 1973). An attractive aspect of these approaches is that a single principle makes predictions for a variety of sentence types, and some variants gain additional theoretical mileage by linking this preference for recent constituents to independently established recency effects in memory (Gibson et al., 1996).

However, there is evidence that experience plays a central role in interpretation of these ambiguities. The most telling findings are that the local modification preference varies across languages, as Mitchell and colleagues have shown for the relative clause modification ambiguities as in (3) (Cuetos & Mitchell, 1988; Mitchell, Cuetos, Corley, & Brysbaert, 1995; see Thornton, MacDonald, & Gil, 1999 for cross-linguistic differences in prepositional phrase modification as in (2)). Focusing on the adverb modifications in (1), MacDonald & Thornton (2009) examined how the interpretation preferences could arise from comprehenders' prior experience, in this case the relative frequency of distant vs. local modification interpretations for these structures. Using corpus data (see also Sturt, Costa, Lombardo, & Frasconi, 2003), they found that while local modification interpretations were common in English, distant modification interpretations are rare. They described biases in the production system that promote use of alternative forms to convey the same meaning as a distant modification structure, as in *Maria will say tomorrow that her cousins left* (cf. example 1c). MacDonald and Thornton argued that comprehenders learn from these input patterns to interpret ambiguous modification sentences in favor of the more frequent local modification. Of course, an innate local modification bias and an experience-based approach are not inherently inconsistent, as there could be an innate bias (perhaps owing to a recency advantage in memory, Gibson et al., 1996), and this bias could be modulated by prior experience. However, there is also evidence that in some languages, distant modification is both more frequent and easier than local modification (Mitchell et al., 1995), which suggests that any inherent bias here can be overcome by experience with distant modifications. These results suggest that whatever one's position on innate syntactic processing operations, experience with prior linguistic and non-linguistic input strongly shapes online interpretation of these ambiguous sentences.

8.3.2 Syntactic complexity, memory, and experience

Dating from Miller and Chomsky (Chomsky & Miller, 1963; Miller & Chomsky, 1963), the link between syntactic complexity and comprehension difficulty has been via memory—syntactically more complex sentences are thought to place higher memory burdens on the comprehender, leading to higher comprehension difficulty. The classic contrast involves subject relative (also known as right-branching) clauses, as in (4a), and center-embedded or object relative clauses (4b). In English and most other languages studied to date, subject relatives are more difficult than object relatives (e.g., Gibson, 1998; King & Just, 1991; Traxler et al., 2002; see O'Grady, 2011, for review of some of the cross-linguistic and developmental data). Both syntactic complexity (via memory burdens) and experience explanations have been offered for these patterns.

(4a) Subject Relative: The girl$_i$ [that ___$_i$ kissed the woman] was ...
(4b) Object Relative: The girl$_i$ [that the woman kissed ___$_i$] was ...

Gibson (1998, 2002) hypothesized that memory is taxed when the head of a relative clause (*girl* in 4) must be linked to the "gap" in the relative clause, the position (shown with underlines in 4) where the head is extracted and where the head must be integrated with the verb *kissed*. Gibson's Dependency Locality Theory holds that the memory load to maintain the information of the unresolved dependencies varies with the distance between the head and the gap—longer intervals lead to larger memory burdens, and therefore higher processing difficulty. In (4), information of the head noun must be maintained over more intervening elements in object relatives than in subject relatives, and this additional memory load is hypothesized to be the source of the additional comprehension difficulty.

Another approach emphasizes severe restrictions on the size of working memory so that integration of different parts of a sentence during comprehension relies on rapid retrieval of information from long-term memory (Lewis & Vasishth, 2005; Lewis, Vasishth, & van Dyke, 2006; Martin, 2016; van Dyke & Johns, 2012; van Dyke & McElree, 2006). Sentence components serve as retrieval cues, for example *kissed* in (4) is a cue for retrieving *girl*. This characterization of memory predicts difficulty for long-distance dependencies as in (4), particularly when cues available at retrieval are not easily distinguishable from one another (e.g., *girl* and *woman* in (4b) are semantically similar and both related to *kissed*). Conflicts are alleviated when cues of the antecedents are made highly accessible at retrieval (Fedorenko, Woodbury, & Gibson, 2013). A related similarity-based interference account comes from Gordon and colleagues (Gordon, Hendrick, & Johnson, 2004; Gordon, Hendrick, Johnson, & Lee, 2006), who suggest that interference is lower when the two noun phrases involved in the relative clause are of different grammatical types (e.g., one a full noun and another a pronoun, as in *the girl that you kissed*). It is less clear that similarity-based interference extends to phonological similarity; some studies have found evidence that phonological similarity between sentence nouns or verbs can impair comprehension (Acheson & MacDonald, 2011), while other studies have suggested that phonological interference is not a major factor in comprehension difficulty (Kush, Johns, & van Dyke, 2015). Because phonological form, grammatical category, and meaning are all intercorrelated to some degree (e.g., Dikker et al., 2010), it is likely that similarity-based interference is multifaceted.

An experience-based approach to sentence complexity effects suggests that comprehenders have less experience interpreting syntactically more complex sentences than simpler ones, and that this difference in experience affects comprehension difficulty. Experience-based accounts were initially associated with ambiguity resolution, as just described; because relative clauses were often thought to be unambiguous, experience did not immediately suggest itself as a possible explanation for processing difficulty in relative clauses. More recently, however, ambiguities in relative clauses have been identified in several languages, including English (Gennari & MacDonald, 2008), Mandarin (Y. Hsiao & MacDonald, 2013, 2016; Jäger, Chen, Li, Lin, & Vasishth, 2015), Korean (Kwon, Gordon, Lee, Kluender, & Polinsky, 2010) and Japanese (Miyamoto & Tsujino, 2016). These findings show that that relative clauses cannot be a pure testing ground for effects of syntactic complexity. More generally, information theoretic accounts have noted that there is always uncertainty about upcoming sentence input (Hale, 2006; Levy, 2008), and in that sense we can never set aside ambiguity resolution processes as a potential explanation for comprehension difficulty. On this view, the x-axis in Figure 8.1, rather than being a continuum between ambiguity and complexity, could be seen as a range of different types of ambiguity.

Various types of complex sentences do differ substantially in their frequency and ambiguity in different languages. For example, English object relative clauses like (4b) are less common than subject relatives like (4a) (Roland et al., 2007). They are also more ambiguous: the start of the sentence in *The girl that the woman . . .* might continue as an object relative clause as in (4b) but might instead turn out to be some other structure, such as *The girl that the woman said was leaving/had been kissed by/wanted to give the prize to*. Both frequency and ambiguity affect comprehension difficulty (Gennari & MacDonald, 2008). More generally, much like more widely recognized syntactic ambiguities (MacDonald & Seidenberg, 2006), there is strong lexico-syntactic covariation in relative clauses that affects comprehension ease (Gennari & MacDonald, 2008; Reali, 2014; Reali & Christiansen, 2007; Wiechmann, 2015), meaning that there are ample routes for experience to influence relative clause comprehension.

Mandarin Chinese relative clauses have also been the subject of extensive work concerning their frequency, ambiguity, and memory demands. Mandarin and English relative clauses form an interesting comparison that unconfounds type of relative clause (subject vs. object) and the distance between dependent nouns and verbs: Whereas subject relatives have shorter dependency distance than object relatives in English, subject relatives have longer dependency distances than object relatives in Mandarin. If dependency distance is a key factor in comprehension difficulty, then Mandarin, with its reversed pattern of dependency distance, should also reverse the pattern of difficulty. Some studies have found exactly this reversal, with subject relatives being harder than object relatives (e.g., F. Hsiao & Gibson, 2003), even though subject relatives are more frequent than object relatives in Mandarin. Other studies have cast doubt on these results and have suggested that difficulty is not straightforwardly related to dependency distance. Instead ambiguity in the various relative clauses and comprehenders' experience with these sentences strongly affect comprehension difficulty (Y. Hsiao & MacDonald, 2013, 2016; Jäger et al., 2015; Lin & Bever, 2006). These results suggest that despite the strikingly different structure across Mandarin and English relative clauses, comprehenders' patterns of sensitivity to ambiguity and frequency may not be so different.

The debates between experience- and memory-based accounts are evolving to the point that researchers recognize that both experience and memory constraints will shape processing (Demberg & Keller, 2008; Staub, 2010). That development is a good one, because memory-only or experience-only approaches were never tenable hypotheses, given enormous evidence that readers (and comprehenders more generally) improve with experience, and considering the basic reasons why learning and practice are necessary to become a skilled language user: if computational (working memory) capacity were infinite, every sentence would be trivial to comprehend, and there would be no need to learn from past experience. Instead, comprehension is capacity-constrained, and longer-term learning is necessary to overcome the limitations on processing capacity.

This more ecumenical approach to working memory and experience still leaves numerous issues to investigate, however. A key question is whether the limitations on computational capacity are separable from effects of experience, yielding two independent effects on comprehension difficulty, or whether computational limitations such as attention, retrieval speed from the system's local traffic manager (LTM), and temporary maintenance, are themselves shaped by experience. Dating from Miller's (1956) discussion of chunking, where frequent sequences can be grouped together to form a single "unit" in temporary memory, we have known that experience can expand effective working memory capacity. Perhaps because chunking has often been viewed as reflecting deliberate practice (as in memorizing a telephone number), psycholinguists haven't always considered the extent to which the act of sentence comprehension itself could be expanding capacity, ultimately affecting subsequent sentence processing (though these ideas have long been at the heart of connectionist accounts of language processing, e.g., Elman, 1990; McClelland & Elman, 1986). Several developments suggest that this situation may change. First, there is now active consideration of the role of chunking in comprehension (Christiansen & Chater, 2016, and commentaries), where input is rapidly grouped into larger units—words, phrases, clauses, and so on. All sentence processing theories have assumed that such groupings form a principal component of sentence interpretation, but the explicit use of the term *chunking* may provide a more transparent link between effects of memory and comprehension experience. Second, there is now ample evidence of the effect of experience in sentence processing, as just documented. Third, prior exposure to sequences (regular patterns) also affects the capacity of working memory, even without any attempts to learn sequences or even awareness of them (Botvinick & Bylsma, 2005; G. Jones & Macken, 2015). Specifically, for the relative clauses we have just discussed, computational models and training studies with both natural and artificial languages show how experience with these sentences (MacDonald & Christiansen, 2002; Wells, Christiansen, Race, Acheson, & MacDonald, 2009) and other constructions with long-distance relationships (Amato & MacDonald, 2010; Elman, 1990; Wonnacott, Newport, & Tanenhaus, 2008) can change the effective capacity of a sentence processing network.

A related positive development is a growing consideration of the nature of both working memory and long-term memory retrieval processes in theories of sentence processing. While most comprehension research has drawn on a small number of approaches to working memory (e.g., Baddeley, 1992; Just & Carpenter, 1992), the range of working memory accounts is quite broad in that field, and there is actually significant controversy concerning the nature of verbal working memory, including effects of linguistic experience and other factors with important consequences for language use (Acheson & MacDonald, 2009; Cowan, 2005; Gupta & Tisdale, 2009; D. M. Jones, Macken, & Nicholls, 2004; G. Jones & Macken, 2015; Klem et al., 2015; MacDonald, 2016; MacDonald & Christiansen, 2002). Similarly, the nature of retrieval from long-term memory is a crucial component of interpreting language, but again, there has been relatively little attention to how theories of retrieval must shape models of sentence processing (McElree et al., 2003). Some sentence processing researchers now explicitly identify the memory framework being assumed and interpret comprehension data in that context (Fedorenko, Gibson, & Rohde, 2006; Lewis & Vasishth, 2005; Lewis et al., 2006; MacDonald & Christiansen, 2002; Martin, 2016; Patil, Vasishth, & Lewis, 2016; van Dyke & McElree, 2006). Given the centrality of memory or computational capacity in explanations of difficulty, a precise characterization of memory demands and the role of experience is crucial for any approach to individual differences in comprehension processes (Farmer et al., 2012; MacDonald & Christiansen, 2002; Misyak, Christiansen, & Tomblin, 2010; Prat, 2011; van Dyke, Johns, & Kukona, 2014). There are still significant disagreements here, but the explicit linking of the comprehension and memory work is an important step.

8.3.3 Learning mechanisms, probabilistic models, and computational models

The relationship between memory and sentence processing must incorporate accounts of learning. Encountering language or events in the world entails forming long-term memories (learning), and subsequently using this knowledge to understand language input requires retrieval of what has previously been learned. There are relatively few studies of learning in sentence processing, which is surprising given the centrality of experience in theories of comprehension processes. The focus on adult comprehension of relatively complex sentences means that child language acquisition studies focusing on very simple sentences are of limited use, but there are increasingly studies of comprehension in older children and more complex sentences, which can be integrated with adult research (O'Grady, 2011). Learning can also be studied in adults. Several researchers have used short-term training studies that manipulate people's experience with a natural or artificial language to investigate what can be learned from brief linguistic experience. Many of these studies have found that adults rapidly learn distributional information in their linguistic input, with downstream effects on subsequent sentence comprehension (Amato & MacDonald, 2010; Fine, Jaeger, Farmer, & Qian, 2013; Fraundorf & Jaeger, 2016; Kaschak & Glenberg, 2004; Perek & Goldberg, 2015; Wells et al., 2009; Wonnacott et al., 2008). Researchers have also asked about non-linguistic learning relevant to sentence processing, such as the statistics of events in the world, and the relationship between learning about events in the world and learning about the language that describes them (Altmann & Mirković, 2009; McRae & Matsuki, 2009; Willits, Amato, & MacDonald, 2015). While there has been comparatively little attention to precise learning mechanisms that support language learning and comprehension, studies of the role of sleep in implicit learning of language statistics (e.g., Mirković & Gaskell, 2016) may offer a route to further identify these mechanisms, because sleep processes may be more heavily involved in some kinds of learning than others.

A related learning question concerns the "grains" of learning and the time course of application of this knowledge: each new sentence changes a perceiver's linguistic experience at many levels—the abstract sentence structure, words, intonation contours, the discourse, the co-occurrences of these, and other factors. Which of these experiences yield a measurable change in online sentence processing and final sentence interpretation? Researchers have taken different positions here. Mitchell et al. (1995) argued that for the modification ambiguities like those in (1–3), online measures show evidence only of syntax-level learning (the frequency of alternative structures), independent of words in sentences. The claim of abstract syntactic learning can be linked to findings of syntactic priming in comprehension, in which comprehension of a given sentence type is slightly speeded after prior presentation of the same sentence structure (Kim, Carbary, & Tanenhaus, 2013; Tooley & Traxler, 2010). Since the effect can arise without overlap of words, it can be interpreted as implicit learning and generalization over abstract structures, with consequences for online sentence processing (Chang, Dell, Bock, & Griffin, 2000; Fine & Jaeger, 2013).

Of course, the existence of learning at one level does not exclude learning at other levels, and constraint-based models (or "experience-based accounts") have emphasized the fine-grained nature of learning and the interplay of information at many levels (see Spivey-Knowlton & Sedivy, 1995, for discussion of the modification ambiguities as in (1–3) and MacDonald & Seidenberg, 2006, for review more generally). The notion that so many factors have rapid effects on comprehension has led to objections that constraint-based accounts seem more like a laundry list of factors rather than a theory of sentence parsing mechanisms (Frazier, 1995). Put another way, "It is one thing to suggest that all of these different information sources interact ... but quite another to specify a psychologically plausible hypothesis about how they interact" (Rumelhart, 1977, p. 588). This point returns us to the multiplicity of theoretical positions in Figure 8.1 and range of phenomena addressed by each, recognizing that every theory emphasizes certain claims and phenomena and sets other issues aside. Researchers approach the question of integrating prior experience in sentence processing in several different ways.

On the one hand, proponents of constraint-based accounts use experiments and computational simulations to focus on learning and weighing of many probabilistic constraints, emphasizing how error-correcting learning algorithms gradually place greater weight on more informative information in the input, leading to increased accuracy of interpretation (Elman, 1990; MacDonald & Christiansen, 2002; Mayberry, Crocker, & Knoeferle, 2009; Tabor & Tanenhaus, 1999). These computational models aim to address online language comprehension but can seem divorced from empirical sentence processing studies with humans, because the models require simplifying assumptions or implementations such as limited vocabulary or impoverished semantics. An alternative is probabilistic accounts in which sentence interpretation proceeds via (unconscious) Bayesian rational inference to choose the most likely interpretation of the current input (see Jurafsky, 2003). Like constraint-based accounts, this approach assumes that abundant probabilistic information is learned from past experience, but the emphasis is different: Compared to constraint-based accounts, the probabilistic models have comparatively less focus on processing mechanisms, emphasizing instead comprehension as rational decision making (Anderson, 1989). Here, the linking hypothesis to comprehension data is via prediction: Bayes' rule, an equation for predicting the probability of input given prior context, provides "a principled and well-understood algorithm for weighing and combining evidence to choose interpretations in comprehension" (Jurafsky, 2003, p. 41). Bayesian accounts such as this are aimed at a computational level of analysis of cognition (Marr, 1982) that characterizes computations necessary for comprehension but without commitments to specific hypothesized processes at Marr's algorithmic level (see Lewis, Howes, & Singh, 2014 for discussion of these levels and intermediate cases). The relative value of Bayesian vs. more algorithmic-level theory development is a point of controversy (e.g., M. Jones & Love, 2011, and commentaries there; see also Jurafsky, 2003, specifically for language processes), but in some respects, the accounts may prove to be very similar (McClelland, 2013). Indeed, several researchers are developing approaches that are intermediate between computational and algorithmic levels, stemming from a consideration of the role of processing capacity in cognitive processes (Griffiths, Lieder, & Goodman, 2015; Lewis et al., 2014). That is, while in principle an infinite amount of data could be considered in making a rational inference, in practice humans' behavior likely reflects a much more restricted range of information. On this *bounded rationality* view (a term initially owing to Simon, 1955), theorizing must consider computational limitations, and attention to this perspective is another example of how theories of memory and computational capacity are central to accounts of sentence interpretation.

8.3.4 Information theoretic approaches

An important development in sentence comprehension is the application of Shannon's (1948) Information Theory to account for comprehension difficulty. This work is generally associated with Bayesian accounts, but as Hale (2016) notes, it is also compatible with other frameworks. Researchers who use this framework to investigate sentence comprehension seek to develop a linking hypothesis between uncertainty, specified by Shannon's original equation or related equations, and human behavior, typically measures of comprehension difficulty such as reading time. Experience is often a factor in calculations of uncertainty, in the sense that prior experience with sequences reduces uncertainty about what is likely upcoming in the linguistic signal, but these approaches do not necessarily commit to particular accounts of learning or sentence processing mechanisms. They are instead working at Marr's (1982) computational level of analysis, aiming to bring the rigor of a mathematical characterization of comprehension behavior to the study of sentence processing, without commitments to specific algorithmic-level processes such as ambiguity resolution or thematic role assignment.

Surprisal and Entropy Reduction are two approaches that make incremental (that is, word by word) predictions about online processing difficulty. A word's surprisal, its negative log probability given a prior context, is a mathematically specified linking hypothesis between comprehension difficulty and behavior such as reading times (Hale, 2001; Levy, 2008; Smith & Levy, 2013). Various formulations of surprisal exist, as researchers may choose different methods to specify the context (e.g., a probabilistic grammar, a corpus; see discussion in Hale, 2016) and a level over which surprisal is calculated, where unlexicalized surprisal is calculated over part of speech (e.g., the probability of a noun given a previous part-of-speech context), or lexicalized surprisal, in which the exact word is predicted from exact word context (Demberg & Keller, 2008; Frank, 2009). These decisions can reflect different theoretical commitments to claims about what "grain" of experience is a primary driver of comprehenders' reading behavior; Demberg and Keller found that unlexicalized surprisal made superior predictions of reading time patterns for English newspaper texts. Frank (2009) observed that an SRN making predictions on upcoming input (Elman, 1990) provides another calculation of surprisal, with better fits to human reading patterns in some types of constructions than at least some other formulations.

An alternative approach, not mutually exclusive with surprisal, is *entropy reduction*, which characterizes uncertainty in a different way (Hale, 2006, 2016). As comprehenders encounter new words in a sentence, these words can disambiguate the prior input; in that they are inconsistent with alternative syntactic parses that were viable earlier in the sentence. Constraining words thus reduce entropy (uncertainty) about upcoming input in the sentence. Words that eliminate many alternative parses and thus strongly reduce entropy are associated with higher comprehension difficulty, reflecting the view that these words require more parsing "work."

8.4 INCREMENTALITY, SETTLING, AND PREDICTION

In Charles Dickens' *A Christmas Carol*, Ebenezer Scrooge was visited by the ghosts of Christmas Past, Christmas Present, and Christmas Yet to Come. Each one gave Scrooge critical information, which, together with the knowledge that future events were not certain, transformed the lives of Scrooge and other characters. The processes in everyday sentence processing are more prosaic, but they too are controlled by representations of the past, present, and (uncertain) future. The linguistic signal arrives over time, meaning that interpretation processes could be operating at three time scales: (a) interpreting and integrating information that is just arriving into the developing representation of the input; (b) revising or elaborating the representation of past input in light of newly encountered information; and (c) predicting or preparing for future input. All researchers likely believe that these three processes all affect interpretations to some degree, but there has been a significant shift in theorizing over the years concerning the relative emphasis on past, present, and future processing.

8.4.1 Interpreting the present

The term incrementality is used in comprehension to refer to claims that the current input is being interpreted as soon as possible, and to the fullest extent possible. The "as soon as possible" component is seen as necessary to avoid decay of information in memory (see Christiansen & Chater, 2016, for review). Earlier proposals had suggested that processing was delayed until a clause boundary was reached, but these delay approaches faded in the face of evidence for extremely rapid speech processing (see Marslen-Wilson, Tyler, & Seidenberg, 1978). Modular processing perspectives have also implied certain amounts of processing delay, in that they hypothesize restrictions on information flow. For example, the Garden Path model (Frazier, 1987) posited two processing stages, so that syntactic information was processed first, and semantic and discourse information was delayed in its influence. Most accounts of lexical and syntactic interpretation have since done away with rigid processing stages. Instead, the relative time course in which various types of information are brought to bear on interpretation can be seen as a function of how rapidly they can be computed and their informativity (see Brown-Schmidt & Heller in this volume for a review on perspective-taking in incremental sentence comprehension). A useful illustration can be seen in Kawamoto's (1993) connectionist model of lexical ambiguity resolution, in which both bottom-up information and information from prior context exert constraint on the interpretation of the input immediately, and yet the effects of context tend to be weaker and delayed relative to bottom-up information. The bottom-up information tends to be inherently more constraining about the identity of a word, and Kawamoto's simulation illustrates how effects of informativeness can make a continuous process seem to have distinct stages.

8.4.2 Updating the past

The second aspect of incrementality is the degree to which the input is processed to the "fullest extent" possible. Initially controversy about this claim was tied to strictly serial and deterministic accounts, in which a single syntactic structure was adopted for the input, and where building a structure would be a full commitment and failing to build one (or building several, in parallel), would be the absence of commitment. In current probabilistic models, the interpretive mechanisms are thought to be in a probabilistic state, with belief updating as information accrues (Levy, Bicknell, Slattery, & Rayner, 2009). This view is consistent with earlier evidence that downstream context can refine the interpretation of earlier input (Connine & Clifton, 1987; MacDonald, 1994; Warren & Sherman, 1974). There is also good evidence that for both lexical and syntactic ambiguities, this updating does not completely obliterate interpretations that become highly unlikely in the face of new input, such as disambiguating words favoring another interpretation (Barton & Sanford, 1993; Ferreira et al., 2002; Patson, Darowski, Moon, & Ferreira, 2009; Sanford & Sturt, 2002; Slattery et al., 2013).

Indeed, we can ask whether interpretations are ever fully settled. An early example of this idea arose in interpretation of quantifier scope ambiguities, such as in *Every girl climbed a tree*, in which the mapping between girls and trees is uncertain—did every girl climb a different tree, all climb the same tree, or some other mapping? Fodor (1982) suggested that in the absence of strong context that demanded one interpretation, these ambiguities were not necessarily fully resolved. Intuitively, a similar phenomenon happens in interpretation of reference; if we overhear a bit of conversation containing *Tanya didn't say when she would leave*, it is possible to remain in a permanent state of uncertainty about who *Tanya* is or whether *she* refers to *Tanya* or someone else. Probabilistic models (Jurafsky, 2003; Levy et al., 2009) extend these ideas to all ambiguities. This state of affairs represents a contrast with language production, where the utterance plan must be settled by the time of execution, with a choice for one form over another (e.g., implicitly choosing to say *sofa* instead of *couch*).

Noisy channel. One reason why uncertainty about the past persists is that mistakes happen—people do misread or mishear input, and that possibility could shape behavior (Levy et al., 2009). Indeed, the possibility of mistakes and other "noise" in the communicative process (both literal noise and more metaphorical noise, such as inattention, misinterpretation, and so on) could itself be a factor in belief updating about sentence interpretation (Gibson et al., 2013).

8.4.3 Predicting the future

In the same way that there is a degree of uncertainty about the interpretation of prior input, there can be some degree of uncertainty about the nature of upcoming input; this is the sense in which many researchers use terms such as *prediction, expectation,* or *pre-activation* (Altmann & Mirković, 2009; Clark, 2013; Huettig & Mani, 2016; Kuperberg & Jaeger, 2016). Earlier approaches to prediction focused on the degree to which exact words could be predicted; since exact words were predicted very poorly except under very unusual circumstances, researchers were skeptical that prediction could be a major force in comprehension processes (see MacDonald & Seidenberg, 2006). However, prediction is much more than guessing upcoming words: the act of settling into an interpretation for previously encountered input amounts to a prediction that the upcoming input will be consistent with the ongoing probabilities (Kuperberg & Jaeger, 2016; Levy, 2008). Kuperberg and Jaeger also note that updating of the ongoing interpretation is happening at many more levels than the next word; there can be probabilistic predictions for upcoming phonemes, grammatical categories, prosodies, pitches, and many other types of information. The predictions need not be strictly linguistic, and Altmann and Mirković (2009) discuss how sentence comprehension is influenced by predictions over events in the world (e.g., after visits from two ghosts, Scrooge suspected a third was coming). The current focus on prediction in the literature, with a few exceptions (e.g., Ferreira & Lowder, 2016; Huettig & Mani, 2016) ascribes an increasingly important role to prediction, which may be in need of some error correction of its own. That is, brains may indeed be "prediction machines" (Clark, 2013, p. 181), but this does not mean that the central *goal* of the system is prediction. The goal is to interpret the actual input, and prediction is a component of the comprehender's toolkit that aids in that goal. This point is illustrated by a connectionist model developed by Allen and Seidenberg (1999), which was not trained to predict upcoming input but simply to represent the current input. Placed under time pressure, the network began to develop predictions of future input in the service of efficient interpretation of that input when it became the present.

8.5 THE RELATIONSHIP BETWEEN SENTENCE COMPREHENSION AND PRODUCTION

An important trend in sentence comprehension research is a revised consideration of the relationship between comprehension and production. As Meyer, Huettig, and Levelt (2016) note in their introduction to a special issue of *Journal of Memory and Language* on this topic, comprehension and production processes have traditionally been studied independently, but there are now several research approaches directly investigating the interaction between comprehension and production (see Chapter 20, this volume, for review). One possibility here is in the role of language production in verbal working memory, where some researchers have hypothesized that the maintenance and ordering of verbal information in working memory tasks are accomplished by the language production system, not some dedicated temporary memory store (Acheson & MacDonald, 2009; MacDonald, 2016). On this view, memory that is essential to interpreting language input could also be supported by internal production processes.

Another approach investigates the role of language production in prediction processes. In the previous section, prediction was seen as emergent from comprehension processes settling into an interpretation of the current and past input, but Pickering and Garrod (2007) have argued that the language production system has a central role in prediction during language comprehension. As Dell and Chang (2014) note, prediction of future input on the basis of the semantic representation of prior input is a top down process very like language production, in which a message guides the generation of words for an utterance. The claim here must be that the production system *supports* predictions during comprehension rather than production being the sole route of prediction, because our perceptual systems can generate predictions for actions that we cannot produce, as when we predict the trajectory of a bird's flight.

Prediction via language production can be seen as a specific example of prediction of others' actions more generally, and several groups have suggested that prediction of others' actions emerges from one's own action planning (Pickering & Garrod, 2014; Wolpert, Doya, & Kawato, 2003). Other traditions in joint action research hold that coordinated action, including expectations for others' actions, does not require full prediction via action or language production processes (Vesper, Butterfill, Knoblich, & Sebanz, 2010). Continued work in joint action should be informative about the role of production in comprehension, and this work should also be useful in expanding comprehension research, so often limited to reading texts, to more interactive processes involved in the joint action of conversation.

Another claim for interactions between comprehension and production is the Production, Distribution Comprehension (PDC) account (MacDonald, 1999, 2013), which links comprehension behavior to aspects of the production process over time. The PDC draws on production research to observe that there are typically many viable alternative forms (words, sentences, intonations, and so on) to convey a producer's message. The form that is actually settled on is driven in part by biases toward more easily produced forms, with the consequence that aspects of the language production architecture shape the distribution of sentences that are produced. This distribution in turn shapes comprehenders' linguistic experience, which affects comprehenders' interpretations of ambiguities and complex sentences such as relative clauses (Gennari & MacDonald, 2009; Y. Hsiao & MacDonald, 2016; Humphreys, Mirković, & Gennari, 2016; MacDonald & Thornton, 2009). On this view, if we want to understand comprehension processes via experience and patterns of sentence comprehension difficulty, then we must also address the nature of language production processes, where difficulty of production shapes distribution and ultimately difficulty of comprehension (see commentaries to MacDonald, 2013, for critiques and future directions).

8.6 Sentence processing yet to come

In an analysis of research trends in cognitive science, Cohen Priva and Austerweil (2015) developed models of publishing topics based on 34 years of papers in the journal *Cognition*. Their topics, extracted by a computational model using word patterns in the papers' titles and abstracts, identify some methodological shifts in the journal, such as the rise of eye-tracking methods with the introduction of the visual world paradigm in language comprehension research (Tanenhaus et al., 1995), and they chart interesting changes in how research is framed, with declining references to theories in abstracts, replaced by increasing mention of prior empirical results. The popularity of various research areas has also changed, and one of the most dramatic is "the fall of sentence processing," (p. 4), as evidenced by a sharp decline in articles aligning with the sentence processing topic that the model identified. This trend would seem to be very bad news for the field we have just been reviewing, but we think news of sentence processing's demise is premature, most obviously because it is implausible that a field would be disappearing just as one of its central methodologies (eye-tracking) is soaring. As always, it is important to check the linking hypotheses. Cohen Priva and Austerweil interpret the decline in the "theory" topic as a shift in how authors *frame* their research; the decline of use of words in the "theory" topic is not evidence of theories themselves leaving the pages of *Cognition*. We can apply a similar analysis to the "sentence processing" topic, namely that the field hasn't gone away but is now framed differently, so that the words that cohered to form the original topic (e.g., *sentence, syntactic, verb, structure, language, noun, processing*) no longer are dominant in the titles and abstracts of publications that are focused on the central themes of sentence comprehension identified in this chapter. The decline of specific topic words does likely reflect reduced focus on one theoretical approach: comprehension as requiring an explicit phrase structure during interpretation. We suspect that words capturing some of the other theoretical framings described in this chapter are likely to rise to the fore (e.g., *probabilistic, dependency, expectation, prediction, constraint, information, corpus*, and so on). If so, we could ask whether this different framing reflects different conceptualizations about what sentence processing research seeks to explain. Our impression is that researchers increasingly aim to investigate sentence-level comprehension in connection with other information or constraints, including reference, interactive conversations, event representations, production processes, memory limitations, learning, bilingualism, and others. These areas represent some primary future directions of the field; rather than a decline in sentence processing, we instead see a greater inclusiveness and interaction among comprehension processes.

References

Acheson, D. J., & MacDonald, M. C. (2009). Verbal working memory and language production: Common approaches to the serial ordering of verbal information. *Psychological Bulletin*, 135(1), 50–68.

Acheson, D. J., & MacDonald, M. C. (2011). The rhymes that the reader perused confused the meaning: Phonological effects during on-line sentence comprehension. *Journal of Memory and Language*, 65(2), 193–207.

Allen, J., & Seidenberg, M. S. (1999). The emergence of grammaticality in connectionist networks. In: MacWhinney, B. (Ed.), *The Emergence of Language* (pp. 115–51). Lawrence Erlbaum Associates, Mahwah, NJ.

Altmann, G. T. M., & Mirković, J. (2009). Incrementality and prediction in human sentence processing. *Cognitive Science*, 33(4), 583–609.

Altmann, G. T. M., van Nice, K. Y., Garnham, A., & Henstra, J.-A. (1998). Late closure in context. *Journal of Memory and Language*, 38(4), 459–84.

Amato, M. S., & MacDonald, M. C. (2010). Sentence processing in an artificial language: Learning and using combinatorial constraints. *Cognition*, 116(1), 143–8.

Anderson, J. R. (1989). A rational analysis of human memory. In: Roediger, H. L.III, & Craik, F. I. M. (Eds.), *Varieties of Memory and Consciousness: Essays in Honour of Endel Tulving* (pp. 195–210). Lawrence Erlbaum Associates, Hillsdale, NJ.

Baddeley, A. (1992). Working memory. *Science*, 255(5044), 556–9.

Barton, S. B., & Sanford, A. J. (1993). A case study of anomaly detection: Shallow semantic processing and cohesion establishment. *Memory & Cognition*, 21(4), 477–87.

Bever, T. G. (1970). The cognitive basis for linguistic structures. In: Hayes, J. R. (Ed.), *Cognition and the Development of Language* (pp. 279–362). John Wiley, New York, NY.

Botvinick, M., & Bylsma, L. M. (2005). Regularization in short-term memory for serial order. *Journal of Experimental Psychology: Learning, Memory, and Cognition*, 31(2), 351–8.

Chang, F., Dell, G. S., Bock, K., & Griffin, Z. M. (2000). Structural priming as implicit learning: A comparison of models of sentence production. *Journal of Psycholinguistic Research*, 29(2), 217–30.

Chomsky, N., & Miller, G. A. (1963). Introduction to the formal analysis of natural languages. In: Luce, R., Bush, R., & Galanter, E. (Eds.), *Handbook of Mathematical Psychology* (Vol. 2, pp. 269–322). Wiley, New York, NY.

Christiansen, M. H., & Chater, N. (2001). Finite models of infinite language: A connectionist approach to recursion. In: Christiansen, M. H., & Chater, N. (Eds.), *Connectionist Psycholinguistics*. (pp. 138–76). Ablex Publishing, Westport, CT.

Christiansen, M. H., & Chater, N. (2016). The now-or-never bottleneck: A fundamental constraint on language. *Behavioral and Brain Sciences*, 39, e62.

Christianson, K., Hollingworth, A., Halliwell, J. F., & Ferreira, F. (2001). Thematic roles assigned along the garden path linger. *Cognitive Psychology*, 42(4), 368–407.

Clark, A. (2013). Whatever next? Predictive brains, situated agents, and the future of cognitive science. *The Behavioral and Brain Sciences*, 36(3), 181–204.

Cohen Priva, U., & Austerweil, J. L. (2015). Analyzing the history of cognition using topic models. *Cognition*, 135, 4–9.

Connine, C. M., & Clifton, C. J. (1987). Interactive use of lexical information in speech perception. *Journal of Experimental Psychology: Human Perception and Performance*, 13(2), 291–9.

Cowan, N. (2005). *Working Memory Capacity*. Taylor & Francis, Oxford.

Cuetos, F., & Mitchell, D. C. (1988). Cross-linguistic differences in parsing: Restrictions on the use of the Late Closure strategy in Spanish. *Cognition*, 30(1), 73–105.

Dell, G. S., & Chang, F. (2014). The P-chain: Relating sentence production and its disorders to comprehension and acquisition. *Philosophical Transactions of the Royal Society of London B: Biological Sciences*, 369(1634), 20120394.

Demberg, V., & Keller, F. (2008). Data from eye-tracking corpora as evidence for theories of syntactic processing complexity. *Cognition*, 109(2), 193–210.

Dikker, S., Rabagliati, H., Farmer, T. A., & Pylkkänen, L. (2010). Early occipital sensitivity to syntactic category is based on form typicality. *Psychological Science*, 21, 629–34.

Elman, J. L. (1990). Finding structure in time. *Cognitive Science*, 14, 179–211.

Farmer, T. A., Misyak, J. B., Christiansen, M. H., Spivey, M., Joannisse, M., & McRae, K. (2012). Individual differences in sentence processing. In: Spivey, M., McRae, K., & Joanisse, M. (Eds.), *The Cambridge Handbook of Psycholinguistics* (Cambridge Handbooks in Psychology, pp. 353–64). Cambridge University Press, Cambridge.

Fedorenko, E., Gibson, E., & Rohde, D. (2006). The nature of working memory capacity in sentence comprehension: Evidence against domain-specific working memory resources. *Journal of Memory and Language*, 54(4), 541–53.

Fedorenko, E., Woodbury, R., & Gibson, E. (2013). Direct evidence of memory retrieval as a source of difficulty in non-local dependencies in language. *Cognitive Science*, 37(2), 378–94.

Ferreira, F., Bailey, K. G. D., & Ferraro, V. (2002). Good-enough representations in language comprehension. *Current Directions in Psychological Science*, 11(1), 11–15.

Ferreira, F., & Lowder, M. W. (2016). Prediction, information structure, and good-enough language processing. In: Ross, B. (Ed.), *Psychology of Learning & Motivation* (pp. 218–41). Elsevier, Amsterdam.

Fine, A. B., & Jaeger, T. F. (2013). Evidence for implicit learning in syntactic comprehension. *Cognitive Science*, 37(3), 578–91.

Fine, A. B., Jaeger, T. F., Farmer, T. A., & Qian, T. (2013). Rapid expectation adaptation during syntactic comprehension. *PloS One*, 8(10), e77661.

Fodor, J. D. (1982). The mental representation of quantifiers. In: Peters, S., & Saarinen, E. (Eds.), *Processes, Beliefs, and Questions* (pp. 129–164). Springer Netherlands, Amsterdam.

Foraker, S., & McElree, B. (2011). Comprehension of linguistic dependencies: Speed-accuracy tradeoff evidence for direct-access retrieval from memory. *Language and Linguistics Compass*, 5(11), 764–83.

Fossum, V., & Levy, R. (2012). Sequential vs. hierarchical syntactic models of human incremental sentence processing. In: *Proceedings of the 3rd Workshop on Cognitive Modeling and Computational Linguistics* (pp. 61–69). Association for Computational Linguistics. Available at: http://dl.acm.org.ezproxy.library.wisc.edu/citation.cfm?id=2390313

Frank, S. L. (2009). Surprisal-based comparison between a symbolic and a connectionist model of sentence processing. In: *Proceedings of the 31st Annual Conference of the Cognitive Science Society* (pp. 1139–1144). Citeseer. Available at: http://citeseerx.ist.psu.edu/viewdoc/download?doi=10.1.1.412.7397&rep=rep1&type=pdf

Frank, S. L., & Bod, R. (2011). Insensitivity of the human sentence-processing system to hierarchical structure. *Psychological Science*, 22(6), 829–34.

Fraundorf, S. H., & Jaeger, T. F. (2016). Readers generalize adaptation to newly-encountered dialectal structures to other unfamiliar structures. *Journal of Memory and Language*, 91, 28–58.

Frazier, L. (1987). Sentence processing: A tutorial review. In: Coltheart, M. (Ed.), *Attention and Performance XII* (pp. 559–86). Lawrence Erlbaum Associates, Inc. Available at: http://doi.apa.org/psycinfo/1987-98557-025

Frazier, L. (1995). Constraint satisfaction as a theory of sentence processing. *Journal of Psycholinguistic Research*, 24(6), 437–68.

Frazier, L., & Clifton, C. (1996). *Construal*. The MIT Press, Cambridge, MA.

Frazier, L., & Fodor, J. D. (1978). The sausage machine: A new two-stage parsing model. *Cognition*, 6(4), 291–325.

Frazier, L., & Rayner, K. (1982). Making and correcting errors during sentence comprehension: Eye movements in the analysis of structurally ambiguous sentences. *Cognitive Psychology*, 14(2), 178–210.

Friederici, A. D. (2002). Towards a neural basis for auditory sentence processing. *Trends in Cognitive Sciences*, 6(2), 78–84.

Gahl, S., Jurafsky, D., & Roland, D. (2004). Verb subcategorization frequencies: American English corpus data, methodological studies, and cross-corpus comparisons. *Behavior Research Methods, Instruments, & Computers*, 36(3), 432–43.

Gennari, S. P., & MacDonald, M. C. (2008). Semantic indeterminacy in object relative clauses. *Journal of Memory and Language*, 58(4), 161–87.

Gennari, S. P., & MacDonald, M. C. (2009). Linking production and comprehension processes: The case of relative clauses. *Cognition*, 111(1), 1–23.

Gibson, E. (1998). Linguistic complexity: Locality of syntactic dependencies. *Cognition, 68*, 1–76.

Gibson, E., Bergen, L., & Piantadosi, S. T. (2013). Rational integration of noisy evidence and prior semantic expectations in sentence interpretation. *Proceedings of the National Academy of Sciences of the United States of America, 110*(20), 8051–6.

Gibson, E., Pearlmutter, N., Canseco-Gonzalez, E., & Hickok, G. (1996). Recency preference in the human sentence processing mechanism. *Cognition, 59*(1), 23–59.

Gordon, P. C., Hendrick, R., & Johnson, M. (2004). Effects of noun phrase type on sentence complexity. *Journal of Memory and Language, 51*(1), 97–114.

Gordon, P. C., Hendrick, R., Johnson, M., & Lee, Y. (2006). Similarity-based interference during language comprehension: Evidence from eye tracking during reading. *Journal of Experimental Psychology: Learning, Memory, and Cognition, 32*(6), 1304.

Griffiths, T. L., Lieder, F., & Goodman, N. D. (2015). Rational use of cognitive resources: Levels of analysis between the computational and the algorithmic. *Topics in Cognitive Science, 7*(2), 217–29.

Gupta, P., & Tisdale, J. (2009). Does phonological short-term memory causally determine vocabulary learning? Toward a computational resolution of the debate. *Journal of Memory and Language, 61*(4), 481–502.

Hale, J. (2001). A probabilistic Earley parser as a psycholinguistic model. In: *Proceedings of the second meeting of the North American Chapter of the Association for Computational Linguistics on Language Technologies* (pp. 1–8). Association for Computational Linguistics. Available at: http://dl.acm.org.ezproxy.library.wisc.edu/citation.cfm?id=1073357

Hale, J. (2006). Uncertainty about the rest of the sentence. *Cognitive Science, 30*(4), 643–72.

Hale, J. (2016). Information-theoretical complexity metrics: Information-theoretical complexity metrics. *Language and Linguistics Compass, 10*, 397–412.

Henderson, J. M., & Ferreira, F. (2004). *The Interface of Language, Vision, and Action: Eye Movements and the Visual World*. Psychology Press, New York, NY.

Hockett, C. F. (1954). Two models of grammatical description. *Word, 10*(2–3), 210–34.

Hockett, C. F. (1961). Grammar for the hearer. In: *Proceedings of Symposia in Applied Mathematics* (Vol. 12, pp. 220–236). New York, NY.

Hsiao, F., & Gibson, E. (2003). Processing relative clauses in Chinese. *Cognition, 90*(1), 3–27.

Hsiao, Y., & MacDonald, M. C. (2013). Experience and generalization in a connectionist model of Mandarin Chinese relative clause processing. *Frontiers in Psychology, 4*, 767.

Hsiao, Y., & MacDonald, M. C. (2016). Production predicts comprehension: Animacy effects in Mandarin relative clause processing. *Journal of Memory and Language, 89*, 87–109.

Huettig, F., & Mani, N. (2016). Is prediction necessary to understand language? Probably not. *Language, Cognition and Neuroscience, 31*(1), 19–31.

Humphreys, G. F., Mirković, J., & Gennari, S. P. (2016). Similarity-based competition in relative clause production and comprehension. *Journal of Memory and Language, 89*, 200–21.

Jäger, L., Chen, Z., Li, Q., Lin, C.-J. C., & Vasishth, S. (2015). The subject-relative advantage in Chinese: Evidence for expectation-based processing. *Journal of Memory and Language, 79*, 97–120.

Jones, D. M., Macken, W. J., & Nicholls, A. P. (2004). The phonological store of working memory: Is it phonological and is it a store? *Journal of Experimental Psychology: Learning, Memory, and Cognition, 30*(3), 656–74.

Jones, G., & Macken, B. (2015). Questioning short-term memory and its measurement: Why digit span measures long-term associative learning. *Cognition, 144*, 1–13.

Jones, M., & Love, B. C. (2011). Bayesian fundamentalism or enlightenment? On the explanatory status and theoretical contributions of Bayesian models of cognition. *Behavioral and Brain Sciences, 34*(4), 169–88.

Jurafsky, D. (2003). Probabilistic modeling in psycholinguistics: Linguistic comprehension and production. In: Bod, R., Hay, J., & Jannedy, S. (Eds.), *Probabilistic Linguistics* (pp. 39–95). MIT Press, Cambridge.

Just, M. A., & Carpenter, P. A. (1992). A capacity theory of comprehension: Individual differences in working memory. *Psychological Review, 99*(1), 122.

Just, M. A., Carpenter, P. A., & Woolley, J. D. (1982). Paradigms and processes in reading comprehension. *Journal of Experimental Psychology: General, 111*(2), 228–38.

Kaan, E. (2007). Event-related potentials and language processing: A brief overview. *Language and Linguistics Compass, 1*(6), 571–91.

Kaschak, M. P., & Glenberg, A. M. (2004). This construction needs learned. *Journal of Experimental Psychology: General, 133*(3), 450.

Kawamoto, A. H. (1993). Nonlinear dynamics in the resolution of lexical ambiguity: A parallel distributed processing account. *Journal of Memory and Language, 32*(4), 474–516.

Kennedy, A., Hill, R., & Pynte, J. (2003). The Dundee corpus. In: *Proceedings of the 12th European conference on eye movement*. University of Dundee, Dundee.

King, J., & Just, M. A. (1991). Individual differences in syntactic processing: The role of working memory. *Journal of Memory and Language, 30*(5), 580–602.

Kim, C. S., Carbary, K. M., & Tanenhaus, M. K. (2013). Syntactic priming without lexical overlap in reading comprehension. *Language and Speech, 57*(Pt 2), 181–95.

Kimball, J. (1973). Seven principles of surface structure parsing in natural language. *Cognition, 2*(1), 15–47.

Klem, M., Melby-Lervåg, M., Hagtvet, B., Lyster, S.-A. H., Gustafsson, J.-E., & Hulme, C. (2015). Sentence repetition is a measure of children's language skills rather than working memory limitations. *Developmental Science, 18*, 146–54.

Kuperberg, G. R. (2007). Neural mechanisms of language comprehension: Challenges to syntax. *Brain Research, 1146*, 23–49.

Kuperberg, G. R., & Jaeger, T. F. (2016). What do we mean by prediction in language comprehension? *Language, Cognition and Neuroscience, 31*(1), 32–59.

Kush, D., Johns, C. L., & van Dyke, J. A. (2015). Identifying the role of phonology in sentence-level reading. *Journal of Memory and Language, 79–80*, 18–29.

Kutas, M., & Federmeier, K. D. (2011). Thirty years and counting: Finding meaning in the N400 component of the event related brain potential (ERP). *Annual Review of Psychology, 62*, 621.

Kwon, N., Gordon, P. C., Lee, Y., Kluender, R., & Polinsky, M. (2010). Cognitive and linguistic factors affecting subject/object asymmetry: An eye-tracking study of prenominal relative clauses in Korean. *Language, 86*(3), 546–82.

Levy, R. (2008). Expectation-based syntactic comprehension. *Cognition, 106*(3), 1126–77.

Levy, R., Bicknell, K., Slattery, T., & Rayner, K. (2009). Eye movement evidence that readers maintain and act on uncertainty about past linguistic input. *Proceedings of the National Academy of Sciences of the United States of America, 106*(50), 21086–90.

Lewis, R. L., Howes, A., & Singh, S. (2014). Computational rationality: Linking mechanism and behavior through bounded utility maximization. *Topics in Cognitive Science, 6*(2), 279–311.

Lewis, R. L., & Vasishth, S. (2005). An activation-based model of sentence processing as skilled memory retrieval. *Cognitive Science, 29*(3), 375–419.

Lewis, R. L., Vasishth, S., & van Dyke, J. A. (2006). Computational principles of working memory in sentence comprehension. *Trends in Cognitive Sciences*, *10*(10), 447–54.

Lin, C.-J. C., & Bever, T. G. (2006). Subject preference in the processing of relative clauses in Chinese. In: Baumer, D., Montero, D., & Scanlon, M. (Eds.), *Proceedings of the 25th West Coast Conference on Formal Linguistics* (pp. 254–60). Cascadilla Proceedings Project, Somerville, MA.

MacDonald, M. C. (1994). Probabilistic constraints and syntactic ambiguity resolution. *Language and Cognitive Processes*, *9*(2), 157–201.

MacDonald, M. C. (1999). Distributional information in language comprehension, production, and acquisition: Three puzzles and a moral. In: MacWhinney, B. (Ed.), *The Emergence of Language* (pp. 177–96). Lawrence Erlbaum Associates, Mahwah, NJ.

MacDonald, M. C. (2013). How language production shapes language form and comprehension. *Frontiers in Psychology*, *4*, 226.

MacDonald, M. C. (2016). Speak, act, remember: The language-production basis of serial order and maintenance in verbal memory. *Current Directions in Psychological Science*, *25*(1), 47–53.

MacDonald, M. C., & Christiansen, M. H. (2002). Reassessing working memory: Comment on Just and Carpenter (1992) and Waters and Caplan (1996). *Psychological Review*, *109*(1), 35–54; discussion 55–74.

MacDonald, M. C., Pearlmutter, N. J., & Seidenberg, M. S. (1994). The lexical nature of syntactic ambiguity resolution. *Psychological Review*, *101*(4), 676–703.

MacDonald, M. C., & Seidenberg, M. S. (2006). Constraint satisfaction accounts of lexical and sentence comprehension. In: Traxler, M. J., & Gernsbacher, M. A. (Eds.), *Handbook of Psycholinguistics* (2nd Edition) (pp. 581–611). Academic Press, New York, NY.

MacDonald, M. C., & Thornton, R. (2009). When language comprehension reflects production constraints: Resolving ambiguities with the help of past experience. *Memory & Cognition*, *37*(8), 1177–86.

Marr, D. (1982). *Vision: A Computational Investigation into the Human Representation and Processing of Visual Information*. The MIT Press, Cambridge, MA.

Marslen-Wilson, W. D. (1975). Sentence perception as an interactive parallel process. *Science*, *189*(4198), 226–8.

Marslen-Wilson, W. D., Tyler, L. K., & Seidenberg, M. (1978). Sentence processing and the clause boundary. In: Levelt, W. J. M., & Flores D'Arcais, G. B. (Eds.), *Studies in the Perception of Language* (pp. 219–46). John Wiley & Sons, Chichester.

Marslen-Wilson, W., & Tyler, L. K. (1975). Processing structure of sentence perception. *Nature*, *257*, 784–6.

Martin, A. E. (2016). Language processing as cue integration: Grounding the psychology of language in perception and neurophysiology. *Language Sciences*, *7*, 120.

Mayberry, M. R., Crocker, M. W., & Knoeferle, P. (2009). Learning to attend: A connectionist model of situated language comprehension. *Cognitive Science*, *33*(3), 449–96.

McClelland, J. L. (2013). Integrating probabilistic models of perception and interactive neural networks: A historical and tutorial review. *Frontiers in Language Sciences*, *4*, 503.

McClelland, J. L., & Elman, J. L. (1986). The TRACE model of speech perception. *Cognitive Psychology*, *18*(1), 1–86.

McElree, B., Foraker, S., & Dyer, L. (2003). Memory structures that subserve sentence comprehension. *Journal of Memory and Language*, *48*(1), 67–91.

McRae, K., & Matsuki, K. (2009). People use their knowledge of common events to understand language, and do so as quickly as possible. *Language and Linguistics Compass*, 3(6), 1417–29.

McRae, K., Spivey-Knowlton, M. J., & Tanenhaus, M. K. (1998). Modeling the influence of thematic fit (and other constraints) in on-line sentence comprehension. *Journal of Memory and Language*, 38(3), 283–312.

Meyer, A. S., Huettig, F., & Levelt, W. J. (2016). Same, different, or closely related: What is the relationship between language production and comprehension? *Journal of Memory and Language*, 89, 1–7.

Miller, G. A. (1956). The magical number seven, plus or minus two: Some limits on our capacity for processing information. *Psychological Review*, 63(2), 81–97.

Miller, G. A., & Chomsky, N. (1963). Finitary models of language users. In R. Luce, R. Bush, & Galanter (Eds.), *Handbook of Mathematical Psychology* (Vol. 2, pp. 419–91). Wiley, New York, NY.

Mirković, J., & Gaskell, M. G. (2016). Does sleep improve your grammar? Preferential consolidation of arbitrary components of new linguistic knowledge. *PloS One*, 11(4), e0152489.

Misyak, J. B., Christiansen, M. H., & Tomblin, J. B. (2010). On-line individual differences in statistical learning predict language processing. *Frontiers in Psychology*, 1, 31.

Mitchell, D. C., Cuetos, F., Corley, M. M. B., & Brysbaert, M. (1995). Exposure-based models of human parsing: Evidence for the use of coarse-grained (nonlexical) statistical records. *Journal of Psycholinguistic Research*, 24(6), 469–88.

Miyamoto, E. T., & Tsujino, K. (2016). Subject relative clauses are easier in Japanese regardless of working memory and expectation. Presented at the The Japanese Society for Language Sciences 2016 Conference.

O'Grady, W. (2011). Relative clauses: Processing and acquisition. In: Kidd, E. (Ed.), *The Acquisition of Relative Clauses: Processing, Typology and Function* (pp. 13–38). John Benjamins, Amsterdam.

Osterhout, L., Kim, A., & Kuperberg, G. R. (2012). The neurobiology of sentence comprehension. In: Spivey, M., Joannisse, M., McCrae, K. (Eds.), *The Cambridge Handbook of Psycholinguistics* (pp. 365–89). Cambridge University Press, Cambridge.

Patil, U., Vasishth, S., & Lewis, R. L. (2016). Retrieval interference in syntactic processing: The case of reflexive binding in English. *Frontiers in Psychology*, 7, 329.

Patson, N. D., Darowski, E. S., Moon, N., & Ferreira, F. (2009). Lingering misinterpretations in garden-path sentences: Evidence from a paraphrasing task. *Journal of Experimental Psychology: Learning, Memory, and Cognition*, 35(1), 280–5.

Perek, F., & Goldberg, A. E. (2015). Generalizing beyond the input: The functions of the constructions matter. *Journal of Memory and Language*, 84, 108–27.

Pickering, M. J., & Garrod, S. (2007). Do people use language production to make predictions during comprehension? *Trends in Cognitive Sciences*, 11(3), 105–10.

Pickering, M. J., & Garrod, S. (2014). Self-, other-, and joint monitoring using forward models. *Frontiers in Human Neuroscience*, 8, 132.

Prat, C. S. (2011). The brain basis of individual differences in language comprehension abilities. *Language and Linguistics Compass*, 5(9), 635–49.

Preston, C. J. (2005). Pluralism and naturalism: Why the proliferation of theories is good for the mind. *Philosophical Psychology*, 18(6), 715–35.

Radach, R., & Kennedy, A. (2013). Eye movements in reading: Some theoretical context. *The Quarterly Journal of Experimental Psychology*, 66(3), 429–52.

Rayner, K., Carlson, M., & Frazier, L. (1983). The interaction of syntax and semantics during sentence processing: Eye movements in the analysis of semantically biased sentences. *Journal of Verbal Learning and Verbal Behavior*, 22(3), 358–74.

Reali, F. (2014). Frequency affects object relative clause processing: Some evidence in favor of usage-based accounts. *Language Learning*, 64(3), 685–714.

Reali, F., & Christiansen, M. H. (2007). Word chunk frequencies affect the processing of pronominal object-relative clauses. *Quarterly Journal of Experimental Psychology (2006)*, 60(2), 161–70.

Roland, D., Dick, F., & Elman, J. L. (2007). Frequency of basic English grammatical structures: A corpus analysis. *Journal of Memory and Language*, 57(3), 348–79.

Roland, D., & Jurafsky, D. (2002). Verb sense and verb subcategorization probabilities. In: Merlo, P., & Stevenson, S. (Eds.), *The Lexical Basis of Sentence Processing: Formal, Computational, and Experimental Issues* (Vol. 4, pp. 325–45). John Benjamins Publishing, Amsterdam.

Rumelhart, D. E. (1977). Toward an interactive model of reading. In: Dornic, S. (Ed.), *Attention and Performance VI* (pp. 572–603). Lawrence Erlbaum Associates, Hillsdale, NJ.

Sanford, A. J., & Sturt, P. (2002). Depth of processing in language comprehension: Not noticing the evidence. *Trends in Cognitive Sciences*, 6(9), 382–6.

Sanz, M., Laka, I., & Tanenhaus, M. K. (2013). Sentence comprehension before and after 1970: Topics, debates, and techniques. *Language Down the Garden Path: The Cognitive and Biological Basis for Linguistic Structures*, 4, 81.

Shannon, C. E. (1948). A mathematical theory of communication. *Bell System Technical Journal*, 27, 379–423, 623–56.

Simon, H. A. (1955). A behavioral model of rational choice. *The Quarterly Journal of Economics*, 69(1), 99.

Slattery, T. J., Sturt, P., Christianson, K., Yoshida, M., & Ferreira, F. (2013). Lingering misinterpretations of garden path sentences arise from competing syntactic representations. *Journal of Memory and Language*, 69(2), 104–20.

Smith, N. J., & Levy, R. (2013). The effect of word predictability on reading time is logarithmic. *Cognition*, 128(3), 302–19.

Spivey-Knowlton, M., & Sedivy, J. C. (1995). Resolving attachment ambiguities with multiple constraints. *Cognition*, 55(3), 227–67.

St. John, M. F., & McClelland, J. L. (1990). Learning and applying contextual constraints in sentence comprehension. *Artificial Intelligence*, 46(1), 217–57.

Staub, A. (2010). Eye movements and processing difficulty in object relative clauses. *Cognition*, 116(1), 71–86.

Sturt, P., Costa, F., Lombardo, V., & Frasconi, P. (2003). Learning first-pass structural attachment preferences with dynamic grammars and recursive neural networks. *Cognition*, 88(2), 133–69.

Sturt, P., Sanford, A. J., Stewart, A., & Dawydiak, E. (2004). Linguistic focus and good-enough representations: An application of the change-detection paradigm. *Psychonomic Bulletin & Review*, 11(5), 882–8.

Tabor, W., & Tanenhaus, M. K. (1999). Dynamical models of sentence processing. *Cognitive Science*, 23(4), 491–515.

Tanenhaus, M. K., Magnuson, J. S., Dahan, D., & Chambers, C. (2000). Eye movements and lexical access in spoken-language comprehension: Evaluating a linking hypothesis between fixations and linguistic processing. *Journal of Psycholinguistic Research*, 29(6), 557–80.

Tanenhaus, M. K., Spivey-Knowlton, M. J., Eberhard, K. M., & Sedivy, J. C. (1995). Integration of visual and linguistic information in spoken language comprehension. *Science, 268*(5217), 1632–4.

Tanenhaus, M. K., & Trueswell, J. C. (1995). Sentence comprehension. In: Miller, J. L., & Eimas, P. D. (Eds.), *Handbook of Perception and Cognition* (Vol. 11: Speech Language and Communication, pp. 217–62). Academic Press, San Diego, CA.

Taraban, R., & McClelland, J. L. (1988). Constituent attachment and thematic role assignment in sentence processing: Influences of content-based expectations. *Journal of Memory and Language, 27*(6), 597–632.

Thornton, R., MacDonald, M. C., & Gil, M. (1999). Pragmatic constraint on the interpretation of complex noun phrases in Spanish and English. *Journal of Experimental Psychology: Learning, Memory, and Cognition, 25*(6), 1347–65.

Tooley, K. M., & Traxler, M. J. (2010). Syntactic priming effects in comprehension: A critical review. *Language and Linguistics Compass, 4*(10), 925–37.

Traxler, M. J., Morris, R. K., & Seely, R. E. (2002). Processing subject and object relative clauses: Evidence from eye movements. *Journal of Memory and Language, 47*(1), 69–90.

Trueswell, J. C., & Tanenhaus, M. K. (2005). *Approaches to Studying World-Situated Language Use*. MIT Press, Cambridge, MA.

Trueswell, J. C., Tanenhaus, M. K., & Garnsey, S. M. (1994). Semantic influences on parsing: Use of thematic role information in syntactic ambiguity resolution. *Journal of Memory and Language, 33*(3), 285–318.

Tyler, L. K., & Marslen-Wilson, W. D. (1977). The on-line effects of semantic context on syntactic processing. *Journal of Verbal Learning and Verbal Behavior, 16*(6), 68392.

van Dyke, J. A., & Johns, C. L. (2012). Memory interference as a determinant of language comprehension. *Language and Linguistics Compass, 6*(4), 193–211.

van Dyke, J. A., Johns, C. L., & Kukona, A. (2014). Low working memory capacity is only spuriously related to poor reading comprehension. *Cognition, 131*(3), 373–403.

van Dyke, J. A., & McElree, B. (2006). Retrieval interference in sentence comprehension. *Journal of Memory and Language, 55*(2), 157–66.

Vesper, C., Butterfill, S., Knoblich, G., & Sebanz, N. (2010). A minimal architecture for joint action. *Neural Networks: The Official Journal of the International Neural Network Society, 23*(8–9), 998–1003.

Vosse, T., & Kempen, G. (2000). Syntactic structure assembly in human parsing: A computational model based on competitive inhibition and a lexicalist grammar. *Cognition, 75*(2), 105–43.

Vosse, T., & Kempen, G. (2009). The Unification Space implemented as a localist neural net: Predictions and error-tolerance in a constraint-based parser. *Cognitive Neurodynamics, 3*(4), 331–46.

Warren, R. M., & Sherman, G. L. (1974). Phonemic restorations based on subsequent context. *Perception & Psychophysics, 16*(1), 150–6.

Wells, J. B., Christiansen, M. H., Race, D. S., Acheson, D. J., & MacDonald, M. C. (2009). Experience and sentence processing: Statistical learning and relative clause comprehension. *Cognitive Psychology, 58*(2), 250–71.

Wiechmann, D. (2015). *Understanding Relative Clauses: A Usage-Based View on the Processing of Complex Constructions* (Vol. 268). Walter de Gruyter GmbH & Co KG, Berlin.

Willits, J. A., Amato, M. S., & MacDonald, M. C. (2015). Language knowledge and event knowledge in language use. *Cognitive Psychology, 78*, 1–27.

Wolpert, D. M., Doya, K., & Kawato, M. (2003). A unifying computational framework for motor control and social interaction. *Philosophical Transactions of the Royal Society of London B: Biological Sciences, 358*(1431), 593–602.

Wonnacott, E., Newport, E. L., & Tanenhaus, M. K. (2008). Acquiring and processing verb argument structure: Distributional learning in a miniature language. *Cognitive Psychology, 56*(3), 165–209.

CHAPTER 9

TEXT COMPREHENSION

EVELYN C. FERSTL

9.1 Introduction

In our everyday lives we are constantly engaged in language comprehension, and most of it takes place in an extended context. We skim a newspaper article, listen to the radio, watch a movie, engage in a dinner conversation, study a textbook chapter, or read a novel for entertainment. Thus, what we hear or read in a particular moment needs to be interpreted in light of what was said before or what we already know about the topic. In psycholinguistics, these comprehension processes are subsumed under the label text comprehension or discourse comprehension.

The goal of this chapter is to give an overview of the field and to point the interested reader to recent developments. In the first part, I will provide the theoretical background and introduce basic concepts that explicate how text comprehension differs from language processing on the word and sentence level. For the second part, I have selected three of the most vital research domains within text comprehension research that reflect its multidisciplinary nature. The first subsection is devoted to cognitive psychology, particularly to the question of how memory and attention influence text comprehension. The second subsection is concerned with educational research, an ever-expanding applied field whose importance is beyond question. The ability to extract information from written text and spoken discourse is the basis of advanced learning. The third research domain is the neuroscience of text comprehension. The availability of neuroimaging methods has greatly extended the experimental toolbox, and some neuroscientific findings have the potential to make us reconsider previous theoretical distinctions. To conclude the chapter, I provide a short sketch of recent methodological advances that provide novel approaches for future research.

9.2 Concepts and theoretical background

Text or discourse comprehension is often used synonymously with "higher level language comprehension" or "language processing in context," indicating that the current sentence or utterance is to be understood embedded in a discourse context or a communicative context. Defined as such, linguistic phenomena traditionally put into the domain of pragmatics, for example metaphors, verbal humor, irony, or dialogue, are also part of text comprehension research. These topics are covered in separate chapters in this volume (Chapters 26 and 27).

Texts are defined as (written) language units of more than one sentence that have a coherent structure and that serve a communicative function. *Discourse*, in contrast, is often used when texts are presented auditorily, or as the more general term including both written and spoken language. Text genres include narrative texts (e.g., stories, verbal jokes, fairy tales, novels), expository texts (e.g., newspaper articles, textbook chapters), or procedural texts (e.g., recipes, manuals). Other genres, such as argumentative texts (e.g., essays, commentaries, political speeches, sermons) or literary texts (e.g., poems, short stories, novels) have been studied as well, but are also beyond the scope of this chapter (Busselle & Bilandzic, 2008; Willems & Jacobs, 2016).

A vast majority of studies on text comprehension use visual materials (i.e., written texts). However, most researchers make the assumption (at least implicitly), that the processes contributing to comprehension are in principle modality general and apply both during the comprehension of spoken and written language. In cross-modal lexical decision tasks, for instance, the researcher combines spoken texts with written probe words for methodological reasons only, not because there are modality-specific hypotheses about processing. Neuroimaging studies directly comparing the comprehension of written and spoken language confirm that in addition to modality-specific activations of the perceptual systems, there are specific regions associated with the interpretation and integration of text information on a higher level (Regev, Honey, Simony, & Hasson, 2013).

Psycholinguistic research on text comprehension is concerned with describing the interaction between the text and the comprehender. Comprehension goes beyond the decoding of words in reading, or the phonological analysis of words during listening. Comprehension takes place when people can build a mental representation of the text information that can be used for recall, question answering, knowledge acquisition, information exchange—or merely entertainment. Successful comprehension requires comprehensible texts, appropriate background knowledge, and the utilization of cognitive resources, such as working memory or attention.

9.2.1 Text structure

A classical issue is how longer texts, such as stories, newspaper articles, or textbook chapters are processed. One of the first attempts to tackle this question was the description of *text structure*. Rumelhart (1980) introduced the term *story grammar*, in analogy to grammar on the sentence level, and attempted to formulate similar principles for texts as for sentences. A story, according to this approach, consists of several mandatory and optional elements. For example, there is a setting in which the protagonists and the location are introduced, the story contains a goal the protagonists set for themselves, a complication, and finally the resolution at the end. All of these story elements can be recursively embedded in a hierarchical structure (by adding subepisodes, and so on). Similarly, the template for a story describing a standard event (e.g., going to a restaurant), follows a script-like structure which is filled in a particular text with specific actors and events (Rizzella & O'Brien, 2002). Readers use such templates to form expectations about the content of texts, which, in turn, facilitates comprehension. Kintsch and van Dijk (1978; van Dijk & Kintsch, 1983) used a more general approach and defined the macrostructure of a text in analogy as the text's semantic structure on a global level, distinct from the microstructure describing the relationships between subsequent sentences, to which we now turn.

9.2.2 Cohesion, coherence, and inference

Cohesion refers to the connection between sentences that is directly signaled by linguistic units, the cohesive markers, or *ties* (Halliday & Hasan, 1976). The most important cohesive ties are word repetitions, pronouns, anaphoric expressions, and conjunctions (Garrod & Sanford, 1977). In general, cohesion facilitates text comprehension. Explicit cues to connections between phrases and sentences reduce misunderstandings and provide information not only about the existence of a connection but also about the specific relation. Consider the sentences: "The man crossed the street. The dog started to bark." Without explicit information about whether the two events are related, we cannot be sure about the correct reading. In contrast, both versions: "Because the man crossed the street, the dog started to bark," or "The man crossed the street, because the dog started to bark" are plausible, but describe rather different states of affairs. Similarly, the use of pronouns facilitates comprehension. They reduce cognitive complexity, because discourse protagonists are explicitly marked as given or new information (Garrod & Sanford, 1999).

In contrast to lexical cohesion, *coherence* refers to the content-based connection between utterances. For example, the sentence pair: "Lilly and her friend Suzie jumped into the swimming pool. The weather was really warm." is perfectly coherent, although there are no lexical cohesive ties present. Since readers and listeners assume a coherent connection, they access their world knowledge to infer that the swimming pool was probably an outdoor pool and the event took place on a summer day. In contrast, when the second sentence is "The water was really warm.", the knowledge that a pool contains water provides a more direct connection between the sentences via an anaphoric reference.

These examples illustrate that *coherence*, which refers to a property of the text, depends on *inferences* (i.e., the cognitive processes the comprehender employs for establishing coherence). Inferences are defined as the enhancement of text information by prior knowledge. The issue of inferencing has long been one of the pillars of text comprehension research, and this research area is still going strong (O'Brien, Cook, & Lorch, 2015). Inferences have been classified according to their content (e.g., goal related, instrumental, temporal), to their function (e.g., bridging, elaborative), to the information needed (e.g., local: based on information in the current sentence, or global: integrating information from two or more positions within the text), and, most importantly, their status in the cognitive system (e.g., mandatory or automatic, goal-directed, or strategic). The debate about which types of inferences are a necessary component of comprehension (minimalist hypothesis: McKoon & Ratcliff, 1992; vs. constructionist approach: Graesser, Singer, & Trabasso, 1994) has inspired decades of experimental research and the development of a multitude of sophisticated experimental paradigms. A more thorough treatment of this topic is found in Chapter 26, Garnham, this volume.

Current theorizing about inferences adds the dimension of time to the aforementioned classifications. Rather than asking the question whether an inference is *made* online, during comprehension, or offline, for instance in the context of a probe task, recent research distinguishes prediction (Kuperberg & Jaeger, 2016), generation (Yeari & van den Broek, 2015), and validation of inferences (Schroeder, Richter, & Hoever, 2008; Singer, 2013). Using these dissociable phases (and functions) allows the researcher to focus on the respective aspects of the inferencing process (Cook & O'Brien, 2017).

9.2.3 Situation model

The result of comprehension is the *situation model* or mental model of a text (van Dijk & Kintsch, 1983). The situation model is a representation in the comprehender's mind that integrates the text information with prior knowledge. Thus, the situation model is a general idea of what the text is about, but it also includes details, associations, and elaborations from general world knowledge. It combines information from the text with the results of inferences and elaborations. Importantly, it is assumed that the situation model goes beyond a verbal, propositional or symbolic format, and can include non-verbal information, reflecting the specific content of a text (e.g., a visualization, a map, odors, or auditory scenes). For instance, the situation model representation of an article about a football game might include a spatial layout of the field, or an imagination of the fans' chants. Experimental studies on situation model building often use the inconsistency paradigm (Albrecht & O'Brien, 1993; Ferstl, Rinck, & von Cramon, 2005). Consistent texts are compared with an inconsistent version, in which a word or sentence is replaced by a piece of information that is still grammatical and consistent on a local level (e.g., a story about a couple going to a restaurant, where the woman orders a hamburger), but becomes inconsistent or implausible when the global discourse context is taken into account (e.g., when the woman had been introduced as a vegetarian). The results show that such inconsistencies are noticeable, and processing times for inconsistent information increase.

The most specific theory of situation model building has been developed for narrative texts. Taking up some aspects of story grammar, Zwaan, Magliano, and Graesser (1995) assume that situation models of stories contain information about the protagonists, their goals and emotions, and about the time and location of the story events. These dimensions are tracked continuously during comprehension and updated as needed. Empirical evidence for the model is abundant (see Zwaan & Radvansky, 1998, for review). Methods used for testing it include probe verification or priming tasks, in which the reaction times are compared for conditions in which an object is still present in the situation model (e.g., a runner wearing a sweatshirt), or not (when the runner has taken it off and put it on a bench). In other studies, reading times are measured when a narrative shift (i.e., a noticeable change in one of the dimensions) takes place (e.g., Speer & Zacks, 2005).

Importantly, situation model building does not depend on text length. Even when hearing or reading a single sentence, comprehenders immediately set up a situation model. While this model is much less complex and detailed than that of a textbook chapter or a novel, the fundamental comprehension processes are the same. Neuroscientific results, both using event-related potentials (ERPs), as well as neuroimaging, are very comparable for shorter and longer texts, as soon as similar interpretative demands are posed (see van Berkum, 2012, for discussion of this issue).

9.2.4 Models of text comprehension

Three-level theories of text comprehension (most notably: Kintsch, 1998; van Dijk & Kintsch, 1983) propose the parallel construction of representations on three levels. First, the words and phrases in the text are represented in some linguistic format, preserving the grammatical structure and the lexical entities. This *surface level* is needed whenever the verbatim form is relevant (e.g., for memorization), but it is retained only for a short amount of time. Text cohesion is represented on this level. The second level of representation is the *textbase* or text representation. This level is still close to the words in the text, but it abstracts from the verbatim form. Kintsch and van Dijk (1978) used a propositional notation, borrowed from logic, as a short-cut for representing idea units or phrases of the text and their interrelations. In this notation, predicates (such as verbs or relations) are combined with the respective arguments. For example, the sentence "Mary ordered a hamburger at the restaurant" would consist of two propositions: P1: order[Mary, hamburger], and P2: location[P1, restaurant]. In this representational form, neither the exact grammatical structure, nor the choice of words plays a role, but only the semantic meaning on a phrasal level. In addition to these text propositions, the textbase is enriched by inferences and associations from general world knowledge. For the construction-integration model (Kintsch, 1988), the textbase is the crucial component, because it also contains an algorithm for simulating activation and de-activation of context relevant information. Adding associative connections between the textbase elements (based on the strength of their association in general world knowledge or on argument overlap of the propositions) and inhibitory connections between incompatible units, a spreading-activation process gives rise to an activation pattern that represents the comprehender's current interpretation, based on prior discourse context and idiosyncratic background knowledge. Memory functions are included via a working-memory buffer that carries the propositions with the strongest activation level over to the next processing cycle (e.g., the next sentence).

Despite some criticisms, the construction-integration model has inspired most current models of text comprehension, such as the *Landscape Model* (Tzeng, van den Broek, Kendeou, & Lee, 2005), *RI-Val*, (Cook & O'Brien, 2014, 2017) or the *Reading Systems Framework* (Perfetti & Stafura, 2014) (see McNamara & Magliano, 2009, for review). It spells out computationally specific mechanisms for knowledge activation and integration at the interface between the surface structure and the textbase. In contrast, the interface between the elaborated textbase and the situation model is less clear. This is, of course, due to the content dependence of the situation model and the richness and variability of the knowledge representations. Drawing on the fact that situation models are not necessarily verbal but may include perceptual features (see above), Zwaan (2004; cf. Glenberg & Kaschak, 2002) proposed a two-level model of comprehension (the *Immersed Experiencer*) without a propositional textbase representation. Rather, the situation model is conceptualized as an embodied representation reflecting the experiential traces of language in its respective perceptual context (cf. Barsalou, 2008; de Vega, Glenberg, & Graesser, 2008). Situation model building is seen as resonance of words and sentences with perceptual experiences, similar to neuroscientific conceptions of semantic processing as neuronal resonance of domain specific brain regions (e.g., activations of the (pre-)motor cortex elicited by action verbs; Hauk, Johnsrude, & Pulvermüller, 2004). Psycholinguistic evidence for this approach comes from sentence-picture verification tasks, in which the visual Gestalt of probe pictures matches or mismatches the objects in sentences, or from studies using the action-compatibility effect (ACE; Glenberg & Kaschak, 2002; Kaup, Yaxley, Madden, Zwaan, & Ludtke, 2007), in which the compatibility between the required response (e.g., a finger movement away from or toward oneself) and the meaning of the presented sentence (e.g., a present given away or being received) predicts response times.

As with the event-indexing model, the hypothesis of the *Immersed Experiencer* has inspired empirical text comprehension research and helped to identify many perceptually grounded features of situation models. However, from a psycholinguistic viewpoint, the question remains how the particular wording of a text gives rise to these representations. And, in fact, the importance of linguistic cues and grammatical structure is starting to enter the picture once more. It is being recognized that the complexity of language, including abstractions and strong influences of the exact wording on the contents of representations, cannot merely be explained by perceptual resonance on the word level (de Vega, Glenberg, & Graesser, 2008).

The focus on situation model building and inferencing has for some time put the surface and textbase levels in the background, although syntactic, lexical, or semantic variations of the exact wording can greatly influence the intended interpretation. Based on more detailed linguistic theories, psycholinguistics has again begun to tackle this issue. Although many of these studies are on the sentence level, they are still highly relevant for text comprehension research. For example, using the concept of information structure Schumacher and Hung (2012) investigated the interaction between word order in German and givenness of the presented information (Gernsbacher, 1990). Brennan et al. (2012) studied the process of combining words into idea units on the phrasal level (similar to Kintsch's propositionalizing) based on the linguistic concept of composition, and Mak and Sanders (2013) evaluated how the specificity of conjunctions facilitates causal inferences. Finally, Perfetti and Stafura (2014) proposed a theoretical framework to bring into focus the role of word knowledge for local text comprehension.

The challenge for future theories of text comprehension will be to bring together these rather disparate research strands, moving from subtle linguistic distinctions on the word level to a fuzzy, enriched situation model, considering memory representations of the discourse context and background knowledge. In addition, as suggested by Graesser and McNamara (2011), a full theory of text comprehension needs to include levels representing the text genre, the rhetorical structure, and aspects of pragmatic communication.

9.3 Research topics and recent developments

Basic research, and specifically the theoretical developments and conceptual definitions, were in the focus of text comprehension research before the turn of the century. When inspecting the ten most cited papers (in *Web of Science*) published between 1985 and 2000, all except for one early neuroimaging study (Fletcher, Happé, Frith et al., 1995) were on theories of text comprehension, on inferencing, or on situation model building. In the second part of the chapter, I will now move on to sketch various research issues that have since been in the focus of research. Of course, the coverage must be selective. This part is divided into three subsections including partly overlapping disciplinary directions (cognitive psychology, education, neuroscience), followed by a short section on recent methodological advances.

9.3.1 Contributions of cognitive functions to text comprehension

Research on text comprehension from a cognitive psychology perspective has focused on the role of non-linguistic, cognitive processes during text comprehension, most prominently on memory functions.

Short-term memory has never been a good predictor for language comprehension ability, although it seems obvious that keeping verbal context information in mind during listening or reading of subsequent utterances is necessary. In the early model by Kintsch and van Dijk (1978), short-term memory was included in the form of a buffer with variable storage capacity for carrying over information from one processing cycle to the next. However, there are few studies showing a relationship between, let's say, the digit span and text comprehension performance. In line with the development of Baddeley's working memory model (Gathercole & Baddeley, 2014), Daneman and Carpenter (1983) developed the reading span measure. In addition to assessing storage capacity, the reading span test and its variations include a domain specific processing component (e.g., reading sentences while memorizing their final words). The reading span has proven an invaluable predictor of comprehension tasks such as pronoun resolution or syntactic disambiguation. By now, the reading span test is the gold standard for evaluating individual differences whenever working memory plays a role during text comprehension (Dutke & von Hecker, 2011; Virtue, Parrish, & Jung-Beeman, 2008). However, the measure has been criticized as well. In particular, there is doubt that the reading span assesses memory independently of language comprehension ability. Evidence for circular reasoning is the correlation of reading experience with both reading span and comprehension performance (Farmer, Fine, Misyak, & Christiansen, 2017).

Long-term memory and comprehension are so closely intertwined that it is almost impossible to disentangle their respective roles. For instance, in many studies on text understanding, comprehension questions are posed after reading, or recall protocols are analyzed. These off-line memory measures are useful given the assumption that successful memory for text contents cannot be achieved without comprehension, but they do not shed light on online processes taking place during reading or listening. In addition to memory as a result of comprehension, background knowledge stored in long-term memory is a prerequisite for building appropriate text representations. In a classic study Bartlett (1932) presented a Native American legend to British people, who lacked this cultural background. In addition to missing important information, the comprehenders also distorted other statements to fit into their prior schemata. This finding has been replicated numerous times. For instance, it is almost impossible to infer missing cohesive ties without knowledge about likely relationships between content units, incoherent texts cannot be understood without an appropriate topic or an illustration, readers with appropriate domain knowledge comprehend and recall more information, and situation models contain information that was not stated in the text but retrieved from long-term memory (e.g., Bransford & Johnson, 1972;

Dooling & Lachman, 1971). Importantly, a lack of appropriate background knowledge restricts comprehensibility and cannot be compensated by providing additional information after reading or listening. Taken together, the function of background knowledge is to provide access to word meanings, to general facts needed for inferencing, and to templates for situation models in which the incoming information can be integrated.

An extension of the work on situation model updating is research on the comprehension of *multiple texts* (Perfetti, 1997). With the reliance on hypertext systems, such as the *World Wide Web*, it has become crucial to understand how information is integrated across information sources, to identify strategies for information search, and to assess the source memory of readers for pieces of their resulting knowledge representation. This is particularly important when conflicting information is encountered (Beker, Jolles, Lorch, & van den Broek, 2016), or when an integrated opinion is to be based on prior beliefs and information provided in several texts (Bråten, Britt, Strømsø, & Rouet, 2011).

Compared to memory, less is known about the role of attention during text comprehension. Although it is intuitively obvious that concentration and focus is important for getting the most out of the reading experience, experimental studies manipulating attentional factors are few and far between (e.g., Sanford, Sanford, Molle, & Emmott, 2006). Recently, *mind wandering* during reading has become a research topic. Mind wandering refers to the experience of being distracted during a task by intruding thoughts. The prerequisite for this type of study is a reliable measure. Most studies use self reports which are then validated using a variety of comprehension and recall tasks. The most important results are that mind wandering occurs more frequently during easy tasks, and that self-reported mind wandering does indeed predict reading behavior and comprehension scores (Feng, D'Mello, & Graesser, 2013; McVay & Kane, 2012; Reichle, Reineberg, & Schooler, 2010).

9.3.2 Applied educational research

Educational research is concerned with the development and improvement of text comprehension skill, both across the life span and during language learning. The goal is to understand individual differences and thereby to improve the chances for successful learning from text. The populations of interest include adults of various age groups (see Thornton & Light, 2006), children and adolescents at different educational levels, and second language learners. Much of the research in this domain is concerned with the development and evaluation of interventions (Oakhill, Cain, & Ebro, 2015; Rapp, van den Broek, McMaster, Kendeou, & Espin, 2007).

One prerequisite for successful reading comprehension is appropriate text difficulty. To tailor texts to a particular age or skill group, readability measures have been developed (see Benjamin, 2012, for review). Many of them are based on word length and frequency, and on syntactic complexity. Recently, automated systems, such as *Coh-Metrix* (Graesser, McNamara, Louwerse, & Cai, 2004) have been used for assessing global features of texts, particularly cohesion and coherence. While these measures predict reading comprehension better than previous measures, it is important to consider the individuals' background knowledge. In a seminal study, McNamara, Kintsch, Songer, and Kintsch (1996) showed that cohesion helps readers with little background knowledge. However, for readers with more background knowledge a less cohesive text encourages inference generation and thus yields better comprehension and memory performance.

A second topic is the question of component processes of text comprehension. While most cognitive theories take for granted that readers and listeners have the required decoding skills and sufficient vocabulary knowledge, this is not necessarily the case for children or language learners. Thus, one strand of research is the interaction between different levels of language processing, including the word and sentence level, as well as the text level. For example, Oakhill, Cain, and Bryant (2003) analyzed data from a longitudinal study in children and showed that word reading was related to phonological awareness, but inferencing skills were related to vocabulary size. Thus, basic decoding skills are clearly separable from higher level language comprehension.

Interventions on the text level include teaching programs that induce structuring and inferencing in readers, but also meta-cognition and monitoring of comprehension success (Gersten, Fuchs, Williams, & Baker, 2001). One well-known strategy for learning from expository texts is the SQ3R technique (Robinson, 1946), in which the readers are encouraged to survey the relevant content domain before reading, pose questions during reading, recite the information and, finally, review the text. The results of controlled evaluations of such interventions are mixed. While some researchers document improvements in comprehension scores (Bos, Koning, Wassenburg, & van der Schoot, 2016), others do not. As an example, pointing readers to the importance of monitoring narrative shifts increases reading times and improves memory for these shifts, but not necessarily comprehension scores (Bohn-Gettler, 2014). Neuroscientific studies accompanying teaching schemes have not yet been conducted but could shed light on the development of reading comprehension skills.

Another means for improving comprehension skill is to provide additional information. Extensively studied are the effects of illustrations and pictures to accompany and guide comprehension (Glenberg & Langston, 1992; see Bransford & Johnson, 1972). Advance organizers are used as an aid to structure incoming information in expository texts (i.e., tables of content, or explicit introductions; e.g., Gurlitt, Dummel, Schuster, & Nückles, 2012), and textbook writers have used tools such as boxes or comments in the margins to highlight and weigh information during comprehension. In all these cases, of course, the text information is changed or enriched. To assess the success of such measures for a sustainable improvement of skills, it would be important to ensure that improvements in comprehension scores cannot be due to memory of this additional information, but to improved comprehensibility of the verbal information.

A recently widely studied topic in applied text comprehension research is the comparison of reading in digital form, for example, on computers or tablets, to traditional reading of books or papers. From a psycholinguistic point of view, however, there is no reason to predict a qualitative difference. Effects might be caused by motivational factors, or by perceptual properties of the medium (e.g., tablet computers can be adjusted to individual viewing preferences; Kretzschmar et al., 2013).

9.3.3 Neuroscience of text comprehension

Neuroscience has greatly enhanced our understanding of language comprehension in context. The description of acquired language deficits after brain damage confirms a dissociation between word- and sentence level deficits and higher-level language processing. While many patients with aphasia (i.e., with acquired language deficits after lesions of the dominant, usually left hemisphere of the brain; cf. Chapter 11, this volume), are surprisingly adept at utilizing the communicative context, some brain lesions cause problems on the discourse level. Text comprehension deficits have been observed in patients after brain injury, particularly after frontal lobe lesions, right hemisphere lesions (Beeman & Chiarello, 1998), or closed head injury (Ferstl, Walther, Guthke, & von Cramon, 2005), in which diffuse neuronal disconnections occur. Crucially, these patients are not aphasic, that is, they are relatively unimpaired in basic language tasks (such as lexico-semantic or syntactic processing). These non-aphasic deficits appear on the level of discourse production and text comprehension. Symptoms include incoherent discourse, the failure to draw inferences, an inability to distinguish main ideas from details, or problems with non-literal language and pragmatic language use. Although these deficits are also referred to as *cognitive communication impairments* (Coelho, 2013), relating higher level language comprehension to basic cognitive deficits (such as working memory, attention, or inhibition) has yielded mixed results (e.g., Barbey, Colom, & Grafman, 2014; Ferstl, Walther et al., 2005). Text comprehension is such a complex skill that it cannot be reduced to a collection of basal subprocesses.

The occurrence of non-aphasic language deficits suggests that higher level language processing engages brain regions beyond the perisylvian language cortex. Electrophysiological and neuroimaging methods shed light on this issue. Starting with the seminal work by Kutas and colleagues on the integration of words into a sentence context (Kutas & Hillyard, 1980; for review see Kutas & Federmeier, 2011; Chapter 40, this volume), the use of electroencephalography (EEG), and in particular, of ERPs opened up a whole new window into the brain (van Berkum, 2012). Because of their excellent temporal resolution, ERPs can dissociate qualitatively different subprocesses of comprehension during reading or listening. In particular, the N400 component provides information about the contextual fit of words into a context. It is sensitive to word level associations, to inference demands and to global discourse context (e.g., Lau, Holcomb, & Kuperberg, 2013; St. George, Mannes, & Hoffman, 1997). Furthermore, pronoun resolution and anaphoric processes elicit a frontal negative shift, interpreted as a specific index for referential processes during discourse comprehension (Nieuwland & van Berkum, 2008; van Berkum, 2012).

Neuroimaging methods, in particular positron emission tomography (PET) and functional magnetic resonance imaging (fMRI), have also been used to study text comprehension (see Ferstl, Neumann, Bogler, & von Cramon, 2008; Zacks & Ferstl, 2016). By now there is considerable convergence regarding the key players in the brain. Several regions—which I have dubbed the extended language network (ELN; Ferstl et al., 2008)—are consistently involved during text comprehension and higher-level language processing (cf. Xu, Kemeny, Park, Frattali, & Braun, 2005). As an illustration, Figure 9.1 shows the results from a meta-analysis comparing the comprehension of coherent text to control conditions of unconnected sentences or words (Ferstl et al., 2008). Besides the perisylvian language cortex in the dominant, usually left, hemisphere (Broca's area: left inferior gyrus; Wernicke's area: posterior superior temporal lobe; Geschwind area: angular gyrus, AG), the ELN includes the anterior temporal lobes (aTL) bilaterally, the temporo-parietal junction (TPJ) on the right, the dorsomedial prefrontal cortex (dmPFC) and the posterior cingulate cortex (PCC). With increasing task demands, various regions in the dorso-lateral prefrontal cortex are also activated.

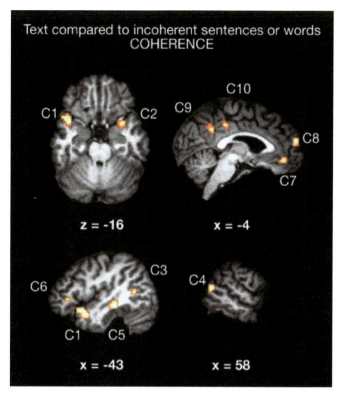

FIG. 9.1 The results of a meta-analysis comparing connected, coherent text to unconnected language stimuli. The regions consistently activated across studies are: C1: left anterior temporal lobe (aTL), C2: right aTL, C3: left posterior superior temporal sulcus (pSTS), C5: right pSTS, C5: mid-middle temporal gyrus (MTG), C6: left inferior frontal gyrus (IFG), opercular part, C7: ventro-medial prefrontal cortex (vmPFC); C8: dorso-medial prefrontal cortex (dmPFC), C9, C10: inferior precuneus, posterior cingulate cortex (prec/PCC).

Reproduced from Evelyn C. Ferstl, Jane Neumann, Carsten Bogler, and D. Yves von Cramon, The extended language network: A meta-analysis of neuroimaging studies on text comprehension, *Human Brain Mapping*, 29 (5), pp. 581–93, doi: 10.1002/hbm.20422, Copyright © 2008, Wiley Periodicals, Inc.

What are the putative roles of the components of the ELN? The network overlaps to some degree with regions implicated for Theory-of-Mind processes (see Ferstl & von Cramon, 2002), that is, regions that are important when the mental state, the beliefs, and emotions of other people need to be evaluated (Frith & Frith, 1999). Interestingly, the right hemisphere (RH) does not play as much of a role as proposed in the neuropsychological literature (cf. Long & Baynes, 2002; Jung-Beeman, 2005). Instead, brain imaging brought attention to regions previously not thought to be involved during language comprehension. Most prominently, the two medial regions (dmPFC and PCC) have been shown to be particularly sensitive to cognitive demands related to inferencing and situation model building (Zacks & Ferstl, 2016). For instance, Speer and Zacks (2005) found PCC activation at the locations of narrative shifts in situation model building, Ferstl and von Cramon (2001, 2002) reported both dmPFC and PCC activations for coherent compared to incoherent textoids, and recently, Helder et al. (2017) argued that these medial structures were particularly important for the detection of coherence breaks. None of these regions are language specific, however. For example, posterior medial regions have been implicated in general world knowledge retrieval, in visualization, or in attention shifting; fronto-medial regions play a role in processing of self-relevant information, in emotion processing, or in the self-guided evaluation of stimuli.

Particularly interesting is the role of the left inferior frontal gyrus. This anatomic structure includes Broca's area (opercular part; BA44), with an important function for syntactic and phonological processing, but also the triangular part (BA45), a region consistently activated when semantic selection or disambiguation is needed. Finally, the left inferior frontal gyrus (IFG) has been reported to be active in many studies on inferencing (e.g., Virtue et al., 2008), in line with the proposal by Hagoort (2013) who stressed this region's importance for *unification* (i.e., the process of assembling meaning from linguistic building blocks), a process clearly resembling propositionalization as postulated in early text comprehension models. It is interesting to note that other researchers stress the role of the aTL for similar functions (Ferstl et al., 2008), for example, Pylkkänen and colleagues (Brennan et al., 2012; Zhang & Pylkkänen, 2015) for combinatorial processes in the semantic domain.

Few theoretical proposals have been put forward for integrating these and other findings with previous psycholinguistic or textlinguistic models (e.g., Hagoort, 2013; Mason and Just, 2006). Ferstl and colleagues (Ferstl et al., 2008; Ferstl, Rinck, & von Cramon, 2005) argued that the pattern of reactivating context and background knowledge needed for reinstatement search was consistent with activation in the PCC (see also Egidi & Caramazza, 2016, for task effects), and that aTL activation reflected propositionalization (Kintsch & van Dijk, 1978). Mason and Just (2006) include a mechanism for protagonist monitoring, reminiscent of one of the dimensions postulated in the event-indexing model. These and other attempts to map the components of the ELN to subprocesses of text comprehension, and thus, to couple psycholinguistic theory and neurolinguistic models, will enhance our understanding of the neurobiology of language. Predictions from such a comprehensive theory would help to design further neuroimaging studies, which could in turn be used to evaluate and refine concepts from text comprehension research.

In addition to psycholinguistic attempts to describe and delineate processes of comprehension, in particular the interplay between text features and comprehension processes, imaging research has moved into using text materials as the means to study other psychological processes. For example, text-based studies have been conducted on such varied topics as suspense (Lehne et al., 2015), argumentation (Schmaelzle, Haecker, Honey, & Hasson, 2015), Theory of Mind (Altmann, Bohrn, Lubrich, Menninghaus, & Jacobs, 2012), or moral reasoning (Kaplan et al., 2016). While these and similar studies provide interesting insights into higher level cognition, the operationalizations are rarely based on a linguistic analysis of the text materials. Instead, the researchers use empirical assessments (e.g., ratings) to define the conditions of study. This approach is clearly useful. However, it would be desirable to integrate the findings with psycholinguistic theory. If we understand which cognitive demands the linguistic features of the texts impose, confounds can be avoided, and a differentiated interpretation of the results becomes possible. Specifically, it is important to dissociate the processes of interest (e.g., morality, suspense) from those needed to comprehend the experimental texts (see Ferstl & von Cramon, 2002). This is particularly important given the overlap between social cognition and higher-level language processing.

Taken together, neuroscience has already made considerable contributions to text comprehension research. The multidimensional data are particularly useful for dissociating qualitatively different processes. Neuroimaging provides direct insight into the interplay between linguistic and domain specific or embodied representations built during comprehension (e.g., de Vega et al., 2014). And finally, neuroscientific results have broadened the scope of text comprehension research by showing that language comprehension is inseparable from social communication.

9.3.4 Recent methodological developments

The development of neuroscientific methods is fast and will provide a vast array of tools in the future (see Chapters 41 and 42, this volume). In the domain of text comprehension research, ERPs and fMRI are by now almost standard (see van Berkum, 2012; Zacks & Ferstl, 2016). In the future, transcranial magnetic stimulation (TMS) and magneto-encephalography (MEG), now employed mainly on the word and sentence level, will become more important. TMS is used to simulate the effects of circumscribed brain lesions and can thus shed light on whether certain regions are necessary for comprehension (Acheson & Hagoort, 2013; Franzmeier, Hutton, & Ferstl, 2012). MEG is useful whenever very fine-grained temporal and spatial resolution is needed (e.g., Zhang & Pylkkänen, 2015). Finally, large-scale analyses of brain activation during the processing of naturalistic texts without the need for stringent experimental design can provide information about building complex situation model representations, and they can be an informative tool for understanding features of texts beyond word and sentence level descriptions (e.g., by using intersubject correlations, Wilson, Molnar-Szakacs, & Iacoboni, 2008; or regression analyses, see Hasson & Egidi, 2015; Yarkoni, Speer, Balota, McAvoy, & Zacks, 2008).

Besides neuroscientific methods, eye tracking is one of the most promising new methodological advances (Hyönä, Lorch, & Rinck, 2003; Mak & Sanders, 2013; Richardson, Dale, & Kirkham, 2007). Unfortunately, only few theorists have attempted to describe reading strategies within a discourse context (Just & Carpenter, 1980). In addition to measures of eye movements during reading, which provide information about reading strategies and a dissociation between immediate effects and later rereading patterns, visual world paradigms have become more and more useful for studying the contents of text representations. Viewing patterns for pictorial representations of alternative scenarios shed light on the time course of situation model building and updating. However, the results from reading and visual world studies do not always converge (Ferstl & Israel, 2016; Ferstl, Israel, & Putzar, 2016). Thus, it is important to accumulate converging evidence from reading and listening, as well as from various paradigms and tasks. Such empirical comparisons will enable researchers to further develop theories of how eye movements and text comprehension processes are interwoven.

Statistical methods can also extend the toolbox for text comprehension research (see Chapter 39, this volume). In the last few years, mixed effects modeling has proven particularly useful (Baayen, Davidson, & Bates, 2008; Richter, 2006). This method, borrowed from linguistics, was originally developed for the analysis of complex data that lacks a stringent experimental design (e.g., of naturally occurring corpus data). Mixed effects models have the advantage that variability by subjects and items can be included in one model, and, at the same time, covariates for both participants (e.g., age, reading skill) and items (e.g., word frequencies, sentence length, trial order) can account for various sources of heterogeneity. This is especially useful when the materials are variable, and it enables the researcher to develop paradigms that are less restrictive than perfectly controlled factorial designs. Recent examples for applications of these methods in text comprehension research include reading times (Bohn-Gettler, 2014), and eye-tracking data (Ferstl et al., 2016; Mayerhofer & Schacht, 2015). Even ERPs can now be analyzed taking into account trial-by-trial variability (Canal, Garnham, & Oakhill, 2015).

A further methodological step taken is the use of big data as a research tool in text comprehension research. Corpus analyses (e.g., *Linguistic Inquiry and Word Count*, LIWC; Tausczik & Pennebaker, 2010) and the assessment of semantic relationships, for example, using latent semantic analysis (LSA; Landauer, Kireyev, & Panaccione, 2011; Landauer, McNamara, Dennis, & Kintsch, 2007) provide up-to-date information about naturally occurring discourse. Estimates of association strengths, such as needed for cognitive modeling, can now be derived from large-scale corpora, rather than from an empirical assessment. A comparison of corpus data with comprehension variables can shed light on the impact of frequency on one hand, and on the felicity of certain usages on the other.

Similarly, computer models and AI systems are increasingly important in the classroom. The development of automatized grading systems (Wade-Stein & Kintsch, 2004) or computerized assessments of discourse coherence (Graesser et al., 2004), are based on the results of text comprehension research. Given the fast developments of AI methods in other domains, it is likely that educational applications of cognitive models of reading and comprehension will enter the classrooms of the future.

9.4 Conclusions

Research on text and discourse comprehension becomes ever more important in a society in which information exchange by verbal communication is ubiquitous. Reading and writing, comprehending, and integrating knowledge from different sources, all require processes of inferencing and situation model building. These basic concepts are by now well understood and there is wide-spread agreement about their importance. However, even after many decades of empirical research, there are still many open questions regarding individual differences in comprehension skills and the optimal way to enhance comprehension success. Neuroscientific research has added to our understanding of text comprehension by highlighting the overlap with extralinguistic functions, such as Theory-of-Mind processing and executive functions.

References

Acheson, D. J., & Hagoort, P. (2013). Stimulating the brain's language network: Syntactic ambiguity resolution after TMS to the inferior frontal gyrus and middle temporal gyrus. *Journal of Cognitive Neuroscience*, 25(10), 1664–77.

Albrecht, J. E., & O'Brien, E. J. (1993). Updating a mental model: Maintaining both local and global coherence. *Journal of Experimental Psychology: Learning, Memory, and Cognition*, 19(5), 1061–70.

Altmann, U., Bohrn, I. C., Lubrich, O., Menninghaus, W., & Jacobs, A. M. (2012). The power of emotional valence—from cognitive to affective processes in reading. *Frontiers in Human Neuroscience*, 6, 192.

Baayen, R. H., Davidson, D. J., & Bates, D. M. (2008). Mixed-effects modeling with crossed random effects for subjects and items. *Journal of Memory and Language*, 59(4), 390–412.

Barbey, A. K., Colom, R., & Grafman, J. (2014). Neural mechanisms of discourse comprehension: A human lesion study. *Brain*, 137, 277–87.

Barsalou, L. W. (2008). Grounded cognition. *Annual Review of Psychology*, 59, 617–45.

Bartlett, F. C. (1932). *Remembering: A Study in Experimental and Social Psychology*. Cambridge University Press, Cambridge, UK.

Beeman, M., & Chiarello, C. (Eds.). (1998). *Right Hemisphere Language Comprehension: Perspectives from Cognitive Neuroscience*. Erlbaum, Mahwah, NJ.

Beker, K., Jolles, D., Lorch, R. F., JR, & van den Broek, P. (2016). Learning from texts: Activation of information from previous texts during reading. *Reading and Writing*, 29, 1161–78.

Benjamin, R. G. (2012). Reconstructing readability: Recent developments and recommendations in the analysis of text difficulty. *Educational Psychology Review*, 24(1), 63–88.

Bohn-Gettler, C. M. (2014). Does monitoring event changes improve comprehension? *Discourse Processes*, 51(5–6), 398–425.

Bos, L. T., Koning, B. B. de, Wassenburg, S. I., & van der Schoot, M. (2016). Training inference making skills using a situation model approach improves reading comprehension. *Frontiers in Psychology*, 7, 116.

Bransford, J. D., & Johnson, M. K. (1972). Contextual prerequisites for understanding: Some investigations of comprehension and recall. *Journal of Verbal Learning and Verbal Behavior*, 11(6), 717–26.

Bråten, I., Britt, M. A., Strømsø, H. I., & Rouet, J.-F. (2011). The role of epistemic beliefs in the comprehension of multiple expository texts: Toward an integrated model. *Educational Psychologist*, 46(1), 48–70.

Brennan, J., Nir, Y., Hasson, U., Malach, R., Heeger, D. J., & Pylkkänen, L. (2012). Syntactic structure building in the anterior temporal lobe during natural story listening. *Brain and Language*, 120(2), 163–73.

Busselle, R., & Bilandzic, H. (2008). Fictionality and perceived realism in experiencing stories: A model of narrative comprehension and engagement. *Communication Theory*, 18(2), 255–80.

Canal, P., Garnham, A., & Oakhill, J. (2015). Beyond gender stereotypes in language comprehension: Self sex-role descriptions affect the brain's potentials associated with agreement processing. *Frontiers in Psychology*, 6, 1953.

Coelho, C. A. (2013). Cognitive-communication deficits following traumatic brain injury. In: Zasler, H. D., Katz, D. I., & Zafonte, R. D. (Eds.), *Brain Injury Medicine: Principles and Practice* (pp. 1119–32). Demos Medical, New York, NY.

Cook, A. E., & O'Brien, E. J. (2014). Knowledge activation, integration, and validation during narrative text comprehension. *Discourse Processes*, 51 (1–2), 26–49.

Cook, A. E., & O'Brien, E. J. (2017). Fundamentals of inferencing during reading. *Language and Linguistics Compass*, 11, e12246.

Daneman, M., & Carpenter, P. A. (1983). Individual differences in integrating information between and within sentences. *Journal of Experimental Psychology: Learning, Memory, and Cognition*, 9(4), 561–84.

de Vega, M., Glenberg, A. M., & Graesser, A. C. (Eds.). (2008). *Symbols and Embodiment: Debates on Meaning and Cognition*. Oxford University Press, Oxford.

de Vega, M., Leon, I., Hernández, J. A., Valdes, M., Padron, I., & Ferstl, E. C. (2014). Action sentences activate sensory motor regions in the brain independently of their status of reality. *Journal of Cognitive Neuroscience, 26*(7), 1363–76.

Dooling, D. J., & Lachman, R. (1971). Effects of comprehension on retention of prose. *Journal of Experimental Psychology, 88*(2), 216–22.

Dutke, S., & von Hecker, U. (2011). Comprehending ambiguous texts: A high reading span helps to constrain the situation model. *Journal of Cognitive Psychology, 23*(2), 227–42.

Egidi, G., & Caramazza, A. (2016). Integration processes compared: Cortical differences for consistency evaluation and passive comprehension in local and global coherence. *Journal of Cognitive Neuroscience, 28*, 1568–83.

Farmer, T. A., Fine, A. B., Misyak, J. B., & Christiansen, M. H. (2017). Reading span task performance, linguistics experience and the processing of unexpected syntactic events. *Quarterly Journal of Experimental Psychology, 70*(3), 413–433.

Feng, S., D'Mello, S., & Graesser, A. C. (2013). Mind wandering while reading easy and difficult texts. *Psychonomic Bulletin & Review, 20*(3), 586–92.

Ferstl, E. C., & von Cramon, D. Y. (2001). The role of coherence and cohesion in text comprehension: An event-related fMRI study. *Cognitive Brain Research, 11*(3), 325–40.

Ferstl, E. C., & von Cramon, D. Y. (2002). What does the frontomedian cortex contribute to language processing: Coherence or theory of mind? *NeuroImage, 17*(3), 1599–612.

Ferstl, E. C., & Israel, L. (2016, July). *The comprehension of verbal jokes: A visual world study*. 26th Annual Meeting of the Society of Text and Discourse, Kassel, Germany.

Ferstl, E. C., Israel, L., & Putzar, L. (2016). Humor facilitates text comprehension: Evidence from eye movements. *Discourse Processes, 54*, 259–84.

Ferstl, E. C., Neumann, J., Bogler, C., & von Cramon, D. Y. (2008). The extended language network: A meta-analysis of neuroimaging studies on text comprehension. *Human Brain Mapping, 29*(5), 581–93.

Ferstl, E. C., Rinck, M., & von Cramon, D. Y. (2005). Emotional and temporal aspects of situation model processing during text comprehension: An event-related fMRI study. *Journal of Cognitive Neuroscience, 17*(5), 724–39.

Ferstl, E. C., Walther, K., Guthke, T., & von Cramon, D. Y. (2005). Assessment of story comprehension deficits after brain damage. *Journal of Clinical and Experimental Neuropsychology, 27*(3), 367–84.

Fletcher, P. C., Happé, F., Frith, U., Baker, S. C., Dolan, R. J., Frackowiak, R. S. J., & Frith, C. D. (1995). Other minds in the brain: A functional imaging study of "theory of mind" in story comprehension. *Cognition, 57*, 109–28.

Franzmeier, I., Hutton, S. B., & Ferstl, E. C. (2012). The role of the temporal lobe in contextual sentence integration: A single-pulse transcranial magnetic stimulation study. *Cognitive Neuroscience, 3*(1), 1–7.

Frith, C. D., & Frith, U. (1999). Interacting minds—a biological basis. *Science, 286*(5445), 1692–5.

Garrod, S., & Sanford, A. (1977). Interpreting anaphoric relations: The integration of semantic information while reading. *Journal of Verbal Learning and Verbal Behavior, 16*(1), 77–90.

Garrod, S. C., & Sanford, A. J. (1999). Resolving sentences in a discourse context: How discourse representation affects language understanding. In: Gernsbacher, M. A. (Ed.), *Handbook of Psycholinguistics*, 3rd Edition (pp. 675–698). Academic Press, San Diego, CA.

Gathercole, S. E., & Baddeley, A. D. (2014). *Working Memory and Language Processing: Essays in Cognitive Psychology*. Taylor and Francis, Hoboken.

Gernsbacher, M. A. (1990). *Language Comprehension as Structure Building*. Erlbaum, Hillsdale, NJ.

Gersten, R., Fuchs, L. S., Williams, J. P., & Baker, S. (2001). Teaching reading comprehension strategies to students with learning disabilities: A review of research. *Review of Educational Research*, 71(2), 279–320.

Glenberg, A. M., & Kaschak, M. P. (2002). Grounding language in action. *Psychonomic Bulletin & Review*, 9(3), 558–65.

Glenberg, A. M., & Langston, W. E. (1992). Comprehension of illustrated text: Pictures help to build mental models. *Journal of Memory and Language*, 31(2), 129–51.

Graesser, A. C., & McNamara, D. S. (2011). Computational analyses of multilevel discourse comprehension. *Topics in Cognitive Science*, 3, 371–98.

Graesser, A. C., McNamara, D. S., Louwerse, M. M., & Cai, Z. (2004). Coh-Metrix: Analysis of text on cohesion and language. *Behavior Research Methods, Instruments, & Computers*, 36(2), 193–202.

Graesser, A. C., Singer, M., & Trabasso, T. (1994). Constructing inferences during narrative text comprehension. *Psychological Review*, 101(3), 371–95.

Gurlitt, J., Dummel, S., Schuster, S., & Nückles, M. (2012). Differently structured advance organizers lead to different initial schemata and learning outcomes. *Instructional Science*, 40(2), 351–69.

Hagoort, P. (2013). MUC (Memory, Unification, Control) and beyond. *Frontiers in Psychology*, 4, 416.

Halliday, M.A.K., & Hasan, R. (1976). *Cohesion in English*. Longman Group, London.

Hasson, U., & Egidi, G. (2015). What are naturalistic comprehension paradigms teaching us about language? In: Willems, R. M. (Ed.), *Cognitive Neuroscience of Natural Language Use* (pp. 228–55). Cambridge University Press, Cambridge, UK.

Hauk, O., Johnsrude, I., & Pulvermüller, F. (2004). Somatotopic representation of action words in human motor and premotor cortex. *Neuron*, 41(2), 301–7.

Helder, A., van den Broek, P., Karlsson, J. & van Leijenhorst, L. (2017). Neural correlates of coherence-break detection during reading of narratives. *Scientific Studies of Reading*, 21, 463–79.

Hyönä, J., Lorch, R. F., JR, & Rinck, M. (2003). Eye movement measures to study global text processing. In: Radach, R., Hyönä, J., & Deubel, H. (Eds.), *The Mind's Eye: Cognitive and Applied Aspects of Eye Movement Research*, 1st Edition (pp. 313–34). North Holland.

Jung-Beeman, M. (2005). Bilateral brain processes for comprehending natural language. *Trends in Cognitive Sciences*, 9(11), 512–18.

Just, M. A., & Carpenter, P. A. (1980). A theory of reading: From eye fixations to comprehension. *Psychological Review*, 87(4), 329–54.

Kaplan, J. T., Gimbel, S. I., Dehghani, M., Immordino-Yang, M. H., Sagae, K., Wong, J. D., ... Damasio, A. (2016). Processing narratives concerning protected values: A cross-cultural investigation of neural correlates. *Cerebral Cortex*, 27, 1428–38.

Kaup, B., Yaxley, R. H., Madden, C. J., Zwaan, R. A., & Ludtke, J. (2007). Experiential simulations of negated text information. *Quarterly Journal of Experimental Psychology*, 60(7), 976–90.

Kintsch, W. (1988). The role of knowledge in discourse comprehension: A construction-integration model. *Psychological Review*, 95(2), 163–82.

Kintsch, W. (1998). *Comprehension: A Paradigm for Cognition*. Cambridge University Press, Cambridge, UK.

Kintsch, W., & van Dijk, T. A. (1978). Toward a model of text comprehension and production. *Psychological Review*, 85(5), 363–94.

Kretzschmar, F., Pleimling, D., Hosemann, J., Fussel, S., Bornkessel-Schlesewsky, I., & Schlesewsky, M. (2013). Subjective impressions do not mirror online reading effort: Concurrent EEG-eyetracking evidence from the reading of books and digital media. *PloS One, 8*(2), e56178.

Kuperberg, G. R., & Jaeger, T. F. (2016). What do we mean by prediction in language comprehension? *Language, Cognition and Neuroscience, 31*(1), 32–59.

Kutas, M., & Federmeier, K. D. (2011). Thirty years and counting: Finding meaning in the N400 component of the event-related brain potential (ERP). *Annual Review of Psychology, 62,* 621–47.

Kutas M., & Hillyard S. A. (1980). Reading senseless sentences: Brain potentials reflect semantic incongruity. *Science, 207,* 203–205.

Landauer, T. K., Kireyev, K., & Panaccione, C. (2011). Word maturity: A new metric for word knowledge. *Scientific Studies of Reading, 15*(1), 92–108.

Landauer, T., McNamara, D. S., Dennis, S., & Kintsch, W. (Eds.) (2007). *Handbook of Latent Semantic Analysis.* Erlbaum, Mahwah, NJ.

Lau, E. F., Holcomb, P. J., & Kuperberg, G. R. (2013). Dissociating N400 effects of prediction from association in single-word contexts. *Journal of Cognitive Neuroscience, 25*(3), 484–502.

Lehne, M., Engel, P., Rohrmeier, M., Menninghaus, W., Jacobs, A. M., & Koelsch, S. (2015). Reading a suspenseful literary text activates brain areas related to social cognition and predictive inference. *PloS One, 10*(5), e0124550.

Long, D. L., & Baynes, K. (2002). Discourse representation in the two cerebral hemispheres. *Journal of Cognitive Neuroscience, 14*(2), 228–42.

Mak, W. M., & Sanders, T. J. M. (2013). The role of causality in discourse processing: Effects of expectation and coherence relations. *Language and Cognitive Processes, 28*(9), 1414–37.

Mar, R. A. (2011). The neural bases of social cognition and story comprehension. *Annual Review of Psychology, 62,* 103–34.

Mason, R. A., & Just, M. A. (2006). Neuroimaging contributions to the understanding of discourse processes. In: Traxler, M. J., & Gernsbacher, M. A. (Eds.), *Handbook of Psycholinguistics,* 2nd Edition (pp. 765–99). Elsevier, Amsterdam.

Mayerhofer, B., & Schacht, A. (2015). From incoherence to mirth: Neuro-cognitive processing of garden-path jokes. *Frontiers in Psychology, 6,* 550.

McKoon, G., & Ratcliff, R. (1992). Inference during reading. *Psychological Review, 99*(3), 440–6.

McNamara, D., Kintsch, E., Songer, N. B., & Kintsch, W. (1996). Are good texts always better? Interactions of text coherence, background knowledge, and levels of understanding in learning from text. *Cognition and Instruction, 14*(1), 1–43.

McNamara, D. S., & Magliano, J. (2009). Toward a comprehensive model of comprehension. In: Ross, B. (Ed.), *The Psychology of Learning and Motivation* (Vol. 51, pp. 297–384). Elsevier Science, New York, NY.

McVay, J. C., & Kane, M. J. (2012). Why does working memory capacity predict variation in reading comprehension? On the influence of mind wandering and executive attention. *Journal of Experimental Psychology: General, 141*(2), 302–20.

Nieuwland, M. S., & van Berkum, J. J. A. (2008). The neurocognition of referential ambiguity in language comprehension. *Language and Linguistics Compass, 2*(4), 603–30.

Oakhill, J. V., Cain, K., & Bryant, P. E. (2003). The dissociation of word reading and text comprehension: Evidence from component skills. *Language and Cognitive Processes, 18*(4), 443–68.

Oakhill, J., Cain, K., & Ebro, C. (2015). *Understanding and Teaching Reading: A Handbook.* Routledge, Oxon.

O'Brien, E. J., Cook, A. E., & Lorch, R. F., JR. (2015). *Inferences During Reading.* Cambridge University Press, Cambridge.

Perfetti, C. A. (1997). Sentence, individual differences, and multiple texts: Three issues in text comprehension. *Discourse Processes, 23*(3), 337–55.

Perfetti, C., & Stafura, J. (2014). Word knowledge in a theory of reading comprehension. *Scientific Studies of Reading, 18,* 22–37.

Rapp, D. N., van den Broek, P., McMaster, K. L., Kendeou, P., & Espin, C. A. (2007). Higher-order comprehension processes in struggling readers: A perspective for research and intervention. *Scientific Studies of Reading, 11*(4), 289–312.

Regev, M., Honey, C. J., Simony, E., & Hasson, U. (2013). Selective and invariant neural responses to spoken and written narratives. *Journal of Neuroscience, 33*(40), 15978–88.

Reichle, E. D., Reineberg, A. E., & Schooler, J. W. (2010). Eye movements during mindless reading. *Psychological Science, 21*(9), 1300–10.

Richardson, D. C., Dale, R., & Kirkham, N. Z. (2007). The art of conversation is coordination: Common ground and the coupling of eye movements during dialogue. *Psychological Science, 18*(5), 407–13.

Richter, T. (2006). What is wrong with ANOVA and multiple regression? Analyzing sentence reading times with hierarchical linear models. *Discourse Processes, 41*(3), 221–50.

Rizzella, M. L., & O'Brien, E. J. (2002). Retrieval of concepts in script-based texts and narratives: The influence of general world knowledge. *Journal of Experimental Psychology: Learning, Memory, and Cognition, 28*(4), 780–90.

Robinson, F. P. (1946). *Effective Study,* Revised edition. Harper, New York, NY.

Rumelhart, D. E. (1980). On evaluating story grammars. *Cognitive Science, 4*(3), 313–16.

Sanford, A. J. S., Sanford, A. J., Molle, J., & Emmott, C. (2006). Shallow processing and attention capture in written and spoken discourse. *Discourse Processes, 42*(2), 109–30.

Schmaelzle, R., Haecker, F. E. K., Honey, C. J., & Hasson, U. (2015). Engaged listeners: Shared neural processing of powerful political speeches. *Social, Cognitive and Affective Neuroscience, 10*(8), 1137–43.

Schroeder, S., Richter, T., & Hoever, I. (2008). Getting a picture that is both accurate and stable: Situation models and epistemic validation. *Journal of Memory and Language, 59*(3), 237–55.

Schumacher, P. B., & Hung, Y.-C. (2012). Positional influences on information packaging: Insights from topological fields in German. *Journal of Memory and Language, 67*(2), 295–310.

Singer, M. (2013). Validation in reading comprehension. *Current Directions in Psychological Science, 22*(5), 361–6.

Speer, N. K., & Zacks, J. M. (2005). Temporal changes as event boundaries: Processing and memory consequences of narrative time shifts. *Journal of Memory and Language, 53*(1), 125–40.

St George, M., Mannes, S., & Hoffman, J. E. (1997). Individual differences in inference generation: An ERP analysis. *Journal of Cognitive Neuroscience, 9*(6), 776–87.

Tausczik, Y. R., & Pennebaker, J. W. (2010). The psychological meaning of words: LIWC and computerized text analysis methods. *Journal of Language and Social Psychology, 29*(1), 24–54.

Thornton, R., & Light, L. L. (2006). Language comprehension and production in normal aging. In: Birren, J. E., & Warner Schaie, K. (Eds.), *Handbook of the Psychology of Aging* (pp. 261–87). Elsevier Academic Press, Burlington, MA.

Tzeng, Y., van den Broek, P., Kendeou, P., & Lee, C. (2005). The computational implementation of the landscape model: Modeling inferential processes and memory representations of text comprehension. *Behavior Research Methods*, 37(2), 277–86.

van Berkum, J. (2012). The electrophysiology of discourse and conversation. In: Spivey, M., McRae, K., & Joanisse, M. (Eds.), *The Cambridge Handbook of Psycholinguistics* (pp. 589–612). Cambridge University Press, Cambridge.

van Dijk, T. A., & Kintsch, W. (1983). *Strategies of Discourse Comprehension*. Academic Press, New York, NY.

Virtue, S., Parrish, T., & Jung-Beeman, M. (2008). Inferences during story comprehension: Cortical recruitment affected by predictability of events and working memory capacity. *Journal of Cognitive Neuroscience*, 20(12), 2274–84.

Wade-Stein, D., & Kintsch, E. (2004). Summary street: Interactive computer support for writing. *Cognition and Instruction*, 22(3), 333–62.

Willems, R. M., & Jacobs, A. M. (2016). Caring about Dostoyevsky: The untapped potential of studying literature. *Trends in Cognitive Sciences*, 20(4), 243–5.

Wilson, S. M., Molnar-Szakacs, I., & Iacoboni, M. (2008). Beyond superior temporal cortex: Intersubject correlations in narrative speech comprehension. *Cerebral Cortex*, 18(1), 230–42.

Xu, J., Kemeny, S., Park, G., Frattali, C., & Braun, A. (2005). Language in context: Emergent features of word, sentence, and narrative comprehension. *NeuroImage*, 25(3), 1002–15.

Yarkoni, T., Speer, N. K., Balota, D. A., McAvoy, M. P., & Zacks, J. M. (2008). Pictures of a thousand words: Investigating the neural mechanisms of reading with extremely rapid event-related fMRI. *NeuroImage*, 42(2), 973–87.

Yeari, M., & van den Broek, P. (2015). The role of textual semantic constraints in knowledge-based inference generation during reading comprehension: A computational approach. *Memory*, 23(8), 1193–214.

Zacks, J. M., & Ferstl, E. C. (2016). Discourse comprehension. In: Hickok, G., & Small, S. L. (Eds.), *Neurobiology of Language* (pp. 661–73). Academic Press, Amsterdam.

Zhang, L., & Pylkkänen, L. (2015). The interplay of composition and concept specificity in the left anterior temporal lobe: An MEG study. *NeuroImage*, 111, 228–40.

Zwaan, R. A. (2004). The immersed experiencer: Toward an embodied theory of language comprehension. *Psychology of Learning and Motivation: Advances in Research and Theory*, 44, 35–62.

Zwaan, R. A., Magliano, J. P., & Graesser, A. C. (1995). Dimensions of situation model construction in narrative comprehension. *Journal of Experimental Psychology: Learning, Memory, and Cognition*, 21(2), 386–97.

Zwaan, R. A., & Radvansky, G. A. (1998). Situation models in language comprehension and memory. *Psychological Bulletin*, 123(2), 162–85.

CHAPTER 10

BILINGUAL SENTENCE PROCESSING

ARTURO E. HERNÁNDEZ, EVA M. FERNÁNDEZ,
AND NOEMÍ AZNAR-BESÉ

10.1 INTRODUCTION

BILINGUALS live, by definition, in two linguistic worlds. Given the different demands of each language, one might think that each system functions independently. However, as Grosjean (1992) and Paradis (1987) have pointed out, bilinguals do not behave like two monolingual speakers/listeners housed in a single brain. Instead, the evidence to date suggests that the characteristics of bilingual language processing may appear to be "in-between" an individual's two codes (Cutler et al., 1992; Hernández et al., 1994; Kilborn, 1987; Kilborn & Ito, 1989; Liu et al., 1992; Vaid & Pandit, 1991).

Studies in bilingual sentence processing have focused on phenomena related to how semantic or syntactic representations are built. This chapter reviews data consistent with the view of interdependence between the two languages of the bilingual, using evidence from the literature on bilingual sentence processing. To do this, we will discuss processing at the semantic and syntactic level. Studies in both the semantic and syntactic domains reveal that bilinguals almost always use a unitary mechanism that accesses two separately represented grammars. We will also see that the study of bilingual sentence processing can offer insights to our understanding of human language processing in general, because bilinguals offer opportunities to examine sentence processing effects in within-participant designs impossible to carry out with monolinguals, and the coexistence of two codes within an individual leads to questions regarding the nature of sentence processing impossible to ask with monolinguals.

10.2 SEMANTIC PROCESSING

One of the fundamental questions for researchers studying bilingual sentence processing is the nature of language representation. We begin with a brief overview of lexical representations, because sentence processing relies on these heavily. Does a bilingual store both sets of words in the same lexicon or there is a separate lexicon for each language? For many years, researchers addressed this issue by using traditional memory methodologies involving free recall or recognition (see Heredia & Maclaughlin, 1992, for a review) and it wasn't until the 1990s that investigators turned to the semantic priming paradigm. At the single-word level, researchers looked at whether cross-language priming is an automatic process and in line with the view that there are strong interconnections between words in each language. These studies found that, depending on circumstances, priming across languages may either be automatic (Altarriba, 1992; Tzelgov & Eben-Ezra, 1992), controlled (Grainger & Beauvillain, 1988), or both (Hernández et al., 1996; Keatley & de Gelder, 1992), providing thus insufficient evidence to clearly resolve the one- or two-lexicon debate.

One factor that has emerged as a strong predictor of the strength of within- or between-language priming is order of acquisition. For example, Kroll and Sholl (1992) looked at the size of lexical priming from bilinguals' first language to their second language (L1 to L2) and from bilinguals' second language to their first language (L2 to L1) across a set of studies. In general, most such studies demonstrate that the priming effect is larger from L1 to L2 than vice versa. Kroll and colleagues (Kroll, 1994; Kroll & Sholl, 1992; Kroll & Stewart, 1994) suggest that the results from studies investigating within- and between-language lexical priming fit very well within their *Revised Hierarchical Model*, a model initially designed to address the nature of second-language acquisition. The model posits that there are two lexical stores and a common conceptual store. These stores are interconnected via weighted bidirectional links between both the L1 and L2 lexicons and between the conceptual store and each particular lexicon as well. Lexical links are stronger from L2 to L1 than from L1 to L2, a product of second-language acquisition. However, conceptual links are stronger to L1 than to L2. This model has been supported through a series of studies (Kroll, Van Hell, Tokowicz, & Green, 2010) which have found that conceptual processing is stronger from L1 to L2 than from L2 to L1 while translation is faster from L2 to L1 than from L1 to L2 (i.e., translation asymmetry).

Evidence from subsequent studies has found that the semantic feature of concreteness (presumably specified lexically) may mediate the presence or absence of translation or naming asymmetries (Heredia, 1996). Thus, it is not clear that a bilingual's two lexicons can be so neatly divided, a view that has received support from de Groot and colleagues (de Groot, 1994; de Groot & Nas, 1991), among many others. Heredia also found that L1 and L2 are not equivalent to the more dominant and less dominant language for Spanish-English bilinguals in the United States. To account for these differences, Heredia proposed a re-revised Hierarchical Model in which dominance and not order of acquisition determines the nature of language asymmetries (see also Heredia, 1997). Studies of lexical priming have also found that dominance may not be directly related to order of acquisition. For example, Altarriba (Altarriba, 1992) found larger priming from L2 to L1 than from L1 to L2. Thus, studies of bilingualism should consider profoundly the age at which the second language was acquired as well as the domains and frequency of use of each language, two variables that lead to different language dominance profiles. In the case of Hispanics in southern Florida and in the Southwest of the United States, the second language (English) ends up being the dominant language since it is the language in which most formal education occurs.

Thus, studies of semantic priming in bilinguals must consider that in certain populations the second language is the dominant language. A final criticism of the Revised Hierarchical Model is the distinction between lexical and conceptual processing of items in a second language. In fact, many have proposed that translation equivalents may be conceptually mediated both in acquisition (Altarriba & Mathis, 1997) and in usage (de Groot et al., 1994; de Groot & Hoeks, 1995) suggesting that dominance effects need careful consideration. The notion of dominance continues to be the topic of considerable research more recently. For example, research has found that proficiency may play a stronger role in the magnitude of cross-language priming when the scripts differ. Nakayama, Ida, and Lupker (2016) found that bilinguals with low proficiency in their L2 showed no significant cross-language priming. However, those with high proficiency did show it. Thus, priming can occur across languages for non-cognates in languages that differ in their script.

While a substantial amount of work has been done with lexical priming and single-word naming, relatively little work has been done with sentence priming in bilinguals to study shared lexical representations (but see below for discussion of studies of sentence priming to study shared syntactic representations). Kroll and Borning (1987) looked at the effects of English sentences on lexical decisions to English and Spanish target words. Lexical decisions were slower to Spanish targets, but the magnitude of priming did not vary systematically with the target language. Similarly, Hernández et al. (1996) further explored the nature of within- and between-language sentence priming in a group of Spanish-English bilinguals. The participants in the study reported Spanish to be their L1 although English, their L2, was the dominant language. Like Kroll and Borning, Hernández et al. did not observe language asymmetries under normal viewing conditions. However, language asymmetries were found for targets which were visually degraded and for which the language was not predictable. In fact, these differences were larger in both conditions: the cross-language condition (English-Spanish priming > Spanish-English priming) and in the within-language condition (English-English priming > Spanish-Spanish priming). The results from Hernández et al. (1996) extend findings in the single-word priming literature with bilinguals by showing that sentence priming may be larger when a target is in L2 and the L2 has become the dominant language. This confirms other research which shows that language proficiency is the biggest determinant of the magnitude of cross-language priming.

Researchers have noted that lexical priming effects are unable to capture the "real-world" nature of priming. Specifically, researchers suggested that cross-language priming in a sentence context would be more robust and approximate the code-switching nature of natural bilingual speech. Altarriba et al. (1996) found that, under certain conditions, sentence context effects can produce surprising results in bilinguals. Fixation durations and naming latencies were recorded when bilinguals read sentences that contained high- and low-frequency Spanish and English words in high- and low-constraint sentences. Reaction times were faster and fixation durations were shorter for low-frequency targets in high-constraint sentences when compared to performance for these targets in low-constraint sentences across both languages. For high-frequency targets, however, an asymmetry was found. English high-frequency targets showed the same constraint effect observed for low-frequency targets, being faster in high-constraint sentences. On the other hand, Spanish high-frequency targets showed slower reaction times and longer fixation durations in high-constraint sentences. Altarriba et al. suggest that high-frequency Spanish words in high-constraint English sentences led to slower reaction times because of violations of lexical expectations. That is, there may be some lexical-level competition for a high-frequency Spanish word when the sentence provides a strong form of constraint for its English translation. The fact that this competition occurred even during first fixation durations suggests that this effect is a product of delays in word recognition.

The results obtained by Altarriba et al., are confirmed by studies using event-related potentials (ERPs) (Moreno, Federmeier, & Kutas, 2002). Moreno and colleagues asked participants to listen to sentences (e.g., *Each night the campers built a . . .*) which either had a congruent completion (*fire*), a lexical switch (*blaze*), or a code-switch (*fuego*). Participants were also tested with idiomatic phrases (e.g., *Out of sight, out of . . .*), which are much more highly constrained. Lexical switches revealed greater N400 effects than congruent completions for both sentences and idiomatic phrases, suggesting that participants had more difficulty integrating these lower constraint items into a semantic context. Code-switches, however, did not produce an increased N400. Rather, these items yielded an enhanced late positive complex (LPC) which has been associated with task-relevant improbable events (Donchin & Coles, 1988; Johnson, 1986). The LPC was also modulated by proficiency in Spanish. Specifically, higher vocabulary scores in Spanish were predictive of LPC's that were smaller and peaked earlier. Given that code-switches are more likely to be present in the auditory modality and are modulated by the proficiency in the language, Moreno et al. posit that the enhanced LPC is due to a physical mismatch with the stimulus. This result reveals an interesting parallel with Altarriba et al.'s results which show slower processing of target items in the less dominant language in high-constraint sentences than in the dominant language (for comparable results using a different methodology see Hernández, 2002).

The cost of integrating code-switched words in sentences was examined by Ng, Gonzalez, and Wicha (Ng, Gonzalez, & Wicha, 2014) in a study also measuring ERPs while bilinguals read code-switched nouns and verbs in short stories. The study compared responses to switched nouns and verbs and found that switched words elicited larger late anterior negativity (LAN) and LPC amplitude than non-switched words, similarly to the study by Moreno and colleagues. Ng and colleagues also report that nouns have a higher integration cost than verbs, suggesting discourse-processing effects: nouns are referential elements that might be harder to integrate into discourse than verbs, which are relational elements.

The importance of context can also be observed in a study by Elston-Guettler et al. (2005) in which German-English bilinguals were presented with a short film in either German or English. After the film, participants were presented with a set of sentences (i.e., *The woman gave her friend an expensive gift*) and asked to press a "yes" button when they were finished reading each item. Two hundred milliseconds after pressing the button, participants were asked to make a lexical decision to a visually presented probe word (e.g., *poison*) or a control prime (*shell*) which remained on a computer screen for a maximum of 3,000 ms. The visual probes were "false friends": interlingual homographs which are spelled the same but have entirely different meanings (*Gift* means "poison" in German). In order to create strong context effects that would bias against any German meaning, the sentences were all in English and the target words were all legal English words. Items were presented in separate blocks to assess whether the language of the film was constant across a longer session or dissipated over time. Activation of the German meaning of the homograph, for both reaction times and ERP measures, appeared but only after the German film was viewed and only in the first two blocks. By the third block after the presentation of the German film there was no priming of the German meaning of the homographs. Finally, there was no semantic priming after presentation of the English film. One finding of interest was the lack of proficiency effects. The authors interpret these findings as supporting a model in which strong contexts allow L2 speakers to zoom into a particular language and essentially cut off access to another language. The use of discourse contexts has shown similar elimination of cross-language semantic priming in certain conditions (Hernández et al., 1996).

More recent studies also support the findings from previous studies. For example, Duyck et al. (2007) used eye tracking to test whether words in the first language were activated when participants read sentences in L2. Dutch-English bilinguals were asked to read low-constraint sentences with embedded cognate or control words (e.g., *Hilda bought a new RING; cognate or Hilda bought a new COAT; control*). Norming of the materials ensured that both the cognate and control conditions were comparable regarding predictability. A cognate facilitation effect was found starting at 249 ms after first encountering the target, but only for true cognates (*ring–ring*) but no facilitation effect was found for non-identical cognates (*schip-ship*). The fact that the cognate effect only appeared when the visual words were identical suggests that similarity between translation equivalent words is not enough. Finally, the cognate facilitation effect is quite early as evidenced by the presence of this effect during the first fixation of the target. Further studies have also found that degree of similarity moderates priming effects (Sánchez-Casas & García-Albea, 1992; van Assche, Drieghe, Duyck, Welvaert, & Hartsuiker, 2011).

Libben and Titone (2009) conducted a study with slightly different findings and came to a different conclusion. French-English bilinguals were presented with identical cognates as well as homographs in English in low- and high-constraint sentences. Results revealed facilitation for cognates but interference for homographs on all measures in low-constraint sentences. However, in high-constraint sentences, these cross-lingual interaction effects were only observed during early stage reading but not late stage reading. Libben and Titone concluded that lexical access in bilinguals is non-selective during early word processing, but that this dual-language activation is rapidly resolved by top-semantic factors at later stages of comprehension.

Peeters, Dijkstra, and Grainger (2013) looked at how French-English cognates that were orthographically identical were processed at both at the behavioral and at the electrophysiological level. The main question was whether these identical cognates were processed as part of the dominant or non-dominant language. To accomplish their goal, Peeters et al. used the fact that the N400 is sensitive to word frequency manipulations and examined the processing of identical cognates, by performing an orthogonal word frequency manipulation of both readings of cognates. Identical cognates that had either high or low word frequencies in both French and English as well as cognates whose frequencies differed across their French and English readings were compared against English non-cognate words. Behavioral responses showed larger for facilitation for cognates with low English word frequency. The authors also found word frequency effects for English words. The electrophysiological data were in the same direction, showing cognate facilitation effects (i.e., more negative-going waves for non-cognates) as well as a widely distributed English word frequency effect (i.e., more negative-going waves for identical cognates with low English frequency as compared to those with high English frequency) and a shorter French word frequency effect for the N400. In addition, cognates produced more positive waveforms in the 600–900 ms time-window than control words. These ERP differences helped to disambiguate whether word frequency effects in English (L2) and French (L1) played a role in the processing of identical cognates. The authors suggest that bilinguals have common orthographic and semantic representations shared by identical cognates but two distinct phonological and morphemic representations, one for each of the two readings of a cognate.

The results from studies which have investigated semantic processing at the sentence level reveal greater cross-talk between languages. Priming from sentences in L1 does cross over to L2. One possible interpretation is that sentence processing is evidence for a single conceptual system. However, the magnitude of these effects can vary depending on proficiency of the language or the strength of the context. Thus, it is also possible that these effects are due to information from one language to another.

10.3 Syntactic processing through the lens of the Competition Model

Work on syntactic processing with bilinguals has involved two different paradigms. In some paradigms participants are asked to make explicit judgments about grammar (a practice very common in research on second-language acquisition). Others, on the other hand, test the nature of grammar in a more implicit manner. One paradigm that has been used in a great number of bilingual studies is the sentence interpretation paradigm developed by Bates and MacWhinney (for a review, see Bates & MacWhinney, 1989). This paradigm has been used extensively to test predictions of the Competition Model of Bates and MacWhinney (Bates & MacWhinney, 1982, 1987, 1989). The *Competition Model* is a functionalist approach to language, in which linguistic representations are viewed not as a set of discrete and autonomous rules, but as a set of probabilistic mappings between form and meaning. The model begins with the assumption that all listeners (bilingual and monolingual) must deal with two important but occasionally conflicting tasks. On the one hand, listeners must know in advance which pieces of information in the input language carry valuable information and merit attentional priority. On the other hand, they must be sensitive to the processing costs and timing parameters of a language to deploy resources in the most efficient way. Bates and MacWhinney (1989) have referred to these two dimensions of language processing with the terms cue validity (the information value associated with particular linguistic forms) and cue cost (the processing costs involved in using those forms, including demands on perception and memory). Sentence comprehension is viewed as a process of interactive activation, a form of constraint satisfaction in which linguistic forms or cues compete and converge in order to lead to a particular interpretation, (i.e., the interpretation that provides the best fit to this particular configuration of inputs).

Within this framework, languages can vary not only in terms of the presence or absence of specific form types (e.g., case-marking on nouns), but also in terms of the relative strength of form-function mappings. In other words, there are quantitative as well as qualitative differences between language types. To illustrate, consider languages such as Spanish, French, Italian, German, or Russian. Compared to English, these languages offer a rich set of markings for subject-verb agreement and, as a result, subject-verb agreement is a strong cue to agent–object relations. At the same time, Spanish and Italian are pro-drop languages and therefore permit null subjects in free-standing declarative sentences like *Ü bebo agua* ("I drink water"), where the subject pronoun is omitted. Pro-drop languages are generally quite tolerant of word order variation, permitting strings which depart from the canonical subject-verb-object (SVO) word order preferred for pragmatically neutral sentences: a sentence like *María se comió una galleta* ("María ate a cookie") can also be realized with the subject noun phrase (NP) in sentence-medial (*Se comió María una galleta*), or sentence-final position (*Se comió una galleta María*). These languages offer a variety of other cues that can aid in identifying the thematic roles of the constituents, cues including clitic agreement, the accusative preposition *a* used with animate direct objects, and gender and case markings on determiners and adjectives that must agree with the nouns they modify. As a result, word order is a relatively weak and unreliable cue to semantic roles while other cues are much stronger.

English behaves quite differently. There are very few contrasts in verb morphology to agree with the subject (*I eat, you eat, they eat*), subject pronouns cannot be omitted in free-standing declarative sentences, and the canonical SVO word order is rigidly preserved in most sentence types. Hence, in English, subject-verb agreement is a weak cue while word order is a very strong cue to agent–object roles. Note that all the languages previously described have the same basic word order as English (SVO), and all have at least some form of subject-verb agreement. The primary difference here is, then, a matter of degree: which cues to meaning should the listener trust in assigning semantic roles when processing sentences in two different languages?

The Competition Model predicts that Spanish listeners, for instance, will rely primarily on morphological cues in sentence interpretation, ignoring word order if the two sources of information do not agree. By contrast, English listeners should rely primarily on word order cues at the expense of morphological information. Three previous studies have confirmed this prediction for Spanish and English (Hernández & Bates, 1994; Kail, 1989; Wulfeck, Juarez, Bates, & Kilborn, 1986). Similar confirmations of cue validity and cue strength have been reported for Italian, German, French, Hungarian, Serbo-Croatian, Dutch, Hebrew, Hindi, Turkish, Warlpiri, Japanese, and Chinese (for a review, see Bates & MacWhinney, 1989). This research employs a sentence interpretation task in which participants are presented with strings consisting of two nouns and a verb, representing various competing and converging combinations of word order, morphology, semantic information (e.g., animate vs. inanimate nouns), and pragmatic information (e.g., topicalization and/or contrastive stress). In this type of experiment, the participants' task is to choose the agent of the sentence. Results from these studies have consistently confirmed that speakers of different languages can have radically different configurations of cue strengths, in accord with predictions based on cue validity. When cues are set into competition, the strongest cues prevail, determining the assignment of agent–object roles.

A somewhat different interpretation of the range of effects just described would propose that during sentence interpretation, the processing mechanisms merely perform routines that involve accessing the competence repositories where such cues are represented, based on their validity and processing cost. Thus, the cross-linguistic differences observed in sentence interpretation tasks can be interpreted as reflecting not how actual sentence processing strategies are deployed, but instead how aspects of the grammar (in the competence repositories) are represented. One consequence of such a model is unitary and language-independent sentence processing routines where the same sentence processor can work for any language, and cross-linguistic differences in performance are caused by language-specific grammatical representations.

Kilborn (1987) performed one of the first studies of sentence interpretation with bilinguals. Bilingual subjects listened to digitized auditory sentence stimuli in German and English, in separate sessions, administered in a counterbalanced order across participants. As a group, Kilborn's German-English bilingual subjects displayed strong patterns of forward transfer (transfer from L1 to L2) in their assignment of agent–object roles. In both languages they showed strong effects of agreement and animacy, and relatively weak effects of word order. The reaction time findings were in general in accord with these results.

Another of the earliest implementations of the sentence interpretation paradigm with bilinguals was carried out by Vaid and Pandit (1991). In this study, 48 Hindi-English bilinguals who used Hindi at home and English at school were asked to perform the sentence interpretation paradigm. Despite having very similar profiles of use, individuals in this group showed variable patterns of dominance: 7 participants exhibited Hindi dominant profiles in both languages, 19 exhibited Hindi dominant profiles in Hindi but a mixture of strategies in English (partial forward transfer), and 17 displayed patterns of amalgamation in both languages. Only five subjects (11% of the total), showed patterns of differentiation between the two languages. This suggests that most bilinguals tend to mix their processing strategies.

Hernández et al. (1994) manipulated word order, verb agreement, and animacy in a sentence interpretation paradigm with bilingual and monolingual English and Spanish speakers. Data for percent first noun choice and reaction times for making this choice were collected. The results revealed an amalgamated, in-between pattern of results for percent first noun choice in the bilingual college-age group when compared to each monolingual group. Whereas monolinguals in Spanish relied almost exclusively on verb agreement, and monolinguals in English relied almost exclusively on word order, bilinguals relied on an amalgam of word order and verb agreement strategies in both languages. This suggests that speakers of two languages may combine aspects of grammar from both languages even when interpreting.

So far, the work that we have reviewed has dealt with adult bilinguals who are in a relatively steady state. However, the Competition Model was proposed to account for much more dynamic and variable patterns of performance. Two particular studies have captured this dynamic aspect with adult bilinguals. The first study conducted by McDonald (McDonald, 1989) looked at late English-French bilinguals who were in their first and second year of college French. McDonald found a clear pattern of forward transfer almost from the beginning of L2 learning. By the fourth semester, bilinguals exhibited sentence interpretation profiles that were very similar to those seen in adult bilinguals in other studies. In short, even L2 learners show relatively quick developmental changes in their L2 strategies (McLaughlin, Osterhout, & Kim, 2004).

A second study of interest conducted by Liu et al. (1992), investigated the nature of Chinese-English and English-Chinese bilinguals' performance when L2 is learned early or late in life. The results revealed a complex pattern related to the age of L2 acquisition and other possible factors. While late L2 learners showed the expected patterns of forward transfer, early bilinguals exposed to English between the ages of 6 and 10 showed patterns of differentiation. In addition, those who learned English before the age of four, showed patterns of backward transfer (transfer from L2 to L1), as did individuals who had arrived in the US between 12 and 16 years of age. These results demonstrate that the direction of transfer is linked to age of L2 acquisition (perhaps instead to language dominance), and that differentiation between L1 and L2 is the least common pattern. However, that early L2 acquirers exhibited patterns of forward transfer is an interesting finding which is no doubt related to language dominance rather than age of exposure.

The results from studies using sentence interpretation tasks within the Competition Model's framework, clearly lead to the important generalization that bilinguals do not function with two independent language systems. Rather, there is a considerable amount of interaction between these two systems in the form of transfer (backward and forward) as well as, in some cases, an amalgamation of strategies. This can be understood as linked to the dynamic properties of the bilingual's internalized grammars. The two grammatical components must be represented separately in the bilingual's competence repositories, but certain aspects of each might be given more prominence and are therefore more salient during the interpretation of sentences. Prominence is in part determined by the language-specific grammar which, for instance, permits or disallows word order variation. If the bilingual's grammar in either of the languages is close enough to the monolingual grammar, performance will be monolingual-like. If, instead, the internal representation of the grammar of one of the languages is not rich enough and either contains elements from the other languages or elements that do not match either of the languages, performance will reflect transfer or amalgamation (for a similar argument see Hernández, Sierra, & Bates, 2000).

10.4 Emergent Properties of Bilingual Sentence Processing

Early work in the framework of the Competition Model considered bilingualism to be fundamentally different from monolingual sentence processing. However, MacWhinney's Unified Model of Language Learning (UMLL) conceptualizes language learning as an emergent process (MacWhinney, 2004, 1999). In this view, L1 and L2 learning is a process in which representations are formed as language functions compete. As L2 learning progresses, increased proficiency results in sharpening of the underlying language representations. As functions become more automatized and representations are molded to the underlying linguistic input, L2 processing will experience reduced interference from L1.

Compared with monolinguals in both languages, bilinguals demonstrate an in-between pattern with regard to how they perceive and attend to different cues in each language (Hernández et al., 1994). The ways in which bilingual development can be considered as an extension of monolingual development were examined by Reyes and Hernández (2006). In this study, early Spanish-English bilingual children performed somewhere in-between English and Spanish monolingual children in making use of word-order strategies (local cues) before subject-verb agreement. That is, bilinguals attended to subject-verb agreement cues at a later age than the typical Spanish monolingual speaker but at an earlier age than the typical English monolingual speaker. Furthermore, bilinguals' use of a second-noun strategy for interpreting NNV and VNN sentences was delayed in comparison to both English and Spanish monolinguals. Whereas English monolinguals have a defined pattern of choosing the second noun as the agent of VNN sentences by age seven, and of NNV sentences by age nine (Von Berger, Wulfeck, Bates, & Fink, 1996), for Spanish monolinguals the second-noun strategy does not appear until age 11 for both VNN and NNV sentences (Reyes & Hernández, 2006). However, in this study bilinguals did not show evidence of this strategy until the ages of 14 to 16. The effect of competing strategies also increased with age as the participants attempted to sort and integrate cues to arrive at the most efficient processing strategy. These results support the idea that bilingual language acquisition, complex though it may be, involves a process that not only resembles but also transpires within the same time frame as monolingual first language acquisition (Paradis, 2009).

The UMLL also makes predictions about the role of overlap in language learning: functions which overlap between L1 and L2 should be easier to learn in a second language due to cross-language transfer. If ease of processing is related to less neural activity, the model would predict that neural activity should be reduced for items which overlap across languages. It is important to note that the concept of overlap differs from transfer in one important respect. Specifically, overlap exists at the level of linguistic description whereas transfer is the process of using functions in one language to guide processing in a second language.

The importance of overlap has been noted in several studies. At the phonological level, there is evidence that higher similarity between a native language and English leads to better perception and production of English vowels in non-native speakers (E. Flege, Bohn, & Jang, 1997). At the lexical level, words that are orthographically similar across languages (*tomato-tomate*) are easier to process (Costa, Caramazza, & Sebastián-Gallés, 2000; de Groot & Nas, 1991; Gollan, Forster, & Frost, 1997; Sánchez-Casas, Davis, & García-Albea, 1992) and show fewer differences in neural activity than those which are not (de Blesser et al., 2003). Linguistic similarity also affects neural activity produced by grammatical features across languages. Li et al. (2004) asked Chinese monolinguals to perform a lexical decision task on nouns, verbs, or class ambiguous items and analyzed fMRI scans to identify the regions of neural activity while the participants were performing this task. Verbs in Chinese are not inflected to indicate number/person distinctions, while English inflects the third person singular (e.g., *run/runs*). In addition, the form of many Chinese verbs is identical to related nouns, while in English the few forms that exist are distinguishable by lexical stress (e.g., *conflict*). Results revealed strong overlapping regions of activity for both nouns and verbs, agreeing with the idea that syntactical characteristics do influence neuronal activation. Similarly, in a subsequent study by Chan et al. (2004) Chinese-English bilinguals were asked to perform lexical decisions on nouns and verbs in each language. As in the case of Chinese monolinguals, neuroimaging data from Chinese-English bilinguals during processing of Chinese items revealed large areas of overlapping activity for processing of nouns and verbs, although the processing of English terms resulted in increased activity in different brain regions.

Work by Tokowicz and MacWhinney (2005) sheds light on the nature of transfer in late second language learners. In that study, English-Spanish bilinguals were asked to make grammaticality judgments on sentences which varied in the extent to which syntactic functions overlapped across languages. Participants' brain activity was measured using ERPs. The first type of functions involved tense marking, a feature which is similar across the two languages. The second type of function involved determiner-noun agreement (*las*[pl] *casas*[pl] vs. **las*[sg] *casas*[sg]). Like in Spanish, number in English is marked on the noun (*houses*). However, unlike in Spanish, there is no need in English for the noun to agree with the definite determiner (*the houses*). Participants were also asked to make decisions about sentences which manipulated gender agreement, a function which exists in Spanish but not in English (*la*[f] *casa*[f] vs. **el*[m] *casa*[f]). The results revealed increased activity for noun-verb agreement—a function which is similar across languages, as well as for determiner-noun gender agreement. In contrast, no ERP differences for gender or number agreement in Spanish were found. However, the distribution of the signal was diffuse, suggesting that it involved multiple neural generators. Taken together, these results suggest that properties of the grammar of L1 influence brain responses to L2 during the early stages of learning. Furthermore, it suggests that functions which overlap across languages are easier to track in L2 than those which don't, and that the effects of overlap are present in both semantic and syntactic tasks.

Overlap is a crucial factor to consider in L2 acquisition. The objective of the L2 learner is to develop a representational system which contains both overlapping and functionally distinct components. The language system builds L2 by bootstrapping from L1. Hence, overlap assists by making the first steps into L2 easier. As automaticity and learning settle, the system becomes less dependent on L1. Eventually, as the two systems become more stable, order of acquisition may no longer be as important a predictor as language dominance.

10.5 PARSING

Traditional models which suggest that monolinguals assign syntactic structure to a linearly ordered string of lexical items, propose that the syntactic processor, or parser, computes structure by applying minimal effort strategies (Frazier & Clifton, 1996; Frazier & Fodor, 1978; Kimball, 1973; Mitchell, 1994). These strategies, also referred to as routines or heuristics, are best understood as originating in the limitations imposed by human cognition: computing the simplest structure requires less computational resources and places less demands on working memory. One such strategy, *Minimal Attachment*, accounts for the difficulty experienced when reading the classic garden path sentence *The horse raced past the barn fell* (Bever, 1970). Here, the verb *raced*, in the reduced relative clause, is initially taken to be the matrix sentence verb, because this is the simplest structure for an input string like *The horse raced* . . . This interpretation persists (the reader is led "up the garden path") until the last word in the string is reached, at which point the reader (or listener) either re-analyzes the complete string to arrive at the correct syntactic structure or deems the sentence to be ungrammatical. By another such strategy, *Late Closure*, the parser prefers to attach incoming material locally, to the most recently built constituent. In a sentence like *Peter said the boss will call yesterday*, the final constituent *yesterday* is initially attached inside the more local clause, *the boss will call*, even though the verb, *will call*, is temporally incompatible with it. The operation of these parsing routines can be observed by examining listeners' or readers' preferences with linguistic stimuli that contain local or global ambiguities. Preference can be measured using a range of psycholinguistic techniques, including examining the proportion of preferred interpretations in pencil-and-paper questionnaires using globally ambiguous materials, or by examining reaction times, eye-gaze times, and ERP responses in tasks that contain materials forcing disambiguation one way or another.

If parsing strategies, like Minimal Attachment and Late Closure, are derived from the inherent properties of human cognition, there is no reason to suppose that bilinguals will parse sentences in ways that are qualitatively different from the ways monolinguals do, as argued, for example, in Fernández (2003). Studies that have compared the preferences of bilinguals and monolinguals when dealing with locally or globally ambiguous sentences find precisely this: evidence of similar parsing preferences for speakers of one or more languages. Frenck-Mestre and Pynte (1997) examined the eye movement patterns of monolinguals and bilinguals, reading sentences with local syntactic ambiguities resolved downstream in the sentence. The bilinguals were English-L1-dominant speakers of French as L2. The materials tested included sentence pairs like *Elle protège les enfants du danger/du village . . .* ("She protects the children from danger/of the village"), in which attaching the prepositional phrase to the matrix sentence verb, as with *du danger*, results in a simpler structure (thus the version of the pair with prepositional phrase *du village* modifying *les enfants* is dispreferred). Also tested were sentence pairs like *Whenever the dog barked/obeyed the pretty little girl showed her approval*, for which the simplest structure incorrectly takes the noun phrase *the little girl* to be the direct object of the verb in the subordinate clause –this is far more likely to happen with an optionally transitive verb like *obeyed* than with an intransitive verb like *barked*. Frenck-Mestre and Pynte observed that while the bilinguals had longer second-pass reading times than the monolingual participants, the patterns of preference for the resolution of the local ambiguities were identical for both types of participants: reading times were increased for the constructions that involved building more complex structure.

Frenck-Mestre (2005) examined how monolinguals and bilinguals read sentences involving the classic garden path reduced relative clause construction described earlier. The structurally equivalent sentence *The submarine destroyed during the war sank in a few seconds* might not be nearly as difficult to process as *The horse raced past the barn fell*, because the disambiguation point is reached earlier: the critical verb *destroy* is obligatorily transitive. The flexible word order of French, compared to English, and the likeness in form between the past participle and present indicative form of verbs like *détruire* permit a comparison of sentences like *Le sous-marin détruit pendant la guerre a coulé en quelques secondes*, equivalent to the English sentence above, and *Le sous-marin détruit pendant la guerre un navire de la marine royale* ("The submarine destroys during the war a ship from the royal navy"). Monolingual readers showed a preference for the structurally simpler sentences—those without a reduced relative clause, though this preference was not immediate. The bilingual readers, in contrast, exhibited difficulty throughout the prepositional phrase region and showed a preference for the more complex structure—the reduced relative clause version of the sentences. Clearly, the native language affected how the bilinguals processed these strings: the prepositional phrase following the verb *détruit* rules out, for the bilinguals, the possibility of this verb being anything other than a participle.

Evidence of forward transfer in sentence processing has been offered by a number of studies that examine how bilinguals process relative clause attachment ambiguities, as in the sentence *Peter fell in love with the sister of the psychologist who lives in California*. Here, the relative clause *who lives in California* could be interpreted as referring to *the sister* or to *the psychologist*. By a principle such as Late Closure, the relative clause should be preferably interpreted as referring to the low, more recent noun, *the psychologist*. This is indeed the preferred interpretation of the construction for speakers of English (Cuetos & Mitchell, 1988; Fernández, 2003). Yet, speakers of languages like Spanish as well as French, Portuguese, and several others, prefer to attach the relative clause high, to the more distant noun, *the sister* (Carreiras & Clifton, 1993, 1999; Cuetos & Mitchell, 1988; Fernández, 2003). The earliest explanations of this difference in preference attributed this effect to language-specificity in the parser (Mitchell & Cuetos, 1991). Alternative accounts of this cross-linguistic difference propose that the language-specific effects are not based in the sentence processing mechanisms, but rather driven by information outside of the parser; for example, the default prosodic phrasing imposed by a language's phonology (Fodor, 1998), or the language-specific application of pragmatic principles (Frazier & Clifton, 1996). Whether the cross-linguistic difference is sourced in the parser or the grammar is a matter beyond the scope of this discussion; the fact that cross-linguistic differences have been widely documented in monolinguals raises the question of how bilinguals behave in each of their languages.

Experiments comparing the relative clause attachment preferences of speakers of two languages for which monolinguals exhibit cross-linguistic differences in preferred interpretations have demonstrated that patterns of attachment very typically match those of monolinguals of the bilingual's L1 or the bilingual's dominant language. Frenck-Mestre (Frenck-Mestre, 1997) reports that beginner L2 learners of French (whose L1 was English) show patterns of attachment that resemble those of English monolinguals, with a preference for the low-attachment interpretation. Similar results involving forward transfer for Portuguese-English and English-Portuguese bilinguals are reported by Maia and Maia (2005). A more complex set of findings is reported by Dussias (2001), who examined the patterns of preference for early Spanish/English bilinguals who learned both languages before age six, and late Spanish/English bilinguals whose L2 was either Spanish or English. The late L2-Spanish bilinguals showed the same type of forward transfer pattern as in the Frenck-Mestre study, a preference for low attachment in both English and Spanish whereas the late L2-English bilinguals showed differentiation (L1 high, L2 low). Additionally, the early bilinguals exhibited no clear preference for attaching to the low or to the high noun, in either language.

A second study conducted by Dussias (2003) examined the relative clause attachment preferences of Spanish-English bilinguals who are highly proficient in both languages. Their proficiency was determined by a careful screening procedure that identified speakers with higher levels of L2 competence. In a series of experiments, both L2-Spanish and L2-English bilinguals exhibited low-attachment preferences in both languages, like their English monolingual counterparts, but unlike their Spanish monolingual counterparts. Dussias contemplates an explanation for this finding that hinges on the idea that the cognitive demands placed on bilinguals might promote the use of minimal effort strategies, like Late Closure. An alternative explanation, but one that, as Dussias acknowledges, contends that language exposure is crucial in determining preferences: the bilinguals in this study were living in an environment where English is the majority language. Dussias and Sagarra (2007) examined the variable of exposure directly, by comparing attachment preferences in Spanish monolinguals, Spanish-English bilinguals with limited exposure to English, and bilinguals with extensive exposure to English. Their results indicate that immersion experience affects attachment preferences: bilinguals with extensive exposure had more English-monolingual-like attachment preferences.

Dussias and Sagarra's (2007) findings offer strong empirical support to the idea that immediate linguistic environment can determine the type of preferences that bilinguals have when processing the relative clause attachment construction. Yet, the factor that actually drives such preferences might not be the environment directly, but rather a variable influenced by the environment: proficiency or language dominance. Fernández (2003) examined the attachment preferences of early Spanish/English bilinguals, grouped as English- or Spanish-dominant (all were native speakers of Spanish or native speakers of both languages), and found an effect of language dominance. Spanish-dominant bilinguals had preference profiles that resembled those of Spanish monolinguals, while English-dominant bilinguals showed preferences similar to those of their English monolingual counterparts.

To conclude this section, we turn to a set of findings from syntactic processing in bilinguals which measure syntactic priming effects in production rather than perception (see also Branzi, Calabria, and Costa, this volume). In these studies, participants are placed in discourse contexts where both languages must be activated, as the tasks involve moving from one language (in which a prime sentence is presented), to another (in which a target sentence is produced by the participant). The primes can be presented either auditorily or in writing, and participants are sometimes required to repeat the primes, others not. The results of these priming experiments are all quite similar: a structure provided in one language primes itself in the other. Similarly to how studies of lexical priming (discussed earlier in this chapter) examine questions related to shared versus separate lexical representations, studies of structural priming offer empirical testbeds for questions related to shared versus separate syntactic representations.

One of the earliest such studies, Loebell and Bock (2003) asked participants to repeat a sentence heard in L1 (German) or L2 (English) and subsequently describe a picture in the other language. The materials included dative alternation and active/passive alternation constructions. Loebell and Bock report reliable priming effects for double object primes, prepositional object primes, and active primes. Another study conducted by Hartsuiker et al. (2004) also examined the active/passive alternation by employing a picture description task in which a confederate participant presented primes in Spanish while describing a picture, and a naïve participant described a picture in English. Hartsuiker et al. observe a reliable priming effect with both active and passive primes.

Desmet and Declercq (2006) administered a sentence completion task to a group of Dutch-English bilinguals whose task was to complete the relative clause. The materials included primes in which a relative clause attachment was forced either high or low by the gender agreement of the relative pronoun. Prime and target items were sentence fragments presented through the relative pronoun, and fillers were sentence completion items of different forms. In the targets, the resolution of the attachment was identified by the verb produced by the participants, which matched in number to either the high or low noun in the complex NP. Desmet and Declerq found a reliable priming effect with relative clause attachment primes forced to attach low.

The simplest explanation for these effects, though certainly not the only possible explanation, invokes shared representations for generating and recovering syntactic structure in both languages. One complication for priming experiments is the unavoidable fact that both languages are activated during the experimental trial, thus plausibly reducing the possibility to observe language-specific behavior. This concern can be addressed by examining contrasts between languages which are predicted to have varying degrees of shared representations.

Fernández, de Souza, and Carando (2016) collected data from Spanish-English bilinguals using a structural priming paradigm where the prime was in English or in Spanish, and the target was in Spanish. Carando contrasted three alternations: the active/passive voice alternation (*The dancer pushed the janitor/The janitor was pushed by the dancer*), reciprocal alternation (*The chef and the policeman hugged/The chef hugged the policeman*), and dative alternation (*The doctor gave a suitcase to the waiter/The doctor gave the waiter a suitcase*). The first two alternation types are structurally very similar in both languages, but the dative alternation involves different structures in the two languages. All three alternations elicited priming effects both within language (Spanish-to-Spanish) and between languages (English-to-Spanish), but the last alternation, with dative constructions, produced reduced priming English-to-Spanish compared to Spanish-to-Spanish.

10.6 ON AGE OF ACQUISITION AND PROFICIENCY

Although work from Tokowicz and MacWhinney (2005) reveals that overlap can transfer between a bilingual's two languages, it also reveals that syntactic functions which do not overlap between languages can be learned. Hence, some syntactic information overlaps across languages whereas some does not. However, semantic processing especially when it is reliant on concepts that exist in the real world (e.g., dog) is relatively language-independent and thus does overlap across languages in a more consistent manner. The fact that overlap across languages is modulated by the type of function makes an interesting prediction about the difference between semantic and syntactic processing. Specifically, semantic processing should transfer more easily from one language to the other and should be less affected by variables that are traditionally known to modulate language processing in bilinguals.

Work investigating sentence processing using neuroimaging methods suggests that age of acquisition plays a more critical role than proficiency in determining the neural activity associated with grammatical processing (Wartenburger et al., 2003; Weber-Fox & Neville, 1996). A seminal study by Weber-Fox and Neville (1996) found that ERPs to syntactic anomalies differed between L1 and L2 speakers even when the latter began L2 acquisition between one and three years of life. However, differences in the electrophysiological signatures to semantic anomalies differed in individuals who learned L2 after the age of 11. More recently, Wartenburger et al. (2003) asked participants to detect syntactic anomalies (violations of case, gender, or number) or semantic anomalies in a set of visually presented sentences. The groups included one early high-proficiency group, one late high-proficiency group, and one late low-proficiency group. For semantic judgments, there were differences between the high- and low-proficiency late bilinguals. However, there were no differences in brain activity for semantic processing even in high-proficiency groups that differed in second language age of acquisition (AoA). For syntactic anomalies there were significant differences between the two high-proficiency groups which differed on AoA but no differences between the two low-proficiency groups. In short, we could assert that proficiency plays a stronger role in semantic processing (Moreno & Kutas, 2005) whereas AoA plays a stronger role in syntactic processing.

The differential effects of AoA (Birdsong, 1992, 1999; Birdsong & Flege, 2001; Flege, Yeni-Komshian, & Liu, 1999; Izura & Ellis, 2004) and proficiency levels in the processing of a second language (Miyake & Friedman, 1998; Moreno & Kutas, 2005; Perani et al., 1998; Snodgrass, 1993) has been the discussion of a number of articles and is beyond the scope of this article. However, there is one interesting aspect of the debate that fits in with the notion of overlap discussed earlier. Specifically, because semantic processing relies on conceptual information, it overlaps to a greater extent across languages (Kroll & de Groot, 2005; Kroll & Tokowicz, 2005; Kroll, Tokowicz, & Nicol, 2001). Syntactic and morphological information shows relatively less overlap across languages and hence transfers much less easily. Results from the studies cited above suggest that overlap can help to mitigate maturational differences that appear during language transfer. Interestingly, this is a topic that has received more attention in the bilingual imaging literature than in the psycholinguistic literature.

Recent work by Steinhauer suggests that language proficiency plays an important role in syntactic processing (White, Genesee, & Steinhauer, 2012). For example, work has found that as participants improve in their second-language proficiency their ERP wave signatures change from being dominated by a semantic mode of processing to a more syntactic mode of processing. Specifically, participants who were shown grammatically incorrect sentences showed stronger N400's during early stages of learning but began to show a stronger P600 as proficiency improved. As noted earlier, N400's are associated with lexical processing and are greater under a variety of conditions that make processing of a word more difficult (Kutas & Federmeier, 2011). The P600 is found when participants are presented with sentences that have syntactic errors (Friederici, 2011; Sassenhagen, Schlesewsky, & Bornkessel-Schlesewsky, 2014).

Recent work by Tanner, Osterhout and colleagues has followed up on this finding (Tanner, Mclaughlin, Herschensohn, & Osterhout, 2013). Specifically, they have found that variance in second-language proficiency can be clearly correlated along an N400-P600 continuum. Thus, lower language proficiency can be associated with a more lexically based strategy for interpreting syntactic errors. Higher language proficiency can be associated with a more syntactic based strategy. Finally, recent studies have found that those with the highest proficiency can actually show more native-like ERP components including a left anterior negativity which is sensitive to morphosyntactic violations as well as a P600 (Bowden, Steinhauer, Sanz, & Ullman, 2013). These results suggest that acquisition of a second language can result in very high levels of language proficiency that approximate those seen in native speakers of a language (Kotz, 2009; Steinhauer, White, & Drury, 2009).

10.7 Conclusion

Taken together, results from the bilingual sentence processing literature suggest that "bilinguals are not two monolinguals in one head." Specifically, many studies have shown that bilinguals use sentence processing strategies that are sometimes L1-like, sometimes L2-like, and sometimes in-between, when processing linguistic stimuli in one or the other language. This has been shown to be true across both semantic and syntactic processing. Furthermore, we found evidence that this was also true for both explicit and implicit measures of syntactic processing. Altogether, these results support a model in which multiple constraints play a role in determining the nature of bilingual sentence processing. These constraints include the nature of a speaker's language, proficiency, and language acquisition history. In general, the more dominant language will influence the processing of the less dominant language across both semantic and syntactic processing domains. The nature of sentence processing in bilinguals is also determined by the particular characteristics of the languages being learned. For example, there is evidence that similarity in lexical forms and grammatical forms can result in increased transfer in both the semantic and syntactic domains respectively. Bilinguals navigate this multidimensional landscape in order to arrive at a unique language system. Understanding the role of both speaker and language constraints on this process requires further inquiry.

Given the complexity of the task facing a bilingual, one would expect incredible amounts of interference between the languages, or an over-reliance on other cognitive systems in order to mediate between the two languages. We find evidence of neither of these. Understanding how the bilingual can take advantage of similarities between languages while they avoid catastrophic interference is one that should keep researchers occupied for many years to come.

References

Altarriba, J. (1992). The representation of translation equivalents in bilingual memory. In: Harris, R. J. (Ed.), *Cognitive Processing in Bilinguals, Vol. 83* (pp. 157–174). North-Holland, Amsterdam.

Altarriba, J., Kroll, J. F., Sholl, A., & Rayner, K. (1996). The influence of lexical and conceptual constraints on reading mixed-language sentences: Evidence from eye fixations and naming times. *Memory & Cognition, 24*(4), 477–92.

Altarriba, J., & Mathis, K. M. (1997). Conceptual and lexical development in second language acquisition. *Journal of Memory and Language, 36*, 550–68.

Bates, E., & MacWhinney, B. (1982). Functionalist approaches to grammar. In: Wanner, E., & Gleitman, L. R. (Eds.), *Language Acquisition: The State of the Art*. Cambridge University Press, New York, NY.

Bates, E., & MacWhinney, B. (1987). Competition, variation and language learning. In: MacWhinney, B. (Ed.), *Mechanisms of Language Acquisition*. Erlbaum, Hillsdale, NJ.

Bates, E., & MacWhinney, B. (1989). *The Crosslinguistic Study of Sentence Processing*. Cambridge University Press, New York, NY.

Bever, T.G. (1970). The cognitive basis for linguistic structures. In: Hayes, R. (Ed.), *Cognition and Language Development* (pp. 277–360). Wiley & Sons, Inc, New York, NY.

Birdsong, D. (1992). Ultimate attainment in 2nd language acquisition. *Language, 68*(4), 706–55.

Birdsong, D. (Ed.) (1999). *Second Language Acquisition and the Critical Period Hypothesis*. Lawrence Erlbaum Associates, Mahwah, NJ.

Birdsong, D., & Flege, J. E. (2001). *Regular-irregular dissociations in the acquisition of English as a second language*. Paper presented at the BUCLD 25: Proceedings of the 25th Annual Boston University Conference on Language Development, Boston, MA.

Bowden, H. W., Steinhauer, K., Sanz, C., & Ullman, M. T. (2013). Native-like brain processing of syntax can be attained by university foreign language learners. *Neuropsychologia, 51*(13), 2492–511.

Carreiras, M., & Clifton, C. (1993). Relative clause interpretation preferences in Spanish and English. *Language and Speech, 36*, 353–72.

Carreiras, M., & Clifton, C. (1999). Another word on parsing relative clauses: Eyetracking evidence from Spanish and English. *Memory & Cognition, 27,* 826-33.

Chan, A. H. D., Li, G., Li, P., & Tan, L. H. (2004). Neural correlates of nouns and verbs in early bilinguals. *NeuroImage,* MO11.

Costa, A., Caramazza, A., & Sebastián-Gallés, N. (2000). The cognate facilitation effect: Implications for models of lexical access. *Journal of Experimental Psychology: Learning, Memory, and Cognition, 26*(5), 1283-96.

Cuetos, F., & Mitchell, D. C. (1988). Cross-linguistic differences in parsing: Restrictions on the use of the Late Closure strategy in Spanish. *Cognition, 30,* 73-105.

Cutler, A., Mehler, J., Norris, D., & Segui, J. (1992). The monolingual nature of speech segmentation by bilinguals. *Cognitive Psychology, 24,* 381-410.

de Blesser, R., Dupont, P., Postler, J., Bormans, G., Speelman, D., Mortelmans, L., & Debrock, M. (2003). The organisation of the bilingual lexicon: A PET study. *Journal of Neurolinguistics, 16,* 439-56.

de Groot, A. M. B. (1994). Word-type effects in bilingual processing tasks: Support for a mixed-representational system. In: Schreuder, R., & Weltens, B. (Eds.), *The Bilingual Lexicon* (pp. 27-51). John Benjamins, Amsterdam.

de Groot, A. M. B., & Nas, G. L. (1991). Lexical representation of cognates and noncognates in compound bilinguals. *Journal of Memory and Language, 30,* 90-123.

de Groot, A. M. B., Dannenburg, L., & van Hell, J. G. (1994). Forward and backward word translation. *Journal of Memory and Language, 33,* 600-29.

de Groot, A. M. B., & Hoeks, J. C. J. (1995). The development of bilingual memory: Evidence from word translation by trilinguals. *Language Learning, 45,* 683-724.

Desmet, T., & Declercq, M. (2006). Cross-linguistic priming of syntactic hierarchical configuration information. *Journal of Memory and Language, 54*(4), 610-32.

Donchin, E., & Coles, M. G. (1988). Is the P300 component a manifestation of context updating? *Behavioral and Brain Sciences, 11*(3), 357-427.

Dussias, P. (2001). Sentence parsing in fluent Spanish-English bilinguals. In: Nicol, J. L. (Ed.), *One Mind, Two Languages: Bilingual Language Processing* (pp. 159-76). Blackwell, Oxford.

Dussias, P. (2003). Syntactic ambiguity resolution in L2 learners: Some effects of bilinguality on L1 and L2 processing strategies. *Studies in Second Language Acquisition, 25,* 529-57.

Dussias, P. E., & Sagarra, N. (2007). The effect of exposure on syntactic parsing in Spanish-English bilinguals. *Bilingualism: Language and Cognition, 10*(1), 101-16.

Duyck, W., Assche, E. V., Drieghe, D., & Hartsuiker, R. J. (2007). Visual word recognition by bilinguals in a sentence context: Evidence for nonselective lexical access. *Journal of Experimental Psychology: Learning, Memory, and Cognition, 33*(4), 663-79.

Elston-Guettler, K. E., Paulmann, S., & Kotz, S. A. (2005). Who's in control? Proficiency and L1 influence on L2 processing. *Journal of Cognitive Neuroscience, 17*(10), 1593-610.

Fernández, E. M. (2003). *Bilingual Sentence Processing: Relative Clause Attachment in English and Spanish.* John Benjamins, Amsterdam.

Fernández, E. M., Souza, R. A., & Carando, A. (2016). Bilingual innovations: Experimental evidence offers clues regarding the psycholinguistics of language change. *Bilingualism: Language and Cognition, 20*(2), 251-68.

Flege, E., Bohn, O., & Jang, S. (1997). Effects of experience on non-native speakers' production and perception of English vowels. *Journal of Phonetics, 25,* 437-70.

Flege, J. E., Yeni-Komshian, G. H., & Liu, S. (1999). Age constraints on second language acquisition. *Journal of Memory and Language, 41,* 78-104.

Fodor, J. D. (1998). Learning to parse? *Journal of Psycholinguistic Research, 27*, 285–319.
Frazier, L., & Clifton, C. (1996). *Construal*. MIT Press, Cambridge, MA.
Frazier, L., & Fodor, J. D. (1978). The sausage machine: A new two-stage parsing model. *Cognition, 6*, 294–325.
Frenck-Mestre, C. (1997). Examining second language reading: An on-line look. In: Sorace, A., Heycock, C., & Shillcock, R. (Eds.), *Language Acquisition, Knowledge Representation and Processing: GALA 1997* (pp. 444–448). HCRC, Edinburgh, UK.
Frenck-Mestre, C. (2005). Ambiguities and anomalies: What can eye movements and event-related potentials reveal about second language sentence processing? In: Kroll, J. F., & de Groot, A. M. B. (Eds.), *Handbook of Bilingualism: Psycholinguistic Approaches* (pp. 268–81). Oxford University Press, New York.
Frenck-Mestre, C., & Pynte, J. (1997). Syntactic ambiguity resolution while reading in second and native languages. *Quarterly Journal of Experimental Psychology, 50A*, 119–48.
Friederici, A. D. (2011). The brain basis of language processing: From structure to function. *Physiological Reviews, 91*(4), 1357–92.
Gollan, T. H., Forster, K. I., & Frost, R. (1997). Translation priming with different scripts: Masked priming with cognates and noncognates in Hebrew-English bilinguals. *Journal of Experimental Psychology: Learning, Memory, and Cognition, 23*(5), 1122–39.
Grainger, J., & Beauvillain, C. (1988). Associative priming in bilinguals: Some limits of interlingual facilitation effects. *Canadian Journal of Psychology, 42*, 261–73.
Grosjean, F. (1992). Another view of bilingualism. In: Harris, R. (Ed.), *Cognitive Processing in Bilinguals*. Elsevier, New York, NY.
Hartsuiker, R. J., Pickering, M. J., & Veltkamp, E. (2004). Is syntax separate or shared between languages? *Psychological Science, 15*(6), 409–14.
Heredia, R., & Maclaughlin, B. (1992). Bilingual memory revisited. In: Harris, R. J. (Ed.), *Cognitive Processing in Bilinguals, Vol. 83* (pp. 91–103). North-Holland, Amsterdam.
Heredia, R. R. (1996). Bilingual memory: A re-revised version of the hierarchical model of bilingual memory. *CRL Newsletter, 10*(3).
Heredia, R. R. (1997). Bilingual memory and hierarchical models: A case for language dominance. *Current Directions in Psychological Science, 6*(2), 34–9.
Hernández, A. E. (2002). The effects of language asymmetries on lexical and sentential priming in Spanish-English bilinguals. In: Heredia, R., & Altarriba, J. (Eds.), *Bilingual Sentence Processing*. Elsevier/Academic Press, Amsterdam.
Hernández, A. E., & Bates, E. (1994). Interactive-activation in normal and brain-damaged individuals: Can context penetrate the lexical module? *Linguitiche Berichte, 6*, 145–67.
Hernández, A. E., Bates, E., & Avila, L. X. (1994). Sentence interpretation in Spanish-English bilinguals: What does it mean to be in-between? *Applied Psycholinguistics, 15*(n4), 417–66.
Hernández, A. E., Bates, E., & Avila, L. X. (1996). Processing across the language boundary: A cross modal priming study of Spanish-English bilinguals. *Journal of Experimental Psychology: Learning, Memory, and Cognition, 22*, 846–64.
Hernández, A. E., Sierra, I., & Bates, E. (2000). Sentence interpretation in bilingual and monolingual Spanish speakers: Grammatical processing in a monolingual mode. *Spanish Applied Linguistics, 4*, 179–213.
Izura, C., & Ellis, A. W. (2004). Age of acquisition effects in translation judgement tasks. *Journal of Memory and Language, 50*(2), 165.
Johnson, R. (1986). A triarchic model of P300 amplitude. *Psychophysiology, 23*(4), 367–84.

Kail, M. (1989). Cue validitiy, cue cost, and processing types in sentence comprehension in French and Spanish. In: MacWhinney, B., & Bates, E. (Eds.), *The Crosslinguistic Study of Sentence Processing*. Cambridge University Press, New York, NY.

Keatley, C., & de Gelder, B. (1992). The bilingual primed lexical decision task: Cross-language priming disappears with speeded responses. *European Journal of Cognitive Psychology*, 4, 273–92.

Kilborn, K. (1987). *Sentence Processing in a Second Language: Seeking a Performance Definition of Fluency* (Ph.D. Dissertation). University of California, San Diego, CA.

Kilborn, K., & Ito, T. (1989). Sentence processing strategies in adult bilinguals. In: Bates, E., & MacWhinney, B. (Eds.), *The Crosslinguistic Study of Sentence Processing* (pp. 257–91). Cambridge University Press, New York, NY.

Kimball, J. (1973). Seven principles of surface structure parsing in natural language. *Cognition*, 2(1), 15–47.

Kotz, S. A. (2009). A critical review of ERP and fMRI evidence on L2 syntactic processing. *Brain and Language*, 109(2–3), 68–74.

Kroll, J. F. (1994). Accessing conceptual representations for words in a second language. In: Schreuder, R., & Weltens, B. (Eds.), *The Bilingual Lexicon* (pp. 53–81). John Benjamins, Amsterdam.

Kroll, J. F., & Borning, L. (1987, November). Shifting language representations in novice bilinguals: Evidence from sentence priming. Paper presented at the Twenty-Seventh Annual Meeting of the Psychonomic Society, Seattle, WA.

Kroll, J. F., & de Groot, A. M. B. (2005). *Handbook of Bilingualism: Psycholinguistic Approaches*. Oxford University Press, New York, NY.

Kroll, J. F., & Sholl, A. (1992). Lexical and conceptual memory in fluent and nonfluent bilinguals. In: Harris, R. J. (Ed.), *Cognitive Processing in Bilinguals* (pp. 191–204). Elsevier, Amsterdam.

Kroll, J. F., & Stewart, E. (1994). Category inference in translation and picture naming: Evidence for asymmetric connections between bilingual memory representations. *Journal of Memory and Language*, 33, 149–74.

Kroll, J. F., & Tokowicz, N. (2005). Models of bilingual representation and processing: Looking back and to the future. In: Kroll, J. F., & DeGroot, A. M. B. (Eds.), *Handbook of Bilingualism: Psycholinguistic Approaches.* (pp. 531–33). Oxford University Press, New York, NY.

Kroll, J. F., Tokowicz, N., & Nicol, J. L. (2001). The development of conceptual representation for words in a second language. In: Nicol, J. L. (ed.), *One Mind, Two Languages: Bilingual Language Processing* (pp. 49–71). Blackwell Publishing, Hoboken, NJ.

Kroll, J. F., Van Hell, J. G., Tokowicz, N., & Green, D. W. (2010). The Revised Hierarchical Model: A critical review and assessment. *Bilingualism: Language and Cognition*, 13(3), 373–81.

Kutas, M., & Federmeier, K. D. (2011). Thirty years and counting: finding meaning in the N400 component of the event-related brain potential (ERP). *Annual Review of Psychology*, 62, 621–47.

Li, P., Jin, Z., & Tan, L. H. (2004). Neural representations of nouns and verbs in Chinese: An fMRI study. *NeuroImage*, 21(4), 1533–41.

Libben, M. R., & Titone, D. A. (2009). Bilingual lexical access in context: evidence from eye movements during reading. *Journal of Experimental Psychology: Learning, Memory, and Cognition*, 35(2), 381–90.

Liu, H., Bates, E., & Li, P. (1992). Sentence interpretation in bilingual speakers of English and Chinese. *Applied Psycholinguistics*, 13, 451–84.

Loebell, H., & Bock, K. (2003). Structural priming across languages. *Linguistics*, 41, 791–824.

MacWhinney, B. (2004). A unified model of language acquisition. In: Kroll, J. F., & DeGroot, A. M. B. (Eds.), *Handbook of Bilingualism: Psycholinguistic Approaches*. Oxford University Press, New York, NY.

MacWhinney, B. (Ed.) (1999). *Emergence of Language*. Lawrence Erlbaum Associates, Hillsdale, NJ.

Maia, M., & Maia, J. M. (2005). A compreensão de orações relativas por falantes monolíngües e bilíngües de pertuguês e de inglês. In: Maia, M., & Finger, I. (Eds.), *Processamento da linguagem* (pp. 163–78). Brazil, Educ. Pelotas.

McDonald, J. L. (1989). *The Acquisition of Cue-category Mappings*. Cambridge University Press, New York, NY.

McLaughlin, J., Osterhout, L., & Kim, A. (2004). Neural correlates of second-language word learning: Minimal instruction produces rapid change. *Nature Neuroscience*, 7(7), 703–4.

Mitchell, D. C. (1994). Sentence parsing. In: Gernsbacher, M. (Ed.), *Handbook of Psycholinguistics* (pp. 375–409). Academic Press, New York, NY.

Mitchell, D. C., & Cuetos, F. (1991). The origins of parsing strategies. In: Smith, C. (Ed.), *Current Issues in Natural Language Processing* (pp. 1–12). University of Texas Center for Cognitive Science, Austin, TX.

Miyake, A., & Friedman, N. P. (1998). Individual differences in second language proficiency: Working memory as language aptitude. In: Healy, A. F., & Bourne, L. E. Jr (Eds.), *Foreign Language Learning: Psycholinguistic Studies on Training and Retention* (pp. 339–64). Psychology Press, Mahwah, NJ.

Moreno, E. M., Federmeier, K. D., & Kutas, M. (2002). Switching languages, switching Palabras (words): An electrophysiological study of code switching. *Brain and Language*, 80(2), 188–207.

Moreno, E. M., & Kutas, M. (2005). Processing semantic anomalies in two languages: an electrophysiological exploration in both languages of Spanish-English bilinguals. *Cognitive Brain Research*, 22(2), 205–20.

Nakayama, M., Ida, K., & Lupker, S. J. (2016). Cross-script L2-L1 noncognate translation priming in lexical decision depends on L2 proficiency: Evidence from Japanese–English bilinguals. *Bilingualism: Language and Cognition*, 19(5), 1001–22.

Ng, S., Gonzalez, C., & Wicha, N. Y. (2014). The fox and the cabra: an ERP analysis of reading code switched nouns and verbs in bilingual short stories. *Brain Research*, 1557, 127–40.

Paradis, M. (1987). *The Assessment of Bilingual Aphasia*. Erlbaum, Hillsdale, NJ.

Paradis, M. (2009). *Declarative and Procedural Determinants of Second Languages*. John Benjamins Publishing, Amsterdam/Philadelphia.

Peeters, D., Dijkstra, T., & Grainger, J. (2013). The representation and processing of identical cognates by late bilinguals: RT and ERP effects. *Journal of Memory and Language*, 68(4), 315–32.

Perani, D., Paulesu, E., Galles, N. S., Dupoux, E., Dehaene, S., Bettinardi, V., . . . Mehler, J. (1998). The bilingual brain: Proficiency and age of acquisition of the second language. *Brain*, 121(10), 1841–52.

Reyes, I., & Hernández, A. E. (2006). Sentence interpretation strategies in emergent bilingual children and adults. *Bilingualism: Language and Cognition*, 9, 51–69.

Sánchez-Casas, R. M., Davis, C. W., & García-Albea, J. E. (1992). Bilingual lexical processing: Exploring the cognate/noncognate distinction. *European Journal of Cognitive Psychology*, 4(4), 293–310.

Sassenhagen, J., Schlesewsky, M., & Bornkessel-Schlesewsky, I. (2014). The P600-as-P3 hypothesis revisited: Single-trial analyses reveal that the late EEG positivity following linguistically deviant material is reaction time aligned. *Brain and Language*, 137, 29–39.

Snodgrass, J. G. (1993). Translating versus picture naming: Similarities and differences. In: Schreuder, R., & Weltens, B. (Eds.), *The Bilingual Lexicon: Studies in Bilingualism* (Vol. 6, pp. 83–114). John Benjamins Publishing, Amsterdam.

Steinhauer, K., White, E. J., & Drury, J. E. (2009). Temporal dynamics of late second language acquisition: Evidence from event-related brain potentials. *Second Language Research*, 25(1), 13–41.

Tanner, D., Mclaughlin, J., Herschensohn, J., & Osterhout, L. (2013). Individual differences reveal stages of L2 grammatical acquisition: ERP evidence. *Bilingualism: Language and Cognition*, 16(2), 367–82.

Tokowicz, N., & MacWhinney, B. (2005). Implicit vs. explicit measures of sensitivity to violations in L2 grammar: An event-related potential investigation. *Studies in Second Language Acquisition*, 27, 173–204.

Tzelgov, J., & Eben-Ezra, S. (1992). Components of the between-language priming effect. *European Journal of Cognitive Psychology*, 4, 253–72.

Vaid, J., & Pandit, R. (1991). Sentence interpretation in normal and aphasic Hindi speakers. *Brain and Language*, 41(n2), 250–74.

van Assche, E., Drieghe, D., Duyck, W., Welvaert, M., & Hartsuiker, R. J. (2011). The influence of semantic constraints on bilingual word recognition during sentence reading. *Journal of Memory and Language*, 64(1), 88–107.

Von Berger, E., Wulfeck, B., Bates, E., & Fink, N. (1996). Developmental changes in real-time sentence processing. *First Language*, 16(47), 193–222.

Wartenburger, I., Heekeren, H. R., Abutalebi, J., Cappa, S. F., Villringer, A., & Perani, D. (2003). Early setting of grammatical processing in the bilingual brain. *Neuron*, 37(1), 159–70.

Weber-Fox, C., & Neville, H. J. (1996). Maturational constraints on functional specializations for language processing: ERP and behavioral evidence in bilingual speakers. *Journal of Cognitive Neuroscience*, 8, 231–56.

White, E. J., Genesee, F., & Steinhauer, K. (2012). Brain responses before and after intensive second language learning: Proficiency-based changes and first language background effects in adult learners. *PLoS One*, 7(12), e52318.

Wulfeck, B., Juarez, L., Bates, E., & Kilborn, K. (1986). Sentence interpretation strategies in healthy and aphasic bilingual adults. In: Vaid, J. (Ed.), *Language Processing in Bilinguals: Psycholinguistic and Neuropsychological Perspectives*. Erlbaum, Hillsdale, NJ.

CHAPTER 11

SENTENCE LEVEL APHASIA

DAVID CAPLAN

11.1 INTRODUCTION

SENTENCES convey relationships between the meanings of words, such as who is accomplishing an action or receiving it. These aspects of meaning—collectively known as the propositional content of a sentence—extend the power of language beyond what is available through single words and word formation processes to allow language to represent events and states of affairs. Propositions are used to update semantic memory, to reason, and for many other purposes, and thus constitute a vital link between language and other cognitive processes.

Syntactic structures are the means whereby the meanings of individual words are combined to represent propositional meaning. Individual lexical items are marked for syntactic category (e.g., *cat* is a noun [N]; *kill* is a verb [V]; *a* is a determiner [DET]). These categories combine hierarchically to create phrasal categories such as noun phrase (NP), verb phrase (VP), sentence (S), and so on, and specific relations between the syntactic categories in these hierarchical structures determine different aspects of sentence meaning. Consider, for instance, sentence one, whose syntactic structure is shown in very schematic form in Figure 11.1.

11.2 THE DOG THAT SCRATCHED THE CAT KILLED THE MOUSE

Sentence one conveys the proposition that the dog killed the mouse. Figure 11.1 shows how they are related in the hierarchical structure of the sentence. The NP *the dog that scratched the cat* is immediately dominated by the sentence node (S), which also directly dominates the VP *killed the mouse*. An NP immediately dominated by an S is the subject of the sentence, and the subject of the sentence has a thematic role related to the verb of the VP of the sentence. In sentence one, *the dog* (actually, *the dog that scratched the cat*) is the subject of the sentence and is the agent of the verb *killed*.

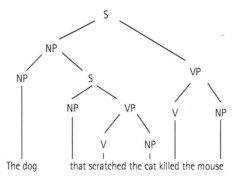

FIG. 11.1 Simplified syntactic structure of the sentence, *The dog that scratched the cat killed the mouse*, showing the hierarchical organization of syntactic categories that determine thematic roles.

There is a sequence of words in sentence one—*the cat killed the mouse*—in which an NP (*the cat*) immediately precedes a V (*killed*) in the linear structure of the sentence but does not play a thematic role around *killed*. This is because of the position of these words in the hierarchical syntactic structure of this sentence. *The cat* is the object of the verb *scratched* in the relative clause *that scratched the cat* and is the theme of *scratched*. The path over the hierarchical structure between *the cat* and *killed* has no semantic interpretation.

The fact that syntactic structures relate word meanings by rules, not inferentially, allows language to express relations among items, properties, and actions that are unlikely, false, or impossible. This ability is crucial to reasoning counterfactually (e.g., "If John were here, he would agree with me"), an ability that is critical to both planning individuals' actions and to collective enterprises such as science, law, management, and so on.

Difficulties using syntax to encode or to decode messages are common in aphasia. Disturbances affecting the ability to construct syntactic structure in production were recognized relatively early (Pick; see Brown, 1973). Disturbances affecting comprehension that required syntactic processing were first described much later (in 1976) but research into disorders of syntactic comprehension has progressed much further than has work on syntactic disorders in production, especially through the use of online measures to assess performance. In this chapter, I briefly review behavioral aspects of disorders of syntactic comprehension and production, and neural issues related to these disorders.

11.3 Disorders of syntactic comprehension

Caramazza and Zurif (1976) first documented the existence of syntactic comprehension in people with aphasia (PWA). They found that PWA could not reliably match sentences such as 2 to pictures, but could match sentences such as 3:

2. The apple the boy is eating is red.
3. The girl the boy is chasing is tall.

They interpreted the results as indicating that some PWAs (those with Broca's and conduction aphasia) could assign thematic roles inferentially but not by constructing and interpreting syntactic structures. This study established the criteria still in use to diagnose such a disorder—the PWAs cannot demonstrate understanding of sentences whose meaning cannot be inferred from word meaning and real-world knowledge or by the application of a heuristic (e.g., taking the noun immediately preceding each verb as the agent of that verb).

At least 12 models of the psycholinguistic and/or cognitive deficits that produce these disorders have been proposed. Box 11.1 lists them and classifies them in relation to different mechanisms. I will not review all these models here. I will discuss specific deficit models, resource reduction models, slowed processing models, and interference models, which are representative of work in the field and for which most evidence has accumulated.

The first theories of syntactic comprehension deficits were specific deficit models. My colleagues and I advocated these analyses in our earlier work (see Caplan & Hildebrandt, 1988, for a detailed study of a series of PWAs within this framework; also Hildebrandt et al., 1987). Researchers who advocate specific deficit accounts of aphasic disturbances have claimed that certain PWAs' patterns of performance indicate that specific representations and processes specified in linguistics and in psycholinguistic models of parsing and sentence interpretation are deficient. For instance, the "trace deletion hypothesis" (Grodzinsky, 2000) maintains that

---

Box 11.1 Models of Syntactic Comprehension Deficits

Group 1—Global parsing or interpretive failure
Model 1: *Global parsing failure* (Caramazza & Zurif, 1976)
Model 2: *Mapping failure* (Linebarger et al., 1983; Linebarger, 1995)
Model 3: *Noisy channel* (Gibson et al., 2013; Warren et al., 2014)

Group 2: Selective parsing or interpretive failure
Model 4: *Selective parsing deficits* (Beretta & Munn, 1998; Caplan & Hildebrandt, 1988; Fyndanis et al., 2010; Garraffa & Grillo, 2008; Grodzinsky, 1990; Grodzinsky, 2000; Mauner et al., 1993; Varlokosta et al., 2014)
Model 5: *Task-parsing/interpretation interaction deficits* (Cupples & Inglis, 1993; Caplan et al. 1997, 2006, 2007, 2013a)

Group 3: Resource reduction
Model 6: *Resource reduction* (Caplan et al., 1985, 2007a; Caplan, 2012; Gutman et al., 2010, 2011)
Model 7: *Resource reduction with noise* (Caplan et al., 2006, 2007a)

Group 4: Slowed processing
Model 8: *Slowed lexical access* (Love et al., 2008; Prather et al., 1992; Swinney & Zurif, 1995; Zurif et al., 1993)
Model 9: *Slowed syntactic processing* (Burkhardt et al., 2003; Friederici & Kilborn, 1989; Haarmann & Kolk, 1991a, b; Sullivan et al., 2014).

Group 5: Increased interference
Model 10: *Heightened susceptibility to interference* (Dickey et al., 2007; Dickey & Thompson, 2009; Hanne et al., 2011; Meyer et al., 2012; MacKenzie et al., 2014; Thompson & Choy, 2009)

Group 6: Late delayed operations
Model 11: *Delayed lexical integration* (Choy & Thompson, 2010; Mack et al., 2013; Meyer et al., 2012)
Model 12: *Insensitivity to predictions* (Dickey et al., 2014; Mack et al., 2013)

individual PWAs cannot process sentences that Chomsky's theory maintains contain a certain type of moved item (the term "trace deletion hypothesis" refers to an earlier version of Chomsky's theory in which these items were moved and left a "trace").

Evidence for such deficits would come from the finding that a PWA had an impairment restricted to processing those sentences that required that structure or operation to be understood. Proponents of these models have argued that data of this sort are derived from aphasic studies. For instance, Grodzinsky (2000) reviewed studies in several languages that he claimed show that PWAs with Broca's aphasia have abnormally low performances on sentences in which these movement operations have taken place, and where simple heuristics cannot lead to a normal interpretation.

There are serious problems with specific deficit models. First, adequate linguistic controls have not been run that would show that the deficit is restricted to the structures claimed. For instance, the trace deletion hypothesis maintains that PWAs with the deficit in question can co-index items other than traces, such as pronouns and reflexives. None of the papers in the literature that has been taken as supporting the trace deletion hypothesis have reported PWAs' performance on both sentences with traces and sentences with reflexives (or other referentially dependent items, such as pronouns; see Caplan 1995; Caplan et al., 2007b).

A second problem with specific deficit analyses is that the data in support of the analysis overwhelmingly consist of measures of accuracy in one task, usually sentence–picture matching. However, it has been well documented that performance dissociates over tasks (Caplan et al., 1997; Cupples & Inglis 1993). Analysis of the largest series of single cases currently available (Caplan et al., 2006, 2007a, 2013a) failed to find a single PWA who had a deficit affecting comprehension of sentences with a certain structure or that required a particular operation that was found in all tasks on which the PWA was tested, and no other deficit. On the contrary, many PWAs had deficits affecting sentences with a certain structure or that required a particular operation in one task only. These task-dependent, construction-specific deficits were found in both sentence–picture matching and enactment. These results point to most deficits being due to a deficit in the ability to combine parsing and interpretive operations with the operations needed to perform a task. Understanding these deficits will require a deeper understanding of tasks such as sentence–picture matching or enactment that are performed.

An alternative view is that deficits of aphasic syntactic comprehension consist of reductions of processing capacity. Five arguments have been made in support of this suggestion:

1. Some PWAs can understand sentences that contain certain structures or operations in isolation but not sentences that contain combinations of those structures and operations (Caplan & Hildebrandt, 1988; Hildebrandt et al., 1987).
2. In large groups of PWAs, as PWAs' performances deteriorate, more complex sentence types are affected more than less complex ones (Caplan et al., 1985, 2007a).
3. In factor analyses of performance of such PWA groups in syntactic comprehension tasks, first factors on which all sentence types load account for most of the variance (Caplan et al., 1985, 1996, 2007a).
4. The best fitting Rasch models of accuracy of responses in tests of syntactic comprehension in PWAs have included factors that affect all sentences (Gutman et al., 2011).
5. Simulations of the effect of resource reductions on syntactic comprehension in normal subjects using speeded presentation (Miyake et al., 1994), concurrent tasks (King & Just, 1991), and other methods mimic aphasic performance.

The fundamental question that arises about resource reduction models is what "resources" are. A widely held view is that they are the mechanisms that support short-term, or working, memory. These mechanisms have been thought to include a phonological store, a subvocal rehearsal process, a "central store" that maintains multidimensional representations, a "central executive" that maintains these representations and operates on them, and an executive attention controller that schedules entry and removal of items in these stores. Our work with both normal individuals, PWAs with Alzheimer's Disease, and PWAs does not support the view that these mechanisms are the "resource" that supports the memory requirements of parsing and interpretation (see Caplan & Waters, 1999, 2013, for reviews) or the view that disorders of these mechanism lead to syntactic comprehension disorders (see Caplan et al., 2013b, for recent work with PWAs). The basic findings supporting this conclusion come from individual differences studies and interference studies. In both, evidence for a role for working memory in syntactic comprehension would consist of a disproportionate effect of low working memory, or a memory load, on online behaviors in comprehension tasks at points at which there is an increase in parsing load; a simple effect of low working memory or load throughout a sentence could be due to a role for working memory in any number of processes (e.g., lexical access). While there are many results showing interactions, or working memory capacity and syntactic complexity, and of concurrent memory load and syntactic complexity, in end-of-sentence measures of comprehension, there are no results showing such interactions in online measures (see reviews cited above). We have concluded that working memory plays a role in maintaining *interpreted* materials in memory in order to perform a task, but not in assigning structure and deriving meaning in-line. Comparable studies that focus on other cognitive capacities, such as executive attention, inhibition, and others, have not been performed; to the extent that some measures of working memory used in the studies referred to above, such a complex span tasks, measure executive functions, existing data suggest that online parsing and interpretation is also not under direct executive control. To our knowledge, another postulated short duration memory system—short-term semantic memory (Martin & He, 2004)—has never been considered to be the "resource" that supports all syntactic comprehension; its role has been limited to particular structures.

A second mechanism that could reduce the "resources" needed for syntactic comprehension is an increase in the level of random noise that exists in the parser/interpreter. Caplan et al. (2006) provided evidence that noise affects performances of PWAs in the form of statistically better performance of some PWAs on a baseline than an experimental sentence in a task, which can only happen if random disruptions of the parser/interpreter occasionally affect baseline sentences more than related experimental sentences. Caplan et al. (2006) suggested that the only factors that determine performance of PWAs in syntactic comprehension tasks may be the level of noise each PWA's parser/interpreter is subject to and the demands of each sentence type. Our Rasch models suggested this model is too simple (Gutman et al., 2010, 2011), but noise and sentence complexity may account for a great deal of the variance in performance.

A second view of resource reduction constitutes the third type of model I shall review— the view that what appears as resource reduction reflects a slower speed of processing, either affecting lexical access with secondary effects of parsing and interpretation or directly affecting parsing and interpretation itself. Data supporting these models come from measures of online syntactic processing—the centisecond-by-centisecond assignment of syntactic structure as a sentence unfolds auditorily or is inspected visually.

One series of online studies uses the cross-modal lexical priming (CMLP) task. In this task, a subject listens to a sentence and, at some point in the sentence, a series of letters appears on a computer screen; the subject must push a button to indicate if the letter string is or is not a word (a lexical decision task). Unbeknown to the subject, in half the cases in which the letter string is a word, it is semantically related or associated with a word that was previously presented in the sentence. In these cases, reaction times are typically faster than when the real-word stimuli are not related to previously presented words. Using this technique, Zurif et al. (1993) and Swinney and Zurif (1995) found priming for words related to the noun retrieved at relative clause verbs in four Wernicke's aphasics but not in four Broca's aphasics. Love et al. (2008) showed that eight Broca's aphasics showed CMLP for nouns retrieved by verbs of object-extracted relative clauses when speaking rate was slow (3.4 syllables/second; exp 2) but not when it was fast (4.47 syllables/second; exp 1), which they took as evidence for delayed activation of the antecedent of the trace at the relative clause verb in Broca's aphasics. These results are consistent with slowed lexical access or syntactic processing in agrammatic PWA. However, there are discrepant data regarding slowing in PWA. Blumstein et al. (1998) reported normal cross-modal priming at the verb of object-extracted relative clauses in Broca's aphasics (see discussion in Balogh et al., 1998, and Caplan, 2001).

The final model of syntactic comprehension I shall review is the interference model. This model also is based on online data, in this case from the use of the "visual world paradigm" task, developed by Tanenhaus et al. (1995). In this paradigm, a participant listens to a sentence while viewing a display containing pictures of nouns referred to in the sentence and distracters. Fixations on pictures are interpreted as indications that the concept corresponding to the picture is active at the point of the fixation. Several studies have studied fixations on pictures representing items that have to be retrieved by a verb, pronoun, or reflexive at the point that these words occur in agrammatic PWA and normal controls (Dickey et al., 2007 (n = 12); Dickey & Thompson, 2009 (n = 8); Thompson & Choy, 2009 (n = 8)). Normal increases in fixations on the picture corresponding to the retrieved item occurred at the point of the word that triggered retrieval both when PWAs responded correctly and when they made errors. As Dickey et al. (2007) wrote, "The index of automatic comprehension in wh- questions, increased looks to the object during the verb, appeared equally early for aphasic and control participants. This seems surprising . . . under slowed-processing accounts (p. 14)."

In these studies, PWA's errors were associated with abnormally high numbers of looks to a competitor picture late in the presentation of the sentence (after the word triggering retrieval had passed). Eye-tracking studies using sentence–picture matching (SPM) have shown differences in fixations for correct and incorrect responses early in the presentation of a sentence in two groups of PWAs with Broca's aphasia (Meyer et al., 2012; n = 10; Hanne et al., 2011; n = 7). These results suggest that increased susceptibility to interference from thematic roles that are not licensed by the syntactic structure of the sentence may be a mechanism for syntactic comprehension deficits. The difference in the time course of abnormal looks to foils in the visual world paradigm and sentence–picture matching is consistent with thematic roles presented in foil pictures being available, and affecting comprehension, early in SPM and thematic roles derived from the use of heuristics being available, and affecting comprehension, late in the visual world paradigm.

Results of studies using self-paced listening are consistent with the eye fixation data in showing effects that are attributable to different time course of potentially interfering thematic roles in different tasks. Caplan et al. (2007a) used self-paced listening with SPM, in which thematic roles were available from foils at the onset of the sentence. For PWAs whose performances were at chance, listening times for object relative verbs were normally elevated in correct responses and did not show the normal prolongation in errors. In contrast, using a plausibility judgment task, in which thematic roles were available only at the end of a relative clause, Caplan and Waters (2003) found equivalent, and normal, increases in listening times at the verbs of object relatives and clefts in both errors and correct responses in PWAs whose performances were at chance.

To summarize, a variety of models of aphasic syntactic comprehension have been proposed. I have reviewed four: that syntactic comprehension disorders arise from (1) deficits in the ability to apply particular parsing or interpretive operations; (2) reduction in resources needed to parse and interpret sentences; (3) slowing of lexical access or parsing; (4) increased susceptibility to thematic roles derived non-syntactically. They all require further study.

11.3.1 Disorders of syntactic production

Studies of syntactic processing in sentence production have explored two aphasic disturbances of production that have been described clinically—agrammatism and paragrammatism. Agrammatism is a component of the syndrome of Broca's aphasia. The most noticeable deficit in agrammatism is the widespread omission of function words and affixes and the greater retention of content words. Paragrammatism is marked by substitutions of function words and morphological elements. Although separate disorders, agrammatism and paragrammatism often co-occur (de Bleser, 1987; Heeschen, 1985; Menn & Obler, 1990).

The class of words that are affected in agrammatism and paragrammatism has been described in a psychological and in a linguistic framework. According to the psychological account, the words that are affected in agrammatism are those that belong to the closed class of vocabulary elements—categories other than nouns, verbs, adjectives, and derived adverbs, to which words are not added. The linguistic approach to the characterization of agrammatism has been explored by several researchers (e.g., Kean (1977) proposed that the elements affected in this syndrome were ones that could not be assigned stress in English).

There are many patterns of agrammatism and paragrammatism (Berndt, 1987; Goodglass, 1973; Luria, 1973; Menn & Obler, 1990; Miceli et al., 1989; Miceli et al., 1983; Parisi, 1987; Tissot et al., 1973). However, there are some general features of these disorders. The loss of affixes and function words tends to mirror their developmental sequence of acquisition in reverse, although there are important exceptions to this effect (de Villiers, 1974). Goodglass (1973) suggested that words that are less "salient" are more difficult for an agrammatic PWA. Salience is the "psychological resultant of stress, of the informational significance, of the phonological prominence, and of the affective value of a word" (Goodglass, 1973, p. 204). Kean (1977) proposed that agrammatic PWAs are constrained to produce real words; this would explain the retention of affixes in languages in which roots without affixes are not well-formed words, such as Hebrew (Grodzinsky, 1984) and Italian (Miceli et al., 1983). Infinitives and gerunds tend to be overproduced in paragrammatism. Lapointe (1983) suggested that this is because they are the basic forms in the verbal system and are the first to be accessed by PWAs with limited resources available for accessing verb forms. In other cases, substitutions are closely related to the inferred target (Miceli et al.,1990). In almost all cases, errors are paradigm internal; that is, they do not violate the word formation and even the syntactic processes of the language.

There seem to be two broad sources of agrammatism: an inability to access these lexical forms per se, and a disturbance of using them in sentence production. Some PWAs who omit function words and bound morphemes have disturbances affecting the production or processing of these items in isolation. Many PWAs with agrammatism have deep dyslexia and cannot read function words and bound morphemes aloud. Others, such as F.S. (Miceli & Caramazza, 1988), have problems repeating some morphological forms. In these cases, several authors have suggested that the omission of function words and bound morphemes seen in sentence production is related to these processing disturbances at the single-word level.

In other PWAs, however, agrammatism occurs only in relationship to sentence planning and production, without any disturbance of processing function words or bound morphemes in isolation. For example, Caramazza and Hillis (1988) reported a PWA with this form of the disorder. In one PWA, M.M., this phenomenon was quite dramatic. Nespoulous et al. (1988) asked M.M. to read words written vertically, one to a page. M.M. did so perfectly, turning the pages over and reading each word, until he quite suddenly realized that the sequence of words formed a sentence. From that point on, he had difficulty with the items in these affected groups of words.

Several models of disturbances in producing syntactic structures have been proposed. These have some similarities to models of syntactic comprehension deficits.

Ostrin (1982) suggested that some agrammatic PWAs have what might be considered a form of resource reduction. She reported the performance of four agrammatic PWAs in repeating sentences with a variable number of NPs, prepositional phrases, and adjectives modifying nouns. She found that the PWAs had a strong tendency to repeat either a determiner and a noun (*the man*) or an adjective and a noun (*old man*), but did not produce both (*the old man*). Similarly, in sentences with both an NP and a prepositional phrase (PP) in the VP (*The woman is showing the dress to the man*), the PWAs showed a tendency to produce either the NP or the PP but not both. The PWAs' multiple attempts to repeat the target sentences often produced all the elements of the sentence, one on each attempt. Ostrin suggested that these PWAs retained the entire semantic content of the presented sentence but could not produce all the elements they retained. She suggested that these PWAs have a reduced number of "planning frames" that they can use.

Ostrin and Schwartz (1986) proposed a different deficit, of the "resource reduction" type. They had six agrammatic PWAs repeat semantically reversible, semantically plausible, and semantically implausible sentences in the active and passive voice. Errors to plausible sentences were primarily lexical substitutions. Many errors to implausible sentences reversed the thematic roles in the sentence to render the resulting utterance plausible. The PWAs tended to retain the order of nouns and verbs in the presented sentence and made many errors that the authors interpreted as efforts to produce passive forms (mixed morphology errors, such as *The bicycle is riding by the boy* for *The bicycle is riding the boy*). The authors argued that their PWAs had a memory deficit—that they produced plausible sentences from an incomplete memory trace that contained the grammatical roles (subject, object) of the NPs in the presented sentence.

Analyses more akin to specific deficits have also been developed. Friedman and Grodzinsky (1999) argued that agrammatic PWAs cannot construct full syntactic trees, and nodes that are higher in a syntactic tree are pruned in agrammatism. Specifically, in some versions of Chomsky's theory, abstract nodes in trees mark subject–verb agreement and tense, with the latter higher than the former. The "tree pruning hypothesis" maintains that agrammatics can construct trees with the node for agreement, but not tense; evidence for this comes from observations that tense markers on verbs are more often omitted than are agreement markings. However, the pattern of retained ability to produce correct agreement and not tense marking has not always been replicated. Not producing the highest nodes in a syntactic structure could also be thought of as a form of resource reduction.

Several researchers have suggested that there is a more profound disturbance of sentence production in certain PWAs. This disturbance has been said to affect the PWA's ability to use the basic word order of English to convey propositional features, such as thematic roles. Saffran et al. (1980) presented data regarding the order of nouns around verbs in sentences produced by five agrammatic PWAs describing simple pictures of actions. The authors noted a strong effect of animacy upon the position of the nouns around the verbs. The authors suggested that thematic roles were not mapped onto the established noun-verb-noun word order of English, and that animacy determined the position of nouns around verbs in these PWAs. They concluded that agrammatic PWAs have either lost the basic linguistic notions of thematic roles (Agency, Theme) or else cannot use even the basic word order of the language to express this sentential semantic feature.

The ability to produce utterances that convey thematic roles is closely linked to the ability to produce verbs. Many agrammatic PWAs have particular difficulties with the production of verbs. These difficulties do not entirely consist of trouble producing the correct inflectional and derivational forms of a verb in a given context. They also affect the ability to produce verbs themselves, resulting in omissions, paraphrases, and nominalizations of verbs.

Several studies have investigated this disturbance of verb production in agrammatic PWAs, with comparable results. Miceli et al. (1984) compared five agrammatic, five anomic, and ten normal subjects on tests requiring naming objects (The Boston Naming Test; Kaplan, Goodglass, & Weintraub, 1976) or actions (The Action Naming Test; Obler & Albert, 1979). They found that the agrammatic PWAs were better at naming objects than actions, whereas the anomic PWAs and normal controls showed the opposite pattern. The agrammatic PWAs' difficulties in naming actions did not appear to arise at the level of achieving the concept of the action, since many erroneous responses were nouns, phrases, and nominalizations that were related to the intended verbs. Miceli and his colleagues concluded that their agrammatic PWAs had a sort of anomia for verbs—a disturbance separate from the other aspects of their output.

A recent set of studies has examined unaccusative verbs such as *freeze*, which differ from unergative verbs such as *cough* in assigning the thematic role of theme to their subjects (in *The pond froze*, the pond becomes frozen; in *The boy coughed*, the boy does the coughing). Linguists in the Chomskian framework posit an underlying structure for sentences with unaccusative verbs in which the surface subject appears in underlying object position, as for passives. The similarity of unaccusatives to passives, and the fact that both these sentence types have moved constituents in Chomsky's theory, has led researchers to ask if some PWAs might have specific deficits affecting the ability to produce sentences with unaccusative verbs, as is the case for passives.

Thompson (2003) found that agrammatic aphasic subjects were significantly more accurate in a picture-naming task when targets were unergative rather than unaccusative verbs.

Lee and Thompson (2004) found that aphasic subjects produced correct sentences at a significantly higher rate for unergative than for unaccusative verbs. Bastiaanse and van Zonneveld (2005) found that agrammatic aphasic subjects produced unaccusative verbs more accurately in a transitive frame, in which movement does not take place, than in the intransitive form. These authors assumed that the PWAs had specific deficits affecting the production of sentences with moved constituents, but a study from our lab (McAllister et al., 2009) tells a different story. Single-word naming, sentence production, and sentence–picture matching tests using unaccusative, unergative, and passive structures were administered to a group of nine unselected aphasic subjects and 12 age- and education-matched control subjects. The difference between unaccusatives and non-movement constructions was significant for age-matched control subjects, as well as for aphasic PWAs. This finding supports the hypothesis that the unaccusative construction imposes higher processing costs than non-movement constructions, and that PWAs do not have the resources needed to meet these costs.

Given the crucial role that verbs play in sentences, one would expect that a disturbance affecting the ability to use information regarding verbs would severely affect many other aspects of sentence production and comprehension. McCarthy and Warrington (1985) have argued that this is the case. Their PWA, R.O.X., had a severe disturbance in naming actions and matching verbs to pictures. The authors argued that this disturbance was the result of a category-specific degradation of the meaning of verbs that also resulted in almost no production of verbs in speech and in difficulties in syntactic comprehension. However, the relationship between an inability to produce verbs and other abnormalities in the speech of agrammatic PWAs is not always so clear. In the Miceli et al. study, PWAs' inabilities to produce verbs were only partially responsible for the shortened phrase length found in their speech, since the overall correlation between the noun-to-verb ratio and phrase length in the five agrammatic PWAs was not high. Berndt et al. (1997) also found that disturbances in verb production were variably related to disturbances in producing syntactic structures. It thus appears that some agrammatics have a disturbance affecting their ability to produce verbs, and that this disturbance can affect their ability to accomplish some sentence processing tasks, such as spontaneously producing a normal range of syntactic structures. Other PWAs can build at least some phrasal structures despite poor verb production, whereas others cannot produce normal phrase structure despite relatively good verb production.

It is also not clear whether agrammatic disturbances affecting syntactic forms are related to PWAs' omission of function words and bound morphemes. There is no clear connection between the disturbances in production of function words and bound morphemes seen in individual PWAs and their syntactic abnormalities. Although many agrammatic PWAs show severe reductions in the production of syntactic structures, not all PWAs do so. Miceli et al. (1983), Berndt (1987), and others have documented PWAs who omit disproportionally high numbers of function words and bound morphemes, but who produce an apparently normal range of syntactic structures.

Turning to paragrammatic PWAs, several studies suggest that the syntactic production of these PWAs differs from that found in agrammatic PWAs. Butterworth and Howard (1987) described five paragrammatic PWAs who each produced many "long and complex sentences, with multiple interdependencies of constituents" (p. 23). Errors in paragrammatism include incorrect tag question formation, illegal noun phrases in relative clauses, and illegal use of pronouns to head relative clauses (Butterworth & Howard, 1987). A particular type of error that has often been commented on in paragrammatism is a *blend*, in which the output seems to reflect two different ways of saying the same thing. These features of the speech of paragrammatic PWAs are not found in agrammatic PWAs—at least not with the same frequency as in paragrammatism—and they suggest that differences exist in the ability of these different PWAs to construct syntactic structures.

Butterworth (1982, 1985; Butterworth & Howard, 1987) has argued that the syntactic and morphological errors in paragrammatism result from the failure of these PWAs to monitor and control their own output. If this is correct, the basic locus of the syntactic errors in paragrammatism may differ from those in agrammatism. Agrammatism would reflect a disturbance of one basic aspect of the sentence building process—the construction of syntactic form—whereas paragrammatism would result from a disturbance of control mechanisms that monitor the speech planning process. Butterworth's analysis assumes that normal subjects often generate erroneous utterances unconsciously, and that these errors are filtered out by control processes.

11.3.2 Relation of production and comprehension deficits

Studies of aphasic PWAs are relevant to the question of whether there is a single mechanism that computes syntactic structure in both input and output tasks. The discussion focuses on the fact that PWAs with expressive agrammatism often have syntactic comprehension disturbances (Caplan & Futter, 1986; Grodzinsky, 1986; Heilman & Scholes, 1976; Schwartz et. al., 1980). Several authors have argued that the co-occurrence of deficits in sentence production and comprehension seen in these PWAs indicates the presence of "central" or "overarching" syntactic operations, used in both comprehension and production tasks (Berndt & Caramazza, 1980; Grodzinsky, 1986; Zurif, 1984).

However, although deficits in syntactic comprehension frequently co-occur with expressive agrammatism, it does not appear that the two are due to a single functional impairment. Patients with agrammatism show a wide variety of performances in syntactic comprehension tasks. As noted above, several PWAs with expressive agrammatism have shown no disturbances of syntactic comprehension whatsoever (Kolk & van Grunsven, 1985; Miceli et. al., 1983; Nespoulous et al., 1984), and some PWAs without agrammatism have syntactic comprehension disorders that are indistinguishable from those seen in agrammatic PWAs (Caplan et al., 1985; Caramazza & Zurif, 1976; Martin, 1987; Schwartz et al., 1987). To the extent that disturbances of syntactic comprehension and expressive agrammatism can be assessed in terms of degree of severity, there seems to be no correlation between the severity of a syntactic comprehension deficit and the severity of expressive agrammatism in an individual PWA. These data constitute an argument against the view that only one impairment produces expressive agrammatism that necessarily entails a disturbance of syntactic comprehension. They are consistent with a model that has separate mechanisms dealing with the construction of syntactic form in input- and output-side processing, and with the view that these mechanisms can be separately disturbed. This conclusion is reflected in the theoretically oriented work of researchers such as Grodzinsky (2000), who has postulated specific deficits in agrammatic production and comprehension—the trace deletion hypothesis and the tree pruning hypothesis—that are unrelated to one another. The different deficits in production and comprehension in agrammatism are not such that one could cause the other. One implication of these analyses is that PWAs with agrammatism have two deficits, and that the area of the brain in which the lesion occurs supports separate functions in comprehension and production.

11.3.3 Aphasia and the functional neuroanatomy of syntactic processing

I will conclude with a brief review of results from lesion studies and their implications for the neural organization that supports syntactic processing. The logic behind relating deficits and lesion is that, if a function cannot be performed normally after a lesion, it follows that the area of the brain that is lesioned is necessary for the normal exercise of that function. All of the detailed work in this area applies to comprehension.

There is good evidence that syntactic processing in sentence comprehension involves the perisylvian association cortex—the pars triangularis and opercularis of the inferior frontal gyrus (Brodmann's areas (BA) 45, 44: Broca's area), the angular gyrus (BA39), the supramarginal gyrus (BA40), and the superior temporal gyrus (BA22: Wernicke's area)—in the dominant hemisphere. We have estimated that over 90% of PWAs with aphasic disorders who have lesions in this region have disturbances of syntactic comprehension (Caplan, 1987a). Disorders affecting syntactic comprehension after perisylvian lesions have been described in all languages that have been studied, in PWAs of all ages, with written and spoken input, and after a variety of lesion types, indicating that this cortical region is involved in syntactic processing, independent of these factors (see Caplan, 1987b, for review). Regions outside the perisylvian association cortex that activation studies suggest support syntactic processing include the left inferior anterior temporal lobe (Bavelier et al., 1997; Mazoyer et al., 1993; Noppeney & Price, 2004), the cingulate gyrus and nearby regions of medial frontal lobe (Caplan et al., 1998, 1999, 2000), left superior temporal lobe (Caplan et al., 1998; Carpenter et al., 1999), and left and right posterior inferior temporal lobe (Cooke et al., 2001). The non-dominant hemisphere may also be involved in syntactic comprehension (Ben-Shachar et al., 2003; Caplan et al., 1996; Just et al., 1996).

A major focus of investigation has been how the perisylvian association cortex is organized to support syntactic comprehension. However, the evidence regarding the effect of lesions in PWA with chronic stroke on syntactic comprehension is limited. Studies have generally enrolled a small number of participants and/or used a small number of sentence types studied and/or examples of each sentence type. Tyler et al. (2010, 2011) reported 14 PWAs; Caplan et al. (1996) reported 18. Thothathiri et al. (2012) reported 79 subjects, but only presented five examples of each sentence type, which is likely to miss reliable but slight differences in performance of different PWAs. Caplan et al. (2007c) is intermediate in both regards, presenting 10 examples of each sentence type to 42 PWAs. With two exceptions (Tyler et al., 2010), one of which is hard to interpret, the results are based on accuracy in end-of-sentence tasks, not online observations. The most widely used approaches to analyzing lesions and their relation to deficits have significant problems. For instance, voxel-based lesion deficit mapping, in which the number of PWAs with normal and abnormal performances are compared as a function of lesions in each voxel, has generally not considered the effects of lesions in other voxels on performance.

The results of these studies are inconsistent. Of the six studies that identify syntactic comprehension deficits and use modern neuroimaging, two report null results (Caplan et al., 1996; Warren et al., 2009). Positive findings differed in different studies. Tyler et al. (2011) reported effects of lesion size in left inferior frontal gyrus (LIFG), left posterior middle temporal gyrus (LpMTG), left superior temporal gyrus (LSTG) and left supramarginal gyrus (LSMG) on comprehension of passives and Thothathiri et al. (2012) reporting an effect of lesion size only in the left inferior parietal lobe on comprehension of passive and object relative sentences. Caplan et al. (2007c) found yet another pattern—there was no effect of lesion size in specific ROIs on syntactic complexity scores that were similar to the measure in Thothathiri et al. (2012) in SPM, and fluorodeoxyglucose (FDG)-positron emission tomography (PET) activity in the insula predicted these scores in SPM. Tasks affected results. In Caplan et al. (2007c), lesion volume in Wernicke's area, the inferior parietal lobe, and the anterior inferior temporal lobe and PET activity in the inferior parietal lobe predicted syntactic complexity scores in an object manipulation task, but not in a sentence–picture matching task. There is no evidence for an equivalent effect of a focal lesion on syntactic comprehension performance in more than one task (Caplan et al., 2016). Tyler et al. (2010, 2011) reported correlations of lesion size in Broca's area with performance of PWA in three tasks, but results are hard to interpret in two of the three tasks. The limited available data thus suggest that focal lesions affect syntactic comprehension performance differently as a function of task.

Four studies report syntactic comprehension following acute stroke. Three measured both infarct size using diffusion weighted imaging (DWI) and the apparent diffusion coefficient (ADC) and perfusion using perfusion weighted imaging (PWI). One defined areas of infarction using DWI imaging. These studies are also limited. All data consist of end-of-sentence accuracy measures and two studies used small numbers of sentences. The results were not consistent across studies. Davis et al. (2008) reported effects of hypoperfusion in BA 44/45 on answering reversible questions, not seen in Race et al. (2013); Magnusdottir et al. (2012) found that lesions in superior temporal gyrus (STG) and middle temporal gyrus (MTG) were most predictive of disturbances of comprehension that required syntactic processing.

Overall, the most consistent finding in both chronic and acute stroke is that posterior lesions and hypoperfusion, in the inferior parietal, superior, and middle temporal lobe, affect syntactic comprehension, but much remains to be learned about the effects of lesions on this function. Analyses in which multiple areas are assessed for the patterns of their interactions, might show common networks underlying deficits; whole brain analyses might be revealing in such studies, rather than focusing on specific regions. A better understanding of compensatory strategies that lead to comprehension of some sentence types might serve to account for some of the behavioral variance and reduce interstudy differences.

11.4 CONCLUSION

This review highlights some of the progress made in understanding syntactic deficits in PWA. Advances have been made in theory development and in the adaptation of experimental techniques that allow online observations for use with PWA. It also illustrates some of the challenges facing research in this field. Much more work needs to be done using online methods, especially to study sentence production. There are challenges in image analysis and regarding the statistical methods used to relate lesions to performance. Researchers find it hard to recruit enough participants to achieve adequate power for many studies. One can hope that these challenges will be confronted successfully and that doing so will lead to better understanding of these deficits and their neural correlates.

REFERENCES

Balogh, J., Zurif, E., Prather, P., Swinney, D., & Finkel, L. (1998). Gap-filling and end-of-sentence effects in real-time language processing: Implications for modeling sentence comprehension in aphasia. *Brain and Language, 61*, 169–82.

Bastiaanse, R., & van Zonneveld, R. (2005). Sentence production with verbs of alternating transitivity in agrammatic Broca's aphasia. *Journal of Neurolinguistics, 18*, 57–66.

Bavelier, D., Corina, D., & Jezzard, P. (1997). Sentence reading: A functional MRI study at 4 Tesla. *Journal of Cognitive Neuroscience, 9*(5), 664–86.

Ben-Shachar, M., Hendler, T., Kahn, I., Ben-Bashat, D., & Grodzinsky, Y. (2003). The neural reality of syntactic transformations: Evidence from fMRI. *Psychological Science, 14*, 433–40.

Beretta, A., & Munn, A. (1998). Double-agents and trace-deletion in agrammatism. *Brain and Language, 65*, 404–21.

Berndt, R. S. (1987). Symptom co-occurrence and dissociation in the interpretation of agrammatism. In: Coltheart, M., Sartori, G., & Job, R. (Eds.), *The Cognitive Neuropsychology of Language* (pp. 221–32). Lawrence Erlbaum, London.

Berndt, R. S., & Caramazza, A. (1980). A redefinition of the syndrome of Broca's aphasia. *Applied Psycholinguistics, 1*, 225–78.

Berndt, R. S., Haendiges, A. N., Mitchum, C. C., & Sandson, J. (1997). Verb retrieval in aphasia 2: Relationship to sentence processing. *Brain and Language, 56*, 107–37.

Blumstein, S., Byma, G., Hurowski, K. Huunhen, J., Brown, T., & Hutchison, S. (1998). On-line processing of filler-gap constructions in aphasia. *Brain and Language, 61*(2), 149–69.

Brown, J. W. (1973). *Aphasia*, trans. of A. Pick, *Aphasie*. Thomas, Springfield, IL.

Burkhardt, P., Piñango, M. M., & Wong, K. (2003). The role of the anterior left hemisphere in real-time sentence comprehension: evidence from split intransitivity. *Brain and Language, 86*, 9–22.

Butterworth, B. (1982). Speech errors: Old data in search of new theories. In: Cutler, A. (Ed.), *Slips of the Tongue in Language Production* (pp. 73–108). Mouton, The Hague.

Butterworth, B. L. (1985). Jargon aphasia: Processes and strategies. In: Newman, S., & Epstein, R. (Eds.), *Current Perspectives in Dysphasia*. Churchill Livingstone, Edinburgh.

Butterworth, B., & Howard, D. (1987). Paragrammatisms. *Cognition, 26*, 1–38.

Caplan, D. (1987a). Discrimination of normal and aphasic subjects on a test of syntactic comprehension. *Neuropsychologia, 25*, 173–84.

Caplan, D. (1987b). *Neurolinguistics and Linguistic Aphasiology*. Cambridge University Press, Cambridge, UK.

Caplan, D. (1995). Issues arising in contemporary studies of disorders of syntactic processing in sentence comprehension in agrammatic PWAs. *Brain and Language, 50*, 325–38.

Caplan, D. (2001). The measurement of chance performance in aphasia, with specific reference to the comprehension of semantically reversible passive sentences: A note on issues raised by Caramazza, Capitani, Rey and Berndt (2000) and Drai, Grodzinsky and Zurif (2000). *Brain and Language, 76*, 193–201.

Caplan, D. (2012). Resource reduction accounts of syntactic comprehension disorders. In: Bastiaanse, R., & Thompson, C. K. (Eds.), *Perspectives on Agrammatism* (pp. 34–48). Psychology Press, New York, NY.

Caplan, D., & Futter, C. (1986). Assignment of thematic roles to nouns in sentence comprehension by an agrammatic PWA. *Brain and Language, 27*, 117–34.

Caplan, D., & Hildebrandt, N. (1988). *Disorders of Syntactic Comprehension*. MIT Press (Bradford Books), Cambridge, MA.

Caplan, D., & Waters, G. S. (1999). Verbal working memory and sentence comprehension. *Behavioral and Brain Sciences, 22*, 77–94.

Caplan, D., & Waters, G. S. (2003). On-line syntactic processing in aphasia: Studies with auditory moving windows presentation. *Brain and Language, 84*(2), 222–49.

Caplan, D., & Waters, G. (2013). Memory mechanisms supporting syntactic comprehension. *Psychonomic Bulletin & Review, 20*(2), 243–68.

Caplan, D., Baker, C., & Dehaut, F. (1985). Syntactic determinants of sentence comprehension in aphasia. *Cognition, 21*, 117–75.

Caplan, D., Hildebrandt, N., & Makris, N. (1996). Location of lesions in stroke PWAs with deficits in syntactic processing in sentence comprehension. *Brain, 119*, 933–49.

Caplan, D., Waters, G., & Hildebrandt, H. (1997). Determinants of sentence comprehension in aphasic PWAs in sentence-picture matching tasks. *Journal of Speech and Hearing Research, 40*, 542–55.

Caplan, D., Alpert, N., & Waters, G. (1998). Effects of syntactic structure and propositional number on patterns of regional cerebral blood flow. *Journal of Cognitive Neuroscience, 10*, 541–52.

Caplan, D, Alpert, N., & Waters, G. S. (1999). PET studies of sentence processing with auditory sentence presentation. *NeuroImage, 9*, 343–51.

Caplan, D., Alpert, N., Waters, G. S., & Olivieri, A. (2000). Activation of Broca's area by syntactic processing under conditions of concurrent articulation. *Human Brain Mapping, 9*, 65–71.

Caplan, D., DeDe, G., & Michaud, J. (2006). Task-independent and task-specific syntactic deficits in aphasic comprehension. *Aphasiology, 20*, 893–920.

Caplan, D., Michaud, J., & Hufford, R. (2013a). Dissociations and associations of performance in syntactic comprehension in aphasia and their implications for the nature of aphasic deficits. *Brain and Language, 127*(1), 21–33.

Caplan, D., Michaud, J., & Hufford, R. (2013b). A study of the relation of short term memory and syntactic comprehension in aphasia. *Cognitive Neuropsychology, 30*(2), 77–109.

Caplan, D., Michaud, J., Hufford, R., & Makris, N. (2016). Deficit-lesion correlations in syntactic comprehension in aphasia. *Brain and Language, 152*, 14–27.

Caplan, D., Waters, G., DeDe, G., Michaud, J., & Reddy, A. (2007a). A study of syntactic processing in aphasia I: Psycholinguistic aspects. *Brain and Language, 101*, 103–50.

Caplan, D., Waters, G. S., & DeDe, G. (2007b). Specialized verbal working memory for language comprehension. In: Conway, A., Jarrold, C., Kane, M., Miyake, A., & Towse, J. (Eds.), *Variation in Working Memory*. Oxford University Press, Oxford, UK.

Caplan, D., Waters, G., Kennedy, D., Alpert, N., Makris, N., DeDe, G., ... Reddy, A. (2007c). A study of syntactic processing in aphasia II: Neurological aspects. *Brain and Language, 101*, 151–77.

Caramazza, A., & Hillis, A. (1988). The disruption of sentence production: A case of selected deficit to positional level processing. *Brain and Language, 35*, 625–50.

Caramazza, A., & Zurif, E. B. (1976). Dissociation of algorithmic and heuristic processes in language comprehension: Evidence from aphasia. *Brain and Language*, 3, 572–82.

Carpenter, P. A., Just, M. A., Keller, T. A., Eddy, W. F., & Thulborn, K. R. (1999). Time course of fMRI-activation in language and spatial networks during sentence comprehension. *NeuroImage*, 10, 216–24.

Choy, J. J., & Thompson, C. K. (2010). Binding in agrammatic aphasia: Processing to comprehension. *Aphasiology*, 24(5), 551–79.

Cooke, A., Zurif, E. B., DeVita, C., Alsop, D., Koenig, P., Detre, J., . . . Grossman, M. (2001). Neural basis for sentence comprehension: Grammatical and short-term memory components. *Human Brain Mapping*, 15, 80–94.

Cupples, L., & Inglis, A. L. (1993). When task demands induce "asyntactic" sentence comprehension: A study of sentence interpretation in aphasia. *Cognitive Neuropsychology*, 10, 201–34.

Davis, C., Kleinman, J. T., Newhart, M., Gingis, L., Pawlak, M., & Hillis, A. E. (2008). Speech and language functions that require a functioning Broca's Area. *Brain and Language*, 105, 50–8.

de Bleser, R. (1987). From agrammatism to paragrammatisms: German aphasiological traditions and grammatical disturbances. *Cognitive Neuropsychology*, 4, 187–256.

de Villiers, J. G. (1974). Quantitative aspects of agrammatism in aphasia. *Cortex*, 10, 36–54.

Dickey, M. W., & Thompson, C. K. (2009). Automatic processing of wh- and NP-movement in agrammatic aphasia: Evidence from eyetracking. *Journal of Neurolinguistics*, 22(6), 563–83.

Dickey, M., Choy, J., & Thompson (2007). Real time comprehension of wh-movement in aphasia: Evidence from eyetracking, while listening. *Brain and Language*, 100, 1–22.

Dickey, M. W., Warren, T., Hayes, R., & Milburn, E. (2014). Prediction during sentence comprehension in aphasia. *Frontiers in Psychology*, Conference Abstract, Academy of Aphasia—52nd Annual Meeting. Miami, FL, United States, October 5–7, 2014.

Friederici, A. and Kilborn, K. (1989). Temporal constraints on language processing: Syntactic priming in Broca's aphasia. *Journal of Cognitive Neuroscience*, 1, 262–72.

Friedman, N., & Grodzinsky, Y. (1999). Tense and agreement in agrammatic production: Pruning the syntactic tree. *Brain and Language*, 56, 397–425.

Fyndanis, V., Varlokosta, S., & Tsapkini, K. (2010). Exploring *wh*-questions in agrammatism: Evidence from Greek. *Journal of Neurolinguistics*, 23, 644–62.

Garraffa, M., & Grillo, N. (2008). Canonicity effects as grammatical phenomena. *Journal of Neurolinguistics*, 21(2), 177–97.

Gibson, E., Sandberg, C., Fedorenko, E., & Kiran, S. (2013). *A rational inference approach to aphasic language comprehension*. Talk presented at the CUNY Sentence Comprehension Conference, Columbia, SC.

Goodglass, H. (1973). Studies on the grammar of aphasics. In: Goodglass, H., & Blumstein, S. (Eds.), *Psycholinguistics and Aphasia*. Johns Hopkins University Press, Baltimore, MD.

Grodzinsky, Y. (1984). The syntactic characterization of agrammatism. *Cognition*, 16, 99–120.

Grodzinsky, Y. (1986). Language deficits and the theory of syntax. *Brain and Language*, 27, 135–59.

Grodzinsky, Y. (1990). Theoretical perspectives on language deficits. MIT Press, Cambridge, MA.

Grodzinsky, Y. (2000). The neurology of syntax: Language use without Broca's area. *Behavioral and Brain Sciences*, 23, 47–117.

Gutman, R., DeDe, G., Michaud, J., Liu, J. S., & Caplan, D. (2010). Rasch models of aphasic performance on syntactic comprehension tests. *Cognitive Neuropsychology*, 27, 230–44.

Gutman, R., DeDe, G., Caplan, D., & Liu, J. S. (2011). Rasch model and its extensions for analysis of aphasic deficits in syntactic comprehension. *Journal of the American Statistical Association*, 106, 1304–16.

Haarmann, H. J., & Kolk, H. H. J. (1991a). A computer model of the temporal course of agrammatic sentence understanding: the effects of variation in severity and sentence complexity. *Cognitive Science*, 15, 49–87.

Haarmann, H. J., & Kolk, H. H. J. (1991b). Syntactic priming in Broca's aphasics: Evidence for slow activation. *Aphasiology*, 5, 247–63.

Hanne, S., Sekerina, I. A., Vasishth, S., Burchert, F., & De Bleser, R. (2011). Chance in agrammatic sentence comprehension: What does it really mean? Evidence from eye movements of German agrammatic aphasic PWAs. *Aphasiology*, 25, 221–44.

Heeschen, C. (1985). Agrammatism vs. paragrammatism: A fictitious opposition. In: Kean, M. L. (Ed.), *Agrammatism* (pp. 207–48). Academic Press, London.

Heilman, K. M., & Scholes, R. J. (1976). The nature of comprehension errors in Broca's, conduction, and Wernicke's aphasics. *Cortex*, 12, 258–65.

Hildebrandt, N., Caplan, D., & Evans, K. (1987). The mani lefti without a trace: A case study of aphasic processing of empty categories. *Cognitive Neuropsychology*, 4(3), 257–302.

Just, M. A., Carpenter, P. A., Keller, T. A., Eddy, W. F., & Thulborn, K. R. (1996). Brain activation modulated by sentence comprehension. *Science*, 274, 114–16.

Kaplan, E., Goodglass, H., & Weintraub, S. (1976). *The Boston Naming Test*. Veterans Administration, Boston, MA.

Kean, M. L. (1977). The linguistic interpretation of aphasic syndromes: Agrammatism in Broca's aphasia, an example. *Cognition*, 5, 9–46.

King, J. W., & Just, M. A. (1991). Individual difference in syntactic processing: The role of working memory. *Journal of Memory and Language*, 30, 580–602.

Kolk, H. H. J., & van Grunsven, J. J. F. (1985). Agrammatism as a variable phenomenon. *Cognitive Neuropsychology*, 2, 347–84.

Lapointe, S. (1983). Some issues in the linguistic description of agrammatism. *Cognition*, 14, 1–39.

Lee, M., & Thompson, C. L. (2004). Agrammatic aphasic production and comprehension of unaccusative verbs in sentence contexts. *Journal of Neurolinguistics*, 17(4), 315–30.

Linebarger, M. C. (1995). Agrammatism as evidence about grammar. *Brain and Language*, 50, 52–91.

Linebarger, M. C., Schwartz, M. F., & Saffran, E. M. (1983). Sensitivity to grammatical structure in so-called agrammatic aphasics. *Cognition*, 13, 361–92.

Love, T., Swinney, D., Walenski, M., & Zurif, E. (2008). How left inferior frontal cortex participates in syntactic processing: Evidence from aphasia. *Brain and Language*, 107, 203–19.

Luria, A. R. (1973). *The Working Brain*. Basic Books, New York, NY.

Mack, J. E., Ji, W., & Thompson, C. K. (2013). Effects of verb meaning on lexical integration in agrammatic aphasia: Evidence from eyetracking. *Journal of Neurolinguistics*, 26(6), 619–36.

MacKenzie, S., Walenski, M., Love, T., Ferrill, M., Engel, S., Sullivan, N., . . . & Shapiro, L. (2014). The impact of similarity-based interference in processing wh-questions in aphasia. *Frontiers in Psychology.* Available at: http://www.frontiersin.org/Journal/FullText.aspx?f=69&name=psychology&ART_DOI=10.3389/conf.fpsyg.2014.64.00080

Magnusdottir, S., Fillmore, P., den Ouden, D. B., Hjaltason, H., Rorden, C., Kjartansson, O., & Fridriksson, J. (2012). Damage to left anterior temporal cortex predicts impairment of complex syntactic processing: a lesion-symptom mapping study. *Human Brain Mapping,* 34, 2715–23.

Martin, R. C. (1987). Articulatory and phonological deficits in short-term memory and their relation to syntactic processing. *Brain and Language,* 32, 159–92.

Martin, R. C., & He, T. (2004). Semantic short-term memory and its role in sentence processing: a replication. *Brain and Language,* 89(1), 76–82.

Mauner, G., Fromkin, V., & Cornell, T. (1993). Comprehension and acceptability judgments in agrammatism: Disruptions in the syntax of referential dependency. *Brain and Language,* 45, 340–70.

Mazoyer, B. M., Tzourio, N., Frak, V., Syrota, A., Murayama, N., Levrier, O., & Mehler, J. (1993). The cortical representation of speech. *Journal of Cognitive Neuroscience,* 5(4), 467–79.

McAllister, T., Bachrach, A., Waters, G. S., Michaud, J., & Caplan, D. (2009). Production and comprehension of unaccusatives in aphasia. *Aphasiology,* 23, 989–1004.

McCarthy, R., & Warrington, E. M. (1985). Category specificity in an agrammatic PWA: The relative impairment of verb retrieval and comprehension. *Neuropsychologia,* 23, 709–27.

Menn, L., & Obler, L. (Eds.). (1990). *Agrammatic Aphasia: A Cross-Language Narrative Sourcebook.* John Benjamins, Philadelphia, PI.

Meyer, A. M., Mack, J. E., & Thompson, C. K. (2012). Tracking passive sentence comprehension in agrammatic aphasia. *Journal of Neurolinguistics,* 25, 31–43.

Miceli, G., & Caramazza, A. (1988). Dissociation of inflectional and derivational morphology. *Brain and Language,* 35, 24–65.

Miceli, G., Mazzucchi, A., Menn, L., & Goodglass, H. (1983). Contrasting cases of Italian agrammatic aphasia without comprehension disorder. *Brain and Language,* 19, 65–97.

Miceli, G., Silveri, M., Villa, G., & Caramazza, A. (1984). On the basis for the agrammatic's difficulty in producing main verbs. *Cortex,* 20, 207–20.

Miceli, G., Silveri, M. C., Romani, C., & Caramazza, A. (1989). Variation in the pattern of omissions and substitutions of grammatical morphemes in the spontaneous speech of so-called PWAs. *Brain and Language,* 36, 447–92.

Miceli, G., Guistolisi, L., & Caramazza, A. (1990). *The Interaction of Lexical and Non-lexical Processing Mechanisms: Evidence from Anomia.* The Cognitive Neuropsychology Laboratory, The Johns Hopkins University, Baltimore, MD.

Miyake, A. K., Carpenter, P., & Just, M. (1994). A capacity approach to syntactic comprehension disorders: Making normal adults perform like brain-damaged PWAs. *Cognitive Neuropsychology,* 11, 671–717.

Nespoulous, J. L., Dordain, M., Perron, C., Ska, B., Bub, D., Caplan, D., et al. (1988). Agrammatism in sentence production without comprehension deficits: Reduced availability of syntactic structures and/or of grammatical morphemes? A case study. *Brain and Language,* 33, 273–95.

Nespoulous, J. L., Joanette, Y., Beland, R., Caplan, D., & Lecours, A. R. (1984). Phonological disturbances in aphasia: Is there a "markedness" effect in aphasic phonemic errors? In: Rose, F. C. (Ed.), *Progress in Aphasiology: Advances in Neurology* (Vol. 42). Raven Press, New York, NY.

Noppeney, U., & Price, C. J. (2004). An fMRI study of syntactic adaptation. *Journal of Cognitive Neuroscience, 16,* 702–13.

Obler, L. K., & Albert, M. L. (1979). *Action Naming Test*, experimental ed. VA Medical Center, Boston, MA.

Ostrin, R. (1982). *Framing the Production Problem in Agrammatism*. [Unpublished paper, Department of Psychology]. University of Pennsylvania, Philadelphia, PA.

Ostrin, R., & Schwartz, M. F. (1986). Reconstructing from a degraded trace: A study of sentence repetition in agrammatism. *Brain and Language, 28,* 328–45.

Parisi, D. (1987). Dual coding: Theoretical issues and empirical evidence. In: Scandura, J. M., & Brainerd, C. J. (Eds.), *Structure/process Models of Complex Human Behavior*. Nordhoff, Leiden.

Prather, P., Zurif, E., Stern, C., & Rosen, T. J. (1992). Slowed lexical access in nonfluent aphasia: a case study. *Brain and Language, 43*(2), 336–48.

Race, D. S., Tsapkini, K., Crinion, J., Newhart, M., Davis, C., Gomez, Y., ... & Faria, A. V. (2013). An area essential for linking word meanings to word forms: evidence from primary progressive aphasia. *Brain and Language, 127*(2), 167–76.

Saffran, E. M., Bogyo, L. C., Schwartz, M. F., & Marin, O. S. M. (1980). Does deep dyslexia reflect right-hemisphere reading? In: Coltheart, M., Patterson, K., & Marshall, J. C. (Eds.), *Deep Dyslexia* (pp. 381–406). Routledge, London.

Schwartz, M. F., Linebarger, M. C., Saffran, E. M., & Pate, D. S. (1987). Syntactic transparency and sentence interpretation in aphasia. *Language and Cognitive Processes, 2,* 85–113.

Schwartz, M., Saffran, E., & Marin, O. (1980). The word order problem in agrammatism. I: Comprehension. *Brain and Language, 10,* 249–62.

Sullivan, N., Walenski, M., MacKenzie, S., Ferrill, M., Love, T., & Shapiro, L. P. (2014). The time-course of lexical reactivation of unaccusative verbs in Broca's aphasia. *Frontiers of Psychology*, Conference Abstract, Academy of Aphasia—52nd Annual Meeting, October 5–7, 2014, Miami, FL. DOI=10.3389/conf.fpsyg.2014.64.00058

Swinney, D., & Zurif, E. (1995). Syntactic processing in aphasia. *Brain and Language, 50,* 225–39.

Tanenhaus, M. K., Spivey-Knowlton, M. J., Eberhard, K. M., & Sedivy, J. E. (1995). Integration of visual and linguistic information in spoken language comprehension. *Science, 268,* 1632–4.

Thompson, C. (2003). Unaccusative verb production in agrammatic aphasia: The argument structure complexity hypothesis. *Journal of Neurolinguistics, 16,* 151–67.

Thompson, C. K., & Choy, J. (2009). Pronominal resolution and gap-filling in agrammatic aphasia: Evidence from eyetracking. *Journal of Psycholinguistic Research, 38,* 255–83.

Thothathiri, W., Kimberg, D., Schwartz, M. (2012). The neural basis of reversible sentence comprehension: Evidence from voxel-based lesion symptom mapping in aphasia. *Journal of Cognitive Neuroscience, 24*(1), 212–22.

Tissot, R. J., Mounin, G., & Lhermitte, F. (1973). *L'agrammatisme*. Dessart, Brussels.

Tyler, L. K., Marslen-Wilson, W. D., Randall, B., Wright, P., Devereux, B. J., Zhuang, J., ... & Stamatakis, E. A. (2011). Left inferior frontal cortex and syntax: Function, structure and behaviour in left-hemisphere damaged PWAs. *Brain, 134*(2), 415–31.

Tyler, L. K., Wright, P., Randall, B., Marslen-Wilson, W. D., & Stamatakis, E. A. (2010). Reorganisation of syntactic processing following LH brain damage: Does RH activity preserve function? *Brain, 133*(11), 3396–408.

Varlokosta, S., Nerantzini, M., Papadopolou, D., Bastiaanse, R., & Beretta, A. (2014). Minimality effects in agrammatic comprehension: The role of lexical restriction and feature impoverishment. *Lingua*, 148, 80–90.

Warren, J. E., Crinion, J. T., Lambon Ralph, M. A., & Wise, R. J. S. (2009). Anterior temporal lobe connectivity correlates with functional outcome after aphasic stroke. *Brain*, 132 (12), 3428–42.

Warren, T., Liburd, T., & Dickey, M. W. (2014). Sentence comprehension in aphasia: A noisy channel approach. *Frontiers of Psychology*, Conference Abstract: Academy of Aphasia—52nd Annual Meeting, October 5–7, 2014, Miami, FL. DOI=10.3389/conf. fpsyg.2014.64.00068

Zurif, E. B. (1984). Psycholinguistic interpretation of the aphasias. In: Caplan, D., Lecours, A. R., & Smith, A. (Eds.), *Biological Perspectives on Language* (pp. 158–71). MIT Press, Cambridge, MA.

Zurif, E., Swinney, D., Prather, P., Solomon, J., & Bushell, C. (1993). An on-line analysis of syntactic processing in Broca's and Wernicke's aphasia. *Brain and Language*, 45, 448–64.

CHAPTER 12

LANGUAGE IN DEAF POPULATIONS
Signed language and orthographic processing

DAVID P. CORINA AND LAUREL A. LAWYER

12.1 INTRODUCTION

THE field of psycholinguistics strives to explicate processes involved in the comprehension and production of language. Although psycholinguistics has been an active and fruitful research discipline for more than 70 years, research on signed languages is still in its infancy. Indeed, it was not until the late 1960s and early 1970s that the idea that signed languages were autonomous and linguistically complex languages gained credence.

Initial studies of American Sign Language (ASL) acquisition, recognition, and memory were reported in the seminal work by Klima and Bellugi (1979). Studies exploring the psychological and neurological ramifications of sign language processing began to emerge thereafter, and have had a profound impact on our understanding of the core principles guiding the expression and understanding of human languages (Corina 1998; Emmorey, 2002; Poizner, Klima, & Bellugi, 1990). A prominent focus in these early studies was in showing how processes that affect the memory, recognition, and expression of signed languages mirror processes observed in spoken languages. For example, the finding that memory for lists of signs shows differential effects of semantic and form-based (aka *phonological*) manipulations indicates that the encoding and retrieval of signs is fundamentally analogous to processes described for spoken languages (Bellugi, Klima, & Siple, 1974). Subsequently, the discovery that left hemisphere damage results in aphasic syndromes in signed languages that parallel those found in spoken languages illustrated the core neural similarities between speech and sign language (Poizner, Klima, & Bellugi, 1990). These studies helped established the legitimacy of signed languages as both natural languages and valid objects of psychological exploration.

Since this time, the field of signed language and deafness research has blossomed. Descriptions and formal analyses of signed languages from around the world have emerged, rapidly broadening the sign language linguistics landscape (see for example: Brentari, 2001; de Vos & Pfau, 2015; Sandler & Lillo-Martin, 2006; Zeshan & de Vos, 2012). The discovery and documentation of emerging signed languages has allowed scientists to demonstrate the contributions of intergenerational reanalysis of linguistic systems that underlie language evolution (Meir, Sandler, Padden, & Aronoff, 2010; Senghas, 2003; Senghas, Senghas, & Pyers, 2005). The expansion of new online databases (e.g., ASL-LEX; Caselli, Sehyr, Cohen-Goldberg, & Emmorey (2017); Asian Sign Bank, http://cslds.org/asiansignbank/; DGS-KORPUS, http://www.sign-lang.uni-hamburg.de/dgs-korpus/index.php/welcome.html; British Sign Language Corpus Project, http://www.bslcorpusproject.org/), notational systems and cataloging tools (e.g., Hamburg Sign Language Notation System HamNoSys (Hanke, 2004), ELAN, http://tla.mpi.nl/tools/tla-tools/elan/ (Crasborn & Sloetjes, 2008; Lausberg & Sloetjes, 2009)), and compendiums of research methods and practices (Orfanidou, Woll, & Morgan, 2015) have facilitated psycholinguistic research on signed languages across the globe.

The appreciation that the audiological and language experiences of deaf individuals are highly heterogeneous has added new complexities to accounts of psycholinguistic processing in this population. Sensory loss due to deafness is not only graded in degree (i.e., mild, moderate, severe, profound), but may change over time, impacting the acquisition of spoken and/or signed language. Moreover, most deaf individuals are born to parents with normal hearing, who do not typically know a signed language. As such, a deaf child's exposure to and acquisition of an accessible language like ASL may not occur until preschool or later. About 5% of the deaf population has parents who are fluent signers, and only these individuals (often termed "native" signers) will be exposed to a signed language as a native language within the normative developmental period. Deaf non-native learners of sign language, while often highly fluent users of sign, may nevertheless experience subtle processing inefficiencies (Mayberry & Fischer, 1989; Mayberry, Lock, & Kazmi, 2002; Morford et al., 2008; Newport, 1990). On top of this, most deaf individuals will ultimately develop competencies in both signed language and accessible forms of spoken language during their education. The recognition of deaf signers as bilinguals has led to new characterizations of language processing in signers, particularly in expanding our understanding of how deaf individuals process written forms of spoken language (see for example Cates, 2015; Emmorey, Giezen, & Gollan, 2016; Piñar, Carlson, Morford, & Dussias, 2016). Finally, the acknowledgment that the sensory consequences of early deafness can have an impact on the remaining sensory systems, such as vision, adds an additional factor in accounts of language and cognitive processing in the deaf.

Advances in psycholinguistic and cognitive neuroscience investigations have allowed researchers to probe not only the commonalities between spoken and signed languages, but to begin to broach the very real possibility that the modality of expression uniquely impacts the cognitive and neural processing of signed languages (Corina, Lawyer, & Cates, 2013). In this chapter, rather than providing an exhaustive review of the burgeoning psycholinguistic studies in signed language, we outline some fundamental linguistic properties of signed languages and report on selected studies that illustrate psycholinguistic properties governing the earliest stages of sign language recognition. The studies chosen highlight how processes of lexical sign recognition appear similar to those reported in spoken language as well as provide an opportunity to examine how signed languages may diverge from spoken languages. We also take this opportunity to report on a growing number of studies that have examined how deaf adults engage in reading of a language they cannot hear. This work illustrates the efficacy of a bilingual perspective and at the same time reveals how reading strategies may be affected by modifications to visual attentional systems as a result of deafness. Prior reviews of sign language psycholinguistics can be found in studies by Corina and Knapp (2006a, b) and Emmorey (2002). A review of sign language production studies appears in Corina, Gutiérrez, and Grosvald (2014).

12.2 THE LINGUISTIC STRUCTURE OF SIGNS

In his seminal works, William Stokoe classified each ASL sign according to the shape of the hand (*handshape*), the *location* in relation to the body, and the *movement* in space (Stokoe, Casterline, & Croneberg, 1976). These separate dimensions of sign formation came to be known as "parameters." Subsequent work by Battison (1978) argued for the inclusion of the *orientation* of the hand as an additional parameter. In comparison to the segmental features of spoken languages, these parameters are often considered to exhibit greater simultaneity of patterning. This characterization recognizes that most signs typically express one unique place of articulation (i.e., location) rather than sequentially patterned sequences and that handshape information is expressed throughout a sign's articulation. These four parameters of sign formation have been widely adopted in cross-linguistic studies of signed languages, though psycholinguistic investigations tend to ignore orientation, as it remains difficult to vary in a systematic fashion.

Over the last few decades, researchers have elaborated on these initial descriptions of sign structure, proposing models that encompass phonological, morphological, syntactic, and prosodic properties of these languages (for a review, see Sandler & Lillo-Martin, 2006). Descriptions cast within these formal linguistic models help elucidate those properties of signed languages that are common to all human languages, as well as isolate those properties that reflect the unique structure of a human language that is manually articulated and perceived through the eyes.

12.3 LEXICAL RECOGNITION OF SIGNS

Models of spoken and written word recognition traditionally conceptualize lexical access as a matching process between the perceptual signal that accrues over time and potential lexical candidates stored in memory (e.g., Cohort model, Neighborhood Activation model, and TRACE. For a review see Jusczyk & Luce, 2002). More recent accounts posit active predictive processes guiding language understanding (Huettig, 2015; Norris, McQueen, & Cutler 2016; Willems et al., 2016). As with spoken language, research with signed languages has questioned how the physical properties of the sign language signal affect the way in which the lexicon is initially accessed en route to word recognition, and what organizational principles dictate how signs are stored within the lexicon. Psycholinguistic investigations using signed languages have revealed properties of lexical organization through effects of lexicality and frequency, as well as contextual effects including semantic priming, form-based priming, and neighborhood effects.

Lexicality effects refer to the finding that words are categorized faster than non-words. This basic finding suggests that presence of a mental representation (i.e., a known word or sign) provides a target for a search through the lexicon, whereas the lack of a representation requires an exhaustive and unfulfilled search which incurs a processing disadvantage (Forster & Chambers, 1973; Rubenstein et al, 1970). There is a growing body of literature confirming that lexical factors which affect spoken word recognition can also be observed in the recognition of signed languages. For example, when participants are required to make a lexical decision about a sign, reaction times are significantly slower to formationally possible but non-existing ASL signs (i.e., pseudosigns) relative to real signs (Bosworth & Emmorey, 2010; Corina & Emmorey, 1993; Dye and Shih, 2006).

Electrophysiological studies have extended these findings to include effects of preceding context on lexical recognition and gestural processing. For instance, Grosvald et al. (2012) demonstrate that in a sentential context such as "BOY SLEEP IN HIS XXX," electrophysiological responses to formationally possible but non-existing pseudosigns are distinguished both from semantically incongruous signs (i.e., LEMON) and self-grooming gestures (i.e., the model scratching her face). For the semantically incongruous and pseudosign stimuli, greater negative potentials were observed in the N400 time window (400–600 msec. after the onset of the final word), relative to the baseline condition. The graded N400 effects, (pseudosign > semantically incongruent > baseline), mirrors numerous studies using similar paradigms with spoken language stimuli (Bentin, 1987; Bentin, McCarthy, & Wood, 1985; Hagoort & Kutas, 1995; Kutas et al., 1987). These data are consistent with the notion that the N400 indexes semantic integration processes (Brown & Hagoort, 1993; Hagoort & van Berkum, 2007), and demonstrates that N400 effects generalize across language modality.

In this study, electrophysiological responses to gestures were also distinct from pseudosigns, semantically incongruent signs, and baselines signs, in this case showing no N400 effect. This suggests that non-linguistic manual gestures (such as scratching one's face, rubbing your eyes, and so on), even when observed in the context of a signed sentence, are not incorporated into the accruing linguistic interpretation. This is important because it demonstrates that signers are uniquely sensitive to the linguistic properties of signs and are quick to distinguish possible linguistic forms from non-language manual gestures. These data suggest that there may be predictive processes guiding sign language recognition that qualitatively differs from the processing of spontaneous everyday non-linguistic and non-communicative manual gestures.

Such studies raise questions concerning the potential separability and interplay between the neural systems mediating sign language and gestures more generally. Neuroimaging studies reveal distinct patterns of neural activation in deaf signers during the processing of sign language forms relative to non-linguistic gestures and human actions (Corina et al., 2007; Emmorey et al., 2010; MacSweeney et al., 2004; Okada et al., 2016). For example, Emmorey et al. (2011) reported differences in brain activation during the production of ASL verb forms that resemble actions (e.g., BRUSH-HAIR) versus pantomimes. Generation of ASL verbs induced activation in left hemisphere inferior frontal regions, while pantomimed actions engaged bilateral superior parietal cortex. Studies of deaf aphasics have also reported impaired sign language processing with preserved pantomime recognition and use (Corina & Emmorey, 1993; Marshall et al., 2004).

However, it is interesting to note that the processing of co-speech gestures in hearing users of spoken language often involve left inferior frontal and posterior superior temporal regions, and bilateral middle temporal gyrus. These regions are typically implicated in spoken language perception (Dick et al., 2014; Willems, Özyürek, & Hagoort, 2006, 2009) and signed language comprehension (e.g., Emmorey, 2015; MacSweeney et al., 2006; MacSweeney et al., 2008; Neville et al., 1998; Petitto et al., 2000). Indeed, the functional and anatomical relationship between neural systems that come to support sign language processing and those that normally support gesture processing (in its many forms) in hearing individuals remains an active area of research (see for example Corina, Grosvald, & Lachaud, 2011; Corina & Grosvald, 2012; Emmorey & Özyürek, 2014; Özyürek, 2014).

12.3.1 Sublexical properties of the lexicon

Research across distinct signed languages using a variety of paradigms has demonstrated that signers are sensitive to sublexical properties of signs. An emerging literature also indicates the lexical recognition processes may be differentially affected by particular phonological parameters, such as location or handshape. For example, in a gating study by Emmorey and Corina (1990), signs were partitioned into 33 millisecond parts and presented to participants cumulatively. Participants were able to identify the location of the sign first, followed quickly by the handshape, and finally the movement. Signs located in neutral space were recognized before those located upon the face, presumably because the target location of the sign was achieved earlier for neutral space signs. In addition, it was observed that signers could anticipate handshape changes in signs prior to full articulation of the handshape. These data are important as they demonstrate that in sign recognition, as is seen with spoken language, coarticulatory factors may assist word identification. In addition, these studies confirmed that signs were identified very quickly. In contrast to spoken English, in which approximately 83% of a word must be heard before identification occurs (Grosjean, 1980), sign identification occurred only after approximately 35% of the sign form had been seen. Two factors that may account for this finding include the relatively greater simultaneous packaging of phonological information within a sign and the fact that few signs share an initial phonological shape, leading to a reduced number of competing lexical items (i.e., reduced initial cohort size).

Another well-known factor influencing lexical access across both written and spoken language modalities is the composition of the candidate set of lexical entries from which a single target form must emerge. In spoken languages these effects are conceptualized as owing to competition among formationally similar lexical entries—so-called neighborhood effects. The metric of lexical neighborhood similarity has been traditionally defined in terms of phonological properties in studies of spoken words and orthographic properties in studies of written words. For example, Luce and Pisoni (1998) derive neighborhood similarity by considering the number of words that could be obtained by a single phoneme substitution, addition, or deletion. Numerous studies have demonstrated that these similarity properties influence word recognition, as shown in the accuracy of perceptual identification, latencies in naming and lexical decision tasks, and priming effects in both spoken and visual word recognition (for discussion, see Jusczyk & Luce, 2002).

Carreiras et al. (2008) investigated the construct of lexical neighborhoods in sign language. They operationalized sign neighborhoods based on phonological grounds, defined as a collection of signs that were phonetically similar to a given stimulus sign by virtue of sharing one phonological parameter. Carreiras and colleagues examined the recognition of signs in sparse or dense neighborhoods defined on the basis of either handshape or location. Signs articulated at locations with sparse neighborhoods, that is, locations shared by few other phonetically similar signs, were recognized more quickly and more accurately than signs that were articulated at locations with dense neighborhoods. These data provide some of the first evidence that the mental lexicon for signed languages reflects compositional sublexical structure.

Lexical decision studies have also used priming to examine whether prior exposure to a phonological feature of a sign influences the subsequent processing of signs sharing the same features. For example, in ASL the signs MOTHER (a five-handshape articulated on the chin with a brief tapping motion) and CANDY (a one-handshape articulated on the chin with a twisting motion) share the articulatory property of location, while they differ in the remaining parameters. SORRY (an S handshape signed on the chest with a circular motion) has no featural overlap with either sign. Comparing the time it takes to recognize signs like MOTHER when preceded by similar signs like CANDY, relative to unrelated signs like SORRY provides an indication of whether the location parameter affects lexical activation. Using the same logic, one can test signs that share the same handshape, but differ in location and movement (e.g., THINK vs. TELL) or share only movement (e.g., CONSIDER vs. DISGUST), and so on.

Studies using priming paradigms show that different sublexical features in signs produce different patterns of behavioral responses. Numerous studies have shown that signs sharing location produce inhibitory effects in recognition (Carreiras et al., 2008; Corina & Emmorey, 1993; Corina & Hildebrandt, 2002; see also Baus et al., 2008). In contrast, signs sharing handshape and movement parameters have yielded mixed results, with some research reporting facilitation (Carreiras et al., 2008), while others show no reliable effects (Corina & Emmorey, 1993). Using electrophysiological measures, Gutiérrez et al. (2012a) showed that location overlap in Spanish Sign Language (LSE) signs elicited a higher amplitude N400 than an unrelated form condition, with no N400 effects observed for handshape overlap, again suggesting that location may serve a privileged role in sign language processing.

The special status of location is supported by work in numerous other domains. For instance, studies of sign language acquisition have shown that location is more accurately produced than handshape or movement in children's early signs (Cheek et al., 2001; Clibbens & Harris, 1993; Karnopp, 2002; Marentette & Mayberry, 2000; Morgan et al., 2007; Siedlecki & Bonvillian, 1997; Takkinen, 2003; von Tetzchner, 1994). Location is the first phonological parameter of signs to be accessed in gating studies (Emmorey & Corina, 1990; Grosjean, 1980) and also serves as a common feature in the representation of iconic-semantic properties of sign languages (Cates et al., 2013). Aphasia studies have also shown location more resistant to errors in persons with neurological damage than any of the other phonological parameters (Corina, 2000).

One of the factors contributing to the special status of location might be that there are relatively few possible realizations of location in comparison to handshape. Gutiérrez and Carreiras (2009) reported that LSE had 130 phonetically different handshapes while only 26 distinct locations (note, however, this count likely reflects allophonic variants as distinct handshapes). Location is proposed to be equivalent to syllable onset, and is less influenced by sequentiality than, for example, movement, which requires a certain amount of time from the initiation of the movement to be perceived (Brentari, 2002). An alternative conception posits that during sign recognition signers make use of abstract postural targets that reflect holistic specifications of proprioceptive and somatosensory states of the articulators and body configurations. Articulatory location may serve as particularly reliable proxy for such internal representations.

More work is needed to better understand the contributions of sign form to sign recognition (see for example Gutiérrez et al., 2012b). For example, we do not fully understand why different phonological parameters have different processing consequences. Much of the work in this area has tacitly presupposed that lexical recognition of a sign requires decomposition into its constituent parts (i.e., separate specifications of handshape, location, movement, and orientation), mirroring linguistically motivated phonological parameters. Existing experiments may be formulated to amplify these effects but run the risk of not reflecting more naturalistic processing of sign forms. In addition, there is mounting evidence that combinations of single parameters may not be strictly additive. Several experiments have shown that the combination of location and movement information in a sign may be a privileged processing unit (Baus et al., 2014; Corina & Knapp, 2006a, b; Dye & Shih, 2006; Gutiérrez, 2008; Hildebrandt & Corina, 2002). Linguistic models of sign structure have described movement and location as the main syllabic building blocks (e.g., Brentari, 1998; Corina & Emmorey, 1993; Sandler, 1989) with handshape being represented on a separate structural tier (e.g., Sandler, 1986).

12.4 SEMANTIC MAPPING IN SIGNED LANGUAGES

A fascinating issue raised in psycholinguistic studies of sign languages concerns the relation between form-based and meaning-based properties of signed languages. The notion that language forms (phonology) are arbitrarily related to language meaning (semantics) is often considered a central tenet of human language (Hockett, 1959). Spoken languages tend to favor a clear separation between properties of form and meaning, that is, the same concept adopts different forms in different languages (e.g., "dog" in English, "perro" in Spanish, "chien" in French, "cane" in Italian). Accordingly, theories of lexical access have maintained clear separations between form properties of the input/output representations and meaning representations (Fodor et al., 1974; Levelt, 1989).

While arbitrary mappings between form and meaning exist in signed languages, it is frequently observed that many signs show a tighter coupling between form and meaning. The visual-manual modality affords many more opportunities for non-arbitrary mappings (e.g., Taub, 2000) and across signed languages, a high proportion of lexical signs are iconic. Iconicity is not only prevalent in signs referring to concrete objects and actions, but also in abstract domains like cognition, emotion, and communication (Vinson et al., 2015). The prevalence of these iconic forms may derive from the close historical relationship between gestures and formal sign languages, where it is generally accepted that sign languages arise, in part, from gestural and pantomimic forms that afford clear conveyance of meaning within communities of users (Armstrong et al., 1995; Armstrong & Wilcox, 2007; Corballis, 1999, 2003; Kendon, 1997, 2000, 2004; Tomasello, 2005; Wilcox, 2004).

Iconicity extends beyond the lexical level and factors prominently in multisign utterances. For example, signed languages make extensive use of depictive classifier forms.

Classifiers are a special class of predicates used to encode motion in space, with handshapes representing objects, moving in ways that map onto the real-world motion (e.g., Emmorey, 2002; Schembri, 2003). Signed languages also make extensive iconic use of space, such as reflecting literal arrangements of physical scenes, or representing persons or objects in space in order to express more abstract relations among them iconically (e.g., Perniss, 2012).

An important question is whether iconicity in signed languages has processing consequences, including whether the relatively greater iconicity leads to differences in the acquisition of signed language. Here, researchers ask whether the more transparent coupling between a sign and its referent might serve to boost the learning of sign forms in infancy. Early work indicated that iconic signs were not overly represented in children's earliest signs (Morgan et al., 2006; Orlansky & Bonvillian, 1984), and that children are more likely to produce errors that favor ease of articulation over preserving iconic relationship between a sign and its referent. For example, a child may produce the ASL sign COW with the simpler "S" handshape (a closed fist) at the head, rather than with the target "Y" handshape, which eliminates the iconic mapping between the extended fingers and the horns of a cow (Meier et al., 2008). However, Thompson, Vinson, Woll, and Vigliocco (2012) recently reported that iconic signs were more prevalent than expected in the vocabularies of very young BSL signing children (aged 11–20 months) and that the proportion of iconic signs increased relatively rapidly for older children (aged 20–30 months). Thompson et al. (2012) suggest iconicity could provide an imitative, embodied mechanism to earliest sign acquisition, highlighting motor and perceptual similarity between actions and signs. That the advantage for iconic signs was found to increase with children's age may reflect an emerging cognitive system that is able to capitalize upon meaningful form-meaning mappings. Iconicity has been shown to help adult learners in mastering signed languages (Campbell, Martin, & White, 1992).

In psycholinguistic studies with adult signers, iconicity effects have been shown both in sign language recognition and in production. For example, in sign-picture matching experiments, researchers have shown that subjects are faster at matching signs and pictures when a pictured object's salient features mirror the iconic properties of a sign (for example a picture of a bird highlighting the bird's beak, which mirrors the ASL sign for BIRD which uses the index and thumb to depict a bird beak) (Thompson, Vinson, & Vigliocco, 2009; Vinson et al., 2015). Iconicity effects were also observed when subjects had to make phonological decisions about path movements in signs which were either more iconic (e.g., ROCKET, made with an upward vertical movement) or less iconic (e.g., BOTTLE, made with an upward path movement which does not signify motion). BSL signers were faster at classifying the direction of movement in more iconic signs, whereas non-signing controls did not discriminate between more and less iconic categories.

In a picture naming experiment, Vinson et al. (2015) also report effects of iconicity on production. Here they report an interaction between age of acquisition and iconicity, whereby signs which were acquired early showed no effect of iconicity. However, among later acquired signs, subjects were faster at producing iconic signs. Vinson et al. (2015) note that in spoken language, phonological retrieval has been shown to be slower and more difficult for later-learned words (e.g., Belke et al., 2005; Hernández & Fiebach, 2006; Kittredge et al., 2008; Navarrete et al., 2013). Vinson et al. (2015) suggest that the iconic link between conceptual features and phonological form serves to mitigate this effect in late acquired signs.

Emmorey (2014) proposed a model to account for many of the reported effects of iconicity in signed languages, based on work by Gentner (1983) on the interpretation of analogies and metaphors. Here, it is suggested that processing iconicity involves a structured comparative process, whereby connections are made between alignable features of mental objects (i.e., signs and images). Alignment is thought to facilitate processing, thus providing an explanation for the effects of iconicity reported by Thompson et al. (2009, 2012). Structure mapping theory provides an explanation for the lack of iconicity effects observed in some other studies, such as Bosworth and Emmorey, 2010, where the authors reported no facilitation in lexical decision response times nor in semantic priming effects for iconic signs. Emmorey suggests this may be due to the fact that lexical decisions can be made solely on the basis of form or meaning and do not engage the comparative structure mapping process. However, it remains less clear how such an account would explain iconicity effects reported in sign language production (e.g., Vinson et al., 2015). Additional work is required to fully explore the conditions under which iconicity effects may be observed in sign recognition.

12.5 THE ROLE OF SPACE IN SIGN GRAMMAR

A notable property of all signed languages is the prominent use of spatialized devices in the conveyance of complex meanings including grammatical roles (such as subject/object), prepositional meaning, locative relations, and speaker viewpoint in ways that may not have direct parallels in spoken languages. For example, in signed languages like ASL, a signer may associate a noun with a specific location in articulatory space (typically on a horizontal plane in front of the signer) with a later indexic point to this space signaling a co-referential relationship. Thus, in the sentence "*John bought a new guitar*," the proper noun John may be articulated in a right-sided location in neural space, and a subsequent point to that same location would signal the antecedent "John." In many theories of sign language grammar this pointing sign is considered a pronoun. Spoken language studies have found evidence that the antecedent noun is "reactivated" when a pronoun is encountered in a sentence. Using a probe recognition technique, Emmorey et al. (1991) found evidence for antecedent reactivation during sign comprehension that was like that observed for spoken languages. In this study, a semantically related probe sign that followed the pronoun was recognized faster than a semantically inconsistent sign. They extended these findings by investigating several sign language-specific aspects of co-reference. For example, the reactivation was noted even when the grammatical co-reference was signaled by verb agreement rather than by an overt pronoun, further providing a psycholinguistic validation of the theoretically motivated analysis of null-pronoun phenomena in ASL (Emmorey & Lillo-Martin, 1995).

Emmorey, Corina, and Bellugi (1995) examined whether the spatial location of the probe also interacted with entailed semantic relationships. They found that the consistency of the spatial location of the probe item did not influence response times. That is, while a semantically (and co-referentially) appropriate probe sign was recognized faster than a semantically inconsistent sign, these recognition times were not modulated by absolute spatial location of the probe (which could appear in the same location as the pronoun [and antecedent] or a different location). Interestingly, this lack of spatial effect was observed only in sentences in which the spatial locations signaled grammatical relations. In contrast, when the spatialization of the nouns and pronouns referred to actual topographic relationships (i.e., real-world space, as in "chair located to the left of a table") the consistency between the probes and the spatially established referents did positively influence reaction times. This finding is consistent with a theoretically motivated distinction between grammatical space and topographic use of space in sign. In sum, these studies have found that the same processing mechanisms are required to interpret coreference in signed and spoken languages, but for signed languages, the type of information represented by the spatial location can influence how coreference relations are processed (Emmorey, 2002).

Capek et al. (2009) used ERPs to examine the processing of syntactic and semantic information in ASL sentences, including conditions relating to spatial grammar processing. Subjects viewed complex signed sentences that either were well-formed or exhibited one of two different types of syntactic spatial violations. For example, in the well-formed sentence "I washed the car," the referent for car can be established at a particular location in signing space (e.g., by signing CAR and then "placing" the car to the right of the signer), and subsequently the verb is articulated with a movement from the location of the subject (i.e., the signer) to the location of the object. Reversed verb agreement violations were formed by reversing the direction of the verb such that the verb moved toward the subject instead of the object (i.e., "the car washed me"). Unspecified verb agreement violations were formed by directing the verb toward a location in space that had not been defined previously as the subject or object.

Analysis of the results showed that these two agreement errors resulted in somewhat different electrophysiological response patterns. Reversed verb agreement errors showed a negativity which was largest over left frontal electrode sites, similar to what has been found in studies of syntactic violations in spoken languages (Friederici, 2002). In contrast, unspecified verb agreement violations resulted in a negativity which was unexpectedly largest over right frontal sites. Capek et al. (2009) suggest that the unspecified verb agreement violations likely place different demands on the system involved in processing spatial syntax than the reversed verb agreement violations. The unspecified verb agreement violations refer to a spatial location at which no referent had previously been located. In these cases, the viewer is forced to either posit a new referent whose identity is unknown (and will perhaps be introduced later in the discourse) or infer that the intended referent is one that was previously placed at a different spatial location. Either way, this is functionally different than the processing required for reversed verb agreement violations, where subject and object referents are properly placed, but the relationship between them is anomalous. Though both violations involve spatial syntax in ASL, these results implicate distinguishable neural subsystems depending on the processing demands, and suggest a more complex organization for the neural basis of syntax than a unitary "grammatical processing" system (Capek et al., 2009).

In summary, studies of lexical recognition in signed languages reveal that factors of lexicality and lexical neighborhood density influence the time course of recognition in signed languages. These studies show that basic principles of lexical organization are common across signed and spoken languages. However, lexical access in signed languages also shows signal-driven modality-specific recognition properties that are unique to signed languages. For example, the differential effects of sublexical properties of handshape and location (and formational parameter combinations) on recognition and the affordance of sign forms to convey iconic meaning reflect the unique properties of signed languages that do not have obvious spoken language analogs. Studies of sentence processing reveal that while global patterns of activation during syntactically driven referencing occur in both signed and spoken language, spatial devices used in sign language syntax may place unique demands on the language processor.

12.6 Neuroimaging studies of sign language processing

Functional neuroimaging studies of deaf signers have revealed language networks that are highly similar to those that have been proposed for spoken languages. For example, studies of sentence processing in signed languages have repeatedly reported left hemisphere activations that parallel those found for spoken languages. These activation patterns include inferior frontal gyrus (including Broca's area and insula), precentral sulcus, superior and middle temporal cortical regions, posterior superior temporal sulcus (STS), angular gyrus (AG), and supramarginal gyrus (SMG) (e.g., Lambertz, Gizewski, de Greiff, & Forsting, 2005; MacSweeney et al., 2002; MacSweeney et al., 2006; Neville et al., 1998; Newman et al., 2002; Petitto et al., 2000; Sakai, Tatsuno, Suzuki, Kimura, & Ichida, 2005). The majority of functional imaging studies of sign language confirm the importance of the left hemisphere in sign processing and emphasize the similarity of patterns of activation for signed and spoken languages.

12.6.1 Reading in the deaf

The question of how profoundly deaf individuals acquire the ability to read has important pedagogical and theoretical ramifications. Long standing reports of a reading achievement gap between hearing and deaf readers (cf. Allen, 1986; Gallaudet Research Institute, 2005; Holt, 1994; Karchmer & Mitchell, 2003; Traxler, 2000; Wauters, van Bon, & Tellings, 2006) is a concern of educators. At the same time, evidence of successful reading ability in some profoundly deaf individuals challenges current theories of orthographic processing which suggest that access to spoken language phonology is a cornerstone in the mapping between print and meaning.

12.6.2 Deaf readers as bilinguals

Increasingly, psychologists and educators have been moving away from a deficit model of deaf reading which argues that remediation of reading skills requires providing the deaf reader with the same capacities of normally hearing readers, principally the development of spoken language phonological awareness. The growing appreciation that deaf individuals who rely upon signed languages may approach the reading process like second-language users has ushered in new studies that examine the relationships between lexical representations of signed languages and orthographic forms.

Research on bilingual language processing has demonstrated that bilinguals do not "turn off" the language not in use, even when it might be beneficial to do so. An increasing number of studies with spoken language show that both languages are active when bilinguals listen (Marian & Spivey, 2003), speak (Kroll, Bobb, & Wodniecka, 2006), and read (Dijkstra, 2005) each language. For instance, Thierry and Wu (2007) demonstrated cross-language effects in reading with Chinese-English bilinguals. Their study utilized pairs of words in English, half of which contained repeated characters when translated into Chinese. In making semantic judgments, subjects showed effects of both semantic relatedness in English and of character repetition, regardless of whether the English words were read or heard. These data indicate that Chinese-English bilinguals spontaneously access Chinese translations when reading or listening to English words.

This effect has been replicated by Morford et al. (2011), who adapted the semantic relatedness paradigm from Thierry and Wu (2007) to ask whether deaf readers activate the ASL translations of English words. They asked deaf signers to judge the semantic relatedness of English word pairs whose translations shared several formational parameters, and compared responses to English words whose ASL translations were unrelated. As excepted, participants were significantly faster to respond to semantically related than unrelated English pairs. Critically they also observed an interaction between semantic decisions and the presence of the implicit ASL phonological manipulation. Participants were faster to accept semantically related words with phonologically related ASL translations than with phonologically unrelated ASL translations, but slower to reject semantically unrelated words with phonologically related translations than with phonologically unrelated translations. These effects were not observed in a group of spoken language bilinguals for whom English served as their L2. These results provide compelling evidence that deaf bilinguals activate signs while processing written words of a spoken language. Subsequent research has further demonstrated implicit sign language phonological effects on word reading in German deaf bilinguals who use DGS as their native language (Kubus et al., 2015) and in Dutch deaf children (Ormel et al., 2012).

While these results demonstrate the explanatory utility of approaching deaf readers from a bilingual perspective, these studies raise a number of additional questions, for instance regarding the exact nature of the sign language phonological overlap. Each of these studies has used different metrics for composing their "phonologically related" forms. Indeed, it is noteworthy that in the ASL study of Morford et al. (2011), the effects of phonological overlap were faciliatory on semantic decisions, while in the case of the DGS study of Kubus et al. (2015) shared phonological effects were inhibitory on semantic relatedness judgments. As noted by Kubus et al., the Morford study defined ASL phonological overlap largely based upon shared movement and location parameters while the DGS sign translations of the stimuli generally overlapped in handshape and location. That such difference might impact the valence of interference effects is perhaps not surprising given the evidence discussed earlier for differential effects of phonological parameters in lexical decisions.

These studies also leave open questions about the relationship between English word form activation and ASL activation. In contrast to the electrophysiological studies of Thierry and Wu (2007) the behavioral reaction time paradigms used in the sign studies above do not permit a deep understanding of the time course of these effects. Whether sign phonology mediates the retrieval of the meanings of written words or is activated after access to the meaning remains an open question for further investigation. Finally, we may also ask whether studies conducted using single word lexical decision experiments generalize to more naturalistic text-based reading behaviors. To address some of these issues, several studies have begun to explore the time course of reading behaviors using self-paced reading procedures and eye-tracking methodologies. These techniques provide an opportunity to evaluate how deaf readers weigh and integrate different types of cues during reading of texts.

12.6.3 Perceptual span

Eye-tracking measures of reading behavior have provided a basic understanding of the fundamental properties of the eye movements during reading (Rayner, 1998, 2009). Readers move their eyes with a series of alternating fixations and saccades. During fixations, which last on the average of 200–250 milliseconds, visual information from the text is obtained. Saccades are periods of rapid eye movements (20–40 ms) during which time eye movement spans seven to nine letter spaces. During these brief movements visual information uptake is suppressed because of the extreme speed at which the eyes move (Matin, 1974). Readers do not fixate on all words, and skip about 30% of the words in a text (mainly short and frequent words). Although most saccades travel in the direction of reading (left to right for English), 10–15% of saccades are regressions to revisit text that was previously read. The time spent fixating on a word is highly variable among readers but is largely determined by lexical factors, such as a word's frequency, length, and predictability (Rayner, 1998, 2009). Text difficulty and reading skill also influence fixation durations. Skilled readers have shorter fixations overall than less-skilled readers (Bélanger et al., 2012; Rayner, 1986). Reading skill also affects eye movements such that beginning readers and less-skilled readers (even college-level readers) make fewer skips, and have shorter saccades, more fixations within a sentence, more regressions back in the text, and more within-word refixations (Blythe, 2014).

In a series of studies, Bélanger and colleagues have characterized eye movements in adult deaf readers and have reported differences between skilled deaf and hearing readers, as well as between skilled and less-skilled deaf readers (see Bélanger & Rayner, 2015, for a review). For instance, Bélanger et al. (2012) reported that skilled deaf readers had a wider perceptual span (up to 18 letter spaces to the right of fixation) than did the skilled hearing readers matched on reading level and less-skilled deaf readers (both with a span of 14 letter spaces). This finding accords with reported differences in the distribution of visual attention which indicates enhanced attentional allocation to the periphery, relative to hearing individuals, in low-level visual perception tasks (Bavelier, Dye, & Hauser, 2006; Proksch & Bavelier, 2002). This suggests that the size of the perceptual span in deaf readers is not determined solely by reading skill, but that it may be wider than expected because of the added influence of a differential spread of attention across the visual field that is specific to deafness (Bélanger & Rayner, 2015).

12.7 THE INFLUENCE OF SPOKEN LANGUAGE PHONOLOGY

Phonological awareness (PA) commonly refers to a metalinguistic awareness of the sound structure of a language: our conscious ability to detect and manipulate language sounds

(Liberman & Shankweiler, 1985; Wagner & Torgesen, 1987). Since Wagner and Torgesen's (1987) seminal review which supported a causal role for PA in learning to read, a plethora of research continues to document the relationships between phonological skills, especially PA, and the acquisition of reading (but see Castles & Coltheart, 2004). A recent meta-review examined relationships among three of the most widely studied measures of children's phonological skills (phonemic awareness, rhyme awareness, and verbal short-term memory) and reports a pivotal role of phonemic awareness as a predictor of individual differences in reading development (Melby-Lervåg, Lyster, & Hulme, 2012). Anthony and Francis (2005) stated that PA and its relation to literacy exists in all alphabetic languages that have been examined (see also Goswami, 2008).

The question of how and whether deaf and hard of hearing children develop a sound-based PA and whether this is causally related to the development of reading in this population has been an area of active research (see, e.g., del Giudice & Lieberman, 2011; Easterbrooks, Lederberg, Miller, Bergeron, & Connor, 2008; McQuarrie & Parilla, 2009; Mayberry, del Giudice, & Lieberman, 2011; Miller, 1997; Sterne & Goswami, 2000; Trezek & Malmgren, 2005; Wang, Trezek, Luckner, & Paul, 2008). Given the great heterogeneity in language experiences, educational instruction, and so on, it is perhaps not surprising that there is a wide range of data and inferences drawn about the importance of spoken language PA in learning to read.

For example, Mayberry, del Giudice, and Lieberman (2011) in a meta-review observed that phonological coding and awareness skills predicted 11% of the variance in reading proficiency in deaf participants. Other possible modulating factors, such as task type and reading grade level, did not explain the remaining variance. Rather language ability, broadly defined, emerged as the factor most highly correlated with reading ability in deaf readers, accounting for 35% of the variance in reading proficiency. Language ability was measured using a wide range of assessments, including both spoken and signed vocabulary production and comprehension measures.

An individual differences study reported by Cates (2015) of 78 adult deaf readers provides further confirmation that factors such as vocabulary comprehension and reading volume are stronger predictors of reading ability than PA. A novel aspect of this study was the inclusion of a control group of hearing Chinese-English bilingual university students who learned English as a second language (a monolingual hearing English control group was also tested). In a PA task, deaf and hearing subjects were asked to determine which of two words, if pronounced, would be a homophone of an existing English word (e.g., *khat* versus *kift*). Performance on this measure requires knowledge of rules of orthographic to phonemic mappings. As expected, hearing monolingual controls were near ceiling on this measure. However, both the deaf readers and the Chinese-English bilinguals scored significantly worse on this measure and did not differ from one another. This finding demonstrates that PA awareness may not be a predictor of reading achievement in individuals who approach reading as second-language learners, regardless of whether they are deaf or hearing.

In a separate study, Corina et al. (2014) investigated the role of PA for ASL and its relation to PA in English. In this paradigm, deaf signing subjects examined two ASL pseudosign forms and were asked to combine the phonological parameters from these forms to generate a possible ASL sign. An analogous experiment in English might ask subjects to listen to two pseudowords; "*krom*" and "*leete*," and using components of these pseudowords create a possible common English word. For example, one could take the onset of the first word /kr/, the nucleus of the second word /i/, and the coda consonant of the first word /m/ to create the word /krim/ "cream." Corina and colleagues reported that deaf signers who were exposed to ASL from birth (i.e., native signers) performed better than early signers (deaf subjects who were first exposed to ASL in elementary school) and late signers (deaf subjects who learned ASL as teenagers). These data suggest that early ASL exposure affords advantages in the mental manipulation of sublexical properties of ASL sign formation.

Deaf subjects also participated in a PA test for English, using a picture-based rhyming task. While late and early deaf signers outperformed the native deaf signers on this English-based test, native signers nevertheless showed a strong positive correlation ($r = 0.66$) between performance on the ASL PA test and the English rhyme judgment test. This relationship was not found for late or early signers. This finding may reflect cross-language transfer of PA which has been shown in spoken language bilinguals for structurally similar languages like Spanish and English (e.g., Dickinson, McCabe, Clark-Chiarelli, & Wolf, 2004; Durgunoglu, Nagy, & Hancin-Bhatt, 1993), but also for structurally dissimilar languages such as Dutch and Turkish (Verhoeven, 2007) and Chinese and English (Chen et al., 2010). The data from native ASL signers suggest that PA, as measured by these tests, may be a metalinguistic skill that transcends language modality.

Recent work by Bélanger et al. (2013) has expanded on the use of phonological information in deaf reading by investigating the combined use of orthographic and phonological codes in parafoveal vision. Skilled reading is inherently a predictive process, and skilled hearing readers make use not only of visual information falling in the fixated high-acuity foveal region (the central 2 degrees around the center of fixation) but are able to make use of upcoming pre-fixated information that falls within the parafoveal region (approximately 5–7 degrees of visual angle from fixation). This information speeds the processing of the word when it is subsequently fixated (Pollatsek, Lesch, Morris, & Rayner, 1992; Schotter, Angele, & Rayner, 2012).

Bélanger et al. (2013) used a gaze-contingent boundary paradigm where preview words are presented in the parafovea and targets replace them after an invisible boundary is crossed. The authors compared fixation times in preview-target pairs which were either homophones (e.g., week-weak) or orthographically related (wear-weak) to a baseline condition with identical items (weak-weak). The results showed that hearing readers, as expected, showed early activation of both orthographic and phonological codes in parafoveal vision, but that deaf readers showed only effects of orthographic information and no effects of phonological information, regardless of their reading level (skilled or less skilled). These data add to a growing literature which indicates that sound-based phonological processing may play a less-central role in the development of reading, even in skilled deaf readers.

12.7.1 Syntactic and semantic influences

Eye-tracking studies have also been used to evaluate the influence of syntactic and semantic factors in sentence-level reading in deaf readers. In normally hearing readers, sentence processing is primarily led by general syntactic parsing principles, with lexico-semantic, sense-semantic, and contextual cues modulating the outcome (e.g., Altmann & Steedman, 1988; Ferreira & Clifton, 1986; Traxler & Pickering, 1996). Researchers have routinely made use of sentences that vary in structural complexity to make inference about the interplay of factors that influence reading. For example, the processing of English subject and object relative clauses have provided a fertile testing ground for the interplay of syntactic and semantic factors in reading as well as the role of cognitive variables such as working memory capacity and perspective-taking (e.g., Traxler, 2000; Traxler et al., 2005). Recent studies have begun to evaluate these same issues in second-language learners, and have suggested that whether L2 learners' processing strategies differ from those in the L1 is largely determined by individual variables such as working memory (Dussias & Piñar, 2010), proficiency in the L2 (Frenck-Mestre, 2002; Hopp, 2006; Hoshino, Dussias & Kroll, 2010; Kilborn, 1992), and other experience-based factors (Dussias, 2003; Dussias & Sagarra, 2007; McDonald, 2006).

Piñar and colleagues (2016) have extended these investigations to skilled and less-skilled deaf readers. Here they made use of eye tracking to examine how deaf readers use syntactic and semantic cues when they read English sentences and whether individual variables, such as the reader's experience in English and in ASL, might affect their sentence parsing strategies. Using material adapted from Traxler et al. (2005), they quantified eye movements while readers encountered subject and object relative clauses. A reliable finding in the literature on sentence processing is that object relative clauses in English (ORCs, e.g., *The hiker that the avalanche buried appeared in the six o'clock news.*) are typically harder to process than equivalent subject relative clauses (SRCs, e.g., *The hiker that fled the avalanche appeared in the six o'clock news.*). Importantly, available semantic cues, such as the animacy of the noun phrases (NPs), modulate the subject/object relative contrast effect (e.g., Mak, Vonk, & Schriefers, 2002; Traxler et al., 2002; Traxler et al., 2005; Weckerly & Kutas, 1999). Thus, when the relativized NP is inanimate, and therefore a more likely object, the processing difficulty in object relative clauses disappears. These data show that English L1 readers can weigh and effectively integrate both syntactic and semantic cues in the processing of relative clause structures.

Piñar and colleagues evaluated common dependent variables such as first-pass and total reading times for the relative clause, the likelihood of a regression from the relative clause to the left of the relative clause, and the regression path (RP) reading time in deaf readers. Consistent with what has been found in previous studies involving hearing native English speakers, eye-tracking fixation patterns of deaf readers reveal the interplay of syntactic and semantic cues in the online processing of relative clauses. Overall, participants are faster to read subject than object relative clauses, indicating effects of syntactic complexity on fixation times. Total reading times also indicate that deaf readers capitalize on useful animacy cues in the condition that poses the most structural difficulty, namely, in ORCs.

Group differences between deaf readers and hearing English monolingual readers were also observed. Deaf readers evidenced a high degree of word skipping, primarily failing to fixate on constituents critical to the interpretation of the relative clause (e.g., the antecedent NP, relative clause verb, and so on). This finding accords well with Bélanger and Rayner (2015), who also reported differences in gross patterns of eye movements in their studies. In this case, skilled deaf readers showed fewer regressions back in the text (rereading) and more skipped words than did skilled hearing readers. One explanation for this strategy, offered by Bélanger & Rayner (2015), is that deaf readers may be more efficient visual word processors, with tighter connections between orthography and semantics. Deaf readers are thought to be extremely attuned to the visual-orthographic makeup of words and can quickly detect precise word forms within a single fixation even while words are still in the parafovea.

Another important finding to emerge from the Piñar et al. (2016) study was the indication that self-rated ASL proficiency may influence English syntactic processing. Specifically, that the difficulty associated with animate ORCs may be smaller for individuals with greater ASL self-ratings. This finding adds to growing evidence that early sign language experience enhances English literacy development (Chamberlain & Mayberry, 2008; Corina et al., 2014; Mayberry, 1989). Here, Piñar and colleagues show that effects of ASL experience may afford processing advantages for parsing syntactic forms in an unrelated language such as English. However, the mechanism by which such cross-language effects occur and a definitive accounting of the experiential factors that may drive these effects remains elusive.

In summary, psycholinguistic studies of eye movements have provided new insights into how deaf individuals with reduced access to the acoustic properties of spoken English navigate the reading of English orthography. Accruing data indicates that despite less reliance on phonological encoding, deaf readers can develop efficient visual-based strategies for mapping orthographic forms to meaning and develop sensitivities to syntactic properties of English. Evidence indicates that deaf individuals activate ASL forms during text comprehension. Envisioning the deaf reader from a bilingual perspective rather than through a deficiency model, and understanding the visual strategies utilized by deaf readers may lead to the development of more effective pedagogical innovations that will lead to increased literacy rates for deaf children.

12.8 Conclusions

Although research in signed languages is still very much under development within psycholinguistics, the past 40 years of research following Klima and Bellugi's seminal work has expanded our understanding of what human language processing looks like, regardless of modality. Current research not only highlights the commonalities observed in language processing across signed and spoken languages, but also illuminates the many ways in which languages expressed in the visual/manual domain engender unique cognitive and neural processing constraints. At the same time, a broadening acknowledgment of the complexities of the deaf language experience has led to new insights into deaf reading and signed language processing. In particular, the appreciation of deaf readers as bilingual language users highlights similarities between deaf individuals and second-language users, while also showing the ways in which deafness itself shapes perceptual and attentional systems.

Acknowledgments

This work was support by the following grants: NIH NIDCD R01 DC011538 and R01 DC014767.

References

Allen, T. (1986). Patterns of academic achievement among hearing impaired students: 1974 and 1973. In: Schildroth, A. N., & Karchmer, M. A. (Eds.), *Deaf Children in America* (pp. 161–206). College-Hill Press, San Diego, CA.

Altmann, G., & Steedman, M. (1988). Interaction with context during human sentence processing. *Cognition, 30*, 191–238.

Anthony, J. L., & Francis, D. J. (2005). Development of phonological awareness. *Current Directions in Psychological Science, 14*(5), 255–59.

Armstrong, D. F., Stokoe, W. C., & Wilcox, S. E., (1995). *Gesture and the Nature of Language*. Cambridge University Press, Cambridge, MA.

Armstrong, D. F., & Wilcox, S. E. (2007). *The Gestural Origin of Language*. Oxford University Press, New York, NY.

Battison, R. (1978). *Lexical Borrowing in American Sign Language*. Linstok Press, Silver Spring, MD.

Baus, C., Gutiérrez-Sigut, E., Quer, J., & Carreiras, M. (2008). Lexical access in Catalan signed language (LSC) production. *Cognition, 108*(3), 856–65.

Baus, C., Gutiérrez, E., & Carreiras, M. (2014). The role of syllables in sign language production. *Frontiers of Psychology, 5*, 1254.

Bavelier, D., Dye, M. W. G., & Hauser, P. (2006). Do deaf individuals see better? *Trends in Cognitive Sciences, 10*, 512–18.

Bélanger, N. N., Mayberry, R. I., & Rayner, K. (2013). Orthographic and phonological preview benefits: Parafoveal processing in skilled and less-skilled deaf readers. *Quarterly Journal of Experimental Psychology, 66*, 2237–52.

Bélanger, N. N., Slattery, T. J., Mayberry, R. I., & Rayner, K. (2012). Skilled deaf readers have an enhanced perceptual span in reading. *Psychological Science, 23*, 816–23.

Bélanger, N. N., & Rayner, K. (2015). What eye movements reveal about deaf readers. *Current Directions in Psychological Science, 24*(3) 220–6.

Belke, E., Brysbaert, M., Meyer, A. S., & Ghyselinck, M. (2005). Age of acquisition effects in picture naming: Evidence for a lexical-semantic competition hypothesis. *Cognition, 96*(2005), B45–B54.

Bellugi, U., Klima, E. S., & Siple, P. (1974). Remembering in signs. *Cognition, 3*(2), 93–125.

Bentin, S. (1987). Event-related potentials, semantic processes, and expectancy factors in word recognition. *Brain and Language, 31*, 308–27.

Bentin, S., McCarthy, G., & Wood, C. C. (1985). Event-related potentials, lexical decision, and semantic priming. *Electroencephalography & Clinical Neurophysiology, 60*, 353–5.

Blythe, H. (2014). Developmental changes in eye movements and visual information encoding associated with learning to read. *Current Directions in Psychological Science, 23*, 201–7.

Bosworth, R. G., & Emmorey, K. (2010). Effects of iconicity and semantic relatedness on lexical access in American Sign Language. *Journal of Experimental Psychology: Learning, Memory, and Cognition, 36*(6), 1573.

Brentari, D. (2001). *Foreign Vocabulary in Sign Languages: A Cross-linguistic Investigation of Word Formation*. Lawrence Erlbaum Associates, Mahwah, NJ.

Brentari, D. A. (1998). *Prosodic Model of Sign Language Phonology*. MIT Press, Cambridge, MA.

Brentari, D. (2002). Modality differences in sign language phonology and morphophonemics. In: Meier, R. P., Cormier, K., Quinto-Pozos, D. (Eds.), *Modality and Structure in Signed and Spoken Languages* (pp. 35–64). Cambridge University Press, New York, NY.

Brown, C., & Hagoort, P. (1993). The processing nature of the N400: Evidence from masked priming. *Journal of Cognitive Neuroscience, 5*, 34–44.

Campbell, R., Martin, P., & White, T. (1992). Forced choice recognition of sign in novice learners of British Sign Language. *Applied Linguistics, 13*, 185–201.

Capek, C. M., Grossi, G., Newman, A. J., McBurney, S. L., Corina, D., Roeder, B., & Neville, H. J. (2009). Brain systems mediating semantic and syntactic processing in deaf native signers: Biological invariance and modality specificity. *Proceedings of the National Academy of Sciences of the United States of America, 106*, 8784–9.

Carreiras, M., Gutiérrez-Sigut, E., Baquero, S., & Corina, D. (2008). Lexical processing in Spanish sign language (LSE). *Journal of Memory and Language, 58*(1), 100–22.

Caselli, N. K., Sehyr, Z. S., Cohen-Goldberg, A. M., & Emmorey, K. (2017). ASL-LEX: A lexical database of American Sign Language. *Behavior Research Methods, 49*(2), 784–801.

Castles, A., & Coltheart, M. (2004). Is there a causal link from phonological awareness to success in learning to read? *Cognition, 91*(1), 77–111.

Cates, M. D. (2015). Predictors of reading comprehension skill in deaf and hearing bilingual readers. University of California, Davis, ProQuest Dissertations Publishing. Available at: https://search.proquest.com/openview/02b4413e17f097e2748b367751b98ecc/1.pdf?pq-origsite=gscholar&cbl=18750&diss=y

Cates, D., Gutiérrez, E., Hafer, S., Barrett, R., & Corina, D. (2013). Location, location, location. *Sign Language Studies, 13*(4), 433–61.

Chamberlain, C., & Mayberry, R. I. (2008). ASL syntactic and narrative comprehension in skilled and less skilled adult readers: Bilingual-bimodal evidence for the linguistic basis of reading. *Applied Psycholinguistics, 28*, 537–49.

Cheek, A., Cormier, K., Repp, A., & Meier, R. P. (2001). Prelinguistic gesture predicts mastery and error in the production of early signs. *Language, 77*(2001), 292–323.

Chen, X., Xu, F., Nguyen, T., Hong, G., & Wang, Y. (2010). Effects of cross-language transfer on first-language phonological awareness and literacy skills in Chinese children receiving English instruction. *Journal of Educational Psychology, 102*, 712–28.

Clibbens, J., & Harris, M. (1993). Phonological processes and sign language development. In: Messer, D., & Turner, G. (Eds.), *Critical Influences on Child Language Acquisition and Development*, Macmillan/St. Martin's Press, London.

Corballis, M. C. (1999). The gestural origins of language. *American Scientist, 87*(2), 138.

Corballis, M. C. (2003). *From Hand to Mouth: The Origins of Language*. Princeton University Press, Princeton, NJ.

Corina, D. P. (1998). Aphasia in users of signed languages. In: Coppens, P., Lebrun, Y., & Basso, A. (Eds.), *Aphasia in Atypical Populations* (pp. 261–309). Lawrence Erlbaum Associates, Mahwah, NJ.

Corina, D. P. (2000). Some observations regarding paraphasia in American Sign Language. In: Emmorey K., & Lane, H. (Eds.), *The Signs of Language Revisited: An Anthology to Honor Ursula Bellugi and Edward Klima* (pp. 418–31). Lawrence Erlbaum Associates, Mahwah, NJ.

Corina, D., Chiu, Y. S., Knapp, H., Greenwald, R., San Jose-Robertson, L., & Braun, A. (2007). Neural correlates of human action observation in hearing and deaf subjects. *Brain Research, 1152*, 111–29.

Corina, D. P., & Emmorey, K. (1993). Lexical priming in American Sign Language. Paper presented at the Linguistic Society of American Conference, Philadelphia, PA.

Corina, D. P., & Grosvald, M. (2012). Exploring perceptual processing of ASL and human actions: Effects of inversion and repetition priming, *Cognition, 122*(3), 330–45.

Corina, D., Grosvald, M., & Lachaud, C. (2011). Perceptual invariance or orientation specificity in American Sign Language: Evidence from repetition priming for signs and gestures. *Language and Cognitive Processes, 26*(8), 1102–35.

Corina, D. P., Gutiérrez, E., & Grosvald, M. (2014). Sign language production: An overview. In: Goldrick, M., Ferreira, V., & Miozzo, M. (Eds.), *The Oxford Handbook of Language Production* (pp. 393–416). Oxford University Press, Oxford.

Corina, D. P., Hafer, S., & Welch, K. (2014). Phonological awareness for American Sign Language. *Journal of Deaf Studies and Deaf Education, 19*(4), 530–45.

Corina, D. P., & Knapp, H. P. (2006a). Sign language psycholinguistics. In: Brown, K. (Ed.), *Encyclopedia of Language and Linguistics* (pp. 343–9). Elsevier, London.

Corina, D. P., & Knapp, H. P. (2006b). Lexical retrieval in American Sign Language Production. In: Goldstein, L., Whalen, D., & Best, C., (Eds.), *Laboratory Phonology, 8: Varieties of Phonological Competence* (pp. 213–39). Mouton de Gruyter, Berlin.

Corina, D., Lawyer, L., & Cates, D. (2013). Cross-linguistic differences in the neural representation of human language: Evidence from users of signed languages. *Frontiers in Psychology, 3*, 587.

Corina, D. P., & Hildebrandt, U. C. (2002). Psycholinguistic investigations of phonological structure in ASL. In: Meier, R., Cormier, K., & Quinto-Pozos, D. (Eds.), *Modality and Structure in Signed and Spoken Languages* (pp. 88–111). Cambridge University Press, Cambridge.

Crasborn, O., & Sloetjes, H. (2008). Enhanced ELAN functionality for sign language corpora. In: *Proceedings of LREC 2008, Sixth International Conference on Language Resources and Evaluation*.

de Vos, C., & Pfau, R. (2015). Sign language typology: The contribution of rural sign languages. *Annual Review of Linguistics, 1*, 265–88.

Dick, A. S., Mok, E. H., Beharelle, A. R., Goldin-Meadow, S., & Small, S. L. (2014). Frontal and temporal contributions to understanding the iconic co-speech gestures that accompany speech. *Human Brain Mapping, 35*(3), 900–17.

Dickinson, D. K., McCabe, A., Clark-Chiarelli, N., & Wolf, A. (2004). Cross-language transfer of phonological awareness in low-income Spanish and English bilingual preschool children. *Applied Psycholinguistics, 25*, 323–47.

Dijkstra, T. (2005). Bilingual visual word recognition and lexical access. In: Kroll, J. F., & de Groot, A. M. B. (Eds.), *Handbook of Bilingualism: Psycholinguistic Approaches* (pp. 179–201). Oxford University Press, New York.

Durgunoglu, A. Y., Nagy, W. E., & Hancin-Bhatt, B. J. (1993). Cross-language transfer of phonological awareness. *Journal of Educational Psychology, 85*, 453–65.

Dussias, P. E. (2003). Syntactic ambiguity resolution in L2 learners. *Studies in Second Language Acquisition, 25*, 529–57.

Dussias, P. E., & Piñar, P. (2010). Effects of reading span and plausibility in the reanalysis of wh-gaps by Chinese-English second language speakers. *Second Language Research, 26*, 443–72.

Dussias, P. E., & Sagarra, N. (2007). The effect of exposure on syntactic parsing in Spanish-English L2 speakers. *Bilingualism: Language and Cognition, 10*, 101–16.

Dye, M., & Shih, K. (2006). Mock attitudes and old chairs: Phonological priming in British Sign Language. In: Goldstein, L., Whalen, D. W., & Best, C. T. (eds.), *Papers in Laboratory Phonology 8: Varieties of Phonological Competence*. Mouton de Gruyter, Berlin.

Easterbrooks, S. R., Lederberg, A. R., Miller, E. M., Bergeron, J. P., & McDonald Connor, C. (2008). Emergent literacy skills during early childhood in children with hearing loss: Strengths and Weaknesses. *The Volta Review, 108*(2), 91–114.

Emmorey, K. (2002). *Language, Cognition, and the Brain: Insights from Sign Language Research*. Lawrence Erlbaum and Associates, Mahwah, NJ.

Emmorey, K. (2014). Iconicity as structure mapping. *Philosophical Transactions of the Royal Society B, 369*, 20130301. http://dx.doi.org/10.1098/rstb.2013.0301

Emmorey, K. (2015). The neurobiology of sign language. In: Toga, A. W. (Ed.), *Brain Mapping: An Encyclopedic Reference, Vol. 3*. (pp. 475–9). Academic Press, Waltham.

Emmorey, K., & Corina, D. (1990). Lexical recognition in sign language: Effects of phonetic structure and morphology. *Perceptual and Motor Skills, 71*, 1227–52.

Emmorey, K. Corina, D., and Bellugi, U. (1995). Differential processing of topographic and referential functions of space. In: Emmorey, K., & Reilly, J. (Eds), *Language, Gesture, and Space* (pp. 43–62). Lawrence Erlbaum Associates, Hillsdale, NJ.

Emmorey, K., Giezen, M., & Gollan, T. (2016). Psycholinguistic, cognitive, and neural implications of bimodal bilingualism. *Bilingualism: Language and Cognition, 19*(2), 223–42.

Emmorey, K., & Lillo-Martin, D. (1995). Processing spatial anaphora: Referent reactivation with overt and null pronouns in American Sign Language. *Language and Cognitive Processes, 10*(6), 631–64.

Emmorey, K., McCullough, S., Mehta, S., Ponto, L. B. L., & Grabowski, T. (2011). Sign language pantomime production differentially engage frontal and parietal cortices. *Language and Cognitive Processes, 26*(7), 878–901.

Emmorey, K., Norman, F., & O'Grady, L. (1991). The activation of spatial antecedents from overt pronouns in American Sign Language. *Language and Cognitive Processes, 6*(3), 207–28.

Emmorey, K., & Özyürek, A. (2014). Language in our hands: Neural underpinnings of sign language and co-speech gesture. In: Gazzaniga, M. S., & Mangun, G. R. (Eds.), *The Cognitive Neurosciences*, 5th Edition (pp. 657–66). MIT Press, Cambridge, MA.

Emmorey, K., Xu, J., Gannon, P., Goldin-Meadow, S., & Braun, A. (2010). CNS activation and regional connectivity during pantomime observation: No engagement of the mirror neuron system for deaf signers. *NeuroImage, 49*(1), 994–1005.

Ferreira, F., & Clifton Jr, C. (1986). The independence of syntactic processing. *Journal of Memory and Language, 25*, 348–68.

Fodor, J. A., Bever, T. G., & Garrett, M. F. (1974). *The Psychology of Language: An Introduction to Psycholinguistics and Generative Grammar*. McGraw-Hill, New York, NY.

Forster, K. I., & Chambers, S. M. (1973). Lexical access and naming time. *Journal of Verbal Learning and Verbal Behavior, 12*(6), 627–35.

Frenck-Mestre, C. (2002). An on-line look at sentence processing in the second language. In: Heredia, R., & Altarriba, J. (Eds.), *Bilingual Sentence Processing* (pp. 217–36). Elsevier, New York, NY.

Friederici, A. D. (2002). Towards a neural basis of auditory sentence processing. *Trends in Cognitive Science, 6*(2),78–84.

Gallaudet Research Institute. (2005). Regional and national summary report of data from the 2003–2004 annual survey of deaf and hard of hearing children and youth. GRI, Washington, DC.

Gentner, D. (1983). Structure mapping: A theoretical framework for analogy. *Wiley Interdisciplinary Review of Cognitive Science, 7*, 155–70.

Goswami, U. (2008). Reading, dyslexia and the brain. *Educational Research, 50*(2),135–48.

Grosjean, F. (1980). Spoken word recognition processes and the gating paradigm. *Perception & Psychophysics, 28*, 267–83.

Grosvald, M., Gutiérrez, E., Hafer, S., & Corina, D. (2012). Dissociating linguistic and non-linguistic gesture processing: Electrophysiological evidence from American Sign Language. *Brain and Language*, 121(1), 12–24.

Gutiérrez, E. (2008). *El Papel de Los Parámetros Fonológicos en el Procesamiento de la Lengua de Signos Española* [Unpublished doctoral dissertation]. University of la Laguna, Tenerife, Spain.

Gutiérrez, E., & Carreiras, M. (2009). El papel de los parámetros fonológicos en el procesamiento de los signos de la lengua de signos española. Available at: http://www.fundacioncnse.org/imagenes/Las%20portadas/pdf/El_papel_de_los_Parametros.pdf

Gutiérrez, E., Müller, O., Baus, C., & Carreiras, M. (2012a). Electrophysiological evidence for phonological priming in Spanish Sign Language lexical access. *Neuropsychologia*, 50(7), 1335–46.

Gutiérrez, E., Williams, D., Grosvald, M., & Corina, D. P. (2012b). Lexical access in American Sign Language: An ERP investigation of effects of semantics and phonology. *Brain Research*, 1468, 63–83.

Hagoort, P., & Kutas, M. (1995). Electrophysiological insights into language deficits. In: Boller, F., & Grafman, J. (Eds.), *Handbook of Neuropsychology* (pp. 105–34). Elsevier, Amsterdam.

Hagoort, P., & van Berkum, J. (2007). Beyond the sentence given. *Philosophical Transactions of the Royal Society of London. Series B: Biological Sciences*, 362, 801–11.

Hanke, T. (2004). HamNoSys —representing sign language data in language resources and language processing contexts. In: Streiter, O., & Vettori, C. (Eds.), *LREC 2004, Workshop proceedings: Representation and Processing of Sign Languages* (pp. 1–6.). ELRA, Paris.

Hernández, A. E., & Fiebach, C. J. (2006). The brain bases of reading late learned words: Evidence from functional MRI. *Visual Cognition*, 13, 1027–43.

Hildebrandt, U. C., & Corina, D. P. (2002). Phonological similarity in American Sign Language. *Language and Cognitive Processes*, 6, 593–612.

Hockett, C. F. (1959). Animal "languages" and human language. In: Spuhler, J. N. (Ed.), *The Evolution of Man's Capacity for Culture* (pp. 32–9). Wayne State University Press, Detroit, MI.

Holt, J. A. (1994). Classroom attributes and achievement test scores for deaf and hard of hearing students. *American Annals of the Deaf*, 139, 430–7.

Hopp, H. (2006). Syntactic features and reanalysis in near-native processing. *Second Language Research*, 22, 369–97.

Hoshino, N., Dussias, P. E., & Kroll, J. K. (2010). Processing subject-verb agreement in a second language depends on proficiency. *Bilingualism: Language and Cognition*, 13, 87–98.

Huettig, F. (2015). Four central questions about prediction in language processing. *Brain Research*, 1626, 118–35.

Jusczyk, P. W., & Luce, P. A. (2002). Speech perception. [References]. In: Pashler, H., & Yantis, S. (Eds.), *Steven's Handbook of Experimental Psychology*, 3rd Edition (Vol. 1: Sensation and perception, pp. 493–536). John Wiley & Sons, New York, NY.

Karchmer, M. A., & Mitchell, R. E. (2003). Demographic and achievement characteristics of deaf and hard-of-hearing students. In: Marschark, M., & Spencer, P. E. (Eds.), *Oxford Handbook of Deaf Studies, Language, and Education* (pp. 21–37). Oxford University Press, New York, NY.

Karnopp, L. B. (2002). Phonology acquisition in Brazilian Sign Language. In: Morgan, G., & Woll, B. (Eds.), *Directions in Sign Language Acquisition* (pp. 29–53). John Benjamins, Amsterdam.

Kendon, A. (1997). Gesture. [Review]. *Annual Review of Anthropology*, 26(1), 109–28.

Kendon, A., (2000). Language and gesture: Unity or duality. In: McNeill, D. (Ed.), *Language and Gesture: Window into Thought and Action* (pp. 47–63). Cambridge University Press, Cambridge.

Kendon, A. (2004). *Gesture: Visible Action as Utterance*. Cambridge University Press, Cambridge.

Kilborn, K. (1992). On-line integration of grammatical information in a second language. *Advances in Psychology*, 83, 337–50.

Kittredge, A. K., Dell, G. S., Verkuilen, J., & Schwartz, M. F. (2008). Where is the effect of frequency in word production? Insights from aphasic picture naming errors. *Cognitive Neuropsychology*, 25, 463–92.

Klima, E., & U. Bellugi. (1979). *The Signs of Language*. Harvard University Press, Cambridge, MA.

Kroll, J. F., Bobb, S. C., & Wodniecka, Z. (2006). Language selectivity is the exception, not the rule: Arguments against a fixed locus of language selection in bilingual speech. *Bilingualism: Language and Cognition*, 9, 119–35.

Kubus, O., Villwock, A., Morford, J. P., & Rathmann, C. (2015). Word recognition in deaf readers: Cross-language activation of German Sign Language and German. *Applied Psycholinguistics*, 36(4), 831–54.

Kutas, M., Neville, H. J., & Holcomb, P. J. (1987). A preliminary comparison of the N400 response to semantic anomalies during reading, listening, and signing. *Electroencephalography and Clinical Neurophysiology*, 39(Suppl), 325–30.

Lambertz, N., Gizewski, E. R., de Greiff, A., & Forsting, M. (2005). Cross-modal plasticity in deaf subjects dependent on the extent of hearing loss. *Cognitive Brain Research*, 25(3), 884–90.

Lausberg, H., & Sloetjes, H. (2009). Coding gestural behavior with the NEUROGES-ELAN system. *Behavior Research Methods, Instruments, & Computers*, 41(3), 841–9.

Levelt, W. J. M. (1989). Models of word production. *Trends in Cognitive Sciences*, 3, 223–32.

Liberman, I. Y., and Shankweiler, D. (1985). Phonology and the problems of learning to read and write. *Remedial Special Education*, 6, 8–17.

Luce, P. A., & Pisoni, D. B. (1998). Recognizing spoken words: The neighborhood activation model. *Ear and Hearing*, 19, 1–36.

MacSweeney, M., Campbell, R., Woll, B., Giampietro, V., David, A. S., McGuire, P. K., . . . Brammer, M. J. (2004). Dissociating linguistic and nonlinguistic gestural communication in the brain. *NeuroImage*, 22(4), 1605–18.

MacSweeney, M., Campbell, R., Woll, B., Brammer, M. J., Giampietro, V., David, A. S., . . . & McGuire, P. K. (2006). Lexical and sentential processing in British Sign Language. *Human Brain Mapping*, 27(1), 63–76.

MacSweeney, M., Capek, C. M., Campbell, R., & Woll, B. (2008). The signing brain: the neurobiology of sign language. *Trends in Cognitive Sciences*, 12(11), 432–40.

MacSweeney, M., Woll, B., Campbell, R., McGuire, P. K., David, A. S., Williams, S. C. R., . . . & Brammer, M. J. (2002). Neural systems underlying British Sign Language and audio-visual English processing in native users, *Brain*, 125, (7), 1583–93.

Mak, W. M., Vonk, W., & Schriefers, H. (2002). The influence of animacy on relative clause processing. *Journal of Memory and Language*, 47, 50–68.

Marentette, P. F., & Mayberry, R. I. (2000). Principles for an emerging phonological system: A case study in early American Sign Language acquisition. In: Chamberlain, C., Morford, J., & Mayberry, R. (Eds.), *Language Acquisition by Eye* (pp. 71–90). Erlbaum, Mahwah, NJ.

Marian, V., & Spivey, M. J. (2003). Competing activation in bilingual language processing: Within- and between-language competition. *Bilingualism: Language and Cognition*, 6, 97–115.

Marshall, J., Atkinson, J., Smulovitch, E., Thacker, A., & Woll, B. (2004). Aphasia in a user of British Sign Language: Dissociation between sign and gesture. *Cognitive Neuropsychology*, 21(5), 537–54.

Matin, E. (1974). Saccadic suppression: A review and an analysis. *Psychological Bulletin*, 81, 899–917.

Mayberry, R. I. (1989). *Deaf children's reading comprehension in relation to sign language structure and input*. Paper presented at the Society for Research in Child Development, Kansas City.

Mayberry, R. I., del Giudice, A. A., & Lieberman, A. M. (2011). Reading achievement in relation to phonological coding and awareness in deaf readers: A meta-analysis. *Journal of Deaf Studies and Deaf Education*, 16, 164–88.

Mayberry, R. I., & Fischer, S. D. (1989). Looking through phonological shape to lexical meaning: The bottleneck of non-native sign language processing. *Memory and Cognition*, 17(6), 740–54.

Mayberry, R. I., Lock, E., & Kazmi, H. (2002). Development: Linguistic ability and early language exposure. *Nature*, 417(6884), 38.

McDonald, J. L. (2006). Beyond the critical period: Processing based explanations for poor grammaticality judgment performance by late second language learners. *Journal of Memory and Language*, 55, 381–401.

McQuarrie, L., & Parilla, R. (2009). Phonological representations in deaf children: Rethinking the "functional equivalence" hypothesis. *Journal of Deaf Studies and Deaf Education*, 14, 137–54.

Meier, R. P., Mauk, C. E., Cheek, A., Moreland, C. J. (2008). The form of children's early signs: Iconic or motoric determinants? *Language Learning and Development*, 4, 63–98.

Meir, I., Sandler, W., Padden, C., & Aronoff, M. (2010). Emerging sign languages. In: Marschark, M., & Spencer, P. E. (Eds.), *Oxford Handbook of Deaf Studies, Language, and Education*, Vol. 2 (pp. 267–80). Oxford University Press, Oxford.

Melby-Lervåg, M., Lyster, S. A, Hulme, C. (2012). Phonological skills and their role in learning to read: A meta-analytic review. *Psychological Bulletin*, 138(2), 322–52.

Miller, P. (1997). The effect of communication mode on the development of phonemic awareness in prelingually deaf students. *Journal of Speech Language and Hearing Research*, 40, 1151–63.

Morford, J. P., Grieve-Smith, A. B., MacFarlane, J., Staley, J., & Waters, G. (2008). Effects of language experience on the perception of American Sign Language. *Cognition*, 109(1), 41–53.

Morford, J. P., Wilkinson, E., Villwock, A., Piñar, P., & Kroll, J. F. (2011). When deaf signers read English: Do written words activate their sign translations? *Cognition*, 118(2), 286–92.

Morgan, G., Barrett-Jones, S., & Stonehan, H. (2007). The first signs of language: Phonological development in British Sign Language. *Applied Psycholinguistics*, 28, 3–22.

Morgan, G., Barrière, I., & Woll, B. (2006). The influence of typology and modality on the acquisition of verb agreement morphology in British Sign Language. *First Language*, 26, 19–43.

Navarrete, E., Scaltritti, M., Mulatti, C., & Peressotti, F. (2013). Age-of-acquisition effects in delayed picture-naming tasks. *Psychonomic Bulletin & Review*, 20, 148–53.

Neville, H. J., Bavelier, D., Corina, D., Rauschecker, J., Karni, A., Lalwani, A., . . . & Turner, R. (1998). Cerebral organization for language in deaf and hearing subjects: biological constraints and effects of experience. *Proceedings of the National Academy of Sciences*, 95(3), 922–9.

Newman, A. J., Bavelier, D., Corina, D. P., Jezzard, P., & Neville, H. J. (2002). A critical period for right hemisphere recruitment in American Sign Language processing. *Nature Neuroscience*, 5, 76–80.

Newport, E. (1990). Maturational constraints on language learning. *Cognitive Science*, 14, 11–28.

Norris, D., McQueen, J. M., & Cutler, A. (2016). Prediction, Bayesian inference and feedback in speech recognition. *Language, Cognition and Neuroscience*, 31(1), 4–18.

Okada, K., Rogalsky, C., O'Grady, L., Hanaumi, L., Bellugi, U., Corina, D., & Hickok, G. (2016). An fMRI study of perception and action in deaf signers. *Neuropsychologia*, 82, 179–88.

Orfanidou, E., Woll, B., & Morgan, G. (2015). *Research Methods in Sign Language Studies: A Practical Guide*. Wiley-Blackwell, London.

Orlansky, M., & Bonvillian, J. D. (1984). The role of iconicity in early sign language acquisition. *Journal of Speech and Hearing Disorders*, 49 (1984), 287–92.

Ormel, E., Hermans, D., Knoors, H., & Verhoeven, L. (2012). Cross-language effects in written word recognition: The case of bilingual deaf children. *Bilingualism: Language and Cognition*, 15(2), 288–303.

Özyürek, A. (2014). Hearing and seeing meaning in speech and gesture: Insights from brain and behavior. *Philosophical Transactions of the Royal Society B: Biological Sciences*, 369, 20130296.

Perniss, P. M. (2012). Use of sign space. In: Pfau, R., Steinbach, M., & Woll, B. (Eds.), *Sign Language: An International Handbook* (pp. 412–31). Mouton de Gruyter, Berlin.

Petitto, L. A., Zatorre, R. J., Gauna, K., Nikelski, E. J., Dostie, D., & Evans, A. C. (2000). Speech-like cerebral activity in profoundly deaf people processing signed languages: Implications for the neural basis of human language. *Proceedings of the National Academy of Sciences*, 97(25), 13961–6.

Piñar, P., Carlson, M. Y., Morford, J. P., & Dussias, P. (2016). Bilingual deaf readers' use of semantic and syntactic cues in the processing of English relative clauses. *Bilingualism: Language and Cognition*. doi:10.1017/S1366728916000602

Poizner, H., Klima, E. S., & Bellugi, U. (1990). *What the Hands Reveal About the Brain*. MIT Press, Cambridge, MA.

Pollatsek, A., Lesch, M., Morris, R. K., & Rayner, K. (1992). Phonological codes are used in integrating information across saccades in word identification and reading. *Journal of Experimental Psychology: Human Perception and Performance*, 18, 148–62.

Proksch, J., & Bavelier, D. (2002). Changes in the spatial distribution of visual attention after early deafness. *Journal of Cognitive Neuroscience*, 14, 687–701.

Rayner, K. (1986). Eye movements and the perceptual span in beginning and skilled readers. *Journal of Experimental Child Psychology*, 41, 211–36.

Rayner, K. (1998). Eye movements in reading and information processing: 20 years of research. *Psychological Bulletin*, 124, 372–422.

Rayner, K. (2009). The 35th Sir Frederick Bartlett Lecture: Eye movements and attention during reading, scene perception, and visual search. *Quarterly Journal of Experimental Psychology*, 62, 1457–506.

Rubenstein, H., Garfield, L., & Millikan, J. A. (1970). Homographic entries in the internal lexicon. *Journal of Verbal Learning and Verbal Behavior*, 9, 487–92.

Sakai, K. L., Tatsuno, Y., Suzuki, K., Kimura, H., & Ichida, Y. (2005). Sign and speech: Amodal commonality in left hemisphere dominance for comprehension of sentences. *Brain*, 128(6), 1407–17.

Sandler, W. (1986). The spreading hand autosegment of ASL. *Sign Language Studies*, 15, 1–28.

Sandler, W. (1989). *Phonological Representation of the Sign: Linearity and Nonlinearity in American Sign Language*. Foris, Dordrecht.

Sandler, W., & Lillo-Martin, D. (2006). *Sign Language and Linguistic Universals*. Cambridge University Press, Cambridge.

Schembri, A. (2003). Rethinking "classifiers" in signed languages. In: Emmorey, K. (Ed.), *Perspectives on Classifier Constructions in Sign Languages* (pp. 3–34). Lawrence Erlbaum Associates, Mahwah, NJ.

Schotter, E. R., Angele, B., & Rayner, K. (2012). Parafoveal processing in reading. *Attention, Perception, & Psychophysics*, 74, 5–35.

Senghas, A. (2003). Intergenerational influence and ontogenetic development in the emergence of spatial grammar in Nicaraguan Sign Language. *Cognitive Development*, 18(4), 511–31.

Senghas, R. J., Senghas, A., & Pyers, J. E. (2005). The emergence of Nicaraguan Sign Language: Questions of development, acquisition, and evolution. In: Parker, S. T., Langer, J., & Milbrath, C. (Eds.), *Biology and Knowledge Revisited: From Neurogenesis to Psychogenesis* (pp. 287–306). Lawrence Erlbaum, Mahwah, NJ.

Siedlecki, T., & Bonvillian, J. D. (1997). Young children's acquisition of the handshape aspect of American Sign Language: Parental report findings. *Applied Psycholinguistics*, 18, 17–31.

Sterne, A., & Goswami, U. (2000). Phonological awareness of syllables, rhymes, and phonemes in deaf children. *Journal of Child Psychological Psychiatry*, 41, 609–25.

Stokoe, W., Casterline, D. C., & Croneberg, C. G. (1976). *A Dictionary of American Sign Language on Linguistic Principles*. Galluadet University Press, Washington, DC.

Takkinen, R. (2003). Variation of handshape features in the acquisition process. In: Baker, A., van den Bogaerde, B., & Crasborn, O. (Eds.), *Cross-linguistic Perspectives in Sign Language Research* (pp. 81–94). Signum, Hamburg.

Taub, S. (2000). Iconicity in American Sign Language: Concrete and metaphorical applications. *Spatial Cognition and Computation*, 2, 31–50.

Thierry, G., & Wu, Y. J. (2007). Brain potentials reveal unconscious translation during foreign language comprehension. *Proceedings of National Academy of Sciences*, 104, 12530–5.

Thompson, R. L., Vinson, D. P., & Vigliocco, G. (2009). The link between form and meaning in American Sign Language: Lexical processing effects. *Journal of Experimental Psychology: Language, Memory, and Cognition*, 35, 550–7.

Thompson, R. L., Vinson, D. P., Woll, B., & Vigliocco, G. (2012). The road to language learning is iconic: Evidence from British Sign Language. *Psychological Science*, 23(2012), 1443–8.

Tomasello, M. (2005). *Constructing a Language: A Usage-Based Theory of Language Acquisition*. Harvard University Press, Cambridge, MA.

Traxler, C. B. (2000). The Stanford Achievement Test, 9th Edition: National norming and performance standards for deaf and hard-of-hearing students. *Journal of Deaf Studies and Deaf Education*, 5, 337–48.

Traxler, M. J., Morris, R. K., & Seely, R. E. (2002). Processing subject and object-relative clauses: Evidence from eye movements. *Journal of Memory and Language*, 47, 69–90.

Traxler, M. J., & Pickering, M. J. (1996). Plausibility and the processing of unbounded dependencies: An eye-tracking study. *Journal of Memory and Language*, 35, 454–75.

Traxler, M. J., Williams, R. S., Blozis, S. A., & Morris, R. K. (2005). Working memory, animacy, and verb class in the processing of relative clauses. *Journal of Memory and Language*, 53, 204–24.

Trezek, B., & Malmgren, K. W. (2005). The efficacy of utilizing a phonics treatment package with middle school deaf and hard-of-hearing students. *Journal of Deaf Studies and Deaf Education, 10*, 256–71.

Verhoeven, L. (2007). Early bilingualism, language transfer, and phonological awareness. *Applied Psycholinguistics, 28*, 425–39.

Vinson, D., Thompson, R. L., Skinner, R., & Vigliocco, G. (2015). A faster path between meaning and form? Iconicity facilitates sign recognition and production in British Sign Language. *Journal of Memory and Language, 82*, 56–85.

von Tetzchner, S. (1994). First signs acquired by a Norwegian deaf child with hearing parents. *Sign Language Studies, 44*, 225–57.

Wagner, R. K., & Torgesen, J. K. (1987). The nature of phonological processing and its causal role in the acquisition of reading skills. *Psychological Bulletin, 101*, 192–212.

Wang, Y., Trezek, B. J., Luckner, J. L., & Paul, P. V. (2008). The role of phonology and phonologically related skills in reading instruction for students who are deaf or hard of hearing. *American Annals of the Deaf, 153*(4), 396–407.

Wauters, L. N., van Bon, W. H., & Tellings, A. E. (2006). Reading comprehension of Dutch deaf children. *Reading and Writing, 19*(1), 49–76.

Weckerly, J., & Kutas, M. (1999). An electrophysiological analysis of animacy effects in the processing of object relative sentences. *Psychophysiology, 36*, 559–70.

Wilcox, S. E. (2004). Language from gesture. *Behavioral and Brain Sciences, 27*(4), 525–6.

Willems, R. M., Frank, S. L., Nijhof, A. D., Hagoort, P., & van den Bosch, A. (2016). Prediction during natural language comprehension. *Cerebral Cortex, 26*(6), 2506–16.

Willems, R. M., Özyürek, A., & Hagoort, P. (2006). When language meets action: The neural integration of gesture and speech. *Cerebral Cortex, 17*(10), 2322–33.

Willems, R. M., Özyürek, A., & Hagoort, P. (2009). Differential roles for left inferior frontal and superior temporal cortex in multimodal integration of action and language. *NeuroImage, 47*(4), 1992–2004.

Zeshan, U., & de Vos, C. (Eds.) (2012). *Sign Languages in Village Communities: Anthropological and Linguistic Insights*. Mouton de Gruyter, Berlin.

PART II

LANGUAGE PRODUCTION

SECTION I
Sublexical level

SECTION I

CHAPTER 13

SPEECH PRODUCTION
Integrating psycholinguistic, neuroscience, and motor control perspectives

GRANT WALKER AND GREGORY HICKOK

SPEECH production is the process that starts with a message that one wishes to communicate and ends with a set of coordinated vocal tract gestures that produce the sequence of hums, buzzes, whooshes, and chirps that we call speech. Research on speech production aims to understand the computational mechanisms and stages involved in traversing from message to gesture. Research over the last 40 years has revealed that the process is multistage (Dell, 1986; Fromkin, 1971; Garrett, 1975; Levelt, 1989; Levelt, Roelofs, & Meyer, 1999), minimally involving access to (1) abstract word representations called "lemmas" or "lexemes," (2) grammatical structures for sequencing the words and morphemes, a stage called "grammatical encoding," (3) the phonological pattern (sequence of sounds) associated with the words, sometimes called "phonological encoding," and (4) motor planning for articulation. Each of these speech production stages has been studied independently, engendering their own burgeoning literatures. Because excellent reviews already exist on these topics, we will merely provide a small sampling of the issues and data that have been investigated under each scope.

Word-level research has focused on the components that define individual words, particularly their morphological and grammatical properties. Morphemes are the basic sets of phonemes that cannot be subdivided further without losing their meaning—such as prefixes, stems, or suffixes—which can be combined to form words. Grammatical properties include things, like part-of-speech—such as a noun, verb, or adjective—which govern, in part, how morphemes combine into words and how words combine into sentences. Other grammatical properties include number (singular or plural) or gender (masculine, feminine, or neuter). The terms *lexeme* and *lemma* were coined to refer to the morphology part of a word representation and its grammatical properties, respectively (Kempen & Huijbers, 1983; Kempen & Hoenkamp, 1987; Levelt, 1989), although the terms are not always used consistently across the literature. Whether these representations are indeed separable in the process of speech production has been a popular topic of discussion (Roelofs, Meyer, & Levelt, 1998). Some of the data that have been marshaled in support of one position or another include: decisions about grammatical properties during tip-of-the-tongue states when the phonological form of the word is not available (Caramazza & Miozzo, 1997; Miozzo & Caramazza, 1997); morphological substitution errors within and between phrases or grammatical categories in large corpora of natural speech (Garrett, 1975, 1980, 1988); chronometric measures from experimental tasks requiring production of words with high- or low-complexity morphology (Roelofs, 1996a,b, 1998); and chronometric measures from tasks requiring production of high- and low-frequency homophone words (e.g., more/moor) matched on phonological and syllabic frequency (Jescheniak & Levelt, 1994).

Research on grammatical encoding has focused on the structures and procedures for generating phrases and sentences. Issues regarding the incrementality of planning have been investigated, such as the details of planning frames and slots that can be filled by words that have the appropriate grammatical properties (Dell, Chang, & Griffin, 1999). A major source of relevant data here are word substitution errors in large corpora of natural speech, which respect grammatical category boundaries (Garrett, 1975). That is, nouns substitute for other nouns, and verbs substitute for other verbs, demonstrating that these properties are already determined prior to the selection of words. Another well-studied phenomenon related to sentence planning is *structural priming*. Under both natural and experimental conditions, speakers tend to reuse sentence structures that they previously produced, such as active or passive voice, even when the sentences differ in lexical, prosodic, and conceptual content (Bock, 1986; Bock & Loebell, 1990). Verb structure has been another important avenue of research for sentence production. Data from brain-damaged individuals with agrammatism and non-brain-damaged individuals performing confrontation and elicitation tasks show that the complexity of verb structures, such as transitive versus intransitive, influences sentence planning and production (Thompson, 2003; Thompson, Lange, Schneider, & Shapiro, 1997).

Research at the phonological level has focused on the sound segments that are sequenced to produce a word. At this level as well, *frame-and-slot* models address the incrementality of word production (Shattuck-Hufnagel, 1979), with phonemes being inserted into canonical arrangements of consonants and vowels, such as the consonant-vowel-consonant sequence (CVC). Once again, speech error phenomena in natural speech corpora provide relevant evidence: phonological errors tend to respect the phonotactic rules of the language, producing "legal" strings; syllable onsets are more prone to slips than other parts of the syllable, revealing the importance of syllable structure; and phoneme exchanges between words respect the syllable positions. The tongue twister paradigm, in which participants repeat a small set of words intentionally designed to elicit phonological slips, has been used to demonstrate that phoneme similarity and reiteration are properties that challenge the phonological encoding system (Wilshire, 1999). Production of consonant clusters has provided another avenue for research, particularly from second language learners and individuals with dyslexia or specific language impairment (SLI). For example, non-word repetition performance by these individuals revealed that word position and stress influence the accuracy of consonant cluster productions (Marshall & van der Lely, 2009). Another issue regarding consonant clusters is the apparent insertion of vowels, and whether this represents an additional gesture or the mistiming of flanking gestures during articulation (Davidson & Stone, 2003).

Whereas psycholinguists are primarily concerned with how conceptual information is transformed into a properly structured and sequenced set of linguistic representations, motor control researchers often take as their starting point the problem of how the system coordinates the approximately 100 muscles in the respiratory, laryngeal, and oral motor systems during articulation. Here the concerns revolve around kinematic forces, movement trajectories, and sensory feedback control (Fairbanks, 1954; Guenther, Hampson, & Johnson, 1998; Houde & Jordan, 1998). The role of sensory information in motor control is a particularly important topic in this approach, because it has been discovered that movement is dependent on sensory information. Intuitively, one can appreciate that in order to reach for an object, it is necessary to perceive its location, shape, and orientation, as well as the current position of the limb; without this information, it is impossible even to initiate an appropriate action. Experimental work has found that blocking somatosensory feedback from a monkey's limb (while leaving motor fibers intact) causes the limb to slump. With training, the monkey can learn to reuse it clumsily, but only with visual feedback; blindfold the animal, and motor control degrades dramatically (Sanes, Mauritz, Dalakas, & Evarts, 1984). A similar problem can be found in humans suffering from large-fiber sensory neuropathy, which deafferents the body sense while leaving motor fibers intact (Sanes et al., 1984).

Speech scientists have studied the role of sensory information in speech motor control with altered auditory feedback paradigms. Participants are asked to generate some speech, which is digitally processed and played back to the talker in near real time, but altered in one way or another. One common setup involves shifting the pitch of the fundamental frequency (Burnett, Freedland, Larson, & Hain, 1998; Burnett, Senner, & Larson, 1997), which makes the voice sound higher or lower than what was produced. Another setup involves shifting the first formant (Houde & Jordan, 1998), which can make one vowel sound like another. In both cases, participants will quickly, and often unconsciously, compensate for the altered feedback, such that what they hear themselves producing matches what they intended to produce in the first place. Similar experiments have been conducted in the somatosensory domain using various intraoral devices to manipulate feedback from sensory receptors in the vocal tract; again, participants readily compensate under such conditions (Tremblay, Shiller, & Ostry, 2003). Importantly, models that have emerged from this approach emphasize the role of sensory feedback in the control of speech motor planning (Houde & Nagarajan, 2011; Tourville & Guenther, 2011).

As should be clear from this discussion, there is an obvious subdivision between research into the first three stages and the last stage of speech production (i.e., the psycholinguistic and the motor control approaches). While the psycholinguistic approach focuses on symbolic manipulation within frames and slots, the motor control approach focuses on the manipulation of speech effectors and acoustic properties in dynamic physical models. These lines of investigation are generally carried out quite independently of one another and typically by researchers with very different training: engineering, kinematics, and anatomy compared with linguistics and psychology. This division of labor and of process assumptions has been justified, at least implicitly, by the idea that there is a fundamental distinction between (psycho)linguistic processes and motor-articulatory processes. However, recent research has suggested that the chasm is narrower than imagined, reflecting theoretical and methodological approaches more than fundamental computational and system architecture differences (Hickok, 2012a, 2012b, 2014a, 2014b; Hickok, Houde, & Rong, 2011). Our aim in the present chapter is to highlight some of this progress and to provide an example of what research under a unified approach might look like, by describing the development of a computational model of aphasic picture naming. Next, we examine how the assumed separation between the disciplines has masked some of their potentially important similarities.

13.1 Psycholinguistic and Motor Control Approaches Overlap

1. **Representations.** Psycholinguists make use of phoneme representations in their models. Phonemes, according to dominant linguistic theories, are bundles of articulatory features including voicing, place of articulation, and manner of articulation (Chomsky & Halle, 1968), exactly the objects that motor control models aim to control. Further, motor control theorists understand that actions are not planned in small incremental bits, but rather in sequences of movements. When we start thinking about sequences of speech sounds, the planning units become syllables or words (Bohland & Guenther, 2006), which crosses well over into psycholinguistic theory territory.
2. **Processes.** Both approaches have discovered and make use of the same processes in their models. Both psycholinguistic and motor control approaches have independently discovered that sensory feedback is an important factor in speech production and that it can come in external and internal forms (Houde & Jordan, 1998; Houde & Nagarajan, 2011; Levelt, 1983). The two fields give different names to the process, *state feedback control* versus *self-monitoring* for motor control and psycholinguistics, respectively, and differ in how much theoretical weight is given to it, but the concepts are essentially the same.
3. **Computational models.** Both approaches use artificial neural networks (ANN) and spreading activation to model the flow of information through processing systems, although the inputs and outputs typically correspond to different phenomena between the approaches. In ANN models, pairs of nodes (a.k.a., units) are connected in a network. Each unit is assigned a value quantifying its *activation*, while each connection is assigned a value quantifying its *strength* (a.k.a., *weight*). These connection strengths can be assigned manually or through a learning procedure, such as *backpropagation of error*. Once the input nodes of the network are supplied with activation values, the activation value of each node is updated iteratively on each *timestep*, according to a function that depends on the activation of the other nodes in the network, their connection strengths, and possibly noise or decay of activation. In the psycholinguistic approach, nodes (or groups of nodes) often correspond with symbols, and their selection and manipulation are governed by activation levels and thresholds (Dell, 1986; Dell et al., 1997; Foygel & Dell, 2000; Levelt, Roelofs, & Meyer, 1999; Plaut & Kello, 1999; Roelofs, 2014; Ueno, Saito, Rogers, & Ralph, 2011). In the motor control approach, nodes often correspond with positions and velocities of articulators or the response levels of auditory sensors, and their coordination is managed through excitatory and inhibitory interactions (Guenther, 1995; Guenther, Ghosh, & Tourville, 2006; Tourville & Guenther, 2011), although networks that include both symbolic and effector node representations have been investigated as well (Bohland, Bullock, & Guenther, 2010).
4. **Brain circuits.** The neural correlates of the models overlap. Modern brain imaging and brain lesion-to-symptom mapping studies have identified neural regions that are associated with components of the models put forward by the two approaches. There is much overlap, including in Broca's area, sensorimotor cortex, and the

temporal-parietal junction (Bohland & Guenther, 2006; Dell, Schwartz, Nozari, Faseyitan, & Coslett, 2013; Golfinopoulos et al., 2011; Golfinopoulos, Tourville, & Guenther, 2010; Schwartz, Faseyitan, Kim, & Coslett, 2012), suggesting they are studying the same neurocomputational processes.

13.2 What can the approaches learn from each other?

The motor control approach emphasizes the central role of sensorimotor feedback in guiding action, whereas the psycholinguistic approach considers it closer to an appendage to the main processing chain. Sensory feedback is critical to controlling action generally and there is much evidence for the role of sensory feedback in speech motor control (Perkell, 2012). For example, delayed auditory feedback can disrupt speech fluency (Yates, 1963) and altered speech feedback such as shifting the pitch or a speech formant produces a reflexive, automatic compensatory response in articulation (Burnett et al., 1998; Houde & Jordan, 1998). Relatedly, motor control models of speech emphasize the role of sensory representations as the targets for action (Guenther, Hampson, & Johnson, 1998). These observations suggest that psycholinguistic models might benefit from considering feedback mechanisms and sensorimotor interaction as more central to speech production.

13.3 An attempt at integration

The state feedback control (SFC) theory, and its extended hierarchical version (HSFC), represent an attempt to synthesize the psycholinguistic, neuroscience, and motor control perspectives on speech production (Hickok, 2012a, 2012b, 2014a, 2014b; Hickok, Houde, & Rong, 2011). A primary goal is to challenge some of the widely held assumptions that lead to these fields being studied in isolation. In particular, the theory assumes that the same feedback control scheme that is used in motor control models can also apply to higher levels of speech planning (i.e., during retrieval of phonemes, the targets for production). A similar architecture may apply to even higher levels of representation, but this possibility has not yet been explored in any depth. The goal of this line of work is not intended to minimize or eliminate abstract linguistic representations, but rather to consider motor control-like architectures underlying their realization and usage.

Figure 13.1 shows a *box-and-arrow* schematic of the SFC theory. The components in the vertical direction map onto traditional psycholinguistic levels of representation: conceptual (message), lexical (lemma), and phonological. The phonological level, however, has been broken down into two representational components, auditory-phonological and motor-phonological, as well as a computational component in-between that maps from auditory to motor-phonological representations. This phonological-level architecture is more characteristic of motor control models, which emphasize sensorimotor interaction in coordinating gestures. An elaborated version breaks down the phonological level into a hierarchy of its

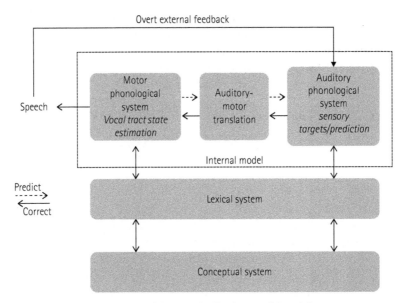

FIG. 13.1 Box-and-arrow schematic of the state feedback control (SFC) theory.

own, including a higher-level auditory-motor loop and a lower-level somatosensory-motor loop (Hickok, 2012a).

What the sensorimotor phonological architecture offers is a mechanism for predicting the auditory consequences of selected motor-phonological plans and for correcting them when the motor plans do not match the sensory targets. The idea is that lexical level activation leads to simultaneous activation of both a motor-phonological plan and an auditory-phonological target. These are then checked against one another via motor-to-sensory prediction to ensure that the motor plan will actually hit the target. If there is a match, then the motor plan can be executed; if there is a mismatch, then a correction can be generated.

There is evidence for such a predictive/corrective mechanism. The neural response to one's own speech is reduced compared with listening to the same speech at the same level played back via a recording, suggesting that the predicted consequences of producing speech attenuates the response in auditory cortex (Aliu, Houde, & Nagarajan, 2009; Houde, Nagarajan, Sekihara, & Merzenich, 2002). Furthermore, behavioral work shows that errors are detected and corrections made even before speech is overtly produced (Baars, Motley, & MacKay, 1975; Motley, Camden, & Baars, 1982).

Perhaps the best evidence for this architecture is conduction aphasia. People with conduction aphasia have fluent speech and make frequent phonological paraphasias which they often detect and try to correct (Baldo, Klostermann, & Dronkers, 2008; Damasio & Damasio, 1980; Goodglass, 1992) in a kind of verbal groping behavior similar to what is found in manual sensorimotor deficits such as optic ataxia (Perenin & Vighetto, 1988). Because speech fluency and comprehension are preserved in conduction aphasia, the syndrome cannot be readily explained in terms of either an auditory or a motor deficit and is best explained as an auditory-motor transformation deficit (the middle box in Fig. 13.1). More specifically, fluent production is explained by the normal activation of motor-phonological plans from the lexical level, but because the system cannot check the accuracy of the plans against the auditory target, an increase in phonological error rates is the result. Once an error is produced, it is readily detected as an error, because auditory targets are activated normally via the lexical level. Correction attempts fail, however, because of the disrupted auditory-motor translation system. The model also explains other surprising findings in conduction aphasia, such as the reduced disruption that delayed auditory feedback has on fluency in people with conduction aphasia compared with healthy controls (Boller, Vrtunski, Kim, & Mack, 1978). In healthy speakers, delayed auditory feedback interferes with the current targets for production, but the disconnection of auditory targets from motor plans in conduction aphasia prevents this potentially disruptive effect. Neurological evidence supports this view of conduction aphasia as well, since the lesion patterns associated with the syndrome encompass an area (Spt) at the temporal-parietal boundary that exhibits auditory-motor response properties (Buchsbaum et al., 2011; Hickok, Buchsbaum, Humphries, & Muftuler, 2003; Hickok, Okada, & Serences, 2009; Pa & Hickok, 2008). Lesions in this area have been associated specifically with the symptom of repetition errors for both words and non-words, providing strong evidence for its role in auditory-motor translation (Rogalsky et al., 2015).

If this integrated motor control/psycholinguistic approach is on the right track, we should be able to use its basic tenets to generate better explanations and predictions for speech production data. One possibility is to simulate speech production with a computational model that uses a standard psycholinguistic architecture compared with a model that uses a sensorimotor architecture. We report on such a comparison immediately next, starting with a description of a highly successful psycholinguistic model of single word production.

13.4 THE SEMANTIC-PHONOLOGICAL MODEL (SP)

The SP model (Foygel & Dell, 2000) is a two-step, interactive, spreading activation model of the lexical retrieval process that was developed primarily to explain speech errors in healthy and aphasic speakers. The model describes an "intermediate" stage of speech production, following successful conceptual processing but prior to overt articulation, and consists of three layers of representational units: semantic, lexical, and phonological (Fig. 13.2). A very small lexical network is simulated with fixed connections between the representations, which approximates the statistical error opportunities in English. Picture naming is simulated by delivering a boost of activation to the semantic units, and the activation cascades through the network in both directions. In the first step of the retrieval process, lexical units compete for selection, with the winner receiving an activation boost; in the second step of the process, phonological units compete for selection, and the output sequence is categorized according to its relation to the target. The model can make errors during either selection step, due to the presence of noise in the activation of each unit, although strong connection weights mitigate this risk by improving the signal-to-noise ratio. The maximum connection weights are set to mimic the healthy speech pattern, which includes infrequent errors that typically bear a semantic relation to the target; aphasic speech patterns can then be simulated by reducing the connection strength between semantic and lexical units (S) or between lexical and phonological units (P). This rather simple model has been used to explain an abundance of effects in the observed speech of healthy and aphasic speakers.

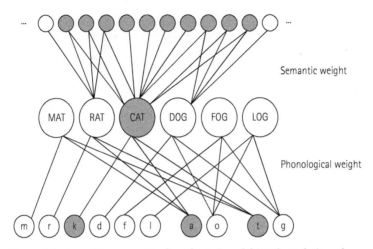

FIG. 13.2 The architecture of the semantic-phonological model (SP) lexical network.

Reproduced from *Psychonomic Bulletin & Review*, Bridging computational approaches to speech production: The semantic–lexical–auditory–motor model (SLAM), 23 (2), p. 340, Figure 2, Grant M. Walker and Gregory Hickok, DOI: doi.org/10.3758/s13423-015-0903-7 Copyright © 2015, Psychonomic Society, Inc. With permission of Springer.

The SP model has had a substantial impact on research and clinical practice, especially because there is an accompanying standardized picture naming test (Roach et al., 1996), an online interface to run the model and fit data (Dell, Lawler, Harris, & Gordon, 2004; Walker & Hickok, 2016), and an online database of healthy and aphasic picture naming responses (Mirman et al., 2010). The naming test has been translated into German (Abel, Huber, & Dell, 2009), and the computational model was used to predict clinical diagnostic information. The model has also been used to characterize the locus of lexical frequency effects (Kittredge, Dell, Verkuilen, & Schwartz, 2008), error patterns associated with different types of aphasia (Schwartz, Dell, Martin, Gahl, & Sobel, 2006), errors of omission (Dell et al., 2004), patterns of recovery (Schwartz & Brecher, 2000), and interactive error effects (Foygel & Dell, 2000). SP has been used to explain performance on other tasks as well, such as word repetition (Dell, Martin, & Schwartz, 2007), and to predict the location of neurological damage seen in clinical imaging (Dell et al., 2013). The SP model has been useful for interpreting many qualitative patterns in speech production data; meanwhile, there has been substantial progress in neuroscience and motor control research on speech that has yet to be integrated with this approach.

13.5 THE SEMANTIC-LEXICAL-AUDITORY-MOTOR MODEL (SLAM)

The SLAM model (Walker & Hickok, 2016) was developed to test the assumption that two kinds of phonological representations play a role in speech production, with auditory representations serving as targets for motor programs. The SP model's simple yet robust explanations of speech production provided an opportunity to implement and test our hypothesis: if auditory representations act as targets during speech planning, then adding them to the SP model should improve explanations of speech production behavior. The effect should be especially noticeable for conduction aphasia, where the theory suggests that auditory targets may be activated but are disconnected from their corresponding motor programs.

SLAM therefore maintains many of SP's essential processing assumptions, including the two steps and interactivity. SLAM simply augments the model's structure with two copies of the phonological units, one designated as auditory and the other as motor, which are connected to each other in a one-to-one fashion (Fig. 13.3). An additional processing constraint is that the lexical-auditory weight (LA) is always stronger than the lexical-motor weight (LM). This constraint has both empirical and theoretical motivations. From an empirical standpoint, the LA connections presumably develop first, because children comprehend single words before they produce them (Benedict, 1979). Additionally, the LA connections are also more resilient to damage, with comprehension typically showing greater recovery after stroke (Lomas & Kertesz, 1978). From a theoretical standpoint, the SFC theory stipulates that auditory targets must be activated to guide motor production (Hickok, 2012b; Hickok, Houde, & Rong, 2011), so the LA weights must activate the auditory units as a precondition for the LM weights to simultaneously activate the corresponding motor units. Finally, this constraint distinguishes the SLAM parameter space from the SP parameter space; if the LA weight could be set to zero while the LM weight is allowed to freely vary, the SLAM model would reduce to the SP model and make identical predictions. The constraint prevents this possibility and thus ensures that when we compare SP and SLAM fits to an individual speaker, we are comparing different models.

We compared the SLAM and SP model fits to archived picture naming data from 255 aphasic patients. To do this, we found the connection strengths in each model that generated the most similar naming response distribution to each patient's observed naming responses. We obtained a distance measure of the model's simulated data from the observed data, using the root mean square error (RMSE), and used these values to quantify the model's fit. Given the models' shared processing assumptions, it was unsurprising that they made similar predictions for most patients; however, the SLAM model fit significantly better for the conduction patients. Additionally, the best-fitting connection weights for this group were strong lexical-auditory weights, and weak lexical-motor and auditory-motor weights; in accordance with the SFC theory's assumptions, the auditory targets are activated but are disconnected from their corresponding motor programs. Figure 13.4 presents data and model fits from an example conduction patient. Further analyses demonstrated that the preserved phonological feedback from the auditory targets to the lexical level makes formal errors more likely during lexical selection, and combined with weak activation of the motor units, this leads to an increase in errors that are phonologically related to the target. The separation of phonological codes, with auditory representations serving as targets for motor plans, thus finds support in the speech errors of aphasic patients.

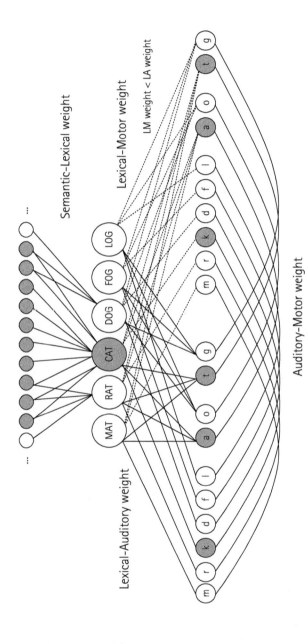

FIG. 13.3 Semantic-lexical-auditory-motor (SLAM) model architecture.

Reproduced from *Psychonomic Bulletin & Review*, Bridging computational approaches to speech production: The semantic–lexical–auditory–motor model (SLAM), 23 (2), p. 342, Figure 3, Grant M. Walker and Gregory Hickok, DOI: doi.org/10.3758/s13423-015-0903-7 Copyright © 2015, Psychonomic Society, Inc. With permission of Springer.

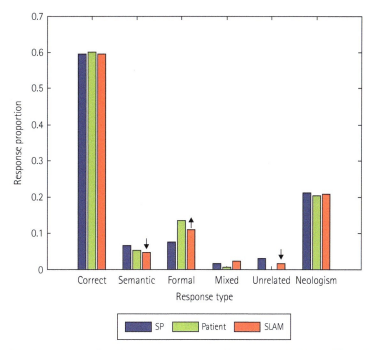

FIG. 13.4 Naming response distribution from an example patient with Conduction aphasia, along with the corresponding SP and SLAM model fits. Arrows indicate how SLAM improves the fit to data, increasing Formal at the expense of Semantic and Unrelated errors. The SLAM model reduced fit error for this patient by 0.0135 RMSD.

Reproduced from *Psychonomic Bulletin & Review*, Bridging computational approaches to speech production: The semantic–lexical–auditory–motor model (SLAM), 23 (2), p. 349, Figure 8, Grant M. Walker and Gregory Hickok, DOI: doi.org/10.3758/s13423-015-0903-7 Copyright © 2015, Psychonomic Society, Inc. With permission of Springer.

13.6 Conclusion

Psycholinguistics focuses on the mental symbols and processes that support language use, while motor control theorists focus on the implementation of these processes in physical systems. Although these fields can be, and often are, studied independently, there appear to be some opportunities for cross-pollination of ideas. As we have discussed here, the extension of sensory and motor divisions to higher levels of linguistic representations is one such possibility. Other possibilities that we did not explore include the role of inhibition, the interaction between auditory and somatosensory systems, and the implications of a hierarchical gradient of representations. As a subfield of cognitive science, it naturally follows that psycholinguistics should benefit from the interdisciplinary approaches that are characteristic of the field.

References

Abel, S., Huber, W., & Dell, G. S. (2009). Connectionist diagnosis of lexical disorders in aphasia. *Aphasiology*, 23(11), 1353–78.

Aliu, S. O., Houde, J. F., & Nagarajan, S. S. (2009). Motor-induced suppression of the auditory cortex. *Journal of Cognitive Neuroscience*, 21(4), 791–802.

Baars, B. J., Motley, M. T., & MacKay, D. G. (1975). Output editing for lexical status in artificially elicited slips of the tongue. *Journal of Verbal Learning and Verbal Behavior*, 14, 382–91.

Baldo, J. V., Klostermann, E. C., & Dronkers, N. F. (2008). It's either a cook or a baker: Patients with conduction aphasia get the gist but lose the trace. *Brain and Language*, 105(2), 134–40.

Benedict, H. (1979). Early lexical development: Comprehension and production. *Journal of Child Language*, 6(2), 183–200.

Bock, J. K. (1986). Syntactic persistence in language production. *Cognitive Psychology*, 18(3), 355–87.

Bock, K., & Loebell, H. (1990). Framing sentences. *Cognition*, 35(1), 1–39.

Bohland, J. W., Bullock, D., & Guenther, F. H. (2010). Neural representations and mechanisms for the performance of simple speech sequences. *Journal of Cognitive Neuroscience*, 22(7), 1504–29.

Bohland, J. W., & Guenther, F. H. (2006). An fMRI investigation of syllable sequence production. *NeuroImage*, 32(2), 821–41.

Boller, F., Vrtunski, P. B., Kim, Y., & Mack, J. L. (1978). Delayed auditory feedback and aphasia. *Cortex*, 14(2), 212–26.

Buchsbaum, B. R., Baldo, J., Okada, K., Berman, K. F., Dronkers, N., D'Esposito, M., & Hickok, G. (2011). Conduction aphasia, sensory-motor integration, and phonological short-term memory–an aggregate analysis of lesion and fMRI data. *Brain and Language*, 119(3), 119–28.

Burnett, T. A., Freedland, M. B., Larson, C. R., & Hain, T. C. (1998). Voice F0 responses to manipulations in pitch feedback. *Journal of the Acoustical Society of America*, 103(6), 3153–61.

Burnett, T. A., Senner, J. E., & Larson, C. R. (1997). Voice F0 responses to pitch-shifted auditory feedback: A preliminary study. *Journal of Voice*, 11(2), 202–11.

Caramazza, A., & Miozzo, M. (1997). The relation between syntactic and phonological knowledge in lexical access: Evidence from the "tip-of-the-tongue" phenomenon. *Cognition*, 64(3), 309–43.

Chomsky, N., & Halle, M. (1968). *The Sound Pattern of English*. Harper & Row, New York, NY.

Damasio, H., & Damasio, A. R. (1980). The anatomical basis of conduction aphasia. *Brain*, 103(2), 337–50.

Davidson, L., & Stone, M. (2003). Epenthesis versus gestural mistiming in consonant cluster production: an ultrasound study. In: *Proceedings of the West Coast Conference on Formal Linguistics*, Vol. 22, pp. 165–78.

Dell, G. S. (1986). A spreading-activation theory of retrieval in sentence production. *Psychological Review*, 93(3), 283.

Dell, G. S., Chang, F., & Griffin, Z. M. (1999). Connectionist models of language production: Lexical access and grammatical encoding. *Cognitive Science*, 23(4), 517–42.

Dell, G. S., Lawler, E. N., Harris, H. D., & Gordon, J. K. (2004). Models of errors of omission in aphasic naming. *Cognitive Neuropsychology*, 21(2–4), 125–45.

Dell, G. S., Martin, N., & Schwartz, M. F. (2007). A case-series test of the interactive two-step model of lexical access: Predicting word repetition from picture naming. *Journal of Memory and Language*, 56(4), 490–520.

Dell, G. S., Schwartz, M. F., Martin, N., Saffran, E. M., & Gagnon, D. A. (1997). Lexical access in aphasic and nonaphasic speakers. *Psychological Review*, 104(4), 801.

Dell, G. S., Schwartz, M. F., Nozari, N., Faseyitan, O., & Coslett, H. B. (2013). Voxel-based lesion-parameter mapping: Identifying the neural correlates of a computational model of word production. *Cognition, 128*(3), 380–96.

Fairbanks, G. (1954). Systematic research in experimental phonetics: 1. A theory of the speech mechanism as a servosystem. *Journal of Speech & Hearing Disorders, 19*, 133–9.

Foygel, D., & Dell, G. S. (2000). Models of impaired lexical access in speech production. *Journal of Memory and Language, 43*(2), 182–216.

Fromkin, V. A. (1971). The non-anomalous nature of anomalous utterances. *Language, 47*, 27–52.

Garrett, M. F. (1975). The analysis of sentence production. *Psychology of Learning and Motivation, 9*, 133–77.

Garrett, M. F. (1980). Levels of processing in sentence production. In: Butterworth, B. (Ed.), *Language Production. Vol. 1. Speech and talk* (pp. 177–220). Academic Press, New York, NY.

Garrett, M. F. (1988). Processes in language production. In: Nieuwmeyer, F. J. (Ed.), *Linguistics: The Cambridge Survey. Vol. III. Biological and Psychological Aspects of Language* (pp. 69–96). Harvard University Press, Cambridge, MA.

Golfinopoulos, E., Tourville, J. A., Bohland, J. W., Ghosh, S. S., Nieto-Castanon, A., & Guenther, F. H. (2011). fMRI investigation of unexpected somatosensory feedback perturbation during speech. *NeuroImage, 55*(3), 1324–38.

Golfinopoulos, E., Tourville, J. A., & Guenther, F. H. (2010). The integration of large-scale neural network modeling and functional brain imaging in speech motor control. *NeuroImage, 52*(3), 862–74.

Goodglass, H. (1992). Diagnosis of conduction aphasia. In: Kohn, S. E. (Ed.), *Conduction Aphasia* (pp. 39–49). Lawrence Erlbaum Associates, Hillsdale, NJ.

Guenther, F. H. (1995). Speech sound acquisition, coarticulation, and rate effects in a neural network model of speech production. *Psychological Review, 102*(3), 594.

Guenther, F. H., Ghosh, S. S., & Tourville, J. A. (2006). Neural modeling and imaging of the cortical interactions underlying syllable production. *Brain and Language, 96*(3), 280–301.

Guenther, F. H., Hampson, M., & Johnson, D. (1998). A theoretical investigation of reference frames for the planning of speech movements. *Psychological Review, 105*, 611–33.

Hickok, G. (2012a). Computational neuroanatomy of speech production. *Nature Reviews Neuroscience, 13*(2), 135–45.

Hickok, G. (2012b). The cortical organization of speech processing: feedback control and predictive coding the context of a dual-stream model. *Journal of Communication Disorders, 45*(6), 393–402.

Hickok, G. (2014a). The architecture of speech production and the role of the phoneme in speech processing. *Language, Cognition and Neuroscience, 29*(1), 2–20.

Hickok, G. (2014b). Toward an integrated psycholinguistic, neurolinguistic, sensorimotor framework for speech production. *Language, Cognition and Neuroscience, 29*(1), 52–9.

Hickok, G., Buchsbaum, B., Humphries, C., & Muftuler, T. (2003). Auditory–motor interaction revealed by fMRI: Speech, music, and working memory in area Spt. *Journal of Cognitive Neuroscience, 15*(5), 673–82.

Hickok, G., Houde, J., & Rong, F. (2011). Sensorimotor integration in speech processing: Computational basis and neural organization. *Neuron, 69*(3), 407–22.

Hickok, G., Okada, K., & Serences, J. T. (2009). Area Spt in the human planum temporale supports sensory-motor integration for speech processing. *Journal of Neurophysiology, 101*(5), 2725–32.

Houde, J. F., & Jordan, M. I. (1998). Sensorimotor adaptation in speech production. *Science, 279*, 1213–16.

Houde, J. F., & Nagarajan, S. S. (2011). Speech production as state feedback control. *Frontiers in Human Neuroscience, 5.* DOI:10.3389/fnhum.2011.00082

Houde, J. F., Nagarajan, S. S., Sekihara, K., & Merzenich, M. M. (2002). Modulation of the auditory cortex during speech: An MEG study. *Journal of Cognitive Neuroscience, 14*(8), 1125–38.

Jescheniak, J. D., & Levelt, W. J. (1994). Word frequency effects in speech production: Retrieval of syntactic information and of phonological form. *Journal of Experimental Psychology: Learning, Memory, and Cognition, 20*(4), 824.

Kempen, G., & Huijbers, P. (1983). The lexicalization process in sentence production and naming: Indirect election of words. *Cognition, 14*(2), 185–209.

Kempen, G., & Hoenkamp, E. (1987). An incremental procedural grammar for sentence formulation. *Cognitive Science, 11*(2), 201–58.

Kittredge, A. K., Dell, G. S., Verkuilen, J., & Schwartz, M. F. (2008). Where is the effect of frequency in word production? Insights from aphasic picture-naming errors. *Cognitive Neuropsychology, 25*(4), 463–92.

Levelt, W. J. (1983). Monitoring and self-repair in speech. *Cognition, 14*(1), 41–104.

Levelt, W. J. (1989). *Speaking: From Intention to Articulation.* MIT Press, Cambridge, MA.

Levelt, W. J., Roelofs, A., & Meyer, A. S. (1999). Multiple perspectives on word production. *Behavioral and Brain Sciences, 22*(01), 61–9.

Lomas, J., & Kertesz, A. (1978). Patterns of spontaneous recovery in aphasic groups: A study of adult stroke patients. *Brain and Language, 5*(3), 388–401.

Marshall, C. R., & van der Lely, H. K. (2009). Effects of word position and stress on onset cluster production: Evidence from typical development, specific language impairment, and dyslexia. *Language, 85*(1), 39–57.

Miozzo, M., & Caramazza, A. (1997). Retrieval of lexical–syntactic features in tip-of-the-tongue states. *Journal of Experimental Psychology: Learning, Memory, and Cognition, 23*(6), 1410.

Mirman, D., Strauss, T. J., Brecher, A., Walker, G. M., Sobel, P., Dell, G. S., & Schwartz, M. F. (2010). A large, searchable, web-based database of aphasic performance on picture naming and other tests of cognitive function. *Cognitive Neuropsychology, 27*(6), 495–504.

Motley, M. T., Camden, C. T., & Baars, B. J. (1982). Covert formulation and editing of anomalies in speech production: Evidence from experimentally elicited slips of the tongue. *Journal of Verbal Learning and Verbal Behavior, 21,* 578–94.

Pa, J., & Hickok, G. (2008). A parietal–temporal sensory–motor integration area for the human vocal tract: Evidence from an fMRI study of skilled musicians. *Neuropsychologia, 46*(1), 362–8.

Perenin, M. T., & Vighetto, A. (1988). Optic ataxia: A specific disruption in visuomotor mechanisms. *Brain, 111*(3), 643–74.

Perkell, J. S. (2012). Movement goals and feedback and feedforward control mechanisms in speech production. *Journal of Neurolinguistics, 25*(5), 382–407.

Plaut, D. C., & Kello, C. T. (1999). The emergence of phonology from the interplay of speech comprehension and production: A distributed connectionist approach. *The Emergence of Language,* 381–415. http://psycnet.apa.org/record/1999-02258-014

Roach, A., Schwartz, M. F., Martin, N., Grewal, R. S., & Brecher, A. (1996). The Philadelphia naming test: Scoring and rationale. *Clinical Aphasiology, 24,* 121–34.

Roelofs, A. (1996a). Morpheme frequency in speech production: testing WEAVER. In: Booij, G. E., van Marle, J. (Eds.), *Yearbook of Morphology* (pp. 135–54). Kluwer Academic, Dordrecht.

Roelofs, A., (1996b). Serial order in planning the production of successive morphemes of a word. *Journal of Memory and Language, 35,* 854–876.

Roelofs, A. (1998). Rightward incrementality in encoding simple phrasal forms in speech production: Verbparticle combinations. *Journal of Experimental Psychology: Learning, Memory, and Cognition*, 24, 904–21.

Roelofs, A. (2014). A dorsal-pathway account of aphasic language production: The WEAVER++/ARC model. *Cortex*, 59, 33–48.

Roelofs, A., Meyer, A. S., & Levelt, W. J. (1998). A case for the lemma/lexeme distinction in models of speaking: Comment on Caramazza and Miozzo (1997). *Cognition*, 69(2), 219–230.

Rogalsky, C., Poppa, T., Chen, K. H., Anderson, S. W., Damasio, H., Love, T., & Hickok, G. (2015). Speech repetition as a window on the neurobiology of auditory–motor integration for speech: A voxel-based lesion symptom mapping study. *Neuropsychologia*, 71, 18–27.

Sanes, J. N., Mauritz, K. H., Dalakas, M. C., & Evarts, E. V. (1984). Motor control in humans with large-fiber sensory neuropathy. *Human Neurobiology*, 4(2), 101–14.

Schwartz, M. F., & Brecher, A. (2000). A model-driven analysis of severity, response characteristics, and partial recovery in aphasics' picture naming. *Brain and Language*, 73(1), 62–91.

Schwartz, M. F., Dell, G. S., Martin, N., Gahl, S., & Sobel, P. (2006). A case-series test of the interactive two-step model of lexical access: Evidence from picture naming. *Journal of Memory and Language*, 54(2), 228–64.

Schwartz, M. F., Faseyitan, O., Kim, J., & Coslett, H. B. (2012). The dorsal stream contribution to phonological retrieval in object naming. *Brain*, 135(12), 3799–814.

Shattuck-Hufnagel, S. (1979). Speech errors as evidence for a serial-ordering mechanism in sentence production. In: *Sentence Processing: Psycholinguistic Studies Presented to Merrill Garrett* (pp. 295–342). L. Erlbaum, Hillsdale NJ.

Thompson, C. K. (2003). Unaccusative verb production in agrammatic aphasia: The argument structure complexity hypothesis. *Journal of Neurolinguistics*, 16(2), 151–67.

Thompson, C. K., Lange, K. L., Schneider, S. L., & Shapiro, L. P. (1997). Agrammatic and non-brain-damaged subjects' verb and verb argument structure production. *Aphasiology*, 11(4-5), 473–90.

Tourville, J. A., & Guenther, F. H. (2011). The DIVA model: A neural theory of speech acquisition and production. *Language and Cognitive Processes*, 26(7), 952–81.

Tremblay, S., Shiller, D. M., & Ostry, D. J. (2003). Somatosensory basis of speech production. *Nature*, 423(6942), 866–69.

Ueno, T., Saito, S., Rogers, T. T., & Ralph, M. A. L. (2011). Lichtheim 2: Synthesizing aphasia and the neural basis of language in a neurocomputational model of the dual dorsal-ventral language pathways. *Neuron*, 72(2), 385–96.

Walker, G. M., & Hickok, G. (2016). Bridging computational approaches to speech production: The semantic–lexical–auditory–motor model (SLAM). *Psychonomic Bulletin & Review*, 23(2), 339–52.

Wilshire, C. E. (1999). The "tongue twister" paradigm as a technique for studying phonological encoding. *Language and Speech*, 42(1), 57–82.

Yates, A. J. (1963). Recent empirical and theoretical approaches to the experimental manipulation of speech in normal subjects and in stammerers. *Behaviour Research and Therapy*, 1(2), 95–119.

CHAPTER 14

LINKS BETWEEN PERCEPTION AND PRODUCTION

Examining the roles of motor and premotor cortices in understanding speech

CAROLYN MCGETTIGAN AND PASCALE TREMBLAY

14.1 INTRODUCTION

SPEECH is a hugely important signal in human behavior, allowing individuals to share thoughts and emotions with others as part of complex social interactions. As an action, or rather a set of actions (involving highly coordinated movements of the larynx, tongue, jaw, lips, and soft palate), speech production is a highly complex sensorimotor behavior, from the perspectives of both the speaker and the listener. Though historically seen as distinct, the neural mechanisms controlling speech perception and speech production are now conceptualized as largely interacting and possibly overlapping. Indeed, from the very first months of life, speech perception and production are closely related. Speaking requires learning to map the relationships between oral movements and the resulting acoustical signal, which demands a close interaction between perceptual and motor systems.

In the mid-twentieth century, a Motor Theory of Speech Perception (MTSP) was proposed, which suggested a strong link between speech production and perception mechanisms; through a series of empirical tests, the theory was tested, strongly contested, and largely abandoned. However, following the late-century discovery of mirror neurons in macaques, and in the context of a developing field of human neuroscience research interested in the interactions between sensory and motor systems and the grounding of cognitive processes in the motor system (a field often referred to as "cognitive embodiment"), the theory enjoyed an unexpected revival. In this chapter, we outline the empirical basis for the original MTSP, describing its main tenets. We then discuss how, equipped with modern methods to probe neuromotor systems, researchers in cognitive neuroscience first described the involvement of the motor system in non-motor tasks such as auditory speech processing.

Focusing on research published in the last decade, we highlight the ways in which authors have since elaborated theoretical accounts to clarify whether this motor involvement is at the foundation of language comprehension. In particular, we draw attention to the use of multivariate analyses of functional MRI responses to speech that allow more detailed descriptions of the content of motor responses to speech, and the refinement of experimental designs to address the specificity and possible predictive/causal roles for motor cortical involvement in speech perception.

14.2 Motor Theories of Speech Perception in the Twentieth Century

The MTSP was developed at the Haskins Laboratories in the United States in the 1950s (Liberman, 1957) and revised in 1985 (Liberman & Mattingly, 1985), in the midst of infructuous attempts at developing a machine that would read aloud text for the blind (a scientific endeavor that would have tremendous impact on the way that we understand the nature of the speech signal; for a review, see Shankweiler and Fowler, 2015). These machines operated by producing sequences of discrete sounds associated with alphabetic segments— however, this is not representative of natural speech, where sequences of vowels and consonants are produced as smooth integrated sequences instead of concatenations of individually produced sounds. Largely as a consequence of this phenomenon of "coarticulation," the same speech sound (e.g., /d/) becomes associated with different acoustic realizations depending on the phonetic and prosodic context—for example, the /d/ sounds in /di/, /da/ and /du/ are acoustically different because of the different neighboring vowels (Liberman, 1957). This essentially eliminates the possibility of phoneme- or alphabet-like discrete acoustic segments in speech, and this complicated the development of reading machines because they could not generate speech that was intelligible to listeners when produced at a natural rate. This observation also posed a theoretical problem—how does human speech communication successfully establish parity between receivers and senders in the face of such acoustical variability? The MTSP was developed to account for this well-known "lack of invariance problem" in speech perception, which is still often considered one of the main goals of speech perception research (Galantucci, Fowler, & Turvey, 2006; Liberman, Cooper, Shankweiler, & Studdert-Kennedy, 1967).

One of the main tenets of the MTSP was that speech perception and production are intimately linked. Indeed, Liberman and colleagues wrote, in 1967, that "[. . .] *the perceiver is also the speaker and must be supposed, therefore, to possess all the mechanisms for putting language through the successive coding operations that result eventually in the acoustic signal*" (p. 452). The MTSP thus proposes that there must exist a link between perceptual and motor codes for speech. Though the idea of coupling between perceptual and motor systems was shared by numerous researchers across a range of fields beyond language (see Prinz, 1997), in its revised form (Liberman & Mattingly, 1985), the MTSP focused only on speech-related mechanisms, with one of its main claims being that the conversion from the speech acoustic signal to a speech motor gesture occurred within a biologically specialized "speech" (phonetic) module in the brain. According to the MTSP, each speech sound (phoneme) is associated with a specific combination of motor commands, such as "tongue elevation" or "lip protrusion." Thus, another main tenet of the MTSP was that the ability to categorize the speech sounds in the incoming speech stream into phonemes and syllables is accomplished by tracking the intended articulatory patterns—that is, recovering the intended (invariant) motor gesture from the interlocutor's own motor repertoire (a process often referred to as analysis-by-synthesis). This suggestion was based upon the finding that whenever articulation and the resulting acoustic patterns diverge, perception tracks the intended articulation (in our example, a closure of the vocal tract between the tongue and the alveolar ridge to form /d/). In other words, the relation between phonemes and articulation is closer to a one-to-one relationship than the relationship between phonemes and the acoustic signal. Thus, according to the theory, the intended articulatory patterns represent the elemental objects of speech perception.

The theory was, and still is to some extent, highly controversial (Fowler, Shankweiler, & Studdert-Kennedy, 2015; Fowler, 1996; Galantucci et al., 2006; Lane, 1965; Rizzolatti & Arbib, 1998; Stasenko, Garcea, & Mahon, 2013). The main points of contention were (and still are), (1) the idea of a specialized speech module and the focus on speech-specific processes, (2) the notion of motor invariants. In particular, the notion of an innate vocal-tract synthesizer that would be used to derive motor invariants from the acoustic signal has been contested and various alternatives proposed. However, there has not been a clear replacement for the MTSP, and the idea of a close interaction between perceptual and motor systems remains. As will become clear in the following sections, the MTSP, despite its shortcomings, continues to have a major influence on the field of speech perception research.

14.3 Cognitive neuroscience of speech perception in the twenty-first century

14.3.1 The advent of Mirror Neurons and motoric accounts of perception

In the last decade of the twentieth century, work from the laboratory of Giacomo Rizzolatti at the University of Parma made a huge impression on the field of neuroscience. In studies of awake macaques, Rizzolatti and colleagues described single cells in the premotor cortex (area F5 of the frontal lobe) that fire during performance of an action (e.g., grasping a piece of food) and when observing the same action performed by another individual (in this case, researchers in the laboratory; e.g., Gallese, Fadiga, Fogassi, & Rizzolatti, 1996; Rizzolatti & Craighero, 2004). This one-to-one mapping of perception and production led these authors (and many others) to posit a role for such "mirror neurons" in action understanding—that is, the suggestion that an individual learns how to make sense of the actions of others by simulating these actions in their own motor cortex. This finding was taken up with great enthusiasm, with many authors in the field of human cognitive neuroscience seeking evidence for equivalent mechanisms in the human brain. Respected neuroscientists such as Vilayanur S. Ramachandran even went as far as to declare that "mirror neurons will do for psychology what DNA did for biology" (Ramachandran, 2000). Notably, the lack of scope for single cell recordings in humans meant that such endeavors could only claim to identify mirror *systems* in the brain, typically those showing topographical overlap between perception and execution of actions (e.g., Decety et al., 1997; di Pellegrino, Fadiga, Fogassi, Gallese, & Rizzolatti, 1992; Grafton, Arbib, Fadiga, & Rizzolatti, 1996).

Alongside the work on visual observation and its correspondence with action (motor) programs, the Rizzolatti group had also explored observation-execution in the auditory modality. Kohler et al. (2002) reported the discovery of neurons in F5 that fired when the monkey performed actions such as ripping paper and vocalizing, and when hearing the sounds produced by those actions. In their paper, Kohler et al. suggest that the location of these mirror neurons in the non-human homologue of "Broca's area" [1]—a region associated with speech production since seminal neuropsychological case reports from the mid-nineteenth century—might support an account of language evolution based on the representations of actions and their auditory consequences in inferior frontal cortex.

The idea behind motor theories of speech perception is that the same neural tissue (at least in part) that is involved in producing speech is also involved in perceiving speech. However, because the production of speech is an intricate, multistage process involving control of dozens of muscles distributed in the abdomen, neck, and face, and requiring both speed and precision, there is more than one candidate region for such sensorimotor interactions. The "core" cortical speech network involves large parts of the human brain, including the ventral part of the central sulcus (which contains the primary motor area or $M1_v$), the precentral gyrus and sulcus (which contains the ventral lateral premotor cortex or PMv), the medial aspect of the superior frontal gyrus (which contains the medial premotor areas, which are composed of the pre-supplementary motor area and supplementary motor area (SMA)), the cingulate motor area (CMA), and the inferior frontal gyrus (IFG) (see Fig. 14.1). Subcortical motor areas implicated in speech production include the cerebellum, basal ganglia, and thalamus (e.g., Bohland & Guenther, 2006; Tremblay, Deschamps, Baroni, & Hasson, 2016; Tremblay & Small, 2011b). Anatomically, $M1_v$, PMv, SMA, and CMA contribute to descending (motor) pathways, meaning that these regions have direct control over lower motor neurons located in the brainstem and, ultimately, over the muscles of phonation and articulation (Breshears, Molinaro, & Chang, 2015; Dum & Strick, 1991; Jenabi, Peck, Young, Brennan, & Holodny, 2015; Jurgens, 2002, 2009). The IFG, in contrast, does not, and it is also not involved in the cortico-striatal motor loop implicated in motor planning for speech (Alexander, Crutcher, & DeLong, 1990).

Depending on their architecture and connectivity, the different parts of the motor system contribute to different operations such as sequencing, motor initiation and execution, and may not be the most likely targets for perceptual-motor integration. Instead, regions believed to contain motor representations for speech may be the ideal sites. The *Directions into Velocities of Articulators* (DIVA) model of speech production (Guenther, Ghosh, & Tourville, 2006), a dominant neurobiological model in the field, proposes that the ventral part of the lateral premotor cortex (PMv) contains speech motor programs. Interestingly, the PMv, along with surrounding tissue in $M1_v$ and the pars opercularis of the IFG (IFG_{op}), has been the target of most investigations into the motor theories of speech perception. However, there remain questions about the extent to which the different regions exhibit mirror-like properties, and whether these reflect functional differences between these cortical sites.

---

[1] The term "Broca's area" refers to an anatomically ill-defined portion of the inferior frontal region that often includes pars triangularis and pars opercularis. For a discussion of this topic, see Tremblay and Dick, 2016.

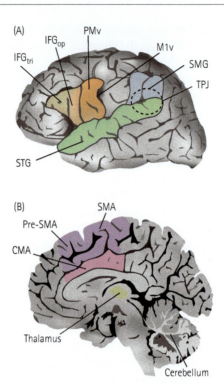

FIG. 14.1 Illustration of the main regions involved in the perception and production of speech. A. Lateral view of a human brain. B. Sagittal view of a human brain. IFG$_{tri}$, inferior frontal gyrus, pars triangularis; IFG$_{op}$, inferior frontal gyrus, pars opercularis; PMv, ventral premotor cortex; M1$_v$, ventral primary motor cortex; SMG, supramarginal gyrus; TPJ, temporoparietal junction; STG, superior temporal gyrus; CMA, cingulate motor area; Pre-SMA, pre-supplementary motor area; SMA, supplementary motor area. Note that the primary auditory cortex and planum temporale are not visible from the surface as they are located medial to the STG. Other deep structures involved in speech processes are the basal ganglia and insula.

As human cognitive neuroscience began to produce reports of "mirror"-like perception-production links for hand and arm actions, so authors in the cognitive neuroscience of speech began to investigate the possibility of common involvement of the IFG$_{op}$ and adjacent PMv in the perception and production of speech. Two key functional magnetic resonance imaging studies (fMRI) provided some of the earliest evidence for overlap of brain responses during perception and production of simple syllables such as "ba" and "da" (Wilson, Saygin, Sereno, & Iacoboni, 2004), as well as a suggestion that these responses were somatotopically organized[2] (Pulvermüller et al., 2006). Specifically, it was shown that the perception of distinct speech sounds (phonemes[3]) recruits motor areas varying spatially according to involvement of different speech articulators (e.g., phonemes involving lip movements, such

---

[2] Somatotopy is the point-for-point correspondence of an area of the body to a specific area in the brain. Such organization is found, with different levels of precision, throughout the sensorimotor system.

[3] The smallest unit of speech that can be used to make one word different from another word. For example, the difference in meaning between the English words cat and bat is a result of the exchange of the phoneme /k/ for the phoneme /b/.

as /p/, engaged relatively non-overlapping parts of the precentral gyrus as compared to phonemes requiring tongue movements, such as /t/). The latter finding was used to argue for a specific involvement of the motor/premotor[4] cortex in the perception of heard speech, rather than a general or non-specific sound-to-action response. Similarly, transcranial magnetic stimulation (TMS) of M1 to generate motor-evoked potentials (MEPs) in lip and hand muscles showed that lip MEPs were enhanced during perception of audio and visual speech, but this was not the case for hand MEPs, supporting the notion of a somatotopic involvement of the motor system in speech perception (Watkins, Strafella, & Paus, 2003). In a study further probing somatotopy using TMS, it was shown that hearing words requiring pronounced tongue movements (i.e., words including /r/) was associated with stronger tongue MEPs compared to words involving less pronounced movements of this articulator (Fadiga, Craighero, Buccino, & Rizzolatti, 2002). However, none of these studies addressed a key theoretical issue at the heart of any motoric account of speech perception, in that they did not show any causal or mechanistic role for motor/premotor cortex in speech perception accuracy or sensitivity. Further, the studies on MEP modulation targeted $M1_v$, which controls the execution of movements, rather than PMv and IFG_{op} that are associated with the representation of speech motor plans (Guenther et al., 2006). As discussed previously here, PMv and IFG_{op} are more likely targets for perception-production interactions; it is possible, however, that stimulation of M1 cascades to premotor areas with which it is connected.

Later studies employed TMS to modulate activation in motor and premotor cortical sites and examine the effects on speech perception performance. Here, authors reported impaired syllable recognition in noise performance after TMS to premotor cortex (Meister, Wilson, Deblieck, Wu, & Iacoboni, 2007). This finding was developed by a later TMS study (D'Ausilio et al., 2009) reporting a somatotopic double dissociation, where stimulation of lip M1 selectively *enhanced* syllable recognition performance for consonant-vowel plosives beginning with a bilabial closure (e.g., /pa/, /ba/), while stimulation of tongue cortex impaired recognition for other syllables (e.g., /ta/, /da/). A point to note in these studies was that they almost invariably involved an active task, in which participants were, for example, required to make fine-grained phonemic judgments (e.g., discriminating /ba/ from /pa/), to segment the incoming speech stream into phonemic constituents (e.g., breaking down "cat" into /k/, /æ/ and /t/), or to identify syllables against noise. Active tasks such as these may not be representative of the manner in which speech is naturally processed in day-to-day situations—this point was raised by a number of critics (e.g., Scott, McGettigan, & Eisner, 2009; see next) who claimed that there was therefore insufficient evidence that motor representations are engaged in an automatic or obligatory fashion in the service of everyday speech perception as posited by MTSP (otherwise such effects should be seen also for passive listening in quiet).

The overall viewpoint emerging from these studies (and many others) was one that leaned at times toward a strong interpretation of the Motor Theory—that the perception of speech gestures is fundamental to the understanding of speech. However, responses to these claims were mixed, and provoked a series of influential opinion and review papers (Hickok, 2009, 2010; Lotto, Hickok, & Holt, 2009; Scott, McGettigan, & Eisner, 2009). The next section offers an overview of some of the arguments on both sides, and summarizes what we see as

---

[4] In this chapter, we use the expression "(pre)motor cortex" to refer to the ventral central sulcus (M1), ventral precentral gyrus and sulcus (PM), and posterior part of the IFG (pars opercularis).

the three prominent theoretical standpoints on the role of motor cortex in speech perception, as they stood at the end of the first decade of the millennium.

14.3.2 The new Motor Theory of Speech Perception: Support and criticisms

Initially, studies investigating motor contributions to speech perception tended to make positive assertions about the importance of motoric representations—indeed, some authors claimed an "essential" role for motor/premotor cortex in the recognition of speech (Meister et al., 2007; Pulvermüller & Fadiga, 2010).

Other authors presented a view that cautioned a limited interpretation of the motor involvement in speech perception and emphasized the paucity of evidence for this in the face of overwhelming data suggesting a primary role for a ventral processing stream in temporal cortex supporting speech perception (Scott, Blank, Rosen, & Wise, 2000; Scott & Johnsrude, 2003). In a critique of the posited "action understanding" interpretation of mirror neurons (and mirror systems), Hickok (2009) sets out eight problems for the field to consider, including concerns about the empirical evidence for an action understanding role in non-human primates, raising criticism of the neuroanatomical parallels between macaque F5 and human "Broca's area," and presenting evidence for dissociations between action production and perception deficits in human patients. Most relevant for our current discussion, Hickok invokes perception-production dissociation data from aphasic patients to argue that there is little evidence that mirror theories of action understanding generalize to speech perception. Like other critics of the Motor Theory, Hickok acknowledges that motor systems may well have some role in supporting speech perception, particularly when this places large demands on executive, attentional or working memory processes (e.g., through requiring phonemic segmentation) or when the process is challenged by noise: "However, this influence is modulatory, not primary" (Hickok, 2009, p. 1240).

Scott and colleagues (2009) offer a detailed critique of experimental methods, pointing out the lack of suitable acoustic control conditions in fMRI studies (or, the lack of statistical comparison with these control conditions; see Wilson et al., 2004), the presence of challenging listening conditions and/or demanding phoneme segmentation tasks in behavioral and TMS work, and the lack of evidence for an essential role of speech production for successful perception during development or in the patient literature. Responding to the strong claim of a specialized speech "module" in the brain, they point out that IFG (including the opercular part [IFG$_{op}$]), PMv, and M1$_v$ respond to passive listening to a wide range of sounds, including tool sounds, music, and non-verbal emotional vocalizations. Instead of being essential to speech perception, Scott et al. rather argue that there could be an alternative role for motor knowledge in the perception of auditory stimuli, which might reflect a more general sound-to-action response. Specifically, they call upon behavioral data showing that turn-taking behavior in human conversation happens with very low latencies, using this evidence to propose that auditory-motor connections in the brain might be particularly crucial in supporting smooth transitions in communicative interactions.

Pulvermüller and Fadiga (2010) make a claim for the importance of perception-action networks in supporting language comprehension, from speech recognition to semantic and syntactic processing of words and sentences. In terms of speech perception at the phonemic and syllabic level (our focus for this chapter), their main arguments center around evidence for specificity of perceptual responses in motor cortex through somatotopy. While they acknowledge criticisms for a context dependency on responses in terms of the importance of noisy or degraded listening conditions, they make the argument that such contexts are in fact much more representative of normal everyday speech perception, and as such, the evidence from these studies is still valid in the evaluation of the MTSP. Galantucci, Fowler, and Turvey (2006) were similarly encouraged by mirror neuron accounts, but concluded that the limitations of the original MTSP included having too strong a focus on speech: they argue that general cognition shows many indications of the importance of motor systems for comprehension. While rejecting the tenet of the MTSP that there should be a specialized module in the brain for speech, they remain strongly in favor of gestures as the primary objects of perception. In contrast, Massaro and Chen (2008) have claimed that their Fuzzy Logical model, which describes perception in terms of prototypical pattern recognition based on the integration of several sources of input information (e.g., voice, face) can account for some of the most important experimental evidence for the MTSP (e.g., the invariance of /d/ despite variation in formant transitions depending on the following vowel; see Liberman, Delattre, & Cooper, 1952). Crucially, where the emergence of mirror neurons encouraged Galantucci et al. (2006) as supporting evidence for some form of MTSP, Massaro & Chen rather pose the question of how a mirror mechanism can actually explain perception: " . . . mirror neurons cannot account for perception, because they would overgeneralize. The macaque certainly experiences the difference between seeing a conspecific action and performing its own action, but the same mirror neurons are activated by these very different events and experiences" (Massaro & Chen, 2008, p. 456).

14.3.3 Motor cortex and speech: Prominent viewpoints

Thus, by the end of the last decade, several dissenting voices had emerged on the topic of the "revived" version of the MTSP, yet some quite fervent and strong-form support remained. The concerns raised by critics presented clear challenges for the field—namely, to better describe the perceptual representations of speech sounds in motor cortex (i.e., Are these equivalent in perception and production of speech? At what level of abstraction are they encoded?), and to further characterize when and how these representations might contribute to speech perception (and crucially, to assess the *importance* of those contributions for language comprehension). While there remained some authors still arguing for an essential role (e.g., Pulvermüller & Fadiga, 2010), there were two main viewpoints contesting this. First, some argued that motor knowledge is not essential for speech perception, but may play a significant role in supporting this process under certain circumstances. The second main viewpoint extended this stance, suggesting that a focus on basic phonemic/syllabic perception mechanisms might have distracted from a more important role for motor responses in spoken communication as an interactive, social process (e.g., in turn-taking; Scott et al., 2009). In one form of this view, Pickering and Garrod (2013) advocate something superficially more aligned with MTSP, which proposes the use of forward models in spoken communication to allow a conversational agent to make predictions during both production and comprehension at several levels in the linguistic hierarchy. Here, however, they allow both for "prediction-by-simulation" and "prediction-by-association" mechanisms; while clearly characterizing speech comprehension as action perception, their main argument is for mechanisms that smooth the coordination and alignment of communicative processes in dialogue, and thus allow for relatively more flexibility in how this might be achieved.

In the next sections, we turn to the experimental evidence that emerged around the time of, and after, the publication of these influential review papers. We consider the extent to which these studies addressed the two challenges described here: 1) to describe the nature of speech representations in motor cortex, and 2) to identify their precise role in speech perception and language comprehension, as well as more general social interactions.

14.4 Gathering evidence: Recent developments in the cognitive neuroscience of motor theories of speech perception

Several highly cited papers in the initial resurgence of interest in MTSP and its potential neural bases contributed supporting evidence from fMRI (Pulvermüller et al., 2006; Wilson et al., 2004) and TMS (D'Ausilio et al., 2009; Fadiga et al., 2002; Meister et al., 2007; Watkins et al., 2003) in healthy young listeners. In this section, we consider how these methods, and related experimental designs, have been advanced in recent years to progress our understanding of motoric responses to speech. We also include newer evidence emerging from other methods— electroencephalography (EEG) and magnetoencephalography (MEG) have allowed for closer inspection of the dynamics of motor involvement in perception, while electrocorticography (ECoG) has provided greater spatial resolution and specificity than the former techniques by measuring directly from the cortical surface.

14.4.1 Perceptual representations of speech in the cortical motor system

The studies of Wilson and colleagues (2004) and Pulvermüller and colleagues (2006) offered thought-provoking indications of perception-production links in passive listening to speech. As described here, the observations of somatotopic overlap in these responses argued for a specificity in representation, suggestive of underlying mirror-like activity: perception of speech sounds involves activation of the corresponding motor plans (or gestures; Galantucci et al., 2006) used to produce those sounds. However, spatial overlap of responses offers limited insights into whether the activations actually reflect matching underlying representations, and whether the responses code for physical (articulatory) or more abstract properties of speech.

Recent fMRI studies have provided more nuanced evidence, and perhaps because of their milder stance, they have received far less attention. A strong MTSP view would predict a preferential and selective response to speech over other sounds in motor cortex—if perception is dependent on the activation of corresponding motor programs, this should be specific to sounds within the listeners' native speech repertoire. However, Wilson and Iacoboni (2006) had found contradictory evidence, showing greater responses of the motor system to non-native syllables compared with native, and showing correlations between response magnitude and sound producibility only in superior temporal regions. In a more refined approach, a passive perception paradigm in fMRI using native speakers of English showed that there was no difference in the magnitude of premotor responses to English plosive consonants compared with producible ingressive click sounds (used communicatively, but not linguistically, in English). These sounds were, however, differentiated by the posterior superior temporal sulcus (Agnew, McGettigan, & Scott, 2011), lending support to the view that the extraction of meaningful linguistic percepts in speech is predominately a process carried out in the ventral auditory processing stream (Scott & Johnsrude, 2003). Allowing for a softer version of the theory, where motor activations to sound are not necessarily speech selective in terms of the magnitude of the BOLD response, there should nonetheless be evidence for common representations of motor-related information in perception and production. However, this has not been the case. It has been shown in fMRI that while PMv is active in both speech perception and production, it is only sensitive to phonetic details (syllable structure) in speech production/rehearsal and not in passive speech perception (e.g., Tremblay & Small, 2011b). This stands in contrast to evidence from studies directly measuring the movements of the articulators, using techniques such as electropalatography (measuring tongue contact with the hard palate) and Doppler ultrasound imaging (measuring tongue kinematics), which have shown that hearing speech can evoke corresponding movements of the tongue in a "mirroring" fashion (D'Ausilio et al., 2014; Yuen, Davis, Brysbaert, & Rastle, 2010). This speaks to another essential element of MTSP—that motor knowledge should be used in an obligatory fashion during speech perception.

It can be argued that fMRI bears insufficient resolution, in time or space, to fully address the question of whether motor knowledge is used in the perception of speech. In recent years, multivariate analyses of the BOLD response have allowed descriptions of speech representations during perception at a finer granularity. Moving beyond the relatively coarse subtraction analyses of earlier studies, researchers have employed machine learning techniques to classify the responses to stimuli and speakers based on the spatial patterning of activation (multivoxel pattern analysis; MVPA) in a brain region of interest or within a "searchlight" volume passing through the brain (e.g., Formisano, De Martino, Bonte, & Goebel, 2008). This has afforded greater sensitivity in the classification of perceptual responses to speech, often revealing areas of activation that were obscured by regional averaging for subtraction (e.g., Abrams et al., 2013). With regard to the possibility of a motor involvement in speech perception, multivariate statistics also present a means of characterizing the *content* of neural representations. Representational Similarity Analysis (RSA; Kriegeskorte, Mur, & Bandettini, 2008) uses cross-correlation of the neural responses to different stimulus categories within a region of interest to generate a representational dissimilarity matrix (RDM)—this RDM can be compared with matrices constructed from responses in other brain regions, participant groups, or data types (e.g., perceptual ratings, correlations of stimulus properties) to identify the nature of the representations in the region of interest. RSA was recently employed to describe the content of representations in regions of cortex showing overlapping activation in the production and perception of both clean and degraded spoken syllables (Evans & Davis, 2015). Significant correlations were found between neural responses and searchlight RDMs describing the acoustic form of speech, as well as those describing the categorical identity of the syllables. This revealed abstract (i.e., categorical), and not form-related, representation of syllabic identity and phonemic content within left somatomotor cortex (extending over pre and postcentral gyrus) during passive listening to speech, but no evidence for motor representation of phonetic features, such as place of articulation.

Other work has argued in favor of feature-level representations, although the findings have not been consistent across studies. MVPA of passive responses to spoken syllables was used to identify context-independent encoding of phonetic features, by testing for generalization across an orthogonal feature (e.g., testing representation of place of articulation by training a classifier on /p/ versus /t/ and testing for generalization to /f/ vs. /s/; Correia et al., 2015). This revealed representation of phonetic features across perisylvian cortex, including $M1_v$, PMv, IFG_{op}, STG, and somatosensory sites. However, there was variation in the topography of feature representation, where information on place and manner of articulation was identified in regions such as IFG, while voicing information was largely contained within superior temporal and somatosensory cortices. Another study used MVPA to examine the location of consonant articulatory features during a passive syllable processing task, and found that articulatory features were represented in superior temporal cortex but predominately not within motor or premotor areas (Arsenault & Buchsbaum, 2015).

The inconsistent involvement of motor/premotor regions in the description of articulatory features in perception argues against an obligatory engagement of motor representations or mechanisms, as might be expected if there were an essential motor response in speech perception. Previous investigations claiming strong somatotopic representation of speech in motor cortex have used plosive stimuli varying in place of articulation (see Pulvermüller et al., 2006; Wilson et al., 2004), which is a feature that in such contexts may strongly engage the motor system (consider the contrastive tongue positions for /t/ versus /k/, and compare with the relatively consistent tongue configurations in a fricated /s/ and a plosive /t/) but is not reflective of the perceptual separability of heard phonemes across a wider range of sounds and feature combinations (Arsenault & Buchsbaum, 2015). However, the evidence does suggest that premotor cortex can represent some specialization for speech motor programs, in a way that the brain does not represent other, non-speech, sounds (e.g., birdsong; see Tremblay, Baroni, & Hasson, 2013). To the extent that motor regions are involved in the perceptual representation of speech, the challenge remains to account for when, and how, such representations might be engaged in the service of speech comprehension.

Despite such advances, one of the main limitations of the fMRI method is its low temporal resolution and indirect measure of brain activity. In recent years, several compelling studies of speech perception and production have emerged from work using electrocorticography (ECoG), which involves direct recordings of electrical activity from the cortical surface typically obtained from patients awaiting resection of tissue for the treatment of epilepsy (Bouchard, Mesgarani, Johnson, & Chang, 2013; Cheung, Hamilton, Johnson, & Chang, 2016; Mesgarani, Cheung, Johnson, & Chang, 2014; see also Flinker, Piai, & Knight, this volume). Unlike fMRI, ECoG, and electrophysiological approaches in general have a high temporal resolution (≥1,000 Hz). And yet, like findings with fMRI, ECoG studies have also suggested a relatively inconsistent profile for motor representations of speech articulatory information. Brain responses sensitive to the acoustic features of speech were found in the superior temporal cortex during passive listening to connected speech—specifically, these were predominantly organized with respect to manner of articulation rather than place (Mesgarani et al., 2014). In contrast, responses during speech production found in the pre- and postcentral gyrus (i.e., including PMv and M1) were organized according to place of articulation (Bouchard et al., 2013). Greater similarity in the organization of responses across temporal and somatomotor sites during perception, compared with that between perception and articulation within somatomotor cortex itself, suggested that the content of somatomotor responses during perception and production is not equivalent (Cheung et al., 2016), consistent with some of the earlier fMRI evidence (Tremblay & Small, 2011a, b).

How can these findings be tied together? The current body of evidence, although mixed, certainly suggests some capacity for articulatory information to be represented in the brain's perceptual responses to speech. Thus, we cannot accept a strong "anti-Motor Theory" argument that motor/premotor cortex is only involved in basic sound-to-action behaviors, such as tracking the rhythm of a repeating sound or in conversational turn-taking. However, the variability in the extent to which certain features are accessed during speech perception, in the consistency of activation and informational content across perception and production responses, and in the distribution of this information across somatomotor and sensory regions of cortex, raises problems for the interpretation that articulatory information forms the basis for speech perception. Thus, we turn to the second challenge: if articulatory information *can* be present in motor/premotor cortex during perception, when does this occur, and how does it contribute to the success of speech comprehension?

14.4.2 Functional roles of motor responses to speech: Task-dependency, environmental factors, taking turns?

A major criticism of the neurobiological studies arguing for an MT interpretation of motor responses to speech pointed out that these were often identified under particular stimulus and task contexts (e.g., Scott et al., 2009). Many empirical studies have since supported a context-dependent role for motor and premotor cortex in speech perception. These studies largely follow two main themes: investigating the role of task demands on phonological processes, and modeling perception of connected speech under challenging listening conditions.

A view gaining increasing support is that representations in motor cortex may be redundant in basic speech comprehension but useful for challenging listening conditions, for example in the presence of noise or distortion, or under specific task demands. A series of TMS experiments provide interesting evidence in support of a task- and environment-dependent role for the PMv in speech processing. Meister and colleagues reported that TMS applied to the PMv interferes with participants' ability to discriminate sublexical speech sounds in the presence of noise (Meister et al., 2007). Interestingly, however, it was later demonstrated that the effect of TMS to PMv during sublexical speech processing in the absence of ambient noise is dependent upon phonological processing demands, with only the most demanding phonological task being affected by TMS (Sato, Tremblay, & Gracco, 2009). Indeed, in that study, out of three phonological tasks—phoneme identification, syllable discrimination (same/different), and phoneme discrimination (same/different)—only phoneme discrimination (which required segmentation and comparison of the first phoneme of two syllables) was affected by TMS. Thus, the evidence suggested that the contribution of the premotor cortex to speech perception varies as a function of both task demands and environmental conditions (e.g., quiet vs. presence of noise). A recent TMS study compared TMS applied to PMv and STG during the processing of partially degraded auditory words in the context of a semantic task (semantic judgments, e.g., "man-made or natural?") and a phonological task consisting in phoneme identification and requiring segmentation (Krieger-Redwood, Gaskell, Lindsay, & Jefferies, 2013). Consistent with previous studies, the results demonstrate that the phonological task is affected by TMS to PMv; however, they show no effect of TMS for the semantic task, which the authors interpret as suggesting that the PMv is not necessary for speech comprehension but only in explicit phonological processes. The authors thus suggest that PMv is not involved, or at least not crucially so, in mapping sounds to meaning (or more generally in semantic processing). In contrast to the PMv results, TMS to STG interfered with both the phonological task and the semantic task, thereby suggesting a role for mapping sound to meaning for the STG, but not the PMv.

In their seminal fMRI study of sentence comprehension employing a range of degraded speech forms, Davis and Johnsrude (2003) identified a particularly elevated response to noise-vocoded sentences in the left IFG_{op}, relative to undistorted speech and a noise baseline condition; this was replicated in a later study of noise-vocoded word perception (Hervais-Adelman, Carlyon, Johnsrude, & Davis, 2012). A more nuanced aspect to this finding is that premotor and IFG engagement is enhanced in particular for speech that is degraded but still partially intelligible (e.g., for moderate to high levels of noise masking; Du, Buchsbaum, Grady, & Alain, 2014; Osnes, Hugdahl, & Specht, 2011). Thus, there has gradually emerged a view that a variety of regions including motor and premotor sites might form a compensatory mechanism in the support of degraded speech perception. It is posited that this involves top-down guidance or constraint of auditory processes during perception, dependent on task context (e.g., Davis & Johnsrude, 2007; Skipper, Goldin-Meadow, Nusbaum, & Small, 2007).

Investigating the nature, and consequences of, context dependency allows comparison of competing theoretical standpoints—for example, where a direct realist account would claim that the contents of motor activations during speech processing should represent the articulatory information available in the signal, a constructivist account would instead posit that such correspondence is not necessary and that motor activations might instead assist perception in a predictive and task-dependent fashion (see Callan, Callan, Gamez, Sato, & Kawato, 2010)[5]. In line with the latter view, an effective connectivity analysis (using dynamic causal modeling) on fMRI data collected during a speech-in-noise task reported top-down connections from premotor cortex to auditory regions, but only for listening to (partially) intelligible speech and not for non-speech control sounds (Osnes et al., 2011). Similarly, premotor regions have been specifically implicated in the response to training-related feedback during a speech perceptual learning paradigm (Hervais-Adelman et al., 2012). A speech-in-noise study including MEG and MRI experiments indicated that such involvement was not only correlated with task outcome, but might be predictive of it—within left IFG and premotor cortex sites showing responses during perception and production of speech, there were significant differences in BOLD and in pre-stimulus event-related synchronizations and desynchronizations (in the alpha, beta, and

---

[5] For a more detailed explanation of these competing theoretical positions, see Samuel (2011).

gamma ranges), when comparing correct and incorrect trials of a speech categorization task (Callan et al., 2010). Complementary findings from EEG identified mu suppressions localized to left and right pre- and postcentral gyrus during syllable discrimination in noise, but only for active listening—furthermore, only suppression in the left hemisphere was predictive of performance (Bowers, Saltuklaroglu, Harkrider, & Cuellar, 2013). Studies of MEPs and tongue kinematics have further shown that expectation of a phoneme can increase excitability of the tongue during perception (D'Ausilio et al., 2009), and that the degree to which individuals exhibit specific "mirroring" articulatory engagement during passive listening to speech is predictive of their success in categorizing syllables in noise (D'Ausilio et al., 2014). Notably, a multivariate analysis of BOLD responses to speech in noise showed that classification of phoneme identity in premotor cortex (including IFG) was successful from signal-to-noise ratios (SNRs) as low as -6 dB, whereas superior temporal cortex showed classification when the speech signal was much more audible (at + 8 dB SNR; Du et al., 2014). Thus, it appears that the speech motor system acts to constrain perception through the top-down communication of predictions to auditory cortex during sensory stimulation. There may, however, also be domain-general aspects to the engagement of PM and IFG by speech perception. Wild and colleagues (2012) explicitly tested the hypothesis that modulations of the BOLD response in a range of brain regions expressly index effortful listening, and found that regions including IFG and PMv tended to be implicated more strongly under conditions where speech is both degraded *and* attended.

To date, there has been little work explicitly testing the prediction of Scott and colleagues (2009), that motor cortex may be predominately associated with other forms of sound-to-action responses such as conversational turn-taking, and not with mechanisms for comprehension. Studies of spoken and musical interaction have aimed to characterize the neural basis of turn-taking and have presented affirmative evidence for a motor involvement in supporting the fine timing of communicative interactions (Bögels, Magyari, & Levinson, 2015; Foti & Roberts, 2016; Hadley, Novembre, Keller, & Pickering, 2015). In a study of piano duet playing, TMS-induced disruption of dorsal PM (associated with motor simulation in a variety of tasks) caused delays in turn-taking, which were more marked for sequences in which the partner's turn (preceding the delay) was familiar because the participant had also previously rehearsed it—this effect was not found for SMA (associated with motor imagery), thus suggesting a role for online simulation in the execution of smooth interactions during joint behavior (Hadley et al., 2015). During listening to spoken conversation, sustained EEG responses between turns, localized to PM (and inferior parietal cortex), were associated with hearing an unexpectedly long delay before a speaker's response to a request (usually associated with reluctance or hesitation), while activity associated with the speaker's response itself was localized to superior temporal cortex (Foti & Roberts, 2016). The authors argue that their findings align well with Scott et al.'s (2009) proposition that ventral and dorsal auditory processing streams perform differing functions during the perception of speech sounds.

Taken together, the findings from cognitive neuroscience studies in healthy young adults have allowed for developing a more detailed account of motor processing in speech perception, which suggests a role for motor/premotor areas in task- and environment-dependent phonological processing during speech perception, and more complex coordinated actions such as turn-taking.

14.5 WIDENING THE SCOPE: EVIDENCE FROM PATIENTS AND HEALTHY AGING

The study of special populations offers a unique opportunity to examine the effect of damage to motor/premotor regions, either normal or pathological, on speech perception. However, one difficulty with this approach is that there have been very few reports of focal damage to these regions. Another difficulty is related to the fact that, following stroke, the brain reorganizes itself, which obscures the study of brain-behavior relationships. Nevertheless, case studies have traditionally suggested that inferior frontal/premotor damage leads to a deficit in speech production in the absence of a deficit in speech perception, a clinical presentation usually referred to as non-fluent aphasia (or Broca's aphasia). Non-fluent aphasia has been viewed as opposite to fluent (Wernicke's) aphasia, defined as an auditory comprehension deficit in the absence of speech production deficits, which is associated with lesions to posterior superior temporal areas. It should be noted, however, that mild speech perception symptoms have repeatedly been documented in non-fluent aphasics, and that this has been a subject of contention since the nineteenth century in the field of aphasiology (see Lecours, Chain, Poncet, Nespoulous, & Joanette, 1992, for an account of a debate at the 1908 Neurology Society in Paris).

Several studies conducted on non-fluent patients with left-hemisphere stroke have reported no deficit to speech perception (Hickok, Costanzo, Capasso, & Miceli, 2011; Rogalski, Peelle, & Reilly, 2011; Stasenko et al., 2015). For example, Hickok et al. (2011) studied 24 patients with a left-hemisphere ischemic stroke affecting (at least) the IFG (pars triangularis [IFG_{tri}] and/or opercularis [IFG_{op}]), using a set of same-different discrimination tasks involving non-word and word comprehension in quiet. In an auditory-visual discrimination task, patients showed impaired performance, but there was no relationship between the severity of their fluency disorder and their perceptual discrimination skills. One potential issue with these studies, however, is that in many of them performance is at (or near) ceiling, suggesting that perhaps the tasks used are unsuitable to detect subtle changes to speech processing skills. In the neurostimulation literature, these types of tasks do not tend to be affected by TMS to premotor cortex or IFG. One study used a more challenging auditory word-picture matching task with normal and degraded auditory stimuli to measure performance in aphasic patients and normal controls (Moineau, Dronkers, & Bates, 2005). The results demonstrate a deficit in the degraded auditory condition for both fluent and non-fluent aphasics, suggesting an impact of frontal lobe damage on speech processing (though the site of the lesion was not examined, warranting prudence in interpreting these results). Using a different approach focusing on lesion location instead of behavioral symptoms, Schwartz et al (Schwartz, Faseyitan, Kim, & Coslett, 2012) correlated brain lesions to auditory comprehension errors in a large sample of 106 post-stroke patients with different types of aphasia and found that errors were correlated with lesions located mainly in the superior temporal area, as was expected, but also, to a limited extent, in the left posterior IFG. Hence, there is some clinical evidence, though relatively limited, supporting the notion that posterior IFG may play a role in auditory speech comprehension.

The study of normal aging provides an alternative framework to test at least two non-mutually exclusive hypotheses about the motor theories of speech perception. The first hypothesis is that, if the motor/premotor cortex is key to speech perception, an age-related decline in the anatomy and functioning of these regions would be expected to lead to a difficulty processing speech. The second hypothesis is that presbycusis—the decline in the peripheral hearing system associated with aging—should be associated with a compensatory action of the motor/premotor cortex to help maintain performance by relying more strongly on preserved motor knowledge, similar to the hypothesis that a degraded auditory signal is associated with stronger recruitment of the motor/premotor cortex.

Several studies have examined brain activity using fMRI during sentence comprehension tasks at various levels of intelligibility in young and older adults (Eckert et al., 2008; Erb & Obleser, 2013; Harris, Dubno, Keren, Ahlstrom, & Eckert, 2009; Hwang, Li, Wu, Chen, & Liu, 2007). None of these studies reported an age-related increase in activation during the processing of sentences in low intelligibility in the motor/premotor cortex. However, it is possible that sentence comprehension does not require access to detailed motor representations; it is a simple task that may rely on top-down cognitive and linguistic processes to recover the missing information, rather than on motor knowledge, and this higher-order information may be more important when there is less available context. Consistent with this notion, Peelle et al. examined the relationship between hearing and brain activity during a sentence comprehension task at various intelligibility levels in older adults. The results show no evidence of a motor/premotor modulation as a function of hearing thresholds (Peelle, Troiani, Grossman, & Wingfield, 2011). One exception is a brain morphometry study, in which performance during a sentence comprehension task presented at different intelligibility levels was compared in young and older adults. Results demonstrated a positive correlation between performance and gray matter volume in the left IFGtri (Wong, Ettlinger, Sheppard, Gunasekera, & Dhar, 2010). However, it is unlikely that IFGtri, which lies immediately anterior to the frontal operculum and is not classified as premotor cortex, contains motor knowledge of speech sounds. Speech tasks providing less linguistic context (e.g., using word-level instead of sentence-level stimuli) provide a slightly different picture. For instance, using a picture-word matching task performed under various intelligibility levels, Wong et al. (2009) found an increase in the activation of the premotor cortex (in a broadly defined region encompassing the middle frontal gyrus (MFG) and M1) that was positively correlated with performance. Similarly, a recent MRI study combining structural and functional measures found that the structure of the left premotor cortex mediates the negative effect of age on BOLD signal during a speech perception task consisting of passive audio-visual word presentation (videos of a talking female producing words; Tremblay, Dick, & Small, 2013). In contrast, a study examining simple word repetition performed by adults ranging in age from 20 to 65 years showed no age-related modulation in activity in the PM or the IFG during the task (Manan, Franz, NazlimYusoff, & Mukari, 2015).

Sublexical speech perception tasks, which presumably represent the greatest level of difficulty from a speech perception perspective since they offer no lexical or contextual information to aid speech perception, are rarer in the literature. In a recent study examining the relation between age and speech perception, it was found that, when controlling for hearing, speech perception declines with age. This behavioral decline was examined using a mediation approach, to determine whether age-related speech decline is mediated by structural or functional brain changes. No direct or indirect relationship between speech perception and the function and structure of the premotor cortex or IFG was found (Bilodeau-Mercure,

Lortie, Sato, Guitton, & Tremblay, 2015). An age-related decline in the cortical thickness of the PMv was found, but it did not influence speech perception. However, the intelligibility of the speech stimuli was associated with a modulation of the activity in the left PMv, in an age-independent fashion (though the relationship between BOLD and speech intelligibility was positive, which is inconsistent with a compensatory function).

Taken together, the aging literature on speech perception, as well as the clinical literature reviewed at the beginning of this section, provides relatively inconclusive evidence in support of a role for the motor/premotor cortex in speech perception. There is a tendency for the results to suggest that more difficult tasks, such as sublexical perception and tasks involving degraded auditory stimuli, might engage the premotor cortex more strongly in elderly individuals and lead to a decline in performance in patients. However, the only study of sublexical processing with aging did not report such an effect. Additional studies are needed to examine a wider range of tasks in line with the context-dependent motor theory of speech hypothesis.

14.6 FURTHER PERSPECTIVES

14.6.1 From motor theories of speech perception to embodied theories of language

The discovery of mirror neurons in the monkey, and the subsequent discovery of a system in humans exhibiting mirror-like properties, not only served as a catalyst for the study of speech perception/production interactions but also triggered a parallel research bloom in other fields of cognitive neuroscience. The discovery that premotor areas were engaged in goal-oriented action observation (e.g., Decety et al., 1997; di Pellegrino et al., 1992; Grafton et al., 1996) and motor imagery (Roth et al., 1996) was soon followed by the discovery that action words (e.g., Hauk, Johnsrude, & Pulvermüller, 2004; Pulvermüller, Härle, & Hummel, 2001), and action sentences (Aziz-Zadeh, Wilson, Rizzolatti, & Iacoboni, 2006; Tettamanti et al., 2005) also activated premotor areas. The finding of motor/premotor cortex activation during language comprehension has been interpreted to suggest that specific action representations are activated during action language understanding. This phenomenon is often referred to as *language embodiment*. This is contrast with the classical "disembodied" view that cognition is mediated, at least in part, by symbolic representations. Just as the MTSP has generated extensive discussion, so has the question as to whether motor/premotor representations are necessary or accessory to language comprehension more broadly (e.g., Fernandino & Iacoboni, 2010; Hickok, 2009; Mahon, 2015). As is the case for speech perception, several studies have shown that motor/premotor cortex responses during action language processing are context-sensitive (e.g., Alemanno et al., 2012; Schuil, Smits, & Zwaan, 2013; Tettamanti et al., 2008; Tomasino, Weiss, & Fink, 2010). Thus, the two fields of research shared some similar issues with interpretation of the evidence. Only limited clinical evidence favors the embodied language hypothesis—for example, it has been shown that processing of action verbs is impaired in patients with motor disorders such as Parkinson's disease (Boulenger et al., 2008) and motor neuron disease (Bak & Hodges, 2004), supporting the notion of a role for the motor system in action language comprehension. Moreover, Fazio et al. examined the ability of aphasic patients with lesions to the posterior IFG, and no apraxia, to perform an action comprehension task and showed that, compared to age-matched controls, action comprehension was reduced (Fazio et al., 2009), establishing a link between language and action comprehension deficits. A Voxel-based Lesion Symptom Mapping approach (VLSM), has further identified linguistic and non-linguistic action comprehension deficits in aphasia (Saygin, Wilson, Dronkers, & Bates, 2004). Behaviorally, the results demonstrated that both behaviors were impaired. However, the lesion mapping analysis revealed distinct lesion foci, with a focus in the IFG/PM for non-linguistic action understanding and more distributed and non-overlapping lesioned site for linguistic action processing. This is consistent with fMRI studies conducted in healthy subjects showing that distinct parts of the premotor cortex were active during action observation compared to processing of action sentences (Tremblay & Small, 2011a) or action word processing (Postle, McMahon, Ashton, Meredith, & de Zubicaray, 2008).

In sum, the MTSP and the language embodiment hypothesis suggest that hearing language (e.g., "kick") activates motor representation for at least two distinct purposes: to retrieve the motor programs associated with the sounds being processed (here the phonemes /k/, /I/, /k/), but only under specific conditions and depending on the task, and to retrieve those associated with the meaning of the words (here, the action of kicking with the foot). However, recent studies examining the implication motor/premotor cortex in language comprehension did not provide support for a causal role, as TMS had no effect on comprehension per se (Krieger-Redwood et al., 2013; Tremblay & Small, 2011b); although, in the Krieger-Redwood et al. study, the focus was not specifically on action language, but on word comprehension more generally. Alternative interpretations have been put forward, for example, a unifying role for PM in "motor syntax" (Fazio et al., 2009), but this suggestion awaits empirical support. It will be important, in the future, to study these two questions together to better understand the roles of the motor system in speech perception and language comprehension, and how these relate to each other.

14.6.2 Perception-production links beyond motor cortex: sensorimotor transformations in posterior cortical fields

In developing more integrated models of speech, we should consider a growing literature that has described consistent perception-production links *outside* motor/premotor cortex. An important requirement of successful spoken language use is the existence of parity, such that signalers and receivers can exchange roles (Fitch, 2010); this necessitates some capacity for conversion between input and output signals. Overlapping activations have been observed for speech perception and production, throughout superior temporal cortex and extending medially and posteriorly toward the parietal lobe (McGettigan et al., 2011; Tremblay & Small, 2011b). Some studies have reported equivalent activation in posterior fields on the planum temporale (PT) and around the temporoparietal junction or TPJ (including the supramarginal gyrus; SMG) during input and output (Tremblay & Small, 2011a, b), or indeed stronger responses during imagined/covert speech than during listening to speech (Buchsbaum, Hickok, & Humphries, 2001; Hickok, Buchsbaum, Humphries, & Muftuler, 2003). These latter findings are suggestive of a role in sensorimotor transformations and representations rather than basic auditory perception or imagery, and some authors have presented PT and the temporoparietal junction as a candidate region for the phonological store in working memory (e.g., Buchsbaum & D'Esposito, 2008). Such regions are potentially more central to speech sensorimotor processes than motor/premotor cortex: in a study of pseudoword perception and production, it was found that the magnitude of the BOLD response in PM was not modulated by syllabic complexity in perception, but that right PT did show such a sensitivity (Tremblay & Small, 2011b). In this case, the authors suggested context-dependent involvement of motor cortex in their study, where performance of the tasks required only a coarse-grained representation of articulatory detail, whereas this engaged PT in a more obligatory fashion (see also Deschamps & Tremblay, 2014, for passive sensitivity to syllabic structure in PT). Existing findings suggest a functional heterogeneity within subregions of the PT, where the caudal part in particular is insensitive to auditory feedback during speech yet is activated by tasks requiring auditory-to-motor conversion (whether for reading aloud or silently; Tremblay et al., 2013)—elaboration of the representations and processes subserved by these cortical fields, as well as their anatomical and functional connections with other frontotemporal nodes of the language system, will be integral to the future development of neurobiological models of speech (Dick & Tremblay, 2012).

14.7 Conclusion

Which is the most likely role for motor cortex in speech perception? We have described progress in the field of cognitive neuroscience in its quest to elaborate the role(s) of motor/premotor cortical fields in the perception of spoken language. Drawing together findings from neuroimaging, electrophysiology, and brain stimulation in healthy participants, as well as considering the evidence from brain injury and healthy aging, we acknowledge that motor processes and/or representations are involved in speech understanding, but that this is strongly dependent on context. As it stands, the empirical evidence suggests that while motor/premotor involvement in speech perception is neither fundamental nor essential, it cannot be dismissed as fully redundant. By now, many studies have demonstrated the online engagement of motor/premotor cortex by heard speech, with causal implications for perceptual performance. The degree to which these "motor responses" extract and represent the articulatory information in the signal is yet unclear—in the same way that the detectability of motor cortical activations appears to be dependent on the task and the listening situation, it may also be the case that similar factors modulate the granularity of representations within these sites. While there are interesting data emerging that support a qualitatively different role for motor cortex in the timing of conversational interactions—surely the natural habitat of speech—these are still few in number, and it remains to be seen whether these really are more fundamental to the evolution of spoken communicative behaviors across humanity.

Accepting that the motor/premotor cortex performs a variety of roles in speech perception, it is appropriate that neurocognitive models of speech processing should more keenly reflect the overlap and integration of processes within the input and output systems that have previously received rather independent treatment. Going forward, it will become increasingly important to model and measure the engagement of neural systems during contextualized and dynamic communicative interactions, rather than continuing to focus almost exclusively on speech as the disembodied and unilateral transmission of signals from talkers to listeners (McGettigan, 2015; Pickering & Garrod, 2013; Schilbach et al., 2013). This brings methodological challenges, for example in designing fMRI paradigms and analyses that can mitigate factors such as speech-related head movements associated with free conversation. When studying both perception and production of speech and considering the extensive and overlapping regions of the brain involved, it also becomes increasingly important to consider neural responses at the level of networks as well as local cortical representations—techniques such as independent components analysis can reveal the independent modulation of overlapping cortical nodes by task and condition, and the separation of domain-specific from domain-general contributions to task performance (see e.g., Geranmayeh et al., 2014). The comparison of speech and non-speech sound processing could also provide useful information to understand underlying computations and distinguish domain general from (potentially) speech-specific ones. Thus, a combination of more naturalistic designs and analyses combining region and network approaches might be key to furthering current understanding of the neural interactions underpinning perception and production.

Acknowledgments

P. T. holds a career award from the Fonds Québécois de la Recherche—Santé (FRQ-S); her research is funded by the Natural Sciences and Engineering Research Council of Canada (NSERC) (#195812603). C. M. is funded by the UK Economic and Social Research Council (ES/L01257X/1) and The Leverhulme Trust (RL-2016-013).

References

Abrams, D. A., Ryali, S., Chen, T., Balaban, E., Levitin, D. J., & Menon, V. (2013). Multivariate activation and connectivity patterns discriminate speech intelligibility in Wernicke's, Broca's, and Geschwind's areas. *Cerebral Cortex*, 23(7), 1703–14.

Agnew, Z., McGettigan, C., & Scott, S. (2011). Discriminating between auditory and motor cortical responses to speech and nonspeech mouth sounds. *Journal of Cognitive Neuroscience*, 23(12), 4038–47.

Alemanno, F., Houdayer, E., Cursi, M., Velikova, S., Tettamanti, M., Comi, G., ... Leocani, L. (2012). Action-related semantic content and negation polarity modulate motor areas during sentence reading: An event-related desynchronization study. *Brain Research*, 1484, 39–49.

Alexander, G. E., Crutcher, M. D., & DeLong, M. R. (1990). Basal ganglia-thalamocortical circuits: Parallel substrates for motor, oculomotor, "prefrontal" and "limbic" functions. *Progress in Brain Research, 85*, 119–46.

Arsenault, J. S., & Buchsbaum, B. R. (2015). Distributed neural representations of phonological features during speech perception. *The Journal of Neuroscience, 35*(2), 634–42.

Aziz-Zadeh, L., Wilson, S. M., Rizzolatti, G., & Iacoboni, M. (2006). Congruent embodied representations for visually presented actions and linguistic phrases describing actions. *Current Biology, 16*(18), 1818–23.

Bak, T. H., & Hodges, J. R. (2004). The effects of motor neurone disease on language: Further evidence. *Brain and Language, 89*(2), 354–61.

Bilodeau-Mercure, M., Lortie, C. L., Sato, M., Guitton, M. J., & Tremblay, P. (2015). The neurobiology of speech perception decline in aging. *Brain Structure & Function, 220*(2), 979–97.

Bögels, S., Magyari, L., & Levinson, S. C. (2015). Neural signatures of response planning occur midway through an incoming question in conversation. *Scientific Reports, 5*(12881), 1–11.

Bohland, J. W., & Guenther, F. H. (2006). An fMRI investigation of syllable sequence production. *NeuroImage, 32*(2), 821–41.

Bouchard, K. E., Mesgarani, N., Johnson, K., & Chang, E. F. (2013). Functional organization of human sensorimotor cortex for speech articulation. *Nature, 495*(7441), 327–32.

Boulenger, V., Mechtouff, L., Thobois, S., Broussolle, E., Jeannerod, M., & Nazir, T. A. (2008). Word processing in Parkinson's disease is impaired for action verbs but not for concrete nouns. *Neuropsychologia, 46*(2), 743–56.

Bowers, A., Saltuklaroglu, T., Harkrider, A., & Cuellar, M. (2013). Suppression of the mu rhythm during speech and non-speech discrimination revealed by independent component analysis: Implications for sensorimotor integration in speech processing. *PLoS One, 8*(8), e72024.

Breshears, J. D., Molinaro, A. M., & Chang, E. F. (2015). A probabilistic map of the human ventral sensorimotor cortex using electrical stimulation. *Journal of Neurosurgery, 123*(August), 340–9.

Buchsbaum, B. R., & D'Esposito, M. (2008). The search for the phonological store: From loop to convolution. *Journal of Cognitive Neuroscience, 20*(5), 762–78.

Buchsbaum, B. R., Hickok, G., & Humphries, C. (2001). Role of left posterior superior temporal gyrus in phonological processing for speech perception and production. *Cognitive Science, 25*(5), 663–78.

Callan, D., Callan, A., Gamez, M., Sato, M., & Kawato, M. (2010). Premotor cortex mediates perceptual performance. *NeuroImage, 51*(2), 844–58.

Cheung, C., Hamilton, L. S., Johnson, K., & Chang, E. F. (2016). The auditory representation of speech sounds in human motor cortex. *eLife, 5*, pii e12577.

Correia, J. M., Jansma, B. M., & Bonte, M. (2015). Decoding articulatory features from fMRI responses in dorsal speech regions. *Journal of Neuroscience, 35*(45), 15015–25.

D'Ausilio, A., Maffongelli, L., Bartoli, E., Campanella, M., Ferrari, E., Berry, J., & Fadiga, L. (2014). Listening to speech recruits specific tongue motor synergies as revealed by transcranial magnetic stimulation and tissue-Doppler ultrasound imaging. *Philosophical Transactions of The Royal Society: B, 369*, 20130418.

D'Ausilio, A., Pulvermüller, F., Salmas, P., Bufalari, I., Begliomini, C., & Fadiga, L. (2009). The motor somatotopy of speech perception. *Current Biology, 19*(5), 381–5.

Davis, M. H., & Johnsrude, I. S. (2003). Hierarchical processing in spoken language comprehension. *Journal of Neuroscience, 23*(8), 3423–31.

Davis, M. H., & Johnsrude, I. S. (2007). Hearing speech sounds: Top-down influences on the interface between audition and speech perception. *Hearing Research*, 229(1–2), 132–47.

Decety, J., Grezes, J., Costes, N., Perani, D., Jeannerod, M., Procyk, E., . . . & Fazio, F. (1997). Brain activity during observation of actions. Influence of action content and subject's strategy. *Brain*, 120(Pt 1), 1763–77.

Deschamps, I., & Tremblay, P. (2014). Sequencing at the syllabic and supra-syllabic levels during speech perception: An fMRI study. *Frontiers in Human Neuroscience*, 8, 1–14.

di Pellegrino, G., Fadiga, L., Fogassi, L., Gallese, V., & Rizzolatti, G. (1992). Understanding motor events: A neurophysiological study. *Experimental Brain Research*, 91(1), 176–80.

Dick, A. S., & Tremblay, P. (2012). Beyond the arcuate fasciculus: Consensus and controversy in the connectional anatomy of language. *Brain*, 135(Pt 12), 3529–50.

Du, Y., Buchsbaum, B. R., Grady, C. L., & Alain, C. (2014). Noise differentially impacts phoneme representations in the auditory and speech motor systems. *Proceedings of the National Academy of Sciences of the United States of America*, 111(19), 7126–31.

Dum, R. P., & Strick, P. L. (1991). The origin of corticospinal projections from the premotor areas in the frontal lobe. *The Journal of Neuroscience*, 11(3), 667–89.

Eckert, M. A., Walczak, A., Ahlstrom, J., Denslow, S., Horwitz, A., & Dubno, J. R. (2008). Age-related effects on word recognition: Reliance on cognitive control systems with structural declines in speech-responsive cortex. *JARO—Journal of the Association for Research in Otolaryngology*, 9(2), 252–9.

Erb, J., & Obleser, J. (2013). Upregulation of cognitive control networks in older adults' speech comprehension. *Frontiers in Systems Neuroscience*, 7, 116.

Evans, S., & Davis, M. H. (2015). Hierarchical organization of auditory and motor representations in speech perception: Evidence from searchlight similarity analysis. *Cerebral Cortex*, 25(12), 4772–88.

Fadiga, L., Craighero, L., Buccino, G., & Rizzolatti, G. (2002). Speech listening specifically modulates the excitability of tongue muscles: a TMS study. *European Journal of Neuroscience*, 15(2), 399–402.

Fazio, P., Cantagallo, A., Craighero, L., D'Ausilio, A., Roy, A. C., Pozzo, T., . . . & Fadiga, L. (2009). Encoding of human action in Broca's area. *Brain*, 132(Pt 7), 1980–8.

Fernandino, L., & Iacoboni, M. (2010). Are cortical motor maps based on body parts or coordinated actions? Implications for embodied semantics. *Brain and Language*, 112(1), 44–53.

Fitch, W. T. (2010). *The Evolution of Language*. Cambridge University Press, Cambridge.

Formisano, E., De Martino, F., Bonte, M., & Goebel, R. (2008). "Who" is saying "what"? Brain-based decoding of human voice and speech. *Science*, 322(5903), 970–3.

Foti, D., & Roberts, F. (2016). The neural dynamics of speech perception: Dissociable networks for processing linguistic content and monitoring speaker turn-taking. *Brain and Language*, 157–158, 63–71.

Fowler, C. A. (1996). Listeners do hear sounds, not tongues. *The Journal of the Acoustical Society of America*, 99(3), 1730–41.

Fowler, C. A., Shankweiler, D., & Studdert-Kennedy, M. (2015). Perception of the speech code revisited: Speech is alphabetic after all. *Psychological Review*, 123(2), 125–50.

Galantucci, B., Fowler, C. A., & Turvey, M. T. (2006). The motor theory of speech perception reviewed. *Psychonomic Bulletin Review*, 13(3), 361–77.

Gallese, V., Fadiga, L., Fogassi, L., & Rizzolatti, G. (1996). Action recognition in the premotor cortex. *Brain*, 119(Pt 2), 593–609.

Geranmayeh, F., Wise, R. J., Mehta, A., & Leech, R. (2014). Overlapping networks engaged during spoken language production and its cognitive control. *Journal of Neuroscience*, 34(26), 8728–40.

Grafton, S. T., Arbib, M. A., Fadiga, L., & Rizzolatti, G. (1996). Localization of grasp representations in humans by positron emission tomography. 2. Observation compared with imagination. *Experimental Brain Research*, 112(1), 103–111.

Guenther, F. H., Ghosh, S. S., & Tourville, J. A. (2006). Neural modeling and imaging of the cortical interactions underlying syllable production. *Brain and Language*, 96(3), 280–301.

Hadley, L. V., Novembre, G., Keller, P. E., & Pickering, M. J. (2015). Causal role of motor simulation in turn-taking behavior. *The Journal of Neuroscience: The Official Journal of the Society for Neuroscience*, 35(50), 16516–20.

Harris, K. C., Dubno, J. R., Keren, N. I., Ahlstrom, J. B., & Eckert, M. A. (2009). Speech recognition in younger and older adults: A dependency on low-level auditory cortex. *The Journal of Neuroscience: The Official Journal of the Society for Neuroscience*, 29(19), 6078–87.

Hauk, O., Johnsrude, I., & Pulvermüller, F. (2004). Somatotopic representation of action words in human motor and premotor cortex. *Neuron*, 41(2), 301–7.

Hervais-Adelman, A. G., Carlyon, R. P., Johnsrude, I. S., & Davis, M. H. (2012). Brain regions recruited for the effortful comprehension of noise-vocoded words. *Language and Cognitive Processes*, 27(7–8), 1145–66.

Hickok, G. (2009). Eight problems for the mirror neuron theory of action understanding in monkeys and humans. *Journal of Cognitive Neuroscience*, 21(7), 1229–43.

Hickok, G. (2010). The role of mirror neurons in speech perception and action word semantics. *Language and Cognitive Processes*, 25(6), 749–76.

Hickok, G., Buchsbaum, B., Humphries, C., & Muftuler, T. (2003). Auditory-motor interaction revealed by fMRI: Speech, music, and working memory in area Spt. *Journal of Cognitive Neuroscience*, 15(5), 673–82.

Hickok, G., Costanzo, M., Capasso, R., & Miceli, G. (2011). The role of Broca's area in speech perception: Evidence from aphasia revisited. *Brain and Language*, 119(3), 214–20.

Hwang, J. H., Li, C. W., Wu, C. W., Chen, J. H., & Liu, T. C. (2007). Aging effects on the activation of the auditory cortex during binaural speech listening in white noise: An fMRI study. *Audiology and Neurotology*, 12(5), 285–94.

Jenabi, M., Peck, K. K., Young, R. J., Brennan, N., & Holodny, A. I. (2015). Identification of the corticobulbar tracts of the tongue and face using deterministic and probabilistic DTI fiber tracking in patients with brain tumor. *American Journal of Neuroradiology*, 36(11), 2036–41.

Jurgens, U. (2002). Neural pathways underlying vocal control. *Neuroscience and Biobehavioral Reviews*, 26(2), 235–58.

Jurgens, U. (2009). The neural control of vocalization in mammals: A review. *Journal of Voice*, 23(1), 1–10.

Kohler, E., Keysers, C., Umilta, M. A., Fogassi, L., Gallese, V., & Rizzolatti, G. (2002). Hearing sounds, understanding actions: action representation in mirror neurons. *Science*, 297(5582), 846–8.

Krieger-Redwood, K., Gaskell, M. G., Lindsay, S., & Jefferies, E. (2013). The selective role of premotor cortex in speech perception: a contribution to phoneme judgements but not speech comprehension. *Journal of Cognitive Neuroscience*, 25(12), 2179–88.

Kriegeskorte, N., Mur, M., & Bandettini, P. A. (2008). Representational similarity analysis— connecting the branches of systems neuroscience. *Frontiers in Systems Neuroscience*, 2, 4.

Lane, H. (1965). The Motor Theory of speech perception: A critical review. *Psychological Review*, 72(4), 275–309.

Lecours, A., Chain, F., Poncet, M., Nespoulous, J., & Joanette, Y. (1992). Paris 1908: The hot summer of aphasiology or a season in the life of a chair. *Brain and Language, 42*(2), 105–52.

Liberman, A. M. (1957). Some results of research on speech perception. *The Journal of the Acoustical Society of America, 29*(1), 117.

Liberman, A. M., Cooper, F. S., Shankweiler, D. P., & Studdert-Kennedy, M. (1967). Perception of the speech code. *Psychological Review, 74*(6), 431–61.

Liberman, A. M., Delattre, P., & Cooper, F. S. (1952). The role of selected stimulus-variables in the perception of the unvoiced stop consonants. *The American Journal of Psychology, 65*(4), 497–516.

Liberman, A. M., & Mattingly, I. G. (1985). The motor theory of speech perception revised. *Cognition, 21*(1), 1–36.

Lotto, A. J., Hickok, G. S., & Holt, L. L. (2009). Reflections on mirror neurons and speech perception. *Trends in Cognitive Sciences, 13*(3), 110–14.

Mahon, B. Z. (2015). What is embodied about cognition? *Language, Cognition and Neuroscience, 30*(4), 420–9.

Manan, H. A., Franz, E. A., NazlimYusoff, A., & Mukari, S. Z.-M. S. (2015). Aging effects on working memory: Fronto-parietal network involvement on tasks involving speech stimuli. *Neurology, Psychiatry and Brain Research, 21*(1), 64–72.

Massaro, D., & Chen, T. (2008). The motor theory of speech perception revisited. *Psychonomic Bulletin & Review, 15*, 453–7.

McGettigan, C. (2015). The Social Life of Voices: Studying the neural bases for the expression and perception of the self and others during spoken communication. *Frontiers in Human Neuroscience, 9*, 129.

McGettigan, C., Warren, J. E., Eisner, F., Marshall, C. R., Shanmugalingam, P., & Scott, S. K. (2011). Neural correlates of sublexical processing in phonological working memory. *Journal of Cognitive Neuroscience, 23*, 961–77.

Meister, I. G., Wilson, S. M., Deblieck, C., Wu, A. D., & Iacoboni, M. (2007). The essential role of premotor cortex in speech perception. *Current Biology, 17*(19), 1692–6.

Mesgarani, N., Cheung, C., Johnson, K., & Chang, E. F. (2014). Phonetic feature encoding in human superior temporal gyrus. *Science (New York, N.Y.), 343*(6174), 1006–10.

Moineau, S., Dronkers, N. F., & Bates, E. (2005). Exploring the processing continuum of single-word comprehension in aphasia. *Journal of Speech, Language, and Hearing Research: JSLHR, 48*(4), 884–96.

Osnes, B., Hugdahl, K., & Specht, K. (2011). Effective connectivity analysis demonstrates involvement of premotor cortex during speech perception. *NeuroImage, 54*(3), 2437–45.

Peelle, J. E., Troiani, V., Grossman, M., & Wingfield, A. (2011). Hearing loss in older adults affects neural systems supporting speech comprehension. *The Journal of Neuroscience, 31*(35), 12638–43.

Pickering, M. J., & Garrod, S. (2013). An integrated theory of language production and comprehension. *Behavioral and Brain Sciences, 36*(4), 329–47.

Postle, N., McMahon, K. L., Ashton, R., Meredith, M., & de Zubicaray, G. I. (2008). Action word meaning representations in cytoarchitectonically defined primary and premotor cortices. *NeuroImage, 43*(3), 634–44.

Prinz, W. (1997). Perception and action planning. *European Journal of Cognitive Psychology, 9*(2), 129–54.

Pulvermüller, F., & Fadiga, L. (2010). Active perception: Sensorimotor circuits as a cortical basis for language. *Nature Reviews Neuroscience, 11*(5), 351–60.

Pulvermüller, F., Härle, M., & Hummel, F. (2001). Walking or talking? Behavioral and neurophysiological correlates of action verb processing. *Brain and Language, 78*(2), 143–68.

Pulvermüller, F., Huss, M., Kherif, F., Moscoso del Prado Martin, F., Hauk, O., & Shtyrov, Y. (2006). Motor cortex maps articulatory features of speech sounds. *Proceedings of the National Academy of Sciences of the United States of America, 103*(20), 7865–70.

Ramachandran, V. S. (2000). MIRROR NEURONS and imitation learning as the driving force behind the great leap forward in human evolution. Available at: https://www.edge.org/conversation/mirror-neurons-and-imitation-learning-as-the-driving-force-behind-the-great-leap-forward-in-human-evolution

Rizzolatti, G., & Arbib, M. A. (1998). Language within our grasp. *Trends in Neurosciences, 21*(5), 188–94.

Rizzolatti, G., & Craighero, L. (2004). The mirror-neuron system. *Annual Review of Neuroscience, 27*, 169–92.

Rogalski, Y., Peelle, J. E., & Reilly, J. (2011). Effects of perceptual and contextual enrichment on visual confrontation naming in adult aging. *Journal of Speech, Language, and Hearing Research: JSLHR, 54*(5), 1349–60.

Roth, M., Decety, J., Raybaudi, M., Massarelli, R., Delon-Martin, C., Segebarth, C., . . . & Jeannerod, M. (1996). Possible involvement of primary motor cortex in mentally simulated movement: A functional magnetic resonance imaging study. *NeuroReport, 7*(7), 1280–4.

Samuel, A. G. (2011). Speech Perception. *Annual Review of Psychology, 62*, 49–72.

Sato, M., Tremblay, P., & Gracco, V. L. (2009). A mediating role of the premotor cortex in phoneme segmentation. *Brain and Language, 111*(1), 1–7.

Saygin, A. P., Wilson, S. M., Dronkers, N. F., & Bates, E. (2004). Action comprehension in aphasia: Linguistic and non-linguistic deficits and their lesion correlates. *Neuropsychologia, 42*(13), 1788–804.

Schilbach, L., Timmermans, B., Reddy, V., Costall, A., Bente, G., Schlicht, T., & Vogeley, K. (2013). Toward a second-person neuroscience. *Behavioral and Brain Sciences, 36*(4), 393–414.

Schuil, K. D. I., Smits, M., & Zwaan, R. A. (2013). Sentential context modulates the involvement of the motor cortex in action language processing: An FMRI study. *Frontiers in Human Neuroscience, 7*(April), 100.

Schwartz, M. F., Faseyitan, O., Kim, J., & Coslett, H. B. (2012). The dorsal stream contribution to phonological retrieval in object naming. *Brain, 135*(12), 3799–814.

Scott, S. K., Blank, C. C., Rosen, S., & Wise, R. J. (2000). Identification of a pathway for intelligible speech in the left temporal lobe. *Brain, 123*, 2400–6.

Scott, S. K., & Johnsrude, I. S. (2003). The neuroanatomical and functional organization of speech perception. *Trends in Neuroscience, 26*(2), 100–7.

Scott, S. K., McGettigan, C., & Eisner, F. (2009). A little more conversation, a little less action— candidate roles for the motor cortex in speech perception. *Nature Reviews Neuroscience, 10*(4), 295–302.

Shankweiler, D., & Fowler, C. A. (2015). Seeking a reading machine for the blind and discovering the speech code. *History of Psychology, 18*(1), 78–99.

Skipper, J. I., Goldin-Meadow, S., Nusbaum, H. C., & Small, S. L. (2007). Speech-associated gestures, Broca's area, and the human mirror system. *Brain and Language, 101*(3), 260–77.

Stasenko, A., Bonn, C., Teghipco, A., Garcea, F. E., Sweet, C., Dombovy, M., . . . & Mahon, B. Z. (2015). A causal test of the motor theory of speech perception: A case of impaired speech production and spared speech perception. *Cognitive Neuropsychology, 32*(2), 38–57.

Stasenko, A., Garcea, F. E., & Mahon, B. Z. (2013). What happens to the motor theory of perception when the motor system is damaged? *Language and Cognition*, 5(2-3), 225-38.

Tettamanti, M., Buccino, G., Saccuman, M. C., Gallese, V., Danna, M., Scifo, P., . . . & Perani, D. (2005). Listening to action-related sentences activates fronto-parietal motor circuits. *Journal of Cognitive Neuroscience*, 17(2), 273-81.

Tettamanti, M., Manenti, R., Della Rosa, P. A., Falini, A., Perani, D., Cappa, S. F., & Moro, A. (2008). Negation in the brain: Modulating action representations. *NeuroImage*, 43(2), 358-67.

Tomasino, B., Weiss, P. H., & Fink, G. R. (2010). To move or not to move: Imperatives modulate action-related verb processing in the motor system. *Neuroscience*, 169(1), 246-58.

Tremblay, P., Baroni, M., & Hasson, U. (2013). Processing of speech and non-speech sounds in the supratemporal plane: Auditory input preference does not predict sensitivity to statistical structure. *NeuroImage*, 66, 318-32.

Tremblay, P., Deschamps, I., Baroni, M., & Hasson, U. (2016). Neural sensitivity to syllable frequency and mutual information in speech perception and production. *NeuroImage*, 136(1), 106-21.

Tremblay, P., & Dick, A. (2016). Broca and Wernicke are dead, or moving past the classic model of language neurobiology. *Brain and Language*, 162, 60-71.

Tremblay, P., Dick, A. S., & Small, S. L. (2013). Functional and structural aging of the speech sensorimotor neural system: Functional magnetic resonance imaging evidence. *Neurobiology of Aging*, 34(8), 1935-51.

Tremblay, P., & Small, S. L. (2011a). From language comprehension to action understanding and back again. *Cerebral Cortex*, 21(5), 1166-77.

Tremblay, P., & Small, S. L. (2011b). On the context-dependent nature of the contribution of the ventral premotor cortex to speech perception. *NeuroImage*, 57(4), 1561-71.

Watkins, K. E., Strafella, A. P., & Paus, T. (2003). Seeing and hearing speech excites the motor system involved in speech production. *Neuropsychologia*, 41(8), 989-94.

Wild, C. J., Yusuf, A., Wilson, D. E., Peelle, J. E., Davis, M. H., & Johnsrude, I. S. (2012). Effortful listening: The processing of degraded speech depends critically on attention. *Journal of Neuroscience*, 32(40), 14010-21.

Wilson, S. M., & Iacoboni, M. (2006). Neural responses to non-native phonemes varying in producibility: Evidence for the sensorimotor nature of speech perception. *NeuroImage*, 33(1), 316-25.

Wilson, S. M., Saygin, A. P., Sereno, M. I., & Iacoboni, M. (2004). Listening to speech activates motor areas involved in speech production. *Nature Neuroscience*, 7(7), 701-2.

Wong, P. C., Jin, J. X., Gunasekera, G. M., Abel, R., Lee, E. R., & Dhar, S. (2009). Aging and cortical mechanisms of speech perception in noise. *Neuropsychologia*, 47(3), 693-703.

Wong, P. C. M., Ettlinger, M., Sheppard, J. P., Gunasekera, G. M., & Dhar, S. (2010). Neuroanatomical characteristics and speech perception in noise in older adults. *Ear and Hearing*, 31(4), 471-9.

Yuen, I., Davis, M. H., Brysbaert, M., & Rastle, K. (2010). Activation of articulatory information in speech perception. *Proceedings of the National Academy of Sciences of the United States of America*, 107(2), 592-7.

SECTION II
Lexical level

CHAPTER 15

SPOKEN WORD PRODUCTION
Representation, retrieval, and integration

LINDA R. WHEELDON
AND AGNIESZKA E. KONOPKA

15.1 INTRODUCTION

Spoken word production has been in the spotlight of psycholinguistic research since the publication of Levelt's classic work, *Speaking: From intention to articulation* (1989). The result is now hundreds of studies on the sequence and timing of processes involved in the production of individual words, beginning with activation of the conceptual information needed to retrieve words and ending with articulation. Here, we outline research that focuses on two distinct stages of processing: semantic and lexical aspects of word production, followed by morphological and phonological processing. In both cases, we first outline questions that have received the most attention in the field: we briefly summarize models of *lexical representation* and models of *lexical selection* that have focused on the retrieval of single words. These models agree that access to lexical information is not holistic but that different kinds of information become available at different points in time during production, with access to semantic and syntactic information preceding access to information about lexical form (e.g., Caramazza, 1997; Dell, 1986; Garrett, 1980; Levelt, Roelofs, & Meyer, 1999). The structure of our review reflects this dichotomy. At each level of processing we also address the question of *lexical integration* (i.e., the process of producing and integrating words into longer sentences). Integration encompasses the goal of all production research: in everyday language use, words are produced in the company of other words, as nearly everything we say after the age of three consists of multiword phrases or full sentences. Thus, comprehensive production models must be able to account for the sequencing and timing of lexical processing in multiword utterances and for the effects of utterance context on the planning of lexical forms. Nevertheless, lexical integration has been the focus of many fewer studies to date. We describe work in this area from different paradigms: single-object naming paradigms, interference paradigms, and paradigms eliciting full sentences.

15.2 Semantic and lexical processing

15.2.1 Representation: Words in networks

Questions regarding lexical representation focus on two properties of words: semantic and syntactic properties. Words are linguistic units conveying meaning, so discussions of their *semantic* properties fall within the purview of models of semantic representation. These models address two main questions: what are word meanings and how are words interconnected? The *syntactic* properties of words are in turn described in language production models, and questions addressed by these models concern the nature and storage of syntactic information.

With respect to word meanings, two different perspectives are outlined in models that assume *non-decompositional* and *decompositional* conceptual representations (see Leshinskaya & Caramazza, 2014; Vigliocco & Vinson, 2007; Vinson, Andrews, & Vigliocco, 2014, for reviews and discussions). In *non-decompositional* models, word meanings are represented holistically, and words correspond roughly to *lexical concepts*, i.e., to conceptual units for which lexicons have unique linguistic terms (e.g., the word *"mouse"* for the concept *mouse* in English). In contrast, *decompositional* models assume distributed representations: word meanings are decomposed into features and these features can be shared across concepts (e.g., the concept *mouse* shares features with other small, furry animals). Individual concepts are thus defined in terms of unique feature combinations, and individual words are "pointers" to distributed semantic representations.

Both types of models propose that concepts in semantic memory are organized in a network. Similarity between concepts is operationalized in terms of connection strength between concepts (non-decompositional models) or feature overlap across concepts (compositional models). The main architectural assumptions of these models, such as the plausibility of a one-to-one relationship between entities in the external world and individual lexical concepts, have been debated at length. Cross-linguistic differences in lexicalization have also fueled debates about the relationship between prelinguistic and linguistic representations, and about the degree of language-specificity in these representations (e.g., Vigliocco & Kita, 2006). Importantly, whatever the nature of concept-to-word mappings, psycholinguistic models agree, that the mental lexicon largely reflects the organization of concepts in semantic memory: activation of one word entails coactivation of its semantic neighbors (a lexical *cohort*), modulated by semantic distance (Caramazza, 1997; Dell, 1986; Levelt et al., 1999; Vigliocco, Vinson, Damian, & Levelt, 2002).

The syntactic properties of words are described in models of lexical access (i.e., models concerned with the structure of *linguistic* representations). The most detailed account is Levelt et al.'s (1999) WEAVER++ model (also see Dell & O'Séaghdha, 1992; Garrett, 1975; Indefrey & Levelt, 2004; Jescheniak & Levelt, 1994). The model proposes a dual-stage structure for lexical representations: lexical concepts are linked to *lemmas* (linguistic units or nodes that include language-specific syntactic information) and lemmas are linked to *lexemes* (linguistic units or nodes that include language-specific, phonological word forms).

Syntactic information stored at the lemma level includes, for example, grammatical class, gender, and number for nouns, and tense and aspect for verbs. Nodes that specify this information are shared across lemmas with the same syntactic properties. From the point of view of representation, lemmas lie at the interface of concepts and language, so these syntactic properties convey a combination of conceptual and linguistic information. For nouns and verbs, grammatical class is heavily dependent on meaning: there is a relatively transparent relationship (marked either via word order or morphology) between a word's meaning and its grammatical function in any multiword utterance. The conceptual basis of grammatical gender for nouns is more controversial, although there is some consensus that gender categories are largely symbolic (see Baron, 1971; Corbett, 1991; Kousta et al., 2008; Sera et al., 2002; Vigliocco et al., 2005; Vigliocco & Franck, 1999, for discussions). The evidence is mixed for grammatical number, as some aspects of grammatical number may be conceptually motivated (see, e.g., Bock et al., 2006; Middleton et al., 2004).

The existence of the lemma/lexeme distinction is disputed by Caramazza (1997; also see Caramazza & Miozzo, 1997) who proposed that the lemma level is superfluous in models of lexical access. The argument is based on evidence from patients suggesting that prior access to syntactic information is not required for access to phonological information. On this account, lemmas can thus be replaced with modality-specific lexical nodes, and syntactic and phonological information can be stored in independent networks (see Roelofs, Meyer, & Levelt, 1998, for a response).

15.2.2 Selection and retrieval: Words and their neighbors

Speakers produce language to communicate complex meanings, and doing so requires fast and error-free retrieval of words from the mental lexicon. We summarize studies focusing on single word retrieval and then turn to the effects of word neighbors on the retrieval process.

15.2.2.1 *Individual words*

In classic word production paradigms, speakers see and name pictures of objects as quickly and accurately as possible. The ease of object naming varies with conceptual, object-specific variables (such as the ease of object recognition and conceptual accessibility) and word-specific variables (such as lexical frequency, age of acquisition, codability, and name agreement; see e.g., Brysbaert et al., 2016, for a recent review). It is generally agreed that word activation levels reflect experience and familiarity. Recent use of a word temporarily boosts its activation levels: retrieval times are approximately 600 ms when unprimed (estimated by Indefrey & Levelt, 2004; also see Bates et al., 2003; Shao & Stiegert, 2016; Snodgrass & Yuditsky, 1996) and approximately 100 ms faster when primed (Wheeldon & Monsell, 1992). Repeated use of a particular concept-to-word retrieval pathway also produces a longer-lasting cumulative decrease in retrieval speed (e.g., the word *cat* is retrieved more quickly than *possum*; Jescheniak & Levelt, 1994).

Research in this domain focused largely on two challenges in estimating the effects of cumulative experience on retrieval. The first of these challenges is finding an appropriate index of frequency (see Brysbaert & New, 2009). On different accounts, word frequency or familiarity may depend on the "solidification" of lexical representations, their place in lexical networks, or the ease of accessing information at the lemma and lexeme levels. The key candidates for frequency measures have been, traditionally, word frequency counts and age-of-acquisition estimates. These measures are highly correlated, and there is mixed evidence concerning the extent to which they account for unique variance in word retrieval times (Barry et al., 2001; Belke et al., 2005; Brown & Watson, 1987; Brysbaert et al., 2000; Ellis & Lambon Ralph, 2000; Kittredge et al., 2008; Lewis et al., 2001; Morrison & Ellis, 1995; Shao & Stiegert, 2016). It is thus also debatable whether they tap into different aspects of the retrieval process: frequency effects may be specific to *lexical* access (instead of prelexical processing; Almeida et al., 2007), while age of acquisition may better reflect ease of access to either *semantic* information (Belke et al., 2005) or *phonological* information during lexical access (Barry et al., 2001; Kittredge et al., 2008; see Johnston & Barry, 2006, for a review). Estimating word frequency is also complicated by the fact that, in practice, infrequently used words can nevertheless be retrieved quickly because differences in word use need not imply differences in word knowledge. A recently developed index that can eschew this problem is *word prevalence* (Brysbaert, Stevens, Mandera, & Keuleers, 2016; Keuleers, Stevens, Mandera, & Brysbaert, 2015). Word prevalence captures overall word knowledge or familiarity; thus, it quantifies word familiarity in terms of subjective word frequency, and has so far been shown to account for variance in lexical decision times not explained by traditional predictors.

A second challenge in this area has been to determine the locus of frequency effects: frequency differences between words may emerge at the level of lexical representations or at a prelexical, perceptual stage (Almeida et al, 2007; Bates et al., 2003; Caramazza, 1997; Jescheniak & Levelt, 1994; Levelt, Roelofs, & Meyer, 1999; Kittredge, Dell, Verkuilen, & Schwartz, 2008; Roelofs, 1997). Jescheniak & Levelt's (1994) classic study showed that tasks engaging lexical processing (like word translation) show reaction time (RT) differences between high- and low-frequency words (i.e., high-frequency words are produced more quickly), while tasks requiring object categorization or grammatical gender judgments do not. This places frequency differences as originating during retrieval of lexical forms. However, a variety of inconsistent findings have since called this conclusion into question (see Kittredge et al., 2008, for a review). Kittredge et al.'s (2008) analysis of aphasic naming errors suggests that frequency can influence retrieval of both semantic and phonological information, but with stronger consequences at the phonological level.

15.2.2.2 *Words in networks*

A key property of lexical retrieval is, naturally, that words are retrieved *from* a rich mental lexicon: production of any word always occurs in the context of activation of other words. This context may be implicit: activating a word (e.g., *mouse*) entails automatic activation of semantic and phonological neighbors (e.g., *rat, house*) as well as thematic associates (e.g., *cheese*), and word retrieval times are sensitive to semantic and phonological neighborhood density (see next for a discussion of phonological effects). A context may also be provided explicitly, as in picture-word interference paradigms where speakers name a pictured object presented with a superimposed distractor word (the name of an object that is semantically or phonologically related to the target object). In both cases, this context is "hard-wired" in the lexicon due to speakers' lifelong accumulation of semantic and lexical knowledge.

Picture-word interference paradigms are now standard tools for testing hypotheses about the nature of lexical access (competitive vs. non-competitive access) and the time-course of lexical access (serial vs. interactive retrieval models; see Glaser, 1992, and Vigliocco & Hartsuiker, 2002, for reviews).

Is lexical access competitive or non-competitive? Retrieval of words from a network requires a fast selection mechanism, one able to retrieve the target word out of a sea of activation of related words. The fact that non-target words can slow down word retrieval lead to the development of competitive lexical access theories: many studies reported semantic interference when objects are named in the presence of semantic distractors (e.g., naming a picture of a *sheep* in the presence of the word *goat*). By hypothesis, the semantic distractors delay naming latencies for the target object as they compete for selection, and competition is assumed to increase with semantic similarity of targets and distractors (Abdel-Rahman & Aristei, 2010; Abdel-Rahman & Melinger, 2009; Belke, Meyer, & Damian, 2005; Bloem & La Heij, 2003; Bloem et al., 2004; Damian & Bowers, 2003; Damian, Vigliocco, & Levelt, 2001; Glaser & Düngelhoff, 1984; Piai, Roelofs, & Schriefers, 2011; Schriefers, Meyer, & Levelt, 1990; Roelofs, 1992, 2003; Roelofs & Piai, 2015; Schriefers et al., 1990; Wheeldon & Monsell, 1994). Damian and Bowers (2003) place the locus of semantic interference effects specifically at the lexical level (i.e., at the level of competing lexical items): interference effects are observed in picture-word interference paradigms but not picture-picture interference paradigms, ruling out the possibility of semantic interference indexing competition between prelexical representations.

The controversy over competitive lexical access arises because semantic distractors do not generate consistent interference effects; for example, close semantic associates as well as thematic associates have also been shown to facilitate, instead of interfere with, object naming (Mahon et al., 2007). The proposal of non-competitive accounts is that naming delays are produced only by distractors that meet response-selection criteria (e.g., words that are part of a trial-specific response set). Naming delays occurring with more distant semantic associates may then be reinterpreted as originating from a postlexical selection process that requires time to remove non-target words from a temporary buffer (the response exclusion hypothesis; Caramazza, 1997; Costa et al., 2005; Dhooge & Hartsuiker, 2010; Finkbeiner & Caramazza, 2006; Janssen et al., 2008; Kuipers, La Heij, & Costa, 2006; Mahon, Costa, Peterson, Vargas, & Caramazza, 2007; Mahon, Garcea, & Navarrete, 2012; Miozzo & Caramazza, 2003).

Is lexical retrieval serial or interactive? In theory, models of lexical representation with a multilevel architecture (i.e., links from concepts to lemmas, to lexemes, and to phonology) allow for multiple plausible possibilities of information flow during production. Indefrey and Levelt (2004) describe the overall sequence of events with time-windows derived from behavioral and imaging studies (also see Bürki & Laganaro, 2014), and lexical access models make more specific assumptions about the directionality of information flow between stages.

One proposal is that retrieval processes occur in discrete stages. In *serial* models, activation is assumed to flow from higher levels in the production system to lower levels unidirectionally, and all processing at one level must be completed before information is passed down to the next level (Levelt, Roelofs, & Meyer, 1999; Roelofs, 1992, 1997). For example, retrieving the word *couch* begins with activation of the lexical concept *couch* and possible coactivation of the lexical concept *sofa*, but is followed by selection of the lemma for *couch* alone and retrieval of the phonological form for *couch* alone. Other serial models allow cascading, that is, the possibility of activation spreading down from a higher level to the next level before processing is completed at the higher level (Costa, Caramazza, & Sebastián-Gallés, 2000;

Cutting & Ferreira, 1999; Jescheniak & Schriefers, 1998; Peterson & Savoy, 1998). For example, in these models, activation of the lexical concept *couch* and coactivation of the lexical concept *sofa* will result in activation of the lemmas for *couch* and (to a lesser extent) *sofa*, followed by activation of the phonology of *couch* and (again to a lesser extent) *sofa*. A shared feature of serial and cascading models is that they do not allow the possibility of information at lower levels influencing processing at higher levels.

In contrast, *interactive* models assume that activation can flow bidirectionally, with feedback from lower levels to higher levels. Thus, while information flows down from conceptual to lexical to phonological levels, activation at the lemma level can also feed back to influence activation of conceptual nodes, and activation at the phonological level can feed back to influence lexical selection (Dell et al., 1997). Thus, for example, in these models, selection of the word *couch* can be influenced by phonological neighbors of *sofa*, as phonological information from a competitor word can feed back to the lemma level to influence selection of the target word.

A middle-ground in this debate is provided by the proposal that the production system is "globally modular and locally interactive" (Dell & O'Séaghdha, 1991; Vigliocco & Hartsuiker, 2002; see Dell et al., 2014, for a summary). Activation in the mental lexicon must flow down from the conceptual level to phonological processes (Schriefers et al., 1990), and is largely constrained by the speaker's communicative intent. Evidence of interactivity suggests some cross-talk between levels, but the magnitude of these effects is relatively small, as expected in a system where the goal is to select *specific* words from a large lexicon.

15.2.3 Producing sequences of words: How words influence the retrieval of other words

The next layer of complexity in establishing effects of context on lexical retrieval is in the production of multiple words in succession (i.e., word sequences). Resting word activation levels are sensitive to subtle changes in recent word usage, such as recent production of the target word or production of related words. Two classic examples are repetition effects and cumulative semantic interference effects.

Possibly the simplest type of context for a word is exact repetition: reductions in speech onsets are observed with immediate as well as delayed repetition (e.g., Meyer, Wheeldon, van der Meulen, & Konopka, 2012; Wheeldon & Monsell, 1992), showing long-lasting cumulative repetition effects. These effects arise from repetition of a specific semantic-lexical mapping as well as a phonological representation, rather than repetition of phonology alone (Wheeldon & Monsell, 1992). Repetition priming studies have also shown, for example, stronger repetition priming for low-frequency than high-frequency words (e.g., Wheeldon & Monsell, 1992), suggesting that the "benefit" of exact repetition is greater for words with lower baseline activation levels.

Another paradigm uses blocked naming to study retrieval of multiple semantic neighbors. Lexical retrieval becomes progressively harder with retrieval of each new word from the same semantic category, resulting in increasingly slow retrieval times and high error rates (Belke et al., 2005; Damian et al., 2001; Howard et al., 2006; Kroll & Stewart, 1994; Navarrete, Mahon, & Caramazza, 2010; Oppenheim, Dell, & Schwartz, 2010; Runnqvist et al., 2012; Schnur et al., 2006). One explanation for the growing naming delays involves inhibition: the name of each new category member becomes progressively harder to retrieve because retrieving each word requires inhibiting other same-category words (Roelofs & Piai, 2011; Shao et al., 2013, 2014). A related account, however, predicts blocking effects in object naming without making recourse to inhibitory mechanisms. Oppenheim, Dell, and Schwartz (2010) describe a model with a learning algorithm that dynamically updates semantic-to-lexical mappings in the mental lexicon with each retrieval attempt: repeated use of a specific concept-to-word mapping strengthens that mapping at the expense of the semantic-to-lexical mappings of related words. Thus, on this account, lexical retrieval implies continuous and incremental "learning" and "unlearning" of concept-to-word mappings, and this process can be responsible for experience-driven fluctuations in the ease of word retrieval in blocked naming paradigms.

Notably, recent experience can also modulate competition effects by creating new category structures. Production contexts can be manipulated by providing novel ad-hoc categories (such as the category of objects used on a fishing trip; Abdel-Rahman & Melinger, 2011). The emergence of cumulative interference in such contexts demonstrates that contexts can be task-specific and can change dynamically to add new constraints on word activation (also see Abdel-Rahman & Melinger, 2009). This finding has broad implications for language processing in real-life settings, where the cohort of competitors that can plausibly influence production of a target word can vary from one production setting to another. Furthermore, since the content and structure of the mental lexicon is not stable but changes over time, the ease of lexical retrieval is also continuously subject to changes in word activation levels and network connections.

15.2.4 Integration during production of full sentences: Going beyond the word

Finally, an important goal is to explain how lexical retrieval unfolds when words are produced in multiword utterances that obey the grammatical rules of the target language. Which aspects of word selection are shaped by *sentence* context, and how? Naturally, sentences provide a stronger context for the retrieval of individual words than the narrow, hard-wired context of semantic or phonological neighbors in the mental lexicon. Studies exploiting categorical relations between words capture only a restricted range of plausible between-word relations that speakers encounter during everyday language production. As such, the constraints imposed by sentence contexts on word activation are not easily captured by lexical norms: context can eliminate some competitors but also introduce new, context-specific ones. Research in this domain has two main goals: understanding how context influences word selection, and understanding how far ahead context exerts its influence in spontaneous production.

15.2.4.1 *Producing words in sentences*

How does a sentence context change the time-course and specificity of lexical activation? In language comprehension, typical effects of context include the generation of highly specific predictions (e.g., Altmann & Kamide, 1999) and faster processing of reduced or ambiguous word forms (e.g., Schvaneveldt et al., 1976; Tabossi, 1988; Tanenhaus et al., 1979). Context has an analogous effect on production, because multiword utterances provide information that narrows down the cohort of word candidates. For example, Griffin and Bock (1998) tracked the effects of local context on production of individual words in highly predictive and less predictive sentences: speakers read sentences and saw objects corresponding to the missing sentence-final concepts that they had to name. Highly predictive sentences facilitated object naming, and constraining activation of candidate words eliminated effects of lexical frequency that are normally observed in single-object naming studies.

Even though production in Griffin and Bock's (1998) study was limited to single words, such paradigms are a closer analog to natural language production than retrieval of the same words out of context. In reality, context may have a stronger effect on lexical retrieval when speakers generate messages from scratch. Unlike comprehension, where listeners work out what a speaker is intending to say word by word and thus can generate a range of predictions, speakers *know* what they want to communicate: the speaker's communicative intent quickly limits the make-up of the relevant lexical cohort. It is therefore plausible that studies of single word production overestimate the degree to which selection of a word entails activation of its neighbors in the mental lexicon.

Context can also motivate finer-grained lexical decisions, such as the choice to produce the full or reduced form of a word. The outcome may depend on word *informativity*. Words can contribute different amounts of new information in different contexts: in an efficient processing system, words that are less expected (i.e., more informative) are more likely to be produced in their full forms, while more expected (i.e., less informative) words may be omitted or produced in orthographically reduced forms (Jaeger's uniform density account; see Jaeger, 2010; also see Mahowald, Fedorenko, Piantadosi, & Gibson, 2013). We also review the consequences of informativity at the phonological level below.

15.2.4.2 *Planning scope*

Producing multiword sentences from scratch adds another parameter to the production process: it requires speakers to plan ahead to activate the words they intend to produce. How far ahead are speakers able to plan? Put differently, how many words can speakers activate in parallel and what constrains their activation at any point in time? In principle, word activation in an efficient system should be dynamic: words should be activated as and when they are needed. Thus, ideally, speakers should prepare some of the words they will produce immediately after the current word, largely to avoid having to pause in between words after speech onset, but not so many words as to require storage in a short-term buffer (Levelt, 1989; Ferreira & Swets, 2002; Wheeldon, 2012). On some accounts, planning scope may be a flexible parameter that is under a speaker's control (Ferreira & Swets, 2002). On other accounts, flexibility in planning scope may be bounded: planning scope may depend on the ease of lexical encoding, it may be grammatically constrained, it may be subject to limitations in processing capacity, and it may be sensitive to conversational pressures.

On one hand, some studies show a very narrow planning scope: in some production contexts, speakers may build up their utterances word by word. For example, when naming objects in a predetermined sequence (e.g., *The A and the B are above the C*), speakers can focus resources on retrieving object names sequentially. Specifically, they fixate each object in turn until they complete conceptual, lexical, and phonological encoding of this object name, and fixation durations on each object are unaffected by properties of the next object or by object repetition (Griffin, 2001: Meyer et al., 1998; also see Meyer et al., 2012). The systematicity of this process suggests that speakers can control what information they encode when, and thus that they can manage word activation strategically. One advantage of this word-by-word encoding strategy is that it minimizes interference between words during production. On the other hand, however, this type of production context is unusual in real-life language use, where speakers produce longer utterances and must meet multiple production constraints.

Indeed, the production of object names in utterances with less predictable structures or with more complex structures shows activation of more than one object name at a time. For example, speech onsets are longer for sentences beginning with complex noun phrases (e.g., *The car and the book are* . . .) than simple noun phrases (e.g., *The car is* . . .; Smith & Wheeldon, 1999). Thus, while lexical retrieval generally proceeds "left-to-right," speakers do devote some resources to a later-named object (*book*) before the onset of the first word (*car*). Importantly, lexical coactivation is modulated by properties of both objects: speakers preactivate the second object name when the first object is easy to recognize and to name, but this preactivation is only observed when the second object is also easy to name (Malpass & Meyer, 2010; Morgan & Meyer, 2005; also see Wheeldon et al., 2011). Such findings suggest that planning scope is highly sensitive to the ease of lexical processing (also see Konopka, 2012) and that adjustments in planning scope may support efficient encoding.

A second constraint on word activation is structural in nature: planning increments generally coincide with grammatical units, such as phrases (Martin et al., 2010; Smith & Wheeldon, 1999, 2001) or functional phrases (Allum & Wheeldon, 2007, 2009). Within a complex noun phrase (e.g., *The car and the book are* . . .), planning scope also varies with the ease of generating the required phrasal structure: planning scope is limited to one object when this structure takes longer to generate but extends to two objects when speakers can generate the required syntactic structure more quickly (Konopka, 2012). Facilitating planning of *simple* noun phrase structures does not extend planning scope to the next phrase, confirming that planning does not "cross" grammatical boundaries.

Cognitive constraints on planning include individual differences in working memory and sustained attention. For example, speakers with higher working memory capacity may plan sentences in larger increments (Swets, Jacovina, & Gerrig, 2014). Similarly, word production speed in complex noun phrases varies with individual differences in attention: speakers who are less able to maintain attention for longer periods of time show longer naming times, plausibly because of the increased demands of coordinating planning of two object names (Jongman et al., 2015a, 2015b). More broadly, inherent limitations in processing capacity may create constraints that favor a planning strategy biased toward generating small, economically feasible increments (Christiansen & Chater's, 2016, *now-or-never* proposal). From a language learnability perspective, an interesting question is whether grammatical constraints on planning scope follow from more general cognitive constraints on processing.

A final constraint on planning scope in everyday language use is conversational pressure. Speakers generally prefer to avoid long gaps between phrases or clauses in their speech, as these may be interpreted as the end of a conversational turn. When given the floor, interlocutors also tend to respond very quickly: turn-taking gaps are short cross-linguistically (200 ms on average). The speed of conversation thus leaves little time for extended planning and implies that speakers must be planning what they want to say while still listening to their interlocutors (Levinson, 2016). Confirming this hypothesis, object naming studies suggest that speakers begin conceptual and linguistic planning only shortly before it is their turn to speak (Boiteau et al., 2014; Sjerps & Meyer, 2015), while the length of turn-taking gaps during production of full sentences is additionally sensitive to factors such as utterance length (an index of conceptual complexity; e.g., Roberts et al., 2015; Torreira et al., 2016).

15.2.4.3 *Controlling lexical access*

The studies discussed so far used contexts that narrow down the range of lexical candidates for a particular sentence slot. A related question is how speakers manage to produce the right word *in the right slot* and how they can do so efficiently. As shown repeatedly, retrieval of one word entails coactivation of multiple competitors, both when speakers perform a task that requires naming of objects in isolation and when producing the same words in longer utterances. A striking example of lexical activation being relatively unconstrained is activation of words from two lexicons in bilingual speakers, even in a monolingual task context (e.g., Costa, Miozzo, & Caramazza, 1999). So, what are the mechanisms that control which word gets activated when during sentence production?

One answer is again that lexical activation may be driven by some degree of linearity in sentence planning. Since language output is linear, an efficient way of managing lexical access is to activate words in a particular order, ideally shortly before production, as required by the speaker's communicative goals. In other words, it is possible that linear activation is a direct result of speakers planning what they want to say linearly—that is, in an order that is isomorphic with word order—and thus that lexical activation is constrained by conceptual planning (Brown-Schmidt & Konopka, 2008; Brown-Schmidt & Tanenhaus, 2006; Konopka & Brown-Schmidt, 2014; also see Levinson, 2016, for a conversation-based view of this possibility).

A complementary perspective is that controlling lexical activation during sentence production is the responsibility of syntax. Dell, Oppenheim, and Kittredge (2008) describe the problem faced by the production system in terms of paradigmatic and syntagmatic interference. *Paradigmatic* interference occurs between words competing for the same slot, for example when speakers retrieve an object name in the presence of a distractor in picture-word interference paradigms (such as naming a picture of a *cat* with the superimposed word *dog*). As outlined here, the production system may deal with paradigmatic interference via inhibition or via changes in individual concept-to-word retrieval pathways. A different problem concerns interference between words that are coactivated by virtue of being produced in the same utterance (such as the words *cat* and *mat* in the sentence "The cat is on the mat"). To deal with this type of *syntagmatic* interference, Dell et al. (2008) propose the existence of a "syntactic traffic cop" (also see Gordon & Dell, 2003): sentence production requires generation of a sentence frame with a number of syntactic slots, and this frame restricts lexical activation to structurally suitable lexical candidates at various points during production. Indeed, data from speech errors and aphasic patients show that word activation is subject to a syntactic constraint: only words from the same grammatical class compete for the same slot (i.e., *cat* and *mat* will compete, but *cat* and *on* will not). It is thus plausible that the "syntactic traffic cop" may have developed as a mechanism to control the *timing* of word activation.

Experimental support for this position also comes from cross-linguistic production studies showing strong effects of word order on lexical activation, suggesting that lexical activation is constrained by grammatical boundaries (Konopka, 2009; Martin et al., 2004; Wheeldon et al., 2011, 2013). For example, production of noun phrases like *The kite above the dog* in English shows word activation in the order of mention, and production of the same phrase in Japanese (roughly: *dog above kite*) also shows activation of words in the initial noun phrase before the sentence-final head noun phrase (Allum & Wheeldon, 2007, 2009). Similarly, production of subject-verb-object (SVO) sentences in languages like English and Dutch shows that, once speakers have completed some degree of conceptual encoding and are ready to begin linguistic encoding, words are retrieved in the order of mention (Gleitman et al., 2007; Griffin & Bock, 2000; Konopka & Meyer, 2014; Kuchinsky, 2009). Analogous word order effects are observed in sentences with VSO/VOS structures (such as in Korean, Tzeltal, and Tagalog; see Hwang & Kaiser, 2014; Norcliffe et al., 2015; Sauppe et al., 2013): speakers engage in early encoding of the sentence verb, showing a pattern of lexical retrieval that reflects the grammatical requirements of the target language.

15.3 Morphological and phonological processing

15.3.1 Representation: The morphological and phonological form of words

The retrieval and integration of lemmas into grammatical structures is followed by the generation of lexical forms. The consensus view is that this involves the construction of an abstract morpho-phonological representation (henceforth word-form encoding) and that the generation of this representation intervenes between word selection and the construction of the phonetic representations that guide articulation (e.g., Dell, 1986; Garrett, 1980; Goldrick, Folk, & Rapp, 2010; Levelt, Roelofs, & Meyer, 1999; Shattuck-Hufnagel, 1979; see Buchwald, 2014, and Goldstein & Pouplier, 2014, for reviews of the generation of phonetic structure). This view is supported by evidence that speakers can retrieve word-form information in the absence of overt articulation (e.g., Morgan & Wheeldon, 2003; Wheeldon & Levelt, 1995; Wheeldon & Morgan, 2002) and produce inner speech errors which show less sensitivity to detailed featural information than overt speech errors (Oppenheim & Dell, 2008, 2010). The distinction between an abstract morpho-phonological and a more detailed phonetic processing stage during word production is also consistent with evidence from patterns of deficits in aphasia (e.g., Goldrick & Rapp, 2007; Romani & Galluzzi, 2005) and patterns of neurological activity in intact speakers (e.g., Indefrey & Levelt, 2004; Indefrey, 2011; Ziegler & Ackermann, 2014; see Goldrick, 2014 for a review).

As discussed earlier (in section 15.2.2), the input to the process of word-form encoding comes from activated semantic (e.g., Caramazza, 1997) or syntactic lexical representations (e.g., Levelt et al., 1999). The phonological structure for the word is then assembled from these components. There are different claims about the levels of representation involved in word-form encoding. In some models, lexical-semantic representations directly activate their constituent phonological segments. Such models either focus on the production of morphologically simple words or propose unified lexical representations of complex words (e.g., Caramazza, 1997; Dell, Chang, & Griffin, 1999; Dell & O'Séaghdha, 1992; Dell, Nozari, & Oppenheim, 2014). In other models, a lexicon of morpho-phonological form representations intervenes between lexical representations and sublexical phonological units (e.g., Dell, 1986; Levelt et al, 1999; Rapp & Goldrick, 2006).

15.3.1.1 *Morphological structure*

Compared to language comprehension research, the *production* of morphologically complex words has received scant attention. The issues that have been addressed in the production domain are like those for language comprehension. First and foremost, is there an independent representation of morphological structure that cannot be reduced to the interaction of meaning and form (Aronoff, 1976, 1994), or can the effects of morphological structure be explained in terms of a direct mapping between meaning and phonological representations (e.g., Davis, van Casteren, & Marslen-Wilson, 2003; Plaut & Gonnerman, 2000)? Second, are complex words accessed in a compositional or non-compositional manner (e.g., Butterworth, 1983; Caramazza, 1997; Dell, 1986; Levelt et al., 1999)?

Theoretical positions range from a mental lexicon in which complex words are listed in full (e.g., Butterworth, 1983; Caramazza, 1997; Janssen, Bi, & Caramazza, 2008) to a fully decomposed lexicon from which morphemes are retrieved in order to construct complex words. In WEAVER++ (Levelt et al. 1999; Roelofs, 1992, 1997), morphemes are stored as decomposed phonological units in the word-form lexicon. They are activated by their lemmas, which represent morphosyntactic information critical to word-form encoding, such as number, tense, and person. During word-form encoding, the morphemes that represent this information are retrieved in parallel and are phonologically encoded in a sequential manner from left to right. Existing derived words (e.g., *argument*) and compounds (e.g., *teddy-bear*) have their own lemma representations marked for syntactic class but activate their component morphemes in the same way as inflected words. A similar compositional approach is taken in the interactive activation model of Dell (1986). In this model, lexical information is represented in a network of nodes through which activation spreads. A complex word like *swimmer* has a single lemma node, which marks it as a noun. However, at the morphological level, it must be constructed from separate nodes for stems and affixes (*swim + er*). Activation of the lemma triggers the construction of a morphological frame with slots for stems and affixes to which the morpheme nodes are attached.

A fully listed mental lexicon, devoid of any representation of morphological structure, is untenable for many of the world's languages, which show a huge variety in the complexity and productivity of their morphological systems (e.g., see Blevins, 2014; Waksler, 2000, for reviews). Of course, the representation of morphological structure may differ across languages, depending on the characteristics of their morphological systems (Chen & Chen, 2006; Janssen et al., 2008). In addition, there may be differences in the representation of subsets of complex words within a language. Factors critical for the representation of morphologically complex words include the nature of the morphological process (inflectional or derivational; e.g., Janssen et al., 2008; Janssen, Roelofs, & Levelt, 2002, 2004), the productivity of the affixation process (e.g., Baayen, 1994; Badecker, 2001), the semantic transparency and phonological regularity of complex words (e.g., Badecker & Caramazza, 1991; Badecker, 2001; Blanken, 2000; Cholin, Rapp, & Miozzo, 2010), and the frequency of words and their constituent morphemes (e.g., Bien, Levelt, & Baayen, 2006; Bien, Baayen, & Levelt, 2011; Stemberger & MacWhinney, 1986). In general, the proposal is that decomposed representations are more likely to occur for highly productive and transparent morphological processes, and for low-frequency but not for high-frequency complex words. Many of these factors are of course related, as both inflectional processes (e.g., number: *boy, boys;* intensity: *big, bigger*), and productive derivational processes (e.g., adjective + ness: *happiness;* verb + er: *writer*), tend to be both semantically transparent and phonologically regular (e.g., Aronoff, 1976, 1994).

Evidence for the distinct representation of morphological forms comes from a variety of disciplines. Morphemes have been observed to function as units in speech errors produced by unimpaired speakers; errors such as *slicely thinned* for *thinly sliced*, arguably involve the movement of morpho-phonological representations as the interacting units share no semantic or syntactic characteristics (e.g., Stemberger, 1982). Similar errors have been observed in aphasic speech, for example *youthly* for *youthful* (Badecker & Caramazza, 1991), which are also consistent with morphologically decomposed phonological forms, rather than more abstract morpho-syntactic representations (e.g., Allen & Badecker, 1999; see Rapp & Goldrick, 2006, for a review).

Experimental evidence that morphemes are represented independently has come from the implicit priming paradigm (Meyer, 1990, 1991). In this paradigm, the production latency for sets of words with overlapping representations is compared to that of mixed sets of words. Facilitation is observed when words share initial phonological information. Moreover, larger facilitatory effects of shared initial segments are observed when those segments also constitute a morpheme of the target words (e.g., for *bij* in *bijrol*—"supporting role" compared to *bijbel*—"bible"; Roelofs, 1996a, b, 1998). In line with a sequential encoding process, no facilitation is observed for word sets with non-initial overlapping morphemes. Using the picture-word interference technique, Zwitserlood, Bölte, and Dohmes (2000) demonstrated that the naming of pictures with simple German names (e.g., *blume*—"flower") is facilitated by related complex words (e.g., *blumen*—"flowers," *blumig*—"flowery," *blumentopf*—"flower pot"). The morphological primes facilitated naming and did so to a greater degree than purely phonological primes (e.g., *bluse*—"blouse"), while semantically related distractors inhibited naming. These effects generalize to the production of morphologically complex target words such as *strawberry* (Lüttmann, Zwitserlood, Böhl, & Bölte, 2011). Moreover, in a delayed version of the task in which the prime and targets were separated by 7–10 unrelated trials, only the effects of morphological primes survived and were insensitive to the position of the morpheme in the prime (*rosebud* and *tea-rose* facilitated the naming of a rose to the same extent; Zwitserlood, Bölte, & Dohmes, 2002). This finding suggests that this task might tap into processes involved in the retrieval of morphemes rather than in their sequential encoding.

Experimental evidence also contradicts the claim that semantic transparency dictates how morphemes are represented. The implicit priming benefit observed for word initial morpheme overlap occurs to the same extent for semantically transparent (e.g., *in + put*) and opaque (e.g., *in + voice*) complex words compared to simple words (e.g., *insect*; Roelofs & Baayen, 2002). Delayed morphological priming effects in compound words also occur irrespective of the semantic transparency of the primes (e.g., Dohmes, Zwitserlood, & Bölte, 2004; Koester & Schiller, 2008). In addition, semantic relatedness does not affect the rate of occurrence of experimentally induced derivational morpheme exchange errors (Melinger, 2003). These findings are consistent with the representation of morphological structure at a level that is independent from semantics, and therefore with models that incorporate representations for morphemes at the word-form level.

However, some evidence from studies examining the effects of word and morpheme frequency on spoken production is inconsistent with a fully compositional approach to the representation of morphologically complex words. Janssen et al. (2008; Janssen, Pajtas, & Caramazza, 2014) observed effects of whole word frequency but not morpheme frequency on the production of compound picture names in Mandarin and English, consistent with a full listing account (see also Chen & Chen, 2006). Other studies have found more complex relationships between a range of frequency measures and complex word production latencies. Bien et al. (2006) demonstrated frequency effects for both constituents of Dutch compounds (modifier and head) but no significant effect of whole compound frequency, although there was some evidence of facilitation in the lower frequency ranges. However, latency was also predicted by frequency measures that incorporated structural information about the position of the constituents in compounds, such that constituents with higher frequencies in a given structural position were produced faster. Bien et al. (2011) found evidence of decomposition for deverbal adjectives (e.g., *lees-baar*, "readable"), while inflected verb production showed effects related to the frequencies of their inflectional variants. Effects of phonological overlap were also observed, suggesting interactions with phonological neighborhoods (discussed next). Bien et al. (2011) proposed an intermediate representational option, which they termed structural storage, in which compounds are stored with their internal structure represented and with links between morphologically related forms.

A key challenge in this area is to determine the level at which morpheme frequencies have their effects. The frequency effect observed for heads (i.e., non-initial morphemes; Bien et al., 2006) is not consistent with strict incrementality in encoding, although there was some evidence for an inhibitory effect of head frequency (second element), while all effects of modifier frequency (first element) were facilitatory. This suggests that the selection of the first element of a morphologically complex word is more difficult when the second element is high-frequency. However, incrementality may operate following morpheme selection and there is evidence that complex words are encoded as single prosodic units during phonological encoding (Jacobs & Dell, 2014; Wheeldon & Lahiri, 2002; Wynne, Wheeldon, & Lahiri, 2017) and that a whole complex word can be phonologically encoded prior to the onset of articulation (Wheeldon & Lahiri, 1997; see discussion of phonological planning scope below). Nevertheless, the data reviewed here is most consistent with the storage of many complex words at a level of morpho-phonological form that reflects both the details of the morphological relations between the constituents of complex words and their relationship to the other words that share them.

15.3.1.2 *Phonological structure*

A more consistent picture exists of the critical phonological representations involved in word-form encoding. Much of the relevant research is informed by theoretical linguistics, particularly theories of autosegmental (Goldsmith, 1990) and prosodic phonology (Selkirk,

1982, 1984), in which distinctive features, segments, and suprasegmental representations (such as syllables, feet, moras, stress, and tone) form distinct but related levels within the representation of lexical and utterance form (e.g., Goldrick, 2014; Levelt, 1989). Once again early evidence for the role of such representations in spoken word production came from the analysis of speech error corpora. Errors involving segments account for the vast majority of sublexical speech errors and the occurrence of segmental errors is influenced by a variety of factors (e.g., Fromkin, 1973; Shattuck-Hufnagel, 1979; Stemberger, 1982). Segments that share phonological features are more likely to interact in errors than dissimilar segments. While syllables rarely function as error units, syllable structure and stress strongly influence segmental errors such that segments are significantly more likely to be misplaced to similar syllable positions, and to syllables with similar stress assignments. Misplaced segment clusters also tend to correspond to syllable constituents (e.g., *face-spood*; see Meyer, 1991, for a detailed review). Similar factors have also been shown to operate in aphasic speech errors (e.g., Rapp & Goldrick, 2006; Romani & Galluzzi, 2005). These data lead to the development of frame-filling theories of phonological encoding, in which segmental content is associated to metrical frames (Dell, 1986; Garrett, 1975; Levelt, 1989; Levelt et al, 1999; Shattuck-Hufnagel, 1979).

Despite broad agreement about the nature of the critical information to be represented and the processing stages involved, current models of phonological encoding diverge in their details. In particular, there is controversy about the role of syllables during phonological encoding. While there is good evidence that syllables and segments have independent but related representations, claims about the nature of the relationship between them differ. Based on the preservation of syllable structure in aphasic errors, Romani et al. (2011) give syllables a significant role, storing syllable and segmental structure in an integrated fashion in the lexicon. Syllables also play a vital role in Dell's (1986) spreading activation model of speech error production, which contains nodes for syllables and syllabic constituents, and these nodes connect to segmental nodes marked for syllable position. During phonological encoding, segments are activated in parallel and then assigned to syllabic slots within a metrical frame. In WEAVER++ (Levelt et al., 1999; Roelofs, 1992, 1997), syllables are not stored in the lexicon but are computed online during phonological encoding and then retrieved as phonetic units. Morpheme selection triggers the parallel release of their constituent phonemic segments and a minimally specified metrical frame comprising a representation of the number of syllables marked as weak or strong—but only for words which do not conform to lexical stress rules of the language (but see Schiller, Fikkert, & Levelt, 2004). Following the release of this information, there is a sequential process of prosodification, during which syllables are constructed, assigned metrical structure (e.g., relative stress), and combined into phonological words. Numbered links between segment and morpheme nodes fix the serial order of this process. Phonetic syllables are then retrieved and assembled for output (Cholin, Dell, & Levelt, 2011; Cholin, Levelt, & Schiller, 2006; Levelt & Wheeldon, 1994).

What has persisted, despite the differences in detail, is the idea of a sequential frame-filling process for phonological encoding. More recent research has turned to questions about the universality of this process and there has been an increase in the number of studies examining phonological encoding in non-Indo-European languages. These studies demonstrate language-specific differences in the phonological frame and the units that attach to them. For example, for implicit priming to be observed in Chinese, the overlap must be at least the initial syllable (Chen & Chen, 2013; Chen, Chen, & Dell, 2002; Chen, O'Séaghdha,

& Chen, 2016; O'Séaghdha, Chen, & Chen, 2010; but see Qu, Damian, & Kazanina, 2012). In contrast, Japanese studies show the implicit priming effect is based on moras (Kureta, Fushimi, & Tatsumi, 2006; see O'Séaghdha, 2015; Roelofs, 2015, for reviews). Nevertheless, the development of theory remains hampered by limitations in the range of phonological processes and languages that have been investigated to date (Baković, 2014). In particular, the interface between morphology and phonology has received little attention (see Cohen-Goldberg, Cholin, Miozzo, & Rapp, 2013, for a recent exception), and this remains an important topic for future research. Lahiri (2000) provides a detailed review of the morphological systems of the world's languages and their repercussions for the generation of phonological structure.

15.3.2 Selection: Words and their phonological neighbors

The complexity of the processes involved in generating the morpho-phonological form of spoken words is compounded by the fact that activation also spreads to non-target form representations during this process. The speed and accuracy with which a word is processed is affected by its phonological neighborhood density (PND, Luce & Pisoni, 1998). PND is defined as the number of alternative words that can be made by changing, deleting, or adding a phoneme in any position in the target word. In spoken word comprehension, the effects of increasing neighborhood density are inhibitory and are modeled by the activation of multiple candidates based on form information and competition between them for selection (e.g., Luce & Pisoni, 1998; Vitevitch & Luce, 2016).

In contrast, larger neighborhoods have been shown to have largely faciliatory effects on the accuracy of spoken word production. Words with larger neighborhoods are less likely to occur in speech errors (Stemberger, 2004; Vitevitch, 1997, 2002) and tip-of-the-tongue states (e.g., Vitevitch & Sommers, 2003), and are more likely to be correctly produced by aphasic speakers (Gordon, 2002; Middleton & Schwartz, 2010; but see Laganaro, Chetelat-Mabillard, & Frauenfelder, 2013, for evidence of some detrimental effects of PND). There is evidence that PND is a lexical level effect, as it affects patients with lexical but not with postlexical processing deficits (Goldrick & Rapp, 2007; Goldrick et al., 2010). PND effects are also found when phonotactic probability is controlled for (Vitevitch, 2002; Vitevitch, Armbrüster, & Chu, 2004). Other studies have examined in more detail the critical features that determine the nature of phonological neighborhoods, demonstrating that multiple dimensions of similarity contribute to the activation of a target word's neighborhoods, including position-dependent segmental overlap, shared initial phonemes, lexical frequency, and grammatical class (e.g., Goldrick et al., 2010).

Explanations for these facilitatory effects differ. In interactive activation spreading models, the underlying mechanism is feedback between lexical and segmental representations (e.g., Dell, 1986; Goldrick et. al., 2010; Rapp & Goldrick, 2000). An activated word spreads activation to all its constituent segments, which in turn feed activation back to all of the words in which they occur. This spread of activation means that the representations for words in large phonological neighborhoods will become more strongly activated and therefore more readily accessible during phonological encoding (Dell & Gordon, 2003). Phonological neighborhoods can also become activated in feed-forward models such as WEAVER++, without the need for production internal feedback links. An internal speech monitoring loop feeds the sequential output of the phonological encoding process into the speech comprehension system, which in turn activates compatible segmental, morphological, and lemma representations in the production system (Roelofs, 2004a, 2004b).

A number of studies have also reported facilitatory effects of neighborhood density on production *latency*, such that words with larger neighborhoods are produced more quickly than those with smaller neighborhoods in picture naming tasks (e.g., Baus, Costa, & Carreiras, 2008; Dell & Gordon, 2003; Vitevitch, 2002). However, these latency effects have proven unreliable. Sadat, Martin, Costa, and Alario (2014) conducted a mega study of the effects of PND on production latencies and demonstrated a high degree of variability in findings across studies. Their reanalysis of the data, using regression models at the single trial level, found inhibitory effects of large neighborhoods on spoken word production latencies. They suggested that neighbors typically inhibit normal word retrieval processes by competing with the target word. However, when the process of lexical retrieval is compromised, the extra activation may aid word retrieval. A related hypothesis suggested by Chen and Mirman (2012), predicts different effects of PND depending of the strength of neighborhood activation: they present a model in which weak neighborhood activation results in facilitation, whereas strong neighborhood activation results in competition.

The precise parameters that govern the swing from facilitatory to inhibitory effects of PND remain to be determined, as does the level of representation at which these effects play out. As already mentioned, in some models there are intervening morpho-phonological representations or lexemes to which segmental nodes attach (e.g., Dell, 1986; Levelt et al., 1999). In such models, PND based competition for retrieval would occur within the form lexicon. In this case, interactions between PND, morpheme frequency, and morphological neighborhood density would be predicted (e.g., Bien, Baayen, & Levelt, 2011; Caselli, Caselli, & Goldberg, 2015) and the patterning of these effects should vary depending on the morpho-phonological systems of different languages (e.g., Vitevitch & Stamer, 2006).

Finally, PND has also been shown to influence the phonetic properties of words, such as aspects of word duration (e.g., Caselli et al., 2015; Gahl, Yao, & Johnson, 2012) and voice-onset time (VOT) to initial consonants (e.g., Goldrick, Vaughn, & Murphy, 2013). It has been proposed that such effects reflect the direct influence of lexical retrieval processes on articulation such that increased ease of retrieval results in phonetic reduction (e.g., Gahl et al., 2012) and this is an issue we return to next. However, the exact nature of the relationship between PND and the phonetic properties of words is unclear (see Gahl, 2015; Gahl & Strand, 2016) and other researchers have argued for the independence of lexical retrieval and phonetic planning (e.g., Buz & Jaeger, 2015). We therefore remain some way from understanding the nature of PND effects on spoken word production and the mechanisms by which PND affects the accuracy, latency, and articulation of spoken words.

15.3.3 Producing sequences of words: how word forms influence the retrieval of other words

Similarities in sound structure also affect the sequential production of spoken words. In the tasks that have been frequently used to investigate phonological encoding in the production literature, such as the picture-word interference task (e.g., Meyer & Schriefers, 1991) and the implicit priming task (Meyer, 1990, 1991), the effect of phonological overlap (e.g., *dog-doll*) has been shown to be predominantly facilitatory, speeding production and reducing error rates. Phonological priming has also been shown to facilitate aphasic word production (e.g., Lee & Thompson, 2015; Wilshire & Saffran, 2005).

In contrast, interference effects of phonological form repetition have been demonstrated on spoken word production. Bock (1987) found that when participants produce descriptions of simple pictures, they place form-primed words later in the sentence and are less likely to use them at all. Several studies have demonstrated interference effects of phonological overlap in tongue-twister style tasks (e.g., Meyer & Gordon, 1985; O'Séaghdha, Dell, Peterson, & Juliano, 1992). For example, Sevald and Dell (1994) used a speeded syllable repetition task in which they varied the repetition of consonants. They found that repeated initial consonants increased error rates (e.g., *pick, pun, puck, pin*), while repeated final consonants decreased error rates (e.g., *pick, tuck, puck, tick*). They modeled these effects in terms of competition between activated shared segments for the same position in a metrical frame (see also O'Séaghdha et al., 1992; O'Séaghdha & Marin, 2000). Similar patterns of form priming have been observed using more standard speech production paradigms. Wheeldon (2003) demonstrated an inhibitory effect of a single spoken phonological prime in a simple picture naming task in Dutch, but only for pairs on consecutive trials that shared onset segments (e.g., *hond-hoed*, "dog-hat"; see also Damian & Dumay, 2009). Primes that shared offset segments with the target picture names facilitated naming (e.g., *kurk-jurk*, "cork-dress"). Moreover, inhibition was only observed for prime target pairs with mismatching segments. Sullivan and Riffel (1999) reported inhibitory effects on picture naming latencies of both onset and rhyme overlap, although the effect was reduced for rhymes. More recently, Breining, Nozari, and Rapp (2015) demonstrated inhibitory effects of phonological overlap in a cyclic blocked picture naming task (e.g., *cat* with *mat, cot, cap, map, mop*; see also, Nozari, Freund, Breining, Rapp, & Gordon, 2016).

As we have mentioned, onset overlap effects have also been documented in studies of PND. Goldrick et al. (2010) reported that initial segments were shared between target and error words more often than other position, and Vitevitch et al. (2004) reported an inhibitory effect onset density on picture naming latencies. Another similarity between the effects of sequential form priming and PND effects is that sequential form priming has also been shown to affect the phonetic properties of words. Initial overlap between words can result in longer word durations than final overlap (Yiu & Watson, 2015; but also see Damian & Dumay, 2009). These results have also been explained in terms of a direct link between the speed of sequential phonological encoding and articulatory planning (e.g., Watson, Buxó-Lugo, & Simmons, 2015).

Position-dependent interference effects of form overlap suggest that their locus is the sequential encoding of phonological structure during which segments activate their related lexical representations. However, they are consistent with both lexically conditioned segmental competition (e.g., Sevald & Dell, 1994) and segmentally conditioned lexical competition (e.g., Stemberger, 1985), the latter being similar to the modeling of the PND effects reviewed here earlier. Other models do not employ direct competition between lexical representations but propose a competitive incremental learning mechanism in which connections to activated non-target items are weakened, slowing their subsequent retrieval (e.g., Breining et al., 2015).

What is clear from the phonological priming data reviewed in this section and the PND effects reviewed here, is that an accurate model of phonological encoding must incorporate mechanisms that allow for the activation of multiple words based on their phonological overlap and that can account for both facilitation and interference effects of form similarity during spoken word production (e.g., Breining et al., 2015; Wheeldon, 1999). Such a model must also account for the time-course and control of these effects during sequential word production (e.g., Nozari et al., 2016) as, in the end, an unimpaired speaker is able to select and encode the correct word for output from a sea of activated alternatives with a high success rate and at an impressive speed.

15.3.4 Integration during the production of sentences: Word forms in context

We now turn to the generation of the phonological form of words during connected speech production. The questions we address are the same as those addressed for the retrieval of words during the generation of syntactic structure. First, how is word-form generation influenced by aspects of the context in which it occurs, including the semantic, syntactic, and prosodic structure of a sentence and, in the larger context, by the parameters of the discourse in which it is produced? And second, what degree of advanced planning of phonological structure is required for the generation of fluent sentences?

15.3.4.1 Effects of sentential context on spoken word production

Following the retrieval of word-form information, the phonological and phonetic structure of the utterance must be constructed prior to articulation. Sentences are produced with rhythmic structure realized in duration, pitch, amplitude, and pauses. Many aspects of utterance structure can alter the relative prominence of syllables within a word and of words within a sentence (e.g., contrastive focus, *No, JOAN caught the ball*). Moreover, the segmental and syllabic structure of words can also be altered in context-dependent ways (e.g., *what do you want to eat* can become *wa-je-wan-teet*). Such changes often cross syntactic and lexical boundaries and, within linguistic theory, they have led to the postulation of a hierarchy of prosodic constituents that intervenes between the morphosyntactic representation of an utterance and its phonological and phonetic realization (e.g., Nespor & Vogel, 1986; Selkirk, 1996). Levelt's (1989) theory of language production accounts for such effects within a prosody generator, which takes as input information about the intonational meaning of an utterance (illocutionary force, emotions, and attitudes), the unfolding syntactic structure, and lexical metrical and segmental information. It then generates (via a sequential phonological process) new context-dependent syllables, specified for duration, amplitude, and pitch. According to this approach, the phonetic properties of a word are determined by its place in the structure of the message to be conveyed and are encoded in an intermediate prosodic representation.

An increasing body of experimental work has examined effects of prosodic structure during sentence production (see Wagner & Watson, 2010, and Wheeldon, 2000, for reviews). Much of the relevant research has focused on the phonetic realization of words in context and has demonstrated that aspects of word duration are influenced by the word's position within the constituents of the prosodic hierarchy (e.g., Ferreira, 1993, 2007; Wightman, Shattuck-Hufnagel, Ostendorf, & Price, 1992). However, word duration is also influenced by probabilistic factors. The predictability of occurrence of a word in both utterance and in discourse contexts has been shown to affect spoken word durations, such that less predictable words are articulated with a longer duration (e.g., Aylett & Turk, 2004; Bell, Brenier, Gregory, Girand, & Jurafsky, 2009; Gahl & Garnsey, 2004; Gahl, Yao, & Johnson, 2012; Jurafsky, Bell, Gregory, & Raymond 2001; Tily et al. 2009; Watson, Arnold, & Tanenhaus, 2008, see also Arnold & Watson, 2015; Shattuck-Hufnagel 2014, for recent reviews). One explanation for such effects is that they are driven by the speaker's aim to facilitate information processing for the listener (e.g., Aylett & Turk, 2004). An alternative hypothesis relates these reductions to effects of facilitated processing, such that predictable words can be accessed and planned more quickly, like the accounts of PND and form priming on word duration mentioned here (e.g., Watson et al., 2015). Related to this proposal is evidence that longer word durations are also associated with production difficulties and disfluencies (Bell et al., 2003; Clark & Fox Tree, 2002). Such performance-based explanations seem diametrically opposed to the structurally driven account of Levelt (1989). However structural and performance factors are often related, in that words in certain structural positions can also be easier to retrieve (see Arnold & Watson, 2015, for a detailed review). Adequate models of connect speech production require mechanisms for both structural and performance factors. The challenge is to clarify the relationship between them, and to specify the production mechanisms underlying articulatory reduction.

15.3.4.2 *Scope of activation and planning during phonological encoding*

The assumption of cascading of activation from lemma to lexical-form representations entails word-form activation not just for words related to the target word but also for upcoming words in the utterance to be produced. Two related questions have been addressed about the scope of planning during phonological encoding. First, what is the window of advanced activation for the phonological representation of words during phonological encoding? Second, how much phonological code must be constructed before articulation can commence?

Evidence from speech error corpora suggests that the scope of advanced planning at the level of phonological encoding is smaller than that for the lexical representations required for the generation of syntax. Segmental errors tend to involve adjacent words occurring within the same phrase, suggesting a relatively limited planning scope (e.g., Garrett, 1975, 1980). Several experimental studies have addressed this issue using the picture-word interference task during the production of phrases and sentences. Facilitation is observed for distractors phonologically related to utterance initial words (e.g., Meyer, 1996; Schriefers, Teruel, & Meinshausen, 1998) but also non-initial words (e.g., *car* in *the red car*, e.g., Alario & Caramazza, 2002; Costa & Caramazza, 2002; Jescheniak, Schriefers, & Hantsch, 2003; Miozzo & Caramazza, 1999; see also Damian & Dumay, 2007, 2009; Smith & Wheeldon, 2004). Moreover, Schnur, Costa, and Caramazza (2006) demonstrated phonological facilitation for words much further downstream. Utterance initiation for sentences such as *The girl jumps* and *The orange girl jumps*, were facilitated by distractors phonologically related to the verb (e.g., *jug*). These data are consistent with advanced retrieval of the phonological form of words beyond the first phrase of a sentence.

However, there is also evidence that the advanced retrieval of lexical form can disadvantage planning. Jescheniak et al. (2003) found inhibitory effects of phonological distractors for nouns in complex noun phrases (e.g., *The big red car*, see also Meyer, 1996; Oppermann, Jescheniak, & Schriefers, 2010). Jescheniak et al. (2003) propose a graded activation account, in which the linearization of lemmas during syntactic encoding leads to the graded activation of their corresponding lexemes, with the utterance initial word forms being most highly activated. The effect of a phonological distractor is facilitatory unless it disturbs the correct serial position encoded by graded activation. When this happens, a word that should be produced later in an utterance can interfere with the encoding of the current element.

It is clear from the research to date that the phonological form of words can be activated some time before they are due to be articulated. However, the way in which this activation relates to *planning* is not yet understood, as the effect of such activation is not always to facilitate production. There is evidence that the activation of the phonological form of words can occur automatically during the processing of visual information, even for aspects of the image that are not to be named (e.g., Meyer & Damian, 2007; Morsella & Miozzo, 2002). Therefore, picture description tasks may overestimate the advanced planning of lexical form. Oppermann, Jescheniak, and Schriefers (2010) addressed this issue by using a picture of the sentence subject (e.g., *mouse*) to cue production of a learned sentence (e.g., *The mouse eats the cheese*) and demonstrated interference when the object of the sentence (*cheese*) was primed. However, it is not clear how sentence memorization affects the activation of phonological forms in this task. Future work is required to clarify the factors that determine the pattern of advanced activation of lexical form, the effects of conceptual and syntactic structure on word-form activation, as well as the mechanisms underlying the facilitation and interference effects that have been observed.

Finally, how much phonological and phonetic code is constructed before articulation commences? While the advanced activation of lexical form can be quite extensive, it does not follow that these words have also been phonologically and phonetically encoded prior to utterance onset (e.g., Damian et al., 2010). It has been claimed that speakers can start to articulate a word as soon as the first phoneme has been retrieved (Dell, Juliano, & Govindjee, 1993; Kawamoto, Kello, Jones, & Bame, 1998). However, this claim cannot account for the coarticulation effects observed in speech planning (e.g., Lehiste, 1970), nor can it account for effects of whole syllable frequency on production latencies, in some cases including the frequency of the second syllable of bisyllabic words (Cholin, Dell, & Levelt, 2011; Wheeldon & Levelt, 1995). There is also evidence that at least a whole word is phonologically encoded prior to output. Word length can affect production latencies (e.g., Meyer, Belke, Häcker, & Mortensen, 2007; Meyer, Roelofs, & Levelt, 2003; see also Damian, Bowers, Stadthagen-Gonzalez, & Spalek, 2010). Moreover, distractors related to word final syllables can facilitate word production (Damian et al., 2010), and the length of a word can affect the planning of upcoming words (Griffin, 2003).

As mentioned here earlier, the syllable structure of words can change in connected speech (e.g., *gave it* becoming *gay-vit*). To account for such resyllabification effects, WEAVER++ proposes the phonological word as the minimal unit of phonological and phonetic encoding. The phonological word is defined as minimally a stressed foot and maximally a lexical word and any unstressed syllables that follow it (e.g., [king of the]ω [castle]ω) and it functions as the domain of syllabification in several languages (e.g., Lahiri, Jongman, & Sereno, 1990). There is also evidence of the construction of such units prior to utterance onset, from both delayed and online speech production tasks (Wheeldon & Lahiri, 1997, 2002; Lahiri & Wheeldon, 2011; Wynne et al., 2017). WEAVER++ generates phonological words with minimal look-ahead. However, languages differ in the scope of their phonological dependencies. Lahiri (2000) discusses several examples of dependencies at the level of the phonological phrase that are difficult to accommodate within a strictly incremental model phonological encoding. The structural factors that influence look-ahead during phonological and phonetic encoding remain to be determined, as does the nature of their relationship to the processing effects discussed earlier.

15.4 Summary and future directions

We have reviewed studies on the production of individual spoken words, the production of sequences of words, and the production of words in full sentences. Many of these studies examine word production in *context*—a context that can be as small as a single word (e.g., a distractor that is presented at the same time as the stimulus eliciting the target word), a sequence of words from the same category (e.g., related in meaning or form), or a sequence of words that together make up grammatical and prosodic units in phrases or sentences. The general finding is that lexical retrieval in longer utterances depends as much on a word's unique properties and its relationship to other similar words, as it does on the context in which the word is produced. However, as the complexity of the context increases, so does the impact of context on lexical retrieval, both in terms of structural constraints and ease of processing.

At the same time, our aim has been to highlight limitations in the current body of empirical work and theory. Traditionally, word production research has been narrow, in terms of the range of languages and linguistic structures that have been investigated. In the field of linguistics, theories are tested in terms of their ability to capture generalizations both within and across the world's languages. Modern psycholinguistics research is increasingly adopting this approach and is also investigating word production processes in the minds of multilingual speakers (see Chapters 9 and 14 in this *Handbook* for reviews).

The available theories also focus either on the breakdown of word production or on the fluent production of words by a limited section of the population (often female undergraduate students). However, more recent research has extended investigation to changes in word production process across the life span (see Mortensen, Meyer, & Humphreys, 2006, for a review). Moreover, we are now beginning to learn more about individual differences in word production processes. One well-documented finding concerns the relationship between linguistic and non-linguistic operations: namely, the efficiency of lexical processing may be bounded by the cognitive constraints of attention and executive control (e.g., Ferreira & Pashler, 2002) and by individual differences in components of these skills (e.g., Piai & Roelofs, 2013; Shao et al., 2013, 2014, 2015).

Finally, a growing area of research concerns learning. What is beyond doubt is that, for every speaker, the mental representation of words and the processes by which they are retrieved and integrated are never in a fixed state, but are continually changed by experience (also see Brehm & Goldrick, this volume). While aspects of the spoken word production processes we have reviewed have been modeled in systems designed to learn, the field lacks a fully articulated learning model of word production.

References

Abdel-Rahman, R., & Aristei, S. (2010). Now you see it . . . and now again: Semantic interference reflects lexical competition in speech production with and without articulation. *Psychonomic Bulletin & Review*, 17, 657–61.

Abdel-Rahman, R., & Melinger, A. (2009). Semantic context effects in language production: A swinging lexical network proposal and a review. *Language and Cognitive Processes*, 24, 713–34.

Abdel-Rahman, R., & Melinger, A. (2011). The dynamic microstructure of speech production: Semantic interference built on the fly. *Journal of Experimental Psychology: Learning, Memory, and Cognition*, 37, 149–61.

Alario, F.-X., and Caramazza, A. (2002). The production of determiners: evidence from French. *Cognition*, 82, 179–223.

Allen, M., & Badecker, W. (1999). Stem homograph inhibition and stem allomorphy: Representing and processing inflected forms in a multi-level lexical system. *Journal of Memory and Language*, 41, 105–23.

Allum, P. H., & Wheeldon, L. R. (2007). Planning scope in spoken sentence production: The role of grammatical units. *Journal of Experimental Psychology: Learning, Memory, and Cognition*, 33, 791–810.

Allum, P. H., & Wheeldon, L. (2009). Scope of lexical access in spoken sentence production: Implications for the conceptual–syntactic interface. *Journal of Experimental Psychology: Learning, Memory, and Cognition*, 35, 1240–55.

Almeida, J., Knobel, M., Finkbeiner, M., & Caramazza, A. (2007). The locus of the frequency effect in picture naming: When recognizing is not enough. *Psychonomic Bulletin & Review*, 14, 1177–82.

Altmann, G. T., & Kamide, Y. (1999). Incremental interpretation at verbs: Restricting the domain of subsequent reference. *Cognition*, 73, 247–64.

Arnold, J. E., & Watson, D. G. (2015). Synthesizing meaning and processing approaches to prosody: Performance matters. *Language, Cognition, and Neuroscience*, 30, 88–102.

Aronoff, M. (1976). *Word Formation in Generative Grammar*. MIT Press, Cambridge, MA.

Aronoff, M. (1994). *Morphology by Itself: Stems and Inflectional Classes.* (Linguistic Inquiry Monograph, 22.), MIT Press, Cambridge, MA.

Aylett, M., & Turk, A. (2004). The smooth signal redundancy hypothesis: A functional explanation for relationships between redundancy, prosodic prominence, and duration in spontaneous speech. *Language and Speech*, 47, 31–56.

Baayen, R. H. (1994). Productivity in production. *Language and Cognitive Processes*, 9, 447–69.

Badecker, W. (2001). Lexical composition and the production of compounds: Evidence from errors in naming. *Language and Cognitive Processes*, 16, 337–66.

Badecker, W., & Caramazza, A. (1991). Morphological composition in the lexical output system. *Cognitive Neuropsychology*, 8, 335–67.

Baković, E. (2014). Phonology and phonological theory. In: Ferreira, V., Goldrick, M., & Miozzo, M. (Eds.), *The Oxford Handbook of Language Production* (pp. 199–209). Oxford University Press, Oxford.

Baron, N. S. (1971). A reanalysis of English grammatical gender. *Lingua*, 27, 113–40.

Barry, C., Hirsh, K. W., Johnston, R. A., & Williams, C. L. (2001). Age of acquisition, word frequency, and the locus of repetition priming of picture naming. *Journal of Memory and Language*, 44, 350–75.

Bates, E., D'Amico, S., Jacobsen, T., Székely, A., Andonova, E., Devescovi, A., . . . & Tzeng, O. (2003). Timed picture naming in seven languages. *Psychonomic Bulletin & Review, 10*, 344–80.

Baus, C., Costa, A., & Carreiras, M. (2008). Neighbourhood density and frequency effects in speech production: A case for interactivity. *Language and Cognitive Processes, 23*, 866–88.

Belke, E., Meyer, A. S., & Damian, M. F. (2005). Refractory effect in picture naming as assessed in a semantic blocking paradigm. *Quarterly Journal of Experimental Psychology: Human Experimental Psychology, 58*, 667–92.

Bell, A., Brenier, J. M., Gregory, M., Girand, C., & Jurafsky, D. (2009). Predictability effects on durations of content and function words in conversational English. *Journal of Memory and Language, 60*, 92–111.

Bell, A., Jurafsky, D., Fosler-Lussier, E., Girand, C., Gregory, M., & Gildea, D. (2003). Effects of disfluencies, predictability, and utterance position on word form variation in English conversation. *The Journal of the Acoustical Society of America, 113*, 1001–24.

Bien, H., Baayen, H. R., & Levelt, W. J. M. (2011). Frequency effects in the production of Dutch deverbal adjectives and inflected verbs. *Language and Cognitive Processes, 27*, 683–715.

Bien, H., Levelt, W. J. M., & Baayen, H. R. (2006). Frequency effects in compound production. *Proceedings of the National Academy of Sciences, 102*(49), 17876–81.

Blanken, G. (2000). The production of nominal compounds in aphasia. *Brain and Language, 74*, 84–102.

Blevins, J. P. (2014). The morphology of words. In: Ferreira, V., Goldrick, M., & Miozzo, M. (Eds.), *The Oxford Handbook of Language Production* (pp. 152–64). Oxford University Press, Oxford.

Bloem, I., & La Heij, W. (2003). Semantic facilitation and semantic interference in word translation: Implications for models of lexical access. *Journal of Memory and Language, 48*, 468–88.

Bloem, I., van den Boogaard, S., & La Heij, W. (2004). Semantic facilitation and semantic interference in language production: Further evidence for the conceptual selection model of lexical access. *Journal of Memory and Language, 51*, 307–23.

Bock, K. (1987). An effect of the accessibility of word forms on sentence structures. *Journal of Memory and Language, 26*, 119–37.

Bock, K., Cutler, A., Eberhard, K. M., Butterfield, S., Cutting, J. C., & Humphreys, K. R. (2006). Number agreement in British and American English: Disagreeing to agree collectively. *Language, 82*(1) 64–113.

Boiteau, T. W., Malone, P. S., Peters, S. A., & Almor, A. (2014). Interference between conversation and a concurrent visuomotor task. *Journal of Experimental Psychology: General, 143*, 295–311.

Breining, B., Nozari, N., & Rapp, B. (2015). Does segmental overlap help or hurt? Evidence from blocked cyclic naming in spoken and written production. *Psychonomic Bulletin & Review, 23*(2), 500–6.

Brown, G. D., & Watson, F. L. (1987). First in, first out: Word learning age and spoken word frequency as predictors of word familiarity and word naming latency. *Memory & Cognition, 15*, 208–16.

Brown-Schmidt, S., & Konopka, A. E. (2008). Little houses and casas pequeñas: Message formulation and syntactic form in unscripted speech with speakers of English and Spanish. *Cognition, 109*, 274–80.

Brown-Schmidt, S., & Tanenhaus, M. K. (2006). Watching the eyes when talking about size: An investigation of message formulation and utterance planning. *Journal of Memory and Language, 54*, 592–609.

Brysbaert, M., & New, B. (2009). Moving beyond Kučera and Francis: A critical evaluation of current word frequency norms and the introduction of a new and improved word frequency measure for American English. *Behavior Research Methods*, 41, 977–90.

Brysbaert, M., Stevens, M., Mandera, P., & Keuleers, E. (2016). The impact of word prevalence on lexical decision times: Evidence from the Dutch Lexicon Project 2. *Journal of Experimental Psychology: Human Perception and Performance*, 42, 441–58.

Brysbaert, M., Van Wijnendaele, I., & De Deyne, S. (2000). Age-of-acquisition effects in semantic processing tasks. *Acta Psychologica*, 104, 215–26.

Buchwald, A. (2014). Phonetic processing. In: Ferreira, V., Goldrick, M., & Miozzo, M. (Eds.), *The Oxford Handbook of Language Production* (pp. 245–58). Oxford University Press, Oxford.

Bürki, A., & Laganaro, M. (2014). Tracking the time course of multi-word noun phrase production with ERPs or on when (and why) cat is faster than the big cat. *Frontiers in Psychology*, 5, 586.

Butterworth, B. (1983). Lexical representation. In: Butterworth, B. (Ed.), *Language Production: Vol 2. Development, Writing and other Language Processes* (pp. 257–94). Academic Press, London.

Buz, E., & Jaeger, T. F. (2015). The (in) dependence of articulation and lexical planning during isolated word production. *Language, Cognition and Neuroscience*, 31, 404–24.

Caramazza, A. (1997). How many levels of processing are there in lexical access? *Cognitive Neuropsychology*, 14, 177–208.

Caramazza, A., & Miozzo, M. (1997). The relation between syntactic and phonological knowledge in lexical access: Evidence from the "tip-of-the-tongue" phenomenon. *Cognition*, 64, 309–43.

Caselli, N. K., Caselli, M. K., & Cohen-Goldberg, A. (2015). Inflected words in production: Evidence for a morphologically rich lexicon. *Quarterly Journal of Experimental Psychology*, 69, 1–53.

Chen, J.-Y., Chen, T.-M., & Dell, G. S. (2002). Wordform encoding in Mandarin Chinese as assessed by the implicit priming task. *Journal of Memory and Language*, 46, 751–81.

Chen, J-Y., O'Séaghdha, P. G., & Chen, T-M. (2016). The primacy of abstract syllables in Chinese word production. *Journal of Experimental Psychology: Learning, Memory, and Cognition*, 42, 825–36.

Chen, Q., & Mirman, D. (2012). Competition and cooperation among similar representations: toward a unified account of facilitative and inhibitory effects of lexical neighbors. *Psychological Review*, 199, 417–30.

Chen, T-M., & Chen, J-Y. (2006). Morphological encoding in the production of compound words in Mandarin Chinese. *Journal of Memory and Language*, 54, 491–514.

Chen, T.-M., & Chen, J.-Y. (2013). The syllable as the proximate unit in Mandarin Chinese word production: An intrinsic or accidental property of the production system? *Psychonomic Bulletin & Review*, 20, 154–62.

Cholin, J., Dell, G., & Levelt, W. J. M. (2011). Planning and articulation in incremental word production: Syllable-frequency effects in English. *Journal of Experimental Psychology: Learning, Memory, and Cognition*, 37, 109–22.

Cholin, J., Levelt, W. J. M., & Schiller, N. O. (2006). Effects of syllable frequency in speech production. *Cognition*, 99, 205–35.

Cholin, J., Rapp, B., & Miozzo, M. (2010). When do combinatorial mechanisms apply in the production of inflected words? *Cognitive Neuropsychology*, 27, 334–59.

Christiansen, M. H., & Chater, N. (2016). The now-or-never bottleneck: A fundamental constraint on language. *Behavioral and Brain Sciences*, 39, e62.

Clark, H. H., & Fox Tree, J. E. (2002). Interpreting pauses and ums at turn exchanges. *Discourse Processes*, 34, 37–55.

Cohen-Goldberg, A. M., Cholin, J., Miozzo, M., & Rapp, B. (2013). The interface between morphology and phonology: Exploring a morpho-phonological deficit in spoken production. *Cognition*, 127, 270–86.

Corbett, G. S. (1991). *Gender*. Cambridge University Press, Cambridge.

Costa, A., & Caramazza, A. (2002). The production of noun phrases in English and Spanish: Implications for the scope of phonological encoding in speech production. *Journal of Memory and Language*, 46, 178–98.

Costa, A., Alario, F. X., & Caramazza, A. (2005). On the categorical nature of the semantic interference effect in the picture-word interference paradigm. *Psychonomic Bulletin & Review*, 12, 125–31.

Costa, A., Caramazza, A., & Sebastián-Gallés, N. (2000). The cognate facilitation effect: implications for models of lexical access. *Journal of Experimental Psychology: Learning, Memory, and Cognition*, 26, 1283–96.

Costa, A., Miozzo, M., & Caramazza, A. (1999). Lexical selection in bilinguals: Do words in the bilingual's two lexicons compete for selection? *Journal of Memory and Language*, 41, 365–97.

Cutting, J. C., & Ferreira, V. S. (1999). Semantic and phonological information flow in the production lexicon. *Journal of Experimental Psychology: Learning, Memory, and Cognition*, 25, 318–44.

Damian, M. F., & Bowers, J. S. (2003). Locus of semantic interference in picture-word interference tasks. *Psychonomic Bulletin & Review*, 10, 111–17.

Damian, M. F. E., Bowers, J. S., Stadthagen-Gonzalez, H., & Spalek, K. (2010). Does word length affect speech onset latencies in single word production? *Journal of Experimental Psychology: Learning, Memory, and Cognition*, 36, 892–905.

Damian, M. F., & Dumay, N. (2007). Time pressure and phonological advance planning in spoken production. *Journal of Memory and Language*, 57, 195–209.

Damian, M. F., & Dumay, N. (2009). Exploring phonological encoding through repeated segments. *Language & Cognitive Processes*, 24, 685–712.

Damian, M. F., Vigliocco, G., & Levelt, W. J. M. (2001). Effects of semantic context in the naming of pictures and words. *Cognition*, 81, B77–B86.

Davis, M. H., van Casteren, M., Marslen-Wilson, W. D. (2003). Frequency effects in processing inflected Dutch nouns: A distributed connectionist account. In: Baayen, R. H., & Schreuder R. (Eds.), *Morphological Structure in Language Processing* (pp. 427–62). Mouton de Gruyter, Berlin.

Dell, G. S. (1986). A spreading-activation theory of retrieval in sentence production. *Psychological Review*, 93, 283–321.

Dell, G. S., Chang, F., & Griffin, Z. M. (1999). Connectionist models of language production: Lexical access and grammatical encoding. *Cognitive Science*, 23, 517–42.

Dell, G. S., & Gordon, J. K. (2003). Neighbors in the lexicon: Friends or foes?. In: Schiller, N. O., & Meyer, A. S. (Eds.) *Phonetics and Phonology in Language Comprehension and Production: Differences and Similarities*. Mouton de Gruyter, New York, NY.

Dell, G. S., Juliano, C., & Govindjee, A. (1993). Structure and content in language production: A theory of frame constraints in phonological speech errors. *Cognitive Science*, 17, 149–95.

Dell, G. S., Nozari, N., & Oppenheim, G. M. (2014). Lexical access: Behavioral and computational considerations. In: Ferreira, V., Goldrick, M., & Miozzo, M. (Eds.), *The Oxford Handbook of Language Production* (pp. 88–104). Oxford University Press, Oxford.

Dell, G. S., & O'Séaghdha, P. G. (1991). Mediated and convergent lexical priming in language production: A comment on Levelt et al. (1991). *Psychological Review, 98*, 604–14.

Dell, G. S., & O'Séaghdha, P. G. (1992). Stages of lexical access in language production. *Cognition, 42*, 287–314.

Dell, G. S., Oppenheim, G. M., & Kittredge, A. K. (2008). Saying the right word at the right time: Syntagmatic and paradigmatic interference in sentence production. *Language and Cognitive Processes, 23*, 583–608.

Dell, G. S., Schwartz, M. F., Martin, N., Saffran, E. M., & Gagnon, D. A. (1997). Lexical access in aphasic and nonaphasic speakers. *Psychological Review, 104*, 801–33.

Dhooge, E., & Hartsuiker, R. J. (2010). The distractor frequency effect in picture–word interference: Evidence for response exclusion. *Journal of Experimental Psychology: Learning, Memory, and Cognition, 36*, 878–91.

Dohmes, P., Zwitserlood, P., & Bölte, J. (2004). The impact of semantic transparency of morphologically complex words on picture naming. *Brain and Language, 90*, 203–12.

Ellis, A. W., & Lambon Ralph, M. A. (2000). Age of acquisition effects in adult lexical processing reflect loss of plasticity in maturing systems: insights from connectionist networks. *Journal of Experimental Psychology: Learning, Memory, and Cognition, 26*, 1103–23.

Ferreira, F. (1993). The creation of prosody during sentence processing. *Psychological Review, 100*, 233–53.

Ferreira, F. (2007). Prosody and performance in language production. *Language and Cognitive Processes, 22*, 1151–77.

Ferreira, V. S., & Pashler, H. (2002). Central bottleneck influences on the processing stages of word production. *Journal of Experimental Psychology: Learning, Memory, and Cognition, 28*, 1187–99.

Ferreira, F., & Swets, B. (2002). How incremental is language production? Evidence from the production of utterances requiring the computation of arithmetic sums. *Journal of Memory and Language, 46*, 57–84.

Finkbeiner, M., & Caramazza, A. (2006). Now you see it, now you don't: On turning semantic interference into facilitation in a Stroop-like task. *Cortex, 42*, 790–6.

Fromkin, V. (1973). *Speech Errors as Linguistic Evidence*. Mouton, The Hague.

Gahl, S. (2015). Lexical competition in vowel articulation revisited: Vowel dispersion in the Easy/Hard database. *Journal of Phonetics, 49*, 96–116.

Gahl, S., & Garnsey, S. M. (2004). Knowledge of grammar, knowledge of usage: Syntactic probabilities affect pronunciation variation. *Language, 80*, 748–75.

Gahl, S., & Strand, J. F. (2016). Many neighborhoods: Phonological and perceptual neighborhood density in lexical production and perception. *Journal of Memory and Language, 89*, 162–78.

Gahl, S., Yao, Y., & Johnson, K. (2012). Why reduce? Phonological neighborhood density and phonetic reduction in spontaneous speech. *Journal of Memory and Language, 66*, 789–806.

Garrett, M. F. (1975). The analysis of sentence production. In: Bower, G. (Ed.), *Psychology of Learning and Motivation*, Vol. 9 (pp. 133–77). Academic Press, New York, NY.

Garrett, M. F. (1980). Levels of processing in sentence production. In: Butterworth, B. (Ed.), *Language Production*, Vol. 1 (pp. 177–220). Academic Press, London.

Glaser, W. R. (1992). Picture naming. *Cognition, 42*, 61–105.

Glaser, W. R., & Düngelhoff, F. J. (1984). The time course of picture-word interference. *Journal of Experimental Psychology: Human Perception and Performance, 10*, 640–54.

Gleitman, L. R., January, D., Nappa, R., & Trueswell, J. C. (2007). On the give and take between event apprehension and utterance formulation. *Journal of Memory and Language, 57*, 544–69.

Goldrick, M. (2014). The retrieval and encoding of word information in speech production. In: Ferreira, V., Goldrick, M., & Miozzo, M. (Eds.), *The Oxford Handbook of Language Production* (pp. 228–44). Oxford University Press, Oxford.

Goldrick, M., & Rapp, B. (2007). Lexical and postlexical phonological representations in spoken production. *Cognition, 102*, 219–60.

Goldrick, M., Folk, J., & Rapp, B. (2010). Mrs. Malaprop's neighborhood: Using word errors to reveal neighborhood structure. *Journal of Memory and Language, 62*, 113–34.

Goldrick, M., Vaughn, C., & Murphy, A. (2013). The effects of lexical neighbors on stop consonant articulation. *The Journal of the Acoustical Society of America, 134*, EL172–7.

Goldsmith, J. (1990). *Autosegmental and Metrical Phonology*. Basil Blackwell, Oxford.

Goldstein, L., & Pouplier, M. (2014). The temporal organization of speech. In: Ferreira, V., Goldrick, M., & Miozzo, M. (Eds.), *The Oxford Handbook of Language Production* (pp. 210–27). Oxford University Press, Oxford.

Gordon, J. K. (2002). Phonological neighborhood effects in aphasic speech errors: Spontaneous and structured contexts. *Brain and Language, 82*, 113–45.

Gordon, J. K., & Dell, G. S. (2003). Learning to divide the labor: An account of deficits in light and heavy verb production. *Cognitive Science, 27*, 1–40.

Griffin, Z. M. (2001). Gaze durations during speech reflect word selection and phonological encoding. *Cognition, 82*, B1–B14.

Griffin, Z. M. (2003). A reversed length effect in coordinating the preparation and articulation of words in speaking. *Psychonomic Bulletin & Review 10*, 603–9.

Griffin, Z. M., & Bock, K. (1998). Constraint, word frequency, and the relationship between lexical processing levels in spoken word production. *Journal of Memory and Language, 38*, 313–38.

Griffin, Z. M., & Bock, K. (2000). What the eyes say about speaking. *Psychological Science, 11*, 274–9.

Howard, D., Nickels, L., Coltheart, M., & Cole-Virtue, J. (2006). Cumulative semantic inhibition in picture naming: Experimental and computational studies. *Cognition, 100*, 464–82.

Hwang, H., & Kaiser, E. (2014). The role of the verb in grammatical function assignment in English and Korean. *Journal of Experimental Psychology: Learning, Memory, and Cognition, 40*, 1363–73.

Indefrey, P. (2011). The spatial and temporal signatures of word production components: A critical update. *Frontiers in Psychology, 2*, 255.

Indefrey, P., & Levelt, W. J. (2004). The spatial and temporal signatures of word production components. *Cognition, 92*, 101–44.

Jacobs, C. L., & Dell, G. S. (2014). "hotdog" not "hot" "dog": The phonological planning of compound words. *Language, Cognition, and Neuroscience, 29*, 512–23.

Jaeger, T. F. (2010). Redundancy and reduction: Speakers manage syntactic information density. *Cognitive Psychology, 61*, 23–62.

Janssen, N., Bi, Y., and Caramazza, A. (2008). A tale of two frequencies: Determining the speed of lexical access in Mandarin Chinese and English compounds. *Language and Cognitive Processes, 23*, 1191–223.

Janssen, N., Pajtas, P. E., & Caramazza, A. (2014). Task influences on the production and comprehension of compound words. *Memory & Cognition, 42*, 1–14.

Janssen, D. P., Roelofs, A., & Levelt, W. J. M. (2002). Inflectional frames in language production. *Language and Cognitive Processes, 17*, 209–36.

Janssen, D. P., Roelofs, A., & Levelt, W. J. M. (2004). Stem complexity and inflectional encoding in language production. *Journal of Psycholinguistic Research, 33*, 365–81.

Janssen, N., Schirm, W., Mahon, B. Z., & Caramazza, A. (2008). Semantic interference in a delayed naming task: Evidence for the response exclusion hypothesis. *Journal of Experimental Psychology: Learning, Memory, and Cognition, 34*, 249–56.

Jescheniak, J. D., & Levelt, W. J. M. (1994). Word frequency effects in speech production: Retrieval of syntactic information and of phonological form. *Journal of Experimental Psychology: Learning, Memory, and Cognition, 29*, 432–8.

Jescheniak, J. D., & Schriefers, H. (1998). Discrete serial versus cascaded processing in lexical access in speech production: Further evidence from the coactivation of near-synonyms. *Journal of Experimental Psychology: Learning, Memory, and Cognition, 24*, 1256–74.

Jescheniak, J. D., Schriefers, H., & Hantsch A. (2003). Utterance format affects phonological priming in the picture–word task: Implications for models of phonological encoding in speech production. *Journal of Experimental Psychology: Human Perception and Performance, 29*, 441–54.

Johnston, R. A., & Barry, C. (2006). Age of acquisition and lexical processing. *Visual Cognition, 13*, 789–845.

Jongman, S. R., Roelofs, A., & Meyer, A. S. (2015a). Sustained attention in language production: An individual differences investigation. *The Quarterly Journal of Experimental Psychology, 68*, 710–30.

Jongman, S. R., Meyer, A. S., & Roelofs, A. (2015b). The role of sustained attention in the production of conjoined noun phrases: An individual differences study. *PloS One, 10*, e0137557.

Jurafsky, D, Bell, A., Gregory, M., & Raymond, W. D. (2001). Probabilistic relations between words: Evidence from reduction in lexical production. In: Bybee, J., & Hopper, P. (Eds.), *Frequency and the Emergence of Linguistic Structure* (pp. 229–54). John Benjamins, Amsterdam.

Kawamoto, A. H., Kello, C. T., Jones, R., & Bame, K. (1998). Initial phoneme versus whole word criterion to initiate pronunciation: Evidence based on response latency and initial phoneme duration. *Journal of Experimental Psychology: Learning, Memory, and Cognition, 24*, 862–85.

Keuleers, E., Stevens, M., Mandera, P., & Brysbaert, M. (2015). Word knowledge in the crowd: Measuring vocabulary size and word prevalence in a massive online experiment. *The Quarterly Journal of Experimental Psychology, 68*, 1665–92.

Kittredge, A. K., Dell, G. S., Verkuilen, J., & Schwartz, M. F. (2008). Where is the effect of frequency in word production? Insights from aphasic picture-naming errors. *Cognitive Neuropsychology, 25*, 463–92.

Koester, D., and Schiller, N. O. (2008). Morphological priming in overt language production: Electrophysiological evidence from Dutch. *NeuroImage 42*, 1622–30.

Konopka, A. E. (2009). *Variability in the scope of planning for simple and complex noun phrases: Effects of experience with messages, structures, and words*. Poster presented at the 22nd CUNY Human Sentence Processing Conference, Davis, CA, USA.

Konopka, A. E. (2012). Planning ahead: How recent experience with structures and words changes the scope of linguistic planning. *Journal of Memory and Language, 66*, 143–62.

Konopka, A. E., & Brown-Schmidt, S. (2014). Message encoding. In: Ferreira, V., Goldrick, M., Miozzo, M. (Eds.), *The Oxford Handbook of Language Production* (pp. 3–20). Oxford University Press, Oxford.

Konopka, A. E., & Meyer, A. S. (2014). Priming sentence planning. *Cognitive Psychology*, 73, 1–40.

Kousta, S. T., Vinson, D. P., & Vigliocco, G. (2008). Investigating linguistic relativity through bilingualism: The case of grammatical gender. *Journal of Experimental Psychology: Learning, Memory, and Cognition*, 34, 843–58.

Kroll, J. F., & Stewart, E. (1994). Category interference in translation and picture naming: Evidence for asymmetric connections between bilingual memory representations. *Journal of Memory and Language*, 33, 149–74.

Kuchinsky, S. E. (2009). *From Seeing to Saying: Perceiving, Planning, Producing* [Unpublished doctoral dissertation]. University of Illinois at Urbana-Champaign, Champaign, IL.

Kuipers, J. R., La Heij, W., & Costa, A. (2006). A further look at semantic context effects in language production: The role of response congruency. *Language and Cognitive Processes*, 21, 892–919.

Kureta, Y., Fushimi, T., & Tatsumi, I. F. (2006). The functional unit in phonological encoding: Evidence for moraic representation in native Japanese speakers. *Journal of Experimental Psychology: Learning, Memory, and Cognition*, 32(5), 1102–19.

Laganaro, M., Chetelat-Mabillard, D., & Frauenfelder, U. H. (2013). Facilitatory and interfering effects of neighborhood density on speech production: Evidence from aphasic errors. *Cognitive Neuropsychology*, 30, 127–46.

Lahiri, A. (2000). Phonology: structure, representation and process. In: Wheeldon, L. R. (Ed.), *Aspects of Language Production* (pp. 165–247). Psychology Press/Taylor and Francis, Hove.

Lahiri, A., Jongman, A., & Sereno, J. (1990). The pronominal clitic [der] in Dutch. *Yearbook of Morphology*, 3, 115–27.

Lahiri, A., & Wheeldon, L. R. (2011). Phonological trochaic grouping in language planning and language change. In: Frota, S. (Ed.), *Prosodic Categories: Production, Perception and Comprehension*. Springer, London.

Lee, J., & Thompson, C. K. (2015). Phonological facilitation effects on naming latencies and viewing times during noun and verb naming in agrammatic and anomic aphasia. *Aphasiology*, 29, 1164–88.

Lehiste, I. (1970). *Suprasegmentals*. MIT Press, Cambridge, MA.

Leshinskaya, A., & Caramazza, A. (2014). Organization and structure of conceptual representations. In: Ferreira, V., Goldrick, M., & Miozzo, M. (Eds.), *The Oxford Handbook of Language Production* (pp. 118–33). Oxford University Press, Oxford.

Levelt, W. J. M. (1989). *Speaking: From Intention to Articulation*. Cambridge, MA, MIT Press.

Levelt, W. J. M., Roelofs, A., & Meyer, A. S. (1999). A theory of lexical access in speech production. *Behavioral & Brain Sciences*, 22, 1–38.

Levelt, W. J. M., & Wheeldon, L. R. (1994). Do speakers have access to a mental syllabary? *Cognition*, 50, 239–69.

Levinson, S. C. (2016). Turn-taking in human communication–origins and implications for language processing. *Trends in Cognitive Sciences*, 20, 6–14.

Lewis, M. B., Gerhand, S., & Ellis, H. D. (2001). Re-evaluating age-of-acquisition effects: are they simply cumulative-frequency effects? *Cognition*, 78, 189–205.

Luce, P. A., & Pisoni, D. B. (1998). Recognizing spoken words: The Neighborhood Activation Model. *Ear & Hearing*, 19, 1–36.

Lüttmann, H., Zwitserlood, P., Böhl, A., & Bölte, J. (2011). Evidence for morphological composition at the form level in speech production. *Journal of Cognitive Psychology*, 23, 818–36.

Mahon, B. Z., Garcea, F. E., & Navarrete, E. (2012). Picture-word interference and the response-exclusion hypothesis: A response to Mulatti and Coltheart. *Cortex*, 48, 373–7.

Mahon, B. Z., Costa, A., Peterson, R., Vargas, K. A., & Caramazza, A. (2007). Lexical selection is not by competition: A reinterpretation of semantic interference and facilitation effects in the picture-word interference paradigm. *Journal of Experimental Psychology: Learning, Memory, and Cognition*, 33, 503–35.

Mahowald, K., Fedorenko, E., Piantadosi, S. T., & Gibson, E. (2013). Info/information theory: Speakers choose shorter words in predictive contexts. *Cognition*, 126, 313–18.

Malpass, D., & Meyer, A. S. (2010). The time course of name retrieval during multiple-object naming: Evidence from extrafoveal-on-foveal effects. *Journal of Experimental Psychology: Learning, Memory, and Cognition*, 36, 523–37.

Martin, R. C., Crowther, J. E., Knight, M., Tamborello, F. P., & Yang, C. L. (2010). Planning in sentence production: Evidence for the phrase as a default planning scope. *Cognition*, 116, 177–92.

Martin, R. C., Miller, M., & Vu, H. (2004). Lexical-semantic retention and speech production: further evidence from normal and brain-damaged participants for a phrasal scope of planning. *Cognitive Neuropsychology*, 21, 625–44.

Melinger, A. (2003). Morphological structure in the lexical representation of prefixed words: evidence from speech errors. *Language and Cognitive Processes*, 18, 335–62.

Meyer, A. S. (1990). The time course of phonological encoding in language production: the encoding of successive syllables of a word. *Journal of Memory and Language* 29, 524–45.

Meyer, A. S. (1991). The time course of phonological encoding in language production: phonological coding inside a syllable. *Journal of Memory and Language*, 30, 69–89.

Meyer, A. S. (1996). Lexical access in phrase and sentence production: Results from picture–word interference experiments. *Journal of Memory and Language*, 35, 77–496.

Meyer, A. S., Belke, E., Häcker, C., & Mortensen, L. (2007). Use of word length information in utterance planning. *Journal of Memory and Language*, 57, 210–31.

Meyer, A. S., & Damian, M. F. (2007). Activation of distractor names in the picture–picture interference paradigm. *Memory & Cognition*, 35, 494–503.

Meyer, A. S., Roelofs, A., & Levelt, W. J. M. (2003). Word length effects in object naming: The role of a response criterion. *Journal of Memory and Language*, 48, 131–47.

Meyer, A. S., & Schriefers, H. (1991). Phonological facilitation in picture-word interference experiments: Effects of stimulus onset asynchrony and types of interfering stimuli. *Journal of Experimental Psychology: Learning, Memory, and Cognition*, 17, 1146–60.

Meyer, A. S., Sleiderink, A. M., & Levelt, W. J. (1998). Viewing and naming objects: Eye movements during noun phrase production. *Cognition*, 66, B25–B33.

Meyer, A. S., Wheeldon, L., Van der Meulen, F., & Konopka, A. (2012). Effects of speech rate and practice on the allocation of visual attention in multiple object naming. *Frontiers in Psychology*, 3, 39.

Meyer, D. E., & Gordon, P. C. (1985). Speech production: Motor programming of phonetic features. *Journal of Memory and Language*, 224, 3–26.

Middleton, E. L., & Schwartz, M. F. (2010). Density pervades: An analysis of phonological neighbourhood density effects in aphasic speakers with different types of naming impairment. *Cognitive Neuropsychology*, 27, 401–27.

Middleton, E. L., Wisniewski, E. J., Trindel, K. A., & Imai, M. (2004). Separating the chaff from the oats: Evidence for a conceptual distinction between count noun and mass noun aggregates. *Journal of Memory and Language, 50*, 371–94.

Miozzo, M., & Caramazza, A. (1999). The selection of determiners in noun phrase production. *Journal of Experimental Psychology: Learning, Memory, and Cognition, 25*, 907–22.

Miozzo, M., & Caramazza, A. (2003). When more is less: a counterintuitive effect of distractor frequency in the picture-word interference paradigm. *Journal of Experimental Psychology: General, 132*, 228–51.

Morgan, J. L., & Meyer, A. S. (2005). Processing of extrafoveal objects during multiple-object naming. *Journal of Experimental Psychology: Learning, Memory, and Cognition, 31*, 428–42.

Morgan, J. L., & Wheeldon, L. R. (2003). Syllable monitoring in internally and externally generated English words. *Journal of Psycholinguistic Research, 32*, 269–96.

Morrison, C. M., & Ellis, A. W. (1995). Roles of word frequency and age of acquisition in word naming and lexical decision. *Journal of Experimental Psychology: Learning, Memory, and Cognition, 21*, 116–33.

Morsella, E., & Miozzo, M. (2002). Evidence for a cascade model of lexical access in speech production. *Journal of Experimental Psychology: Learning, Memory, and Cognition, 28*, 555–63.

Mortensen, L., Meyer, A. S., & Humphreys, G. W. (2006). Age-related effects on speech production: A review. *Language and Cognitive Processes, 21*, 238–90.

Navarrete, E., Mahon, B. Z., & Caramazza, A. (2010). The cumulative semantic cost does not reflect lexical selection by competition. *Acta Psychologica, 134*, 279–89.

Nespor, M., & Vogel, I. (1986). *Prosodic Phonology*. Foris, Dordrecht, the Netherlands.

Norcliffe, E., Konopka, A. E., Brown, P., & Levinson, S. C. (2015). Word order affects the time course of sentence formulation in Tzeltal. *Language, Cognition and Neuroscience, 30*, 1187–208.

Nozari, N., Freund, M., Breining, B., Rapp, B., & Gordon, B. (2016). Cognitive control during selection and repair in word production, *Language, Cognition and Neuroscience, 31*(7), 886–903.

Oppenheim, G. M., & Dell, G. S. (2008). Inner speech slips exhibit lexical bias, but not the phonemic similarity effect. *Cognition, 106*, 528–37.

Oppenheim, G. M., & Dell, D. S. (2010). Motor movement matters: The flexible abstractness of inner speech. *Memory & Cognition, 38*, 1147–60.

Oppenheim, G. M., Dell, G. S., & Schwartz, M. F. (2010). The dark side of incremental learning: A model of cumulative semantic interference during lexical access in speech production. *Cognition, 114*, 227–52.

Oppermann, F., Jescheniak, J. D., & Schriefers, H. (2010). Phonological advance planning in sentence production. *Journal of Memory and Language, 63*, 526–40.

O'Séaghdha, P. G. (2015). Across the great divide: Proximate units at the lexical-phonological interface. *Japanese Psychological Research, 57*, 4–21.

O'Séaghdha, P. G., Chen, J.-Y., & Chen, T.-M. (2010). Proximate units in word production: Phonological encoding begins with syllables in Mandarin Chinese but with segments in English. *Cognition, 115*, 282–302.

O'Séaghdha, P. G., Dell, G. S., Peterson, R. R., & Juliano, C. (1992). Modelling form-related priming effects in comprehension and production. In: Reilly, R., & Sharkey, N. E. (Eds.), *Connectionist Approaches to Language Processing* (*Vol. 1*). Lawrence Erlbaum Associates Inc, Hillsdale, NJ.

O'Séaghdha, P. G., & Marin, J. W. (2000). Phonological competition and cooperation in form-related priming: Sequential and nonsequential processes in word production. *Journal of Experimental Psychology: Human Perception & Performance*, 26(1), 57–73.

Peterson, R. R., & Savoy, P. (1998). Lexical selection and phonological encoding during language production: Evidence for cascaded processing. *Journal of Experimental Psychology: Learning, Memory, and Cognition*, 24, 539–57.

Piai, V., Roelofs, A., & Schriefers, H. (2011). Semantic interference in immediate and delayed naming and reading: Attention and task decisions. *Journal of Memory and Language*, 64, 404–23.

Piai, V., & Roelofs, A. (2013); Piantadosi, S. T., Tily, H., & Gibson, E. (2010). Word lengths are optimized for efficient communication. *Proceedings of the National Academy of Sciences*, 108, 3526–9.

Plaut, D. C., & Gonnerman, L. M. (2000). Are non-semantic morphological effects incompatible with a distributed connectionist approach to lexical processing? *Language and Cognitive Processes*, 15, 445–85.

Qu, Q., Damian, M. F., & Kazanina, N. (2012). Soundsized segments are significant for Mandarin speakers. *Proceedings of the National Academy of Sciences of the United States of America*, 109, 14265–70.

Rapp, B., & Goldrick, M. (2000). Discreteness and interactivity in spoken word production. *Psychological Review*, 107, 460–99.

Rapp, B., & Goldrick, M. (2006). Speaking words: Contributions of cognitive neuropsychological research. *Cognitive Neuropsychology*, 23, 39–73.

Roberts, S. G., Torreira, F., & Levinson, S. C. (2015). The effects of processing and sequence organization on the timing of turn taking: A corpus study. *Frontiers in Psychology*, 6, 509.

Roelofs, A. (1992). A spreading-activation theory of lemma retrieval in speaking. *Cognition*, 42, 107–142.

Roelofs, A. (1996a). Morpheme frequency in speech production: Testing WEAVER. In: Booij, G. E., & van Marle, J. (Eds.), *Yearbook of Morphology* (pp. 135–54). Kluwer, Dordrecht.

Roelofs, A. (1996b). Serial order in planning the production of successive morphemes of a word. *Journal of Memory and Language*, 35, 854–76.

Roelofs, A. (1997). The WEAVER model of word-form encoding in speech production. *Cognition*, 64, 249–84.

Roelofs, A. (1998). Rightward incrementality in encoding simple phrasal forms in speech production: Verb–particle combinations. *Journal of Experimental Psychology: Learning, Memory, and Cognition*, 24, 904–21.

Roelofs, A. (2003). Goal-referenced selection of verbal action: Modeling attentional control in the Stroop task. *Psychological Review*, 110, 88–125.

Roelofs, A. (2004a). Error biases in spoken word planning and monitoring by aphasic and nonaphasic speakers: Comment on Rapp and Goldrick (2000). *Psychological Review*, 111, 561–72.

Roelofs, A. (2004b). Comprehension-based versus production-internal feedback in planning spoken words: A rejoinder to Rapp and Goldrick (2004). *Psychological Review*, 111, 579–80.

Roelofs, A. (2015). Modeling of phonological encoding in spoken word production: From Germanic languages to Mandarin Chinese and Japanese. *Japanese Psychological Research*, 57, 22–37.

Roelofs, A., & Baayen, H. (2002). Morphology by itself in planning the production of spoken words. *Psychonomic Bulletin & Review*, 9, 132–8.

Roelofs, A., Meyer, A. S., & Levelt, W. J. (1998). A case for the lemma/lexeme distinction in models of speaking: Comment on Caramazza and Miozzo (1997). *Cognition*, 69, 219–30.

Roelofs, A., & Piai, V. (2011). Attention demands of spoken word planning: A review. *Frontiers in Psychology*, 2, 307.

Roelofs, A., & Piai, V. (2015). Aspects of competition in word production: Reply to Mahon and Navarrete. *Cortex*, 64, 420–4.

Romani, C., & Galluzzi, C. (2005). Effects of syllabic complexity in predicting accuracy of repetition and direction of errors in patients with articulatory and phonological difficulties. *Cognitive Neuropsychology*, 22, 817–50.

Romani, C., Galluzzi, C., Bureca, I., & Olson, A. (2011). Effects of syllable structure in aphasic errors: Implications for a new model of speech production. *Cognitive Psychology*, 62, 151–92.

Runnqvist, E., Strijkers, K., Alario, F. X., & Costa, A. (2012). Cumulative semantic interference is blind to language: Implications for models of bilingual speech production. *Journal of Memory and Language*, 66, 850–69.

Sadat, J., Martin, C. D., Costa, A., & Alario, F. X. (2014). Reconciling phonological neighborhood effects in speech production through single trial analysis. *Cognitive Psychology*, 68, 33–58.

Sauppe, S., Norcliffe, E., Konopka, A. E., & Levinson, S. C. (2013). Dependencies first: eye tracking evidence from sentence production in Tagalog. In: *The 35th Annual Meeting of the Cognitive Science Society* (pp. 1265–70). Cognitive Science Society.

Schiller, N. O., Fikkert, P., & Levelt, C. C. (2004). Stress priming in picture naming: An SOA study. *Brain and Language*, 90, 231–40.

Schnur, T. T., Costa, A., & Caramazza, A. (2006). Planning at the phonological level during sentence production. *Journal of Psycholinguistic Research*, 35, 189–213.

Schnur, T. T., Schwartz, M. F., Brecher, A., & Hodgson, C. (2006). Semantic interference during blocked-cyclic naming: Evidence from aphasia. *Journal of Memory and Language*, 54, 199–227.

Schriefers, H., Meyer, A. S., & Levelt, W. J. (1990). Exploring the time course of lexical access in language production: Picture-word interference studies. *Journal of Memory and Language*, 29, 86–102.

Schriefers, H., Teruel, E., & Meinshausen, R. M. (1998). Producing simple sentences: Results from picture–word interference experiments. *Journal of Memory and Language*, 39, 609–32.

Schvaneveldt, R. W., Meyer, D. E., & Becker, C. A. (1976). Lexical ambiguity, semantic context, and visual word recognition. *Journal of Experimental Psychology: Human Perception and Performance*, 2, 243.

Selkirk, E. (1982). The syllable. In: van der Hulst, H., & Smith, N. (Eds.), *The Structure of Phonological Representations II* (pp. 337–83). Foris, Dordrecht.

Selkirk, E. (1984). *Phonology and Syntax: The Relation Between Sound and Structure*. MIT Press, Cambridge, MA/London.

Selkirk, E. O. (1996). Sentence prosody: Intonation, stress and phrasing. In: Goldsmith, J. A. (Ed.), *The Handbook of Phonological Theory* (pp. 550–69). Blackwell, Cambridge, MA.

Sera, M., Selieff, C., Burch, M., Forbes, J., & Rodriguez, W. (2002). When language affects cognition and when it does not: An analysis of grammatical gender and classification. *Journal of Experimental Psychology: General*, 131, 377–97.

Sevald, C. A., & Dell, G. S. (1994). The sequential cuing effect in speech production. *Cognition*, 53, 91–127.

Shao, Z., Meyer, A. S., & Roelofs, A. (2013). Selective and nonselective inhibition of competitors in picture naming. *Memory & Cognition, 41,* 1200–11.

Shao, Z., Roelofs, A., Acheson, D. J., & Meyer, A. S. (2014). Electrophysiological evidence that inhibition supports lexical selection in picture naming. *Brain Research, 1586,* 130–42.

Shao, Z., Roelofs, A., Martin, R. C., & Meyer, A. S. (2015). Selective inhibition and naming performance in semantic blocking, picture-word interference, and color–word Stroop tasks. *Journal of Experimental Psychology: Learning, Memory, and Cognition, 41,* 1806–20.

Shao, Z., & Stiegert, J. (2016). Predictors of photo naming: Dutch norms for 327 photos. *Behavior Research Methods, 48,* 577–84.

Shattuck-Hufnagel, S. (1979). Speech errors as evidence for a serial ordinary-insertion-filterer mechanism in sentence production. In: Cooper, W. E., & Walker, E. C. T. (Eds.), *Sentence Processing: Psycholinguistic Studies Presented to Merrill Garrett* (pp. 295–342). Erlbaum, Hillsdale, NJ.

Shattuck-Hufnagel, S. (2014). Phrase-level phonological and phonetic encoding. In: Ferreira, V., Goldrick, M., & Miozzo, M. (Eds.), *The Oxford Handbook of Language Production* (pp. 259–74). Oxford University Press, Oxford.

Sjerps, M. J., & Meyer, A. S. (2015). Variation in dual-task performance reveals late initiation of speech planning in turn-taking. *Cognition, 136,* 304–24.

Smith, M., & Wheeldon, L. (1999). High level processing scope in spoken sentence production. *Cognition, 73,* 205–46.

Smith, M., & Wheeldon, L. (2001). Syntactic priming in spoken sentence production–an on-line study. *Cognition, 78,* 123–64.

Smith, M. C., & Wheeldon L. R. (2004). Horizontal information flow in spoken sentence production. *Journal of Experimental Psychology: Learning Memory and Cognition, 30,* 675–86.

Snodgrass, J. G., & Yuditsky, T. (1996). Naming times for the Snodgrass and Vanderwart pictures. *Behavior Research Methods, 28,* 516–36.

Stemberger, J. P. (1982). *The Lexicon in a Model of Language Production* [Doctoral dissertation]. University of California, San Diego, CA.

Stemberger, J. P. (1985). An interactive activation model of language production. In: Ellis, A. (Ed.), *Progress in the Psychology of Language* (pp. 143–86). Lawrence Erlbaum and Associates, London.

Stemberger, J. P. (2004). Neighbourhood effects on error rates in speech production. *Brain and Language, 90,* 413–22.

Stemberger, J., & MacWhinney, B. (1986). Frequency and the lexical storage of regularly inflected forms. *Memory & Cognition, 14,* 17–26.

Sullivan, M. P., & Riffel, B. (1999). The nature of phonological encoding during spoken word retrieval. *Language and Cognitive Processes, 14,* 15–45.

Swets, B., Jacovina, M. E., & Gerrig, R. J. (2014). Individual differences in the scope of speech planning: evidence from eye-movements. *Language and Cognition, 6,* 12–44.

Tabossi, P. (1988). Accessing lexical ambiguity in different types of sentential contexts. *Journal of Memory and Language, 27,* 324–40.

Tanenhaus, M. K., Leiman, J. M., & Seidenberg, M. S. (1979). Evidence for multiple stages in the processing of ambiguous words in syntactic contexts. *Journal of Verbal Learning and Verbal Behavior, 18,* 427–40.

Tily, H., Gahl, S., Arnon, N., Snider, N., Kothari, A., & Bresnan, J. (2009). Syntactic probabilities affect pronunciation variation in spontaneous speech. *Language and Cognition, 1,* 147–65.

Torreira, F. J., Bögels, S., & Levinson, S. C. (2016). Breathing for answering. The time course of response planning in conversation. *Frontiers in Psychology, 6*, 284.

Vigliocco, G., & Franck, J. (1999). When sex and syntax go hand in hand: Gender agreement in language production. *Journal of Memory and Language, 40*, 455–78.

Vigliocco, G., & Hartsuiker, R. J. (2002). The interplay of meaning, sound, and syntax in sentence production. *Psychological Bulletin, 128*, 442–72.

Vigliocco, G., & Kita, S. (2006). Language-specific properties of the lexicon: Implications for learning and processing. *Language and Cognitive Processes, 21*, 790–816.

Vigliocco, G., & Vinson, D. P. (2007). Semantic representation. In: Garkell, M. G. (Ed.), *The Oxford Handbook of Psycholinguistics* (pp. 195–215). Oxford University Press, Oxford.

Vigliocco, G., Vinson, D. P., Damian, M. F., & Levelt, W. (2002). Semantic distance effects on object and action naming. *Cognition, 85*, B61–9.

Vigliocco, G., Vinson, D. P., Paganelli, F., & Dworzynski, K. (2005). Grammatical gender effects on cognition: Implications for language learning and language use. *Journal of Experimental Psychology, 134*, 501–20.

Vinson, D., Andrews, M., & Vigliocco, G. (2014). Giving words meaning: Why better models of semantics are needed in language production research. In: Goldrick, M., Ferreira, V., & Miozzo, M. (Eds.), *The Oxford Handbook of Language Production* (pp. 134–51). Oxford University Press, Oxford.

Vitevitch, M. S. (1997). The neighborhood characteristics of malapropisms. *Language & Speech, 40*, 211–28.

Vitevitch, M. S. (2002). The influence of phonological similarity neighborhoods on speech production. *Journal of Experimental Psychology: Learning, Memory, and Cognition, 28*, 735–47.

Vitevitch, M. S., Armbrüster, J., Chu, S. (2004). Sublexical and lexical representations in speech production: Effects of phonotactic probability and onset density. *Journal of Experimental Psychology: Learning, Memory, and Cognition, 30*, 514–29.

Vitevitch, M. S., & Luce, P. A. (2016). Phonological neighborhood effects in spoken word perception and production. *Annual Review of Linguistics, 2*, 75–94.

Vitevitch, M. S., & Sommers, M. (2003). The facilitative influence of phonological similarity and neighborhood frequency in speech production. *Memory & Cognition, 31*, 491–504.

Vitevitch, M. S., & Stamer, M. K. (2006). The curious case of competition in Spanish speech production. *Language and Cognitive Processes, 21*, 760–70.

Wagner, M., & Watson, D. G. (2010). Experimental and theoretical advances in prosody: A review. *Language and Cognitive Processes, 25*, 905–45.

Waksler, R. (2000). Morphological systems and structure in language production. In: Wheeldon, L. R. (Ed.), *Aspects of Language Production* (pp. 227–47). Psychology Press/Taylor and Francis, Hove.

Watson, D. G., Arnold, J. E., & Tanenhaus, M. K. (2008). Tic Tac Toe: effects of predictability and importance on acoustic prominence in language production. *Cognition, 106*, 1548–57.

Watson, D. G., Buxó-Lugo, A., & Simmons, D. C. (2015). The effect of phonological encoding on word duration: Selection takes time. In: Frazier, L., & Gibson, E. (Eds.), *Explicit and Implicit Prosody in Sentence Processing: Studies in Honor of Janet Dean Fodor*. Springer International, New York, NY.

Wheeldon, L. R. (1999). Competitive processes during word form encoding. Comment on "A theory of lexical access in speech production" by W. J. M. Levelt, A. Roelofs & A. S. Meyer. *Behavioral and Brain Sciences, 22*, 59–60.

Wheeldon, L. R. (2000). Generating prosodic structure. In: Wheeldon, L. (Ed.), *Aspects of Language Production* (pp. 165–226). Psychology Press, Hove.

Wheeldon, L. R. (2003). Inhibitory form priming of spoken word production. *Language and Cognitive processes, 18*, 81–109.

Wheeldon, L. R. (2012). Producing spoken sentences: The scope of incremental planning. In: Fuchs, S., Weirich, M., Pape, D., & Perrier, P. (Eds.), *Speech Production and Perception, Vol. 1: Speech Planning and Dynamics* (pp. 97–118). Peter Lang, Frankfurt.

Wheeldon, L. R., & Lahiri, A. (1997). Prosodic units in speech production. *Journal of Memory and Language, 37*, 356–81.

Wheeldon, L. R., & Lahiri, A. (2002). The minimal unit of phonological encoding: prosodic or lexical word. *Cognition, 85*, B31–B41.

Wheeldon, L. R., & Levelt, W. J. M. (1995). Monitoring the time course of phonological encoding. *Journal of Memory and Language, 34*, 311–34.

Wheeldon, L. R., & Monsell, S. (1992). The locus of repetition priming of spoken word production. *Quarterly Journal of Experimental Psychology, 44*, 723–61.

Wheeldon, L. R., & Monsell, S. (1994). Inhibition of spoken word production by priming a semantic competitor. *Journal of Memory and Language, 33*, 332–56.

Wheeldon, L. R., & Morgan, J. L. (2002). Phoneme monitoring in internal and external speech. *Language and Cognitive Processes, 17*, 503–35.

Wheeldon, L. R., Ohlson, N., Ashby, A., & Gator, S. (2013). Lexical availability and grammatical encoding scope during spoken sentence production. *The Quarterly Journal of Experimental Psychology, 66*, 1653–73.

Wheeldon, L. R., Smith, M. C., & Apperly, I. A. (2011). Repeating words in sentences: effects of sentence structure. *Journal of Experimental Psychology: Learning, Memory, and Cognition, 37*, 1051–64.

Wightman C. W., Shattuck-Hufnagel, S., Ostendorf, M., & Price, P. J. (1992). Segmental durations in the vicinity of prosodic phrase boundaries. *Journal of the Acoustical Society of America, 9*, 1707–17.

Wilshire, C. E., & Saffran, E. M. (2005). Contrasting effects of phonological priming in aphasic word production. *Cognition, 95*, 31–71.

Wynne, H., Wheeldon, L. R., & Lahiri, A. (2017). Compounds, phrases and clitics in connected speech. *Journal of Memory and Language, 98*, 45–48.

Yiu, L. K., & Watson, D. G. (2015). When overlap leads to competition: Effects of phonological encoding on word duration. *Psychonomic Bulletin & Review, 22*, 1701–8.

Ziegler, W., & Ackermann, H. (2014). Neural basis of phonological and articulatory processing. In: Ferreira, V., Goldrick, M., & Miozzo, M. (Eds.), *The Oxford Handbook of Language Production* (pp. 275–91). Oxford University Press, Oxford.

Zwitserlood, P., Bölte, J., & Dohmes, P. (2000). Morphological effects on speech production: evidence from picture naming. *Language and Cognitive Processes, 15*, 563–91.

Zwitserlood, P., Bölte, J., & Dohmes, P. (2002). Where and how morphologically complex words interplay with naming pictures. *Brain and Language, 81*, 358–67.

CHAPTER 16

CONNECTIONIST PRINCIPLES IN THEORIES OF SPEECH PRODUCTION

LAUREL BREHM AND MATTHEW GOLDRICK

16.1 INTRODUCTION

IN psycholinguistics, speech production refers broadly to the processes mapping a message the speaker intends to communicate onto its form. If a speaker wishes to tell someone "The picture I'm looking at is an animal—a feline pet," these processes allow the speaker to generate the spoken form "cat." Psycholinguistic theories have focused on *formulation* processes—the construction/retrieval of a plan to produce an utterance. This plan specifies the phonological structure of the utterance (e.g., an accented syllable composed of three segments /k/ /ae/ /t/). Subsequent articulatory/motoric processes execute this plan, producing the actual movements of the speech organs. Theories of these post-formulation processes are not reviewed here (see Byrd & Saltzmann, 2003, for discussion).

Since the mid-1980s (e.g., Dell, 1986; MacKay, 1987; Stemberger, 1985) connectionist architectures have served as the dominant paradigm for characterizing theories of formulation processes. The first section of this chapter examines how two connectionist principles (localist representations and spreading activation) have influenced the development of speech production theories. The use of these principles in framing theories of speech production is discussed, followed by an illustration of how the principles have been used to account for three sets of empirical observations. Although this work has been quite successful in explaining a variety of empirical phenomena, it has failed to incorporate two principles that are central to connectionist research in many other domains: learning and distributed representations. The second section of the chapter reviews three examples of more recent work that incorporate these principles into theories of speech production.

16.2 Spreading activation between localist representations

16.2.1 Localist connectionist principles

Two general connectionist processing principles (after Smolensky, 2000) have guided the bulk of connectionist research in speech production:

1. *Representations are activation patterns.* Mental representations are patterns of numerical activity.
2. *Processing is spreading activation.* Mental processes are transformations of activity patterns by patterns of numerical connections.

To instantiate the first principle, many connectionist speech production theories have assumed that different types of linguistic information are encoded using localist representations (see Page, 2000, for a detailed discussion of the use of such representational structures in connectionist networks). The two basic types of representations are illustrated in Figure 16.1. The first representational type, shown at the top of Figure 16.1, is strictly local; each linguistic object is represented by a single processing unit (e.g., each word has an independent unit such as <CAT>). The second representational type is feature-based (or "semi-local"). In such representations, a small, discrete group of processing units represents each linguistic object (e.g., each word is encoded by a small set of discrete phonemes such as /k/ /ae/ /t/).

To instantiate the second principle, the most basic element of processing in connectionist systems (localist as well as non-localist) is spreading activation. Suppose a numerical pattern of activity is imposed on some set of representational units (e.g., in Fig. 16.1, the word unit <CAT>'s activation is set to 100; all other word units are inactive). This activation can then be spread to other units via a set of weighted connections (e.g., in Fig. 16.1, <CAT>

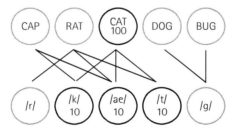

FIG. 16.1 Illustration of spreading activation between strictly local (top layer) and featural (bottom layer) representations in speech production theories. Lines denote connections between units (here, all connection weights are set to 0.1). Numbers within units denote activation (units without numbers have zero activation).

is linked to the phoneme units /k/ /ae/ /t/ by connections with weights of 0.1). The amount of activation a unit transmits to other units is simply the product of its activation and the weight on the connection between the units (e.g., 100 * 0.1). The activation of the target units is the sum of this incoming activation (e.g., 100 * 0.1 = 10 for each phoneme unit connected to <CAT>).

16.2.2 A generic localist connectionist framework

Following Rapp and Goldrick (2000), Figure 16.2 provides a generic representational and processing framework to illustrate how these two connectionist principles are instantiated within theories of single word production. First, three broad levels of linguistic structure are represented by numerical patterns of activity over localist representational units. At the top of the figure are semantic representations, specifying the meaning of lexical items in a particular language. Here, a set of semantic features represents each lexical concept (e.g., {animal, feline, pet} for lexical concept {CAT}). These representations provide an interface between more general (non-linguistic) conceptual processing and those processes that specify the linguistic form of an intended message. The bottom of the figure depicts phonological representations; stored, sublexical representations of the spoken form of lexical items. Here, a set of phonemes represents each word's form (e.g., /k/ /ae/ /t/ for the lexical item <CAT>). The relationship between these two representations is mediated by a lexical representation; here, a unitary word-size node (e.g., <CAT>).

Most current theories of speech production (Garrett, 1980; Levelt, 1992 inter alia) assume that formulation processes are implemented via two stages of activation spreading between these localist representations. The first stage begins with activation of a set of

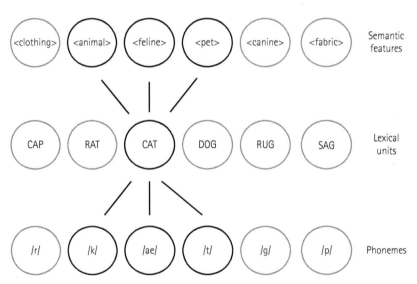

FIG. 16.2 A generic representational framework for speech production. The top layer represents word meaning; the middle, mediating lexical representations; and the bottom, sublexical representations of form. Lines show connections between the representational units for target "cat."

semantic feature units; activation spreads from these units, and the stage ends with the selection of the most strongly activated lexical unit (discussed in more detail next). This corresponds to selecting a lexical item to express the intended message. The second stage begins with the selection of a lexical unit, which spreads activation throughout the production network. This stage ends with the selection of the most strongly activated phoneme units. This corresponds to the construction of an utterance plan for the selected lexical item. It is important to note that these two stages may not be strictly separated; they may interact and overlap in time (e.g., Dell, 1986; a discussion of the interactive mechanisms follows).

As shown by the description here, processing in localist connectionist architectures involves not only the simple spreading of activation between connected units, but also the *selection* of units at particular points in processing. This refers to processes that enhance the activation of units corresponding to one representation relative to that of other units (e.g., enhancement of a single lexical unit; enhancement of a set of phoneme units). By increasing the relative amount of activation that a unit (or group of units) can send on to other representational levels, this enhancement process allows the selected unit(s) to dominate subsequent processing. A variety of spreading activation mechanisms have been used to enhance selected representations. First, some theories propose that the selected representation's activation is simply boosted by adding extra activation to it (e.g., Dell, 1986; Dell, Schwartz, Martin, Saffran, & Gagnon, 1997; Rapp and Goldrick, 2000). For example, in Dell's (1986) theory, at selection points the most highly activated node (or nodes) has its activation boosted to a preset high level. The node is then much more active than its competitors, allowing it to dominate processing. The second selection mechanism involves inhibiting the activation of competitors (see Dell & O'Seaghdha, 1994, for a review; for recent discussion of contrasting views of the role of inhibition in production models, see Abdel Rahman & Melinger, 2009; Mahon & Caramazza, 2009). This mechanism is most often realized computationally via lateral inhibitory connections among units of a similar representational type (e.g., Harley, 1995). With the activation of competitors greatly reduced, the target representation can dominate subsequent processing. A final prominent proposal for enhancing relative activation involves "gating" activation flow. In such systems, representations are not allowed to spread activation to other processing stages until they meet some activation-based response criterion (e.g., a threshold of activation: Laine, Tikkala, & Juhola, 1998; or a relative activation level sufficiently greater than that of competitors: Levelt, Roelofs, & Meyer, 1999). Since only selected representations can influence subsequent processes, they completely dominate processing at these levels.

These selection mechanisms detail how a representation comes to dominate processing. But how does the production system determine which representation to select? Generally, it is assumed that selection processes target a representation that is structurally appropriate. At the lexical level, words must be able to fit into the syntactic structure of the sentence being produced. When producing the head of a noun phrase, it is crucial that a noun (not a verb) be selected. At the phonological level, the selected segments must fit into the appropriate metrical structure. When producing the first segment of <CAT>, it is crucial that an onset consonant (not a vowel, nor a coda consonant such as /ng/) be selected. These structural influences are commonly incorporated into localist connectionist architectures by postulating distinct planning representations. One approach uses structural frames with categorically specified slots to guide selection (e.g., Dell, Burger, & Svec, 1997). Each frame activates its slots in the appropriate sequence. When a slot is active, it enhances the activation of all units within the specified category. This activation boost ensures that structurally appropriate units are selected. For example, at the lexical level, a structural frame for noun phrases would first activate a determiner slot, enhancing the activation of all determiners. Once the determiner has been selected, the frame would activate a noun slot, enhancing the activation of all noun units. This activation support ensures that the most highly activated noun (and not a verb) is selected for production.

It should be noted that the detailed structure of this generic architecture differs from that of many prominent localist connectionist theories. Although these details do not affect the account of the empirical results discussed next, they are briefly reviewed here due to their important implications for other aspects of speech production. First, note that this framework omits any representation of the grammatical properties of lexical items (e.g., grammatical category, number, gender, and so on) which play an important role in speech production (see Ferreira & Morgan, this volume, for further discussion). Second, many theories assume the existence of different numbers and types of localist representations in the production system. With respect to semantic representations, some proposals make use of unitary semantic concept nodes, not sets of features (e.g., {CAT}, instead of {animal, feline, pet}; see Levelt et al., 1999; Roelofs, 1992, for discussion). With respect to phonological representations, many theories assume that in addition to phoneme identity, multiple dimensions of phonological structure are represented (e.g., features, such as [-voice] for /k/; consonant/vowel structure (CVC), such as CVC for "cat"; and metrical structure such as location of stress; see e.g., Dell, 1988; Levelt et al., 1999). Finally, some theories assume that multiple levels of lexical representation are present (e.g., Dell, 1986, 1990; Levelt et al., 1999). A related debate concerns modality specificity: whether a given level of lexical representation is specific to the spoken modality (e.g., Caramazza, 1997) or shared across writing and speaking (e.g., Dell, Schwartz et al., 1997). Theories with two levels of lexical representations generally assume a distinction between modality independent lexical representations (typically referred to as lemmas, which link to grammatical information) and modality dependent representations (typically referred to as lexemes, which link to form information). Those with a single level either assume a single, amodal lexical representation (linking to both grammatical and form information), or distinct lexical representations for spoken and written production (which link to shared grammatical information but distinct form information). (For detailed discussions of the pros and cons of particular proposals for lexical representation(s), see Caramazza, 1997; Caramazza and Miozzo, 1997, 1998; Caramazza, Bi, Costa, & Miozzo, 2004; Caramazza, Costa, Miozzo, & Bi, 2001; Jescheniak, Meyer, & Levelt, 2003; Levelt et al., 1999; Rapp and Caramazza, 2002; Roelofs, Meyer, & Levelt, 1998.)

In spite of differences in the detailed structure of the system, this generic processing framework reflects two core assumptions shared by most speech production theories (see Wheeldon & Konopka, this volume, for a deeper review). First, it makes use of three processing levels that are shared across all current theories (conceptual, lexical, and phonological). Second, it adopts the general assumption (discussed previously) that formulation involves two stages of processing. These core assumptions are sufficient to frame the discussion of the empirical results discussed next.

16.2.3 Applying localist connectionist principles to empirical data

Localist representations and spreading activation mechanisms have been used to account for a wide variety of empirical phenomena. The discussion in this section uses three specific sets of observations to illustrate the influence of these principles on speech production theories. Table 16.1 provides an overview. First, accounts of the contrasting influence of semantic and phonological similarity in picture naming illustrate how connectionist representational principles have influenced production theories. The next section discusses how connectionist processing principles play a crucial role in the explanation of mixed error

Table 16.1 Three sets of empirical observations that have been explained using connectionist principles in theories of speech production

Empirical phenomenon	*Connectionist account*
Semantic interference vs. phonological facilitation in picture naming.	Effect of spreading activation depends on representational structure.
In picture-word interference experiments, words in the same semantic category as the target interfere with picture naming more than unrelated controls. In contrast, words phonologically related to the target facilitate naming relative to controls.	Spreading activation from semantic representations leads to competition between strictly local lexical representations.
	Spreading activation from lexical representations converges on overlapping feature-based phonological representations.
Mixed error effect.	Spreading activation allows processes at distinct representational levels to interact.
Word errors that overlap with the target in both meaning and form (e.g., "cat"→"rat") are more likely to occur than predicted based on the rates of purely semantic (e.g., "cat"→"dog") and purely phonological (e.g., "cat"→"cab") errors.	Cascading activation allows semantic neighbors to activate their phonological representations, making mixed errors more likely than purely phonological errors at the phoneme level.
	Feedback allows phonological representations to influence the activation of lexical representations, making mixed errors more likely than purely semantic errors at the lexical level.
Disruptions to speech production.	Spreading activation between and/or within specific representational levels is disrupted by brain damage.
Following brain damage, individuals produce varying distributions of error types in speech production.	Disrupting spreading activation lowers activation levels, allowing noise to overwhelm the target representation.
	Local damage provides a superior account of error patterns compared to global disruptions of processing.

biases. The final section examines how neurobiologically inspired connectionist principles have been used to understand the consequences of neurological damage.

16.2.3.1 Semantic interference versus phonological facilitation in picture naming

An important technique for studying speech production processes has been the picture-word interference task (for a historical overview of this research, and discussion of the importance of this paradigm in the development of theoretical accounts, see Levelt, 1999; Levelt et al., 1999). In this paradigm, participants are presented with pictures (typically, black and white line drawings) depicting common objects and asked to name them. At some point in time close to the presentation of the picture, an interfering stimulus is presented. Either a written word is superimposed on the picture, or an auditory stimulus is presented while participants look at the picture. Although participants are instructed to ignore the interfering stimulus, it can influence the time it takes them to initiate production of the picture's name. In particular, two distinct effects on naming latency are observed depending on the linguistic relationship between the interfering stimulus and the target. (Latencies are also influenced by the time difference between picture and word onset; these effects are not discussed here.)

First, semantic category relationships produce interference. In the seminal study of Schriefers, Meyer, & Levelt (1990), auditory distractor words from the same semantic category as the picture name slowed response times. If the word "dog" was presented prior to the presentation of a picture of a cat, the time to initiate the response "cat" was significantly slower (compared to trials where an unrelated word such as "mop" was presented). However, in contrast to interference from semantically related items, Schriefers et al. found that phonological relationships facilitate picture naming. If the word "cap" was presented at the same time or following presentation of target picture "cat," the response time was significantly faster compared to unrelated trials. Many studies have replicated the basic patterns of facilitation from similar-sounding words (see Starreveld, 2000, for a review) and inhibition from semantic category members (see Abdel Rahman & Melinger, 2009; Roelofs, 1992, for reviews; but see Costa, Alario, & Caramazza, 2005; Costa, Mahon, Savova, & Caramazza, 2003; Mahon & Caramazza, 2009; Mahon, Costa, Peterson, Vargas, & Caramazza, 2007, for discussion of alternative accounts).

Many connectionist theories of speech production have used localist representational principles to account for these effects. Specifically, these theories attribute contrasting effects of semantic and phonological distractors to differences in the structure of lexical and phonological representations (see, e.g., Levelt et al., 1999; Roelofs, 1992). Figure 16.1 illustrates the general properties of this account. As shown in Figure 16.3A, when a semantic distractor is presented, spreading activation from the target and competitor's semantic features diverges onto two distinct lexical representations (e.g., <CAT> and <DOG>). Because lexical representations are strictly local, this spreading activation increases the activation of competitor representations, slowing the selection of the target. As shown in Figure 16.3B, a different situation occurs for phonological distractors. Spreading activation from the target and competitor's lexical representations[1] converges onto shared phonemes (/k/, /ae/

---

[1] An additional source of activation from word distractors is via sublexical conversion procedures that directly activate phonological representations from orthographic or acoustic input (e.g., Roelofs, Meyer, & Levelt, 1996). In fact, Costa, Miozzo, & Caramazza (1999) argue that these sublexical processes drive

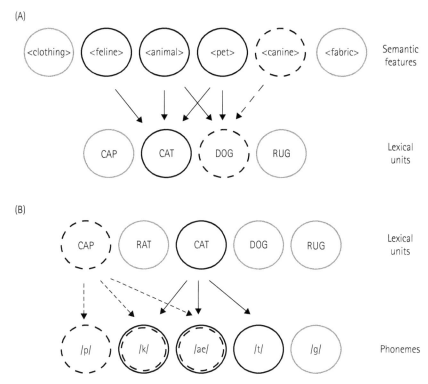

FIG. 16.3 Semantic interference and phonological facilitation in the picture-word interference task reflect the structure of localist representations. Dashed lines denote activation from the distractor word. (A) Semantic interference stems from competition between coactive unitary lexical representations. (B) Phonological facilitation arises due to the activation of overlapping feature-based phonological representations.

); unshared phonemes receive activation from only one lexical representation. The activation of these shared phonemes can enhance the target's representation, speeding selection of the target's phonological structure compared to a case where no phonemes are shared. By assuming that the degree of localist representation for linguistic structure varies across levels, connectionist theories can account for the distinct patterns of semantic and phonological distractors.

16.2.3.2 The mixed error effect

Errors in speech production are often classified in terms of their linguistic relationship to the target. Purely semantic errors (e.g., "cat"→ "dog") are similar in meaning, but not form; purely phonological errors (e.g., "cat"→"cap") share form, but not meaning. The term mixed error is generally used to refer to errors that overlap along both of these dimensions (e.g.,

the phonological facilitation effect. Regardless of the source of the activation, the presence of facilitation (as opposed to inhibition) derives from the use of feature-based localist representations (such that target and distractor overlap in structure).

"cat"→"rat"). Many studies have observed that mixed errors occur more often than would be predicted by the simple sum of the rates of purely semantic (e.g., "cat"→"dog") and purely phonological (e.g., "cat"→ "cap") errors. This has been observed in studies of spontaneous speech errors (e.g., Harley & MacAndrew, 2001), experimentally induced speech errors (e.g., Brédart & Valentine, 1992), and the production errors of many aphasic individuals (e.g., Rapp & Goldrick, 2000).

This result is unexpected under a fully discrete version of the two-stage framework of speech production discussed here. If we assume that the two stages have a strictly serial relationship, mixed errors should simply be the sum of (independently occurring) semantic and phonological errors. During the first stage, a lexical representation is selected solely based on the intended message. Both mixed and purely semantic competitors should therefore be equally active (e.g., for target "cat," <DOG> should be just as active as <RAT>). If processing is serial and discrete, during the second stage only the phonemes of the selected lexical item are activated. Both mixed and purely phonological competitors should therefore be equally active (e.g., /k/ /ae/ /p/ should be just as active as /r/ /ae/ /t/). Since at neither level of processing are mixed errors more likely than "pure" semantic or phonological errors, this discrete theory cannot account for the mixed error effect.

To produce the mixed error effect, many theories have relied on the connectionist principle of spreading activation. Specifically, the discrete architecture is enhanced by adding two spreading activation mechanisms (e.g., Dell, 1986). These are illustrated in Figure 16.4. The first is cascading activation (Fig. 16.4A). Cascade allows non-selected lexical representations to exert an influence on processing at the phonological level. For example, semantic neighbors (activated via spreading activation from semantic features) are allowed to activate their phonemes (e.g., <RAT> activates /r/). This activation boost makes mixed errors more likely than purely phonological errors (e.g., /r/ is more active than /p/, meaning that "rat" is more active than "cap").

The second mechanism is feedback (Fig. 16.4B). Feedback systems allow activation from phonological representations to spread back to lexical representations (e.g., /ae/ /t/ activate <RAT>). This can combine with top-down activation from shared semantic features, boosting the activation of mixed competitors relative to that of purely semantic competitors (e.g., because it shares phonemes with the target, <RAT> is more active than <DOG>). By influencing the first stage of processing (i.e., the selection of a lexical item), feedback makes mixed error outcomes more likely to occur than purely semantic errors. The relative contributions and strength of cascading activation and feedback within the speech production system is a matter of some debate (see Goldrick, 2006; Rapp & Goldrick, 2000, for discussion).

Other theories have attributed the mixed error effect not to spreading activation within the production system but to the influence of response monitoring—what could be considered feedback from external processes. One such monitoring system is based in a perceptual loop (e.g., Levelt, 1983). This could halt speech prior to articulation, preventing some of the errors arising during formulation processes from being overtly produced. According to such accounts, since mixed errors are both phonologically and semantically like the target, they are less likely to be detected by the perceptual monitor than corresponding "pure" error types. Mixed errors are therefore more likely to be overtly produced, producing the mixed error effect (for discussion, see Levelt et al., 1999; Roelofs, 2004).

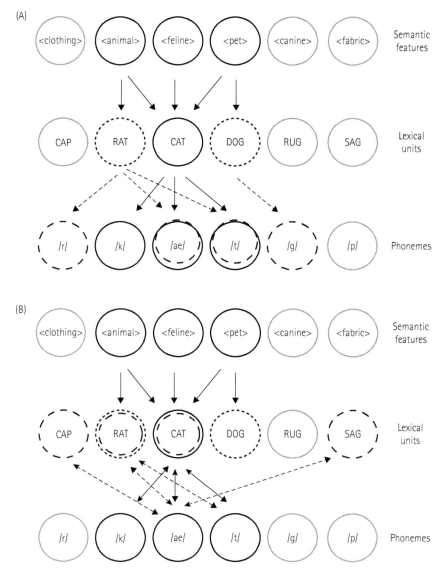

FIG. 16.4 Interaction between levels of processing in speech production produces the mixed error effect. (A) Overlapping semantic features activate semantic neighbors of the target (depicted with dotted lines). Cascade allows these lexical units to activate their phonological representations (shown with dashed lines), producing an advantage for mixed errors. (B) Feedback allows phonological representations to activate lexical representations. Illustrated here is the first step of feedback: the target's phonological representation reactivates the target as well as its lexical neighbors (depicted by dashed lines). (Note that these lexical representations could then, in turn, activate their non-target phonological representations; e.g., SAG could activate /g/.) Feedback from the phonology of the target combines with activation of the target's semantic neighbors (shown by dotted lines), producing an advantage for mixed errors.

16.2.3.3 *Connectionist accounts of speech production impairments*

As a consequence of brain damage, many individuals suffer from impaired speech production abilities (see, e.g., the contribution of Schwartz to this volume). Given that connectionist principles reflect (in part) neurobiological processing principles, connectionism may provide a very useful framework for understanding these impairments. Most commonly, researchers have conceptualized impaired speech production performance as reflecting the distortion of the spread of activation within the production network. Theories of damage can be broadly divided into two types: those that involve global alteration of spreading activation, and those that involve alterations that are specific to particular representational levels.

Global damage mechanisms. In a series of papers, Dell, Martin, Saffran, Schwartz, and colleagues (Dell, Schwartz et al., 1997; Martin, Dell, Saffran, & Schwartz, 1994; Martin & Saffran, 1992; Martin, Saffran, & Dell, 1996; Schwartz & Brecher, 2000) proposed that global alterations to activation spreading could account for the range of patterns of impairment to speech production processes. They proposed two specific damage mechanisms. The first was a reduction of the ability of representational layers in the network to spread activation to one another (the "connection weight" parameter of Dell, Schwartz et al., 1997). If this type of activation spreading is reduced, less activation flows between representational levels. Due to lower levels of activation, noise on processing units can then overwhelm the representation of the correct response, leading to errors. The second mechanism involved a reduction of the ability of units to retain activation over time ("decay" in Dell, Schwartz et al., 1997). Typically, the activation of a unit at a given time step is not just determined by the activation flowing into it from other representational levels but also by its activation at previous time steps. (Note that this can be conceived of as a unit spreading activation back onto itself.) Increasing decay—that is, decreasing the amount of activation that units retain over time—can therefore serve to lower levels of activation, allowing random noise to disrupt the target and produce errors (for further discussion of the potential influence of decay on impairments to speech production, see Harley & MacAndrew, 1992; Wright and Ahmad, 1997).

To test the ability of these two mechanisms of global damage to account for aphasic naming patterns, Dell, Schwartz et al. (1997) constructed a simulation of the formulation processes of English speakers. For 21 individuals with aphasia, the connection strength and decay parameters of this simulation were globally adjusted to see if the simulation could reproduce their error patterns. Specifically, for each of the 21 patients, the simulation's parameters were globally altered so that it matched (as closely as possible) the patient's relative proportion of: correct responses; phonologically related (e.g., cat → rat) and unrelated (e.g., cat → dog) semantic errors; phonologically related (e.g., cat → cap) and unrelated (e.g., cat → rug) word errors; and non-word errors (e.g., cat → zat). The results of this parameter-fitting procedure provided some quantitative support for the global damage theory. The simulation was able to fairly closely approximate the individual error distributions (but see Ruml & Caramazza, 2000, for a criticism of the simulation's fit to the data, and Dell, Schwartz, Martin, Saffran, & Gagnon, 2000, for a response to these criticisms).

Not only was the global damage simulation able to reproduce the patients' error patterns, but the parameter fits used to account for the error distributions were able to derive novel predictions about patient performance. As just discussed, the presence of a mixed error effect requires the presence of spreading activation between phonological and lexical representations (either due to lexical to phonological cascade or phonological to lexical feedback). If an individual's error pattern is fit by reducing connection strength, the spreading activation theory of mixed errors predicts an associated reduction of the mixed error effect. Consistent with this prediction, Dell et al. (1997) found that as a group, individuals whose pattern was fit by high connection weights showed a significant mixed error effect, while individuals whose pattern was fit by low connection weights did not.

Local damage mechanisms. Other theoretical accounts of neurologically impaired speech production have proposed that deficit patterns result from distinct disruptions to specific processes (see, e.g., Ruml, Caramazza, Capasso, & Miceli, 2005, for discussion). Connectionist theories have realized this claim in several diverse ways. One proposal simulates neurological damage by increasing the strength of noise at particular representational levels (Laine et al., 1998; Rapp and Goldrick, 2000). Increased noise can overwhelm target's activation at a particular processing level, producing errors. Another proposal uses localist instantiations of disruption to lexical selection processes (e.g., reducing the amount by which the activation of the selected representation is enhanced: Goldrick & Rapp, 2002; Harley & MacAndrew, 1992; Rapp & Goldrick, 2000; or manipulations of the threshold for lexical selection: Dell, Lawler, Harris, & Gordon, 2004; Laine et al., 1998). Disrupting selection interferes with the normal flow of activation in the production system, leading to phonological and semantic errors.

More recent work within Dell, Schwartz et al.'s two-step model framework implements localist damage by independently weakening the strength of connections between semantic and lexical vs. lexical and phonological levels (Foygel & Dell, 2000; see also Harley & MacAndrew, 1992). Weakening connection strength produces errors by lowering activation levels, allowing noise to overwhelm the activation of the target. This model accounts for the novel predictions made by the parameter fits of Dell, Schwartz et al. (1997) and later work from the same group (Dell, Martin, & Schwartz, 2007; Schwartz, Dell, Martin, Gahl, & Sobel, 2006) shows local damage to have a small but reliable advantage over global mechanisms for capturing word naming errors (see also Hanley, Dell, Kay, & Baron, 2004).

Finally, and perhaps most problematic for global damage proposals, local damage can account for empirically observed error patterns that simply cannot be produced by global damage. Rapp and Goldrick (2000) reviewed the performance of two individuals with deficits to formulation processes (i.e., their comprehension and articulation were intact; their deficits were in mapping messages onto form). These individuals produced only semantic errors in picture naming. As shown by a number of studies (cited next), this pattern of only semantic errors cannot be produced by simulations incorporating global damage. Similarly, Caramazza, Papagno, and Ruml (2000) review cases where individuals with formulation deficits produce only phonologically related errors (see Goldrick, 2016, for discussion). Global damage simulations also fail to produce this pattern of performance. Global damage predicts that "pure" error patterns should never occur—damage always results in the production of a mixture of error types (e.g., not just semantic errors, but phonologically related word and non-word errors as well). In contrast, simulations with local damage can account for these patterns of errors (so long as there is an appropriate degree of interaction between representational levels; see Goldrick & Rapp, 2002; Rapp & Goldrick, 2000; for discussion). For more detailed qualitative and quantitative critiques of global damage theories, see: Caramazza et al. (2000); Cuetos, Aguado, and Caramazza (2000); Foygel and Dell, (2000); Goldrick (2011); Hanley, Dell, Kay, and Baron (2004); Rapp and Goldrick (2000); Ruml et al. (2005); Ruml, Caramazza, Shelton, and Chialant, (2000); Walker and Hickok (2016). This large body of work leads to the conclusion that impairments to speech production processes are the consequence of local, not global disruptions to processing.

16.3 Distributed representations: Learning and processing

16.3.1 Connectionist principles outside the traditional localist framework

As noted in the introduction, the work reviewed in the previous section differs in two ways from the bulk of connectionist research in other domains. First, these are mainly localist networks which assume that connection weights (specifying how activation spreads in the production system) are largely fixed to values set by the simulation designer. In contrast, learning has played a crucial role in other domains of connectionist research (e.g., Elman et al., 1998). The process of learning is in fact seen as a third general principle of connectionist theories (after Smolensky, 2000).

3. *Learning is innately guided modification of spreading activation by experience.* Knowledge acquisition results from the interaction of:
   a. innate learning rules
   b. innate architectural features
   c. modification of connection strengths with experience

A second divergence is that the research reviewed in the previous section makes use of localist representations, whereas most connectionist research assumes that mental representations are highly distributed patterns of activity as evidenced by the title of the seminal connectionist work *Parallel Distributed Processing* (PDP; see Rumelhart, McClelland, & the PDP Research Group, 1986); for recent reviews, see special issues of *Frontiers in Psychology* (Mayor, Gomez, Chang, & Lupyan, 2014) and *Cognitive Science* (Rogers & McClelland, 2014). In such approaches, the first principle of connectionist processing can be reformulated as:

1. *Representations are distributed activation patterns.* Mental representations are highly distributed patterns of numerical activity.

In fact, learning and distributed representations are often closely connected in connectionist architectures. Many connectionist networks learn using error correction algorithms. In these simulations, the designer specifies the structure of input and output representations and a learning algorithm. The network is then trained using a set of examples pairing input and output patterns (e.g., the network is taught to map the pattern <animal, feline, pet> to /k/ /ae/ /t/). To allow networks to learn complex input-output mappings, many connectionist theories assume the presence of additional internal representations. These are realized using "hidden" units that mediate the relationship between the input and output units (much like the lexical level in Figure 16.2). The structure of these representations is not prespecified in the simulation design. Instead, the representations (i.e., the response patterns of the hidden units) develop over the course of learning the mapping between input and output representations (most prominently via the method of backpropagation of error; see Rumelhart, Durbin, Golden, & Chauvin, 1996; Rumelhart, Hinton, & Williams, 1986, for overviews). Of particular relevance here is that these learned internal representations are often highly distributed (see, e.g., Plaut, McClelland, Seidenberg, & Patterson, 1996). Rather than a single unit or a small discrete set of units responding to input patterns, inputs to these trained networks evoke a highly distributed pattern of activity over the hidden units. In this way, learning and distributed representations are often intertwined in connectionist theories.

These two principles, so crucial to connectionist accounts in other domains, were not incorporated into the localist architectures discussed in the first section. This may in part be a historical artifact. The highly influential model of Dell (1986; the foundation of work such as Dell, Schwartz et al., 1997) was grounded in localist models developed in the early 1980s (Dell's 1980 thesis, as well as McClelland & Rumelhart, 1981). Such work predated the foundational work in the learning-centered PDP approach (Rumelhart et al., 1986) It may also be due to the nature of the problem: for example, it is more tractable to pose questions regarding relative degrees of interactivity in a network with designer-specified vs. learned connection weights (e.g., Rapp & Goldrick, 2000). Recent work has begun to bridge this gap; the remainder of this chapter considers several examples in detail. The application of connectionist learning mechanisms to problems in sentence production is reviewed first, followed by discussions of processing and selection in distributed representational structures.

16.3.2 Learning and syntactic priming

The term syntactic priming is used here to refer to the observation that speakers repeat the same syntactic structures in successive utterances (this is also referred to as structural priming in the sentence production literature). A typical experimental paradigm for inducing this effect has participants repeat a prime sentence aloud and then describe (on a subsequent trial) a picture depicting an event. Many studies have found that participants' picture descriptions tend to reflect the structure of the prime sentence. For example, if participants repeat a passive prime sentence (e.g., "The building manager was mugged by a gang of teenagers"), they are more likely to describe subsequent pictures using passive constructions (e.g., "The man was stung by a bee") compared to active constructions (e.g., "The bee stung the man"). This priming is syntactic in that it does not appear to rely on the prime and target sentences overlapping in other aspects of linguistic structure such as lexical semantics, argument structure, or prosody, nor does it require explicit memory for the previous utterance (see Pickering & Ferreira, 2008, for a review of the paradigm and basic results).

What processing mechanism gives rise to this effect? As noted here, many connectionist theories assume that some activation persists on representational units over time (e.g., Dell, Schwartz et al.'s (1997) decay parameter). One view of syntactic priming is that it is influenced by this persistence; representational units (such as slots in a structural frame) are preactivated by previous productions, allowing them to be more quickly and easily retrieved (e.g., Branigan, Pickering, & Cleland, 1999). However, since units retain only a fraction of their activation, smaller and smaller amounts of activation persist across time steps. The influence of this mechanism is therefore necessarily limited in time. In contradiction to this prediction, Bock and Griffin (2000) found that syntactic priming effects can persist across extremely long lags (e.g., 10 intervening sentences; but see Branigan et al., 1999, for evidence of decay). They interpreted this as support for an alternative account of syntactic priming based on implicit learning. According to this view, syntactic priming is a consequence of learning processes which make longer-term adjustments to the sentence production system—learning processes that might be an extension of the abilities that allowed us to acquire language in the first place Importantly, learning has a natural interpretation within connectionist architectures. In the third connectionist principle detailed here, learning is seen as the adjustment of connection weights. Instead of relying solely on persistent activation, the system can rely on experience-driven changes to the way in which activation flows[2].

A learning-based account of syntactic priming has been examined in simulation experiments by Chang and colleagues (e.g., Chang, 2002; Chang, Dell, & Bock, 2006; Chang, Dell, Bock, & Griffin, 2000). They utilized the simple recurrent network architecture (Elman, 1990; Jordan, 1986), setting up separate pathways for processing meaning and sequencing words that both contribute to the incremental production of a sentence. A simplified version of Chang et al. (2006)'s network is depicted in Figure 16.5.

To produce an utterance, activation of the message units is fixed to a pattern representing a sentence's meaning. The message system relies upon distributed semantic representations that separate event semantics (representing argument number, tense, and aspect) and lexical semantics; lexical semantics are themselves composed of event roles (*where*) and lexical semantics (*what*). The intended message and the learned semantics give rise to the model's sequencing system, such that the selection and sequencing of words for production is based on thematic roles assigned to the message.

At each time step, the activation of the hidden units in the sequencing system (the learned internal representations just discussed) is influenced by this message representation and by a set of context units that are a copy of the hidden units' activation pattern from the previous time step. This recurrence of hidden unit activation patterns allows previous states of the network to influence processing; in effect, providing the network with a memory for what has been already said. The combination of memory for the past and a top-down message allows the model to be flexible in instantiating alternative plans, allowing incremental production of utterances and allowing the model to produce syntactic alternations (e.g., the dative and active/passive alternations) which have multiple possible word orders.

Since the model's internal representations are sensitive to previous states, and since there are separate components for messages, structures, and words, the network can be trained to produce novel sequences of outputs by comparing model predictions to an externally generated utterance (see Elman, 1990; Jordan, 1986, for further discussion). In this case, the network learns to activate, in sequence, the word units corresponding to the intended sentence (e.g., first activating <THE>, then <CAT>, then <WALKS>) with training using the

---

[2] Note that this account is also capable of using persistent activation effects to account for other priming effects that occur only over short lags. However, it does not currently specify why different effects have different priming lags (e.g., in single word production, why repetition priming is found over long lags while semantic priming is not; Barry, Hirsh, Johnston, & Williams, 2001).

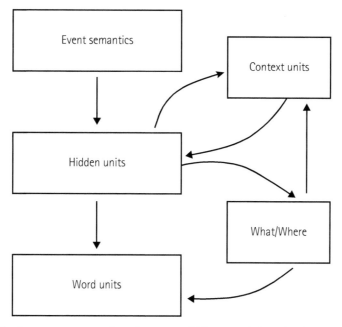

FIG. 16.5 Simple recurrent network architecture of Chang et al. (2006). The meaning system is comprised of two parts: event semantics represent propositional structure; what/where units represent the binding between concepts (what); and their event structure roles (where). Word units represent the words that make up the sentence the network produces (the network is trained to activate sequences of word units). A set of hidden units is used to mediate the mapping between these representations. To allow for the production of word sequences, context units (containing copies of the hidden unit activations and what/where units from the previous time step) are allowed to influence the activation of the hidden units.

backpropagation algorithm mentioned here. Chang et al. (2006) argue that these changes to hidden units allow the network to acquire language in a human-like fashion, providing evidence that it can simulate a variety of phenomena in child language acquisition.

To simulate syntactic priming, the network received further training corresponding to prime sentences, changing the flow of activation within the network as fast-changing weights were updated. Following this additional training, the simulation was tested using new message inputs. In response to these inputs, the stimulation tended to produce the same structure as the prime sentence, replicating the syntactic priming effect. This influence extended across long intervening lags (e.g., 10 sentences) and across differing prepositions and different tenses, showing that the learning-based theory can account for Bock and Griffin's (2000) results.

These results illustrate how the third principle of connectionist architectures (experience-driven modification of connection weights) can serve as the basis for a theoretical account for speech production behavior, capturing generalizations about changes to the language system in the short term (priming) and across the long term (acquisition). Such generalizations form the foundation of emerging work, where incorporation of a learning mechanism serves to capture other aspects of language production.

One line of this work focuses on sequencing in production, asking how items (words, phonemes) are selected in the right order. With respect to sentence production, Gordon and Dell (2003) and Dell, Oppenheim, and Kittredge (2008) use syntactic frame constraints (a "syntactic traffic cop") to govern selection and ordering of lexical items; this model can be trained using error-based learning to mirror typical and aphasic production. Rohde (2002) instantiates a model that is conceptually like the Chang et al. model discussed here; prediction and learning mechanisms provide a bridge between production and comprehension and this allows the model to account for a variety of classic psycholinguistic findings. Models incorporating error-based learning have also been highly successful in word-level production: Warker and Dell (2006) model the acquisition of novel phonotactic constraints; Gupta and Tisdale (2009) model the learning of novel phonological sequences. In both models, error-based learning provides strong coverage for empirical phenomena.

The interplay between short-term and long-term learning is another area of ongoing work. Oppenheim, Dell, and Schwartz (2010) use error-based learning in a simple network to elegantly account for two empirical phenomena: cumulative semantic interference, where retrieval of a word from a set of semantic competitors becomes more difficult over time, and repetition priming, where the second repetition of a word is faster and less-error prone. On the theoretical side, such generalizations about the nature of adaptation of the language system over time also provide the basis for unified theories of language mechanisms (e.g., the *P-Chain*; Dell & Chang, 2013).

16.3.3 Selection in distributed representations

As noted in the first section, localist connectionist architectures commonly incorporate categorically specified planning representations that guide selection of content units (e.g., a noun phrase frame guides selection of a lexical unit representing a determiner <THE> followed by a unit representing a noun <CAT>). Theories making use of learned internal representations (such as the simple recurrent network just described) often eschew such explicit planning representations (for "frame"-less approaches to phonological processing, see Dell, Juliano, & Govindjee, 1993; Gupta & Dell, 1999). Alternative approaches explored in recent work do not eliminate distinct planning representations but do utilize more distributed representations of structure. Such models require attention to the problem of selection over distributed, componential representations. Next, we walk through two frameworks that involve distributed structural representations and use them to highlight the role of selection in capturing several empirical phenomena. The first framework is an oscillator model based in control signal theory (Harris, 2002; Hartley & Houghton, 1996; Vousden, Brown, & Harley, 2000); the second is Gradient Symbolic Computation (Cho & Smolensky, 2016; Goldrick & Chu, 2014; Goldrick, Putnam, & Schwarz, 2016; Smolensky, Goldrick, & Mathis, 2014).

16.3.3.1 *Oscillator models*

Vousden et al. (2000) focused on the selection of sublexical phonological structure (e.g., selecting onset /k/, vowel /ae/, and coda /t/ for target <CAT>). They posit that selection is controlled by a distributed representation of syllable structure generated by a set of oscillators (based on a more general theory of serial order proposed by Brown, Preece, and Hulme, 2000). A set of repeating oscillators sweep through the same series of values during each syllable, just as on a clock a minute hand sweeps through the same digits every hour (e.g., in every syllable, 15 minutes past represents "onset," 30 minutes past represents "vowel," 45 minutes past represents "coda"). This repeating component represents structural similarity across syllables. "Non-repeating" oscillators (i.e., oscillators with extremely long periods) take on distinct values for each syllable, allowing their system to represent the distinction between syllables. This is similar to the hour hand on a clock, which allows one to distinguish 3:30 from 4:30.

This distributed representation of structure is then used to control selection of phonological content. The time-varying oscillator states (both repeating and non-repeating) are combined to generate a dynamic control signal. The system learns a set of weights[3] on connections associating control signal states to phonological structures (following the clock analogy, this means learning that 3:15 corresponds to /k/, 3:30 to /ae/, and so on). During retrieval, the appropriate control signal is provided to the system; the oscillators then automatically generate the sequence of control signal states that cue retrieval of the stored phonological sequence with a winner-take-all selection algorithm.

This proposal shares many properties with localist connectionist planning frames. Both frameworks assume a division between structure and content with categorically specified structural representations (e.g., the repeating oscillator states are predefined to be the same across all syllables). This allows both frameworks to account for structural similarity effects on speech errors, where segments in similar positions are more likely to interact than those in dissimilar positions (e.g., onset consonants are more likely to interact with onset consonants as compared to those in coda; Vousden et al., 2000). By assuming categorically specified structural representations, the effect can be explained as a consequence of representational overlap between segments in similar positions. For example, in virtue of their shared structural representations, onset /k/ will be more like onset /g/ than coda /g/. This similarity leads to a greater likelihood of segments interacting in errors.

Despite the properties shared by the two frameworks, there are important distinctions. As noted by Vousden et al. (2000), the oscillator mechanism provides an explicit account of how successive states of the planning representation are generated—oscillators will cycle through their states automatically, just like a clock that has been wound up will automatically cycle through the minutes of each hour. In contrast, many localist frame-based theories have failed to provide detailed sequencing mechanisms (but see Dell, Burger, et al., 1997).

A second difference stems specifically from properties of distributed representations. As shown by Vousden et al. (2000), speech errors are influenced by distance—all else being equal, closer segments are more likely to interact with one another than more distant segments, meaning that errors occur from the improper selection of an element appearing within a certain time window of the target. This phenomenon is a natural consequence of the use of distributed representations. Vousden et al.'s control signal specifies slots in the planning representation using a time-varying signal. The time-dependence of this signal entails that slots that are temporally close will also have a similar structure. For example, consider a three-syllable word such as "subjective" using the clock face analogy just discussed. Each

---

[3] See Harris (2002) for discussion of the limitations of Vousden et al.'s (2000) method and a distributed associative memory proposal for more efficiently storing the relationship between control signals and phonological structure.

syllable will be associated with a distinct state of the hour hand on the clock (e.g., "sub" will be 4, "jec" will be 5, and "tive" will be 6), while their internal segments are associated with distinct states of the minute hand (e.g., "s" will be 4:15, "u" will be 4:30, and so on). Because these states are generated by time-varying oscillators, the temporally close first and second syllables will be associated with closer values on the hour hand (e.g., 4, 5) than the first and third syllables (4, 6). This overlap means that errors will be more likely to occur between the first and second syllables than between the first and third. In contrast, localist frame units do not represent similarity in time as an inherent component of the representation. In many of these theories, slots in planning representations are specified by discrete, atomic units equal in similarity, allowing the system to represent, for example, the distinction between the onsets of the first, second, and third syllables but not to encode the fact that the first and second are produced closer in time than the first and third.

Though to date, the control signal theory has been used only for word-level production, the computational principles are domain-general and should transfer to other levels of production. For example, the example of a three-phoneme word <CAT> has a parallel to a three-constituent sentence such as [$_S$ [$_{NP}$ Mary] [$_{VP}$ [$_V$ loves] [$_{NP}$ John]]]. A similar model could be implemented to produce this sentence. As in the phonological model, a set of long-period oscillators could represent the order of elements within a string (here: word order, vs. phoneme order). As in the phonological model, oscillators with a shorter period could represent elements belonging to the same class (here: "Mary" and "John," vs. /k/ and /t/). Then, the combination of oscillators instantiates hierarchical structure, as in the multisyllabic example ("subjective"). In the example [$_S$ [$_{NP}$ Mary] [$_{VP}$ [$_V$ loves] [$_{NP}$ John]]], one-hour oscillators might represent subject NP and VP, while 30-minute oscillators might represent V and object NP. As such, applying sequencing mechanisms from control signal theory to other levels of language production is likely to be a promising area for future research.

In principle, then, control signal theories incorporate the positive aspects of frame-based representations (i.e., categorically specified slots, accounting for positional similarity effects) while increasing their empirical coverage (i.e., accounting for distance effects in errors). This increased empirical coverage can be directly attributed to relying on a connectionist processing principle—distributed representations—during selection of linguistic structure.

16.3.3.2 Gradient Symbolic Computation

Another recent formalism, Gradient Symbolic Computation (GSC; Smolensky, Goldrick, & Mathis, 2014) incorporates distributed representations of both structural positions (as in the oscillator representations of syllable structure) and the elements that fill such structural positions (the sounds occupying a syllable position; the words occupying a syntactic position). This allows for graded activation in all aspects of linguistic representational structure. While this increased representational power allows GSC to capture a variety of empirical phenomena (as discussed next), it also requires a novel approach to selection. The question is how to allow graded activation while regulating it to match the observed limited levels of graded activation in language production.

Unlike the localist selection mechanisms reviewed in §2.2 (e.g., increasing activation to a target, inhibiting activation to competitors), selection in the GSC architecture arises via optimization of a *quantization* constraint that pushes outcomes toward discrete states. This operates in parallel with constraints on structure retrieval and planning. Quantization starts low in the beginning of a simulation, allowing the network to enter in to intermediate processing states with graded activation of a variety of possible outcomes. For example, during lexical access, the network might begin with the desired onset /k/ /ae/ and would activate the various words beginning with those sounds (cat, cab, cap . . .) to graded degrees. Similarly, during syntactic planning, the network might begin with the words "The cat" and then would activate the various sentences beginning with those words ("The cat naps," "The cat chases the mouse" . . .) to graded degrees. Over the course of processing, the strength of quantization is increased. This pushes the model toward a state that discretely selects one of these outcomes out of the many possibilities.

Although the quantization constraint pushes the system *toward* a discrete outcome, it is crucially violable. Allowing these non-discrete final states lets GSC capture some novel empirical phenomena. For example, it has been shown that speech errors retain acoustic and articulatory properties of the original target. When a /k/ is produced in error instead of the target /t/ (i.e., top kop → *k*op kop), it is distinguishable from a /k/ produced as a correct target; the error /k/ exhibits articulatory movements specific to the target /t/ (e.g., Goldrick & Chu, 2014). Goldrick and Chu (2014) analyze this phenomenon using the GSC framework. In their model, when errors occur there is graded coactivation of the target (e.g., /t/) and the error outcome (/k/), reflecting the influence of planning constraints that prefer target properties be retained during production. When this blended phonological plan is mapped onto articulation, the result is a blend of the two representations—a response that might be dominated by one representation (the error) but still retains aspects of another (the original target). In essence, coactivation pushes the final state slightly away from a discrete outcome, though errors and correct targets alike remain identifiable as tokens of (discrete) English phonemes (i.e., they are very close to one phonological representation and distant from another). This limited gradience—or in other words, violable discreteness—is captured inherently by the GSC architecture.

Another phenomenon that might best be described by a non-discrete selection mechanism is code-switching, where bilingual speakers use two languages within a single sentence (see Kroll & Gollan, 2014 for a recent review). Goldrick et al. (2016) outline a GSC analysis of an extreme case of code-switching—doubling constructions. In these, a word and its translation equivalent both appear in a single sentence. In languages that have different constraints on word ordering, the repeated word tokens surround a point of commonality between the two languages. For example, English uses a subject-verb-object (SVO) structure, while Tamil uses a subject-object-verb (SOV) structure. An English-Tamil doubling construction might take the form $S_{English}$ $V_{English}$ $O_{English}$ V_{Tamil}, fulfilling the local constraints of the two languages (VO for English; OV for Tamil) in a global blend. An observed example is the utterance "They gave me a grant *koḍutaa*," which has two synonymous verbs (the English "*gave*" and the Tamil "*koḍutaa*") sandwiching the objects "me a grant." Goldrick et al. analyze this as a blend of an SVO *and* an SOV sentence, resulting from planning constraints (preferring the presence of both verbs in the utterance) overriding the preferences of quantization.

These results show how GSC's quantization constraint provides a novel means of specifying how speakers regulate the degree of coactivation of linguistic representations. GSC preserves the ability to account for structure-sensitive language processing while also allowing for fully distributed representations of structural positions and the elements that fill them; these parallel considerations give GSC the power to describe previously uncaptured data within a connectionist framework.

16.4 Conclusions: Connectionist principles in speech production theories

Connectionist principles have had a profound impact on speech production research. For three decades, production theories have framed their discussion of behavioral data using two assumptions: mental representations are numerical patterns of activity; and processing is spreading activation between these representations. This has not only allowed specific accounts of a variety of empirical phenomena (as illustrated here) but has also supported the development of unified theories of single word production (e.g., WEAVER++; Levelt et al., 1999). As documented in the second section, more recent work has examined how speech production phenomena can be accounted for by using connectionist principles that are quite prominent in other empirical domains (learning and distributed representations). Importantly, much of this new research is cumulative in that it attempts to build on the insights of previous localist approaches. For example, in both syntax (Chang, 2002; Chang et al., 2006) and phonology (Harris, 2002), many distributed, learning-based theories have incorporated the localist theories' distinction between mechanisms that control sequencing (e.g., structural frames) and mechanisms specifying representational content, where distributed architectures which lack this distinction can have great difficulty accounting for the empirical data. A challenge for future work is to determine the crucial features of localist connectionist theories of production and how best to incorporate them within a dynamic, distributed representational framework. One such framework that we believe holds promise for instantiating structure and representational similarity in an integrated way is GSC (Smolensky et al., 2014).

Acknowledgment

Supported by a grant from the National Science Foundation (NSF) (BCS1344269). Any opinions, findings, and conclusions or recommendations expressed in this material are those of the authors and do not necessarily reflect the views of the NSF.

References

Abdel Rahman, R., & Melinger, A. (2009). Semantic context effects in language production: A swinging lexical network proposal and a review. *Language and Cognitive Processes*, 24, 713–34.

Barry, C., Hirsh, K. W., Johnston, R. A., & Williams, C. L. (2001). Age of acquisition, word frequency, and the locus of repetition priming of picture naming. *Journal of Memory and Language*, 44, 350–75.

Bock, K., & Griffin, Z. M. (2000). The persistence of structural priming: Transient activation or implicit learning? *Journal of Experimental Psychology: General*, 129, 177–92.

Branigan, H. P., Pickering, M. J., & Cleland, A. A. (1999). Syntactic priming in written production: Evidence for rapid decay. *Psychonomic Bulletin & Review, 6*, 635–40.

Brédart, S., & Valentine, T. (1992). From Monroe to Moreau: An analysis of face naming errors. *Cognition, 45*, 187–223.

Brown, G. D. A., Preece, T., & Hulme, C. (2000). Oscillator-based memory for serial order. *Psychological Review, 107*, 127–81.

Byrd, D., & Saltzmann, E. (2003). Speech production. In: Arbib, M. (Ed.), *The Handbook of Brain Theory and Neural Networks*, 2nd Edition (pp. 1072–6). MIT Press, Cambridge, MA.

Caramazza, A. (1997). How many levels of processing are there in lexical access? *Cognitive Neuropsychology, 14*, 177–208.

Caramazza, A., Bi, Y., Costa, A., Miozzo, M. (2004). What determines the speed of lexical access: Homophone or specific-word frequency? A reply to Jescheniak et al. (2003). *Journal of Experimental Psychology: Learning, Memory, and Cognition, 30*, 278–82.

Caramazza, A., Costa, A., Miozzo, M., & Bi, Y. (2001). The specific-word frequency effect: Implications for the representation of homophones in speech production. *Journal of Experimental Psychology: Learning, Memory, and Cognition, 27*, 1430–50.

Caramazza, A., & Miozzo, M. (1997). The relation between syntactic and phonological knowledge in lexical access: Evidence from the "tip-of-the-tongue" phenomenon. *Cognition, 64*, 309–43.

Caramazza, A., & Miozzo, M. (1998). More is not always better: A response to Roelofs, Meyer, and Levelt. *Cognition, 69*, 231–41.

Caramazza, A., Papagno, C., & Ruml, W. (2000). The selective impairment of phonological processing in speech production. *Brain and Language, 75*, 428–50.

Chang, F. (2002). Symbolically speaking: A connectionist model of sentence production. *Cognitive Science, 26*, 609–51.

Chang, F., Dell, G. S., & Bock, K. (2006). Becoming syntactic. *Psychological Review, 113*(2), 234–72.

Chang, F., Dell, G. S., Bock, K., & Griffin, Z. M. (2000). Structural priming as implicit learning: A comparison of models of sentence production. *Journal of Psycholinguistic Research, 29*, 217–29.

Cho, P.-W., & Smolensky, P. (2016). Bifurcation analysis of a Gradient Symbolic Computation model of incremental processing. In: Papafragou, A., Grodner, D., Mirman, D., & Trueswell, J. (Eds.), *Proceedings of the 38th Annual Conference of the Cognitive Science Society* (pp. 1487–92). Cognitive Science Society, Austin, TX.

Costa, A., Alario, F.-X., & Caramazza, A. (2005). On the categorical nature of the semantic interference effect in the picture-word interference paradigm. *Psychonomic Bulletin & Review, 12*, 125–31.

Costa, A., Mahon, B., Savova, V., & Caramazza, A. (2003). Levels of categorization effect: A novel effect in the picture-word interference paradigm. *Language and Cognitive Processes, 18*, 205–33.

Costa, A., Miozzo, M., & Caramazza, A. (1999). Lexical selection in bilinguals: Do words in the bilingual's two lexicons compete for selection? *Journal of Memory and Language, 41*, 365–97.

Cuetos, F., Aguado, G., & Caramazza, A. (2000). Dissociation of semantic and phonological errors in naming. *Brain and Language, 75*, 451–60.

Dell, G. S. (1980). *Phonological and Lexical Encoding in Speech Production: An Analysis of Naturally Occurring and Experimentally Elicited Speech Errors* [Unpublished doctoral dissertation]. University of Toronto, Toronto, ON.

Dell, G. S. (1986). A spreading activation theory of retrieval in sentence production. *Psychological Review, 93,* 283–321.

Dell, G. S. (1988). The retrieval of phonological forms in production: Tests of predictions from a connectionist model. *Journal of Memory and Language, 27,* 124–42.

Dell, G. S. (1990). Effects of frequency and vocabulary type on phonological speech errors. *Language and Cognitive Processes, 4,* 313–49.

Dell, G. S., Burger, L. K., & Svec, W. R. (1997). Language production and serial order: A functional analysis and a model. *Psychological Review, 104,* 123–47.

Dell, G. S., & Chang, F. (2013). The P-chain: Relating sentence production and its disorders to comprehension and acquisition. *Philosophical Transactions of the Royal Society of London B: Biological Sciences, 369,* 20120394.

Dell, G. S., Juliano, C., & Govindjee, A. (1993). Structure and content in language production: A theory of frame constraints in phonological speech errors. *Cognitive Science, 17,* 149–95.

Dell, G. S., Lawler, E. N., Harris, H. D., & Gordon, J. K. (2004). Models of errors of omission in aphasic naming. *Cognitive Neuropsychology, 21,* 125–45.

Dell, G. S., Martin, N., & Schwartz, M. F. (2007). A case-series test of the interactive two-step model of lexical access: Predicting word repetition from picture naming. *Journal of Memory and Language, 56,* 490–520.

Dell, G. S., & O'Seaghdha, P. G. (1994). Inhibition in interactive activation models of linguistic selection and sequencing. In: Dagenbach, D., & Carr, T. H. (Eds.), *Inhibitory Processes in Attention, Memory, and Language* (pp. 409–53). Academic Press, San Diego, CA.

Dell, G. S., Oppenheim, G. M., & Kittredge, A. K. (2008). Saying the right word at the right time: Syntagmatic and paradigmatic interference in sentence production. *Language and Cognitive Processes, 23,* 583–608.

Dell, G. S., Schwartz, M. F., Martin, N., Saffran, E. M., & Gagnon, D. A. (1997). Lexical access in aphasic and nonaphasic speakers. *Psychological Review, 104,* 801–38.

Dell, G. S., Schwartz, M. F., Martin, N., Saffran, E. M., & Gagnon, D. A. (2000). The role of computational models in neuropsychological investigations of language: Reply to Ruml and Caramazza (2000). *Psychological Review, 107,* 635–645.

Elman, J. L. (1990). Finding structure in time. *Cognitive Science, 14,* 179–211.

Elman, J. L., Bates, E. A., Johnson, M. H., Karmiloff-Smith, A., Parisi, D., & Plunkett, K. (1998). *Rethinking Innateness.* MIT Press, Cambridge, MA.

Foygel, D., & Dell, G. S. (2000). Models of impaired lexical access in speech production. *Journal of Memory and Language, 43,* 182–216.

Garrett, M. F. (1980). Levels of processing in sentence production. In: Butterworth, B. (Ed.), *Language Production: Speech and Talk, Vol. I* (pp. 177–220). Academic Press, New York, NY.

Goldrick, M. (2006). Limited interaction in speech production: Chronometric, speech error, and neuropsychological evidence. *Language and Cognitive Processes, 21,* 817–55.

Goldrick, M. (2011). Theory selection and evaluation in case series research. *Cognitive Neuropsychology, 28,* 451–65.

Goldrick, M. (2016). Integrating SLAM with existing evidence: Comment on Walker and Hickok (2016). *Psychonomic Bulletin & Review, 23,* 648–52.

Goldrick, M., & Chu, K. (2014). Gradient co-activation and speech error articulation: Comment on Pouplier and Goldstein (2010). *Language, Cognition and Neuroscience, 29,* 452–8.

Goldrick, M., Putnam, T., & Schwarz, L. (2016). Coactivation in bilingual grammars: A computational account of code mixing. *Bilingualism: Language and Cognition, 19,* 857–76.

Goldrick, M., & Rapp, B. (2002). A restricted interaction account (RIA) of spoken word production: The best of both worlds. *Aphasiology*, 16, 20–55.

Gordon, J. K., & Dell, G. S. (2003). Learning to divide the labor: An account of deficits in light and heavy verb production. *Cognitive Science*, 27, 1–40.

Gupta, P., & Dell, G. S. (1999). The emergence of language from serial order and procedural memory. In: MacWhinney, B. (Ed.), *Emergentist Approaches to Languages*, pp. 447–81. Erlbaum, Mahweh, NJ.

Gupta, P., & Tisdale, J. (2009). Does phonological short-term memory causally determine vocabulary learning? Toward a computational resolution of the debate. *Journal of Memory and Language*, 61, 481–502.

Hanley, J. R., Dell, G. S., Kay, J., & Baron, R. (2004). Evidence for the involvement of a nonlexical route in the repetition of familiar words: A comparison of single and dual route models of auditory repetition. *Cognitive Neuropsychology*, 21, 147–58.

Harley, T. A. (1995). Connectionist models of anomia: A comment on Nickels. *Language and Cognitive Processes*, 10, 47–58.

Harley, T. A., & MacAndrew, S. B. G. (1992). Modelling paraphasias in normal and aphasic speech. In: *Proceedings of the 14th Annual Meeting of the Cognitive Science Society* (pp. 378–83). Lawrence Erlbaum Associates, Hillsdale, NJ.

Harley, T. A., & MacAndrew, S. B. G. (2001). Constraints upon word substitution speech errors. *Journal of Psycholinguistic Research*, 30, 395–417.

Harris, H. D. (2002). Holographic reduced representations for oscillator recall: A model of phonological production. In: Gray, W. D., & Schunn, C. D. (Eds), *Proceedings of the 24th Annual Meeting of the Cognitive Science Society* (pp. 423–8). Lawrence Erlbaum Associates, Hillsdale, NJ.

Hartley, T., & Houghton, G. (1996). A linguistically constrained model of short-term memory for nonwords. *Journal of Memory and Language*, 35, 1–31.

Jescheniak, J. D., Meyer, A. S., & Levelt, W. J. M. (2003). Specific-word frequency is not all that counts in speech production: Comments on Caramazza, Costa, et al. (2001) and new experimental data. *Journal of Experimental Psychology: Learning, Memory, and Cognition*, 29, 432–8.

Jordan, M. I. (1986). *Serial Order: A Parallel Distributed Processing Approach*. Institute for Cognitive Science Report 8604. University of California, San Diego, CA. Reprinted (1997) in Donahoe, J. W., & Dorsel, V. P. (Eds.), *Neural-Network Models of Cognition: Biobehavioral Foundations*, pp. 221–77. Elsevier Science Press, Amsterdam.

Kroll, J. F., & Gollan, H. (2014). Speech planning in two languages: What bilinguals tell us about language production. In: Goldrick, M., Ferreira, V., & Miozzo, M. (Eds.), *The Oxford Handbook of Language Production*, pp. 165–81. Oxford University Press, Oxford.

Laine, M., Tikkala, A., & Juhola, M. (1998). Modelling anomia by the discrete two-stage word production architecture. *Journal of Neurolinguistics*, 11, 275–94.

Levelt, W. J. M. (1983). Monitoring and self-repair in speech. *Cognition*, 14, 41–104.

Levelt, W. J. M. (1992). Accessing words in speech production: Stages, processes, and representations. *Cognition*, 42, 1–22.

Levelt, W. J. M. (1999). Models of word production. *Trends in Cognitive Sciences*, 3, 223–32.

Levelt, W. J. M., Roelofs, A., & Meyer, A. S. (1999). A theory of lexical access in speech production. *Behavioral and Brain Sciences*, 22, 1–38.

MacKay, D. G. (1987). *The Organization of Perception and Action: A Theory for Language and Other Cognitive Skills*. Springer-Verlag, New York, NY.

Mahon, B. Z., & Caramazza, A. (2009). Why does lexical selection have to be so hard? Comment on Abdel Rahman and Melinger's swinging lexical network proposal. *Language and Cognitive Processes, 24,* 735–48.

Mahon, B. Z., Costa, A., Peterson, R., Vargas, K. A., & Caramazza, A. (2007). Lexical selection is not by competition: A reinterpretation of semantic interference and facilitation effects in the picture-word interference paradigm. *Journal of Experimental Psychology: Learning, Memory, and Cognition, 33,* 503.

Martin, N., Dell, G. S., Saffran, E. M., & Schwartz, M. F. (1994). Origins of paraphasias in deep dysphasia: Testing the consequences of a decay impairment to an interactive spreading activation model of lexical retrieval. *Brain and Language, 47,* 609–60.

Martin, N., & Saffran, E. M. (1992). A computational study of deep dysphasia: Evidence from a single case study. *Brain and Language, 43,* 240–74.

Martin, N., Saffran, E. M., & Dell, G. S., (1996). Recovery in deep dysphasia: Evidence for a relation between auditory-verbal STM capacity and lexical errors in repetition. *Brain and Language, 52,* 83–113.

Mayor, J., Gomez, P., Chang, F., & Lupyan, G. (2014). Connectionism coming of age: Legacy and future challenges. *Frontiers in Psychology, 5,* 187.

McClelland, J. L., & Rumelhart, D. E. (1981). An interactive activation model of context effects in letter perception: Part 1. An account of basic findings. *Psychological Review, 88,* 375–407.

Oppenheim, G. M., Dell, G. S., & Schwartz, M. F. (2010). The dark side of incremental learning: A model of cumulative semantic interference during lexical access in speech production. *Cognition, 114,* 227–52.

Page, M. (2000). Connectionist modeling in psychology: A localist manifesto. *Behavioral and Brain Sciences, 23,* 443–512.

Pickering, M. J., & Ferreira, V. S. (2008). Structural priming: A critical review. *Psychological Bulletin, 134*(3), 427.

Plaut, D. C., McClelland, J. L., Seidenberg, M. S., & Patterson, K. (1996). Understanding normal and impaired word reading: Computational principles in quasi-regular domains. *Psychological Review, 103,* 56–115.

Rapp, B., & Caramazza, A. (2002). Selective difficulties with spoken nouns and written verbs: A single case study. *Journal of Neurolinguistics, 15,* 373–402.

Rapp, B., & Goldrick, M. (2000). Discreteness and interactivity in spoken word production. *Psychological Review, 107,* 460–99.

Roelofs, A. (1992). A spreading-activation theory of lemma retrieval in speaking. *Cognition, 42,* 107–42.

Roelofs, A. (2004). Error biases in spoken word planning and monitoring by aphasic and nonaphasic speakers: Comment on Rapp and Goldrick (2000). *Psychological Review, 111,* 561–72.

Roelofs, A., Meyer, A. S., & Levelt, W. J. M. (1996). Interaction between semantic and orthographic factors in conceptually driven naming: Comment on Starreveld and La Heij (1995). *Journal of Experimental Psychology: Learning, Memory, and Cognition, 22,* 246–51.

Roelofs, A., Meyer, A. S., & Levelt, W. J. M. (1998). A case for the lemma-lexeme distinction in models of speaking: Comment on Caramazza and Miozzo (1997). *Cognition, 69,* 219–30.

Rogers, T., & McClelland, J. (Eds.) (2014). 2010 Rumelhart Prize Special Issue Honoring James L. McClelland. [Special issue] *Cognitive Science, 38*(6), 1286–315.

Rohde, D. L. T. (2002). *A Connectionist Model of Sentence Comprehension and Production* [Unpublished PhD thesis]. School of Computer Science, Carnegie Mellon University, Pittsburgh, PA.

Rumelhart, D. E., Durbin, R., Golden, R., & Chauvin, Y. (1996). Backpropagation: The basic theory. In: Smolensky, P., Mozer, M. C., & Rumelhart, D. E. (Eds.), *Mathematical Perspectives on Neural Networks*, pp. 533-66. Lawrence Erlbaum Associates, Mahwah, NJ.

Rumelhart, D. E., Hinton, G. E., & Williams, R. J. (1986). Learning internal representations by error propagation. In: Rumelhart, D. E., McClelland, J. L., & the PDP Research Group (Eds.), *Parallel Distributed Processing: Explorations in the Microstructure of Cognition: Vol. 1, Foundations* (pp. 318-62). MIT Press, Cambridge, MA.

Rumelhart, D. E., McClelland, J. L., & the PDP Research Group (1986). *Parallel Distributed Processing: Explorations in the Microstructure of Cognition: Vol. 1, Foundations*. MIT Press, Cambridge, MA.

Ruml, W., & Caramazza, A. (2000). An evaluation of a computational model of lexical access: Comment on Dell et al. (1997). *Psychological Review, 107*, 609-34.

Ruml, W., Caramazza, A., Capasso, R., & Miceli, G. (2005). Interactivity and continuity in normal and aphasic language production. *Cognitive Neuropsychology, 22*, 131-68.

Ruml, W., Caramazza, A., Shelton, J. R., & Chialant, D. (2000). Testing assumptions in computational theories of aphasia. *Journal of Memory and Language, 43*, 217-48.

Schriefers, H, Meyer, A. S., & Levelt, W. J. M. (1990). Exploring the time course of lexical access in language production: Picture-word interference studies. *Journal of Memory and Language, 29*, 86-102.

Schwartz, M. F., & Brecher, A. (2000). A model-driven analysis of severity, response characteristics, and partial recovery in aphasics' picture naming. *Brain and Language, 73*, 62-91.

Schwartz, M. F., Dell, G. S., Martin, N., Gahl, S., & Sobel, P. (2006). A case-series test of the interactive two-step model of lexical access: Evidence from picture naming. *Journal of Memory and Language, 54*, 228-64.

Smolensky, P. (2000). Grammar-based connectionist approaches to language. *Cognitive Science, 23*, 589-613.

Smolensky, P., Goldrick, M., & Mathis, D. (2014). Optimization and quantization in gradient symbol systems: A framework for integrating the continuous and the discrete in cognition. *Cognitive Science, 38*, 1102-38.

Starreveld, P. (2000). On the interpretation of phonological context effects in word production. *Journal of Memory and Language, 42*, 497-525.

Stemberger, J. P. (1985). An interactive activation model of language production. In: Ellis, A. W. (Ed.), *Progress in the Psychology of Language, Vol. 1* (pp. 143-86). Erlbaum, Hillsdale, NJ.

Vousden, J. I., Brown, G. D. A., & Harley, T. A. (2000). Serial control of phonology in speech production: A hierarchical model. *Cognitive Psychology, 41*, 101-75.

Walker, G. M., & Hickok, G. (2016). Bridging computational approaches to speech production: The semantic–lexical–auditory–motor model (SLAM). *Psychonomic Bulletin & Review, 23*, 339-52.

Warker, J. A., & Dell, G. S. (2006). Speech errors reflect newly learned phonotactic constraints. *Journal of Experimental Psychology: Learning, Memory, and Cognition, 32*, 387.

Wright, J. F., & Ahmad, K. (1997). The connectionist simulation of aphasic naming. *Brain and Language, 59*, 367-89.

CHAPTER 17

FROM THOUGHT TO ACTION
Producing written language

BRENDA RAPP AND MARKUS F. DAMIAN

17.1 SPELLING/WRITING: A CORE LANGUAGE PROCESS?

WRITTEN language is *un*like other language components—phonological, syntactic, semantic, morphological processing—in several important ways. Written language (reading and spelling) is evolutionarily recent, a human invention that entered our repertoire only a few thousand years ago and has become widespread in the global population only in the past 100 years. As a result, unlike spoken language, written language has not had the opportunity to shape the human genome to provide a blueprint for its neural processing. Also, unlike other language skills, reading and spelling typically require explicit instruction; mere exposure during a sensitive period is usually not sufficient. Furthermore, written language acquisition in the individual follows spoken language acquisition and relies on it heavily. Nonetheless, in the literate adult, written language knowledge and processes become neurally and cognitively autonomous components of the language system, interacting in complex ways with the other language components to produce fluent spoken and written language production. Not only does spoken language knowledge influence orthographic processing (Bonin, Fayol, & Chalard, 2001; Zhang & Damian, 2010), but orthographic knowledge may also influence spoken language processing (Damian & Bowers, 2003; Seidenberg & Tanenhaus, 1979). It is hard to imagine a complete understanding of the psycholinguistics of language that does not include written language. Although reading has received considerable research attention and interest in psycholinguistics, written language production, unfortunately, has been the "neglected" language modality. This is despite the fact that in this age of written electronic communication via email, texting, messaging, and so on, increasing numbers of people are processing written language as much or more than spoken language and everywhere we are bombarded by people producing written language by typing into their phones. In this chapter, we review some of the central issues in the psycholinguistics of single word written language production with the goal of providing the reader with an understanding of the cognitive and neural bases of this vital component of our language expertise.

17.2 THE MAJOR COGNITIVE PROCESSES OF SPELLING AND THEIR NEURAL SUBSTRATES

Written word production most often occurs in response to a thought or idea one wants to write down (e.g., a text message, a poem, a grocery list) or words one is hearing (e.g., taking lecture notes or a phone message). In the laboratory, these everyday activities are typically simulated using the written picture naming and writing to dictation tasks. Research on written production has identified four major orthography-specific processes (with their associated representations): orthographic long-term memory (O-LTM), phoneme-grapheme conversion (PGC), orthographic working memory (O-WM), and letter-shape selection. We describe these briefly here, and go into more detail for certain components in subsequent sections.

Orthographic long-term memory (also referred to as the orthographic lexicon) refers to the stored knowledge of learned word spellings and the processes involved in their retrieval/selection/encoding (see Fig. 17.1).

Phoneme-grapheme conversion refers to the knowledge and processes involved in converting a phonological representation to a plausible orthographic representation. Sublexical PGC knowledge is developed based on one's experiences in spelling words and, therefore, is assumed to represent phoneme-grapheme mappings based on their frequency in the language. This process is especially necessary when one needs to spell an unfamiliar word (e.g., taking a phone message from a Mr. /floup/). Given that there is no corresponding spelling in O-LTM, a plausible spelling (FLOPE, FLOAP, and so on) is generated by the PGC system. This system can, of course, be used to spell familiar words, and will likely be accurate with words with common, predictable spellings (e.g., "cat"→ CAT) but produce phonologically plausible errors with words with less predictable spellings (e.g., "once"→ WUNCE). Once a spelling is either retrieved from O-LTM or generated via the PGC system, the representation of letters is processed by **orthographic working memory** (also referred to as the graphemic buffer) and serially selected in their appropriate order for downstream production processes that produce letters in a specific format. Like other working memory systems, O-WM is a limited capacity system. The letters held in the graphemic buffer are assumed to be abstract, symbolic letter representations without form or sound. Spellings can be expressed in a variety of formats: letter shapes, letter names typing, or even Morse code or finger spelling. Letter-form selection involves selecting, in the correct order, the specific letter forms corresponding to the abstract letters held in the graphemic buffer. For handwriting, letter-form selection will involve retrieval of a relatively abstract motor plan for each letter in a specific case (upper or lower); for oral spelling, the letter names must be selected, and so on. These will then be passed along to motor planning and production processes that produce appropriate muscle movements.

Cognitive neuropsychological research has been pivotal in establishing the dissociability of these primary components from one another by documenting patterns of performance after brain damage that indicate that each of these components can be independently damaged (for a review, see Rapp & Fischer-Baum, 2015). Damage to either results in characteristic

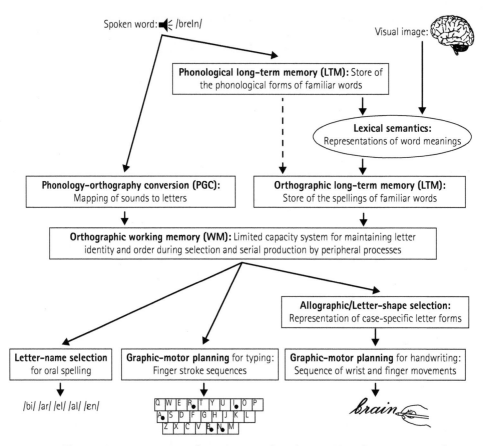

FIG. 17.1 The cognitive operations used in written word production. Note that components that are specifically involved in spelling are bolded.

Reproduced from Rapp, B. and Purcell, J., "Understanding how we produce written words: Lessons from the brain," in G. de Zubicaray & N. Schiller (Eds.), *The Oxford Handbook of Neurolinguistics*, in press. Reproduced by permission of Oxford University Press.

performance and error profiles that are useful both for clinical diagnostic purposes, but also for research directed at understanding the processes and representations handled by each of these components. In cognitive neuropsychological research, these deficits have served as "windows" into the inner workings of the components of the spelling system. Subsequent sections will review research carried out with both brain-damaged and neurotypical individuals directed at understanding the nature of these processes, their interactions, and the various representational types that they manipulate. In the remainder of this section we focus on the distinction between O-LTM and O-WM and the neural substrates of these fundamental processes.

Building on much previous work by other researchers, Buchwald and Rapp (2009) examined the performance profiles of four individuals with damage to O-LTM or O-WM and confirmed their predicted distinctiveness. Because O-LTM is a long-term memory store, damage/disruption is expected to result in difficulty in orthographic word form retrieval which: a) is sensitive to lexical variables such as word frequency and age-of-acquisition or AoA (e.g., greater difficulty in the retrieval, selection, and encoding of lower vs. higher frequency words) and b) results in a specific error profile: word errors are expected (semantic or form-related neighbors of the target word) and also phonologically plausible spellings of the target words. The latter are expected when the PGC system is intact. If a word's spelling is not identified in O-LTM (e.g., "sauce"), the PGC system may generate a plausible spelling (SOSS). In contrast, damage/disruption to O-WM is expected to exhibit a very different profile because of its very different functional characteristics. As indicated, O-WM is a limited capacity system that is responsible for maintaining orthographic representations active while letters are serially selected and passed along for subsequent motor planning and execution. Damage/disruption is expected to result in: 1) sensitivity to the number of letters, such that letters in longer vs. shorter words should be more susceptible to error, and 2) letter errors characteristic of WM failure are expected, namely: letter substitutions, deletions, movement, and additions. Buchwald and Rapp (2009) confirmed these predictions.

The striking behavioral dissociation between these deficit types is a strong indication that O-LTM and O-WM are instantiated in distinct neural substrates. Rapp, Purcell, Hillis, et al. (2016) sought to test this expectation, using a voxel-based lesion mapping approach to examine the distribution of lesions of 33 individuals identified—based on the behavioral profiles just described —as having deficits affecting O-LTM, O-WM, or both. Figure 17.2 depicts in blue/pink the brain areas associated with O-WM but not O-LTM impairment. Depicted in orange/red are regions associated with O-LTM but not O-WM impairment. The results show a clear neurotopographic dissociation between the substrates supporting these

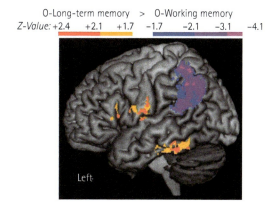

FIG. 17.2 Voxel-based lesion mapping comparison of the lesions of individuals with orthographic long-term memory (O-LTM) and working memory (O-WM) deficits, from Rapp et al. (2016). Depicted are the results of testing (at each voxel) for differences in presence/absence of lesion for individuals with deficits affecting O-LTM or O-WM. Clusters of significant difference are rendered on a left hemisphere standard brain template. All clusters are FDR (false discovery rate) corrected for multiple comparisons at $p < 0.05$. The color scale reflects the z-values of the significant clusters. Positive z-values (orange/red) indicate O-LTM deficit clusters; negative z-values (blue/pink) indicate O-WM deficit clusters.

Reproduced from Rapp, B. and Purcell, J., "Understanding how we produce written words: Lessons from the brain," in G. de Zubicaray & N. Schiller (Eds.), *The Oxford Handbook of Neurolinguistics*, in press. Reproduced by permission of Oxford University Press.

cognitive functions: O-WM is supported by a left hemisphere parietal region centered on the intraparietal sulcus, while O-LTM is supported by two left hemisphere regions: one in the ventral temporal, fusiform region (near the Visual Word Form Area (VWFA); Cohen, Lehéricy, Chochon, et al., 2002) and the other in the posterior inferior frontal gyrus. These findings not only shed light on the neural substrates of these spelling processes, they are relevant for the broader issues regarding the relationship between LTM and WM processes beyond the domain of spelling. In that regard, there has been much debate regarding whether LTM and WM are independent or "embedded" processes (Cowan, 2008). While this is not the place to elaborate on this issue, the Rapp et al. (2016) findings generally favor the independent processes position. Furthermore, the fact that individuals with O-WM deficits were also shown not to have difficulties with phonological or visuo-spatial WM supports the domain-specificity of the O-WM system. For a more complete review of the neural substrates of spelling/writing, see Purcell, Jiang, and Eden (2017) and Planton, Jucla, Roux, and Démonet (2013).

17.3 THE RELATIONSHIP BETWEEN WRITTEN LANGUAGE PRODUCTION AND OTHER LANGUAGE PROCESSES

17.3.1 Writing and speaking

Both written and spoken production tasks convert thought into overt form. Hence, it is likely that writing and speaking share several representational stages, and perhaps only diverge into modality-specific forms at a relatively advanced stage of preparation. The question of which stages are shared, and which are modality-specific has attracted some attention. Models of language production (e.g., Levelt, Roelofs, & Meyer, 1999) commonly assume that conceptual preparation is followed by a stage of access to abstract lexical presentations (i.e., "lemmas"), and that lemma retrieval is followed by form encoding. According to this view, lemmas are abstract lexical-syntactic representations that are shared across input and output tasks, and so it is plausible that writing and speaking should also involve access to the same lemmas, and that only subsequently are modality-specific codes accessed. This notion is for instance embedded in van Galen's (1991) model of handwritten production, and it receives support from recent studies that have used electroencephalography (EEG) to explore handwriting. Perret and Laganaro (2012) compared EEG activity associated with spoken and written picture naming directly, and found very similar electrophysiological activity associated with naming in either modality until approximately 260 ms after stimulus onset, with activity diverging thereafter into modality-specific components. The figure of 260 ms roughly matches the time estimates provided by Indefrey (2011; Indefrey & Levelt, 2004) for spoken word-form encoding; in turn, this implies that "lemma" access is indeed shared between speaking and writing. Further, although less direct, evidence for this claim comes from the observation that frequency effects in both modalities show a similar time course (see section 17.3.1.3, next), which is consistent with the notion that frequency-sensitive lemmas are shared between the two modalities. It should be noted that Caramazza (1997;

see also Caramazza & Miceli, 1990; Rapp & Caramazza, 2002) proposed that lemma representations may not be needed to explain the existing data suggesting, instead, that conceptual representation is followed by parallel access to modality-specific lexemes and syntactic information. Regardless of how the "lemma dilemma" (Rapp & Goldrick, 2006) is eventually resolved, understanding the specific characteristics of the processing and representational relationships between spoken and written word production is key to understanding language in the literate mind/brain.

17.3.1.1 *Orthographic autonomy*

Given the fact that written language follows and builds upon spoken language, both in the species and in the individual, an important question concerns the relationship between written and spoken language in the literate adult. In this regard the key question concerns the relationship between orthographic forms and word meaning. Given that a speaker comes to the task of learning to read and spell with strong links between word meanings and their spoken forms, the question is: Does literacy involve developing direct (autonomous) links between meanings and orthographic forms or is there obligatory mediation by spoken word forms? In reading, there has been considerable research on what is referred to as "phonological recoding": Is a written word necessarily converted to its phonological form to access its meaning? The corresponding question in spelling is: Is a word meaning necessarily first converted to its phonological form to access its written form for production?

The cognitive neuropsychological data are the strongest and most compelling in terms of adjudicating between these hypotheses. The prediction of the *obligatory phonological mediation hypothesis* is that a person who cannot access spoken word forms (e.g., as a result of brain damage) should also not be able to access their orthographic forms, while the *orthographic autonomy* hypothesis posits that, access to orthographic word forms should be possible despite failure to access spoken word forms. Rapp, Benzing, and Caramazza (1997) described a brain-damaged individual who, when presented with pictures of objects, for example a tiger, orally produced a semantically related word such as "lion" while at the same time correctly writing TIGER. Responses such as these cannot be explained in a cognitive architecture in which the phonological form necessarily forms the basis for orthographic retrieval. However, they are predicted in a language system in which orthographic forms can be independently retrieved from lexical-semantic representations (see Figure 17.1). In fact, this pattern supporting orthographic autonomy has been reported numerous times and in a variety of languages, both in those with opaque orthographies such as English (e.g., Hillis & Caramazza, 1995) and Chinese (Law, Wong, & Kong, 2006) and transparent orthographies such as Italian (Miceli, Benvegnù, Capasso, & Caramazza, 1997), Spanish (Cuetos & Labos, 2001), and Welsh (Tainturier & Rapp, 2001).

In addition to this strong cognitive neuropsychological evidence, there is also psycholinguistic evidence from neurotypical individuals. These investigations typically seek to determine if activation of phonological forms necessarily has an influence on the production of the related written words. For example, Bonin, Fayol, and Peereman (1998) found that, contrary to the predictions of the obligatory phonological mediation hypothesis, priming conditions that facilitate the production of spoken words do not necessarily facilitate the production of their corresponding written forms. For example, a written pseudohomophone (DANT) facilitates the subsequent spoken naming of the picture "dent" (tooth) but not the written picture naming of the same word. Also, Zhang and Damian (2010; Experiment 2) used a picture-word interference paradigm that involved writing the names of pictures presented with superimposed distractor words. They found that under conditions of articulatory suppression, the degree of phonological similarity of distractor words to the picture name (e.g., picture of a hand, distractor SAND/WAND) did not affect writing response times. These findings are all consistent with the predictions of the orthographic autonomy hypothesis.

In sum, there is clear and convincing evidence favoring a system in which word meanings are directly linked to orthographic word forms. However, this does not preclude the possibility that phonological mediation is an option (see Fig. 17.1). In fact, given the developmental dependence of written language on spoken, this would be the most plausible hypothesis. What will be most interesting is understanding the conditions under which phonological mediation and orthographic autonomy are most likely to occur, and the time course and contributions of these two pathways to written word production.

17.3.1.2 *Phonology in written word production*

Over the last 20 or so years, a growing number of studies have been devoted to understanding the degree to which phonological codes contribute to written production, and many if not most of them have made use of inexpensive digital graphic tablets that allow straightforward collection of written latencies and other features of written production. Hence, experimental tasks that are well-established in research on spoken production can be adapted to the written domain. As will be shown in this section, although the question is far from resolved, there is substantial evidence from a variety of experimental tasks that phonological codes are often activated and influence written responses.

Table 17.1 provides an overview of the dozen or so available studies, roughly sorted by experimental task. As will become clear, the bulk of these studies have adapted tasks which are well-used in research on spoken production, to the generation of written responses. For instance, the so-called "picture-word interference" paradigm is immensely popular in work on speech production (e.g., Schriefers, Meyer, & Levelt, 1990; Mahon, Costa, Peterson, et al., 2007). In this task, participants name objects while instructed to ignore "distractor" words presented simultaneously or in close temporal proximity. A central observation is that form-related distractors (picture: cat; distractor: cap) tend to lead to faster object naming times than unrelated distractors (picture: cat; distractor: top, e.g., Glaser & Düngelhoff, 1984; Lupker & Katz, 1981; Schriefers, Meyer, & Levelt, 1990; Starreveld & La Heij, 1996). This implies that target preparation and distractor processing engage in "cross-talk," which provides insight into how speakers prepare spoken responses. Several studies have now adapted this task for use with written, rather than spoken responses, and one of the questions that can be addressed is whether phonologically related, but orthographically unrelated (or less related) distractors provide priming. The answer appears to be that they can; for example, Zhang and Damian (2010) showed more priming from phonologically related distractors (hand-sand) than from orthographically equally related, but phonologically less related (hand-wand) distractors, relative to an unrelated condition. As will be appreciated from these examples, orthographic and phonological overlap cannot easily be dissociated in an alphabetic script, even in a language with irregular spelling such as English. By contrast, in Chinese this dissociation is easier to achieve, and for this reason some recent

Table 17.1 Overview of studies which have studied the potential role of phonology in written production

Task	Target language	Sample size	Effect of phonology?
Picture-word interference			
Zhang & Damian (2011)	English	30	✓
Qu, Damian, Zhang, & Zhu (2011)	Chinese (Mandarin)	30	✓
Zhang & Wang (2015)	Chinese (Mandarin)	24	✓
Picture-picture priming			
Roux & Bonin (2011)	French	30 in Exp. 3	✗
Implicit priming			
Afonso & Álvarez (2011)	Spanish	18 in Exp. 1; 48 in Exp. 2	✓
Shen, Damian, & Stadthagen-Gonzalez (2013)	English	20 in Exp. 4 & 5	✗
Picture naming			
Bonin, Peereman, & Fayol (2001)	French	36 in Exp. 3	✓
Masked priming			
Bonin, Fayol, & Peereman (1998)	French	27 in Exp. 1–3	✗
Qu, Damian, & Li (2016)	Chinese (Mandarin)	16 in Exp. 1–2	✓
Cross-modal long-lasting repetition priming			
Damian, Dorjee, & Stadthagen-Gonzalez (2011)	English	18	✓
Stroop task			
Damian & Qu (2013)	Chinese (Mandarin)	37	✓
Written picture naming; copying of written words			
Bonin, Méot, Lagarrigue, & Roux (2015)	French	34	✗
Spelling-to-dictation			
Bonin, Méot, Lagarrigue, & Roux (2014)	French	34	✓

studies have examined Chinese writers as participants. For instance, Qu, Damian, Zhang, and Zhu (2011) asked Chinese individuals to write the names of objects on a tablet, and compared priming from distractors which were orthographically and phonologically related, to priming from distractors which were phonologically related (but orthographically unrelated). Importantly, priming was found for the latter (compared to an unrelated condition), which makes a rather compelling case for the influence of phonology on writing. Comparable results were reported by Zhang and Wang (2015) in a picture-word task, again conducted with Chinese writers.

Although studies using PWI reveal the influence of phonology, some have also reported important conflicting evidence. They varied the onset of the distractor relative to the target dimension (stimulus-onset asynchrony, or SOA), a manipulation assumed to yield information about the time course of processing. In doing so, Zhang and Damian (2010) with English speakers, and Qu et al. (2011) with Mandarin speakers demonstrated a characteristic time course such that phonology appeared primarily relevant at an "early" stage of orthographic encoding, but at a "later" SOA, only orthographic overlap appeared relevant. This might be interpreted as the "primacy" of phonological access in object naming. Interestingly, however, the opposite pattern was found by Zhang and Wang (2015): in their study, early SOAs showed exclusively orthographic priming, and phonological priming only emerged at later SOAs. According to the authors, early orthographic priming reflects the direct route from meaning to orthography, whereas the later phonologically based priming indicates activation via the indirect phonologically based pathway. The reason for the discrepancy between Zhang and Damian's and Zhang and Wang's findings in otherwise very similar tasks and designs needs to be determined. It also highlights the need for future research to employ innovative tasks and online measures to tackle the issue, such as electroencephalography (e.g., Qu, Li, & Damian, 2014).

As is evident in Table 17.1, a range of other experimental tasks have also been used to explore the issue, such as masked priming (Bonin, Fayol, & Peereman, 1998; Qu, Damian, & Li, 2016), Stroop (Damian & Qu, 2013), and long-lasting repetition priming between spoken and written naming (Damian, Dorjee, & Stadthagen-Gonzalez, 2011). In assessing the results available to date (summarized in Table 17.1), it is apparent that the evidence supporting phonological effects is rather substantial. Nevertheless, a number of null findings are acknowledged, pointing to the possibility that there are task- and (perhaps) language-specific aspects which might benefit or discourage the emergence of phonological effects.

Many of the tasks summarized in Table 17.1 merely demonstrate a phonological impact on writing, but they do not speak to the level at which such an effect could occur. However, Bonin, Peereman, & Fayol (2001) manipulated sound-to-print consistency of picture names, and found that consistency manipulated at the lexical level (heterographic homophones vs. non-homophones; e.g., cygne/signe) did not affect naming latencies, but that sublexical PGC inconsistency did (e.g., cloche, where the initial /k/ could be spelled as qu, c, k, or ch) but only when located in word-initial position. This pattern suggests that phonology affects orthographic encoding mainly by the sublexical PGC route (see Alario, Schiller, Domoto-Reilly, & Caramazza, 2003; Miceli, Capasso, & Caramazza, 1999, for neuropsychological evidence supporting this claim). Interestingly, however, effects of phonology have also been shown in Chinese (e.g., Qu, Damian, Zhang, & Zhu, 2011), an orthographic system which does not represent such sublexical sound-to-spelling correspondences at the phoneme/grapheme level (see also section 17.4.3, next).

17.3.1.3 *Frequency and AoA*

One of the best-documented variables affecting language processing is the frequency with which a word occurs, demonstrating that language processing is sensitive to the distribution of information in the environment. Frequency effects are found in spoken production tasks such as object naming (e.g., Almeida, Knobel, Finkbeiner, & Caramazza, 2007; Jescheniak & Levelt, 1994; Oldfield & Wingfield, 1965) and they also appear in written object naming, both in studies using multiple regression (e.g., Bonin, Chalard, Méot, & Fayol, 2002) and in factorial designs (e.g., Bonin & Fayol, 2002). Interestingly, frequency effects are (at least sometimes) absent in spelling-to-dictation and immediate copying tasks (Bonin, Méot, Lagarrigue, & Roux, 2015), suggesting that these orthographic production tasks are mainly carried out via sublexical PGC pathways.

In research on spoken production, a long-standing issue has been to identify the exact locus of frequency effects. An early prominent claim that frequency affects retrieval of phonological word forms (Jescheniak & Levelt, 1994) has now been superseded by the idea that frequency mainly affects prephonological (perhaps "lemma") retrieval (Bonin & Fayol, 2002; Caramazza, Bi, Costa, & Miozzo, 2004; Caramazza, Costa, Miozzo, & Bi, 2001; Cuetos, Bonin, Alameda, & Caramazza, 2010; Finocchiaro & Caramazza, 2006). This inference dovetails with the observation that in EEG studies of spoken word production, frequency effects emerge in a relatively "early" time window, starting 150–200 ms after picture onset (Strijkers, Costa, & Thierry, 2010; Strijkers, Holcomb, & Costa, 2011; Strijkers, Baus, Runnqvist, FitzPatrick, & Costa, 2013), which highlights a lexical-semantic rather than a phonological locus. As regards written word production, the behavioral evidence also favors a lexical-semantic locus (e.g., Bonin & Fayol, 2002). EEG evidence is still scant, but Qu, Zhang, and Damian (2016) also reported a word frequency effect in Chinese writers, which emerged in a similar "early" time window (~160 ms post stimulus onset) as observed in spoken production. However, note that with typed (rather than handwritten) responses, Baus, Strijkers, and Costa (2013) recently reported a frequency effect which emerged at a much later point in time (330–430 ms). The reason for this discrepancy is at present unclear, and further research is clearly needed to resolve the issue.

A related variable is AoA, or the average age at which a particular word or concept has been acquired. Over the last few decades, AoA has emerged as a major influence on latencies in various language tasks (e.g., Ellis & Lambon Ralph, 2000; Morrison, Ellis, & Quinlan, 1992), including spoken (e.g., Barry, Morrison, & Ellis, 1997; Bonin, Barry, Méot, & Chalard, 2004) and written (Bonin, Fayol, & Chalard, 2001) word production. Like frequency, an extensive controversy exists concerning the processing stage (or stages) at which AoA effects emerge. AoA effects have been claimed to affect the level of word-form encoding (e.g., Morrison, Ellis, & Quinlan, 1992), the semantic level (Belke, Brysbaert, Meyer, & Ghyselinck, 2005; Brysbaert, van Wijnendaele, & de Deyne, 2000; Johnston & Barry 2005), or perhaps the entire system (e.g., Ellis & Lambon Ralph, 2000). An EEG-based study of spoken object naming (Laganaro & Perret, 2011) suggested AoA effects at a time window starting approximately 350 ms post picture onset, which points to a lexical-phonological locus. Perret, Bonin, and Laganaro (2014) directly compared written and spoken picture naming, and found similar AoA effects in both modalities, starting at around 400 ms post onset. These studies point toward a word-form encoding locus of AoA.

Overall, both frequency and AoA effects are reliably obtained not only in spoken, but also in written production. The—admittedly scant—evidence from EEG points toward a lexical-semantic locus of frequency effects, and a word-form locus of AoA effects.

17.3.2 The relationship between spelling and reading

For written language there has been considerable interest in understanding the relationship between perception and production: reading and spelling. This is part of a long-standing broader debate on the role of the motor system in perception (e.g., in speech there is the motor theory of speech perception). Specifically, one can ask whether one or more of the major components of spelling are also used for reading. Most research has considered whether or not reading and spelling share O-LTM and, therefore, our review will focus on this specific issue. Three types of studies have been brought to bear on this question: psycholinguistic, cognitive neuropsychological, and functional neuroimaging. The basic logic of all the approaches has been to try to determine if there are compelling similarities (associations) or differences (dissociations) in performance or activation patterns for reading and spelling that can be localized to O-LTM. While the logic appears straightforward, the interpretative difficulties have turned out to be quite complex.

Psycholinguistic studies with neurotypical individuals carried out by Monsell (1987) found significant repetition priming in reading words that had been earlier spelled (without visual feedback). Consistent with the notion of shared lexical orthographic representations, Holmes and Carruthers (1998), and also Burt and Tate (2002) found that specific words that individuals could not spell correctly, were also responded to more slowly or less accurately in reading tasks (such as lexical decision or visual spelling accuracy judgments). These findings provide support for the hypothesis that both reading and spelling share LTM lexical orthographic representations which, if they are incorrect/incomplete will affect both reading and spelling and which exhibit priming when repeatedly activated in spelling and reading. However, this interpretation can be challenged by concerns that the shared reading/spelling errors result from a correlation due to some third factor or that episodic memory traces from one task (e.g., spelling) may affect performance on the other (e.g., reading).

The cognitive neuropsychological evidence has also been subject to interpretative difficulties. There have been several cases of associated reading and spelling impairments that seem to originate in O-LTM (Philipose, Gottesman, Newhart, et al., 2007; Rapcsak & Beeson, 2004) but also cases of dissociations in which either reading or spelling are intact in the face of O-LTM damage in the other modality (Hillis, Rapp, & Caramazza, 1999). The interpretive difficulty arises because associated deficits could either indicate a shared process or, alternatively, be the result of damage that just happens to affect O-LTM components for reading and spelling that are instantiated in nearby neural areas. Dissociations are also subject to multiple interpretations; they could either be the result of damage to distinct O-LTM memory components, or they could arise from lesions affecting modality-specific *access* to a shared O-LTM system.

On this issue, the neuroimaging data are perhaps the most compelling. Again, the logic is one of association/dissociation: do reading and spelling activate the same neural substrates? There have been a small number of fMRI studies that have examined the neural substrates of both reading and spelling in the same individuals (Purcell et al., 2017; Rapp & Dufor, 2011; Rapp & Lipka, 2011) and all found coactivation for reading and spelling in the left mid-fusiform gyrus and the left inferior frontal gyrus. The left mid-fusiform region has sometimes been referred to as the VWFA (Cohen et al., 2002) and has been argued to play a role in orthographic word processing. Consistent with that characterization, both Rapp and Lipka (2011) and Rapp and Dufor (2011) found these areas to be sensitive to the lexical frequency of the words that were read and spelled. However, the fact that this evidence consists of overlapping activation for reading and spelling, leaves open the possibility that there are, in fact, distinct O-LTM components for reading and spelling supported by different subpopulations of neurons within this region. Purcell et al. (2017) provided the strongest evidence to date refuting this interpretation and providing evidence of shared O-LTM for reading and spelling. They used the neural adaptation approach to address the question of shared substrates for reading and spelling. The logic of neural adaptation is like that of behavioral priming. It is based on the empirically supported assumption that repeated activation of a neural population leads to a decreasing response. Because of this, it provides a powerful tool for investigating whether or not the same neural population is engaged in different tasks. Just as Monsell (1987; just described) tested for priming for words first spelled and then read, Purcell et al. (2017) examined neural adaptation for pairs of the same vs. different words first spelled and then read, and also for same vs. different words first repeated and then read. The repeat-READ condition provides a control to determine if any observed adaptation in the spell-READ condition is due simply to shared non-orthographic processes, such as phonological or semantic ones. Figure 17.3 depicts the neural adaptation results for the VWFA region, showing adaptation when the same (vs. different) word is spelled and then read (spell-READ) but not when it is repeated and then read (repeat-READ). These findings, therefore, provide robust evidence that reading and spelling share orthographic processes/representations in this brain area. These findings constitute the strongest evidence to date that the same neural population is involved in some aspect of O-LTM for both reading and spelling.

17.4 LEVELS OF REPRESENTATION IN THE WRITING SYSTEM AND THEIR INTERACTIONS

17.4.1 Orthographic representations

What do we know when we know the spelling of a word? In other words, what is the content of the representations of word spellings that are stored in O-LTM? The default hypothesis is that these representations consist of a set of letter identities and their position/order—the "letter-string" hypothesis. While this information must certainly be represented, an alternative is that orthographic representations have more complex and rich internal structure and organization; this is sometimes referred to as the "multidimensional hypothesis" (Caramazza & Miceli, 1990). Research has provided strong evidence in favor of the multidimensional hypothesis and in this section, we provide an overview of the units of orthographic representation and the different types of information that form an orthographic representation. Figure 17.4 schematizes the representation of the word THICKNESS and serves as a summary and guide to the rest of this section (see Rapp & Fischer-Baum, 2014, for a more detailed discussion).

First, a fundamental question concerns the nature/format of the letter identities in orthographic representations. As already indicated, spellings can be expressed in a variety of

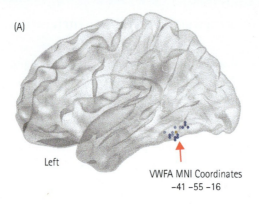
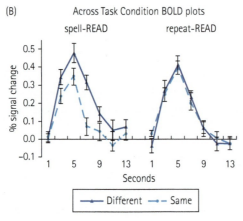
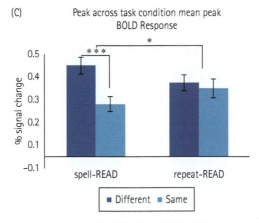

FIG. 17.3 Neural adaptation in the left Visual Word Form Area (VWFA) region of interest demonstrating orthographic representations/processes shared across spelling and reading. (A) The mean location of the participant-specific VWFA regions projected onto a transparent left hemisphere standard brain. Red dot refers to the mean location across subjects (-41 -55 -16); the blue dots refer to the individual subject peak locations. (B) Blood Oxygenation Level Dependent (BOLD) responses for the spell-READ and the repeat-READ consecutive task pairs of either different words (solid lines) or the same words (dotted lines). Error bars correspond to standard error. (C) Average peak BOLD response (4–8 sec post stimulus) differences for each condition. Positive values refer to an adaptation effect (i.e., different>same). Error bars are standard error. P-values: ***$p < 0.0001$; *$p < 0.01$. These results reveal a significant effect for the spell-READ conditions, but critically not for the repeat-READ condition, indicating shared orthographic representations *across* spelling and reading (but not for repetition and reading) within the left VWFA.

Reprinted from NeuroImage, 147, Jeremy J. Purcell, Xiong Jiang, and Guinevere F. Eden, Shared orthographic neuronal representations for spelling and reading, pp. 554–567, doi.org/10.1016/j.neuroimage.2016.12.054 © 2016 Elsevier Inc. All rights reserved.

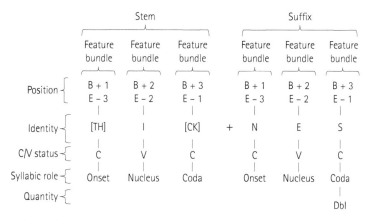

FIG. 17.4 Orthographic representation for the word THICKNESS. The bolded elements represent the content and structure of the representation. Five features of orthographic unit representation are depicted: letter position, letter identity, consonant vowel status (C/V status), syllabic role, and letter quantity. For example, one orthographic unit has S in the identity dimension. Another feature associated with this unit is its position represented as both three after the beginning of the morpheme (B+3) and one before the end of the morpheme (E-1). Also represented is the CV status of consonant (C), the syllabic role of coda, and the quantity of double (Dbl). Note that the digraphs TH and CK are each represented within a single feature bundle. The brackets around [TH] and [CK] depict that these digraphs are single units in the letter identity dimension. Feature bundles are further organized into higher-level morphological units. The first three feature bundles combine to form the stem morpheme THICK, while the final three feature bundles combine to form the suffix morpheme NESS. The plus symbol (+) between the two morphemes indicates processes that combine multiple morphemes into whole word representations.

Reproduced from Rapp, B. and Fischer-Baum, S., "Representation of Orthographic Knowledge," in M. Goldrick, V. Ferreira, and M. Miozzo (Eds.), *The Oxford Handbook of Language Production*, Figure 21.3, p. 342 © Oxford University Press, 2014. Reproduced by permission of Oxford University Press.

formats with written letter shapes, spoken letter names, and typing being the most common. There are two alternative hypotheses regarding the nature of letter representations processed by the central spelling processes (O-LTM, PGC, and O-WM). One is that letters are represented in a specific format (e.g., letter shapes) and then converted into other formats by downstream processes. The other is that letters are represented as abstract, symbolic entities with no format, which are then assigned a format by downstream processes. The format-specific hypothesis predicts that an individual who has difficulty generating spellings in the critical format (not due to motor deficits) should also have difficulty in all other formats. For example, if letters are represented in a spatial format used for handwriting, then an individual with difficulties in written spelling should also have difficulties in oral spelling (and typing, and so on). Similarly, if letters are represented as letter names, an individual with difficulties with letter-name retrieval should also have difficulties in written spelling (and typing, and so on). In contrast, according to the abstract letter identity hypothesis, damage to the central processes should produce comparable error patterns in all output modalities, and selective deficits in a specific modality (e.g., oral or written spelling) should be possible if letter-shape or letter-name conversion processes are selectively affected. The cognitive neuropsychological evidence clearly favors the abstract letter identity hypothesis. Several cases have been reported of individuals with difficulties retrieving the spoken names of letters, but who are able to spell words accurately in writing (Kinsbourne & Warrington, 1965) as well as the complementary dissociation involving individuals who have difficulty retrieving the correct shapes of letters and produce errors in written spelling, but are correct in oral spelling (Rapp, Benzing, & Caramazza, 1997). In addition, the prediction regarding deficits affecting central components of the spelling process has been upheld in cases of individuals with near identical accuracies and error distributions in both written and oral spelling (Caramazza & Miceli, 1990; Hillis & Caramazza, 1989; Jónsdóttir, Shallice, & Wise, 1996; Katz, 1991; McCloskey, Badecker, Goodman-Schulman, & Aliminosa, 1994). Finally, Dufor and Rapp (2013), using an fMRI neural adaptation paradigm with letter writing, found a region in the left mid-fusiform gyrus (near the VWFA) that responded to letter identity in a way that could not be explained by letter size, shape, or case, indicating abstract, symbolic letter representations.

Having established that orthographic representations are encoded in terms of abstract graphemes one can ask how these letter representations are organized—as a linear string of letter identities or into larger, more complex units? Several lines of evidence, both cognitive neuropsychological (Tainturier & Rapp, 2004) and psycholinguistic (e.g., Kandel & Spinelli, 2010; Shen, Damian, & Stadthagen-Gonzalez, 2013) indicate that letters are organized into digraph units that correspond to phonemes (e.g., a word such as WREATH contains three digraphs: WR, EAT, and TH). Perhaps one of the most compelling lines of evidence comes from Fischer-Baum and Rapp (2014) who reported on a cognitive neuropsychological case who produced a sizeable number of perseveration errors in which letters from previous responses were produced in later responses ("motel"→ MOLD*EL*, followed by "under"→ UND*EL*). With regard to digraphs, they compared the rate of digraph (TH) and consonant cluster (TR) perseverations to the rate of single consonant perseverations. If digraphs form a single orthographic unit, the letters that form a digraph should (a) "travel together" in a perseveration more often than the two independent letters of a cluster and (b) they should do so at rates comparable to single letters. This is exactly what was found.

While there have been many studies investigating the morphological decomposition of multimorphemic words in reading, there have been relatively few that have considered this issue in spelling. Hillis and Caramazza (1989) reported on an individual whose dysgraphia resulted from an O-WM deficit, who showed the characteristic pattern of producing more errors on letters in longer words than in shorter words. They also found that he produced fewer errors on multimorphemic words than matched monomorphemic words. They proposed that the WM burden was lessened in multimorphemic words if we assume that orthographic representations are morphologically decomposed, allowing for the separate processing of constituent morphemes. In fact, Rapp, Fischer-Baum, and Miozzo (2015) proposed the *morpho-orthography hypothesis*, according to which, in addition to morpho-phonological processes, there are morpho-orthographic ones that operate over morphologically complex orthographic representations. In support of this hypothesis they presented four individuals who exhibited specific difficulties (deletion and/or substitution errors) that primarily affected their writing of inflectional morphemes (e.g., "slicing" → SLICES, "drives"→ DRIVER, "perplexed" → PERPLEXES; picture of two cats → TWO CAT) while their spoken production of inflectional morphemes was relatively preserved. Importantly, these cases contrast with others who show either a selective difficulty with inflectional morphemes in spoken but not written production (Rapp et al., 2015) and others who show selective difficulty with stems but affixes in spelling (Badecker, Rapp, & Caramazza, 1996). Finally, also supportive of the internal morphological organization of orthographic representations, Kandel, Spinelli, Tremblay, et al. (2012) reported that writing times for neurologically intact individuals are longer for letters preceding morpheme boundaries in suffixed (PRUN/EAU) vs. pseudo-suffixed words (PINC/EAU). These findings reveal the morphological organization of orthographic representations and that high-level language operations operate over orthographic representations

In addition to being internally structured into units such as diagraphs and morphemes, there is the claim that letter representations are complex feature bundles that not only include information about abstract letter identity and order, but also other features such as consonant vowel status and quantity (Rapp & Fischer-Baum, 2014). While consonant/vowel are phonological categories, the claim is that these categories have been incorporated into the orthographic system. In the reading literature, some (e.g., Berent, Shimron, & Vaknin, 2001) have argued that, during letter identification, the consonant/vowel status of each letter is identified and contributes to the orthotactic processing required to identify strings as legal vs. illegal. A similar claim has been made for spelling, based largely on cognitive neuropsychological data. First, there are the cases that make up a double dissociation with deficits selectively affecting either consonants or vowels in spelling (Cotelli, Abutalebi, Zorzi, & Cappa, 2003; Cubelli, 1991; Miceli, Capasso, Benvegnù, & Caramazza, 2004). These cases indicate that consonants and vowels are represented with sufficient neural independence that they can be selectively affected by brain damage. The fact that these individuals did not have similar deficits in spoken production, underscores that the consonant-vowel (CV) distinction applies to orthographic representations. More specific support for the independent representation of letter identity and CV status comes from the letter substitution errors of individuals with deficits affecting O-WM. Caramazza and Miceli (1990) reported on an Italian case in which 99% of substitution errors preserved the CV status of the target letter (e.g., "fanale" → FARALE, "maschi" → MASGHI). They argued that this pattern can be understood if we assume the independence of letter identity and CV information such that letter identity can be disrupted, leaving intact CV info. For example, in Figure 17.4, if the letter identity H were disrupted, the system could generate a response consistent with the remaining information (e.g., T*P*ICKNESS). Buchwald and Rapp (2006) specifically examined the hypothesis that these substitutions were based on orthographic rather than phonological information, or could be accounted for by the constraints of the local orthographic environment rather than requiring the explicit representation of CV information. Among other things, they examined CV preservation rates for substitutions in which there was a mismatch between phonological and orthographic CV status. For example, the CV structure of the phonological representation of a word such as "sleigh" is CCV, whereas its orthographic CV structure is CCVVCC. The question they considered is: What happens when the G or H are substituted in individuals with O-WM deficits? The phonological representation indicates the word ends in a V, whereas the orthographic representation indicates a C. Buchwald and Rapp found that the substitutions matched the orthographic category 91 and 70% of the time for the two individuals they reported on and that these rates were significantly greater than would be expected by chance.

Finally, with respect to the representation of letter quantity there are two possibilities: one is that double letters are represented as are any pair of adjacent letters (O + D + D and O + L + D), while another is that doubling is a distinct piece of orthographic information, (O + D$^{+\text{double}}$) which is independent and separable from the letter identity it is associated with. Lashley (1951) and later Rumelhart and Norman (1982) discussed the significance of typing errors in which the doubling of a letter is misplaced ODD → OOD claiming that they revealed that doubling is represented independently from letter identity such that the doubling information can occasionally be attached to the wrong identity. Since then, cognitive neuropsychological cases have provided critical data localizing doubling information not only to motor representations, but to higher-level orthographic ones as well. The evidence comes from individuals with deficits at the level of O-WM where the reduction in WM capacity produces omissions, substitutions, transpositions, and so on of the elements processed by the O-WM system. Caramazza and Miceli (1990) reported on an Italian individual who made errors which could be understood if there was a doubling feature that could be deleted ("marrone" → MAZZONE), moved to a different letter (MARONNE), or duplicated (MARRONNE). Importantly they failed to find errors that were predicted not to occur if double letters consist of a single letter identity with a double marker. In other words, they found no errors in which doubles were separated (e.g., MARORNE) and very few errors in which only one letter of a double was substituted (e.g., MALRONE) (for additional cases in other languages, see McCloskey et al., 1994). Finally, additional support for the claim that doubling information is independent of letter identity came from Fischer-Baum and Rapp (2014), who presented evidence that the doubling feature can independently perseverate into subsequent responses. They found that double letter intrusion errors ("tragic"→ TRRACE) were preceded by trials containing a different double letter (e.g., "excess"→ EXCESS) at rates far greater than would be predicted by chance. These "quantity but not identity" perseverations indicate that quantity information can persist from one response to another and they are difficult to explain without positing an independent doubling feature. These errors provide further evidence of the rich internal content and organization of orthographic representations.

17.4.2 Interaction and cascadedness

Spoken and written word production involve a series of processing states: conceptual selection; abstract lexical ("lemma") access; retrieval of form-related lexical information, phonological, or orthographic encoding; and so on. The way activation is transmitted across these stages has been the focus of much research attention for a long time. Many early models of spoken production tended to be strictly serial (Garrett, 1976; Levelt, Schriefers, Vorberg, et al., 1991). However, recent evidence favors a "cascaded" view of production. Cascadedness implies that access to phonology begins before semantic-syntactic retrieval has been completed, and that all candidates which are activated at the semantic level, and not just the target, can influence phonological encoding (see Rapp & Goldrick, 2000, for extensive analysis). Empirical support for this assumption comes from several recent studies which have shown that in various experimental tasks, speakers appear to phonologically encode "non-target properties," such as the names of to-be-ignored objects (Görges, Oppermann, Jescheniak, & Schriefers, 2013; Meyer & Damian, 2007; Morsella & Miozzo, 2002; Navarrete

& Costa, 2005; Oppermann, Jescheniak, & Schriefers, 2008; Oppermann, Jescheniak, Schriefers, & Görges 2010). Although the exact circumstances under which cascadedness is found remains controversial (e.g., Roux & Bonin, 2016) most researchers now accept the view that spoken production is unlikely to be "strictly serial." Cascadedness has also been suggested not just at the semantics-phonology interface, but also between phonology and articulation (e.g., McMillan & Corley, 2010).

A similar question can be raised regarding written production: is information transmission "serial," or does activation "cascade" from one processing level to another? Care should be taken not to generalize from one mode of production (spoken) to another (written), because the two modes conceivably differ in their processing demands. Yet, the existing evidence also favors a cascaded view in written production. For instance, Roux and Bonin (2012) adapted the spoken production task introduced by Morsella and Miozzo (2002) in which two pictures were superimposed on each other in two colors, and participants named the one cued by one color, and attempted to ignore the other. Roux and Bonin asked French participants to write (rather than say) the target picture name, and found that phonologically and orthographically related distractor pictures (bougie-banc; "candle-bench") generated facilitation in writing latencies, compared to an unrelated condition. This finding suggests that, as for spoken production, with written responses the form properties of the to-be-ignored object "cascaded" to the orthographic level. Facilitation was also found when target and distractor picture names shared the initial grapheme but started with a different phoneme (cigare-camion, "cigar-truck"), but not when they shared the initial phoneme but not the initial grapheme (souris-citron, "mouse-lemon") (note that the latter finding is one of the null effects regarding the role of phonology in writing; cf. Table 17.1). Converging evidence was reported in Qu and Damian (2015): Chinese participants were presented with colored line drawings of objects and wrote the name of the color while attempting to ignore the object. Compared to an unrelated condition, facilitation was found when target color and object name shared an orthographic radical.

The inference that written production is cascaded was to some extent qualified in work reported by Bonin, Roux, Barry, and Canell (2012). Rather than using a task in which an unattended dimension "cascaded" activation to the target dimension, the authors employed "additive factors logic" (Sternberg, 1969) and crossed, in a written object naming task, two experimental dimensions pertaining to two underlying processing stages (e.g., perceptual: clear vs. blurred; conceptual: contextual constraint arising from a preceding sentence; lexical: frequency of occurrence). Perceptual and lexical variables exerted additive effects, but conceptual and lexical variables statistically interacted. In combination, the results were interpreted as supporting a "limited cascading" view in which cascading takes place only between the conceptual and the form level.

A parallel question is whether activation cascades from the lexical to the letter/grapheme level. Evidence from neuropsychological patients suggests that this might be the case. For instance, Sage and Ellis (2004) reported a patient with hypothesized impairment to the graphemic buffer, whose spelling accuracy depended to some extent on lexical properties such as word frequency. Buchwald and Rapp (2009) also showed in multiple graphemic buffer cases that lexical properties significantly predicted accuracy over that predicted by letter length. Buchwald and Falconer (2014) reported a case study of an individual with damage to both lexical and graphemic levels, and showed that for lexemes which were only weakly activated (as evidenced by lexical-semantic errors), letter accuracy was reduced, again suggesting cascadedness between the two levels. Indeed, feedback interactivity from graphemic and lexical levels (rather than just cascadedness) between the two levels was suggested by results from a study by Falconer and Buchwald (2013), showing that written semantically related word errors produced by a dysgraphic individual exhibited greater-than-chance orthographic overlap to the target word (see also McCloskey, Macaruso, & Rapp, 2006 for other evidence regarding feedback interactivity).

Finally, one can explore the temporal processing relationship between central and "peripheral" components of written production. A growing body of literature suggests that motor processes are directly affected by more abstract properties of the output. For instance, Roux et al. (2013) showed that in the written production of French words, letter durations were longer for irregular than regular words, and the duration effect was modulated by the position of the irregularity. Hence, movement execution is evidently affected by lexical and sublexical variables that regulate spelling. This suggests that movement begins before central planning is completed, and the latter affects the former via cascadedness (see also Delattre, Bonin, & Barry, 2006, for a similar inference drawn from a spelling-to-dictation task). Interletter interval durations are sensitive to the position of syllabic (Álvarez, Cottrell, & Afonso, 2009; Kandel, Álvarez, & Vallée, 2006) and morphological boundaries (Kandel et al., 2006; Kandel, Spinelli, Tremblay, Guerassimovitch, & Álvarez, 2012), and are affected by the presence of complex graphemes (Kandel & Spinelli, 2010) or double letters (Kandel, Peereman, & Ghimenton, 2014). These and related findings clearly demonstrate that the multidimensional structure of orthographic representations has an impact on peripheral processes (Kandel & Perret, 2015; Roux, McKeeff, Grosjacques, et al., 2013).

In summary, the currently available evidence makes a rather convincing case for a cascaded principle of activation transmission in orthographic production: between semantic and lexical levels, between lexical and graphemic representations, and between central and peripheral levels.

17.4.3 Cross-script similarities and differences

Research on spelling has, until relatively recently, largely involved English, an alphabetic language with a non-transparent (opaque) orthographic code in which many word spellings are not predictable from their pronunciations. There are many orthographic codes that are either non-alphabetic (e.g., Chinese) or highly transparent (e.g., Finnish), or both (e.g., Japanese Kana). Therefore, it is important to understand the extent to which findings for English hold for other orthographies. Specifically, we can ask: How broadly does the architecture depicted in Figure 17.1 apply? Does the internal content and organization of orthographic representations depicted in Figure 17.4 apply to other types of orthographies?

In terms of the cognitive architecture depicted in Figure 17.1, the most researched question has been whether spellers of transparent orthographies develop an O-LTM system. Word spellings that are unpredictable (irregular) in non-transparent orthographies are those that cannot be spelled reliably by the sublexical PGC system. Consequently, the only way to consistently spell them correctly is to store them in memory, hence the basis for O-LTM. However, is this necessary in transparent orthographies such as Spanish, Italian, Turkish, German, and so on? One possibility is that in these languages, word spellings are always generated via PGC and there is no O-LTM system. This does not seem to be the case, however. The primary source of evidence that even spellers of transparent codes store word spellings in O-LTM comes from neuropsychology. There have been several case reports of individuals who have acquired impairments in writing pseudowords—indicating damage to the sublexical PGC system—but who, nonetheless, are very accurate in spelling words (e.g., Spanish: Iribarren, Jarema, & Lecours, 2001; Italian: Miceli, Capasso, & Caramazza, 1994; Turkish: Raman & Weekes, 2005). This pattern of performance is difficult to account for without positing the O-LTM (and PGC) processes depicted in Figure 17.1.

In terms of orthographic representation, as reviewed in section 17.4.1.1, in alphabetic languages, they consist of a series of abstract letter representations, together with suprasegmental information such as syllables, morphemes, and so on. An interesting and so far largely unexplored issue is the extent to which this also holds for non-alphabetic languages such as Chinese. Chinese implements a logographic writing script in which a Chinese character (also called "Han zi" or Han character) maps onto a spoken syllable and most of the time maps onto a morpheme. Rather than consisting of letters and graphemes (as in Western orthographies), written Chinese words are composed of characters, themselves containing radicals that are, in turn, composed of strokes. Strokes, as the "atoms" of Chinese orthography, correspond to a single movement during writing, beginning when the pen touches the paper and terminating when the pen lifts off (Law & Leung, 2000). Eight basic strokes form 29 compound strokes. Each character is executed in a specific stroke order, and children are explicitly taught strokes and stroke order rules before being taught full characters.

Chinese readers appear to decompose characters into subcharacter components (e.g., Ding, Peng, & Taft, 2004; Taft, Zhu, & Peng, 1999; Zhou & Marslen-Wilson, 1999). Research on written production similarly suggests that Chinese character writing involves the automatic activation of embedded radicals. This inference is based on the spelling errors of dysgraphic patients (e.g., Law, 1994, 2004; Law & Caramazza, 1995; Law, Yeung, Wong, & Chiu, 2005), as well as on experimental evidence from healthy writers, who exhibit radical-sized priming effects of several types (e.g., Qu, Damian, Zhang, & Zhu, 2011; Qu & Damian, 2015; Qu, Damian, & Li, 2016). A recent discussion concerns the possibility of a further, intermediate-sized representational unit, the "logographeme" (or "stroke pattern"). Evidence from the spelling errors generated by dysgraphic patients indeed suggests that logographemes might be relevant in Chinese writing (Law & Leung, 2000), and a recent set of experiments reported by Chen and Cherng (2013) provides converging evidence that logographemes might also be relevant planning units for healthy writers, and indeed, that they might constitute "proximate units" (most salient form-related units; O'Seaghdha, Chen, & Chen, 2010) in Chinese written production. Research on orthographic production in non-alphabetic languages is still in its infancy, and we expect major progress in this domain soon.

17.5 LEARNING HOW TO SPELL AND WRITE

17.5.1 The normal trajectory

Learning how to write requires the acquisition of orthographic processes and representations (depicted in Figs. 17.1 and 17.4), as well as motor plans required to form letters. These processes naturally build on spoken language skills and knowledge and develop in close relationship with reading. With regard to the latter, Bryant and Bradley (1980), in their study of six- and seven-year-olds and the characteristics of words they could spell but not read and vice versa, concluded that in reading there is greater reliance on visual processes, while in spelling there is greater reliance on phonological ones. This relationship represents an under-researched topic that certainly warrants further study.

Regarding the acquisition of orthographic representations and processes, a number of stage theories have been proposed (e.g., Gentry, 1982; Ehri, 1986; Henderson, 1981). While there are differences among them, they generally posit some type of preliterate stage during which children realize that written marks—other than drawings—are used to represent meanings, followed by a phonological stage during which letters/letter names are used to represent sounds, and then there is an orthographic stage/s in which letters, letter groups, orthographic regularities, and eventually morphological units/information are incorporated into the spelling process. Importantly, however, in an extensive series of papers, Treiman and colleagues determined that children begin to use knowledge types earlier than stage theories would predict, with children who would be classified as phonetic spellers showing clear evidence that they are familiar with orthographic conventions for things such as letter doubling (Treiman, 2003), morphological boundaries, and so on (for reviews see Pollo, Kessler, & Treiman, 2009; Treiman, 1993; Treiman & Bourassa, 2000; Treiman & Kessler, 2014). Treiman and colleagues conclude that spelling development is not strictly stage-like, but rather that multiple knowledge types are used across time points with periods marked by the predominant use of certain processes.

The motor control required to write is quite demanding, and unsurprisingly, letter production is initially very slow and variable, and only with extensive practice, around age 10–11 years, does letter production become automatized, fast (e.g., Halsband & Lange, 2006), and less variable (van Galen et al., 1993). Once writing is automatized, children can devote resources to other aspects of writing, such as sentence construction and text elaboration (Maggio, Lété, Chenu, et al., 2012; Pontart, Bidet-Ildei, Lambert, et al., 2013). Furthermore, Kandel and Perret (2015) argued that with increasing automatization, the cascaded interaction between higher orthographic levels of processes and more peripheral motor aspects develops and gradually approaches the adult state (see section 17.4.1.1), with several studies supporting the claim of a qualitative shift in writing at around age 10 or so.

Several studies have provided a more fine-grained insight into the developmental trajectory of handwriting acquisition. In terms of the involvement of O-LTM and PGC processes, for instance, Kandel and Valdois (2006) asked French first and second graders to write regular and irregular words on a digitizer, and varied the position of the irregularity within the word, as well as the AoA of the word itself. Their results revealed that early acquired regular and irregular words were accessed from the orthographic lexicon. By contrast, late-acquired words were written via a phonological recoding strategy involving PGC processes. Regarding orthographic representations, Kandel and Valdois (2006) asked first to fifth graders to copy words and non-words on a digitizer, and found that the younger children utilized a syllable-by-syllable strategy to copy the stimuli (as indicated by a gaze lift following execution of the initial syllable), whereas the older children copied items as orthographic units. Children of all age groups revealed an influence of syllabic structure, such that the second syllable was planned during execution of the first syllable. Further research showed that children planned their responses based on orthographic, rather than phonological, syllables (Kandel, Hérault, Grosjacques, et al., 2009; see also Kandel, Peereman, Grosjacques, & Fayol, 2011).

17.5.2 Developmental deficits

While developmental dyslexia has received a great deal of research attention, developmental dysgraphia has received scarcely any at all (Peterson & Pennington, 2015). However, it is not rare to find difficulties in learning to spell and write in children who have normal IQ, no sensory impairments, and have had adequate schooling opportunities, with prevalence estimates in the range of 7–15% for school aged children (Döhla & Heim, 2015). It is important to point out that there are two senses of the term developmental dysgraphia—one refers specifically to motoric handwriting difficulties and the other to spelling/written language production difficulties. Here we will focus on difficulties in acquiring spelling/written language production knowledge and skills. Nonetheless it is important to note that while handwriting and spelling difficulties often co-occur, they do not necessarily do so (Berninger, 2004). This brings up the issue of other co-occurring deficits, most commonly: dyslexia, ADHD (Adi-Japha, Landau, Frenkel, et al., 2007), and/or spoken language difficulties. Despite these commonly occurring clusters of disorders, there is increasing evidence that dysgraphia can occur as an independent disorder. In that regard, dysgraphia has been documented in the context of intact rapid spoken naming (e.g., Roncoli & Masterson, 2016) and in the absence of ADHD and more specific visual attentional deficits (e.g., Valdois, Bosse, Ans, et al., 2003). However, it is indeed the case that it very commonly co-occurs with developmental dyslexia and that a close relationship between reading and spelling skill levels has been documented (Ehri, 2000; Holmes, Malone, & Redenbach et al., 2008; Kohnen, Nickels, Coltheart, & Brunsdon, 2008). Nonetheless, there are now several cases documenting apparently excellent reading in the context of dysgraphia (Burden, 1992; Roncoli & Masterson, 2016). It will be important for future research to determine if the cases of associated deficits are simply coincidental or if there are forms of developmental dysgraphia that necessarily co-occur with other deficits because of a shared underlying disorder or etiology. Understanding this is not only clinically relevant, but may provide essential information about the nature and development of cognitive processes.

In discussing causes of developmental disorders, Coltheart (2015) made a useful distinction between *proximal* and *distal* causes. Proximal causes refer to abnormalities in the cognitive system involved in the skill. In the case of dysgraphia, for example, they refer to the components of cognitive architecture depicted in Figure 17.1. Failure of one or more of these components to develop normally would result in developmental dysgraphia. Distal causes, on the other hand, refer to causes outside the cognitive system of interest, ranging from genetic causes to poor teaching. Very often these are referred to as "underlying causes." In the following paragraphs, we will provide a brief review of what is known about both proximal and distal causes of developmental dysgraphia.

Regarding proximal causes, in the context of developmental disorders there has been considerable debate regarding whether or not it is appropriate to characterize developmental deficits in terms of the component processes of the adult system. The concern has been that since learning is a dynamic process without a good understanding of the learning trajectories of the cognitive processes of interest it cannot be assumed that disruptions during learning can be meaningfully related to the adult-state system. Similarly, the concern has been raised that perhaps we should not expect developmental deficits to be analogous to those acquired as a result of damage to the adult system (Bishop,

1997; Karmiloff-Smith & Thomas, 2003; but see Castles, Kohnen, Nickels, & Brock, 2014). These are reasonable concerns that need to be addressed empirically, asking if we actually see patterns of developmental dysgraphia that map onto the component processes of the adult spelling system. With regard to developmental dysgraphia (and dyslexia), the answer seems to be that there are many developmental cases with performance patterns that seem highly similar to deficits acquired in adulthood and that can be understood as failures to adequately develop the major components of the spelling process (see Castles & Coltheart, 1993, for similar claims for developmental dyslexia). Despite the fact that the research on developmental dysgraphia is, as we said, still quite limited, cases have been reported where performance can be well-accounted for by assuming selective difficulty in developing: O-LTM, PGC, or O-WM. With regard to O-LTM, several cases have been described of individuals who have difficulty spelling irregular words (producing phonologically plausible errors) and have little or no difficulty in spelling pseudowords. This pattern is sometimes referred to as "developmental surface dysgraphia" (Brunsdon, Coltheart, & Nickels, 2005; Coltheart, Masterson, Byng, et al., 1983; Goulandris & Snowling, 1991; Hanley & Gard, 1995; Hanley & Kay, 1992; Romani, Ward, & Olson, 1999; Seymour, 1986; Seymour & Evans, 1993; Temple 1985). The reported cases primarily involve English, but also involve other languages such as German (Cholewa, Mantey, Heber, & Hollweg, 2010) and Italian (Angelelli, Judica, Spinelli, et al., 2004). The complementary pattern, sometimes referred to as "developmental phonological dysgraphia," is attributed to difficulty in developing the PGC system. This involves better spelling of words (including irregular words) compared to pseudowords (Campbell & Butterworth, 1985; Funnell & Davison, 1989; Snowling, Goulandris, Bowlby, & Howell, 1986; Temple, 1986; Temple & Marshall, 1983). Recently there have also been a few reports of selective impairment in the development of O-WM. Roncoli and Masterson (2016; see also Yachini & Friedmann, 2010, for Hebrew cases) described a 10-year old boy with impaired spelling but excellent (87th percentile) reading. Also intact were his phonological abilities, verbal working memory, and visual memory. Consistent with an O-WM deficit, he had comparable difficulty spelling regular and irregular words, accuracy was related to the length of the word but not its frequency, and he made many letter errors.

Why should developmental deficits map onto components of the adult, expert system? Interestingly, Bates, Castles, Luciano, et al. (2007), in a study of 1,382 mono and dizygotic twins, proposed a common genetic basis for the acquisition of reading and spelling and found evidence that distinct genes influence the acquisition of O-LTM and the sublexical OPC/POC systems. The possibility of genetic bases focuses attention on understanding the nature of underlying or distal cognitive causes that might be supported by different genes, since we assume that these are not specific to written language (given its evolutionary recency). Three prominent distal causes that we will briefly review are deficits in phonological processing/awareness, visual memory, and order encoding/learning. What we find is that there is evidence supporting each of these as a distal cause, but that there are also cases where the process appears to be unimpaired.

As is the case for developmental dyslexia, the most commonly proposed distal underlying cause of developmental dysgraphia is a deficit in phonological processing/awareness, supported by reports of the association of dysgraphia with phonological deficits (Campbell & Butterworth, 1985; Snowling et al., 1986). The proposal is that phonological failures make it difficult to parse and maintain active phonological material, a skill required to develop the

PGC system and build orthographic lexical representations. However, despite the reported association, there have been numerous reports of dysgraphic individuals with intact phonological processing skills (Frith, 1978, 1980; Hanley & Kay, 1992; Holmes & Quinn, 2009; Masterson, Laxon, Lovejoy, & Morris, 2007; Romani et al., 1999; Roncoli & Masterson, 2016). With regard to underlying deficits in the visual domain, Goulandris and Snowling (1991) described an individual with an impairment in visual memory and reasoned that this would make it difficult to retain information needed to build lasting orthographic representations. However, Romani et al. (1999) did not find evidence of a visual memory deficit in the case they reported (see also, Roncoli & Masterson, 2016). Instead, they presented evidence of a specific deficit in encoding and learning letter position/serial order. The adult individual they reported on had difficulty spelling irregular words but no difficulties in reading, phonological processing, configurational visual memory, or lexical-semantic memory. Instead, he had difficulties on tasks that involved detecting or learning the order of letters or complex visual characters.

What this review of proximal and distal causes of developmental dysgraphia underscores is that developmental dysgraphia (like developmental dyslexia) is a heterogeneous category, with no single underlying causal factor. This should not come as a surprise because, as we have seen, the cognitive architecture of spelling is complex, and composed of multiple interacting processes that undoubtedly require the healthy development of a host of functions. There is no reason to assume that there would only be one way to disrupt the development of such a complex component of the language system.

Acknowledgments

We gratefully acknowledge the support for B.R. from the multisite NIH grant DC006740 directed at examining the neurobiology of language recovery in aphasia.

References

Adi-Japha, E., Landau, Y. E., Frenkel, L., Teicher, M., Gross-Tsur, V., & Shalev, R. S. (2007). ADHD and dysgraphia: Underlying mechanisms. *Cortex*, *43*, 700–9.

Afonso, O., & Álvarez, C. J. (2011). Phonological effects in handwriting production: Evidence from the implicit priming paradigm. *Journal of Experimental Psychology: Learning, Memory, and Cognition*, *37*, 1474–83.

Alario, F., Schiller, N. O., Domoto-Reilly, K., & Caramazza, A. (2003). The role of phonological and orthographic information in lexical selection. *Brain and Language*, *84*, 372–98.

Almeida, J., Knobel, M., Finkbeiner, M., & Caramazza, A. (2007). The locus of the frequency effect in picture naming: When recognizing is not enough. *Psychonomic Bulletin & Review*, *14*, 1177–82.

Álvarez, C. J., Cottrell, D., & Afonso, O. (2009). Writing dictated words and picture names: Syllabic boundaries affect execution in Spanish. *Applied Psycholinguistics*, *30*, 205–23.

Angelelli, P., Judica, A., Spinelli, D., Zoccolotti, P., & Luzzatti, C. (2004). Characteristics of writing disorders in Italian dyslexic children. *Cognitive and Behavioral Neurology*, *17*, 18–31.

Badecker, W., Rapp, B., & Caramazza, A. (1996). Lexical morphology and the two orthographic routes. *Cognitive Neuropsychology*, 13, 161–75.

Barry, C., Morrison, C. M., & Ellis, A. W. (1997). Naming the Snodgrass and Vanderwart pictures: Effects of age of acquisition, frequency, and name agreement. *The Quarterly Journal of Experimental Psychology: Section A*, 50, 560–85.

Bates, T. C., Castles, A., Luciano, M., Wright, M. J., Coltheart, M., & Martin, N. G. (2007). Genetic and environmental bases of reading and spelling: A unified genetic dual route model. *Reading and Writing*, 20, 147–71.

Baus, C., Strijkers, K., & Costa, A. (2013). When does word frequency influence written production? *Frontiers in Psychology*, 4, 963.

Belke, E., Brysbaert, M., Meyer, A. S., & Ghyselinck, M. (2005). Age of acquisition effects in picture naming: Evidence for a lexical-semantic competition hypothesis. *Cognition*, 96, B45–B54.

Berent, I., Shimron, J., & Vaknin, V. (2001). Phonological constraints on reading: Evidence from the Obligatory Contour Principle. *Journal of Memory and Language*, 44, 644–65.

Berninger, V. (2004). Understanding the graphia in dysgraphia. In: Dewey, D., & Tupper, D. (Eds.), *Developmental Motor Disorders: A Neuropsychological Perspective* (pp. 328–50). Guilford, New York, NY.

Bishop, D. V. (1997). Cognitive neuropsychology and developmental disorders: Uncomfortable bedfellows. *The Quarterly Journal of Experimental Psychology: Section A*, 50, 899–923.

Bonin, P., Barry, C., Méot, A., & Chalard, M. (2004). The influence of age of acquisition in word reading and other tasks: A never ending story? *Journal of Memory and Language*, 50, 456–76.

Bonin, P., Chalard, M., Méot, A., & Fayol, M. (2002). The determinants of spoken and written picture naming latencies. *British Journal of Psychology*, 93, 89–114.

Bonin, P., & Fayol, M. (2002). Frequency effects in the written and spoken production of homophonic picture names. *European Journal of Cognitive Psychology*, 14, 289–313.

Bonin, P., Fayol, M., & Chalard, M. (2001). Age of acquisition and word frequency in written picture naming. *The Quarterly Journal of Experimental Psychology*, 54A, 469–89.

Bonin, P., Fayol, M., & Peereman, R. (1998). Masked form priming in writing words from pictures: Evidence for direct retrieval of orthographic codes. *Acta Psychologica*, 99, 311–28.

Bonin, P., Méot, A., Lagarrigue, A., & Roux, S. (2015). Written object naming, spelling to dictation, and immediate copying: Different tasks, different pathways? *The Quarterly Journal of Experimental Psychology*, 68, 1268–94.

Bonin, P., Peereman, R., & Fayol, M. (2001). Do phonological codes constrain the selection of orthographic codes in written picture naming? *Journal of Memory and Language*, 45, 688–720.

Bonin, P., Roux, S., Barry, C., & Canell, L. (2012). Evidence for a limited-cascading account of written word naming. *Journal of Experimental Psychology: Learning, Memory, and Cognition*, 38, 1741–58.

Brunsdon, R., Coltheart, M., & Nickels, L. (2005). Treatment of irregular word spelling in developmental surface dysgraphia. *Cognitive Neuropsychology*, 22, 213–51.

Bryant, P. E., & Bradley, L. (1980). Why children sometimes write words which they do not read. In: Frith, U. (Ed.), *Cognitive Processes in Spelling* (pp. 355–70). Academic Press, London, UK.

Brysbaert, M., van Wijnendaele, I., & de Deyne, S. (2000). Age-of-acquisition effects in semantic processing tasks. *Acta Psychologica*, 104, 215–26.

Buchwald, A., & Falconer, C. (2014). Cascading activation from lexical processing to letter-level processing in written word production. *Cognitive Neuropsychology*, 31, 606–21.

Buchwald, A., & Rapp, B. (2006). Consonants and vowels in orthographic representations. *Cognitive Neuropsychology, 23*, 308–37.

Buchwald, A., & Rapp, B. (2009). Distinctions between orthographic long-term memory and working memory. *Cognitive Neuropsychology, 26*, 724–51.

Burden, V. (1992). Why are some "normal" readers such poor spellers? In: Sterling, C. M., & Robson, C. (Eds.), *Psychology, Spelling and Education* (pp. 200–14). Multilingual Matters, Clevedon, UK.

Burt, J. S., & Tate, H. (2002). Does a reading lexicon provide orthographic representations for spelling? *Journal of Memory and Language, 46*, 518–43.

Campbell, R., & Butterworth, B. (1985). Phonological dyslexia and dysgraphia in a highly literate subject: A developmental case with associated deficits of phonemic processing and awareness. *The Quarterly Journal of Experimental Psychology, 37*, 435–75.

Caramazza, A. (1997). How many levels of processing are there in lexical access? *Cognitive Neuropsychology, 14*, 177–208.

Caramazza, A., Bi, Y., Costa, A., & Miozzo, M. (2004). What determines the speed of lexical access: Homophone or specific-word frequency? A reply to Jescheniak et al. (2003). *Journal of Experimental Psychology: Learning, Memory, and Cognition, 30*, 278–82.

Caramazza, A., Costa, A., Miozzo, M., & Bi, Y. (2001). The specific-word frequency effect: Implications for the representation of homophones in speech production. *Journal of Experimental Psychology: Learning, Memory, and Cognition, 27*, 1430–40.

Caramazza, A., & Miceli, G. (1990). The structure of graphemic representations. *Cognition, 37*, 243–97.

Castles, A., & Coltheart, M. (1993). Varieties of developmental dyslexia. *Cognition, 47*, 149–80.

Castles, A., Kohnen, S., Nickels, L., & Brock, J. (2014). Developmental disorders: What can be learned from cognitive neuropsychology? *Philosophical Transactions of the Royal Society B: Biological Sciences, 369*, 20130407.

Chen, J. Y., & Cherng, R. J. (2013). The proximate unit in Chinese handwritten character production. *Frontiers in Psychology, 4*, 3389.

Cholewa, J., Mantey, S., Heber, S., & Hollweg, W. (2010). Developmental surface and phonological dysgraphia in German 3rd graders. *Reading and Writing, 23*, 97–127.

Cohen, L., Lehéricy, S., Chochon, F., Lemer, C., Rivaud, S., & Dehaene, S. (2002). Language-specific tuning of visual cortex? Functional properties of the Visual Word Form Area. *Brain, 125*, 1054–69.

Coltheart, M. (2015). What kinds of things cause children's reading difficulties? *Australian Journal of Learning Difficulties, 20*, 103–12.

Coltheart, M., Masterson, J., Byng, S., Prior, M., & Riddoch, J. (1983). Surface dyslexia. *Quarterly Journal of Experimental Psychology, 35*, 469–95.

Cotelli, M., Abutalebi, J., Zorzi, M., & Cappa, S. F. (2003). Vowels in the buffer: A case study of acquired dysgraphia with selective vowel substitutions. *Cognitive Neuropsychology, 20*, 99–114.

Cowan, N. (2008). What are the differences between long-term, short-term, and working memory? *Progress in Brain Research, 169*, 323–38.

Cubelli, R. (1991). A selective deficit for writing vowels in acquired dysgraphia. *Nature, 353*, 258–260.

Cuetos, F., Bonin, P., Alameda, J. R., & Caramazza, A. (2010). The specific-word frequency effect in speech production: Evidence from Spanish and French. *The Quarterly Journal of Experimental Psychology, 63*, 750–71.

Cuetos, F., & Labos, E. (2001). The autonomy of the orthographic pathway in a shallow language: Data from an aphasic patient. *Aphasiology, 15*, 333–42.

Damian, M. F., & Bowers, J. S. (2003). Effects of orthography on speech production in a form-preparation paradigm. *Journal of Memory and Language, 49*, 119–32.

Damian, M. F., Dorjee, D., & Stadthagen-Gonzalez, H. (2011). Long-term repetition priming in spoken and written word production: Evidence for a contribution of phonology to handwriting. *Journal of Experimental Psychology: Learning, Memory, and Cognition, 37*, 813–26.

Damian, M. F., & Qu, Q. Q. (2013). Is handwriting constrained by phonology? Evidence from Stroop tasks with written responses and Chinese characters. *Frontiers in Psychology, 4*, 765.

Delattre, M., Bonin, P., & Barry, C. (2006). Written spelling to dictation: Do irregularity effects persist on writing durations? *Journal of Experimental Psychology: Learning, Memory, and Cognition, 32*, 1330–40.

Ding, G., Peng, D.-L., & Taft, M. (2004). The nature of the mental representation of radicals in Chinese: A priming study. *Journal of Experimental Psychology: Learning, Memory, and Cognition, 30*, 530–9.

Döhla, D., & Heim, S. (2015). Developmental dyslexia and dysgraphia: What can we learn from the one about the other? *Frontiers in Psychology, 6*, 2045.

Dufor, O., & Rapp, B. (2013). Letter representations in writing: An fMRI adaptation approach. *Frontiers in Psychology, 4*, 781.

Ehri, L. C. (1986). Sources of difficulty in learning to spell and read words. In: Wolraich, M., & Routh, D. (Eds.), *Advances in Developmental and Behavioral Pediatrics, Vol. 7* (pp. 121–95). JAI Press, Greenwich, CT.

Ehri, L. C. (2000). Learning to read and learning to spell: Two sides of a coin. *Topics in Language Disorders, 20*, 19–36.

Ellis, A. W., & Lambon Ralph, M. A. (2000). Age of acquisition effects in adult lexical processing reflect loss of plasticity in maturing systems: Insights from connectionist networks. *Journal of Experimental Psychology: Learning, Memory, and Cognition, 26*, 1103–23.

Falconer, C., & Buchwald, A. (2013). Do activated letters influence lexical selection in written word production? *Aphasiology, 27*, 849–66.

Finocchiaro, C., & Caramazza, A. (2006). The production of pronominal clitics: Implications for theories of lexical access. *Language and Cognitive Processes, 21*, 141–80.

Fischer-Baum, S., & Rapp, B. (2014). The analysis of perseverations in acquired dysgraphia reveals the internal structure of orthographic representations. *Cognitive Neuropsychology, 31*, 237–65.

Frith, U. (1978). From print to meaning and from print to sound, or how to read without knowing how to spell. *Visible Language, 12*, 43–54.

Frith, U. (1980). Unexpected spelling problems. In: Frith, U. (Ed.), *Cognitive Processes in Spelling* (pp. 495–515). Academic Press, London.

Funnell, E., & Davison, M. (1989). Lexical capture: A developmental disorder of reading and spelling. *The Quarterly Journal of Experimental Psychology, 41*, 471–87.

Garrett, M. F. (1976). Syntactic processes in sentence production. In: Wales, R., & Walker, E. (Eds.), *New Approaches to Language Mechanisms*. North-Holland, Amsterdam.

Gentry, J. R. (1982). An analysis of developmental spelling in "GNYS AT WRK." *The Reading Teacher, 36*, 192–200.

Glaser, W. R., & Düngelhoff, F. (1984). The time course of picture-word interference. *Journal of Experimental Psychology: Human Perception and Performance, 10*, 640–54.

Görges, F., Oppermann, F., Jescheniak, J. D., & Schriefers, H. (2013). Activation of phonological competitors in visual search. *Acta Psychologica, 143*, 168–75.

Goulandris, N. K., & Snowling, M. (1991). Visual memory deficits: A plausible cause of developmental dyslexia? Evidence from a single case study. *Cognitive Neuropsychology, 8*, 127–54.

Halsband, U., & Lange, R. K. (2006). Motor learning in man: A review of functional and clinical studies. *Journal of Physiology – Paris, 99*, 414–24.

Hanley, J. R., & Gard, F. (1995). A dissociation between developmental surface and phonological dyslexia in two undergraduate students. *Neuropsychologia, 33*, 909–14.

Hanley, J. R., & Kay, J. (1992). Does letter-by-letter reading involve the spelling system? *Neuropsychologia, 30*, 237–56.

Henderson, E. H. (1981). *Learning to Read and Spell: The Child's Knowledge of Words*. Northern Illinois University Press, DeKalb, IL.

Hillis, A. E., & Caramazza, A. (1989). The graphemic buffer and attentional mechanisms. *Brain and Language, 36*, 208–35.

Hillis, A. E., & Caramazza, A. (1995). Representation of grammatical categories of words in the brain. *Journal of Cognitive Neuroscience, 7*, 396–407.

Hillis, A. E., Rapp, B. C., & Caramazza, A. (1999). When a rose is a rose in speech but a tulip in writing. *Cortex, 35*, 337–56.

Holmes, V. M., & Carruthers, J. (1998). The relation between reading and spelling in skilled adult readers. *Journal of Memory and Language, 39*, 264–89.

Holmes, V. M., Malone, A. M., & Redenbach, H. (2008). Orthographic processing and visual sequential memory in unexpectedly poor spellers. *Journal of Research in Reading, 31*, 136–56.

Holmes, V. M., & Quinn, L. (2009). Unexpectedly poor spelling and phonological-processing skill. *Scientific Studies of Reading, 13*, 295–317.

Indefrey, P. (2011). The spatial and temporal signatures of word production components: A critical update. *Frontiers in Psychology, 2*, 255.

Indefrey, P., & Levelt, W. J. (2004). The spatial and temporal signatures of word production components. *Cognition, 92*, 101–44.

Iribarren, I. C., Jarema, G., & Lecours, A. R. (2001). Two different dysgraphic syndromes in a regular orthography, Spanish. *Brain and Language, 77*, 166–75.

Jescheniak, J. D., & Levelt, W. J. (1994). Word frequency effects in speech production: Retrieval of syntactic information and of phonological form. *Journal of Experimental Psychology: Learning, Memory, and Cognition, 20*, 824–43.

Johnston, R. A., & Barry, C. (2005). Age of acquisition effects in the semantic processing of pictures. *Memory & Cognition, 33*, 905–12.

Jónsdóttir, M. K., Shallice, T., & Wise, R. (1996). Phonological mediation and the graphemic buffer disorder in spelling: Cross-language differences? *Cognition, 59*, 169–97.

Kandel, S., Álvarez, C. J., & Vallée, N. (2006). Syllables as processing units in handwriting production. *Journal of Experimental Psychology: Human Perception and Performance, 32*, 18–31.

Kandel, S., Hérault, L., Grosjacques, G., Lambert, E., & Fayol, M. (2009). Orthographic vs. phonologic syllables in handwriting production. *Cognition, 110*, 440–4.

Kandel, S., Peereman, R., Grosjacques, G., & Fayol, M. (2011). For a psycholinguistic model of handwriting production: Testing the syllable-bigram controversy. *Journal of Experimental Psychology: Human Perception and Performance, 37*, 1310–22.

Kandel, S., Peereman, R., & Ghimenton, A. (2014). How do we code the letters of a word when we have to write it? Investigating double letter representation in French. *Acta Psychologica, 148*, 56–62.

Kandel, S., & Perret, C. (2015). How does the interaction between spelling and motor processes build up during writing acquisition? *Cognition, 136*, 325–36.

Kandel, S., & Spinelli, E. (2010). Processing complex graphemes in handwriting production. *Memory & Cognition, 38*, 762–70.

Kandel, S., Spinelli, E., Tremblay, A., Guerassimovitch, H., & Álvarez, C. J. (2012). Processing prefixes and suffixes in handwriting production. *Acta Psychologica, 140*, 187–95.

Kandel, S., & Valdois, S. (2006). Syllables as functional units in a copying task. *Language and Cognitive Processes, 21*, 432–52.

Karmiloff-Smith, A., & Thomas, M. (2003). What can developmental disorders tell us about the neurocomputational constraints that shape development? The case of Williams syndrome. *Development and Psychopathology, 15*, 969–90.

Katz, R. B. (1991). Limited retention of information in the graphemic buffer. *Cortex, 27*, 111–19.

Kinsbourne, M., & Warrington, E. K. (1965). A case showing selectively impaired oral spelling. *Journal of Neurology, Neurosurgery & Psychiatry, 28*, 563–6.

Kohnen, S., Nickels, L., Coltheart, M., & Brunsdon, R. (2008). Predicting generalization in the training of irregular-word spelling: Treating lexical spelling deficits in a child. *Cognitive Neuropsychology, 25*, 343–75.

Laganaro, M., & Perret, C. (2011). Comparing electrophysiological correlates of word production in immediate and delayed naming through the analysis of word age of acquisition effects. *Brain Topography, 24*, 19–29.

Lashley, K. S. (1951). The problem of serial order in behavior. In: Jeffress, L. A. (Ed.), *Cerebral Mechanisms in Behavior* (pp. 112–36). Wiley, New York, NY.

Law, S. P. (1994). The structure of orthographic representations of Chinese characters: From the perspective of the cognitive neuropsychological approach. *Bulletin of Institute of History and Philology, 65*, 81–130.

Law, S. P. (2004). Writing errors of a Cantonese dysgraphic patient and their theoretical implications. *Neurocase, 10*, 132–40.

Law, S. P., & Caramazza, A. (1995). Cognitive processes in writing Chinese characters: Basic issues and some preliminary data. In: de Gelder B., & Morais J. (Eds.), *Speech and Reading: A Comparative Approach* (pp. 143–90). Psychology Press, Hove.

Law, S. P., & Leung, M. T. (2000). Structural representations of characters in Chinese writing: Evidence from a case of acquired dysgraphia. *Psychologia, 43*, 67–83.

Law, S. P., Wong, W., & Kong, A. (2006). Direct access from meaning to orthography in Chinese: A case study of superior written to oral naming. *Aphasiology, 20*, 565–78.

Law, S. P., Yeung, O., Wong, W., & Chiu, K. M. Y. (2005). Processing of semantic radicals in writing Chinese characters: Data from a Chinese dysgraphic patient. *Cognitive Neuropsychology, 22*, 885–903.

Levelt, W. J., Roelofs, A., & Meyer, A. S. (1999). A theory of lexical access in speech production. *Behavioral and Brain Sciences, 22*, 1–38.

Levelt, W. J., Schriefers, H., Vorberg, D., Meyer, A. S., Pechmann, T., & Havinga, J. (1991). The time course of lexical access in speech production: A study of picture naming. *Psychological Review, 98*, 122.

Lupker, S. J., & Katz, A. N. (1981). Input, decision, and response factors in picture–word interference. *Journal of Experimental Psychology: Human Learning and Memory, 7*, 269-82.

Maggio, S., Lété, B., Chenu, F., Jisa, H., & Fayol, M. (2012). Tracking the mind during writing: Immediacy, delayed, and anticipatory effects on pauses and writing rate. *Reading and Writing, 25*, 2131–51.

Mahon, B. Z., Costa, A., Peterson, R., Vargas, K. A., & Caramazza, A. (2007). Lexical selection is not by competition: A reinterpretation of semantic interference and facilitation effects in the picture-word interference paradigm. *Journal of Experimental Psychology: Learning, Memory, and Cognition*, 33, 503.

Masterson, J., Laxon, V., Lovejoy, S., & Morris, V. (2007). Phonological skill, lexical decision and letter report performance in good and poor adult spellers. *Journal of Research in Reading*, 30, 429–42.

McCloskey, M., Badecker, W., Goodman-Schulman, R. A., & Aliminosa, D. (1994). The structure of graphemic representations in spelling: Evidence from a case of acquired dysgraphia. *Cognitive Neuropsychology*, 11, 341–92.

McCloskey, M., Macaruso, P., & Rapp, B. (2006). Grapheme-to-lexeme feedback in the spelling system: Evidence from a dysgraphic patient. *Cognitive Neuropsychology*, 23, 278–307.

McMillan, C. T., & Corley, M. (2010). Cascading influences on the production of speech: Evidence from articulation. *Cognition*, 117, 243–60.

Meyer, A. S., & Damian, M. F. (2007). Activation of distractor names in the picture-picture interference paradigm. *Memory & Cognition*, 35, 494–503.

Miceli, G., Benvegnù, B., Capasso, R., & Caramazza, A. (1997). The independence of phonological and orthographic lexical forms: Evidence from aphasia. *Cognitive Neuropsychology*, 14, 35–69.

Miceli, G., Capasso, R., & Caramazza, A. (1994). The interaction of lexical and sublexical processes in reading, writing and repetition. *Neuropsychologia*, 32, 317–33.

Miceli, G., Capasso, R., & Caramazza, A. (1999). Sublexical conversion procedures and the interaction of phonological and orthographic lexical forms. *Cognitive Neuropsychology*, 16, 557–72.

Miceli, G., Capasso, R., Benvegnù, B., & Caramazza, A. (2004). The categorical distinction of vowel and consonant representations: Evidence from dysgraphia. *Neurocase*, 10, 109–21.

Monsell, S. (1987). On the relation between lexical input and output pathways for speech. In: Allport, A., MacKay, D. G., & Prinz, W. (Eds.), *Language Perception and Production: Relationships Between Listening, Speaking, Reading and Writing* (pp. 273–311). Academic Press, San Diego, CA.

Morrison, C. M., Ellis, A. W., & Quinlan, P. T. (1992). Age of acquisition, not word frequency, affects object naming, not object recognition. *Memory & Cognition*, 20, 705–14.

Morsella, E., & Miozzo, M. (2002). Evidence for a cascade model of lexical access in speech production. *Journal of Experimental Psychology: Learning, Memory, and Cognition*, 28, 555–63.

Navarrete, E., & Costa, A. (2005). Phonological activation of ignored pictures: Further evidence for a cascade model of lexical access. *Journal of Memory and Language*, 53, 359–77.

O'Seaghdha, P. G., Chen, J.-Y., & Chen, T.-M. (2010). Proximate units in word production: Phonological encoding begins with syllables in Mandarin Chinese but with segments in English. *Cognition*, 115, 282–302.

Oldfield, R. C., & Wingfield, A. (1965). Response latencies in naming objects. *The Quarterly Journal of Experimental Psychology*, 17, 273–81.

Oppermann, F., Jescheniak, J., & Schriefers, H. (2008). Conceptual coherence affects phonological activation of context objects during object naming. *Journal of Experimental Psychology: Learning, Memory, and Cognition*, 34, 587–601.

Oppermann, F., Jescheniak, J. D., Schriefers, H., & Görges, F. (2010). Semantic relatedness among objects promotes the activation of multiple phonological codes during object naming. *The Quarterly Journal of Experimental Psychology*, 63, 356–70.

Perret, C., Bonin, P., & Laganaro, M. (2014). Exploring the multiple-level hypothesis of AoA effects in spoken and written object naming using a topographic ERP analysis. *Brain and Language, 135,* 20–31.

Perret, C., & Laganaro, M. (2012). Comparison of electrophysiological correlates of writing and speaking: A topographic ERP analysis. *Brain Topography, 25,* 64–72.

Peterson, R. L., & Pennington, B. F. (2015). Developmental dyslexia. *Annual Review of Clinical Psychology, 11,* 283–307.

Philipose, L. E., Gottesman, R. F., Newhart, M., Kleinman, J. T., Herskovits, E. H., Pawlak, M. A., & Hillis, A. E. (2007). Neural regions essential for reading and spelling of words and pseudowords. *Annals of Neurology, 62,* 481–92.

Planton, S., Jucla, M., Roux, F. E., & Démonet, J. F. (2013). The "handwriting brain": A meta-analysis of neuroimaging studies of motor versus orthographic processes. *Cortex, 49,* 2772–87.

Pollo, T. C., Kessler, B., & Treiman, R. (2009). Statistical patterns in children's early writing. *Journal of Experimental Child Psychology, 104,* 410–26.

Pontart, V., Bidet-Ildei, C., Lambert, E., Morisset, P., Flouret, L., & Alamargot, D. (2013). Influence of handwriting skills during spelling in primary and lower secondary grades. *Frontiers in Psychology, 4,* 818.

Purcell, J. J., Jiang, X., & Eden, G. F. (2017). Shared Orthographic neuronal representations for spelling and reading. *NeuroImage, 147,* 554–67.

Qu, Q., & Damian, M. F. (2015). Cascadedness in Chinese written word production. *Frontiers in Psychology, 6,* 1271.

Qu, Q., Damian, M. F., & Li, X. (2016). Phonology contributes to writing: Evidence from a masked priming task. *Language, Cognition and Neuroscience, 31,* 251–64.

Qu, Q. Q., Li, X., & Damian, M. F. (2014). An electrophysiological analysis of the time course of phonological and orthographic encoding in written word production. Poster presented at the International Workshop on Language Production, July 2014, Geneva.

Qu, Q. Q., Damian, M. F., Zhang, Q., & Zhu, X. B. (2011). Phonology contributes to writing: Evidence from written word production in a nonalphabetic script. *Psychological Science, 22,* 1107–12.

Qu, Q., Zhang, Q., & Damian, M. F. (2016). Tracking the time course of lexical access in orthographic production: An event-related potential study of word frequency effects in written picture naming. *Brain and Language, 159,* 118–26.

Raman, I., & Weekes, B. S. (2005). Deep dysgraphia in Turkish. *Behavioural Neurology, 16,* 59–69.

Rapcsak, S. Z., & Beeson, P. M. (2004). The role of left posterior inferior temporal cortex in spelling. *Neurology, 62,* 2221–9.

Rapp, B., Benzing, L., & Caramazza, A. (1997). The autonomy of lexical orthography. *Cognitive Neuropsychology, 14,* 71–104.

Rapp, B., & Caramazza, A. (2002). Selective difficulties with spoken nouns and written verbs: A single case study. *Journal of Neurolinguistics, 15,* 373–402.

Rapp, B., & Dufor, O. (2011). The neurotopography of written word production: An fMRI investigation of the distribution of sensitivity to length and frequency. *Journal of Cognitive Neuroscience, 23,* 4067–81.

Rapp, B., & Fischer-Baum, S. (2014). Representation of orthographic knowledge. In: Goldrick, M. A., Ferreria, V., & Miozzo, M. (Eds.), *Oxford Handbook of Language Production* (pp. 338–57). Oxford University Press, New York, NY.

Rapp, B., & Fischer-Baum, S. (2015). Uncovering the cognitive architecture of spelling. In: Hillis, A. (Ed.), *Handbook on Adult Language Disorders: Integrating Cognitive Neuropsychology, Neurology and Rehabilitation*, 2nd Edition. Psychology Press, Philadelphia, PA.

Rapp, B., Fischer-Baum, S., & Miozzo, M. (2015). Modality and morphology: what we write may not be what we say. *Psychological Science, 26*, 892–902.

Rapp, B., & Goldrick, M. (2000). Discreteness and interactivity in spoken word production. *Psychological Review, 107*, 460.

Rapp, B., & Goldrick, M. (2006). Speaking words: Contributions of cognitive neuropsychological research. *Cognitive Neuropsychology, 23*, 39–73.

Rapp, B., & Lipka, K. (2011). The literate brain: The relationship between spelling and reading. *Journal of Cognitive Neuroscience, 23*, 1180–97.

Rapp, B., Purcell, J., Hillis, A. E., Capasso, R., & Miceli, G. (2016). Neural bases of orthographic long-term memory and working memory in dysgraphia. *Brain, 139*, 588–604.

Rapp, B., & Purcell, J. (in press). Understanding how we produce written words: Lessons from the brain. To appear in: de Zubicaray, G., & Schiller, N. (Eds.), *The Oxford Handbook of Neurolinguistics*. Oxford University Press, Oxford.

Romani, C., Ward, J., & Olson, A. (1999). Developmental surface dysgraphia: What is the underlying cognitive impairment? *The Quarterly Journal of Experimental Psychology: Section A, 52*, 97–128.

Roncoli, S., & Masterson, J. (2016). "Unexpected" spelling difficulty in a 10-year-old child with good reading skills: An intervention case study. *Writing Systems Research, 8*, 143–66.

Roux, S., & Bonin, P. (2012). Cascaded processing in written naming: Evidence from the picture-picture interference paradigm. *Language and Cognitive Processes, 27*, 734–69.

Roux, S., & Bonin, P. (2016). "RED" matters when naming "CAR": The cascading activation of nontarget properties. *Journal of Experimental Psychology: Learning, Memory, and Cognition, 42*, 475.

Roux, S., McKeeff, T. J., Grosjacques, G., Afonso, O., & Kandel, S. (2013). The interaction between central and peripheral processes in handwriting production. *Cognition, 127*, 235–41.

Rumelhart, D. E., & Norman, D. A. (1982). Simulating a skilled typist: A study of skilled cognitive-motor performance. *Cognitive Science, 6*, 1–36.

Sage, K., & Ellis, A. W. (2004). Lexical influences in graphemic buffer disorder. *Cognitive Neuropsychology, 21*, 381–400.

Schriefers, H., Meyer, A. S., & Levelt, W. J. (1990). Exploring the time course of lexical access in language production: Picture-word interference studies. *Journal of Memory and Language, 29*, 86–102.

Seidenberg, M. S., & Tanenhaus, M. K. (1979). Orthographic effects on rhyme monitoring. *Journal of Experimental Psychology: Human Learning and Memory, 5*, 546–54.

Seymour, P. H. (1986). *Cognitive Analysis of Dyslexia*. Routledge, London.

Seymour, P. H., & Evans, H. M. (1993). The visual (orthographic) processor and developmental dyslexia. In: Willows, D. M., Kruk, R. S., & Corcos, E. (Eds.), *Visual Processes in Reading and Reading Disabilities* (pp. 317–46). Lawrence Erlbaum Associates, Hillsdale, NJ.

Shen, X. R., Damian, M. F., & Stadthagen-Gonzalez, H. (2013). Abstract graphemic representations support preparation of handwritten responses. *Journal of Memory and Language, 68*, 69–84.

Snowling, M., Goulandris, N., Bowlby, M., & Howell, P. (1986). Segmentation and speech perception in relation to reading skill: A developmental analysis. *Journal of Experimental Child Psychology, 41*, 489–507.

Starreveld, P. A., & La Heij, W. (1996). Time-course analysis of semantic and orthographic context effects in picture naming. *Journal of Experimental Psychology: Learning, Memory, and Cognition, 22*, 896–918.

Sternberg, S. (1969). The discovery of processing stages: Extensions of Donders' method. *Acta Psychologica, 30*, 276–315.

Strijkers, K., Baus, C., Runnqvist, E., FitzPatrick, I., & Costa, A. (2013). The temporal dynamics of first versus second language production. *Brain and Language, 127*, 6–11.

Strijkers, K., Costa, A., & Thierry, G. (2010). Tracking lexical access in speech production: Electrophysiological correlates of word frequency and cognate effects. *Cerebral Cortex, 20*, 912–28.

Strijkers, K., Holcomb, P. J., & Costa, A. (2011). Conscious intention to speak proactively facilitates lexical access during overt object naming. *Journal of Memory and Language, 65*, 345–62.

Taft, M., Zhu, X., & Peng, D. (1999). Positional specificity of radicals in Chinese character recognition. *Journal of Memory and Language, 40*, 498–519.

Tainturier, M., & Rapp, B. (2001). The spelling process. In: Rapp, B. (Ed.), *The Handbook of Cognitive Neuropsychology: What Deficits Reveal About the Human Mind* (pp. 263–89). Psychology Press, Hove.

Tainturier, M., & Rapp, B. (2004). Complex graphemes as functional spelling units: Evidence from acquired dysgraphia. *Neurocase, 10*, 122–31.

Temple, C. M. (1985). Reading with partial phonology: Developmental phonological dyslexia. *Journal of Psycholinguistic Research, 14*, 523–41.

Temple, C. M. (1986). Developmental dysgraphias. *The Quarterly Journal of Experimental Psychology, 38*, 77–110.

Temple, C. M., & Marshall, J. C. (1983). A case study of developmental phonological dyslexia. *British Journal of Psychology, 74*, 517–33.

Treiman, R. A. (1993). *Beginning to Spell: A study of first-grade children*. Oxford University Press, New York, NY.

Treiman, R. (2003). Phonology and spelling. In: Nunes, T., & Bryant, P. (Eds.), *Handbook of Children's Literacy* (pp. 31–42). Kluver, Dordrecht, Netherlands.

Treiman, R., & Bourassa, D. C. (2000). The development of spelling skill. *Topics in Language Disorders, 20*, 1–18.

Treiman, R., & Kessler, B. (2014). *How Children Learn to Write Words*. Oxford University Press, Oxford.

Valdois, S., Bosse, M., Ans, B., Carbonnel, S., Zorman, M., David, D., & Pellat, J. (2003). Phonological and visual processing deficits can dissociate in developmental dyslexia: Evidence from two case studies. *Reading and Writing, 16*, 541–72.

van Galen, G. P. (1991). Handwriting: Issues for a psychomotor theory. *Human Movement Science, 10*, 165–91.

van Galen, G. P., Portier, S. J., Smits-Engelsman, B. C., & Schomaker, L. R. (1993). Neuromotor noise and poor handwriting in children. *Acta Psychologica, 82*, 161–78.

Yachini, M., & Friedmann, N. (2010). Developmental graphemic buffer dysgraphia. *Procedia-Social and Behavioral Sciences, 6*, 148–9.

Zhang, Q., & Damian, M. (2010). Impact of phonology on the generation of handwritten responses: Evidence from picture-word interference tasks. *Memory & Cognition, 38,* 519–28.

Zhang, Q., & Wang, C. (2015). Phonology is not accessed earlier than orthography in Chinese written production: Evidence for the orthography autonomy hypothesis. *Frontiers in Psychology, 6,* 448.

Zhou, X., & Marslen-Wilson, W. (1999). The nature of sublexical processing in reading Chinese characters. *Journal of Experimental Psychology: Learning, Memory, and Cognition, 25,* 819–37.

CHAPTER 18

GRAMMATICAL ENCODING

VICTOR S. FERREIRA, ADAM MORGAN, AND L. ROBERT SLEVC

18.1 INTRODUCTION

AT the heart of the faculty of language are the processes of grammatical encoding. Grammatical encoding has the task of selecting and retrieving the syntactic and lexical forms that can convey non-linguistic thoughts (Meteyard & Vigliocco, this volume), and then determining the morphological forms and their constituent ordering in preparation for their phonological spell-out (Wheeldon & Konopka, this volume), and eventual externalization by the oral (Walker & Hickok, this volume) or manual (Corina & Lawyer, this volume) articulators. As such, grammatical encoding processes most directly determine the gross characteristics of our individual utterances. Therefore, it is only a minor indulgence to claim that to understand why and how grammatical encoding carries out its duties is to understand a significant part of the why and how of language itself.

In this chapter, we describe the state of the field by describing the major debates that current research on grammatical encoding addresses. To situate these debates, section 18.2 broadly describes a consensus view of the general architecture of grammatical encoding (illustrated in Fig. 18.1). This consensus holds that grammatical encoding consists of two component sets of subprocesses, one that deals with content and the other that deals with structure. Each set of subprocesses proceeds through two phases or stages, the first involving selection and the second involving retrieval. Section 18.3 then describes ongoing debates that operate within (or question aspects of) this consensus view, beginning with debates over this content and structure and selection-then-retrieval character of grammatical encoding. Next, section 18.4 describes two debates that have maintained a relatively elevated level of visibility, attesting to their fundamental status in the grammatical encoding literature: the first concerns the *incrementality* or *scope* of grammatical encoding (how far do we plan ahead in an utterance before beginning it?), and the second concerns the factors that influence syntactic choice (given an idea to express, why do we say what we say?). In section 18.5, we look forward to emerging debates in the field that are likely to receive increased attention in the coming years, largely due to the confluence of their central questions with other prominent

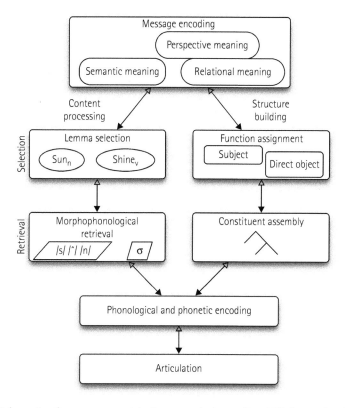

FIG. 18.1 Schematic of consensus model of grammatical encoding. Filled arrowheads mark direction of primary information flow, open arrowheads mark possible feedback information flow.

and topical issues in cognitive science. These debates concern rational or optimal production, effects of ongoing learning, and dialogue. With all this discussion of debate, it is easy to lose sight of the insights that the field has made and how our knowledge of the way grammatical encoding works has accumulated, and so section 18.6 closes on a constructive note, by highlighting two fundamental insights that we have gained as a field along the way.

18.2 Grammatical encoding: A consensus model

Producing linguistic expressions involves encoding non-linguistic meanings, termed preverbal messages (Levelt, 1989) or interfacing representations (Bock, 1982), into a set of linguistic representations that can ultimately be phonologically encoded. We will start our description of grammatical encoding at the beginning, by describing what theories of grammatical encoding generally require preverbal messages to represent.

18.2.1 Message encoding

Preverbal messages are derived from conceptual representations; that is, they are not *thought*, but the collection of semantic and pragmatic information that the language system needs so that it can encode the meaning that the speaker aims to express. The information in preverbal messages will typically be a superset of the information that a speaker wishes to convey, a necessary consequence of the fact that in order to make a sentence, languages often require a speaker to specify features like tense, aspect, number, perspective, animacy, and definiteness, any number of which may be irrelevant to the communicative goal (e.g., a speaker's communicative intention may be fulfilled even without the expression of the meaning features that express definiteness, but because the production of certain noun phrases requires that definiteness be specified, the speaker's message will often include such information regardless).

The processes that formulate preverbal messages have been termed *message encoding* processes or the *message component* (Bock, 1995b; V. S. Ferreira, in press), *conceptualization* processes (Levelt, 1989), or *referential arena* processes (Bock, 1982). The first step of message encoding is to specify the goal to be achieved by producing an utterance—whether to request something, provide information, guide action, and so forth. Any such *speech act* can only be carried out by expressing a meaning, and so the next step is to encode this meaning into the preverbal message. Meanings are encoded into what are here termed *events*, which represent the "who did what to whom" that is to be expressed by linguistic utterances. Events include three specific aspects of meaning: *semantic meaning* represents the *who, what*, and *whom* themselves the semantic features of the expressed entities, states, actions, events, and so on. *Relational meaning* represents how the who, what, and whom in the event relate to one another—who/what is performing which action or is in which state, who/what is having which action performed on it, and so forth. *Perspective meaning* represents which semantic or relational aspects of the event are more or less important; for example, which aspects are foreground or background, which are topic or comment, and which aspects have meaning added to them, and which aspects are the added meaning.

For example, take the utterance "In San Diego, it's always sunny." Someone might express this utterance to inform his or her interlocutor of a relevant observation (say, if they were discussing cities in southern California). This observation corresponds to an event in which the semantic meaning includes a representation of a geographical location that has the proper name "San Diego" and a state that is a weather condition brought on by unobstructed exposure to the sun. The relational meaning in the event involves attributing the state corresponding to the weather condition to the geographical location. The perspective meaning encodes that it is the geographical location that is the topic and the weather-state that is the added information (compared to, say, the meaning expressed by "It's always sunny in San Diego").

18.2.2 Grammatical encoding

Once semantic, relational, and perspective meanings are encoded into at least part of a preverbal message, grammatical encoding can begin. Grammatical encoding consists of separable subprocesses that deal with formulating the content and specifying the structure of the eventual utterance. In turn, the content and structure subprocesses each proceed through two phases or stages (sometimes termed functional and positional processing; Bock, 1995b; Garrett, 1975, 1982, 1988), where linguistic features are selected from a candidate set, and then the properties of those selected linguistic features are retrieved.

18.2.2.1 Content subprocesses

Though possibly an oversimplification, the function of the content subprocesses of grammatical encoding is to select and then retrieve the details of the meaning-carrying or *content* words in an utterance. The first step of content processing is *lexical selection* (Bock, 1995b): picking a set of words that "covers" (i.e., conveys a sufficient extent of) the semantic meaning represented in the preverbal message. A counterintuitive finding is that there are at least two separate types of representation for every word: one, termed a *lemma* (Kempen & Huijbers, 1983; Levelt, 1989; Levelt, Roelofs, & Meyer, 1999) or a *lexical entry* (Bock, 1995b), which encodes grammatical properties of the word like its form class (e.g., noun, verb, and so on) and grammatical gender, and another encoding metrical and phonological information.

Lemma selection is the first step in content processing. Lemmas in turn point to morphological, segmental, and metrical information necessary for spell-out of the word. The retrieval of this morphophonological knowledge forms the second step of content processing, namely *lexical retrieval* (Bock, 1995b). Most theories of grammatical encoding claim that access to this metrical and phonological knowledge is mediated by distinct whole-word representations, which are sometimes termed *lexemes* (Kempen & Huijbers, 1983; Levelt, 1989; Levelt et al., 1999) or *word forms* (see also Garrett, 1975).

For example, take the utterance, "the sun shines." Content subprocesses select and then retrieve the syntactic, morphological, and phonological details of the words "sun" and "shine," but not the word "the" nor the suffix "-s" (which are not primary meaning-carrying words and so are termed *function* words). Lexical selection must determine the word that expresses the semantic meaning of the large gaseous body that warms the earth, and thereby select the lemma for "sun" (and not, say, "moon"), as constrained by the grammatical category membership of candidate lemmas (which in turn comes from structure subprocesses). As the lemma for "sun" is accessed, lexical retrieval retrieves the singular count-noun morpheme for "sun" as well as its segmental content (/s/, /^/, and /n/) and metrical specification (a single stressed syllable). A similar lexical-selection-then-lexical-retrieval process occurs for the word "shine."

18.2.2.2 Structure subprocesses

While content subprocesses select and retrieve content words that convey semantic meaning, structure subprocesses select and retrieve the syntactic representations necessary to convey relational and perspective meaning. Like content processing, this occurs through two stages; first selecting *grammatical functions* (Garrett, 1975), and then retrieving the *positional* (Garrett, 1975) or *constituent* (Bock, 1995b) structures necessary to realize those grammatical functions. For ease of description, we focus on the expression of relational meaning, returning to the role of perspective meaning, described next.

The first step in structure building has been termed *function assignment* (Bock, 1995b). It involves selecting grammatical functions—representations that relate one aspect of a linguistically encoded event to another—in accordance with the relational meaning represented in the preverbal message. For example, the *subject, direct object*, and *indirect object* grammatical functions relate entities in events expressed by nouns to actions or states in events expressed by verbs. Different *modifier* functions might relate a simple property in an event expressed by an adjective or a complex property expressed by a full clause to an entity expressed by a noun. Thus, function assignment involves consulting the relational meaning in a preverbal message and determining which grammatical functions must be selected to cover that relational meaning.

Once selected, grammatical functions proceed through the second step of structure building, which has been termed *constituent assembly* (Bock, 1995b). This involves the retrieval of constituent structures that can express the grammatical functions selected at function assignment. In *fixed word order* languages like English, this primarily involves arriving at a sequential ordering of words that convey the represented relational meanings. For example, in most English sentences, one of the nouns before a verb is the subject of that verb, and so a constituent structure must be assembled that specifies that sequential ordering. That is, to communicate "the sun shines," constituent assembly processes must make sure "sun" is mentioned before "shines." This can be complicated because most sentences simultaneously express several aspects of relational meaning. For example, in "the bright sun that warms the earth shines," both "bright" and "warms the earth" bear a relational meaning to "sun," which in turn bears a relational meaning to "shines" (not to mention the relational meanings encoded in "that warms the earth"). For these multiple relations to be conveyed by a single sequence, constituent assembly structures must appeal to hierarchical principles that determine how simultaneously expressed relational meanings can be embedded in one another so that an addressee can recover relational meaning from the resulting linear sequence. *Free word order* languages like Japanese place less burden on sequential ordering, instead relying more heavily on affixes or *case-markers* that use phonological content to convey relational meaning (e.g., the suffix "-o" applied to a noun indicates that it is the object of a verb, relatively independently of the positions of that noun and verb). The role of such affixes in structure building implies that function words and affixes (e.g., "the" and "-s" from "the sun shines") are included as parts of constituent frames, rather than retrieved by content subprocesses (e.g., most especially, Garrett, 1975). In short, relational meaning is expressed by an appropriate set of grammatical functions in an appropriate affixed sequence, as selected in the function assignment and constituent assembly stages of structure building, respectively.

This description of structure building has so far considered exclusively relational meaning, but perspective meaning also influences structure building in important ways that are often described as the *information structure* of an utterance (e.g., Lambrecht, 1994). This can be seen from the fact that a given relational meaning can be expressed with more than one combination of function assignments and constituent structures. Consider "In San Diego, it's always sunny" versus "It's always sunny in San Diego." Though these sentences express the same relational meanings, the different sequential orderings convey different perspective meanings, in that the first sentence is about San Diego and the second sentence is about always being sunny. Thus, perspective differences influence structure-building mechanisms by affecting both function assignment and constituent assembly processes. An example of perspective meaning primarily affecting function assignment is the difference between a sentence in the active and passive voice (which, for a verb like "kick," respectively, assign the kicker or "kickee" to the subject function), whereas an example of perspective meaning primarily affecting constituent assembly is the difference between the examples presented here ("In San Diego, it's always sunny" and "It's always sunny in San Diego"). Of course, perspective meaning could influence both stages of structure building, resulting in the production of complex perspective-communicating structures (e.g., clefts like "It is San Diego that is always sunny").

18.2.3 On dividing and uniting

Together, the operations of the content and structure subprocesses of grammatical encoding, proceeding through their respective selection and retrieval stages, determine the gross-level characteristics of speakers' linguistic utterances. But the assumption that sentences are produced by independent content and structure subprocesses raises two thorny issues. First, why process content and structure separately? Second, if content and structure are processed separately, how are they brought together again?

The answer to the first question has to do with the sheer expressive power of language, in that we can describe with language almost any thought we can conceive, at least at some level of coarseness. This implies that the devices that create linguistic expressions must be systematic—they must be able to cover a comprehensive range of possible meanings—and they must be productive—they must be able to create, in principle, an infinity of possible linguistic expressions. This systematicity and productivity of language derives directly from the separation of content and structure. That is, because a linguistic expression is a combination of two relatively independent devices (content and structure), each of which expresses relatively independent aspects of meaning (semantic and relational/perspective meaning), these devices can be freely combined to express any semantic meaning arranged in any relational or perspective manner. If structure and content were not independent, then even if the separate semantic, relational, and perspective properties of an event were known, any previously unexperienced combination of those properties would not necessarily have a linguistic device for its expression. In short, it is the independent combination of content and structure that allows two bounded systems to systematically express boundless meanings (for a similar argument with respect to thought processes, see Fodor & Pylyshyn, 1988).

But, if structure and content are processed separately, they must be brought together again if speakers are to produce a single utterance that combines content and structure. And of course, the combination of content and structure must be the *right* combination—the word that is used to express the subject of the verb to better express the semantic features of the subject rather than say, the object (a process that sometimes goes awry in speech errors; for seminal observations, see Garrett, 1975). This has been dubbed the *coordination problem* (Bock, 1987a), and is a version of the more general *binding problem* in information science. (Another well-known example of the binding problem is that, because the identity and location of visually perceived objects are processed separately (e.g., Ungerleider & Haxby, 1994), perception processes must somehow keep track of which location corresponds to which identity.) At the present, no complete solution to the coordination problem exists. Grammatical category labels (noun, verb, and so on) are likely to be critical, as are something akin to event- or thematic-role representations (agents, themes, goals, and so on). A different solution is to avoid the coordination problem altogether by claiming that content and structure are *not* represented separately, a point of view approaching that expressed by lexically based theories of syntax (e.g., F. Ferreira, 2000; Levelt, 1989; see section 18.3 next for further discussion on this debate). Progress on this issue awaits not only further research, but likely, revolutionary insights into the way that cognitive mechanisms work.

18.3 Fundamental debates: On stages and structures

"Consensus" should not be confused with "unanimous." This section describes some of the challenges to the view just characterized that make it a consensus view and not a unanimous one. Along the way, we hope to show that, with some flexibility, enough semblance of the consensus framework can usually be maintained that its spirit survives (which has directed and structured research on grammatical encoding for over 40 years).

Both major divisions in the consensus model have been questioned. We first discuss challenges to the idea that grammatical encoding consists of two separable stages (both regarding content and to structure subprocesses), and then discuss challenges to the idea that content and structure are processed relatively separately.

18.3.1 Does grammatical encoding proceed through two stages?

The debate over the extent to which grammatical encoding can be characterized as involving staged mechanisms has played out mostly separately with respect to content and structure subprocesses, and so each is discussed in turn.

18.3.1.1 *Content processing*

The original modern-day view of lexical production (Garrett, 1975) and views that followed up on it (Levelt, 1989; Levelt et al., 1999) claimed that word production consults two stages of lexical representation. The first stage includes lexically specific representations that are critically syntactic in nature (i.e., one representation per word in the language, defined especially with respect to its form-class membership). This became the lemma level in current theoretical discourse. The second stage includes full word-form representations whose critical characteristic is a morphophonological nature. That this level was at least partly phonological in nature led to the claim that these representations are sound-form specific (e.g., *sun* and *son*, in all their meanings, share one of these representations), so that they became the *lexeme* level in current theoretical discourse. The syntactic-versus-phonological distinction between these levels naturally leads to the view that the lemma level is modality general (so that the same level is consulted in speaking or writing, hearing, or reading), whereas the lexeme level is modality specific.

A long-standing debate about these lexical representations concerns a detail of processing: Is access to these stages *discrete* (Levelt, 1989; Levelt et al., 1999), in that lemmas must be fully selected before lexemes begin to be retrieved? Or is access *interactive*, so that lexemes begin to be retrieved even before a lemma is fully selected (*cascading*), possibly even allowing partially retrieved lexemes to influence lemma selection (*feedback*; Cutting & Ferreira, 1999; Dell, 1986; Dell et al., 1997; Rapp & Goldrick, 2000)? This debate has maintained prominence due to its association with the modularity debate (Fodor, 1983) in psycholinguistics and cognitive science generally. It is worth noting, however, that even if processing is interactive, this leaves intact a fundamentally staged character to lexical production that Dell and O'Seaghdha (1991) termed "globally modular but locally interactive"—processing still proceeds through stages of lexical selection and lexical retrieval; it is simply a debate concerning whether the dynamics of retrieval are influenced by the intermediate products of selection (*cascading*), and whether the dynamics of retrieval influence the timing or nature of selection (*feedback*).

Another challenge to the original view poses that only one lexical stage operates during lexical production (for initial volleys, see Caramazza, 1997; Roelofs, Meyer, & Levelt, 1998). Some previous models have assumed only one lexical level, either for reasons of substance or convenience (see, e.g., Dell et al., 1997); however, these models typically assumed the sole level to be the lemma level. The new challenge suggests that the sole level of lexical representation has properties that cross-cut the distinctions between lemma and lexeme: On the one hand, like lemmas, the representations are lexically specific (so "sun" and "son" have different lexical representations), but on the other hand, like lexemes, they are modality specific (with different representations for speaking, writing, hearing, or reading). Implications of this different organization have led to tests of alternative predictions, leading to the current disagreement (Caramazza, Bi, Costa, & Miozzo, 2004; Caramazza, Costa, Miozzo, & Bi, 2001; Jescheniak, Meyer, & Levelt, 2003).

It is important, however, to view this debate for what it is and what it is not. This challenge does not hold that production has anything other than a selection-then-retrieval character. Indeed, the one-level view is compatible with the claim that processing is discrete rather than interactive, and so in some ways is *more* staged than some versions of the two-lexical-level view. The entire debate can be summarized with the question of whether lemmas are modality specific—an important question that does not undermine the fundamental character of the aforementioned consensus model.

An interestingly different approach to lexical production comes from a series of experiments and theoretical proposals from Strijkers and colleagues (see especially Strijkers & Costa, 2016). This approach stems from electrophysiological evidence (i.e., changes in the electrical field given off by brain activity), showing that remarkably early changes in the electrophysiological record can be observed as a function of differences among words that, according to traditional theoretical approaches, should not arise until later in the time course of processing. Most striking is evidence showing that within 200 ms of seeing a to-be-named picture, systematic differences can be observed in the physiological record when bilingual speakers name pictures of objects that have *cognate* names (i.e., names that sound similar in the bilingual speakers' two languages) versus non-cognate names (Strijkers, Costa, & Thierry, 2010). The difference between cognates and non-cognates is entirely phonological, and according to standard theories, phonology is not accessed until the last step of lexical selection (note that according to some estimates within traditional frameworks, phonological access does not even begin until 250 ms after picture onset, unfolding over the subsequent 350 ms; Indefrey & Levelt, 2004). Evidence like this has led Strijkers and colleagues to propose a quite different time course of information access, whereby an initial *ignition* stage involves parallel activation of neurons coding any information that is relevant to producing a word, followed by *reverberations*, or sequential activation of components of words' representations, ordered so that each component is available as it is needed. On the one hand, this alternative framework for lexical production represents a significant departure from the sequential, selection-then-retrieval nature of modal models of word production. On the other, especially given the reverberatory phase's similarity to sequential staged production, it is unclear whether the departure is a significant one at the level of information-processing (as opposed to the level of neural implementation, for which the implications are clearly profound).

This does raise the question of what kind of architecture *would* undermine the fundamental character of the consensus model. Two aspects of the consensus view are central to its selection-then-retrieval character. One is that it involves lexically specific representations—symbols of the content words in a speaker's vocabulary. The second is that these lexically specific representations mediate meaning and form. If lexical production requires moving through lexically specific representations to access phonological and eventually articulatory knowledge, then a selection-then-retrieval character is preserved (for a challenge to these kinds of assumptions in the domain of word reading, see Plaut, McClelland, Seidenberg, & Patterson, 1996; Seidenberg & McClelland, 1989).

18.3.1.2 Structure building

Beginning three decades ago, the discreteness-versus-interactivity debate flared with respect to structure building, just as it had with lexical production. The question was whether function assignment could be influenced by the dynamics of constituent assembly. Some evidence suggested not (Bock, 1986a; Bock & Warren, 1985), whereas other evidence suggested so, at least indirectly (Bock, 1987b; Levelt & Maassen, 1981). Like the corresponding debate in lexical production, however, this question concerns an important processing detail of the consensus model that is relevant to its staged character, but not a fundamental challenge to that staged character.

A subsequent challenge to this staged characterization comes from evidence gleaned from an especially powerful methodology for investigating structure building, namely *syntactic persistence* (which has also been termed *syntactic priming, structural persistence*, or *structural priming*—a neat 2 × 2 nomenclature design). Briefly, speakers tend to persist in the use of previously processed structures. This is typically investigated by assessing the effect of the structure of a *prime* sentence upon the subsequent production of a *target* sentence. For example, speakers who hear or say passive prime structures are likely to describe a subsequent picture with passive target descriptions, relative to if they had heard or said active prime descriptions (for recent reviews, see Mahowald, James, Futrell, & Gibson, 2016; Pickering & Ferreira, 2008).

One research thread assessing syntactic persistence has explored whether constituent assembly has its own staged nature. That is, after the functional structure of an impending utterance is specified, do speakers first determine dominance relations in a constituent structure, and only afterward *linearize* that structure into a specific word order? Evidence for this possibility is that mere word order appears to exhibit syntactic persistence (e.g., the difference in Dutch sentences like "On the table is a ball" and "A ball is on the table"; Hartsuiker, Kolk, & Huiskamp, 1999; Hartsuiker & Westenberg, 2000; see also Vigliocco & Nicol, 1998). Alternatively, constituent structure may be undifferentiated, specifying dominance relations and linear order with a single integrated process. Evidence for this is that dominance relations by themselves do not exhibit persistence (e.g., structures like "The driver showed to the mechanic the overalls" does not cause the persistence of structures like "The patient showed the injury to the doctor"; Pickering, Branigan, & McLean, 2002).

A more fundamental challenge to the staged nature of structure building comes from recent modeling work by Chang (Chang, 2002; Chang, Dell, & Bock, 2006; Chang, Dell, Bock, & Griffin, 2000), demonstrating that much of the evidence from syntactic persistence can be simulated by architecturally complex computational models that learn to generate sequences of words. These architectures do not work through a straightforward sequence of function assignment then constituent assembly. Instead, they work by developing sequencing representations akin to syntactic constructions that are triggered by a combination of lexical and event-semantic knowledge (as well as previous learning, leading to persistence). To the extent that these models can describe grammatical encoding successfully, they represent a very different way of construing the structure-building process.

18.3.2 Where is the line between content and structure?

In cognitive science broadly, it is controversial to claim that structure and content are separately processed (see Fodor & Pylyshyn, 1988; Rumelhart & McClelland, 1986). Interestingly, this distinction is more firmly established within the subfield of language production. Instead, the controversy with respect to theories of grammatical encoding has concerned the nature of the content and structure systems' representations.

The aforementioned consensus model proposes a very neat line between content and structure: content subprocesses select and retrieve content words; structure subprocesses assign functions and build constituent structures. This view is often termed *frame-based*, because it assumes structures that are strictly independent of content-word content (although structure building must be influenced by selected content words; for an initial proposal, see Garrett, 1975). A recurring challenge to this neat division comes from *lexically based* models of grammatical encoding (see especially Levelt, 1989), which claim that content words belong in the structure system, indeed forming the fundamental basis of the process of structure building.

One explicitly developed lexically based account of structure building comes from F. Ferreira (2000). This approach grounds structure building in a linguistic formalism called *lexicalized tree-adjoining grammar* (Joshi, Levy, & Takahashi, 1975; Schabes, Abeille, & Joshi, 1988). Briefly, the approach argues that grammatical encoding builds structure by retrieving content words that include elementary trees—component bits of syntactic structure that are unified by operations including *substitution, adjoining,* and more recently, *overlay* (F. Ferreira, Lau, & Bailey, 2004). This kind of approach has the obvious advantage that it can straightforwardly account for how structure-building processes operate so that only certain grammatical options are used with certain content words. In a frame-based view, such lexical dependencies must either derive from distinctions represented in the preverbal message (which is not ideal, given that many such dependencies have little or no basis in meaning), or they must arise during the coordination process described here. On the other hand, lexically based accounts require additional processing machinery to explain lexically independent structure-building effects, most especially evidence that syntactic persistence occurs completely independently of lexical content (e.g., Pickering & Branigan, 1998).

A different view of the content-structure distinction comes from Pickering and Branigan (1998). This approach represents structure with *combinatorial nodes* that specify how content words can combine into constituent structures. Such nodes are viewed as like the traditional lemma nodes that are selected by content subprocesses; in fact, combinatorial nodes and lemma nodes form a kind of seamless network of grammatical-encoding knowledge. Thus, this approach allows for the representation of the just-described lexical dependencies as well as the independence of constituent structure that is implied by patterns of syntactic persistence. From the perspective of the distinction between structure and content, this approach is mixed. Unlike the consensus view presented here, structure and content freely intermingle, but unlike lexically based approaches, structure knowledge (as represented by combinatorial nodes) and content knowledge (as represented by traditional lemmas) are fully distinct. The combinatorial-node-based approach is in principle compatible with a view of structure building that separates function assignment and constituent assembly, so long as function assignment can influence baseline activations of combinatorial nodes directly and constituent assembly is informed by the grammatical knowledge embodied by combinatorial nodes.

18.4 Ongoing debates: Incrementality and syntactic choice

Two particularly persistent debates in the literature on grammatical encoding concern the scope of grammatical planning and the factors influencing syntactic choice.

18.4.1 Incrementality and the scope of planning

Production is at least to some extent *incremental* (a property termed Wundt's principle by Levelt, 1989). This implies grammatical encoding has two critical characteristics: It creates structure piecemeal and it does so unidirectionally. Basic evidence for incrementality is the influence of *accessibility* on grammatical encoding. Specifically, grammatical encoding processes tend to build sentence structures such that more accessible content words (e.g., ones that have been semantically primed; Bock, 1986a) are mentioned earlier than less accessible content words (more on this next). Given that more accessible words can be processed sooner, it makes sense that they would be mentioned earlier under two assumptions: First, grammatical encoding must create structures piecemeal, otherwise, grammatical encoding processes would have to wait for all parts of the sentence to become accessible anyway. Second, grammatical encoding must operate unidirectionally, otherwise, an accessible content word could be processed sooner even by assigning it to a later sentence position.

Whereas little evidence disputes the unidirectional nature of grammatical encoding (but see Momma, Slevc, & Phillips, 2016, discussed next), evidence for the piecemeal nature of grammatical encoding is less coherent. This is closely tied to the question of the *scope* of grammatical encoding—with respect to the eventually spoken utterance, how far ahead does the grammatical encoding process specify structure before production begins? The answer to this question is complicated by two factors. First, the scope of grammatical encoding likely varies by level of encoding, so that as production proceeds from "higher" levels (e.g., message encoding) to "lower" ones (e.g., phonological encoding), the scope of encoding narrows (for an elegant demonstration, see Dell, 1986). This can be seen in Garrett's (1975) original model, where the scope of planning at function assignment is a full clause and at constituent assembly is more phrase-like. Additional evidence supporting the idea that the highest levels of grammatical encoding involve a clause-sized scope of planning include patterns of elicited errors of subject-verb agreement (Bock & Cutting, 1992) and of pauses and hesitation during speech (Ford, 1982; Ford & Holmes, 1978). Other evidence shows that speakers can detect upcoming difficulty in a sentence surprisingly early, again suggesting substantial advance planning (F. Ferreira & Swets, 2005). There is also evidence that the scope of planning narrows at later stages of encoding. For example, Meyer (1996) showed that when speakers produce short sentences, semantic distractors related to either subject or object nouns affected initiation times, suggesting that both nouns were semantically planned to some extent. However, phonological distractors only affected initiation times when related to subject nouns, suggesting that only the subject noun was phonologically planned (see also Wheeldon & Lahiri, 1997).

All of that said, other evidence suggests that the scope of planning at early levels of grammatical encoding can sometimes be narrower than the clause. In a pictures-description task, Smith and Wheeldon (1999) showed that speakers began utterances more slowly when the subject noun phrase was complex and the object noun phrase simple rather than vice versa. This suggests that more planning occurs for the subject noun phrase than the object noun phrase before utterance onset. Similarly, Griffin (2001) measured speech onset times and eye-movement patterns during a pictures-description task, and showed that lemma-level properties of names produced in direct object phrases did not affect performance; this suggests that those lemmas were not accessed prior to speech onset. Brown-Schmidt and Konopka (2008) contrasted English and Spanish production, providing evidence suggesting that even production within a phrase can show evidence of incrementality. These different degrees of planning scope, especially for earlier stages of grammatical encoding, probably occur because the degree to which speakers produce sentences incrementally appears to be strategically sensitive. That this is so explicitly is illustrated directly by evidence from F. Ferreira and Swets (2002), who showed that speakers produced sentences more incrementally when under a production deadline, and implicitly by Swets, Jacovina, and Gerrig (2014), who showed that scope of planning is affected by speakers' working memory span.

A potentially interesting new wrinkle concerning incrementality comes from Momma et al. (2016) and related work. Momma et al. asked Japanese speakers to describe pictures using either subject-verb sentences (e.g., the Japanese translation of "The dog howls") or object-verb sentences (e.g., the Japanese translation of "pets the cat," which is ordered "cat pet" in Japanese; note that in Japanese, arguments such as subjects can be omitted). The pictures had superimposed upon them distractor words that were related in meaning to the verb (e.g., "rub" for "pets the cat"). Results showed that distractors related to the verb slowed the initiation of picture description—an interference effect regularly observed in production—but only for object-verb sentences and not for subject-verb sentences. Related evidence from English points to analogous results, whereby distractor words semantically related to verbs slow the initiation of passive sentences (i.e., sentences where the thematic object begins the sentence) but not active sentences (i.e., sentences where the thematic subject begins the sentence), and for sentences with unaccusative verbs (ones that begin with a thematic object, like "the ship sank") but not unergative verbs (ones that begin with a thematic subject, like "the man ran"). Together, this is compelling evidence that speakers do not begin to articulate the thematic objects of sentences until they have selected the lemma for the verb, but they can begin to articulate the thematic subjects of sentences before they select the lemma for the verb. In turn, this may be because thematic objects form an integral part of the predicate that is expressed by a sentence in a way that thematic subjects do not (as illustrated by the fact that aspects of verb meaning are determined by thematic objects, as in the difference between "hit the ball" and "hit the road").

18.4.2 Syntactic choice

The way that language works requires sentences that differ in meaning to also differ in form (setting aside ambiguity). Interestingly, the opposite claim is not so; sentences that differ in form do not always differ in meaning, at least not obviously. For example, the sentences "I know that San Diego is always sunny" and "I know San Diego is always sunny" differ, yet the difference in meaning between the two is extremely difficult to discover (as illustrated by the fact that papers appear every few years purporting to have done so; see, e.g., Bolinger, 1972; Dor, 2005; Thompson & Mulac, 1991; Yaguchi, 2001). This raises an important question about grammatical encoding: When meaning does not guide speakers to produce one sentence form versus another, what does?

The answer is that many factors seem to affect grammatical encoding relatively independently of meaning. Based on current research, we restrict the present analysis to just three. The first is the aforementioned syntactic persistence: given a choice between two roughly meaning-equal syntactic structures, speakers tend to produce structures they have just experienced. Syntactic persistence is evident both in laboratory settings (Bock, 1986b) and in naturalistic production (Szmrecsanyi, 2004), in spoken as well as in written production (Pickering & Branigan, 1998), in isolated production as well as in dialogue (Branigan, Pickering, & Cleland, 2000; Levelt & Kelter, 1982), in English, Dutch (Hartsuiker & Kolk, 1998), German (Scheepers, 2003), American Sign Language (Hall, Ferreira, & Mayberry, 2015), and even from one language to another (Hartsuiker, Pickering, & Veltkamp, 2004; Loebell & Bock, 2003). The reason why speakers persist in their production of syntactic structure is a matter of active debate (see V. S. Ferreira & Bock, 2006; Pickering & Ferreira, 2008), but it likely is motivated by reasons of efficiency (Bock & Loebell, 1990; Smith & Wheeldon, 2001), communication (see next; Pickering & Garrod, 2004), or is a signal of learning (Chang et al., 2006).

The second set of factors relate to the aforementioned accessibility effects: given a choice between two roughly meaning-equal structures, speakers tend to produce the one that allows for the earlier mention of more accessible sentence material. The range of factors that condition accessibility effects is impressively broad, including semantic priming (Bock,

1986a), phonological interference (Bock, 1987b), imageability (Bock & Warren, 1985; James, Thompson, & Baldwin, 1973), prototypicality (Kelly, Bock, & Keil, 1986), coreference (V. S. Ferreira & Dell, 2000), and salience or prominence (Prat-Sala & Branigan, 2000). (For additional review, see Bock, 1982; McDonald, Bock, & Kelly, 1993.)

One important type of effect that brings about accessibility effects appears to be grounded in semantic interference. One demonstration of this is V. S. Ferreira and Firato (2002), who showed that proactive interference—when a later noun in a sentence is similar in meaning to earlier nouns in the sentence—compels speakers to produce the optional "that" more in sentences. A series of studies have looked at relative clause production, including by looking at the choice between active object relative clauses versus passive subject-relative clauses. Across a series of papers (e.g., Gennari, Mirković, & MacDonald, 2012; Hsiao, Gao, & MacDonald, 2014; Hsiao & MacDonald, 2016; Humphreys, Mirković, & Gennari, 2016), MacDonald and colleagues have shown that with inanimate head nouns, speakers tend to produce active object relative clauses (*the sandbag that the woman is punching*), but with animate head nouns, they tend to produce passive subject relatives (*the man who is being punched by the woman*). Such effects appear to be due to semantic interference between the head noun and the full noun phrase in the relative clause (e.g., *sandbag-woman* vs. *man-woman*), because the strength of the tendency to use passives with animate heads is correlated with the rated semantic similarity of the two nouns.

One explanation for accessibility effects is that they make grammatical encoding proceed more efficiently. The idea is that if grammatical encoding is incremental, then producing accessible content sooner allows speakers to dispatch it sooner. This presumably circumvents the need to buffer that accessible content and buys time to access the remaining less accessible content. V. S. Ferreira (1996) provided evidence consistent with this possibility, by showing that speakers began to produce sentences more quickly and produced them with fewer errors when grammatical encoding had more structural options available.

Under this explanation, accessibility effects might infringe on the influence of perspective meaning on grammatical encoding. That is, recall that speakers will produce different structures depending on what perspective they take on a situation, as represented by the perspective meaning represented in their preverbal message ("San Diego is always sunny" vs. "It's always sunny in San Diego"). At least some such effects might be due to raw accessibility rather than to perspective meaning per se. An illustration of this distinction comes from Cowles and Ferreira (2012), who suggested that speakers mentioned one kind of argument earlier in sentences (*given* arguments) because of accessibility, whereas they mentioned another kind of argument earlier in sentences (*topic* arguments) independent of accessibility.

A third set of factors that can influence grammatical encoding relatively independently of meaning are *audience design* factors. Here, given a choice between two roughly meaning-equal structures, speakers might choose the one that would be easier for their addressee to understand (for review, see V. S. Ferreira & Dell, 2000). The most heavily investigated factor in this set has been ambiguity: All things equal, does grammatical encoding select a less ambiguous rather than a more ambiguous syntactic form?

Evidence concerning the effect of ambiguity on grammatical encoding has been mixed (for review, see Ferreira, 2008). Some evidence has shown that grammatical encoding processes do not preferentially select unambiguous structures, neither in spoken (V. S. Ferreira & Dell, 2000) nor written (Elsness, 1984) production, nor in dialogue (Kraljic & Brennan, 2005), nor with various kinds of structures (Arnold, Wasow, Asudeh, & Alrenga,

2004), nor with prosody (Allbritton, McKoon, & Ratcliff, 1996; Schafer, Speer, Warren, & White, 2000). Other evidence suggests that grammatical encoding might select unambiguous structures in highly interactive dialogue (Haywood, Pickering, & Branigan, 2005), or in written form (Temperley, 2003), or with prosody (Snedeker & Trueswell, 2003). Keys to sorting out these mixed results likely include taking into account the effects of ambiguity-independent factors on syntactic choice (see V. S. Ferreira & Dell, 2000), and separating non-linguistic-ambiguity avoidance and linguistic-ambiguity avoidance (V. S. Ferreira, Slevc, & Rogers, 2005).

18.5 Emerging debates: Rationality, learning, and dialogue

Within grammatical encoding, certain current research threads have special promise for progress, due largely to their tight relationships to areas of active investigation in psycholinguistics or cognitive science. This includes work investigating rationality, learning, and dialogue.

18.5.1 Rational models of sentence production

Across the behavioral sciences, a new focus of research has been on *rational* or *optimal* models of behavior. Many such accounts are Bayesian in nature. The general idea behind rational accounts of behavior is that when the various contextual factors that are relevant to a behavioral domain are considered, individuals' behaviors can be seen as maximizing or optimizing some set of desirable outcomes.

In the domain of sentence production, the most prominent rational account of behavior is likely *Uniform Information Density* (Jaeger, 2010). According to Uniform Information Density, speakers aim to smoothly express an optimal amount of information across an utterance. To do so, they use whatever flexibility is available to them to dilute stretches of language that may be too informative, or compress stretches of language that may be too uninformative. In this way, a speaker can avoid overwhelming their listeners' comprehension system by providing too much information in too little time, or wasting time by producing a sequence that could have been more informative.

A straightforward example of such information smoothing arises with the mention of the optional *that* in certain sentence structures. For example, in a *verb-* or *sentence-complement structure*, the main verb in a sentence takes a clausal complement that (in English) can optionally be introduced with the complementizer *that*, as in *The proud mother announced (that) the wedding would be a big event*. As already noted, the complementizer carries little (if any) semantic or relational meaning, but it can convey a valuable bit of information, specifically, that a clausal complement is upcoming (rather than, say, a direct object as in *The proud mother announced the wedding yesterday*). According to Uniform Information Density, such an optional element can be used to smooth the rate of information delivery. In particular, if a comprehender already anticipates the arrival of an upcoming clausal complement, then the *that* only contributes redundant information, and so its mention only serves to create a stretch of uninformative language. But if the upcoming clause is less expected, including *that* will reduce the spike in information density that would otherwise arrive when the clausal complement is eventually inferred. Consistent with such a prediction, speakers are in fact less likely to mention the optional *that* after verbs that usually are followed by clausal complements (as in *The proud mother announced the wedding would be a big event*), but are more likely to mention it after verbs that are rarely followed by clausal complements (as in *The talented photographer accepted the money could not be spent yet*; Ferreira & Schotter, 2013; Jaeger, 2010).

18.5.2 Ongoing learning effects

With the exception of the Chang et al. (2006) model described here, most investigations of language production up through the 2000s assumed that our linguistic knowledge is relatively static. However, starting in the 2000s, a series of experimental programs have investigated whether ongoing experience has enduring effects on our representation of linguistic knowledge; that is, whether we are constantly learning about the language we experience in ways that affect speakers' productions.

One such program has already been described (twice): Syntactic persistence. Although syntactic persistence has been viewed as due to residual accessibility of structural information (Pickering & Branigan, 1998) or as a communicative effect (Pickering & Garrod, 2004), another well-developed approach views it as a learning effect. As mentioned, Chang et al. (2006) presents a comprehensive model of sentence production that explains syntactic persistence as due to learning, an account that has been extended into the rational domain by Jaeger and Snider (2013).

Another form of learning that has been heavily investigated can be termed *phonotactic learning*. First reported by Dell, Reed, Adams, and Meyer (2000), phonotactic learning refers to the fact that producers seem to notice the fact that certain speech sounds can be restricted to certain syllable positions. Such restrictions occur naturally in language. For example, the "h" sound in English can only happen at the beginnings of syllables, and the "ng" sound can only happen at the end. This is not due to physical or biological constraints, as other languages do not have such restrictions (e.g., Vietnamese permits the "ng" sound to begin syllables and [h] appears in syllable-final position in many dialects of Brazilian Portuguese). Dell et al. showed that if speech sounds in English that are normally unrestricted are instead restricted to specific syllable positions, people's productions will reflect this.

To show this, Dell et al. exploited a speech-error phenomenon called the *syllable-position constraint*: when a speaker slips in their production of a speech sound, the erroneously placed sound will usually be positioned in the intended syllable position (but in the wrong syllable). For the English sounds "h" and "ng," the syllable-position constraint is observed 100% of the time (so, a speaker intending to say, "the man sa*ng*" might say, "the ma*ng*...," but will never say, "the *ng*an"). For unrestricted English sounds like "s" and "f," the syllable-position constraint is observed about 70% of the time (so, a speaker intending to say, "the man sang" might say, "the *s*an ... " 70% of the time, but "the ma*s* ... " 30% of the time). Dell et al. discovered that if speakers are asked to produce sequences of seemingly random syllables, but where normally unrestricted sounds like "s" and "f" are in fact restricted to either the beginnings or ends of syllables—like "h" and "ng" are in English—then like "h" and "ng" in English, when speakers made speech errors with "s" and "f," they observed the syllable-position constraint almost 100% of the time. That is, speakers learned a brand new phonotactic restriction as a function of their recent linguistic experience.

18.5.3 Dialogue

For decades, two lines of work in psycholinguistics have proceeded mostly separately. One, in which the aforementioned consensus view is situated, views psycholinguistic theorizing as a branch of cognitive psychology, where the nature of general mechanisms is inferred from summary measures of performance during highly controlled tasks. The other line views psycholinguistic performance as language use (Clark, 1996)—as a set of tools that people use to accomplish goals in socially coordinated fashion. This work relies more on the logic and techniques used in the philosophy of language and linguistic pragmatics, observing and cataloging performance to analyze language as a system of strategies. Study within this line focuses on *dialogue* contexts in which more than one interlocutor interact, usually in the performance of some game or task. The separation between these lines emerged partly from the heavy emphasis in the 1970s and 1980s on the study of reading—a socially impoverished setting for language use, to say the least. But valuably, in the last two decades, the increasing prominence of research on language production and on spoken-language comprehension has encouraged a synthesis of these heretofore more independent lines.

Research on grammatical encoding has figured prominently in this synthesis. One relevant angle is the aforementioned debate concerning the effects of audience design on syntactic choice (see also Brennan & Clark, 1996; Horton & Keysar, 1996; Schober & Brennan, 2003). Another angle that has become relevant to controlled research using dialogue is syntactic persistence. Branigan, Pickering, and Cleland (2000) reported robust syntactic persistence in a laboratory-based dialogue task, and the numerical size of these persistence effects was larger than that observed in previous, monologue-based demonstrations (e.g., Bock, 1986b). Pickering and Garrod (2004) brought this dialogue-based persistence effect together with research on similar semantic coordination effects (Garrod & Anderson, 1987) to propose a broad view of language use as alignment driven. The idea is that in dialogue, interlocutors aim to coordinate their use of linguistic devices at all possible levels, so they use corresponding pronunciations, locutions (e.g., Clark & Wilkes-Gibbs, 1986), framing (Garrod & Anderson, 1987), and most innovatively, syntactic structures (Branigan et al., 2000) during conversation. The function of such alignment is to ultimately achieve corresponding *situation models*, which can be considered analogous to preverbal messages in production theories, thereby achieving successful communication. In turn, this alignment approach to linguistic performance has come together with work in cognitive science more broadly on imitation (e.g., Iacoboni et al., 1999), embodiment (where cognitive representation is seen as critically "external" in nature; e.g., Barsalou, 1999), and "mirror-neuron" systems (whereby perception and action involve the same neural substrates; e.g., Rizzolatti, Fadiga, Gallese, & Fogassi, 1996) to form a distinct but prominent subfield within psycholinguistics. The resulting promise for cross-disciplinary interaction and unification is an extremely valuable strength of this view.

More recently, frameworks that aim to advance understanding of language production in dialogue have adopted insights from theories of action control in cognitive science and cognitive neuroscience (Grush, 2004; Wolpert, 1997). In particular, according to a number of accounts (Pickering & Garrod, 2007, 2013), successful dialogue comes from the coordination of the mechanisms typically thought to underlie language comprehension and production (e.g., semantic and lexical representations). Such coordination has been argued to underlie predictions as to the features of language that will be heard or produced during dialogue, and by comparing the predicted language against what is actually heard or produced, interlocutors in dialogue can monitor whether language was accurately produced, and learn about linguistic features so as to inform future acts of production and comprehension.

18.6 Fundamental insights

Like any area of active inquiry, research on grammatical encoding is more easily characterized in terms of debates and disagreement than in terms of consensus and agreement. Nonetheless, the field has come a long way in the short 40 (or so) years of its current incarnation. Next, we briefly mention two specific points for which little debate exists in mainstream theories of grammatical encoding, but for which there was at least uncertainty (if not outright rancor) in other areas or in times past.

18.6.1 Linguistic knowledge and non-linguistic knowledge are both different

Every current approach to grammatical encoding postulates distinct non-linguistic and linguistic representational systems. Indeed, this separation was vital for the initial growth of the field, so that theories of grammatical encoding could develop without the burden of accounting for the nature of thought more generally. The assumption of linguistic-non-linguistic separation is not trivial. For language production, even Fodor (1983) once rejected it. In other areas, there are several well-known incursions on this assumption that have not managed to get a foothold in accounts of grammatical encoding. For example, the popularity of the Whorf-Sapir hypothesis has ebbed and flowed in the broader study of language over the twentieth century (see Boroditsky, 2001; Lucy, 1992; Whorf, 1956). According to this class of views, the nature of the linguistic devices offered by a language critically determine the thought patterns of those who use that language. Yet, approaches to grammatical encoding have generally found it useful to postulate distinct representational systems for conceptual constructs versus linguistic constructs (although a valuable middle ground comes from Slobin's (1996) "thinking-for-speaking" approach and related work). Similarly, views of psychological performance deriving from the behaviorist perspective (Skinner, 1957) aimed to reduce grammatical patterns to patterns of instrumental responses ingrained by reinforcement and punishment contingencies. Some connectionist and parallel-distributed-processing frameworks (Rumelhart & McClelland, 1986) could be viewed as neobehaviorist in nature, yet it is notable that connectionist accounts of grammatical encoding of any comprehensiveness (e.g., Chang, 2002; Chang et al., 2000, 2006; Dell, 1986) involve a much richer and structured cognitive architecture than comparably comprehensive accounts of, say, single-word reading (Plaut et al., 1996; Seidenberg & McClelland, 1989). Finally, the aforementioned embodied approaches to cognition (e.g., Barsalou, 1999) promise a different way to blur the distinction between language and thought, namely by driving at least the perceptual characteristics of language into thought. Nonetheless, the account of grammatical encoding that is most embodied in nature (Pickering & Garrod, 2004) still includes independent and distinct representational systems for thought and for language. In short, among students of grammatical encoding, it is almost universally held that thinking and talking are different, and so are based on distinct systems of representation.

18.6.2 Syntax is in there somewhere

A constant tension in approaches to language acquisition and language comprehension is the status of syntactic representations. Some approaches (e.g., Frazier, 1988; Pinker, 1989) view syntactic knowledge as the irreducible basis of our grammatical knowledge (even if, of course, non-syntactic knowledge can be bootstrapped to acquire it). Others (e.g., MacDonald, Pearlmutter, & Seidenberg, 1994; Tomasello, 2000) view syntactic knowledge as derived from or reducible to other forms of knowledge, including conceptual and perceptual knowledge.

Among approaches to grammatical encoding, this tension is far less prominent, largely because some form of syntactic knowledge is seen as fundamental to how grammatical encoding works (as represented by the aforementioned consensus model). Three lines of empirical work have led to this standpoint. The first comes from the speech-error observations that pioneered research on language production (Fromkin, 1971, 1973; Garrett, 1975). Specifically, it is notable that most speech-error investigations explore the fact that errant productions maintain their syntactic integrity, even when semantic integrity is compromised (for discussion, see Bock, 1990). For example, because about 85% of word-exchange errors involve exchanging words that belong to the same grammatical categories (Garrett, 1975; Stemberger, 1985), the syntactic structures of errant utterances will conform to speakers' intentions (and will be well formed), even when their meanings do not (e.g., "that log could use another *fire*," V. S. Ferreira & Humphreys, 2001; "she *sings* everything she *writes*," Garrett, 1975). The second line is syntactic persistence: Most early work on syntactic persistence (see especially Bock, 1986b, 1989; Bock & Loebell, 1990; Bock, Loebell, & Morey, 1992) determined that syntactic contributions to persistence are separate from conceptual, semantic, lexical, or phonological contributions. Thirty years later, the research landscape suggests that while a more general type of *plan reuse* (MacDonald, 2013) arises such that persistence of clearly non-syntactic effects can be observed (e.g., Scheepers et al., 2011), when non-syntactic factors influence syntactic production they do so either independently of syntactic factors (e.g., Bock et al., 1992; Pickering & Branigan, 1998), or only when syntactic factors are neutralized (see especially Chang, 2002; Griffin & Weinstein-Tull, 2003). The third line is work on the production of agreement (e.g., in English, verbs agree with the grammatical number of their subject). Specifically, patterns of agreement errors show that performance is heavily influenced by grammatical features (see Bock, 1995a) and hierarchical representation (e.g., Franck, Vigliocco, & Nicol, 2002), with non-syntactic influences (see Haskell & MacDonald, 2003; Thornton & MacDonald, 2003) of limited scope (Eberhard, Cutting, & Bock, 2005). Together, observations like these suggest that syntactic structures form the foundation of spoken utterances, in accordance with the approach described here.

18.7 Summary

How and why do speakers say what they say? The consensus model that opened this chapter provides a sketch of how: independent but mutually influential component systems that process structure and content proceed through stages of selecting linguistic features and then retrieving their details. How staged these processes are and where the line should be drawn between structure and content are subjects of active debate. The remaining debates outlined in this chapter provide a sketch of why speakers say what they say: In addition to the expression of meaning, speakers' utterances are influenced by incrementality of processing, the accessibility or persistence of linguistic features, audience design, rational behavioral goals, ongoing learning, and influences during dialogue. Ongoing research will play out these debates, resolving some and spawning others. Through all of this, this research trajectory is providing fundamental insights into the way that language works.

References

Allbritton, D. W., McKoon, G., & Ratcliff, R. (1996). Reliability of prosodic cues for resolving syntactic ambiguity. *Journal of Experimental Psychology: Learning, Memory, and Cognition*, 22(3), 714–35.

Arnold, J. E., Wasow, T., Asudeh, A., & Alrenga, P. (2004). Avoiding attachment ambiguities: The role of constituent ordering. *Journal of Memory and Language*, 51, 55–70.

Barsalou, L. W. (1999). Perceptual symbol systems. *Behavioral & Brain Sciences*, 22(4), 577–660.

Bock, J. K. (1982). Toward a cognitive psychology of syntax: Information processing contributions to sentence formulation. *Psychological Review*, 89, 1–47.

Bock, J. K. (1986a). Meaning, sound, and syntax: Lexical priming in sentence production. *Journal of Experimental Psychology: Learning, Memory, and Cognition*, 12, 575–86.

Bock, J. K. (1986b). Syntactic persistence in language production. *Cognitive Psychology*, 18, 355–87.

Bock, J. K. (1987a). Coordinating words and syntax in speech plans. In: Ellis, A. (Ed.), *Progress in the Psychology of Language, Vol. 3* (pp. 337–90). Erlbaum, London.

Bock, J. K. (1987b). An effect of the accessibility of word forms on sentence structures. *Journal of Memory and Language*, 26, 119–37.

Bock, J. K. (1989). Closed-class immanence in sentence production. *Cognition*, 31, 163–86.

Bock, J. K. (1990). Structure in language: Creating form in talk. *American Psychologist*, 45, 1221–36.

Bock, J. K. (1995a). Producing agreement. *Current Directions in Psychological Science*, 8, 56–61.

Bock, J. K. (1995b). Sentence production: From mind to mouth. In: Miller, J. L., & Eimas, P. D. (Eds.), *Handbook of Perception and Cognition. Vol 11: Speech, Language, and Communication* (pp. 181–216). Academic Press, Orlando, FL.

Bock, J. K., & Cutting, J. C. (1992). Regulating mental energy: Performance units in language production. *Journal of Memory and Language, 31*, 99–127.

Bock, J. K., & Loebell, H. (1990). Framing sentences. *Cognition, 35*, 1–39.

Bock, J. K., Loebell, H., & Morey, R. (1992). From conceptual roles to structural relations: Bridging the syntactic cleft. *Psychological Review, 99*, 150–71.

Bock, J. K., & Warren, R. K. (1985). Conceptual accessibility and syntactic structure in sentence formulation. *Cognition, 21*, 47–67.

Bolinger, D. (1972). *That's That*. Mouton, The Hague.

Boroditsky, L. (2001). Does language shape thought? Mandarin and English speakers' conceptions of time. *Cognitive Psychology, 43*(1), 1–22.

Branigan, H. P., Pickering, M. J., & Cleland, A. A. (2000). Syntactic co-ordination in dialogue. *Cognition, 75*(2), B13–B25.

Brennan, S. E., & Clark, H. H. (1996). Conceptual pacts and lexical choice in conversation. *Journal of Experimental Psychology: Learning, Memory, and Cognition, 22*(6), 1482–93.

Brown-Schmidt, S., & Konopka, A. E. (2008). Little houses and casas pequeñas: Message formulation and syntactic form in unscripted speech with speakers of English and Spanish. *Cognition, 109*, 274–80.

Caramazza, A. (1997). How many levels of processing are there in lexical access? *Cognitive Neuropsychology, 14*, 177–208.

Caramazza, A., Bi, Y. C., Costa, A., & Miozzo, M. (2004). What determines the speed of lexical access: Homophone or specific-word frequency? A reply to Jescheniak et al. (2003). *Journal of Experimental Psychology: Learning Memory, and Cognition, 30*(1), 278–82.

Caramazza, A., Costa, A., Miozzo, M., & Bi, Y. (2001). The specific-word frequency effect: Implications for the representation of homophones in speech production. *Journal of Experimental Psychology: Learning, Memory, and Cognition, 27*(6), 1430–50.

Chang, F. (2002). Symbolically speaking: A connectionist model of sentence production. *Cognitive Science, 26*, 609–51.

Chang, F., Dell, G. S., & Bock, K. (2006). Becoming syntactic. *Psychological Review, 113*, 234–72.

Chang, F., Dell, G. S., Bock, J. K., & Griffin, Z. M. (2000). Structural priming as implicit learning: A comparison of models of sentence production. *Journal of Psycholinguistic Research, 29*(2), 217–29.

Clark, H. H. (1996). *Using Language*. Cambridge University Press, Cambridge, England.

Clark, H. H., & Wilkes-Gibbs, D. (1986). Referring as a collaborative process. *Cognition, 22*, 1–39.

Cowles, H. W., & Ferreira, V. S. (2012). The influence of topic status on written and spoken sentence production. *Discourse Processes, 49*, 1–28.

Cutting, J. C., & Ferreira, V. S. (1999). Semantic and phonological information flow in the production lexicon. *Journal of Experimental Psychology: Learning, Memory, and Cognition, 25*(2), 318–44.

Dell, G. S. (1986). A spreading-activation theory of retrieval in sentence production. *Psychological Review, 93*, 283–321.

Dell, G. S., & O'Seaghdha, P. G. (1991). Mediated and convergent lexical priming in language production: A comment on Levelt et al. *Psychological Review, 98*(4), 604–14.

Dell, G. S., Reed, K. D., Adams, D. R., & Meyer, A. S. (2000). Speech errors, phonotactic constraints, and implicit learning: A study of the role of experience in language production. *Journal of Experimental Psychology: Learning, Memory, and Cognition, 26*, 1355–67.

Dell, G. S., Schwartz, M. F., Martin, N., Saffran, E. M., & Gagnon, D. A. (1997). Lexical access in aphasic and nonaphasic speakers. *Psychological Review, 104*(4), 801–38.

Dor, D. (2005). Toward a semantic account of that-deletion in English. *Linguistics, 43*(2), 345–82.

Eberhard, K. M., Cutting, J. C., & Bock, K. (2005). Making syntax of sense: Number agreement in sentence production. *Psychological Review, 112*(3), 531–59.

Elsness, J. (1984). That or zero? A look at the choice of object clause connective in a corpus of American English. *English Studies, 65*, 519–33.

Ferreira, F. (2000). Syntax in language production: An approach using tree-adjoining grammars. In: Wheeldon, L. (Ed.), *Aspects of Language Production* (pp. 291–330). Psychology Press/Taylor & Francis, Philadelphia, PA.

Ferreira, F., Lau, E., & Bailey, K. (2004). *A Model of Disfluency Processing Based on Tree-Adjoining Grammar*. Paper presented at the Seventeenth Annual CUNY Conference on Human Sentence Processing, College Park, MD.

Ferreira, F., & Swets, B. (2002). How incremental is language production? Evidence from the production of utterances requiring the computation of arithmetic sums. *Journal of Memory and Language, 46*(1), 57–84.

Ferreira, F., & Swets, B. (2005). The production and comprehension of resumptive pronouns in relative clause "island" contexts. In: Cutler, A. (Ed.), *Twenty-first Century Psycholinguistics: Four Cornerstones*. Erlbaum, Hove.

Ferreira, V. S. (1996). Is it better to give than to donate? Syntactic flexibility in language production. *Journal of Memory and Language, 35*(5), 724–55.

Ferreira, V. S. (in press). How are speakers' linguistic choices affected by ambiguity? In: Meyer, A. S., Krott, A., & Wheeldon, L. R. (Eds.), *Language Processes and Executive Function*. Psychology Press, London.

Ferreira, V. S. (2008). Ambiguity, accessibility, and a division of labor for communicative success. *Psychology of Learning and Motivation, 49*, 209–46.

Ferreira, V. S., & Bock, J. K. (2006). The functions of structural priming. *Language and Cognitive Processes, 21*, 1011–29.

Ferreira, V. S., & Dell, G. S. (2000). Effect of ambiguity and lexical availability on syntactic and lexical production. *Cognitive Psychology, 40*(4), 296–340.

Ferreira, V. S., & Firato, C. E. (2002). Proactive interference effects on sentence production. *Psychonomic Bulletin & Review, 9*, 795–800.

Ferreira, V. S., & Humphreys, K. R. (2001). Syntactic influences on lexical and morphological processing in language production. *Journal of Memory and Language, 44*(1), 52–80.

Ferreira, V. S., & Schotter, E. R. (2013). Do verb bias effects on sentence production reflect sensitivity to comprehension or production factors? *Quarterly Journal of Experimental Psychology, 66*, 1548–71.

Ferreira, V. S., Slevc, L. R., & Rogers, E. S. (2005). How do speakers avoid ambiguous linguistic expressions? *Cognition, 96*, 263–84.

Fodor, J. A. (1983). *The modularity of mind*. MIT Press, Cambridge, MA.

Fodor, J. A., & Pylyshyn, Z. W. (1988). Connectionism and cognitive architecture: A critical analysis. *Cognition, 28*, 3–71.

Ford, M. (1982). Sentence planning units: Implications for the speaker's representation of meaningful relations underlying sentences. In: Bresnan, J. (Ed.), *The Mental Representation of Grammatical Relations*. MIT Press, Cambridge, MA.

Ford, M., & Holmes, V. M. (1978). Planning units and syntax in sentence production. *Cognition*, 6, 35–53.

Franck, J., Vigliocco, G., & Nicol, J. (2002). Subject-verb agreement errors in French and English: The role of syntactic hierarchy. *Language & Cognitive Processes*, 17(4), 371–404.

Frazier, L. (1988). Grammar and language processing. In: Newmeyer, F. J. (Ed.), *Linguistics: The Cambridge Survey (iii) Linguistic theory: Extensions and implications* (pp. 15–34). Cambridge University Press, Cambridge.

Fromkin, V. A. (1971). The non-anomalous nature of anomalous utterances. *Language*, 47, 27–52.

Fromkin, V. A. (Ed.) (1973). *Speech Errors as Linguistic Evidence*. Mouton, The Hague.

Garrett, M. F. (1975). The analysis of sentence production. In: Bower, G. H. (Ed.), *The Psychology of Learning and Motivation, Vol. 9* (pp. 133–77). Academic Press, New York, NY.

Garrett, M. F. (1982). Production of speech: Observations from normal and pathological language use. In: Ellis, A. (Ed.), *Normality and Pathology in Cognitive Functions* (pp. 19–76). Academic Press, London.

Garrett, M. F. (1988). Processes in language production. In: Newmeyer, F. J. (Ed.), *Linguistics: The Cambridge Survey, Vol. 3: Language: Psychological and Biological Aspects* (pp. 69–96). Cambridge University Press, Cambridge.

Garrod, S., & Anderson, A. (1987). Saying what you mean in dialogue: A study in a conceptual and semantic co-ordination. *Cognition*, 27, 181–218.

Gennari, S. P., Mirković, J., & MacDonald, M. C. (2012). Animacy and competition in relative clause production: A cross-linguistic investigation. *Cognitive Psychology*, 65(2), 141–76.

Griffin, Z. M. (2001). Gaze durations during speech reflect word selection and phonological encoding. *Cognition*, 82(1), B1–B14.

Griffin, Z. M., & Weinstein-Tull, J. (2003). Conceptual structure modulates structural priming in the production of complex sentences. *Journal of Memory and Language*, 49(4), 537–55.

Grush, R. (2004). The emulation theory of representation: Motor control, imagery, and perception. *Behavioral and Brain Sciences* 27, 377–96.

Hall, M. L., Ferreira, V. S., & Mayberry, R. I. (2015). Syntactic priming in American Sign Language. *PloS One*, 10(3), e0119611.

Hartsuiker, R. J., & Kolk, H. H. J. (1998). Syntactic persistence in Dutch. *Language & Speech*, 41(2), 143–84.

Hartsuiker, R. J., Kolk, H. H. J., & Huiskamp, P. (1999). Priming word order in sentence production. *Quarterly Journal of Experimental Psychology: Human Experimental Psychology*, 52(1), 129–47.

Hartsuiker, R. J., Pickering, M. J., & Veltkamp, E. (2004). Is syntax separate or shared between languages? Cross-linguistic syntactic priming in Spanish-English bilinguals. *Psychological Science*, 15(6), 409–14.

Hartsuiker, R. J., & Westenberg, C. (2000). Word order priming in written and spoken sentence production. *Cognition*, 75(2), B27–B39.

Haskell, T. R., & MacDonald, M. C. (2003). Conflicting cues and competition in subject-verb agreement. *Journal of Memory and Language*, 48(4), 760–778.

Haywood, S. L., Pickering, M. J., & Branigan, H. P. (2005). Do speakers avoid ambiguity during dialogue? *Psychological Science*, 16, 362–6.

Horton, W. S., & Keysar, B. (1996). When do speakers take into account common ground? *Cognition*, 59(1), 91–117.

Hsiao, Y., Gao, Y., & MacDonald, M. C. (2014). Agent-patient similarity affects sentence structure in language production: Evidence from subject omissions in Mandarin. *Frontiers in Psychology*, 5, 1015.

Hsiao, Y., & MacDonald, M. C. (2016). Production predicts comprehension: Animacy effects in Mandarin relative clause processing. *Journal of Memory and Language, 89*, 87–109.

Humphreys, G. F., Mirković, J., & Gennari, S. P. (2016). Similarity-based competition in relative clause production and comprehension. *Journal of Memory and Language, 89*, 200–21.

Iacoboni, M., Woods, R. P., Brass, M., Bekkering, H., Mazziotta, J. C., & Rizzolatti, G. (1999). Cortical mechanisms of human imitation. *Science, 286*(5449), 2526–8.

Indefrey, P., & Levelt, W. J. M. (2004). The spatial and temporal signatures of word production components. *Cognition, 92*, 101–44.

Jaeger, T. F. (2010). Redundancy and reduction: Speakers manage syntactic information density. *Cognitive Psychology, 61*, 23–62.

Jaeger, T. F., & Snider, N. E. (2013). Alignment as a consequence of expectation adaptation: Syntactic priming is affected by the prime's prediction error given both prior and recent experience. *Cognition, 127*, 57–83.

James, C. T., Thompson, J. G., & Baldwin, J. M. (1973). The reconstructive process in sentence memory. *Journal of Verbal Learning and Verbal Behavior, 12*, 51–63.

Jescheniak, J. D., Meyer, A. S., & Levelt, W. J. M. (2003). Specific-word frequency is not all that counts in speech production: Comments on Caramazza, Costa, et al. (2001) and new experimental data. *Journal of Experimental Psychology: Learning, Memory, and Cognition, 29*(3), 432–8.

Joshi, A. K., Levy, L., & Takahashi, M. (1975). Tree adjunct grammars. *Journal of the Computer and System Sciences, 10*, 136–63.

Kelly, M. H., Bock, J. K., & Keil, F. C. (1986). Prototypicality in a linguistic context: Effects on sentence structure. *Journal of Memory and Language, 25*, 59–74.

Kempen, G., & Huijbers, P. (1983). The lexicalization process in sentence production and naming: Indirect election of words. *Cognition, 14*, 185–209.

Kraljic, T., & Brennan, S. E. (2005). Prosodic disambiguation of syntactic structure: For the speaker or for the addressee? *Cognitive Psychology, 50*, 194–231.

Lambrecht, K. (1994). *Information Structure and Sentence Form*. Cambridge University Press, Cambridge.

Levelt, W. J. M. (1989). *Speaking: From Intention to Articulation*. MIT Press, Cambridge, MA.

Levelt, W. J. M., & Kelter, S. (1982). Surface form and memory in question answering. *Cognitive Psychology, 14*, 78–106.

Levelt, W. J. M., & Maassen, B. (1981). Lexical search and order of mention in sentence production. In: Klein, W., & Levelt, W. (Eds.), *Crossing the Boundaries in Linguistics* (pp. 221–52). Reidel, Dordrecht.

Levelt, W. J. M., Roelofs, A., & Meyer, A. S. (1999). A theory of lexical access in speech production. *Behavioral & Brain Sciences, 22*(1), 1–75.

Loebell, H., & Bock, K. (2003). Structural priming across languages. *Linguistics, 41*(5), 791–824.

Lucy, J. A. (1992). *Grammatical Categories and Cognition: A Case Study of the Linguistic Relativity Hypothesis*. Cambridge University Press, Cambridge, England.

MacDonald, M. C. (2013). How language production shapes language form and comprehension. *Frontiers in Psychology, 4*, 226.

MacDonald, M. C., Pearlmutter, N. J., & Seidenberg, M. S. (1994). The lexical nature of syntactic ambiguity resolution. *Psychological Review, 101*(4), 676–703.

Mahowald, K., James, A., Futrell, R., & Gibson, E. (2016). A meta-analysis of syntactic priming in language production. *Journal of Memory and Language, 91*, 5–27.

McDonald, J. L., Bock, J. K., & Kelly, M. H. (1993). Word and world order: Semantic, phonological, and metrical determinants of serial position. *Cognitive Psychology, 25*(2), 188–230.

Meyer, A. S. (1996). Lexical access in phrase and sentence production: Results from picture-word interference experiments. *Journal of Memory and Language*, 35(4), 477–96.

Momma, S., Slevc, L. R., & Phillips, C. (2016). The timing of verb selection in Japanese sentence production. *Journal of Experimental Psychology: Learning, Memory, and Cognition*, 42, 813–24.

Pickering, M. J., & Branigan, H. P. (1998). The representation of verbs: Evidence from syntactic priming in language production. *Journal of Memory and Language*, 39(4), 633–51.

Pickering, M. J., Branigan, H. P., & McLean, J. F. (2002). Constituent structure is formulated in one stage. *Journal of Memory and Language*, 46(3), 586–605.

Pickering, M. J., & Ferreira, V. S. (2008). Structural priming: a critical review. *Psychological Bulletin*, 134, 427–59.

Pickering, M. J., & Garrod, S. (2004). Toward a mechanistic psychology of dialogue. *Behavioral and Brain Sciences*, 27(2), 169–226.

Pickering, M. J., & Garrod, S. (2007). Do people use language production to make predictions during comprehension? *Trends in Cognitive Sciences*, 11, 105–10.

Pickering, M. J., & Garrod, S. (2013). An integrated theory of language production and comprehension. *Behavioral and Brain Sciences*, 36, 329–47.

Pinker, S. (1989). *Learnability and Cognition: The Acquisition of Argument Structure*. MIT Press Cambridge, MA.

Plaut, D. C., McClelland, J. L., Seidenberg, M. S., & Patterson, K. (1996). Understanding normal and impaired word reading: Computational principles in quasi-regular domains. *Psychological Review*, 103(1), 56–115.

Prat-Sala, M., & Branigan, H. P. (2000). Discourse constraints on syntactic processing in language production: A cross-linguistic study in English and Spanish. *Journal of Memory and Language*, 42(2), 168–82.

Rapp, B., & Goldrick, M. (2000). Discreteness and interactivity in spoken word production. *Psychological Review*, 107(3), 460–99.

Rizzolatti, G., Fadiga, L., Gallese, V., & Fogassi, L. (1996). Premotor cortex and the recognition of motor actions. *Cognitive Brain Research*, 3(2), 131–41.

Roelofs, A., Meyer, A. S., & Levelt, W. J. M. (1998). A case for the lemma/lexeme distinction in models of speaking: Comment on Caramazza and Miozzo (1997). *Cognition*, 69, 219–30.

Rumelhart, D. E., & McClelland, J. L. (1986). On learning the past tenses of English verbs. In: McClelland, J. L., & Rumelhart, D. E. (Eds.), *Parallel Distributed Processing, Vol. 2: Psychological and Biological Models* (pp. 216–71). MIT Press, Cambridge, MA.

Schabes, Y., Abeille, A., & Joshi, A. K. (1988). *New parsing strategies for tree adjoining grammars*. Paper presented at the 12th International Conference on Computational Linguistics.

Schafer, A. J., Speer, S. R., Warren, P., & White, S. D. (2000). Intonational disambiguation in sentence production and comprehension. *Journal of Psycholinguistic Research*, 29(2), 169–82.

Scheepers, C. (2003). Syntactic priming of relative clause attachments: Persistence of structural configuration in sentence production. *Cognition*, 89(3), 179–205.

Scheepers, C., Sturt, P., Martin, C. J., Myachykov, A., Teevan, K., & Viskupova, I. (2011). Structural priming across cognitive domains: From simple arithmetic to relative-clause attachment. *Psychological Science*, 22, 1319–26.

Schober, M. F., & Brennan, S. E. (2003). Processes of interactive spoken discourse: The role of the partner. In: Graesser, A. C., & Gernsbacher, M. A. (Eds.), *Handbook of Discourse Processes* (pp. 123–64). Lawrence Erlbaum Associates, Mahwah, NJ.

Seidenberg, M. S., & McClelland, J. L. (1989). A distributed, developmental model of word recognition and naming. *Psychological Review, 96,* 523–68.

Skinner, B. F. (1957). *Verbal Behavior.* McGraw-Hill, New York, NY.

Slobin, D. I. (1996). From "thought and language" to "thinking for speaking". In: Gumperz, J., & Levinson, S. C. (Eds.), *Rethinking Linguistic Relativity* (pp. 70–96). Cambridge University Press, Cambridge.

Smith, M., & Wheeldon, L. (1999). High level processing scope in spoken sentence production. *Cognition, 73*(3), 205–46.

Smith, M., & Wheeldon, L. (2001). Syntactic priming in spoken sentence production: An on-line study. *Cognition, 78*(2), 123–64.

Snedeker, J., & Trueswell, J. (2003). Using prosody to avoid ambiguity: Effects of speaker awareness and referential context. *Journal of Memory and Language, 48*(1), 103–30.

Stemberger, J. P. (1985). An interactive activation model of language production. In: Ellis, A. (Ed.), *Progress in the Psychology of Language, Vol. 1* (pp. 143–86). Erlbaum, London.

Strijkers, K., & Costa, A. (2016). The cortical dynamics of speaking: Present shortcomings and future avenues. *Language, Cognition and Neuroscience, 31,* 484–503.

Strijkers, K., Costa, A., & Thierry, G. (2010). Tracking lexical access in speech production: Electrophysiological correlates of word frequency and cognate effects. *Cerebral Cortex, 20,* 912–28.

Swets, B., Jacovina, M. E., & Gerrig, R. J. (2014). Individual differences in the scope of speech planning: evidence from eye-movements. *Language and Cognition, 6*(1), 12–44.

Szmrecsanyi, B. (2004). *Persistence Phenomena in the Grammar of Spoken English* [Unpublished Ph. D. dissertation]. Albert-Ludwigs-Universität Freiburg, Freiburg, Germany.

Temperley, D. (2003). Ambiguity avoidance in English relative clauses. *Language, 79,* 464–84.

Thompson, S. A., & Mulac, A. (1991). The discourse conditions for the use of the complementizer *that* in conversational English. *Journal of Pragmatics, 15,* 237–51.

Thornton, R., & MacDonald, M. C. (2003). Plausibility and grammatical agreement. *Journal of Memory and Language, 48*(4), 740–59.

Tomasello, M. (2000). Do young children have adult syntactic competence? *Cognition, 74*(3), 209–53.

Ungerleider, L. G., & Haxby, J. V. (1994). "What" and "where" in the human brain. *Current Opinion in Neurobiology, 4,* 157–65.

Vigliocco, G., & Nicol, J. (1998). Separating hierarchical relations and word order in language production: Is proximity concord syntactic or linear? *Cognition, 68*(1), B13–B29.

Wheeldon, L., & Lahiri, A. (1997). Prosodic units in speech production. *Journal of Memory and Language, 37,* 356–81.

Whorf, B. L. (1956). The relation of habitual thought and behavior to language. In: Carroll, J. B. (Ed.), *Language, Thought, and Reality: Selected Writings of Benjamin Lee Whorf* (pp. 134–59). MIT Press, Cambridge, MA.

Wolpert, D. M. (1997). Computational approaches to motor control. *Trends in Cognitive Sciences, 1,* 209–16.

Yaguchi, M. (2001). The function of the non-deictic *that* in English. *Journal of Pragmatics, 33*(7), 1125–55.

SECTION III
Sentence and discourse level

CHAPTER 19

CROSS-LINGUISTIC/ BILINGUAL LANGUAGE PRODUCTION

FRANCESCA M. BRANZI, MARCO CALABRIA, AND ALBERT COSTA

19.1 The bilingual language control system: On the origin of the "hard problem"

It is largely known that even when they want to speak in one language alone, bilinguals experience the parallel activation of the two languages, during which a shared semantic representation simultaneously activates two possible lexical candidates (e.g., Colomé, 2001; Costa et al., 2000; Hermans, Bongaerts, De Bot, & Schreuder, 1998; Macizo, Bajo, & Martín, 2010; Poulisse, 1999; Thierry & Wu, 2007; Wu & Thierry, 2010, 2012). The evidence for such a phenomenon comes from different studies, such as those that have shown cognate effects[1] in naming latencies for bilinguals but not for monolinguals (Costa et al., 2000), studies that have revealed translation effects during phoneme monitoring tasks (Colomé, 2001), and other studies that have demonstrated that when accessing the intended language during comprehension tasks, bilinguals cannot avoid unconscious translation into the non-intended language (e.g., Thierry & Wu, 2007).

Importantly, the parallel activation of the two languages seems to have some consequences on bilingual language production. One of them is that language production in the non-dominant language (L2) is generally less efficient compared to that in the dominant language (L1), even in high-proficient bilinguals and in contexts in which only one language is used (e.g., Ivanova & Costa, 2008). Bilinguals are also slower in articulating

---

[1] "Cognate effects" are referred to in experimental comparisons between cognate and non-cognate words. *Cognates* are those translation words that have similar orthographic-phonological forms in the two languages of a bilingual (e.g., *tomato*—English, *tomate*—Spanish). *Non-cognates* are those translations that only share their meaning in the two languages (e.g., *apple*—English, *manzana*—Spanish).

complete words and sentences, and they often speak with a more or less perceptible foreign accent (Gollan, Fennema-Notestine, Montoya, & Jernigan, 2007; Gollan, Montoya, Cera, & Sandoval, 2008; Gollan & Silverberg, 2001; Ivanova & Costa, 2008; Kohnert, Hernández, & Bates, 1998; Roberts, Garcia, Desrochers, & Hernández, 2002). More surprisingly, in comparison to monolinguals, bilinguals also have speech production disadvantages when they speak in their L1. These effects have been observed in word naming latencies (Gollan et al., 2008; Gollan, Montoya, Fennema-Notestine, & Morris, 2005; Ivanova & Costa, 2008; Sadat, Martin, Alario, & Costa, 2012), in the amount of lexical items produced in standardized naming tests (e.g., Boston naming test) (Gollan et al., 2007; Kohnert, Hernández, & Bates, 1998; Roberts et al., 2002), and in timed verbal fluency tasks (Bialystok, Craik, & Luk, 2008; Gollan, Montoya, & Werner, 2002). Moreover, bilinguals, as compared to monolingual speakers, are more likely to encounter "tip of the tongue" states (i.e., the inability of retrieving a known word) (e.g., Gollan & Acenas, 2004; Gollan & Silverberg, 2001; Sandoval, Gollan, Ferreira, & Salmon, 2010). These observations suggest that lexicalization processes for bilingual speakers are harder in comparison to those of monolinguals, likely because of the simultaneous activation of two language systems.

However, this "problematic" situation seems to be somehow negotiable. In fact, cross-language intrusions are very rare in bilingual language production (e.g., Gollan, Sandoval, & Salmon, 2011). Moreover, even if lexical selection should be harder for high-proficient bilinguals than for low-proficient bilinguals—since in the former group the two lexical candidates for a given concept should be activated by the semantic systems with the same strength (e.g., Kroll & Stewart, 1994)—nevertheless, high-proficient bilinguals do not experience more difficulty speaking in one language instead of the other.

Therefore, the "hard problem" (see Finkbeiner, Gollan, & Caramazza, 2006) in bilingual speech production arises because a given semantic representation equally activates two translation equivalent lexical nodes and because, at the same time, the decision of speaking in one language cannot completely switch off the other language. In turn, these considerations have prompted the questions of how lexical selection in the intended language is achieved by bilinguals and how the interference from the non-intended language is avoided. As we will see, different models of bilingual language production have been proposed and empirically tested to answer these questions. In this chapter, we will first provide a critical overview of the most important models of bilingual language production. Then we will describe the most relevant evidence in support of them.

19.2 THE MECHANISMS OF BILINGUAL LANGUAGE PRODUCTION

To understand how spoken word production is accomplished in bilinguals when two or more alternatives are available, it is necessary to characterize the nature of cross-language activity and to specify the selection mechanisms. Various models of bilingual language production have been provided in the more than 20 years of research on bilingualism. These models can be divided into two main groups: language-specific vs. language-non-specific selection models. With a few exceptions, rather than differing in the extent to which the non-response language is activated, these models differ regarding the extent to which the two languages enter into competition (cross-language competition) and the nature of the selection mechanisms (language-specific vs. domain-general). In what follows, we will try to characterize the most important views on bilingual language production.

19.2.1 Language-specific selection models of bilingual language production

Some models have proposed that lexical selection in bilinguals is qualitatively similar to that of monolinguals (Costa & Caramazza, 1999; Costa, Miozzo, & Caramazza, 1999; Finkbeiner, Gollan, & Caramazza, 2006; La Heij, 2005). Within this category, a model of bilingual language production proposes that lexical selection is not a competitive process, either in monolingual or in bilingual language production (see "differential activation account" in Finkbeiner, Gollan, & Caramazza, 2006). According to this model, the ease with which a given word is selected is independent from the relative activation of competitors (Finkbeiner & Caramazza, 2006; Janssen et al., 2008; Mahon et al., 2007; Miozzo & Caramazza, 2003; Navarrete, Mahon, & Caramazza, 2010), and lexical selection is achieved by means of a "selection by threshold" mechanism that determines whether and how fast a given word is selected.

Other models propose that lexical access is a competitive process, but just within languages. In other words, competition during lexical access would arise only between semantic competitors but not between translation equivalents. One of these accounts, the "concept selection account," proposes that the activation levels of translation equivalents will never approximate each other since the intended language is already specified at the conceptual level. That is, the lexical nodes of the intended language are activated by the semantic system to a substantially higher level than lexical nodes in the non-intended language (La Heij, 2005). This account, however, is difficult to reconcile with evidence suggesting that language production is not fully serial (e.g., Caramazza, 1997; Dell, 1986; Levelt, Roelofs, & Meyer, 1999; Miozzo et al., 2015; Morsella & Miozzo, 2002; Navarrete & Costa, 2005; see also Strijkers, 2016) and with evidence showing the presence of languages' coactivation in bilinguals, even when they want to speak only in one language (e.g., Colomé, 2001; Costa et al., 2000).

Another influential model proposes that although an active conceptual representation and those related to it are simultaneously activated in the two languages, a lexicon-external device enables bilinguals to select the lexical representations of the intended language without considering those of the non-intended language (Costa et al., 1999; Costa & Caramazza, 1999). This account, like that proposed by La Heij (2005), assumes that "selection" is language-specific. However, in this model the "selection" has its effects at the lexical level instead of at the conceptual level (La Heij, 2005).

Finally, another view implemented in the WEAVER++ model of spoken word production suggests that language selection is guided by condition-action rules that make explicit reference to behavioral goals (see Roelofs & Verhoef, 2006). In particular, these condition-action rules would determine what is selected from the activated lexical information depending on the intended language (e.g., <IF the concept is HOUSE(X) and the target language is Spanish,

THEN select "casa">). Hence, similarly to Costa et al. (1999), linguistic representations of the intended language can be selected without considering those of the non-intended language.

19.2.2 Language-non-specific selection models of bilingual language production: The inhibitory control model

According to other models, not only are the two lexical systems simultaneously activated during bilingual language production, but such systems also enter into competition (e.g., de Bot, 1992; Green, 1986, 1998; Hermans et al., 1998; Lee & Williams, 2001; Poulisse & Bongaerts, 1994). This competition is then resolved by an inhibitory mechanism that suppresses the activation of the lexical items belonging to the non-intended language.

To date, the inhibitory control model (ICM; Green, 1986, 1998) has been the one within this view that has received the most experimental attention (e.g., Levy, McVeigh, Marful, & Anderson, 2007; Linck, Kroll, & Sunderman, 2009; Misra, Guo, Bobb, & Kroll, 2012; Philipp, Gade, & Koch, 2007). The ICM (Green, 1986, 1998) proposes that during lexicalization the two languages of a bilingual become concurrently activated and that such activation leads to cross-language competition. To cope with the competition, an inhibitory control mechanism operates over the lexical representations of the non-intended language to reduce or suppress their activation.

Hence, when a bilingual wants to speak in a given language (e.g., English), the inhibition of the non-intended language (e.g., Spanish) is achieved through lexicon-external task-schemas that allow control of output goals (e.g., "name in English"). The specific way in which this operation is achieved is by projecting inhibitory signals from the task-schemas to all the lexical representations that contain a language tag of the non-intended language (i.e., Spanish). Consequently, the level of activation of Spanish is reduced, and therefore cross-language interference is also reduced. According to the ICM, this process allows bilinguals to select the lexical items from the intended language. For example, when an English-Spanish bilingual plans to name a picture in English (e.g., *chair*), the language schemas will suppress the activation of all the lemmas with an incorrect language tag. Therefore, in our example *silla* will be inhibited, in addition to all the semantically related words in Spanish (e.g., *mesa*).

This view also posits three important assumptions regarding the functioning of the inhibitory control system. First, the amount of inhibition applied to a given language depends on the strength with which its representations are activated to begin with. Hence, when trying to speak in the L2, the inhibition applied to the L1 is higher than vice versa. This assumption comes from the reactive nature of the inhibitory system, in the sense that inhibitory control is applied only after the lexical representations of the non-intended language have been activated. Second, the activation of previously inhibited representations (i.e., overcoming inhibition) requires time. Hence, the stronger the inhibition applied, the more time is needed to overcome it. Taken together, these assumptions lead to predicting that recovering from L1 inhibition will require more time and cognitive sources than in the case of L2 inhibition. Third, according to this model bilingual language control is considered an instantiation of motor action. Thus, those cognitive and neural processes underlying language control (i.e., inhibitory control) are recruited from those of action control (see Abutalebi & Green, 2007, 2008). Hence, if bilingual language control mechanisms are not language-specific, one should expect that the performance of the same bilinguals in language control and domain-general executive control tasks should be somehow related. In the following section we present some experimental studies that have put to the test the models of bilingual language production.

19.3 Testing accounts of bilingual language selection

Regardless of the specific experimental task employed, the two groups of models reviewed here might lead to the formulation of different predictions. For instance, according to language-specific selection models one should expect to find a lack of cross-language competition during bilingual language production. Rather, if language-specific models are correct, one should find qualitatively similar effects when comparing the mechanisms of lexical access within or between languages. In addition, if language selection processes in bilinguals are language-specific, as Costa et al. (1999) have proposed, the continuous use of them (i.e., during language switching) should affect just the domain of language and not be transferred to other domains of cognition. In other words, if we were to compare the control mechanisms involved in language selection and those involved in domain-general response selection in the same bilingual participants, we should not find any overlap.

Conversely, according to language-non-specific models of language production, and specifically the ICM (Green, 1998), one should expect to find experimental support for the presence of cross-language competition and for the presence of inhibitory control in the task. Furthermore, since according to this model inhibition is a domain-general mechanism, we should expect to find evidence of an overlap between mechanisms involved in language control and those involved in non-linguistic control.

Next, we critically review the behavioral, neurophysiological, and neuroimaging evidence supporting one or the other view on bilingual language production. In doing so, we particularly focus on the findings issued from the picture-word interference and language switching paradigms. Beyond that, we also provide some evidence coming from other experimental designs that have tried to disentangle the language-specific and language-non-specific models.

19.3.1 Picture-word interference paradigm

A consistent set of evidence in support of the first group of models (language-specific selection models) comes from the picture-word interference (PWI) paradigm (Glaser & Glaser, 1989; Lupker, 1979). The monolingual version of this task requires participants to name pictures and, at the same time, to ignore a superimposed distractor word. A common finding is that naming a picture (e.g., *cat*) takes longer when the distractor is semantically related to the picture to be named (e.g., *dog*), as compared to when the distractor is not semantically related to it (e.g., *spoon*). This is the result that one would expect if lexical selection involves competition between semantically related items. In fact, in the semantically related condition, the lexical representation corresponding to the distracter word (*dog*) would receive activation from two sources, that is, from the distractor and from the picture (of a *cat*) to be named. Instead, in the semantically unrelated condition, the lexical representation that corresponds to the distractor word (*spoon*) would receive activation from the written word only. This would result in different activation levels for lexical representations of distractors in semantically related and unrelated conditions. That is, following the previous example, the interference effect would be observed because the related distracter word *dog* becomes a stronger competitor than *spoon*, in that the activation level of its lexical representation (*dog*) is higher than that of *spoon*.

Various researchers interested in studying how bilinguals manage cross-language activation have employed a bilingual version of this paradigm. This has been done according to the idea that lexical selection is a competitive mechanism, and therefore the PWI effect would be greatest when pictures are displayed with translation equivalent distractors. In fact, by definition translation equivalents are different lexical representations that share the same conceptual representation. Therefore, they might be considered as even more closely related than semantically related words within a single language. Hence, if a Spanish-English bilingual has to name a picture of a *cat* in Spanish (*gato*), the English translation equivalent (*cat*) should slow down naming latencies more than the case in which the same bilingual has to name the same picture (*gato*), but this time superimposed with a semantically related distractor within the same language (*dog*).

Even if this is a reasonable hypothesis, various studies have found that rather than increasing the interference effect, the translation equivalent distractors facilitate naming latencies during picture naming (Costa et al., 1999; Costa & Caramazza, 1999). In other words, when a given picture to be named is superimposed with a word that corresponds to its translation equivalent, bilinguals name that picture faster as compared to when this picture is superimposed with an unrelated distractor. This facilitatory effect has been explained as resulting from a priming effect at the lexical level. That is, in the previous example the distractor word *cat* would have primed the activation level of the lexical representations of *gato* via the conceptual system.

These results suggest that translation equivalents facilitate access to the other language rather than impair its retrieval. Hence, one might be tempted to conclude that bilingual language selection does not involve cross-language competition (see Costa et al., 1999) and that it is qualitatively similar to that of monolinguals; that is, language selection would be competitive just within languages.

Nonetheless, these findings have received some criticism, since the facilitatory effect observed when the distractor word is the strongest (cross-language) competitor of the target response (Costa et al., 1999) could be embraced by alternative explanations that the PWI design is not able to parse. In detail, it has been questioned whether this facilitation occurs mainly at the lexical or at the conceptual level (e.g., Abutalebi & Green, 2007; Hermans, 2004). Indeed, the facilitatory effect observed by Costa et al. (1999) might have been determined by a strong priming effect occurring at the conceptual level rather than by an effect occurring at the lexical level (e.g., Hermans et al., 1998). Some authors have argued that this facilitatory effect might be stronger than the cost of resolving cross-language competition (see Abutalebi & Green, 2007; Hermans, 2004), in that lexical inhibition might occur at the lexical level, but then it would be over-ruled by a stronger priming effect originating at the conceptual level.

In respect to these considerations and beyond, a group of successive studies has suggested the limitations of the PWI paradigm to test how language selection is achieved in bilinguals and monolinguals (e.g., Costa, Alario, & Caramazza, 2005; Dhooge & Hartsuiker, 2010, 2011; Finkbeiner & Caramazza, 2006; Janssen, Schirm, Mahon, & Caramazza, 2008; Mahon et al., 2007; Miozzo & Caramazza, 2003). For instance, it has been suggested that the PWI paradigm, rather than constraining lexical access processes, would implicate general response selection processes (see Finkbeiner et al., 2006). For all the reasons mentioned here, this paradigm has become less popular for tackling questions related to the mechanisms of bilingual language production. In the following, we will review evidence coming from the language switching literature.

19.3.2 Language switching

A consistent set of evidence in support of the second group of models (language-non-specific models of language production) comes from different instantiations of the language switching paradigm (e.g., Branzi et al., 2015; Branzi, Calabria, Boscarino, & Costa, 2016; Branzi, Martin, Abutalebi, & Costa, 2014; Costa & Santesteban, 2004; Costa, Santesteban, & Ivanova, 2006; Guo, Liu, Misra, & Kroll, 2011; Jackson, Swainson, Cunnington, & Jackson, 2001; Meuter & Allport, 1999; for recent reviews see Baus, Branzi, & Costa, 2015; Costa, Branzi, & Ávila, 2016). Despite the differences between the different instantiations (i.e., trial-by-trial or blocked switching tasks), they all involve speakers using their two languages in such a way that it is possible to measure the after-effects of using one language on the subsequent use of the other language.

19.3.2.1 *The trial-by-trial language switching task*

The trial-by-trial language switching task (e.g., Christoffels, Firk, & Schiller, 2007; Jackson et al., 2001; Meuter & Allport, 1999; Wang, Xue, Chen, Xue, & Dong, 2007) is likely the most used instantiation of the language switching paradigm. This version of the task comes from the domain-general task switching literature (e.g., Allport, Styles, & Hsieh, 1994; Allport & Wylie, 1999; Jersild, 1927; Monsell, 2003). Most of the studies using this paradigm assume a tight relationship between the bilingual language control mechanisms and those involved in domain-general executive control (e.g., Meuter & Allport, 1999). In the trial-by-trial language switching task, bilinguals are required to name some pictures in one language and some other pictures in the other language, with the presentation of these pictures mixed. The language in which a given picture must be named is indicated by a cue (e.g., color of the picture). Generally, in these tasks there are two types of trials: trials in which the language to be used is the same as that of the previous trial ("repeat" trials; AA language sequences) and trials in which the language to be used is different from that of the previous trial ("switch" trials; BA task sequences). The difference between naming latencies of switch and repeat trials results in the "switch cost" or "n-1 shift cost." One possible interpretation of the origin of this switch cost is the deployment of inhibitory control on the non-response language (or task) (Green, 1986, 1998; Meuter & Allport, 1999). For example, in a BA language sequence, naming in the language B would entail the inhibition of the language A. Hence, when the language A needs to be produced in the successive trial, more time is needed to activate the previously inhibited representations. This interpretation is consistent with the main assumptions of the ICM (Green, 1986, 1998), although this is not the only possible explanation of the phenomenon (e.g., Koch, Gade, Schuch, & Philipp, 2010; Yeung & Monsell, 2003; see also Branzi et al., 2014). One of the most highly considered indices of the presence of inhibitory control in the task is probably the "asymmetrical switch cost" (Calabria et al., 2012; Costa et al., 2006; Costa & Santesteban, 2004; Jackson et al., 2001; Linck, Schwieter, & Sunderman, 2012; Macizo, Bajo, & Paoleri, 2012; Meuter & Allport, 1999; Philipp et al., 2007; Schwieter & Sunderman, 2008; Wang et al., 2007). This refers to the observation of larger switch costs when switching to the dominant language as compared to when switching to the non-dominant language (e.g., Jackson et al., 2001; Meuter & Allport, 1999). Similarly, asymmetrical switch costs are found in non-linguistic versions of the switching task, if tasks of different difficulty/strength are involved (e.g., Martin et al., 2011).

The evidence of asymmetries in linguistic switch costs is in accord with the ICM, since it proposes that the amount of inhibition applied on one language is proportional to its strength (level of activation). Hence, in the case of a difference of strength between the two languages (e.g., unbalanced bilinguals), one would expect that more inhibition would be necessary to inhibit L1 during L2 production than to inhibit L2 during L1 production. Since the switch cost is a measure of the after-effects of this inhibition, these after-effects are supposed to be more detrimental when the switch is to L1 (due to the need of recovering from a strong inhibition) than when the switch is to L2 (e.g., Costa et al., 2006; Costa & Santesteban, 2004; Jackson et al., 2001; Meuter and Allport, 1999). Moreover, it has also been found that bilinguals with equal strength in the two languages (high-proficient and balanced bilinguals) show symmetrical switch costs, likely because the same amount of inhibition is deployed on the non-intended language when speaking in L1 or in L2 (e.g., Costa & Santesteban, 2004).

Electrophysiology literature provides some evidence in accord with the idea that bilingual language control is implemented through inhibition. The critical component of event related potentials (ERPs) is a negative deflection typically observable in switch trials when compared to repeat trials (e.g., Jackson et al., 2001). This enhanced negativity peaks around 200–250 ms after stimulus presentation (N200). In the context of domain-general executive control tasks (e.g., Go/NoGo tasks), this component has often been interpreted as revealing inhibitory processes, although other interpretations have been advanced (e.g., Nieuwenhuis, Yeung, van den Wildenberg, & Ridderinkhof, 2003). In a trial-by-trial language switching task, Jackson et al. (2001) found that switch trials elicited an increased N200 relative to repeat trials. Interestingly, this N200 modulation associated with language switching was only present when switching into the L2. Such asymmetry was interpreted as revealing that the L1 must be strongly inhibited when accessing lexical representations in the L2.

Neuroimaging studies on language switching have revealed asymmetries in brain activation like those found in behavioral and electrophysiological studies. For example, in a functional magnetic resonance imaging (fMRI) study, Wang et al. (2007) tested a group of late Chinese-English bilinguals in a trial-by-trial language switching task and found a behavioral asymmetry in switch costs (i.e., larger switch costs for L1 than for L2) like that reported in previous studies (see Jackson et al., 2001; Meuter & Allport, 1999). Along with this finding, Wang et al. (2007) also observed that switching into L2 only activated brain areas involved in executive control and inhibition, such as frontal areas, the anterior cingulate cortex (ACC), and the supplementary motor area (SMA) (e.g., Garavan, Ross, Murphy, Roche, & Stein,

2002; Garavan, Ross, & Stein, 1999). This asymmetry was interpreted as a result of increased demands on the domain-general executive control system, to allow successful L2 production and avoid competition from the L1, an explanation clearly in line with the ICM (for similar results in language comprehension, see van Heuven, Schriefers, Dijkstra, & Hagoort, 2008).

All in all, the results reviewed here contrast with the PWI findings provided by Costa et al. (1999). In fact, they suggest that producing a given word in a given language does not facilitate the successive retrieval of its translation equivalent. Rather, they indicate that speaking in one language hampers the access to the lexicon of the other language, therefore suggesting a certain degree of cross-language competition.

In respect to the question of the domain-generality of the mechanisms involved in bilingual language control, the neuroimaging literature suggests that the brain network involved in language switching overlaps, at least to some extent, the network involved in non-linguistic task switching (Abutalebi & Green, 2007, 2008; Branzi et al., 2015; de Baene, Duyck, Brass, & Carreiras, 2015; de Bruin, Roelofs, Dijkstra, & Fitzpatrick, 2014; see also Luk, Green, Abutalebi, & Grady, 2012, for a meta-analysis of brain areas involved in language switching). In other words, switching between languages and switching between non-linguistic tasks elicit similar brain activations. Therefore, these observations are in accord with the tenets of language-non-specific models of bilingual language production that propose that bilingual language control functioning is achieved through the same mechanisms and brain areas of domain-general executive control (Abutalebi & Green, 2007; Green, 1998). Moreover, this seems consistent with lesion studies in bilingual patients presenting deficits of language control. That is, bilingual speakers with pathological language mixing and switching following damage over the fronto-striatal network also have executive control deficits (e.g., Leemann, Laganaro, Schwitter, & Schnider, 2007; Mariën, Abutalebi, Engelborghs, & de Deyn, 2005) or pathological performance in non-linguistic switching tasks (Calabria et al., 2014). These results suggest that bilingual language control is just an instance of the functioning of a domain-general executive control system.

Even though the evidence reviewed here dovetails quite well with various assumptions of the ICM (Green, 1986, 1998), another series of studies has reported results that are hardly reconcilable with this view. One clear example is provided in Costa and Santesteban (2004; see also Costa et al., 2006), where high-proficient bilinguals were required to switch between two languages of different strength (their L1 and a much weaker L3). Results revealed an unexpected pattern: symmetrical rather than asymmetrical switch costs (Costa et al., 2006; Costa & Santesteban, 2004). These results are problematic for the ICM, since switching between languages of different strengths should lead to asymmetrical switch costs. Hence, the authors proposed an explanation that represents a feasible way out for the ICM: high-proficient bilinguals are a "special case" of bilingual language control. That is, in contrast to low-proficient bilinguals, they do not need to resort to inhibition to control their languages. As previously described, there are other models of bilingual language control that propose mechanisms different from inhibition (see Costa et al., 1999). Hence, Costa and Santesteban (2004) have argued that in high-proficient bilinguals the simple intention to speak in the intended language allows these "language-specific selection mechanisms" to select the intended language while ignoring the activation of the lexicon of the non-intended language. Importantly, once these "language-specific selection mechanisms" are developed in high-proficient bilinguals, they can also be applied to languages with different strengths (Costa et al., 2006; Costa & Santesteban, 2004; Schwieter & Sunderman, 2008). Unfortunately, such an interesting proposal has been undermined by multiple observations. First, high-proficient bilinguals also show asymmetrical switch costs when switching between an L3 and an L4 or between L1 and a newly learned language (Costa et al., 2006). Second, symmetrical switch costs have also been revealed in low-proficient bilinguals (e.g., Christoffels et al. 2007; Prior & Gollan, 2011).

Moreover, it has also been found that switch cost patterns are affected by experimental variables that are not related to bilingualism at all, such as task predictability (Gollan & Ferreira, 2009), preparation times (Ma, Li, & Guo, 2016; Verhoef, Roelofs, & Chwilla, 2009), or the type of stimuli involved in the task (Finkbeiner, Almeida, Janssen, & Caramazza, 2006). In addition to this evidence that is problematic for the ICM, Finkbeiner et al. (2006) reported asymmetrical switch costs and a lack of switch costs depending on the type of stimuli involved in the task. In this experiment, participants named digits either in L1 or L2, according to the language cue. The experiment also included some pictures that had to be named only in L1. Naming latencies for the digits revealed an asymmetrical switch cost, with longer naming latencies for switching into L1. Conversely, there was no switch cost for picture naming. In other words, picture naming in L1 was not affected by the language in which the previous digit was named (the same or not), but rather it depended on whether the items used in the experiment needed to be named in the two languages (bivalent stimulus) or not (univalent stimulus).

Beyond behavioral findings, some electrophysiological and neuroimaging evidence is inconsistent with the ICM. For instance, in assorted studies the modulation of the N200 has behaved rather differently than the original findings of Jackson et al. (2001). Sometimes the modulation of the N200 was present for the L1, but only for repeat trials rather than for switch trials (Christoffels et al., 2007). Moreover, Verhoef et al. (2009) showed that the N200 component related to inhibition was sensitive to preparation times but not to language switch effects. This suggests that some caution should be exercised when interpreting the N200 modulation as an unequivocal index of inhibition in bilingual speech production.

When going to the neuroimaging evidence, the interpretation of asymmetries/symmetries in the language switching tasks is no simpler. In fact, if in low-proficient bilinguals the asymmetrical involvement of executive control brain areas (e.g., frontal areas, the SMA, and the ACC) reflects L1 inhibition in the linguistic switching task (see Wang et al., 2007), a symmetrical neural switch cost for high-proficient bilinguals should be observable. That is, we might expect to observe in high-proficient bilinguals a similar involvement of the aforementioned areas, regardless of the direction of the language switch. However, Garbin et al. (2011) found that in high-proficient bilinguals, switches from the L1 to the L2 activated the left caudate. Instead, the reverse switches activated other areas involved in executive control, such as the presupplementary motor area (pre-SMA). Arguably, it is possible that the involvement of different neural substrates in language switching does not correspond directly to the magnitude of the behavioral switch cost (see Garbin et al., 2011). Interestingly, such directionality is also observed in patients who make pathological switching; that is, in many cases the cross-language intrusions are always from one to the other language and not in the opposite direction. Moreover, in language switching tasks, such patients make more cross-language errors when required to switch from their L2 to their L1 (Calabria et al., 2014).

All in all, the aforementioned evidence poses some challenges to the ICM (Green, 1998) and highlights how the evidence for cross-language competition and inhibitory control based on the patterns of switch costs is rather unstable. Consequently, it has been questioned whether asymmetries of switch costs reflect the effects of inhibitory control in linguistic switching tasks. In fact, switch costs and asymmetries do not necessarily reflect the workings of inhibitory control processes (see Koch et al., 2010). For example, switch costs might be caused by a carryover effect of the previously activated language (or task) that negatively affects the current switch trial (see Philipp et al., 2007; Yeung & Monsell, 2003). Thus, the asymmetries of linguistic switch costs could be explained by assuming that during production, the L2 needs to be overactivated as compared to the L1. This language activation might interfere during switch trials more when switching to L1 than when switching to L2 (e.g., Yeung & Monsell, 2003; see also Koch et al., 2010), leading to the same asymmetrical switch cost.

Therefore, to shed light on the origin of asymmetrical switch costs, researchers have tested another type of switch cost which has been proposed to measure inhibitory control only. This cost is the "n-2 repetition cost" (e.g., Mayr & Keele, 2000), and it is measured in switching tasks in which participants are required to switch among three tasks (e.g., A, B, C). The general observation is that response times (RTs) for ABA task sequences are slower than those for CBA task sequences. Hence, the presence of the n-2 repetition cost proves that the execution of task B during an ABA task sequence elicits the inhibition of the just executed task (A). In fact, if this were not the case, faster RTs would be observed in ABA task sequences as compared to CBA ones.

The ICM hence would predict the following pattern of n-2 repetition costs: larger for the L1 than for the L2. Interestingly, Philipp et al. (2007) found an asymmetrical n-2 repetition cost that was larger for the L1 rather than for two non-dominant languages (L2 and L3). This finding is clearly consistent with the ICM. However, according to the ICM, the magnitude of the n-2 repetition cost should have been larger for the L2 as compared to the L3. Indeed, the authors found that the n-2 repetition cost was larger for the L3 than for the L2, a result that is clearly at odds with the ICM. Further attempts of detecting any modulation of the n-2 repetition cost associated with language proficiency have not produced the expected results (Guo, Liu, Chen, & Li, 2013; Philipp & Koch, 2009) or have failed to detect n-2 repetition costs at all (Guo, Ma, & Liu, 2013), leading to the conclusion that the evidence for the n-2 repetition cost in support of the ICM seems to be unsteady and does not provide a consistent picture of the mechanisms involved in bilingual language control. Nevertheless, the fact that the large majority of the studies reviewed here have reported significant switch costs suggests that the nature of cross-language activity might be competitive.

In respect to the assumption about the domain-generality of language selection mechanisms, although some studies have suggested some overlap between linguistic and non-linguistic mechanisms, recent findings have undermined these conclusions. For instance, in a recent study we demonstrated that the involvement of inhibitory control measured through the n-1 shift cost and the n-2 repetition cost is different in linguistic and non-linguistic tasks (Branzi et al., 2016; see also Babcock & Vallesi, 2015). Precisely, we failed to reveal any correlation between the n-1 shift cost and the n-2 repetition cost between language switching and domain-general task switching. This finding, along with other previous ones (Babcock & Vallesi, 2015; Calabria et al., 2012, 2015; Cattaneo et al., 2015; Prior & Gollan, 2013) is clearly at odds with the prediction of the ICM.

Finally, it has been suggested that the workings of bilingual language production may be better tested by employing other kinds of paradigms that do not require continuous allocation of attention for language selection, such as in trial-by-trial language switching paradigms, but that rather allow restriction of production to one language alone (e.g., Costa, La Heij, & Navarrete, 2006; Finkbeiner, Almeida, Janssen, & Caramazza 2006; Finkbeiner, Gollan, & Caramazza, 2006). This is particularly relevant for assessing issues related to cross-language competition and domain-generality of the mechanisms. In fact, in trial-by-trial switching, between-language competition might be artificially triggered by the need for continuous switching between languages. However, this competition might not arise in all naming contexts, leaving open the possibility that trial-by-trial switching paradigms measure response selection processes, not necessarily lexical access processes.

For these reasons, the mechanisms of bilingual language control have recently been investigated through another instantiation of the language switching paradigm that does not require switching continuously between languages. In the following section we provide a description of this instantiation along with the most important findings.

19.3.2.2 *The blocked language switching task*

Beyond the switch cost that measures the after-effects of one language on the other one in a mixed context, there is a way to measure the after-effects of one language on the other one in single naming contexts (e.g., Branzi et al., 2014, 2015; Misra et al., 2012; Strijkers et al., 2013). In this design, participants are typically required to name an entire block of pictures in one language and then another block of pictures in the other language. Hence, the comparison of RTs for the same language after and before naming in the other language allows measurement of the after-effects of one language on the other one in single naming contexts.

Some evidence suggests that only L1 production is affected by previous naming in the other language. For example, it has been shown that naming a set of pictures in L1 was hampered when the very same pictures were previously named in L2, as compared to naming them in L1 first. This was indicated by the absence of a behavioral priming effect that is generally observed when the same pictures are repeated in a task. Conversely, this priming effect was observed when naming a set of pictures in L2 after L1, as compared to naming them in L2 first (Branzi et al., 2014; Misra et al., 2012). Interestingly, in the study by Misra and collaborators (2012), these behavioral asymmetries were accompanied by ERP effects related to inhibitory control (N200 enhanced negativity; see Falkenstein, Hoormann, & Hohnsbein, 1999; Jodo & Kayama, 1992). In an fMRI study implementing a similar design, Guo et al. (2011) did not find the same behavioral asymmetries between languages. However, the lack of this effect in the behavioral responses was somehow compensated by the fact that these asymmetries were observable in the brain activations. That is, compared to naming in L1 first, naming in L1 after L2 elicited the activation of a brain network of frontal, parietal, and temporal areas known to be involved in bilingual language control (see Abutalebi & Green, 2007, 2008; Green & Abutalebi, 2013). Instead, compared to naming in L2 first, naming in L2 after L1 elicited a completely different pattern of brain activations, since only visual processing areas were involved. All in all, these results might be considered in accord with the idea that in order to produce the intended language bilinguals inhibit the non-intended language (e.g., Green, 1986, 1998), likely a consequence of cross-language competition.

19.3.3 Other experimental evidence

Several other experiments have been conducted to investigate how performance in one language is affected by the previous use of a different language (e.g., Lee & Williams, 2001; Levy, McVeigh, Marful, & Anderson, 2007; Runnqvist & Costa, 2012). For instance, among the literature on memory, Levy and collaborators (2007) showed that naming pictures in L2 negatively affects the subsequent recall of the corresponding L1 translations (the so-called retrieval-induced forgetting [RIF] effect across languages). The RIF effect was interpreted as reflecting an inhibitory mechanism that suppresses the strong interference of the L1 lexical entry when the L2 correspondent must be retrieved from memory. Because of this L1 inhibition during L2 retrieval, the subsequent recall of L1 is hindered. However, the existence of this effect has recently been questioned by Runnqvist and Costa (2012). In their study, the authors tested three diverse groups of bilinguals (low-, medium- and high-proficient in the L2) in an RIF paradigm like the one used by Levy et al. (2007). They found a result opposite to Levy et al. (2007): naming a picture in the L2 facilitated the subsequent recall of the translation in the L1, so no RIF effect was present. Thus, the hypothetical inhibition of the L1 during L2 retrieval is still unresolved.

Other relevant evidence comes from studies in which the models of bilingual language production have been tested by measuring the effect of cumulative semantic interference (CSI). This effect refers to the finding that when naming pictures belonging to the same semantic category (e.g., *cat, dog, pig*), RTs increase linearly every time a new member of the same category is named (e.g., Brown, 1981; Canini et al., 2016; Costa, Strijkers, Martin, & Thierry, 2009; Howard et al., 2006; Navarrete et al., 2010; Oppenheim et al., 2010). In detail, in the monolingual version of this task, the CSI is measured in a paradigm in which several members of various categories are intermixed with a varying lag between them (e.g., the category members may be separated by 2, 4, 6, or 8 intervening items). Hence, authors manipulate the semantic category membership and the ordinal position of the pictures to be named. Generally, it is observed that, independently of lag, naming latencies increase by approximately 20 ms every time a new semantic category member is named. As in the PWI tasks, the presence of CSI has been interpreted as a consequence of lexical competition (the activation level of *cat* affects the retrieval of *dog*). Runnqvist et al. (2012) implemented a bilingual version of this task to disentangle language-specific and language-non-specific models of bilingual language production. Specifically, they compared one experiment in which they measured CSI without language alternation (language invariant) with another experiment in which they asked participants to alternate between the two languages (language alternating). According to language-non-specific selection models, the inhibition of a complete language system should have erased the presence of CSI effects both between and within languages during the language alternating as compared to the language invariant condition. However, according to the language-specific selection model, the CSI effect in the language alternating condition should have had a different magnitude as compared to that measured in the language invariant condition. In fact, the language-specific selection model predicts the presence of two parallel cumulative effects in the language alternating condition, one for each language. This is because the lexical activation of the two languages will never enter into competition. Therefore, semantic interference should not accumulate across languages but only within languages, and the magnitude of the CSI effect in the language alternating condition should be half that of the language invariant condition.

The predictions of the two models were clearly at odds with the results provided by Runnqvist et al. (2012). In fact, the authors found that the CSI effect was indistinguishable in both conditions (i.e., alternating and invariant), indicating that CSI is not sensitive to naming context. All in all, the data from the RIF and CSI literature does not help to clarify the questions related to the nature of cross-language activity and selection mechanisms.

19.4 CONCLUSION

In this chapter we have provided a critical overview of the most prominent psycholinguistic models on bilingual language production. In doing so, we have tackled different theoretical issues that are currently controversial in this field. The first one has to do with the consequences of languages coactivation on lexical selection; that is, whether it leads to cross-language competition. The second one has to do with the nature of the mechanisms of language production, that is, whether they are domain-general or specific to language.

Two different groups of models have provided different views on these issues. Promoters of language-specific mechanisms assume that during language selection the two languages of bilinguals do not enter into competition and that selection mechanisms are language-specific. Alternately, other researchers assume that the two languages of a bilingual compete during lexical access and that language selection mechanisms are non-specific to language.

Given the contrasting sets of evidence, providing an answer to these questions becomes quite challenging, if not imprudent. In fact, the current theories do not fully account for the available data. Even those studies that tested language-specific and language-non-specific accounts of bilingual language production within the very same experiment (Costa et al., 1999; Runnqvist et al., 2012) were not able to provide results supporting one or the other group of models.

In an attempt to deal with this situation, some researchers have proposed revised versions or even new models of bilingual language production (Declerck et al., 2015; Runnqvist et al., 2012; for a model based on electrophysiological data, see also Strijkers, 2016). Many of these models, however, have been designed to account for specific findings and have not been properly tested so far (e.g., Declerck et al., 2015; Runnqvist et al., 2012). Hopefully, future investigations will undertake the arduous task of validating them.

Regardless, the majority of available evidence (see switching studies and particularly evidence from blocked language switching) might suggest that cross-language competition is likely to occur during bilingual language production, even when naming in single naming contexts. This would confer some support to the language-non-specific accounts of lexical selection in bilinguals. However, some caution must be taken because experimental evidence of such cross-language competition has not been consistently replicated. Moreover, the domain-generality of the mechanisms predicted by these models has been called into question by a set of recent findings. Indeed, it has been consistently shown that certain indices of cross-language interference and inhibition (i.e., switch costs) are not related to similar indices in non-linguistic domains. In this regard, further research is needed to clarify in more detail the exact mechanisms of control that are shared between the two domains and those that are specific. For instance, some researchers recently went beyond the assessment of measurements related to reactive control (e.g., switch costs) only by measuring the overlap between language control and domain-general executive control for proactive control (e.g., mixing costs) (e.g., Cattaneo et al., 2015; Prior & Gollan, 2013). Therefore, understanding the extent to which reactive and proactive control mechanisms are involved in language and related to non-linguistic domains might be one potential way to improve the existing models of bilingual language production.

References

Abutalebi, J., & Green, D. W. (2007). Bilingual language production: The neurocognition of language representation and control. *Journal of Neurolinguistics, 20*(3), 242–75.

Abutalebi, J., & Green, D. W. (2008). Control mechanisms in bilingual language production: Neural evidence from language switching studies. *Language and Cognitive Processes, 23*(4), 557–82.

Allport, A., Styles, E. A., & Hsieh, S. (1994). Shifting intentional set: Exploring the dynamic control of tasks. In: Umilta, C., & Moscovitch, M. (Eds.), *Attention and Performance XV: Concious and Nonconcious Information Processing, Vol. 15* (pp. 421–52). Erlbaum, Hillsdale, NJ.

Allport, A., & Wylie, G. (1999). Task switching: Positive and negative priming of task-set. In: Humphreys, G. W., Duncan, J., & Treisman, A. M. (Eds.), *Attention, Space and Action: Studies in Cognitive Neuroscience* (pp. 273–96). Oxford University Press, Oxford.

Babcock, L., & Vallesi, A. (2015). Language control is not a one-size-fits-all languages process: Evidence from simultaneous interpretation students and the n-2 repetition cost. *Frontiers in Psychology, 6*, 1622.

Baus, C., Branzi, F., & Costa, A. (2015). On the mechanism and scope of language control in bilingual speech production. In: Schwieter, J. W., (Ed.), *The Cambridge Handbook of Bilingual Processing* (pp. 508–26). [Online]. *Cambridge Handbooks in Language and Linguistics.* Cambridge University Press, Cambridge. Cambridge Books Online. Available at: http://dx.doi.org/10.1017/CBO9781107447257.022.

Bialystok, E., Craik, F., & Luk, G. (2008). Cognitive control and lexical access in younger and older bilinguals. *Journal of Experimental Psychology: Learning, Memory, and Cognition, 34*(4), 859–73.

Branzi, F. M., Calabria, M., Boscarino, M. L., & Costa, A. (2016). On the overlap between bilingual language control and domain-general executive control. *Acta Psychologica, 166*, 21–30.

Branzi, F. M., Della Rosa, P. A., Canini, M., Costa, A., & Abutalebi, J. (2015). Language control in bilinguals: Monitoring and response selection. *Cerebral Cortex,* doi: 10.1093/cercor/bhv052.

Branzi, F. M., Martin, C. D., Abutalebi, J., & Costa, A. (2014). The after-effects of bilingual language production. *Neuropsychologia, 52*, 102–16.

Brown, A. S. (1981). Inhibition in cued retrieval. *Journal of Experimental Psychology: Human Learning and Memory, 7*(3), 204.

Calabria, M., Branzi, F. M., Marne, P., Hernández, M., & Costa, A. (2015). Age-related effects over bilingual language control and executive control. *Bilingualism: Language and Cognition, 18*(01), 65–78.

Calabria, M., Hernández, M., Branzi, F. M., & Costa, A. (2012). Qualitative differences between bilingual language control and executive control: Evidence from task-switching. *Frontiers in Psychology*, 2, 399.

Calabria, M., Marne, P., Romero-Pinel, L., Juncadella, M., & Costa, A. (2014). Losing control of your languages: A case study. *Cognitive Neuropsychology*, 31(3), 266–86.

Canini, M., Della Rosa, P. A., Catricalà, E., Strijkers, K., Branzi, F. M., Costa, A., & Abutalebi, J. (2016). Semantic interference and its control: A functional neuroimaging and connectivity study. *Human Brain Mapping*, 37(11), 4179–96.

Caramazza, A. (1997). How many levels of processing are there in lexical access? *Cognitive Neuropsychology*, 14(1), 177–208.

Cattaneo, G., Calabria, M., Marne, P., Gironell, A., Abutalebi, J., & Costa, A. (2015). The role of executive control in bilingual language production: A study with Parkinson's disease individuals. *Neuropsychologia*, 66, 99–110.

Christoffels, I. K., Firk, C., & Schiller, N. O. (2007). Bilingual language control: An event-related brain potential study. *Brain Research*, 1147, 192–208.

Colomé, A. (2001). Lexical activation in bilinguals' speech production: Language-specific or language-independent? *Journal of Memory and Language*, 45(4), 721–36.

Costa, A., Alario, F. X., & Caramazza, A. (2005). On the categorical nature of the semantic interference effect in the picture-word interference paradigm. *Psychonomic Bulletin & Review*, 12(1), 125–31.

Costa, A., Branzi, F. M., & Ávila, C. (2016). Bilingualism: Switching. In: Hickok, G., & Small, S. L. (Eds.), *Neurobiology of Language* (pp. 419–30). Academic Press, San Diego, CA.

Costa, A., & Caramazza, A. (1999). Is lexical selection in bilingual speech production language-specific? Further evidence from Spanish–English and English–Spanish bilinguals. *Bilingualism: Language and Cognition*, 2(3), 231–44.

Costa, A., Caramazza, A., & Sebastián-Gallés, N. (2000). The cognate facilitation effect: Implications for models of lexical access. *Journal of Experimental Psychology: Learning, Memory, and Cognition*, 26(5), 1283–96.

Costa, A., La Heij, W., & Navarrete, E. (2006). The dynamics of bilingual lexical access. *Bilingualism: Language and Cognition*, 9(2), 137–51.

Costa, A., Miozzo, M., & Caramazza, A. (1999). Lexical selection in bilinguals: Do words in the bilingual's two lexicons compete for selection? *Journal of Memory and Language*, 41(3), 365–97.

Costa, A., & Santesteban, M. (2004). Lexical access in bilingual speech production: Evidence from language switching in highly proficient bilinguals and L2 learners. *Journal of Memory and Language*, 50(4), 491–511.

Costa, A., Santesteban, M., & Ivanova, I. (2006). How do highly proficient bilinguals control their lexicalization process? Inhibitory and language-specific selection mechanisms are both functional. *Journal of Experimental Psychology: Learning, Memory, and Cognition*, 32(5), 1057–74.

Costa, A., Strijkers, K., Martin, C., & Thierry, G. (2009). The time course of word retrieval revealed by event-related brain potentials during overt speech. *Proceedings of the National Academy of Sciences*, 106(50), 21442–6.

de Baene, W., Duyck, W., Brass, M., & Carreiras, M. (2015). Brain circuit for cognitive control is shared by task and language switching. *Journal of Cognitive Neuroscience*, 27(9), 1752–65.

de Bot, K. (1992). A bilingual production model: Levelt's speaking model adapted. *Applied Linguistics*, 13(1), 1–24.

de Bruin, A., Roelofs, A., Dijkstra, T., & Fitzpatrick, I. (2014). Domain-general inhibition areas of the brain are involved in language switching: FMRI evidence from trilingual speakers. *NeuroImage*, *90*, 348–59.

Declerck, M., Koch, I., & Philipp, A. M. (2015). The minimum requirements of language control: Evidence from sequential predictability effects in language switching. *Journal of Experimental Psychology: Learning, Memory, and Cognition*, *41*, 377–94.

Dell, G. S. (1986). A spreading-activation theory of retrieval in sentence production. *Psychological Review*, *93*(3), 283–321.

Dhooge, E., & Hartsuiker, R. J. (2010). The distractor frequency effect in picture-word interference: Evidence for response exclusion. *Journal of Experimental Psychology: Learning, Memory, and Cognition*, *36*(4), 878–91.

Dhooge, E., & Hartsuiker, R. J. (2011). The distractor frequency effect in a delayed picture-word interference task: Further evidence for a late locus of distractor exclusion. *Psychonomic Bulletin & Review*, *18*(1), 116–22.

Falkenstein, M., Hoormann, J., & Hohnsbein, J. (1999). ERP components in Go/NoGo tasks and their relation to inhibition. *Acta Psychologica*, *101*(2), 267–91.

Finkbeiner, M., Almeida, J., Janssen, N., & Caramazza, A. (2006). Lexical selection in bilingual speech production does not involve language suppression. *Journal of Experimental Psychology: Learning, Memory, and Cognition*, *32*(5), 1075–89.

Finkbeiner, M., & Caramazza, A. (2006). Now you see it, now you don't: On turning semantic interference into facilitation in a Stroop-like task. *Cortex*, *42*(6), 790–6.

Finkbeiner, M., Gollan, T. H., & Caramazza, A. (2006). Lexical access in bilingual speakers: What's the (hard) problem? *Bilingualism: Language and Cognition*, *9*(2), 153–66.

Garavan, H., Ross, T. J., Murphy, K., Roche, R. A. P., & Stein, E. A. (2002). Dissociable executive functions in the dynamic control of behavior: Inhibition, error detection, and correction. *NeuroImage*, *17*(4), 1820–9.

Garavan, H., Ross, T. J., & Stein, E. A. (1999). Right hemispheric dominance of inhibitory control: An event-related functional MRI study. *Proceedings of the National Academy of Sciences of the United States of America*, *96*(14), 8301–6.

Garbin, G., Costa, A., Sanjuan, A., Forn, C., Rodriguez-Pujadas, A., Ventura, N., . . . , & Avila, C. (2011). Neural bases of language switching in high and early proficient bilinguals. *Brain and Language*, *119*(3), 129–35.

Glaser, W. R., & Glaser, M. O. (1989). Context effects in stroop-like word and picture processing. *Journal of Experimental Psychology: General*, *118*(1), 13.

Gollan, T. H., & Acenas, L. A. (2004). What is a TOT? Cognate and translation effects on tip-of-the-tongue states in Spanish-English and Tagalog-English bilinguals. *Journal of Experimental Psychology: Learning, Memory, and Cognition*, *30*(1), 246–69.

Gollan, T. H., & Ferreira, V. S. (2009). Should I stay or should I switch? A cost-benefit analysis of voluntary language switching in young and aging bilinguals. *Journal of Experimental Psychology: Learning, Memory, and Cognition*, *35*(3), 640–65.

Gollan, T. H., Fennema-Notestine, C., Montoya, R. I., & Jernigan, T. L. (2007). The bilingual effect on Boston Naming Test performance. *Journal of the International Neuropsychological Society: JINS*, *13*(2), 197–208.

Gollan, T. H., Montoya, R. I., Cera, C., & Sandoval, T. C. (2008). More use almost always means a smaller frequency effect: Aging, bilingualism, and the weaker links hypothesis. *Journal of Memory and Language*, *58*(3), 787–814.

Gollan, T. H., Montoya, R. I., Fennema-Notestine, C., & Morris, S. K. (2005). Bilingualism affects picture naming but not picture classification. *Memory and Cognition*, *33*(7), 1220–34.

Gollan, T. H., Montoya, R. I., & Werner, G. A. (2002). Semantic and letter fluency in Spanish-English bilinguals. *Neuropsychology, 16*(4), 562–76.

Gollan, T. H., Sandoval, T., & Salmon, D. P. (2011). Crosslanguage intrusion errors in aging bilinguals reveal the link between executive control and language selection. *Psychological Science, 22*(9), 1155–64.

Gollan, T. H., & Silverberg, N. B. (2001). Tip-of-the-tongue states in Hebrew–English bilinguals. *Bilingualism: Language and Cognition, 4*(1), 63–83.

Green, D. W. (1986). Control, activation, and resource: A framework and a model for the control of speech in bilinguals. *Brain and Language, 27*(2), 210–23.

Green, D. W. (1998). Mental control of the bilingual lexicosemantic system. *Bilingualism: Language and Cognition, 1*(2), 67–81.

Green, D. W., & Abutalebi, J. (2013). Language control in bilinguals: The adaptive control hypothesis. *Journal of Cognitive Psychology, 25*(5), 515–30.

Guo, T., Liu, F., Chen, B., & Li, S. (2013). Inhibition of non-target languages in multilingual word production: Evidence from Uighur-Chinese-English trilinguals. *Acta Psychologica, 143*(3), 277–83.

Guo, T., Liu, H., Misra, M., & Kroll, J. F. (2011). Local and global inhibition in bilingual word production: fMRI evidence from Chinese-English bilinguals. *NeuroImage, 56*(4), 2300–9.

Guo, T., Ma, F., & Liu, F. (2013). An ERP study of inhibition of non-target languages in trilingual word production. *Brain and Language, 127*(1), 12–20.

Hermans, D. (2004). Between-language identity effects in picture-word interference tasks: A challenge for language-nonspecific or language-specific models of lexical access? *International Journal of Bilingualism, 8*(2), 115–25.

Hermans, D., Bongaerts, T., De Bot, K., & Schreuder, R. (1998). Producing words in a foreign language: Can speakers prevent interference from their first language? *Bilingualism: Language and Cognition, 1*(3), 213–29.

Howard, D., Nickels, L., Coltheart, M., & Cole-Virtue, J. (2006). Cumulative semantic inhibition in picture naming: Experimental and computational studies. *Cognition, 100*(3), 464–82.

Ivanova, I., & Costa, A. (2008). Does bilingualism hamper lexical access in speech production? *Acta Psychologica, 127*(2), 277–88.

Jackson, G. M., Swainson, R., Cunnington, R., & Jackson, S. R. (2001). ERP correlates of executive control during repeated language switching. *Bilingualism: Language and Cognition, 4*(2), 169–78.

Janssen, N., Schirm, W., Mahon, B. Z., & Caramazza, A. (2008). Semantic interference in a delayed naming task: Evidence for the response exclusion hypothesis. *Journal of Experimental Psychology: Learning, Memory, and Cognition, 34*(1), 249–56.

Jersild, A. T. (1927). Mental set and shift. *Archives of Psychology, 14*(89), 81.

Jodo, E., & Kayama, Y. (1992). Relation of a negative ERP component to response inhibition in a Go/No-go task. *Electroencephalography and Clinical Neurophysiology, 82*(6), 477–82.

Koch, I., Gade, M., Schuch, S., & Philipp, A. M. (2010). The role of inhibition in task switching: A review. *Psychonomic Bulletin & Review, 17*(1), 1–14.

Kohnert, K. J., Hernández, A. E., & Bates, E. (1998). Bilingual performance on the Boston naming test: Preliminary norms in Spanish and English. *Brain and Language, 65*(3), 422–40.

Kroll, J. F., & Stewart, E. (1994). Category interference in translation and picture naming: Evidence for asymmetric connections between bilingual memory representations. *Journal of Memory and Language, 33*(2), 149–74.

La Heij, W. (2005). Selection processes in monolingual and bilingual lexical access. In: Kroll, J. F., & de Groot, A. M. B. (Eds.), *Handbook of Bilingualism: Psycholinguistic Approaches* (pp. 289–307). Oxford, New York, NY.

Lee, M. W., & Williams, J. N. (2001). Lexical access in spoken word production by bilinguals: Evidence from the semantic competitor priming paradigm. *Bilingualism: Language and Cognition*, 4(3), 233–48.

Leemann, B., Laganaro, M., Schwitter, V., & Schnider, A. (2007). Paradoxical switching to a barely-mastered second language by an aphasic patient. *Neurocase*, 13, 209–13.

Levelt, W. J. M., Roelofs, A., & Meyer, A. S. (1999). A theory of lexical access in speech production. *Behavioral and Brain Sciences*, 22(1), 1–38.

Levy, B. J., McVeigh, N. D., Marful, A., & Anderson, M. C. (2007). Inhibiting your native language: The role of retrieval induced forgetting during second-language acquisition. *Psychological Science*, 18(1), 29–34.

Linck, J. A., Kroll, J. F., & Sunderman, G. (2009). Losing access to the native language while immersed in a second language: Evidence from the role of inhibition in second language learning. *Psychological Science*, 20(12), 1507–15.

Linck, J. A., Schwieter, J. W., & Sunderman, G. (2012). Inhibitory control predicts language switching performance in trilingual speech production. *Bilingualism: Language and Cognition*, 15(3), 651–62.

Luk, G., Green, D. W., Abutalebi, J., & Grady, C. (2012). Cognitive control for language switching in bilinguals: A quantitative meta-analysis of functional neuroimaging studies. *Language and Cognitive Processes*, 27(10), 1479–88.

Lupker, S. J. (1979). The semantic nature of response competition in the picture-word interference task. *Memory & Cognition*, 7(6), 485–95.

Ma, F., Li, S., & Guo, T. (2016). Reactive and proactive control in bilingual word production: An investigation of influential factors. *Journal of Memory and Language*, 86, 35–59.

Macizo, P., Bajo, T., & Martín, M. C. (2010). Inhibitory processes in bilingual language comprehension: Evidence from Spanish–English interlexical homographs. *Journal of Memory and Language*, 63(2), 232–44.

Macizo, P., Bajo, T., & Paolieri, D. (2012). Language switching and language competition. *Second Language Research*, 28(2), 131–49.

Mahon, B. Z., Costa, A., Peterson, R., Vargas, K. A., & Caramazza, A. (2007). Lexical selection is not by competition: A reinterpretation of semantic interference and facilitation effects in the picture-word interference paradigm. *Journal of Experimental Psychology: Learning, Memory, and Cognition*, 33(3), 503–35.

Mariën, P., Abutalebi, J., Engelborghs, S., & de Deyn, P. P. (2005). Pathophysiology of language switching and mixing in an early bilingual child with subcortical aphasia. *Neurocase*, 11(6), 385–98.

Martin, C. D., Barcelo, F., Hernández, M., & Costa, A. (2011). The time course of the asymmetrical "local" switch cost: Evidence from event-related potentials. *Biological Psychology*, 86(3), 210–18.

Mayr, U., & Keele, S. W. (2000). Changing internal constraints on action: The role of backward inhibition. *Journal of Experimental Psychology: General*, 129(1), 4–26.

Meuter, R. F. I., & Allport, A. (1999). Bilingual language switching in naming: Asymmetrical costs of language selection. *Journal of Memory and Language*, 40(1), 25–40.

Miozzo, M., & Caramazza, A. (2003). When more is less: A counterintuitive effect of distractor frequency in the picture-word interference paradigm. *Journal of Experimental Psychology: General*, 132(2), 228–52.

Miozzo, M., Pulvermüller, F., & Hauk, O. (2015). Early parallel activation of semantics and phonology in picture naming: Evidence from a multiple linear regression MEG study. *Cerebral Cortex*, 25(10), 3343–55.

Misra, M., Guo, T., Bobb, S. C., & Kroll, J. F. (2012). When bilinguals choose a single word to speak: Electrophysiological evidence for inhibition of the native language. *Journal of Memory and Language*, 67(1), 224–37.

Monsell, S. (2003). Task switching. *Trends in Cognitive Sciences*, 7(3), 134–40.

Morsella, E., & Miozzo, M. (2002). Evidence for a cascade model of lexical access in speech production. *Journal of Experimental Psychology: Learning, Memory, and Cognition*, 28(3), 555–63.

Navarrete, E., & Costa, A. (2005). Phonological activation of ignored pictures: Further evidence for a cascade model of lexical access. *Journal of Memory and Language*, 53(3), 359–77.

Navarrete, E., Mahon, B. Z., & Caramazza, A. (2010). The cumulative semantic cost does not reflect lexical selection by competition. *Acta Psychologica*, 134(3), 279–89.

Nieuwenhuis, S., Yeung, N., van den Wildenberg, W., & Ridderinkhof, K. R. (2003). Electrophysiological correlates of anterior cingulate function in a go/no-go task: Effects of response conflict and trial type frequency. *Cognitive, Affective, & Behavioral Neuroscience*, 3(1), 17–26.

Oppenheim, G. M., Dell, G. S., & Schwartz, M. F. (2010). The dark side of incremental learning: A model of cumulative semantic interference during lexical access in speech production. *Cognition*, 114, 227–52.

Philipp, A. M., Gade, M., & Koch, I. (2007). Inhibitory processes in language switching: Evidence from switching language defined response sets. *European Journal of Cognitive Psychology*, 19(3), 395–416.

Philipp, A. M., & Koch, I. (2009). Inhibition in language switching: What is inhibited when switching between languages in naming tasks? *Journal of Experimental Psychology: Learning, Memory, and Cognition*, 35(5), 1187–95.

Poulisse, N. (1999). *Slip of the Tongue: Speech Errors in First and Second Language Production*. John Benjamins, Amsterdam/Philadelphia.

Poulisse, N., & Bongaerts, T. (1994). First language use in second language production. *Applied Linguistics*, 15(1), 36–57.

Prior, A., & Gollan, T. H. (2011). Good language-switchers are good task-switchers: Evidence from Spanish–English and Mandarin–English bilinguals. *Journal of the International Neuropsychological Society*, 17(4), 682–91.

Prior, A., & Gollan, T. H. (2013). The elusive link between language control and executive control: A case of limited transfer. *Journal of Cognitive Psychology*, 25(5), 622–45.

Roberts, P. M., Garcia, L. J., Desrochers, A., & Hernández, D. (2002). English performance of proficient bilingual adults on the Boston Naming Test. *Aphasiology*, 16(4–6), 635–45.

Roelofs, A., & Verhoef, K. (2006). Modeling the control of phonological encoding in bilingual speakers. *Bilingualism: Language and Cognition*, 9(2), 167–76.

Runnqvist, E., & Costa, A. (2012). Is retrieval-induced forgetting behind the bilingual disadvantage in word production?. *Bilingualism: Language and Cognition*, 15(2), 365–77.

Runnqvist, E., Strijkers, K., Alario, F.-X., & Costa, A. (2012). Cumulative semantic interference is blind to language: Implications for models of bilingual speech production. *Journal of Memory and Language*, 66(4), 850–69.

Sadat, J., Martin, C. D., Alario, F. X., & Costa, A. (2012). Characterizing the bilingual disadvantage in noun phrase production. *Journal of Psycholinguistic Research*, 41(3), 159–79.

Sandoval, T. C., Gollan, T. H., Ferreira, V. S., & Salmon, D. P. (2010). What causes the bilingual disadvantage in verbal fluency? The dual-task analogy. *Bilingualism: Language and Cognition*, 13(2), 231–52.

Schwieter, J. W., & Sunderman, G. (2008). Language switching in bilingual speech production: In search of the language-specific selection mechanism. *The Mental Lexicon*, 3(2), 214–38.

Strijkers, K. (2016). A neural assembly–based view on word production: The bilingual test case. *Language Learning*, 66(S2), 92–131.

Strijkers, K., Baus, C., Runnqvist, E., Fitzpatrick, I., & Costa, A. (2013). The temporal dynamics of first versus second language production. *Brain and Language*, 127(1), 6–11.

Thierry, G., & Wu, Y. J. (2007). Brain potentials reveal unconscious translation during foreign-language comprehension. *Proceedings of the National Academy of Sciences of the United States of America*, 104(30), 12530–5.

van Heuven, W. J. B., Schriefers, H., Dijkstra, T., & Hagoort, P. (2008). Language conflict in the bilingual brain. *Cerebral Cortex*, 18(11), 2706–16.

Verhoef, K., Roelofs, A., & Chwilla, D. J. (2009). Role of inhibition in language switching: Evidence from event-related brain potentials in overt picture naming. *Cognition*, 110(1), 84–99.

Wang, Y., Xue, G., Chen, C., Xue, F., & Dong, Q. (2007). Neural bases of asymmetric language switching in second-language learners: An ER-fMRI study. *NeuroImage*, 35(2), 862–70.

Wu, Y. J., & Thierry, G. (2010). Chinese-English bilinguals reading English hear Chinese. *The Journal of Neuroscience*, 30(22), 7646–51.

Wu, Y. J., & Thierry, G. (2012). Unconscious translation during incidental foreign language processing. *NeuroImage*, 59(4), 3468–73.

Yeung, N., & Monsell, S. (2003). Switching between tasks of unequal familiarity: The role of stimulus-attribute and response set selection. *Journal of Experimental Psychology: Human Perception and Performance*, 29(2), 455.

CHAPTER 20

THE RELATIONSHIP BETWEEN SYNTACTIC PRODUCTION AND COMPREHENSION

PETER INDEFREY

20.1 INTRODUCTION

LANGUAGE production and language comprehension are traditionally treated as separate areas within psycholinguistics, reflecting obvious differences between the processes involved in speaking on the one hand and listening or reading on the other hand. In speaking, we start with a prelinguistic thought that we want to convey to a listener, a "conceptual message" in the terminology of Levelt's (1989; Levelt et al., 1999) theory of language production. If that message is about some "giving" event, for example, it will include concepts such as the person who is the "giver" (e.g., *Peter*), the person who is the "receiver" (e.g., *Mary*), the thing that is given (e.g., *book*), and the action of giving itself. We will retrieve words ("lemmas") in our mental lexicon that correspond to these concepts. Retrieving the lemmas will make their grammatical properties available, such as word category (noun, verb, and so on), gender (e.g., masculine, feminine, neuter in a language with a three-way gender distinction), or the arguments a verb requires. Upon selection of a lemma we can retrieve its speech sounds and insert them into the syllables that constitute a phonological word. For articulation, the phonological words will be translated into phonetic representations and finally motor representations that steer our speech musculature.

For the production of sentences retrieving the words alone is insufficient, because we have to choose between different grammatical options to express the giving event. Among other options we could say *Peter gives a book to Mary* (active, prepositional object), *Peter gives Mary a book* (active, double object), or the corresponding passive sentences *A book is being given to Mary (by Peter)/ Mary is being given a book (by Peter)*. Although all these sentences express the giving event, they reflect different perspectives on this event and hence are not all felicitous under all circumstances. The conceptual message, therefore, must take into account the so-called information structure, in particular what is "old" information (i.e., known to the addressee), what is new information, and who or what is the topic of the message (*Do I want to make a statement about Peter, about Mary, or about the book?*). If, for example, the book is old information and the topic of our statement, we will choose the definite determiner *the* instead of the indefinite determiner *a* and a passive sentence structure in which *the book* is the subject. In Levelt's (1989) theory, the information structure contained in the conceptual message is used to build the grammatical structure of a sentence. This structure does not yet contain the words *Peter, Mary, book*, or *give*, but instead empty slots, for example a subject slot that is marked "noun, definite" and a slot for a verb with a passive argument structure. It is only after the words have been retrieved from the lexicon that they are inserted in the appropriate slots. Levelt took the notion of an empty syntactic structure that is then filled with content words over from earlier work by Garrett (1975, 1980, 1988), whose theory is based on the study of speech errors. He proposed an empty grammatical structure ("functional level representation") to account for certain speech error phenomena, for example the fact that word exchange errors (e.g., saying *Mary gives Peter a book* when *Peter gives Mary a book* was intended) tend to preserve the word category (i.e., nouns are exchanged with nouns). Assuming a process of inserting words into the slots of an empty but grammatically specified structure explains why exchange errors can happen (the word *Mary* is erroneously inserted in the wrong slot) and why they tend to preserve the word category (the slot is marked as a "noun" slot and *Mary* is lexically specified as a noun).

Whereas speakers thus encode a single syntactic structure based on a complex conceptual message, the situation is quite different for listeners and readers. They are faced with an incoming stream of words from which they have to derive a conceptual message. In many cases a short-cut going directly from the word meanings to the meaning of the sentence may be sufficient (Ferreira et al., 2002). For example, in the sentence *The cat chases a mouse* there is little doubt who does what to whom. However already in the sentences describing the "giving" event mentioned here, listeners have to perform a syntactic analysis ("parsing") to understand who is the giver and who is the receiver. Sentence comprehension theories agree that syntactic parsing is incremental (parsing begins with the first word and the syntactic structure grows word by word) and that parsing uses the lexically specified information of the incoming words. Theories differ with respect to the point in time at which different kinds of lexical information are used. Some assume that in a first step only syntactic information such as word category is taken into account (Bornkessel & Schlesewsky, 2006; Friederici, 2002; Frazier & Fodor, 1978). Others assume that non-syntactic lexical information, such as semantic information (e.g., animacy), general world knowledge, or even statistical knowledge about how often a particular verb occurs with a particular argument structure, immediately influences the build-up of the syntactic structure (Altmann & Steedman, 1988; MacDonald et al., 1994; Trueswell et al., 1994).

Crucially, due to the incrementality of parsing there is, most pronounced at the beginning of sentences, a great deal of uncertainty about the syntactic structure of the incoming sentence ("syntactic ambiguity"). For example, a sentence beginning with *Mary*... might evolve to an active sentence (*Mary gives a book to Peter*) or a passive sentence (*Mary is being given a book by Peter*). At points of ambiguity, parsers may wait for more information (i.e., the next words), compute several possible structures, or commit to one of several possible structures. The evidence provided by so-called "garden-path" sentences shows that at least to some degree parsers commit to one structure that may turn out to be wrong at a later point in the sentence (point of disambiguation). When encountering the morpho-syntactically ambiguous word *floated* in the sentence *The boat floated down the river sank* (Sturt & Crocker, 1996), for example, the parser tends to prefer a past tense reading and build a corresponding structure with *floated* as the head of the verb phrase of a simple main clause. The alternative reading as a passive participle and head of the verb phrase in a reduced relative clause is only considered when *sank* is encountered and cannot be accommodated in the originally preferred syntactic structure.

In sum, listeners and readers incrementally build up a syntactic structure based on the syntactic (but at some point influenced by non-syntactic) properties of the incoming words. Due to lexical ambiguities, intermediate tentative syntactic structures may have to be revised. In parallel, they build up a semantic structure based on word meanings (Kuperberg et al., 2007) which often may be sufficient to understand the sentence (Ferreira et al., 2002).

Hence quite different processes are involved in building up the syntactic structure of a sentence in language production and comprehension and some of their properties suggest that not only the processes but also their output representations are modality-specific. First of all, there is the fundamental difference that in comprehension a complete syntactic representation is not always necessary for understanding, whereas the "production system must get the details of form 'right' in every instance, whether those details are germane to sentence meaning or not" (Garrett, 1980, p. 216). Note, furthermore, that because syntactic parsing in comprehension is driven by the incoming words, there is no place for an abstract or empty syntactic representation that is assumed for production in the models of Levelt (1989) and Garrett (1988). In consequence, the production model of Levelt (1989) assumes a separate comprehension pathway. It is this pathway that speakers use to monitor their own speech. Both their inner speech (a phonetic representation in Levelt, 1989, a phonological representation in Levelt et al., 1999) and their overt speech are fed into the comprehension system where they are processed up to the conceptual level just like external speech ("perceptual loop"). As the self-monitoring loop has no access to processing stages before phonological encoding, this architecture requires a comprehension-specific syntactic representation.

Although there are thus very good reasons to assume modality-specific syntactic representations, it is nonetheless conceivable that there is only one representation of the syntactic structure of a sentence, which, depending on whether we speak or listen (read), is the output of syntactic encoding or parsing processes. If that was the case, we would expect activation of a syntactic structure in one modality to have an immediate impact on the processing of that structure in the other modality. There is indeed experimental evidence for such cross-modal influences. Bock (1986) introduced a syntactic priming paradigm in which participants were asked to describe pictures. Bock showed that the syntactic structure (e.g., active or passive) that was chosen by the participants was influenced by the structure of their preceding utterance (which was manipulated by the experimenter). Crucially, in later studies, Bock and collaborators showed that listening to a preceding sentence with a particular structure also made this structure more likely to be used in a subsequent sentence production (e.g., Bock et al., 2007). Similar effects are also found as one kind of "alignment" in natural dialogue. Branigan et al., (2000) observed that interlocutors tend to use the same syntactic structures (see also Garrod, Tosi, & Pickering, this volume). Such cross-modal syntactic influences are easily accounted for under the assumption that syntactic representations are shared between production and comprehension. Going a step further, Pickering and Garrod (2007) propose that the two modalities do not only share the same representations but are also functionally interleaved. Starting from the observation that listeners can and do predict grammatical properties of upcoming words (e.g., their grammatical gender; van Berkum et al., 2005), they suggest that during language comprehension simultaneous language production may act as a forward model predicting the upcoming input.

A recent experiment by Kempen et al. (2012) provided compelling evidence for production-based predictions influencing syntactic parsing in comprehension. Kempen et al. (2012) used a simultaneous reading and speaking paradigm to study how syntactic encoding and decoding interact during overlapping time intervals. In a "paraphrasing" task, they presented participants with sequential fragments of sentences including direct speech ending with a correct or incorrect reflexive pronoun (*The lottery winner said: "I have decided to buy a red car for myself/*himself"*). The participants were asked to change the sentences to indirect speech (*The lottery winner said that he had decided to buy a red car for himself*). In a "proofreading" task, they presented participants with indirect speech sentences ending with a correct or incorrect reflexive pronoun (*The lottery winner said that he had decided to buy a red car for *myself/himself*). The participants were asked to read out the sentences and to correct them when necessary, so that they produced the same responses as in the paraphrasing task (i.e., *The lottery winner said that he had decided to buy a red car for himself*). In both tasks, participants were also asked to judge the correctness of the input. Kempen et al. (2012) found that, not surprisingly, incorrect input resulted in prolonged voice onset times for the reflexive pronoun in the proofreading task. In the paraphrasing task, however, incorrect input facilitated the responses, presumably because the reflexive pronoun that was incorrect in direct speech was the correct pronoun in the paraphrasing indirect speech sentence. In addition, the participants' ability to judge the correctness of the input sentences was greatly reduced (i.e., they did not notice that the reflexive pronoun of the input was incorrect). These results suggest that the encoded syntax of the produced sentences overwrote the decoded syntactic representation of the input sentences and predicted the incorrect rather than the correct pronoun. Kempen et al. (2012) conclude that language production and comprehension cannot operate on different syntactic structures during overlapping time intervals and take this result as indicating that syntactic processing is shared by production and comprehension.

To sum up, considering the behavioral evidence there are very good arguments for as well as against shared syntactic representations for production and comprehension. In the remainder of this chapter, I will review the evidence from neurocognitive studies. To answer the question of whether syntactic parsing and encoding use the same neural resources I will first present the current evidence on the brain structures subserving sentence comprehension summarizing the results of a recent large-scale meta-analysis of language comprehension studies (Hagoort & Indefrey, 2014, henceforth known as H&I). For comparison, I will then conduct a meta-analysis of the much smaller number of studies investigating sentence production. To the extent that syntactic encoding and parsing rely on the same resources the observed brain networks should overlap. Finally, I will present the results of studies seeking to demonstrate direct interactions between syntactic parsing and encoding by testing for cross-modal functional magnetic resonance imaging (fMRI) syntactic adaptation effects. If the neural response to the production of a particular grammatical structure is affected by the preceding comprehension of the same structure (and vice versa), then it can be assumed that the neural populations representing that structure are shared between modalities.

20.2 BRAIN AREAS INVOLVED IN SENTENCE COMPREHENSION

In a recent meta-analysis of 151 hemodynamic studies on sentence processing, H&I investigated whether the neural activations related to syntactic aspects of sentence comprehension can be distinguished from neural activations related to semantic aspects of sentence comprehension. The activation foci and the spatial extent of 198 contrasts were coded in an anatomical reference system of 112 regions on the basis of the stereotaxic atlas of Talairach and Tournoux (1988) (for details, see Indefrey & Levelt 2000, 2004). For any particular region the reliability of its activation was assessed using the following estimate: The average number of activated regions reported per experiment divided by the number of regions (112) corresponds to the probability for any particular region to be reported in an experiment, if reports were randomly distributed over regions. Assuming this probability, the chance level for a region to be reported as activated in a certain number of experiments is given by a binomial distribution. The possibility that the agreement of reports about a certain region was coincidental was rejected if the chance level was below 5% (uncorrected for the number of regions). Regions with a chance level below 0.0004 survived a Bonferroni correction for 112 regions and were reported as 0.05 (corrected). This estimate considers that not all studies covered the whole brain owing to the heterogeneity of techniques and analysis procedures (for example, analyzing only regions of interest). The procedure also controls for the fact that the average number of activated regions per study differs between contrasts. In contrasts comparing sentences to low-level control conditions, the number of activated regions is typically higher than in contrasts comparing syntactically demanding to less demanding sentences; thus, the chances of coincidental agreements between studies are also higher.

About one-third of the studies compared sentences to non-sentential stimuli, ranging from word lists to cross-hair fixation or rest conditions (see Table 20.1 for a list of all contrasts and Table 20.2 for the studies reporting hemodynamic activations for the respective contrasts). The resulting brain activations could be expected to include whichever brain regions are involved in sentence-level syntactic and semantic processing. However, in these types of contrasts neural activation due to many other processes may also show up. About two-thirds of the studies compared syntactically or semantically demanding sentences to less demanding sentences. The latter studies controlled much more tightly for lower-level (e.g., lexical) differences between stimuli so that the resulting activations could be considered relatively specific to syntactic or semantic unification. Note, however, that these studies not only may have missed neural correlates of sentence-level processing that were shared between demanding and less demanding sentences, but also may have induced processes related to higher general cognitive demands, such as attention or error-related processes.

Frequent manipulations for increasing syntactic demands are the use of sentences containing syntactic violations or word-class ambiguities (e.g., *watch* as noun or verb) and the use of structurally more complex sentences, such as those containing object relative clauses (*The reporter who the senator attacked admitted the error*) compared to subject relative clauses (*The reporter who attacked the senator admitted the error*; Just et al., 1996). Manipulations for increasing semantic demands are semantic violations (e.g., *Dutch trains are sour...*; Hagoort et al., 2004) and lexical-semantic ambiguities (e.g., *bank*) that

Table 20.1 Types of contrasts used in hemodynamic studies on sentence comprehension and production. For each type of contrast, the last four columns give the number of studies included in the meta-analysis and the distribution of presentation modalities (see Table 20.2 for the complete list of studies)

Contrast no.	Condition of interest	Control condition	No. Studies	Reading	Listening	Both
Sentence comprehension						
1	Sentence comprehension	Below sentence level	53	21	30	2
2	Sentence comprehension	Words	15	6	8	1
3	Sentence reading	Below sentence level	22	22	0	0
4	Sentence listening	Below sentence level	31	0	31	0
5	Passive sentence reading	Below sentence level	13	13	0	0
6	Passive sentence listening	Below sentence level	20	0	20	0
7	Syntax demanding	Syntax less demanding	57	39	15	3
8	Syntax demanding	Semantics demanding	6	3	3	0
9	Syntactic violation	No violation	18	13	3	2
10	Syntactic ambiguity	No ambiguity	4	3	1	0
11	Syntax complex	Syntax less complex	33	22	9	2
12	Complex relative clauses	Simpler relative clauses	20	14	5	1
13	Non-canonical word order	Canonical word order	7	4	2	1
14	Syntactic repetition	No repetition	5	2	2	1
15	Semantics demanding	Semantics less demanding	51	36	14	1
16	Semantics demanding	Syntax demanding	10	5	5	0
17	Semantic violation	No violation	19	12	6	1
18	Lexical constraint violation	No violation	14	8	6	0
19	World knowledge violation	No violation	7	4	2	1

(continued)

Table 20.1 Continued

Contrast no.	Condition of interest	Control condition	No. Studies	Reading	Listening	Both
20	Semantic ambiguity	No ambiguity	10	4	6	0
21	Semantics complex	Less complex	30	28	2	0
22	Metaphoric sentence	Literal sentence	17	17	0	0
23	Familiar metaphor	Literal sentence	7	7	0	0
24	Novel metaphor	Literal sentence	11	11	0	0
25	Additional semantic operations	No additional semantic operations	3	3	0	0
26	Speaker meaning	Literal sentence	11	9	2	0
27	Irony	Literal sentence	8	7	1	0
28	Indirect utterance	Literal sentence	3	2	1	0

Sentence production

Contrast no.	Condition of interest	Control condition	No. Studies	Reading	Listening	Both
29	Sentence production	Word production	7			
30	More/complex syntactic production	Less/simpler syntactic production	7			
31	Syntactic repetition in production	No repetition	5			

Table 20.2 Studies included in the meta-analysis. The numbers in column 4 refer to the contrast numbers in column 1 of Table 20.1. For example, the study of Ahrens et al. (2007) contributed hemodynamic activation data for the contrasts 15 (semantics demanding—semantics less demanding), 21 (semantics complex—semantics less complex), 22 (metaphoric sentence—literal sentence), 23 (familiar metaphor—literal sentence), and 24 (novel metaphor—literal sentence)

Study	Year	Journal	Contrasts
Ahrens et al.	2007	Brain Lang	15, 21, 22, 23, 24
Argyropoulos et al.	2013	NeuroImage	30
Bahlmann et al.	2004	Hum Brain Mapp	1, 3, 5, 7, 11, 13
Bambini et al.	2011	Brain Res Bull	15, 21, 22
Bašnáková et al.	2014	Cereb Cortex	15, 21, 26, 28
Bavelier et al.	1997	J Cogn Neurosci	1, 3, 5
Bavelier et al.	1998	NeuroReport	1, 3
Bekinschtein et al.	2011	J Neurosci	15, 20
Ben-Shachar et al.	2003	Psychol Sci	7, 11
Ben-Shachar et al.	2004	NeuroImage	7(2×), 11(2×), 13
Bornkessel & Schlesewsky	2005	NeuroImage	7, 11, 13
Borofsky et al.	2010	J Neuroling	8, 16
Bottini et al.	1994	Brain	1, 2, 3, 15, 21, 22, 24
Braze et al.	2011	Cortex	7, 9, 15, 17, 19
Capek et al.	2004	Cogn Brain Res	1, 3
Caplan et al.	1998	J Cogn Neurosci	7, 11, 12
Caplan et al.	1999	NeuroImage	7, 11, 12
Caplan et al.	2000	Hum Brain Mapp	7, 11, 12
Cardillo et al.	2004	J Cogn Neurosci	15, 17, 18
Chee et al.	1999	Neuron	1, 3
Chen et al.	2006	Cortex	7, 11, 12
Chen et al.	2008	Brain Lang	15, 21, 22, 23
Chou et al.	2012	Neuropsychologia	7, 9
Christensen & Wallentin	2011	NeuroImage	7, 9, 11, 13
Collina et al.	2014	PLoS ONE	29
Constable et al.	2004	NeuroImage	1, 3, 4, 11, 12
Cooke et al.	2001	Hum Brain Mapp	7, 11, 12
Cooke et al.	2006	Brain Lang	7, 9
Dapretto & Bookheimer	1999	Neuron	7, 8, 16
Davis et al.	2007	Proc Natl Acad Sci USA	1, 4, 6
Den Ouden et al.	2008	Brain Lang	30

(continued)

Table 20.2 Continued

Study	Year	Journal	Contrasts
Desai et al.	2011	J Cogn Neurosci	15, 21, 22
Devauchelle et al.	2009	J Cogn Neurosci	14
Diaz et al.	2011	Neuropsychologia	15, 21, 22, 24
Diaz & Hogstrom	2011	J Cogn Neurosci	15, 21, 22, 24
Dien & O'Hare	2008	Brain Research	16
Embick et al.	2000	Proc Natl Acad Sci USA	7, 9
Eviatar & Just	2006	Neuropsychologia	21, 26, 27
Fiebach et al.	2004	J Cogn Neurosci	7, 10, 11
Fiebach et al.	2005	Hum Brain Mapp	7, 11
Friederici et al.	2000	Brain Lang	1, 4, 6
Friederici et al.	2003	Cereb Cortex	7, 9, 15, 16, 17, 18
Friederici et al.	2009	NeuroReport	7, 11
Gennari et al.	2007	NeuroImage	15, 20
Giraud et al.	2000	Brain	1, 4, 6
Golestani et al.	2006	Neuropsychologia	29
Grande et al.	2012	NeuroImage	30
Grewe et al.	2007	NeuroImage	7, 11, 13
Groen et al.	2010	Cereb Cortex	15, 17, 18, 19
Grossman et al.	2002	NeuroImage	7, 11, 12
Hagoort et al.	2004	Science	15, 17, 18, 19
Haller et al.	2005	Neuropsychologia	29
Hashimoto & Sakai	2002	Neuron	1, 2, 3
Hoen et al.	2006	Cortex	7, 9
Hoenig & Scheef	2005	Hippocampus	15, 20
Homae et al.	2002	NeuroImage	1, 4
Humphreys & Gennari	2014	NeuroImage	30
Humphries et al.	2001	NeuroReport	1, 4, 6
Humphries et al.	2005	Hum Brain Mapp	1, 2, 4, 6
Humphries et al.	2006	J Cogn Neurosci	1, 2, 4
Husband et al.	2011	J Cogn Neurosci	7, 9, 15, 16, 17, 21, 25
Indefrey et al. a	2001	Proc Natl Acad Sci USA	29, 30
Indefrey et al. b	2001	NeuroImage	1, 3
Indefrey et al.	2004	Brain Lang	1, 2, 4, 29, 30
Inui et al.	1998	NeuroReport	7, 11, 12
Jobard et al.	2007	NeuroImage	1, 2
Just et al.	1996	Science	7, 11, 12

Table 20.2 Continued

Study	Year	Journal	Contrasts
Kambara et al.	2013	*Language Sciences*	7, 9
Kang et al.	1999	*NeuroImage*	1, 3, 5
Kiehl et al.	2002	*NeuroImage*	15, 17, 18
Kinno et al.	2008	*Hum Brain Mapp*	7, 11, 13
Kircher et al.	2005	*British J Psychiatry*	30
Kircher et al.	2007	*NeuroImage*	15, 21, 22, 24
Kircher et al.	2009	*Neuropsychologia*	1, 4, 6
Koeda et al.	2006	*Biol Psychiatry*	1, 4, 6
Kuperberg et al.	2000	*J Cogn Neurosci*	1, 2, 4, 7, 9, 15, 17, 18, 19
Kuperberg et al.	2003	*J Cogn Neurosci*	7, 9
Kuperberg et al.	2006	*NeuroImage*	15, 21, 25
Kuperberg et al. a	2008	*Biol Psychiatry*	15, 17, 18
Kuperberg et al. b	2008	*NeuroImage*	7, 9, 15, 17, 19
Love et al.	2006	*Cortex*	7, 11, 12
Maguire & Frith	2004	*NeuroImage*	1, 2, 4, 6
Mashal et al.	2009	*Brain Cogn*	15, 21, 22, 24
Mason & Just	2007	*Brain Res*	15, 20
Mazoyer et al.	1993	*J Cogn Neurosci*	1, 4, 6
Meltzer et al.	2010	*Cereb Cortex*	7, 11, 12
Menenti et al.	2011	*Psychol Sci*	14, 31
Menenti et al.	2012	*Brain Lang*	31
Meyer et al.	2000	*Cogn Brain Res*	7
Meyer et al.	2002	*Hum Brain Mapp*	1, 4
Meyer et al.	2003	*J Neurolinguistics*	1, 4
Michael et al.	2001	*Hum Brain Mapp*	7, 11 (2×), 12 (2×)
Moore-Parks et al.	2010	*Brain Lang*	15, 17, 18
Moro et al.	2001	*NeuroImage*	7, 9
Muller et al.	1997	*NeuroReport*	1, 4, 6
Naito et al.	2000	*Hear Res*	1, 4, 6
Nakai et al.	1999	*Neurosc Lett*	1, 4, 6
Nathaniel-James et al.	1997	*Neuropsychologia*	1, 3, 5
Neville et al.	1998	*Proc Natl Acad Sci USA*	1, 3, 5
Newman et al.	2001	*J Psycholinguist Res*	16
Newman et al.	2003	*Brain Res Cogn Brain Res*	7, 11, 12
Newman et al.	2010	*Brain Lang*	7, 11, 12
Ni et al.	2000	*J Cogn Neurosci*	1, 4, 15, 16, 17, 18

(continued)

Table 20.2 Continued

Study	Year	Journal	Contrasts
Nichelli et al.	1995	Brain Lang	7, 9
Nieuwland et al.	2012	Hum Brain Mapp	7, 9, 15, 16, 17, 18
Noguchi et al.	2002	Hum Brain Mapp	7, 8
Noppeney & Price	2004	J Cogn Neurosci	1, 3, 5, 14
Ozawa et al.	2000	NeuroReport	1, 4, 6
Pallier et al.	2011	Proc Natl Acad Sci USA	1 (2x), 2, 3 (2x), 5 (2x)
Peck et al.	2004	NeuroImage	29
Peelle et al.	2004	Brain Lang	7, 11, 12
Pylkkänen et al.	2014	Cognition	29
Raettig et al.	2010	Cortex	7, 9
Rapp et al.	2004	Brain Res Cogn Brain Res	1, 3, 15, 21, 22, 24
Rapp et al.	2010	Brain Lang	21, 26, 27
Rapp et al.	2011	Brain Lang	15, 21, 25
Robertson et al.	2000	Psychol Sci	1, 3
Rodd et al.	2005	Cereb Cortex	1(2×), 4(2×), 6, 15(2×), 20(2×)
Rodd et al.	2010	Neuropsychologia	1, 4, 7, 10, 15, 16, 20
Rodd et al.	2012	Cereb Cortex	15, 20
Röder et al.	2002	NeuroImage	7, 11, 13
Rogalsky & Hickok	2009	Cereb Cortex	1, 2, 4, 6
Ruschemeyer et al.	2006	NeuroImage	7, 8, 16
Salvi et al.	2002	Hear Res	1, 4, 6
Sanjuan	2010	Eur Radiol	1, 4
Schlosser et al.	1998	Hum Brain Mapp	1, 4, 6
Schmidt & Seger	2009	Brain Cogn	15, 21, 22
Schoot et al.	2014	Frontiers Psychology	31
Scott et al.	2000	Brain	1, 4, 6
Segaert et al.	2012	Cereb Cortex	14, 31
Segaert et al.	2013	Brain Lang	31
Shibata et al.	2007	Brain Res	15, 21, 22, 24
Shibata et al.	2010	Brain Res	21, 26, 27
Shibata et al.	2011	Neuropsychologia	15, 21, 26, 28
Shibata et al.	2012	Brain Lang	15, 21, 22, 24
Snijders et al.	2009	Cereb Cortex	1–3, 5, 7, 10
Spotorno et al.	2012	NeuroImage	15, 21, 26, 27
Stowe et al.	1994	J Psychol Res	1, 3, 5, 7
Stowe et al.	1998	Cereb Cortex	11

Table 20.2 Continued

Study	Year	Journal	Contrasts
Stowe et al.	2004	Brain Lang	7, 10
Stringaris et al.	2006	NeuroImage	15, 21, 22, 23
Stringaris et al.	2007	Brain Lang	15, 17, 18, 21, 22, 23
Stromswold et al.	1996	Brain Lang	7, 11, 12
Suh et al.	2007	Brain Res	7, 11, 12
Suzuki & Sakai	2003	Brain Res	7, 8
Uchiyama et al.	2006	Brain Res	21, 26, 27
Uchiyama et al.	2008	Neurosci Res	1, 2, 4, 6, 7, 9
Uchiyama et al.	2012	Cortex	15, 21, 22, 23, 26, 27
van Ackeren et al.	2012	J Cogn Neurosci	15, 21, 26, 28
Vandenberghe et al.	2002	J Cogn Neurosci	1, 2, 3, 5, 15, 17, 18
Wakusawa et al.	2007	NeuroImage	21, 26, 27
Wang et al.	2006	Soc Cogn Affect Neurosci	21, 26, 27
Wang et al.	2008	Neuropsychologia	7, 8
Wartenburger et al.	2003	J Neurolinguistics	7, 9
Waters et al.	2003	NeuroImage	7(2×), 11(2×), 12(2×)
Weber & Indefrey	2009	NeuroImage	1, 3, 5, 14
Wong et al.	1999	Hear Res	1, 2, 4, 6
Xu et al.	2005	NeuroImage	1, 2, 3, 5
Yang et al.	2009	Brain Lang	23, 24
Yang et al.	2010	Neuropsychologia	15, 21, 22, 23, 24
Ye & Zhou	2009	NeuroImage	15, 17, 19
Zempleni et al.	2007	NeuroImage	15, 20
Zhu et al.	2009	NeuroImage	15, 17, 19
Zhu et al.	2012	NeuroImage	15, 17, 18
Zhu et al.	2013	NeuroImage	15, 17, 18

did not affect the syntactic structure in comparing with the correct control sentences. Other instances of higher semantic demands were experimental manipulations that complicated the listener's ability to assign an overall meaning without inducing a syntactic difference. These instances included sentences with a metaphoric meaning (e.g., *A sailboat is a floating leaf*; Diaz & Hogstrom, 2011); sentences inducing semantic operations such as coercion (*The novelist began/wrote the book*; Husband et al. 2011), metonymy (*Africa is hungry/arid*; Rapp et al., 2011), and sentences making connections to the previous discourse context (*The boys were having an argument. They became more and more angry/They began hitting each other. The next day they had bruises*; Kuperberg et al.,

2006). These instances also included sentences requiring listeners to assess speakers' intentions (irony, indirect replies, or requests, e.g., *Did you like my presentation?/How hard is it to give a good presentation? It is hard to give a good presentation*; Bašnáková et al., 2014).

20.2.1 Sentences compared with control conditions below the sentence level

H&I found that, compared with control conditions below sentence level, the comprehension of sentences reliably activates the temporal lobes and the posterior inferior frontal gyrus (IFG) bilaterally, albeit with a clear left hemisphere dominance. There were some differences among the regions involved in processing written and spoken sentences. Some right hemisphere temporal regions were not reliably found in reading, and posterior frontal regions were less frequently found in listening. Interestingly, when the participants just listened or read for comprehension without performing any additional tasks, or when sentence processing was compared with the processing of word lists, the most dorsal part of the IFG (pars opercularis, Brodmann area, BA 44) was not found to be reliably activated (see Fig. 20.1A).

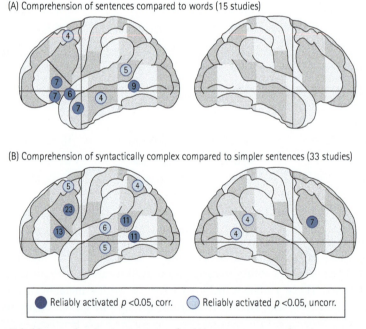

FIG. 20.1 Reliable neural activation increases for (A) sentence comprehension compared to word comprehension and (B) syntactically complex compared to simpler sentences.

Reproduced from Peter Hagoort and Peter Indefrey, The Neurobiology of Language Beyond Single Words, *Annual Review of Neuroscience*, 37 (1), pp. 347–62 © 2014, Annual Reviews. Reproduced with permission of Annual Review http://www.annualreviews.org.

20.2.2 Sentences with higher demands on syntactic or semantic processing

In studies comparing syntactically or semantically more demanding sentences with simpler sentences confounding non-syntactic or non-semantic differences between conditions are typically much better controlled. A contribution of such differences to the resulting brain activations can hence be largely excluded. H&I found that higher syntactic processing demands most reliably activate the more dorsal parts of posterior left inferior frontal gyrus (LIFG) (BA 44/45), the right posterior IFG, and the left posterior superior and middle temporal gyri (STG, MTG). In addition, the left precuneus, the left inferior parietal lobule, and the right posterior MTG were all reliably activated. Higher semantic processing demands most reliably activate all parts of posterior LIFG (but BA 45/47 are reported twice as often as is BA 44), the right posterior IFG, and the left middle and posterior MTG. In addition, the data indicate a reliable activation of the medial prefrontal cortex that is not seen for higher syntactic processing demands and demonstrate activations of the left anterior insula, angular gyrus, and the posterior inferior temporal gyrus (ITG).

The results of 16 studies directly comparing sentences with high syntactic and high semantic processing demands confirmed that the medial prefrontal cortex is involved in processing sentences with high semantic processing demands. Direct comparisons also demonstrated a syntactic/semantic gradient in LIFG: a reliably stronger activation of BA 44 is seen for syntactically, compared with semantically, demanding sentences; a reliably stronger activation of BA 45/47 is observed for semantically, compared with syntactically, demanding sentences.

H&I furthermore analyzed in which way different kinds of increased syntactic and semantic demands contributed to the overall result. Studies comparing sentences with syntactic violations (mostly agreement violations and phrase-structure/word-category violations) with correct sentences most reliably found BA 44/45 activation. Studies comparing sentences containing semantic violations with correct sentences most reliably found activation of all parts of the left posterior IFG, but activation of BA 45/47 was reported more often than was BA 44. Both semantic and syntactic violations generally activate the posterior temporal cortex less frequently than other kinds of demanding sentences do. Compared to unambiguous sentences, sentences containing local syntactic ambiguities (mostly word-class ambiguities, e.g., *He noticed that landing planes frightens some new pilots*) or semantic ambiguities (*The reporter commented that modern compounds react unpredictably*; examples from Rodd et al., 2010) activate the posterior IFG bilaterally and the left posterior MTG. For syntactic ambiguities, activation in the left posterior IFG was confined to BA 44. Semantic ambiguities activated the left posterior inferior medial temporal lobe.

Most studies manipulating syntactic complexity compared sentences containing complex relative clauses with simpler relative clauses. The main manipulation in the remaining studies was the use of non-canonical word order. Studies inducing semantic complexity typically used a condition in which understanding the meaning of the sentence required some additional effort compared with that required for syntactically identical control sentences. In most of the studies this goal was achieved by comparing sentences containing a metaphoric meaning with sentences containing a literal meaning. Another subset of studies used ironic/sarcastic sentences or indirect replies/requests. Both syntactic and semantic complexity reliably induced stronger activation of the posterior IFG bilaterally and the left mid and posterior MTG (see Fig. 20.1B). Left posterior IFG activation again showed a gradient with activation of BA 44 for syntactic but not semantic complexity, and activation of BA 47 for semantic but not syntactic complexity. The posterior STG seemed to show additional activation only for syntactic complexity. Conversely, semantic complexity induced medial prefrontal activations that were not reliably seen for syntactic complexity manipulations.

Separate analyses of the two main kinds of syntactic complexity yielded results that were like the overall activation patterns induced by syntactic complexity; therefore, the mechanism that drives these activations seems to be shared by non-canonical word orders and relative clause complexity. Separate analyses of different kinds of semantic complexity, however, yielded differential activation patterns. Sentences with metaphoric meaning contributed most to the overall activation of BA 45/47 and left posterior MTG, replicating the findings of a recent voxel-based meta-analysis on metaphor processing (Bohrn et al., 2012). By contrast, sentences that required the listener to assess the speaker's intentions (irony, indirect requests/utterances) did not reliably activate BA 45 or the left posterior temporal lobe. These kinds of sentences most frequently activated the medial prefrontal cortex (also reliably reported for metaphoric sentences but in a relatively smaller number of studies) and the right temporoparietal cortex (mainly observed in studies using indirect utterances).

In sum, H&I's meta-analysis yielded several important results. The most robust result was a distinctive activation pattern in the posterior LIFG: syntactic demands activated more dorsal parts (BA 44/45) and semantic demands activated more ventral parts (BA 45/47) across all kinds of increased processing demands (violations, ambiguity, complexity). This pattern was corroborated by studies performing direct comparisons of high syntactic and semantic processing demands. In particular, BA 44 activation is clearly driven more strongly by syntactic than by semantic demands, suggesting that this region contains neuronal populations involved in syntactic operations as such or that the semantic consequences of syntactic demands (difficulty of thematic role assignment) are processed by neuronal populations that differ from those processing other kinds of semantic unification. This dorsal/ventral gradient observed in the left posterior IFG seems to be mirrored in the left posterior temporal lobe. Higher syntactic demands reliably activate STG and MTG, and higher semantic demands reliably activate MTG and ITG. These gradients in posterior frontal and temporal regions are remarkably consistent with a functional connectivity pattern found by Xiang et al. (2010), which links seed regions in BA 44, BA 45, and BA 45/47 to left posterior STG, MTG, and ITG, respectively. This finding clearly supports the idea that sentence-level unification relies on the coactivation of neuronal populations in a network of posterior frontal and temporal regions, with a similar functional gradient in both parts of the brain.

Another important observation is the degree to which posterior temporal lobe activation differs between violations and other kinds of higher processing demands. Syntactic violations do not seem to elicit posterior temporal lobe activations reliably, and reports about such activations are relatively infrequent for semantic violations. I will come back to the potential relevance of this observation after the discussion of the neural activations patterns observed for sentence production.

20.3 Brain areas involved in sentence production

Due to problems with motion artifacts in functional MRI there are far less studies on sentence production than there are on sentence comprehension. To avoid these problems the earliest studies either used the positron emission tomography (PET) technique (Indefrey et al., 2001, 2004) or covert sentence production (Golestani et al., 2006; Peck et al., 2004). Meanwhile, however, fMRI scanning and analysis techniques have been developed that allow for overt articulation in the scanner (see Willems & van Gerven, this volume) so that over the last years a sufficient number of studies on sentence production have been published to allow for a tentative meta-analytic assessment of the reliability of findings across studies. Using the same procedures as for the sentence comprehension studies here, I analyzed the activation foci reported in 17 studies with altogether 350 participants. Seven of these compared sentence or phrase production to word list production (Contrast 29 in Tables 20.1 and 20.2). Seven studies compared more/complex syntactic production to less/simpler syntactic production (Contrast 30 in Tables 20.1 and 20.2). Five studies used an fMRI syntactic adaptation paradigm (Contrast 31 in Tables 20.1 and 20.2) and will be discussed in section 4.

20.3.1 Sentence production compared with word production

Studies comparing sentence production to word production used two main paradigms. In one type of paradigm participants were presented with pictures or visual scenes and instructed to describe the visual stimuli in different conditions with sentences or word lists (Indefrey et al., 2001; Indefrey et al., 2004; Peck et al., 2004; Pylkkänen et al., 2014). In the other type of paradigm participants were visually presented with lists of words. They were instructed to generate sentences from these words or, in the baseline condition, to simply read them out (Collina et al., 2014; Golestani et al., 2006; Haller et al., 2005).

As can be seen in Figure 20.2A, there was a highly reliable agreement between studies with respect to stronger activation of the left posterior IFG (pars opercularis, BA 44) in the sentence production task compared to word production. Surrounding regions (left ventral precentral gyrus, posterior MFG, superior frontal gyrus (SFG) and IFG, pars triangularis, BA 45) as well as left inferior parietal and precuneus activation were found less often but are still reliable at an uncorrected threshold. Note, however, that sentence and word production were not always well matched with respect to the required degree of conceptual planning and the amount of material to be uttered. The latter point particularly raises serious concerns about the interpretation of the observed posterior IFG activations because this region is known to be recruited for single word production as well (Indefrey & Levelt, 2004; Indefrey, 2011a). For this reason, Indefrey et al. (2001, 2004) additionally manipulated the rate of visual scene presentation, such that the increase in syllables or words per minute between the faster rate and the slower rate corresponded to the difference between the sentence and the word list conditions, which was due to the additional grammatical morphemes and function words in the sentences. They found the higher word production rate to result in stronger activation of the bilateral auditory cortices and an adjacent part of left IFG but not in stronger activation

(A) Production of sentences compared to words (seven studies)

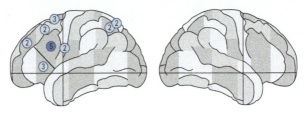

(B) Production of syntactically more complex compared to simpler sentences (seven studies)

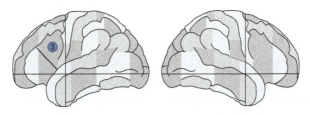

(C) fMRI syntactic adaptation in sentence production and comprehension (five studies)

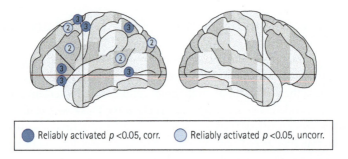

● Reliably activated $p <0.05$, corr.　○ Reliably activated $p <0.05$, uncorr.

FIG. 20.2 Reliable neural activation increases for (A) sentence production compared to word production and (B) production of syntactically more compared to less demanding sentences. (C) Reliable fMRI adaptation for the production and comprehension of sentences preceded by sentences with identical syntactic structures compared to sentences preceded by sentences with different syntactic structures.

of the region that was sensitive to the sentence/word list contrast suggesting that the hemodynamic response observed in BA 44 was indeed due to the increased demand on syntactic encoding rather than to changes in the number of syllables or words per minute.

20.3.2. Production of syntactically more versus less demanding sentences

In this group of studies, the degree of syntactic encoding was manipulated in different ways. Most studies compared grammatically more complex sentences to simpler ones (Den

Ouden et al., 2008; Humphreys & Gennari, 2014; Kircher et al., 2005). Indefrey et al. (2001, 2004) compared the production of sentences with the production of noun phrases. Argyropoulos et al. (2013) compared the generation of sentences with the repetition of sentences. Grande et al. (2012) used a very interesting and unusual paradigm: participants were asked to freely describe pictures while being scanned. The resulting speech samples were coded for (among other things) the syntactic completeness of sentences so that the hemodynamic activity of the brain during the production of syntactically complete and incomplete sentences could be compared post-hoc.

As can be seen in Figure 20.2B, there was only one region showing reliable agreement across studies. Three of the seven studies (Grande et al., 2012; Humphreys & Gennari, 2014; Indefrey et al., 2001) reported stronger activation of the left posterior IFG (BA 44) for the syntactically more demanding condition (see Fig. 20.2B). No other region was reported more than once.

20.3.3 Comparison of sentence comprehension and production activation patterns

The logic for presenting the evidence on reliable activation pattern for sentence comprehension and production was to test a prediction following from the assumption of shared processing resources for syntactic parsing and encoding: if that assumption is true, there should be some degree of overlap of the neural activation patterns. Figure 20.3 summarizes the most relevant findings from sentence comprehension and production studies. Unfortunately, at first sight our results do not seem to provide a clear answer, at least when looking at the activation patterns for the production and comprehension of simple sentences compared to words (Figs. 20.1A and 20.2A). In production the most reliably activated region is BA 44 and in comprehension just this region is not reliably observed (see also previous meta-analyses with the same finding; e.g., Indefrey, 2011b; Indefrey, 2012; Indefrey & Cutler, 2004). Instead, comprehension seems to recruit posterior temporal regions not found in production studies and more ventral parts of the left posterior IFG.

The picture looks different when comparing the outcome of studies that targeted syntactic processing more directly. Here the only reliably activated region in sentence production is BA 44 and just this region is also most frequently reported in comprehension studies (Figs. 20.1B and 20.2B). Again, however, highly reliable posterior temporal activations that are observed in comprehension are not observed in production. Note, that also in comprehension we found a dissociation between IFG and posterior temporal activations: syntactic violations activated the former but not the latter. This dissociation suggests a functional difference between the two regions that may also be relevant for the dissociation between production and comprehension. A tentative explanation accommodating all findings could be based on a distinction between Broca's area subserving sentence-level compositional processes, and the posterior temporal lobe subserving the retrieval of lexical syntactic and semantic information (Hagoort, 2005; Snijders et al., 2009). Syntactic violations only arise at a compositional processing stage and hence do not result in increased activation of posterior temporal cortex. Conversely, understanding simple spoken sentences does not necessarily require parsing their grammatical

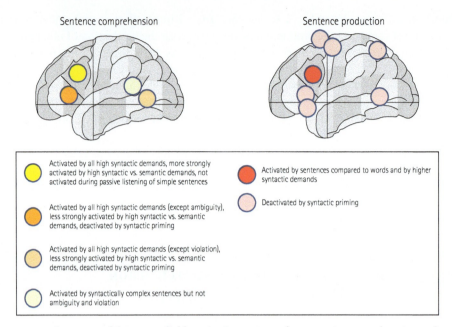

FIG. 20.3 Summary of the most reliable activation patterns for syntactic comprehension and sentence production.

Reproduced from Peter Hagoort and Peter Indefrey, The Neurobiology of Language Beyond Single Words, *Annual Review of Neuroscience*, 37 (1), pp. 347–62 © 2014, Annual Reviews. Reproduced with permission of Annual Review http://www.annualreviews.org.

structure, because their meaning can be derived from the word meanings ("good-enough representations," Ferreira et al., 2002). Hence, the neural activation we observe may not reflect syntactic processing at all but rather word and sentence level semantic processing and, indeed, the activation pattern corresponds best to what H&I identified as the pattern for semantic processing. Sentence production of even the simplest sentences, by contrast, cannot do without syntax, because speakers need to express the syntactic relationships between words in the ways required by their language. On the other hand, compared to listeners, speakers have the advantage of not having to deal with lexical ambiguities. As they know which word of which syntactic category to retrieve from the lexicon there may not be much difference between the word retrieval effort for sentences and word lists and hence no observable posterior temporal activation for sentence processing. In this view, syntactic processing resources may well be shared between production and comprehension but the differential affordances of expressing a message and deriving it from acoustic input nonetheless result in differences in neural activation patterns.

As far as our considerations have been based on correspondences between activated regions for the production and comprehension of sentences, they remain speculative as long as it cannot be shown that activation of the same region really means activations of the same neuronal population. This type of evidence can in principle be provided by studies using the fMRI adaptation paradigm. We, therefore, now turn to the set of studies that used this paradigm to study the relationship between syntactic encoding and parsing.

20.4 WITHIN- AND BETWEEN-MODALITY SYNTACTIC REPETITION EFFECTS

The fMRI adaptation paradigm exploits the fact that the activation of a neuronal population decreases with repeated presentations of the stimuli that initially activated these neurons (Henson & Rugg, 2003). By manipulating which aspect of a stimulus is repeated, this technique allows to identify neuronal populations that are tuned to ("interested in") this particular aspect. In a series of studies, Menenti, Segaert, Schoot, Hagoort, and colleagues orthogonally manipulated semantic, syntactic, and word repetition during the production and comprehension of sentences. As shown in Figure 20.2C, reliable syntactic adaptation effects across studies were found in left posterior IFG, MFG, and SFG (supplementary motor area), as well as the left posterior temporal cortex and the inferior parietal cortex, replicating both earlier syntactic adaptation findings for comprehension (Weber & Indefrey, 2009) and the pattern of regions activated by syntactic processing in classic subtraction studies reported here. The surplus of this series of studies lies in the fact that the syntactic adaptation effects did not differ between speaking and listening (Menenti et al., 2011; Menenti et al., 2012, see also Tooley & Bock, 2014, for recent corresponding behavioral results), and, most importantly, were even found between modalities (Segaert et al., 2012; Segaert et al., 2013; Schoot et al., 2014). These results provide convincing evidence for shared neuronal populations engaged in syntactic processing in both sentence production and comprehension. Some caveats, however, should be mentioned. A close inspection of the results of Segaert et al. (2012) shown in Schoot et al. (2014) suggests that between-modality syntactic repetition suppression was mainly found from production to comprehension, much less from comprehension to production. It seems, therefore, possible that the participants' comprehension of their own utterances contributed to the priming effect. Furthermore, production priming effects were comparatively small in left posterior temporal cortex. This latter observation may help to reconcile the apparent contradiction between fMRI adaptation effects suggesting an involvement of left posterior MTG in syntactic processing in production and classic subtraction studies not reporting reliable activation of this region. As suggested here, there may be relatively little effort for the retrieval of lexical syntactic information in production. This is also reflected in the fMRI adaptation data. Nonetheless, this technique may be just sensitive enough to detect a small facilitation of the retrieval of lexical syntactic information, in particular, when the retrieval of a dispreferred argument structure such as the passive argument frame of a verb (Segaert et al., 2013) is primed.

20.5 CONCLUSIONS

The question investigated in this article was whether there is one syntactic system that is shared by language production and comprehension or whether there are two separate systems. The available evidence from hemodynamic studies suggests that the answer is: there is one system consisting of at least two functionally distinct cortical regions, the pars opercularis of the left posterior IFG (BA 44) and the left posterior temporal cortex. This answer is mainly motivated by the compelling evidence from recent fMRI syntactic adaptation studies, showing cross-modal adaptation effects. There are differences in the activation patterns observed in classic subtraction fMRI studies between (a) sentence production and comprehension, (b) the comprehension of simple and syntactically complex sentences, and (c) syntactic violations and other types of syntactically demanding conditions. These differences can be accounted for by assuming a particular relevance of left posterior IFG for compositional syntactic processing and a particular relevance of the posterior temporal region for the retrieval of lexical syntactic information. Sentence production, the comprehension of simple and complex sentences, and the parsing of sentences containing grammatical violations tax these two functional components differently.

References

Altmann, G. T. M., & Steedman, M. (1988). Interaction with context during human sentence processing. *Cognition, 30*, 191–238.

Argyropoulos, G. P., Tremblay, P., & Small, S. L. (2013). The neostriatum and response selection in overt sentence production: An fMRI study. *NeuroImage, 82*, 53–60.

Bašnáková, J., Weber, K., Petersson, K. M., van Berkum, J., & Hagoort, P. (2014). Beyond the language given: The neural correlates of inferring speaker meaning. *Cerebral Cortex, 24*(10), 2572–8.

Bock, J. K. (1986). Syntactic persistence in language production. *Cognitive Psychology, 18*, 355–87.

Bock, J. K., Dell, G. S., Chang, F., & Onishi, K. H. (2007). Persistent structural priming from language comprehension to language production. *Cognition, 104*, 437–58.

Bohrn, I. C., Altmann, U., & Jacobs, A. M. (2012). Looking at the brains behind figurative language—a quantitative meta-analysis of neuroimaging studies on metaphor, idiom, and irony processing. *Neuropsychologia, 50*, 2669–83.

Bornkessel, I., & Schlesewsky, M. (2006). The extended argument dependency model: A neurocognitive approach to sentence comprehension across languages. *Psychological Review, 113*, 787–821.

Branigan, H. P., Pickering, M. J., & Cleland, A. A. (2000). Syntactic co-ordination in dialogue. *Cognition, 75*, B13–B25.

Collina, S., Seurinck, R., & Hartsuiker, R. J. (2014). Inside the syntactic box: The neural correlates of the functional and positional level in covert sentence production. *PLoS One, 9*(9), e106122.

Den Ouden, D.-B., Hoogduin, H., Stowe, L. A., & Bastiaanse, R. (2008). Neural correlates of Dutch Verb Second in speech production. *Brain and Language, 104*, 122–31.

Diaz, M. T., & Hogstrom, L. J. (2011). The influence of context on hemispheric recruitment during metaphor processing. *Journal of Cognitive Neuroscience, 23*, 3586–97.

Ferreira, F., Bailey, K. G. D., & Ferraro, V. (2002). Good-enough representations in language comprehension. *Current Directions in Psychological Science, 11*, 11–15.

Frazier, L., & Fodor, J. D. (1978). The sausage machine: A new two-stage parsing model. *Cognition, 6*, 291–326.

Friederici, A. (2002). Towards a neural basis of auditory sentence processing. *Trends in Cognitive Sciences, 6*, 78–84.

Garrett, M. F. (1975). The analysis of sentence production. In: Bower, G. (Ed.), *Psychology of Learning and Motivation*, Vol. 9 (pp. 133–77). Academic Press, New York, NY.

Garrett, M. F. (1980). Levels of processing in sentence production. In: Butterworth, B. (Ed.), *Language Production*, Vol. 1 (pp. 177–220). Academic Press, London.

Garrett, M. F. (1988). Processes in language production. In: Nieuwmeyer, F. J. (Ed.), *Linguistics: The Cambridge Survey, Vol. III: Biological and Psychological Aspects of Language* (pp. 69–96). Harvard University Press, Harvard, MA.

Garrod, S., Tosi, A., & Pickering, M. J. (2018). Alignment during interaction. In: Rueschemeyer, S. A., & Gaskell, M. G. (Eds.), *The Oxford Handbook of Psycholinguistics*, 2nd Edition (pp. 575–93). Oxford University Press, Oxford.

Golestani, N., Alario, F.-X., Meriaux, S., Le Bihan, D., Dehaene, S., & Pallier, C. (2006). Syntax production in bilinguals. *Neuropsychologia*, 44, 1029–40.

Grande, M., Meffert, E., Schoenberger, E., Jung, S., Frauenrath, T., Huber, W., Hussmann, K., Moormann, M., & Heim, S. (2012). From a concept to a word in a syntactically complete sentence: An fMRI study on spontaneous language production in an overt picture description task. *NeuroImage*, 61, 702–14.

Hagoort, P. (2005). On Broca, brain, and binding: A new framework. *Trends in Cognitive Sciences*, 9, 416–23.

Hagoort, P., Hald, L., Bastiaansen, M., & Petersson, K. M. (2004). Integration of word meaning and world knowledge in language comprehension. *Science*, 304, 438–41.

Hagoort, P., & Indefrey, P. (2014). The neurobiology of language beyond single words. *Annual Review of Neuroscience*, 37, 347–62.

Haller, S., Radue, E. W., Erb, M., Grodd, W., & Kircher, T. (2005). Overt sentence production in event-related fMRI. *Neuropsychologia*, 43, 807–14.

Henson, R. N. A., & Rugg, M. D. (2003). Neural response suppression, haemodynamic repetition effects and behavioural priming. *Neuropsychologia*, 41, 263–70.

Humphreys, G. F., & Gennari, S. P. (2014). Competitive mechanisms in sentence processing: Common and distinct production and reading comprehension networks linked to the prefrontal cortex. *NeuroImage*, 84, 354–66.

Husband, E. M., Kelly, L. A., & Zhu, D. C. (2011). Using complement coercion to understand the neural basis of semantic composition: Evidence from an fMRI Study. *Journal of Cognitive Neuroscience*, 23, 3254–66.

Indefrey, P. (2011a). The spatial and temporal signatures of word production components: A critical update. *Frontiers in Psychology*, 2, 255.

Indefrey, P. (2011b). Neurobiology of syntax. In: Hogan, P. C. (Ed.), *The Cambridge Encyclopedia of the Language Sciences* (pp. 835–8). Cambridge University Press, Cambridge/New York.

Indefrey, P. (2012). Hemodynamic studies of syntactic processing. In: Faust, M. (Ed.), *The Handbook of the Neuropsychology of Language* (pp. 209–28). Blackwell, Malden, MA.

Indefrey, P., Brown, C. M., Hellwig, F., Amunts, K., Herzog, H., Seitz, R. J., & Hagoort, P. (2001). A neural correlate of syntactic encoding during speech production. *Proceedings of the National Academy of Sciences of the United States of America*, 98, 5933–6.

Indefrey, P., & Cutler, A. (2004). Prelexical and lexical processing in listening. In: Gazzaniga, M. (Ed.), *The Cognitive Neurosciences III* (pp. 759–74). MIT Press, Cambridge, MA.

Indefrey, P., Hellwig, F., Herzog, H., Seitz, R. J., & Hagoort, P. (2004). Neural responses to the production and comprehension of syntax in identical utterances. *Brain and Language*, 89, 312–19.

Indefrey, P., & Levelt, W. J. M. (2000). The neural correlates of language production. In: Gazzaniga, M. S. (Ed.), *The New Cognitive Neurosciences* (pp. 845–65). MIT Press, Cambridge, MA.

Indefrey, P., & Levelt, W. J. M. (2004). The spatial and temporal signatures of word production components. *Cognition, 92*, 10–44.

Just, M. A., Carpenter, P. A., Keller, T. A., Eddy, W. F., & Thulborn, K. R. (1996). Brain activation modulated by sentence comprehension. *Science, 274*, 114–16.

Kempen, G., Olsthoorn, N., & Sprenger, S. (2012). Grammatical workspace sharing during language production and language comprehension: Evidence from grammatical multitasking. *Language and Cognitive Processes, 27*, 345–80.

Kircher, T. T. J., Oh, T. M., Brammer, M., J., & McGuire, P. K. (2005). Neural correlates of syntax production in schizophrenia. *British Journal of Psychiatry, 186*, 209–14.

Kuperberg, G. R., Kreher, D. A., Sitnikova, T., Caplan, D. N., & Holcomb, P. J. (2007). The role of animacy and thematic relationships in processing active English sentences: Evidence from event-related potentials. *Brain and Language, 100*, 223–37.

Kuperberg, G. R., Lakshmanan, B. M., Caplan, D. N., & Holcomb, P. J. (2006). Making sense of discourse: An fMRI study of causal inferencing across sentences. *NeuroImage, 33*, 343–61.

Levelt, W. J. M. (1989). *Speaking: From Intention to Articulation*. MIT Press, Cambridge, MA.

Levelt, W. J. M., Roelofs, A., & Meyer, A. S. (1999). A theory of lexical access in speech production. *Behavioral and Brain Sciences, 22*, 1–38.

MacDonald, M. C., Pearlmutter, N. J., & Seidenberg, M. S. (1994). Lexical nature of syntactic ambiguity resolution. *Psychological Review, 101*, 676–703.

Menenti, L., Gierhan, S. M. E., Segaert, K., & Hagoort, P. (2011). Shared language: Overlap and segregation of the neuronal infrastructure for speaking and listening revealed by functional MRI. *Psychological Science, 22*, 1173–82.

Menenti, L., Segaert, K., & Hagoort, P. (2012). The neuronal infrastructure of speaking. *Brain and Language, 122*, 71–80.

Peck, K. K., Wierenga, C. E., Bacon Moore, A., Maher, L. M., Gopinath, K., Gaiefsky, M., . . . & Crosson, B. (2004). Comparison of baseline conditions to investigate syntactic production using functional magnetic resonance imaging. *NeuroImage, 23*, 104–10.

Pickering, M. J., & Garrod, S. (2007). Do people use language production to make predictions during comprehension? *Trends in Cognitive Sciences, 11*, 105–10.

Pylkkänen, L., Bemis, D. K., & Blanko Elorrieta, E. (2014). Building phrases in language production: An MEG study of simple composition. *Cognition, 133*, 371–84.

Rapp, A. M., Erb, M., Grodd, W., Bartels, M., & Markert, K. (2011). Neural correlates of metonymy resolution. *Brain and Language, 119*, 196–205.

Rodd, J. M., Longe, O. A., Randall, B., & Tyler, L. K. (2010). The functional organisation of the fronto-temporal language system: Evidence from syntactic and semantic ambiguity. *Neuropsychologia, 48*, 1324–35.

Schoot, L., Menenti, L., Hagoort, P., & Segaert, K. (2014). A little more conversation—the influence of communicative context on syntactic priming in brain and behavior. *Frontiers in Psychology, 5*, 208.

Segaert, K., Kempen, G., Petersson, K. M., & Hagoort, P. (2013). Syntactic priming and the lexical boost effect during sentence production and sentence comprehension: An fMRI study. *Brain and Language, 124*, 174–83.

Segaert, K., Menenti, L., Weber, K., Petersson, K. M., & Hagoort, P. (2012). Shared syntax in language production and language comprehension—an FMRI study. *Cerebral Cortex*, 22, 1662–70.

Snijders, T. M., Vosse, T., Kempen, G., van Berkum, J. J. A., Petersson, K. M., & Hagoort, P. (2009). Retrieval and unification of syntactic structure in sentence comprehension: An fMRI study using word-category ambiguity. *Cerebral Cortex*, 19, 1493–503.

Sturt, P., & Crocker, M. W. (1996). Monotonic syntactic processing: A cross-linguistic study of attachment and reanalysis. *Language and Cognitive Processes*, 11, 449–94.

Talairach, J., & Tournoux, P. (1988). *Co-Planar Stereotaxic Atlas of the Human Brain: 3-D Proportional System: An Approach to Cerebral Imaging*. Thieme, Stuttgart.

Tooley, K. M., & Bock, K. (2014). On the parity of structural persistence in language production and comprehension. *Cognition*, 132, 101–36.

Trueswell, J. C., Tanenhaus, M. K., & Garnsey, S. M. (1994). Semantic influences on parsing: Use of thematic role information in syntactic disambiguation. *Journal of Memory and Language*, 33, 285–318.

van Berkum, J. J., Brown, C. M., Zwitserlood, P., Kooijman, V., & Hagoort, P. (2005). Anticipating upcoming words in discourse: Evidence from ERPs and reading times. *Journal of Experimental Psychology: Learning, Memory, and Cognition*, 31, 443–67.

Weber, K., & Indefrey, P. (2009). Syntactic priming in German-English bilinguals during sentence comprehension. *NeuroImage*, 46, 1164–72.

Willems, R. M., & van Gerven, M. A. J. (2018). New fMRI methods for the study of language. In: Rueschemeyer, S. A., & Gaskell, M. G. (Eds.), *The Oxford Handbook of Psycholinguistics*, 2nd Edition (pp. 977–93). Oxford University Press, Oxford.

Xiang, H. D., Fonteijn, H. M., Norris, D. G., & Hagoort, P. (2010). Topographical functional connectivity pattern in the Perisylvian language networks. *Cerebral Cortex*, 20, 549–60.

CHAPTER 21

WORD PRODUCTION AND RELATED PROCESSES
Evidence from aphasia

MYRNA F. SCHWARTZ

21.1 INTRODUCTION

OUR ability to speak fluently and informatively rests on the timely and accurate retrieval of information from an extensive lexicon of known words. Speech errors—the retrieval of a word or pronunciation different from what the speaker intended—have yielded invaluable clues about the stages and process that underlie language production. Speech errors are quite rare in neurologically healthy ("neurotypical") speakers but they occur far more often in those who experience aphasia—the disruption of language processing by stroke or other brain damage. Speaking and naming errors from people with aphasia (PWA) have featured importantly in the development and evaluation of cognitive models of production.

This chapter provides a selective review of research carried out in this speech error tradition. We begin by considering how and why brain lesions in aphasia exaggerate the normal tendency to err. Subsequent sections describe new lines of research on aphasia that expose and explore points of contact between processes involved in word production, incremental lexical learning, and self-monitoring of errors.

The framework that unifies these diverse lines of research is the interactive two-step model of word production (Fig. 21.1). This simple, connectionist model was developed to explain certain speech error phenomena found in neurotypical speakers (Dell, 1986) and to reconcile interactive, spreading-activation theories with modular two-stage accounts (Dell & O'Seaghdha, 1991; Levelt et al., 1991). In subsequent years, variants of this model have been used to simulate and explain a wide range of speech production phenomena in both neurotypical speakers and PWA. I will describe the original or "base" model first, then turn to variants of the base model that are of present interest: the semantic-phonological model of aphasia (Foygel & Dell, 2000; Nozari, Kittredge, Dell, & Schwartz, 2010; Schwartz et al., 2006); the conflict model of monitoring (Nozari, Dell, & Schwartz, 2011); and the dark side

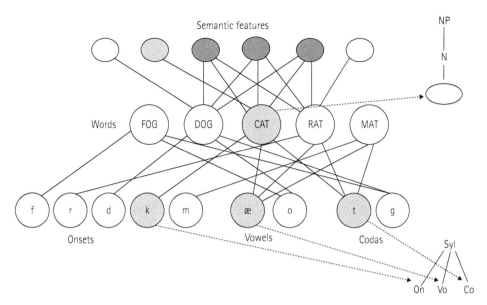

FIG. 21.1 The interactive two-step model of naming, with CAT as the target.

Reprinted from *Journal of Memory and Language*, 54 (2), Myrna F. Schwartz, Gary S. Dell, Nadine Martin, Susanne Gahl, and Paula Sobel, A case-series test of the interactive two-step model of lexical access: Evidence from picture naming, pp. 228–64, doi.org/10.1016/j.jml.2005.10.001, Copyright © 2005 Elsevier Inc., with permission from Elsevier.

model of cumulative semantic interference and incremental learning (Oppenheim, Dell, & Schwartz, 2010).

21.2 THE INTERACTIVE, TWO-STEP MODEL OF NAMING

The base model contains a three-level lexical network consisting of semantic features, words, and phonemes, with weighted connections that transmit activation both top-down and bottom-up (Fig. 21.1). All activation is positive; there is no inhibition. All words are consonant-vowel-consonant (CVC) syllables, with phonemes marked for syllable position. This is a model of a stable system after learning has been completed. Connection weights are comparable and fixed for all words (semantic-, or s-weights) and all phonemes (phonological, or p-weights) and the base model does not represent variations in lexical frequency (but see Nozari et al., 2010). A naming trial begins with external activation supplied to the target's semantic features. The spread of activation is stochastic, so target selection is not guaranteed. The one-to-many mapping from features to words generates semantic competition for word selection and sets the stage for word substitution errors. The paradigmatic word substitution error is related to the target in meaning and not form (e.g., cat → "dog") (semantic error). Other types of word substitution errors are formal errors, which resemble the target in form and not meaning (cat → "mat"); mixed errors, which resemble the target in both meaning and form (e.g, cat → "rat"); and unrelated errors, bearing no obvious resemblance to the target (cat → "fog"). The model's explanation of formal and mixed errors rests on interactivity. Prior to word selection, activation flows top-down and bottom-up, allowing phonological feedback to influence the competition for word selection. Other features of the model, though, limit the interactive flow of information to ensure that semantic information dominates step 1 and phonological information dominates step 2 (Dell & O'Seaghdha, 1991; Rapp & Goldrick, 2000). Such limited interactivity is one distinctive feature of the model. Another is its mechanism of selection. The interactive two-step model implements a non-competitive selection threshold: Activation flows for a fixed amount of time, after which the most active word is selected, ending step 1. Other models implement some form of competitive selection, whereby strongly activated neighbors impede or slow the selection of target words (e.g., Howard et al., 2006; Levelt, Roelofs, & Meyer, 1999). The nature of selection features importantly in the literature on cumulative semantic interference and will be taken up again below, in the context of the dark side model.

Step 2 of lexical access begins with a jolt of activation supplied to the selected word unit and ends with selection of position-specified phonemes (e.g., onset /k/; coda /t/). The effect of the jolt is to privilege the phonemes of the selected word over the phonemes of strongly activated semantic competitors. Although this limits competition at step 2, it does not eliminate it, and sometimes the wrong phoneme or phonemes will be selected. While phoneme substitution can by chance create a real word, the paradigmatic step 2 error is a phonologically related non-word (cat → "dat") (non-word error).

21.3 THE APHASIA MODELS

Efforts to adapt the base model to explain word production impairments in PWA began in the mid-1990s (Dell et al., 1997; Martin, Dell, Saffran, & Schwartz, 1994). Since then, variants of the base model have been used to quantitatively fit the individualized naming-error data from more than 200 PWA. The procedure is to have each participant perform a standardized 175-item naming test (*Philadelphia Naming Test*; Roach et al., 1996), results of which are expressed in terms of the proportions (relative to total trials) of correct responses and five types of error: *semantic, formal, mixed, unrelated,* and *non-words*. The six proportions (comprising the PWA's "naming pattern") are then fit to the model, with measured goodness-of-fit, using procedures described in subsequent paragraphs.

From the start, the model implementations were guided by two facts about naming patterns in aphasia. Firstly, key error types pattern differently with respect to severity. I will say more about this "severity/error type interaction" shortly. Second, not all between-patient variation in error types can be explained by severity. In particular, some patients are more prone to produce word substitutions (typically semantic), while others at the same level of severity are more prone to produce sublexical substitutions (typically non-words). Table 21.1 shows data from two patients, both of whom were 77% correct on the Philadelphia Naming Test (PNT). Patient 1 produced 4% semantic and 13% non-words, whereas Patient 2 produced 12% semantic and 1% non-words. (For discussion and additional examples, see Rapp & Goldrick, 2000; Ruml & Caramazza, 2000; Schwartz et al., 2006.)

Table 21.1 (Top) Naming response proportions from two patients with equal levels of correctness but different error patterns. (Bottom) These same patients' error patterns are better fit by the semantic–phonological model than the weight–decay model

Patient	Naming response category					
	Correct	Semantic	Formal	Mixed	Unrelated	Non-word
1	0.77	0.04	0.02	0.04	0.01	0.13
2	0.77	0.12	0.03	0.04	0.03	0.01

Source	Model diagnosis		Naming response category						Model fit	
	wt/sem	decay/phon	Correct	Semantic	Formal	Mixed	Unrelated	Non-word	Chi-squared	RMSD
Patient 1										
Naming response prop.			0.77	0.04	0.02	0.04	0.01	0.13		
Weight-decay model	0.01	0.55	0.74	0.07	0.05	0.02	0.02	0.11	12.51	0.025
Semantic–phonological model	0.03	0.02	0.77	0.05	0.04	0.01	0.01	0.12	6.88	0.013
Patient 2										
Naming response prop.			0.77	0.12	0.03	0.04	0.03	0.01		
Weight-decay model	0.05	0.71	0.74	0.1	0.05	0.04	0.01	0.06	12.45	0.027
Semantic–phonological model	0.02	0.04	0.79	0.09	0.05	0.02	0.04	0.01	6.86	0.021

Returning to the severity/error type interaction: Put simply, PWA who make many errors have response proportions dominated by non-words, formals, and unrelated errors. These can be thought of as "high opportunity" errors; if one were to try to select a target word by randomly selecting from the lexicon, the errors would mostly be of this type. At the other end of the severity continuum, in PWA who make few errors overall, the predominant error types are semantic and mixed. These semantically related word substitutions have low probability of being selected at random but the errors are those most likely to be made by neurotypical speakers. The aphasia models envision a continuum stretching between the normal state and the fully impaired, random state, with individual PWA situated along the continuum. The models start with a lexicon (inherited from the base model) in which the statistical error opportunities match those in natural speech; and they are parameterized such that the default (normal) model outputs response proportions that match the naming pattern of typical speakers, and at maximal break-down (lowest signal-to-noise ratio) the model outputs the random pattern, dominated by high opportunity errors. What differentiates one aphasia model from others is which model parameters are allowed to vary (i.e., which parameters are "lesionable"). The choice affects how severity and error type interact in the model, and, thus, how well the model fits the data. The fitting process essentially compares a PWA's naming response proportions to the proportions produced by the model at different combinations of lesionable parameters, finds the combination that best matches the PWA's proportions, and measures the goodness-of-fit of the match (Dell, Lawler, Harris, & Gordon, 2004). This process is then repeated for the next PWA, and so on.

Dell et al. (1997) achieved reasonably good success with the weight-decay model. The two lesionable parameters in this model—connection strength and decay rate—are both global in that they affect all connections and/or all units to the same degree. Subsequently, Foygel and Dell (2000) developed a model in which semantic and phonological connections are governed by two different parameters, and lesions in aphasia alter either the s-weights or the p-weights, or both; this is known as the semantic-phonological model.

Schwartz et al. (2006) fit the naming data from 94 PWA with diverse types of aphasia using both the weight-decay and semantic-phonological models. Both models were generally successful, but the semantic-phonological model produced superior results, accounting for 94.5% of the total variance and closely matching the individual response proportions (mean root mean squared deviation = 0.034). By exploring the similarities and differences across the two models, the authors were able to identify which properties are most important for simulating naming data from aphasia: (1) *Continuity thesis*—as stated in the paper: "Any model that correctly fits the normal pattern, correctly characterizes the random pattern, and places patients on a continuum between these two patterns, will fit [PWA] reasonably well" (Schwartz et al., 2006, p. 258). (2) *Two-step assumption*—Both aphasia models follow the base model in separating lexical and sublexical retrieval steps, so both make possible the two main errors types—semantic and non-words. The semantic-phonological model allows these error types to dissociate more fully than the alternative approach and so is better able to fit the data better (see Table 21.1, bottom). (3) *Interactivity*—Investigators continue to debate what extent and degree of interactivity is required to fit PWAs' naming response proportions (Goldrick & Rapp, 2002; Ruml, Caramazza, Capasso, & Miceli, 2005). Schwartz et al.'s (2006) model comparisons did not resolve that issue, but other results they presented (see also Dell et al., 1997; Gagnon, Schwartz, Martin, Dell, & Saffran, 1997) provide compelling evidence that feedback from phonology plays a role in the genesis of PWAs' formal and mixed errors.

The case series data that went into developing and testing the aphasia models have enabled other types of analyses, with interesting results (for critical discussion of case series methods in neuropsychology, see Schwartz & Dell, 2010, and related commentary). For example, the fitted s- and p-weight parameters have been analyzed for their distribution and association with other measures. One study demonstrated that p-weights determined from picture naming strongly predict word repetition performance, thus providing evidence that the second (lexical-phonological) step of naming is shared with repetition (Dell, Martin, & Schwartz, 2007; see also Nozari et al., 2010). Other studies have combined case series methods with voxel-based lesion-symptom mapping (VLSM; Bates, Wilson, Saygin, et al., 2003) to map the brain lesions that predict model parameters (s-weights, p-weights, and the non-lexical repetition parameter; Dell et al., 2013; Schwartz, 2014) or actual semantic and phonological error rates (Schwartz, Kimberg, Walker, et al., 2009; Schwartz, Kimberg, Walker, et al., 2011; Walker, Schwartz, Kimberg, et al., 2011). These anatomical investigations support and extend contemporary dual-route accounts of word production processes in the brain (e.g., Hickok & Poeppel, 2004; 2007; Ueno, Saito, Rogers, & Lambon Ralph, 2011) and provide additional evidence for the semantic-phonological model.

Nevertheless, the semantic-phonological account of word production continues to generate healthy debate and counterproposals, arguably accounting better for the quantitative error patterns of particular subtypes of aphasia (Romani & Galluzzi, 2005; Walker & Hickok, 2016), and dissociations at the level of individual patients (Goldrick, 2011, 2016; Goldrick & Rapp, 2007). For example, it seems quite likely that phonological errors do not arise solely from selection failure at step 2 of lexical access, but rather have additional loci in one or more postlexical stages of phonological-phonetic encoding (Galluzzi, Bureca, Guariglia, & Romani, 2015; Goldrick & Rapp, 2007; Kohn & Smith, 1994; Romani & Galluzzi, 2005; Schwartz, Wilshire, Gagnon, & Polansky, 2004). This is in keeping with the anatomical investigations mentioned earlier, which located the lesions responsible for phonological errors and reduced p-weights to frontoparietal, sensorimotor regions of the left peri-Sylvian region (Dell et al., 2013; Schwartz et al., 2012). There is also considerable evidence favoring a more expansive view of how semantic errors in aphasia arise, with behavioral and anatomical evidence implicating deficits in semantic representations (e.g., DeLeon, Gottesman, Kleinman, et al., 2007; Dell et al., 2013; Mesulam et al., 2013) and semantic regulation (Jefferies, Baker, Doran, & Lambon Ralph, 2007; Jefferies & Lambon Ralph, 2006; Jefferies, Patterson, & Lambon Ralph, 2008; Schnur et al., 2009) in addition to damaged s-weights (Schwartz et al., 2009; Walker et al., 2011).

Ongoing investigations into these and related questions are facilitated by the open access publication of relevant resources, including a database of the item-level naming and repetition responses that were used to develop and test the aphasia models (Mirman, Strauss, Brecher, et al., 2010) and the automated programs that can be used to fit and compare the weight-decay and semantic-phonological models (http://langprod.cogsci.illinois.edu/cgi-bin/webfit.cgi) as well as a related, alternative model developed by Walker and Hickok (2016) (http://www.cogsci.uci.edu/~alns/webfit).

21.4 Error monitoring, incremental learning, and a possible link between them

21.4.1 The conflict model of monitoring

In both speech and naming, production deficits in aphasia manifest in hesitations, editing terms, and self-correction, in addition to overt errors. The standardized coding procedures used to calculate naming response proportions take the first complete response on each trial and ignore all utterances preceding and following that response, much of which constitutes evidence of spontaneous error monitoring. There are risks in studying errors apart from monitoring. If speakers can detect and edit their errors prior to articulation of the first complete response, the error proportions we strive to fit with our models will underrepresent the true proportions. And, indeed, evidence for pre-articulatory monitoring is strong in both neurotypical speakers (Baars, Motley, & MacKay, 1975; Hartsuiker, Corley, & Martensen, 2005; Motley, 1980; Motley, Camden, & Baars, 1982;) and PWA (Oomen, Postma, & Kolk, 2001; Schlenk, Huber, & Wilmes, 1987). Moreover, if, as has been proposed, the status of monitoring in PWA relates directly to the integrity of production processes (Stark, 1988; Nozari et al., 2011), then by excluding monitoring, we ignore a potentially important source of information about production.

Bridging the divide, Nozari et. al. (2011) used the semantic-phonological naming model as the basis for an account of spontaneous monitoring of word production. Their conflict-monitoring model proposes that the competing activations among candidate responses at the word and phoneme layers of lexical access constitute a conflict signal that is the basis for detecting errors generated at that layer. They supported this thesis with model simulations showing, first, that activation vectors at the word and phoneme layers predicted the occurrence of semantic and non-word errors, respectively, and, second, that stronger s-weights produced a more reliable signal of semantic errors, and analogously for p-weights and non-word errors. The next step was to show that PWA with stronger weights actually had better error detection. For this, Nozari et al. (2011) drew on the archived transcriptions of PWAs' naming responses on the 175-item PNT (Roach et al., 1996), which included all disfluencies, pauses, repetitions, tangents, and incomplete responses produced on each trial. Nozari et al. (2011) established a reliable method for coding whether a given trial did or did not contain evidence of spontaneous error detection and then correlated PWAs' detection rates for semantic and phonological errors with their fitted s-and p-weights. The predictions were confirmed: PWA with stronger s-weights detected a higher proportion of their semantic errors ($r = 0.59$; $n = 29$; $p = 0.001$); those with stronger p-weights detected a higher proportion of their phonological errors ($r = 0.43$; $n = 29$; $p = 0.021$). The cross correlations (s-weight with phonological error detection; p-weight with semantic error detection) had significant negative coefficients.

The conflict model of speech error monitoring grew out of the well-supported thesis that in motor and other tasks, states of high conflict recruit cognitive control, typically associated with increased activity in the anterior cingulate cortex (Botvinick et al., 1999, 2001; Carter et al., 1998). Extrapolating from this, and from related studies of the error-related negativity component of the electroencephalography (EEG) signal (e.g., Yeung, Botvinick, & Cohen,

2004), Nozari et al. (2011) postulated that the conflict signals generated by the speech production system are read and acted upon by that same general-purpose conflict monitor.

The pre-eminent theory of speech monitoring is Levelt's (1983, 1989) Perceptual Loop Theory, which situates the monitor within the so-called conceptualizer component of the language system. This is the component that generates the prelinguistic message and passes it to the speech formulator for linguistic encoding. The function of the monitor is to compare the prelinguistic message (what was intended) to what the production system produces, *as processed through the comprehension system*. The result of this comparison determines whether the conceptualizer plans further speech acts of a clarifying or corrective nature. Levelt's theory does not address whether this is a dedicated or general-purpose monitor. The theory's most controversial claim is the importance it assigns to the comprehension system. In keeping with prior negative evidence from aphasia (e.g., Nickels & Howard, 1995; Marshall Robson, Pring, & Chiat, 1998), Nozari et al., (2011) found no significant correlations between the PWAs' semantic and phonological error-detection scores and their scores on relevant comprehension measures, and there were abundant examples of dissociations in both directions (e.g., poor semantic error detection with good semantic comprehension, and the reverse). These findings, alongside the positive evidence linking detection rates to production processes, pose difficulties for the Perceptual Loop Theory. Nevertheless, this theory's rich and detailed characterization of monitoring processes in speech is without parallel and we will have occasion to draw upon that characterization later in the chapter.

21.4.2 The dark side model

Oppenheim, Dell, and Schwartz's (2010) dark side model enhanced the base model's lexical-semantic architecture with the capacity to adaptively adjust connection weights in the service of learning. This allowed them to explore a learning-based account of cumulative semantic interference in naming. By way of background: it is well known that retrieving a name from meaning facilitates the later retrieval of that same name on the order of seconds and minutes (so-called repetition priming; e.g., Wheeldon & Monsell, 1992). Meaning-based name retrieval also impacts the subsequent retrieval of a semantically related name, both positively (semantic priming) and negatively (semantic interference). Wheeldon and Monsell (1994) famously showed that whereas semantic priming is transitory, semantic interference is longer lasting and persists across intervening, unrelated trials. Building on this, as well as earlier work by Brown (1981), Howard et al. (2006) demonstrated that the degree of interference, as manifested in naming latencies, increased linearly across successive category-related objects in a naming list and was unaffected by the presence and number of unrelated fillers between 2–8. They developed a model for this so-called cumulative semantic interference effect, which incorporated three essential properties: (1) naming an object (e.g., SHARK) persistently primes its future retrieval by strengthening its lexical-semantic connections; (2) such priming increases the potency of SHARK as a competitor for words that share its semantic features (e.g., WHALE); (3) SHARK's heightened potency impacts the latency and accuracy to name WHALE, and other related objects through a competitive selection mechanism (e.g., lateral inhibition, in their model).

Oppenheim et al. (2010) proposed that the first of these properties—persistent priming of lexical-semantic connection weights—might be a consequence of incremental, use-dependent learning. Their model derives its name, "dark side," from the authors' contention that cumulative semantic interference and long-term repetition priming are, respectively, the dark and light sides of the same learning process. To test their learning account, they implemented (only) the first, lexical access, step of naming in the manner of the interactive two-step model but using trainable s-weights. They then used this model to simulate data from semantic interference experiments with neurotypical speakers (e.g., Belke, Meyer, & Damian, 2005; Howard et al., 2006) and speakers with aphasia (Hsiao, Schwartz, Schnur, & Dell, 2009; Schnur, Schwartz, Brecher, & Hodgson, 2006). Each simulation experiment was run in two phases: The first phase—training—simulated participants' acquisition of pre-experimental lexical-semantic knowledge; the second phase—testing—simulated the incremental learning that took place throughout the experiment. The details of vocabulary varied across the phases but, critically, the learning process was the same in both: upon retrieving a word from semantics, a supervised, error-based learning rule ("delta rule") was applied. In this type of learning (e.g., Rumelhart, McClelland, & the PDP research group, 1986), connection weights (here, s-weights) are adjusted post-selection based on the discrepancy between a node's desired activation value on that trial and what the system actually produced. This desired-actual activation discrepancy is the "error" that drives learning. The delta rule functions as a teacher, or "supervisor," implementing post-selection weight changes that strengthen the desired target and weaken strong competitors, thereby reducing the likelihood of error on future trials.

After demonstrating that the dark side model was generally successful in reproducing the experimental findings, Oppenheim et al. (2010) went on to investigate the specific role played by delta rule learning. To quote the authors, "The important aspect of this algorithm is that it creates both strengthening of the connections to the target, and the weakening of the connections to competitors. Connection strengthening is clearly required for repetition priming, and connection weakening appears to explain at least a component of semantic interference" (p. 248). Their simulations revealed that the component of semantic interference explained by connection weakening is what could alternatively be achieved by replacing the dark side model's non-competitive lexical selection mechanism (inherited from the interactive two-step model) with a mechanism that introduced competition into the selection process itself. In other words, to account for semantic interference, competition must be allowed to influence performance, either during lexical selection (as in the Howard et al. 2006 model) or through delta rule learning, as implemented in the dark side model.

21.4.3 Learning and monitoring

Let us turn now to another feature of the learning rule implemented in the dark side model: the supervisory knowledge it instantiated. That the algorithm "knew" the correct answer on each trial was important for the simulations because it allowed the model to correct its errors during the first, training phase of each experiment[1]. But is this a psychologically

---

[1] Unpublished simulations run by Gary Oppenheim confirmed that with an unsupervised form of delta rule learning, where the selected response is assumed to be correct, and therefore strengthened, performance that starts out error-prone quickly becomes overwhelmed by errors. I am grateful to Dr. Oppenheim and Dr. Gary Dell for the very helpful discussions of these and related issues discussed in this section.

plausible mechanism of incremental, use-dependent learning? An interesting possibility is that such supervisory knowledge derives from or equates to what the central monitor knows about the produced versus intended response. That is, the knowledge that a speaker manifests in disavowing a naming response (SHARK → "whale, no") may directly or indirectly direct the choice of which weights to weaken (those of WHALE). Similarly, the knowledge that is manifested in an error repair (SHARK → "whale ... uh ... shark") may direct which weights to strengthen (those of SHARK). If this suggestion has merit, it should be possible to use error monitoring to predict incremental learning. A recent study provides some evidence to this effect (Schwartz et al., 2016).

The Schwartz et al. (2016) study sought to answer this question: Absent experimenter feedback, does spontaneous detection and/or repair of an error increase the probability of its being named correctly at a later time? Twelve PWA named a large set of items (n = 615) twice. The two tests were separated by at least a week, and extrinsic feedback was withheld on both tests. For each participant, on each trial of each test, both naming performance and monitoring performance were scored. The outcome of interest was how often errors at time 1 changed to correct at time 2 as a function of the associated monitoring behavior. The learning prediction was that compared to undetected errors, detected errors would be more likely to change to correct (because the learning process has access to relevant supervisory information). Using undetected errors as the baseline condition controlled for a variety of other factors that were likely to impact change from time 1 to 2, e.g., re-exposure to the target pictures, practice gains, and the stamping in of errors through Hebbian learning. It did not, however, control for the possibility that errors that are monitored are simply stronger items to begin with (i.e., closer to the normal threshold). On this possibility—call it the strength hypothesis—whether or not an error is detected is itself an indication of the target's strength and thus its likelihood of being correct at a different point in time, be it earlier or later. The test of the strength hypothesis involved a *backward* analysis. Consider: if items A and B are both misnamed at time 2, and the speaker spontaneously detects the error to A but not B, then according to the strength hypothesis, A is a stronger item than B and thus more likely to have been named correctly at the earlier test (time 1). The backward analysis thus measured correctness at time 1 for items that were incorrectly named at time 2, with the expectation that those of the A-type (detected error) would have higher correctness than those of the B-type (undetected error). This backward analysis provided a measure of the strength effect, as well as the means to control for its contribution to the forward analysis. In particular, the measure of the *learning effect* was whether the detected/not detected difference in the forward direction exceeded that in the backward direction; such an asymmetry would indicate a causal relationship between monitoring and future naming accuracy (i.e., learning).

Schwartz et al.'s (2016) actual study design was a bit more complicated. First, detected errors were subdivided according to whether the detected error was or was not repaired (i.e., corrected) before the end of the trial. So, there were three detection conditions: Detected–Repaired, Detected–Not Repaired, and Not Detected. Second, forward and backward analyses were conducted separately for three types of errors: semantic, phonological, and fragments (see Table 21.2 for definitions and examples). The analyses involved mixed effects logit regression modeling with crossed random effects.

Moving on to the results, there were consistent differences observed between the Detected–Repaired and baseline conditions. In no analysis did Detected–Not Repaired differ from baseline. Thus, the positive findings from this study all centered on error *repair*,

Table 21.2 Definitions of terms, with examples, from the study by Schwartz et al. (2006) that investigated the monitoring learning link

	Semantic error	Phonological error	Fragments	Detection	Repair
Definition	Noun response that conveys a conceptual mismatch in the form for a near-synonym, category coordinate, thematic associate, or incorrect but related superordinate or subordinate. Semantic errors could also resemble the target phonologically.	Non-target response that did not meet criteria for Semantic Error but has ≥.50 phonological overlap with the target, inclusive of non-words. Phonological errors included non-words as well as real-word nouns, adjectives, adverbs, or verbs.	Self-interrupted response comprising minimally a consonant + vowel (CV) or vowel + consonant (VC) sequence that is non-repetitious with the subsequent response. In cases where the following response repeated the fragment (goose >*/dʌ-/, duck'), the fragment.	Verbal response on the same trial as the error that signals its disavowal through a negation response, changes naming attempted, or changed affixation of a free or bound morpheme (exclusive of plural morpheme). Filled pauses ("oh" "eh" "umm") do not count as detection responses.	Detected errors were classified as repaired if the correct response was produced immediately after the error as the last of multiple attempts. All other detected errors were classified as detected without repair.
Example	notebook > "copybook"; trumpet > "tuba"; pirate > "treasure"; lemon > "lime"; apple > "vegetable"; shoe > "slipper."	banana > "/ɔnæn/"; stool > "sit"; chair > "care"; flower > "/saʊər/ (sour).	shoe > "***" (fragment error); goose > /dʌ-/ duck (semantic error; self-interruption ignored)."	shoe > "slipper, *no*" (or, "*that's not it*," "*it's not that*" "*nope*," and so on); duck > "goose, *duck*"; banana >"/ bi-/, *banana*."	

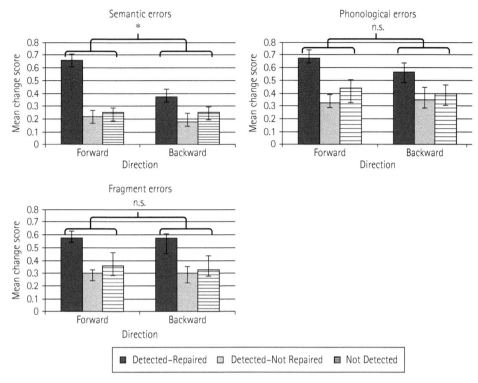

FIG. 21.2 Proportion mean change score as a function of detection/repair event and direction for each error type.

Reprinted from *Neuropsychologia*, 84, Myrna F. Schwartz, Erica L. Middleton, Adelyn Brecher, Maureen Gagliardi, and Kelly Garvey, Does naming accuracy improve through self-monitoring of errors?, pp. 272–81, doi.org/10.1016/j.neuropsychologia.2016.01.027, Copyright © 2016 Elsevier Ltd., with permission from Elsevier.

not error detection. Repaired errors of all three types (semantic, phonological, fragments) exhibited the strength effect; in the backward analysis, errors that were repaired at time 2 were more likely to be correct at time 1, relative to baseline. This is convincing evidence that items that are misnamed with repair are stronger items than those that are misnamed without repair.

There was also support for the all-important learning effect, but only in the case of semantic errors. For semantic errors, the repaired/not repaired difference was greater in the forward than backward analysis, indicating a causal relationship between repair of a semantic error and its future correctness. Figure 21.2 shows the data in the form of proportions. For details of the mixed models analyses used to determine significance, readers should consult the original paper.

From the perspective of delta rule learning, the evidence from this monitoring study suggests that learning requires knowing the correct response: what to strengthen. But is that really what's critical? Maybe when an error is repaired, the learning system can compare activation vectors for the correct response (the repair) with those for the original response (the error), and this comparison is what drives learning. Of course, this requires that relevant traces of the error response remain available to the system, rather than being overwritten or suppressed. This requirement is consistent with existing accounts, which characterize the repair process as "reprogramming," subject to contextual priming from lingering traces of the original response (Hartsuiker & Kolk, 2001; Levelt, 1983; and for experimental support, Hartsuiker, Pickering, & de Jong, 2005). Let us pursue this idea a bit further.

Hartsuiker and Kolk (2001) formalized the Perceptual Loop Theory to account for experimental data on the time course of self-interruptions and repair of errors in connected speech. Relevant to the present discussion, their model assumed that the timing of phonological repair benefits from earlier attempts at the same word to a greater extent than semantic and grammatical errors. First, reprogramming of a phonological error benefits from the lingering trace of the correct, higher level representations. Second, the repair is primed by the phonological overlap with the error response.

Schuchard, Middleton, & Schwartz (2017) obtained support for these timing assumptions in an analysis of the time course of semantic and phonological error monitoring in the data from Schwartz et al. (2016). Latencies were measured from the onset of error to the onset of the first overt evidence of detection. In some cases, the first evidence of detection was a negation response (Fig. 21.3.A). In other cases, the first evidence of detection was a repair attempt, which could be successful (Fig. 21.3B) or unsuccessful (Fig. 21.3C). Thus, with detection latency as the outcome variable, the predictors of interest were error type (semantic or phonological) and detection type (negation, successful repair, unsuccessful repair). Data were analyzed with mixed effects regression models, using a model comparisons approach.

Results showed that phonological error detection was faster than semantic error detection, and this was due primarily to successful repairs. As is evident in Table 21.3 and Figure 21.4, phonological errors were repaired more quickly than semantic errors were repaired. The statistical analysis confirmed that repair latencies were speeded by error-response phonological overlap. Importantly, though, the timing advantage for phonological error repair remained significant after controlling for such overlap. This is as expected if the original (correct) products of step 1 remain available to prime or otherwise influence step 2's reprogramming.

So, returning to the earlier discussion, it does appear that products of the original response persist long enough to impact the time course of repair, at least. Important questions for the future are whether these lingering traces function in the service of a supervised learning process, for example, supporting comparison between the correct (reprogrammed) activations and those that produced the error and whether this is indeed the basis for the monitoring learning effect obtained by Schwartz et al. (2016).

21.5 Conclusion

This chapter has touched on multiple lines of research framed around the family of lexical access models created by Dell and colleagues. An overarching goal has been to illustrate the cycle of influence whereby a theoretical model developed for normal language processing and adapted for aphasia generates new hypotheses and new data leading to novel theoretical insights and further model development. This is a widely used strategy in cognitive neuropsychology, familiar to many from the body of work on the "distributed-plus-hub" theory of semantic memory and semantic dementia (Lambon Ralph, Sage, Jones, & Mayberry, 2010;

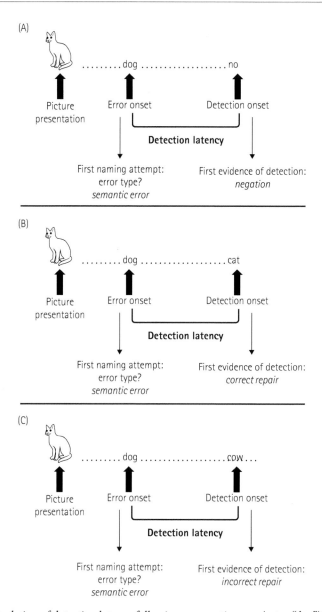

FIG. 21.3 Calculation of detection latency following a semantic error (cat → "dog"), where the first evidence of detection is a negation response (panel A), a correct repair (B), or an incorrect repair (C).

Reprinted from Schuchard, J., Middleton, E. L., & Schwartz, M. F. (2017). The timing of spontaneous detection and repair of naming errors in aphasia. *Cortex, 93*, 79–91.

Patterson, Nestor, & Rogers, 2007; Rogers, Lambon Ralph, Garrard, et al., 2004; Woollams et al., 2008).

The unique aspect of the interactive two-step model of aphasia is that it is designed to fit quantitative data from individual patients. This enabled Dell, Schwartz, and their colleagues to evaluate the model for how well it captured the wide variation in naming patterns observed in unselected samples of PWA, compare variants of the base model, and identify

Table 21.3 Individual detection rates and latencies

Participant	Phonological errors (proportion detected)	Semantic errors (proportion detected)	Detection latency: Negation	Detection latency: Phonological error repair	Detection latency: Semantic error repair
1	50 (0.44)	236 (0.41)	2.137	4.188	2.918
2	177 (0.74)	111 (0.38)	1.739	3.040	3.413
3	105 (0.26)	85 (0.13)	4.496	1.949	2.610
4	69 (0.35)	263 (0.38)	0.891	2.439	2.847
5	62 (0.53)	168 (0.49)	2.034	1.099	3.077
6	81 (0.06)	148 (0.23)	3.381	4.274	3.422
7	74 (0.43)	132 (0.24)	1.476	1.007	3.729
8	24 (0.13)	147 (0.06)	1.241	2.302	3.182
9	87 (0.08)	114 (0.06)	0.870	1.028	1.547
10	28 (0.79)	129 (0.16)	1.628	1.091	1.727
11	54 (0.17)	149 (0.17)	2.541	1.481	4.386
12	100 (0.33)	169 (0.34)	2.038	2.531	4.548
Mean	76 (0.36)	154 (0.25)	1.759	2.377	3.238

Note: Detection latencies represent the mean time in seconds from the onset of the error to the onset of the detection response.

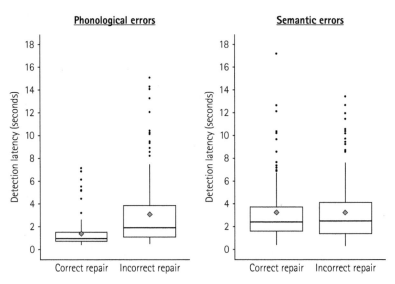

FIG. 21.4 Distributions of detection latencies for repair attempts. The bottom, middle, and top of each box represent the 25th, 50th, and 75th percentiles, respectively. Points represent outliers greater than 1.5 times the interquartile range. The diamond overlaid on each plot represents the mean.

Reprinted from Schuchard, J., Middleton, E. L., & Schwartz, M. F. (2017). The timing of spontaneous detection and repair of naming errors in aphasia. *Cortex, 93,* 79–91.

naming patterns that are systematically observed but not adequately explained by the model (see Schwartz et al., 2006 for examples). In addition, because each PWA fit by the naming model receives a "diagnosis" estimating the severity of the affected process (e.g., degree to which the s-weights and p-weights are compromised), predictions could be made and tested as to how well the PWA would perform on other, related language measures, such as word repetition (Dell et al., 1997) or spontaneous error detection (Nozari et al., 2010).

In applied research on naming impairments in aphasia, a PWA's model diagnosis, or, more commonly, naming response proportions, is frequently used as a basis for assignment to treatment group and/or to explain differences in response to treatment (e.g., Abel, Willmes, & Huber, 2007; Martin, Fink, Laine, & Ayala, 2004). In the early days of cognitive neuropsychology, there was optimism that model-driven diagnosis of impaired and spared lexical access process could serve as the basis for devising treatment plans. This optimism has been tempered somewhat by the mix of negative and positive findings from multiple individual and small group studies (Lorenz & Ziegler, 2009; Nickels, 2002). Today, there is greater awareness of the confluence of factors that influence a PWA's response to treatment, including how the damaged language system responds to its errors.

Interest in the impact of errors stems from several lines of inquiry. On the one hand, we have evidence suggesting that naming errors can be learned (Humphreys, Menzies, & Lake, 2010; Middleton & Schwartz, 2013) and encouraging errorless approaches to treatment (for history and review, Middleton & Schwartz, 2012). On the other hand, it has been shown that treatments that combine name retrieval (an errorful procedure) with feedback promote more enduring gains compared to an errorless approach (Friedman, Jones, & Snider, 2017; Middleton, 2016; Middleton, Schwartz, Rawson, & Garvey, 2015; Middleton, Schwartz, Rawson, et al., 2016). Finally, there is the now abundant evidence of lifelong, user-based, incremental language learning that is neither derailed by errors nor dependent on other-produced corrective feedback. The dark side model (Oppenheim et al., 2010) simulates such learning using a supervised, error-based learning algorithm. The search for a psychologically plausible account of the "supervisor" motivated the search for a monitoring learning link, with encouraging results.

Schwartz et al.'s (2016) monitoring study took advantage of the fact that the lexical access difficulties in aphasia result from lesions that reduce the efficiency of signaling activation relative to noise, which renders lexical access highly variable within subject and items; that is, a given item is frequently named correctly on one occasion but not another (for contrast with semantic dementia, see Jefferies & Lambon Ralph, 2006). As the test for the monitoring learning effect depended on this within-item variable performance, the study would have been difficult, if not impossible, to carry out in a different population. Nevertheless, the results, if replicated, promise to advance the understanding of incremental lexical learning in all types of speakers. The important takeaway lesson is that model-based investigations of atypical speakers open the door to new types of experimental inquiry and new insights into general processes in language production.

Acknowledgments

This chapter was written with support from the NIH NIDCD, grant #DC000191-35. The ideas presented in this chapter draw upon the work and insights of many colleagues and students, and the author wishes to acknowledge especially the contributions of Gary Dell, Erica Middleton, Bonnie Nozari, Gary Oppenheim, and Julia Schuchard.

References

Abel, S., Willmes, K., & Huber, W. (2007). Model-oriented naming therapy: Testing predictions of a connectionist model. *Aphasiology*, 5, 411–47.

Baars, B. J., Motley, M. T., & MacKay, D. G. (1975). Output editing for lexical status in artificially elicited slips of the tongue. *Journal of Verbal Learning & Verbal Behavior*, 14, 382–91.

Bates, E., Wilson, S. M., Saygin, A. P., Dick, F., Sereno, M. I., Knight, R. T., & Dronkers, N. F. (2003). Voxel-based lesion-symptom mapping. *Nature Neuroscience*, 6, 448–50.

Belke, E., Meyer, A. S., & Damian, M. F. (2005). Refractory effects in picture naming as assessed in a semantic blocking paradigm. *Quarterly Journal of Experimental Psychology Section A: Human Experimental Psychology*, 58, 667–92.

Botvinick, M. M., Braver, T. S., Carter, C. S., Barch, D. M., & Cohen, J. D. (2001). Evaluating the demand for control: Anterior cingulate cortex and crosstalk monitoring. *Psychological Review*, 108, 624–52.

Botvinick, M. M., Nystrom, L. E., Fissell, K., Carter, C. S., & Cohen, J. D. (1999). Conflict monitoring versus selection-for-action in anterior cingulate cortex. *Nature*, 402, 179–81.

Brown, A. S. (1981). Inhibition in cued retrieval. *Journal of Experimental Psychology: Human Learning and Memory*, 7(3), 204–15.

Carter, C. S., Braver, T. S., Barch, D., Botvinick, M. M., Noll, D., & Cohen, J. D. (1998). Anterior cingulate cortex, error detection, and the online monitoring of performance. *Science*, 280, 747–9.

DeLeon, J., Gottesman, R. F., Kleinman, J. T., Newhart, M., Davis, C., Heidler-Gary, J., . . . & Hillis, A. E. (2007). Neural regions essential for distinct cognitive processes underlying picture naming. *Brain*, 130, 1408–22.

Dell, G. S. (1986). A spreading-activation theory of retrieval in sentence production. *Psychological Review*, 93, 283–321.

Dell, G. S., Lawler, E. N., Harris, H. D., & Gordon, J. K. (2004). Models of errors of omission in aphasic naming. *Cognitive Neuropsychology*, 21(2–4), 125–45.

Dell, G. S., Martin, N., & Schwartz, M. F. (2007). A case-series test of the interactive two-step model of lexical access: Predicting word repetition from picture naming. *Journal of Memory and Language*, 56, 490–520.

Dell, G. S., & O'Seaghdha, P. G. (1991). Mediated and convergent lexical priming in language production: A comment on Levelt et al. (1991). *Psychological Review*, 98, 604–14.

Dell, G. S., Schwartz, M. F., Martin, N., Saffran, E. M., & Gagnon, D. A. (1997). Lexical access in aphasic and nonaphasic speakers. *Psychological Review*, 104, 801–38.

Dell, G. S., Schwartz, M. F., Nozari, N., Faseyitan, O., & Coslett, H. B. (2013). Voxel-based lesion-parameter mapping: Identifying the neural correlates of a computational model of word production in aphasia. *Cognition*, 128, 380–96.

Foygel, D., & Dell, G. S. (2000). Models of impaired lexical access in speech production. *Journal of Memory and Language*, 43, 182–216.

Friedman, R., Jones, K. T., & Snider, S. F. (2017). Leveraging the test effect to improve maintenance of the gains achieved through cognitive rehabilitation. *Neuropsychology*, 31(2), 220–28.

Gagnon, D. A., Schwartz, M. F., Martin, N., Dell, G. S., & Saffran, E. M. (1997). The origins of formal paraphasias in aphasics' picture naming. *Brain and Language, 59*, 450–72.

Galluzzi, C., Bureca, I., Guariglia, C., & Romani, C. (2015). Phonological simplifications, apraxia of speech and the interaction between phonological and phonetic processing. *Neuropsychologia, 71*, 64–83.

Goldrick, M. (2011). Theory selection and evaluation in case series research. *Cognitive Neuropsychology, 28*, 451–65.

Goldrick, M. (2016). Integrating SLAM with existing evidence: Comment on Walker and Hickok (2015). *Psychonomic Bulletin & Review, 23*, 648–52.

Goldrick, M., & Rapp, B. (2002). A restricted interaction account (RIA) of spoken word production: The best of both worlds. *Aphasiology, 16*, 20–55.

Goldrick M., & Rapp B. (2007). Lexical and post-lexical phonological representations in spoken production. *Cognition, 102*, 219–60.

Hartsuiker, R. J., Corley, M., & Martensen, H. (2005). The lexical bias effect is modulated by context, but the standard monitoring account doesn't fly: Related reply to Baars et al. (1975). *Journal of Memory and Language, 52*, 58–70.

Hartsuiker, R. J., & Kolk, H. H. J. (2001). Error monitoring in speech production: A computational test of the perceptual loop theory. *Cognitive Psychology, 42*, 113–57.

Hartsuiker, R. J., Pickering, M. J., & de Jong, N. H. (2005). Semantic and phonological context effects in speech error repair. *Journal of Experimental Psychology: Learning, Memory, and Cognition, 31*, 921–32.

Hickok, G., & Poeppel, D. (2004). Dorsal and ventral streams: a framework for understanding aspects of the functional anatomy of language. *Cognition, 92*(1–2), 67–99.

Hickok, G., & Poeppel, D. (2007). The cortical organization of speech processing. *Nature Reviews Neuroscience, 8*, 393–402.

Howard, D., Nickels, L., Coltheart, M., & Cole-Virtue, J. (2006). Cumulative semantic inhibition in picture naming: Experimental and computational studies. *Cognition, 100*, 464–82.

Hsiao, E. Y., Schwartz, M. F., Schnur, T. T., & Dell, G. S. (2009). Temporal characteristics of semantic perseverations induced by blocked-cyclic picture naming. *Brain and Language, 108*, 133–44.

Humphreys, K. R., Menzies, H., & Lake, J. K. (2010). Repeated speech errors: Evidence for learning. *Cognition, 117*, 151–65.

Jefferies, E., & Lambon Ralph, M. A. (2006). Semantic impairment in stroke aphasia versus semantic dementia: A case-series comparison. *Brain, 129*, 2132–47.

Jefferies, E., Baker, S. S., Doran, M., & Lambon Ralph, M. A. (2007). Refractory effects in stroke aphasia: A consequence of poor semantic control. *Neuropsychologia, 45*, 1065–79.

Jefferies, E., Patterson, K. A., & Lambon Ralph, M. A. (2008). Deficits of knowledge versus executive control in semantic cognition: Insights from cued naming. *Neuropsychologia, 46*, 649–58.

Kohn, S. E., & Smith, K. L. (1994). Distinctions between two phonological output deficits. *Applied Psycholinguistics, 15*, 75–95.

Lambon Ralph, M. A., Sage, K., Jones, R. W., & Mayberry, E. J. (2010). Coherent concepts are computed in the anterior temporal lobes. *Proceedings of the National Academy of Sciences, 107*, 2717–22.

Levelt, W. J. M. (1983). Monitoring and self-repair in speech. *Cognition, 14*, 41–104.

Levelt, W. J. M. (1989). *Speaking: From Intention to Articulation.* MIT Press, Cambridge, MA.

Levelt, W. J. M., Roelofs, A., & Meyer, A. S. (1999). A theory of lexical access in speech production. *Behavioral and Brain Sciences, 22*, 1–38.

Levelt, W. J. M., Schriefers, H., Vorberg, D., Meyer, A. S., Pechmann, T., & Havinga, J. (1991). The time course of lexical access in speech production: A study of picture naming. *Psychological Review, 98*, 122–42.

Lorenz, A., & Ziegler, W. (2009). Semantic vs. word-form specific techniques in anomia treatment: A multiple single-case study. *Journal of Neurolinguistics, 22*, 515–37.

Marshall, J., Robson, J., Pring, T., & Chiat, S. (1998). Why does monitoring fail in jargon aphasia? Comprehension, judgment, and therapy evidence. *Brain and Language, 63*, 79–107.

Martin, N., Dell, G. S., Saffran, E. M., & Schwartz, M. F. (1994). Origins of paraphasias in deep dysphasia: Testing the consequences of a decay impairment to an interactive spreading activation model of lexical retrieval. *Brain And Language, 47*, 609–60.

Martin, N., Fink, R., Laine, M., & Ayala, J. (2004). Immediate and short-term effects of contextual priming on word retrieval in aphasia. *Aphasiology, 18*, 867–98.

Mesulam, M., Wieneke, C., Hurley, R., Rademaker, A., Thompson, C. K., Weintraub S., & Rogalski, E. J. (2013). Words and objects at the tip of the left temporal lobe in primary progressive aphasia. *Brain, 136*, 601–18.

Middleton, E. (2016). *Retrieval Practice and Spacing Effects in Naming Rehabilitation: A Theory of Learning*. Frontiers of Psychology. Conference Abstract: 54th Annual Academy of Aphasia Meeting. doi: 10.3389/conf.fpsyg.2016.68.00040

Middleton, E. L., & Schwartz, M. F. (2012). Errorless learning in cognitive rehabilitation: A critical review. *Neuropsychological Rehabilitation, 22*, 138–68.

Middleton, E. L., & Schwartz, M. F. (2013). Learning to fail in aphasia: An investigation of error learning in naming. *Journal of Speech, Language, and Hearing Research, 56*, 1287–97.

Middleton, E. L., Schwartz, M. F., Rawson, K. A., & Garvey, K. (2015). Test-enhanced learning versus errorless learning in aphasia rehabilitation: Testing competing psychological principles. *Journal of Experimental Psychology: Learning, Memory, and Cognition, 41*, 1253–61.

Middleton, E. L., Schwartz, M. F., Rawson, K. A., Traut, H., & Verkuilen, J. (2016). Towards a theory of learning for naming rehabilitation: Retrieval practice and spacing effects. *Journal of Speech, Language, and Hearing Research, 59*(5), 1111–22.

Mirman, D., Strauss, T. J., Brecher, A., Walker, G. M., Sobel, P., Dell, G. S., & Schwartz, M. F. (2010). A large, searchable, web-based database of aphasic performance on picture naming and other tests of cognitive function. *Cognitive Neuropsychology, 27*, 495–504.

Motley, M. T. (1980). Verification of "Freudian slips" and semantic prearticulatory editing via laboratory induced spoonerisms. In: Fromkin, V. A. (Ed.), *Errors in Linguistic Performance: Slips of the Tongue, Ear, Pen, and Hand* (pp. 133–48). Academic Press, New York, NY.

Motley, M. T., Camden, C. T., & Baars, B. J. (1982). Covert formulation and editing of anomalies in speech production: evidence from experimentally elicited slips of the tongue. *Journal of Verbal Learning and Verbal Behavior, 21*, 578–94.

Nickels, L. (2002). Therapy for naming disorders: Revisiting, revising, and reviewing. *Aphasiology, 16*, 935–79.

Nickels, L., & Howard, D. (1995). Phonological errors in aphasic naming: Comprehension, monitoring and lexicality. *Cortex, 31*, 209–37.

Nozari, N., Dell, G. S., & Schwartz, M. F. (2011). Is comprehension necessary for error detection? A conflict-based account of monitoring in speech production. *Cognitive Psychology, 63*, 1–33.

Nozari, N., Kittredge, A. K., Dell, G. S., & Schwartz, M. F. (2010). Naming and repetition in aphasia: Steps, routes, and frequency effects. *Journal of Memory and Language, 63*, 541–59.

Oomen, C. C. E., Postma, A., & Kolk, H. H. J. (2001). Prearticulatory and postarticulatory self-monitoring in Broca's aphasia. *Cortex, 37*, 627–41.

Oppenheim, G. M., Dell, G. S., & Schwartz, M. F. (2010). The dark side of incremental learning: A model of cumulative semantic interference during lexical access in speech production. *Cognition, 114*, 2.

Patterson, K., Nestor, P. J., & Rogers, T. T. (2007). Where do you know what you know? The representation of semantic knowledge in the human brain. *Nature Reviews Neuroscience, 8*, 976–87.

Rapp, B. C., & Goldrick, M. (2000). Discreteness and interactivity in spoken word production. *Psychological Review, 107*, 460–99.

Roach, A., Schwartz, M. F., Martin, N., Grewal, R. S., & Brecher, A. (1996). The Philadelphia Naming Test: Scoring and rationale. *Clinical Aphasiology, 24*, 121–33.

Rogers, T. T., Lambon Ralph, M. A., Garrard, P., Bozeat, S., McClelland, J. L., Hodges, J. R., & Patterson, K. (2004). Structure and deterioration of semantic memory: A neuropsychological and computational investigation. *Psychological Review, 111*, 205–35.

Romani, C., & Galluzzi, C. (2005). Effects of syllabic complexity in predicting accuracy of repetition and direction of errors in patients with articulatory and phonological difficulties. *Cognitive Neuropsychology, 22*, 817–50.

Rumelhart, D. E., McClelland, J. L., & the PDP Research Group (1986). *Parallel Distributed Processing: Explorations in the Microstructure of Cognition (Vol. I)*. MIT Press, Cambridge, MA.

Ruml, W., & Caramazza, A. (2000). An evaluation of a computational model of lexical access: Comment on Dell et al. (1997). *Psychological Review, 107*, 609–34.

Ruml, W., Caramazza, A., Capasso, R., & Miceli, G. (2005). Interactivity and continuity in normal and aphasic language production. *Cognitive Neuropsychology, 22*, 131–68.

Schlenk, K., Huber, W., & Wilmes, K. (1987). "Prepairs" and repairs: different monitoring functions in aphasic language production. *Brain and Language, 30*, 226–44.

Schnur, T. T., Schwartz, M. F., Brecher, A., & Hodgson, C. (2006). Semantic interference during blocked-cyclic naming: Evidence from aphasia. *Journal of Memory and Language, 54*, 199–227.

Schnur, T. T., Schwartz, M. F., Kimberg, D. Y., Hirshorn, E., Coslett, H. B., & Thompson-Schill, S. L. (2009). Localizing interference during naming: Convergent neuroimaging and neuropsychological evidence for the function of Broca's area. *Proceedings of the National Academy of Sciences, 106*, 322–7.

Schuchard, J., Middleton, E. L., & Schwartz, M. F. (2017). The timing of spontaneous detection and repair of naming errors in aphasia. *Cortex, 93*, 79–91.

Schwartz, M. F. (2014). Theoretical analysis of word production deficits in adult aphasia. *Philosophical Transactions of the Royal Society B: Biological Sciences, 369*, 20120390.

Schwartz, M. F., & Dell, G. S. (2010). Case series investigations in cognitive neuropsychology. *Cognitive Neuropsychology, 27*, 477–94.

Schwartz, M. F., Dell, G. S., Martin, N., Gahl, S., & Sobel, P. (2006). A case-series test of the interactive two-step model of lexical access: Evidence from picture naming. *Journal of Memory and Language, 54*, 228–64.

Schwartz, M. F., Faseyitan, O., Kim, J., & Coslett, H. B. (2012). The dorsal stream contribution to phonological retrieval in object naming. *Brain, 135*, 3799–814.

Schwartz, M. F., Kimberg, D. Y., Walker, G. M., Brecher, A., Faseyitan, O., Dell, G. S., ... & Coslett, H. B. (2011). Neuroanatomical dissociation for taxonomic and thematic knowledge in the human brain. *Proceedings of the National Academy of Sciences, 108*, 8520–4.

Schwartz, M. F., Kimberg, D. Y., Walker, G. M., Faseyitan, O., Brecher, A., Dell, G. S., & Coslett, H. B. (2009). Anterior temporal involvement in semantic word retrieval: VLSM evidence from aphasia. *Brain, 132*, 3411–27.

Schwartz, M. F., Middleton, E. L., Brecher, A., Gagliardi, M., & Garvey, K. (2016). Does naming accuracy improve through self-monitoring of errors? *Neuropsychologia, 84*, 272–81.

Schwartz, M. F., Wilshire, C. E., Gagnon, D. A., & Polansky, M. (2004). Origins of nonword phonological errors in aphasic picture naming. *Cognitive Neuropsychology, 21*, 159–86.

Stark, J. (1988). Aspects of automatic versus controlled processing, monitoring, metalinguistic tasks, and related phenomena in aphasia. In: Dressler, W., & Stark, J. (Eds.), *Linguistic Analyses of Aphasic Language* (pp. 179–223). Springer-Verlag, New York, NY.

Ueno, T., Saito, S., Rogers, T. T., & Lambon Ralph, M. A. (2011). Lichtheim 2: Synthesising aphasia and the neural basis of language in a neurocomputational model of the dual dorsal-ventral language pathways. *Neuron, 72*, 385–96.

Walker, G. M., & Hickok, G. (2016). Bridging computational approaches to speech production: The semantic–lexical–auditory–motor model (SLAM). *Psychonomic Bulletin & Review, 23*, 339–52.

Walker, G. M., Schwartz, M. F., Kimberg, D. Y., Faseyitan, O., Brecher, A., Dell, G. S., & Coslett, H. B. (2011). Support for anterior temporal involvement in semantic error production in aphasia: New evidence from VLSM. *Brain and Language, 117*, 110–22.

Wheeldon, L. R., & Monsell, S. (1992). The locus of repetition priming of spoken word production. *Quarterly Journal of Experimental Psychology Section A: Human Experimental Psychology, 44*, 723–61.

Wheeldon, L. R., & Monsell, S. (1994). Inhibition of spoken word production by priming a semantic competitor. *Journal of Memory and Language, 33*, 332–56.

Woollams, A., Cooper-Pye, E., Hodges, J. R., & Patterson, K. (2008). Anomia: A doubly typical signature of semantic dementia. *Neuropsychologia, 46*, 2503–14.

Yeung, N., Botvinick, M. M., & Cohen, J. D. (2004). The neural basis of error detection: Conflict monitoring and the error-related negativity. *Psychological Review, 111*, 931–59.

CHAPTER 22

ATTENTION AND STRUCTURAL CHOICE IN SENTENCE PRODUCTION

ANDRIY MYACHYKOV, MIKHAIL POKHODAY, AND RUSSELL TOMLIN

22.1 INTRODUCTION

THE world that we perceive and describe changes constantly. If we believe our descriptions of the world to be accurate and consistent, we must assume that the content and the structure of individual sentences accurately and consistently reflect the world's constantly changing nature. A comprehensive production system must therefore portray a sentence generation process that considers this basic assumption: words, their linear arrangement, and the structures they are inserted in must somehow reflect corresponding parameters of the described event. This system should include representation of *salience* as one integral component of the perceived world. Constant interplay between perception and language involves constant, regular, and automatic mappings between elements of a visual scene, their varying salience, and the structural arrangement of the sentence constituents and the grammatical relations between them. By affecting the speaker's attentional state, salience provides the most basic perceptual input for further conceptual, lexical, and grammatical encoding. However, this basic perceptual input is not processed in an unconstrained fashion; instead, it is systematically filtered, selected, and relayed based on a regular interface between the general content of the described event and the corresponding conceptual and linguistic categories and structures. As a result, linguistic output reflects in a regular way the event's conceptual organization including the attentional state of the speaker. This chapter will consider theoretical and empirical knowledge concerning the correspondence between the speaker's *attentional state* and the *structural choices* made during sentence production.

First, we need to consider how attention features in commonly accepted sentence production frameworks. One of the most enduring models (Levelt, 1989) starts with a *conceptualizer* that allows mapping the observed event onto a preverbal *message*. Processing at this stage leads to the formulation of the event's conceptual plan. Among other parameters, the conceptual plan codes the event's perceptual properties including the relative salience of its integral components. Then the *utterance formulator* takes over by selecting *lemmas*, or the words with their grammatical properties, leading to a *structural assembly*: the process of prescribing structural configuration and a word order according to the rules of a given grammar. Finally, the *articulator* operates on this input producing spoken (or written) output. Operations at the message stage encompass *non-linguistic* processing of the content to be described. The stages that follow are referred to as *linguistic* stages as operations within them involve lexical, morphological, syntactic, and phonological access. Levelt's model is optimal in detailing what happens at the linguistic stages. At the same time, it is quite general about the organization of the message or, indeed, whether the message itself has any internal organization at all. It also has relatively little to say about the mapping mechanisms that translate the content of the message into the corresponding linguistic categories and structures. In order to describe how the message may affect the content and the organization of a sentence, we need to consider two important theoretical questions that will help us to properly understand the empirical literature we review next. To situate these questions in context, consider an event, in which *a policeman is chasing a burglar*. In English, this event can be described by using multiple structural alternatives including the following:

(a) *The policeman is chasing the burglar.*
(b) *The burglar is chased by the policeman.*

Although these two options do not exhaust the available structural inventory, they occur most frequently. They also allow us to identify two distinct structural alternatives:

(a) An active clause with *the policeman* as syntactic *subject* and the sentential *starting point* with *the burglar* as *object* in *final position*.
(b) A passive clause with *the burglar* as syntactic *subject* and the sentential *starting point* and *by the policeman* as *adverbial* in *final position*.

How can attention *in principle* bias the speaker to favor one of these alternatives? The obvious null hypothesis about the role for attention in the choice between these two alternatives is that it has none. We will entertain and reject this hypothesis in the first section of our empirical data review. If we consider any positive role for attention, we then need to break down our original question in two parts:

(1) What motivates the speaker to arrange the sentence in such a way that the referents assume a specific linear ordering?
(2) What motivates the speaker to assign specific structural roles (e.g., subject or object/adverbial) within a specific syntactic structure (e.g., active or passive voice)?

These two questions reflect two corresponding processes in sentence production: word order selection and grammatical-role assignment.

In principle, attention can play a role in either or both of these two processes: First, by ordering constituents according to their corresponding referents' salience; second, by mapping referents onto specific structural elements: subject, object, and so on. Correspondingly, a *positional* view (see also Bock, Irwin, & Davidson, 2004) suggests that the preference for (b), for example, predominantly reflects the tendency to *start* a sentence with a more salient *burglar* regardless of its grammatical role. In contrast, a *grammatical-role* account (Tomlin, 1995, 1997) suggests that different languages may use different *grammatical* strategies to accomplish the end of conveying the most salient referent to a listener. As a result, a speaker of English may choose (b) by mapping the more salient *burglar* onto the grammatical relation of the subject in the sentence.

The importance of sentential starting points was pointed out by MacWhinney (1977) who suggested that salient referents tend to occupy initial positions in spoken sentences thus triggering both its linear and structural organization. However, structural importance of starting points varies from language to language. This is true because, while some languages generally conflate linear and structural arrangement (e.g., English), others do not (e.g., Russian). As a result, the starting point will not always correspond to the most prominent grammatical role (e.g., subject) making it difficult to explain how and why the prominent starting point will sometimes diverge from the structurally prominent subject role. Next, we review evidence from flexible word order languages that contradicts a strong positional view.

According to the grammatical-role account there are two theoretical possibilities. First, mapping events' referents onto their grammatical roles in a sentence may require a *syntactic structure* to code a corresponding *thematic structure* making the underlying mapping mechanism more holistic. According to this scenario, the mapping mechanism treats the to-be-described event as one holistic gist rather than a structured conceptual map with differing prominence statues of the individual components. Alternatively, the selected sentence frame may signal the interacting referents' *individual* conceptual and/ or perceptual *statuses*. According to this scenario, perceptually salient or preferentially attended referents will be prescribed "salient" grammatical roles (e.g., subject) while less perceptually prominent referents will receive less prominent grammatical roles. These two possibilities will become very important when we derive specific contrasting experimental predictions.

As just described, potential biases from event relations and from referents' statuses/roles are not necessarily mutually exclusive; they just attribute priority for linguistic encoding to various aspects of the conceptual organization of the *same* event. In other words, aboutness (a relationship between the referents or who-does-what-to-whom) and salience/prominence (who is bigger/brighter/more animate/more important) are part of the same conceptual structure and, as such, can (at least in principle) be simultaneously coded by specific sentence parameters. Although there is a distinct lack of research that systematically teases apart contributions from the relational and the role-related forces, some studies indeed find that while certain event descriptions promote salience-based structural selections, others tend to focus on how easy it is to conceptualize the relational structure of the event itself (Konopka, 2012; Kuchinsky & Bock, 2010). Note that a priori neither salience nor "aboutness" has anything to do with why active is preferred to passive, for example. All it shows is that various non-linguistic event parameters can bias the resulting structural choice—sometimes speakers rely more on attentional relations, at other times on the nature of the event itself. In fact, many other perceptual and conceptual event parameters were shown to motivate structural choice. These include animacy (Prat-Sala & Branigan, 2000), an event's referential complexity (Griffin & Weinstein-Tull, 2003), referential definiteness (Grieve & Wales, 1973), imageability (Bock & Warren, 1985), givenness (Arnold et al., 2000; Bock, 1977), and prototypicality (Kelly, Bock, & Keil, 1986).

It makes more sense, and it is theoretically more relevant, to differentiate between *linguistic* and *non-linguistic* predictors of structural selection instead. The theoretical counterposition should therefore be about what comes first: the intention to use a particular linguistic form or the conceptualization of the event that motivates the selection of the linguistic forms, categories, and units. From this point of view, the diagnostic principle is simple. For language-driven theories to be correct, message-level effects including those related to salience should only predict linguistic (e.g., structural) choices when there are no linguistic predictors available or when such linguistic predictors are too vague. For message-driven theories to be correct, message-level biases must "survive" even in the presence of simultaneously presented linguistic cues. Next, we will assess existing empirical evidence against the abovementioned theoretical scenarios. We will first outline the general role of attention in language and in structural choice, in particular. We will then review experimental evidence demonstrating that (1) a referent's accessibility status and (2) its relative salience can successfully predict structural choice thus reflecting the speaker's attentional state. Next, we will focus on studies in languages other than English to better understand how the assignment of the grammatical roles and linear ordering of the constituents in the sentence reflect the speaker's attentional state. Finally, we will review evidence demonstrating the robustness of attentional biases in structural choice in the presence of linguistic ones suggesting that any sentence production architecture needs to incorporate a mapping mechanism that codes perceptual salience of the described event's constituents.

22.2 ATTENTION AND STRUCTURAL CHOICE

Existing literature provides (1) neuroanatomical, (2) developmental, and (3) behavioral reasons to conclude that linguistic performance relies upon allocation of attentional resources. The neuroanatomical argument includes evidence that the human brain is flexibly organized so that the same cortical region often supports a variety of mental operations. For example, neuroimaging studies in reading identify brain areas involved in chunking visual letters into words, associating letters with sounds, and providing entry into a distributed lexicon. Chunking visual letters into words takes place in a posterior visually specific area of the left fusiform gyrus (McCandliss et al., 2003). In the right hemisphere, similar areas are involved in the perception and individuation of faces (Kanwisher et al., 1997). While these areas were first thought to be word and face specific, more recent conceptualizations argue that they are related more to the process of chunking of visual elements or individuation of complex forms and can be performed on other inputs (Gauthier et al., 1999). This same principle of localized mental operations over domain-specific representations may explain why Broca's area seems important for forms of non-speech motor activity (e.g., Pulvermüller & Fadiga, 2010). At the same time, event-related potential (ERP) research has shown a large area of activation in the anterior cingulate gyrus during lexical search (Abdullaev & Posner, 1998; Raichle et al., 1994); the same area is known to be involved in conflict resolution and executive attention (Fan et al., 2002; Petersen & Posner, 2012; Posner & Petersen, 1990). fMRI research (Newman et al., 2001) revealed that syntactic violations elicit significantly greater activation in the superior frontal cortex—the area largely involved in attentional control. ERP studies of syntactic violations confirm the existence of two electrophysiological brain signatures of syntactic processing: an early left anterior negativity (LAN) and/or a late positive wave with a peak at 600 ms (P600) (Hagoort et al., 1993). Hahne and Friederici (1999) hypothesized that the LAN is a highly automated process whereas the P600 involves more attention. They tested this hypothesis in a study manipulating the proportion of correct sentences and sentences with structural violations in them. Syntactically incorrect sentences appeared in a low (20% violation) or a high (80% violation) proportion conditions. Both conditions led to the elicitation of the LAN effect while only low proportion of incorrect sentences resulted in P600. These results support the idea that LAN is an automated first-pass sentence parsing mechanism accompanying syntactic processing while the P600 component is a second-pass parsing that requires a deliberate deployment of executive attention. Together these findings demonstrate that the brain localizes *processes* or mental operations not particular *representations* (either linguistic or non-linguistic). Sharing processing regions may lead to sharing resources between domain-specific and domain-general operations computed in the same area.

Developmental research provides additional reasons to hypothesize that attention and language are intimately linked (Matthews & Krajewski, 2015). Several studies suggest that attentional amplification of visual input is actively used by caretakers during the early stages of language development. Consistent pairing of attentional focus to real-world objects and events with the corresponding names and structures helps the infant build firm associations between the perceived world and the language about it. Experiments show for example that both individual and joint gazes of infants and caretakers can serve as indicators of current learning processes such as matching names to their referent objects (Baldwin, 1995; Carpenter et al., 1998; Dominey & Dodane, 2004; Estigarribia & Clark, 2007). The establishment of the attention-language interface is a starting point in the development of a more complex linking system, one mapping event semantics onto sentence structure. Surprisingly, the rudiments of this system are in place already by two to three years of age. Research has shown that children regularly scan visual referents of transient events following the way they are described in auditorily perceived sentences (Arunachalam & Waxman, 2010; Yuan & Fisher, 2009). In this learning process, the associations between event semantics and syntax are regulated by directing the child's attention to the structurally relevant elements of the described scene. The ability to successfully represent the perceptual details in the syntactic structure has been recently reported for children as young as three to four years old (Ibbotson et al., 2013). Some theorists (e.g., Mandler, 1992) proposed that after initial visual analysis perceptual information in the child's mind becomes represented in the form of image schemas that support development of more abstract conceptual representations and derived thematic and structural relationships. Overall, the role of attentional control in language development suggests an early and a potentially strong coupling between the distribution of attention in the environment and the organization of the language about this environment.

The link between attending to objects and acting on them remains strong in adults. People tend to look at objects regardless of whether they linguistically describe these objects or the interactions between them (Ballard et al., 1997). Understanding linguistic processing as a subsystem of other behavioral tasks suggests that a similar link can be expected between attending to objects and naming them in a sentence. Indeed, some theoretical proposals claim that perceptual regularities are represented in the syntactic system. For example, Landau and Jackendoff (1993; also see Jackendoff, 1996) suggested that representing objects in the human mind (*what*) and locations (*where*) maps directly onto the distinction between nouns and prepositions.

Attention in experimental tasks is often manipulated through a cueing paradigm (Posner, 1980). A cue in this context is something that regulates the salience of stimuli. It can be an independent marker "pointing" to the stimulus (e.g., an arrow) or it can be a feature of the stimulus itself (e.g., a stimulus' size or luminance). Cues can be exogenous or endogenous, and they can be explicit or implicit; their presence can result in either overt or covert deployment of attention (Posner, Raichle, & Goldman-Rakic, 1994). Exogenous cues are external to the perceiver's mind. Endogenous cues originate from within the perceiver's mind and are guided by internally generated plans and/or intentions. An explicit cue is a clearly noticeable and, therefore, consciously processed marker (e.g., an arrow pointing toward a location on the screen presented long enough to be noticed and looked at). An implicit cue directs attention in a subtler manner; it is usually presented for duration shorter than would be necessary for conscious processing (e.g., 50 msec.). An implicit cue is typically not consciously processed but its display succeeds in attracting attention and directing the focus of attention and the gaze toward a cued location. Importantly, gaze does not necessarily accompany attentional shifts although they typically follow the allocation of attention (Fischer, 1998). This property underlies the difference between overt and covert deployment of attention. An overt attentional shift occurs when the eyes move to align the visual focus with the attended object. A covert shift directs the focus of attention outside of the visual focus making the two foci dissociable (Posner, 1980).

One aspect of attention that is often addressed in psycholinguistic research is how selective it is (Bock & Ferreira, 2014; Langacker, 2015). The world around us provides us with an excessive amount of perceptual information, which is available for processing at any given moment. Attention commands the selection of the information, which is most relevant to the given task (e.g., Chun & Wolfe, 2001). This selection or "filtering" of information is central to many definitions of attention. According to Corbetta (1998, p. 831), *"Attention defines the mental ability to select stimuli, responses, memories, or thoughts that are behaviorally relevant among the many others that are behaviorally irrelevant."* Selecting different stimuli leads to selection between competing responses (Fan et al., 2002) and linguistic behavior is not an exception. Speakers must choose between different names to refer to the same entity, and they must select among different available syntactic structures when describing the same event.

22.2.1 Referential priming

Much of early psycholinguistic reports on the role of attention in the sentence production used versions of a *referential priming* paradigm. In a typical experiment, participants preview one of the visual referents for some time prior to the presentation of a target event. It is generally predicted that the information about the referent extracted during the preview will facilitate its accommodation in the produced sentence. This often causes the speaker to choose the primed referent as the starting point of a sentence describing the target event. In one of his studies, Prentice (1967) investigated how referent preview biases attention and affects elicitation of active and passive voice English sentences. Participants described pictures of transitive events involving two characters, agent and patient (e.g., *a fireman kicking a cat*), after previewing one of them. In half of the trials, participants previewed agents of the events and in the other half patients. When the previewed referent was the agent, participants were more likely to produce active voice sentences (e.g., *The fireman is kicking a cat*). When the previewed referent was the patient, they were more likely to produce passive voice sentences (e.g., *The cat is being kicked by the fireman*). Prentice concluded that the speakers were primed to place the previewed referent first and make it the sentential subject. This effect was not equally strong in the agent-preview and the patient-preview trials: while agent-cued trials resulted in almost 100% of active voice sentences, the patient-cued trials elicited about 40–50% of passive voice sentences. This shows how preference for active voice in English can act as a factual constraint on the degree to which perceptual biases may affect linguistic choices.

In Turner and Rommetveit (1968), children memorized active- and passive voice sentences for subsequent recall. These original sentences were presented together with a picture of the agent, the patient, the whole event, or a blank screen. The same pictures were shown at the time of sentence recall. The recalled sentences were compared to the stored sentences and analyzed as correct or incorrect. The data showed, among other things, that the children remembered the active voice sentences better if the storage sentence was presented to them with a picture of the agent. Conversely, the passive voice sentences were better recalled when they were presented with a picture of the patient. A more recent study (Myachykov et al., 2012) looked at how informative and uninformative visual cues affect structural choice in English transitive sentence production. Two types of cues were used: (1) a pointer to the subsequent referent's location or (2) a picture of the corresponding referent (i.e., referent preview) in the same location. Results showed that cueing the agent or the patient prior to presenting the target event reliably predicted the likelihood of selecting this referent as the sentential subject and triggered the associated choice between active and passive voice. However, there was no difference in the magnitude of the general cueing effect between the informative (preview) and uninformative cueing conditions (location pointer). This suggests that attentionally driven structural choices rely on a direct and automatic mapping from attention to sentence and that this mechanism is independent of the degree of the referent's conceptual accessibility provided by referent preview.

To summarize, the studies using referential priming paradigm indicate that the speaker's attentional state, manipulated via referent preview, may affect preferential assignment of constituents in sentence production or recall by improving the chances of the cued referent becoming the initial constituent or the subject of the sentence. Nevertheless, one should note that referent preview is not a "purely" attentional manipulation as it provides the speaker with both perceptual and semantic information about the referent. Thus, the final structural choice may reflect both the endogenously driven attentional focus to the previewed referent and an increase in its conceptual accessibility. As a result, the question about the *specific* role of attention during structural choice is left unanswered. To answer these questions studies using a perceptual priming paradigm are discussed in the next section.

22.2.2 Perceptual priming

In a typical *perceptual priming* experiment, speakers describe visually perceived events while their attention is directed to one of the event's referents by a cue unrelated to (and uninformative about) the cued referent. In its essence, therefore, the perceptual priming paradigm is a psycholinguistic adaptation of a visual cueing paradigm (Posner, 1980). One of the earliest perceptual priming studies used a very strong version of the paradigm known as the "FishFilm" (Tomlin, 1995). Participants observed and described an animated interaction between two fish in which one fish always ended up eating the other. In half of the trials an explicit visual cue (arrow pointer) was presented above the agent fish and in the other half of trials above the patient fish. The results demonstrated that in virtually 100% of the agent-cued trials participants produced an active voice sentence (e.g., *The red fish ate the blue fish*). When the cue was on the patient participants nearly always produced a passive voice sentence (e.g., *The blue fish was eaten by the red fish*). Tomlin concluded that attentional cueing promotes the assignment of the subject-role (to either the agent or the patient) in an English transitive sentence thereby triggering the choice between active and passive voice.

Although Tomlin's results were very persuasive, the paradigm itself received significant methodological criticism (e.g., Bock et al., 2004). The most critical points were (1) the repetitive use of the same event without filler materials, (2) the explicit nature of the visual cue (and related experimental instructions), and (3) the joint presentation of the cue and its target. Obviously in real life, visual salience can be subtler; hence a more tacit manipulation of the attentional focus may be necessary to further substantiate the role of perceptual priming on structural choice. Gleitman and colleagues (Gleitman et al., 2007) conducted a study that avoided the methodological problems of the FishFilm paradigm. In this study, participants observed and described interactions between two referents portrayed in still pictures. Speakers' attention was directed to the location of one of the referents by means a visual cue (a black square). The cue appeared on the screen *before* the target picture in the place of one of the subsequently presented referents. The cue was presented for only 65 msec. and participants remained largely unaware of its presence. This *implicit* cueing procedure was nevertheless successful in directing attention to the cued area of the screen (as revealed by eye movement data) and subsequently to one of the referents (e.g., agent or patient). The use of filler materials minimized the probability of using event-specific linguistic strategies. In addition to the active/passive alternation, the experiment included picture materials for a variety of other structural choices including symmetrical predicates (e.g., *X meets Y/Y meets X/X and Y meet*), verbs of perspective (e.g., *X chases Y/Y flees X*), and conjoined noun-phrases (e.g., *X and Y . . . /Y and X . . .*). Gleitman et al.'s syntactic alternation results largely confirmed Tomlin's findings, yet their effects were much weaker due to the far more subtle perceptual cueing manipulation: Speakers were 10% more likely to produce passive voice sentences when the cue attracted their attention to the patient location. In the remaining 90% of the patient-cued trials, speakers still produced the established active voice structure.

Perceptual priming studies using other structures came to similar conclusions. For example, Forrest (1996) explored the visually cued production of locative sentences in English. As in Gleitman et al. (2007) speakers' attentional focus was attracted not to the cued referent itself but to its location prior to the target event presentation. The experimental materials were line drawings of locative events (e.g., *a star left of a heart*). Prior to target display presentation an explicit visual cue appeared in the location of either the star or the heart. As a result, speakers tended to produce sentences like *A star is left of a heart* when the star's location was cued, and *A heart is right of a star* when the heart's location was cued.

Finally, a recent study by Pokhoday, Shtyrov, and Myachykov (2016) addressed the question of whether attentionally motivated structural choice is limited to the visual modality or whether the attentional system subserving structural choice is more general. Results of a number of recent studies corroborate this universalist view (e.g., Spence, 2010; Kostov & Janyan, 2012). For example, in their study of manipulation affordances, Kostov and Janyan (2012) found that using a lateral auditory cue leads to the establishment of a lateral affordance effect typically observed in studies using visual input and attention manipulations. Similarly, Spence (2010) studied unimodal and bimodal sensory cues from auditory, visual, and motor modalities. Results of this study suggested that unimodal (one cue from one modality at a time), as well as bimodal (two cues from two different modalities), successfully orient attention to the source of the cue. In Pokhoday, Shtyrov, and Myachykov (2016), the visual cue was replaced by a lateral auditory cue or a motor cue (a button press corresponding to the referent's position). Results demonstrate that in concordance with visual cueing studies the shift of attention by means of auditory and motor cues biased structural choice: Participants produced more passive voice structures when the cue was on the patient of the event. Another important finding was that there was a significant difference in effectiveness of attentional manipulation with a motor cue having a stronger effect in comparison to an auditory cue suggesting a hierarchy of modalities in an otherwise general attentional system underlying structural choice.

The perceptual priming literature reviewed in this section demonstrates that the structure of English sentences in part reflects the speaker's attentional focus; that is, the referent's salience predicts the speaker's structural choice. The explicitness of the cue and the strength of association between the cue and the referent improve this priming effect. Finally, most recent findings suggest that the attentional system supporting the interface between referential salience and structural choice may be relatively universal and not limited to the visual modality.

22.2.3 Attention and the positional vs. grammatical-role hypotheses

The studies reviewed thus far used English as the target language, a subject-verb-object (SVO) language with a highly constrained word order. For example, in describing a transitive event the speaker of English primarily selects between active voice and passive voice SVO options[1]. Hence, the grammatical subject in English usually coincides with the sentential starting point. This feature makes it difficult to distinguish between assignment of the grammatical roles and linear ordering of constituents. As a result, they have little to say about the possible *mechanisms* of attention-structure interplay; they only indicate that attention matters during structural selection. Interestingly, the symmetrical predicate data in Gleitman et al. (2007) provide some insights in this respect. When describing a symmetrical event, speakers may choose among various authorized active voice options. For example: (1) *The man kissed the woman*; (2) *The woman kissed the man*; (3) *The man and woman kissed*; and (4) *The woman and the man kissed*. Structural variants (1) and (2) rely on a canonical SVO-frame and the choice between them may reflect both positional (starting point)

---

[1] There is an order-only alternative possible, so-called topicalization, but this is not used for these descriptions.

and grammatical-role (subject) preferences for the most salient referent. The choice between structures (3) and (4) involves only positional mappings as the two referents are part of the same conjoined noun phrase (CNP) in the subject. Participants in Gleitman et al. (2007) produced all four possible alternatives. Moreover, they tended to assign the visually cued referent to an early position in the sentence, that is, to the subject-position when choosing an SVO-frame (1 or 2) and to the first element when choosing a CNP-frame (3 or 4). Most interestingly, the perceptual cueing effect was stronger when participants used an SVO-frame (31%) than when they used a CNP-frame (23%). This could suggest a *hybrid* system of attention-driven structural choice either with a stronger bias toward the grammatical-role assignment component or with additive effects of perceptual cueing on both linear positioning and grammatical-role assignment.

Some languages differ from English in that they allow for a more flexible organization of sentences. Three recent studies analyzed perceptually primed structural choice in Russian (Myachykov & Tomlin, 2008), Finnish (Myachykov et al., 2011), and Korean (Hwang & Kaiser, 2009) sentence production. Unlike English, these three languages permit flexible word ordering making at least some permutations of subject, verb, and object grammatical. Russian and Finnish, like English, are SVO languages but, unlike English, they permit both object-initial and verb-initial constructions and thus allow a wider range of topicalization constructions. Korean is a subject-object-verb (SOV) language that permits placement of subject and object before the verb (which always follows its arguments). Although topicalization is possible in these languages it is not freely licensed. For example, factors related to discourse context (e.g., contrast of given/new information) were shown to predict ordering of sentential constituents in Russian (Comrie, 1989, 2009; Yokoyama, 1986), Finnish (Kaiser & Trueswell, 2004; Vilkuna, 1989), and Korean (Choi, 1996; Jackson, 2008). The same, however, is true for English (e.g., Chafe 1976; Downing & Noonan, 1995; Givón, 1992; Halliday, 1967; *inter alia*). More importantly, the role of discourse-level factors does not preclude the possibility that speakers of these other languages also accommodate referential salience in structural choice. The lack of corresponding evidence makes perceptual priming research in flexible word order languages very useful. Importantly, voice-based alternations are also possible in these three languages, but they are greatly dispreferred and less frequent (e.g., Siewierska, 1988; Vilkuna, 1989; Zemskaja, 1979) than in English (e.g., Svartvik, 1966). In a perceptual priming task, speakers of flexible word order languages could map the salient referent either onto the subject or onto the sentential starting point without subject-role assignment. Such languages provide an optimal test-bed for independent predictions from the linear ordering and the grammatical-role accounts of perceptually driven structural choice.

Myachykov and Tomlin (2008) conducted an analysis of Russian language transitive events using the FishFilm paradigm (see Tomlin, 1997). They hypothesized that if the visually cued referent becomes the sentential subject Russian speakers, like their English-speaking counterparts, should be more likely to alternate between active and passive voice when describing FishFilm events. Alternatively, they may choose to use topicalization, which in the patient-cued condition would result in an increased percentage of object-initial active voice structures. This would support a linear-ordering account of perceptual priming effect on structural choice. The results supported the latter view: Russian speakers produced 20% more object-initial (OVS or OSV) active voice structures (plus ca. 2% passive voice sentences) when the perceptual cue was on the patient. This perceptual priming effect is noticeably smaller than in Tomlin's (1995) study with English speakers who produced passive voice sentences in nearly 100% of the patient-cued trials. This is especially noteworthy given the fact that Myachykov and Tomlin (2008) employed exactly the same manipulations as Tomlin (1995).

Myachykov et al. (2011) compared perceptual priming effects between English and Finnish. Similarly to Gleitman et al. (2007) participants described pictures of transitive events after their attention was directed to the location of either the agent or the patient by an implicit (70 ms) visual cue. The data from the English participants replicated earlier findings (Gleitman et al., 2007): there was a reliable main effect of Cue Location with participants producing 94% active voice sentences in the agent-cued trials and 74% active voice sentences in the patient-cued trials. One difference between the form of the passive voice in Russian and in Finnish is that the passive voice in Finnish is not only infrequent but also always realized without an explicit structural analogue to the English *by*-phrase (Kaiser & Vihman, 2006). Hence, it may be difficult to induce passivization in a study using events that always involved two protagonists. Topicalization however is equally possible in Finnish and in Russian. Therefore, one could expect a reduced yet noticeable effect of perceptual priming in Finnish through topicalization like Russian. However, there was no reliable word order alternation in Finnish although the cueing manipulation was equally effective (as revealed in saccades to the cued locations). Virtually the same result was observed in Hwang and Kaiser (2009) who used an implicit cueing paradigm in a study with Korean: participants described transitive events (e.g., *dog biting policeman*) after their attention was directed to either the agent or the patient via the presentation of an implicit visual cue. Similar to the results of Myachykov et al. (2011), the cueing manipulation was successful (in terms of attracting initial fixations); however, this did not lead to any perceptual priming effect affecting structural choice.

Together these results suggest the existence of language-specific differences in how visual cueing affects structural choice. The exact nature of these differences is not yet clear. It is possible that the largely dispreferred status of the passive voice in languages like Russian and Finnish makes mapping of a salient patient referent onto the subject role problematic. The same explanation is offered by Hwang and Kaiser who proposed that Korean has a strong bias toward actives with canonical word order (SOV) and that passives in Korean are more marked than in English. However, it is important to remember that the decrease in the cue power was responsible for the decrease of the overall perceptual priming effect observed in Gleitman et al. (2007) as compared to Tomlin (1995). At the same time a FishFilm experiment with Russian (Myachykov & Tomlin, 2008) also revealed a reliable yet greatly decreased perceptual priming effect compared to Tomlin (1995). Put together these studies suggest that in flexible word order languages the extent of perceptual priming is consistently weaker than in the fixed word order languages. An important question is why is this so? We propose that the grammatical-role assignment mechanism operates as the primary syntactic device responsible for representing the speaker's attentional focus while linear ordering of the constituents is only employed when the grammatical-role assignment mechanism is not easily available. In English transitive sentence production, the two routes coincide making the overall perceptual priming effect stronger. In languages like Russian and Finnish only the linear-ordering route is available (because of the unavailability of the passive); hence there is a much weaker effect in Russian (Myachykov & Tomlin, 2008) and, respectively, null effects in Finnish (Myachykov et al., 2011) and Korean (Hwang & Kaiser, 2009). Supporting the grammatical-role assignment view a recent FishFilm study using a VOS-language (Malagasy) demonstrated that speakers of Malagasy consistently assign the cued referent to the subject role; but in Malagasy, the subject role shows up in the *final* position (Rasolofo, 2006). This provides further support for the dominance of the grammatical-role mechanism over the linear-ordering one: availability of structures that allow for direct mapping between the salient referent and the subject makes the importance of linear ordering for the accommodation of referential salience in structural choice irrelevant.

22.2.4 Interactive properties of perceptual priming

The assignment of grammatical roles in a spoken sentence and the resulting structural configurations do not depend solely on the salience characteristics of the described event. Note that natural sentence production unfolds in a rich context where multiple sentence production cues are available simultaneously. Some of these cues are linguistic and others are not. Prior lexical and syntactic contexts are also known to affect the likelihood of selecting one structure over another. Lexical priming studies using nouns consistently show that primed referents tend to become sentential starting points and/or subjects triggering the resulting structural choice (Bates & Devescovi, 1989; Bock & Irwin, 1980; Ferreira & Yoshita, 2003; Flores d'Arcais, 1975; Osgood & Bock, 1977; Prat-Sala & Branigan, 2000). Priming studies using verbs show similar effect (Melinger & Dobel, 2005). Finally, syntactic priming studies show that speakers tend to recycle entire syntactic configurations they previously encountered or produced (Bock, 1986; Ferreira, Morgan, & Slevc, this volume). Some accounts of structural choice rely upon the interaction between lexical and syntactic components (e.g., Pickering & Branigan, 1998, but see Bock & Loebell, 1990; Bock et al., 1992; Desmet & Declercq, 2006; Scheepers, 2003). One could naturally assume that the final choice of structure is a product of many interacting forces including perceptual, lexical, and syntactic priming effects. Comprehensive sentence production architecture needs to model how perceptual priming interacts with other priming parameters known to influence the speaker's choice of syntax, including both *lexical* and *syntactic* priming.

As we noted in the Introduction, some existing theoretical proposals (e.g., Bock & Ferreira, 2014; Kuchinsky & Bock, 2010) suggest that structural choice is largely insensitive to the perceptual details of the described scene and is primarily motivated by the speaker's decision to describe the event in a particular way. This decision, in the view of the authors, emerges from the event's "*aboutness*" rather than from the more minute details of the event itself and its integral parts (e.g., referents' salience). The structural choice process, therefore, is a result of a very coarse conceptual analysis that tends to ignore referents' salience. Just now, we referred to this proposal as a *language-* or *structure-driven* hypothesis. The alternatives include (1) a *message-driven* and (2) an *interactive* hypothesis. According to (1), the referents' salience is accommodated in the structural choices regardless of the presence or absence of other biasing cues. According to (2), multiple cues may interact with the resulting structural choice reflecting a combination of processes—linguistic and non-linguistic.

Independent of these theoretical differences, interactive properties of the distinct priming effects established at different production stages remain largely unknown. This has motivated the experiments reported in Myachykov, Garrod, and Scheepers (2012). These experiments investigated structural choice in English transitive sentence production by combining priming manipulations at both linguistic and non-linguistic levels. In each of the three reported experiments, participants described visual events after receiving combinations of the following priming manipulations: (1) perceptual priming; (2) lexical (verb match); and (3) syntactic priming. Across all three experiments, there were clear and robust perceptual priming effects even in the presence of concurrent linguistic manipulations (syntactic priming and verb match). These findings provide further evidence that perceptual information about the referents (e.g., referential salience) plays an integral and distinct role during the assignment of syntactic roles alongside available lexical and syntactic information. As such, these findings are problematic for structure-driven accounts (Bock et al., 2004; Kuchinsky & Bock, 2010). Importantly, the simultaneously observed syntactic priming effect *did not* interact with the perceptual priming effect suggesting that interactions between priming effects are constrained by a *neighborhood* principle, according to which only immediately *neighboring* processing stages (e.g., message and lemma; lemma and syntax) can interact with one another in determining structural choice while non-neighboring stages (message and syntax) cannot. The ubiquitous presence and comparable magnitude of the perceptual and the syntactic priming effects hint at the existence of a dual-path mapping mechanism akin to Chang (2002). According to a dual-path logic, mapping non-linguistic effects (such as perceptual salience) and linguistic effects (such as syntactic and lexical accessibility) can affect subject assignment independently and in parallel, each offering its individual biases.

One important additional finding was that the perceptual priming effect interacted with the verb-match effect. The visual cueing effect (the increase in the proportion of passive voice responses in the patient-cued condition) remained relatively unaffected by the verb match manipulation. This may indicate that speakers have a general tendency to use salient patients as subjects of their sentences (and correspondingly select a passive voice frame) regardless of the co-presence of linguistic cues competing for the same choice. The verb-match effect in this scenario would result from a relatively higher activation of the otherwise dispreferred passive voice frame when the prime verb matches the target event (cf. Melinger & Dobel (2005) who found that isolated verbs can indeed prime syntactic frames). Importantly, this passive promoting verb-match effect was only observed when the visual cue was on the agent or in the situation when the visual cue did not simultaneously compete for the choice of passive. One possibility is that matching prime verbs can only make the passive voice alternative to the canonical active more available in the absence of a visual cue competing for the same choice: In the agent-cued condition (supporting active voice) the verb cue is informative as it provides a cue toward the alternative (passive voice); in the patient-cued condition (supporting passive voice) the verb cue is uninformative as it supports the same response as the patient-cue itself. If this interpretation is correct then it follows that lexical information (whether the prime verb matches the target event or not) is considered only after perceptual information (visual cueing) has already been integrated into the grammatical encoding process. Thus, perceptual information would take priority over lexical information (at least in the current experimental setup where the visual cue was always delivered most recently, i.e., immediately before the target event). This theoretical scenario entails an interesting prediction, namely that it should be possible to register an independent transitive verb-match effect (more passive voice target descriptions after presenting a matching prime verb) in the absence of any visual cues to either agent or patient.

To this moment however, it remains unclear how non-linguistic and linguistic information becomes integrated in sentence production. We assume that sentence production begins with the creation of a message, a conceptual representation of the event to be encoded linguistically (Bock & Levelt, 1994). Availability of non-linguistic information about the protagonists extracted at this stage (including their perceptual salience) may vary (Bock & Warren, 1985). This perceptual asymmetry may bias the speaker to process the more salient referents ahead of the less salient ones making it likely that the salient referent becomes encoded earlier. In English, this may lead to the salient referent mapping onto the subject. This suggestion is supported by findings from several studies. Participants are more likely to assign the subject role to the agent and choose the corresponding active voice frame when the agent is cued, and they are likewise more likely to assign the subject to the patient and select the corresponding passive voice frame when the cue is on the patient. It should be noted that the visual cueing used in the experiments discussed here were often uninformative of the referent's identity or its semantic properties. Hence, simply directing visual attention toward the location of the referent is enough to affect speakers' likelihood of producing an active or a passive voice sentence (cf. Gleitman et al., 2007; Myachykov et al., 2012; Tomlin, 1995, 1997).

22.3 Conclusions

In this chapter, we reviewed evidence for the existence of a regular interface between attention and structural choice in visually mediated sentence production. Several reviewed studies demonstrate how speakers regularly choose between structural alternatives as a consequence of attentional shift to one of the referents of the described events. The persistence of such an attentionally driven assignment of syntactic roles confirms that the attentionally detected referents appear earlier in a spoken sentence and they are often assigned to prominent syntactic roles (i.e., subject). The exact mechanism supporting representation of the speaker's attentional state in linguistic structure in different languages is far from certain. One possibility is that different languages' grammars provide speakers with *different* means for grammatical encoding of perceptual properties of the described world. Another possibility is that the link between attentional focus and structural choice via the assignment of subject *is* more or less universal in that speakers always *try* to map the salient referent onto the subject. However, the likelihood of this mapping varies (1) between specific languages and (2) specific structures. When a direct mapping is less accessible (e.g., passive in Russian), the attempt to map the visually focused referent onto subject appears to be discontinued. In this case, a "second-best" mapping may be used, one that *is not* syntactically coded in the language's grammar. One example is Russian speakers' tendency to resort to topicalization instead of activating the theoretically available passive when they attempt to preferentially position the salient patient in their transitive sentences. This assignment through topicalization, however, is secondary to a more preferred and automated direct mapping mechanism; hence, its use is associated with slower sentence production rates and inflated eye movement measurements, such as eye-voice spans (see Myachykov, 2007). We propose that the grammatical-role assignment mechanism and the positional assignment mechanism form a hierarchical dual-path system that allows grammatical representation of the perceptually salient referent in a sentence.

This system is hierarchical in two ways. First, while the grammatical-role mapping mechanism is a common but language-specific mapping based on syntactic coding, the positional mapping may in principle be available regardless of the existence of the corresponding grammatical-role mapping mechanism. It is undoubtedly easier to freely arrange the constituents in a language that licenses topicalization grammatically (e.g., via case marking), but it is still quite impossible to use "semi-legal" positioning devices like dislocations in languages that do not normally permit topicalization. Second, these two mapping mechanisms are hierarchically related in that in languages like English grammatical-role assignment dominates positional assignment. For example, speakers try to activate structural alternatives that permit direct mapping from attentional focus to the subject before they (1) abandon this attempt in favor of a more dominant structure that requires remapping (e.g., the use of active voice in patient-salient situations) or (2) using topicalization as the second-best mapping alternative.

All this does not generally mean that *subjecthood* only reflects attentional focus on a referent. What it means is that when attentional focus needs to be represented, the speaker tries to do it by assigning the subject role to the most salient referent in the scene. The problem is that the corresponding structural contrast may not always be available, as in languages like Russian and Finnish, because passives are rare or largely dispreferred. When the grammatical-role assignment mechanism is not easily available the speaker looks for an alternative. In flexible word order languages, this alternative is topicalization. As a result, a linear-ordering mechanism is used to accommodate referential salience in terms of word order but with detrimental effects on the speed of processing and the strength of the overall perceptual priming effect.

References

Abdullaev, Y. G., & Posner, M. I. (1998). Event-related brain potential imaging of semantic encoding during processing single words. *NeuroImage*, 7(1), 1–13.

Arnold, J. E., Losongco, A., Wasow, T., & Ginstrom, R. (2000). Heaviness vs. newness: The effects of structural complexity and discourse status on constituent ordering. *Language*, 76(1), 28–55.

Arunachalam, S., & Waxman, S. R. (2010). Meaning from syntax: Evidence from 2-year-olds. *Cognition*, 114(3), 442–6.

Baldwin, D. A. (1995). Understanding the link between joint attention and language. In: Moore, C., & Dunham, P. J. (Eds.), *Joint Attention: Its Origins and Role in Development* (pp. 131–58). Lawrence Erlbaum, Hillsdale, NJ.

Ballard, D. H., Hayhoe, M. M., Pook, P. K., & Rao, R. P. (1997). Deictic codes for the embodiment of cognition. *Behavioral and Brain Sciences*, 20(4), 723–42.

Bates, E., & Devescovi, A. (1989). Crosslinguistic studies of sentence production. *Cognition*, 54(2), 169–207.

Bock, J. K. (1977). The effect of pragmatic presupposition on syntactic structure in question answering. *Journal of Verbal Learning and Verbal Behavior*, 16(6), 723–34.

Bock, J. K. (1986). Syntactic persistence in language production. *Cognitive Psychology, 18*(3), 355–87.
Bock, K., & Ferreira, V. (2014). Syntactically speaking. In: Goldrick, M. A., Ferreira, V., & Miozzo, M. (Eds.), *The Oxford Handbook of Language Production* (pp. 21–46). Oxford University Press, New York, NY.
Bock, J. K., & Irwin, D. E. (1980). Syntactic effects of information availability in sentence production. *Journal of Verbal Learning and Verbal Behavior, 19*(4), 467–84.
Bock, K., Irwin, D. E., & Davidson, D. J. (2004). Putting first things first. In: Henderson, J., & Ferreira, F. (Eds.), *The Interface of Language, Vision, and Action: Eye Movements and the Visual World* (pp. 249–78). Psychology Press, Hove.
Bock, K., & Levelt, W. J. M. (1994). Language production: Grammatical encoding. In: Gernsbacher, M. (Ed.), *Handbook of Psycholinguistics* (pp. 945–84). Academic Press, New York, NY.
Bock, K., & Loebell, H. (1990). Framing sentences. *Cognition, 35*(1), 1–39.
Bock, K., Loebell, H., & Morey, R. (1992). From conceptual roles to structural relations: Bridging the syntactic cleft. *Psychological Review, 99*(1), 150.
Bock, J. K., & Warren, R. K. (1985). Conceptual accessibility and syntactic structure in sentence formulation. *Cognition, 21*(1), 47–67.
Carpenter, M., Nagell, K., Tomasello, M., Butterworth, G., & Moore, C. (1998). Social cognition, joint attention, and communicative competence from 9 to 15 months of age. *Monographs of the Society for Research in Child Development, 63*(4), 1–174.
Chafe, W. L. (1976). Givenness, contrastiveness, definiteness, subjects, topics, and point of view. In: Li, C. N. (Ed.), *Subject and Topic*, (pp. 25–55). Academic Press, New York, NY.
Chang, F. (2002). Symbolically speaking: A connectionist model of sentence production. *Cognitive Science, 26*(5), 609–51.
Choi, H.-W. (1996). *Optimizing Structure in Context: Scrambling and Information Structure* [Dissertation]. Stanford University, Stanford, CA.
Chun, M., & Wolfe, J. (2001). Visual attention. In: Goldstein, E. B. (Ed.), *Blackwell Handbook of Perception* (pp. 272–310). Blackwell Publishers Ltd., Oxford, UK.
Comrie, B. (1989). *Language Universals and Linguistic Typology: Syntax and Morphology*. University of Chicago Press, Chicago, IL.
Comrie, B. (Ed.) (2009). *The World's Major Languages*. Routledge, London.
Corbetta, M. (1998). Frontoparietal cortical networks for directing attention and the eye to visual locations: Identical, independent, or overlapping neural systems? *Proceedings of the National Academy of Sciences, 95*(3), 831–8.
Desmet, T., & Declercq, M. (2006). Cross-linguistic priming of syntactic hierarchical configuration information. *Journal of Memory and Language, 54*, 610–32.
Dominey, P., & Dodane, C. (2004). Indeterminacy in language acquisition: The role of child-directed speech and joint attention. *Journal of Neurolinguistics, 17*, 121–45.
Downing, P. A., & Noonan, M. (Eds.) (1995). *Word Order in Discourse, Vol. 30*. John Benjamins Publishing, Amsterdam.
Estigarribia, B., & Clark, E. V. (2007). Getting and maintaining attention in talk to young children. *Journal of Child Language, 34*(4), 799–814.
Fan, J., McCandliss, B. D, Sommer, T., Raz, A., & Posner M. I. (2002). Testing the efficiency and independence of attentional networks. *Journal of Cognitive Neuroscience, 14*(3), 340–7.
Ferreira, V. S., & Yoshita, H. (2003). Given-new ordering effects on the production of scrambled sentences in Japanese. *Journal of Psycholinguistic Research, 32*(6), 669–92.

Fischer, B. (1998). Attention in saccades. In: Wright, R. D. (Ed.), *Visual Attention* (pp. 289–305). Oxford University Press, New York, NY.

Flores d'Arcais, G. B. (1975). Some perceptual determinants of sentence construction. In: Flores d'Arcais, G. B. (Ed.), *Studies in Perception: Festschrift for Fabio Metelli* (pp. 344–73). Aldo Martello-Giunti, Milan.

Forrest, L. B. (1996). Discourse goals and attentional processes in sentence production: The dynamic construal of events. In: Goldberg, A. E. (Ed.), *Conceptual Structure, Discourse and Language* (pp. 149–62). CSLI Publications, Stanford, CA.

Gauthier, I., Tarr, M. J., Anderson, A. W., Skudlarski, P., & Gore, J. C. (1999). Activation of the middle fusiform 'face area' increases with expertise in recognizing novel objects. *Nature Neuroscience*, 2(6), 568–73.

Givón, T. (1992). The grammar of referential coherence as mental processing instructions. *Linguistics*, 30(1), 5–56.

Gleitman, L. R., January, D., Nappa, R., & Trueswell, J. C. (2007). On the give and take between event apprehension and utterance formulation. *Journal of Memory and Language*, 57(4), 544–69.

Grieve, R., & Wales, R. J. (1973). Passives and topicalization. *British Journal of Psychology*, 64(2), 173–82.

Griffin, Z. M., & Weinstein-Tull, J. (2003). Conceptual structure modulates structural priming in the production of complex sentences. *Journal of Memory and Language*, 49(4), 537–55.

Hagoort, P., Brown, C., & Groothusen, J. (1993). The syntactic positive shift (SPS) as an ERP measure of syntactic processing. *Language and Cognitive Processes*, 8(4), 439–83.

Hahne, A., & Friederici, A. D. (1999). Electrophysiological evidence for two steps in syntactic analysis: Early automatic and late controlled processes. *Journal of Cognitive Neuroscience*, 11(2), 194–205.

Halliday, M. A. K. (1967). Notes on transitivity and theme in English: Part 2. *Journal of Linguistics*, 3(2), 199–244.

Hwang, H., & Kaiser, E. (2009). *The Effects of Lexical vs. Perceptual Primes on Sentence Production in Korean: An On-Line Investigation of Event Apprehension and Sentence Formulation*. 22nd CUNY Conference on Human Sentence Processing, Davis, CA.

Ibbotson, P., Lieven, E. V. M., & Tomasello, M. (2013). The attention-grammar interface: Eye-gaze cues structural choice in children and adults. *Cognitive Linguistics*, 24(3), 457–81.

Jackendoff, R. (1996). The architecture of the linguistic-spatial interface. In: Bloom, P., Peterson, M., Nadel, L., & Garrett, M. (Eds.), *Language and Space* (pp. 1–30). MIT Press, Cambridge, MA.

Jackson, K. H. (2008). *The Effect of Information Structure on Korean Scrambling* [Dissertation]. University of Hawai'i, Honolulu, HI.

Kaiser, E., & Trueswell, J. C. (2004). The role of discourse context in the processing of a flexible word-order language. *Cognition*, 94(2), 113–47.

Kaiser, E., & Vihman, V.-A. (2006). Invisible arguments: Effects of demotion in Estonian and Finnish. In: Solstad, T., & Lyngfelt, B. (Eds.), *Demoting the Agent: Passive and Other Voice-Related Phenomena* (p. 111–41). John Benjamins, Amsterdam.

Kanwisher, N., McDermott, J., & Chun, M. M. (1997). The fusiform face area: A module in extrastriate visual cortex specialized for face perception. *Journal of Neuroscience*, 17, 4302–11.

Kelly, M. H., Bock, J. K., & Keil, F. C. (1986). Prototypicality in a linguistic context: Effects on sentence structure. *Journal of Memory and Language*, 25(1), 59–74.

Konopka, A. E. (2012). Planning ahead: How recent experience with structures and words changes the scope of linguistic planning. *Journal of Memory and Language*, 66(1), 143–62.

Kostov, K., & Janyan, A. (2012). The role of attention in the affordance effect: Can we afford to ignore it? *Cognitive Processing*, 13(1), 215–18.

Kuchinsky, S., & Bock, K. (2010). *From Seeing to Saying: Perceiving, Planning, Producing*. Presented at the 23rd CUNY Sentence Processing Conference, New York, NY.

Landau, B., & Jackendoff, R. (1993). Whence and whither in spatial language and spatial cognition? *Behavioral and Brain Sciences*, 16(2), 255–65.

Langacker, R. W. (2015). Descriptive and discursive organization in cognitive grammar. *Change of Paradigms–New Paradoxes: Recontextualizing Language and Linguistics*, 31, 205.

Levelt, W. J. M. (1989). *Speaking*. MIT Press, Cambridge, MA.

MacWhinney, B. (1977). Starting points. *Language*, 53, 152–68.

Mandler, J. M. (1992). How to build a baby: II. Conceptual primitives. *Psychological Review*, 99(4), 587.

Matthews, D., & Krajewski, G. (2015). Early child development. In: Dabrowska, E., & Divjak, D. (Eds.), *Handbook of Cognitive Linguistics*, Vol. 39 (p. 587). Walter de Gruyter GmbH & Co KG.

McCandliss, B. D., Cohen, L., & Dehaene, S. (2003). The visual word form area: Expertise for reading in the fusiform gyrus. *Trends in Cognitive Sciences*, 7(7), 293–9.

Melinger, A., & Dobel, C. (2005). Lexically-driven syntactic priming. *Cognition*, 98(1), B11–B20.

Myachykov, A. (2007). *Integrating Perceptual, Semantic and Syntactic Information in Sentence Production* [Dissertation]. University of Glasgow, Scotland.

Myachykov, A., & Tomlin, R. S. (2008). Perceptual priming and structural choice in Russian sentence production. *Journal of Cognitive Science*, 6(1), 31–48.

Myachykov, A., Garrod, S., & Scheepers, C. (2011). Perceptual priming of structural choice during English and Finnish sentence production. In: Mishra, R. K., & Srinivasan, N. (Eds.), *Language and Cognition: The State of the Art* (pp. 53–71). Lincom Europa, Munich.

Myachykov, A., Garrod, S., & Scheepers, C. (2012). Determinants of structural choice in visually-situated sentence production. *Acta Psychologica*, 141(3), 304–15.

Myachykov, A., Thompson, D., Garrod, S., & Scheepers, C. (2012). Referential and visual cues to structural choice in sentence production. *Frontiers in Psychology*, 2, 396.

Newman, A. J., Pancheva, R., Ozawa, K., Neville, H. J., & Ullman, M. T. (2001). An event-related fMRI study of syntactic and semantic violations. *Journal of Psycholinguistic Research*, 30(3), 339–64.

Osgood, C., & Bock, K. (1977). Salience and sentencing: Some production principles. In: Rosenberg, S. (Ed.), *Sentence Production: Developments in Research and Theory* (pp. 89–140). Erlbaum, Hillsdale, NJ.

Petersen, S. E., & Posner, M. I. (2012). The attention system of the human brain: 20 years after. *Annual Review of Neuroscience*, 35, 73.

Pickering, M. J., & Branigan, H. P. (1998). The representation of verbs: Evidence from syntactic priming in language production. *Journal of Memory and Language*, 39(4), 633–51.

Pokhoday, M., Shtyrov, Y., & Myachykov, A. (2016). *The Role of Attention in Sentence Production: Beyond the Visual Modality*. Poster presented at the 22nd AMLaP Conference, Bilbao, Spain.

Posner, M. I. (1980). Orienting of attention. *Quarterly Journal of Experimental Psychology*, 32(1), 3–25.

Posner, M., & Petersen, S. (1990). The attention system of the human brain. *Annual Review of Neuroscience, 13,* 25–42.

Posner, M. I., Raichle, M. E., & Goldman-Rakic, P. (1994). *Images of Mind.* Scientific American Library, New York, NY.

Prat-Sala, M., & Branigan, H. P. (2000). Discourse constraints on syntactic processing in language production: A cross-linguistic study in English and Spanish. *Journal of Memory and Language, 42*(2), 168–82.

Prentice, J. L. (1967). Effects of cuing actor vs cuing object on word order in sentence production. *Psychonomic Science, 8*(4), 163–64.

Pulvermüller, F., & Fadiga, L. (2010). Active perception: Sensorimotor circuits as a cortical basis for language. *Nature Reviews Neuroscience, 11*(5), 351–60.

Raichle, M. E., Fiez, J. A., Videen, T. O., MacLeod, A. M., Pardo, J. V., Fox, P. T., & Petersen, S. E. (1994). Practice-related changes in human brain functional anatomy during nonmotor learning. *Cerebral Cortex, 4*(1), 8–26.

Rasolofo, A. (2006). *Malagasy Transitive Clause Types and Their Functions.* ProQuest. Available at: http://www.proquest.com/

Scheepers, C. (2003). Syntactic priming of relative clause attachments: Persistence of structural configuration in sentence production. *Cognition, 89*(3), 179–205.

Siewierska, A. (1988). The passive in Slavic. In: Shibatani, M. (Ed.), *Passive and Voice* (pp. 243–89). John Benjamins, Amsterdam.

Spence, C. (2010). Crossmodal spatial attention. *Annals of the New York Academy of Sciences, 1191*(1), 182–200.

Svartvik, J. (1966). *On Voice in the English Verb.* Mouton & Co, The Hague/Paris.

Tomlin, R. (1995). Focal attention, voice, and word order: An experimental, cross-linguistic study. *Word Order in Discourse, 30,* 517–54.

Tomlin, R. (1997). Mapping conceptual representations into linguistic representations: The role of attention in grammar. In: Nuyts, J., & Pederson, E. (Eds.), *Language and Conceptualization* (pp. 162–89). Cambridge University Press, Cambridge.

Turner, E. A., & Rommetveit, R. (1968). Focus of attention in recall of active and passive sentences. *Journal of Verbal Learning and Verbal Behavior, 7*(2), 543–8.

Vilkuna, M. (1989). *Free Word Order in Finnish: Its Syntax and Discourse Functions.* Suomalaisen kirjallisuuden seura, Helsinki.

Yokoyama, O. T. (1986). *Discourse and World Order (Pragmatics and Beyond Companion Series, 6).* John Benjamins Publishing Company, Amsterdam.

Yuan, S., & Fisher, C. (2009). "Really? She blicked the baby?" Two-year-olds learn combinatorial facts about verbs by listening. *Psychological Science, 20*(5), 619–26.

Zemskaja, E. A. (1979). *Russkaja razgovornaja reč: lingvističeskij analiz i problemy obučenija.* Russkij jazyk.

PART III
INTERACTION AND COMMUNICATION

CHAPTER 23

PERSPECTIVE-TAKING DURING CONVERSATION

SARAH BROWN-SCHMIDT AND DAPHNA HELLER

23.1 INTRODUCTION

WHEN people come together to communicate, they each bring their own unique set of life experiences, beliefs, and background knowledge. Communicating with another person depends on your own representations of that person's knowledge and beliefs, which is known as their "perspective." During conversation, this representation is relevant to language use at different levels: from the choice of what to say (which determines sentence structure), to the selection of specific words, and even to the way in which words are acoustically realized at a fine-grain level. For example, when conversing with your dentist, it is appropriate to *inquire* about proper tooth-brushing technique, but making an assertion (i.e., stating new information) on the same topic would be more appropriate when talking to your five-year-old. Furthermore, a term such as *carious lesion* may be appropriate in a conversation between dentists, but when addressing a patient, a dentist may have more success using the everyday term *cavity* (see Bromme, Jucks, & Wagner, 2005; Clark & Murphy, 1982; Isaacs & Clark, 1987). Finally, the prosodic realization of words may depend, for example, on whether information is considered new to the partner, in which case one may choose to emphasize that word, to accommodate the addressee's unfamiliarity with the term (Galati & Brennan, 2010; cf., Bard et al., 2000).

The process whereby people consider their partner's perspective during conversation is known as *perspective-taking*. In our examples above, we focused on the process of perspective-taking in language production, also known as *audience design* (Clark & Murphy, 1982). Perspective information is also relevant to language comprehension, as the addressee often needs to take into consideration the speaker's perspective at each of these levels of representation as well. When your dentist opens a conversation (see Schegloff, 1968), with the question, *How are you doing today?*, it is an invitation to talk about your dental health. But if a friend were to ask the same question, the response, *Well one of my fillings seems to be loose* would be rather odd. In each case, the addressee must use their knowledge of the speaker's background and perspective to interpret the question in the appropriate way.

The idea that felicitous language use depends on perspective information has been recognized in the philosophical literature since the late 1960s. Lewis (1969) was a pioneer in conceptualizing communication as intentional actions performed by rational agents, and in pointing out the relevance of common knowledge to these actions. The role of common knowledge took on central importance in the work of Stalnaker, who coined the now widely-used term *common ground*: common knowledge that is mutually recognized as such (Stalnaker, 1970, 1973, 1974). Stalnaker pointed out that all conversational moves are performed in relation to common ground: assertions need to contain information that is *not* already in common ground, and, similarly, questions are about information that is *not* in common ground. By contrast, definite referring expressions are based on information that *is* in common ground. It has since been widely recognized in both philosophy and formal linguistics that common ground plays a central role in interpretation. The formal properties of common ground have been studied in connection to many linguistic phenomena, including presuppositions (see e.g., Heim, 1983, 1992; Potts, 2005; Roberts, 2012; Stalnaker, 1973; von Fintel, 2004), implicatures (see e.g., Grice, 1967; Levinson, 2000; Sperber & Wilson, 1995), anaphora (see e.g., Asher & Lascarides, 2003; Kaplan, 1989), and many others.

In psycholinguistics, the focus of most research concerns *language processing*; namely, when and how perspective information influences language use. The fact that adult interlocutors *represent* information about the perspectives of others *in some form* is generally taken for granted (contrasting with the developmental trajectory by which the young child comes to have such representations: Baillargeon, Scott, & He, 2010; Perner & Ruffman, 2005). Thus, the main research questions concern whether perspective-taking behavior relies on the same mechanisms across language comprehension and production, and across the various levels of linguistic representations (e.g., sound, structure, meaning).

The study of perspective-taking in language processing should be considered against the backdrop of two other lines of inquiry within psychology.

One intellectual tradition explores the development of *theory of mind*, or the capacity to attribute to other individuals belief states that are different than one's own. Level 1 theory of mind allows one to understand that another person may perceive different objects than you do, and includes the capacity to attribute the *absence of belief* (e.g., *Sally does not know about the toy*); this capacity is thought to emerge early in development, prior to age four (Carlson, Mandell, & Williams, 2004; Flavell, Everett, Croft, & Flavell, 1981). Level 2 theory of mind is a more complex capacity that allows one to understand that another person may have *different* knowledge, and includes the ability to attribute *false* beliefs to others. For example, it allows one to understand that the same object may be perceived differently by another person (e.g., Sally thinks this is her toy, but it is not really her toy). With respect to this more complex ability, there is an ongoing debate regarding the developmental trajectory: classic research using the *false belief task* (Baron-Cohen, Leslie, & Frith, 1985; Wimmer & Perner, 1983) concludes that children develop this ability only around age four, whereas more recent work using implicit response measures finds that children as young as 13–15 months already exhibit behavior indicating that they can represent the false beliefs of others (Onishi & Baillargeon, 2005; Surian, Caldi, & Sperber, 2007). In the adult perspective-taking literature in psycholinguistics, the central question is not whether adults *represent* the belief states of others, but instead when and how these representations guide *real-time language processing*. It is interesting to note that the adult processing literature we discuss in this chapter has mostly focused on cases of level 1 knowledge, with only a handful of studies targeting the more complex level 2 knowledge (e.g., Hanna, Tanenhaus, & Trueswell, 2003; Mozuraitis, Chambers, & Daneman, 2015; Mozuraitis, Stevenson, & Heller, 2018).

A second tradition that has influenced the study of perspective-taking in language processing is the study of *egocentrism in social psychology and decision-making*. A consistent finding in social psychology studies has been that when individuals are asked to estimate what others know, their estimates are biased toward their own knowledge (Epley, Keysar, Van Boven, & Gilovich, 2004; Fussell & Krauss, 1991; Ross, Greene, & House, 1977). Such egocentric influences have been observed both in non-linguistic domains (e.g., estimates of how much housework you complete; Ross & Sicoly, 1979), and in the domain of language, including measurements of what information a speaker tends to repeat in a conversation (Knutsen & Le Bigot, 2012, 2014), and one's memory for the discourse history (Isaacs, 1990; Yoon, Benjamin, & Brown-Schmidt, 2016; cf. Stafford & Daly, 1984; see discussion in Caruso, Epley, & Bazerman, 2006). These effects are likely to be tied to the greater memory availability for one's own actions and beliefs (Fischer, Schult, & Steffens, 2015; Isaacs, 1990; Ross & Sicoly, 1979). Theories that judgments begin with egocentric estimation processes that are incrementally adjusted (see Epley et al., 2004; Epley & Gilovich, 2006; Tversky & Kahneman, 1974) have informed a view of perspective-taking in language processing that posited an initial egocentrism phase, followed by incremental adjustment away from this egocentric perspective (Horton & Keysar, 1996; Savitsky, Keysar, Epley, Carter, & Swanson, 2011). As we will see, this intellectual inheritance has influenced research on perspective-taking in language use from the early days until today.

In what follows, we describe approaches to the study of perspective-taking in conversation from the *past* and the *present*. We then speculate about the *future* directions this research will take.

23.2 THE PAST

An influential experimental paradigm for studying perspective-taking has been the *referential communication task* (Krauss & Glucksberg, 1977; Krauss & Weinheimer, 1964). In this task, two individuals collaborate to arrange or rearrange a set of objects or pictures in a workspace (or, in recent years, on a computer screen). This setup creates a situation where participants need to produce and interpret referring expressions with respect to a restricted set of candidate referents. In the domain of perspective-taking, this setup allows controlled manipulations of the knowledge mismatch between the conversational partners. Such mismatches are created using their visual perspective (e.g., Keysar, Barr, Balin, & Brauner, 2000, and many others), by linguistic mention (e.g., Brown-Schmidt, 2012; Hanna et al., 2003) or by the background experiences of participants, both experiences in the lab (e.g., Wu & Keysar, 2007), as well as prior experiences (e.g., Isaacs & Clark, 1987). What is shared between participants is taken to be in common ground, whereas information available to only one partner is considered to be in that partner's *privileged ground*. To measure perspective-taking, the literature has focused on the referential forms produced by speakers, and on the real-time interpretation of referential forms by listeners as reflected by their eye movements (i.e., using the visual world paradigm; see Tanenhaus, Spivey-Knowlton, Eberhard, & Sedivy, 1995).

As worked out in detail by Clark and Marshall (1978), for communication to be successful, it is not sufficient for one to assume that their partner knows a certain piece of information, but they must also assume that their partner assumes that *they* know this piece of information too. A problem with this logic arises because this recursion should logically continue ad infinitum, but, clearly, infinite recursions could not be represented in our mind. Instead, Clark and Marshall (1978) argue that interlocutors rely on *heuristics* to estimate mutual knowledge, or common ground (also see Clark & Marshall, 1981). On this view, interlocutors combine evidence for mutual knowledge with reasonable assumptions to estimate common ground. The evidence can come from different sources (Clark, 1996). These include visual or other sensory cues (we both see a certain object or hear a certain sound; *physical co-presence*), linguistic cues (we talked about something; *linguistic co-presence*), and cultural cues (Americans are usually assumed to know who the US president is; the Canadian Prime Minister ... uh ... not so much common ground; *community membership*). Clark and Marshall point out that the stronger the *evidence* for mutual knowledge is, the weaker the *assumption* needs to be that the information is indeed shared. They use a diary-like metaphor for one's memory for life's experiences, and introduce a "reference diaries" model to explain partner-specific effects in definite reference, such as *the candle* or *that flower*; such referring expressions require there to be a uniquely identifiable object that fits the description in the context. In this model, the relevant context is the common ground that the partners share.

The idea that the production and comprehension of definite reference involves a memorial representation linked to a specific conversational partner inspired a body of work seeking to document the influence of these representations on language use. Evidence that the particular conversational partner affects the *production* of referring expressions comes from the study of how referential forms change over the course of a conversation, with repeated reference to the same entity triggering shorter referring expressions (Clark & Wilkes-Gibbs, 1986), and, conversely, with referring expressions becoming comparatively detailed when there is a lack of common ground (Wilkes-Gibbs & Clark, 1992). Other evidence comes from how speakers adapt their referential forms when talking to a partner who they assess to be an expert or a novice with respect to a certain topic (Bromme et al., 2005; Isaacs & Clark, 1987; Wilkes-Gibbs & Clark, 1992), how speakers continue to use a certain way of talking about an object, even when it is relatively atypical, because it was introduced earlier in the conversation (Bortfeld & Brennan, 1997), and how speakers adapt to a new partner with whom they do not share the same common ground (Brennan & Clark, 1996). Knowledge of common ground is also used to *hinder* understanding by certain persons, as when bilinguals switch to a language not shared by eavesdroppers, or when speakers use terms unfamiliar to certain listeners to prevent their understanding (e.g., spelling P-I-Z-Z-A in front of a preliterate child; Clark & Schaefer, 1987). On the *comprehension* side, hearers who actively participate in the conversational exchange perform better on a task than overhearers who are not active participants (Schober & Clark, 1989). This finding has been linked to the conversational process of *grounding*, where hearers actively mark the addition of information to the common ground, with either silence or with short phrases like *yes* and *ok* (Clark & Schaefer, 1989; Clark & Brennan, 1991; Clark & Krych, 2004). In sum, this body of work has led to the documentation of many natural language phenomena that attest to the fact that conversational partners represent the perspective of others, and that these knowledge representations, in some form, guide language use.

In the late 1990s, the emphasis in the literature shifted away from language use at the macro level toward asking how representations of common ground guide real-time use, and in particular, *real-time (online) language comprehension*. This research was influenced by the dominant view in social psychology where reasoning and decision-making were thought to begin from egocentrically-biased estimations. One early paper examined participants' eye movements during real-time referential processing to contrast a *restricted search hypothesis* in which the initial search for a referent is restricted to entities in common ground, with an *unrestricted search hypothesis*, in which all referents are initially considered as candidates, independent of their ground status (Keysar, Barr, Balin, & Paek, 1998). The authors took the eye-movement patterns they observed to reflect an early unrestricted search process coupled with a later stage of error-checking that would correct for violations of common ground. While the hypothesis that language comprehension is initially egocentric with a delayed effect of correction (Barr & Keysar, 2002; Keysar et al., 2000; Keysar, Lin, & Barr, 2003) was originally inspired by work in social psychology (e.g., Tversky), it is reminiscent of debates concerning the role of contextual information in other areas of language processing that were taking place at around the same time. In the 1980s and 1990s, a dominant view in cognitive psychology was the *modular conceptualization of the mind* (Fodor, 1983). Under modularity, basic cognitive systems, including language and its subsystems (e.g., lexicon, syntax), are informationally encapsulated, meaning that processing in each module operates independent of the influence of other (especially higher-level) modules. In domains such as lexical access or syntactic parsing, the initial stage of processing was argued to be independent of top-down contextual expectations, which were only integrated at a later point (e.g., Ferreira & Clifton, 1986; Frazier, 1979; Swinney, 1979). Similarly, common ground can be viewed as high-level knowledge that would be too effortful and resource-intensive to be incorporated into the initial, rapid first-stage process of language comprehension. Indeed, some have argued that theory of mind, while available for deliberative and explicit reasoning, is not routinely incorporated into the processes by which we interpret the behavior of other people (Apperly, et al., 2010; Keysar et al., 2003).

However, subsequent work provided evidence from a variety of domains that counters the idea that language processing is encapsulated from higher-level knowledge representations. Evidence of cross-domain interaction in language processing included the influence of visual and linguistic context on lexical access (Dahan & Tanenhaus, 2004; Federmeier & Kutas, 1999; van Berkum, van den Brink, Tesink, Kos, & Hagoort, 2008) and on syntactic parsing (Altmann & Steedman, 1988; Chambers, Tanenhaus, & Magnuson, 2004; Tanenhaus et al. 1995). An alternative theoretical approach—*constraint-based lexicalist theories*—emerged at this time. These theories postulated that multiple probabilistic constraints simultaneously guide the moment-by-moment processing of language (MacDonald, Pearlmutter, & Seidenberg, 1994; Trueswell & Tanenhaus, 1994). The earliest evidence in support of the constraint-based approach to sentence processing came from studies of how lexical and syntactic processing are influenced by multiple simultaneous cues provided by properties of verbs and their arguments, including their meaning and distributional patterns (Garnsey, Pearlmutter, Myers, & Lotocky, 1997; Trueswell, Tanenhaus, & Kello, 1993; Wilson & Garnsey, 2009), as well as by the visual context (Eberhard, Spivey-Knowlton, Sedivy, & Tanenhaus, 1995; Spivey, Tanenhaus, Eberhard, & Sedivy, 2002; Tanenhaus et al., 1995). Other work extended these findings to the literature on perspective-taking, showing that the listener's knowledge about the perspective of the speaker is one of the cues that affects referential interpretation from the earliest moments of processing (Brown-Schmidt, Gunlogson, & Tanenhaus, 2008; Hanna et al., 2003; Heller, Grodner, & Tanenhaus, 2008; Hanna & Tanenhaus, 2004; Nadig & Sedivy, 2002).

For example, Heller et al. (2008) show that when listeners interpret a temporarily-ambiguous referring expression, they use information about the perspective of the speaker in choosing between potential referents, before overt disambiguating information becomes available in the speech stream. This study examined listeners' interpretation in a context where potential referents were objects on a shelf (see Fig. 23.1). The listener (participant) followed an instruction to move objects that was provided by a (confederate) speaker who was sitting on the other side of the display (see Keysar et al., 2000, for an earlier use of this type of experimental set-up). Heller et al. build on the finding that listeners expect modified expressions with size adjectives (e.g., *the big bowl*) in contexts where a noun alone would be insufficient (e.g., when a big and a small bowl are present: Sedivy, Tanenhaus, Chambers, & Carlson, 1999). Of interest were contexts like the example in Figure 23.1 containing two pairs of size-contrasting objects (e.g., two bowls and two cars), where the two bowls and the big car were visible to both partners, and were thus in common ground, but the small car was hidden from the speaker's view. Because the small car is hidden, the speaker should not

FIG. 23.1 Example display modeled after Heller et al. (2008), shown from the listener's perspective (the speaker would be sitting on the other side of the display). The two bowls and the big car are visible from both sides of the display, and thus are in common ground, whereas the small car is in a cubbyhole that is hidden from the speaker's perspective by an opaque panel, and is thus only known to the listener. The speaker will instruct the listener to *"pick up the big bowl..."*

be aware of it. A listener who appreciates the speaker's perspective should therefore take this into account. Heller et al. reasoned that if referential processing is initially egocentric, then upon hearing an unfolding referring expression like *the big . . .* , listeners will consider both the big bowl *and* the big car as potential referents, as both have a contrasting object in the display. However, if listeners consider the fact that the small car is not known to the speaker, they should rule out the big car as a potential referent, even though that object, in and of itself, *is* in common ground and matches the unfolding expression (they should expect the speaker to simply call it *the car*). Indeed, upon hearing *the big* and before any information from the noun was available in the speech stream (a short interval of about 300 ms), listeners developed the expectation that the speaker would refer to the big bowl and not the big car. These findings were since replicated by Ryskin, Benjamin, Tullis, and Brown-Schmidt (2015), and also by Heller, Parisien, and Stevenson (2016). This work provides critical evidence against egocentric-first theories of the role of common ground in language processing (e.g., Keysar et al., 2003), because it shows that listeners integrate information about the common vs. privileged distinction continuously during processing, and not just at a stage when a decision needs to be made (i.e., choice of referent), possibly correcting an initially egocentric interpretation. These findings also provide evidence against a later, more nuanced version of egocentricity—anticipation-without-integration (Barr, 2008)—which argues that listeners distinguish common and privileged referents but do not use this information in interpreting language in the earliest moments (for discussion, see Heller et al., 2016).

In the domain of *language production*, early research on the process of audience design was similarly influenced by findings from social psychology about egocentric biases. For example, Horton and Keysar (1996) proposed a *monitoring and adjustment model*, where common ground does not play a role in initial utterance planning, and instead only comes into play at a delayed second stage. This proposal was based on an analysis of referential forms in a situation where a size-contrasting object was only visible to the speaker and not the addressee (e.g., the speaker would be looking at a display like that shown in Fig. 23.1, and will describe to the addressee an object like the big car, for which the contrasting object, namely the small car, is hidden from the view of the addressee). In situations like this, Horton and Keysar found that speakers, when under time pressure, used an unnecessary adjective in the description (e.g., *the big car*) 43% of the time. Interestingly, Nadig and Sedivy (2002) similarly find that in situations like this, where a size-contrasting object is privileged to the speaker, five- to six-year-old children (and adults) include an unnecessary adjective about half of the time. However, Nadig and Sedivy interpret this finding differently, taking it as evidence that adults and children *do* take perspective in language production. One reason for the different conclusions may be the theoretical backdrop: Horton and Keysar's conclusion is in line with arguments that decision-making is egocentrically biased and therefore deviates from rationality (Tversky & Kahneman, 1974, 1981). By contrast, Nadig and Sedivy's conclusion may have been influenced by their developmental perspective, where achieving the adaptive behavior half the time is a substantive change over a baseline condition where both objects were available to both partners and children produced a modifier 75% of the time (see Brown-Schmidt & Hanna, 2011 for a related discussion regarding the use of baseline conditions in studies of language comprehension). More recent studies have shown that speakers often exhibit adaptation to the perspective of the addressee, along with a simultaneous influence of the speaker's privileged perspective (Heller, Gorman, & Tanenhaus, 2012;

Gorman, Gegg-Harrison, Marsh, & Tanenhaus, 2013; Vanlangendonck, Willems, Menenti, & Hagoort, 2016; Wardlow Lane & Ferreira, 2008; Wardlow Lane, Groisman, & Ferreira, 2006). For example, when referring to unfamiliar objects whose names were learned by a speaker but are unknown to an addressee, speakers rarely use these names on their own (e.g., uttering *click on the fluliket*: 5% in Heller et al., 2012), but they do sometimes use these names coupled with a description (e.g., *Fluliket, with the arms*: 18% in Heller et al., 2012; see also Isaacs & Clark, 1987; Gorman et al., 2013). The influence of privileged information may be more apparent when the speaker is under time pressure (Horton & Keysar, 1996), when speakers are describing a state of affairs to their addressee rather than requesting something from them (Yoon, Koh, & Brown-Schmidt, 2012), and when privileged ground is salient in the task (Wardlow Lane et al., 2006; Wardlow Lane & Ferreira, 2008). Thus, while speakers show a remarkable ability of tracking common ground and in using this information in their referring expressions, they do not seem to completely adapt to the addressee's knowledge. Interestingly, in most studies, the intrusion of privileged ground on language production has been used as a litmus test for whether speakers fail in audience design. However, this misses the fact that speakers are regularly required to draw on privileged information in order to make felicitous contributions to conversation. Indeed, Mozuraitis et al. (2018) propose that the simultaneous consideration of both the speaker's and the addressee's perspectives is a design feature of the system. It remains an open question, then, whether the "incomplete" nature of audience design reflects inherent limits in speakers' ability to avoid egocentrism, or whether it instead reflects a communicative system that is operating in relative balance.

23.3 THE PRESENT

As noted earlier, the notion that language processing might be initially egocentric arose from certain perspectives in social psychology and assumptions about cognitive effort, where contextual information was expected to have a delayed effect on interpretation. With conclusive evidence now showing that listeners *can* use information about the knowledge state of the speaker from the earliest moments of processing, the research question has shifted from *whether* people can use perspective information to *when and how* they use this type of information.

This shift has driven researchers to begin cataloging the ways in which perspective influences language processing. One important line of research investigates phenomena that are characteristic of *situated conversation*, such as the role of conversational grounding in establishing common ground (Brown-Schmidt, 2012; Brown-Schmidt & Fraundorf, 2015), the influence of shared experiences in object labeling (Gorman et al., 2013; Heller et al., 2012; Wu & Keysar, 2007), the role of spatial language and spatial cognition (Galati & Avraamides, 2013; Garrod & Sanford, 1988; Ryskin, Wang, & Brown-Schmidt, 2016), the cognitive and communicative forces that shape attention to common vs. privileged ground (Wardlow, 2013; Wardlow Lane & Ferreira, 2008; Wardlow Lane & Liersch, 2012; Yoon, Koh, & Brown-Schmidt, 2012), as well as mechanisms of multiparty conversation (Yoon & Brown-Schmidt, 2014) and multimodal communication (Galati & Brennan, 2013; Hilliard & Cook, 2016). A second line of work investigates how *characteristics of one's conversational partner* influence language processing, including stereotypical beliefs about the behavior of individuals from different social groups (van Berkum et al., 2008), and cases where the partner is believed to have a cognitive or linguistic deficit (Arnold, Kam, & Tanenhaus, 2007; Grodner & Sedivy, 2005). Additional work has focused on representations of the partner's *goals and beliefs*, including false beliefs (Ferguson, Scheepers, & Sanford, 2010; Mozuraitis et al., 2015), the actions that the partner can make in the setting (Hanna & Tanenhaus, 2004), and the partner's desire to keep a secret (Ferguson & Breheny, 2011; Wardlow Lane et al., 2006). Taken together, this body of work has identified a wide range of factors that influence how perspective guides language processing.

A related question concerns the *cognitive differences* that guide or limit how information is brought to bear on language processing. Proposed system-level constraints include capacity-limited memory and cognitive control processes (e.g., Just & Carpenter, 1992; Novick, Trueswell, & Thompson-Schill, 2005). Note that an alternative view holds that individual differences are linked to differences in *language experience* between individuals (MacDonald & Christiansen, 2002; Mishra, Singh, Pandey, & Huettig, 2012; Wells et al., 2009). In the domain of perspective-taking, there have been several reports of links between individual differences in working memory and executive function processes, and perspective-taking behavior (Brown-Schmidt, 2009a; Lin, Keysar, & Epley, 2010; Wardlow, 2013). According to one view, these findings provide support for the idea that language users need to resolve competition between competing constraints (Brown-Schmidt, 2009a). Others argue instead that such links reveal that the use of perspective is too effortful to routinely influence language processing, particularly in children (Epley, Morewedge, & Keysar, 2004; Lin et al., 2010). There is, however, evidence that young children *do* represent—and in some cases use—perspective information successfully (Nadig & Sedivy, 2002; Nilsen, Graham, Smith, & Chambers, 2008; Scott, He, Baillargeon, & Cummins, 2012). Furthermore, the developing executive function in young children has been linked to children's ability to use perspective in language processing (Nilsen & Graham, 2009; Nilsen, Varghese, Xu, & Fecica, 2015). In sum, links between executive function and perspective-taking have been demonstrated in both children and adults. However, it is important to note in this context that more recent studies fail to find substantive links between individual differences in adults' cognitive function and perspective-taking during language comprehension (Brown-Schmidt, 2012; Brown-Schmidt & Fraundorf, 2015; Ryskin et al., 2014; Ryskin, Benjamin, Tuillis, & Brown-Schmidt, 2015), questioning the magnitude or generalizability of the earlier findings. When the reliability of the measures of individual differences in perspective-taking have been reported, they have been low (Brown-Schmidt & Fraundorf, 2015; Ryskin et al., 2015); this places an upper limit on the size of a correlation one could expect with other measures (e.g., working memory). Thus, to make further progress on this question, it will be necessary to first identify internally-reliable measures of individual differences in listeners' perspective-taking ability.

While the era of cataloging has significantly advanced our understanding of what influences perspective-taking behavior, the demise of the egocentric-first approach has left the field searching for a new framework. Several candidate approaches have emerged.

One influential framework has been *interactive alignment*, which proposes that during conversation speakers and listeners align to each other (Pickering & Garrod, 2004, 2013). Alignment is hypothesized to operate at all levels of representation, ranging from syntactic priming (where communicative partners become more likely to reuse previously produced or previously heard structures), to phonetic accommodation (where partners become more similar in terms of the acoustic properties of their speech). Pickering and Garrod (2004) suggest that perspective-taking behavior emerges through this same mechanism of priming, and this leads speakers and listeners to arrive at similar understanding of a linguistic exchange without having to continuously calculate and integrate explicit representations of common ground. What makes this approach attractive is that it buys perspective-taking behavior "for free" from more general mechanisms, such as the activation of linguistic forms in memory.

The alignment approach can be used to account for certain phenomena in conversation. Here we consider *conceptual pacts*, a tacit agreement about the conceptualization of an object that is reflected in the use of entrained referential phrases (e.g., whether to call a certain object *the shiny cylinder* or *the silver pipe*). Entrained terms tend to persist in conversation, such that speakers continue to use these terms when talking to the same partner, but do so to a lesser extent when interacting with a new partner (Brennan & Clark, 1996; Wilkes-Gibbs & Clark, 1992). This behavior is mirrored in comprehension: listeners interpret a referring expression faster when their partner continues to use a term they developed earlier (Barr & Keysar, 2002; Brown-Schmidt, 2009b), but interpretation is slowed if the speaker refers to a previously-mentioned object in a new way (Kronmüller & Barr, 2007; Matthews, Lieven, & Tomasello, 2010; Metzing & Brennan, 2003). Under alignment, when a speaker produces a certain referring expression, this linguistic form creates activation at all levels of representation for both the speaker herself and for her addressee. This can explain why speakers reuse entrained terms (because the term is already activated), and why such reuse is observed less with a new partner (because the term is tied to the partner with whom the pact was forged). Alignment can also account for certain partner-specific effects in comprehension. For example, the facilitation observed when the same speaker reuses a referring expression, such as *the shiny cylinder,* is explained as a result of the activation of the linguistic representation in the addressee's mind. The penalty observed when the same speaker "breaks" the pact, compared to a new speaker, can be attributed to preactivation of the previous term (*shiny cylinder*) with the same speaker (but not a new speaker). In sum, effects associated with the use of conceptual pacts can be explained by conceptual alignment, offering an explanation of how perspective-taking behavior can be obtained without the complex process of calculating explicit common ground. There are, however, limits to the explanatory power of the alignment approach. Recall that alignment does not just operate at the conceptual level, but at all levels of linguistic representation. Parallel to the conceptual level, interactive alignment predicts that the *syntactic structure* of referring expressions is activated (and reactivated) and thus should be preserved over the course of the conversation. This prediction is not borne out: not only is such preservation not observed, but, in fact, the structure of a referring expression normally *changes* over time, becoming shorter as the conversation progresses (e.g., from *the person ice skating that has two arms* to *the ice skater*; Clark & Wilkes-Gibbs, 1986; Isaacs & Clark, 1987). It is unclear whether and how the alignment approach can be developed to capture the *change* in the syntactic form that referring expressions undergo over time (also see Heller & Chambers, 2014 for a discussion of other phenomena that cannot be captured using alignment).

A different mechanism is presented in Horton and Gerrig (2005a, 2005b, 2016) who propose that effects of perspective-taking can arise from *ordinary memory processes*. Horton and Gerrig propose that through shared experiences, we form memory traces that link specific partners with the contents of that shared experience. On this view, when a speaker prepares a referring expression, the addressee serves as a memory cue which resonates with information in memory that is already associated with that addressee. This process leads the speaker to use shared information in the referring expression, such as calling an object by its shared name (*shiny cylinder*), rather than a non-shared name (*silver pipe*). This aspect of the memory approach is attractive because, like alignment, it derives perspective-taking behavior as a result of general mechanisms that are not specific to common ground.

There is evidence that perspective-taking behavior is indeed linked to shared experiences (Gorman et al., 2013; Heller et al., 2012; Horton & Gerrig, 2005b). For example, one set of findings showed that speakers were better at distinguishing shared and privileged labels when shared information was acquired through a shared learning experience with the addressee, compared to when speakers were simply *told* that the addressee shared this information (Gorman et al., 2013). However, not all cases of shared information are based on direct experience. For example, Isaacs and Clark (1987) examined common ground that is based on community membership: they had New Yorkers ("experts") and non-New Yorkers ("novices") perform a task of ordering postcards of New York City landmarks. The task was performed six times; each time they arranged the postcards into a different order. Even though participants were *not* told that they may have different knowledge of New York City, already on the first time through the task, expert speakers tended to use unadorned names when interacting with other experts (e.g., *Rockefeller Center*), whereas they tended to include descriptions in their utterances when interacting with a novice partner (e.g., *Rockefeller Center, with all the flags*). Strikingly, this sensitivity to the partner's expertise (or lack thereof) emerged very early in the interaction, even before all the cards had been discussed for the first time (see Table 2 in the original paper). This pattern reveals that speakers inferred—and adapted to—the knowledge state of their partner rapidly, possibly based on the partner's accent, or perhaps based on their reaction to the first card description (only six out of thirty-two pairs of participants explicitly discussed their familiarity with New York City). As noted by Horton and Gerrig (2005a), cases where common ground is *inferred* based on community membership cannot be handled by associative memory mechanisms, and instead require *strategic* use of memory representations. Understanding how, and when, speakers calculate what type of referential form will be successful with a given addressee, remains an open question. Resolving this issue would require a better understanding of how representations of others' knowledge are stored, and how they are accessed during language production (Brown-Schmidt & Duff, 2016; Clark & Marshall, 1978).

We have seen that some linguistic phenomena that are taken to reflect perspective-taking behavior can arise "for free" from general, non-dedicated cognitive processes that do not require explicit computation of common ground. However, it seems unlikely that these non-dedicated processes alone can be developed to explain *all* aspects of perspective-taking that have been observed in the literature to date. Furthermore, the two mechanisms discussed here focus on *shared* information, and are silent with respect to the phenomena that rely on *non-shared* (or private) information, which, as we will consider in the next section, also plays a central—yet neglected—role in perspective-taking.

23.4 THE FUTURE

Perspective-taking is complex. Because there is no direct access to another person's perspective, the process requires estimating what others know, likely by using inferences based on multiple probabilistic cues in the situational context. To maintain relevance over time, these estimates must be continuously updated when new information becomes available. At the same time, however, it is clear that language comprehension and production are remarkably rapid and efficient. Earlier research attempted to explain how perspective-taking is accomplished in real time by saying that it isn't: that the effects we observe are due to heuristics such as using one's own knowledge in lieu of calculating another person's (Keysar et al., 1998). More recent attempts take a different direction, by acknowledging that perspective-taking does happen, but arguing that it is a by-product of other, non-dedicated cognitive processes (Horton & Gerrig, 2005a, 2005b, 2016; Pickering & Garrod, 2004). Such approaches are appealing, as they offer ways of understanding how seemingly complex mental representations nonetheless entail rapid language processing. However, it is unlikely that these processes alone would be able to account for all aspects of perspective-taking behavior. Moving forward, it will be necessary to develop in more detail the full range of mechanisms that explain perspective-taking behavior.

One essential line of inquiry is the development of implemented *computational models*. First, from the idea that multiple probabilistic constraints guide language comprehension comes the prediction that various sources of information will vary in the degree to which they allow the listener to make a prediction about upcoming structure. A class of computational models that has been emerging in the literature on pragmatics are probabilistic *Bayesian models* (e.g., Frank & Goodman, 2012; Goodman & Stuhlmüller, 2013; Kehler & Rohde, 2013). In these models, listeners develop an interpretation that is based on reasoning about the most likely context that would have caused the speaker to say what she said. These models have several important properties. First, their probabilistic nature captures the fact that interpretation inherently involves uncertainty: a listener infers what the speaker meant, but never has access to that meaning directly. Second, their probabilistic nature further allows taking noisy context into account, calculating specific predictions about language use, which can then be tested against human behavior in context. Finally, these models reflect a clear hypothesis about the relationship between comprehension and production, where the experience with past production patterns are the basis of the comprehender's inferences about current speaker meaning (cf. MacDonald, 2013). The first such model in the domain of perspective-taking is presented in Heller et al. (2016), which models the comprehension of referring expressions under varying situations of knowledge mismatch between the conversational partners. This work demonstrates how a probabilistic approach can account for different results that were previously interpreted as support for qualitatively-different mechanisms (specifically, Heller et al., 2008, and Keysar et al., 2000). One limitation of current Bayesian models is that they deal with highly simplified situations that abstract away from many aspects of conversation. However, developing a framework to quantify perspective knowledge will allow us to make *qualitative and quantitative predictions* about perspective-taking in language use. Doing so might also provide forward momentum for the cataloging approach and offer a way of corralling these findings within a unified theoretical framework, allowing us to test competing computational frameworks. One important issue is whether humans are "rational" (Frank & Goodman, 2012) or whether rationality is in fact bounded when processing language (e.g., Ferreira & Patson, 2007). Furthermore, what constitutes rational behavior in the domain of conversation deserves further inquiry. For example, Brown-Schmidt (2012) and Brown-Schmidt and Fraundorf (2015) found very little evidence for an influence of conversational grounding on the degree to which mentioned information was treated as common ground in language comprehension. Yet these grounding phenomena, such as nodding and saying *uh-huh* when listening to your partner, are evident in conversational interactions, suggesting that listeners may be failing to appreciate a useful source of information—a type of bounded rationality. In the domain of perspective-taking, then, resolving the issues of if, when, and *how* language users are rational, would likely benefit from a modeling approach.

Current computational approaches, however, do not directly speak to the *cognitive* mechanisms that underlie perspective-taking behavior. Thus, another goal for future work will be understanding the cognitive mechanisms that support the *representation of perspective in memory* and how these representations are brought to bear during language processing. Such an endeavor could address, for example, questions about whether one-bit representations of common ground (e.g., representing common ground as either my partner "does" or "does not know"; Galati & Brennan, 2010), or gradient representations (e.g., representing how likely it is that my partner knows something; Brown-Schmidt, 2012; Gorman, 2012; Mozuraitis et al., 2018) provide a better account of the data. Other representational questions include whether common ground representations are uni-dimensional, or are instead represented in a multidimensional matrix which is indexed according to the different sources of evidence about common ground (e.g., physical co-presence, linguistic mention, community membership). Understanding the neurobiological systems that support several different types of perspective-taking processes (e.g., Brown-Schmidt & Duff, 2016; Duff & Brown-Schmidt, 2012;, Rubin et al., 2011; Rueschemeyer, Gardner, & Stoner, 2015; van Ackeren et al., 2012, 2016) may also offer insights into when and how perspective representations will guide language use. Considerations of memory mechanisms, such as contextual reinstatement (Godden & Baddeley, 1975, 1980; Mulligan, 2011; Smith, Glenberg, & Bjork, 1978) may provide guidance (for discussion see Brown-Schmidt & Fraundorf, 2015; Horton & Gerrig, 2005b). For example, a well-known finding in the memory literature, *the generation effect*, refers to the finding that generating information, such as producing a word based on a three-letter cue, produces better memory than simply studying that word silently (Jacoby, 1978; Slamecka & Graf, 1978; also see the *production effect*, MacLeod, Gopie, Hourihan, Neary, & Ozubko, 2010). Studies of recognition memory for conversational referents show that speakers indeed exhibit better item memory than listeners (McKinley, Brown-Schmidt, & Benjamin, 2017; Yoon, Benjamin, & Brown-Schmidt, 2016; also see Isaacs, 1990; Knutsen & Le Bigot, 2014). These findings suggest that there may be memorial limitations on the degree to which speakers and listeners can become aligned in conversation. Further, it raises the question of whether and when speakers and listeners are aware of one another's memory or lack of memory for the past. Promising lines of inquiry will examine the interface of language and memory in the service of perspective-taking. These findings pose the question of whether an ideal perspective-taking process is based on joint experience (Clark & Marshall, 1978), or alternatively, is sensitive to the fact that speakers' and listeners' memory of the discourse history is unlikely to be symmetrical (e.g., Fischer, Schult, & Steffens, 2015).

Another important direction for future research is *expanding the range of phenomena investigated*. To illustrate, let us first consider a situation where there are two objects from the same basic level object category (e.g., two trees), and the listener knows both their names (e.g., a Sycamore tree and an Osage Orange tree), but is able to assume that the speaker only knows one of those names (e.g., the Sycamore). When the speaker says *the tree*, then despite the fact that there are two trees, the listener can infer that she is referring *not* to the Sycamore, but how will the listener arrive at this interpretation? If the listener accesses their memory representation of the entities, both entities are good candidate referents, as both fit the description *tree*. To find the correct referent, the listener must not just access their memory representations of the entities and locate memory traces related to the speaker, but also perform a computation of how *this particular speaker* would have referred to each of the two potential referents, comparing this computation to what the speaker actually said. To do this, listeners do not just need to decide which referents would be most likely for the speaker in the situation (cf. Hanna & Tanenhaus, 2004), but instead must compute the different linguistic forms that the speaker would have used for each referent. This is a complex computation that seems to require explicit inference based on access to past episodes that established common ground, and that could not be explained by a priming or associative mechanism.

Like this example, much of the research on perspective-taking has focused on reference, specifically on definite referring expressions, perhaps because of the ease of studying these forms in the lab using the referential communication task. While referential phenomena have taught us a lot about perspective-taking, the fact that referring expressions normally encode shared information has led the field to give disproportionate attention to the role of *shared* information in perspective-taking, whereas the role of *private* information in conversation has been left outside of the range of typically investigated phenomena. Future work will require expanding our investigations of perspective-taking beyond the narrow focus on reference, investigating in detail other linguistic forms, such as verbs (see Chambers & San Juan, 2008) or questions (more to follow next), other aspects of communication, such as gesture (Hilliard & Cook, 2016) and depictions (Clark, 2016), and higher-level decisions such as choosing a partner depending on the goal of the conversation (e.g., calling the dentist if your tooth aches, and the realtor if you want to sell the house), and choosing a language depending on the conversational situation (e.g., speaking Hebrew to your son at home, but English when addressing him in front of his teacher).

Our next example concerns *information questions*, which are characterized by the speaker assuming that the addressee has, in their privileged ground, the answer to the question. Existing research shows that addressees rapidly interpret questions as asking about information in privileged ground (Brown-Schmidt, et al., 2008; Brown-Schmidt, 2009a; Brown-Schmidt & Fraundorf, 2015). Yet many questions about this process remain unanswered, such as how the speaker goes about choosing a relevant addressee for a certain question. Consider a visit to the dentist with your child: you're at the office, the dentist comes to greet you, and you want to know if your son has brushed his teeth that morning. Who do you ask? Your dentist is highly relevant to the topic of tooth-brushing, and in fact most of your conversations with her involve dental hygiene. If questions were designed simply based on past experiences and memory associations, one would be more likely to (erroneously) ask the dentist. But this kind of error virtually never happens, and you would most likely address the question to your son, suggesting that you have mapped out the privileged ground of both potential addressees. This context can be developed even further: Imagine that you've already been talking to the dentist about your son's terrible tooth-brushing habits (rendering the topic in common ground with her), and further, that she has completed your son's dental exam and can therefore infer based on the state of his teeth that he was unlikely to have brushed in the last 24 hours. Even in this case, where the dentist is not only knowledgeable about tooth-brushing, but there is also an immediate conversational record with her about the topic, when it comes time to find out the answer to your question, you ask your son and not the dentist. Why? Because she has no direct evidence as to whether he brushed his teeth this specific morning. This indicates that you can map out their respective privileged grounds and calculate that your son possesses the best evidence for the answer. New frontiers in the research on the use and interpretation of questions would allow us to better understand how privileged information is represented, organized, and accessed in the service of communication. Especially needed are efforts to expand the domain of inquiry to a range of communicative devices that make different demands on privileged information, such as declarative questions, *You didn't brush your teeth?* (Gunlogson, 2003) and contrastive accenting, *It LOOKS like you brushed your teeth*, (Kurumada, Brown, Bibyk, Pontillo, & Tanenhaus, 2014).

Another domain that deserves further attention is the *type of knowledge mismatch* between interlocutors. It is noteworthy that the majority of the studies examining perspective-taking in conversation have involved level 1 knowledge mismatch, namely, situations where one partner knows a certain piece of information that the other does not (e.g., Barr, 2008; Brown-Schmidt et al., 2008; Hanna et al., 2003: Exp. 1; Heller et al., 2008; Keysar et al., 2000, 2003; Nadig & Sedivy, 2002). Yet, this is the type of knowledge that is assumed in the developmental literature to be mastered early in development (Baron-Cohen, Leslie, & Frith, 1985; Wimmer & Perner, 1983). Only a handful of studies have investigated level 2 knowledge mismatch, with mixed results: some have shown adaptive behavior (Hanna et al., 2003: Exp. 2), while others have found that this type of mismatch is much harder to handle (Mozuraitis et al., 2015; Mozuraitis et al., 2018 finds an intermediate pattern). This disparity raises questions about the relationship between theory of mind and perspective-taking behavior in conversation. While some researchers seem to equate perspective-taking processes with theory of mind (Apperly et al., 2010; Keysar et al., 2003), arguments that perspective-taking emerges from ordinary memory processes (Horton & Gerrig, 2005a) or based on simple one-bit cues (Galati & Brennan, 2010) would seem to be at odds with this link. Thus, examining several types of knowledge mismatch would contribute to the development of theories of the relationship between common ground in language processing and representations of theory of mind.

23.5 Conclusion

Everyday language use is guided by our knowledge of what others do and do not know. This knowledge guides who we communicate with, and how. Theoretical and empirical investigations focus on the cognitive processes that support the interfacing of language production and comprehension with representations of privileged and common ground. Our understanding of these processes has been influenced by theoretical traditions in other areas of psychology including cognitive development, social psychology, and decision-making. Early debates about whether or not perspective representations are accessed online have given way to a flood of empirical findings cataloging the factors that influence how perspective is used in language processing. Moving forward, the field will attempt to understand whether language users are integrating information from a noisy signal, or making use of heuristics and other non-dedicated cognitive operations to simplify an otherwise-complex cognitive operation. Achieving forward progress will likely necessitate development of implemented computational models of perspective-taking in language use, considerations of the cognitive mechanisms that encode perspective representations, and expanding the domain of inquiry beyond referential processes. Present approaches provide a viable explanation for how visually-grounded references like *the empty martini glass* are produced and interpreted by conversational partners with distinct perspectives. The next horizon will be explaining how exquisitely canonical exchanges like this, unfold with such ease:

DAPHNA TO SARAH: Another martini?
SARAH TO DAPHNA: [winks, puts down her mocktail], whispers: *"I'm pregnant!"*

Exchanges like this involve making guesses about what the partner does and does not know, and what they think you do and do not know. While these everyday examples seem trivial, we know very little about how they unfold in the mind. We look forward to several more decades of progress in answering this intriguing question.

Acknowledgments

We are grateful to Craig Chambers and Mandy Simons for providing feedback on earlier versions of this chapter. Preparation of this manuscript was supported by National Science Foundation Grant (NSF BCS 15-56700) to Sarah Brown-Schmidt, and a Social Sciences and Humanities Research Council Grant (SSHRC 435-2016-0742) to Daphna Heller.

References

Altmann, G., & Steedman, M. (1988). Interaction with context during human sentence processing. *Cognition, 30*(3), 191–238.

Apperly, I. A., Carroll, D. J., Samson, D., Humphreys, G. W., Qureshi, A., & Moffitt, G. (2010). Why are there limits on theory of mind use? Evidence from adults' ability to follow instructions from an ignorant speaker. *The Quarterly Journal of Experimental Psychology, 63*(6), 1201–17.

Arnold, J. E., Kam, C. L. H., Tanenhaus, M. K. (2007). If you say thee uh you are describing something hard: The on-line attribution of disfluency during reference comprehension. *Journal of Experimental Psychology: Learning, Memory, and Cognition, 33*(5), 914–30.

Asher, N., & Lascarides, A. (2003). *Logics of Conversation*. Cambridge University Press, Cambridge.

Baillargeon, R., Scott, R. M., & He, Z. (2010). False-belief understanding in infants. *Trends in Cognitive Sciences, 14*(3), 110–18.

Bard, E. G., Anderson, A. H., Sotillo, C., Aylett, M., Doherty-Sneddon, G., & Newlands, A. (2000). Controlling the intelligibility of referring expressions in dialogue. *Journal of Memory and Language, 42*, 1–22.

Baron-Cohen, S., Leslie, A. M., & Frith, U. (1985). Does the autistic child have a "theory of mind"? *Cognition, 21*(1), 37–46.

Barr, D. J. (2008). Pragmatic expectations and linguistic evidence: Listeners anticipate but do not integrate common ground. *Cognition, 109*(1), 18–40.

Barr, D. J., & Keysar, B. (2002). Anchoring comprehension in linguistic precedents. *Journal of Memory and Language, 46*(2), 391–418.

Bortfeld, H., & Brennan, S. E. (1997). Use and acquisition of idiomatic expressions in referring by native and non-native speakers. *Discourse Processes, 23*(2), 119–47.

Brennan, S. E., & Clark, H. H. (1996). Conceptual pacts and lexical choice in conversation. *Journal of Experimental Psychology: Learning, Memory, and Cognition, 22*(6), 1482–93.

Bromme, R., Jucks, R., & Wagner, T. (2005). How to refer to "diabetes"? Language in online health advice. *Applied Cognitive Psychology, 19*(5), 569–86.

Brown-Schmidt, S. (2009a). The role of executive function in perspective taking during online language comprehension. *Psychonomic Bulletin & Review, 16*(5), 893–900.

Brown-Schmidt, S. (2009b). Partner-specific interpretation of maintained referential precedents during interactive dialog. *Journal of Memory and Language, 61*(2), 171–90.

Brown-Schmidt, S. (2012). Beyond common and privileged: Gradient representations of common ground in real-time language use. *Language and Cognitive Processes, 27*(1), 62–89.

Brown-Schmidt, S., & Duff, M. C. (2016). Memory and common ground processes in language use. *Topics in Cognitive Science, 8*, 722–36.

Brown-Schmidt, S., & Fraundorf, S. H. (2015). Interpretation of informational questions modulated by joint knowledge and intonational contours. *Journal of Memory and Language, 84*, 49–74.

Brown-Schmidt, S., Gunlogson, C., & Tanenhaus, M. K. (2008). Addressees distinguish shared from private information when interpreting questions during interactive conversation. *Cognition, 107*(3), 1122–34.

Brown-Schmidt, S., & Hanna, J. E. (2011). Talking in another person's shoes: Incremental perspective-taking in language processing. *Dialogue & Discourse, 2*(1), 11–33.

Carlson, S. M., Mandell, D. J., & Williams, L. (2004). Executive function and theory of mind: Stability and prediction from ages 2 to 3. *Developmental Psychology, 40*(6), 1105–22.

Caruso, E. M., Epley, N., Bazerman, M. H. (2006). The costs and benefits of undoing egocentric responsibility assessments in groups. *Journal of Personality and Social Psychology, 91*(5), 857–71.

Chambers, C. G., & San Juan, V. (2008). Perception and presupposition in real-time language comprehension: Insights from anticipatory processing. *Cognition, 108*(1), 26–50.

Chambers, C. G., Tanenhaus, M. K., & Magnuson, J. S. (2004). Actions and affordances in syntactic ambiguity resolution. *Journal of Experimental Psychology: Learning, Memory, and Cognition, 30*, 687–96.

Clark, H. H. (1996). *Using Language*. Cambridge University Press, Cambridge.

Clark, H. H. (2016). Depicting as a method of communication. *Psychological Review, 123*(3), 324–47.

Clark, H. H., & Brennan, S. E. (1991). Grounding in communication. In: Resnick, L., Levine, B., John, M., & Teasley, S. (Eds.), *Perspectives on Socially Shared Cognition* (pp. 127–49). American Psychological Association, Washington, DC

Clark, H. H., & Krych, M. A. (2004). Speaking while monitoring addressees for understanding. *Journal of Memory and Language*, 50(1), 62–81.

Clark, H. H., & Marshall, C. R. (1978). Reference diaries. In: Waltz, D. L. (Ed.), *TINLAP-2: Theoretical Issues in Natural Language Processing-2* (pp. 57–63). Association for Computing Machinery, New York, NY.

Clark, H. H., & Marshall, C. M. (1981). Definite reference and mutual knowledge. In: Joshi, A. K., Webber, B. L., & Sag, I. A. (Eds.), *Elements of Discourse Understanding* (pp. 10–63). Cambridge University Press, Cambridge.

Clark, H. H., & Murphy, G. L. (1982). Audience design in meaning and reference. *Advances in Psychology*, 9, 287–99.

Clark, H. H., & Schaefer, E. F. (1987). Concealing one's meaning from overhearers. *Journal of Memory and Language*, 26(2), 209–25.

Clark, H. H., & Schaefer, E. F. (1989). Contributing to discourse. *Cognitive Science*, 13(2), 259–94.

Clark, H. H., & Wilkes-Gibbs, D. (1986). Referring as a collaborative process. *Cognition*, 22(1), 1–39.

Dahan, D., & Tanenhaus, M. K. (2004). Continuous mapping from sound to meaning in spoken-language comprehension: Immediate effects of verb-based thematic constraints. *Journal of Experimental Psychology: Learning, Memory, and Cognition*, 30(2), 498–513.

Duff, M. C., & Brown-Schmidt, S. (2012). The hippocampus and the flexible use and processing of language. *Frontiers in Human Neuroscience*, 6, 69.

Eberhard, K., Spivey-Knowlton, M., Sedivy, J., & Tanenhaus, M. (1995). Eye movements as a window into real-time spoken language comprehension in natural contexts. *Journal of Psycholinguistic Research*, 24(6), 409–36.

Epley, N., & Gilovich, T. (2006). The anchoring-and-adjustment heuristic. *Psychological Science*, 17(4), 311–18.

Epley, N., Keysar, B., Van Boven, L., Gilovich, T. (2004). Perspective taking as egocentric anchoring and adjustment. *Journal of Personality and Social Psychology*, 87(3), 327–39.

Epley, N., Morewedge, C. K., & Keysar, B. (2004). Perspective taking in children and adults: Equivalent egocentrism but differential correction. *Journal of Experimental Social Psychology*, 40(6), 760–8.

Federmeier, K. D., & Kutas, M. (1999). A rose by any other name: Long-term memory structure and sentence processing. *Journal of Memory and Language*, 41(4), 469–95.

Ferguson, H. J., & Breheny, R. (2011). Eye movements reveal the time-course of anticipating behaviour based on complex, conflicting desires. *Cognition*, 119(2), 179–96.

Ferguson, H. J., Scheepers, C., & Sanford, A. J. (2010). Expectations in counterfactual and theory of mind reasoning. *Language and Cognitive Processes*, 25(3), 297–346.

Ferreira, F., & Clifton, C. Jr. (1986). The independence of syntactic processing. *Journal of Memory and Language*, 25(3), 348–68.

Ferreira, F., & Patson, N. D. (2007). The "Good enough" approach to language comprehension. *Language and Linguistics Compass*, 1(1–2), 71–83.

Fischer, N. M., Schult, J. C., & Steffens, M. C. (2015). Source and destination memory in face-to-face interaction: A multinomial modeling approach. *Journal of Experimental Psychology: Applied*, 21(2), 195–204.

Flavell, J. H., Everett, B. A., Croft, K., & Flavell, E. R. (1981). Young children's knowledge about visual perception: Further evidence for the Level 1–Level 2 distinction. *Developmental Psychology*, 17(1), 99–103.

Fodor, J. A. (1983). *The Modularity of Mind: An Essay on Faculty Psychology*. MIT Press, Cambridge, MA.

Frank, M. C., & Goodman, N. D. (2012). Predicting pragmatic reasoning in language games. *Science*, 336, 998.

Frazier, L. (1979). *On Comprehending Sentences: Syntactic Parsing Strategies*. Indiana University Linguistics Club, Bloomington, IN.

Fussell, S. R., & Krauss, R. M. (1991). Accuracy and bias in estimates of others' knowledge. *European Journal of Social Psychology*, 21(5), 445–54.

Galati, A., & Avraamides, M. (2013). Flexible spatial perspective-taking: Conversational partners weigh multiple cues in collaborative tasks. *Frontiers in Human Neuroscience*, 7, 1–16.

Galati, A., & Brennan, S. E. (2010). Attenuating information in spoken communication: For the speaker, or for the addressee? *Journal of Memory and Language*, 62(1), 35–51.

Galati, A., & Brennan, S. E. (2013). Speakers adapt gestures to addressees' knowledge: Implications for models of co-speech gesture. *Language, Cognition and Neuroscience*, 29(4), 435–51.

Garnsey, S. M., Pearlmutter, N. J., Myers, E., & Lotocky, M. A. (1997). The contributions of verb bias and plausibility to the comprehension of temporarily ambiguous sentences. *Journal of Memory and Language*, 37(1), 58–93.

Garrod, S. C., & Sanford, A. J. (1988). Discourse models as interfaces between language and the spatial world. *Journal of Semantics*, 6(1), 147–60.

Godden, D. R., & Baddeley, A. D. (1975). Context-dependent memory in two natural environments: On land and underwater. *British Journal of Psychology*, 66(3), 325–31.

Godden, D., & Baddeley, A. (1980). When does context influence recognition memory? *British Journal of Psychology*, 71(1), 99–104.

Goodman, N. D., & Stuhlmüller, A. (2013). Knowledge and implicature: Modeling language understanding as social cognition. *Topics in Cognitive Science*, 5(1), 173–84.

Gorman, K. S. (2012). *Investigating Interlocutors' Use of Common Ground During the Comprehension and Production of Referring Expressions* [Unpublished doctoral dissertation]. University of Rochester, New York, NY.

Gorman, K. S., Gegg-Harrison, W., Marsh, C. R., & Tanenhaus, M. K. (2013). What's learned together stays together: Speakers' choice of referring expression reflects shared experience. *Journal of Experimental Psychology: Learning, Memory, and Cognition*, 39(3), 843–53.

Grice, H. P. (1967). Logic and conversation. William James Lectures. Reprinted in: Grice, H. P. (1989), *Studies in the Way of Words* (pp. 1–143). Harvard University Press, Cambridge, MA.

Grodner, D., & Sedivy, J. C. (2005). The effect of speaker-specific information on pragmatic inferences. In: Pearlmutter, N., & Gibson, E. (Eds.), *The Processing and Acquisition of Reference* (pp. 239–72). MIT Press, Cambridge, MA.

Gunlogson, C. (2003). *True to Form: Rising and Falling Declaratives as Questions in English*. Routledge, New York, NY.

Hanna, J. E., & Tanenhaus, M. K. (2004). Pragmatic effects on reference resolution in a collaborative task: Evidence from eye movements. *Cognitive Science*, 28(1), 105–15.

Hanna, J. E., Tanenhaus, M. K., & Trueswell, J. C. (2003). The effects of common ground and perspective on domains of referential interpretation. *Journal of Memory and Language*, 49(1), 43–61.

Heim, I. (1983). On the projection problem for presuppositions. *Second West Coast Conference on Formal Linguistics (WCCFL 2)*, 114–25.

Heim, I. (1992). Presupposition projection and the semantics of attitude verbs. *Journal of Semantics 9*, 183–221.

Heller, D., & Chambers, C. G. (2014). Would a *blue kite* by any other name be just as blue? Effects of descriptive choices on subsequent referential behavior. *Journal of Memory and Language, 70*, 53–67.

Heller, D., Gorman, K. S., Tanenhaus, M. (2012). To name or to describe: Shared knowledge affects referential form. *Topics in Cognitive Science, 4*(2), 290–305.

Heller, D., Grodner, D., & Tanenhaus, M. K. (2008). The role of perspective in identifying domains of reference. *Cognition, 108*(3), 831–6.

Heller, D., Parisien, C., & Stevenson, S. (2016). Perspective-taking behavior as the probabilistic weighing of multiple domains. *Cognition, 149*, 104.

Hilliard, C., & Cook, S. W. (2016). Bridging gaps in common ground: Speakers design their gestures for their listeners. *Journal of Experimental Psychology: Learning, Memory, and Cognition, 42*(1), 91–103.

Horton, W. S., & Gerrig, R. J. (2005a). Conversational common ground and memory processes in language production. *Discourse Processes, 40*(1), 1–35.

Horton, W. S., & Gerrig, R. J. (2005b). The impact of memory demands on audience design during language production. *Cognition, 96*(2), 127–42.

Horton, W. S., & Gerrig, R. J. (2016). Revisiting the memory-based processing approach to common ground. *Topics in Cognitive Science, 8*, 780–95.

Horton, W. S., & Keysar, B. (1996). When do speakers take into account common ground? *Cognition, 59*(1), 91–117.

Isaacs, E. A. (1990). *Mutual Memory for Conversation* [Doctoral dissertation]. Stanford University, Stanford, CA.

Isaacs, E. A., & Clark, H. H. (1987). References in conversation between experts and novices. *Journal of Experimental Psychology: General, 116*(1), 26.

Jacoby, L. L. (1978). On interpreting the effects of repetition: Solving a problem versus remembering a solution. *Journal of Verbal Learning and Verbal Behavior, 17*(6), 649–67.

Just, M. A., & Carpenter, P. A. (1992). A capacity theory of comprehension: Individual differences in working memory. *Psychological Review, 99*(1), 122–49.

Kaplan, D. (1989). Demonstratives. In: Almog, J., Perry, J., & Wettstein, H. (Eds.), *Themes from Kaplan* (pp. 481–563). Oxford University Press, Oxford.

Kehler, A., & Rohde, H. (2013). Aspects of a theory of pronoun interpretation. *Theoretical Linguistics, 39*(3–4), 295–309.

Keysar, B., Barr, D. J., Balin, J. A., & Brauner, J. S. (2000). Taking perspective in conversation: The role of mutual knowledge in comprehension. *Psychological Science, 11*(1), 32–8.

Keysar, B., Barr, D. J., Balin, J. A., & Paek, T. S. (1998). Definite reference and mutual knowledge: Process models of common ground in comprehension. *Journal of Memory and Language, 39*(1), 1–20.

Keysar, B., Lin, S., & Barr, D. J. (2003). Limits on theory of mind use in adults. *Cognition, 89*(1), 25–41.

Knutsen, D., & Le Bigot, L. (2012). Managing dialogue: How information availability affects collaborative reference production. *Journal of Memory and Language, 67*(3), 326–41.

Knutsen, D., & Le Bigot, L. (2014). Capturing egocentric biases in reference reuse during collaborative dialogue. *Psychonomic Bulletin & Review, 21*(6), 1590–9.

Krauss, R. M., & Glucksberg, S. (1977). Social and nonsocial speech. *Scientific American*, 236, 100–5.

Krauss, R. M., & Weinheimer, S. (1964). Changes in reference phrases as a function of frequency of usage in social interaction: A preliminary study. *Psychonomic Science*, 1, 113–14.

Kronmüller, E., & Barr, D. J. (2007). Perspective-free pragmatics: Broken precedents and the recovery-from-preemption hypothesis. *Journal of Memory and Language*, 56(3), 436–55.

Kurumada, C., Brown, M., Bibyk, S., Pontillo, D. F., & Tanenhaus, M. K. (2014). Is it or isn't it: Listeners make rapid use of prosody to infer speaker meanings. *Cognition*, 133(2), 335–42.

Levinson, S. C. (2000). *Presumptive Meanings: The Theory of Generalized Conversational Implicature*. MIT Press, Cambridge, MA.

Lewis, D. (1969). *Convention: A Philosophical Study*. Harvard University Press, Cambridge, MA.

Lin, S., Keysar, B., & Epley, N. (2010). Reflexively mindblind: Using theory of mind to interpret behavior requires effortful attention. *Journal of Experimental Social Psychology*, 46(3), 551–6.

MacDonald, M. C. (2013). How language production shapes language form and comprehension. *Frontiers in Psychology*, 4, 226.

MacDonald, M. C., & Christiansen, M. H. (2002). Reassessing working memory: Comment on Just and Carpenter (1992) and Waters and Caplan (1996). *Psychological Review*, 109(1), 35–54.

MacDonald, M. C., Pearlmutter, N. J., & Seidenberg, M. S. (1994). Lexical nature of syntactic ambiguity resolution. *Psychological Review*, 101(4), 676–703.

MacLeod, C. M., Gopie, N., Hourihan, K. L., Neary, K. R., & Ozubko, J. D., (2010). The production effect: Delineation of a phenomenon. *Journal of Experimental Psychology: Learning, Memory, and Cognition*, 36(3), 671–85.

Matthews, D., Lieven, E., & Tomasello, M. (2010). What's in a manner of speaking? Children's sensitivity to partner-specific referential precedents. *Developmental Psychology*, 46(4), 749–60.

McKinley, G. L., Brown-Schmidt, S., & Benjamin, A. S. (2017). Memory for conversation and the development of common ground. *Memory & Cognition*, 45(8), 1281–94.

Metzing, C., & Brennan, S. E. (2003). When conceptual pacts are broken: Partner-specific effects on the comprehension of referring expressions. *Journal of Memory and Language*, 49(2), 201–13.

Mishra, R. K., Singh, N., Pandey, A., & Huettig, F. (2012). Spoken language-mediated anticipatory eye movements are modulated by reading ability: Evidence from Indian low and high literates. *Journal of Eye Movement Research*, 5(1) 3, 1–10.

Mozuraitis, M., Chambers, C. G., & Daneman, M. (2015). Privileged versus shared knowledge about object identity in real-time referential processing. *Cognition*, 142, 148–65.

Mozuraitis, M., Stevenson, S., & Heller, D. (2018). Modelling reference production as the probabilistic combination of multiple perspectives. *Cognitive Science*, doi: 10.1111/cogs.12582.

Mulligan, N. W. (2011). Generation disrupts memory for intrinsic context but not extrinsic context. *The Quarterly Journal of Experimental Psychology*, 64(8), 1543–62.

Nadig, A. S., & Sedivy, J. C. (2002). Evidence of perspective-taking constraints in children's on-line reference resolution. *Psychological Science*, 13(4), 329–36.

Nilsen, E. S., & Graham, S. A. (2009). The relations between children's communicative perspective-taking and executive functioning. *Cognitive Psychology*, 58(2), 220–49.

Nilsen, E. S., Graham, S. A., Smith, S., & Chambers, C. G. (2008). Preschoolers' sensitivity to referential ambiguity: Evidence for a dissociation between implicit understanding and explicit behavior. *Developmental Science*, 11(4), 556–62.

Nilsen, E. S., Varghese, A., Xu, Z., & Fecica, A. (2015). Children with stronger executive functioning and fewer ADHD traits produce more effective referential statements. *Cognitive Development, 36*, 68–82.

Novick, J., Trueswell, J., & Thompson-Schill, S. (2005). Cognitive control and parsing: Reexamining the role of Broca's area in sentence comprehension. *Cognitive, Affective, & Behavioral Neuroscience, 5*(3), 263–81.

Onishi, K. H., & Baillargeon, R. (2005). Do 15-month-old infants understand false beliefs? *Science, 308*(5719), 255–8.

Perner, J., & Ruffman, T. (2005). Infants' insight into the mind: How deep? *Science, 308*(5719), 214–16.

Pickering, M. J., & Garrod, S. (2004). Toward a mechanistic psychology of dialogue. *Behavioral and Brain Sciences, 27*(2), 169–90.

Pickering, M. J., & Garrod, S. (2013). An integrated theory of language production and comprehension. *Behavioral and Brain Sciences, 36*(4), 329–47.

Potts, C. (2005). *The Logic of Conventional Implicatures*. Oxford University Press, Oxford.

Roberts, C. (2012). Information Structure: Towards an integrated formal theory of pragmatics. *Semantics and Pragmatics, 5*, 1–69.

Ross, L., Greene, D., & House, P. (1977). The "false consensus effect": An egocentric bias in social perception and attribution processes. *Journal of Experimental Social Psychology, 13*(3), 279–301.

Ross, M., & Sicoly, F. (1979). Egocentric biases in availability and attribution. *Journal of Personality and Social Psychology, 37*(3), 322–36.

Rubin, R., Brown-Schmidt, S., Duff, M., Tranel, D., & Cohen, N. (2011). How do I remember that I know you know that I know? *Psychological Science, 22*(12), 1574–82.

Rueschemeyer, S.-A., Gardner, T., & Stoner, C. (2015). The Social-N400 effect: How the presence of other affects language comprehension. *Psychonomic Bulletin & Review, 22*, 128–34.

Ryskin, R. A., Benjamin, A. S., Tullis, J., & Brown-Schmidt, S. (2015). Perspective-taking in comprehension, production, and memory: An individual differences approach. *Journal of Experimental Psychology: General, 144*(5), 898–915.

Ryskin, R. A., Brown-Schmidt, S., Canseco-Gonzalez, E., Yiu, E. K., & Nguyen, E. T. (2014). Visuospatial perspective-taking in conversation and the role of bilingual experience. *Journal of Memory and Language, 74*, 46–76.

Ryskin, R. A., Wang, R. F., & Brown-Schmidt, S. (2016). Listeners use speaker identity to access representations of spatial perspective during online language comprehension. *Cognition, 147*, 75–84.

Savitsky, K., Keysar, B., Epley, N., Carter, T., & Swanson, A. (2011). The closeness-communication bias: Increased egocentrism among friends versus strangers. *Journal of Experimental Social Psychology, 47*(1), 269–73.

Schegloff, E. A. (1968). Sequencing in conversational openings. *American Anthropologist, 70*(6), 1075–95.

Schober, M. F., & Clark, H. H. (1989). Understanding by addressees and overhearers. *Cognitive Psychology, 21*(2), 211–32.

Scott, R. M., He, Z., Baillargeon, R., & Cummins, D. (2012). False-belief understanding in 2.5-year-olds: Evidence from two novel verbal spontaneous-response tasks. *Developmental Science, 15*(2), 181–93.

Sedivy, J. C., Tanenhaus, M. K., Chambers, C. G., & Carlson, G. N. (1999). Achieving incremental semantic interpretation through contextual representation. *Cognition*, 71(2), 109–47.

Slamecka, N. J., & Graf, P. (1978). The generation effect: Delineation of a phenomenon. *Journal of Experimental Psychology: Human Learning and Memory*, 4(6), 592.

Smith, S. M., Glenberg, A., & Bjork, R. A. (1978). Environmental context and human memory. *Memory & Cognition*, 6(4), 342–53.

Sperber, D., & Wilson, D. (1995). *Relevance: Communication and Cognition*, 2nd Edition (pp. 2–9). Blackwell Publishers, Oxford/Cambridge.

Spivey, M. J., Tanenhaus, M. K., Eberhard, K. M., & Sedivy, J. C. (2002). Eye movements and spoken language comprehension: Effects of visual context on syntactic ambiguity resolution. *Cognitive Psychology*, 45(4), 447–81.

Stafford, L., & Daly, J. A. (1984). Conversational memory. *Human Communication Research*, 10(3), 379–402.

Stalnaker, R. C. (1970). Pragmatics. *Synthese: An International Journal for Epistemology, Methodology and Philosophy of Science*, 22, 272.

Stalnaker, R. (1973). Presuppositions. *Journal of Philosophical Logic*, 2, 447.

Stalnaker, R. C. (1974). Pragmatic presuppositions. In: Munitz, M., & Under, P. (Eds.), *Semantics and Philosophy* (pp. 197–213), New York University Press, New York, NY. Reprinted in Davis (1991) and in Stalnaker (1999). Page references to the latter.

Surian, L., Caldi, S., & Sperber, D. (2007). Attribution of beliefs by 13-month-old infants. *Psychological Science*, 18(7), 580–6.

Swinney, D. A. (1979). Lexical access during sentence comprehension: (Re)consideration of context effects. *Journal of Verbal Learning and Verbal Behavior*, 18, 645.

Tanenhaus, M. K., Spivey-Knowlton, M. J., Eberhard, K. M., & Sedivy, J. E. (1995). Integration of visual and linguistic information in spoken language comprehension. *Science*, 268, 632–4.

Trueswell, J. C., & Tanenhaus, M. K. (1994). Toward a lexicalist framework for constraint-based syntactic ambiguity resolution. In: Clifton, C., Frazier, L., & Rayner, K. (Eds.), *Perspectives in Sentence Processing* (pp. 155–79). Lawrence Erlbaum Associates, Hillsdale, NJ.

Trueswell, J. C., Tanenhaus, M. K., & Kello, C. (1993). Verb-specific constraints in sentence processing: Separating effects of lexical preference from garden-paths. *Journal of Experimental Psychology: Learning, Memory, and Cognition*, 19(3), 528–53.

Tversky, A., & Kahneman, D. (1974). Judgment under uncertainty: Heuristics and biases. *Science*, 185(4157), 1124–31.

Tversky, A., & Kahneman, D. (1981). The framing of decisions and the psychology of choice. *Science*, 211(4481), 453–58.

van Ackeren, M., Casasanto, D., Hagoort, P., Bekkering, H., & Rueschemeyer, S.-A. (2012). Pragmatics in action: Indirect requests engage theory of mind areas and the cortical motor network. *Journal of Cognitive Neuroscience*, 24(11), 2237–47.

van Ackeren, Smaragdi A, Rueschemeyer S-A (2016). Neuronal interactions between mentalizing and action systems during indirect request processing. *Social, Cognitive and Affective Neuroscience*, 11 (9), 1402–10.

van Berkum, J. J., van den Brink, D., Tesink, C. M., Kos, M., & Hagoort, P. (2008). The neural integration of speaker and message. *Journal of Cognitive Neuroscience*, 20(4), 580–91.

Vanlangendonck, F., Willems, R. M., Menenti, L., & Hagoort P. (2016). An early influence of common ground during speech planning. *Language, Cognition and Neuroscience*, 31(6), 741–50.

von Fintel, K. (2004). Would you believe it? The king of France is back! Presuppositions and truth-value intuitions. In: Reimer, M., & Bezuidenhout, A. (Eds.), *Descriptions and Beyond* (pp. 315–41). Oxford University Press, Oxford.

Wardlow, L. (2013). Individual differences in speakers' perspective taking: The roles of executive control and working memory. *Psychonomic Bulletin & Review*, 20(4), 766–72.

Wardlow Lane, L., & Ferreira, V. S. (2008). Speaker-external versus speaker-internal forces on utterance form: Do cognitive demands override threats to referential success? *Journal of Experimental Psychology: Learning, Memory, and Cognition*, 34(6), 1466–81.

Wardlow Lane, L., Groisman, M., & Ferreira, V. (2006). Don't talk about pink elephants! *Psychological Science*, 17(4), 273–7.

Wardlow Lane, L., & Liersch, M. J. (2012). Can you keep a secret? Increasing speakers' motivation to keep information confidential yields poorer outcomes. *Language and Cognitive Processes*, 27(3), 462–73.

Wells, J. B., Christiansen, M. H., Race, D. S., Acheson, D. J., & MacDonald, M. C. (2009). Experience and sentence processing: Statistical learning and relative clause comprehension. *Cognitive Psychology*, 58(2), 250–71.

Wilkes-Gibbs, D., & Clark, H. H. (1992). Coordinating beliefs in conversation. *Journal of Memory and Language*, 31(2), 183–94.

Wilson, M. P., & Garnsey, S. M. (2009). Making simple sentences hard: Verb bias effects in simple direct object sentences. *Journal of Memory and Language*, 60(3), 368–92.

Wimmer, H., & Perner, J. (1983). Beliefs about beliefs: Representation and constraining function of wrong beliefs in young children's understanding of deception. *Cognition*, 13(1), 103–28.

Wu, S., & Keysar, B. (2007). The effect of information overlap on communication effectiveness. *Cognitive Science*, 31(1), 169–81.

Yoon, S. O., Benjamin, A. S., & Brown-Schmidt, S. (2016). The historical context in conversation: Lexical differentiation and memory for the discourse history. *Cognition*, 154, 102–17.

Yoon, S. O., & Brown-Schmidt, S. (2014). Adjusting conceptual pacts in three-party conversation. *Journal of Experimental Psychology: Learning, Memory, and Cognition*, 40, 919–37.

Yoon, S., Koh, S., & Brown-Schmidt, S. (2012). Influence of perspective and goals on reference production in conversation. *Psychonomic Bulletin & Review*, 19(4), 699–707.

CHAPTER 24

ALIGNMENT DURING INTERACTION

SIMON GARROD, ALESSIA TOSI, AND MARTIN J. PICKERING

24.1 INTRODUCTION

ACCORDING to Pickering and Garrod (2004), successful dialogue occurs when interlocutors align their representations of relevant aspects of the situation under discussion. For the previous edition of this handbook, we wrote a chapter entitled "Alignment in dialogue" (Garrod & Pickering, 2007), in which we considered various routes to alignment, some more automatic, and some more strategic. However, the central assumption of our interactive-alignment model is that alignment of situation models is primarily driven by automatic processes of alignment at other levels of representation, particularly those relating to language. In this chapter, we consider the extensive and largely new evidence for such processes of alignment and relate them to other processes relevant to communicative success.

According to interactive-alignment accounts, conversation is successful to the extent that participants come to understand the relevant aspects of what they are talking about in the same way as each other. More specifically, they construct mental representations or models of the situation under discussion, and successful conversation occurs when these models become aligned. Such alignment largely occurs as a result of the tendency for conversational partners to align at many different linguistic levels, which they do by repeating each other's choices of words, grammar, and so on (e.g., Brennan & Clark, 1996; Branigan et al., 2000; Garrod & Anderson, 1987). This is a form of imitation. Essentially, conversational partners prime each other to speak about things in the same way, and people who speak about things in the same way are more likely to think about them in the same way as well.

The process of alignment is captured by the horizontal arrows in Figure 24.1 (so-called "channels of alignment"), and assumes that the same representations are involved in production and comprehension (i.e., representational parity). The account assumes that alignment is a consequence of coactivation at multiple distinct levels. For example, at the beginning of a conversation, interlocutors *A* might have the word *chef* activated, and *B* have the word *cook* activated (perhaps because these are the terms that they habitually use), so they would

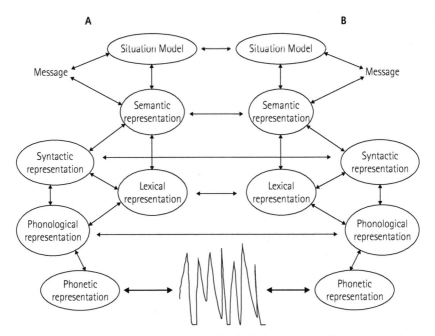

FIG. 24.1 The interactive-alignment account. The links between interlocutors A and B are the "channels of alignment" that lead to transfer of activation. The links within each interlocutor illustrate internal flow of information between level of representation.

Reproduced from Martin J. Pickering and Simon Garrod, Toward a mechanistic psychology of dialogue, *Behavioral and Brain Sciences*, 27 (2), pp. 169–90, doi.org/10.1017/S0140525X04000056, Copyright © 2004 Cambridge University Press.

not be coactivated. But after A uses *chef* in the conversation, B also activates *chef* and as a result this word is coactivated and the interlocutors become more aligned (at the lexical level). Similarly, A might use a syntactic construction such as a passive and this would lead to increased syntactic coactivation and hence syntactic alignment. This process of alignment takes place constantly during conversation, so that A's utterance will lead to both lexical, syntactic, and other forms of alignment, and such alignment persists. Importantly, alignment is defined with respect to mental representations, but the evidence for alignment comes from what interlocutors do, most obviously behavior matching.

For example, if A and B are looking at the New York skyline and A says *Look at the Chrysler Building*, A activates the five words and their phonology, and the syntactic representation for the utterance (including its internal structure). A also activates the meaning of the words, so that the noun phrase *the Chrysler Building* identifies a particular building. In understanding A's utterance, B also activates the same lexical, phonological, and syntactic representations as A whether B knows the building or not. This means that A and B become aligned at these levels of representation—such alignment happens so long as B hears A and knows the same language. Alignment of the situation models will also occur so long as B knows which building A is referring to. So if B thinks that A is referring to what is actually the Empire State Building, they would be misaligned at the level of the situation model. This illustrates how partial alignment can be understood within the interactive-alignment account.

In addition, alignment can also be manifested more broadly (in a way that is more analogous to associative priming than repetition priming). For example, the word *chef* is connected to (upmarket) restaurants and all of their features (e.g., waiters, menus, champagne). Importantly, this network of connections is likely to hold for both interlocutors. In other words, they are already fairly well-aligned with respect to relevant cultural background. These connections are of course highly structured, and might be represented as something like a restaurant "script" (in the sense of Schank & Abelson, 1977). So when interlocutor A utters *chef*, both interlocutors A and B activate *chef* (i.e., alignment via repetition) but also they both activate the network of words, concepts, and relationships associated with upmarket restaurants. This parallel activation across the interlocutors constitutes alignment, and we can say that the alignment *percolates* from *chef* to other aspects of the network. However, most research on alignment has not considered alignment in this broad sense.

This mechanism of alignment assumes that activation flows from the speaker to the addressee as a consequence of the speaker's behavior. In other words, the speaker's activation of *chef* leads to its utterance and hence the listener's activation of *chef* as well. This supports representational parity—the notion that the same representations are used during production and comprehension (Pickering & Garrod, 2004). One question therefore is what are the processes that underlie this transfer of activation. Some of these processes are likely to be linguistic: does activation of one type of linguistic representation (e.g., an aspect of semantics) affect activation of different representations (e.g., syntax)? However, some of it relates to non-linguistic factors that can affect degree of activation (such as attentional or social factors). A second question is whether alignment can come about via alternative routes that are not based on transfer of activation (e.g., via more deliberate or strategic routes).

We now review developments of the understanding of alignment in dialogue. We first briefly consider the evidence (from behavior matching) for alignment of sound, syntax, and meaning, and the extent to which alignment percolates between levels. We then consider the extent to which linguistic alignment leads to successful communication.

This research is primarily based on linguistic and cognitive considerations. Somewhat counterintuitively, we make some reference to studies that involve speaking and listening but not in interactive dialogue; we assume that such studies in effect model communication without feedback from the addressee. We then turn to studies of alignment that are informed by social considerations and which we interpret in terms of the transfer of activation. We also consider routes to alignment that are primarily strategic and where the coactivation is not the consequence of the transfer of activation.

24.2 Linguistic Mechanisms of Alignment

24.2.1 Alignment at different levels

Sound. Evidence for alignment at an articulatory level comes from analyzing the speech of interlocutors discussing routes in the map task (Anderson et al., 1991). Pardo (2006; Pardo et al., 2010) used an AXB matching task (Goldinger, 1998) to demonstrate phonetic convergence between map task players. Independent listeners assessed the perceived similarity of the interlocutors' pronunciation. Interlocutors progressively converged over the interaction, and remained more similar after the interaction. In addition, the degree of convergence was modulated by task role (as receiver or giver of instructions) and sex. Kim, Horton, and Bradlow (2011) also showed convergence between interlocutors who conversed to identify the differences between two depictions of the same scene. Phonetic convergence was observed between native speakers of the same dialect but not between native speakers of different dialects or native/non-native interlocutors. Note that at an acoustic-phonetic level convergence is always approximate: there is presumably never a perfect match of the partner's production (Krauss & Pardo, 2004; Pardo, 2006; Perkell et al., 2002). In addition, evidence suggests that convergence at articulatory and phonetic level is constrained by speakers' phonetic repertoire (Babel, 2009; see also Costa, Pickering, & Sorace, 2008).

Further evidence of sound-based alignment comes from non-interactive, non-social paradigms. Goldinger (1998) had a speaker repeat a word produced by a model. A listener judged the model word to be more similar to the repetition than to another token of the same word produced by the same speaker. He argued that speakers spontaneously imitated the model's speech, and the results also suggest that phonetic representations used in production and comprehension are closely related. The effects were weaker when there was a delay before the speaker repeated the model's word (see also Kappes et al., 2009). If these effects carry over to dialogue, they support sound-based alignment in dialogue, but that it is dependent on the time between utterances. Other studies have used similar repetition tasks or speeded shadowing and have found imitation on two acoustic dimensions, namely voice onset time (Mitterer & Ernestus, 2008; Nielsen, 2011; Sanchez et al., 2010; Shockley et al., 2004), and F0 (Babel & Bulatov, 2012; Bosshardt et al., 1997; Kappes et al., 2009), and there is also evidence for convergence across dialects of French (Delvaux & Soquet, 2007).

There is also evidence that imitative responses are facilitated over non-imitative responses. In other words, speakers produce a speech unit more quickly when they have just perceived the same speech unit than a different unit. This occurs whether the speakers hear the sound or see a silent video showing mouthing (Fowler et al., 2003; Galantucci et al., 2009; Jarick & Jones, 2008; Kerzel & Bekkering, 2000). Interestingly, there is also evidence that phonetic imitation occurs when model utterances are presented only visually (Gentilucci & Bernardis, 2007; Miller et al., 2010).

Syntax. Repetition of syntactic structure in dialogue has been studied (and reviewed) extensively. Very briefly, Levelt and Kelter (1982) found that Dutch shopkeepers tended to say *Om vijf uur* ("At five o'clock") in response to *Om hoe laat gaat uw winkel dicht?* ("At what time does your shop close?"), but *Vijf uur* ("Five o'clock") in response to *Hoe laat gaat uw winkel dicht?* ("What time does your shop close?"). Branigan, Pickering, and Cleland (2000) had a (naïve) participant and a confederate describe cards to each other and to select the appropriate card from an array. If the confederate described a card as *The chef giving the jug to the swimmer*, the participant tended to describe the next card as *The cowboy handing the banana to the burglar*; if the confederate said *The chef giving the swimmer the jug*, the participant tended to say *The cowboy handing the burglar the banana*. The tendency to repeat syntactic form occurred on about four trials out of six when the confederate and the participant used different verbs, and on about five trials out of six when they used the same verb. Similar effects occur for different constructions, languages, and populations from children to second language learners, and largely occur without awareness (Mahowald, James, Futrell, & Gibson, 2016; Pickering & Ferreira, 2008). These large, diverse, and tacit effects motivate our claim that automatic alignment is central to real-life dialogue. In fact, corpus studies suggest that naturalistic syntactic alignment is similar to alignment in laboratory experiments (Gries, 2005), with interlocutors showing tendency for short-term repetition of syntactic rules in both task-oriented and more undirected dialogue (Reitter & Moore, 2014). As syntactic alignment in dialogue is very similar to syntactic priming within a speaker in monologue (Bock, 1986), it is likely that the underlying mechanisms may well be similar too.

Many recent studies have investigated the specific linguistic representations that interlocutors align on (see Mahowald et al., 2016; Pickering & Ferreira, 2008 for references). As one example, Cai, Pickering, and Branigan (2012) found that interlocutors align on representations concerned with grammatical functions (e.g., direct object) as well as representations concerned with constituent structure. Strong alignment occurs between as well as within languages, but the within-language lexical boost is stronger than the boost that sometimes occurs between sentences with verbs that are translation equivalents of each other (Schoonbaert, Hartsuiker, & Pickering, 2007).

24.2.1.1 *Semantics*

Much of the earliest work relating to alignment focused on semantics. In fact, Garrod and Anderson's (1987) principle of output-input coordination was concerned with semantic— and lexical—alignment rather than syntax. In their study, pairs of participants negotiated their way around mazes and tended to use the same "description schemes" as each other and the same key terms with the same interpretations. For example, two partners aligned on a "line" scheme in which they described their positions using expressions such as "top line, fourth box along" (rather than a scheme using paths or coordinates) but initially one used "row" when the other used "line." However, they quickly started to align on using the key term "row" as well (pp. 214–15).

Semantic alignment does not only occur over the course of a whole conversation but also turn by turn, with the use of a certain word by one interlocutor triggering the other interlocutor to use the same word to refer to the same entity in the following utterances. In Branigan et al. (2011) participants took turns at naming pictures for each other. Some pictures had a highly preferred name (e.g., "*chair*" for the picture of a chair) but could also be correctly denoted with an alternative dispreferred name (e.g., "*seat*"). Participants were primed with the dispreferred names by their (real or apparent) dialogue partner; the researchers measured how many times participants converged on the dispreferred name when it was their turn to name the same picture, under the assumption that they would only do so because their partner had done so (and that they would have otherwise used the preferred alternative). Participants did converge on the unusual choice of name introduced by their partner. Moreover, the extent of this convergence was proportional to how poor they perceived their partner's communicative capacity; participants converged more with computers than human partners, and even more so with more obsolete computers.

Other studies support semantic alignment in terms of strengthened activation of linguistic representation, which is independent of the source of this activation. Thus, Foltz, Gaspers, Thiele, Stenneken, and Cimiano (2015b) presented speakers with linguistic input either from an addressee or via instructions over headphones. Speaker and addressee named pictures for each other. Sometimes, the speaker heard different names for the same picture from their addressee and subsequently via headphones (e.g., "*jug*"/"*pitcher*") before they named the picture themselves. Despite doing the task together with the addressee, speakers converged with the lexical choice of the most recent headphone input. Under these circumstance, where mutual understanding was not really at stake (i.e., addressees were able to identify the correct picture whatever label the speaker may have chosen), automatic mechanisms based on enhanced memory activation could overrule adaptation to the co-present addressee.

24.2.2 Integration between levels

So far, we have reviewed the extensive evidence for linguistic behavior matching, which demonstrates that linguistic alignment takes place *within* a level such as syntax or the lexicon. But such alignment does not itself demonstrate that linguistic alignment leads to common situation models and hence understanding. To do this, alignment must "percolate" between levels: alignment at one level must lead to alignment at another level.

As we have noted, Branigan et al. (2000) found a lexical boost to syntactic priming between interlocutors: an interlocutor's tendency to repeat her partner's choice of dative construction is greater if they use the same verb than otherwise. Verb repetition of course means that the interlocutors are lexically aligned, alignment at one level (words) enhances alignment at another level (syntax). Cleland and Pickering (2003) found a similar lexical boost for complex noun phrases (participants said *the sheep that's red* more often after hearing *the sheep that's red* than after *the knife that's red*). They also found a (smaller) semantic boost (participants said *the sheep that's red* more often after hearing *the goat that's red* than after *the knife that's red*), a finding that demonstrates percolation between semantic and syntactic alignment.

Cleland and Pickering (2003) interpreted syntactic priming, the lexical boost, and the semantic boost in terms of an account of lexical representation (Levelt, Roelofs, & Meyer, 1999; Pickering & Branigan, 1998), which they assumed applied to comprehension as well as production (following Branigan et al., 2000). Their account provides a mechanistic basis for interactive alignment. They assume three strata (levels of representation) for each lexical entry: a conceptual (semantic) stratum, a lemma (syntactic) stratum, and a word-form (phonological) stratum, and all information is represented as nodes within these strata. For example, the word *sheep* has a semantic representation (SHEEP) that is linked to its semantic properties (e.g., ANIMAL) and therefore, indirectly, to other semantic representations that share those properties (e.g., GOAT). It also has a syntactic representation (*sheep*) that is linked to its syntactic properties. These include being a noun (i.e., *noun*), but also include its "combinatorial properties" (roughly speaking, grammatical constructions): it can combine with an adjective (A, N; as in *the red sheep*) or a relative clause (N,RC; as in *the sheep that's red*). Finally, it has a word-form representation (<sheep>) that is linked to its phonemes (e.g., /p/) and thus indirectly to other word-form representations with overlapping phonemes (e.g., <ship>).

When an addressee hears an utterance, he activates all the relevant nodes. So, for *the sheep that's red*, he activates SHEEP, *sheep*, and <sheep>, along with *noun* and, importantly, N,RC. This activation of each of these nodes then reduces but does not entirely disappear. Language production also involves activating the same set of nodes (in accord with representational parity). Speakers are more likely to use nodes that have a higher level of activation. Therefore, they are more likely to produce a relative-clause construction after hearing another relative-clause construction than after an adjective-noun construction. This process is represented in the syntactic channel of alignment (Fig. 24.1).

The lexical boost occurs because *the sheep that's red* activates both the *sheep* node and the *N,RC* node. The account assumes strengthening of the link between the nodes based on coactivation (i.e., "Hebbian" learning). The tendency to utter *the knife that's red* after *the sheep that's red* (or vice versa, as in the actual experiment) occurs because of activation of the *N,RC* node alone. But the additional tendency to utter *the sheep that's red* after *the sheep that's red* occurs because of the activation of the *N,RC* node and activation of the link between the *N,RC* node and the *sheep* node. This lexical boost can occur from production to production (i.e., within a speaker) but when it occurs from comprehension to production in dialogue (i.e., between speakers), it demonstrates the percolation of alignment between levels. The semantic boost is explained as follows. After hearing *the sheep that's red*, the addressee activates SHEEP, *sheep*, and *N,RC* as before. But in addition, GOAT activates ANIMAL and GOAT, and GOAT in turn activates *goat*—to a lesser extent than *sheep* but more than *knife*. This means that *goat* and *N,RC* become coactivated (to some extent) and thus the addressee has a stronger tendency to utter *the goat that's red* than *the knife that's red*. These effects enhance the channel of syntactic alignment.

Note that Cleland and Pickering (2003) found no sign of a boost from phonological relatedness (*ship-sheep*). In terms of the model in Figure 24.1, this finding suggests that there is no activation from the word-form stratum to the lemma stratum. Overall, this discussion shows how a psycholinguistically motivated account of representation and processing can provide the mechanisms underlying alignment and in particular the way in which alignment can percolate between levels (and the ways in which it may not be able to). Again, more recent research has extensively investigated the situations in which syntactic alignment can be boosted by other forms of alignment, such as between-language priming involving translation-equivalent verbs (Cai et al., 2011; Schoonbaert et al., 2007).

Neuroscientific studies that compare producing and comprehending the same or related utterances provide evidence for shared patterns of activation and for integration across levels of representation. Menenti et al. (2011) reported an fMRI adaptation study that compared semantic, lexical, and syntactic processes in speaking and listening. They found that repetition of lexical content across heard or spoken sentences induced suppression effects in the same set of areas (left anterior and posterior middle temporal gyrus and left inferior frontal gyrus) in both speaking and listening, although the precuneus additionally showed an adaptation effect in speaking but not listening. Moreover, Segaert et al. (2012) found the same degree of adaptation between speaking and listening within an individual participant as occurred within speaking or listening, a finding that strongly supports shared mechanisms for production and comprehension.

Silbert et al. (2014) scanned participants while they repeatedly produced or comprehended a narrative (see also Stephens et al., 2010). They found that an extensive network of traditionally linguistic brain regions and brain regions relating to non-linguistic activities such as mentalizing was active during both comprehension and production, at the same point in the narrative. Their findings are compatible with shared representations at higher linguistic levels, though there was greater separation at levels concerned with sound. The fact that the regions associated with different linguistic and non-linguistic levels are coactivated supports our proposal that alignment involves the integration of representations across levels, and those levels include non-linguistic ones which may relate to the situation model. For an overview of how the similarity of brain states across individuals relates to shared understanding (alignment of situation models), see Schoot, Hagoort, and Segaert (2016).

24.2.3 Alignment and communicative success

If alignment is related to communicative success, it should be easier to process utterances that reflect aligned than non-aligned representations. In a computer-based confederate-scripting task (Branigan et al., 2000), Ferreira, Kleinman, Kraljic, & Siu (2012) found that participants more rapidly matched a sentence (e.g., *the doctor is handing the apple to the ballerina*) to a picture when they had previously described a different picture using the same verb (*the cowboy handing the shoe to the pirate*) than using a different verb (*the cowboy giving the shoe to the pirate*), and using the same syntactic structure (a PO) than using a different syntactic structure (a DO). Alignment therefore facilitates the process of communication.

But does it make it more successful? More direct evidence for how alignment relates to communicative success comes from a recent psychophysics experiment. Bahrami et al. (2010) had pairs of individuals make first an individual and then a joint judgment (following discussion) about which of two displays contained an oddball Gabor patch stimulus that had a higher luminance contrast than the five others in a circle. Pairs tended to make better joint than individual judgments (i.e., there was a collective benefit to performance). Fusaroli et al. (2012) then analyzed the extent to which each pair locally aligned (i.e., repeated) all lexical items, locally aligned on confidence expressions, and globally aligned (i.e., converged) on confidence expressions throughout the whole of their interaction. They aligned on all lexical items and on confidence expressions (e.g., *completely sure, quite sure, unsure*). Both local and global alignment on confidence expressions strongly enhanced collective benefit (correlations: $r_{(14)}$ = 0.51 and 0.67 respectively) but indiscriminate alignment actually interfered with performance. In other words, they showed that degree of relevant alignment corresponded with communicative success (see also Foltz et al., 2015a, and Nenkova, Gravano, Hirschberg, & Gravano, 2008, for comparable results). We propose that successful pairs routinized confidence expressions at a very fine-grained level, thus establishing their form and meaning in the extended lexicon, and that those expressions then fed into the situation model.

At lexical level, Ward and Litman (2007) found that the extent with which students converged with their physics computer tutor was positively associated with the students' learning outcomes. Participants instructing each other drawing routes on a map produced more accurate representations the stronger their level of lexical and syntactic convergence (Carbary & Tanenhaus, 2011; see also Reitter & Moore, 2007).

Alignment is also affected by communicative role. The strongest effects occur when the speaker has just been addressed, but it also occurs when the speaker previously acted as a side-participant (Branigan, Pickering, McLean, & Cleland, 2007). Much research has investigated the precise conditions under which such priming occurs, as a way of investigating the representations and processes used in language production, and most evidence suggests that priming between interlocutors is broadly similar to priming within a speaker in monologue (see Pickering & Ferreira, 2008).

Other studies have considered the relationship between linguistic alignment and factors relating to social and interactional goals. Social psychologists have long been interested in the role of interpersonal similarity in relationships (e.g., McCrae & Costa, 2008). Moreover, coordination of hand gestures, eye gaze, and posture enhances liking and understanding between people (Chartrand & van Baaren, 2009). Pennebacker and colleagues have shown that people's use of function words is related to aspects of their personality and also that interlocutors tend to align the way that they use these words—a phenomenon that they call *language style matching* or LSM (e.g., Ireland & Pennebaker, 2010). We therefore might expect function word alignment to be predictive of relationship success.

To test this, Ireland et al. (2011) measured LSM between speed daters. For each partner, they counted the percentage of prepositions, impersonal pronouns, and so on. They used a formula to determine how closely matched they were on each of these categories, and then averaged the results from all categories to provide an LSM score for a pair. Thus, well-matched pairs used similar proportions of prepositions, impersonal pronouns, and so on to each other, whereas poorly matched pairs did not. They found that both members of well-matched pairs were much more likely to indicate that they wished to meet again than did poorly matched pairs. In fact, they were more than three times as likely to want to meet again for every standard-deviation increase in LSM. Moreover, the association remained after controlling for mean perceived similarity. A second study showed that LSM between current partners predicted relationship stability three months later. In this case, the association remained after controlling for mean relationship satisfaction.

Assuming that mutual desire-to-meet and relationship stability are related to alignment of situation models, this study nicely suggests a fairly direct relationship between linguistic alignment and situation-model alignment. In fact, people are poor judges of function word alignment (Niederhoffer & Pennebaker, 2002), so the effects are not likely to be mediated by linguistic awareness[1]. The main limitation of the study is of course that the effects are correlational, and it is conceivable that a third factor leads to LSM and positive relationships (or even that the causality is reversed). However, the work provides evidence for a link between linguistic and situation-model alignment and a straightforward explanation is that the linguistic alignment leads to situation-model alignment.

In fact, a closer look at research about the relationship between alignment and cooperative behavior suggests either that the relationship is complex or that the reliance on correlational designs is problematic. Thus, LSM (roughly, function word matching) also predicts successful hostage negotiation (Taylor & Thomas, 2008) and task group cohesiveness (Gonzales, Hancock, & Pennebaker, 2010). But other reports suggest that LSM does not always relate to level of mutual engagement, as measured by mutual gaze, verbal acknowledgments, self-reports of involvement in the interaction, and so on (Babcock, Ta, & Ickes, 2014). Such effects were, however, found for another measure of linguistic alignment based on the similarity of all the language used by each member of a dyad (i.e., using latent semantic analysis; Landauer & Dumais, 1997). Moreover, Manson, Bryant, Gervais, and Kline (2013) had unacquainted dyads have an unstructured conversation for 10 minutes,

---

[1] Note that alignment of function words therefore appears to be a form of priming, but Bock (1986) found no evidence that prepositions affected syntactic priming (in monologue). This needs further research.

then take part in a prisoner's dilemma game as a measure of level of cooperation. LSM correlated with positive evaluations but not cooperative behavior in the game.

Sagi and Diermeier (2017) investigated the relationship between linguistic alignment and success in negotiation. Three participants attempted to negotiate agreements that led to simulated pay-outs. On some occasions two of the participants formed a coalition to the exclusion of the third. Early in the negotiation, participants in a coalition showed the same degree of linguistic alignment (as measured by latent semantic analysis (LSA)) as participants when at least one was not in a coalition. But over time, linguistic alignment increased considerably for participants in a coalition but not for the other participants. Linguistic alignment therefore appears related to communicative "closeness" (being part of an active negotiation) or communicative success. The results provide general evidence for the relationship between linguistic and non-linguistic alignment in an important context (bargaining). The pattern of results gives some weak evidence that success may in part drive linguistic alignment, but it does not give clear evidence about direction of causality.

Swaab, Maddux, and Sinaceur (2011) instructed negotiators (recruiters) to mimic their partner's language. In our terms, they intentionally aligned at various linguistic levels. Negotiators obtained better outcomes when they aligned early in the negotiation (the first 10 minutes) than when they did not align, but no effect occurred when they aligned late (the last 10 minutes). These results therefore indicate that linguistic alignment led to non-linguistic success. Moreover, the negotiators who aligned more (i.e., actually mimicked their partners to a greater extent) early in the negotiation were also more likely to be successful. These findings parallel other studies on behavior mimicry (e.g., van Baaren et al., 2004), and demonstrate a linguistic basis for the effects. They do not, of course, directly tap into mutual understanding, because the outcome measures relate to negotiation rather than understanding (i.e., alignment of situation models).

24.2.4 Social accounts of alignment

Social psychologists have looked at the matching of linguistic and sound-based properties (such as accent) between interlocutors. They primarily discuss such matching in terms of convergence over an extended period (rather than a single pair of utterances). Most evidence in support of social accounts of verbal convergence regards contextual social variables: characteristics of the conversational situation that are linked to how speakers perceive and manage interpersonal relationships (e.g., the interactional goal of the conversation or speakers' impression of each other). Much of the evidence rests on sound-based aspects of speech (e.g., accent, pitch) and, only more recently, syntactic choices. There is no direct evidence at the lexical level, at least in terms of coordination of word choices. Furthermore, most evidence comes from correlational studies making it difficult to determine the directionality of the social-convergence link.

Modulatory routes to alignment. Some of the evidence considered in social accounts suggests that linguistic (and behavioral) convergence is automatic but may be modulated by socioaffective dynamics (*modulatory route*). At a theoretical level, this literature has mostly addressed behavioral (e.g., unintentional motor movements) convergence but the accounts can be extended to linguistic behavior. A person's tendency to match another's behavior is assumed to be a natural consequence of the perceived behavior automatically triggering a matched behavioral response (Bargh & Chartrand, 1999; Dijksterhuis & Bargh, 2001). Social factors then modulate *the degree* of this automatic tendency by strengthening the perception–production link in either of two ways. According to some authors (e.g., Dijksterhuis & Bargh, 2001), the social modulation is goal-independent and mechanistic: when we like or perceive someone positively, we pay more attention to what we perceive of their behavior. The increased attention leads to stronger activation of perceptual representations (e.g., of the incoming speech) and therefore to stronger convergent response (since perceptual and production representations overlap). According to other authors (e.g., Lakin & Chartrand, 2003), the social modulation is goal-driven: when we perceive someone positively, we may wish to minimize social distance or express affiliation; these implicit social goals then reinforce the perception–production links and increase behavioral and linguistic convergence. We note that it may be hard to distinguish empirically between these two different interpretations of the modulatory route. But overall, linguistic convergence is an automatic process whose strength can be moderated by the social context.

That speakers converge more on their partner's verbal behavior when they perceive them positively (e.g., they form a good impression of them) and converge less (or diverge) when they perceive them negatively is supported at an acoustic-phonetic level (e.g., accentedness, vowel pronunciation, speaking rate, F0, intensity; see Pardo, 2013 for a full list of recent investigations). For instance, Welsh speakers who listened to the recording of an English speaker (with whom they never interacted) converged less with his accent if he expressed bias against their culture compared to when he expressed a neutral stance, probably as a way to express disaffiliation (Bourhis & Giles, 1977). Pardo, Gibbons, Suppes, and Krauss (2012) observed that college flatmates, originally unacquainted, showed small but consistent convergence to each other's pronunciation after one semester of cohabitation, an effect that was stronger the closer they felt. In a word shadowing task, the extent with which female speakers converged to the vowel pronunciation of a male talker was modulated by how attractive they found him (Babel, 2012); and in a priming experiment, participants converged to the unusually long voice-onset-times of a narrator toward whom they developed a positive disposition, a factor that reflected the combination of the intrinsic characteristics of the narrator (e.g., sexual orientation), the content of the narrative (e.g., whether the narrator behaved nicely or unpleasantly), and the attitude of the participants themselves, even if in the absence of expectation of interaction (Abrego-Collier, Grove, Sonderegger, & Yu, 2011).

Turning to the content of the speech, Moscoso Del Prado Martin and Du Bois (2015) found that the extent to which interlocutors' words expressed similar high levels of positive affect was correlated with their degree of syntactic convergence. Importantly, the effect was independent of convergence at a lexical level (i.e., it was not a consequence of speakers simply producing the same words). At a lexical level, Gonzales, Hancock, and Pennebaker (2010) observed that speakers who had a similar pattern of use of function words felt more cohesive as a group in a joint information search task: they liked each other more, interacted more effectively, and shared more information.

Taken together, these last studies suggest that degrees of spontaneous coordination in linguistic behavior can reflect underlying social dynamics. However, the evidence was correlational and hence not clear as to the directionality of the effect: did positive affect lead people to converge more as a response (as the modulatory routes would predict), or did people who happened to converge more (for any other reasons, such as perhaps automatic priming mechanisms) end up developing positive rapport? More recent experimental studies manipulated the extent to which a speaker may develop positive affect for another speaker, and measured whether the resulting interpersonal bond predicted their degree of linguistic convergence in a subsequent task. However, these studies produced some puzzling results. Weatherholtz et al. (2014) had participants listen to the recordings of an ideologically charged narrator who produced only one of two alternative syntactic structures (preferred vs. dispreferred, between-subjects). Interpersonal similarity was measured on the basis of political ideological agreement. Participants who heard the narrator using dispreferred syntactic structures converged less on her syntactic choices the more similar they felt to her, while there was no effect of degree of similarity on convergence on the preferred structures. In contrast, the smarter the participants judged the narrator, the less they converged on her use of preferred syntactic structures but there was no effect of perceived smartness on convergence on dispreferred structures. Furthermore, effects were overall very small. In a similar two-stage non-interactive paradigm, Lev-Ari (2015) presented participants with the recording of a (fictitious) previous participant who was presented as either smart or not so smart. The recordings primed participants with one of two syntactic alternatives. Participants then performed a written scrambled sentence task, in which syntactic convergence was measured. The more participants reported liking the speaker, the more they converged on his syntactic choices. However, the effect was restricted to the not-so-smart speaker, arguably because participants were able to empathize with him.

Strategic routes to alignment. Other social accounts of convergence assume a *strategic proactive route* (e.g., the Communicative Accommodation Theory (CAT); Giles & Coupland, 1991), speakers use verbal convergence to meet social psychological goals and to manage social relations. Accordingly, speakers may copy key features of their interlocutors' verbal style (e.g., reusing their choice of words) as a way of pursuing affective goals; for instance, to win trust, create rapport, or foster affiliation as a result of appearing more similar to the interlocutor (Coupland, Coupland, Giles, & Henwood, 1988). Speakers exploit the fact that people prefer others whom they perceive more similar to themselves (e.g., Giles & Smith, 1979). The magnitude of convergence is then proportional to the desire for the other's social approval (Larsen, Martin, & Giles, 1977). Similarly, speakers may use linguistic convergence as a way to mark affiliation or signal identification with their interlocutor (especially at cultural/group-membership level) by sounding more similar to them (Giles & Powesland, 1975).

Evidence that verbal convergence may be used proactively in this way mostly relates to acoustic-phonetic features and focuses on how the interlocutors' perceived social status or dominance determines who is converging with whom and the magnitude of the convergence (Bourhis, Giles, & Lambert, 1975). Results suggest that it is usually the speaker with a perceived lower status who converges toward the speaking style of the higher-status or more dominant interlocutor. For instance, Gregory and Webster (1996) found that guests at a TV show tended to converge on the pitch of higher-status but not lower-status speakers, and bilinguals in industrial settings converged more to the first language of those who were their superiors but not their subordinate (Giles, Coupland, & Coupland, 1991). Interviewees, who are likely to want to be liked, were found to converge to the intensity of pronunciation of interviewers (Natale, 1975). Likewise, speakers may verbally diverge from their interlocutor to signal disaffiliation or mark disassociation. This was observed when speakers interacted with out-group members in ethnically salient contexts (Bourhis, Giles, Leyens, & Tajfel, 1979).

Evidence for proactive convergence of linguistic aspects of speech (i.e., grammar and lexicon) is scantier and less consistent. For example, Coyle and Kaschak (2012) found that male (but not female) speakers converged less with the unusual syntactic choices of a female confederate if the confederate was in her fertile period. This was taken as a sign that males unconsciously yet strategically diverged from their partner's linguistic style to show potential positive mate characteristics (i.e., non-conformity behavior). And a recent study that tried to determine the directionality of syntactic convergence effects by explicitly giving speakers the goal to enhance rapport with their interlocutor in an interview setting (Schoot, Hagoort, & Segaert, 2016) failed to find any effect of speakers' desire to be liked on their degree of syntactic convergence.

24.2.4.1 *The compensatory proactive link*

Finally, other evidence indicates that the link between convergence and socioaffective dynamics may not be as straightforward as the proactive and modulatory routes might suggest: stronger convergence may not consistently relate to positive dynamics and weaker convergence (or absence thereof) may not consistently relate to negative dynamics. There is space for a third route, which we might call the *compensatory strategic route*: speakers may use linguistic convergence as a tool to (re-) establish smooth interaction, particularly when addressing un-cooperative or unfriendly interlocutors. For instance, speakers converged to a greater extent with the lexical choices of an interlocutor that showed annoyance and impatience compared to friendliness and understanding, probably using convergence to ensure a trouble-free interaction with what was perceived as a difficult interlocutor (Balcetis & Dale, 2005).

Importantly, convergence by the strategic proactive or the goal mediated modulatory route need not be conscious or deliberate. For linguistic convergence, deliberation would mean that speakers consciously focus on their partner's linguistic production and adjust features of their own production to match it. Proponents of these strategic routes have argued that even if the goal might be conscious (e.g., being liked by others), the strategy used (e.g., linguistic convergence) can be fully unconscious (Giles et al., 1991); others have proposed that both social goals and their pursuits can operate non-consciously (e.g., Bargh, 1994; Custers & Aarts, 2010). A second point is that both modulatory and strategic social mechanisms concede that speakers may not only converge more when perceiving or wishing affiliation, but may equally converge less, or not at all, when perceiving or wishing disfavor. Specifically, the proactive-route literature recognizes that speakers may diverge from their interlocutors' linguistic style (i.e., maximize the differences) as a form of dissociative tactic: when they wish to dissociate or mark disaffiliation or intergroup vs. outer-group dynamics (Giles & Powesland, 1975).

24.3 CONCLUSION

This chapter updated and developed our previous handbook chapter on *Alignment in Communication* (Garrod & Pickering, 2007). It did so in relation to both psycholinguistic and social psychological approaches to alignment. We first considered work on linguistic alignment that has appeared after publishing the chapter and how such alignment relates to communicative success. We discussed subsequent evidence for alignment of speech sounds, syntax and semantics and how communicative success relates to long-term alignment (especially alignment of task relevant language). We then turned to social accounts both in terms of the social consequences of alignment and its use as a tool in social interaction. In doing so we discussed how social factors may modulate processes of linguistic alignment or be used strategically to bring about the alignment itself.

The chapter illustrates the range of research investigating interactive alignment from perspectives which emphasize either the representation and use of several types of linguistic information, or focusing on how it should be interpreted in terms of social behavior. It seems that there is still a need to bring these perspectives together more, and in particular to further explore the relationship between linguistic alignment and communicative success.

References

Abrego-Collier, C., Grove, J., Sonderegger, M., & Yu, A. C. L. (2011). Effects of speaker evaluation on phonetic convergence. In: *Proceedings of the International Congress of the Phonetic Sciences XVII* (pp. 192–5). International Congress of the Phonetic Sciences, Hong Kong.

Anderson, A., Bader, M., Bard, E., Boyle, E., Doherty, G. M., Garrod, S., . . . & Weinert, R. (1991). The HCRC Map Task Corpus. *Language and Speech, 34*, 351–66.

Babcock, M. J., Ta, V., & Ickes, W. (2014). Latent semantic similarity and language style matching in initial dyadic interactions. *Journal of Language in Social Psychology, 33*, 78–88.

Babel, M. (2009). *Phonetic and Social Selectivity in Speech Accommodation* [Doctoral dissertation]. University of California, Berkeley, CA.

Babel, M. (2012). Evidence for phonetic and social selectivity in spontaneous phonetic imitation. *Journal of Phonetics, 40*(1), 177–89.

Babel, M., & Bulatov, D. (2012). The role of fundamental frequency in phonetic accommodation. *Language and Speech, 55*, 231–48.

Bahrami, B., Olsen, K., Latham, P. E., Roepstorff, A., Rees, G., & Frith, C. D. (2010). Optimally interacting minds. *Science, 329*(5995), 1081–5.

Balcetis, E. E., & Dale, R. (2005). An exploration of social modulation of syntactic priming. In: *Proceedings of the 27th Annual Meeting of the Cognitive Science Society* (pp. 184–89). Lawrence Erlbaum, Mahwah, NJ.

Bargh, J. A. (1994). The four horsemen of automaticity: Awareness, intention, efficiency, and control in social cognition. In: Wyer, R. S., & Srull, T. K. (Eds.), *Handbook of Social Cognition*, Vol. 1 (pp. 1–40). Lawrence Erlbaum, Mahwah, NJ.

Bargh, J. A., & Chartrand, T. L. (1999). The unbearable automaticity of being. *American Psychologist, 54*(7), 462–79.

Bock, J. K. (1986). Syntactic persistence in language production. *Cognitive Psychology, 18*, 355–87.

Bosshardt, H.-G., Sappok, C., Knip-schild, M., and Hölscher, C. (1997). Spontaneous imitation of fundamental frequency and speech rate by nonstutterers and stutters. *Journal of Psycholinguistic Research, 26*, 425–48.

Bourhis, R. Y., & Giles, H. (1977). The language of intergroup distinctiveness. In: Giles, H. (Ed.), *Language, Ethnicity and Intergroup Relations* (pp. 119–35). Academic Press, London.

Bourhis, R. Y., Giles, H., & Lambert, W. E. (1975). Social consequences of accommodating one's style of speech: A cross-national investigation. *International Journal of the Sociology of Language*, 65, 5–71.

Bourhis, R. Y., Giles, H., Leyens, J. P., & Tajfel, H. (1979). Psycholinguistic distinctiveness: Language divergence in Belgium. In: Giles, H., & St-Clair, R. (Eds.), *Language and Social Psychology* (pp. 158–85). Blackwell, Oxford, UK.

Branigan, H. P., Pickering, M. J., & Cleland, A. A. (2000). Syntactic co-ordination in dialogue. *Cognition*, 75(2), 13–25.

Branigan, H. P., Pickering, M. J., McLean, J. F., & Cleland, A. A. (2007). Syntactic alignment and participant role in dialogue. *Cognition*, 104(2), 163–97.

Branigan, H. P., Pickering, M. J., Pearson, J., Mclean, J. F., & Brown, A. (2011). The role of beliefs in lexical alignment: Evidence from dialogs with humans and computers. *Cognition*, 121, 41–57.

Brennan, S. E., & Clark, H. H. (1996). Conceptual pacts and lexical choice in conversation. *Journal of Experimental Psychology: Learning, Memory, and Cognition*, 22(6), 1482–s93.

Cai, Z. G., Pickering, M. J., & Branigan, H. P. (2012). Mapping concepts to syntax: Evidence from structural priming in Mandarin Chinese. *Journal of Memory and Language*, 66, 833–49.

Cai, Z. G., Pickering, M. J., Yan, H., & Branigan, H. P. (2011). Lexical and syntactic representations between closely related languages: Evidence from Cantonese-Mandarin bilinguals. *Journal of Memory and Language*, 65, 431–45.

Carbary, K., & Tanenhaus, M. (2011). Conceptual pacts, syntactic priming, and referential form. In: van Deemter, K., Gatt, A., van Gompel, R., & Krahmer, E. (Eds.), *Proceedings of the CogSci Workshop on the Production of Referring Expressions: Bridging the Gap Between Computational, Empirical and Theoretical Approaches to Reference (PRE-CogSci 2011)*. Cognitive Science Society, Boston, MA.

Chartrand, T. L., & van Baaren, R. B. (2009). Human mimicry. *Advances in Experimental Social Psychology*, 41, 221–2.

Cleland, A. A., & Pickering, M. J. (2003). The use of lexical and syntactic information in language production: Evidence from the priming of noun phrase structure. *Journal of Memory and Language*, 49, 214–30.

Costa, A., Pickering, M. J., & Sorace, A. (2008). Alignment in second language dialogue. *Language and Cognitive Processes*, 23, 528–56.

Coupland, J., Coupland, N., Giles, H., & Henwood, K. (1988). Accommodating the elderly: Invoking and extending a theory. *Language in Society*, 17, 1–41.

Coyle, J. M., & Kaschak, M. P. (2012). Female fertility affects men's linguistic choices. *PLoS One*, 7(2), e27971.

Custers, R., & Aarts, H. (2010). The unconscious will: How the pursuit of goals operates outside of conscious awareness. *Science (New York, N.Y.)*, 329(5987), 47–50.

Delvaux, V., & Soquet, A. (2007). The influence of ambient speech on adult speech productions through unintentional imitation. *Phonetica*, 64, 145–73.

Dijksterhuis, A., & Bargh, J. A. (2001). The perception-behavior expressway: Automatic effects of social perception on social behavior. *Advances in Experimental Social Psychology*, 33, 1–40.

Ferreira, V. S., Kleinman, D., Kraljic, T., & Siu, Y. (2012). Do priming effects in dialogue reflect partner- or task-based expectations? *Psychonomic Bulletin & Review*, 19(2), 309–16.

Foltz, A., Gaspers, J., Meyer, C., Thiele, K., Cimiano, P., & Stenneken, P. (2015a). Temporal effects of alignment in text-based, task-oriented discourse. *Discourse Processes*, 52(8), 609–41.

Foltz, A., Gaspers, J., Thiele, K., Stenneken, P., & Cimiano, P. (2015b). Lexical alignment in triadic communication. *Frontiers in Psychology, 6*, 127.

Fowler, C. A., Brown, J. M., Sabadini, L., Weihing, J. (2003). Rapid access to speech gestures in perception: evidence from choice and simple response time tasks. *Journal of Memory and Language, 49*, 396–413.

Fusaroli, R., Bahrami, B., Olsen, K., Roepstorff, A., Rees, G., Frith, C., & Tylén, K. (2012). Coming to terms quantifying the benefits of linguistic coordination. *Psychological Science, 23*(8), 931–9.

Galantucci, B., Fowler, C. A., & Goldstein, L. (2009). Perceptuomotor compatibility effects in speech. *Attention, Perception, & Psychophysics, 71*, 1138–49.

Garrod, S., & Anderson, A. (1987). Saying what you mean in dialogue: A study in conceptual and semantic co-ordination. *Cognition, 27*(2), 181–218.

Garrod, S., & Pickering, M. J. (2007). Alignment in dialogue. In: Gaskell, M. G. (Ed.), *The Oxford Handbook of Psycholinguistics* (pp. 443–51). Oxford University Press, Oxford.

Gentilucci, M., & Bernardis, P. (2007). Imitation during phoneme production. *Neuropsychologia, 45*, 608–15.

Giles, H., & Coupland, N. (1991). *Accommodating Language: Language: Contexts and Consequences*. Open University Press, Great Britain.

Giles, H., Coupland, N., & Coupland, J. (1991). Accomodation theory: Communication, context, and consequence. *Contexts of Accomodation: Developments in Applied Sociolinguistics*. Cambridge University Press, Cambridge.

Giles, H., & Powesland, P. F. (1975). *Speech Style and Social Evaluation*. Published in cooperation with the European Association of Experimental Social Psychology by Academic Press. London/New York.

Giles, H., & Smith, P. M. (1979). Accommodation theory: Optimal levels of convergence. In: Giles, H., & St. Clair, R. (Eds.), *Language and Social Psychology* (pp. 45–65). Basil Blackwell, Oxford.

Goldinger, S. D. (1998). Echoes of echoes? An episodic theory of lexical access. *Psychological Review, 105*, 251–79.

Gonzales, A. L., Hancock, J. T., & Pennebaker, J. W. (2010). Language style matching as a predictor of social dynamics in small groups. *Communication Research, 37*(1), 3–19.

Gregory, S. W., & Webster, S. (1996). A nonverbal signal in voices of interview partners effectively predicts communication accommodation and social status perceptions. *Journal of Personality and Social Psychology, 70*(6), 1231–40.

Gries, S. Th. (2005). Syntactic priming: A corpus-based approach. *Journal of Psycholinguistic Research, 34*, 365–99.

Ireland, M. E., & Pennebaker, J. W. (2010). Language style matching in writing: Synchrony in essays, correspondence, and poetry. *Journal of Personality and Social Psychology, 99*, 549–71.

Ireland, M. E., Slatcher, R. B., Eastwick, P. W., Scissors, L. E., Finkel, E. J., & Pennebaker, J. W. (2011). Language Style Matching predicts relationship initiation and stability. *Psychological Science, 22*(1), 39–44.

Jarick, M., & Jones, J. A. (2008). Observation of static gestures influences speech production. *Experimental Brain Research, 189*, 221–8.

Kappes, J., Baumgaertner, A., Peschke, C., & Ziegler, W. (2009). Unintended imitation in nonword repetition. *Brain and Language, 111*(3), 140–52.

Kerzel, D., & Bekkering, H. (2000). Motor activation from visible speech: evidence from stimulus response compatibility. *Journal of Experimental Psychology: Human Perception and Performance*, 26, 634–47.

Kim, M., Horton, W. S., & Bradlow, A. R. (2011). Phonetic convergence in spontaneous conversations as a function of interlocutor language distance. *Laboratory Phonology*, 2, 125–56.

Krauss, R. M., & Pardo, J. S. (2004). Is alignment always the result of priming? *Behavioral Brain Sciences*, 27, 203–4.

Lakin, J. L., & Chartrand, T. L. (2003). Using non-conscious behavioral mimicry to create affiliation and rapport. *Psychological Science*, 14, 334–9.

Landauer, T. K., & Dumais, S. T. (1997). A solution to Plato's problem: The Latent Semantic Analysis theory of the acquisition, induction, and representation of knowledge. *Psychological Review*, 104, 211–40.

Larsen, K., Martin, H. J., & Giles, H. (1977). Anticipated social cost and interpersonal accommodation. *Human Communication Research*, 3, 303–8.

Lev-Ari, S. (2015). Selective grammatical convergence: Learning from desirable speakers. *Discourse Processes*, 53(8), 657–74.

Levelt, W. J. M., & Kelter, S. (1982). Surface form and memory in question answering. *Cognitive Psychology*, 14(1), 78–106.

Levelt, W. J., Roelofs, A., & Meyer, A. S. (1999). A theory of lexical access in speech production. *Behavioral and Brain Sciences*, 22, 1–38.

Mahowald, K., James, A., Futrell, R., & Gibson, E. (2016). A meta-analysis of syntactic priming in language production. *Journal of Memory and Language*, 91, 5–27.

Manson, J. H., Bryant, G. A., Gervais, M. M., & Kline, M. A. (2013). Convergence of speech rate in conversation predicts cooperation. *Evolution and Human Behavior*, 34(6), 416–26.

McCrae, R. R., & Costa, Jr., P. T. (2008). The Five-Factor theory of personality. In: John, O. P., Robins, R. W., & Pervin, L. A. (Eds.), *Handbook of Personality: Theory and Research*, 3rd Edition (pp. 159–81). Guilford Press, New York, NY.

Menenti, L., Gierhan, S. M. E., Segaert, K., & Hagoort, P. (2011). Shared language: Overlap and segregation of the neuronal infrastructure for speaking and listening revealed by functional MRI. *Psychological Science*, 22, 1173–82.

Miller, R. M., Sanchez, K., & Rosen-blum, L. D. (2010). Alignment to visual speech information. *Attention, Perception, & Psychophysics*, 72, 1614–25.

Mitterer, H., & Ernestus, M. (2008). The link between perception and production is phonological and abstract: Evidence from the shadowing task. *Cognition*, 109, 168–73.

Moscoso Del Prado Martin, F., & Du Bois, J. W. (2015). Syntactic alignment is an index of affective alignment: An information-theoretical study of natural dialogue. In: Noelle, D. C., Dale, R., Warlaumont, A. S., Yoshimi, J., Matlock, T., Jennings, C. D., & Maglio, P. P. (Eds.), *Proceedings of the 37th Annual Meeting of the Cognitive Science Society*. Cognitive Science Society, Austin, TX.

Natale, M. (1975). Convergence of mean vocal intensity in dyadic communication as a function of social desirability. *Journal of Personality and Social Psychology*, 32(5), 790–804.

Nenkova, A., Gravano, A., Hirschberg, J., & Gravano, A. (2008). High frequency word entertainment in spoken dialogue. In: *46th Annual Meeting of The Association for Computational Linguistics* (pp. 169–72). Available at: http://repository.upenn.edu/cis_papers

Niederhoffer, K. G., & Pennebaker, J. W. (2002). Linguistic style matching in social interaction. *Journal of Language and Social Psychology*, 21(4), 337–60.

Nielsen, K. (2011). Specificity and abstractness of VOT imitation. *Journal of Phonetics, 39*(2), 132–42.

Pardo, J. S. (2006). On phonetic convergence during conversational interaction. *The Journal of the Acoustical Society of America, 119*(4), 2382–93.

Pardo, J. S. (2013). Measuring phonetic convergence in speech production. *Frontiers in Psychology, 4*, 559.

Pardo, J. S., Cajori Jay, I., & Krauss, R. M. (2010). Conversational role influences speech imitation. *Attention, Perception, & Psychophysics, 72*, 2254–64.

Pardo, J. S., Gibbons, R., Suppes, A., & Krauss, R. M. (2012). Phonetic convergence in college roommates. *Journal of Phonetics, 40*(1), 190–7.

Perkell, J. S., Zandipour, M., Matthies, M. L., & Lane, H. (2002). Economy of effort in different speaking conditions. A preliminary study of intersubject differences and modeling issues. *The Journal of the Acoustical Society of America, 112*, 1627–41.

Pickering, M. J., & Branigan, H. P. (1998). The representation of verbs: Evidence from syntactic priming in language production. *Journal of Memory and Language, 39*, 633–51.

Pickering, M. J., & Ferreira, V. S. (2008). Structural priming: A critical review. *Psychological Bulletin, 134*, 427–59.

Pickering, M. J., & Garrod, S. (2004). Toward a mechanistic psychology of dialogue. *The Behavioral and Brain Sciences, 27*, 169–90; discussion 190–226.

Reitter, D., & Moore, J. D. (2007). Predicting success in dialogue. In: *Proceedings of 45th Annual Meeting of the Association for Computational Linguistics* (pp. 808–15). Association for Computational Linguistics, Prague.

Reitter, D., & Moore, J. D. (2014). Alignment and task success in spoken dialogue. *Journal of Memory and Language, 76*, 29–46.

Sagi, E., & Diermeier, D. (2017). Language use and coalition formation in multiparty negotiations. *Cognitive Science, 41*, 259–71.

Sanchez, K., Miller, R. M., & Rosenblum, L. D. (2010). Visual influences on alignment to Voice Onset Time. *Journal of Speech, Language and Hearing Research, 53*, 262–72.

Schank, R. C., & Abelson, R. (1977). *Scripts, Plans, Goals, and Understanding*. Lawrence Earlbaum Associates, Hillsdale, NJ.

Schoonbaert, S., Hartsuiker, R. J., & Pickering, M. J. (2007). The representation of lexical and syntactic information in bilinguals: Evidence from syntactic priming. *Journal of Memory and Language, 56*, 153–71.

Shockley, K., Sabadini, L., & Fowler, C. A. (2004). Imitation in shadowing words. *Attention, Perception, & Psychophysics, 66*, 422–9.

Schoot, L., Hagoort, P., & Segaert, K. (2016). What can we learn from a two-brain approach to verbal interaction? *Neuroscience and Biobehavioral Reviews, 68*, 454–9.

Segaert, K., Menenti, L., Weber, K., Petersson, K. M., & Hagoort, P. (2012). Shared syntax in language production and language comprehension—An fMRI study. *Cerebral Cortex, 22*, 1662–70.

Silbert, L. J., Honey, C. J., Simony, E., Poeppel, D., & Hasson, U. (2014). Coupled neural systems underlie the production and comprehension of naturalistic narrative speech. *Proceedings of the National Academy of Sciences, 111*, E4687–96.

Stephens, G. J., Silbert, L. J., & Hasson, U. (2010). Speaker–listener neural coupling underlies successful communication. *Proceedings of the National Academy of Sciences, 107*(32), 14425–30.

Swaab, R., Maddux, W. W., & Sinaceur, M. (2011). Early words that work: When and how virtual linguistic mimicry facilitates negotiation outcomes. *Journal of Experimental Social Psychology*, 47, 616–21.

Taylor, P. J., & Thomas, S. (2008). Linguistic style matching and negotiation outcome. *Negotiation and Conflict Management Research*, 1(3), 263–81.

van Baaren, R. B., Holland, R. W., Kawakami, K., & Van Knippenberg, A. (2004). Mimicry and prosocial behavior. *Psychological Science*, 15, 71–4.

Ward, A., & Litman, D. (2007). Dialog convergence and learning. In: Luckin, R., Koedinger, K. R., & Greer, J. (Eds.), *Proceedings of the 2007 Conference on Artificial Intelligence in Education: Building Technology Rich Learning Contexts That Work* (pp. 262–9). IOS Press, Amsterdam.

Weatherholtz, K., Campbell-Kibler, K., & Jaeger, T. F. (2014). Socially-mediated syntactic alignment. *Language Variation and Change*, 26(03), 387–420.

CHAPTER 25

ROLE OF GESTURE IN LANGUAGE PROCESSING
Toward a unified account for production and comprehension

ASLI ÖZYÜREK

25.1 INTRODUCTION

Use of language in the face-to-face context involves production and perception of speech using many visual articulators, such as the lips, face, or hand gestures. These visual articulators convey relevant information to what is expressed in speech and at different levels. For example, while lips convey information at the phonological level, hand gestures (and face and head movements to some extent) contribute to semantic, pragmatic, and even syntactic information (e.g., Bavelas et al., 2000; Floyd, 2016; Kendon, 2004; Kita et al.,2007; Krahmer & Swerts, 2007; McNeill, 1992). Gestures can have different forms and functions in communication such as to pick out (e.g., points) or depict concrete or absent referents, action, and motion (e.g., iconic gestures), highlight meaning in the speech channel (e.g., beats), or to coordinate communicative interactions during dialogue such as signaling turn-taking, agreements, and so on (e.g., interactive, pragmatic gestures). Although gestures reveal the information in a different representational format than speech due to radical differences in the visual and auditory modalities, the two are systematically related to each other and convey the speaker's meaning together as a "composite signal" (Clark, 1996; Enfield, 2009). This chapter focuses on the role of hand gestures, and more specifically of iconic gestures, and to some extent of pointing gestures, in the processing of language during production and comprehension based on spontaneous and elicited productions as well as experimental and neural data. The accumulated findings in this domain show that gestures interact with language, both during production and comprehension, and that any model of language processing that tries to account for contextual uses of language needs to consider the role of gesture. Similarities in interactions between speech and gesture during both production and comprehension should be considered in extending the psycholinguistic models of language.

25.2 THE ROLE OF GESTURE IN LANGUAGE PRODUCTION

In considering the role of gesture in language production, it is essential to consider the semantic and temporal relatedness between speech and gesture during spontaneous productions. First, in most cases there is semantic overlap between the representation in gesture and the meaning expressed in concurrent speech. However, gesture usually also encodes additional information that is not expressed in speech due to the affordances of the modality. Consider the example of someone giving directions. He might say in his speech "you walk across the street" accompanied by an iconic hand gesture consisting of the hand moving from left to right while the fingers wiggle repetitively. In this example, a single gesture exhibits simultaneously the manner, the change of location, and the direction of the movement to the right. Speech expresses the manner and the path (walk and across) of the movement, but not the change in direction (left to right). Thus, there is informational overlap between speech and gesture, but also additional/non-overlapping information in the gesture (Holler & Beattie, 2003; Kita & Özyürek, 2003; Özyürek et al., 2005). Secondly, there is systematic temporal relationship between speech and gesture. A gesture phrase has three phases: preparation, stroke (semantically the most meaningful part of the gesture), and retraction or hold. All three phases together constitute a gesture phrase. McNeill (1992) has also shown that in 90% of speech-gesture pairs, the stroke coincides with the relevant speech segment, which might be a single lexical item or a phrase. For example, the stroke phase of the gesture in the aforementioned example is very likely to occur during the phrase "walk across" or "walk across the street" (see examples of spontaneous gestures in Fig. 25.1 from different languages).

25.2.1 Different models of speech and gesture production

Even though speech and gesture seem to be tightly coordinated to achieve semantic and temporal congruity for communicative effectiveness, there is controversy in the literature regarding gesture's underlying origin of representational format, especially of iconic gestures and their interactions with speech during the language production process (see de Ruiter, 2007; Wagner et al., 2014, for a review of different models). Iconic gestures depicting visual, imagistic aspects of actions and referents convey perceptual, motoric, and analogic mappings between gestures and the conceptual content they evoke. While some view and explain the production of such gestures as being generated and executed independent of the spoken linguistic utterances they accompany, others see their processing as intrinsically interwoven with production of spoken language. Another controversy exists regarding the communicative nature of gesture production; that is, whether gestures are produced for the speakers themselves or are designed for the informational needs of the addressees (i.e., with communicative intent or not). These two issues have been crucial for designing different models of gesture production and its relation to processing of spoken language production. These models will be briefly reviewed next.

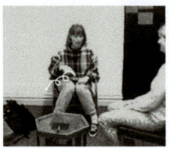

(A) English: *he [rolls down the street]*

 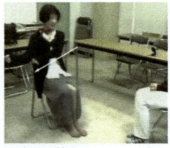

(B) Japanese: *koo [nanka kaiten-shi-nagara booru-mitai-ni] [korogari-ochi-te-t-te]*
Trans: Like somehow as he rotates like ball, (he/she) descends rolling

(C) Turkish: *[yuvarlana yuvarlana]   [gidiyor]*
Trans: rolling, rolling   (he) goes

FIG. 25.1 Differences between English, Japanese, and Turkish speakers' gestures depicting simultaneous manner and path of a motion event paralleling differences in syntactic encoding (brackets indicate where the stroke of the gestures overlap with the speech segment).

According to some views (Krauss et al., 1995; Wesp et al., 2001) speech and iconic gestures originate and are processed independently and are executed in a parallel fashion (i.e., to explain their overt coordination at the behavior level). According to these views iconic gestures are generated and processed directly and solely from the spatial, motoric action representations, whereas speech is generated from abstract propositional representations. This model also assumes that gestures are not communicatively intended, and thus not a necessary part of the speaker's intended message expressed in the spoken utterance. Gestures are generated from spatial representations, "prelinguistically," and independent from how certain information is linguistically formulated. The function of gestures is to keep memories of such representations active and/or facilitate lexical retrieval through cross-modal priming (i.e., from gesture to speech).

Also according to another framework, Gesture as Simulated Action (GSA) (Beilock & Goldin-Meadow, 2010; Cook & Tannenhous, 2009; Hostetter & Alibali, 2008), and a recent Action Generation Hypothesis (Chu & Kita, 2016) gestures *can* arise directly out of simulations of actions (action representations) without requiring explicit interactions between speech and gesture[1]. As such, gestures can be seen as a direct window into "simulated" cognition of speakers. For example, in Cook and Tannenhous (2009), participants were asked to solve a tower of Hanoi problem either by moving real objects with their hands or by moving objects on a computer screen with a mouse. They then described their solutions to a listener who would be solving the same problems later. Participants who solved the problem with real objects produced more gestures with grasping hand shapes and more gestures with higher and more curved trajectories than those who solved the computerized version of the problem. In a recent study, Chu and Kita (2016) have asked participants to imagine mentally rotating "smooth" faced or "spiky" mugs, and to think aloud as they did so in a non-communicative setting. They have found participants to gesture less in the "spiky" mug condition than in the "smooth" mug condition. According to authors these findings reflect speakers' action representations about how they would likely manually interact with the mugs. Finally, a recent study shows gestures being sensitive to "affordances" of objects mentioned in speech (Masson-Carro et al., 2016). Note that in these models no explicit interactions between speech and gesture are *necessary*, but possible (see footnote 1). Finally, the GSA model gestures—even though not inherently communicatively intended—can be suppressed if context does not require it. However, communicative intent does not shape the form or the choice of gesturing or not.

Other models (e.g., Interface Hypothesis, Kita & Özyürek, 2003) on the other hand propose more close interactions between imagistic/action representations that give rise to gestural representations and linguistic conceptualization during the generation and execution of coordinated speech and gesture units (e.g., clause). In this framework, these interactions are almost inevitable due to the notion that gestures function as a communicative device as does language, and that there is close semantic and temporal coordination between the two. As such, gestures are generated from the same communicative intention used during conceptualization of speech production (de Ruiter, 2007; Melinger & Levelt, 2004; Peeters et al., 2015, shown for pointing gesture) and go hand-in-hand taking addressee's knowledge state into account (i.e., common ground such as shared knowledge between interlocutors, visibility of the gestures, or the shared space among the interlocutors) (Alibali et al., 2001; Campisi & Özyürek, 2013; Schubotz et al., 2015; Özyürek, 2002). A recent study manipulating production of pointing gestures accompanying demonstrative speech (e.g., *this, that*) as a function of addressee's knowledge state has also identified possible neural correlates of

---

[1] Note that in the GSA model, gesture's link to speech is seen best as gesture production, helping conceptualization for speech. It does not propose explicit bidirectional communication between speech and gesture unlike what is assumed in other models such as Interface Hypothesis (see next). The GSA model also accepts the possibility that linguistic planning involves simulations of perceptual events, which in turn can influence production of gestures (Hostetter & Alibali, 2008; p. 508).

communicative intent in the brain during the planning of pointing gestures (Peeters et al., 2015). Finally, when one considers the larger discourse context, it is also shown that gesture production is influenced by the accessibility of the referent (i.e., old vs. new) in discourse (e.g., Debreslioska et al., 2013; Perniss & Özyürek, 2015; So et al., 2009), a finding that generalizes across different types of languages. Speakers are more likely to gesture with new or pragmatically marked referents in discourse context paralleling such discourse markers in speech, within and across languages (Azar et al., 2017).

In addition to postulating that gestures are as communicatively intended as speech, the Interface Hypothesis also proposes that speech and gesture processing interact during production. The evidence for this comes from studies showing that iconic gestures of the same event (i.e., similar imagery) differ according the language-specific semantic and grammatical encoding of spatial information in different languages. The independence models mentioned here would predict that the way certain elements of an event are encoded linguistically will *not* change the form of gestures, since gestures are generated from and are shaped *solely* by spatial, imagistic, motoric, action representations (i.e., which would be similar across speakers of different languages with different encoding possibilities). However according to interaction models (i.e., specifically the Interface Model; see Kita & Özyürek, 2003), the linguistic encoding of the event would change the shape of gestures, due to an interaction between linguistically formulating the message (i.e., specific semantic, linguistic, and discourse for requirements of each language) and the spatiomotoric imagery that underlies formation of gesture during the conceptualization phase of the online language production. That is, the spatiomotoric imagery would be influenced by the linguistic conceptualization that is specific for each language, giving rise to differences in gestures (mostly for iconic gestures) for the same event.

One domain where there are particular differences between spoken languages and their corresponding gestures is in the realm of expressions of motion events. Talmy (1985) has proposed a typology in the expression of motion event across the world's languages, based on how path of motion is expressed syntactically: in *satellite-framed languages* (S-languages, English, German, and so on), manner of motion is typically expressed in the verb, while path of motion appears in a particle outside the verb (e.g., "The boy ran down the stairs"). Whereas in *verb-framed languages* (V-languages; Turkish, Spanish, and so on), the main verb usually encodes the path of motion, while manner information is encoded with gerunds (e.g., Spanish), adverbs, or subordinate clauses (e.g., Turkish) outside the verb. In the next example, "*in*" (descend) is the main verb encoding path but manner, "*koş*" (run) is expressed in the subordinate clause. Because of these differences, speakers of V-framed languages express mostly path of motion but omit the manner in speech.

[1] Turkish:

çocuk koş-arak merdiven-den in-di
child run-CONN stairs-ABL descend-PAST
"The boy descended the stairs while running"

Researchers examining speakers' gesture production across a variety of languages show that the content and type of the iconic gestures covary with the aforementioned preferences made in different languages. For example in V-framed languages, adult and child speakers prefer to express only the path of motion both in their speech and gesture; for example, French (Gullberg et al., 2008), and Turkish (Özyürek et al., 2008, 2014). The congruency between speech and gesture patterns is also found in another study where Turkish and English speakers were asked to talk about 10 different motion events that involved different types of manner (jump, roll, spin, rotate) and path (descend, ascend, go around). In cases where only manner or only path was expressed in an utterance in either language, speakers of both languages were more likely to express congruent information in gesture to what is expressed with speech (e.g., he went down the slope: Gesture: index finger moving down expressing just the path information).

Also in line with the view that what can *not* be habitually expressed in speech is also omitted in gesture comes from a study (Kita & Özyürek, 2003) that compares how Japanese, Turkish, and English speakers speak and gesticulate about an event, and where languages differ in the lexical items available to encode a certain part of the event. In this case, speakers of all three languages were shown a Sylvester and Tweety cartoon. In one scene, Sylvester grabs a rope and tries to swing from one building to another to catch Tweety. It was found that English speakers all used the verb *swing across*, and encoded the arc shape of Sylvester's trajectory. On the other hand, Japanese and Turkish speakers used verbs such as *go across*, which does not encode the arc trajectory. In their conceptual planning phase of the utterance describing this event, Japanese and Turkish speakers presumably got feedback from speech formulation processes and created a mental representation of the event that does not include the trajectory shape. If gestures reflect this planning process, the gestural contents should differ cross-linguistically in a way analogous to the difference in speech. It was indeed found that Japanese and Turkish speakers were more likely to produce a straight gesture, which does not encode the trajectory shape, and most English speakers produced just gestures with an arc trajectory.

More evidence demonstrating that what is represented in iconic gestures seems to vary according to verb semantics of the specific language comes from a study comparing French and Dutch speakers' speech and gesture patterns. Placement events are encoded using the simple verb *mettre* "put" in French. In contrast, speakers of Dutch encode these events by using positional verbs such as *leggen* "lay" and *zetten* "set/stand," depending on the shape of the object that is placed. Paralleling these distinctions, adult French speakers have been found to use iconic gestures that encode only the path or direction of movement in their placement descriptions, whereas Dutch speakers' gestures represent the shape of the moved object (i.e., via the hand shape as if holding the object), as well as the direction of movement (Gullberg, 2011; Gullberg & Narasimhan, 2010). Note that these results speak against the idea that action representation system *alone* cannot be the origin of iconic gestures, as assumed by the GSA model of gesture production. Otherwise French speakers would also be expected to gesture, representing the shape of the objects as per Dutch speakers.

Finally, another way linguistic encoding can shape gestural representation has been found in expressions of events that include both manner and path. Here the influence is found not at the lexical level but more at the level of how information is *syntactically* packaged. As mentioned here, verbal descriptions differ cross-linguistically in terms of how manner and path information is lexicalized. English speakers used a manner verb and a path particle or preposition to express the two pieces information within one clause (e.g., he *rolled down* the hill). In contrast, Japanese and Turkish speakers separate manner and path expressions over two clauses; path as in the main clause and manner as in the subordinated clause (e.g., he descended as he rolled). Given the assumption that a clause approximates a unit of processing in speech production (Levelt, 1989) presumably English speakers were likely to process both manner and path within a single processing unit, whereas Japanese and Turkish speakers were likely to need two processing units. Consequently, Japanese and Turkish speakers should be more likely to separate the imagistic representations of manner and path in preparation for speaking so that two pieces of information could be dealt with in turn, unlike as in English speakers. The gesture data confirmed this prediction. In depicting how an animated figure rolled down a hill having swallowed a bowling ball in the cartoon, Japanese and Turkish speakers were more likely to use separate gestures, one for manner and one for path, and English speakers were more likely to use just one gesture to express both manner and path (see Fig. 25.1). Note that as reported in Kita and Özyürek (2003), these patterns are tendencies but not absolute parallels between gesture and speech and might be modulated with what is salient and prominent in the real event or discourse context.

Based on these findings one could argue, however, that gestural variation across speakers of different languages is not due to online interaction between linguistic and imagistic thinking, but rather either due to cultural patterns of gestures learned from others independent of linguist encoding or deep effects of language, which then determine gesture production directly. Two recent studies rule out these possibilities. First of all, Özçalışkan et al. (2016a) have replicated findings from Kita and Özyürek (2003) with blind speakers of English and Turkish –showing that differences in gesture patterns are not learned by seeing others but are influenced by the specific language used. Secondly in another study Özçalışkan et al. (2016b) asked speakers of Turkish and English first to talk about events containing simultaneous manner and path (e.g., an animated figure hopping into a house) and later to depict them with gesture, only without speaking. While in the speech condition gestures have differed as predicted by Kita and Özyürek, in the silent condition, both groups were similar and used conflated gestures. Different patterning of gestures in silent conditions than in accompanying speech context has also been found at the level of ordering of semantic elements such as agent, patient, and action within English (Goldin-Meadow, McNeill, & Singleton, 1996) and also across speakers of different languages that use different word orders (Goldin-Meadow, So, Özyürek, & Mylander, 2008). These experimental findings then argue against the claims that differences in co-speech gestures across different languages arise simply from culturally or prelinguistically shaped conceptualization of events, but rather they point to online influence of linguistic conceptualization on gesture processing.

25.3 Summary: Role of gesture in language production

Gestures that speakers use during multimodal utterances serve multiple functions (i.e., cognitive, communicative) and are shaped by multiple representations (imagery, action simulation, abstract propositional) during production. While much research has emphasized how action, motoric, and spatial representations shape gesture form and content directly and independent of the linguistic processing, there is considerable evidence showing that gesture is shaped also by the speaker's language system and by the communicative needs of the addressee (e.g., to emphasize new and pragmatically marked information, knowledge state, visibility, location of the addressee) and the discourse context. After all, gestures are communicative acts, produced with communicative functions (as language) and are produced to fit semantically and temporally to verbal utterances.

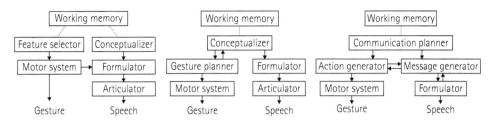

FIG. 25.2 Adapted schematic overview of different models in relation to speech and gesture production (Morrel-Samuels & Krauss, 1992; de Ruiter, 2000; Kita & Özyürek, 2003; from left to right).

Reprinted from *Speech Communication*, 57, Petra Wagner, Zofia Malisz, and Stefan Kopp, Gesture and speech in interaction: An overview, pp. 209–32, doi.org/10.1016/j.specom.2013.09.008, Copyright © 2013 Elsevier B.V., with permission from Elsevier.

Next are some sketches of different models proposed for speech and gesture production, as taken from Wagner, Malisz, and Kopp (2014)) schematizing their link to the language system and to the communicative intent in message formulation (Fig. 25.2).

25.4 THE ROLE OF GESTURE IN LANGUAGE COMPREHENSION

Even though the abovementioned production models of gesture have been split with regard to consideration of gestures as part of speakers' communicative intent and whether they are linked to the language production system, when it comes to comprehension a more unified view emerges. Growing research shows that gestures are interpreted as communicative. As part of a speaker's message, speech and gesture processing mutually influence each other, recruiting similar semantic processing areas in the brain. Furthermore, the perceived communicative intent of the gesture also influences its integration with speech, also at the neural level.

It has been a longstanding finding that addressees pick up semantic information from gestures that accompany speech. That is, gestures are not perceived by comprehenders simply as handwaving or as attracting attention to what is conveyed in speech. For example, Kelly et al. (1999) showed participants video stimuli where gestures conveyed additional information to that conveyed in speech (gesture pantomiming drinking while speech is "I stayed up all night") and asked them to write what they heard. In addition to the speech they heard, participants' written text contained information that was conveyed only in gesture but not in speech (i.e., "I stayed up drinking all night"). In another study, Beattie and Shovelton (1999) showed that listeners answer questions about the size and relative position of objects in a speaker's message more accurately when gestures were part of the description and conveyed additional information than speech.

Furthermore, findings show that gesture is not semantically perceived as an independent system of representation, but it also influences speech comprehension. In a priming study by Kelly et al. (2010) participants were presented with action primes (e.g., someone chopping vegetables) followed by bimodal speech and gesture targets. They were asked to press a button if what they heard in speech or gesture depicted the action prime. Participants related primes to targets more quickly and accurately when they contained congruent information (speech: "chop"; gesture: chop) than when they contained incongruent information (speech: "chop"; gesture: twist). Moreover, the strength of the incongruence between overlapping speech and gesture affected processing, with fewer errors for weak incongruities (speech: "chop"; gesture: cut) than for strong incongruities (speech: "chop": gesture "open"). This indicates that in comprehension, the relative semantic relations between the two channels are considered, providing evidence against independent processing of the two channels. Furthermore and crucially, this effect was bidirectional and was found to be similar when either speech or gesture targets matched or mismatched the action primes. That is, gesture influenced processing of speech and speech influenced processing of gesture. Further research has shown that gestures also show semantic priming effects. Yap et al. (2011) have shown that iconic gestures—shown without speech—(highly conventionalized ones such as flapping both hands on the side meaning bird) prime sequentially presented words.

The evidence for semantic integration between representational gestures and speech has also been corroborated in many neurocognitive studies. They have shown that comprehension of iconic gestures involves brain activations known to be involved in semantic processing of speech (i.e., modulation of the electrophysiological recording component, N400, which is sensitive to the ease of semantic integration of a word to previous context). For example, Wu and Coulson (2007) found that semantically incongruous gestures (shown without speech), when presented after cartoon images, elicited a negative-going event-related potential (ERP) effect around 450 ms, in comparison to gestures that were congruent with the cartoon image. Furthermore, unrelated words followed by gestures (shown without their accompanying speech) also elicited a more negative N400 than related words.

Holle and Gunter (2007) extended the use of the ERP paradigm to investigate the semantic processing of gestures in a speech context. They asked whether manual gestures presented earlier in the sentence could disambiguate the meaning of an otherwise ambiguous word presented later in the sentence and investigated the brain's neural responses to this disambiguation. An electroencephalograph (EEG) was recorded as participants watched videos of a person gesturing and speaking simultaneously. The experimental sentences contained an unbalanced homonym in the initial part of the sentence (e.g., *She controlled the ball* . . .) and were disambiguated at a target word in the subsequent clause (*which during the game* . . . versus *which during the dance* . . .). Coincident with the homonym, the speaker produced an iconic gesture that supported either the dominant or the subordinate meaning. ERPs were time-locked to the onset of the target word. The N400 to target words was found to be smaller after a congruent gesture and larger after an incongruent gesture, suggesting that listeners can use the semantic information from gesture to disambiguate upcoming speech.

In another ERP study, Özyürek et al. (2007) examined directly whether ERPs measured as a response to semantic processing evoked by iconic gestures are comparable to those evoked by words. This ERP study investigated the integration of co-speech gestures and spoken words to a previous sentence context. Participants heard sentences in which a critical word was accompanied by a gesture. Either the word or the gesture was semantically anomalous with respect to the previous sentence context. Both the semantically anomalous gestures and anomalous words to previous sentence context elicited identical N400 effects, in terms of the latency and the amplitude.

fMRI studies also show that perceiving gestures in a speech context involves the recruitment of the left-lateralized frontal-posterior temporal network (left inferior frontal gyrus

(IFG), medial temporal gyrus (MTG), and superior temporal gyrus/sulcus (STG/S)). These brain areas are known to be sensitive to semantic processing linguistic information (see Özyürek, 2014, for a broader overview). Using a functional magnetic resonance imaging (fMRI) method, Straube et al. (2012) isolated the brain's activation in response to iconic gestures to see whether it overlaps with areas involved in processing verbal semantics. fMRI measures brain activity by detecting associated changes in blood flow (i.e., blood-oxygen-level-dependent (BOLD) response), relying on the fact that blood flow and neural activation are coupled. In this study, they compared the brain's activation triggered by meaningful spoken sentences, with sentences from an unknown language, and they also compared activation for co-speech gestures presented without their accompanying speech, and meaningless gestures also without speech. Meaningful iconic gestures activated the left IFG, bilateral parietal cortex, and bilateral temporal areas. The overlap of activations for meaningful speech and meaningful gestures occurred in the left IFG and bilateral MTG. These findings are consistent with another study by Xu et al. (2009) showing that left IFG and posterior MTG are involved in the comprehension of communicative gestures (i.e., pantomimes such as opening a jar without speech) as well as speech glosses of the same gestures (i.e., open jar) presented separately.

Further fMRI studies have attempted to locate the brain areas involved in *integrating* information from speech and gesture. Perceiving iconic gestures mismatching or complementing information or sensitivity to bimodal matching information comparing to speech or gesture alone recruits left IFG, bilateral posterior superior temporal sulcus (STSp), and middle temporal gyrus (MTGp). Interestingly, these are the areas that are also involved when increased semantic processing is required during speech comprehension (see Dick et al., 2012). Dick et al. (2012) for example found left IFG to be sensitive to meaning modulation by iconic gestures; that is, more activation in this area for complementary (speech: "I worked all night"; gesture: type) than redundant gestures accompanying speech (speech: "I typed all night"; gesture: type). Complementary gestures add information and require more semantic processing than redundant gestures. Finally, Skipper et al. (2009, 2015) found that when hand movements (iconic gestures) were related to the accompanying speech, left IFG (pars triangularis and pars opercularis) exhibited a weaker influence on other motor- and language-relevant cortical areas compared with when the hand movements were meaningless (i.e., grooming gestures or "self-adaptors") or when there were no accompanying hand movements. In a recent paper Skipper (2014) has also proposed a model (i.e., NOLB model) according to which gestures can be seen as a predictive context (through their activations of semantic and motor cortices) for speech comprehension, especially for auditory cortex.

If listeners/perceivers are integrating gestures into the speech context, then the next question is how robust is this integration process? Can it be modulated, is it obligatory/automatic, or is this a system unique to gesture? Recent research suggests that this integration can be modulated by several factors. First, the interactions between the two modalities seem to be sensitive to the temporal synchrony of the two channels as well as to the perceived communicative intent of the speakers, and thus seem to be flexible rather than obligatory depending on the communicative context. After all, spontaneous speech is not always accompanied by gestures; gestures might sometimes be asynchronous with the relevant speech segment (Chui, 2005), and the frequency or the informativeness of the representations in gestures can vary depending on the communicative nature of the situation (i.e., whether there is shared common ground between the listener and the addressee or not, and so on).

Habets et al. (2011) investigated the degree of synchrony in speech and gesture onsets that is optimal for semantic integration of the concurrent gesture and speech. Videos of a person gesturing were combined with speech segments that were either semantically congruent or incongruent with the gesture. The onset of the gesture strokes (i.e., the meaningful part of the gesture, but not the preparation) and speech were presented with three different degrees of synchrony: a stimulus onset asynchrony (SOA) 0 condition (the gesture stroke onset and the speech onset were simultaneous) and two delayed SOAs, where speech was delayed by 160 ms (partial overlap with speech) or 360 ms (speech onset presented after gesture stroke was executed; no overlap between the two) in relation to the gesture stroke onset. ERPs time-locked to the speech onset showed a significant difference between semantically congruent versus incongruent gesture—speech combinations for the N400 component with SOAs of 0 and 160 ms, respectively, but not for the 360 ms SOA. Therefore, the closer speech and gesture are temporally to each other (or at least when some temporal overlap is possible), the more likely they are to be integrated with each other

Not only the synchrony, but also the perceived communicative intent of the speakers seems to modulate the speech–gesture integration or the semantic processing of gestures. ERP studies by Kelly et al. (2007) have demonstrated that our brain integrates speech and gesture less strongly when the two modalities are perceived as not intentionally coupled (i.e., gesture and speech being produced by two different persons) than when they are perceived as being produced by the same person. In this study, adults watched short videos of gesture and speech that conveyed semantically congruous and incongruous information. In half of the videos, participants were told that the two modalities were intentionally coupled (i.e., produced by the same communicator), and in the other half, they were told that the two modalities were not intentionally coupled (i.e., produced by different communicators). When participants knew that the same communicator produced the speech and gesture, there was a larger bilateral frontal and central N400 effect to words that were semantically incongruous versus congruous with gesture. However, when participants knew that different communicators produced the speech and gesture—that is, when gesture and speech were not intentionally meant to go together—the N400 effect was present only in right-hemisphere frontal regions. The results demonstrate that pragmatic knowledge about the intentional relationship between gesture and speech modulates neural processes during the integration of the two modalities.

Finally, Holler et al. (2014) have investigated how listeners/viewers comprehend speech–gesture pairs in a simulated triadic communication setting where the speakers' eye gaze is directed at them versus to another addressee (i.e., away from them). Participants were scanned (fMRI) while taking part in triadic communication involving two recipients and a speaker. The speaker uttered sentences that were accompanied by complementary iconic gestures (speech: "she cleaned the house"; gesture: mopping) or with speech only. Crucially, the speaker alternated her gaze direction toward or away from the participant in the experiment, thus rendering him/her in two recipient roles: addressed (direct gaze) versus unaddressed (averted gaze) recipient. "Speech and gesture" utterances, but not "speech only" utterances, produced more activity in the right MTG, one of the brain areas found consistently involved in speech–gesture integration, when participants were addressed than when not addressed. Thus, when the eye gaze of the speaker is averted away from the listener/viewer, indexing decrease in the perception of communicative intent, integration of the two channels and/or semantic processing gesture might be reduced (also see Holler et al., 2014, for similar effects shown by behavioral measures).

Finally, one study has investigated to what extent perception of information from gesture is special by comparing integration of gesture to that of manipulable actions (Kelly et al., 2015). This study shows that listeners/viewers are less likely to integrate overlapping action (e.g., somebody actually drinking from a glass) information to a speech context than a gesture (e.g., someone performing a drink gesture). This suggests that the communicative nature of gesture might be triggering more integration with speech than non-communicative actions, corroborating findings from the aforementioned studies.

25.5 Summary: Role of gesture in language comprehension

When it comes to processing of gestures in speech context, there is a robust involvement of semantic processing, similar to that involved in processing spoken language and recruiting similar brain areas. Studies show further this is not an independent system, but gestures are processed in relation to the speech context they occur in and they in turn influence speech comprehension. The Habets et al. (2011) study also shows that the temporal overlap between speech and gesture is crucial for their integration, pointing to the role of not only gesture in speech processing but also of speech in gesture processing. Thus, one can suggest that there is an incremental meaning interpretation occurring between the two channels. This is in line with the Integrated Systems hypothesis by Kelly et al. (2010) according to which speech and gesture, mutually constrain each other's meaning interpretation in an online manner. Skipper (2014) has also proposed gesture as a predictive context for speech comprehension consistent with this view.

25.6 General conclusions: Toward a unified account of the role of gesture

Both the results of the production and the comprehension studies reported here suggest that information from speech and gesture, is processed in an interactive way during production *and* comprehension; recruiting similar semantic processing and neural correlates in the brain, rather than being processed in a distinct, modular, or modality-specific fashion. Even though many current models view gesture production as mere action simulations and arising originally independent of the language system, postulating gesture processing as linked to language processing seems more plausible when we consider converging evidence from both production and comprehension. Furthermore, this approach is more in line with the genuinely communicative nature of gesture use; that it is sensitive to context, discourse, and the listener's knowledge status. This is not to say that gestures are completely independent of action processing, but any account of gesture processing should consider the interactions between speech and gesture, and their communicative nature both during production and comprehension to give a unified account of their role in language processing. This will offer unique insights into understanding language processing in context in general.

References

Alibali, M. W., Heath, D. C., & Myers, H. J. (2001). Effects of visibility between speaker and listener on gesture production: Some gestures are meant to be seen. *Journal of Memory and Language, 44*, 169–88.

Azar, Z., Backus, A., & Özyürek, A. (2017). Highly proficient bilinguals maintain language-specific pragmatic constraints on pronouns: Evidence from speech and gesture. In: Gunzelmann, G., Howes, A., Tenbrink, T., & Davelaar, E. (Eds.), *Proceedings of the 39th Annual Conference of the Cognitive Science Society* (CogSci 2017) (pp. 81–6). Cognitive Science Society, Austin, TX.

Bavelas, J. B., & Chovil, N. (2000). Visible acts of meaning. An integrated message model of language use in face-to-face dialogue. *Journal of Language and Social Psychology, 19*, 163–94.

Beattie, G., & Shovelton, H. (1999). Do iconic hand gestures really contribute anything to the semantic information conveyed by speech? An experimental investigation. *Semiotica, 123*, 1–30.

Beilock, S. L., & Goldin-Meadow, S. (2010). Gesture changes thought by grounding it in action. *Psychological Science, 21*, 1605–10.

Campisi, E., & Özyürek, A. (2013). Iconicity as a communicative strategy: Recipient design in multimodal demonstrations for adults and children. *Journal of Pragmatics, 47*, 14–27.

Chu, M., & Kita, S. (2016). Co thought and co-speech gestures are generated by the same action generation process. *The Journal of Experimental Psychology: Learning, Memory, and Cognition, 42*(2), 257–70.

Chui, K. (2005). Temporal patterning of speech and iconic gestures in conversational discourse. *Journal of Pragmatics, 37*, 871–87.

Clark, H. (1996). *Using Language*. Cambridge University Press, Cambridge.

Cook, S. W., & Tannenhous, M. K. (2009). Embodied communication: Speakers' gestures affect listeners' actions. *Cognition, 113*, 98–104.

Debreslioska, S., Özyürek, A., Gullberg, M., & Perniss, P. M. (2013). Gestural viewpoint signals referent accessibility. *Discourse Processes, 50*(7), 431–56.

Dick, A. S., Goldin-Meadow, S., Solodkin, A., & Small, S. L. (2012). Gesture in the developing brain. *Developmental Science, 15*, 165–80.

de Ruiter, P. (2007). Postcards from the mind: The relationship between speech, imagistic gesture, and thought. *Gesture, 7*(1), 21–38.

Enfield, N. J. (2009). *The Anatomy of Meaning: Speech, Gesture, and Composite Utterances*. Cambridge University Press, Cambridge, UK.

Floyd, S. (2016). Modally hybrid grammar? Celestial pointing for time-of-day reference in Nheengatú. *Language, 92*(1), 31–64.

Goldin-Meadow, S., McNeill, D., & Singleton, J. (1996). Silence is liberating: Removing the handcuffs on grammatical expression in the manual modality. *Psychological Review, 103*, 34–55.

Goldin-Meadow, S., So, C., Özyürek, A., & Mylander, C. (2008). The natural order of events: How speakers of different languages represent events nonverbally. *Proceedings of the National Academy of Sciences, 105*(27), 9163–8.

Gullberg, M. (2011). Language-specific encoding of placement events in gestures. In: Bohnemeyer, J., & Pederson, E. (Eds.), *Event Representation in Language and Cognition* (pp. 166–88). Cambridge University Press, Cambridge, MA.

Gullberg, M., Hickmann, M., & Hendriks, H. (2008). Learning to talk and gesture about motion in French. *First Language, 28*(2), 2000–236.

Gullberg, M., & Narasimhan, B. (2010). What gestures reveal about how semantic distinctions develop in Dutch children's placement verbs. *Cognitive Linguistics, 21*(2), 239–62.

Habets, B., Kita, S., Shao, Z., Özyürek, A., & Hagoort, P. (2011). The role of synchrony and ambiguity in speech–gesture integration during comprehension. *Journal of Cognitive Neuroscience, 23*, 1845–54.

Holle, H., & Gunter, T. C. (2007). The role of iconic gestures in speech disambiguation: ERP evidence. *Journal of Cognitive Neuroscience, 19*, 1175–92.

Holler, J., Kokal, I., Toni, I., Hagoort, P., Kelly, S., & Özyürek, A. (2014). Eye'm talking to you: Speakers' gaze direction modulates co-speech gesture processing in the right MTG. *Social, Cognitive and Affective Neuroscience, 10*(2), 255–61.

Holler, J., & Beattie, G. (2003). How iconic gestures and speech interact in the representation of meaning: Are both aspects really integral to the process? *Semiotica, 146*, 81–116.

Holler, J., Schubotz, L., Kelly, S., Hagoort, P., Schuetze, M., & Özyürek, A. (2014). Social eye gaze modulates processing of speech and co-speech gesture. *Cognition, 133*, 692–7.

Hostetter, A. B., & Alibali, M. W. (2008). Visible embodiment: Gestures as simulated action. *Psychonomic Bulletin & Review, 15*, 495–514.

Kelly, S. D., Barr, D., Church, R. B., & Lynch, K. (1999). Offering a hand to pragmatic understanding: The role of speech and gesture in comprehension and memory. *Journal of Memory and Language, 40*, 577–92.

Kelly, S. D., Özyürek, A., & Maris, E. (2010). Two sides of the same coin: Speech and gesture mutually interact to enhance comprehension. *Psychological Science, 21*, 260–7.

Kelly, S. D., Ward, S., Creigh, P., & Bartolotti, J. (2007). An intentional stance modulates the integration of gesture and speech during comprehension. *Brain Language, 101*, 222–33.

Kelly, S., Healey, M., Özyürek, A., & Holler, J. (2015). The processing of speech, gesture and action during language comprehension. *Psychonomic Bulletin & Review, 22*, 517–23.

Kendon, A. (2004). *Gesture: Visible Action as Utterance*. Cambridge University Press, Cambridge, MA.

Kita, S., & Özyürek, A. (2003). What does cross-linguistic variation in semantic coordination of speech and gesture reveal? Evidence for an interface representation of spatial thinking and speaking. *Journal of Memory and Language, 48*(1), 16–32.

Kita, S., Özyürek, A., Allen, S., Brown, A., Furman, R., & Ishizuka, T. (2007). Relations between syntactic encoding and co-speech gestures: Implications for a model of speech and gesture production. *Language and Cognitive Processes, 22*(8), 1212–36.

Krahmer, E., & Swerts, M. (2007). The effects of visual beats on prosodic prominence: Acoustic analyses, auditory perception and visual perception. *Journal of Memory and Language, 57*, 396–414.

Krauss, R. M., Dushay, R. A., Chen, Y., & Rauscher, F. (1995). The communicative value of conversational hand gestures. *Journal of Experimental Social Psychology, 31*, 533–52.

Levelt, P. (1989). *Speaking*. MIT Press, Cambridge.

McNeill, D. (1992). *Hand and Mind*. University of Chicago Press, Chicago, IL.

Masson-Carro, I., Goudbeek, M. B., & Krahmer, E. J. (2016). Can you handle this?: The impact of object affordances on how co-speech gestures are produced. *Language, Cognition and Neuroscience*, *31*(3), 430–40.

Melinger, A., & Levelt, W. J. M. (2004). Gesture and the communicative intention of the speaker. *Gesture*, *4*(2), 119–41.

Morrel-Samuels, P., & Krauss, R. M. (1992). Word familiarity predicts the temporal asynchrony of hand gesture and speech. *Journal of Experimental Psychology: Learning, Memory, and Cognition*, *18*, 615–23.

Özçalışkan, S., Lucero, C., & Goldin-Meadow, S. (2016a). Is seeing gesture necessary to gesture like a native speaker? *Psychological Science*, *27*(5), 737–47.

Özçalışkan, S., Lucero, C., & Goldin-Meadow, S. (2016b). Does language shape silent gesture? *Cognition*, *148*, 10–18.

Özyürek, A. (2002). Do speakers design their co-speech gestures for their addresees? The effects of addressee location on representational gestures. *Journal of Memory and Language*, *46*(4), 688–704.

Özyürek, A. (2014). Hearing and seeing meaning in speech and gesture: Insights from brain and behaviour. *Philosophical Transactions of the Royal Society of London, Series B: Biological Sciences*, *369*(1651), 20130296.

Özyürek, A., Kita, S., Allen, S., Furman, R., & Brown, A. (2005). How does linguistic framing of events influence co-speech gestures? Insights from crosslinguistic variations and similarities. *Gesture*, *5*(1/2), 219–40.

Özyürek, A., Kita, S., Allen, S., Furman, R., Brown, A., & Ishizuka, T. (2008). Development of cross-linguistic variation in speech and gesture: Motion events in English and Turkish. *Developmental Psychology*, *44*(4), 1040–54.

Özyürek, A., Willems, R. M., Kita, S., & Hagoort, P. (2007). On-line integration of semantic information from speech and gesture: Insights from event-related brain potentials. *Journal of Cognitive Neuroscience*, *19*(4), 605–16.

Peeters, D., Chu, M., Holler, J., Hagoort, P., & Özyürek, A. (2015). Electrophysiological and kinematic correlates of communicative intent in the planning and production of pointing gestures and speech. *Journal of Cognitive Neuroscience*, *27*(12), 2352–68.

Perniss, P. M., & Özyürek, A. (2015). Visible cohesion: A comparison of reference tracking in sign, speech, and co-speech gesture. *Topics in Cognitive Science*, *7*(1), 36–60.

Schubotz, L., Holler, J., & Özyürek, A. (2015). Age-related differences in multi-modal audience design: Young, but not old speakers, adapt speech and gestures to their addressee's knowledge. In: Ferré, G., & Tutton, M. (Eds.), *Proceedings of the 4th GESPIN—Gesture & Speech in Interaction Conference*. Université of Nantes, Nantes.

Skipper, J. (2014). Echoes of the spoken past: How auditory cortex hears context during speech perception. *Philosophical Transactions of the Royal Society of London. B- Biological Sciences*, *369*(1651), 20130297.

Skipper, J. (2015). The NOLB model: A model of the natural organization of language and the brain. In: Willems, R. (Ed.), *Cognitive Neuroscience of Natural Language Use* (pp. 101–34). Cambridge University Press, Cambridge.

Skipper, J. I., Goldin-Meadow, S., Nusbaum, H. C., & Small, S. L. (2009). Gestures orchestrate brain networks for language understanding. *Current Biology*, *19*, 661–7.

So, W. C., Kita, S., & Goldin-Meadow, S. (2009). Using the hands to identify who does what to whom: Gesture and speech go hand in hand. *Cognitive Science*, *33*, 115–25.

Straube, B., Green, A., Weis, S., & Kircher, T. (2012). A supramodal neural network for speech and gesture semantics: An fMRI study. *PLoS One, 7,* e51207.

Talmy, L. (1985). Lexicalization patterns: Semantic structure in lexical forms. In: Shopen, T. (Ed.), *Language Typology and Semantic Description. Vol. III: Grammatical categories and the lexicon* (pp. 36–149). Cambridge University Press, Cambridge.

Wagner, P., Malisz, Z., & Kopp, S. (2014). Gesture and speech in interaction: An overview. *Speech Communication, 57,* 209–32.

Wesp, R., Hesse, J., Keutmann, D., & Wheaton, K. (2001). Gestures maintain spatial imagery. *The American Journal of Psychology, 114,* 591–600.

Wu, Y., & Coulson, S. (2007). Iconic gestures prime related concepts: An ERP study. *Psychonomic Bulletin & Review, 14*(1), 57–63.

Xu, J., Gannon, P., Emmorey, K., Smith, J. F., & Braun, A. R. (2009). Symbolic gestures and spoken language are processed by a common neural system. *Proceedings of the National Academy of Sciences of the United States of America, 106*(49), 20664–9.

Yap, D. F., So, W. C., Yap, M., & Tan, Y. Q. (2011). Iconic gestures prime words. *Cognitive Science, 35,* 171–83.

CHAPTER 26

PRAGMATICS AND INFERENCE

ALAN GARNHAM

26.1 Introduction

Psycholinguistics deals with all aspects of language processing, as indicated by the scope of this *Handbook*. When considering the meaning (or more generally the interpretation or import) of part of a discourse or text, several things quickly become apparent. In particular, the import of what is said or written does not depend solely on what is explicitly present. It depends also on context, including the previous parts of the discourse or text, and on the knowledge (or beliefs) of the parties to the discourse, which can, itself, be regarded as part of the context.

Linguists, too, are naturally interested in contextual aspects of meaning, and pragmatics is the branch of linguistics that deals with contextual contributions to the meaning, in a broad sense, of utterances. As we will see, linguists' take on these issues is very different from that of the majority of psycholinguists, though the experimental pragmatics movement in psycholinguistics (see Chapter 27) is much more closely aligned with linguistic pragmatics. Linguists identify sets of phenomena that they study under a set of specific headings, the most important of which are readily identified by scanning the contents pages of textbooks on pragmatics. Specific topics include deixis and anaphora, conversational implicature, presupposition, speech acts, conversational structure, information structure, politeness, and the interpretation of figurative language.

Although the contextual effects on meaning investigated by linguists are, in principle, relevant to the questions about language processing studied in psycholinguistics, not all of them have received the same attention in mainstream psycholinguistics as in linguistics, and they are not always identified in the same way in the two disciplines. The questions asked in linguistics are different from those asked in psycholinguistics. For example, linguists may want to specify the presuppositions that particular expressions have; a definite noun phrase (NP) such as "the beer" might presuppose the existence of some relevant beer. Linguists might then claim that an utterance of "the beer is warm" is neither true nor false if no relevant beer can be identified. Psycholinguists are usually interested in the felicitous use of language, and so might present a text containing the phrase "the beer" and assume that readers (or listeners) will take the phrase to be used properly, and hence assume that there is some relevant beer. To put this matter another way, psycholinguists will investigate the inference to the existence of the beer in the context in which the phrase "the beer" is used. For example, on reading "We checked the picnic supplies. The beer was warm," readers typically assume that there was beer among the picnic supplies. However, they might take longer to read "the beer was warm" compared to the case where it had previously been made explicit that there was some beer.

26.2 PRAGMATICS IN LINGUISTICS

The modern study of pragmatics can be traced back to the division, by Charles Morris (1938), of a general theory of signs (semiotic) into syntax, semantics, and pragmatics. Morris defined pragmatics as "the relation of signs to interpreters" (1938, p. 6), though, as indicated here, modern linguistic pragmatics deals with a broader range of contextual effects. Some of the phenomena studied in contemporary pragmatics are clearly related to structural aspects of language, and can be analyzed using techniques like those employed in formal semantics. Others are much less closely related, or perhaps not related at all, to language structure.

One of the most obvious cases of the context-dependence of interpretation is to be found in the use of indexical expressions, such as "I," "you," "here," "there," "now," and "then," whose reference depends on the context in which they are used. And, indeed, some followers of Morris, in particular Bar-Hillel (1954), suggested that pragmatics should be taken to be the study of indexicals. The formal treatment of such expressions was developed in the 1960s at the University of California, Los Angeles (UCLA) by Richard Montague, Dana Scott, David Kaplan, and others. The basic idea was that a formally specified context would allow the reference of an indexical expression to be determined, and then a larger expression containing that indexical could be evaluated, for example as true or false (if it were a declarative sentence) or as asking a question about a particular person (if it were an interrogative with a particular content). A detailed analysis of the word "now" was published by Montague's student Hans Kamp (1971), using a technique called double indexing, in which context is differentiated from the "world" in which contextual effects occur. Kamp (1979; Kamp & Rohrer, 1983) also applied this method of analysis to tense, building on the work of Hans Reichenbach (1947) and Arthur Prior (1968). There has been a great deal of interest, in psycholinguistics, in how children acquire indexicals (e.g., Dent, 1984), though relatively little interest in adults' processing of indexicals. The use of anaphoric expressions, such as third person pronouns of various kinds, and fuller NPs that co-refer with previous expressions in a discourse or text, has been much more thoroughly studied.

Other contextual effects on meaning are much less closely tied to linguistic forms and linguistic structure, but are also standardly studied within pragmatics. Indeed, according to Levinson (1983, p. 9) these disparate elements within pragmatics are "the heart of the definitional problem: the term *pragmatics* covers both context-dependent aspects of language structure and principles of language usage and understanding that have nothing or little to do with linguistic structure." Effects of the second type have been studied in detail from the 1950s onward, often, in the first instance, by philosophers, but increasingly by linguists.

The Oxford philosopher J. L. Austin (1962) observed that analytic philosophy had focused almost entirely on statements and that it had failed to note that many, perhaps most, utterances had other functions than to describe the world, even if, in form, they appear to be statements. Austin called such utterances performatives, and noted that performatives allow us to do things with words. Within pragmatics, this idea has been studied as speech act theory. Speech act was a term of Austin's that was championed by John Searle (1969) in his development of Austin's ideas.

Another Oxford philosopher, Paul Grice (1975) instigated an ambitious program of research in which he hoped to characterize "non-natural" (as opposed to natural) meaning. As part of this program, he introduced the idea of implicature, for what is suggested by an utterance, but not explicitly stated or implied (in the strict logical sense). One type of implicature is associated with indirect speech acts (e.g., the use of an apparent question about an ability, "Can you pass the salt?" as a request—to pass the salt). The notion of implicature allows us to distinguish what is conveyed by an utterance from what is literally said, including simple cases, such as the one just mentioned, and other more complex cases. According to Grice, implicatures are made on the assumption that, in engaging in conversation, people generally adhere to cooperative principles that guide other types of action as well as linguistic exchange. However, this account of implicature has been vigorously debated. The most influential alternative account is Sperber and Wilson's (1986) relevance theory, which claims that the correct interpretation of an utterance is, or should be, the one that is most relevant in the context. The Gricean notion of implicature is closely related to the notion of inference used by psycholinguists (which is not restricted to deductive inference), and so many of the inferences that psycholinguists study would be classified by linguists as implicatures.

The topic of presupposition, in the restricted sense as used in pragmatics, has a longer history in philosophy and has been particularly important in the analysis of referring expressions, such as "the king of France." A presupposition is something that is taken for granted by an utterance, and is usually the same for a negated version of the utterance (e.g., both "the king of France is bald" and "the king of France is not bald" presuppose that there is a king of France). Presuppositions are triggered by particular words or grammatical constructions (presupposition triggers) and the presuppositions of parts of an utterance have complex relations to the presuppositions of the whole utterance (the projection problem). Not surprisingly, questions about the presuppositions of referring expressions were first raised in detail by Frege in *On Sense and Reference* (Frege, 1952/1892). Frege's view was superseded in the minds of many logicians by Bertrand Russell's (1905) theory of descriptions, according to which "the present king of France is bald" asserts the existence of that person. The theory of descriptions was in turn challenged by Peter Strawson (1950), who proposed a theory more akin to Frege's, though, critically, Strawson drew a distinction between statements, which have presuppositions, and sentences, which do not. From this point of view, Strawson's ideas are more akin to those of Grice, Searle, and modern linguistic pragmaticists, than to those of Frege and Russell. As mentioned previously, psycholinguists' take on presuppositions is somewhat different from linguists'. Psycholinguists study inferences to presuppositions, as they assume that readers and listeners typically take utterances to be used felicitously, and hence with their presuppositions satisfied.

Other topics that are, perhaps, less central to pragmatics include information structure, conversation structure, particularly as studied in conversation analysis (Sacks, Schegloff, &

Jefferson, 1974), politeness (Brown & Levinson, 1987; Leech, 1983), and figurative language. Information structure looks at the way sentences are structured to reflect what is currently being talked about. For example, a passive ("the boy was run over by the car") might be more appropriate than the corresponding active ("the car ran over the boy") if the discourse is currently about the boy. There have been a small number of studies of information structure in psycholinguistics (e.g., Cowles, Kluender, Kutas, & Polinsky, 2007), and the notion of information structure may explain why some texts used in psycholinguistic experiments sound awkward. Figurative language has been studied more widely in psycholinguistics, and the main question has been whether computation of the figurative meaning requires prior computation of the literal meaning (see, e.g., Glucksberg, 2001, though many, more recent papers continue to address this question).

26.3 INFERENCE IN PSYCHOLINGUISTICS

Psycholinguists have long been interested in how people go beyond the literal content of a discourse or text, using, among other things, contextual information, either to link information in different parts of the discourse or text, or to elaborate on what is literally presented. Such activity is usually studied under the head of inference, but many of the inferences that psycholinguists are interested in relate to the linguistic phenomena studied in pragmatics. Interpreting anaphoric expressions, such as third person definite pronouns, often depends on inference-making (see Garnham, 2001, for an overview). Implicature is a kind of inference, in a broad sense, and so is working out the presuppositions of an utterance, which will very often not have been explicitly stated in the preceding discourse. Similarly, working out which speech act has been performed, particularly in the case of indirect speech acts, requires inferencing, as does the interpretation of figurative language.

26.3.1 Bransford's three ideas

As has already been mentioned, psycholinguistic work on inference is not usually presented using the technical language of linguistic pragmatics. Nevertheless, the starting points for the two types of work have much in common, particularly the observation that the meaning conveyed by sentences in context, whether uttered or written, goes beyond their literal meaning. This psycholinguistic work is probably best understood as deriving from a set of ideas formulated by John Bransford, around 1970. Bransford thought that the focus on Chomskyan syntax in theories of language processing was not necessarily the best approach when considering broader questions about text and discourse. Bransford's account of comprehension (and he did, indeed, focus on comprehension rather than production, though many of his ideas can be generalized to production) had three main components. The first is the notion that the information extracted from a text, and represented mentally, does not correspond to any of the linguistic representations of the text, or parts of it. As already indicated, Bransford had in mind, primarily, Chomskyan syntactic representations. However, it is now widely acknowledged that the core literal semantic meaning of a sentence usually depends, in a straightforward way, on the meanings of the words in it, and the way they are syntactically assembled. So, the information extracted from a text is not the semantic meaning of the sentences in it. Implicit in Bransford's presentation is the idea that what is represented is part of a real or imaginary world presented in the text, and this idea was later formalized in the theory of mental models (Johnson-Laird, 1983) or situation models (e.g., van Dijk & Kintsch, 1983).

Bransford's other two ideas were that comprehension is an integrative process and that comprehension is a constructive process. By integrative, Bransford meant that to understand a text is to put together the information conveyed by its different parts, not just to extract the meaning of each sentence or utterance separately. Interpreting anaphoric expressions is one critical aspect of integration. By constructive, he meant that the interpretation of a sentence or utterance in context requires the combination of information literally presented with other contextual or background information, a notion clearly linked to the concerns of linguistic pragmatics. What was perhaps not stressed clearly enough in Bransford's original presentation is that constructive processes are often the basis of integration. For example, in the classic Haviland and Clark (1974) psycholinguistic passage:

> We checked the picnic supplies. The beer was warm.

The process of integrating the information in the two sentences into a coherent whole depends on the background knowledge that picnic supplies can include beer. It is perhaps worth reiterating that this classic case of what psycholinguists would call inference in text comprehension reflects the pragmatic phenomenon of presupposition. The use of the definite NP "the beer" as a sentential subject indicates that a particular beer or quantity of beer exists in the context described, and hence can be referred to in the second sentence. The psycholinguistic inference locates this beer in a particular place (among the picnic supplies), and hence makes the passage cohere.

Bransford's best-known demonstration of the process of integration is in his experiments on the so-called linear effect (Bransford & Franks, 1971), in which people recognize a sentence containing four ideas, such as "the ants in the kitchen ate the sweet jelly that was on the table," even though they have only previously encountered sentences presenting one (e.g., "the ants were in the kitchen"), two (e.g., "the ants ate the sweet jelly"), or three (e.g., "the ants ate the sweet jelly that was on the table") of those ideas. However, later work has focused on aspects of integration such as the interpretation of anaphoric expressions (such as pronouns and verbal ellipses) and the computing of coherence relations, such as cause-effect, which may or may not be signaled explicitly by words, for example "because" in the case of cause-effect.

Construction is demonstrated in Bransford's turtles experiment (Bransford, Barclay, & Franks, 1972), in which turtles are described as on or beside a log, and a fish swims beneath the turtles or beneath the log. The results of this experiment (which concern whether the fish is thought to be under the turtles) depend on knowledge about how verbal spatial descriptions map onto spatial relations between objects in the world. Other Bransford studies on the understanding of and memory for text (Bransford & Johnson, 1972), showing striking effects of having or not having a title (the "washing clothes" experiment) or a visual context for a text (the experiment with the picture of balloons lifting a guitar amplifier to a high window for the purposes of serenading the occupant of a room high in an apartment block), also demonstrate constructive effects in comprehension.

Not all integration involves constructive processes, some aspects of integration are guided purely by linguistics features (compare Grice's conventional implicatures, which derive from particular words (e.g., "but" implicates contrast, a coherence relation), Montague's formal pragmatics of indexicals, and Levinson's claim that pragmatics encompasses two different kinds of phenomenon). And not all uses of constructive processes subserve integration. Those that do not are often referred to in the psycholinguistic literature as generating elaborative (or purely elaborative) inferences.

26.3.2 What inferences are made?

Bransford set out a schematic theory of text comprehension, and presented some intriguing demonstration experiments, focusing on the making of inferences, and what can go wrong if inferences are not made. However, the fact that an inference can be made from a text does not mean that it will be. A question that dominated the literature on inference following Bransford (in the 1970s) was that of how to characterize which inferences are made. Bransford's writings implied that many inferences were made and, indeed, later theories describing themselves as constructivist have tended to suggest relatively prolific inferencing. However, most of Bransford's evidence came from memory tests, presented some time after a text had been heard or read. The questions asked in these tests could be thought of as leading questions—questions that led to the inference being made when the question was asked, and, possibly leading people to think they had made the inference as they read the text.

In the decade following Bransford's initial publications, reading time and other more direct measures were applied to the study of whether inferencing occurred as texts were read (most of the work was on written language). Some studies found clear evidence of inference making during reading (e.g., Haviland & Clark, 1974—"the beer was warm" study), though others found evidence against it (e.g., Thorndyke, 1976). One possible conclusion was that inferences necessary for linking together information in different parts of a text— for establishing the coherence of the text—are made during reading, but purely elaborative inferences are not. An a priori argument can be made to support this view. On the one hand, if coherence is not established, the text has not been properly understood. On the other hand, indefinitely many elaborative inferences can be made from a text, and it is difficult to justify the cognitive effort necessary to make any particular one, unless it can be shown to be in some way crucial. From this perspective it should be noted that what appears to be an elaborative inference at one point in a text can be a coherence-creating inference at another point. For example, on reading "We checked the picnic supplies" it is possible to infer, elaboratively, that there is (or might be) beer among the picnic supplies. On subsequently reading "The beer was warm," the inference about beer among the picnic supplies allows a crucial link to be made between the two sentences of the text. Perhaps that is the right point at which to make the inference.

Although the idea that necessary inferences are made and elaborative inferences are not is a plausible one, there was some empirical evidence against it. In addition, although this point was initially relatively unimportant in the core psycholinguistic literature, texts are read for many different reasons, and it is unlikely that the same inferencing regime applies in all cases. Returning to the question of necessary versus elaborative inferences, McKoon and Ratcliff (1992) questioned both sides of the equation. On the one hand, they suggested that some elaborative inferences might require so little effort that they would be made anyway. On the other hand, they suggested that some coherence-creating inferences, particularly where there did not make local links between parts of a text, might not be made. McKoon and Ratcliff called their ideas the Minimalist Hypothesis, and contrasted it with constructivist ideas derived from Bransford's work. However, their dichotomy was a false one (Garnham, 1992), because, on the one hand, and as mentioned before, integration (i.e., establishing coherence) often depends on constructive processes, and, on the other hand, theories that postulate constructive processes need not be committed to the idea that such processes always come into play whenever they can, particularly when they do not contribute to integration.

One problem with McKoon and Ratcliff's idea that inferences are made when they require very little effort or, as they put it, when they are based on readily available information, is giving the theory substance. To do so, one needs to provide a definition of what information is readily available, that is independent empirical tests of whether the inference is made. One possibility is that inferences that depend very closely on the presence of a single word in a text might be made. In some cases, the inference might depend on the definition of the word. So, for example, Garrod and Sanford (1981) found a different pattern of results for "Mary dressed the baby. The clothes were made of pink wool." from those found by Haviland and Clark (1974) for, "We checked the picnic supplies. The beer was warm." In the Haviland and Clark study, the inference appeared to be made in a backward direction, when "beer" was read, as there was a slow down on "beer" compared with the case in which beer had been explicitly mentioned earlier in the text ("We got some beer out of the trunk."). But in the Garrod and Sanford study, it appeared to have been made in a forward direction when "dressed" was read, as there was no slow down on "clothes" compared with the case when the clothes were explicitly mentioned earlier ("Mary put the clothes on the baby."). We have found a similar pattern of results for inferences depending on whether occupants of certain roles, such as nurse or engineer, are typically male or typically female (e.g., Carreiras, Garnham, Oakhill, & Cain, 1996). This latter result cannot be explained by reference to definitions. "To dress" might mean "to put clothes on," but being female is not part of the core definition of "nurse." Furthermore, there are other cases, such as inferences based on implicit causality, where single words do not appear to trigger inferences as they are read (Garnham, Traxler, Oakhill, & Gernsbacher, 1996; though see some more recent results that complicate the picture with implicit causality (Cozijn, Commandeur, Vonk, & Noordman, 2011; Pyykkönen & Järvikivi, 2010)).

McKoon and Ratcliff (1992) explicitly contrasted their ideas with constructivist theories, derived from the work of Bransford, and, according to them, at that time in the ascendant. They did, also, specifically claim that the minimalist account did not apply to inference-making that was the result of specific reading strategies, of which more later. As already mentioned, one response to McKoon and Ratcliff was to point out that minimalism vs. constructivism is, in general terms, a false dichotomy. A different response (Graesser, Singer, & Trabasso, 1994) was to revive the case for constructivism by a systematic presentation of evidence that certain classes of non-minimal inferences were routinely made. Graesser et al. identified 13 types of inference, of which they claimed six were made online, five were not, and for the other two classes there was no clear prediction from their theoretical position. One of Graesser et al.'s points, echoing the claim of Garnham (1992), was that a constructivist theory was not committed to the idea that all classes of inference are generated online.

Graesser et al. did not claim that the 13 types of inference were exhaustive. Indeed, they derived them from the consideration of a very short parable, "How Leisure Came," by Ambrose Bierce. However, the list includes previously studied inference types, such as coreference, instantiation, instrument inferences, causal inferences (antecedent and consequent), and inferences to goals (superordinate and subordinate), as well as inferences about emotions and author's intent. Although the exact details of this taxonomy have not been particularly influential, the taxonomy does point to a potential variety of inference types, and to the possibility that different inferences might be made for different reasons. This observation raises the question of whether a clear distinction can be made between inferences that are made, in some sense, automatically, and those that are made strategically. Nevertheless, as we will see next, the idea of an automatic component to the processes of inference making became an important one in the 1990s.

26.3.3 Mental models and situation models

Before turning to this idea, another important development should be noted. Bransford's three ideas, just discussed, developed into the theories of situation models and mental models that have dominated much work on text and discourse processing in recent years, and which often provide the overarching framework in which processes of inference are considered. The non-linguistic representations constructed during discourse comprehension are situation models or mental models, and the integrative and constructive processes needed to produce those models are both intimately linked to inference-making. Indeed, this framework is particularly suited to modeling processes in which information derived from text is put together with background, or contextual, information, because the two types of information are represented in the same way. Mental models or situation models often contain inferred information: the product of the integrative and constructive processes used to construct them.

Often there are several ways of integrating information, and constructive processes, relying on knowledge about the world, are used to choose between them. For example, in a case of reference resolution, such as:

> John confessed to Bill because he offered a reduced sentence.

The "he" used here could refer to either John or Bill, if only the linguistic form of the pronoun is considered. However, the relationship between confessing and sentencing strongly suggests that "he" must be Bill.

Although the situation model and mental model approaches have much in common, the concerns of people working in the two frameworks have tended to be somewhat different. The situation model approach, which developed primarily in the USA, was strongly influenced by the work of Walter Kintsch, and in particular the line of research first fully articulated in Kintsch and van Dijk's influential 1978 paper "Toward a model of text comprehension and production." Two critical aspects of the model presented in that paper are (i) links with psychological work on memory, and in particular Kintsch's (1974) own earlier work, and (ii) the cyclical nature of text comprehension processes. The notion of a situation model was properly incorporated into this framework in later work by van Dijk and Kintsch, particularly their 1983 book *Strategies of Discourse Comprehension*. An important part of memory research incorporated into this framework is the notion of spreading activation in a semantic network (e.g., Collins & Loftus, 1975), which is an "automatic," passive process set off by initial activation of nodes in a network. In text comprehension, this initial activation typically results from the occurrence (and processing) of specific words in a text, and the spread of activation then takes its course, according to the laws governing the network.

Activation spreads from network nodes specifically associated with words in the text to related nodes not associated with words in the text. This process can, therefore, be thought of as a potential contributor to inferential processes, even if it is not clear how it can determine the eventual content of inferences. For example, spreading activation might explain why beer comes to mind when picnic supplies are mentioned. What it does not explain is the specific content of the supposed inference: these (specifically mentioned) picnic supplies (probably) include (some specific) beer. The reason is that although memory contains general information about picnics and beer supplies, and it may contain information about specific beer and specific picnic supplies, it does not (or at least may well not) contain information about this particular set of picnic supplies and this particular beer, so representations of them have to be constructed, and spreading activation is not the right kind of process to construct structured representations on the fly. Nevertheless, a number of models of text processing, which have as a critical component passive spreading of activation in memory networks, and which include accounts of inference making, have been proposed by people working in the situation models tradition. Typically, these models suggest that networks corresponding to long-term memory, and therefore encoding knowledge about the world, are used together with networks representing information in the text so far. An important set of questions for models of this kind revolves around the additional mechanisms, if any, that are required to explain text comprehension in general, and inference-making in particular.

In Kintsch's own work, his earlier ideas evolved into the Construction-Integration model (1988, 1998). Spreading activation continues to be an important aspect of this model. However, other aspects of the model, such as the initial emphasis on bottom-up processing and the use of constraint satisfaction to resolve ambiguity, a process related to connectionist rather than semantic networks, have received more attention. Note that ambiguity resolution is itself often an inferential process.

A purer version of the spreading activation idea is found in models of so-called memory-based text processing (e.g., Cook, Halleran, & O'Brien, 1998; Gerrig & McKoon, 1998). In this framework, discourse comprehension in general, and inference making in particular, is entirely based on the notion of resonance of nodes in memory with signals transmitted by an automatic passive process that follows from the initial activation of nodes corresponding to ideas in a text. Given that semantic memory networks are postulated for reasons other than discourse comprehension, part of the attraction of these theories is a notion of parsimony. However, as has already been mentioned, McKoon, at least, believes that the strategic making of inferences cannot be explained by this mechanism.

Purely passive models of inference making appear to be at odds with the idea that reading behavior is often directed. Sir Frederic Bartlett, regarded as a precursor of the constructivist approach, proposed the general idea of effort after meaning (Bartlett, 1932), in relation particularly to stories that are difficult to understand (in particular, "The war of the ghosts," a story from a native North American tradition, which has elements unfamiliar to Barlett's early twentieth-century readers in Cambridge). Not surprisingly, given its relation to constructive processes, a large part of the effort after meaning lies in the making of inferences.

More generally, reading often seems to be directed by specific strategic goals. Some models based in a broadly situation model framework have, therefore, incorporated additional (strategic and/or constructivist) processes into models that rely on passive processes of spreading activation. Perhaps the best-known model of this type is the Landscape Model of Paul van den Broek and colleagues (e.g., van den Broek, Risden, Fletcher, & Thurlow, 1996). Van den Broek was drawn to the need for such processes in the explanation of causal inferences, which he had studied earlier with Tom Trabasso (e.g., Trabasso & van den Broek, 1985), and of referential inferences.

A more recent, though in many ways similar, development is the RI-Val model of O'Brien and Cook (2016) in which strategic processing is superimposed on a standard memory-based text comprehension model. The strategic processes can be used, for example, to decide when to respond in a particular experimental task. However, making a response does not stop the automatic processes, such as spreading activation, from running to completion, and hence these processes may produce effects after a response has been executed.

While the situation models approach to text comprehension and inference-making is based firmly in psychology, the mental models approach, which makes many of the same claims at the broadest level, derives from the multiple disciplines of cognitive science, as indicated in the subtitle of Johnson-Laird's 1983 book *Mental Models: Towards a Cognitive Science of Language, Inference, and Consciousness*. The mental models approach, which incorporates reasoning as well as language processing, is strongly influenced by notions of inference from formal logic and related ideas about text and discourse meaning from formal semantics (see, e.g., Garnham, 2001, Ch. 2). Another reflection of the cognitive science orientation of the mental models approach is its concern with the level of explanation provided by the framework itself, and by particular subtheories formulated within the framework. Garnham (1996) discusses this issue in relation to Marr's (1982) three levels of analysis: computational, algorithmic, and implementational. Work in the mental models framework tends to be more concerned with representational detail, than with process, though similar developments can be seen in some work in the situation model framework, particularly that of Rolf Zwaan and colleagues, for example in the event indexing model of Zwaan, Langston, and Graesser (1995).

26.3.4 Embodiment and good-enough representations

Zwaan has also been a pioneer in the field of embodied representation (Zwaan, 1999), as has one of the original contributors to empirical work on mental models, Art Glenberg (Glenberg, Meyer, & Lindem, 1987; for his work on embodiment see, e.g., Glenberg & Kaschak, 2002). Both mental models theory and situation models theory emphasize the similarity of representations derived from text and representations stored in memory, and hence the ease of integrating the two. As we have seen, the situation model approach in particular has emphasized the importance of a passive process of spreading activation, which is typically, though perhaps for mainly historical reasons, conceived of as spreading through an amodal set of representations in a standard semantic network. In various branches of cognitive psychology such amodal representations have come under criticism, for two related reasons. First, they fail to solve the grounding problem (Harnad, 1990) of how symbols in a system such as a natural language relate to (or are grounded in) the physical world. Second, they fail to capture the relations between representations derived from linguistic input and activity in our perceptuo-motor systems. These relations have been documented, both indirectly in behavioral studies such as those of Zwaan and of Glenberg, and more directly in brain imaging studies (e.g., Pulvermüller & Fadiga, 2010), which show the involvement of perceptual and motor areas of the brain in relevant aspects of language processing. At the broadest level, the idea of embodiment does not make much difference to the way that inference in text comprehension is conceived. It is another version of the view that what is expressed in language is closely related to things we perceive as happening in the world and things we do in the world. Representations of the two kinds fit easily together, and hence allow for the constructive processes—the combining of text-based information and background knowledge, general or specific—identified by Bransford in the 1970s, and crucial to inference-making. Of course, the details are different. For example, many studies show that concurrent perceptual or motor activity can interfere with or enhance text comprehension, depending on the particular relations between the activity and the text content (see Chapter 9, this volume). Another set of issues revolves around the question of whether text comprehension depends on mental simulation of the activities described, or on a more abstract manipulation of modality specific representations. A similar debate has occurred in the theory of mind literature.

The idea of representations that are good enough (for particular purposes) is clearly related to the question of whether there is a strategic component to text comprehension. The idea that people extract from text only the information that is needed for the task in hand is, perhaps, an obvious one in pedagogy, and has many precedents in psycholinguistics (e.g., Oakhill, Garnham, & Vonk, 1989). The particular notion of good-enough representations that has come to the fore recently, is primarily associated with the work of Tony Sanford (e.g., Barton & Sanford, 1993; Sturt, Sanford, Stewart, & Dawydiak, 2004) and Fernanda Ferreira (e.g., Ferreira, Bailey, & Ferraro, 2002). A particular focus in the work of Sanford and Ferreira is the construction of representations that fail to "acknowledge" anomalies ("where were the survivors [of an air crash] buried?", "How many animals of each type did Moses take on the ark?"). However, while these phenomena are of interest, they are not directly relevant to questions about inference.

26.4 Conclusion: The present

Where does research on inference in text comprehension now stand? There is general agreement that parts of texts activate in a fairly automatic way, related pieces of information stored in memory. This activation may form the basis for some inferences, but it cannot explain the detailed content of those inferences. Other inferences derive from strategic processing, driven by readers' goals and an effort after meaning. Integrative and constructive processes combine to produce representation of parts of real or imaginary words—mental or situation models. These models may be abstract and amodal, or they may be based on the way we interact, in perception and in action, with the world. In different circumstances they may be one or the other, or a mixture of both. Exactly which inferences are made when remains a matter for debate.

As several chapters in O'Brien, Cook, and Lorch's (2015) recent overview indicate (Gerrig & Wenzel, 2015; Goldman, McCarthy, & Burkett, 2015; Graesser, Li, & Feng, 2015; Lorch, 2015), there is an increasing interest in inference making in real texts, as opposed to the typically very brief texts studied in psycholinguistic experiments. Inferences about emotions are also attracting increasing attention, though they were mentioned in Graesser et al.'s (1994) list of 13 types of inference, and pioneering work was carried out by Gernsbacher, Goldsmith, and Robertson (1992) in the early 1990s. Links with linguistic pragmatics remain, for the most part, tenuous (but see Chapter 27 on experimental pragmatics, this volume), and it is not clear, at least to this author, that the approaches of cognitive neuroscience have yet made any major impact on psycholinguistic thinking about inference.

References

Austin, J. L. (1962). *How to Do Things with Words*, 2nd Edition (Eds. Urmson, J. O. & Sibsà, M.). Oxford University Press, Oxford.

Bar-Hillel, Y. (1954). Indexical expressions. *Mind*, 63, 359–79.

Bartlett, F. C. (1932). *Remembering: A Study in Experimental and Social Psychology*. Cambridge University Press, Cambridge.

Barton, S. B., & Sanford, A. J. (1993). A case study of anomaly detection: Shallow semantic processing and cohesion establishment. *Memory & Cognition*, 21, 477–87.

Bransford, J. D., Barclay, J. R., & Franks, J. J. (1972). Sentence memory: A constructive vs interpretive approach. *Cognitive Psychology*, 3, 193–209.

Bransford, J. D., & Franks, J. J. (1971). The abstraction of linguistic ideas. *Cognitive Psychology*, 2, 331–50.

Bransford, J. D., & Johnson, M. K. (1972). Contextual prerequisites for understanding: Some investigations of comprehension and recall. *Journal of Verbal Learning and Verbal Behavior*, 11, 717–26.

Brown, P., & Levinson, S. C. (1987). *Politeness: Some Universals in Language Usage*. Cambridge University Press, Cambridge.

Carreiras, M., Garnham, A., Oakhill, J. V., & Cain, K. (1996). The use of stereotypical gender information in constructing a mental model: Evidence from English and Spanish. *Quarterly Journal of Experimental Psychology*, 49A, 639–63.

Collins, A. M., & Loftus, E. F. (1975). A spreading-activation theory of semantic processing, *Psychological Review*, 82, 407–28.

Cook, A. E., Halleran, J. G., & O'Brien, E. J. (1998). What is readily available during reading?: A memory-based view of text processing. *Discourse Processes*, 26, 109–29.

Cowles, H. W., Kluender, R., Kutas, M., & Polinsky, M. (2007). Violations of information structure: An electrophysiological study of answers to wh-questions. *Brain and Language*, 102, 228–42.

Cozijn, R., Commandeur, E., Vonk, W., & Noordman, L. G. (2011). The time course of the use of implicit causality information in the processing of pronouns: A visual world paradigm study. *Journal of Memory and Language*, 64, 381–403.

Dent, C. H. (1984). Development of discourse rules: Children's use of indexical reference and cohesion. *Developmental Psychology*, 20, 229–34.

Ferreira, F., Bailey, K. G. D., & Ferraro, V. (2002). Good-enough representations in language comprehension. *Current Directions in Psychological Science*, 11, 11–15.

Frege, G. (1952/1892). On sense and reference. In: Geach, P. T., & Black, M. (Eds.), *Translations from the Philosophical Writings of Gottlob Frege* (pp. 56–78). Blackwell, Oxford [first published in German in 1892 as Über Sinn und Bedeutung, Zeitschrift für Philosophie und Philosophische Kritik, *100*, 25–50].

Garnham, A. (1992). Minimalism versus constructionism: A false dichotomy in theories of inference during reading. *Psycoloquy*, 3(63), reading-inference-1.1.

Garnham, A. (1996). The other side of mental models—theories of language comprehension. In: Oakhill, J., & Garnham, A. (Eds.), *Mental Models in Cognitive Science: Essays in honour of Phil Johnson-Laird* (pp. 32–52). Psychology Press, Hove.

Garnham, A. (2001). *Mental Models and the Interpretation of Anaphora*. Psychology Press, Hove, East Sussex.

Garnham, A., Traxler, M. J., Oakhill, J., & Gernsbacher, M. A. (1996). The locus of implicit causality effects in comprehension. *Journal of Memory and Language*, 35, 517–43.

Garrod, S. C., & Sanford, A. J. (1981). Bridging inferences and the extended domain of reference. In: Long, J., & Baddeley, A. (Eds.), *Attention and Performance IX* (pp. 331–46). Lawrence Erlbaum Associates, Hillsdale, NJ.

Gernsbacher, M. A., Goldsmith, H. H., & Robertson, R. R. W. (1992). Do readers represent characters' emotional states? *Cognition and Emotion*, 6, 89–111.

Gerrig, R. J., & McKoon, G. (1998). The readiness is all: The functionality of memory-based text processing. *Discourse Processes*, 26, 67–86.

Gerrig, R. J., & Wenzel, W. G. (2015). The role of inferences in narrative experiences. In: O'Brien, E. J., Cook, A. E., & Lorch, R. F. Jr. (Eds.), *Inferences during Reading* (pp. 362–85). Cambridge University Press, Cambridge.

Glenberg, A. M., & Kaschak, M. P. (2002). Grounding language in action. *Psychonomic Bulletin & Review*, 9, 558–65.

Glenberg, A. M., Meyer, M., & Lindem, K. (1987). Mental models contribute to foregrounding during text comprehension. *Journal of Memory and Language*, 26, 69–83.

Glucksberg, S. (2001). *Understanding Figurative Language: From Metaphors to Idioms*. Oxford University Press, New York, NY.

Goldman, S. R., McCarthy, K. S., & Burkett, C. (2015). Interpretive inferences in literature. In: O'Brien, E. J., Cook, A. E., & Lorch, R. F. Jr. (Eds.), *Inferences during Reading* (pp. 386–415). Cambridge University Press, Cambridge.

Graesser, A. C., Li, H., & Feng, S. (2015). Constructing inferences in naturalistic reading contexts. In: O'Brien, E. J., Cook, A. E., & Lorch, R. F. Jr. (Eds.), *Inferences during Reading* (pp. 290–320). Cambridge University Press, Cambridge.

Graesser, A. C., Singer, M., & Trabasso, T. (1994). Constructing inferences during narrative text comprehension. *Psychological Review*, 101, 371–395.

Grice, H. P. (1975). Logic and conversation. In: Cole, P., & Morgan, J. (Eds.), *Syntax and Semantics, Vol. 3* (pp. 183–98). Academic Press, New York, NY.

Harnad, S. (1990). The symbol grounding problem. *Physica D*, 42, 335–46.

Haviland, S. E., & Clark, H. H. (1974). What's new? Acquiring new information as a process in comprehension. *Journal of Verbal Learning and Verbal Behavior*, 13, 512–21.

Johnson-Laird, P. N. (1983). *Mental Models: Towards a Cognitive Science of Language, Inference, and Consciousness*. Cambridge University Press, Cambridge.

Kamp, H. (1971). Formal properties of "now". *Theoria*, 37, 227–73.

Kamp, H. (1979). Events, instants and temporal reference. In: Bauerle, R., Egli, U., & von Stechow, A. (Eds.), *Semantics from Different Points of View* (pp. 376–417). Springer Verlag, Berlin.

Kamp, H., & Rohrer, C. (1983). Tense in texts. In: Bauerle, R., Schwarze, C., & von Stechow, A. (Eds.), *Meaning, Use, and Interpretation of Language* (pp. 250–69). Walter de Gruyter, Berlin.

Kintsch, W. (1974). *The Representation of Meaning in Memory*. Lawrence Erlbaum Associates, Hillsdale, NJ.

Kintsch, W. (1988). The role of knowledge in discourse comprehension: A construction-integration model. *Psychological Review, 95*, 163–82.

Kintsch, W. (1998). *Comprehension: A Paradigm for Cognition*. Cambridge University Press, Cambridge.

Kintsch, W., & van Dijk, T. A. (1978). Toward a model of text comprehension and production. *Psychological Review, 85*, 363–94.

Leech, G. N. (1983). *Principles of Pragmatics*. Longman, London.

Levinson, S. C. (1983). *Pragmatics*. Cambridge University Press, Cambridge.

Lorch, R. F., Jr. (2015). What about expository text? In: O'Brien, E. J., Cook, A. E., & Lorch, R. F. Jr. (Eds.), *Inferences during Reading* (pp. 348–61). Cambridge University Press, Cambridge.

McKoon, G., & Ratcliff, R. (1992). Inference during reading. *Psychological Review, 99*, 440–66.

Marr, D. (1982). *Vision: A Computational Investigation into the Human Representation and Processing of Visual Information*. Freeman, New York, NY.

Morris, C. W. (1938). Foundations of the theory of signs. In: Neurath, O., Carnap, R., & Morris, C. (Eds.), *International Encyclopedia of Unified Science* (pp. 77–138). University of Chicago Press, Chicago, IL.

O'Brien, E. J., & Cook, A. E. (2016). Coherence threshold and the continuity of processing. The RI-Val model of comprehension. *Discourse Processes, 53*, 326–38.

O'Brien, E. J., Cook, A. E., & Lorch, R. F., Jr. (Eds.) (2015). *Inferences during Reading*. Cambridge University Press, Cambridge.

Oakhill, J., Garnham, A., & Vonk, W. (1989). The on-line construction of discourse models. *Language & Cognitive Processes, 4*, SI263–86.

Prior, A. N. (1968). *Papers on Time and Tense*. Clarendon Press, Oxford.

Pulvermüller, F., & Fadiga, L. (2010). Active perception: Sensorimotor circuits as a cortical basis for language. *Nature Reviews Neuroscience, 11*, 351–60.

Pyykkönen, P., & Järvikivi, J. (2010). Activation and persistence of implicit causality information in spoken language comprehension. *Experimental Psychology, 57*, 5–16.

Reichenbach, H. (1947). *Elements of Symbolic Logic*. Macmillan, New York, NY.

Russell, B. (1905). On denoting. *Mind, 14*, 479–93.

Sacks, H., Schegloff, E. A., & Jefferson, G. (1974). A simplest systematics for the organization of turn-taking for conversation. *Language, 50*, 696–735.

Searle, J. (1969). *Speech Acts*. Cambridge University Press, Cambridge.

Sperber, D., & Wilson, D. (1986). *Relevance: Communication and Cognition*. Blackwell, Oxford.

Strawson, P. F. (1950). On referring. *Mind, 59*, 320–44.

Sturt, P., Sanford, A., Stewart, A., & Dawydiak, E. J. (2004). Linguistic focus and good-enough representations. An application of the change-detection paradigm. *Psychonomic Bulletin & Review, 11*, 882–8.

Thorndyke, P. W. (1976). The role of inferences in discourse comprehension. *Journal of Verbal Learning and Verbal Behavior, 15*, 436–46.

Trabasso, T., & van den Broek, P. W. (1985). Causal thinking and the representation of narrative events. *Journal of Memory and Language, 24*, 612–30.

van den Broek, P., Risden, K., Fletcher, C. R., & Thurlow, R. (1996). A "landscape" view of reading: Fluctuating patterns of activation and the construction of a stable memory representation. In: Britton, B. K., & Graesser, A. C. (Eds.), *Models of Understanding Text* (pp. 165–87). Lawrence Erlbaum Associates, Hillsdale, NJ.

van Dijk, T. A., & Kintsch, W. (1983). *Strategies of Discourse Comprehension*. Academic Press, New York, NY.

Zwaan, R. A. (1999). Embodied cognition, perceptual symbols, and situation models. *Discourse Processes, 28*, 81–8.

Zwaan, R. A., Langston, M. C., & Graesser, A. C. (1995). The construction of situation models in narrative comprehension: An event-indexing model. *Psychological Science, 6*, 292–7.

CHAPTER 27

EXPERIMENTAL PRAGMATICS

IRA NOVECK

27.1 Introduction

As part of his seminal proposal on language and communication, Paul Grice famously made a distinction between what a sentence *says* and what a sentence *means* when it is expressed as an utterance. The first part of the distinction—sentence meaning—refers to the contribution made by the words in a sentence, as expressed through grammar, that a listener needs to decode. But that is not all there is to *communication* because a listener ultimately needs to understand the speaker's intention and that goes beyond sentence meaning.

To make Grice's distinction clear, consider the following true letter-of-recommendation-request story as recounted in the *New York Times* (Apple, 2016). In the first half of the 20th century, Otto Warburg, a prominent biologist in Berlin, was asked by a colleague to write a letter of recommendation on behalf of a student, George Klein. Warburg accepted and wrote: "George Klein has made a very important contribution to cancer research; He has sent me the cells with which I have solved the cancer problem"[1]. This missive whose two sentences are well constructed and clear, nevertheless prompts the listener to read between the lines. Inferring the writer's intention certainly is central here. Without a Gricean approach, the decoding of the sentence and understanding an utterance's communicative intent would be considered uniformly overlapping. After Grice, sentence meaning can be more readily viewed as at best a clue to the speaker's intent.

His description of intention does not end there. According to Grice, there are (at least) two sorts of intention—what can be called a *that* and a *what* intention. That is, one sort of speaker intention is to indicate *that there is* a message to communicate and another is to indicate *what it is* the speaker intends to communicate. In communication, we use both sorts of intention and accessing them is highly reliant on context. Consider the *non-verbal* communication of car headlights (see Grandy & Warner, 2014). When a driver flashes her

---

[1] This story echoes Grice's well-known example concerning a professor whose pithy letter says, "Mr. Smith has excellent handwriting and is always very punctual."

high beams, it gets your attention (the "speaker" aims to inform her "listener" *that* there is a message to transmit) and its meaning (*what* it intends to inform) is context-dependent and requires inference-making. When a flash is made from high beams to you from a car across the highway divide, it could mean that there is a speed-trap ahead or that your own high beams are irritating; a flash to the back of your car in same-streaming traffic could mean "get out of my way, you're slowing me down"; when a flash comes from a parked car, it could be taken to mean "I'm here."

As these (non-verbal) examples demonstrate, communication involves the listener becoming aware that the speaker is seeking the listener's attention as well as determining the speaker's intended message. Given that inference and context-dependent cues play a fundamental role in ascertaining the speaker's intended meaning, it follows that sentence meaning is not in itself sufficient for calculating it. This observation has led some to argue that the sentences in ALL utterances fall short of being explicit enough for determining the speaker's intention (e.g., see Carston's, 2008, *underdeterminacy hypothesis*).

What accounts for the *experimental* part of the title? There are two major reasons why experimentation is a natural partner for linguistic-pragmatics. One is that in order to account for an utterance's meaning (to understand how a sentence leads a listener to comprehend the speaker's intended meaning), pragmatic theorists inevitably highlight psychological activities, such as inference-making, intention-reading, the application of cognitive effort, and much else. To account for the aforementioned letter-writing scenario, for example, Grice would probably have said that Warburg was flouting a maxim of conversation (more on this next), which in turn leads the letter-reader to infer some novel conclusions about Warburg's intent. Such non-linguistic factors are readily open to experimentation. The second reason is that, while pragmatic accounts—like Grice's—are plausible, they nevertheless rely on armchair theorizing and intuition. This is not a solid basis for drawing valid conclusions about pragmatic processes. A natural next step is to introduce experiments to unsuspecting third-persons, as is done in psychology, in order to evaluate pragmatists' accounts of linguistic-pragmatic phenomena or, better yet, to employ experiments that compare the efficiency of diverging pragmatic accounts. Given the maturity of experimental methods from a multitude of psychological subfields (such as reasoning, psycholinguistics, developmental psychology, and decision making), experimental psychology was poised to play a role in pragmatics. This set the stage for researchers to make genuine discoveries about the way individuals (mostly addressees) process pragmatic phenomena. Ultimately, one can come away with a corpus of data that can seed a field of study (see Noveck, 2018).

This chapter reviews three key topics that are currently being investigated in the experimental pragmatic literature. The first concerns enrichments linked to underinformative terms such as *some* (when and how *some* gets interpreted as *some but not all*), which are typically called *scalar implicatures*. The second concerns reference-making and the extent to which a speaker's perspective (and identity) are taken into account when carrying it out. The third concerns the comprehension of a prototypical pragmatic form: irony. All three topics had benefited from armchair discussions and debates before being considerably advanced by experimentation. Critically, all three experimental pragmatic topics investigate the extent to which *extra-linguistic* information can be attributed to the linguistically encoded meaning of an utterance as a listener aims to appreciate the speaker's intention. As a spoiler alert, the three topics show that understanding a speaker's intended meaning is slightly error-prone (i.e., is not assured) and is nearly always effortful, indicating that it is indeed an isolable aspect of communication[2].

27.2 From Grice to informativeness and inference: Scalar implicature

Grice's program introduced terminology that was quickly taken up by philosophers and linguists. One well-known term is *implicature*, which can be glossed as an utterance's implicit suggested meaning, one that goes beyond its linguistically encoded meaning. Grice actually distinguished between two types of implicature, *conventional implicatures*, and *conversational implicatures*. The former is linked to the meaning of words. For instance, the conjunction *but* in *My daughter's notebooks are incredibly well-organized but her room is a mess* has the same meaning as *and*, however the word *but* pragmatically contrasts the two conjuncts conventionally through language. Conversational implicatures, on the other hand, emerge from a speech act but not directly through the meaning of the speaker's words (Grice, 1989). So, when Warburg wrote his letter of recommendation, there is a conversational implicature of the sort "I do not have a high opinion of Mr. Klein and I do have a high opinion of myself." He further divided conversational implicatures into two sorts: *Generalized Conversational Implicatures* and *Particularized Conversational Implicatures*. The former refers to cases whose implicit meanings can be assumed to occur routinely and the latter to those reliant on more specific aspects of context.

Grice's original proposal described conversational exchanges as forms of cooperative endeavor (expressed as the Cooperative Principle: *Make your contribution such as it is required, at the stage at which it occurs, by the accepted purpose or direction of the talk exchange in which you are engaged*) in which utterances are expected to follow a set of maxims. These expect interlocutors to be truthful (maxim of *Quality*), informative (*Quantity*), relevant (*Relevance*), and efficient (*Manner*). His theory proposed that when a sentence's meaning violates a maxim, it opens possibilities for further interpretation. Thus, an inferential process is guided by an interplay between the linguistically encoded meaning of an utterance and the (violation of) maxims. In this way, an addressee profits from the maxims in order to extract information that was not linguistically encoded. Consider one of Grice's example in (1):

(1) X is meeting a woman this evening.

Given that the speaker was not informative, thus violating the maxim of *Quantity* (not to be underinformative or overinformative), a listener is entitled to come up with a different

---

[2] While these three topics are among the most researched topics in experimental pragmatics, the field as a whole addresses a wide variety of subject matters and issues. Experimental pragmatists investigate, among other things, presuppositions (e.g. Schwarz, 2007), metaphor (e.g., Rubio-Fernández, 2007) and metonymy (see Frisson & Pickering, 1999; Schumacher, 2014; Weiland et al., 2014), conditional inference-making (e.g. Noveck et al., 2011), negations (e.g. Nieuwland & Kuperberg, 2008) and other logical terms, as well as comprehension among those on the autism spectrum (e.g. Chevallier et al., 2009, 2010).

interpretation while maintaining the Cooperative Principle, arguably a narrowing of (1) to mean something akin to *X is meeting a woman who is someone other than X's sister, mother, or wife*.

While Grice's proposal was seminal, it led to many follow-ups as well as debates among philosophers and linguists. I will consider two of the reactions to Grice and show how they laid the groundwork for the experimental pragmatic enterprise. One of the early reactions to Grice's proposal was to make it align with linguistic theory (Horn, 1972, 1984, 1989, 1992; Levinson, 1983, 2000). Neo-Griceans stayed relatively close to Grice's formulation of the maxims by aiming to integrate pragmatic inferences in parallel with syntactic operations. Larry Horn, for example, considered cases such as (2):

(2) (a) Some of the chapters have been completed.
(b) Some but not all the chapters have been completed.

Horn argued that interpreting (2a) relies on linguistic scales that consist in a set of expressions ranked by order of informativeness (e.g., <some, all>), which is based on the notion that the latter entails the former (when *all the x* is true it follows that *some x* are). So, when a speaker uses the weaker term (e.g., *Some*), which is lower in order of informativeness, the speaker can be taken to implicate that the proposition that would have been expressed by the stronger term in the scale (*All*) is false. When hearing (2a), one can deduce that this was done for the purpose of eliminating stronger terms (as seen in 2b).

Importantly, this Hornian approach can be generalized to a host of scales. If a crossword puzzler informs me that the word she is completing *has an A or a B*, it can implicate that it is false that it has both because the speaker would have been more appropriately informative by saying *A and B*. It is the ubiquity of scales in this account and the assumption that this is an extra-linguistic phenomenon that prompted many to dub this kind of narrowing a *scalar implicature*.

Following up on this approach, Stephen Levinson, a fellow neo-Gricean, proposed that these scalar implicatures are generated automatically every time weak terms on the scale are used. He further proposed that they can be cancelled in certain contexts in order to provide the hearer with the semantic meaning. So, according to Levinson's account, an enriched reading of, say, *some* to *some but not all* is the initial go-to reading. Arguably, this sort of account is consistent with adult intuitions. Professors of logic often report that students have difficulty considering the semantic meaning of weak terms as primary (F. J. Pelletier, personal communication).

Note that in each of these examples, the lexical meaning (the semantics) of the weaker-sounding term is *compatible* with the stronger one on the scale. The sentence in (2a) is semantically compatible with the fact that *all the chapters have been completed*. In Relevance Theory (Sperber & Wilson, 1986/1995), an alternative post-Gricean theory, the semantic reading of a term such as *some* (in an utterance) could very well serve as a reading and there is no need to assume that it calls for a *some but not all* reading (Noveck & Sperber, 2007). In other words, according to Relevance Theory, listeners may often be satisfied with the linguistically encoded reading of *Some*; when there is an enrichment it is determined by particular features of the context. Unlike the neo-Griceans who view these cases as generalized implicatures (meaning that these enrichments occur routinely), Relevance Theory views them as particularized because the enrichment depends on context each time. It also follows from Relevance Theory that, all things being equal, a reading of *some* with an enriched meaning would call for extra effort with respect to a reading that maintains its semantic meaning.

27.2.1 The experimental turn

It was in this post-Gricean environment that developmental pragmatic studies began to take root. In a paper that explicitly investigated scalar implicature, Noveck (2001) reported that 7- and 10-year-olds were highly likely to accept *There might be a parrot in the box* as true when background evidence indicated that there *had to be* a parrot in the box (i.e., the children accepted an expression of mere possibility as true when an expression of necessity was called for). In contrast, adults were more likely to enrich the sentence *There might be a parrot in the box* to mean that *There might be, but there does not have to be, a parrot in the box* (which justifies a false response when there is necessarily a parrot in the box). Likewise, when a participant heard that *Some elephants have trunks*, younger participants (8- and 10-year-olds) were more likely to respond true (indicating that *some* was understood as *some and perhaps all*) while adults were more likely to respond false (indicating that *some* was enriched to mean *some but not all* or, to put it another way, to mean *only some*). These kinds of data indicate that pragmatic enrichments evolve with age, but they also show that semantic readings can suffice. The younger children's results also go against most adult intuitions, which is arguably why so many researchers continued to investigate this effect (e.g., Guasti et al., 2005; Huang & Snedeker, 2009a; Katsos & Bishop, 2011; Papafragou & Musolino, 2003; Pouscoulous et al., 2007). The most recent (not to mention massive) replication of this effect comes from a 31-language study (with 768 five-year-old children and 536 adults) that showed, among other things, that five-year-old children accepted underinformative uses of *Some* more often than adults and in all 31 languages (Katsos et al., 2016). For example, when presented a set of five boxes, each having, say, a single apple (without there being other apples anywhere else in view), five-year-olds are more likely than adults to accept *Some of the turtles are in the boxes* as true (49% of the children say true vs. 16% of the adults).

This highly replicable developmental effect captured the attention of different groups and generated the first intensive debate in modern experimental pragmatics. As much as different accounts for developmental findings flourished, they do not provide the kind of evidence that can distinguish between pragmatic accounts. A Gricean could say that children fail to see a violation and answer accordingly and a neo-Gricean such as Levinson could argue that children have not developed a default interpretation yet, whereas adults have. It would take subtler reaction time studies to properly test between pragmatic accounts.

While aiming to edify the theoretical debate about scalar utterances, Bott and Noveck (2004; see also Noveck & Posada, 2003) developed a categorization task that included underinformative statements such as *Some cats are mammals* that included controls such as *All cats are mammals, All mammals are cats*, and *Some mammals are cats*. The underinformative sentences were relevant because we wanted to determine how adults respond (again, the underinformative items are critical because these can be considered true with a semantic *some and perhaps all* reading and false with a narrowed *some but not all* reading). Would participants say true or false? Which of the two interpretations would be faster? Bott and Noveck (2004) reported that false responses to the underinformative statements were significantly slower than true responses. Moreover, the true responses were as fast as all the (true and false) control statements. In another experiment, we found that responses reflecting narrowed interpretations become more frequent when participants are given more time to answer. When participants are limited to a short amount of time (900 msec) to respond, they provide significantly more true responses (indicative of semantic readings) to a statement such as *Some cats are mammals* than when the allowable time to answer is extended to three seconds (i.e., false responses, which point to narrowed readings, increase with time). The main conclusion from this study was that narrowed readings appear to be linked with effort and that there is little evidence indicating that enriched readings can be construed as default, automatic, or ambiguous.

This claim—that enriched readings of scalar terms are effortful—was found to be robust through other tasks employing a variety of methods. I will point to three of the key supporting studies. Through self-paced reading tasks, Breheny et al. (2006) showed that contexts encouraging an enriched reading led to slowdowns. For example, consider one story from their between-subjects experiment in which the dependent measure was the reading time of phrases such as *the class notes or the summary*. For half of the participants, the preceding text indicated that the main character, John, was taking several courses and that he did not have much time to study and so he decided that, depending on the course, he would read *the class notes or the summary*. This interpretation was expected to yield a narrower, exclusive disjunctive interpretation (*class notes or summary, but not both*), which would be expected to be slower than a reading that encourages an inclusive interpretation. The context for the semantic, inclusive construction indicated that John's Geophysics textbook was difficult to understand and that to pass the course he should read *the class notes or the summary*. Indeed, the disjunctive phrase took significantly longer to process when the text encourages an exclusive disjunction interpretation. Second, Huang and Snedeker (2009b), through a visual search paradigm (using sentences such as "Click on the girl who has some of the balloons"), showed that looks to the intended figure (when the choice was between one girl who was shown to have *some but not all* of a set of balloons, while another girl had an entire set of balls) was not resolved at the word *some* (indicating that the enriching of *some* to *some but not all* does not occur upon hearing the existential quantifier) but at the disambiguating word *balloons* (or *balls*). Finally, de Neys and Schaeken (2007), through a dual-task paradigm, showed that prompting participants to apply extra cognitive effort in a secondary task blocks them from carrying out a pragmatic interpretation. Overall, indications from multiple online paradigms showed that enriched readings result when participants can and do apply cognitive effort. It is not the case that extra effort aligns with generating more semantic readings.

Occasionally, data are reported showing that narrowed readings can appear to be as fast as semantic readings (Grodner et al., 2010) or even faster than semantic readings (Bonnefon et al., 2009). But these events occur under particular experimental conditions. To focus on one of these skeptical studies, consider Bonnefon and colleagues' which had participants process a screen containing the utterance *Some people hated your poem* (in a scenario in which a friend is politely informing the participant, a poetry club mate, about the opinions from six other members). Included on the same screen was the test question: "Is it possible that all people hated the poem"? Affirmative responses to this *semantic compatibility* question (meaning that participants agree that *some* is understood as being compatible with *all*) took longer than negative ones, lending credence to their claim that—under these circumstances—the semantic reading of the utterance takes longer than the pragmatic one. However, the data are based on the reading time of an entire screen that includes *both* the scalar utterance and the test question. As Mazzarella et al. (submitted) argue, it is conceivable that all participants, in politeness scenarios, derive the speaker's scalar utterance with its enriched meaning (*Some but not all people hated your poem*) at which point a subsection of participants go on to reject that reading (upon receiving the test question). This occurs because these participants understand that the speaker is being polite and that in fact all the club members presumably hated the poem (see Sperber et al., 2010, on epistemic vigilance and the distinction between *comprehension* and *acceptance*).

Taken together, the findings from the scalar utterance literature indicate that pragmatically enriched meanings are not as common as an adult intuition would suggest nor are they synonymous with default meanings. This sort of empirical claim underlines the importance of doing experiments in the first place. Recently, the claims of non-ubiquity have been reinforced by findings from two corpus studies (Degen, 2015; Larrivée & Duffley, 2015) showing that enriched readings are associated with the meaning of *Some* in less half of the documented cases.

27.2.2 An anti-Gricean reaction

Despite such strong indications showing that the enrichment is extra-linguistic, effortful, non-default-like, and not ubiquitous, one emerging account has doubled down on the claim that enrichments, such as those linked to *some*, are easily available to a listener (Chierchia, 2004; Chierchia, Fox, & Spector, 2008). Chierchia and colleagues' general approach is to say that Levinsonian defaults are not satisfactory and that scalars are actually ambiguous (between the two readings) for the critical terms in its purview. They argue that scalar-like inferences arise *locally* (meaning that *some* is treated as *some but not all* as routinely as *some and perhaps all*) and not as part of an effort to interpret an entire sentence (as Grice argued). The thrust behind their account is to undermine the Gricean enterprise by essentially putting scalar inferences into grammar.

Chierchia and colleagues base their argument on cases in which scalar terms are embedded under another clause, as in sentence (3) next:

(3) George believes that some of his advisors are crooks (Chierchia, 2004).

If one were to adopt a standard pragmatic approach, according to which the listener assumes that the speaker could have said something stronger but did not, the enriched utterance would accord with (4):

(4) It is not the case that George believes that all of his advisors are crooks.

While this seems minimally satisfying, this is, according to Chierchia, too weak. Pragmatic intuition, he argues, agrees better with (5), which is a stronger inference:

(5) George believes that some but not all of his advisors are crooks.

Chierchia and colleagues assume that there is a covert *only* (an exhaustivity operator) that renders *some* as equivalent to *only some*. The upshot is that the operator provides a strengthened meaning, much like default accounts have argued, by negating certain alternative readings. Critically, advocates of a grammatical approach argue *against* the notion that the pragmatic enrichment occurs as part of an effort to interpret the speaker's utterance (i.e., they do not view this as a conceptual process in which a listener effortfully makes further contrasts to understand a speaker's intention). It is simply lurking in the grammar waiting to come out.

Geurts and Pouscoulous (2009), who argue that local scalar enrichments in embedded contexts arise only under exceptional conditions, were skeptical of the grammatical approach. They thereby opened a new round of investigations into scalar terms by asking participants to evaluate complex sentences (as true or false) while presenting participants with rather involved images, such as *Every square is attached to some of the circles*. (Figure 27.1)

According to Geurts and Pouscoulous, if indeed *some of the circles* is taken to locally mean *Every square is connected with some but not all of the circles*, participants would judge the statement false. They did not find a single participant who went with this interpretation. This was not the end of the debate for grammaticalists of course. Chemla and Spector (2011) as well as Potts and colleagues (2016) reacted to the Geurts and Pouscoulous paper by keeping the paradigm but by making it more user-friendly. For example, Potts et al. showed that one can get roughly 50% of participants to answer true to the sentence *Exactly one player hit some of his shots* when presented with the three players mentioned (one who has succeeded in making all his shots, one who has succeeded in none of them, and a third in half of them). Literally, there are two players who have hit at least some of their shots, so participants should say false (Fig. 27.2).

While data such as these are considered positive evidence in favor of a (covert) grammatical operator, there are at least three reasons to consider these data inconclusive. One is that tasks that feature cases in which "local" enrichments are facilitated also include several similarly complex sentences as controls (such as *None of the players hit all of the shots*) so it is not clear whether the mixed answers in this example reveal an on-the-spot interpretation, making it attributable to the grammar, or to the building up of more and more sophisticated

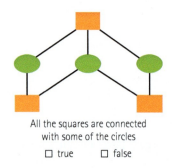

All the squares are connected
with some of the circles

☐ true   ☐ false

FIG. 27.1 The representation of one trial in which a localized reading of *Some* ought to produce a false response.

Adapted from Bart Geurts and Nausicaa Pouscoulous, Embedded implicatures?!?, *Semantics and Pragmatics*, 2 (4), p. 20, Figure 2, doi: 10.3765/sp.2.4 ©2009 Bart Geurts and Nausicaa Pouscoulous. This work is licensed under the Creative Commons Attribution License (CC BY 4.0). It is attributed to the authors Geurts and Pouscoulous.

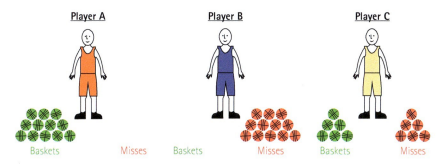

FIG. 27.2 Three basketball players (one who hits all of his shots, one who hits none, and a third who hits half of his shots). A localized reading of *some* in *Exactly one player hit some of his shots* justifies a True response.

Reproduced from Christopher Potts, Daniel Lassiter, Roger Levy, and Michael C. Frank, Embedded Implicatures as Pragmatic Inferences under Compositional Lexical Uncertainty, *Journal of Semantics*, 33 (4), pp. 755–802, Figure 3, doi. org/10.1093/jos/ffv012, Copyright © 2015, Oxford University Press.

strategies that arise from seeing multiple similar trials. A second reason to doubt the findings from the grammatical account is that it does not generalize. Whereas Potts et al.'s *Exactly one* sentence appears to generate a "local implicature" about half the time, there is no evidence of consistent local implicature production in other embedded cases (see von Tiel et al., in press). For example, when shown the sentence *Every player hit some of his shots* (along with two players who were shown to have always succeeded and a third who succeeded half the time), participants overwhelmingly answer with *true* to these types of scenarios, which indicates that they do not routinely make local interpretations (a local interpretation for *some* here should have prompted a false response). Finally, the very same studies that include grammatical approaches also assume, without procuring new data, that scalar implicatures are likely in unembedded cases (Potts et al., 2016, p. 759). When advocates of a new position look past years of carefully collected data, it is difficult to evaluate their newer claims favorably.

While experimental pragmatics evolved to replace a reliance on armchair intuition with experimental data, the apparent ease with which some experts intuit pragmatic enrichments continues to generate accounts in which scalar inferences are practically automatic or even grammatical. Nevertheless, the data show—contrary to intuition—that these pragmatic enrichments are not automatic and that, when they arise, they are typically associated with costs. Given the ubiquity of such online effects, it is difficult to view *only some* interpretations to the word *some* as just the other side of a fair coin.

27.3 Reference: How readily does a listener consider the speaker's view?

Reference resolution is probably one of the most basic of pragmatic acts. Let me quickly provide three examples. (1) When a person points, the observer needs to—not only zero in on one of an unbounded number of possible targets but needs to—understand precisely what is the pointer's purpose. (2) When referring to an object (e.g., as *the small cup*), the speaker is potentially providing a listener with a means to distinguish that object from other similar ones (i.e., *non-small cups*). (3) When a speaker labels an atypical object as the *upside-down funnel*, it is a way for a listener to have common vocabulary with his listener. All of these situations—pointing, adjectival modifications, and the mutual naming of novel objects—fall within the purview of experimental pragmatics, because listeners need to go beyond the linguistically encoded meaning of a referential utterance in order to identify the speaker's intended object.

One central issue in this area concerns the readiness with which a listener considers the speaker's perspective. Like the work on scalars, research focuses on a debate that began with two diametrically opposite views. On one side are those who claim that we automatically and comprehensively consider our interlocutor's perspective. On the other side are those who claim that we have a minimal capacity to access the speaker's perspective and that identifying the speaker's intent is effortful. *Unlike* the work in the scalar literature—where the early experimental findings pointed to a minimal reading before holding off persistent claims that enrichments are automatic—the first studies on reference claimed that perspective-taking was automatic. Only later did challenges appear from those who argued that we are relatively egocentric and that we effortfully consider our interlocutor's perspective. In what follows, I will present the claims and data from the automatic position first and follow this up with the response from those who support the minimal position. I will then present a paradigm that has served as a forum of sorts for the two sides and describe the conclusions it and similar paradigms have generated (see Chapter 23 in this volume, "Perspective-taking during conversation").

27.3.1 Naming objects

Imagine two interlocutors—let's call them a Director and Matcher—who are exchanging descriptions and information to organize their (identical) sets of 12 pictures of basic objects (such as dog, toy, car, and so on) while separated by a short wall. As expected, interlocutors refer to these objects with their common names. However, when an altered second set of 12 pictures is introduced which now includes four objects of the same category (e.g., four cars), the interlocutors are likely to use more specific references (e.g., *sports car* instead of *car*), indicating that the specificity of reference is modified by context. This much is Gricean for the interlocutors have found references that are at levels of informativeness that context calls for. Interestingly, when the exchange returns to the first phase—that is, the one containing 12 different basic objects—participants continue to use the more specific reference they established in the second round (they keep *sports car* instead of returning to *car*). This demonstrates that once a convention is realized, it remains for the duration of the exchange. For Brennan and Clark (1996), this indicates that a *conceptual pact* is "partner-specific" among interlocutors and that it takes precedence over being just informative enough on each occasion. These are important findings showing that shared labeling in a dialogue takes precedence over the particular informational value that a new word in a situation can offer at any instant.

The joint activity between interlocutors is crucial and determinative for labeling and much more so than "solitary choices on the part of the director" (Brennan & Clark, 1996,

p. 1491). *Common ground*, which was first coined by Stalnaker (1970), is a technical term that refers to a set of shared assumptions or shared knowledge that arises through joint actions including conversation (Clark, 1996). For example, when two professional philosophers meet, they share quite a bit already—say, training and technical language—and they can go on to share much more in conversation. Given that memory representations of the speaker's epistemic states are considered to be among the sources of information retained by the listener (Brennan & Hanna, 2009), speaker-specificity becomes an important feature of reference from the earliest moments of interpretation (Brown-Schmidt, 2009a, 2009b). In other words, pragmatic expectations are linked to specific partners in a conversation and that interpretation involves some ready representation of the partner's epistemic states (Brennan & Hanna, 2009; Brown-Schmidt, 2009a, 2009b; E. Clark, 1990; Metzing & Brennan, 2003).

Once a mutually shared term is coined for an object (*entrained* to use technical language) and enters common ground, it *preempts* the expectation that the speaker will come up with another name for it. The *strong common ground view* thus predicts speaker-specific effects. For example, when a single speaker suddenly makes a change to an agreed-upon name, this ought to be surprising. However, when a new (presumably naïve) speaker enters the conversation and comes up with a new name, one should not find evidence of surprise.

27.3.2 The egocentric approach

Being doubtful of the strong common ground view, Boaz Keysar and colleagues (2000) proposed that listeners are egocentric and not readily available to consider their interlocutor's perspective. To make their point, they introduced a seminal paradigm to test between two main possibilities. Imagine a participant (an Addressee responding to requests) who views several objects distributed among the slots of a 4 × 4 grid. Now imagine the speaker (the Director) of this exchange who can only see objects in 12 of the slots (see Fig. 27.3). That is

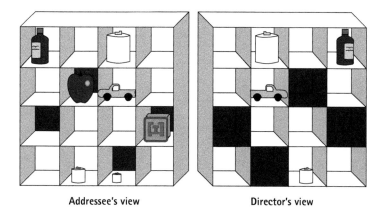

FIG. 27.3 A single 4 × 4 grid containing seven items as viewed by an addressee from one side and by a speaker (the Director) on the other. Four of the slots are screened off from the Director's perspective.

Reproduced from Boaz Keysar, Dale J. Barr, Jennifer A. Balin, and Jason S. Brauner, Taking Perspective in Conversation: The Role of Mutual Knowledge in Comprehension, *Human Brain Mapping*, 11 (1), pp. 32–8, doi: 10.1111/1467-9280.00211, Copyright © 2000, © SAGE Publications. Reprinted by permission of SAGE Publications, Inc.

because the other four slots are obscured by a little curtain, or makeshift wall, that stands between the cubicle and the speaker. This set up allows the Addressee to see all of the objects while also allowing him to infer what the Director can and cannot see (see Fig. 27.3). In the example, there are three differently sized candles from the Addressee's point of view (on the left) but only two (the biggest and second-biggest) from the Director's (on the right). When the Director requests an action on "the small candle" (e.g., "move the small candle . . . ") will the addressee turn her attention to the *Director's* intended "small candle" or to the smallest visible one that is obscured from the Director's point of view?

Keysar et al.'s eye-tracking data indicate that listeners typically focus on the non-intended item (one that matches the speaker's description even though it is out of the speaker's view) before fixating on the intended target. That is, their data show that listeners cannot help but look at the smallest of the three initially. This has given credence to the claim that listeners are egocentric as opposed to being permanently aware of the speaker's perspective. This approach has repercussions for other related referential phenomena. One of them concerns the way conversational partners arrive at common names for (odd, hard-to-name) objects.

27.3.3 An ongoing debate and a meta-analysis

In defending the strong common ground view, Metzing and Brennan (2003) adopted the eye-tracking paradigm (with a Director and a Matcher and a 5 × 5 grid of open cubbyholes). By measuring the duration of time between the onset of a referring expression and first-looks to the target (as well as touches to the target), experimenters could determine how fast a listener makes referential commitments when the same ("original") Director comes up with a new name for a previously named object as opposed to when a new Director does so. In other words, there are four conditions: in the *Same Director-Maintain* condition, reference would be made to the object in the same voice and with the same name throughout; in the *Same Director-Break* condition, a single speaker would introduce a new name for a previously named object; in the *Different Director-Maintain* and the *Different Director-Break* conditions the third trial would be presented by a different voice and would maintain or break with the prior uses. As they predicted, Metzing and Brennan reported slowdowns only when the same Director came up with a new name for a previously named object.

While defending the egocentric view, Barr and Keysar (2002) argued that changing the given name of an object is difficult for listeners generally, irrespective of who appears to make the change. To make their point, they re-introduced the well-known paradigm from Brennan and Clark in which, for example, a car is described as such (as a basic category *car*) early in the task (when it was the only vehicle) and is later described with a subcategory name (as *sports car*), when it was necessary to distinguish that object from a second one. When the experimenters came to the last round, they found that listeners were delayed in finding the target when they heard the basic-level category name *car* once again (even if it had been the only car in the context), no matter who the speaker was (the original speaker or a new speaker). So, while Barr and Keysar found support for the general effect that shows that listeners prefer the entrained name, *recovery-from-preemption* is not linked to a specific speaker.

To re-evaluate Metzing and Brennan's (2003) claims, Kronmüller and Barr (2007) carefully tracked the time course of participants' emerging preference for a target item as they followed instructions from two recorded speakers, one having a male voice and the other female (and participants were told that the two had nothing to do with one another). The task would use eight pictures of unusual objects as participants were required to move them around a computer-generated grid. Participants would hear the same object referred to three times but under the four conditions described here: *Same Speaker-Maintain, Same Speaker-Break, Different Speaker-Maintain*, and *Different Speaker-Break*. Critically, Kronmüller and Barr showed that there were main effects for Maintaining versus Breaking the precedent (regardless of speaker). What remained crucial to listeners was the choice of words. While there was the expected speaker-specific interaction (between the Same Speaker-Break and Different Speaker-Break condition), it was a late-occurring phenomenon (immediate reactions to the two Break conditions were similar and at roughly one and a half seconds, Addressees showed a prolonged reaction to the Same Speaker-Break utterance). In other words, hearing the same voice use a new expression did lead to distinctive results (slowdowns in choosing the intended object), but participants' eye-movements indicated that the delay can be isolated to reactions that occurred late in the trial and not as soon as the speaker began speaking (for more recent work, see Kronmüller et al., 2017).

Given that 10 studies using a similar visual-world paradigm had been carried out, Kronmüller and Barr (2015) were inspired to carry out a meta-analysis. Despite some discrepancies among individual studies, the meta-analysis largely echoes what these authors reported in their (2007) paper. As they put it, the meta-analysis yields three principal effects: (1) when object names are maintained, there is an ("early and fleeting") advantage to locate objects when they come from the same speaker; (2) when a previously named object is given a new label, there is an advantage for locating objects indicated by a different speaker; and (3) there is a "strong and monotonically increasing main effect of precedent," meaning that what is primary is that participants in general expect labels to remain unchanged. While it appears that addressees internally adopt labels from their conversation partners, the identity of that interlocutor does not remain an indelible part of that label. Essentially, object names, once christened, are privately held.

27.4 IRONY

Irony is arguably the most prototypical pragmatic form to investigate because ironic utterances most clearly exhibit how sentence meaning has its limitations for understanding the speaker's intended meaning. When a speaker makes an ironic statement, its literal meaning typically clashes in some way with reality while a mocking attitude emerges. For example, when one opera singer turns to her colleague and says, "Tonight, we gave a superb performance" after the two had sung horribly, it implies, or rather recognizes the fact that, the speaker thinks that they did not sing well at all. Irony has also been subject to Gricean-based explanation, which is typically described as resulting from the speaker flouting the maxim of quality (to tell the truth) and then coming up with implicatures in order to maintain the Cooperative Principle.

This Gricean-inspired account, reminiscent of what we saw with generalized conversational implicatures in (1), has often been referred to in this literature as the Standard Pragmatic Model (or SPM). At its simplest, the SPM is a three-step process that involves

(1) the computation of an utterance's semantic/literal meaning; (2) the recognition of a violation of a maxim; and (3) the computation of an intended meaning through implicature. As Noveck and Spotorno (2013) argued, the SPM did not come from Grice himself but represents an algorithmic application of Grice's (computational) account so it should be taken with a grain of salt (or as a strawman). In any case, Grice's model would assert that a listener computes the speaker's intended meaning after recognizing that the maxim of quality has been violated.

Grice's theory has generated two lines of discussion with respect to irony. One of these questions the SPM. That is, if the SPM is correct, it follows that generating the intended meaning would be time consuming compared, say, to understanding the utterance's literal meaning; after all, the ironic meaning, unlike the literal one, calls on the listener to go through several steps before getting at the intended meaning. To some, this is not a credible claim. Ray Gibbs in particular has strenuously argued that listeners need not go through a set of steps to get indirectly at irony; rather, listeners access ironic interpretations directly. This is why his approach is known as the *Direct Access* view and why it has motivated a set of studies on irony. For example, Gibbs (1994) measured reading times as participants read vignettes (little stories) in which irony was expressed through rather conventional sarcastic remarks (e.g., "You are a fine friend" after that friend disappointed the speaker). The paradigm also included vignettes that used the same phrases to express a literal meaning (as part of a between subject paradigm). Gibbs reported that the reading times of ironic and literal versions of these expressions were comparable (though both were slower than other controls). This ushered in a series of studies that either defended the notion that irony was effortful (Filik & Moxey, 2010; Schwoebel et al., 2000) or that showed that irony was not effortful (e.g., Ivanko & Pexman, 2003).

This debate about effortful processing eventually gave rise to another proposal, Rachel Giora's (1997) *Graded Salience* hypothesis. Giora argues that ironies (and other figurative utterances) generate both literal and figurative meanings, but that the non-literal meaning can essentially compete for most salient status with the literal one. The extent to which a figurative meaning emerges varies as a function of different features, such as familiarity, conventionality, frequency, and prototypicality, of a critical word in the utterance. Much of the original work from the Graded Salience view focuses on irony and to a lesser extent on idioms (Filik & Moxey, 2010; Giora, 1997; Giora & Fein, 1999; Giora, Fein, & Schwartz, 1998).

To give one example with respect to irony, Giora et al. (1998) presented participants with a lexical decision task (*is this a word?*) with the probe word being related either to the literal or the ironic reading of an utterance. Consider the sentence in (6), which could be expressed literally or ironically (to appreciate the ironic reading, imagine the utterance being addressed to a character who is running behind schedule).

(6) "You are just in time."

Two probe words, *punctual* and *late*, were prepared for this trial and presented after (6), with the former compatible with the literal reading and the latter with an ironic reading. With respect to early reactions (after delays of 150 ms and 1,000 ms), Giora et al. showed that probe words linked to the literal interpretation were evaluated significantly faster than those related to the ironic interpretation. After 2,000 msec, however, these differences disappeared, suggesting that the ironic interpretation becomes more salient with time.

As this brief review of the Direct Access and Graded Salience accounts shows, the two provide diametrically opposing predictions. Gibbs, by dismissing the importance of the linguistically encoded meanings, predicts that ironic readings prompt responses that are similar to literal readings. Graded Salience emphasizes that—at least at a lexical level—addressees need to consider the linguistically encoded meaning of a critical word in a figurative utterance. Given that both accounts provide experimental support, it leaves the literature at an impasse.

27.4.1 Reintroducing intention into the irony debate

The second line of discussion considers attitude ascription central to irony understanding. Grice himself had indicated that at least part of understanding irony depends on a "hostile or derogatory judgment or a feeling such as indignation or contempt" (Grice, 1989, p. 53). It would make sense then to assume that ascribing an attitude in itself might figure into the *processing* of irony comprehension. Grice was not alone in underlining the role of attitude in irony comprehension.

Relevance theorists (Sperber & Wilson, 1986/1995) fully weave attitude ascription into the processing of irony. As Wilson writes (2009, page 197), "the point of irony is not to commit the speaker to the truth of the proposition expressed but, on the contrary, to express a certain type of derisory or dissociative attitude to a thought with a similar content." Consider Wilson and Sperber's example about a woman named Mary who says, after a difficult meeting, "That went well." As they wrote, the speaker is expressing an attitude *about* the meeting:

> Mary might use ["That went well"] to communicate that it was ridiculous of her to think that the meeting would go well, stupid of her friends to assure her that it would go well, naïve of her to believe their assurances, and so on. Mary *echoes* a thought or utterance with a similar content to the one expressed in her utterance, in order to express a critical or mocking attitude to it.

This *echoic mention* account also presented one of the seminal cognitive studies on irony. Jorgensen, Miller, & Sperber (1984) presented six stories that each included a remark at the end (e.g., "Tedious, wasn't it"). They showed that the perceived irony of the remark in the experimental stories nearly tripled as a function of the presence of an expectation made explicit earlier in the story. (For example, for the story ending with the aforementioned remark, the irony-facilitative condition had indicated, earlier on, that the speaker and his addressee had expected a lecture to be boring and it turned out to be brilliant.)

The echoic mention account was also not the last proposal to give pride of place to attitude. Clark and Gerrig (1984), in response, proposed that the speaker of an ironical utterance is only *pretending* to perform a speech act in order to convey a mocking, skeptical, or contemptuous attitude. While this proposal generated some heated discussions between the two camps, it has not as yet produced a series of comparative studies. Point is that, from early on in the cognitive literature, there had been proposals, debates, and empirical studies on irony that focus on the attitude ascription, but they ended up being largely overlooked. While promising, both the echoic mention and pretense accounts got largely eclipsed in, and largely forgotten by, the literature by concerns about the role of the literal meaning raised by Gibbs and Giora.

In order to correct for the literature's lasting blindness and to potentially get beyond the "is irony processing effortful?" impasse, Nicola Spotorno and I (along with our colleagues) carried out a series of studies that aimed to substantiate the notion that ascribing attitudes to a speaker is integral to irony processing. One advantage of the long pause (between the time that the attitude-rich accounts first came out in the 1980s and our own recent efforts) is that we were in a position to take advantage of techniques, such as neural imaging, that did not exist back then. That is, by the end of 2010 or so the neuroscience literature had—through the development of dozens of clever tasks—localized brain regions associated with understanding other minds. These regions are the right and left temporal-parietal junction (rTPJ and lTPJ), the medial prefrontal cortex (MPFC), and the precuneus (PC) (see Frith & Frith, 2006; Saxe & Kanwisher, 2003; for meta-analyses, see van Overwalle, 2009, and van Overwalle & Baetens, 2009). We reasoned that if irony relied on capturing the attitude of one's interlocutor, it should follow that interpreting irony should trigger mindreading, or what neuroscience calls *mentalizing*, activity (Spotorno et al., 2012). We thus prepared stories, modeled on Gibbs (1994), that included a line that could be interpreted as either ironic or literal (as a function of slight changes in context). For example, in our flagship story participants read a seven-line long vignette about two opera singers who sang horribly (in its ironic version) or beautifully (in its literal version); this led to a target sentence (mentioned earlier) in which one singer says to the other, "Tonight we gave a superb performance." As we predicted, *Ironic* target sentences, when compared to their *Literal* controls, consistently elicited significant differences and precisely in those neural regions listed above. Moreover, through psycho-physiological analyses, the data showed that there was a functional *connectivity* between mindreading and language networks, namely the ventral part of the medial prefrontal cortex (vMPFC) and the left inferior frontal gyrus (IFG), that increases when participants read a target sentence in the *Ironic* condition as opposed to a *Literal* one[3].

Two follow up studies aimed to better capture how mindreading interacts with processing. In one electroencephalography (EEG) study, our group (Spotorno et al., 2013) used the same paradigm, except that the target sentence was presented word by word (we collected measures from the last word). This work was designed to investigate event-related potentials (namely the P600, which is a recurring index of pragmatic phenomena) and to apply a time frequency analysis (TFA), which can capture more subtle distinctions. As expected, we found an increase in magnitude of the P600, during the *Ironic* condition when compared to the *Literal* one. We also observed an increase of power in the gamma band for the *Ironic*>*Literal* contrast. The TFA result is an intriguing finding because it takes place in the 280–400 ms time window. This indicates that integration operations during irony processing start well before the latency associated with the P600 and that the integration between the linguistic code and the contextual information is *not* obligatorily a late Gricean step in the comprehension of an utterance.

The other follow-up study (Spotorno & Noveck, 2014) used more traditional cognitive techniques to better understand how one can facilitate or delay the understanding of an ironic utterance over the course of an experimental session. For example, we showed that the presence of filler stories called *decoys* (vignettes that invited an ironic remark through

---

[3] Notably, other neuroimaging studies have revealed links between Theory-of-Mind areas and utterance comprehension, especially with respect to indirect requests (van Ackeren et al., 2012, 2016) and indirect replies (Bašnáková et al., 2013, 2015).

a negative event but that ultimately did not present one) prompt readers to take longer to read ironic utterances than their literal controls *throughout* the experimental session. In contrast, when we removed decoys, we again found a significant irony-related slowdown but only during the first half of the experiment. By the time participants got to the second half, the reading times of ironic utterances were comparable to the literal controls. We also found individual differences—as measured by fine differences drawn from the *social skill* score of Baron-Cohen et al.'s (2001) autism quotient (AQ)—that show that socially inclined participants are more likely to anticipate ironic utterances over the course of the task than socially disinclined participants. While there is no rule that says ironic utterances are generally harder or more effortful to process (intervening factors can make ironic utterances easier to process), it is fair to say that unexpected uses of irony (especially its early uses in an experiment) do consistently prompt slowdowns.

27.5 General conclusions

The two words *experimental pragmatics* refer to two largely independent academic traditions that, when brought together, refer to a singular field of study. *Pragmatics* is a subfield of linguistics concerned with determining the intended meaning of an utterance. The word *experimental* refers to the rigorous methodology of experimental psychology whose general aim is to provide data—through controlled studies—that can, in the present case, help us better understand pragmatic phenomena as well as to distinguish between pragmatic theories. Why do we need to insist on doing experiments? The short answer is that the other option—to inspect our own intuitions in order to draw interpretations—is highly suspect. The longer answer is provided in this chapter. Basically, there are many pragmatic (Grice-inspired) theories to consider and experiments serve as a forum to determine which does a better job. But, one can go even further.

Like many scientific projects, *experimental pragmatics* has global goals (e.g., understanding communication, determining the role of language in communication, and describing the semantic/pragmatic border), flagship topics (scalar implicatures), methodological considerations (e.g., discussions about how best to answer a theoretical question), and—importantly—a very wide range of phenomena (see footnote 2). This entry has summarized work on three topics in *experimental pragmatics*—scalar implicature, reference, and irony. As these brief summaries show, research from the three topics has one overlapping interest: To determine the extent to which intention-reading is involved in making pragmatic inferences.

Work on scalar enrichments began by asking whether it is an automatic process (that is practically linguistic) or indeed determined by a listener's effort to access a speaker's intention under particular contexts. The original claim that scalars are occasional enrichments that depend on specific situations has not been undermined despite multiple efforts to view them as default inferences or as part of an ambiguous linguistic meaning. With regard to reference, researchers have taken the opposite tack. The original claim was that perspective-taking was automatic, but that has been hard to document. It appears that gaining an interlocutor's perspective is an effortful step. When it comes to irony, where mindreading appears to be absolutely critical (both theoretically and intuitively), the evidence shows that intention-reading is indeed an effortful step, as many have assumed. Taken together, the three topics reveal that Grice's distinction between sentence meaning and speaker meaning is useful for better understanding how a listener accesses the speaker's intended meaning. Getting at the speaker's intention is not a trivial step. Using the linguistically encoded meaning to get at the speaker's intention is bound to come with gaps that can be bridged with some form of inference making.

References

Apple, S. (2016, May 12). An old idea, revived: Starve cancer to death. *The New York Times Magazine*, p. MM64.

Baron-Cohen, S., Wheelwright, S., Skinner, R., Martin, J., & Clubley, E. (2001). The autism-spectrum quotient (AQ): Evidence from asperger syndrome/high-functioning autism, males and females, scientists and mathematicians. *Journal of Autism and Developmental Disorders*, 31(1), 5–17.

Barr, D. J., & Keysar, B. (2002). Anchoring comprehension in linguistic precedents. *Journal of Memory and Language*, 46, 391–418.

Bašnáková, J., van Berkum, J., Weber, K., & Hagoort, P. (2015). A job interview in the MRI scanner: How does indirectness affect addressees and overhearers? *Neuropsychologia*, 76, 79–91.

Bašnáková, J., Weber, K., Petersson, K. M., van Berkum, J., & Hagoort, P. (2013). Beyond the language given: the neural correlates of inferring speaker meaning. *Cerebral Cortex*, 24(10), 2572–8.

Bonnefon, J. F., Feeney, A., & Villejoubert, G. (2009). When some is actually all: Scalar inferences in face-threatening contexts. *Cognition*, 112(2), 249–58.

Bott, L., & Noveck, I. A. (2004). Some utterances are underinformative: The onset and time course of scalar inferences. *Journal of Memory and Language*, 51, 437–57.

Breheny, R., Katsos, N., & Williams, J. (2006). Are generalised scalar implicatures generated by default? An on-line investigation into the role of context in generating pragmatic inferences. *Cognition*, 100 (3), 434–63.

Brennan, S. E., & Clark, H. H. (1996). Conceptual pacts and lexical choice in conversation. *Journal of Experimental Psychology: Learning, Memory, and Cognition*, 22, 1482–93.

Brennan, S. E., & Hanna, J. E. (2009). Partner-specific adaptation in dialog. *Topics in Cognitive Science*, 1(2), 274–91.

Brown-Schmidt, S. (2009a). Partner-specific interpretation of maintained referential precedents during interactive dialog. *Journal of Memory and Language*, 61, 171–90.

Brown-Schmidt, S. (2009b). The role of executive function in perspective taking during online language comprehension. *Psychonomic Bulletin & Review*, 16, 893–900.

Carston, R. (2008). *Thoughts and Utterances: The Pragmatics of Explicit Communication*. John Wiley & Sons, London.

Chemla, E., & Spector, B. (2011). Experimental evidence for embedded scalar implicatures. *Journal of Semantics*, 28(3), 359–400.

Chevallier, C., Noveck, I., Happé, F., & Wilson, D. (2009). From acoustics to grammar: Perceiving and interpreting grammatical prosody in adolescents with Asperger Syndrome. *Research in Autism Spectrum Disorders*, 3(2), 502–16.

Chevallier, C., Wilson, D., Happé, F., & Noveck, I. (2010). Scalar inferences in autism spectrum disorders. *Journal of Autism and Developmental Disorders, 40*(9), 1104–17.

Chierchia, G. (2004). Scalar implicatures, polarity phenomena, and the syntax/pragmatics interface. In: Belletti, A. (Ed.), *Structures and Beyond* (pp. 39–103). Oxford University Press, Oxford.

Chierchia, G., Fox, D., & Spector, B. (2008). The grammatical view of scalar implicatures and the relationship between semantics and pragmatics [Unpublished manuscript].

Clark, E. V. (1990). Speaker perspective in language acquisition. *Linguistics, 28*(6), 1201–20.

Clark, H. (1996). *Using Language*. Cambridge University Press, Cambridge.

Clark, H. H., & Gerrig, R. J. (1984). On the pretense theory of irony. *Journal of Experimental Psychology. General, 113*(1), 121–6.

Degen, J. (2015). Investigating the distribution of some (but not all) implicatures using corpora and web-based methods. *Semantics and Pragmatics, 8*(11), 1–55.

de Neys, W., & Schaeken, W. (2007). When people are more logical under cognitive load: Dual task impact on scalar implicature. *Experimental Psychology, 54*(2), 128–33.

Filik, R., & Moxey, L. (2010). The on-line processing of written irony. *Cognition, 116*(3), 421–36.

Frisson, S., & Pickering, M. J. (1999). The processing of metonymy: evidence from eye movements. *Journal of Experimental Psychology: Learning, Memory, and Cognition, 25*(6), 1366.

Frith, C. D., & Frith, U. (2006). The neural basis of mentalizing minireview. *NeuroImage*, 531–4.

Geurts, B., & Pouscoulous, N. (2009). Embedded implicatures?!?. *Semantics and Pragmatics, 2*, 4–1.

Gibbs, R. W. (1994). *The Poetics of Mind: Figurative Thought, Language, and Understanding*. Cambridge University Press, Cambridge.

Giora, R. (1997). Understanding figurative and literal language: The graded salience hypothesis. *Cognitive Linguistics, 8*(3), 183–206.

Giora, R., & Fein, O. (1999). Irony: Context and salience. *Metaphor and Symbol, 14*(4), 241–57.

Giora, R., Fein, O., & Schwartz, T. (1998). Irony: grade salience and indirect negation. *Metaphor and Symbol, 13*(2), 83–101.

Grandy, R. E., & Warner, R., "Paul Grice." In: Zalta, E. N. (Ed.), *The Stanford Encyclopedia of Philosophy*, Spring 2014 Edition. Available at: http://plato.stanford.edu/archives/spr2014/entries/grice/

Grice, P. H. (1989). *Studies in the Way of Words*. Harvard University Press, Cambridge, MA.

Grodner, D. J., Klein, N. M., Carbary, K. M., & Tanenhaus, M. K. (2010). "Some," and possibly all, scalar inferences are not delayed: Evidence for immediate pragmatic enrichment. *Cognition, 116*(1), 42–55.

Guasti, M. T., Chierchia, G., Crain, S., Foppolo, F., Gualmini, A., & Meroni, L. (2005). Why children and adults sometimes (but not always) compute implicatures. *Language and Cognitive Processes 20*, 667–96.

Horn, L. (1972). On the semantic properties of logical operators in English. [UCLA dissertation, distributed by Indiana University Linguistics Club, 1976].

Horn, L. (1984). Toward a new taxonomy for pragmatic inference. In: Schiffrin, D. (Ed.), *Meaning, Form and Use in Context: Linguistic Applications, Proceedings of GURT '84* (pp. 11–42). Georgetown University Press, Washington, DC.

Horn, L. R. (1989). *A Natural History of Negation*. Chicago University Press, Chicago, IL.

Horn, L. (1992). The said and the unsaid. In: Barker, C., & Dowty, D. P. (Eds.), *SALT 2: Proceedings of the Second Conference on Semantic and Linguistic Theory* (Ohio State Working Papers in Linguistics 40; pp. 163–92). Ohio State University, Columbus, OH.

Huang, Y. T., & Snedeker, J. (2009a). Semantic meaning and pragmatic interpretation in 5-year-olds: evidence from real-time spoken language comprehension. *Developmental Psychology*, 45(6), 1723.

Huang, Y., & Snedeker, J. (2009b). Semantic meaning and pragmatic interpretation in five-year-olds: Evidence from real time spoken language comprehension. *Developmental Psychology*, 45, 1723–39.

Ivanko, S. L., & Pexman, P. M. (2003). Context incongruity and irony processing. *Discourse Processes*, 35(3), 241–79.

Jorgensen, J., Miller, G., & Sperber, D. (1984). Test of the mention theory of irony. *Journal of Experimental Psychology. General*, 113(1), 112–20.

Katsos, N., & Bishop, D. V. (2011). Pragmatic tolerance: Implications for the acquisition of informativeness and implicature. *Cognition*, 120(1), 67–81.

Katsos, N., Cummins, C., Ezeizabarrena, M.-J., Gavarró, A., Kuvac Kraljevic, J., Hrzica, G., Grohmann, K., ... & Noveck, I. (2016). Cross-linguistic constraints in the order of acquisition of quantifiers. *Proceedings National Academy of Sciences*, 113(33), 9244–9.

Keysar, B., Barr, D. J., Balin, J. A., & Brauner, J. S. (2000). Taking perspective in conversation: The role of mutual knowledge in comprehension. *Psychological Science*, 11, 32–8.

Kronmüller, E., & Barr, D. J. (2007). Perspective-free pragmatics: Broken precedents and the recovery-from-preemption hypothesis. *Journal of Memory and Language*, 56(3), 436–55.

Kronmüller, E., & Barr, D. J. (2015). Referential precedents in spoken language comprehension: A review and meta-analysis. *Journal of Memory and Language*, 83, 1–19.

Kronmüller, E., Noveck, I., Rivera, N., Jaume-Guazzini, F., & Barr, D. (2017). The positive side of a negative reference: The delay between linguistic processing and common ground. *Royal Society Open Science*, 4(2), 160827.

Larrivée, P., & Duffley, P. (2015). The emergence of implicit meaning: Scalar implicatures with some. *International Journal of Corpus Linguistics*, 19(4), 530–47.

Levinson, S. (1983). *Pragmatics*. Cambridge University Press, Cambridge.

Levinson, S. (2000). *Presumptive Meanings*. MIT Press, Cambridge, MA.

Mazzarella, D., Trouche, E., Mercier, H., & Noveck, I. (submitted). Believing what you're told: Politeness and scalar inferences.

Metzing, C., & Brennan, S. E. (2003). When conceptual pacts are broken: Partner-specific effects on the comprehension of referring expressions. *Journal of Memory and Language*, 49, 201–13.

Nieuwland, M. S., & Kuperberg, G. R. (2008). When the truth is not too hard to handle: An event-related potential study on the pragmatics of negation. *Psychological Science*, 19(12), 1213–18.

Noveck, I. A. (2001). When children are more logical than adults. *Cognition*, 86, 253–82.

Noveck, I. A. (2018). *Experimental Pragmatics: The Making of a Cognitive Science*. Cambridge University Press, Cambridge.

Noveck, I., Bonnefond, M., & van der Henst, J. B. (2011). Squib: A deflationary account of invited inferences. *Belgian Journal of Linguistics*, 25(1), 195–208.

Noveck, I. A., & Posada, A. (2003). Characterizing the time course of an implicature: An evoked potentials study. *Brain and Language*, 85, 203–10.

Noveck, I. A., & Sperber, D. (2007). The why and how of experimental pragmatics: the case of "scalar inferences." In: Burton-Roberts, N. (Ed.), *Pragmatics* (pp. 184–212). Palgrave Macmillan, Basingstoke.

Noveck, I. A., & Spotorno, N. (2013). Narrowing. *Brevity*, 280–96.

Papafragou, A., & Musolino, J. (2003). Scalar implicatures: Experiments at the semantics/pragmatics interface. *Cognition, 86*, 253–82.

Potts, C., Lassiter, D., Levy, R., & Frank, M. C. (2016). Embedded implicatures as pragmatic inferences under compositional lexical uncertainty. *Journal of Semantics, 33*(4), 755–802.

Pouscoulous, N., Noveck, I. A., Politzer, G., & Bastide, A. (2007). A developmental investigation of processing costs in implicature production. *Language Acquisition, 14*, 347–76.

Rubio-Fernández, P. (2007). Suppression in metaphor interpretation: Differences between meaning selection and meaning construction. *Journal of Semantics, 24*(4), 345–71.

Saxe, R., & Kanwisher, N. (2003). People thinking about thinking people: the role of the temporo-parietal junction in "theory of mind." *NeuroImage, 19*(4), 1835–42.

Schumacher, P. B. (2014). Content and context in incremental processing: "The ham sandwich" revisited. *Philosophical Studies, 168*(1), 151–65.

Schwarz, F. (2007). Processing presupposed content. *Journal of Semantics, 24*(4), 373–416.

Schwoebel, J., Dews, S., Winner, E., & Srinivas, K. (2000). Obligatory processing of the literal meaning of ironic utterances: further evidence. *Metaphor and Symbol, 15*(1 & 2), 47–61.

Sperber, D., Clément, F., Heintz, C., Mascaro, O., Mercier, H., Origgi, G., & Wilson, D. (2010). Epistemic vigilance. *Mind & Language, 24*(4), 359–93.

Sperber, D., & Wilson, D. (1986/1995). *Relevance: Communication and Cognition*. Blackwell, Oxford.

Spotorno, N., Cheylus, A., van der Henst, J.-B., & Noveck, I. A. (2013). What's behind a P600? Integration operations during irony processing. *PLoS One, 8*(6), e66839.

Spotorno, N., Koun, E., Prado, J., van der Henst, J.-B., & Noveck, I. A. (2012). Neural evidence that utterance-processing entails mentalizing: The case of irony. *NeuroImage, 63*(1), 25–39.

Spotorno, N., & Noveck, I. A. (2014). When is irony effortful? *Journal of Experimental Psychology: General, 143*(4), 1649.

Stalnaker, R. (1970). Pragmatics. *Synthese, 22* (1–2), 272–89.

van Ackeren, M., Casasanto, D., Hagoort, P., Bekkering, H., & Rueschemeyer, S.-A. (2012). Pragmatics in action: Indirect requests engage theory of mind areas and the cortical motor network. *Journal of Cognitive Neuroscience, 24*(11), 2237–47.

van Ackeren, M. J., Smaragdi, A., Rueschemeyer, S.-A. (2016). Neuronal interactions between mentalizing and action systems during indirect request processing. *Social, Cognitive and Affective Neuroscience, 11*(9), 1402–10.

van Overwalle, F. (2009). Social cognition and the brain: A meta-analysis. *Human Brain Mapping, 30*(3), 829–58.

van Overwalle, F., & Baetens, K. (2009). Understanding others' actions and goals by mirror and mentalizing systems: A meta-analysis. *NeuroImage, 48*(3), 564–84.

von Tiel, B., Noveck, I. A., & Khissine, M. (in press). Reasoning with "some." *Journal of Semantics*.

Weiland, H., Bambini, V., & Schumacher, P. B. (2014). The role of literal meaning in figurative language comprehension: Evidence from masked priming ERP. *Frontiers in Human Neuroscience, 8*, 583.

Wilson, D. (2009). Irony and metarepresentation. *UCLWPL, 21*, 183–226.

CHAPTER 28

LANGUAGE COMPREHENSION, EMOTION, AND SOCIALITY
Aren't we missing something?

JOS J. A. VAN BERKUM

28.1. The "psycho" that is missing in psycholinguistics

Some time ago, I was asked to contribute a discourse processing chapter to a 56-chapter 1000-page handbook on the human language faculty. The book explores, in breadth, how language is instantiated in humans. Large sections are about language architecture, processing, and neural realization. There is attention to development and prelinguistic communication, as well as to evolution, genetics, and animal models. There are chapters on iconic communication and home sign systems, on the language-ready organization of motor cortex, on primate vocalization, even various chapters on robots. Yet, a chapter on the relation between language and emotion—the topic that I initially explored—was considered beyond the scope of the book.

This raised an interesting question: Why not talk about emotion in that massive volume on how language is instantiated in humans? Is emotion irrelevant to language, and to its processing? Research in *other* domains of human cognition, such as perception, attention, memory, reasoning, and decision-making, has shown that emotion matters quite a lot there (e.g., Damasio, 1994; Gigerenzer, 2007; Greene, 2014; Haidt, 2012; Kahneman, 2011; Pessoa, 2015; Phelps, Lempert, & Sokol-Hessner, 2014). Wouldn't it be reasonable to assume this holds for language processing too? Furthermore, apart from being just another domain of human cognition, language also happens to be one of the pillars of human sociality, a sociality that is deeply affective. Just like other mammals, we care about such things as dominance, family, and sex. Furthermore, our species is equipped with a vast suite of moral emotions designed to steer us toward within-group cooperation and intergroup distancing (Greene, 2014). Language is a primary channel for expressing these various ingredients of our social life. The power of words is around us everywhere, allowing us to persuade others to do what is good for them (or us), to tell others how much we care about things (e.g., how much we align with them and dislike others, or vice versa), to help or console others, and to share perspectives on the Human Condition. Simple words can cheer us up or put us down, make us angry or empathic, arouse our interest, or make us tune out instead. We use words to influence other people every day, in politics and passion, business and education, art and science, work and play. We even use words to motivate and otherwise influence ourselves.

So here is the puzzle: if language use is about affecting other people, about sharing emotions and evaluations, and about shaping collaboration and conflict, and if much of what people think and do is controlled by emotion anyway, why do we know so little about the interface between language and emotion? Empirical research on language and emotion *has* been growing, over the past decade or so (see, e.g., Majid, 2012). But the impact it is having on the field is relatively marginal, as if that work—although interesting and fun—does not really matter to the core endeavor of psycholinguistics. Why is that? Also, although recent theories explore how language shapes emotion via such things as verbal categorization, construction, and (re)appraisal (Koelsch et al., 2015; Lindquist, Gendron, & Satpute, 2016), the focus there firmly lies on emotion science, with language providing interesting constraints and insights. No theory to date addresses how emotion interfaces with language processing as the latter unfolds, such that we understand why words can yield the power that they do.

Should we worry about this? In this chapter I will argue that we should. Instead of reviewing the empirical research conducted on language and emotion so far (see, e.g., Besnier, 1990; Bohn-Gettler & Rapp, 2014; Lindquist & Gendron, 2013; Majid, 2012, for such reviews), I will make a more general case for why this research is important for psycholinguistics, and present a theoretical framework that should help us think about the interfaces between language and emotion. First, in section 28.2, I lay out some historical reasons for the dominance of a cognitive, non-affective perspective on the human language faculty. Next, for psycholinguists unfamiliar with research on emotion, section 28.3 contains a short primer on the subject. Then, in section 28.4, I present a model for affective language comprehension, explicit enough to at least help us think about the interaction between language and emotion in comprehension. As will be seen in section 28.5, the model can also help clarify the fuzzy concept of "word valence." Finally, section 28.6 contains some conclusions.

28.2 Why emotion is not really on the map

28.2.1 Historical factors

If we examine the history of psycholinguistics, it is not difficult to point to developments in the field that have inhibited the emergence of an affective perspective on language processing (see also Jensen, 2014).

(1) *Technological systems focus.* Just like other disciplines within, or overlapping with, cognitive psychology, psycholinguistics has been heavily shaped by the technology-driven perspective in that larger field. Using the digital computer as a major source of inspiration, cognitive psychology framed the human mind as a symbol-driven

information processing system, whose specialty was to compute accurate representations of the world, and store the invariant aspects of them in long-term memory for better future computation (e.g., Anderson, 1980; Newell & Simon, 1972). Digital computing and the theory behind it (e.g., Turing, 1950) brought in highly useful core ideas about symbols, about internal, mental representations of the outside world and rules operating over them, about static and dynamic memory, and about how to capture processing in flowcharts and computational models. Associated research on communication technology (e.g., Shannon & Weaver, 1949) brought in ideas about limited channels, noise, and bits of information being coded, transmitted, and decoded again. In psycholinguistics, this large cluster of technology-inspired ideas has led to questions about such things as how comprehenders decode noisy acoustic signals, store and retrieve lexical representations, recover syntactic structure, derive a proposition, compute reference, update the situation model, and code their own ideas for subsequent transmission, all questions about retrieving, manipulating, and storing information. As might be expected from an approach inspired by technological systems, it did not readily lead psycholinguists to ask questions about emotions, evaluations, and moods, or the needs of real living organisms that give rise to these affective phenomena.

(2) *Code-cracking focus.* Psycholinguists have always enjoyed the luxury of being able to work from whatever linguists had discovered about nature of language. In terms of a system levels analysis (Chomsky, 1965; Marr, 1982), the arrangement seemed perfect: thanks to quite articulate "competence theories" or "computational theories," psycholinguists to a large extent knew what phenomena to account for, and what distinctions would need to be made, for example, somehow, during actual processing—they simply needed to work out how it was done by the brain. But with that luxury also came subject matter biases that operated in linguistics itself. Mainstream linguistics in the 1970s–1990s focused on language as a generative coding system, and abstracted away from actual usage. The idea that discrete symbols and compositionality are the core of the coding system also pushed the more continuous, gradable aspects of language—such as those at work in affective prosody—to the fringe of the field. Linguistic meaning was acknowledged to have an expressive component (Lyons, 1977), but relatively few people working on syntax, semantics, and pragmatics actually went on to explore the affective side of language. The upshot of all this was that linguistics has inspired a lot of psycholinguistic research on how people crack the linguistic code (cf. all the research on lexical retrieval, syntactic parsing, anaphoric reference, and ambiguity resolution) and how they acquire or lose their code-cracking competence, but has *not* inspired psycholinguists to study how the code actually gets to *affect* people.

(3) *Modularity focus.* Third, even for psycholinguists who did acknowledge the importance of emotion to mental life, nothing of importance seemed to follow for their everyday scientific concerns. After all, wasn't the language system, or at least the most interesting bit of it, "informationally encapsulated" from the rest of mental life anyway? Jerry Fodor's highly influential 1983 book *Modularity of Mind*, where syntactic parsing was construed as a context-free, autonomous computational device, persuaded many psycholinguists to think of language processing in terms of autonomous feed-forward modules. Modularity thinking seemed to fit the psycholinguistic

evidence at the time, and also solved understandable concerns about feasible computation (cf. "combinatorial explosion"). Importantly, it provided an attractive research strategy, allowing researchers to study parts of the system (word recognition, parsing, and so on) without having to worry about other parts. Such modularity thinking also paved the way for thinking about language comprehension as computing what is said and implied *before, and cleanly separate from* computing the affective significance for the reader or listener.

(4) *Uniqueness focus.* As scientists carve up the world between them, it is only natural that people in different disciplines tend to focus on what is unique to "their" chunk of the world. What is obviously unique about human communication is the language code—no other animal has such a powerful discrete combinatorial system for referring to states of affairs at their disposal. What we have recently come to realize as equally unique about human communication is our capability for inferential communication (e.g., Tomasello, 2008), the ability to use *any* signal to communicate with conspecifics by relying on collaborative intentions, perspective-taking skills, and common ground. The unique aspects of human communication have drawn a lot of attention. However, psycholinguistics cannot focus on the unique only. Think about understanding how mountain bikes work, and how they afford transportation and fun. Relative to other types of bikes, a mountain bike is unique in such things as frame shape, gears, tires, suspension, and general robustness. But to understand how such a bike works and what it affords, studying just those features is not enough—you also need to understand how those special features mesh with more mundane ones, like a chain or a set of wheels. And so it is with linguistic communication: yes, the code and inferential machinery is pretty unique, but to understand how the system works, you also need to look at the parts that may *not* be so unique for *Homo Sapiens*, but are critical just the same, such as memory, or emotion.

These factors have shaped psycholinguistics in sometimes very fruitful ways, but they have simultaneously made it hard to see emotion as relevant to the field. As such, they have inadvertently led to a biased view on language use, framing people as dispassionate code users.

28.2.2 The code model position: Emotion is irrelevant to understanding language processing

In the standard code model of communication that dominates psycholinguistics, people are computational devices that exchange information via a fixed communication protocol, a human *TCP-IP* (transmission control protocol/internet protocol, the rules that regulate communication between computers connected via the internet). That protocol allows them to code ideas into utterances and transmit them for subsequent decoding at the other end, with the conversion to or from the code carried out by special language modules. Of course, no psycholinguist will deny that people have emotions, that they talk about them or say things because of them, that addressees or overhearers will have certain emotions as a result of such talk, and that all of this is deeply relevant to everyday life. At the same time, the code model of communication seems to render all of that irrelevant to the endeavor of understanding language processing. After all, just like with the real *TCP/IP* on the Internet, what is conveyed through the code and why, and the impact that that content has "at the other end," is of no importance whatsoever to understanding the nature and processing of the code itself. The logic of this code model position can be articulated as follows:

(1) Language is a code via which we communicate about *everything*, for a principally infinite number of reasons, and to a principally unlimited number of effects.
(2) Psycholinguistics should study the *generic* mechanisms via which people acquire and use that code.
(3) *Other* disciplines, such as emotion science or social psychology, should study what happens when people communicate about the specific things they do, and why they choose to do so.
(4) Although psycholinguistics is connected to those other disciplines in virtue of people using language for everything, there's nothing about the interface that is really of relevance to the task of understanding the *generic* mechanisms via which people acquire and use language.

The logic is intuitively compelling. But is it correct? If human emotion is just a topic, a cause, or a consequent of specific instances of language use, cleanly separated from the machinery that does the language processing, psycholinguistics can just focus on the processing *regardless of emotion*. But is the separation really that clean? To assess this, we need to know more about emotion first.

28.3 Emotion—A Primer for Psycholinguists

Here are some important facts about emotion that psycholinguists should know about, for reasons that will become obvious along the way. The starting point is a working definition that is suitable for current purposes.

> An emotion is a package of relatively reflex-like synchronized motivational, physiological, cognitive, and behavioral changes, triggered by the appraisal of an external or internal stimulus event as relevant to the interests (concerns, needs, values) of the organism, and aimed at generating a prioritized functional response to that stimulus event. The changes involved need not emerge in consciousness, but to the extent that they do, they give rise to feeling.

This definition (which largely follows Scherer, 2005, but also incorporates aspects of other proposals, notably Adolphs, 2017; Damasio, 2010; Frijda, 2008; Lazarus, 1991; Panksepp & Biven, 2012) highlights several core properties of emotion that I will unpack next. To help place those properties in context, Figure 28.1 provides a schematic model of how a specific emotion (or mix of emotions) unfolds in response to a stimulus.

(1) *Emotions are triggered by the appraisal of something as relevant to our concerns.* Emotions emerge when something about a stimulus is appraised as relevant to one's interests, either positively (such as when you win a contest, or see your child do well in a school performance), or negatively (such as when you are insulted, find a huge

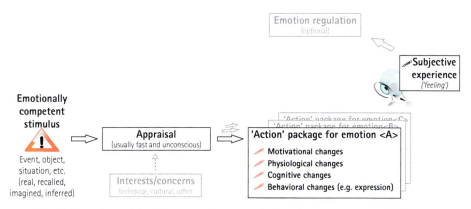

FIG. 28.1 Schematic model of the processing cascade that characterizes an unfolding emotion. Apart from the canonical stimulus → appraisal → action package cascade, the schema also indicates that appraisals always reflect how a stimulus relates to one or more interests or concerns of the perceiver, and that a stimulus can generate more than one emotion simultaneously. To the extent that ingredients of the action package (plus possibly of the appraisal) emerge in consciousness, the emotion at hand is accompanied by a subjective experience or "feeling," which in turn provides people with the possibility to regulate the emotion. The depicted processing cascade also pertains to affective evaluations.

spider in the crib of your two-month old baby, or drop your smartphone on the floor). An emotion is referential (i.e., *about* something). What it is about might be "out there," such as in all these examples, or inside your head, as when you remember or imagine any of these factors, or mentally represent these scenarios in response to language. That is, although examples in the emotion literature are often about concrete events, objects, or situations in our environment, *thoughts* (consciously as well as unconsciously entertained) can just as easily trigger emotion. Following Damasio (2010), I will use the term emotionally competent stimulus or ECS to cover all of this. Appraisal can to some extent be deliberate, (i.e., under slow conscious control), but in line with what emotion is supposed to do for us, it is usually fast, automatic, and unconscious (Adolphs, 2017; Frijda, 2008; Prinz, 2004; Scherer, 2005; Zajonc, 1980)—as every psychotherapist or coach will know, people often don't know what aspect of a situation, person, or event exactly triggered their emotion, and for what reason. Also, as illustrated by research on olfactory and visual perception (e.g., Li, Moallem, Paller, & Gottfried, 2007; Tamietto et al., 2009), people can respond affectively without having consciously *perceived* the stimulus at all.

(2) *Emotions involve a package of relatively automatic, short-lived, synchronized changes in multiple systems.* Emotion is not just about appraising something as relevant to your interests, but also about *doing* something about it. For example, when something makes you angry, your heart beats faster, you sweat a little more, and stress hormones are released, as your body is preparing itself for "combat." You'll momentarily feel a strong urge to act, and perhaps you will strike or yell at something, or someone. Your face will have an angry expression. Attentional focus will briefly narrow, such that you are no longer able to attend to other things in the environment. And finally, you

may become very aware of all of this, giving you the typical "feel" of anger. These specific changes make up the average package for anger. Qualitatively different emotions, such as anger and fear, have different action packages, with some shared ingredients (e.g., both increase sweating), but also some major differences (e.g., in contrast to anger, fear increases the probability of retreat and avoidance). Specific instances of anger may also differ somewhat in their exact "mix" of ingredients, and some mixes will be more prototypical than others. The key observation, however, is that emotions involve relatively automatic, short-lived, and synchronized changes along several different dimensions: (a) *motivational changes* or "action tendencies," the readiness to engage in, or disengage from, particular behavior; (b) *physiological changes* that prepare the body for action or impact; (c) *cognitive changes*, such as increased attention and better memorization; and (d) *behavioral changes*, involving approach or avoidance, as well as more specific actions such as smiling, frowning, shouting, crying, changing posture, stroking, exploring, or playing.

(3) *Emotions briefly take control.* Emotion emerges when something is deemed sufficiently important to relatively automatically engage multiple systems simultaneously, to have "all hands on deck." It is also about doing something *now*. Frijda (2008, p. 72) characterizes emotion as "event-or object-instigated states of action readiness with control precedence." That is, you really have an urge to do something *right now*: strike out or yell at the intruder, or write that email *now*. And that makes sense; after all, emotions are designed to watch over your interests, directly or indirectly rooted in core biological values shaped by evolution. Although culturally conditioned and other personal life experiences construct additional layers of emotional complexity that are unique to humans (Barrett, 2014), emotion is first and foremost about "biological homeostasis," about regulating life within survival-promoting and agreeable ranges (Damasio, 2010; Panksepp & Biven, 2012). Emotions are bits of rapid biological intelligence that have proved useful in the past, reflex-like solutions to recurring problems in the life of the species (and its ancestors), briefly taking control, but—provided that we become aware of them—also open to conscious regulation (Adolphs, 2017).

(4) *Emotions are not necessarily conscious.* A crucial insight in emotion science is that emotion doesn't need to be conscious (Damasio, 2010; Frijda, 2008; Panksepp & Biven, 2012; Scherer, 2005). That is, one can have all of the ingredients (a) to (d) mentioned in (2) without actually being aware of them (i.e., of *feeling* it). This may be counterintuitive, because in daily life we use "emotion" and "feeling" interchangeably. When *strong* emotions are elicited, we will certainly "feel" them. But what holds for other aspects of brain function also holds for emotion: most of the computations are done without us being aware of the process and of what they deliver (Adolphs, 2017). That is, weak emotions may unfold and affect our thoughts and behavior without *any* subjective awareness. If this is hard to imagine, think about moments in life when you suddenly become aware that you have been avoiding someone, or something, or that in particular situations, your neck muscles tend to tighten up. Or about the effort that is sometimes needed to make the relevant appraisals involved in your emotional life explicit, such that you can reflect upon them.

(5) *Emotions have ancient triggers but can hook up to new ones via learning.* For psycholinguists, a particularly critical observation is that there seem to be no limits on the

types of stimuli that can become emotionally competent. For a limited class of biologically significant stimuli (e.g., pain, an unexpected loud noise, signs of decay, being bodily restricted, the anticipation of sex or food, being otherwise cared for, the loss of social bonds, a helpless baby, and the basic emotional displays of conspecifics, such as smiles and frowns, aggression, or playful movement; Panksepp & Biven, 2012), that competence is simply hardwired into your brain. Via "emotional conditioning," however, an *infinite* number of other stimuli can also become emotionally competent (de Houwer, Thomas, & Baeyens, 2001; Hofmann et al., 2010; LeDoux, 1996), as generic categories, or as specific tokens. The amygdalae are crucial to such emotional conditioning, and they are capable of forging emotional associations without any awareness or episodic recollection of the coupling (LeDoux, 1996; Phelps, 2006). So, emotions are sticky little things, value-relevant response packages that can attach themselves to *anything* without you noticing, and with the appraisal that is needed to elicit them consisting of little more than the automatic retrieval of an acquired association from long-term memory.

(6) *Affective evaluation is low-intensity emotion.* In a wide variety of fields, ranging from social psychology (e.g., Zajonc, 1980) to the neuroscience of visual perception (e.g., Barrett & Bar, 2009), research has shown that we hardly ever see things in a neutral way: affective evaluation is part and parcel of how we perceive the world. In the words of Zajonc (1980, p. 154):

> One cannot be introduced to a person without experiencing some immediate feeling of attraction or repulsion and without gauging such feelings on the part of the other. (…) Nor is the presence of affect confined to social perception. (…) We do not just see "a house": we see "a handsome house," "an ugly house," or "a pretentious house." We do not just read an article on attitude change, on cognitive dissonance, or on herbicides. We read an "exciting" article on attitude change, an "important" article on cognitive dissonance, or a "trivial" article on herbicides. And the same goes for a sunset, a lightning flash, a flower, a dimple, a hangnail, a cockroach, the taste of quinine, Saumur, the color of earth in Umbria, the sound of traffic on 42nd Street, and equally for the sound of a 1,000-Hz tone and the sight of the letter Q.

Such automatic affective evaluations of the world around us build on the same affective systems that generate salient emotions like anger, fear, disgust, pride, or joy. With evaluation, however, the intensity of the emotion is so low that the response feels like a quality of the stimulus ("an ugly house"), rather than like a particular state that we are in ("that house made me feel disgusted"; see Barrett & Bar, 2009, for this distinction). Importantly, just like more salient emotions, evaluations have an action component (emphasized by the term "preference"): a more positive evaluation is associated with approach motivation, with—consciously or unconsciously—*preferring* the evaluated item over something else. Furthermore, these affective evaluations are by no means necessarily "*post*-perceptual," or "*post*-conceptual," that is, are not necessary generated only *after* something has been fully identified or conceptualized in cognitive terms. Echoing the classic psychological notion of subjective perception, there is growing evidence in cognitive neuroscience that what something *is* can often not be meaningfully separated from what it means *to me*—perceptions are not objective, and affect can be an intrinsic part of it (Barrett & Bar, 2009; Lebrecht et al., 2012).

(7) *Mood.* Mood differs from short-lived emotion in that it involves a relatively slow-changing affective background state that is not really *about* something (i.e., is not "referential"; Forgas, 1995; Scherer, 2005). Also, whereas short-lived emotions play their role via unique prioritized action packages, mood is believed to play a functional role in signaling the amount of resources available for exploration of the environment (Zadra & Clore, 2011), and/or for signaling that the current course of action is working out well (Clore & Huntsinger, 2007). The effects of this show up in differential patterns of action *and* cognition. For example, in a bad mood we are not only less inclined to climb a steep hill, but also inclined to overestimate the steepness of that hill (Zadra & Clore, 2011). Furthermore, a bad mood narrows the spotlight of visual attention (Rowe, Hirsh, & Anderson, 2007), and reduces such things as the width of associative memory retrieval (Rowe et al., 2007), the use of scripts in episodic memory retrieval (Bless et al., 1996), or the sensitivity to social stereotypes in person judgment (Park & Banaji, 2000). In all, mood tunes cognitive processing in a variety of interesting ways, again without us being aware of it.

Much more can be said about emotion, but for now, the central observation is this: Just like in other mammals, the affective systems that are responsible for emotions, evaluations, and moods are *key to the control of adaptive behavior in a complex environment* (Panksepp & Biven, 2012). Emotions, evaluations, and moods are "motive states," urging or nudging us to approach or avoid, prefer, attend to, explore, grab, attack, submit to, care for, play with, or protect oneself from entities or events out there in the world, all because of how those entities or events relate to our interests. They need not be very strong to exert this control, and we are often not aware of how they tug at us. But they do control what we attend to, what we encode and remember, what we mentally explore, how we reason, what we decide, and what we actually do. Rather than being orthogonal to it, emotion, in all its diversity, is *central* to cognition and action.

28.4 Drawing a first map: The Affective Language Comprehension model

So where exactly are the interfaces between language and emotion? To address this question in a way that is useful for psycholinguists, we need to make explicit the various types of representations that people compute as they produce or comprehend language, as well as the subprocesses involved in computing them, such that we can subsequently ask where emotion might kick in. Such an articulate blueprint is crucial: if we are to make progress on how language processing and emotion interact, we must frame our research questions in ways that honor—and help us orient ourselves within—the real complexity of language processing, and move beyond relatively crude, holistic concepts like "word valence" or "emotional sentences."

Here, I present such a blueprint for language *comprehension*. We know from pragmatics and psycholinguistics that language comprehension is a highly complex business that extends beyond the single utterance, involves several layers of interpretation, and is heavily context-dependent. We also know that language is just one of many simultaneous "channels" or sign systems via which we communicate, and that as we speak or write, such things as a flat voice, raising an eyebrow, a well-chosen emoji, or slightly turning away can make all the difference. The *Affective Language Comprehension* or *ALC* model, illustrated for one specific communicative example in Figure 28.2, is a theoretical model of how emotion can mesh with language comprehension, with the latter unpacked in a way that respects at least some of its complexity and richness. The model captures widely accepted ideas in three research domains: the psycholinguistics of word and sentence processing, the pragmatic analysis of communication, and emotion science. What is new here is that the three are combined.

28.4.1 Comprehending a rude verbal insult

The quickest way to get a feel for the model is to illustrate its claims with a clearly emotion-relevant expression, such as a rude verbal insult. Imagine a face-to-face conversation in which speaker X addresses listener Y by uttering "You are a real bitch!" in a very angry way. What representations does addressee Y retrieve or construct—consciously and unconsciously—in response to this, and how do these active representations move her?

28.4.1.1 *The input: Multimodal, composite signs*

In face-to-face conversation, conversational moves are always implemented as multimodal, composite signs, which include not just words arranged in a certain way, but a wide variety of non-verbal signs as well (Clark, 1996; Goodwin, Cekaite, & Goodwin, 2012; Enfield, 2013; Jensen, 2014). And in writing, we try to replace some of those signs (e.g., emoji, exclamation marks). Those non-verbal signs are *not* peripheral—a particular gaze direction, a specific gesture, bodily orientation, tone of voice, or facial expression may carry much, sometimes all of the speaker's meaning—as can an emoji. For example, speaker X inevitably utters "You are a real bitch!" in a specific manner (e.g., with a very angry voice and matching facial expression). Part of the composite sign, such as a trembling voice, may be unintended (a "symptom"), but for something to count as a communicative move, as least part of the composite sign must be presented deliberately, and this should be recognized *as such*, that is, addressee Y must recognize that X has a communicative intention (Tomasello, 2008).

28.4.1.2 *Recognizing/parsing the signs presented by the speaker*

The conventionalized ingredients of the composite sign will cue representations in long-term memory, traces of stable practices of sign use tracked by an ever-learning brain. For example, the spoken word "bitch" will cue (retrieve, activate) whatever stable memory traces addressee Y has stored for this sign in the mental lexicon, including additional phonological and/or orthographic form properties, its syntactic properties (e.g., singular noun), and its conceptual properties (e.g., that it can single out the class of nasty female persons, as well as the class of female dogs); this is what psycholinguists usually mean when they say a word is recognized. Specific *constellations* of words, such as idiomatic expressions, or other stable constructions, will likewise cue such representations in long-term memory (LTM) (Jackendoff, 2007).

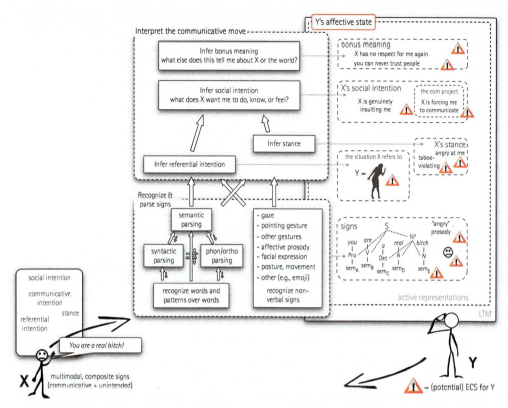

FIG. 28.2 Example processing in the *Affective Language Comprehension* model. Mental processes and the associated retrieved or computed representations are expanded for addressee Y only. Y's computational processes draw upon (and add to) long-term memory traces, and involve currently active dynamic representations that reflect what is currently retrieved from LTM, composed from elements thereof and/or inferred from context, in response to the current communicative move. Y's active representations can be conscious or unconscious. Bonus meaning can be inferred from (or cued by) all other active dynamic representations, and Y's current affective state (e.g., mood) can influence all ongoing computational processes (arrows for these aspects not shown). The basic processing cascade is upward and incremental, starting from the signs, but small downward or sideways arrows between components of parsing and word recognition indicate top-down or sideways prediction or constraint satisfaction; such top-down or lateral contributions to processing can also occur between other components (arrows for the latter not shown). ECS = emotionally competent stimulus; com project = communicative project. *Each* of the illustrated potential ECSs can trigger an emotional processing cascade (see Fig. 28.1) that affects Y's inclinations, physiology, cognitive processing, and actual behavior, plus possibly Y's conscious feeling. Together with mood, these phasic changes also contribute to Y's current affective state, which provides a context for subsequent language processing.

The composite sign "You are a real bitch!" has a grammatical (phonological, syntactic, semantic) structure that Y will at least partially need to recover, a process often referred to as "sentence comprehension." For current purposes, I adopt the psycholinguistic analysis of Jackendoff (2007): addressee Y parses this composite linguistic sign by engaging in a parallel multiple constraint satisfaction process at several levels of grammatical structure simultaneously. Skipping over a lot of complexity here, the effect of this is that the context-free "sentence meaning" of "You are a real bitch!"—a structured semantic representation that reflects the prevailing conventions for using and arranging these verbal signs in the relevant linguistic community—is brought to bear on Y's specific, contextualized analysis of what the signs *really* mean. A rather large part of psycholinguistics has been about how people arrive at this timeless sentence meaning.

28.4.1.3 Interpreting the speaker's communicative move

The goal of language comprehension, however, is not to establish timeless sentence meaning, but to work out the contextualized "speaker meaning": what does X mean, *intend*, by presenting this composite sign to Y *here and now*? As indicated in Figure 28.2, these processes can take their cue from language, but also, and in principle no less powerful, from other types of signs, such as a pointing gesture, a particular glance, or an emoji. And, as forcefully argued by pragmatics researchers (Clark, 1996; Levinson, 2006; Scott-Phillips, 2015; Sperber & Wilson, 1995; Tomasello, 2008), the processes involved do not just tie up a few loose ends after syntactic and semantic processes have done all of the serious work—they are a crucial part of why our species has such powers of communication. In the subsequent sections, I discuss the main types of inferential processes involved, primarily based on Tomasello's (2008) analysis.

28.4.1.3.1 INFERRING THE SPEAKER'S REFERENTIAL INTENTION

One important ingredient of interpreting a communicative move is to infer the speaker's referential intention. For example, the intended referent of "you" may be the addressee but can, depending on exact circumstances, also be somebody else (including the speaker herself). Thus, addressee Y needs to use information that is already in common ground to work out what "you" currently refers to. Similar inferential work is needed to fix the intended meaning of "real" and "bitch," such that, depending on circumstances, the phrase refers to a member of the class of prototypical nasty female persons (rather than, say, of the class of female dogs). The result of all this work is a concrete mental model of the entire situation that speaker X is taken to refer to (e.g., informally: "addressee Y is an *exemplary* member of the class of nasty female persons"). In language processing research, such a referential model is commonly referred to as a *situation model* (Zwaan, 1999).

28.4.1.3.2 INFERRING THE SPEAKER'S STANCE

A second ingredient of interpreting a communicative move is to infer the speaker's stance, his or her orientation to a particular state of affairs or "stance object" under discussion (du Bois, 2007; Kiesling, 2011; Kockelman, 2004). Stance can involve aspects of the speaker's knowledge state, such as the degree to which he or she is certain about something being asserted (so-called "epistemic stance"). Particularly relevant here, however, is the speaker's *affective* orientation toward the stance object, (i.e., his or her emotion(s)). This *affective* stance (or *evaluative* stance, Hunston & Thompson, 2000) can range from full-blown and clearly felt strong emotions (e.g., anger, skepticism, admiration, enthusiasm, playfulness) to very subtle, possibly wholly unconscious evaluations. Stance signals need not have been communicated *deliberately*, and can be part of the automatic, involuntary display of emotion (e.g., a trembling voice, gaze avoidance, a slight turning away of the body). Furthermore, while the stance itself is often detected relatively easily, what the stance is *about* is not always immediately clear. With "You are a real bitch!," the evaluative contents of the expression itself suggest that the person indexed by "you," or something about his or her behavior, is also the object of the negative stance cued by the speaker's angry intonation, angry face, and use of a taboo word. But in many conversational cases, things are less clear—with a mocking "look at *that* guy!" for example, the stance object being mocked might be the guy referred to, but also addressee Y instead[1].

28.4.1.3.3 INFERRING THE SPEAKER'S SOCIAL INTENTION

Addressee Y's mental representation of speaker X's referential intention and (deliberately or accidentally conveyed) stance jointly provide the basis for the third ingredient of interpreting a communicative move, the inferring of X's social intention: What is it that speaker X presumably wants to achieve by making this particular move, here and now? The specific options are unlimited. However, according to Tomasello (2008), speakers have three major types of social motivations for communicating with others, often mixed in the same move, but conceptually distinct: (1) *requesting (or manipulating)*: I want you to do (or know, or feel) something that will help *me*; (2) *informing*: I want you to know something because I think it will help or interest *you*; and (3) *sharing*: I want you to feel something so that we can share feelings together. Obvious verbal examples are "Please close the door," "Hey, you dropped your wallet," and "Isn't that a great view!" In the right context, similar intentions can be expressed by pointing to a specific open door, wallet, or view in a certain manner. Whatever the case might be, addressee Y needs to work out what speaker X wants him or her to do, know, or feel. With our example, addressee Y will most likely infer that X genuinely wants to insult her, and perhaps as such force her to repair or from now on refrain from specific bad behavior (a "request"). If the same expression is uttered in a playful way, however, Y may instead infer that X's intention is not to genuinely insult her at all, but to instead simply "fool around" and have some fun together, in ways that only intimate friends are allowed to do (Irvine, 2013; Jay, 2009).

28.4.1.3.4 THE IMPORTANCE OF RECOGNIZING A COMMUNICATIVE INTENTION

Communication always involves an additional "special" social project: not only has speaker X decided to use language and/or non-verbal signs to realize his or her primary social intention(s), but he or she must somehow make sure that addressee Y recognizes the communicative intention, and (implicitly or explicitly) agrees to the proposed joint *communicative project* for a certain amount of time. The nature of this special type of collaborative has been studied intensely in pragmatics (e.g., Clark, 1996; Enfield, 2013; Levinson, 2006;

---

[1] Situations where we feel compelled to (usually apologetically) explain to our interlocutor that the negative emotions they may pick up "are not about them" also illustrate the ambiguity in what someone's stance is *about*.

Tomasello, 2008), and has among other things led to the famous Conversational Maxims (Grice, 1967), as well as to a deep understanding of the importance of common ground. Interestingly, it also means that when X intends to verbally insult Y, this can only work if Y recognizes X's communicative intention, and assumes that the utterance is "collaboratively" designed by X such that Y can recover the referential and social intention. That is, people need to collaborate even if they want to hurt each other.

28.4.1.3.5 INFERRING BONUS MEANING

Working out speaker X's referential intention, stance, and social intention (and recognizing his or her communicative intention as a special case of the latter) completes the process of inferring or understanding *speaker meaning*, that which the speaker aims to convey or bring about. Some would argue that language processing stops there (e.g., Clark, 1996). But regardless of such discipline-based demarcation lines, *processing* doesn't of course stop there—addressee Y will consciously or unconsciously always infer (via associative memory retrieval or more sophisticated computation) at least some additional "bonus" meaning, things that X did not mean to convey at all, about speaker X (e.g., "she is always so blunt," "she obviously had a bad day"), the relationship between X and Y (e.g., "X doesn't respect me"), and the rest of life (e.g., "they never respect me," "why do people always need to put other people down?"). Although not part of speaker meaning proper, such bonus meaning will usually strongly contribute to whatever Y will think, feel, do, or say next.

28.4.1.4 Other issues

Because the power of language to a large extent resides in its referential precision, it is tempting to assume that *verbal* signs drive inferences about the speaker's referential intention, and *non-verbal* signs drive inferences about the speaker's affective stance. However, this is by no means necessarily the case. Referents can be signaled verbally but also entirely non-verbally, by such means as eye movements, manual pointing, or an iconic gesture (Tomasello, 2008). Also, stance can be expressed through such non-verbal signs as tone of voice, but also by one's choice of words and constructions, in a wide range of subtle and less subtle ways. Examples of the latter (Besnier, 1990; Enfield, 2013; Foolen, 2012, 2015; Kiesling, 2011): using intensifiers (e.g., "very," "horribly"), interjections (e.g., "ugh," "wow," "yeah," "uhh") and swearwords to express strong involvement and positive or negative affect, using specific referential expressions to mark affiliation or distance (e.g., French "tu/vous," first names vs. surnames, demonstrative pronouns as in "I'm fed up with those people next door!"), a diminutive or other suffix to convey affection or express a negative evaluation, constructions such as "Obviously, ... " to express annoyance at somebody else's powers of inference, "dude" to express cool solidarity, or "just" to express non-commitment. The division of labor between how verbal and non-verbal parts of the composite sign signal referents and stance can change with every utterance. In fact, and important to keep in mind, the comprehension process depicted in Figure 28.2 can also work without language (Levinson, 2006; Tomasello, 2008), as when we communicate something with a well-timed silence, a raised eyebrow, an emoji, or a sigh.

Three more things about the inferences involved in interpreting communicative moves. First, although at least some of the inferred intentions (e.g., the presence of a communicative intention) must emerge in the listener's awareness for this to be a model of inferential communication, the "inferring process" itself need not be a conscious, deliberate process, and some of the resulting inferences may also escape awareness; this is simply an echo of the much more general observation that much of the brain's processing is *unconscious* processing. Second, addressees may infer more than a single social intention, and more than a single stance, as well as a whole range of bonus meanings. Third, and important, what the addressee infers is not necessarily correct. Inferential communication is flexible but also vulnerable, in that addressees may be mistaken about the speaker's intended referent, stance (or object of that stance), and/or social intention(s), and may in addition derive all sorts of bonus meanings that are totally unwarranted. In the current context, the upshot is that there is room for a lot more emotion than what "perfect message transfer" would already elicit by itself.

28.4.2 Where are the emotionally competent stimuli, and what do they do?

So, which of the representations retrieved or computed in response to our example utterance can be an ECS to Y? The answer suggested by the ALC model is: *all of them*.

(1) If addressee Y infers that X's *social intention* is to genuinely insult her, this representation of X's communicative move will most certainly be a powerful ECS, capable of triggering various negative emotions (e.g., anger, shame, fear). This is no surprise: the representations that we construct for an interlocutor's social intention are usually emotionally competent, and sometimes very strongly so—after all, it is at *this* level that we deal with each other, where we affiliate ourselves with or distance ourselves from others, as individuals or group members. We warm to the thought that somebody is really trying to help us ("hey, you dropped something"), get annoyed or intimidated if somebody scolds us ("I'd appreciate if you'd be a little more thoughtful next time . . . "), and can resonate to somebody's attempt to connect with us via shared feelings ("Yeah, *Netflix* is really awesome!"). Note that the same utterance can realize very different social intentions. If taken as a genuine insult, "You are a real bitch!" can lead to negative emotions, but if we think the social intention behind the utterance is playful and benign teasing, this can elicit much more positive emotions.

(2) Addressee Y's perception of, or inferences about speaker X's *affective stance* will be a potent ECS as well, independent of the specific social intention ascribed to this particular move. That is, the stance signaled by X's angry prosody, angry facial expression, and use of taboo language will usually by itself already elicit emotional responses in Y, regardless of whether Y has worked out the specific social intention, or even the exact stance *object*. We are immediately sensitive to the emotional displays of our conspecifics, via various evolutionarily sensible routes. These include several aspects involving empathy (Decety & Cowell, 2014)—simple emotional sharing ("resonance," "mirroring," "emotional contagion"), empathic concern ("caring for"), and affective perspective-taking (i.e., more deliberately imagining somebody else's feelings)—as well as various other rapid interpersonal interlockings of social emotions (Fischer & Manstead, 2008), such as when rage

instills fear, admiration instills pride, and contempt instills shame, at least initially. Stance is also a major dimension in affective alignment between speakers in conversation (du Bois, 2007; Kiesling, 2011), and discovering that a speaker clearly shares—or does not share—your stance on something will often elicit non-trivial emotion. Finally, although somebody's inferred affective stance will as a rule act as an ECS, somebody's *epistemic* stance can do so too, as in the case where the speaker's uncertainty over what he or she asserts elicits irritation, or compassion instead.

(3) Independent of the speaker Y's social intention and stance, the *referential situation* that she draws the addressee's attention to can *itself* be emotionally competent. An obvious example is "She drove the knife into her husband's belly and slowly twisted it around," which will for many people lead to an unpleasant model of the situation referred to. The example in Figure 28.2 is similar, in that the description of a state of affairs in which you are depicted as a particularly nasty person is for most people an unpleasant state of affairs to consider. The ALC model predicts that this can generate its own bit of negative emotion. In the case of a negatively construed social intention (X *really* wants to insult me), the impact of the *referential* intention may not be all that noticeable. But in the case where "You are a real bitch!" is construed as an act of playful and benign teasing, the situation referred to (you as a real bitch) can *still* be an ECS for negative affect. This provides an explicit account for why friendly teasing can still sting, and as such lead to mixed emotions[2].

(4) When speaker X uses words to describe a situation to addressee Y, the referential aspects of the meaning of each of those words controls Y's construction of the situation model. However, merely *retrieving word meaning* from long-term memory can itself also activate the addressee's affective system (e.g., Foroni & Semin, 2009), regardless of the specific referential (and other) intentions being inferred. Swearwords are an easy example. Outside of the special conversational domain of dog species and sexes, a word like "bitch" is a taboo word, that is, a word we are not really supposed to use (Jay, 2009). Of course, people use them anyway. But we have all been taught not to, sometimes rather drastically. If you have been raised in a family culture that places a strict ban on the use of swearwords like "bitch" (e.g., you'd be forced to wash your mouth with soap whenever you used it), for example, this is bound to turn those words into emotionally competent stimuli. Furthermore, your ever-learning brain will inevitably track the extent to which particular words are used to express or evoke strong emotion in other people; via emotional conditioning, this too will contribute to the emotional competence of a swearword. The ALC model predicts that swearwords elicit emotion regardless of the current speaker's *specific* referential and social intention, such that even totally benign utterances such as "I'm so glad you are not like that bitch" can trigger a bit of negative emotion, purely because of the emotional component of individual sign meaning. Recent electroencephalography (EEG) evidence that insults with swearwords like "bitch" elicit a very early context- and repetition-insensitive brain response (Struiksma, de Mulder, & van Berkum, 2017), independent

---

[2] Another possible account for the mixed impact of "friendly" teasing that the ALC model allows us to make explicit is that addressee Y discerns *two* simultaneously present social intentions: friendly play mixed with unfriendly criticism. People are complex and layered enough to have such mixed social intentions.

of whether the participant or somebody else is the target (as in "<Participant-name> is a bitch" vs. "<Other-name> is a bitch"), is in line with that prediction. In section 28.5, I return to this issue in a more generic analysis of word valence.

The ALC model allows for two more sources of emotion in addressee Y, as he or she processes X's utterance[3].

(5) One is *the communicative project* proposed by X, which Y may or may not be in the mood for regardless of its contents—if X is bugging Y while she is very tired, or trying to concentrate on something of vital importance (e.g., making a left turn in very heavy traffic), for example, X's proposal to communicate can easily be met with reluctance, or irritation, regardless of the exact social intention. If Y would rather not interact with X at all, X's communicative intention would be similarly evaluated. The example unpacks this in the context of a face-to-face exchange. But emotion over the communicative project is also what controls our willingness to study, say, an information folder, or an annual report.

(6) The other is at the level of *bonus meaning*, additional inferences that are *not* part of the speaker's intended effect, but are simply triggered by the speaker's communicative action anyway. Although heavily context- and person-dependent, "bonus thoughts" like "People like that simply never respect people like me," "Everybody always rejects me," or "I must be doing something wrong again..." provide a rich source of emotion as we communicate with others, perhaps the richest of all potential sources discussed in the ALC model. It is also here where frequent unwarranted thoughts can lead to emotionally dysfunctional habits, and as such can become a useful target for therapeutic interventions (e.g., Greenberger, Padesky, & Beck, 2015).

In all, what the ALC model predicts is that an utterance such as "You are a real bitch!" can generate emotional responses in the addressee (or, for that matter, an overhearer) at *all levels of analysis* exemplified in Figure 28.2. At each of these levels, the emotional response can in turn have a wide variety of specific effects on the addressee, of the types laid out in Figure 28.1, and including such things as an angry reply, a frown, a rise in heart rate, or a vivid memory. *Which* specific effects occur depends on the exact details of the exchange and those involved—the model lays out the complexity, but does not predict the outcome of specific instantiations. In situations where the context does not allow for strong top-down anticipation, the ALC model does predict that (all else equal) an emotional response to retrieving a sign's meaning from the mental lexicon should emerge a little earlier than an emotional response to somebody's referential intention and stance, which should in turn emerge a little earlier than an emotional response to the speaker's social intention[4]. As reviewed before,

---

[3] In the model, "Y's affective state" serves as a reminder that pre-existing mood as well as language-elicited emotions or evaluations can also affect ongoing language processing (see, e.g., van Berkum et al., 2013, for example evidence for mood effects; and van Berkum, 2017, for a corresponding ALC analysis).

[4] The timing of emotional responses that hinge on bonus meaning depends on whether the latter is inferred from, say, the speaker's referential intention (e.g., "what kind of person describes a murder so vividly?"), the social intention (e.g., "what kind of person insults other people?"), or something else in the processing stream.

each of these responses involve changes in action readiness and physiology, changes in such things as attention, memory, and decision-making, and actual behavior (approach or avoidance, frowning, playing, and so on). As such, the ALC model provides us with a detailed map, grounded in psycholinguistics, pragmatics, and emotion science, of where and how the "perlocutionary effects" of an utterance can arise.

28.4.3 The scope of the model

I illustrated the ALC model with an utterance containing a taboo word, because it is the easiest way to make this point. However, the analysis and associated predictions hold for *any* instance of communication, albeit with details that may differ (such as in the strength of the emotional response, and, related, whether the addressee is conscious of it). For example, non-taboo utterances such as "we are out of coffee," "people are talking about you," or "The British people just decided to leave the EU" can be emotionally evocative because of the speaker's referential intention, that is, the situation model, as well as potentially the speaker's social intention (see Lai, Willems, & Hagoort, 2015, for relevant evidence of referentially induced affective systems engagement). Other non-taboo utterances are primarily evocative at the social level, such as when you invite somebody over to restore a relationship that has gone bad, and receive an indirect evasive reply like "I'm kind of busy these days" (see e.g., Bašnáková, van Berkum, Weber, & Hagoort, 2015, for relevant evidence on affective systems engagement induced by face-saving indirect replies, as well as an associated ALC-analysis). Even apparently rather neutral utterances like "The number seven is also a prime number" can elicit traces of emotion at one or more levels of analysis (see van Berkum, 2017, for this example, as well as for an application of the ALC model to several neurocognitive studies).

The model can be applied to spoken or written conversation as well as text (including blogs, information leaflets, news reports, advertisements, and speeches) and also offers a framework in which to analyze the affective impact of such things as emoji in texting, spelling errors in student papers, co-speech gestures, expressions and posture, or the fictional adventures of other people that we can read about in a novel. The latter case is interestingly complex, in that the model not only applies to the communication between author and reader, but also to communication involving characters in the story world (and, possibly, a narrator).

Finally, although the current exposition of the ALC model is focused on exploring the various types of sign-elicited representations that can be emotionally competent stimuli, the model also provides a framework in which to conceptualize more indirect effects related to framing, an important—if somewhat fuzzy—concept in the science of persuasion (Scheufele & Iyengar, 2012). One possibility suggested by the model, for example, is that value framing, the shaping of audience responses by having the message resonate with specific value orientations, does its work via the targeted foregrounding or 'priming' of specific interests/ concerns that thereby increase their impact on the emotional appraisal process (cf. Fig. 28.1), as such changing the particular emotion(s) elicited by the same stimulus. A statement such as, "We need to take action on climate change", for example, could in this way elicit a very different emotional response, depending on whether the previous framing emphasized, say, a fairer world, economic stability, or the security of one's family (all this in interaction with a person's pre-existing value orientation; Corner & Clarke, 2017). Applying the model to framing, or other phenomena studied under the umbrella of rhetoric and persuasion, may well help refine our understanding of those phenomena, and may simultaneously shape and extend the model itself.

28.5 Implications for thinking about word valence

An important claim of the ALC model is that emotion can not only be elicited as soon as the addressee has worked out the current speaker's specific stance, referential, and/or social intention, but also when *the meaning of individual signs is retrieved*, very early in the processing stream. This is where the concept of *word valence* becomes relevant. Psycholinguistics has heeded word valence for a long time (Osgood, Suci, & Tannenbaum, 1957), most often to control for a nuisance factor in code-oriented language processing experiments, but more recently also to study the impact of emotion in language (e.g., Citron et al., 2014; Kuperman, Estes, Brysbaert, & Warriner, 2014; Recio, Conrad, Hansen, & Jacobs, 2014). Word valence is easily quantified in ratings ("rate to what extent these words are positive or negative"), but what it means to say that a word is positive or negative is not all that clear. Because it articulates the various emotionally competent representations that are dynamically computed during comprehension, however, the ALC model provides a principled take on the issue.

As illustrated in Figure 28.3, what follows from the model is that a word or any other communicative sign (e.g., an emoji) can in principle acquire valenced meaning for a particular person P when that sign is sufficiently reliably, and sufficiently selectively:

(1) used by speakers to *refer* to objects, actions, situations, or events that are emotionally competent for P;
(2) used by speakers to signal *stances* that are emotionally competent for P;
(3) used by speakers to signal *social intentions* that are emotionally competent for P;
(4) paired with specific *bonus meanings* that are emotionally evocative for P; and/or
(5) observed by P to intentionally or accidentally elicit emotional responses *in other people*, responses that are in turn emotionally competent for P (with P being an overhearer, or the speaker him/herself).

Sufficiently reliable, selective pairing guarantees that emotions elicited on any of these five grounds in P *at particular occasions* can begin to stick to P's representation of the sign meaning, as an unavoidable consequence of emotional conditioning, and independent of whether P is aware of the relevant appraisal, the elicited emotional response, and/or the learning process that it gives rise to.

Examples of words with clearly valenced *referential* meaning include such words as "torture," "sex," "anger," "holidays," or "love" (for almost all people), "abortion," or "euthanasia" (for a strict Christian), or "dog" (for a dog lover): these words have acquired positive or negative valence for particular language users because their referents are ECSs for positive or negative emotion for those users. A swearword like "bitch," however, exemplifies three

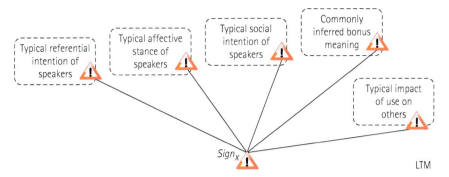

FIG. 28.3 Five potential ingredients of stable (and in four cases possibly conventionalized) affective sign meaning in long-term memory, derived from core elements of the Affective Language Comprehension model.

other types of valenced meaning, where the relevant ECSs involve the speaker's perceived social intentions (often insulting) and stance (strong enough to violate a taboo) as well as the observed consequences of a word's use (e.g., strong rejection from parents, educators, other members of society). Some swearwords seem to derive their stable evocative potential from all just mentioned sources. For example, the Dutch equivalent of the word "cancer" ("kanker") refers to something really bad (a life-threatening disease), most speakers use it as a swearword only when something *really* matters to them, the social intentions in those cases are often interpersonally "violent," and addressees or overhearers often strongly frown upon the disrespectful use of this word. According to the ALC model, all of these ingredients together determine this particular word's valence. More importantly, according to the ALC model, *every* word can accumulate *some* valence along these lines, subtly or obviously, and with us being aware of it or not.

Of course, within a specific linguistic community (or other sign-using community, e.g., those texting with emoticons and emoji), the affective traces accumulated for person P need not be the same as for person Q. For example, whereas the word "bachelor" refers to the set of unmarried men for all speakers of English, and as such has a clear conventionalized referential meaning, the emotional "connotations" will vary across those speakers, and as such fail to show up in lexicosemantic analyses of shared word meaning. Also, commonly inferred bonus meanings will differ wildly for different persons (e.g., a specific word that for whatever reason has often induced emotionally evocative thoughts such as "I'm always doing things wrong" in one person, e.g., "sloppy," may not do so for the next person), and will as such not be conventionalized in a linguistic community. But, importantly: the *brain* doesn't care (see van Berkum, 2010); if a word has stable affective meaning *for you*, you will be affected by it, whether or not that meaning is conventionalized in a wider community. Furthermore, the existence of valence norms for large parts of the mental lexicon of a given language (e.g., Moors et al., 2013; Warriner, Kuperman, & Brysbaert, 2013) suggests that emotional meaning *is* to some extent shared. Again, swearwords are an easy example: they are taboo words by definition (Jay, 2009), and will as such reliably elicit emotion when used, across large parts of a language community. But within certain smaller communities, words like "abortion," "refugee," or "dog" will also elicit shared (i.e., within that community "conventionalized") emotion).

Either way, when speaker S uses a sign X that has stored and relatively unambiguous affective meaning for you, that emotional payload can impact your processing at a very early point in time, as your first guess at (i.e., prediction of) what the sign will mean and bring about in *this* particular context, with *this* particular speaker, and in *this* particular arrangement of other signs. That first memory-based guess will usually be overruled by more precise context-dependent analyses of the speaker's current referential meaning, current social meaning, current stance, as well as of the actual specific impact of the utterance in this situation. However, the ALC model predicts that the rapid retrieval of sign-associated memories of affective meanings computed in past analyses—if available—will nevertheless contribute to the emotional impact of a communicative move, with the effects particularly likely to show up very early in processing (see Struiksma et al., 2017, for an EEG example).

This analysis of the relationship between emotion and language processing at the sign level, clearly situated within a more general framework for grounding meaning (Barsalou, 2008; Glenberg & Kaschak, 2002), makes two important points. The first is that, in fundamental contrast to artificial codes such as *TCP/IP*, the human language code is not a dead, static code. Like its users, the language code is *alive* and self-learning, incorporating emotions and other experiences into sign meaning whenever there is enough regularity. Second, and related, during language comprehension, emotion does not just come into play after the code has done its work. According to the ALC model, words and other signs can inject various types of valenced meaning, and hence emotion, into the processing stream right at the beginning, just like affective predictions can be an intrinsic part of object perception (Barrett & Bar, 2009). The implications for understanding how language influences people as it unfolds, the subject matter of psycholinguistics, are profound.

28.6 Toward a richer psycholinguistics

In this chapter, I have presented a theoretical model of how emotion can mesh with language comprehension, with the latter unpacked in a way that respects at least some of its complexity and richness. I have borrowed widely accepted ideas from three research domains: the psycholinguistics of word and sentence processing, the pragmatic analysis of communication, and emotion science. What is new is just three things: the combination of a psycholinguistic theory of sentence processing (Jackendoff, 2007) with a pragmatics theory of verbal and non-verbal inferential communication (Tomasello, 2008), the subsequent combination of this extended language processing framework with insights about how emotions and evaluations are elicited, and the use of insights about emotional conditioning to derive some implications for stored sign meaning.

In the introduction, I argued that if human emotion would be cleanly separated from the machinery that does the language processing, psycholinguistics could just focus on the processing regardless of emotion. However, the ALC model makes clear that the separation is not that clean at all, and that, as language processing unfolds, emotion can play a role in *every* component of the language comprehension process, all the way down to the retrieval of stable code meaning. Of course, I have not provided much empirical evidence that this core ingredient of the ALC model is correct. However, it does fall out naturally, as soon as well-established ideas on the types of representations retrieved and/or computed as part of language comprehension are combined with well-established ideas on what emotion is, how it can be elicited, and what it can do. The relevant facts about emotion are by no means uniquely human. For instance, we share many emotions with other Great Apes, and our susceptibility to emotional conditioning with Pavlov's dogs, Skinner's pigeons, and the modern lab rat. But that doesn't make emotion less interesting, or less important—quite the contrary. What has gone wrong is that in psycholinguistics, we have implicitly assumed that, thanks to all the referential precision made available by human language, emotion is somehow not so relevant anymore.

Certainly, we are great at computing wildly flexible discrete compositional structures such that we can refer to just about everything with great precision, in fictional worlds or the real one. But we are also something else: alive and highly social, using language to influence each other, and share what we care about. Psycholinguistics may choose to ignore this, and stick to a *lean and mean* definition of the field. But if the research in that field continues to treat people as dispassionate code-crackers, it will never get the bigger picture. Without a proper interface theory, language processing models are as disembodied as the classic models of early-days cognitive science: residing safely in the mind, but with no effective relationship to the real world in which that mind is supposed to operate. Psycholinguists need to understand why language *works* (i.e., how it does not only inform but also *affect* other people). In that puzzle, emotion is not peripheral, but the key.

Acknowledgments

The research in this chapter was supported by NWO Vici grant #277-89-001 to JvB. Thanks to Suzanne Dikker, Björn 't Hart, Hans Hoeken, Anne van Leeuwen, Hannah De Mulder, Hugo Quené, Marijn Struiksma, my anonymous reviewers, and the students in various courses for helpful discussions.

References

Adolphs, R. (2017). How should neuroscience study emotions? By distinguishing emotion states, concepts, and experiences. *Social, Cognitive, and Affective Neuroscience*, 12(1), 24–31.
Anderson, J. R. (1980). *Cognitive Psychology and its Implications*. Macmillan, San Francisco, CA.
Barrett, L. F. (2014). The conceptual act theory: A précis. *Emotion Review*, 6, 292–7.
Barrett, L. F., & Bar, M. (2009). See it with feeling: Affective predictions during object perception. *Philosophical Transactions of the Royal Society B: Biological Sciences*, 364(1521), 1325–34.
Barsalou, L.W. (2008). Grounded cognition. *Annual Review of Psychology*, 59, 617–45.
Bašnáková, J., van Berkum, J. J. A., Weber, K., & Hagoort, P. (2015). A job interview in the MRI scanner: How does indirectness affect addressees and overhearers? *Neuropsychologia*, 76, 79–91.
Besnier, N. (1990). Language and affect. *Annual Review of Anthropology*, 19, 419–51.
Bless, H., Clore, G. L., Schwarz, N., Golisano, V., Rabe, C., & Wölk, M. (1996). Mood and the use of scripts: Does a happy mood really lead to mindlessness? *Journal of Personality and Social Psychology*, 71(4), 665.

Bohn-Gettler, C. M., & Rapp, D. N. (2014). Emotion during reading and writing. In: Pekrun, R., & Linnenbrink-Garcia, L. (Eds.), *International Handbook of Emotions in Education* (pp. 437–57). Routledge, Abingdon.

Chomsky, N. (1965). *Aspects of the Theory of Syntax*. MIT Press, Cambridge, MA.

Citron, F. M., Gray, M. A., Critchley, H. D., Weekes, B. S., & Ferstl, E. C. (2014). Emotional valence and arousal affect reading in an interactive way: Neuroimaging evidence for an approach-withdrawal framework. *Neuropsychologia, 56*, 79–89.

Clark, H. H. (1996). *Using Language*. Cambridge University Press, Cambridge.

Clore, G. L., & Huntsinger, J. R. (2007). How emotions inform judgment and regulate thought. *Trends in Cognitive Sciences, 11*(9), 393–9.

Corner, A., & Clarke, J. (2017). *Talking Climate: From Research to Practice in Public Engagement*. Springer International Publishing, Cham.

Damasio, A. R. (1994). *Descartes' Error: Emotion, Rationality and the Human Brain*. Putnam, New York, NY.

Damasio, A. (2010). *Self Comes to Mind: Constructing the Conscious Mind*. Pantheon, New York, NY.

Decety, J., & Cowell, J. M. (2014). The complex relation between morality and empathy. *Trends in Cognitive Sciences, 18*(7), 337–9.

de Houwer, J., Thomas, S., & Baeyens, F. (2001). Association learning of likes and dislikes: A review of 25 years of research on human evaluative conditioning. *Psychological Bulletin, 127*(6), 853.

du Bois, J. W. (2007). The stance triangle. In: Englebretson, R. (Ed.), *Stancetaking in Discourse: Subjectivity, Evaluation, Interaction* (no. 164; pp. 139–82). John Benjamins Publishing, Amsterdam.

Enfield, N.J. (2013). *Relationship Thinking: Agency, Enchrony, and Human Sociality*. Oxford University Press, New York, NY.

Fischer, A.H., & Manstead, A.S. (2008). Social functions of emotion. In: Lewis, M., Haviland-Jones, J. M., & Barrett, L. F. (Eds.), *Handbook of Emotions* (pp. 456–68). Guilford, New York, NY.

Fodor, J. A. (1983). *The Modularity of Mind: An Essay on Faculty Psychology*. MIT Press, Cambridge, MA.

Foolen, A. (2012). The relevance of emotion for language and linguistics. In: Foolen, A., Lüdtke, U. M., Racine, T. P., & Zlatev, J. (Eds.), *Moving Ourselves, Moving Others: Motion and emotion in intersubjectivity, consciousness and language* (pp. 349–68). John Benjamins Publishing, Amsterdam.

Foolen, A. (2015). Word valence and its effects. In: Lüdtke, U. M. (Ed.), *Emotion in Language* (pp. 241–56). John Benjamins Publishing, Amsterdam.

Forgas, J. P. (1995). Mood and judgment: the affect infusion model (AIM). *Psychological Bulletin, 117*(1), 39.

Foroni, F., & Semin, G. R. (2009). Language that puts you in touch with your bodily feelings: The multimodal responsiveness of affective expressions. *Psychological Science, 20*(8), 974–80.

Frijda, N. H. (2008). The psychologists' point of view. In: Lewis, M., Haviland-Jones, J. M., & Feldman Barrett, L. (Eds.), *Handbook of Emotions* (pp. 68–87). Guilford Publications, New York, NY.

Gigerenzer, G. (2007). *Gut Feelings: The Intelligence of the Unconscious*. Penguin, London.

Glenberg, A. M., & Kaschak, M. P. (2002). Grounding language in action. *Psychonomic Bulletin & Review, 9*(3), 558–65.

Goodwin, M., Cekaite, A., & Goodwin, C. (2012). Emotion as stance. In: Sorjonen, M.-L., & Perakyla, A. (Eds.), *Emotion in Interaction* (pp. 16–41). Oxford University Press, Oxford.

Greenberger, D., Padesky, C. A., & Beck, A. T. (2015). *Mind over Mood: Change how you feel by changing the way you think*. Guilford Publications, New York, NY.

Greene, J. (2014). *Moral Tribes: Emotion, Reason and the Gap between Us and Them*. Atlantic Books, London.

Grice, H. P. (1967). Logic and Conversation [Unpublished manuscript of the William James Lectures]. Harvard University, Cambridge, MA.

Haidt, J. (2012). *The Righteous Mind: Why good people are divided by politics and religion*. Allen Lane, London.

Hofmann, W., De Houwer, J., Perugini, M., Baeyens, F., & Crombez, G. (2010). Evaluative conditioning in humans: A meta-analysis. *Psychological Bulletin*, 136(3), 390.

Hunston, S., & Thompson, G. (Eds.) (2000). *Evaluation in Text: Authorial Stance and the Construction of Discourse*. Oxford University Press, Oxford.

Irvine, W. B. (2013). *A Slap in the Face: Why Insults Hurt—And Why They Shouldn't*. Oxford University Press, Oxford.

Jackendoff, R. (2007). A parallel architecture perspective on language processing. *Brain Research*, 1146, 2–22.

Jay, T. (2009). The utility and ubiquity of taboo words. *Perspectives on Psychological Science*, 4(2), 153–61.

Jensen, T. W. (2014). Emotion in languaging: Languaging as affective, adaptive and flexible behavior in social interaction. *Frontiers in Psychology*, 5, 720.

Kahneman, D. (2011). *Thinking, Fast and Slow*. Farrar, Straus & Giroux, New York, NY.

Kiesling, S. F. (2011, April). Stance in context: Affect, alignment and investment in the analysis of stancetaking. In: iMean conference (Vol. 15). University of the West of England, Bristol.

Kockelman, P. (2004). Stance and subjectivity. *Journal of Linguistic Anthropology*, 14(2), 127–50.

Koelsch, S., Jacobs, A. M., Menninghaus, W., Liebal, K., Klann-Delius, G., von Scheve, C., & Gebauer, G. (2015). The quartet theory of human emotions: an integrative and neurofunctional model. *Physics of Life Reviews*, 13, 1–27.

Kuperman, V., Estes, Z., Brysbaert, M., & Warriner, A. B. (2014). Emotion and language: Valence and arousal affect word recognition. *Journal of Experimental Psychology: General*, 143(3), 1065–81.

Lai, V. T., Willems, R. M., & Hagoort, P. (2015). Feel between the lines: implied emotion in sentence comprehension. *Journal of Cognitive Neuroscience*, 27(8), 1528–41.

Lazarus, R. S. (1991). *Emotion and Adaptation*. Oxford University Press, Oxford.

Lebrecht, S., Bar, M., Barrett, L. F., & Tarr, M. J. (2012). Micro-valences: perceiving affective valence in everyday objects. *Frontiers in Psychology*, 3, 107.

LeDoux, J. (1996). *The Emotional Brain: The Mysterious Underpinnings of Emotional Life*. Simon & Schuster, New York, NY.

Levinson, S. C. (2006). On the human "interaction engine." In: Enfield, N. J., & Levinson, S. C. (Eds.), *Roots of Human Sociality: Culture, Cognition and Interaction* (pp. 39–69). Berg, Oxford.

Li, W., Moallem, I., Paller, K. A., & Gottfried, J. A. (2007). Subliminal smells can guide social preferences. *Psychological Science*, 18(12), 1044–9.

Lindquist, K. A., & Gendron, M. (2013). What's in a word? Language constructs emotion perception. *Emotion Review*, 5(1), 66–71.

Lindquist, K. A., Gendron, M., & Satpute, A. B. (2016). Language and emotion: Putting words into feelings and feelings into words. In: Barrett, L. F., Lewis, M., & Haviland-Jones, J. M. (Eds.), *Handbook of Emotions* (pp. 579–94). Guilford Press, New York, NY.

Lyons, J. (1977). *Semantics* (Vols. I & II). Cambridge University Press, Cambridge.

Majid, A. (2012). Current emotion research in the language sciences. *Emotion Review*, 4(4), 432–43.

Marr, D. (1982). *Vision: A Computational Investigation into the Human Representation and Processing of Visual Information*. MIT Press, Cambridge, MA.

Moors, A., De Houwer, J., Hermans, D., Wanmaker, S., Van Schie, K., Van Harmelen, A. L., . . . & Brysbaert, M. (2013). Norms of valence, arousal, dominance, and age of acquisition for 4,300 Dutch words. *Behavior Research Methods*, 45(1), 169–77.

Newell, A., & Simon, H. A. (1972). *Human Problem Solving*. Prentice-Hall, Englewood Cliffs, NJ.

Osgood, C. E., Suci, G. J., & Tannenbaum, P. H. (1957). *The Measurement of Meaning*. University of Illinois Press, Urbana, IL.

Panksepp, J., & Biven, L. (2012). *The Archaeology of Mind: Neuroevolutionary Origins of Human Emotions*. Norton & Company, New York, NY.

Park, J., & Banaji, M. R. (2000). Mood and heuristics: The influence of happy and sad states on sensitivity and bias in stereotyping. *Journal of Personality and Social Psychology*, 78(6), 1005.

Pessoa, L. (2015). Précis on the cognitive-emotional brain. *Behavioral and Brain Sciences*, 38, e71.

Phelps, E. A. (2006). Emotion and cognition: Insights from studies of the human amygdala. *Annual Review of Psychology*, 57, 27–53.

Phelps, E. A., Lempert, K. M., & Sokol-Hessner, P. (2014). Emotion and decision making: multiple modulatory neural circuits. *Annual Review of Neuroscience*, 37, 263–87.

Prinz, J. J. (2004). *Gut Reactions: A Perceptual Theory of Emotion*. Oxford University Press, Oxford.

Recio, G., Conrad, M., Hansen, L. B., & Jacobs, A. M. (2014). On pleasure and thrill: the interplay between arousal and valence during visual word recognition. *Brain and Language*, 134, 34–43.

Rowe, G., Hirsh, J. B., & Anderson, A. K. (2007). Positive affect increases the breadth of attentional selection. *Proceedings of the National Academy of Sciences*, 104(1), 383–8.

Scherer, K. R. (2005). What are emotions? And how can they be measured? *Social Science Information*, 44(4), 695–729.

Scheufele, D. A., & Iyengar, S. (2012). The state of framing research: A call for new directions. In: Kenski, K., & Jamieson, K. H. (Eds.), *The Oxford Handbook of Political Communication* (pp. 619–32). Oxford University Press, New York, NY.

Scott-Phillips, T. (2015). *Speaking Our Minds: Why Human Communication is Different, and How Language Evolved to Make it Special*. Palgrave MacMillan, New York, NY.

Shannon, C.E., & Weaver, W. (1949). *The Mathematical Theory of Communication*. The University of Illinois Press, Urbana, IL.

Sperber, D., & Wilson. D. (1995). *Relevance: Communication and Cognition*. Blackwell Publishers, Oxford/Cambridge.

Struiksma, M. E., de Mulder, H. N. M., & van Berkum, J. J. A. (2017). The impact of verbal insults: The effects of person-insulted repetition and taboo words [Manuscript submitted for publication].

Tamietto, M., Castelli, L., Vighetti, S., Perozzo, P., Geminiani, G., Weiskrantz, L., & de Gelder, B. (2009). Unseen facial and bodily expressions trigger fast emotional reactions. *Proceedings of the National Academy of Sciences*, 106(42), 17661–6.

Tomasello, M. (2008). *Origins of Human Communication*. MIT Press, Cambridge, MA.

Turing, A. M. (1950). Computing machinery and intelligence. *Mind*, *49*, 433–60.
van Berkum, J. J. A. (2010). The brain is a prediction machine that cares about good and bad—any implications for neuropragmatics? *Italian Journal of Linguistics*, *22*(1), 181–208.
van Berkum, J. J. A. (2017). Language comprehension and emotion: Where are the interfaces, and who cares? In: de Zubicaray, G., & Schiller, N. O. (Eds.), *Oxford Handbook of Neurolinguistics* (in press). Oxford University Press, Oxford.
van Berkum, J. J. A., de Goede, D., van Alphen, P. M., Mulder, E. R., & Kerstholt, J. H. (2013). How robust is the language architecture? The case of mood. *Frontiers in Psychology*, *4*, 505.
Warriner, A. B., Kuperman, V., & Brysbaert, M. (2013). Norms of valence, arousal, and dominance for 13,915 English lemmas. *Behavior Research Methods*, *45*(4), 1191–207.
Zadra, J. R., & Clore, G. L. (2011). Emotion and perception: The role of affective information. *Wiley Interdisciplinary Reviews: Cognitive Science*, *2*(6), 676–85.
Zajonc, R. B. (1980). Feeling and thinking: Preferences need no inferences. *American Psychologist*, *35*(2), 151.
Zwaan, R. A. (1999). Situation models: The mental leap into imagined worlds. *Current Directions in Psychological Science*, *8*(1), 15–18.

PART IV

LANGUAGE DEVELOPMENT AND EVOLUTION

SECTION I
Ontogenetic development

CHAPTER 29

THE DEVELOPMENT OF PROSODIC PHONOLOGY

KATHERINE DEMUTH

29.1 INTRODUCTION

How do children become adult-like speakers of a language? Anyone who has listened to a two-year-old knows that they are young not only due to the high pitch of their voice, but also due to the word-by-word like structure of their early utterances. This is often called "telegraphese" (Brown, 1973), where a target sentence such as "I want to go to the store" might only be produced as "want go store."

Even by the age of three, children's speech begins to sound more "fluent," with an emerging ability to string together longer sequences of words and phrases. They also begin to include more of the grammatical morphemes (e.g., articles, pronouns, prepositions, auxiliaries) that were omitted before, and start to use more complex, multisyllabic words (*banana* instead of truncated form like "nana") and more complex sentences. Some of this emerges along with their growing lexicon and an increasing knowledge of grammar (syntax and semantics). But part of sounding more "adult-like" is due to development at the level of phonology as well.

This raises the question of what phonology is. In general, *phonology* is defined as the "sound system" of language. Much attention has focused at the segmental level of phonology—or the "sounds" that make up a language, how these are "contrastive" or "phonemic" (i.e., lead to creating different meanings in words, such as *cat*/kæt/ vs. *pat*/pæt/). Thus, it has long been common to think of the acquisition of phonology as being about the acquisition of sounds, or segments.

However, linguists have also long realized that there is much more to the sound system of language than segments. Many languages make tonal contrasts, for example, that can change the meaning of a word. This includes many of the languages found in Asia, but also much of the rest of the world, especially Africa and Latin America. But even in a language like English, the placement of stress on one syllable or another can change the meaning of a word, as in re*cord* vs. re*cord*. In this case, the shift in stress from the first syllable to the second syllable results in a noun versus a verb. So, even for English, the placement of stress on one syllable or another can signal a difference in meaning. Researchers have thus begun to explore how and when children master some of these other aspects of the phonological system that can occur above the level of the segment.

The use of tone and stress are part of a much larger class of phonological phenomena that children must learn to become a competent speaker of a language. They must also learn how to produce complex syllables with consonant clusters (e.g., *street*/stɹit/) (cf. Kirk & Demuth, 2005; Kehoe, Hilaire-Debove, Demuth, & Lleó, 2008), long words with both stressed and unstressed syllables (*elephant*/ˈɛləfənt/) (Kehoe & Stoel-Gammon, 1997) and grammatical morphemes (e.g., articles, auxiliary verbs, and so on; see Brown, 1973). They will also need to learn that intonation can be used to signal different meanings. For example, the two utterances *Where are YOU?* vs. *Where ARE you?* have slightly different meanings that involve contrastive focus, which must be mastered to become a competent speaker of English, and many other languages. Finally, children must also learn aspects of prosodic phonology, such as the fact that, in English, unstressed syllables are typically shorter in duration than stressed syllables, and that at the end of a phrase or utterance, the pitch of the utterance will fall in a statement, signaling a phrasal boundary. The last syllable of the phrase/utterance will also be longer in duration than that of the other syllables in the utterance (see next).

Thus, learning the "phonology" of a language entails much more than merely learning the segmental inventory (or phonemes) of a language, and much more than learning just words. Even learning to produce words in an adult-like fashion requires much of what is called "prosodic phonology." One of the ways in which this can be captured is by appealing to the Prosodic Hierarchy in (1) next (Nespor & Vogel, 1986; Selkirk, 1984), where a Prosodic Word (PW) is composed of a foot which contains one or more syllables, and the PW itself is part of a larger Phonological Phrase (PP), Intonational Phrase (IP), and Phonological Utterance (Utt).

(1) The Prosodic Hierarchy

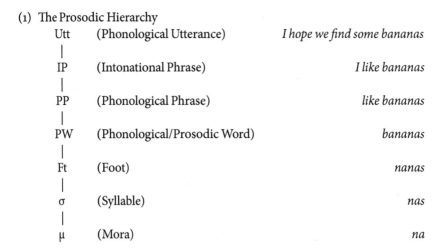

The rest of this chapter will briefly summarize what we know about the acquisition of PWs, what we are beginning to know about the acquisition of higher-level PP and IP structures, how this provides a framework for understanding within-speaker variability in early production, and how this is relevant for understanding the emergence of grammatical morphemes across languages.

29.2 THE ACQUISITION OF PROSODIC WORDS

Researchers and parents alike have long been intrigued by how and when children begin to learn their first words. Although this is often thought to occur when a child first says something like "baba," and a parent thinks they have (obviously) intended "mama" or "papa," the child probably first recognizes their own name around the age of six months (Bortfeld, Morgan, Golinkoff, & Rathbun, 2005), and may have many words in their receptive lexicon before they actually produce their first words, typically between 11 to 16 months. Jakobson (1941) proposed that the period of canonical consonant-vowel (CV) babbling was followed by a silent period before the onset of first words, but this is now no longer thought to be the case. Rather, both babbling and children's first words overlap for several months, with words typically beginning to dominate and babbling diminishing by around one to six years. But even those first words may bear little resemblance to the actual adult form. Consider, for example, the target word *rice*, which one child at one to two years produced as [ˈwʌki] for several months (cf. Demuth, Culbertson, & Alter, 2006). Some precocious children, who produce their first words from around 11 months of age, have been observed to go through this brief stage of development where early monosyllabic target words are produced with an epenthetic vowel, possibly to form a disyllabic "word" (e.g., *clean* [ˈklinə]; one to three years: Demuth et al., 2006, p. 174; see also Vihman & Velleman, 2000). This occurs primarily with those target words that end in a voiced consonant. It is possible that this apparently epenthetic form may be a reflex of voicing articulatory release, ensuring that the final consonant is clearly produced. If one considers that young children have a large tongue and fairly small vocal tract, perhaps it is not surprising that such forms, as well as many well-known early "phonological processes" just as backing (*pack* produced as *pat*), are common around or before the age of two or three (Kent, 1976).

Another way in which young children's word shapes may differ from that of the target form is in the truncation of word-initial unstressed syllables (e.g., *banana* [ˈnænə]) (cf. Demuth, 1996), and the reduction of word medial unstressed syllables (e.g., *telephone* [ˈtɛfon]) (cf., Kehoe & Stoel-Gammon, 1997). This happens not only in English, but also in Dutch (Fikkert, 1994), Spanish (Gennari & Demuth, 1997), and many other languages. Note that the reductions in many of these cases also lead to a disyllabic output form. This led Demuth (1996) to propose that children's early PWs were initially composed of a (disyllabic) Foot. As shown in the following section, this is a common early PW form that many children exhibit.

29.3 MINIMAL WORDS

Well-formed prosodic words in English must contain two moras of structure, that is, either a long/tense vowel or diphthong, or a short vowel and a coda consonant if a disyllable (2b), or be disyllabic (2c). Words with just a short vowel (2a) in English are ill-formed. Nicknames are a productive way to show this: one can shorten Philip to Phil /fɪl/ (containing a short vowel plus coda consonant), and Susan to Sue /su/ (containing a long vowel), but not /fɪ/ or /sʌ/, respectively—both with only a short vowel. But how and when do children learn that English words must have a certain amount of phonological "weight," containing at least a bimoraic or disyllabic Foot? Many other languages have such a constraint as well. For example, Bantu languages like Sesotho (Doke & Mofokeng, 1957), spoken in southern Africa, add another mora to monomoraic words, so that ill-formed *ja!* "eat!" becomes *eja!* or *jaa!* But this is not universal: languages like French have no such constraint, permitting words that contain only one mora of structure, like *o* "water." This gives rise to the various PW structures presented in (2) next.

(2) Prosodic word structures

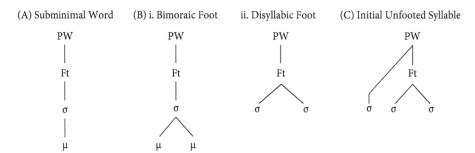

Demuth (2006) proposed that English-speaking children's early words might take the form of phonologically well-formed Minimal Words. This entailed that early words would contain at least two moras of prosodic structure—that is, either a long vowel or diphthong, or a short vowel and a coda consonant—or a Foot. Evidence from children's spontaneous speech productions appeared to suggest that children's early target words containing a short vowel tended to more reliably occur with a coda consonant than those target words containing a long vowel. Thus, learners might have an early sensitivity to this language-specific minimal word constraint.

However, children variably omit coda consonants under the age of 1;6. This also raised the possibility that children might be lengthening a short vowel when a coda was omitted, thus preserving word minimality. If so this would provide additional evidence for an early awareness of this constraint. Song and Demuth (2008) therefore conducted an acoustic study of children's early speech productions, and found that vowels were indeed lengthened in the case of missing codas, but that this occurred for both long and short vowels. Thus, it appeared that processes of compensatory lengthening took place to compensate for the missing consonant, not for mora preservation.

However, all the children in these studies were under the age of two. In a final attempt to address this issue in a more controlled fashion, Miles, Yuen, Cox, and Demuth (2016) conducted an elicited imitation experiment with children aged two to three years. They confirmed that children were more likely to produce coda consonants in the words with short vowels, and to drop codas more often in words with long vowels. This then suggests that, at least for children learning English, coda consonants are more likely to be produced in those prosodic contexts that require them for phonological well-formedness. These English findings then raise many questions about the course of prosodic word development in other languages. We turn now to the case of subminimal words in French.

29.4 Subminimal words

As we have already mentioned, many languages have a word minimality constraint, but this is not universal. Rather, it must be learned. The previous discussion suggests that learners of English have an emerging awareness of this constraint before the age of two, and that it appears fairly stable by two to three years. But what about learners of a language like French, which has submininal words such as *o*, meaning "water"? Do French-learning children produce these as monomoraic, subminimal words? Or do they augment them, as required in Sesotho, adding an epenthetic vowel, or another syllable?

Children often have a limited segmental inventory under the age of two (cf. Smit (1993) for developmental norms for English). Thus, young children may often preserve a syllable, but change the sounds to those they can more easily produce. This often has the effect of replacing late acquired target sounds, such as fricatives, affricates, and liquids, to earlier acquired (and easier to produce) segments, such as stops. French-learning children start by producing PWs that take the shape of disyllabic feet, though these are iambic (weak-strong, final stress), with the more prominent (longer) syllable being the final one (Demuth & Tremblay, 2008). Some of these, as in English and other languages, are reduplicated early on (e.g., *chapeau* "hat" [popo]). But then, at least for some children, there is a stage of development where they not only produce subminimal words like *o* "water," but also truncate longer words to produce subminimal forms (e.g., *chapeau* "hat" [po]) (cf. Demuth & Johnson, 2003). This is quite surprising! Why would a child who is producing disyllabic word forms suddenly start producing them as truncated monosyllables? Such forms then appear to be "subminimal" (monomoraic) words, and are widely attested in other French-learning children under the age of two (cf. Archibald & Carson, 2000).

Why might such truncated forms appear? Why would a child not simply persist with the disyllabic reduplicated form of the word until they can produce the articulatorily more challenging consonants? Demuth and Johnson (2003) suggest that this can be understood in terms of the child's shifting priorities (or, from the perspective of Optimality Theory (Prince & Smolensky, 2004), a "reranking of constraints"). Thus, early on, the child tries to be "faithful" to the number of syllables in the word, producing the same number of syllables as the target word, even at the cost of producing non-target segments. Thus, the two-syllable word *chausson*/ʃosɔ̃/ "slipper" is produced as [tɔtɔ̃], even though the segments of the first syllable are not target-like. At this point in development, this type of approximation is the best the child can do. But a month later, she decides this is "not good enough," that she should produce syllables that are more target-like, with the appropriate consonants and vowels. Thus, at one to five months, though she still cannot produce the fricative /ʃ/, rather than omitting or modifying the consonant, she omits the entire first syllable! This may suggest that the onset consonant and vowel are closely linked in her early phonological representations such that if the consonant is omitted, the vowel must go as well. In this way, children's early phonological "errors" can provide evidence for the nature of their emerging phonological (and lexical) representations. In the phonological grammar of this French child, we can understand her sudden production of monosyllabic forms not as a "regression," but rather the next stage in her developing phonological representation of words. At this point she is no longer prepared to produce segments (and the syllables that contain them) that do not match the target form.

This shows an early sophisticated awareness of segment-specific content in production that is similar, in some ways, to the feature-specific sensitivity to segmental contrasts in infant speech perception mispronunciation tasks (cf. White & Morgan, 2008).

Further confirmation that a developing phonological sensitivity may underlie this type of behavior comes from other studies of infant speech perception as well. In particular, it has been shown that, at one to two years, infants treat a segmental change as mapping onto a different word (Swingley & Aslin, 2000). This type of "switch task" can thus be used to probe children's early phonological representations, showing that they can perceive a language-specific change in phonological features (e.g., place of articulation) as having a different lexical referent. Perhaps then, the French child mentioned here has similar perceptual abilities which then influence her early productions. This suggests that our understanding of children's production of early words, and how this changes over time, may well be much more closely related to developments in perception than often thought. Exploration of both perception and production in the same children, and the role of both with respect to the developing lexicon, is thus an area of research that needs much more investigation.

Most of the word forms just discussed have been very simple, monosyllabic, or disyllable word shapes. In the following section we discuss what happens to longer words, and how these are realized in children's early phonological grammars.

29.5 FEET AND THE EMERGENCE OF UNMARKED PW STRUCTURES

We have seen that early learners of English have an emerging awareness that a well-formed PW must contain at least two moras of structure, as either a heavy monosyllable (with a long vowel or coda consonant), or as a disyllable. In contrast, we have also seen that learners of a language like French, where subminimal, monomoraic PWs are permitted, go through a stage of development where they truncated disyllables extensively, something not typically reported for a language like English. Thus, although children learning English may produce monomoraic CV word forms for target consonant-vowel-consonant (CVC) words when they cannot yet produce coda consonants, it is highly unusual to find disyllables truncated to a monosyllable unless the first syllable is unstressed. So, for example, a word like *giraffe* may be realized as "raf." Note that this is true in early perception for English-learners as well (cf. Jusczyk, Cutler, & Redanz, 2002), where the truncated form "raf" is treated as a word. This is probably due to the fact that the majority of words in English begin with a stressed syllable, and this is even more the case in infant-directed speech.

This raises the question of how young children produce longer words like *banana*? Anyone who has listened to a two-year-old will be well aware of some of the segmental modifications just mentioned, but also that children reduce longer words as well. This results in words such as *banana* being truncated to a disyllabic trochaic foot [ˈnænə]. Since most of the vocabulary young English-speaking children are exposed to contain a trochaic foot (i.e., stress on the first syllable), this tends to also be the form that is most frequently used in their early speech productions. This is the case for other closely related Germanic languages as well, such as Dutch (cf. Fikkert, 1994). Interestingly, Fikkert (1994) provides examples of some children actually shifting stress to the initial syllable at 1;10 years of age, so that a word like *balloon* (ballon

/baˈlon/ is produced with initial stress, as [ˈboːmi]. Thus, the output that these Dutch children produce is similar in form to English children's truncations of words like *banana*: both result in a PW shape that can be characterized as a (disyllabic) trochaic Foot (see (1)).

This led Demuth (1996) to suggest that children's early words were prosodically constrained to take the form of strong-weak (stressed-unstressed) trochaic feet, such as words like *dolly*. This appears to capture the structure of many children's early word productions before the age of two, at least for a language like English, where longer words are truncated to take this form. Thus, words like *banana* are often first realized as *nana*. Around two to six years, children begin to produce unstressed (unfooted) word-initial syllables, finally producing full word forms like *banana*.

Interestingly, some children preserve the word-initial consonant /b/, and produce truncated forms like *bana*, instead of *nana*. This can be thought of in terms of competing "constraints," where the segments of the target word can be mapped into the output in a variety of ways. Thus, *banana* can be realized as either [ˈbænə] or [ˈnænə]. Both are prosodic words that take the shape of a trochaic foot, but the segments that make up that foot are drawn from different parts of the original target word.

Note that the mapping of the initial /b/ of the word *banana* into the output form provides strong evidence that the initial unstressed syllable is actually parsed, and that its omission is not due to a lack of perceiving it. Rather, the disyllabic output seems to be a phonological constraint on output form. Such constraints have been interpreted as the child producing early "unmarked" structures. Thus, early words like *nana* can be thought of as instances of the early "emergence of the unmarked" in child speech (Prince & Smolensky, 2004).

This tendency to truncate words to a disyllable lasts for several months in English and Dutch. But in languages where many more words are longer, as in Spanish or Italian (Roark & Demuth, 2000), these early unmarked forms quickly disappear. Thus, although Spanish-speaking children truncate early words such as *muñeca* "doll" to [ˈmɛka] around one to six years of age (replacing the more challenging nasal with the word-initial /m/), longer words begin to be produced before the age of two (Gennari & Demuth, 1997).

Thus, children's early word shapes gradually become more complex. Words such as *elephant*, with primary stress on the first syllable and secondary stress on the last syllable, tend to be produced by preserving both types of syllables by two years, resulting in word forms such as [ˈɛ.fɑn], in both English (Kehoe & Stoel-Gammon, 1997) and Dutch (Fikkert, 1994). Sometimes such word forms may actually be composed of two feet, e.g., [ˈɛˈfɑn]. Thus, one begins to find an "unfolding" of prosodic structure (cf. Frota, 2012; Frota, Cruz, Matos, & Vigário, 2016), both at the level of the simple PW, but also at higher levels of prosodic structure. To explore this development in more detail, we need to consider the emergence of morphologically complex prosodic words; another fascinating chapter in the development of children's phonological grammar.

29.6 THE ACQUISITION OF HIGHER LEVELS OF PROSODIC STRUCTURE

It has long been known that some children produce what have been called "filler syllables" (e.g., Peters, 1983; Veneziano & Sinclair, 2000). These typically take the form of a reduced vowel that tends to occur where a grammatical morpheme (e.g., article, pronoun, auxiliary verb, and so on) would be expected. Thus, early attempts at multiword utterances might take the form of something like "a go now" for "I'm going now." Such early stages of development suggest that some children attempt forms that they cannot completely produce, and that this may be an area with much individual variation. Critically, the acquisition of these higher levels of prosodic structure involve longer, morphologically, and syntactically more complex utterances. It has therefore often been treated as the domain of morpho-syntax. However, our research reveals that much of the reported within-speaker variability in the apparently gradual emergence of grammatical morphemes is due to principled interactions at the phonology-morphology interface (Demuth, 2015). Thus, as a child's increased complexity at the level of the PW unfolds, so does complexity at the higher levels of the PP and the IP. Different developmental paths are found cross-linguistically because of language-specific PW and higher-level prosodic structures, allowing for predictions to be made about how and when certain structures will be acquired. This can be captured in terms of the Prosodic Licensing Hypotheses (Demuth, 2014), as explained next (see also Lleó, 2003).

Much of this research began in the early 1990s, where researchers began to move beyond the simple word to explore morphologically more complex structures (e.g., Selkirk, 1996). This then was employed to examine how and when children began to produce grammatical function words such as articles, pronouns, and so on. Many of these were either omitted and/or produced as "filler syllables" prior to being produced in their full forms. Yet even filler syllables tend to appear in certain prosodic contexts. Typically, they occur in contexts where they can be prosodified as part of a disyllabic foot. For example, in the southern Bantu language Sesotho, where nouns take a singular/plural noun class prefix, children often truncate a word like *ba-sadi* "women" to *sadi*, appearing to omit the noun class prefix *ba-* (Demuth, 2003). This suggested that this might simply be a problem of knowing which of several noun class prefixes the noun belonged to. However, follow-up corpus analysis found that Sesotho-speaking children did produce noun class prefixes when these occurred on monosyllabic lexical stems (e.g., *ba-tho* "people" was produced in its full form; cf. Demuth, 2001; Demuth & Ellis, 2009). This suggested that children have no problem with noun class prefixes per se, but are merely truncating morphological complex prosodic words to a disyllabic foot—much in the way that English *banana* was reduced to *nana*. This was further confirmed by the fact that nominal agreement was appropriately marked on postnominal modifiers, even when the prefix was omitted on the noun itself (e.g., *ba-sadi ba-ne* produced as [sadi bane] "those women") (Demuth & Weschler, 2012). These findings raise many questions about the nature of phonological and morphological representations, and whether omitted (weak) syllables/morphemes are actually perceived. That is, perhaps they are omitted due to a lack of being perceived. However, the Sesotho data just mentioned again suggest that the morpheme is perceived even though it is not produced, as agreement errors do not occur.

Interestingly, Gerken and McIntosh (1993) showed that English-speaking children under the age of two years show different behavior when presented with a nonce word in a position where "the" should be, even if they consistently omit "the" in their speech productions. This strongly suggests that these function word omissions are due to constraints on production rather than perception. To probe the nature of these limitations further, Gerken (1994, 1996) showed that children are more likely to produce articles before an object when the article is proceeded by a monosyllabic verb rather than a disyllabic verb. That is, when an article can be prosodified as part of a Foot with the proceeding word, as in *Tom [saw the]$_{FT}$ [chickens]$_{FT}$*, it was more likely to be produced than when the article was unfooted, as in *Tom's [washing]$_{FT}$ the [chickens]$_{FT}$*. Unfooted articles then only appear once children have access to higher levels of prosodic structure, such as that of the IP. However, these studies were conducted in an elicited imitation task with two- to three-year-olds, raising questions about what happens in everyday spontaneous speech. Demuth and McCullough (2009), using spontaneous speech productions from children aged one to three in the Providence Corpus (Demuth et al., 2006), then showed exactly the same results over developmental time.

These are very interesting results, for a variety of reasons. Like the results from Sesotho, they point to the fact that much of the variable production of many grammatical morphemes may be prosodically conditioned. That is, grammatical morphemes will be more likely to appear during early stages of development in precisely those contexts where they can be prosodified as part of a Foot. The Prosodic Licensing Hypothesis (Demuth, 2014) therefore provides a principled means of making predictions about the course of early morphological production across languages. If one knows about how different grammatical morphemes are prosodified in the target language, it is then possible to make explicit predictions about which morphemes in which prosodic contexts will be more likely to be acquired first, and which are more likely to appear later, when the syntax and semantics are held constant.

The Prosodic Licensing Hypothesis thus provides a principled explanation for why, once a child has some knowledge of the syntax and the semantic environment in which a grammatical morpheme must be used, the actual use of the morpheme is still highly variable. It also provides a framework for making predictions across speakers, suggesting that similar patterns of use and/or omission will appear.

This can then be tested cross-linguistically. For example, how are articles (and determiners more generally) acquired in Romantic languages such as French, Spanish, and Italian? To test this hypothesis, we need either an experimental paradigm like that used by Gerken (1996), and/or longitudinal data of children's spontaneous speech productions. We are fortunate, as part of the CHILDES database (cf. MacWhinney, 2000), to have French longitudinal data in the form of the Lyon Corpus (Demuth & Tremblay, 2008) and Spanish longitudinal corpora from several sources (cf. Demuth, Patrolia, Song, & Masapollo, 2012). Both studies have explored this issue in detail. As in the Sesotho case, French-speaking 1;10-year-olds were more likely to use articles with monosyllabic (or truncated) nouns (e.g., *la couronne*/ laku'ʀɔn/ > [la'ʀɔn] "the (fem.sg.) crown"), and use articles with disyllabic nouns by around the age of two years (e.g., *les poubelles*/lepu'bɛl/ > [lepu'bel] "the (pl.) garbage"). Thus, despite the fact that French has a very different prosodic system, with phrase-final lengthening (vs. phrase penultimate lengthening in Sesotho (Doke & Mofokeng, 1957)), French- and Sesotho-speaking children showed the same patterns of early inclusion of prenominal morphology with monosyllabic words, and only later inclusion of grammatical morphemes with disyllabic words.

But what about Spanish, with a tendency toward penultimate stress? As mentioned, children under the age of two tend to truncate Spanish words to a disyllable [meka] for *muñeca* "doll"). How and when do articles begin to appear? About a third of the words that a Spanish-speaking child hears contain three or four syllables (Roark & Demuth, 2000). For these longer words, Spanish-speaking children take one of two paths to prosodically incorporate articles. Some add determiners to these truncated forms, producing morphologically complex trisyllabic prosodic words like [a'meka] for *la muñeca* "the doll." (Similar findings are reported for Italian; cf. Giusti & Gozzi, 2006.) However, other Spanish-speaking children prefer not to truncate the lexical item, producing full trisyllabic words like *muñeca* before eventually producing four-syllable morphologically complex prosodic words like *la muñeca* (Demuth et al., 2012; Gennari & Demuth, 1997; Lleó & Demuth, 1999). However, these studies of Spanish have only looked at a few children, as these were the only longitudinal phonemically transcribed data available at the time that allowed for a full assessment of these issues, and the Italian study only looked at one child. It would therefore be very interesting to explore these findings more fully, either with other children with newly available longitudinal data, and/or by conducting cross-sectional experiments similar to that used in Gerken (1996). This would provide further information regarding the nature of children's developing phonology representations, both at the level of the PW, as well as at the higher level of the PP and the IP.

These issues also become highly relevant in considering the variable production of inflectional morphemes as the ends of words, such as English plurals, third person singular, and past tense (e.g., *dogs, hits, washed*). Inspired by research with children with SLI showing worse performance on past tense morphemes with increasingly complex consonant clusters (e.g., *sewed*/sod/, *whipped*/wɪpt/, *danced*/dænst/; see Marshall & van der Lely, 2007), a large body of research has now shown that much of the within-speaker variability found in the production of inflectional morphemes is due to the prosodic context in which they appear. Thus, in addition to being better at producing inflectional morphemes appearing in simple rather than complex coda consonants (e.g., *sees* vs. *hits*), young children are more likely to produce these morphemes utterance-finally compared to utterance medially. This is because the final syllable of the phrase in English is lengthened (phrase-final lengthening), providing ample opportunity to articulate all the consonants (e.g., Kirk & Demuth, 2006) and the inflectional morphemes at the end of the word. Furthermore, children have acquired phrase-final lengthening by the age of two (e.g., Snow, 1994). In contrast, producing these inflectional morphemes is much more challenging utterance medially, where no such lengthening occurs (cf. Song, Sundara, & Demuth, 2009; see also Hsieh, Leonard, & Swanson, 1999). This results in utterance-medial inflectional morphemes being more often omitted during the toddler years, when lexical and morphological representations are still developing (cf. Mealings & Demuth, 2014; Theodore, Demuth, & Shattuck-Hufnagel, 2015). They are also subject to greater omission as function of increased utterance length, so omissions continue to occur even at three years of age, as children's syntax, semantics, and utterance lengths increase (e.g., Song et al., 2009; Valian, 1991).

These results have again raised many questions about how these grammatical morphemes might be perceived. Studies now also show that infants' perception of third person singular –s is much better utterance-finally compared to utterance medially, where the fricative is about half the duration (e.g., *She cries now* vs. *Now she cries*) (Sundara, Demuth, & Kuhl, 2011). This has now also been replicated with adults using online neurological measures employing EEG (Dube et al., 2016). This raises the possibility that increased perceptual salience may play a more important role in understanding both the development of early grammars and variability in production than often thought. For example, recent findings from children's eye-tracking shows that two-year-olds are sensitive to plural –s (e.g., *cats*), but not plural –z (e.g., *dogs*), in a task using novel words (Davies, Xu Rattanasone, & Demuth, 2017). Plural /s/ is not more frequent, but it is longer in duration than /z/, suggesting that this enhances its perceptual salience. However, frequency can also play a role, as in the case of the later acquired –es allomorph in words like *bus-es* (Tomas, Demuth, & Petocz, 2017). Thus, although this allomorph might be thought to be more perceptually salient by virtue of its being an entire syllable (rather than merely a segment), its overall low frequency in the English lexicon (only 5% of the plural input young children hear) appears to contribute to its later acquisition, in both perception and production.

29.7 Discussion

We have outlined in this chapter the course of prosodic word development, and discussed the fact that grammatical morphemes (and unfooted syllables more generally) are often omitted in children's early speech, then slowly begin to appear as children's prosodic representations become more complex. We have also shown how prosodic factors, such as *where* in the utterance grammatical morphemes appear, can contribute to the morpheme's greater perceptual salience, thereby increasing the likelihood that it will be perceived and produced. Appealing to the Prosodic Licensing Hypothesis, as well as frequency factors and perceptual salience, helps to explain much of the within-speaker and cross-linguistic variability in the use of grammatical morphemes that has long been attested, not only in typically developing children's speech, but also in children with language disorders such as SLI (cf. Tomas et al., 2017). Note that much of this research involves not only careful control of the phonological and prosodic context in which early words and grammatical morphemes occur, but also acoustic analysis of the forms themselves in these different prosodic environments (cf. Theodore, Demuth, & Shattuck-Hufnagel, 2012).

What is still not clear is how and when the higher levels of the PP and IP are acquired, especially with respect to the use of prosodic clitics, both within and across languages. These issues have begun to be explored in European Portuguese (Frota et al., 2016), with much more to be done for English and other languages (see Leonard, 2016, for a discussion of nominal morphology).

This research then also raises many questions about how and when other populations (early L2 learners, bilinguals, children with hearing loss) develop perceptual sensitivity to grammatical morphemes, and use them in early speech. A better understanding of prosodic phonology more generally will be needed to inform the processes of speech planning and production, and how these develop over time. It is hoped that this chapter will provide a framework for exploring many of the factors that play a role in acquisition at the prosody/morphology interface, both across populations and languages. The findings will be both theoretically and methodologically important for the field of language development, with important implications for clinical intervention.

Acknowledgments

This work was funded in part by the following grants: ARC FL130100014, ARC CE110001021.

References

Archibald, J., & Carson, J. (2000). The acquisition of Québec French stress. Paper presented at the Annual Meeting of the Canadian Linguistic Association, University of Alberta.

Bortfeld, H., Morgan, J. L., Golinkoff, R. M., & Rathbun, K. (2005). Mommy and me: Familiar names help launch babies into speech stream segmentation. *Psychological Science, 16*, 298–307.

Brown, R. (1973). *A First Language*. Harvard University Press, Cambridge, MA.

Davies, B., Xu Rattanasone, N., & Demuth, K. (2017). Two-year-olds' sensitivity to inflectional plural morphology: Allomorphic effects. *Language, Learning and Development, 13*, 38–53.

Demuth, K. (1996). Alignment, stress and parsing in early phonological words. In: Bernhardt, B., Gilbert, J., & Ingram, D. (Eds.), *Proceedings of the International Conference on Phonological Acquisition* (pp. 113–24). Cascadilla Press, Somerville, MA.

Demuth, K. (2001). Prosodic constraints on morphological development. In: Weissenborn, J., & Höhle, B. (Eds.), *Approaches to Bootstrapping: Phonological, Syntactic and Neurophysiological Aspects of Early Language Acquisition* (pp. 3–21). John Benjamins, Amsterdam.

Demuth, K. (2003). The acquisition of Bantu languages. In: Nurse, D., & Phillipson, G. (Eds.), *The Bantu Languages* (pp. 209–22). Routledge, London.

Demuth, K. (2006). Cross-linguistic perspectives on the development of prosodic words. Guest Editor, Special Issue, *Language and Speech, 49*(2), 129–297.

Demuth, K. (2014). Prosodic licensing and the development of phonological and morphological representations. In: Farris-Trimble, A., & Barlow, J. (Eds.), *Perspectives on Phonological Theory and Acquisition: Papers in Honor of Daniel A. Dinnsen* (pp. 11–24). Language Acquisition and Language Disorders Series, 56. John Benjamins, Amsterdam.

Demuth, K. (2015). The acquisition of prosodic phonology and morphology. In: Bavin, E., & Naigles, L. (Eds.), *Cambridge Handbook on Child Language* (pp. 230–49). Cambridge University Press, Cambridge.

Demuth, K., Culbertson, J., & Alter, J. (2006). Word-minimality, epenthesis, and coda licensing in the acquisition of English. *Language & Speech, 49*, 137–74.

Demuth, K., & Ellis, D. (2009). Revisiting the acquisition of Sesotho noun class prefixes. In: Guo, J., Lieven, E., Budwig, N., Ervin-Tripp, S., Nakamura, K., Ozçalikan, S. (Eds.), *Crosslinguistic Approaches to the Psychology of Language: Festschrift for Dan Slobin* (pp. 93–104). Psychology Press, New York, NY.

Demuth, K., & Johnson, M. (2003). Truncation to subminimal words in early French. *Canadian Journal of Linguistics, 48*, 211–41.

Demuth, K., & McCullough, E. (2009). The prosodic (re)organization of children's early English articles. *Journal of Child Language, 36*, 173–200.

Demuth, K., Patrolia, M., Song, J. Y., & Masapollo, M. (2012). The development of articles in children's early Spanish: Prosodic interactions between lexical and grammatical form. *Linguistic Interfaces and Language Acquisition in Childhood*. Rothman, J., & Guijarro-Fuentes, P. (Eds.), *First Language, 32*, 17–37.

Demuth, K., & Tremblay, A. (2008). Prosodically-conditioned variability in children's production of French determiners. *Journal of Child Language, 35*, 99–127.

Demuth, K., & Weschler, S. (2012). The acquisition of Sesotho nominal agreement. *Morphology, 21*, 67–88.

Doke, C., & Mofokeng, S. (1957). *Textbook of Southern Sotho Grammar*. Longman, Cape Town.

Dube, S., Kung, C., Peter, V., Brock, J., & Demuth, K. (2016). Effects of sentence position and type of violation on the auditory processing of subject-verb agreement: An auditory ERP study. *Frontiers in Psychology*, 7, 1276.

Fikkert, P. (1994). *On the Acquisition of Prosodic Structure* [Dissertation]. University of Leiden, Leiden.

Frota, S. (2012). Prosodic structure, constituents and their representations. In: Cohn, A., Fougeron, C., & Huffman, M. (Eds.), *The Oxford Handbook of Laboratory Phonology* (pp. 255–65). Oxford University Press, Oxford.

Frota, S., Cruz, M., Matos, N., & Vigário, M. (2016). Early prosodic development: Emerging intonation and phrasing in European Portuguese. In: Armstrong, M., Henriksen, N. C., & Vanrell, M. M. (Eds.), *Intonational Grammar in Ibero-Romance: Approaches Across Linguistic Subfields* (pp. 295–324). John Benjamins, Philadelphia, PA.

Gennari, S., & Demuth, K. (1997). Syllable omission in Spanish. In: Hughes, E. M., & Green, A. (Eds.), *Proceedings of the 21st Annual Boston University Conference on Language Development* (pp. 182–93). Cascadilla Press, Somerville, MA.

Gerken, L. A. (1994). Young children's representation of prosodic structure: Evidence from English-speakers' weak syllable omissions. *Journal of Memory and Language*, 33, 19–38.

Gerken, L. (1996). Prosodic structure in young children's language production. *Language*, 72, 683–712.

Gerken, L., & McIntosh, B. (1993). The interplay of function morphemes and prosody in early language. *Developmental Psychology*, 29, 448–57.

Giusti, G., & Gozzi, R. (2006). The acquisition of determiners: Evidence for the full competence hypothesis. In: Belletti, A., Bennati, E., Chesi, C., Di Domenico, E., & Ferrari, I. (Eds.), *Language Acquisition and Development: Proceedings of GALA 2005* (pp. 232–8). Cambridge Scholars Press, Newcastle upon Tyne, UK.

Hsieh, L., Leonard, L. B., & Swanson, L. A. (1999). Some differences between English plural noun inflections and third singular verb inflections in the input: The contribution of frequency, sentence position, and duration. *Journal of Child Language*, 26, 31–543.

Jakobson, R. (1941). *Kindersprache, aphasie und allgemeine lautgesetze*. Almqvist & Wiksells Boktryckeri, Uppsala.

Jusczyk, P. W., Cutler, A., & Redanz, N. J. (2002). Infants' preference for the predominant stress patterns of English words. *Child Development*, 64, 675–87.

Kehoe, M., & Stoel-Gammon, C. (1997). Truncation patterns in English-speaking children's word productions. *Journal of Speech and Hearing Research*, 40, 526–41.

Kehoe, M., Hilaire-Debove, G., Demuth, K., & Lleó, C. (2008). The structure of branching onsets and rising diphthongs: Evidence from the acquisition of French and Spanish. *Language Acquisition*, 15, 5–57.

Kent, R. D. (1976). Anatomical and neuromuscular maturation of the speech mechanism: Evidence from acoustic studies. *Journal of Speech and Hearing Research*, 19, 421–47.

Kirk, C., & Demuth, K. (2005). Asymmetries in the acquisition of word-initial and word-final consonant clusters. *Journal of Child Language*, 32, 709–34.

Kirk, C., & Demuth, K. (2006). Accounting for variability in 2-year-olds' production of coda consonants. *Language Learning and Development*, 2, 97–118.

Leonard, L. B. (2016). Noun-related morphosyntactic difficulties in specific language impairment across languages. *First Language*, 6, 3–29.

Lleó, C. (2003). Prosodic licensing of codas. *Probus*, 15, 257–81.

Lleó, C., & Demuth, K. (1999). Prosodic constraints on the emergence of grammatical morphemes: Crosslinguistic evidence from Germanic and Romance languages. In: Greenhill, A., Littlefield, H., & Tano, C. (Eds.), *Proceedings of the 23rd Annual Boston University Conference on Language Development* (pp. 407–18). Cascadilla Press, Somerville, MA.

Marshall, C., & van der Lely, H. (2007). The impact of phonological complexity on past tense inflection in children with Grammatical-SLI. *Advances in Speech Language Pathology*, 9, 191–203.

MacWhinney, B. (2000). *The CHILDES Project: Tools for Analyzing Talk*. Lawrence Erlbaum, Mahwah, NJ.

Mealings, K., & Demuth, K. (2014). The role of utterance length and position in three-year-olds' production of third person singular -s. *Journal of Speech, Language, and Hearing Research*, 57, 484–94.

Miles, K., Yuen, I., Cox, F., & Demuth, K. (2016). The prosodic licensing of coda consonants in early speech: interactions with vowel length. *Journal of Child Language*, 43, 265–83.

Nespor, M., & Vogel, I. (1986). *Prosodic Phonology*. Foris, Dordrecht/Riverton, NJ.

Peters, A. (1983). *The Units of Language Acquisition, Monographs in Applied Psycholinguistics.* Cambridge University Press, Cambridge.

Prince, A., & Smolensky, P. (2004). *Optimality Theory: Constraint Interaction in Generative Grammar*. Blackwell, Malden, MA.

Roark, B., & Demuth, K. (2000). Prosodic constraints and the learner's environment: A corpus study. In: Howell, S. C., Fish, S. A., & Keith-Lucas, T. (Eds.), *Proceedings of the 24th Annual Boston University Conference on Language Development* (pp. 597–608). Cascadilla Press, Somerville, MA.

Selkirk, E. O. (1984). *Phonology and Syntax: The Relation Between Sound and Structure*. MIT Press, Cambridge, MA.

Selkirk, E. O. (1996). The prosodic structure of function words. In: Morgan, J. L., & Demuth, K. (Eds.), *Signal to Syntax: Bootstrapping from Speech to Grammar in Early Acquisition* (pp. 187–213). Lawrence Erlbaum, Mahwah, NJ.

Smit, A. B. (1993). Phonologic error distributions in the Iowa-Nebraska Articulation Norms Project: Consonant singletons. *Journal of Speech and Hearing Research*, 36, 533–47.

Snow, D. (1994). Phrase-final syllable lengthening and intonation in early child speech. *Journal of Speech, Language, and Hearing Research*, 37, 831–40.

Song, J. Y., & Demuth, K. (2008). Compensatory vowel lengthening for omitted coda consonants: A phonetic investigation of children's early representations of prosodic words. *Language & Speech*, 51, 382–99.

Song, J. Y., Sundara, M., & Demuth, K. (2009). Phonological constraints on children's production of English third person singular -s. *Journal of Speech, Language, and Hearing Research*, 52, 623–42.

Sundara, M., Demuth, K., & Kuhl, P. (2011). Sentence-position effects on children's perception and production of English 3rd person singular –s. *Journal of Speech, Language, and Hearing Research*, 54, 55–71.

Swingley, D., & Aslin, R. N. (2000). Spoken word recognition and lexical representation in very young children. *Cognition*, 76, 147–66.

Theodore, R., Demuth, K., & Shattuck-Hufnagel, S. (2012). Segmental and positional effects on children's coda production: Comparing evidence from perceptual judgments and acoustic analysis. *Clinical Linguistics & Phonetics, 26*, 755–73.

Theodore, R., Demuth, K., & Shattuck-Hufnagel, S. (2015). Examination of the locus of positional effects on children's production of plural –s: Considerations from local and global speech planning. *Journal of Speech, Language, and Hearing Research, 58*, 946–53.

Tomas, E., Demuth, K., & Petocz, P. (2017). The role of frequency in learning morphophonological alternations: Implications for children with specific language impairment. *Journal of Speech, Language, and Hearing Research, 60*, 1316–29.

Valian, V. (1991). Syntactic subjects in the early speech of American and Italian children. *Cognition, 40*, 21–81.

Veneziano, E., & Sinclair, H. (2000). The changing status of "filler syllables" on the way to grammatical morphemes. *Journal of Child Language, 27*, 461–500.

Vihman, M. M., & Velleman, S. L. (2000). The construction of a first phonology, *Phonetica, 57*, 255–66.

White, K. S., & Morgan, J. L. (2008). Sub-segmental detail in early lexical representations. *Journal of Memory and Language, 59*, 114–32.

CHAPTER 30

HOW WELL DOES STATISTICAL LEARNING ADDRESS THE CHALLENGES OF REAL-WORLD LANGUAGE LEARNING?

LUCIA SWEENEY AND REBECCA L. GÓMEZ

30.1 INTRODUCTION

WHEN first faced with a novel language, the input can be overwhelming. Without previous knowledge, fluent speech can sound like a random string of syllables with no individual words or structure. An initial step in learning a language is to extract single words from the continuous input. Learners must also acquire the grammatical and semantic properties of those words to create and comprehend novel word combinations. What mechanisms might learners use to make the initials steps? One proposed mechanism is statistical learning, which is the brain's ability to track regularities in perceptual input (Gómez, 2002; Gómez et al., 2006; Gómez & Gerken, 1999, 2000; Romberg & Saffran, 2010; Saffran, Aslin, & Newport, 1996) including phonotactic constraints of language (Adriaans & Kager, 2010; Jusczyk & Luce, 1994) and phonological rules (Gerken, 2004; Gerken & Bollt, 2008), lexical items (Graf Estes, Evans, Alibali, & Saffran, 2007), and categories with semantic (Lany & Saffran, 2010; Lany & Saffran, 2011) and morpho-syntactic properties (Gerken, Wilson, & Lewis, 2005; Gómez & Lakusta, 2004; Gonzales, Gerken, & Gómez, 2015).

Notwithstanding these discoveries, researchers also raise healthy criticisms of the extent to which learners may be able to rely on statistical learning in light of the challenges of learning a natural language (Johnson & Tyler, 2010; Kidd, 2012; Romberg & Saffran, 2010), individual differences in learning, and the fact that the brain networks processing language develop. We argue here that current research addresses these criticisms and extends statistical learning to increasingly challenging scenarios including natural language and more complex artificial languages. Recent research also points to a broad range of performance among healthy participants in statistical learning tasks. Examining individual differences and what underlies them could shed light on individual cognitive functions that support this type of learning. Finally, advances in neuroimaging open windows into directly investigating the neural bases of statistical learning. We review early and late studies reflecting a role for statistical learning in acquiring a language and we address these important advances. We end by highlighting general conclusions from our review and pointing to open questions.

30.2 STATISTICAL LEARNING OF LANGUAGE

In the following section we review studies that assess statistical learning of artificial and natural language, from infants' and adults' use of statistical information to segment words (Kittleson et al., 2010; Pelucchi, Hay, & Saffran, 2009), map them to referents (Graf Estes et al., 2007; Mirman et al., 2008), and track distributional and phonological statistics of words to construct abstract lexical categories and syntactic rules (Gerken, Wilson & Lewis, 2005; Gómez & Lakusta, 2004; Lany & Saffran, 2011). We explore the relevance of these studies to acquisition of natural language, beginning with word segmentation.

30.2.1 Word segmentation

There are few cues indicating where one word ends and the next begins in fluent speech making this word segmentation a challenging task for infants. How do they accomplish this feat with little knowledge of their language? One approach is for infants to track transitional probabilities (TPs) between syllables (Saffran, Aslin, & Newport, 1996)[1]. Eight-month-olds listened to an artificial language consisting of four trisyllabic words combined so that no word occurred twice in sequence and no cues (e.g., pauses, intonation) indicated boundaries between words. After two minutes of familiarization, infants listened longer at test to part-words (consisting of syllables spanning word boundaries) than to words[2]. Presumably infants computed the probability of the occurrence of one syllable given the occurrence of another syllable and used this information to locate word boundaries in the continuous string of speech. In other words, infants could tell which syllables occurred in sequence—identifying those sequences as words—and distinguish them from syllables that occurred in succession less often. Researchers replicate this ability in a variety of learning contexts, including showing that infants can segment words from a string consisting only of non-native phonemes (Graf Estes, Gluck, & Bastos, 2015), demonstrating the power of statistical learning.

A large literature supports the notion that in an experimental setting, learners can rely on TPs to segment words when they are the only cues to the location of word boundaries. Thus,

---

[1] TPs between syllables X and Y are computed by taking the frequency of the pair XY and dividing it by the frequency of syllable X. TPs can thus range from 0 to 1, 0 being an extremely low TP and 1 being an extremely high TP.
[2] Saffran et al. measured listening time to words and part-words using the head-turn preference procedure, a computer-automated procedure for measuring listening times in infant language studies (Kemler Nelson et al., 1995).

the field generally agrees that TPs are one useful cue to facilitate word segmentation, especially when the learner has little knowledge of the language's dominant stress pattern or phonological rules (Thiessen & Saffran, 2003). However, languages utilized in these experiments are simplified and contain no pauses or changes in pitch or stress, while natural languages contain several cues to the location of word boundaries. It is reasonable, then, to question the usefulness of TPs for segmenting *natural* speech, which is far more complicated than the simplistic languages used in artificial word segmentation studies. In particular, natural language has more variation in word length and more potentially contrasting cues to word boundaries (see Yang, 2004, for an early argument on this point).

Nevertheless, after a short exposure to a natural language, adults can segment words based only on statistical information in the stream (Kittleson et al., 2010). English-speaking participants unfamiliar with Norwegian listened to 60 Norwegian sentences, each containing one of nine disyllabic target words. After the familiarization phase, adults completed a recognition test where they judged test items individually. Test items included the nine target words whose mean internal TP was 0.884 along with two types of illegal items. The first type were part-target non-words containing one syllable from a target word and one syllable from an adjacent word from familiarization (mean internal TP = 0.127). The second type of illegal test items, two-word combinations, contained two monosyllabic words from the familiarization sentences (mean TP = 0.382). Adults endorsed target words significantly more often than both types of illegal items, indicating that they could distinguish the correct words from the non-words. However, this effect was largely due to correct rejection of the non-words; although learners endorsed words at chance level (50%) they endorsed non-words at a rate significantly below chance. This pattern of results reflects an early stage of learning at which adults have more knowledge of what is not a word than what is. Thus, while TPs are informative for word segmentation of a natural language, statistical learning in this context may not yield robust mental representations for word forms in adult learners. Even so, these results demonstrate that TPs are useful cues when segmenting natural languages.

Moreover, Pelucchi et al. (2009) utilized a similar paradigm to assess infants' ability to segment a natural language. Eight-month-olds from native English-speaking homes listened to 12 grammatical Italian sentences containing word forms unfamiliar to them. Infants heard sentences containing two disyllabic target words (TP = 1.0), each occurring six times across the 12 sentences. After familiarization to the sentences, infants entered the testing phase. Half of the test trials contained a repeating target item whose internal TP was 1.0. The other half contained a novel disyllabic item with an internal TP of 0. Infants listened significantly longer to the high-TP compared to the low-TP trials, indicating they were able to discriminate the two; the authors replicated this result with non-target test items with internal TP = 0.33. The success of these eight-month-old infants in using TPs to segment target words from a natural language further demonstrates the application of statistical learning to real-world language. Taking the results of Pelucchi et al. (2009) and Kittleson et al. (2010) into account, it is clear that learners can rely on TPs to segment natural, non-simplified languages.

How robust is statistical learning to other forms of variation? Given that in natural environments infants are likely to hear multiple people talking in sequence, it would be advantageous if learners could track statistics even in the presence of multiple talker voices. Graf Estes and Lew-Williams (2015) found that after listening to an artificial language containing disyllabic words, eight-month-old infants segment a statistical language when the talker voice changes mid-stream, even when the talker changes mid-word. However, segmentation only occurs when there is high talker variability: when infants hear eight voices alternating across the stream, they can distinguish part-words from words at test. When the language alternates between only two talkers, the infants do not properly segment. The authors suggest that the high variability in talker voice draws infants' attention toward what remains constant in the stream—the TPs between syllables—and away from the features that change across talkers such as pitch and articulation. These findings support the idea that variability in the linguistic input supports the tracking of TPs, indicating that statistical learning has a role in word segmentation in real-world settings where variability is unavoidable.

It is possible that other forms of variation may present challenges for learning. In Johnson and Tyler (2010) 5.5- and 8.5-month-old infants listened to a language consisting of concatenated disyllabic and trisyllabic words with no pauses or prosody to indicate word boundaries. At test, words were the disyllabic words from the language. Part-words were the last syllable of one word and the first syllable of another. Infants listened equally to both types of stimuli indicating that they did not segment items from a familiarization language containing words of variable length. The authors argued that when languages are more complex, infants must rely on cues other than TPs to segment speech.

Indeed, infants do segment a language whose word lengths vary if the language is in infant-directed speech (Thiessen, Hill, & Saffran, 2005). Infants aged 6.5 months listened to 12 sentences, each consisting of the same four artificial words arranged in different orders. Two of the words were disyllabic and the other two were trisyllabic. All sentences began with the word /mo/ and ended with /fa/ to ensure infants could not use phrase edges to segment words. Half of the participants heard infant-directed speech during familiarization; the others listened to the same sentences in adult-directed speech. At test, words consisted of one trisyllabic and one disyllabic word from familiarization. Part-words were strings of syllables that spanned a word boundary, one disyllabic and the other trisyllabic. Only the group exposed to infant-directed speech discriminated words from part-words, leading the authors to suggest that the prosodic nature of infant-directed speech draws infants' attention more than adult-directed speech, leading to stronger segmentation. Thus, while variation in word length hinders word segmentation based on TPs, exaggerated prosodic cues can facilitate learning in this context. Perhaps the infants in this study are better able to account for variation in word length when they are more attentive to input. These results support the relevance of statistical learning in infants' acquisition of their native language.

Are there other aspects of infant-directed speech that facilitate word segmentation? For one, utterances in infant-directed speech are shorter and have highly exaggerated pitch contours (Bernstein, 1986; Fernald & Mazzie, 1991), resulting in a greater number of salient utterance boundaries (UBs) compared to adult-directed speech. UBs may potentially aid in word segmentation, to the extent that word edges border a pause. Johnson, Seidl, and Tyler (2014) and Seidl and Johnson (2006) investigated this hypothesis by presenting infants with six English sentences, each containing a target word, novel to the participants. For half of the infants, the target word always occurred sentence medially. For the other half, the word always occurred at an utterance edge (alternating between the first and the final position in a sentence), providing a UB cue for segmentation. Infants who heard the target word in edge positions distinguished it from an unfamiliar word at test but not infants for whom target words occurred in medial sentence positions.

Furthermore, Seidl and Johnson (2008) observed similar results when infants segmented words beginning with a vowel rather than a consonant. Without UB cues to word boundaries, infants do not segment vowel-initial words until age 13–16 months (Nazzi et al., 2005). When the vowel-initial target word is the initial word in a phrase, infants as young as 11 months successfully discriminate the target word from an unfamiliar word they did not hear during familiarization, demonstrating the usefulness of additional prosodic cues (UBs) when it is difficult to segment accurately using TPs alone (Seidl & Johnson, 2008). While the infant-directed speech string in Thiessen et al. (2005) did not include pauses, the results of Johnson et al. (2014), and Seidl and Johnson (2006, 2008) suggest infant-directed speech may, in-part, function to aid word segmentation by providing more UBs in the input. The results of these studies together indicate that the linguistic signal infants hear often (infant-directed speech) supports tracking of TPs when infants would otherwise have difficulty segmenting, as in the cases when the language contains variable word lengths or vowel-initial words.

UBs also facilitate word segmentation in adults. Sohail and Johnson (2016) created three learning conditions. In the TP condition, the experimental language contained only one cue to the location of word boundaries: TPs. In the UB condition, the language had a UB cue and no TP cue, accomplished by concatenating the words of the language in a fixed order so that TPs within and between words were one. The UB cue consisted of a 650 ms pause occurring after every three to five words. In the UB + TP condition, the language contained both UB cues and reliable TPs. On a subsequent two-alternative forced-choice task (2AFC, in which participants listened to one word and one part-word, and had to choose which item occurred in the language heard previously), only adults in the UB and UB + TP conditions performed with above chance (50%) accuracy. This is a surprising finding, as adults often segment strings of speech based on TPs alone. However, this familiarization language contained nine disyllabic words versus the usual four- or six-item lexicon, thus presenting a learning challenge. Even so, adults' inability to segment a language with nine words repeated for approximately nine minutes does not bode well for their ability to use TPs alone to segment natural language, which is incredibly more complex. However, language *does* include multiple cues to word boundaries (as in the UB + TP condition), including the edges of utterances, so the fact that learners can capitalize on congruent cues to segment words is promising for natural language learning.

While UBs clearly aid word segmentation, what about phonotactic cues? Fernandes, Kolinsky, and Ventura (2009) investigated the influence of phonotactics on word segmentation in adults. TPs and legal phonotactic regularities aligned in the congruent condition. In the incongruent condition, items with legal phonotactics spanned a word boundary. After 21 minutes of listening to the artificial language made up of 10 trisyllabic words, participants in the congruent condition selected words over part-words in a 2AFC test. Those in the incongruent condition selected part-words over words based on their legal phonotactics, which overrode TPs, demonstrating that adults rely on phonotactic constraints to segment language more so than they rely on statistical information.

To conclude, statistical learning is certainly useful for word segmentation, even in natural language settings (Graf Estes & Lew-Williams, 2015; Kittleson et al., 2010; Pelucchi, Hay, & Saffran, 2009). However, when word length varies, or the input is less prototypical (e.g., when the words start with vowels) infant learners must rely on prosodic cues such as UBs or those available in infant-directed speech to segment the stream (Johnson et al., 2014; Seidl & Johnson, 2006, 2008; Thiessen et al., 2005). In addition, adults cannot rely on TPs alone to segment an artificial language containing a large lexicon; they must also track UBs (Sohail & Johnson, 2016). The adult population appears to rely on auditory features rather than statistics when listening to a language containing contrasting cues to word boundaries, tending to disregard TPs and segment based on phonotactic constraints (Fernandes et al., 2009). Together, these studies indicate that statistical learning is a robust mechanism for word segmentation in natural language early in life, but as learners acquire more knowledge of the phonotactic rules of their native language they begin to attend to salient auditory cues present in natural speech.

30.2.2 Word learning/lexicalization

If TPs are useful for acquiring language in a real-world setting, what kind of information do learners encode into memory during this process? Research supports the notion that computing the TPs between syllables facilitates the process of word segmentation and aids in discriminating high-TP from low-TP strings, but will learners use these representations as potential words? After exposure to a statistical language, infants fail to use part-words as object labels, but readily map words they segment from an artificial language onto novel objects (Graf Estes et al., 2007). Similarly, adults more readily form label-object mappings between words and novel objects compared to part-words. However, adults learned non-words as labels just as fast as words with high TPs. Because adults are slow to form mappings between objects and part-words yet are fast with words and novel non-words, perhaps part-words inhibit lexical word formation (Mirman et al., 2008). By this view, adults gain potential lexical items for high TPs during segmentation along with knowledge that low-TP items are not likely labels.

Erickson, Thiessen, and Graf Estes (2014) investigated whether statistically segmented words may serve as labels of semantic categories over and above single referents per Graf Estes et al. (2007). Eight-month-old infants first participated in a segmentation phase after Thiessen et al. (2005). Next, during category familiarization they viewed multiple exemplars of a category, one at a time, while hearing either a single word or part-word. Infants then viewed two images side by side in a category test: a novel member of the same category and a member of an untrained category. Infants who heard a word during category familiarization looked longer to the untrained category compared to infants who heard a part-word, suggesting that the words infants extract during statistical learning facilitate categorization of semantically related referents (Erickson et al., 2014). Further research should investigate whether infants are able to perform such mappings after a delay, given that labels for words are not always heard in tandem with the presentation of the associated object.

Lexicalization does not always occur during word segmentation. Fernandes et al. (2009), described earlier, went on to ask whether participants formed lexical entries and whether items would lexicalize based on TPs versus the phonotactics of their native language. The authors utilized a lexical competition paradigm that indicates lexical effects in reaction-time changes in the lexical neighborhood (Gaskell & Dumay, 2003). Syllable sequences with high phonotactics differed from real words—considered "base words" in this experiment—by the final syllable only. If adults segmented these novel items from the artificial language based on their phonotactic properties, they would then be in the form-related neighborhood of the similar base word and would compete for access during the presentation of the shared first two syllables (Gaskell & Dumay, 2003). Lexicalization can thus be measured during a word recognition task: if adults lexicalize newly segmented items, participants would be slower to identify related base words as words compared to control items that did not resemble any syllable sequence in the artificial language. Recalling that the authors asked whether lexicalization would occur based on TPs, phonotactics, or both, they compared lexicalization effects across congruent and incongruent conditions. Learners did not lexicalize in the incongruent condition where TP and phonotactics contrasted, but when phonotactics and statistics aligned in the congruent condition, subjects lexicalized the segmented items. Together these studies provide ample evidence that learners treat the outputs they segment as lexical items.

30.2.3 Syntax

30.2.3.1 *Non-adjacent dependencies*

Infants and adults also use statistical information to learn syntax. One way we acquire knowledge of syntax through statistical regularities is by tracking of non-adjacent dependencies in running speech. In English, the phrase "he is singing" contains a common non-adjacent dependency observed in English verb morphology. Both the auxiliary "is" and the inflectional morpheme "-ing" occur in regular future tense constructions, while the medial item—the verb—varies widely. These morphemes form a "frequent frame," as proposed by Mintz (2003), that potentially aids in syntactic categorization of the medial item. The ability to use frequent frames for categorization depends on learning the frames in the first place, an ability that surfaces in behavior later in development compared to adjacent dependency learning of TPs.

In investigating the trajectory of non-adjacent dependency learning, Gómez and Maye (2005) familiarized 12-, 15-, and 17-month-olds to an artificial language. The language took the form aXc and bXd, where an *a* item always preceded a *c* item, and a *b* item always preceded a *d* item, with a medial X item that came from a class of either 12 or 18 items, depending on the learning condition. Because X items are highly variable, tracking the adjacent TP between *a* and X items will be of little benefit. Gómez (2002) demonstrated the advantages of having a large set of X items so that the medial item is highly variable. In particular, the high variability may draw learner's attention to the consistency of the surrounding items drawn from a smaller set. Infants in Gómez and Maye (2005) listened to repetitions of the aXc and bXd strings to become familiar with the artificial grammar. At test, infants listened to grammatical trials following the grammar of the familiarization language. They also heard ungrammatical trials, in which *a* items paired with *d* items and *b* items paired with *c* items. Importantly, ungrammatical trials violated the non-adjacent dependency from learning. Twelve-month-olds did not distinguish grammatical from ungrammatical trials, demonstrating that infants of this age are not yet rapidly extracting non-adjacent dependencies as measured in behavior. At 15 and 17 months of age, infants discriminated in the large set-size condition. The authors argue that learners focus on TPs between items immediately in sequence. Once learning conditions become more variable and adjacent TPs are very low, learners begin to focus on dependencies over a longer distance (Gómez, 2002; Gómez & Maye, 2005).

However, non-adjacent dependency learning has its constraints. In natural language, long-distance dependencies can be probabilistic in that one *a* element can be paired with multiple *b* items, or vice versa. For example, in the phrase "he *is* danc*ing*," the *a* element "is" and the *b* element "-ing" consistently appear as a non-adjacent dependency surrounding a verb. However, in constructions like "he *was* sing*ing*," the *b* element "-ing" pairs with a different but grammatical *a* element, "was." Therefore, in learning a real-world language, learners must acquire dependencies that are not always deterministic in nature. Evidence that this is a challenge comes from the fact that although 18-month-old infants track "is X-ing" in natural language (Tincoff, Santelmann, & Jusczyk, 2000) they do not track "was X-ing" at this age.

Even adult learners perform at chance when non-adjacent dependencies are probabilistic in the context of an artificial language. Van den Bos, Christiansen, and Misyak (2012) created an aXb language with two *a* items and four *b* items. One *a* element consistently paired with two *b* items. The other *a* element paired with the other two *b* items. A control group listened to a deterministic language with a one-to-one mapping between four *a* items and four *b* items. After a period of listening to this grammar, adults judged whether a test item followed or violated the rules of the language (illegal test items disrupted the non-adjacency relations). Adults in the control condition performed significantly above chance; adults exposed to the probabilistic language performed at chance levels (50%).

The authors next introduced a phonological cue to facilitate acquisition of the probabilistic non-adjacent dependencies in which *a* and *b* items shared a common ending (e.g., the *a* item *puser* shared the *-er* ending with *b* items *meeper* and *skigger*, yielding legal strings such as *puser X meeper* and *puser X skigger*). Adults successfully identified grammatical strings, even when white noise masked the shared endings during the grammaticality judgment test (van den Bos et al., 2012). Masking ensured that the participants were not merely memorizing the rhyming words during familiarization, as reflected in the fact that they discriminated even when they could not hear the rhyme at test. This study highlighted the usefulness of integrating multiple statistical cues in acquiring syntax-like dependencies. When there is no phonological cue linking the *b* items to their respective *a* item, acquiring the dependencies between one *a* item and several *b* items proves difficult for adult learners. However, if there is a phonological cue highlighting the association between *a* and *b* items, this cue aids in adults' acquisition of these long-distance dependencies during learning.

30.2.3.2 *Lexical category acquisition*

Mintz's (2003) proposal that frequent non-adjacent dependencies aid in syntactic category formation is just one in the literature. More complex constellations of cues including adjacent dependencies may also inform learning of syntactic information. For example, in the phrase, "the dog *can* bark," the function word *can* appears before the verb *bark*. Replace "bark" with any other English verb and the sentence remains grammatical. However, replace "bark" with a noun, like "bread," and the sentence becomes ungrammatical. The adjacent dependency here is between the function word "can" and the verb word class. St. Clair, Monaghan, and Christiansen (2010) posit that such adjacent dependencies are beneficial for grammatical category learning, as they often contain a wide variety of items from a given category.

Additionally, phonological and distributional cues may inform category learning, and research suggests a relationship between phonological and distributional cues (Farmer, Christiansen, & Monaghan, 2006). In English, for instance, nouns and verbs differ in syllable length (Kelly, 1992), providing a phonological cue for categorization. Nouns and verbs also pair with different functional items, as already explained; this co-occurrence serves as a distributional cue. Gómez and Lakusta (2004) familiarized 12-month-old infants to an artificial language consisting of two *a* items and two *b* items, each of which were monosyllabic. These distributional cues paired consistently with six disyllabic X items or six monosyllabic Y items (*a* items preceded X items and *b* items preceded Y items with syllable number a phonological cue). In order to fully acquire abstract categories, infants must learn the relationship between *a*/*b* items and the associated cue that marks lexical category (e.g., noun and verb). Once infants make this association, they can form *a*- and *b*-categories based on their associations with the lexical cue and can identify category members based on *a* or *b* items alone. After a three-minute familiarization to the artificial language, infants discriminated novel grammatical phrases containing new X and Y words from illegal phrases in which *b* items preceded X items and *a* items preceded Y items. Infants likely acquired this knowledge through tracking phonological and distributional cues. Gerken et al. (2005) extended this research and found that 17-month-olds generalize based on distributional cues alone when no phonological cue (e.g., syllable length) is present during familiarization, indicating more robust statistical learning at this age.

Lany and Saffran (2010) went on to assess whether infants can map the phrases from Gómez and Lakusta onto lexical categories. Twenty-two-month-old infants first listened to aX and bY phrases. In a control condition, infants heard a language that did not contain reliable statistics where *a* and *b* items preceded X and Y items with equal frequency. After 3.5 minutes of listening, infants entered into a brief referent training phase where they heard a subset of the aX and bY phrases as labels while viewing pictures of animals or vehicles (the category varied depending on which phrase type infants heard on a trial). At test, infants viewed two pictures, one of a vehicle and one of an animal, and heard an aX or bY phrase. The pictures from referent training appeared on familiar trials, whereas infants viewed novel pictures of vehicles and animals on generalization trials. Infants in the experimental group showed looking preferences for the target image on familiar and generalization trials showing that they mapped the phrases successfully onto categories. In order to ensure that infants acquired the semantic properties associated with X and Y words and did not perform the mapping based on the presence of the *a* and *b* items only, Lany and Saffran also assessed memory for specific aX mappings. The familiarization and referent training phases were the same as in the previous experiment, but during the test infants saw two pictures that belonged to the same category (either two animal or two vehicle pictures). As the label paired consistently with only one of the presented pictures during referent training and both items were from the same lexical category, the infants could not use the general association between the *a* and *b* items and their respective semantic category during the test. Rather, infants had to recall the association between the specific X or Y item and its trained referent. Infants in the experimental condition increased their looking to the target picture to a greater degree than control infants, who did not look longer to the target image. As a whole, this study suggests how infants may track correlated distributional (in the form of *a*- and *b*-units) and phonological cues (in the form of word endings), and integrate this statistical knowledge with a visual referent to form a simple lexical category.

Gonzales, Gerken, and Gómez (2015) went on to ask how infants acquire aX and bY categories when statistics in the input are variable. This is the case when children encounter different dialects or language proficiencies in the form of non-native speakers or language learning peers. Gonzales et al. modeled their study after Gómez and Lakusta (2004) who showed that infants tolerate a small degree of inconsistency in the mappings between a, X, b, and Y units in their ability to learn and generalize aX and bY phrases. Gonzales et al. created two streams from these items: a pure stream, containing consistent distributional and phonological statistics (all *a* items preceded X items and *b* items preceded Y items), and a mixed stream containing no reliable statistics because *a* and *b* items preceded X and Y items with equal frequency. Twelve-month-olds segregated the pure and the mixed streams as long as the two occurred minutes apart, even when one stream followed the other with no perceptible break (such as talker voice).

In all, lexical category acquisition appears to begin early, supports mappings between referents and form, and appears robust under challenging learning conditions.

30.3 INDIVIDUAL DIFFERENCES

30.3.1 Variation within typical populations

For an ability that may seem so fundamental in language acquisition, researchers note high variability in statistical learning ranging from very poor to very high performance between individuals in typical populations. In adults, recognition accuracy is often quantified using either a recognition task, where participants hear one item at a time and respond whether they recognize it as a word from the language they heard previously, or a two-alternative forced-choice task in which participants must select which of two items they recognize as a word from the language. In many studies, the worst performer(s) fall within the range of 30–50% recognition accuracy (with one study reporting a low of 15%), while high performers achieve accuracy of 80–100% (as observed in Franco, Cleeremans, & Destrebecqz, 2011; Gabay, Thiessen, & Holt, 2015; Mersad & Nazzi, 2011; Schapiro, Gregory, Landau, McCloskey, & Turk-Browne, 2014; Thiessen, 2010, to name a few). What drives these individual differences in statistical learning?

Misyak and Christiansen (2012) investigated the causes of variance in acquiring adjacent and non-adjacent dependencies. They found no relationship between the ability to learn adjacent and non-adjacent dependencies, with these two types of learning correlating differently with different aspects of cognition. Specifically, acquisition of adjacent dependencies correlated with short-term memory (STM)—measured using a forward digit span task—and verbal working memory (vWM)—measured using a reading span task as created by Waters and Caplan (1996)—whereas learning of non-adjacent dependencies correlated only with vWM. In this study, the STM task measured participants' short-term memory capacity; subjects listened to sequences of numbers ranging from two to nine digits in length. Immediately after each sequence, they were to repeat the numbers in the correct order. In this task they only had to hold the numbers in memory for a maximum of 10 seconds, and they were not required to manipulate the incoming information in any way. The authors quantified STM capacity by recording the number of digits in the last sequence participants successfully repeated before failing twice. Alternatively, the vWM task measured participant's ability to process linguistic information (e.g., make semantic judgments on each sentence as they read) while simultaneously holding other linguistic information in mind across time (i.e., after blocks ranging from two to six sentences long they were to report the last word of each sentence in the block). Thus, vWM in this case requires both retention of presented information and simultaneous online processing of the incoming signal. As Misyak and Christiansen point out, the tendency for learners to primarily attend to adjacent transitions may be due to reliance on STM at the outset of learning. Moreover, constraints on memory may have a role in the late development of non-adjacent dependency acquisition. Gómez and Maye (2005) reported that 12-month-olds do not track non-adjacent dependencies, whereas 15-month-olds do. Perhaps vWM in 12-month-olds is not strong enough to support learning of long-distance dependencies.

Not all studies examining individual differences in statistical learning come to the same findings regarding working memory. A recent investigation failed to observe correlations of adjacent or non-adjacent dependency learning with vWM (Siegelman & Frost, 2015). These authors did not measure STM. The discrepancies between this study and Misyak and Christiansen (2012) may stem from the materials learners acquired during non-adjacent dependency learning. Misyak and Christiansen (2012) had participants learn an aXc bYd grammar similar to that in Gómez (2002), so adults tracked non-adjacent dependencies across words. In contrast, Siegelman and Frost (2015) exposed adults to a language containing 12 words. Each word followed one of three frames: /p_v_g/, /d_k_b/, and /m_t_s/ and each frame appeared in the language with one of four possible combinations of vowels between consonants. Learners could only use non-adjacent dependencies between consonants to acquire the underlying word structure. Learners later discriminated non-words (that did not follow the consonant frame) from novel words that conformed to the frame. In this paradigm, learners track single phonemes versus words in sequence and may not recruit working memory to the same extent as the task Misyak and Christiansen (2012) administered, as these non-adjacent dependencies do not span multiple words.

Individual differences can also influence statistical learning in infancy. Lany and Saffran (2010) demonstrated infants' ability to use distributional, phonological, and semantic information in order to form a new lexical category. They examined whether individual differences in vocabulary size related to learning strategy including a measure of vocabulary and grammatical development: the MacArthur Communicative Development Inventories (CDI). Lany and Saffran (2011) utilized the same methods for familiarization and referent training from their previous study (2010) which involved training infants on semantic referents for aX and bY phrases. During the test phase, there were two types of generalization trials. During distributional cue generalization trials, participants viewed two novel pictures, one of an animal and one of a vehicle, and heard an *a*- or *b*-item in isolation. During phonological cue generalization trials, infants viewed the two novel pictures and heard an X or Y word alone. Infants with larger vocabularies showed preferential looking to the target image on distributional cue trials. Infants with smaller productive vocabularies showed more accurate preferential looking to the target on phonological cue trials.

Recall that use of the distributional cue reflects higher-order knowledge of the aX or bY category to the extent that the *a*- or *b*-item stands in for the phonological cue that attaches to individual words. Lany and Saffran suggest that the patterning of the distributional cue with larger vocabulary instead of smaller vocabulary reflects more taxing processing assuming infants are tracking the co-occurrence frequency between *a* and X items (consistently paired with animals) and between *b* and Y items (consistently paired with vehicles). Alternately, infants could be forming associations between *a/b* items and the visual referents with no attention to distributional cues. In Lany and Saffran (2011), individual *a/b* items occurred 24 times during familiarization, whereas individual X/Y items appeared eight times only. Given that infants are more likely to map a low frequency label to an object than a high frequency label (Hochman, Endress, & Mehler, 2010), it is unlikely that infants are using the frequently occurring *a* and *b* items as labels. Rather, in Lany and Saffran (2011) they truly acquired the distributional relationship between function-like *a/b* items and X/Y items and used this information to acquire lexical categories. Overall, it appears that in infancy and young childhood, vocabulary size is a predictor of statistical learning ability. However, it should be noted that the direction of this association is not clear, as a strong statistical learning mechanism could lead children to acquire more words than their peers who track statistical information to a lesser degree or are less successful in learning from statistical regularities.

30.3.2 Atypical populations

30.3.2.1 *Specific language impairment and language learning delay*

Researchers also investigate atypical language function, as learning in these individuals can inform the cognitive underpinnings of statistical learning. In our discussion of atypical learning we include studies from populations with specific language impairment (SLI) and populations classified as having language learning delay (LLD) given that these groups show similar deficits (Fidler, Plante, & Vance, 2011). Learners with SLI and those with LLD both show impaired STM and vWM (Archibald & Gathercole, 2006; Isaki & Plante, 1997), which are proposed correlates of adjacent and non-adjacent dependency acquisition (Misyak & Christiansen, 2012). These individuals also demonstrate difficulty in word segmentation compared to those with typical language ability (Evans, Saffran, & Robe-Torres, 2009). Moreover, kindergarteners with SLI can segment speech when they have extra exposure, 42 minutes versus the 21-minute exposure adequate for typically developing children (Evans et al., 2009). This finding suggests that the statistical learning mechanism used in this population tracks conditional probabilities at a slower rate.

Participants with LLD also exhibit challenges in acquiring non-adjacent dependencies. Unlike typically developing populations, who benefit from high variability in the X item in a non-adjacent dependency language (Gómez, 2002), participants with LLD do not benefit when the X item is highly variable (Grunow, Spaulding, Gómez, & Plante, 2006). Likewise, Kerkhoff, De Bree, De Klerk, and Wijnen (2013) investigated non-adjacent-dependency learning in 18-month-olds with familial risk of dyslexia using the head-turn preference procedure. These children did not discriminate grammatical from ungrammatical strings compared to infants without familial risk, indicating a deficit in this form of statistical learning in dyslexic populations. Instead, atypical language learners appear to acquire extremely low-variability items. Hsu, Tomblin, and Christiansen (2014) familiarized adolescents with SLI with three non-adjacent dependencies from Gómez (2002) in one of three set-size conditions corresponding to low, medium, and high variability (set-size = 2, 12, and 24, respectively). More participants acquired non-adjacent dependencies in the low-variability condition and this correlated with language proficiency, suggesting that these adolescents learned individual items given their exposure to just six unique strings many times during familiarization.

Similar to the item-based learning indicated in Hsu et al. (2014), Richardson, Harris, Plante, and Gerken (2006) observed evidence of learning of specific phonological patterns in adults with LLD. Participants listened to single-marked and double-marked Russian words during familiarization. Single-marked words contained a suffix marking gender; double-marked words contained a gender suffix and a case marker. Unimpaired adults track the co-occurrence of unique word stems with their gender and case markers and used these cues to generalize to new combinations. LLD and unimpaired learners performed similarly on items heard during familiarization, but LLD learners showed poor discrimination for novel items, endorsing novel grammatical and ungrammatical strings equally. The pattern of results suggested that they responded based on memory for specific stem-suffix combinations that did not permit generalization.

Thus, although learners with impaired language learn specific transitions with sufficient training, more than one study suggests that they focus on specific items over syllable or word combinations.

30.4 IMAGING

Researchers also investigate the neural bases of statistical learning given advances in neuroimaging. Behavioral measurements cannot reveal neural mechanisms supporting statistical learning, while neuroimaging can inform such inquiries. In addition, we can also observe age-related differences in neural activity recruited during statistical learning, which could elucidate behavioral differences between infants and adults. Lastly, event-related potential (ERP) measurements allow researchers to assess neural responses during statistical learning in neonates and very young infants before behavioral evidence of statistical learning surfaces. In the following section we review research covering these topics.

30.4.1 FMRI

In order to assess the neural activity associated with statistical learning of natural language, Plante and colleagues exposed participants to Norwegian sentences during fMRI (Plante et al., 2015). In the "high predictability" condition, each sentence contained one of nine disyllabic target words. Researchers created the "low predictability" stimuli by editing the high predictability sentences so that one syllable from the target word occurred in a random position within the sentence; there was no statistical relationship between the first and second syllables of the target word. Legal items at test were the nine target words, and illegal items were nine non-words created by parsing a syllable pair that included only one syllable from the target word. Participants heard each test item individually and responded via button press whether they recognized it as a word from the language. They completed three scans: during each scan they listened to the two-minute familiarization stimuli and completed a subsequent test. During the familiarization stages, researchers observed different activation patterns in response to high predictability versus low predictability languages, with more widespread activation to the high predictability language. The authors highlight this difference in activation as evidence that learning is "neurobiologically distinct" when statistics at the syllable level are present compared to when the stimuli do not contain regularities.

Plante and colleagues also report positive correlations between recognition accuracy and activation in the left and right frontal lobe, the right temporal lobe, the left parietal lobe, and left dorsolateral prefrontal lobe in the high predictability condition. In particular, the authors draw attention to differences in activation in the temporal lobe between low and high predictability groups, suggesting that this region in particular tracks statistical regularities, among other linguistic functions (Plante et al., 2015).

While others have implicated the inferior frontal gyrus (IFG) in statistical learning of language (Karuza et al., 2013), Plante and colleagues (2015) observe a positive correlation in the high predictability group between dorsolateral prefrontal cortex and correct acceptance of target words during the recognition test. However, this correlation was only present during the first scan, indicating a link between dorsolateral activation and cognitive control rather than tracking of statistical regularities.

Plante and colleagues also observed IFG activation—in the pars opercularis—present during familiarization in scans one and two of the high probability group. The authors consider the possibility that by the third scan the participants may have already segmented the words and were no longer actively tracking statistics. Yet by this point, the participants recognize non-words as correct words from the language approximately 50% of the time, indicating that they were still in the process of segmenting the words from the stream. Given participants' below-ceiling performance by the third test, and the fact that their performance improved between tests two and three, the authors reasoned the participants continued tracking the statistics throughout the last scan despite the lack of activity in the IFG. They thus propose that the lack of activity in the pars opercularis of the IFG during the last scan provides evidence that this region's primary role is *not* related to statistical learning of language (Plante et al., 2015).

Researchers also investigate neural substrates of statistical learning in children, comparing their patterns of activation to adults'. Both 10-year-olds and adults showed activity increases within the superior temporal gyrus (STG) while listening to an artificial language (McNealy, Mazziotta, & Dapretto, 2010). This activation is stronger and left lateralized in adults but bilateral in children. In addition, adults showed significantly greater activation increases than children in the medial temporal gyrus (MTG) bilaterally. These findings point to developmental differences in the statistical learning mechanism. Along similar lines, children and adults showed different activation during testing. In both populations words yielded greater activity than non-words in the left IFG, with adults showing greater activation in both the IFG and MTG. Karuza et al. (2013) suggest the left IFG plays a critical role in statistical learning by computing regularities and generating representations for knowledge gained. However, considering the argument proposed by Plante and colleagues (2015), it is more likely that the IFG activation observed in response to words over part-words relates to processes of working memory, potentially signaling the retrieval of recently segmented word forms from memory. Therefore, difference in activation between adults and children in the IFG (McNealy et al., 2010) may indicate more robust working memory ability in adults. Moreover, as Plante and colleagues (2015) suggested the temporal lobe tracks regularities, and McNealy et al. (2010) found statistical learning in adults yields greater activation in the MTG and STG in comparison to children, a pattern of results further suggesting a stronger statistical learning mechanism in adulthood.

30.4.2 ERP

ERPs also allow us to assess neural responses during word segmentation. Researchers measured ERPs during familiarization to a language consisting of six trisyllabic words (Sanders, Newport, & Neville, 2002). After familiarization, adults completed a 2ACFFC task. The researchers performed a median split based on performance in the 2AFC, grouping participants into high and low learners. High learners showed larger increases across training in the N100 response to word onsets compared to the low learners. As the N100 indicates the identification of a word onset in natural language (Sanders & Neville, 2003), neural responses reveal recognition of word onsets as learners begin to identify the words of the novel language. Sanders et al. (2002) also report increasing N400 responses over learning, time-locked to word onsets. The authors suggest the N400 signals lexical search and is a marker of speech segmentation. Similarly, Cunillera, Toro, Sebastián-Gallés, and Rodríguez-Fornells (2006) report an N400 response during a word segmentation task, but only in adults who listened to a stream containing informative TPs. The N400 in this context provides further evidence for lexicalization of items segmented through statistical learning. Moreover, taking these studies together, the presence of the N100 and the N400 demonstrate the similarities between processing a natural language and processing an artificial language.

Measuring ERPs is also useful for investigating processing very early in development. Neural tracking of sequential structure is present as early as a few days after birth, indicating the potential use of statistical learning in forming early word-form representations. In fact, neonates show greater negativity responses in left hemisphere to word-onset syllables during familiarization to an artificial language (Teinonen et al., 2009).

What kind of neural signatures emerge during acquisition of non-adjacent dependencies? Four-month-old infants listened to natural Italian phrases that followed an aXd cYd pattern (Friederici, Mueller, & Oberecker, 2011). After 13 minutes of listening to grammatically correct phrases, experimenters presented incorrect phrases intermixed with the grammatically correct ones and measured ERPs. A late positivity in response to ungrammatical but not grammatical sentences indicated learning of the non-adjacent dependencies. Research with older children and adults, demonstrating a late positivity effect associated with syntactic processing, corroborates these results (Kaan, Harris, Gibson, & Holcomb, 2000; Oberecker & Friederici, 2006). An unanswered question is what to make of differences between neural (Friederici et al., 2011) and behavioral measures of non-adjacent dependency learning which emerge later in development (Gómez & Maye, 2005). Perhaps eRP measures recorded in early infancy reflect recruitment of a less specialized brain network than that indicated in older learners, as suggested by McNealy et al., (2010). Studies comparing ERP measures of non-adjacent dependency learning in younger and older infants, which might further explain these differences, are absent in the literature. Finally, although the brain may track non-adjacent structure in the short-term, studies investigating their retention may also be useful in understanding the contradictions resulting from different measures.

30.5 Summary

Twenty years after the initial publication of Saffran, Aslin, and Newport (1996) we know a great deal about the scope of statistical learning. Early experiments utilized well-controlled stimuli containing a singular statistic for learners to track. More recent work extends this line of inquiry to contexts more similar to real-world language acquisition with much work suggesting a role for statistical learning in acquiring natural language. Although researchers control input extensively in experimental settings, recent work suggests that converging factors support learning under challenging language-like conditions. For instance, although infants do not readily segment a language with varying word length (Johnson & Tyler, 2010), they do when they hear the language in infant-directed speech (Thiessen et al., 2005). UBs also facilitate segmentation (Johnson et al., 2014; Seidl & Johnson, 2006; Seidl & Johnson, 2008; Sohail & Johnson, 2016). Furthermore, infants and adults gain lexical knowledge through word segmentation (Graf Estes et al., 2007; Mirman et al., 2008) and can use distributional knowledge to learn grammatical rules and form abstract categories (Gerken Wilson & Lewis, 2005; Gómez, 2002; Gómez & Lakusta, 2004; Lany & Saffran).

Statistical learning also has its constraints. When TP cues contrast with phonotactics of their native language, learners segment based on phonotactics rather than TPs. Adults do not represent these segmented items as potential words (Fernandes et al., 2009), yet when no incongruent phonotactic cue is present, learners encode high-TP strings as potential lexical items (Graf Estes et al., 2007; Mirman et al., 2008). This finding demonstrates adults' reliance on non-statistical cues when such cues are perceptually salient, indicating that learners do not always use statistical information even if it is present in the input.

Research on individual differences in statistical learning sheds light on its supporting mechanisms. Successful tracking of adjacent dependencies correlated with STM and vWM, and non-adjacent dependency learning correlated with vWM (Misyak & Christiansen, 2012), potentially indicating a role of these mechanisms in statistical learning. Investigations of atypical learning also support this notion, as individuals with SLI and those with learning difficulties and disabilities (LDD) show deficits in STM and vWM coupled with difficulty tracking both TPs and non-adjacent dependencies. Together these studies point to the importance of STM and vWM for statistical learning. Examining the aspects of cognition that may support statistical learning can inform us of the mechanisms that drive the surfacing of statistical learning ability in infancy. For instance, it could be the case that immature vWM causes 12-month-olds difficulty in acquiring non-adjacent dependencies. In addition, given the reported association between statistical learning in infancy and vocabulary size (Lany & Saffran, 2011) perhaps vocabulary size and vWM (e.g., knowledge of words and ability to hold or manipulate them in memory) work in tandem to assist tracking long-distance dependencies for categorization.

Lastly, neuroimaging in this domain reveals several important discoveries. First, the left temporal and frontal regions activate when adults listen to a language containing reliable statistics (McNealy et al., 2010; Plante et al., 2015), with frontal regions likely contributing to working memory and cognitive control and temporal regions playing a specific role in tracking of statistical regularities (Plante et al., 2015). Secondly, children and adults show significantly different patterns of neural activity during statistical learning (McNealy et al., 2010). Such differences indicate a potential shift in learning mechanism with age that supports more robust statistical learning in adults. Lastly, ERP research illustrates the role of statistical learning in early language acquisition, as ERPs in neonates and young infants suggest successful tracking of both TPs and non-adjacent dependencies. As we develop this theme next, it will be important to connect this work with behavioral evidence of retention to help resolve why neural correlates emerge early in infancy, but behavioral markers emerge later.

30.6 Open questions

30.6.1 Theories of statistical learning

How is statistical learning accomplished? Providing a mechanistic account of statistical learning can further reveal cognitive factors underlying statistical learning, which can then inform therapies to aid populations who show impaired language acquisition. Researchers propose the extraction and integration framework (Erickson & Thiessen, 2015; Thiessen, Kronstein, & Hufnagle, 2013). By this account, learners track conditional relations to extract items from the environment. The extraction mechanism is based in attention and working memory; learners must attend to relevant information in the input (e.g., two high-TP syllables) before working memory binds them together. Correlations between adjacent and non-adjacent dependency acquisition with vWM (Misyak et al., 2010) support the involvement of working memory in this process. Once learners consolidate items (lexical forms, non-adjacent dependencies, and so on) into long-term memory, they may integrate information across a set using distributional statistics and generalize to novel input. In this model integration relies on long-term memory systems such as the hippocampus and associated cortical structures (Erickson & Thiessen, 2015). As such, it assumes learners must consolidate information into long-term memory before generalizing. However, infants with immature brain structures are able to generalize learned rules to novel items immediately after exposure to an artificial language.

Others propose an alternative approach, referred to as the More than One Mechanisms hypothesis (MOM) (Endress & Bonatti, 2007, 2016). In this model, learners come equipped with a rule-learning mechanism, allowing them to take advantage of cues to word boundaries (e.g., pauses, intonation) and track the syllables that appear at word edges. They can then abstract these patterns to acquire rules. Even when no cues are present, learners continue to track TPs between both adjacent and non-adjacent syllables using a statistical learning mechanism. However, learners do not rely on TPs (adjacent or non-adjacent) to acquire word forms or to generalize rules. Rather, they depend on the rule forming mechanism and make generalizations based on syllable position in respect to prosodic markers. Learners use this process to form general rules about phonotactics of the language.

The approaches we have discussed here are similar in multiple ways. Namely, they both entail a dual-process mechanism: one tracks TPs and another serves to generalize. However, the proposed generalization mechanisms differ. While the extraction and integration approach (Thiessen et al., 2013) requires learners to consolidate statistical information into long-term memory before they are able to generalize across multiple exemplars, the MOM hypothesis (Endress & Bonatti, 2016) allows generalization to occur online based on prosodic cues. Given Frost and Monaghan's (2016) report that segmentation occurs in tandem with generalization, a model that favors online generalization better fits the existing literature for adults. In addition, evidence that neonates better track and remember syllables at utterance edges over syllables in the middle of phrases raises challenges for extraction and integration theory (Ferry et al., 2016).

30.6.2 Retention of statistical learning

While experimenters have uncovered much about statistical learning, few examine whether learners retain words or rules they acquire. Simon et al. (2017) asked whether 6.5-month-old infants would remember words they segmented from an artificial language after a delay of approximately 60 minutes. As infants at this age nap regularly, and given the influence of sleep on memory consolidation in adults (Stickgold & Walker, 2007) the authors compared infants who slept after learning to those who remained awake for an identical period of time. Only the infants who slept retained a weak memory for the words they previously segmented. If infants could not remember these words 60 minutes later, how do they go on to successfully form a lexicon through statistical learning? The memory ability of 6.5-month-olds is still maturing; and as infants develop, memory becomes more robust, and it is possible that older infants would retain recently segmented word forms over a longer period of time.

Along these lines, Gómez, Bootzin, and Nadel (2006) found that 15-month-olds who remain awake after learning retain non-adjacent dependencies across a four-hour delay. Therefore, memory for statistical information does improve with age. Those who napped showed a generalization effect. During test, when these infants listened to the first trial type, they seemed to accept it as a legal non-adjacent dependency whether it followed the specific non-adjacencies heard during familiarization. The infants based their listening times off this trial and listened longer to test trials consistent with its non-adjacent dependencies. Researchers replicated this effect testing 24 hours later (Hupbach, Gómez, Bootzin, & Nadel, 2009); infants who napped after learning showed the generalization effect, but those who did not nap after learning showed no memory of the familiarization language. The generalization effect in this study indicates that infants do not remember the specific words from familiarization, rather they remember the abstract relationship between the first and third item.

Frank, Tenenbaum, and Gibson (2013) investigated adults' retention of an artificial language. Participants listened for an hour each day for ten days. On the eleventh day, adults demonstrated knowledge of the words within the language, continuing to retain them three years later. This result indicates that items segmented during statistical learning can be retained across a long delay if adults have sufficient exposure. This study did not establish the minimum exposure required for long-term retention. Researchers should continue this line of research to determine the rate at which statistical information consolidates into long-term memory both in infancy and adulthood. Such research could inform the differences in learning systems recruited across development.

30.6.3 Bilingualism and dialects

The majority of research we review focuses on learning in the context of one language. How do learners cope in an environment with multiple languages? When adults listen to two languages incongruent regularities in alternating two-minute blocks they rely on an indexical cue (e.g., speaker voice) to separate the two sets of statistics (Weiss, Gerfen, & Mitchel, 2009). Infants in a bilingual environment must distinguish one unfamiliar language from another; if they rely on perceptual cues to keep two languages separate this could pose problems in households in which parents are bilingual and produce two languages throughout the day. Gonzales and colleagues (2015) found that 12-month-olds could not generalize the rule of a "pure stream" after they listened to it interleaved randomly with a "mixed stream" with no reliable statistics. However, infants generalized to novel strings successfully after listening to the pure stream for four minutes sandwiched in between two six-minute intervals of mixed streams, even when talker voice remained constant across the two streams. Thus, it appears that infants use the timing of language presentation to keep consistent stimuli separate from inconsistent stimuli, potentially to a greater degree than adults. However, comparing across these two studies is difficult as Weiss and colleagues played each language in intervals of two minutes, which is considerably shorter than the exposure in Gonzales et al. (2015). Researchers should investigate whether infants can generalize when they are exposed to the languages in two-minute intervals and whether they depend on non-statistical cues to do so successfully.

30.6.4 Trajectory of learning

Gómez and Maye (2005) outlined the developmental trajectory of non-adjacent dependency learning, revealing that it surfaces in behavior at about 15 months of age. The locus of this effect could be experience with language or development of memory systems and other neural structures (Gómez, 2016). Research points to the important role of experience in statistical learning. Dawson and Gerken (2009) found that four-month-olds were able to learn sequences of tones that followed an AAB and ABA pattern and generalize to recognize strings of new tones following the same pattern. Seven-month-olds were not able to learn to the same extent. Such an age-related difference is surprising as this is a seemingly simple pattern for seven-month-olds to acquire (Marcus, Vijayan, Rao, & Vishton, 1999). The authors propose that seven-month-olds may have prior expectations for musical sequences given their increasing experience with music. Infants this age may view repetition in tones to be a global property of melodies rather than a property that defines a structural rule. As seven-month-old infants expect chance to govern repetition in music and do not expect it to function as a structural property, these infants do not generalize based off repetition in tonal sequences.

Along similar lines, infants in Gerken and Bollt (2008) heard a language that followed a rule found in natural language (stress syllables end in a consonant) or one that contained a rule not characteristic of natural language (stress words begin with /t/). While nine-month-olds generalized the natural rule to novel strings, they could not generalize the unnatural rule. Infants 7.5 months of age could generalize the unnatural rule, indicating unconstrained generalization in this younger age group. These younger infants may show such generalization as they are less experienced with their native language and have not yet extracted existing relationships between syllable structure and prosody. Nine-month-olds, on the other hand, are aware of the pattern in English that heavy syllables (i.e., syllables ending in a consonant) often receive stress, and use this knowledge to generalize a similar rule in an artificial language. Gerken (2004) also found nine-month-olds to use stress patterns of individual strings they heard during exposure to abstract higher-order prosodic rules that govern the entire language. Together with the results of Gerken and Bollt (2008), these results indicate nine-month-old infants' robust generalization ability when the rules in question are concordant with those in natural languages. Further research should be conducted to establish the developmental trajectory of statistical learning and generalization ability, as these could inform us of learning mechanisms and external cues infants rely on at different ages.

30.7 Concluding remarks

We review significant progress in statistical learning since Saffran et al. (1996), highlighting extensions of statistical learning to infants' and adults' segmentation, their acquisition of word forms, and acquisition of complex rules such as non-adjacent dependencies and abstract lexical categories. We are only beginning to investigate the influence of individual differences on statistical learning ability, but such investigations paired with advanced neuroimaging have the potential to reveal cognitive processes that underlie the statistical learning mechanism. Furthermore, psychologists should continue to consider retention of statistical learning across development along with the influence of experience on statistical learning. By examining these changes across development, we can gain a richer understanding of the significant benchmarks in both development and language acquisition.

References

Adriaans, F., & Kager, R. (2010). Adding generalization to statistical learning: The induction of phonotactics from continuous speech. *Journal of Memory and Language*, 62(3), 311–31.

Archibald, L. M., & Gathercole, S. E. (2006). Short-term and working memory in specific language impairment. *International Journal of Language and Communication Disorders*, 41(6), 675–93.

Bernstein Ratner, N. (1986). Durational cues which mark clause boundaries in mother–child speech. *Journal of Phonetics*, 14, 303–9.

Cunillera, T., Toro, J. M., Sebastián-Gallés, N., & Rodríguez-Fornells, A. (2006). The effects of stress and statistical cues on continuous speech segmentation: An event-related brain potential study. *Brain Research*, 1123(1), 168–78.

Dawson, C., Gerken, L. (2009). From domain-generality to domain-sensitivity: 4-month-olds learn an abstract repetition rule in music that 7-month-olds do not. *Cognition*, 111(3), 378–82.

Endress, A. D., & Bonatti, L. L. (2007). Rapid learning of syllable classes from a perceptually continuous speech stream. *Cognition*, 105(2), 247–99.

Endress, A. D., & Bonatti, L. L. (2016). Words, rules, and mechanisms of language acquisition. *Wiley Interdisciplinary Reviews: Cognitive Science, 7*(1), 19–35.

Erickson, L. C., & Thiessen, E. D. (2015). Statistical learning of language: theory, validity, and predictions of a statistical learning account of language acquisition. *Developmental Review, 37*, 66–108.

Erickson, L. C., Thiessen, E. D., & Graf Estes, K. (2014). Statistically coherent labels facilitate categorization in 8-month-olds. *Journal of Memory and Language, 72*, 49–58.

Evans, J. L., Saffran, J. R., & Robe-Torres, K. (2009). Statistical learning in children with specific language impairment. *Journal of Speech, Language, and Hearing Research, 52*(2), 321–35.

Farmer, T. A., Christiansen, M. H., & Monaghan, P. (2006). Phonological typicality influences on-line sentence comprehension. *Proceedings of the National Academy of Sciences, 103*(32), 12203–8.

Fernald, A., & Mazzie, C. (1991). Prosody and focus in speech to infants and adults. *Developmental Psychology, 27*, 209–21.

Fernandes, T., Kolinsky, R., & Ventura, P. (2009). The metamorphosis of the statistical segmentation output: Lexicalization during artificial language learning. *Cognition, 112*(3), 349–66.

Ferry, A. L., Fló, A., Brusini, P., Cattarossi, L., Macagno, F., Nespor, M., & Mehler, J. (2016). On the edge of language acquisition: Inherent constraints on encoding multisyllabic sequences in the neonate brain. *Developmental Science, 19*(3), 488–503.

Fidler, L. J., Plante, E., & Vance, R. (2011). Identification of adults with developmental language impairments. *American Journal of Speech-Language Pathology, 20*(1), 2–13.

Franco, A., Cleeremans, A., & Destrebecqz, A. (2011). Statistical learning of two artificial languages presented successively: How conscious. *Frontiers in Psychology, 2*, 1–12.

Frank, M. C., Tenenbaum, J. B., & Gibson, E. (2013). Learning and long-term retention of large scale artificial languages. *PloS One, 8*(1), e52500.

Friederici, A. D., Mueller, J. L., & Oberecker, R. (2011). Precursors to natural grammar learning: Preliminary evidence from 4-month-old infants. *PLoS One, 6*(3), e17920.

Frost, R. L., & Monaghan, P. (2016). Simultaneous segmentation and generalisation of non-adjacent dependencies from continuous speech. *Cognition, 147*, 70–4.

Gabay, Y., Thiessen, E. D., & Holt, L. L. (2015). Impaired statistical learning in developmental dyslexia. *Journal of Speech, Language, and Hearing Research, 58*(3), 934–45.

Gaskell, M. G., & Dumay, N. (2003). Lexical competition and the acquisition of novel words. *Cognition, 89*(2), 105–32.

Gerken, L. (2004). Nine-month-olds extract structural principles required for natural language. *Cognition, 93*(3), B89–B96.

Gerken, L., & Bollt, A. (2008). Three exemplars allow at least some linguistic generalizations: Implications for generalization mechanisms and constraints. *Language Learning and Development, 4*(3), 228–48.

Gerken, L., Wilson, R., & Lewis, W. (2005). Infants can use distributional cues to form syntactic categories. *Journal of Child Language, 32*(2), 249–68.

Gómez, R. L. (2016). Do infants retain the statistics of a statistical learning experience? Insights from a developmental cognitive neuroscience perspective. *Philosophical Transactions of the Royal Society B, 372*, 20160054.

Gómez, R. L., & Gerken, L. (2000). Infant artificial language learning and language acquisition. *Trends in Cognitive Sciences, 4*(5), 178–86.

Gómez, R. L. (2002). Variability and detection of invariant structure. *Psychological Science, 13*(5), 431–6.

Gómez, R. L., Bootzin, R. R., & Nadel, L. (2006). Naps promote abstraction in language-learning infants. *Psychological Science, 17*(8), 670–4.

Gómez, R. L., & Gerken, L. (1999). Artificial grammar learning by 1-year-olds leads to specific and abstract knowledge. *Cognition, 70*(2), 109–35.

Gómez, R. L., & Lakusta, L. (2004). A first step in form-based category abstraction by 12-month-old infants. *Developmental Science, 7*(5), 567–80.

Gómez, R., & Maye, J. (2005). The developmental trajectory of nonadjacent dependency learning. *Infancy, 7*(2), 183–206.

Gonzales, K., Gerken, L., & Gómez, R. L. (2015). Does hearing two dialects at different times help infants learn dialect-specific rules? *Cognition, 140*, 60–71.

Graf Estes, K., Evans, J. L., Alibali, M. W., & Saffran, J. R. (2007). Can infants map meaning to newly segmented words? Statistical segmentation and word learning. *Psychological Science, 18*(3), 254–60.

Graf Estes, K., & Lew-Williams, C. (2015). Listening through voices: Infant statistical word segmentation across multiple speakers. *Developmental Psychology, 51*(11), 1517–28.

Graf Estes, K., Gluck, S. C., & Bastos, C. (2015). Flexibility in statistical word segmentation: Finding words in foreign speech. *Language Learning and Development, 11*(3), 252–69.

Grunow, H., Spaulding, T. J., Gómez, R. L., & Plante, E. (2006). The effects of variation on learning word order rules by adults with and without language-based learning disabilities. *Journal of Communication Disorders, 39*(2), 158–70.

Hochmann, J. R., Endress, A. D., & Mehler, J. (2010). Word frequency as a cue for identifying function words in infancy. *Cognition, 115*(3), 444–57.

Hsu, H. J., Tomblin, J. B., & Christiansen, M. H. (2014). Impaired statistical learning of nonadjacent dependencies in adolescents with specific language impairment. *Frontiers in Psychology, 5*, 175.

Hupbach, A., Gómez, R. L., Bootzin, R. R., & Nadel, L. (2009). Nap-dependent learning in infants. *Developmental Science, 12*(6), 1007–12.

Isaki, E., & Plante, E. (1997). Short-term and working memory differences in language/learning disabled and normal adults. *Journal of Communication Disorders, 30*(6), 427–37.

Johnson, E. K., & Tyler, M. D. (2010). Testing the limits of statistical learning for word segmentation. *Developmental Science, 13*(2), 339–45.

Johnson, E. K., Seidl, A., Tyler, M. D. (2014). The edge factor in early word segmentation: Utterance-level prosody enables word form extraction by 6-month-olds. *PLoS One, 9*, e83546.

Jusczyk, P. W., & Luce, P. A. (1994). Infants' sensitivity to phonotactic patterns in the native language. *Journal of Memory and Language, 33*(5), 630–45.

Kaan, E., Harris, A., Gibson, E., & Holcomb, P. (2000). The P600 as an index of syntactic integration difficulty. *Language and Cognitive Processes, 15*(2), 159–201.

Karuza, E. A., Newport, E. L., Aslin, R. N., Starling, S. J., Tivarus, M. E., & Bavelier, D. (2013). The neural correlates of statistical learning in a word segmentation task: An fMRI study. *Brain and Language, 127*(1), 46–54.

Kelly, M. H. (1992). Using sound to solve syntactic problems: The role of phonology in grammatical category assignments. *Psychological Review, 99*(2), 349.

Kemler Nelson, D. G., Jusczyk, P. W., Mandel, D. R., Myers, J., Turk, A., & Gerken, L. (1995). The head-turn preference procedure for testing auditory perception. *Infant Behavior and Development, 18*(1), 111–16.

Kerkhoff, A., De Bree, E., De Klerk, M., & Wijnen, F. (2013). Non-adjacent dependency learning in infants at familial risk of dyslexia. *Journal of Child Language*, *40*(1), 11–28.

Kidd, E. (2012). Implicit statistical learning is directly associated with the acquisition of syntax. *Developmental Psychology*, *48*(1), 171.

Kittleson, M. M., Aguilar, J. M., Tokerud, G. L., Plante, E., & Asbjørnsen, A. E. (2010). Implicit language learning: Adults' ability to segment words in Norwegian. *Bilingualism: Language and Cognition*, *13*(4), 513–23.

Lany, J., & Saffran, J. R. (2010). From statistics to meaning: Infants' acquisition of lexical categories. *Psychological Science*, *21*(2), 284–91.

Lany, J., & Saffran, J. R. (2011). Interactions between statistical and semantic information in infant language development. *Developmental Science*, *14*(5), 1207–19.

Marcus, G. F., Vijayan, S., Rao, S. B., & Vishton, P. M. (1999). Rule learning by seven-month-old infants. *Science*, *283*, 77–80.

McNealy, K., Mazziotta, J. C., & Dapretto, M. (2010). The neural basis of speech parsing in children and adults. *Developmental Science*, *13*(2), 385–406.

Mersad, K., & Nazzi, T. (2011). Transitional probabilities and positional frequency phonotactics in a hierarchical model of speech segmentation. *Memory & Cognition*, *39*(6), 1085–93.

Mintz, T. H. (2003). Frequent frames as a cue for grammatical categories in child directed speech. *Cognition*, *90*(1), 91–117.

Mirman, D., Magnuson, J. S., Estes, K. G., & Dixon, J. A. (2008). The link between statistical segmentation and word learning in adults. *Cognition*, *108*(1), 271–80.

Misyak, J. B., & Christiansen, M. H. (2012). Statistical learning and language: An individual differences study. *Language Learning*, *62*(1), 302–31.

Misyak, J. B., Christiansen, M. H., & Tomblin, J. B. (2010). On-line individual differences in statistical learning predict language processing. *Frontiers in Psychology*, *1*, 31.

Nazzi, T., Dilley, L. C., Jusczyk, A. M., Shattuck-Hufnagel, S., & Jusczyk, P. W. (2005). English-learning infants' segmentation of verbs from fluent speech. *Language and Speech*, *48*(3), 279–98.

Oberecker, R., & Friederici, A. D. (2006). Syntactic event-related potential components in 24-month-olds' sentence comprehension. *NeuroReport*, *17*(10), 1017–21.

Pelucchi, B., Hay, J. F., & Saffran, J. R. (2009). Statistical learning in a natural language by 8-month-old infants. *Child Development*, *80*(3), 674–85.

Plante, E., Patterson, D., Gómez, R., Almryde, K. R., White, M. G., & Asbjørnsen, A. E. (2015). The nature of the language input affects brain activation during learning from a natural language. *Journal of Neurolinguistics*, *36*, 17–34.

Richardson, J., Harris, L., Plante, E., & Gerken, L. (2006). Subcategory learning in normal and language learning-disabled adults: How much information do they need?. *Journal of Speech, Language, and Hearing Research*, *49*(6), 1257–66.

Romberg, A. R., & Saffran, J. R. (2010). Statistical learning and language acquisition. *Wiley Interdisciplinary Reviews: Cognitive Science*, *1*(6), 906–14.

Saffran, J. R., Aslin, R. N., & Newport, E. L. (1996). Statistical learning by 8-month-old infants. *Science*, *274*(5294), 1926–8.

Sanders, L. D., & Neville, H. J. (2003). An ERP study of continuous speech processing: I. Segmentation, semantics, and syntax in native speakers. *Cognitive Brain Research*, *15*(3), 228–40.

Sanders, L. D., Newport, E. L., & Neville, H. J. (2002). Segmenting nonsense: An event-related potential index of perceived onsets in continuous speech. *Nature Neuroscience*, *5*(7), 700–3.

Schapiro, A. C., Gregory, E., Landau, B., McCloskey, M., & Turk-Browne, N. B. (2014). The necessity of the medial temporal lobe for statistical learning. *Journal of Cognitive Neuroscience*, 26(8), 1736–47.
Seidl, A., & Johnson, E. K. (2006). Infant word segmentation revisited: Edge alignment facilitates target extraction. *Developmental Science*, 9(6), 565–73.
Seidl, A., & Johnson, E. K. (2008). Boundary alignment enables 11-month-olds to segment vowel initial words from speech. *Journal of Child Language*, 35(1), 1–24.
Siegelman, N., & Frost, R. (2015). Statistical learning as an individual ability: Theoretical perspectives and empirical evidence. *Journal of Memory and Language*, 81, 105–20.
Simon, K. N., Werchan, D., Goldstein, M. R., Sweeney, L., Bootzin, R. R., Nadel, L., & Gómez, R. L. (2017). Sleep confers a benefit for retention of statistical language learning in 6.5 month old infants. *Brain and language*, 167, 3–12.
Sohail, J., & Johnson, E. K. (2016). How transitional probabilities and the edge effect contribute to listeners' phonological bootstrapping success. *Language Learning and Development*, 12(2), 105–15.
St. Clair, M. C., Monaghan, P., & Christiansen, M. H. (2010). Learning grammatical categories from distributional cues: Flexible frames for language acquisition. *Cognition*, 116(3), 341–60.
Stickgold, R., & Walker, M. P. (2007). Sleep-dependent memory consolidation and reconsolidation. *Sleep Medicine*, 8(4), 331–43.
Teinonen, T., Fellman, V., Näätänen, R., Alku, P., & Huotilainen, M. (2009). Statistical language learning in neonates revealed by event-related brain potentials. *BMC Neuroscience*, 10(1), 21.
Thiessen, E. D. (2010). Effects of visual information on adults' and infants' auditory statistical learning. *Cognitive Science*, 34(6), 1093–106.
Thiessen, E. D., Hill, E. A., & Saffran, J. R. (2005). Infant-directed speech facilitates word segmentation. *Infancy*, 7(1), 53–71.
Thiessen, E. D., Kronstein, A. T., & Hufnagle, D. G. (2013). The extraction and integration framework: A two-process account of statistical learning. *Psychological Bulletin*, 139(4), 792.
Thiessen, E. D., & Saffran, J. R. (2003). When cues collide: Use of stress and statistical cues to word boundaries by 7-to 9-month-old infants. *Developmental Psychology*, 39(4), 706.
Tincoff, R., Santelmann, L., & Jusczyk, P. (2000). Auxiliary verb learning and 18-month-olds' acquisition of morphological relationships. In: Howell, S. C., Fish, S. A., & Keith-Lucas, T. (Eds.), *Proceedings of the 24th Annual Boston University Conference on Language Development*, Vol. 2 (pp. 726–37). Cascadilla Press, Somerville, MA.
van den Bos, E., Christiansen, M. H., & Misyak, J. B. (2012). Statistical learning of probabilistic nonadjacent dependencies by multiple-cue integration. *Journal of Memory and Language*, 67(4), 507–20.
Waters, G. S., & Caplan, D. (1996). The measurement of verbal working memory capacity and its relation to reading comprehension. *The Quarterly Journal of Experimental Psychology: Section A*, 49(1), 51–79.
Weiss, D. J., Gerfen, C., & Mitchel, A. D. (2009). Speech segmentation in a simulated bilingual environment: A challenge for statistical learning? *Language Learning and Development*, 5(1), 30–49.
Yang, C. D. (2004). Universal grammar, statistics or both?. *Trends in Cognitive Sciences*, 8(10), 451–6.

CHAPTER 31

FIRST WORD LEARNING

MARILYN MAY VIHMAN

31.1 INTRODUCTION

WORD learning involves challenges of many different kinds, not only in relation to speech forms and their linked meanings or concepts but also, crucially, to the symbolic nature of those links, the referential principle that unleashes the power and flexibility of language. Furthermore, learning words means, for infants, gaining the ability not only to *understand* what words refer to but also to themselves *produce* identifiable word forms and use those forms to express meaning and make reference. The many kinds of learning involved, as regards comprehension and production, form and meaning and the links between them, must necessarily proceed to some extent in parallel. It is likely that form and meaning crystallize separately out of experience, with familiar word forms providing an attentional filter for novel meanings and often-experienced meanings highlighting recurrent word forms for retention. The first words the child understands—between about six and nine months—will reflect that dual exposure to forms and their situational contexts or meanings, but the first words to be produced will require, in addition, the babbling practice that begins around the same time. The understanding that words have referential meaning, potentially invoking objects and events not present to the senses, will take longer; this is typically seen only in the second year.

This chapter will focus on word learning in the first two years, when word forms and their meanings must first be identified, retained, and represented for long-term access, and when infants typically gain critical insight into the symbolic or referential function of language. It will begin by considering the parallel learning of forms and meanings over the course of the first year. For *word forms*, this will include consideration of the role played by the relatively small proportion of words that infants hear in isolation as compared with those that can only be learned by successfully parsing them out of running speech. We will also review what more is needed for word-form *production* and consider how vocal practice might affect the processing and learning of word forms.

For *word meanings* we will discuss alternative views as to the origins of concepts or categories of meaning and the role of input speech in guiding a child's attention as they form those categories. This will allow us to weigh the evidence for the long-standing claim of several models that links to meaning could not be made without infants being able to "read minds" or understand the communicative intentions of others from early on. We will ask, in short, whether the association of word and referent is learnable from everyday interactions alone, given the social context and infant capacities for attention and memory.

We will then look at the evidence for a shift in the quality of learning in the second year, as the symbolic or referential nature of language comes into focus for the child. The notion of a "vocabulary spurt" in this period has long been taken for granted, although Ganger and Brent (2004) provided evidence to challenge the generality of any such spurt. If there is a shift of this kind, does it relate to a "nominal insight"? Or if a shift in referential understanding and use occurs purely as a function of age or maturation, then what neurophysiological changes underlie it? We will also note studies that suggest, based on experimental research with children aged from one to three years, that word learning itself leads to a qualitative change in the learning process.

31.2 LEARNING WORD FORMS

In order to recognize and eventually produce word forms a child must first retain bits of the speech stream to which they are repeatedly exposed; a fairly rough memory trace of such speech sequences may suffice for the first evidence of word recognition, reported from as early as five months (Delle Luche, Floccia, Granjon, & Nazzi, 2017). However, robust cross-linguistic evidence of long-term word-form recognition has been reported only from 11 months, based on testing, without training in the lab, on a range of early-learned words or phrases likely to be known from everyday life, pitted against phonotactically similar rare words (in French: Hallé & Boysson-Bardies, 1994; British English: Vihman, Nakai, DePaolis, & Hallé, 2004; American English: DePaolis et al., 2012; Dutch: Swingley, 2005; Welsh-English bilinguals: Vihman et al., 2007;[1] Italian: Vihman & Majorano, 2017). The more challenging task of recognizing (segmenting out) the same untrained, familiar lexical forms embedded in passages is achieved at the group level only a month later, at 12 months (British English: DePaolis, Vihman, & Keren-Portnoy, 2014). This gradual growth in reliable long-term memory for word forms is in itself an important step in language development, paving the way to create links between these forms and their meanings or referents (Swingley, 2009).

At the same time, as Saffran, Aslin, and Newport (1996) first demonstrated experimentally, eight-month-old infants are able to learn the regularities of segmental co-occurrences through "statistical" or "distributional learning" from just two minutes of auditory exposure (based on testing with four trisyllabic "words," presented in random sequence and without prosodic modulation). Infants have been shown to be able, in principle, to use distributional

---

[1] The Welsh monolingual infants tested failed to show the expected preferential attention to familiar words even at 12 months, although the bilinguals showed it in both languages at the expected age of 11 months. The anomalous result with children being raised in Welsh-only homes was interpreted as reflecting their constant exposure to the dominant language outside the home, which may make infants particularly responsive to unfamiliar speech forms. The interpretation remains speculative, in the absence of replication in other such communities.

learning, gained through implicit sampling of ambient language structures, to support two basic aspects of phonological learning: (i) the formation of phonological categories, likely based on both the natural clustering of phonetic variants (Maye, Werker, & Gerken, 2002) and the "acquired distinctiveness" that results from repeatedly hearing some variants associated with the same referents (Heitner, 2004; Yeung & Werker, 2009), and (ii) the gaining of familiarity with the sequencing of sounds typical of the language (e.g., Jusczyk et al., 1993; Jusczyk, Luce, & Charles-Luce, 1994; Mattys, Jusczyk, Luce, & Morgan, 1999), which supports the segmentation of words from running speech.

Accounts of word learning continue to emphasize the central role of segmentation. For example, Thorson (2018) succinctly states that "successful word learning in first language acquisition requires … segmentation of the word from the continuous speech stream" (p. 59). The experimental study of segmentation dominated infant speech perception studies throughout the 1990s. It was typically tested, using the Head-turn Preference Procedure (Kemler Nelson et al., 1995), by training infants with a pair of individual words presented in isolation, followed immediately by testing with the trained and comparable untrained words embedded in passages, or the reverse.

The age of successful segmentation has proven variable for different language and dialect groups, however. It has been reported, at the earliest, at 7.5 or 8 months (American English: Jusczyk & Aslin, 1995; Jusczyk, Houston, & Newsome, 1999; Canadian French: Polka & Sundara, 2012), but it may be observed only at nine months (Dutch: Kuijpers, Coolen, Houston, & Cutler, 1998), 10.5 months (British English, but only with use of an uncharacteristically exaggerated infant-directed speech register: Floccia et al., 2016), or even later (12–16 mos.: Parisian French: Nazzi, Iakimova, Bertoncini, Frédonic, & Alcantara, 2006; Nazzi et al., 2014). Whether these differences are due to differences in prosodic structure or are primarily methodological remains unresolved (for discussion see Floccia et al., 2016; Nazzi et al., 2014).

The relative importance for learners of hearing words used on their own in input speech (i.e., "in isolation," or outside of any sentential context, circumventing the segmentation issue) has been a subject of ongoing debate for over 20 years. These words indisputably make up only a minor portion of the speech addressed to infants, although estimates differ as to just how minor this portion is, ranging from a low of 8–10% (English and Japanese: Fernald & Morikawa, 1993; English: Brent & Siskind, 2001) to as much as 40%, based on an intensive diary study of one Dutch child (van de Weijer, 1998). The difference is due to the exclusion, in the former studies, of all but "syntactic words," or words capable of combining with others in sentences (unlike many early-produced words, such as *hello, quack-quack, thank you*, or *uh-oh*).

The logic of the exclusion is clear: If words can't be used in sentences, then how useful are they? Yet non-syntactic words can provide the child with many important points of entry into the linguistic system. That is, although distributional learning may provide a generalized sense of familiarity and thus of what "belongs" in the ambient language and which sounds or sequences therefore merit infant attention, the robust representation of even a few whole word forms can bring that rather abstract knowledge into sharper focus (Vihman, 2017). For example, such English words as *bye, hi, thank you*, onomatopoeia (*baa, moo, quack*) and other words that accompany games with infants (*boo, pattycake*), which seldom occur in full sentences, are among the first that children produce (examples of "non-syntactic" first words from other languages include Estonian *aitäh* "thanks," *tere* "hello"; French *allo*, used when answering the phone, *miam* "yum"; Italian *baubau* "bowwow," *dindon* "dingdong"; Japanese *arigato* "thank you," *ba* "peek-a-boo," *doozo* "please, here you are!," *hai* "yes," *yoisho* "oof!"; Swedish *oj* "oh!," *tacktack* "thanks," *tittut* "peek-a-boo"; Welsh *tata* "bye": See Appendix I, Menn & Vihman, 2011). Repeated exposure to such forms provides a child with solid phonological knowledge regarding the particular sounds, sequences, and structures of their language.

The discovery of an experimental technique that made it possible to identify various clues to segmentation that infants might use led to rapid abandonment, in the 1990s, of the previously held assumption that only exposure, with attention, to words produced on their own could lead to successful word learning (e.g., Ninio, 1985, 1992; Peters, 1983; Pinker, 1984). Furthermore, several studies have now convincingly shown that children with an early ability to segment words from running speech show more rapid lexical advance (Junge, Kooijman, Hagoort, & Cutler, 2012; Newman et al., 2006; Singh, Reznick, & Xuehua, 2012). However, experimental segmentation studies themselves are restricted to very short-term learning. In a dissenting study that involved longer-term analysis and naturalistic data, Brent and Siskind (2001) provided the important finding that the best predictor, from recorded sessions before the end of the first year, of the words children would be producing at 15–18 months was the frequency with which their mothers had used the words *in isolation*, not their overall frequency of use.

Furthermore, however small a proportion of the overall input speech is constituted by words produced in isolation, once any one of those comes to be well established in the child's mind, that word can serve as a crucial wedge into the fast-changing flow of speech. A case in point is the child's own name, which is commonly used in isolation as well as being affectively salient due to its association with the child herself; predictably, the child's name is among the very first word forms to be recognized (Delle Luche et al., 2017; Mandel, Jusczyk, & Pisoni, 1995) and has also been shown to render neighboring words in the input more memorable (Bortfeld, Morgan, Golinkoff, & Rathbun, 2005).

At least two experimental studies have directly demonstrated that children more readily retain words produced in isolation than words heard embedded in passages. Junge et al. (2012) used event-related potentials (ERPs) to test 10-month-old Dutch infants' responses to words presented just once, either in isolation or in running speech. All of the infants showed recognition responses to the words first heard in isolation, whereas not all showed an ability to recognize words presented in sentences. Keren-Portnoy, Vihman, and Dunlop Fisher (2013) provided 11.5-month-old infants with three weeks of exposure, through regular book-reading sessions at home with a caregiver, to eight later-learned animal names, followed by testing in the lab; the words to be read in isolation to one group of infants were contrasted, for another group, with the same words to be read in sentence-final position, which is generally found to be advantageous for learning. Only the words presented in isolation were recognized at test, indicating that, under naturalistic conditions, isolated words are more likely to be remembered than words that occur even in final position in sentences.

Thus, studies of distributional learning and word-form recognition have established a rough timeline for infant accommodation to the sound system of their language and initial word-form learning. These studies have shown that some word forms are likely first learned from hearing them in isolation, although infants must also learn to segment words from running speech, and those who are able to do so earlier are also likely to show the most rapid later lexical advance.

However, neither distributional learning of phonological categories or sequences nor word-form recognition are sufficient in themselves to support word *production*, which additionally requires infants to have gained familiarity with their own phonetic resources and their auditory effects. In fact, the gap between the maturationally based emergence, at about six to eight months (Oller, 1980, 2000), of babbling in adult-like syllables—a reliable milestone that has not been shown to differ in timing or substance by ambient language—and the first word production (typically observed about four months later: Fagan, 2009) can be accounted for in part by infants' need to explore and consolidate their newly formed neuromotor skills through vocal practice before identifiable word production is possible.

Once audio recording became widely available researchers were able to test Jakobson's (1941/68) frequently cited claim, based on early diary studies, of developmental discontinuity between pre-linguistic babble and the *linguistic* period that followed. This led to clear evidence that, to the contrary, the forms of early words resemble babble vocalizations both globally (Oller, Wieman, Doyle, & Ross, 1976) and in terms of the particular sound patterns used by individual children, within the shared constraints of early production (Vihman, Macken, Miller, Simmons, & Miller, 1985).

Following up on the individual differences observed in earlier studies, Vihman and McCune were able to establish "vocal motor schemes" (VMS) as an index of phonetic advance (McCune & Vihman, 2001). The VMS measure requires a simple count of repeated uses of individual consonants, over a series of recorded sessions, to assess stable mastery of phonetic production. With this measure Vihman and colleagues have demonstrated three ways in which production affects speech processing and learning in this period.

First, three experimental studies (with infants exposed to English or Welsh: DePaolis, Vihman, & Nakai, 2013; English: DePaolis, Vihman, & Keren-Portnoy, 2011; or Italian: Majorano, Vihman, & DePaolis, 2014) have shown that once infants have attained mastery of more than a single VMS, their attention is captured by *novel stimuli*, or word forms featuring sounds that they have *not* yet mastered. In addition, Majorano et al. showed that when infants have as yet mastered *only a single VMS*, word forms featuring that sound hold their interest longer. In short, these studies demonstrate an effect of advances in infant phonetic mastery on their attention to speech, with a shift from interest in what is familiar to what is novel as a concomitant of ongoing vocal advances. This corresponds well with the observation that word learning starts slowly, gaining momentum relatively quickly in the second year of life (Bergelson & Swingley, 2012; Oviatt, 1980): The quickening of pace is likely related at least in part to the infants' gradual mastery of speech-like vocal production, which first focuses their interest on familiar patterns in input speech and then, by building the child's phonological memory, provides a critical scaffolding for the retention of novel forms (Keren-Portnoy et al., 2010).

Second, some studies have shown that age at onset of VMS mastery predicts that of first established word use (British English: McGillion et al., 2017), first referential word use (American English: McCune & Vihman, 2001), or overall vocabulary size at 12 months (Italian: Majorano et al., 2014). McGillion et al. showed that vocal mastery predicted early expressive but not receptive lexical advance, while gesture use, along with maternal education, predicted receptive vocabulary only at 18 months.

Finally, DePaolis, Keren-Portnoy and Vihman (2016) showed that children who had mastered more than one VMS by the time of testing at 10 months (i.e., a month earlier than the typical group attainment of this skill) were significantly more likely to show an experimentally measurable preference for either novel or familiar word forms than were children who had not yet achieved such mastery.

Returning to the question of word-form learning, then, it is difficult to avoid the conclusion that vocal advances, which show high individual variability in the first years of life, must be importantly related to the first advances in attending to and retaining word forms, although relatively few studies have attempted to explore speech processing and production from this point of view. It is not implausible to suggest that, in the studies cited here, those prelinguistic infants whose segmentation skills were in advance of those of the group as a whole may well have also had the best-developed production skills; however, since production data are not typically included in segmentation studies, the question remains open.

31.3 LEARNING WORD MEANINGS

Word comprehension begins slowly. Despite experimental evidence that highly frequent words, especially those likely to have been repeatedly heard in isolation, are recognized by six months, the ability to identify word referents is fragile at that age; it may occur only in relation to unique referents (*mommy* or *daddy*: Tincoff & Jusczyk, 1999), or only when the words are presented by a parent (Bergelson & Swingley, 2012). Tincoff and Jusczyk (2012) found that, when presented with *hands* vs. *feet* uttered in isolation, in an unfamiliar voice, in relation to a disembodied image of an unknown woman's hands or feet, six-month-olds could also discriminate these words, which refer to the most frequently named of all body parts. This is evidence that at that early age infants are not restricted to recognizing proper names (such as their own name and *mommy* and *daddy*) but can also recognize at least a few more broadly represented meanings. Going beyond that, Bergelson and Swingley (2012) showed that at six to nine months infants respond by longer looks to images of body parts when these are labeled, by their mothers, at the end of a short phrase ("look at the ear") and contrasted with food-related items (e.g., *ear—spoon, eyes—cookie*). More impressively, under the same conditions, these infants also looked at the matching image in arrays of four within-category items (e.g., *milk, juice, spoon, banana*). However, evidence of word comprehension became much more robust after 14 months.

How might knowledge of word forms interact with the emergence of concepts or categories and the learning of word meanings to support word comprehension? The literature on conceptual development and its relationship to learning word meanings is sharply divided, with two broad positions having been staked out over the past 25 years. One of these can be roughly characterized as "nativist" (or "rationalist": Bloom, 2001, p. 1103), consistent with the notion that a "language acquisition device" or "universal grammar" (UG) must provide "innate knowledge" of linguistic principles. In this view, without such knowledge no child could learn such a complex system as a language (Chomsky, 1965, 1981). A central exemplar of this position is the work of Waxman and her colleagues (e.g., Geraghty, Waxman, & Gelman, 2014; Waxman & Gelman, 2009; Waxman & Markow, 1995), who have steadily maintained that children have "expectations" regarding the link between words and their meanings from early on. For example, in a study that focused on 11-month-olds, Waxman and Booth (2003) maintained that

> Infants begin the task of word learning with *a broad expectation that novel open-class words highlight commonalities among objects*. This initially general expectation guides infants' first word-to-world mappings and supports the early establishment of reference. (p. 128, author's italics)

—although they acknowledge that the source of any such "general expectation" has yet to be identified.

A related approach proposes dedicated "word-learning constraints" (or "biases" or "principles") as a necessary part of learning word meaning and reference (Markman, 1990; Woodward, 2004; Woodward & Markman, 1998; see Golinkoff, Mervis, & Hirsh-Pasek, 1994, but also McMurray, Horst, & Samuelson, 2012). Although Bloom's influential book, *How Children Learn the Meanings of Words* (2000; see also Bloom & Markson, 1998), takes issue with the idea of specific word-learning constraints, Bloom (2001) embraces the "rationalist" view that "children learn words through their sensitivity to the referential intentions of other people, through use of 'theory of mind'" ([or ToM] p. 1099). This view is also supported by Akhtar, Carpenter, and Tomasello (1996) who provide evidence of two-year-olds making use of their understanding of the communicative intent of their interlocutors to deduce word meanings (but see Samuelson & Smith, 1998). On the other hand, as Westbury and Nicoladis (2001) observe in their commentary on Bloom (2000), "ToM stands as much in need of explanation as the learning of word meaning" (p. 1122).

The alternative position, most prominently defended by Sloutsky and Smith and their respective colleagues, holds that perception, memory, and a "dumb attentional mechanism" might suffice to explain word learning (Robinson & Sloutsky, 2004, 2007; Samuelson & Smith, 2000; Sloutsky, 2010; Sloutsky & Robinson, 2008; Smith, Colunga, & Yoshida, 2010; Smith, Jones, & Landau, 1996; for a related study showing the low-level perceptual origins of infant categories, see French, Mareschal, Mermillod, & Quinn, 2004). Gogate and her colleagues have additionally emphasized the importance of intersensory redundancy, especially in the early months of life, as support for attention to and memory for referents, and also the natural propensity of mothers to provide that redundancy by manipulating objects as they talk with infants (Gogate & Bahrick, 1998, 2001; Gogate & Maganti, 2016; Gogate, Walker-Andrews, & Bahrick, 2001).

Each of these approaches has contributed important insights into the process by which language serves to guide child attention to objects and object categories. Studies by Waxman and others have made it clear that word labels are powerful "invitations to form categories" (Waxman & Markow, 1995; cf. also Baldwin & Markman, 1989). In an early study of categorization based on perceptual similarity, Quinn, Eimas, and Rosenkrantz (1993) demonstrated that three- to four-month-olds can already form basic-level categories ("cats," "dogs" vs. "birds": Rosch, 1975; Rosch & Mervis, 1975): Following exposure to photographs of distinct exemplars from one category, the infants looked longer at an exemplar from a *new category* than at a *novel exemplar of a familiarized category*. In a series of studies testing infants aged 6–18 months, Waxman and her colleagues showed that while basic-level categories are formed at all the ages they tested, infants are more likely to form superordinate or "global" categories when objects are presented with an accompanying phrase ("look at the X") than with non-speech sounds (Balaban & Waxman, 1997; Fulkerson & Waxman, 2007; Waxman & Booth, 2003; see also Fulkerson & Haaf, 2003). Conversely, when objects are named with distinct labels they are more likely to be treated as members of distinct categories (Xu, 1999, 2002).

Ferry, Hespos, & Waxman (2010) found a similar effect of words (but not sine waves) as early as three and four months. Here, interestingly, the index of categorization was different for the two age groups: three-month-olds showed a reliable *familiarity* effect, suggesting that processing was underway but incomplete, while four-month-olds showed the *novelty* effect seen in older infants and children. In a striking follow-up study, Ferry, Hespos, and Waxman (2013) showed the same facilitative effect for three-month-olds of "labeling" with the cries of lemurs as with human speech, despite the fact that by this age infants show a strong preference for human vocal signals over those produced by other primates—unlike newborns, whose interest is similarly engaged by both (Shultz & Vouloumanos, 2010; Vouloumanos, Hauser, Werker, & Martin, 2010).

Sloutsky and Robinson, on the other hand, carried out several studies of infants, preschool-age children and adults to investigate the effect of auditory and visual "compounds," or tightly coordinated stimuli involving both modalities. Their goal was specifically to test the language-specificity of the labeling effect identified by Waxman and others. Their basic finding is that, far from being generally facilitative of categorization, auditory stimuli may "overshadow" visual stimuli. This is evidenced by the fact that, in these closely matched compound presentations, a change to the auditory stimulus is generally noticed, whereas a change to the visual stimulus—which elicits a reliable response when presented alone—is not. Robinson and Sloutsky (2004) reported this effect for infants aged 8 and 12 months as well as for four-year-olds; Sloutsky and Robinson (2008) replicated it with 10-month-olds, but found that with 16-month-olds overshadowing occurred only with non-speech sounds, not with non-word forms. In a separate experiment, prefamiliarization with the non-speech sound stimuli was found to facilitate processing of the visual stimuli. In a study designed to challenge these findings, however, Noles and Gelman (2012) tested both four-year-olds and adults with more rigorously controlled comparisons between familiar auditory and visual stimuli; these experiments failed to obtain evidence of auditory dominance.

Robinson and Sloutsky interpret their findings as reflecting low-level effects of familiarity as well as the nature of cross-modal processing. They note that auditory processing functions already before birth and that auditory input is necessarily dynamic and transient. These latter characteristics may account for auditory input having evolved to be automatically and rapidly processed, whereas visual input, which may be static and is necessarily available for longer periods, is processed more slowly. Similarly, familiar stimuli are processed automatically and more quickly than unfamiliar stimuli. The key lesson for conceptual learning would be that repeated exposure to speech forms gradually creates a basis for guiding infant attention, especially in situations in which the child is attending to an object while their interlocutor is talking about it[2].

The work of Gogate and colleagues (see review in Gogate et al., 2001) adds to this the finding that infants are guided to notice and remember objects and events by the intersensory (mainly audiovisual) redundancy that typically obtains, whether in relation to

---

[2] Given the challenge of Noles and Gelman's experiments, which did reveal somewhat more auditory responses in children than in adults, further experimental work with infants, using better matched auditory and visual stimuli, would seem to be called for.

speech or non-speech, as part of the dynamics of their interactions with those objects and events. At three to five months infants detect changes to mismatches in *naturally redundant relations* between auditory and visual stimuli, whereas at seven months they detect changes even in *arbitrary relations*, such as that between the voice and the face of the talker—but only when these relations are marked by temporal synchrony. For older infants, however, a social context is key and intersensory redundancy is no longer required (e.g., 13 mos.: Woodward & Hoyne, 1999; 18–20 mos.: Baldwin et al., 1996).

In the 1990s, experimental studies showed that infants were most likely to learn words provided when their attention was already engaged with the referent (Akhtar, Dunham, & Dunham, 1991; Woodward, Markman, & Fitzsimmons, 1994), consistent with earlier observational studies that found maternal talk to be typically related to their child's focus of attention (e.g., Harris, Jones, & Grant, 1983, 1984). More recently, using a dual head-mounted camera system to track the behaviors of both mothers and their one-year-old children as they play with multiple objects, Yu and Smith (2012, 2013) have validated those findings in a naturalistic setting, providing rich detail on the nature of child attention and adult guidance. For example, although even newborns are capable of following eye-gaze (Farroni, Massaccesi, Pividori, & Johnson, 2004), Yu and Smith (2013) report that in their study children rarely looked at the mother's face as they played but were guided instead by attention to the objects the mother manipulated. In fact, hands, which give more a direct or easily interpreted indication of another's attentional focus than eye gaze, here proved to be the strongest marker of joint attention.

Finally, conceptual learning, including the understanding of others' intentions, can be taken to be largely the outcome of active exploration on the child's part (Woodward, 2009). Woodward argues that "in the infant's world, words are actions, and infants most likely draw on their understanding of action in making sense of words from the very beginning" (2009; p. 150). She notes that infants first begin to understand communicative intent at around nine months, just the age at which they themselves first give evidence of communicative intent through pointing (and also "giving" and "showing": Bates et al., 1979). Furthermore, Woodward and Guajardo (2002) reported that at nine months it was only those infants already using relational points who understood the points of others as relational. In contrast, in another study, seven- to nine-month-olds "seemed unaware of the looker-object relation" (Woodward, 2009, p. 158).

These ideas are in good accord with a fundamental principle of dynamic systems theory, that "categories—the foundations of knowledge—emerge from the infants' ongoing activities and encounters with the world . . . " (Thelen & Smith, 1994, p. 211). The principle is also well exemplified by the findings reviewed in Campos et al. (2000), showing the multiple and dramatic cognitive and social effects of infants' transition to crawling (see also Sommerville & Woodward, 2005; Sommerville, Woodward, & Needham, 2005).

31.4 LEARNING THE REFERENTIAL FUNCTION OF LANGUAGE: A QUALITATIVE SHIFT?

What is needed for the child to pick up on the most essential characteristic of language, the *symbolic relationship between forms and their meanings*? Only a grasp of this principle will permit the child to go beyond primed understanding and use of words embedded in the here and now to begin to apprehend and deploy the full referential function of language. As discussed here, many researchers assume that infant understanding of the principle of reference must be available from the start (e.g., Bloom, 2000; Hollich, Hirsh-Pasek, & Golinkoff, 2000; Macnamara, 1982). However, experimental evidence for access to such a concept is based largely on the responses of children who have already made substantial advances in word learning.

In contrast to developmental psychologists using experimental methods, linguists and others observing infants' earliest word *production or use* have generally assumed that the first words lack symbolic value, being limited to specific situational contexts or functions:

> [Child words] are, at this early stage, essentially vocal signals, and may be compared to adult words which have very limited pragmatic range, like greetings and cries of *ouch*. The meanings of such items, for both adult and child, are best characterized as "what you say when you do X." (Menyuk, Menn, & Silber, 1986, p. 212)

Accordingly, researchers have looked for evidence of children's appreciation of the referential function of language by analyzing referential or generalized child word uses in video recordings (Bates et al., 1979; Harris, Barrett, Jones, & Brookes, 1988; McCune & Vihman, 2001; Vihman & McCune, 1994). As suggested by Menyuk et al., the early "context-limited words" typically *accompany* activities rather than representing them (*boom*, as the child falls; *thank you*, while giving or taking) and may also include words associated with the lifting or feeding situations that recur multiple times a day (*upsydaisy, yumyum*) as well as with common verbal routines, such as naming animal sounds or body parts, in which full symbolic import is hardly assured (for further discussion and examples, see Vihman, 2014).

Following Bates et al., Vihman and McCune (1994) contrast those uses with "context-flexible" words, applied only to nominals and predicates, or relational words (McCune-Nicolich, 1981); the latter include (in English) a variety of word classes (e.g., verb particles, like *up/down, out*, formulaic phrases like *all gone*, adjectives like *stuck/unstuck*, adverbials like *more*, and common "non-syntactic" expressions like *uh-oh*). Context-flexible or generalized (referential) status is established when a child makes multiple more or less appropriate uses of the same form in relation to different situations or referents. For nominals this is straightforward, with uses often occurring with reference to both pictures and real objects, for example (e.g., *shoes*: Harris et al., 1988; Estonian *ahv* "monkey": own puppet and picture-book image: Vihman, 2014, p. 162).

Relational words, which refer to "dynamic and reversible spatial and temporal events" (McCune & Vihman, 2001, p. 674), are commonly found in the single-word period, although they are typically few in number (one or more relationals are listed for twelve out of nineteen 15–16-month-olds who had begun producing words in Vihman & McCune, 1994). To illustrate referential use, the Estonian word *kinni* "closed" was produced, at 14 months, by a child opening and closing her mother's wallet and then, a few days later, on opening and closing the door to the clothes drier (Vihman, 2014, p. 163). Although the meaning of the adult form may not be fully apprehended here, such distinct uses, united by both the child actions involved and the adult words that accompany such actions, provide strong evidence of an adult-like category of relational meaning.

Is the first referential word use pegged to child age or to vocabulary size? That is, is it maturational or experience-dependent? This issue remains unresolved. Vihman and McCune

(1994) reported—for their independent samples of ten American children each, followed with monthly home video recordings from 9 to 16 months—that although the numbers of words produced differed between the two groups (along with differences in research focus and procedure), the age and proportion of referential words identified did not: None of the children showed a start on such use before 13–14 months (see also McCune & Vihman, 2001) and in both groups over half of the word types produced were used referentially by 16 months. On the other hand, Harris et al. (1988) report some referential word use among the first ten words of the four children they followed, at various ages.

A "vocabulary leap" (or burst, spurt, or explosion) is frequently taken to be an established phenomenon for this period, with a specified age of occurrence (e.g., Nazzi & Bertoncini, 2003; Schafer & Plunkett, 1998; Torkildsen et al., 2009). However, efforts to establish such a developmental shift quantitatively, based on larger samples, have identified no such sudden leap in learning rate for all or most children and provide no assurance of a set point—either in terms of age or lexical knowledge—at which such a leap can be expected to occur. For example, from their study of advances in word comprehension in 24 children aged 14–22 months, with additional parental report data on production for 18 children, Reznick and Goldfield (1992) concluded that "vocabulary spurts can occur at almost any point in the second year and . . . some children never experience a vocabulary spurt" (p. 411).

More recently, carrying out more precise quantitative analysis on word production data from 32 children, Ganger and Brent (2004) identified a "spurt" in only five. Ganger and Brent conclude that there is no solid reason to assume, as many have, that a "nominal insight" (McShane, 1979) or some other change in children's understanding of words and their relationship to the world occurs in the second year. Yet the moment of insight noted in diary studies such as Vihman (1976; see Vihman, 2014, p. 162) and Kamhi (1986), both of which report a dramatic increase in rate of word learning soon after the anecdotal observation, suggests that there may indeed be a relationship between a shift in understanding of the function of language and the rate of word learning, although the change is in most cases neither marked behaviorally nor sudden enough to quantify.

Ganger and Brent suggest that what changes, to allow the kind of lexical growth that results in the mean vocabulary size of 300 words reported, at least for American children, by 24 months (Fenson, Dale, Reznick, Bates, & Thal, 1994) may be "many small, unsynchronized changes in both higher cognitive and lower level processing abilities" (p. 631). One such change was identified by McCune, Vihman, Roug-Hellichius, Delery, and Gogate (1996), who observed frequent use, in five children aged 14–16 months, of "communicative grunts," which insistently draw the interlocutor's attention to the child's focus of interest. The first substantial use of communicative grunts was taken to reflect the infants' dawning appreciation of their own capacity to affect their interlocutors through vocal as well as gestural actions; the upturn in use of these vocalizations signaled, for three children with sufficient phonetic skill (i.e., more than a single VMS), the onset of referential word use in the same or the following session and, for the two other children, the onset of referential comprehension as conveyed through gestures. This then again suggests a change in infant communicative understanding that is not experientially but maturationally based.

Research using deferred or elicited imitation has provided additional insight into the gradual shift to less narrowly contextualized, more flexible access to memory over the course of the second year (Taylor, Liu, & Herbert, 2016). Through a series of experimental studies that grew out of Rovee-Collier's pioneering research with very young infants (see, for example, Rovee-Collier, 1995), Hayne, Herbert, and their colleagues have shown that although minor procedural differences affect children's memory for interesting events in this period, the developmental course is continuous rather than involving a shift in the memory systems involved (or discontinuity by cognitive stage, as in Piaget's theoretical approach, 1951, 1952, 1954). These investigators have tracked a gradual developmental liberation of retrieval capacity from dependence on specific cues in either the "nominal event" or the contextual setting (Hayne, MacDonald, & Barr, 1997). For example, once they have observed a three-step action sequence with a puppet, 12-month-olds will imitate one or more of those steps after a 10-minute delay even if the puppet used is in a different color, but not if the puppet has also changed in form (rabbit to mouse or vice versa) and also not a full day later; at 18 months none of these changes block children's ability to imitate the observed actions, although change to a more distinctly different puppet does, while at 21 months not even a radical puppet change blocks recall (Hayne et al., 1997). Verbal cues enhance both retention and the ability to generalize across changes to the target "actor" (Hayne & Herbert, 2004); with 18-month-olds, practice with the action of interest supports memory for the activity after a six-week delay, if a brief reminder is provided the day before testing, and practice also enables children of that age to remember the action they observed the day before (Hayne, Barr, & Herbert, 2003). Later studies have clarified the role of labeling, indicating that labels not only guide attention (Taylor & Herbert, 2014) but also support categorization (Taylor, Liu, & Herbert, 2016), in accord with the studies of Waxman and her colleagues, cited earlier.

Studies using ERPs have provided evidence of a shift in (receptive) semantic processing between 12 and 14 months (Friedrich & Friederici, 2005a, 2005b). Whereas 12-month-olds showed only a phonological priming response to repeated exposure to pseudo-words paired with pictured "pseudo-objects," the older infants also showed a semantic violation response to mismatches, similar to what is found in adults; response to the word-object pairs also persisted in 14-month-olds on retesting after a two-day gap (Friedrich & Friederici, 2008). However, in a follow-up analysis, Friedrich and Friederici (2010) reported that 12 infants with relatively large expressive vocabularies (over four words, with a group mean of 11 and a range from 5 to 29) showed the more mature semantic response already at 12 months, whereas the remaining 40 infants tested did not (mean of 1.7 words, range of 0 to 4). This finding is open to at least two interpretations: (i) neurophysiological maturation advances more quickly in some children and this allows them to learn and produce words earlier than most of their peers; or (ii) knowing and producing several words has in itself readied the brains of the more advanced children to respond to semantic mismatches, whereas children with less experience of lexical processing do not yet respond in that way.

Recent studies of the neurophysiological maturation of the structures that underlie memory and attention provide information that may shed light on the nature of the changes that we see in both word learning and elicited imitation of actions in the second year. Specifically, important advances in "recognition memory," the ability to respond to changes between familiarization and test in visual paired comparison, occur between 12 and 18 months (Robinson & Pascalis, 2004; see the review in Richmond & Nelson, 2007). More generally, Jabès and Nelson (2015) report that relational memory for visual events shows steady improvement over the first two years.

> Infants might learn the relation between items and their context, but ... this relational representation is unitary at first ... such that retrieval is disrupted if components of the learned

> event are changed between the learning and test phases. In other words, relational memory is at first extremely specific to the context in which learning occurs and gradually becomes more "flexible" ... allowing the generalization of learning to other conditions ... This flexibility is a fundamental component of relational memory, which is thought to depend on the integrity of the hippocampal formation. (p. 297)

This account from the field of declarative memory studies provides an intriguing parallel to the observed changes in children's word use as well as in elicited imitation over the same period, providing a promising insight into the neurophysiological changes that affect basic memory processes and thus also learning. However, to our knowledge, research combining direct investigation of those processes with observational or experimental research with children remains to be carried out.

There is also good evidence, both direct and indirect, that increasing word knowledge, or experience with word use, facilitates additional word learning. Specifically, in a range of studies of infants and toddlers aged from one to three years, those with a larger vocabulary show more efficient lexical processing, as regards both familiar and unfamiliar words, than children with smaller vocabularies. For example, 14-month-olds reported to have more than 25 words in their expressive vocabulary were more successful at retaining a minimal difference between non-word stimuli in a Switch task (as shown by their longer looking when the word-form-referent changed in the experimental "switch") than those with fewer words (Werker, Fennell, Corcoran, & Stager, 2002); by 17 months most children gave evidence of having retained the difference. In another study, 16-month-olds with larger expressive vocabularies were more likely to remember two new words after a short nap than were children who were producing fewer words (Horváth, Myers, Foster, & Plunkett, 2015). And in experimental studies with 18- and 21-month-old children, Fernald, Swingley, and Pinto (2001) found that a production lexicon of over 100 words, not age group, was most closely associated with accurate and rapid processing. Similarly, in an ERP study of 20-month-olds Torkildsen et al. (2009) found that children with larger vocabularies required fewer repetitions of a novel word form (a non-word) to show a recognition response than did children with smaller vocabularies.

The conclusion that the more efficient processing seen in these studies is an effect, not a cause, of larger vocabulary size—that is, that efficient processing is not simply an inborn child characteristic, perhaps due to more rapid neurophysiological maturation—was validated in two bilingual studies in which the children proved to be more efficient processors of their dominant language, the one in which they were producing the most words (19–22-month-olds: Conboy & Mills, 2006; 30-month-olds: Marchman, Fernald, & Hurtado, 2010).

Finally, Law and Edwards (2015) tested children aged from 30 to 46 months, using eye-tracking to assess their responses to familiar words, non-words, and mispronunciations; the visual images always included one familiar and one unfamiliar object. Vocabulary size was established through standardized test results rather than the parental report instrument used in studies involving younger children. Here again children with larger vocabularies recognized familiar words more rapidly and consistently than children with smaller vocabularies and looked more quickly to the unfamiliar image when presented with either a one-feature mispronunciation of a familiar word or a non-word. There was no significant effect of age.

There is thus little doubt that through the second year and later, lexical knowledge, and particularly experience with word production and use, strengthens word-processing capacities, as concerns both recognizing familiar words and retaining or representing novel words. This is entirely consistent with the evidence that early vocal practice supports memory for words at the early stages of word learning (Vihman, 2017; Vihman, DePaolis, & Keren-Portnoy, 2014) and that practice with simple action-routines supports memory for those routines in elicited imitation (Taylor et al., 2016). Recall also the finding that the production of intentional communicative gestures may be a necessary step in understanding the intentions of others (Woodward, 2009). In short, learning from self-action, including vocal and lexical production, constitutes a key element in children's representational advances, and thus in word learning in particular.

31.5 Conclusion

The studies reviewed here provide suggestive answers to several questions about the processes involved in first word learning while at the same time raising others. For example, although segmentation studies have shown, albeit with mixed results cross-linguistically, that children are able to find words in running speech by the time they begin to produce words, other studies have provided good evidence that the smaller proportion of isolated words addressed to children are likely to play a more important role in getting the word-learning process well started and, in particular, in providing sufficiently strong representations to support early word production. Complementarily, we have suggested that vocal production itself plays an important role in strengthening such representations and may even support segmentation, although there is as yet little evidence of this.

Turning to the learning of word meanings, we noted the still unresolved debate regarding the extent to which children embark on such learning equipped with either an "expectation" as to the kinds of meanings or categories words will refer to or a precocious, possibly innate understanding of the nature of reference and its role in communication. Attempts to support theoretical models that do or do not assume innate foreknowledge of communicative intention or linguistic structure have resulted in a good deal of detailed information about the chronology of infant understanding of words and word categories and also of the nature of adult interactions that may support and guide infants as they begin to gain knowledge of word meaning. One perspective that seems particularly plausible stresses the child's own initiatives as a grounding for grasping the meaning of others' communicative intentions. We also drew a parallel between evidence of infants learning from their own actions to interpret and represent the actions of others and the effect of the child's advances in vocal production on their perceptual processing of the speech signal.

Finally, we explored what might lie behind the increase in rate of word learning generally observed in the second year of life. Early accounts provided a range of different criteria to substantiate a "lexical spurt"; more recent studies have failed to find reliable quantitative support for such a spurt. However, there appears to be solid evidence that both receptive vocabulary and referential or generalized word use typically begin to increase more rapidly early in the second year, just as children's broader representational capacities gradually begin to be freed up, as suggested by the studies of Hayne and Herbert and their colleagues. Changes related to the maturation of brain structures that have been documented for declarative memory in other domains provide suggestive parallels to the processes of decontextualization of word meaning and reference that we observe early in the second year. Advances in infant intentional communication using vocal signals are also seen just prior to or at about the same time as the first referential word use. Both of these changes seem likely to have a maturational basis. At the same time, studies of children aged from one to three years document clear effects of lexical knowledge and use on the efficiency of further lexical learning. A good deal remains to be discovered about both the maturation of brain structures underlying children's advances in the understanding and use of reference and the nature of the effect of word production and use on the processing of familiar and novel words in relation to their meanings.

REFERENCES

Akhtar, N., Carpenter, M., & Tomasello, M. (1996). The role of discourse novelty in early word learning. *Child Development, 67*, 635–45.

Akhtar, N., Dunham, F., & Dunham, P. (1991). Directive interactions and early vocabulary development: The role of joint attentional focus. *Journal of Child Language, 18*, 1–40.

Balaban, M. T., & Waxman, S. R. (1997). Do words facilitate object categorization in 9-month-old infants? *Journal of Experimental Child Psychology, 64*, 3–26.

Baldwin, D. A., & Markman, E. M. (1989). Establishing word object relations: A first step. *Child Development, 60*, 381–98.

Baldwin, D. A., Markman, E. M., Bill, B., Desjardins, R., Irwin, J. M., & Tidball, G. (1996). Infants' reliance on a social criterion for establishing word-object relations. *Child Development, 67*, 3135–53.

Bates, E., Benigni, L., Bretherton, I., Camaioni, L., & Volterra, V. (1979). *The Emergence of Symbols: Cognition and communication in infancy.* Academic Press, New York, NY.

Bergelson, E., & Swingley, D. (2012). At 6 to 9 months, human infants know the meanings of many common nouns. *Proceedings of the National Academy of Sciences of the USA, 109*, 3253–8.

Bloom, P. (2000). *How Children Learn the Meanings of Words.* MIT Press, Cambridge, MA.

Bloom, P. (2001). Précis of *How Children Learn the Meanings of Words. Behavioral and Brain Sciences, 24*, 1095–103.

Bloom, P., & Markson, L. (1998). Capacities underlying word learning. *Trends in Cognitive Sciences, 2*, 67–73.

Bortfeld, H., Morgan, J. L., Golinkoff, R. M., & Rathbun, K. (2005). Mommy and me: Familiar names help launch babies into speech stream segmentation. *Psychological Science, 16*, 298–304.

Brent, M. R., & Siskind, J. M. (2001). The role of exposure to isolated words in early vocabulary development. *Cognition, 81*, B33–B44.

Campos, J. J., Anderson, D. I., Barbu-Roth, M. A., Hubbard, E. M., Hertenstein, M. J., & Witherington, D. (2000). Travel broadens the mind. *Infancy, 1*, 149–219.

Chomsky, N. (1965). *Aspects of the Theory of Syntax.* MIT Press, Cambridge, MA.

Chomsky, N. (1981). *Lectures on Government and Binding: The Pisa Lectures.* Foris, Dordrecht, Holland.

Conboy, B. T., & Mills, D. L. (2006). Two languages, one developing brain: Event-related potentials to words in bilingual toddlers. *Developmental Science*, 9, F1–F12.

Delle Luche, C., Floccia, C., Granjon, L., & Nazzi, T. (2017). Infants' first words are not phonetically specified: Own name recognition in British English-learning 5-month-olds. *Infancy*, 22(3), 362–88.

DePaolis, R. A., Keren-Portnoy, T., & Vihman, M. M. (2016). Making sense of infant familiarity and novelty responses to words at lexical onset. *Frontiers in Psychology*, 7, 715.

DePaolis, R. A., Seal, B., Kulasr, S, Baird, C., Keren-Portnoy, T., & Vihman, M. M. (2012). The effect of dialect, age, speaker gender, otitis media, and modality on infant word recognition. International Child Phonology Conference, Minneapolis, MN.

DePaolis, R., Vihman, M. M., & Keren-Portnoy, T. (2011). Do production patterns influence the processing of speech in prelinguistic infants? *Infant Behavior and Development*, 34, 590–601.

DePaolis, R. A., Vihman, M. M., & Keren-Portnoy, T. (2014). When do infants begin recognizing familiar words in sentences? *Journal of Child Language*, 41, 226–39.

DePaolis, R., Vihman, M. M., & Nakai, S. (2013). The influence of babbling patterns on the processing of speech. *Infant Behavior and Development*, 36, 642–9.

Fagan, M. K. (2009). Mean length of utterance before words and grammar: Longitudinal trends and developmental implications of infant vocalizations. *Journal of Child Language*, 36, 495–527.

Farroni, T., Massaccesi, S., Pividori, D., & Johnson, M. H. (2004). Gaze following in newborns. *Infancy* 5, 39–60.

Fenson, L., Dale, P. S., Reznick, J. S., Bates, E., & Thal, D. (1994). Variability in early communicative development. *Monographs of the Society for Research in Child Development*, 59(5), 1–173.

Fernald, A., & Morikawa, H. (1993). Common themes and cultural variations in Japanese and American mothers' speech to infants. *Child Development*, 64, 637–56.

Fernald, A., Swingley, D., & Pinto, J. P. (2001). When half a word is enough: Infants can recognize spoken words using partial phonetic information. *Child Development*, 72, 1003–15.

Ferry, A. L., Hespos, S. J., & Waxman, S. R. (2010). Categorization in 3- and 4-month-old infants: an advantage of words over tones. *Child Development*, 81, 472–9.

Ferry, A. L., Hespos, S. J., & Waxman, S. R. (2013). Nonhuman primate vocalizations support categorization in very young human infants. *PNAS*, 110, 15231–5.

Floccia, C., Keren-Portnoy, T., DePaolis, R., Duffy, H., Delle Luche, C., Durrant, S., ... & Vihman, M. (2016). British English infants segment words only with exaggerated infant-directed speech stimuli. *Cognition*, 148, 1–9.

French, R. M., Mareschal, D., Mermillod, M., & Quinn, P. C. (2004). The role of bottom-up processing in perceptual categorization by 3- to 4-month-old infants: Simulations and data. *Journal of Experimental Psychology: General*, 133, 382–397.

Friedrich, M., & Friederici, A. D. (2005a). Phonotactic knowledge and lexical-semantic processing in one-year-olds: Brain responses to words and nonsense words in picture contexts. *Journal of Cognitive Neuroscience*, 17, 1785–802.

Friedrich, M., & Friederici, A. D. (2005b). Lexical priming and semantic integration reflected in the event-related potential of 14-month-olds. *NeuroReport*, 16, 653–6.

Friedrich, M., & Friederici, A. D. (2008). Neurophysiological correlates of online word learning in 14-month-old infants. *NeuroReport*, 19, 1757–1761.

Friedrich, M., & Friederici, A. D. (2010). Maturing brain mechanisms and developing behavioral language skills. *Brain and Language*, 114, 66–71.

Fulkerson, A. L., & Haaf, R. A. (2003). The influence of labels, non-labeling sounds, and source of auditory input on 9- and 15-month-olds' object categorization. *Infancy, 4*, 349–69.

Fulkerson, A. L., & Waxman, S. R. (2007). Words (but not tones) facilitate object categorization: Evidence from 6- and 12-month-olds. *Cognition, 105*, 218–28.

Ganger, J., & Brent, M. R. (2004). Reexamining the vocabulary spurt. *Developmental Psychology, 40*, 621–32.

Geraghty, K., Waxman, S. R., & Gelman, S. A. (2014). Learning words from pictures: 15- and 17-month-old infants appreciate the referential and symbolic links among words, pictures, and objects. *Cognitive Development, 32*, 1–11.

Gogate, L. J., & Bahrick, L. E. (1998). Intersensory redundancy facilitates learning of arbitrary relations between vowel-sounds and objects in 7-month-olds. *Journal of Experimental Child Psychology, 69*, 133–49.

Gogate, L. J., & Bahrick, L. E. (2001). Intersensory redundancy and 7-month-old infants' memory for arbitrary syllable-object relations. *Infancy, 2*, 219–31.

Gogate, L. J., & Maganti, M. (2016). The dynamics of infant attention: Implications for cross-modal perception and word-mapping research. *Child Development, 87*, 345–64.

Gogate, L. J., Walker-Andrews, A. S., & Bahrick, L. E. (2001). The intersensory origins of word comprehension. *Developmental Science, 4*, 1–8.

Golinkoff, R. M., Mervis, C. B., & Hirsh-Pasek, K. (1994). Early object labels: the case for a developmental lexical principles framework. *Journal of Child Language, 21*, 125–55.

Hallé, P., & Boysson-Bardies, B. de. (1994). Emergence of an early lexicon: Infants' recognition of words. *Infant Behavior and Development, 17*, 119–29.

Harris, M., Barrett, M., Jones, D., & Brookes, S. (1988). Linguistic input and early word meaning. *Journal of Child Language, 15*, 77–94.

Harris, M., Jones, D., & Grant, J. (1983). The nonverbal context of mothers' speech to infants. *First Language, 4*, 21–30.

Harris, M., Jones, D., & Grant, J. (1984). The social-interactional context of maternal speech to infants: An explanation for the event-bound nature of early word use? *First Language, 5*, 89–100.

Hayne, H., Barr, R. F., & Herbert, J. S. (2003). The effect of prior practice on memory reactivation and generalization. *Child Development, 74*, 1615–27.

Hayne, H., & Herbert, J. S. (2004). Verbal cues facilitate memory retrieval during infancy. *Journal of Experimental Child Psychology, 89*, 127–39.

Hayne, H., MacDonald, S., & Barr, R. F. (1997). Developmental changes in the specificity of memory over the second year of life. *Infant Behavior and Development, 20*, 233–45.

Heitner, R. M. (2004). The cyclical ontogeny of ontology: An integrated developmental account of object and speech categorization. *Philosophical Psychology, 17*, 45–57.

Hollich, G. J., Hirsh-Pasek, K., & Golinkoff, R. M. (2000). Breaking the language barrier: An emergentist coalition model for the origins of word learning. *Monographs of the Society for Research in Child Development, 65*(3), 1–123.

Horváth, K., Myers, K., Foster, R., & Plunkett, K. (2015). Napping facilitates word learning in early lexical development. *Journal of Sleep Research, 24*, 503–9.

Jabès, A., & Nelson, C. A. (2015). Twenty years after "The ontogeny of human memory: A cognitive neuroscience perspective," where are we? *International Journal of Behavioral Development, 39*, 293–303.

Jakobson, R. (1941/68). *Child Language, Aphasia, and Phonological Universals*. Mouton, The Hague. Eng. tr. of Kindersprache, Aphasie und allgemeine Lautgesetze. Uppsala, 1941.

Junge, C., Kooijman, V., Hagoort, P., & Cutler, A. (2012). Rapid recognition at 10 months as a predictor of language development. *Developmental Science*, 15, 463–73.

Jusczyk, P. W., & Aslin, R. N. (1995). Infants' detection of the sound patterns of words in fluent speech. *Cognitive Psychology*, 29, 1–23.

Jusczyk, P. W., Friederici, A. D., Wessels, J., Svenkerud, V. Y., & Jusczyk, A. M. (1993). Infants' sensitivity to the sound patterns of native language words. *Journal of Memory and Language*, 32, 402–20.

Jusczyk, P. W., Houston, D., & Newsome, M. (1999). The beginnings of word segmentation in English-learning infants. *Cognitive Psychology*, 39, 159–207.

Jusczyk, P. W., Luce, P. A., & Charles-Luce, J. (1994). Infants' sensitivity to phonotactic patterns in the native language. *Journal of Memory and Language*, 33, 630–45.

Kamhi, A. (1986). The elusive first word: The importance of the naming insight for the development of referential speech. *Journal of Child Language*, 13, 155–61.

Kemler Nelson, D. G., Jusczyk, P. W., Mandel, D. R., Myers, J., Turk, A., & Gerken, L. A. (1995). The head-turn preference procedure for testing auditory perception. *Infant Behavior and Development*, 18, 111–16.

Keren-Portnoy, T., Vihman, M. V., & Dunlop Fisher, R. (2013). Babies' first words and parents' speech. Talk presented at International Child Phonology Conference, Nijmegen.

Keren-Portnoy, T., Vihman, M. M., DePaolis, R., Whitaker, C., & Williams, N. A. (2010). The role of vocal practice in constructing phonological working memory. *Journal of Speech, Language, and Hearing Research*, 53, 1280–93.

Kuijpers, C., Coolen, R., Houston, D., & Cutler, A. (1998). Using the head-turning technique to explore the cross-linguistic performance differences. In: Rovee-Collier, C., Lipsitt, L. P., & Hayne, H. (Eds.), *Advances in Infancy Research*, Vol. 12 (pp. 205–20). Ablex Publishing Corporation, Stamford, CT.

Law, F. II, & Edwards, R. (2015). Effects of vocabulary size on online lexical processing by preschoolers. *Language Learning and Development*, 11, 331–55.

Macnamara, J. (1982). *Names for Things*. MIT Press, Cambridge, MA.

Majorano, M., Vihman, M. M., & DePaolis, R. A. (2014). The relationship between infants' production experience and their processing of speech. *Language Learning and Development*, 10, 179–204.

Mandel, D. R., Jusczyk, P. W., & Pisoni, D. B. (1995). Infants' recognition of the sound patterns of their own names. *Psychological Science*, 6, 314–17.

Marchman, V., Fernald, A., & Hurtado, N. (2010). How vocabulary size in two languages relates to efficiency in spoken word recognition by young Spanish–English bilinguals. *Journal of Child Language*, 37, 817–40.

Markman, E. M. (1990). Constraints children place on word meaning. *Cognitive Science*, 14, 57–77.

Mattys, S. L., Jusczyk, P. W., Luce, P. A., & Morgan, J. L. (1999). Phonotactic and prosodic effects on word segmentation in infants. *Cognitive Psychology*, 38, 465–94.

Maye, J., Werker, J. F., & Gerken, L. (2002). Infant sensitivity to distributional information can affect phonetic discrimination. *Cognition*, 82, B101–B11.

McCune, L., & Vihman, M. M. (2001). Early phonetic and lexical development. *Journal of Speech, Language, and Hearing Research*, 44, 670–84.

McCune, L., Vihman, M. M., Roug-Hellichius, L., Delery, D. B., & Gogate, L. (1996). Grunt communication in human infants (*Homo sapiens*). *Journal of Comparative Psychology*, 110, 27–37.

McCune-Nicolich, L. (1981). The cognitive bases of early relational words. *Journal of Child Language*, 8, 15–36.

McGillion, M. M., Matthews, D., Herbert, J., Pine, J., Vihman, M. M., Keren-Portnoy, T., & DePaolis, R. A. (2017). What paves the way to conventional language? The predictive value of babble, pointing and SES. *Child Development*, 88, 156–66.

McMurray, B., Horst, J., & Samuelson, L. K. (2012). Word learning emerges from the interaction of online referent selection and slow associative learning. *Psychological Review*, 119, 831–77.

McShane, J. (1979). The development of naming. *Linguistics*, 17, 879–905.

Menn, L., & Vihman, M. M. (2011). Features in child phonology: inherent, emergent, or artefacts of analysis? In: Clements, N., & Ridouane, R. (Eds.), *Where Do Phonological Features Come From? Cognitive, Physical and Developmental Bases of Distinctive Speech Categories* (pp. 261–301). John Benjamins, Amsterdam.

Menyuk, P., Menn, L., & Silber, R. (1986). Early strategies for the perception and production of words and sounds. In: Fletcher, P., & Garman, M. (Eds.), *Language Acquisition: Studies in First Language Development*, 2nd Edition (pp. 198–222). The University Press, Cambridge.

Nazzi, T., & Bertoncini, J. (2003). Before and after the vocabulary spurt: Two modes of word acquisition? *Developmental Science*, 6, 136–42.

Nazzi, T., Iakimova, G., Bertoncini, J., Frédonie, S., & Alcantara, C. (2006). Early segmentation of fluent speech by infants acquiring French. *Journal of Memory and Language*, 54, 283–99.

Nazzi, T., Mersad, K., Sundara, M., Iakimova, G., & Polka, L. (2014). Early word segmentation in infants acquiring Parisian French: Task-dependent and dialect-specific effects. *Journal of Child Language*, 41, 600–33.

Newman, R. S., Ratner, N. B., Jusczyk, A. M., Jusczyk, P. W., & Dow, K. A. (2006). Infants' early ability to segment the conversational speech signal predicts later language development: A retrospective analysis. *Developmental Psychology*, 42, 643–55.

Ninio, A. (1985). The meaning of children's first words. *Journal of Pragmatics*, 9, 527–46.

Ninio, A. (1992). The relation of children's single word utterances to single word utterances in the input. *Journal of Child Language*, 19, 87–110.

Noles, N. S., & Gelman, S. A. (2012). Preschool-age children and adults flexibly shift their preferences for auditory versus visual modalities but do not exhibit auditory dominance. *Journal of Experimental Child Psychology*, 112, 338–50.

Oller, D. K. (1980). The emergence of the sounds of speech in infancy. In: Yeni-Komshian, G., Kavanagh, J. F., & Ferguson, C. A. (Eds.), *Child Phonology, I: Production*. Academic Press, New York, NY.

Oller, D. K. (2000). *The Emergence of the Speech Capacity*. Lawrence Erlbaum, Mahwah, NJ.

Oller, D. K., Wieman, L. A., Doyle, W. J., & Ross, C. (1976). Infant babbling and speech. *Journal of Child Language*, 3, 1–11.

Oviatt, S. (1980). The emerging ability to comprehend language: An experimental approach. *Child Development*, 50, 97–106.

Peters, A. M. (1983). *The Units of Language Acquisition*. Cambridge University Press, Cambridge.

Piaget, J. (1951). *Play, Dreams and Imitation in Childhood* (translated by M. Cook). Norton, New York.

Piaget, J. (1952). *The Origins of Intelligence* (translated by C. Gattegno & F. M. Hodgson). Heinemann, London.

Piaget, J. (1954). *The Construction of Reality*. New York: Basic Books.

Pinker, S. (1984). *Language Learnability and Language Development*. Harvard University Press, Cambridge, MA.

Polka, L., & Sundara, M. (2012). Word segmentation in monolingual infants acquiring Canadian English and Canadian French: Native language, cross-dialect, and cross-language comparisons. *Infancy*, *17*, 198–232.

Quinn, P. C., Eimas, P. D., & Rosenkrantz, S. L. (1993). Evidence for representations of perceptually similar natural categories by 3-month-old and 4-month-old infants. *Perception*, *22*, 463–75.

Reznick, J. S., & Goldfield, B. A. (1992). Rapid change in lexical development in comprehension and production. *Developmental Psychology*, *28*, 406–13.

Richmond, J., & Nelson, C. (2007). Accounting for change in declarative memory: A cognitive neuroscience perspective. *Developmental Review*, *27*, 349–73.

Robinson, A. J., & Pascalis, O. (2004). Development of flexible visual recognition memory in human infants. *Developmental Science*, *7*, 527–33.

Robinson, C. W., & Sloutsky, V. M. (2004). Auditory dominance and its change in the course of development. *Child Development*, *75*, 1387–401.

Robinson, C. W., & Sloutsky, V. M. (2007). Linguistic labels and categorization in infancy: Do labels facilitate or hinder? *Infancy*, *11*, 233–53.

Rosch, E. (1975). Cognitive representations of semantic categories. *Journal of Experimental Psychology: General*, *104*, 192–233.

Rosch, E., & Mervis, C. (1975). Family resemblances: Studies in the internal structure of categories. *Cognitive Psychology*, *7*, 573–605.

Rovee-Collier, C. (1995). Time windows in cognitive development. *Developmental Psychology*, *31*, 147–69.

Saffran, J. R., Aslin, R. N., & Newport, E. L. (1996). Statistical learning by 8-month-old infants. *Science*, *274*, 1926–8.

Samuelson, L., & Smith, L. (1998). Memory and attention make smart word learning: an alternative account of Akhtar, Carpenter, and Tomasello. *Child Development*, *71*, 98–106.

Samuelson, L., & Smith, L. (2000). Grounding development in cognitive processes. *Child Development*, *69*, 94–104.

Schafer, G., & Plunkett, K. (1998). Rapid word learning by fifteen-month-olds under tightly controlled conditions. *Child Development*, *69*, 309–20.

Shultz, S., & Vouloumanos, A. (2010). Three-month-olds prefer speech to other naturally occurring signals. *Language Learning and Development*, *6*, 241–57.

Singh, L., Reznick, J. S., & Xuehua, L. (2012). Infant word segmentation and childhood vocabulary development: a longitudinal analysis. *Developmental Science*, *15*, 482–95.

Sloutsky, V. M. (2010). From perceptual categories to concepts: what develops? *Cognitive Science*, *34*, 1244–86.

Sloutsky, V. M., & Robinson, C. W. (2008). The role of words and sounds in visual processing: from overshadowing to attentional tuning. *Cognitive Science*, *32*, 342–65.

Smith, L. B., Colunga, E., & Yoshida, H. (2010). Knowledge as process: Contextually-cued attention and early word learning. *Cognitive Science*, *34*, 1287–314.

Smith, L. B., Jones, S. S., & Landau, B. (1996). Naming in young children: A dumb attentional mechanism? *Cognition*, *60*, 143–71.

Sommerville, J. A., & Woodward, A. L. (2005). Pulling out the intentional structure of human action: The relation between action production and processing in infancy. *Cognition*, *95*, 1–30.

Sommerville, J. A., Woodward, A. L., & Needham, A. (2005). Action experience alters 3-month-old infants' perception of others' actions. *Cognition*, *96*, B1–B11.

Swingley, D. (2005). Eleven-month-olds' knowledge of how familiar words sound. *Developmental Science*, 8, 432–43.

Swingley, D. (2009). Contributions of infant word learning to language development. *Philosophical Transactions of the Royal Society, B*, 364, 3617–32.

Taylor, G., & Herbert, J. S. (2014). Infant and adult visual attention during an imitation demonstration. *Developmental Psychobiology*, 56, 770–82.

Taylor, G., Liu, H., & Herbert, J. S. (2016). The role of verbal labels on flexible memory retrieval at 12-months of age. *Infant Behavior & Development*, 45, 11–17.

Thelen, E., & Smith, L. B. (1994). *A Dynamic Systems Approach to the Development of Cognition and Action*. MIT Press, Cambridge, MA.

Thorson, J. (2018). Prosody and word learning. In: Prieto, P., & Esteve Gibert, N. (Eds.), *The Development of Prosody in First Language Acquisition* (pp. 59–72). John Benjamins, Amsterdam.

Tincoff, R., & Jusczyk, P. W. (1999). Some beginnings of word comprehension in 6-month olds. *Psychological Science*, 10, 172–5.

Tincoff, R., & Jusczyk, P. W. (2012). Six-month-olds comprehend words that refer to parts of the body. *Infancy*, 17, 432–44.

Torkildsen, J. V. K., Hansen, H. F., Svangstu, J. M., Smith, L., Simonsen, H. G., Moen, I., & Lindgren, M. (2009). Brain dynamics of word familiarization in 20-month-olds: Effects of productive vocabulary size. *Brain and Language*, 108, 73–88.

van de Weijer, J. (1998). *Language Input for Word Discovery*. Max Planck Institute for Psycholinguistics, Nijmegen.

Vihman, M. M. (1976). From prespeech to speech: on early phonology. *Stanford Papers and Reports on Child Language Development*, 12, 230–44.

Vihman, M. M. (2014). *Phonological Development: The first two years*, 2nd Edition. Wiley-Blackwell, Malden, MA.

Vihman, M. M. (2017). Learning words and learning sounds: Advances in language development. *British Journal of Psychology*, 108, 1–27.

Vihman, M. M., DePaolis, R. A., & Keren-Portnoy, T. (2014). The role of production in infant word learning. *Language Learning*, 64 Suppl. 2, 121–40.

Vihman, M. M., Macken, M. A., Miller, R., Simmons, H., & Miller, J. (1985). From babbling to speech: a reassessment of the continuity issue. *Language*, 61, 395–443.

Vihman, M. M., & Majorano, M. (2017). The role of geminates in infants' early words and word-form recognition. *Journal of Child Language*, 44, 158–84.

Vihman, M. M., & McCune L. (1994). When is a word a word? *Journal of Child Language*, 21, 517–42.

Vihman, M. M., Nakai, S., DePaolis, R. A., & Hallé, P. (2004). The role of accentual pattern in early lexical representation. *Journal of Memory and Language*, 50, 336–53.

Vihman, M. M., Thierry, G., Lum, J., Keren-Portnoy, T., & Martin, P. (2007). Onset of word form recognition in English, Welsh and English-Welsh bilingual infants. *Applied Psycholinguistics*, 28, 475–93.

Vouloumanos, A., Hauser, M. D., Werker, J. F., & Martin, A. (2010). The tuning of human neonates' preference for speech. *Child Development*, 81, 517–27.

Waxman, S., & Booth, A. (2003). The origins and evolution of links between word learning and conceptual organization: New evidence from 11-month-olds. *Developmental Science*, 6, 128–35.

Waxman, S. R., & Gelman, S. A. (2009). Early word-learning entails reference, not merely associations. *Trends in Cognitive Science, 13*, 258–63.

Waxman, S., & Markow, D. (1995). Words as invitations to form categories: evidence from 12- to 13-month-old infants. *Cognitive Psychology, 29*, 257–302.

Werker, J. F., Fennell, C. T., Corcoran, K. M., & Stager, C. L. (2002). Infants' ability to learn phonetically similar words: Effects of age and vocabulary size. *Infancy, 3*, 1–30.

Westbury, C., & Nicoladis, E. (2001). A multiplicity of constraints: How children learn word meaning. *Behavioral and Brain Sciences, 24*, 1122f.

Woodward, A. L. (2004). Infants' use of action knowledge to get a grasp on words. In: Hall, D. G., & Waxman, S. R. (Eds.), *Weaving a Lexicon* (pp. 149–171). MIT Press, Cambridge, MA.

Woodward, A. L. (2009). Infants' grasp of others' intentions. *Current Directions in Psychological Science, 18*, 53–7.

Woodward, A. L., & Guajardo, J. J. (2002). Infants' understanding of the point gesture as an object-directed action. *Cognitive Development, 17*, 1061–84.

Woodward, A. L., & Hoyne, K. L. (1999). Infants' learning about words and sounds in relation to objects. *Child Development, 70*, 65–77.

Woodward, A., & Markman, E. (1998). Early word learning. In: Damon, W. (Ed.), *Handbook of Child Psychology, Vol. 2: Cognition, Perception and Language*, 5th Edition (pp. 371–420). Wiley, Hoboken, NJ.

Woodward, A., Markman, E., & Fitzsimmons, C. (1994). Rapid word learning in 13- and 18-month-olds. *Developmental Psychology, 30*, 553–66.

Xu, F. (1999). Object individuation and object identity in infancy: The role of spatiotemporal information, object property information, and language. *Acta Psychologica, 102*, 113–26.

Xu, F. (2002). The role of language in acquiring object kind concepts in infancy. *Cognition, 85*, 223–50.

Yeung, H. H., & Werker, J. F. (2009). Learning words' sounds before learning how words sound: 9-month-olds use distinct objects as cues to categorize speech information. *Cognition, 113*, 234–43.

Yu, C., & Smith, L. B. (2012). Embodied attention and word learning by toddlers. *Cognition, 122*, 244–62.

Yu, C., & Smith, L. B. (2013). Joint attention without gaze following: Human infants and their parents coordinate visual attention to objects through eye-hand coordination. *PLoS One, 8*, e79659.

CHAPTER 32

LANGUAGE AND CONCEPTUAL DEVELOPMENT

SUSAN A. GELMAN AND STEVEN O. ROBERTS

32.1 INTRODUCTION

A perennial puzzle in the development of thought is the role of language in children's emerging concepts. Concepts and language develop in parallel: as babies learn words such as "mama," "juice," and "more," they are constructing, revising, and refining the concepts to which their words refer—mental representations of people, animals, objects, substances, space, time, actions, properties, relations . . . But does language shape or reflect thought? To what extent does language reveal conceptual structure, and to what extent does it guide conceptual structure? These questions, once squarely within the realm of philosophical speculation, have benefited from recent advances in theory and method that yield new insights on the nature of the learning task, and the capabilities of infants and young children. Thus, a rich body of recent and ongoing research provides answers and directions for the future. By focusing on early childhood processes, research sheds light not only on how children solve the twin inductive puzzles of learning language and making sense of experience, but also on the broader question of how language and thought relate in the human species more broadly. In brief, we can understand adult concepts most clearly by examining their developmental antecedents (Gould, 1983; Karmiloff-Smith, 1994).

This chapter is organized around six themes, each illustrating a different functional relation between language and thought in development: (1) language builds on and reveals conceptual structure; (2) language is a tool for thought; (3) language is a tool for action and attention; (4) language invites categorization; (5) specific languages have specific influences; and (6) language is a social marker. Each of these statements receives empirical support as well as boundary conditions—they certainly do not hold for all aspects of language in all contexts. The first theme indicates how concepts shape language; the other themes indicate distinct ways that language shapes concepts. As will become apparent, there is no single language-thought relation; numerous and varied influences have been documented. Along the way, we will cover examples from different conceptual content (number, space, social kinds, and so on), different forms of language (labels, generics, verbs), and different points in development. Table 32.1 lists the six themes along with some key examples.

Table 32.1 Six themes regarding functional relations between language and concepts

Themes	Examples
Language builds on and reveals conceptual structure	Concepts in infancy; "home signs"; language universals
Language is a tool for thought	"Thinking-for-speaking"; number words as technology; language permits domain cross-talk
Language is a tool for action and attention	Private speech; pedagogical cues; language trains attention; effects of bilingualism on executive functioning
Language invites categorization	Words promote kind concepts, taxonomic categorization, and inductive inferences; generics promote essentialism
Specific languages have specific influences	Spatial categories; count/mass nouns
Language is a social marker	Language, accent, and register as indexes of social status and interactional preferences

32.2 Language Builds on and Reveals Conceptual Structure

To begin, it is important to acknowledge the foundational role of concepts. Concepts do not require language, a point that is clear when considering the mental lives of babies. Decades of research reveal that prelinguistic infants represent a rich range of ideas long before they have learned the corresponding words, including individuals, categories, features, events, and relations. Prior to language, infants distinguish animal species (e.g., dogs from cats; Mareschal & Quinn, 2001), genders (male faces from female faces; Quinn et al., 2002), races (Kelly et al., 2007), colors (Bornstein, 1981), animals vs. vehicles (Mandler & McDonough, 1993), containment vs. occlusion (Hespos & Baillargeon, 2006), and so forth. They note similarity among objects and expect like objects to share non-obvious properties (Baldwin, Markman, & Melartin, 1993). Infants also represent concepts that are difficult to put into words, such as Gestalt principles (Quinn & Bhatt, 2005), or the precise degree of support required before an object falls (Needham & Baillargeon, 1993).

Further evidence for the richness of non-verbal concepts comes from the study of deaf children without exposure to a conventional language. These individuals create a simplified gestural communication system that is language-like in having elements of different grammatical types that are combined with simple rules of recursion (Goldin-Meadow, 2005). They can express ideas such as *I blow bubbles and bubbles go forward*. They can refer to generic kinds of things (e.g., "squirrels" in general, rather than any specific set of squirrels; Goldin-Meadow, Gelman, & Mylander, 2005). Again, a language model is not needed for children to acquire rather sophisticated concepts; instead, a rich conceptual base exists a priori, on which the invented "home sign" language builds.

Recurrent patterns found across unrelated languages also suggest the importance of preexisting concepts guiding language structure. Greenberg (1963), for example, noted that morphological markedness patterns can typically be predicted based on analyses of conceptual simplicity: positive is unmarked relative to negative (do vs. don't; happy vs. unhappy), singular is unmarked relative to plural (cracker vs. crackers), present is unmarked relative to past (walk vs. walked), and so forth. In each of these pairs, one value (e.g., positive, singular) is both conceptually and morphologically simpler than the other (see also Waugh, 1982). Another example of a cross-linguistic recurrent pattern is the organization of words for animals and plants into language hierarchies of approximately three to five levels (Atran, 1993; Berlin, Breedlove, & Raven, 1973). Across unrelated languages, this hierarchical structure permits the same entity to be labeled at multiple levels (animal, bird, swan, trumpeter swan), where the levels are inclusive (all trumpeter swans are swans, all swans are birds, and so on), and the middle level tends to be morphologically simplest (e.g., types of swans are labeled with compound nouns; Gelman, Wilcox, & Clark, 1989). Metaphorical mappings also often reveal cross-linguistic regularities that suggest underlying conceptual bases. For example, many cultures use body parts as the basis for counting systems, even when the particulars of how this is done can be quite variable, ranging for example from a base-10 to a 27-digit system (Saxe, 2015). Body parts are also often the basis for spatial terms (e.g., we speak of the head of a table, the foot of a mountain), and spatial language is often a root metaphor for talking about time (the week ahead, Lakoff & Johnson, 2008). Again, as with counting systems, the particulars are quite variable across languages, but the linking of these domains is a repeated solution across unrelated languages.

Relatedly, patterns of polysemy (using a given word for multiple meanings) appear to reflect conceptual underpinnings. Srinivasan and Rabagliati (2015) noted that certain predictable patterns of polysemy are found in linguistically unrelated languages and emerge early in childhood. For example: the same word can refer to both: an animal and its meat (chicken, fish), a substance and an artifact made from that substance (glass, nickel), or an object and its representational content (book, DVD). The authors tested 14 languages (e.g., Japanese, Hindi, Spanish, Farsi, Turkish, Russian) for their use of 27 distinct types of polysemy. Strikingly, most of the languages were found to express each of the distinct kinds of polysemy that were tested, and only 6% of all possible combinations of polysemy type X language were unattested. These patterns are also generative when people are asked to rate novel polysemous uses. At the same time, in every case there are specific conventions that must be learned (e.g., glass refers to the drinking vessel, not a glass window or glass vase). Srinivasan and Rabagliati (2015) thus dub their model "conventions-constrained-by-concepts." Young children (three to five years of age) can leverage systematic patterns of polysemy to infer new meanings for novel labels (Srinivasan, Al-Mughairy, Foushee, & Barner, 2017).

A final important source of evidence regarding the role of concepts in directing language development comes from language disorders. Although some language disorders suggest some independence of concepts and language (e.g., specific language impairment, in which grammatical deficits are not traceable to any cognitive limitations, Leonard, 2014; Williams Syndrome, in which children are linguistically expressive despite severe cognitive impairments, Wang & Bellugi, 1994; but also see Karmiloff-Smith, 2009), other disorders suggest a tighter link between conceptual limitations and linguistic deficits. Specifically, conceptual differences may result in language differences. For example, individuals with autism spectrum disorder present atypical patterns of intonational use, pragmatic use, word learning, and pronouns which may reflect deficits in theory-of-mind reasoning (Tager-Flusberg, Paul, & Lord, 2005).

32.3 LANGUAGE IS A TOOL FOR THINKING

Although thought does not require language, having language, or having certain ideas expressed conventionally in language, can provide children with a tool for engaging in new kinds of thought. There are at least two distinct ways that language serves this function: language can provide an in-the-moment means of focusing the child on particular dimensions or aspects of thought—what Slobin (1987, 1996), has called "thinking-for-speaking"—and language may exert broader influences by engendering new ways of thinking at key points in development. We discuss each of these influences in turn.

Slobin (1996) notes that language is always more selective than the richness of lived experience, and that in order to produce and comprehend language, one must attend to the relevant conceptual dimensions that one's own language expresses. He thus proposes the notion of "thinking-for-speaking"—that the act of speaking (and comprehending speech) engages a person in ways of thinking that they may not otherwise attempt. One well-worked-out example that can be understood in this framework comes from theory-of-mind reasoning, specifically the concept of false belief (that someone can hold a belief that contradicts reality; e.g., a belief that a certain book is on the shelf, when actually it's on one's desk). Many studies document that an understanding of false belief emerges gradually, primarily between four and five years of age (Wellman, 2014). Critically, however, much of this work has been conducted in English, and languages differ as to whether or not they lexicalize a distinction between "believe" (neutral as to whether the belief is true or false) vs. "believe falsely." This raises the question of whether language may provide a conceptual boost, with better performance on a false belief task among children who speak a language that distinguishes false belief from neutral belief. To test this question, Shatz, Diesendruck, Martinez-Beck, and Akar (2003) studied children speaking four languages: Turkish, Puerto Rican Spanish, English, and Brazilian Portuguese. Turkish and Puerto Rican Spanish have distinct verbs for conveying neutral belief versus false belief (in Turkish, *düşün* means to believe (neutral), whereas *san* means to believe (falsely); in Puerto Rican Spanish, *creer* means to believe (neutral), whereas *creer-se* means to believe (falsely)). In contrast, belief words in English and Brazilian Portuguese are wholly neutral as to whether the belief is true or false (English: *think*; Brazilian Portuguese: *achar*). The authors found that when children were given a false belief task using the relevant false belief terms, Turkish and Puerto Rican Spanish speakers performed better than English and Brazilian Portuguese speakers. Importantly, however, on tasks that did not include the explicit verb for falsely believing, there were no language differences in performance. Thus, theory-of-mind performance is enhanced while listening to language that highlights the relevant concepts, though not when those words are absent.

Another example stems from the domain of number. Frank, Everett, Fedorenko, and Gibson (2008) studied numerical reasoning in the Pirahã of Brazil, an isolated Amazonian hunter-gatherer community. Whereas prior work suggested that the Pirahã have at most three number words (1, 2, many; Gordon, 2004), Frank et al.'s evidence suggests that even the words typically translated as "1" and "2" are only approximate, as each is elicited for a wide range of values. Given that Pirahã thus has no words for precise numbers, Frank et al. (2008) were interested in how well monolingual adult speakers would be able to represent numerosities, on a range of non-verbal reasoning tasks. They found that performance is specifically impaired on task that requires memory for exact large numbers, but not tasks that do not require memory (e.g., matching). This is in striking contrast to languages such as English, with recursive counting systems, where child speakers start to appreciate properties of exact number from an early age (e.g., Izard, Pica, Spelke, & Dehaene, 2008). The results support Frank et al.'s interpretation of number words as a "cognitive technology" that helps speakers to keep track of the precise cardinal value of large sets of items.

In addition to the important yet limited effects of thinking-for-speaking, which take place only in the moment of language use, language may engender certain kinds of conceptual change at different points in development. We return again to theory-of-mind reasoning. Peterson, Wellman, and Liu (2005) proposed that conversational-communicative input regarding mental states enriches a child's theory of mind, and in the absence of such input these developments are significantly delayed (see also Astington & Baird, 2005). Additionally, in order to acquire a full theory of mind, a child needs to hear grammatically sophisticated speech (e.g., sentential complement structures of the sort, "Pat says that X," "John thinks that Y," or "Mary believes that Z") (Schick, De Villiers, De Villiers, & Hoffmeister, 2007). Children typically hear these language forms throughout childhood, mastering their subtleties and using them productively in the preschool years (Nixon, 2005); they also acquire a conceptual distinction between a false belief and reality between roughly four and five years of age. In contrast, deaf signers of non-signing parents typically receive rather simplified language input focused most on the here-and-now, lacking the syntactic sophistication to express these sorts of mental state expressions. Hearing parents are typically non-native signers who may attempt to learn sign but are themselves struggling to acquire its vocabulary and grammar. Without exposure to models of theory-of-mind conversation, these deaf children of speaking parents experience considerable delays in their developmental representation of false belief. Importantly, the difficulty is not deafness per se, as deaf children of deaf parents, who have rich exposure to sign language from birth, acquire false belief understanding on a typical timetable (Peterson et al., 2005).

Language may also serve a foundational role early in development, by allowing children to integrate knowledge across domain-specific modules. Spelke (2003) proposed that natural language serves this role due to two key features: it is a domain-general medium that can express concepts with any content, and it is a combinatorial system that readily allows placing ideas in juxtaposition. To quote Spelke, "Natural languages provide humans with a unique system for combining flexibly the representations they share with other animals. ... natural languages can expand the child's conceptual repertoire to include not just the pre-existing core knowledge concepts but also any new well-formed combination of those concepts" (Spelke, 2003, pp. 291, 306). Spelke and colleagues show that, as young children develop linguistic devices for expressing novel combinatorial concepts, such as "left of X" and "right of X," they become newly able to combine cues that previously had been resolutely encapsulated (e.g., geometric cues and landmarks, in a spatial orientation task; Shusterman, Lee, & Spelke, 2011).

32.4 Language is a Tool for Action and Attention

Language may serve as a tool not only for forming and sustaining concepts, but also for guiding action and attention. One early and prominent view was articulated by Lev Vygotsky (1934/1986), writing in the early twentieth century, who focused on the function of self-directed speech. Young children are often observed to comment on their own behavior, accompanying their actions with a running commentary that does not appear to be directed toward or adapted to others in the speech context. Whereas Piaget (1926) dubbed this "egocentric speech" that reflects a childhood inability to take into account the perspective of others, Vygotsky viewed it instead as socially oriented speech that is self-directed (thus, "private speech"). Vygotsky suggested that private speech serves a self-regulatory function that helps children plan and monitor their mental activities on challenging goal-directed tasks such as puzzles (Frauenglass & Diaz, 1985). More controlled experimental investigations have supported the regulatory functions of this form of language for children as young as four years of age (Alderson-Day & Fernyhough, 2015; Berk, 1992). For example, children given an opportunity to engage in private speech more successfully solve challenging puzzles (Behrend, Rosengren, & Perlmutter, 1989; Fernyhough & Fradley, 2005).

In a very different sort of mechanism, the process of learning certain kinds of words may, over time, train children to attend to certain features or patterns in the environment. Specifically, Smith and colleagues (Gershkoff-Stowe & Smith, 2004; Smith, Jones, Landau, Gershkoff-Stowe, & Samuelson, 2002) suggest that the process of word learning "tunes children's attention to the properties relevant for naming"; for example, learning count nouns may heighten children's focus on shapes, given that count nouns tend to correlate with shape (e.g., *balls* are spherical; *cups* are cylindrical; *pigs* are squat and four-legged), more so than other features such as color or texture. They find that children in the early stages of language learning (e.g., 17 months) become more attuned to shape after receiving intensive experience, over several weeks of training, with word-referent mappings that support shape. Later research suggests that this training operates via children's attention to the correlated feature of object function (Ware & Booth, 2010), and thus language does not direct children's attention in a wholly associative manner but rather interacts with children's conceptual understanding (see also Waxman & Gelman, 2009).

Prior to actual language use, infants are also sensitive to communicative signals from adults, such as direct eye gaze or infant-directed intonation, to guide their attention and learning. Csibra and Gergely (2009) refer to this system of infant-directed cues and infant interpretive understandings as "natural pedagogy," and find that a host of consequences follow from the presence of such signals. Thus, for example, six-month-olds are more likely to follow an adult's gaze after receiving an ostensive signal than not (Senju & Csibra, 2008), nine-month-olds focus more on an object's (enduring) features than its (transient) location after an adult draws their attention to the object via ostensive communicative cues (pointing) than via non-ostensive cues (reaching) (Yoon, Johnson, & Csibra, 2008), and 10-month-olds interpret an adult's action of hiding an object in strikingly different ways depending on whether or not the adult prefaces the action with pedagogical cues (i.e., pedagogical cues signal that the adult is providing general information about properties of the object, whereas non-pedagogical cues signal that the adult is simply providing episodic information about where the object is at the moment; Topál, Gergely, Miklósi, Erdhöhegyi, & Csibra, 2008). Sensitivity to such cues continues past infancy, guiding preschool children's inductive inferences, exploration, and conceptual reorganizations (Butler & Markman, 2012, 2014).

An additional intriguing source of influence on attention, self-regulation, and executive control (including inhibitory control) may be the experience of speaking more than one language (Bialystok, Craik, & Luk, 2012). Several studies show a processing advantage for bilingual children (Carlson & Meltzoff, 2008) as well as changes in the brain mechanisms for attentional control (Arredondo, Hu, Satterfield, & Kovelman, 2015); although the jury is still out on the robustness and generality of the effects on cognitive performance (e.g., Duñabeitia et al., 2014). The mechanism has hypothesized to be the fact that for bilingual speakers, both languages are activated in all contexts (Kroll, Dussias, Bice, & Perrotti, 2015), thus suggesting that executive control processes may be required to inhibit the language that the child is not using in the moment and to attend selectively to the language in use. This is a critically important set of issues that is the focus of much ongoing research.

32.5 LANGUAGE INVITES CATEGORIZATION

We turn now to ways that language guides the formation and use of categories. In a classic paper, Waxman and Markow (1995) suggested that words "invite" children to form categories, by signaling a conceptual space to be analyzed. Thus, hearing different items (duck, bear, elephant, lion) named with the *same* novel word (e.g., "This is a toma, this is a toma, this is a toma, . . . ") prompts children to note similarities among the objects receiving the same label, and to treat the entities as more alike (see also Xu, 2002). In this way, language doesn't just provide category content, but perhaps more importantly, provides a placeholder for a concept whose content can continue to be filled in by the child (see also Carey & Bartlett, 1978, and their notion of fast-mapping). In a programmatic series of studies, Waxman and her colleagues have demonstrated that as early as three to four months of age, infants are attuned to language as indicating a category (Ferry, Hespos, & Waxman, 2010). Over development, this tendency becomes increasingly selective (Lupyan, Rakison, & McClelland, 2007). At first, infants distinguish any speech-like vocalization (including non-human primate calls) from non-speech sounds such as tones, then they distinguish human from non-human language, and later distinguish nouns from other parts of speech (Ferry, Hespos, & Waxman, 2013; Fulkerson & Waxman, 2007; Graham, Keates, Vukatana, & Khu, 2013).

In addition to playing an important role in concept formation, category labels promote inductive inferences (e.g., Gelman & Davidson, 2013; Gelman & Markman, 1986; Graham & Kilbreath, 2007). For example, when children are introduced to a category member marked by a label (e.g., "This is a *bird*"), they generalize a newly learned feature to other members of that category, even when category membership competes with outward perceptual similarity. Thus, after learning that a flamingo ("bird") feeds its baby mashed-up food, and that a bat feeds its baby milk, preschool children infer that a blackbird ("bird") feeds its baby mashed-up food, like the other bird, even though it is more similar to the bat (Gelman & Coley, 1990; Gelman & Markman, 1986; Graham, Kilbreath, & Welder, 2004). These findings extend to novel category labels as well as familiar category labels, but only when those labels have a plausible conceptual basis (Gelman & Davidson, 2013; Jaswal, 2004).

Diesendruck (2003) has proposed that labels may play a more powerful role in certain domains than others. For example, in the animal domain, language cues may not be needed to indicate that a category is richly structured, whereas in the social domain, there is marked cultural variation in which categories are used, and thus language may play a more important role. Consistent with this framework, Diesendruck and Deblinger-Tangi (2014) found language effects on 19-month-old toddlers' categorization of social categories but not animal categories. On their task, they familiarized toddlers (19 and 26 months of age) with instances of categories (e.g., images of *black people*, images of *cows*), followed by two test images, one that was a novel exemplar of the familiarized category (e.g., a black person, a cow), and another that was an exemplar of a contrasting category (e.g., a white person, a horse). Participants were then asked to point to the test image that matched the familiarization pictures. Critically, half of the children were randomly assigned to a condition in which the experimenter provided a novel label during the familiarization phase (e.g., "Look, a Tirpali"), and the other half were given no label at all (i.e., "Look at this"). Thus, those who conceptualized the familiarization images as belonging to the same category should have selected the test image that was a category match, whereas those who did not conceptualize the familiarization images as belonging to the same category should have selected randomly between the two test images. The results provided important insights into the relation between language and concept formation. Irrespective of condition, the younger children made more "correct" matches in the animal domain than in the social domain. Moreover, for 19-month-olds, labels did not increase matches in the animal domain, but they did in the social domain.

Labels also invite essentialism (e.g., the belief that category members share underlying, innate, immutable "essences" that grant them their identity; see Gelman, 2003). For example, Gelman and Heyman (1999) introduced five- to seven-year-old children to exemplars of novel social categories involving a specific attribute (e.g., a person who eats a lot of carrots). For half the children, these categories were given a noun label (e.g., "She is a carrot-eater"); for half, they were given a verbal predicate (e.g., "She eats carrots whenever she can"). Consistent with the notion that children use different kinds of words to elicit different kinds of concepts (Graham, Keates, Vukatana, & Khu, 2013; Waxman & Booth, 2001), and that labels invite essentialism (Gelman, 2003), children who heard a noun label were significantly more likely than those hearing a verbal predicate to judge personality characteristics as stable over time and resistant to change (see also Heyman & Gelman, 2000). Thus, for example, a carrot-eater was judged to be more likely to continue liking carrots into the future, even if others tried to encourage her to stop eating carrots. An important question for the future is whether the use of labels may encourage negative consequences of essentialism for important social categories (ethnic minorities, disability groups), such as stereotyping, stigmatization, or inter-ethnic conflict.

To this point we have focused on labels as inviting categorization and essentialism, but research shows that labels may generate stronger effects on concept formation, inductive reasoning, and essentialism when they appear in generic statements. Generics (e.g., "Cats are four-legged"; "A cat is four-legged") are universally used to express generalizations about kinds, and thus can be distinguished from specific reference ("Those cats are four-legged"; "My cat is four-legged") (Carlson & Pelletier, 1995; Cimpian & Markman, 2008; Gelman

& Bloom, 2007; Leslie, 2008). Semantic analyses of generics suggest at least three reasons why they may promote essentialism: (1) they are timeless and devoid of context (lacking tense, mood, aspect, definiteness, deixis, and so on), thus implying that the information conveyed is itself a timeless truth; (2) they express stable, inherent properties (e.g., "A tiger has stripes"), and indeed are incapable of expressing transient, accidental features (e.g., "A tiger has muddy paws" refers to a particular tiger, not the kind); (3) they minimize variability (e.g., "Birds lay eggs," even though male birds and chicks do not).

Ample evidence indicates that by preschool age, children appropriately *produce* generics ("Does lions crawl?"; "Boys don't ever be ballet dancers") (Gelman, Goetz, Sarnecka, & Flukes, 2008; Gelman, Taylor, & Nguyen, 2004), *comprehend* generics as kind-referring and distinct from specific reference (Brandone, Cimpian, Leslie, & Gelman, 2012; Hollander, Gelman, & Star, 2002), and *recall* whether information was provided using generic or specific language (Gelman & Raman, 2007). By 30 months of age, children make broader inductive inferences from generic than specific language (Graham, Gelman, & Clarke, 2016), and by four to five years of age, children make use of generics to inform their concepts and inductive inferences (Cimpian & Markman, 2009, 2011; Gelman, Star, & Flukes, 2002; Hollander, Gelman, & Raman, 2009). Individual differences in parental and child use of generics predict parental endorsement of essentialism (Gelman, Ware, Kleinberg, Manczak, & Stilwell, 2014). When preschoolers learn a novel category with a series of either generic facts (e.g., "Zarpies sleep in tall trees") or specific facts (e.g., "This Zarpie sleeps in tall trees"), matched for content, they show significantly greater essentialism of the novel category following generic wording (Gelman et al., 2010; Rhodes, Leslie, & Tworek, 2012; Rhodes, Leslie, Bianchi, & Chalik, 2018).

Moreover, preschool children interpret generic statements as having normative implications. For example, after learning that contrasting categories have contrasting properties (e.g., "Hibbles eat this kind of berry, and Glerks eat that kind of berry"), they negatively evaluate a non-conforming individual (e.g., it is bad if a Hibble eats a berry typical of Glerks rather than Hibbles; Roberts, Gelman, & Ho, 2016; Roberts, Ho, & Gelman, 2017; see also Wodak, Leslie, & Rhodes, 2015). Importantly, these normative judgments do not obtain when the information is provided in non-generic statements about individuals.

32.6 Specific languages have specific influences

Concepts and language are distinct representational systems. Human concepts are remarkably rich and varied, yielding enormous flexibility in how we may construe any given experience. Language, in contrast, is selective in what it encodes and expresses, fitting ideas into a linear format with a constrained informational channel (leading to expressions such as "a picture is worth a thousand words"). Furthermore, languages differ from one another in the ease with which a given idea is conventionally expressed. Anything that can be thought, can be expressed in language—but languages differ in the ease with which an idea is encoded in language, and whether or not expressing this concept is optional versus obligatory. For example, the concept "schadenfreude" is lexicalized in German, but requires a phrasal description in English ("pleasure derived by someone from another person's misfortune"), whereas "attitude" is lexicalized in English but requires a longer explanation in German. Likewise, a dimension that is obligatory in one language can be omitted in another (e.g., status/power relations in Japanese; evidentials in Quechua or Korean).

A classic question is whether these language differences have consequences for the young concept-learner. The so-called "Sapir-Whorf" or "Whorfian" hypothesis proposes that the answer is "yes," though claims regarding precisely what these effects might be range from subtle "tweaking" of largely universal concepts, to more foundational differences in ontology (Brown, 1976; Sapir, 1929; Whorf, 1956). We have already covered some influences of language on thought in earlier sections, for example, that words can serve as a technology for enhancing memory or holding in mind a difficult concept, and that labels invite categorization and promote essentialist reasoning. In this section, we turn specifically to the question of how cross-linguistic differences affect children's concepts.

One important finding is that different patterns in how languages organize semantic domains may be acquired surprisingly early in development, suggesting that young children look to the particulars of their language as a guide regarding which conceptual distinctions to attend to. The realm of spatial relationships provides an intriguing test case, as languages differ markedly in how this space is divided up. For example, English makes a distinction between "in" (containment) and "on" (support), whereas Korean makes a distinction between "kkita" (tight-fitting) and "nehta" (loose-fitting) (Bowerman & Choi, 2003). From their earliest language use, children apply these terms in accordance with adult usage. Thus, by the second half of the second year of life (i.e., 18–24 months of age), young Korean speakers divide events into tight- vs. loose-fitting, whereas young English speakers focus on containment vs. support.

Similarly, young children apply novel words differently, depending on whether their language makes a formal distinction between count nouns (e.g., "a book") vs. mass nouns (e.g., "some milk"). English makes such a distinction whereas Japanese does not. Imai and Gentner (1997) were interested in the role of universal conceptual influences and language-specific influences on children's extension of a novel word for a novel item, when presented with a neutral syntactic frame, in children ranging from two to four years of age. Regardless of language spoken, when presented with complex objects, children extended the new word on the basis of shape, and when presented with substances, children extended the new word on the basis of substance. Interestingly, however, when presented with simple objects (e.g., a kidney-shaped piece of paraffin), English-speaking children extended a novel word on the basis of shape, whereas Japanese-speaking children were at chance, not systematically using either shape or substance.

The examples discussed here reveal the early use of language to guide concepts, but do not speak to the issue of whether languages shape concepts on non-linguistic tasks. This continues to be an area of active research, with evidence in support of language-specific influences in areas as diverse as color perception (Regier & Kay, 2009), spatial frames of reference (Majid, Bowerman, Kita, Haun, & Levinson, 2004), gender concepts (Boroditsky, Schmidt, & Phillips, 2003), and time metaphors (Fuhrman et al., 2011), as well as debate regarding the nature and extent of such influences (e.g., Gleitman & Papafragou, 2012; Pinker, 1994). However, much of the current research focuses exclusively on adults, thus leaving open the question that is key to this chapter, regarding the role of language in children's construction of concepts. Examining these issues over development is particularly important, given that some evidence suggests that language effects may not emerge until relatively late in development (e.g., Lucy & Gaskins, 2003, report language effects emerging between seven to nine years of age).

In contrast to the proposal that language-specific variation engenders non-linguistic differences in thought, an alternate idea is that concepts retain their complexity and flexibility, regardless of what is expressed in language, such that speakers select subsets of these representations for the purposes of speech, but this process does not alter their richer conceptual representations. Papafragou and Selimis (2010) refer to this as the "underspecification hypothesis." In line with this view, language differences are not necessarily linked to differences in performance on non-linguistic tasks. For example, although English and Greek verbs differ markedly in their linguistic encoding of events (typically encoding manner vs. path, respectively), and children are sensitive to such distinctions on a language-based task from an early age, there are no differences in their non-linguistic treatment of motion events, such as memory and categorization (Papafragou, Massey, & Gleitman, 2002; Papafragou & Selimis, 2010). Similarly, whether a language does or does not have grammatical encoding of evidentiality (i.e., having to distinguish different means of knowing, such as direct knowledge vs. hearsay, in grammatical morphemes; these are present in Quechua and Korean but not English, for example) does not yield differences in children's reasoning on a non-linguistic task (Papafragou, Li, Choi, & Han, 2007).

32.7 Language is a Social Marker

To this point we have considered the implications of language use for children's concepts. In this final section, we turn to a different way that language contributes to conceptual development, namely, as a social index that allows children to make important inferences about speakers (Kinzler, Shutts, & Correll, 2010). That is, how a person speaks—their language, dialect, accent, and register—provides a wealth of evidence from which children can infer a person's social group membership, such as nationality, region of origin, social status, or ethnicity. People use knowledge of linguistic behavior to predict social kinds, and vice versa. Thus, a variety of indirect evidence suggests that adults make inferences from language to social identity (e.g., a speaker of Chinese-accented English may be assumed to be ethnically Chinese), and from social identity to language (e.g., an Asian professor born in the United States may erroneously be perceived as speaking with an accent; Rubin, 1992), even though language is in reality only an imperfect correlate of social identities (e.g., a speaker of Mandarin need not be ethnically Asian, and vice versa). Language as a social cue is not purely informational, but also may have consequences for judgments of identity. For example, a Black American who does not speak African-American vernacular English (AAVE) may be criticized as "acting white" (Durkee & Williams, 2015).

The use of language as a social index is certainly influenced by familiarity and socialization, yet this phenomenon may be rooted in human evolution. It has been suggested that throughout most of human history, social groups close in physical proximity did not vary much phenotypically (e.g., skin tones typically varied only across wider geographical distances; see also Goodman, 2000), but varied considerably in language and dialect (i.e., languages typically varied even between neighboring tribes), thereby making language a useful predictor of social group membership (Cosmides, Tooby, & Kurzban, 2003). Because of this, humans may be predisposed to pay special attention to language variation when reasoning about others. Consistent with this view, even newborn infants are sensitive to human speech, and they can recognize their native language and their mother's voice, which demonstrate an early emerging capacity to use language as marker of social groups and individuals (DeCasper & Fifer, 1980; Kinzler, Dupoux, & Spelke, 2007; Shutts, Kinzler, McKee, & Spelke, 2009; Vouloumanos & Werker, 2007).

Kinzler and her colleagues have systematically investigated some of the ways that language serves as a social index. Early in development, children make use of how individuals speak when judging who to befriend (Kinzler, Shutts, & Spelke, 2012; Shutts et al., 2009), who to learn from (Corriveau, Kinzler, & Harris 2013; Kinzler, Corriveau, & Harris, 2011), and who to accept food from (Shutts et al., 2009). For example, children indicate that they would rather be friends with someone who speaks their own language versus a different language (e.g., English vs. French), and someone who speaks their language with a native accent vs. a foreign accent (e.g., English spoken with an American vs. French accent). Moreover, young children attend more to language and accent than other important categories, such as race, when reasoning about others. For example, Kinzler, Shutts, DeJesus, and Spelke (2009) presented white five-year-olds with photographs and voice recordings of two children (one black child who spoke English and one white child who spoke French) and asked them to indicate with whom they themselves wanted to be friends. Thus, participants could have selected a friend who matched them on language (but not race), or who matched them on race (but not language). Consistent with the idea that language serves as an early emerging social index, five-year-olds most often selected the language match. Precursors to these propensities develop early in childhood; for example, infants as young as five to six months of age prefer looking at a person who previously had spoken in their native language (Kinzler et al., 2007).

In addition to making use of language variation to guide affiliative behavior, young children also link language to attributions about the speaker. For example, by three years of age, ethnic majority children in the United States expect that people speaking an unfamiliar language are more likely to belong to a racial minority group (e.g., black), to wear unfamiliar clothing (e.g., traditional Mongolian clothing), or to live in an unfamiliar type of dwelling (e.g., a bamboo house with thatched roof) (Hirschfeld & Gelman, 1997). Children have also acquired quite specific expectations of others based on regional dialect. Thus, for example, by 9–10 years of age, children expect those speaking with a Northern US accent to be relatively smarter, and those speaking with a Southern US accent to be relatively nicer (Kinzler & DeJesus, 2013).

Variations in language use also communicate important information about interpersonal relationships. The way we speak shifts as a function of the speaker's social role (e.g., teacher vs. student), the addressee's perceived competence (e.g., baby talk, foreigner talk), and the interactional context (e.g., formal vs. casual). Children appear to have command of multiple, distinct registers from an early age (Andersen, 1990; Shatz & Gelman, 1973; Wagner, Clopper, & Pate, 2014; Wagner, Greene-Havas, & Gillespie, 2010). For example, when assuming a pedagogical role (pretending to be a teacher, or pretending to talk to an alien), preschool children are more likely to express generalizations about kinds of things using generic nouns (Gelman et al., 2013). Certain accents are deployed strategically in children's movies to signal that a character is good or evil (Lippi-Green, 1997), which may contribute to the meaning of dialectal differences for children. These early capacities open up new, unresolved questions;

that is, more work is needed to determine the conceptual implications of these registers for their social evaluations.

32.8 Conclusion

Children are simultaneously learning language and learning to organize experience into conceptual systems. Often these two processes may be seen as the same (e.g., learning language is learning concepts), but that masks the complexity of the phenomenon. We have reviewed in this chapter six distinct ways that language and thought relate in development. In future research, it will be important to extend the developmental implications of these findings, both downward in age to determine the roots in infancy, and upward in age to determine how these patterns interact with children's increasing cognitive sophistication and flexibility.

Acknowledgments

We thank Bruce Mannheim for discussion, and Shirley-Ann Rueschemeyer and an anonymous reviewer for comments on an earlier draft.

References

Alderson-Day, B., & Fernyhough, C. (2015). Inner speech: Development, cognitive functions, phenomenology, and neurobiology. *Psychological Bulletin, 141*, 931–65.
Andersen, E. S. (1990). *Speaking with Style: The Sociolinguistic Skills of Children*. Routledge, New York, NY.
Arredondo, M. M., Hu, X. S., Satterfield, T., & Kovelman, I. (2015). Bilingualism alters children's frontal lobe functioning for attentional control. *Developmental Science, 20*(3), 10.
Astington, J. A., & Baird, J. A. (2005). *Why Language Matters for Theory of Mind*. Oxford University Press, New York, NY.
Atran, S. (1993). *Cognitive Foundations of Natural History: Towards an Anthropology of Science*. Cambridge University Press, New York, NY.
Baldwin, D. A., Markman, E. M., & Melartin, R. L. (1993). Infants' ability to draw inferences about no obvious object properties: Evidence from exploratory play. *Child Development, 64*, 711–28.
Behrend, D. A., Rosengren, K., & Perlmutter, M. (1989). A new look at children's private speech: The effects of age, task difficulty, and parent presence. *International Journal of Behavioral Development, 12*, 305–20.
Berlin, B., Breedlove, D. E., & Raven, P. H. (1973). General principles of classification and nomenclature in folk biology. *American Anthropologist, 75*, 214–42.
Berk, L. (1992). Children's private speech: An overview of theory and the status of research. In: Diaz, R. M., & Berk, L. E. (Eds.), *Private Speech: From Social Interaction to Self-regulation* (pp. 17–53). Erlbaum, Hillsdale, NJ.

Bialystok, E., Craik, F. I., & Luk, G. (2012). Bilingualism: Consequences for mind and brain. *Trends in Cognitive Sciences, 16,* 240–50.

Bornstein, M. H. (1981). Psychological studies of color perception in human infants: Habituation, discrimination and categorization, recognition, and conceptualization. *Advances in Infancy Research, 1,* 1–40.

Boroditsky, L., Schmidt, L., & Phillips, W. (2003). Sex, syntax, and semantics. In: Gentner, D., & Goldin-Meadow, S. (Eds.), *Language in Mind: Advances in the Study of Language and Cognition* (pp. 61–80). Cambridge University Press, New York, NY.

Bowerman, M., & Choi, S. (2003). Space under construction: Language-specific spatial categorization in first language acquisition. In: Gentner, D., & Goldin-Meadow, S. (Eds.), *Language in Mind: Advances in the Study of Language and Thought* (pp. 387–427). Cambridge University Press, New York, NY.

Brandone, A. C., Cimpian, A., Leslie, S., & Gelman, S. A. (2012). Do lions have manes? For children, generics are about kinds rather than quantities. *Child Development, 83,* 423–33.

Brown, R. (1976). Reference in memorial tribute to Eric Lenneberg. *Cognition, 4,* 125–53.

Butler, L. P., & Markman, E. M. (2012). Preschoolers use intentional and pedagogical cues to guide inductive inferences and exploration. *Child Development, 83,* 1416–28.

Butler, L. P., & Markman, E. M. (2014). Preschoolers use pedagogical cues to guide radical reorganization of category knowledge. *Child Development, 130,* 116–27.

Carey, S., & Bartlett, E. (1978). Acquiring a single new word. *Papers and Reports on Child Language Development, 15,* 17–29.

Carlson, S. M., & Meltzoff, A. N. (2008). Bilingual experience and executive functioning in young children. *Developmental Science, 11,* 282–98.

Carlson, G. N., & Pelletier, J. (1995). *The Generic Book.* University of Chicago Press, Chicago, IL.

Cimpian, A., & Markman, E. M. (2008). Preschool children's use of cues to generic meaning. *Cognition, 107,* 19–53.

Cimpian, A., & Markman, E. M. (2009). Information learned from generic language becomes central to children's biological concepts: Evidence from their open-ended explanations. *Cognition, 113,* 14–25.

Cimpian, A., & Markman, E. M. (2011). The generic/nongeneric distinction influences how children interpret new information about social others. *Child Development, 82,* 471–492.

Corriveau, K. H., Kinzler, K. D., & Harris, P. L. (2013). Accuracy trumps accent in children's endorsement of object labels. *Developmental Psychology, 49,* 470–9.

Cosmides, L., Tooby, J., & Kurzban, R. (2003). Perceptions of race. *Trends in Cognitive Sciences, 7,* 173–9.

Csibra, G., & Gergely, G. (2009). Natural pedagogy. *Trends in Cognitive Sciences, 13,* 148–53.

DeCasper, A. J., & Fifer, W. P. (1980). Of human bonding: Newborns prefer their mothers' voices. *Science, 208,* 1174–6.

Diesendruck, G. (2003). Categories for names or names for categories? The interplay between domain-specific conceptual structure and language. *Language and Cognitive Processes, 18,* 759–87.

Diesendruck, G., & Deblinger-Tangi, R. (2014). The linguistic construction of social categories in toddlers. *Child Development, 85,* 114–23.

Duñabeitia, J. A., Hernández, J. A., Antón, E., Macizo, P., Estévez, A., Fuentes, L. J., & Carreiras, M. (2014). The inhibitory advantage in bilingual children revisited: Myth or reality? *Experimental Psychology, 61,* 234–51.

Durkee, M. I., & Williams, J. L. (2015). Accusations of acting White: Links to Black students' racial identity and mental health. *Journal of Black Psychology*, *41*, 26–48.

Fernyhough, C., & Fradley, E. (2005). Private speech on an executive task: Relations with task difficulty and task performance. *Cognitive Development*, *20*, 103–20.

Ferry, A., Hespos, S., & Waxman, S. R. (2010). Categorization in 3- and 4-month-old infants: An advantage of words over tones. *Child Development*, *81*, 472–9.

Ferry, A. L., Hespos, S., & Waxman, S. R. (2013). Nonhuman primate vocalizations support categorization in very young human infants. *Proceedings of the National Academy of Sciences*, *110*, 15231–5.

Frank, M. C., Everett, D. L., Fedorenko, E., & Gibson, E. (2008). Number as a cognitive technology: Evidence from Pirahã language and cognition. *Cognition*, *108*, 819–24.

Frauenglass, M. H., & Diaz, R. M. (1985). Self-regulatory functions of children's private speech. A critical analysis of recent challenges to Vygotsky's theory. *Developmental Psychology*, *21*, 357–64.

Fuhrman, O., McCormick, K., Chen, E., Jiang, H., Shu, D., Mao, S., & Boroditsky, L. (2011). How linguistic and cultural forces shape conceptions of time: English and Mandarin time in 3D. *Cognitive Science*, *35*, 1305–28.

Fulkerson, A. L., & Waxman, S. R. (2007). Words (but not tones) facilitate object categorization: Evidence from 6- and 12-month-olds. *Cognition*, *105*, 218–28.

Gelman, S. A. (2003). *The Essential Child: Origins of Essentialism in Everyday Life*. Oxford University Press, New York, NY.

Gelman, S. A., & Bloom, P. (2007). Developmental changes in the understanding of generics. *Cognition*, *105*, 166–83.

Gelman, S. A., & Coley, J. D. (1990). The importance of knowing a dodo is a bird: Categories and inferences in 2-year-old children. *Developmental Psychology*, *26*, 796–804.

Gelman, S. A., & Davidson, N. S. (2013). Conceptual influences on category-based induction. *Cognitive Psychology*, *66*, 327–53.

Gelman, S. A., & Heyman, G. D. (1999). Carrot-eaters and creature-believers: The effects of lexicalization on children's inferences about social categories. *Psychological Science*, *10*, 489–93.

Gelman, S. A., Goetz, P. J., Sarnecka, B. S., & Flukes, J. (2008). Generic language in parent-child conversations. *Language Learning and Development*, *4*, 1–31.

Gelman, S. A., & Markman, E. M. (1986). Categories and induction in young children. *Cognition*, *23*, 183–209.

Gelman, S. A., & Raman, L. (2007). This cat has nine lives? Children's memory for genericity in language. *Developmental Psychology*, *43*, 1256–68.

Gelman, S. A., Star, J. R., & Flukes, J. (2002). Children's use of generics in inductive inferences. *Journal of Cognition and Development*, *3*, 179–99.

Gelman, S. A., Taylor, M. G., & Nguyen, S. P. (2004). Mother-child conversations about gender: Understanding the acquisition of essentialist beliefs. *Monographs of the Society for Research in Child Development*, *69*, 1–127.

Gelman, S. A., Ware, E. A., & Kleinberg, F. (2010). Effects of generic language on category content and structure. *Cognitive Psychology*, *61*, 273–301.

Gelman, S. A., Ware, E. A., Kleinberg, F., Manczak, E. M., & Stilwell, S. M. (2014). Individual differences in children's and parents' generic language. *Child Development*, *85*, 924–40.

Gelman, S. A., Ware, E. A., Manczak, E. M., & Graham, S. A. (2013). Children's sensitivity to the knowledge expressed in pedagogical and nonpedagogical contexts. *Developmental Psychology*, *49*, 491–504.

Gelman, S. A., Wilcox, S. A., & Clark, E. V. (1989). Conceptual and lexical hierarchies in young children. *Cognitive Development*, 4, 309–26.

Gershkoff-Stowe, L., & Smith, L. B. (2004). Shape and the first hundred nouns. *Child Development*, 75, 1098–114.

Gleitman, L., & Papafragou, A. (2012). New perspectives on language and thought. In: Holyoak, K., & Morrison, B. (Eds.), *Cambridge Handbook of Thinking and Reasoning* (pp. 543–68). Cambridge University Press, New York, NY.

Goldin-Meadow, S. (2005). *The Resilience of Language: What Gesture Creation in Deaf Children Can Tell Us About How All Children Learn Language*. Psychology Press, Hove.

Goldin-Meadow, S., Gelman, S. A., & Mylander, C. (2005). Expressing generic concepts with and without a language model. *Cognition*, 96, 109–26.

Goodman, A. H. (2000). Why genes don't count (for racial differences in health). *American Journal of Public Health*, 90, 1699–702.

Gordon, P. (2004). Numerical cognition without words: Evidence from Amazonia. *Science*, 306, 496–9.

Gould S. J. (1983). *Hen's Teeth and Horse's Toes*. W. W. Norton, New York, NY.

Graham, S. A., Gelman, S. A, & Clarke, J. (2016). Generics license 30-month-olds' inferences about the atypical properties of novel kinds. *Developmental Psychology*, 52(9), 1352–62.

Graham, S. A., Keates, J., Vukatana, E., & Khu, M. (2013). Distinct labels attenuate 15-month-olds' attention to shape in an inductive inference task. *Frontiers in Psychology*, 3, 1–8.

Graham, S. A., & Kilbreath, C. S. (2007). It's a sign of the kind: Gestures and words guide infants' inductive inferences. *Developmental Psychology*, 43, 1111–23.

Graham, S. A., Kilbreath, C. S., & Welder, A. N. (2004). Thirteen- month-olds rely on shared labels and shape similarity for inductive inferences. *Child Development*, 75, 409–27.

Greenberg, J. H. (1963). Some universals of grammar with particular reference to the order of meaningful elements. *Universals of Language*, 2, 73–113.

Hespos, S. J., & Baillargeon, R. (2006). Décalage in infants' knowledge about occlusion and containment events: Converging evidence from action tasks. *Cognition*, 99, B31–B41.

Heyman, G. D., & Gelman, S. A. (2000). Preschool children's use of trait labels to make inductive inferences. *Journal of Experimental Child Psychology*, 19, 1–19.

Hirschfeld, L. A., & Gelman, S. A. (1997). What young children think about the relationship between language variation and social difference. *Cognitive Development*, 12, 213–38.

Hollander, M. A., Gelman, S. A., & Raman, L. (2009). Generic language and judgements about category membership: Can generics highlight properties as central? *Language and Cognitive Processes*, 24, 481–505.

Hollander, M. A., Gelman, S. A., & Star, J. (2002). Children's interpretation of generic noun phrases. *Developmental Psychology*, 38, 883–94.

Imai, M., & Gentner, D. (1997). A cross-linguistic study of early word meaning: Universal ontology and linguistic influence. *Cognition*, 62, 169–200.

Izard, V., Pica, P., Spelke, E. S., & Dehaene, S. (2008). Exact equality and successor function: Two key concepts on the path towards understanding exact numbers. *Philosophical Psychology*, 21(4), 491–505.

Jaswal, V. K. (2004). Don't believe everything you hear: Preschoolers' sensitivity to speaker intent in category induction. *Child Development*, 75, 1871–85.

Karmiloff-Smith, A. (1994). Precis of beyond modularity: A developmental perspective on cognitive science. *Behavioral and Brain Sciences*, 17, 693–707.

Karmiloff-Smith, A. (2009). Nativism versus neuroconstructivism: Rethinking the study of developmental disorders. *Developmental Psychology*, 45, 56–63.

Kelly, D. J., Quinn, P. C., Slater, A. M., Lee, K., Ge, L., & Pascalis, O. (2007). The other-race effect develops during infancy: Evidence of perceptual narrowing. *Psychological Science, 18,* 1084–9.

Kinzler, K. D., Corriveau, K. H., & Harris, P. L. (2011). Children's selective trust in native-accented speakers. *Developmental Science, 14,* 106–11.

Kinzler, K. D., & DeJesus, J. M. (2013). Northern = smart and Southern = nice: The development of accent attitudes in the United States. *The Quarterly Journal of Experimental Psychology, 66,* 1146–58.

Kinzler, K. D., Dupoux, E., & Spelke, E. S. (2007). The native language of social cognition. *Proceedings of the National Academy of Sciences, 104,* 12577–80.

Kinzler, K. D., Shutts, K., & Correll, J. (2010). Priorities in social categories. *European Journal of Social Psychology, 40,* 581–92.

Kinzler, K. D., Shutts, K., DeJesus, J., & Spelke, E. S. (2009). Accent trumps race in guiding children's social preferences. *Social Cognition, 27,* 623–34.

Kinzler, K. D., Shutts, K., & Spelke, E. S. (2012). Language-based social preferences among children in South Africa. *Language Learning and Development, 8,* 215–32.

Kroll, J. F., Dussias, P. E., Bice, K., & Perrotti, L. (2015). Bilingualism, mind, and brain. *Annual Review of Linguistics, 1,* 377–94.

Lakoff, G., & Johnson, M. (2008). *Metaphors We Live By.* University of Chicago Press, Chicago, IL.

Leonard, L. B. (2014). *Children with Specific Language Impairment.* MIT Press, Cambridge, MA.

Leslie, S. (2008). Generics: Cognition and acquisition. *The Philosophical Review, 117,* 1–49.

Lippi-Green, R. (1997). *English with an Accent: Language, Ideology, and Discrimination in the United States.* Psychology Press, Hove.

Lucy, J. A., & Gaskins, S. (2003). Interaction of language type and referent type in the development of nonverbal classification preferences. In: Gentner, D., & Goldin-Meadow, S. (Eds.), *Language in Mind: Advances in the Study of Language and Cognition* (pp. 465–92). Cambridge University Press, New York, NY.

Lupyan, G., Rakison, D. H., & McClelland, J. L. (2007). Language is not just for talking: Redundant labels facilitate learning of novel categories. *Psychological Science, 18,* 1077–83.

Majid, A., Bowerman, M., Kita, S., Haun, D. B., & Levinson, S. C. (2004). Can language restructure cognition? The case for space. *Trends in Cognitive Sciences, 8,* 108–14.

Mandler, J. M., & McDonough, L. (1993). Concept formation in infancy. *Cognitive Development, 8,* 291–318.

Mareschal, D., & Quinn, P. C. (2001). Categorization in infancy. *Trends in Cognitive Sciences, 5,* 443–50.

Needham, A., & Baillargeon, R. (1993). Intuitions about support in 4.5-month-old infants. *Cognition, 47,* 121–48.

Nixon, S. M. (2005). Mental state verb production and sentential complements in four-year-old children. *First Language, 25,* 19–37.

Papafragou, A., Li, P., Choi, Y., & Han, C. H. (2007). Evidentiality in language and cognition. *Cognition, 103,* 253–99.

Papafragou, A., Massey, C., & Gleitman, L. (2002). Shake, rattle, "n" roll: The representation of motion in language and cognition. *Cognition, 84,* 189–219.

Papafragou, A., & Selimis, S. (2010). Lexical and structural biases in the acquisition of motion verbs. *Language Learning and Development, 6,* 87–115.

Peterson, C. C., Wellman, H. M., & Liu, D. (2005). Steps in theory-of-mind development for children with deafness or autism. *Child Development, 76*, 502–17.

Piaget, J. (1926). *The Language and Thought of the Child.* Harcourt Brace, New York, NY.

Pinker, S. (1994). *The Language Instinct.* William Morrow, New York, NY.

Quinn, P. C., & Bhatt, R. S. (2005). Learning perceptual organization in infancy. *Psychological Science, 16*, 511–15.

Quinn, P. C., Yahr, J., Kuhn, A., Slater, A. M., & Pascalis, O. (2002). Representation of the gender of human faces by infants: A preference for female. *Perception, 31*, 1109–21.

Regier, T., & Kay, P. (2009). Language, thought, and color: Whorf was half right. *Trends in Cognitive Sciences, 13*, 439–46.

Rhodes, M., Leslie, S., Bianchi, L., & Chalik, L. (2018). The role of generic language in the early development of social categorization. *Child Development, 89*(1), 148–55.

Rhodes, M., Leslie, S., & Tworek, C. M. (2012). Cultural transmission of social essentialism. *Proceedings of the National Academy of Sciences, 109*, 13526–31.

Roberts, S. O., Gelman, S. A., & Ho, A. K. (2016). So it is, so it shall be: Group regularities license children's prescriptive judgments. *Cognitive Science, 41* Suppl 3, 576–600.

Roberts, S. O., Ho, A. K., & Gelman, S. A. (2017). Group presence, category labels, and generic statements influence children to treat descriptive group regularities as prescriptive. *Journal of Experimental Child Psychology, 158*, 19–31.

Rubin, D. L. (1992). Nonlanguage factors affecting undergraduates' judgments of nonnative English-speaking teaching assistants. *Research in Higher Education, 33*, 511–31.

Sapir, E. (1929). The status of linguistics as a science. *Language, 5*, 207–14.

Saxe, G. B. (2015). *Culture and Cognitive Development: Studies in Mathematical Understanding.* Psychology Press, Hove.

Schick, B., De Villiers, P., De Villiers, J., & Hoffmeister, R. (2007). Language and theory of mind: A study of deaf children. *Child Development, 78*, 376–96.

Senju, A., & Csibra, G. (2008). Gaze following in human infants depends on communicative skills. *Current Biology, 18*, 668–71.

Shatz, M., Diesendruck, G., Martinez-Beck, I., & Akar, D. (2003). The influence of language and socioeconomic status on children's understanding of false belief. *Developmental Psychology, 39*, 717–29.

Shatz, M., & Gelman, R. (1973). The development of communication skills: Modifications in the speech of young children as a function of listener. *Monographs of the Society for Research in Child Development, 38*, 1–38.

Shusterman, A., Lee, S. A., & Spelke, E. S. (2011). Cognitive effects of language on human navigation. *Cognition, 120*, 186–201.

Shutts, K., Kinzler, K. D., McKee, C. B., & Spelke, E. S. (2009). Social information guides infants' selection of foods. *Journal of Cognition and Development, 10*, 1–17.

Slobin, D. (1987). Thinking for speaking. *Proceedings of the Berkeley Linguistic Society, 13*, 435–45.

Slobin, D. (1996). From "thought and language" to "thinking for speaking." In: Gumperz, J., & Levinson, S. (Eds.), *Rethinking Linguistic Relativity* (pp. 70–96). Cambridge University Press, New York, NY.

Smith, L. B., Jones, S. S., Landau, B., Gershkoff-Stowe, L., & Samuelson, L. K. (2002). Creating a shape bias creates rapid world learners. *Psychological Science, 13*, 13–19.

Spelke, E. S. (2003). What makes humans smart? Core knowledge and natural language. In: Gentner, D., & Goldin-Meadow, S. (Eds.), *Language in Mind: Advances in the Study of Language and Cognition* (pp. 277–311). Cambridge University Press, New York, NY.

Srinivasan, M., Al-Mughairy, S., Foushee, R., & Barner, D. (2017). Learning language from within: Children use semantic generalizations to infer word meanings. *Cognition*, *159*, 11–24.

Srinivasan, M., & Rabagliati, H. (2015). How concepts and conventions structure the lexicon: Cross-linguistic evidence from polysemy. *Lingua*, *157*, 124–52.

Tager-Flusberg, H., Paul, R., & Lord, C. (2005). Language and communication in autism. In: Volkmar, F. R., Paul, R., Klin, A., & Cohen, D. (Eds.), *Handbook of Autism and Pervasive Developmental Disorders*, 3rd Edition (pp. 335–64). Wiley and Sons, Hoboken, NJ.

Topál, J., Gergely, G., Miklósi, A., Erdőhegyi, A., & Csibra, G. (2008). Infants' perseverative search errors are induced by pragmatic misinterpretation. *Science*, *321*, 1831–4.

Vouloumanos, A., & Werker, J. F. (2007). Listening to language at birth: Evidence for a bias for speech in neonates. *Developmental Science*, *10*, 159–64.

Vygotsky, L. S. (1986). *Thought and Language*. MIT Press, Cambridge, MA. (Original work published 1934.)

Wagner, L., Clopper, C. G., & Pate, J. K. (2014). Children's perception of dialect variation. *Journal of Child Language*, *41*, 1062–84.

Wagner, L., Greene-Havas, M., & Gillespie, R. (2010). Development in children's comprehension of linguistic register. *Child Development*, *81*, 1678–86.

Wang, P. P., & Bellugi, U. (1994). Evidence from two genetic syndromes for a dissociation between verbal and visual-spatial short-term memory. *Journal of Clinical and Experimental Neuropsychology*, *16*, 317–22.

Ware, E. A., & Booth, A. E. (2010). Form follows function: Learning about function helps children learn about shape. *Cognitive Development*, *25*, 124–37.

Waugh, L. R. (1982). *Marks, Signs, Poems: Semiotics, Linguistics, Poetics*. Toronto Semiotic Circle, Toronto, ON.

Waxman, S. R., & Booth, A. E. (2001). Seeing pink elephants: Fourteen- month-olds' interpretations of novel nouns and adjectives. *Cognitive Psychology*, *43*, 217–42.

Waxman, S. R., & Gelman, S. A. (2009). Early world-learning entails reference, not merely associations. *Trends in Cognitive Sciences*, *13*, 258–63.

Waxman, S. R., & Markow, D. B. (1995). Words as invitations to form categories: evidence from 12- to 13-month-old infants. *Cognitive Psychology*, *29*, 257–302.

Wellman, H. M. (2014). *Making Minds: How Theory of Mind Develops*. Oxford University Press, New York, NY.

Whorf, B. L. (1956). *Language, Thought, and Reality: Selected Writings of Benjamin Lee Whorf*. In: Caroll, J. B. (Ed.). MIT Press, Cambridge, MA.

Wodak, D., Leslie, S., & Rhodes, M. (2015). What a loaded generalization: Generics and social cognition. *Philosophy Compass*, *10*, 625–35.

Xu, F. (2002). The role of language in acquiring object kind concepts in infancy. *Cognition*, *85*, 223–50.

Yoon, J. M. D., Johnson, M. H., & Csibra, G. (2008). Communication-induced memory biases in preverbal infants. *Proceedings of the National Academy of Sciences*, *105*, 13690–5.

CHAPTER 33

ARTIFICIAL GRAMMAR LEARNING AND ITS NEUROBIOLOGY IN RELATION TO LANGUAGE PROCESSING AND DEVELOPMENT

JULIA UDDÉN AND CLAUDIA MÄNNEL

33.1 INTRODUCTION

THE artificial grammar learning (AGL) paradigm enables systematic investigation of acquisition of linguistically relevant structures by exposing participants to examples. The AGL task was first used by Arthur Reber (1967). In AGL, participants acquire a formal grammar on which they are later tested, in a separate testing phase (see Fig. 33.1). In the first acquisition phase, participants are exposed to a sample of sequences generated from a formal grammar. In the standard format for adult human participants, they are informed (after exposure) that sequences were generated according to a complex system of rules and asked to classify novel items as grammatical or not. However, the procedure of testing will inevitably vary depending on the population studied.

There are two basic strengths of the AGL paradigm for use in the language sciences. First, it is used as a model system to study aspects of natural language processing; for example, syntactic or phonological processing, in isolation from semantic influence. Since an artificial language is novel to all participants, prior learning is controlled. AGL has been most widely used as a model system for syntax, but work related to phonology has also appeared (Tessier, 2007). The second strength is the possibility to study a wide range of populations using identical, or at least comparable, paradigms. Populations have ranged from prelinguistic infants to adults, as well as non-human primates and songbirds (a review on comparative animal studies using AGL is, however, outside the focus of this

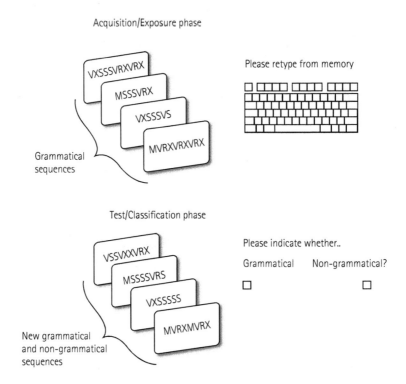

FIG. 33.1 The AGL paradigm was introduced by Reber (1967). Reber separated an acquisition phase, where the participant is exposed to grammatical sequences, from a test phase, where new grammatical and non-grammatical sequences were presented. The participants were asked to indicate whether each test sequence is grammatical or non-grammatical. This figure depicts the original paradigm used by Reber (1967), although the acquisition phase here is adapted for use with a modern keyboard instead of pen and paper. The elements in Reber's experiments (and many experiments since) are consonants only, rendering sequences superficially dissimilar to language stimuli, which naturally include vowels as well. The sequence processing and sequence learning mechanisms at work in AGL are however here explored as relevant for language learning and language processing, independent of the element a particular AGL paradigm uses.

chapter). Comparisons allow contributions to research questions on language acquisition and evolution. These two strengths of the paradigm will be illustrated throughout this chapter, where we will review the state-of-the-art in AGL research, including research with infants, with a particular focus on neuroimaging work. A main limitation of the paradigm, namely the constraints on generalization to natural languages, will also be addressed, through clarifications of some of the main differences between AGL and natural language research.

33.1.1 The AGL key

We will start by introducing a key for understanding variants of AGL experiments. The key is composed of five questions: Which elements? Which grammar? Which simpler features controlled for? Which violations? Which learning?

33.1.1.1 Which elements?

The most common type of presentation in AGL paradigms is visual stimulus presentation. However, auditory paradigms are also frequent, and, furthermore, there are some examples of tactile AGL paradigms (Conway & Christiansen, 2005). Visual, auditory, and tactile paradigms might all use the same grammar, but they differ in the perceptual features of the discrete *elements* that carry the grammar. In principle, the elements of an AGL study can be any stimuli, in any sensory modality, that can be recognized by the participants as a discrete element. The most commonly used elements are (1) spoken or written consonant-vowel (CV) syllables, (2) written consonants, and (3) pseudowords. More unusual elements that have been used include, for example, abstract visual shapes (Fiser & Aslin, 2002; Sturm, 2011) or symbols (Altmann, Dienes, & Goode, 1995), visual tiles (Stobbe, Westphal-Fitch, Aust, & Fitch, 2012), and written symbols from notational systems unknown to the participant (Mei et al., 2014).

While the choice of grammar is usually in focus in AGL studies, the choice of elements will also affect outcomes. For instance, a faster learning speed is expected when using elements known to the participants (e.g., example letters) compared to unknown elements (e.g., letters from other writing systems). We will come back to the influence of using visual versus auditory elements in the section on neuroimaging data, where it will become clear that the underlying neural architecture subserving AGL changes, depending on the sensory modality of the elements.

33.1.1.2 Which grammar? Formal language theory and AGL

Informally, the *grammar* denotes the relation between the discrete elements in some sequences composed of those elements. A powerful illustration of a grammar is a transition graph (see Fig. 33.2—"REBER grammar"). To generate or parse a grammatical sequence such as "VXR," we need to start from the start node, traverse the "V" arrow, followed by "X," "R" and finally the start/end-of-string symbol, # and end up in the end node. The sequence "VRX" is an example of a non-grammatical sequence. This information is contained in the transition graph, because when the "V" arrow connected with the start node has been traversed, we end up in the lower left node where there is no arrow out that is labeled "R." This results in a parsing failure. As soon as the arrows and nodes in this graph are changed, the graph corresponds to a different grammar. Features of the grammar used, such as its size and which class it belongs to, will be the most important factors determining learnability and generalization. In this section, we will introduce classes of grammars that might influence learnability in ways that are interesting for language sciences. Such grammar classes are the topic of study in the field of formal language theory.

The branch of mathematics called formal language theory delineates important principles of sets of sequences (called sets of *strings*). Since the beginning of AGL research, formal

REBER grammar

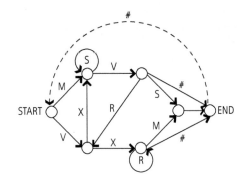

BROCANTO grammar
(flat representation)

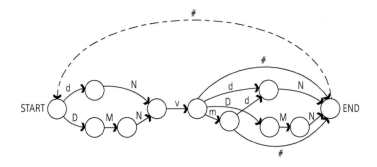

BROCANTO grammar
(hierarchical representation)

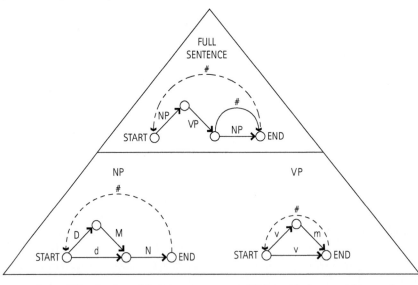

FIG. 33.2 Exemplifies the class of finite state grammars (FSGs) with the transition graph representation of the REBER grammar. In addition, we illustrate (the two topmost layers) of BROCANTO with the same kind of "flat" FSG representation (see also Opitz, 2003). Here, we also illustrate BROCANTO using other (informal) representations to emphasize the hierarchical relation between its phrasal versus sentence layers (see lower panel).

language theory has been its theoretical basis. Formal language theory has been used in AGL research to test whether classes of formal grammars induced by the participant correspond to different levels of behavioral processing difficulties. Formal grammars stipulate a number of rules, for example written down as so-called *rewrite rules* between symbol sequences (see next paragraph). The rules can, however, also be written using other notations. The class of regular grammars for instance (see next paragraph), can alternatively be noted with regular expressions or transition graphs (which are diagrams of so-called finite state automata) as in the top two panels of Figure 33.2. Although transition graphs are commonly used in the empirical AGL literature, we now use rewrite rules, as they show the origin of the names of two more complex grammar classes relevant for AGL.

Formal grammars generate *string sets* that are grammatical. These string sets are the formal languages. If a sequence does not belong to this string set, it is non-grammatical. Formal grammars are finite definitions of possibly infinite formal languages. More precisely, formal grammars are algorithms with a set of instructions. These algorithms are typically non-deterministic, since there is no specified order of how the instructions should be applied. Depending on the form of the rules, formal grammars can be classified into the complexity classes of the Chomsky hierarchy (see Fig. 33.3)[1]. In one version, this hierarchy consists of regular (finite state), context-free, context-sensitive, and general phrase-structure

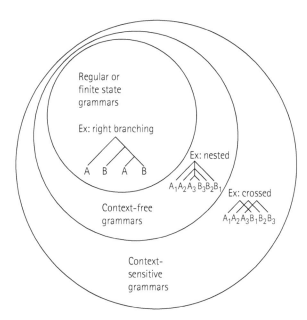

FIG. 33.3 The Chomsky hierarchy.

Reprinted from *Brain and Language*, 120 (2), Karl-Magnus Petersson, Vasiliki Folia, and Peter Hagoort, What artificial grammar learning reveals about the neurobiology of syntax, pp. 83–95, doi.org/10.1016/j.bandl.2010.08.003, Copyright © 2010 Elsevier Inc., with permission from Elsevier.

---

[1] Figure 33.3 and the (informal) description of the Chomsky hierarchy was originally published in the PhD thesis, *Language as structured sequences: a causal role for Broca's region in sequence processing*, written by J. Uddén, 2012, and available at http://hdl.handle.net/10616/40842.

grammars. The relation between classes of rules, classes of grammars, and classes of languages is subtle, since a language can be generated by many different grammars. However, if all grammars G generating the language L contain a context-free rule, for example, then L can be said to be context-free. Informally, regular grammars are built from a collection of production rules of the form S→abS and S→ab (where lower case indicates *terminal symbols* and S a *non-terminal* sentence or start symbol). The non-regular context-free case allows the right-hand side to involve terminal symbols around the sentence symbol in addition, as in S→aSb and S→ab. In the non-regular context-sensitive case, the left hand side has a "context" as exemplified in $a_1a_nSb_1b_n \to a_1a^na_{n+2}Sb_1b^nb_{n+2}$ (cf., Davis, Sigal, & Weyuker, 1994). However, this latter class of grammars overshoots the machinery needed to formalize the structure of natural language. A class of grammars more closely on par with the needs for parsing natural languages is, for example, described by so-called *multiple* context-free grammars (accessibly handled in Clark, 2014, who also discusses the more well-known alternative formalism of mildly context-sensitive grammars), an issue we will return to in this chapter.

Although AGL research inhabits a unique niche in language research, one must remember its limitations. For generalization to natural language to be valid, it is crucial to determine which of the many differences (e.g., between the rules of artificial grammars and natural grammars) are surface differences and which are deeper, so that they actually limit generalizations. One such potential difference is the absence of hierarchical rules in many artificial grammars (see section 33.1). An additional and related difference is that most AGL experiments do not introduce syntactic word categories upon which natural grammar rules can be applied. Here, validation of results from AGL in natural language paradigms, as well as "hybrid" languages is a good way forward. Some AGL paradigms include grammars like BROCANTO (see Fig. 33.2), where the language is more closely modeled on a natural language. BROCANTO is a small language that has words belonging to particular word categories such as nouns, verbs, adjectives, adverbs, and determiners. The nouns refer to objects in a board game, and the verbs refer to particular actions in the game (e.g., push), and so forth. The language is learned via a game in which participants learn the semantic content of the words. Moreover, BROCANTO has grammatical rules mimicking rules of a natural language in the sense that participants are able to build phrases according to separate phrase finite-state grammars (FSGs) for the noun phrase and verb phrase (see Fig. 33.2, lower panel). These are then combined according to a sentence-level FSG. On the other side of the spectrum of artificial grammar learning stimuli, there are simplistic triplet stimuli, for example ABB or AAB patterns. Results obtained with such stimuli are harder to assess in relation to natural language, but are more useful for comparative studies on non-human or infant cognition.

33.1.1.3 *Which simpler features are controlled for?*

AGL paradigms enable sophisticated control of the computational properties of sequential stimuli as well as the simpler features such as letter positions, chunk frequency, repetition patterns, and so forth. To start with, it has been shown that start and terminal positions in a sequence have a salient role, and subjects are more attentive to regularities at these positions (Endress, Nespor, & Mehler, 2009). One possibility is to minimize the role of terminal positions by using stable prefixes and suffixes and by experimental manipulations in the middle part of sequences (Uddén, Ingvar, Hagoort, & Petersson, 2012). The second robust finding is that subjects are highly sensitive to chunks of two or three adjacent letters (so-called bi- and trigrams) that are frequent in the exposure sequences. The sensitivity to these chunks can be viewed as an initial shallow processing of the grammar. It has been shown that bi- and trigram chunk strength predicts classification performance at the beginning of the acquisition phase, rather than at the end, where grammaticality status of the complete string is a better predictor (Forkstam, Elwér, Ingvar, & Petersson, 2008). From one point of view, it is likely that participants become sensitive to n-grams with larger and larger n, with continued exposure. When n is large enough, the whole grammar will be contained in such chunks. However, this gives a highly inflexible representation of the grammar, so it is clear that this does not explain all learning that takes place in an AGL experiment. In particular, for grammars that use multiple non-adjacent dependencies (languages where elements far apart predict each other), pure n-gram representations will be an inflexible processing path. A common way of segregating at least some aspects of pattern- or similarity-based learning from learning the full grammar is to control for the presence of bi- and trigrams, for example in order to match their frequency over grammar and non-grammatical sequences. The procedure when controlling for short n-grams using a measure called associative chunk strength (ACS) has been described previously (Meulemans & Van der Linden, 1997).

Other "similarity-based" or "pattern-based" accounts are also present (Kinder & Lotz, 2009). An influential study (Brooks & Vokey, 1991) presented a *repetition structure account* of AGL, suggesting that the repetitions of elements (globally in the sequence) create a pattern that is learned and used as a template during the test phase. Repetition patterns can be represented in different ways. As two examples, the sequence "ABCDEA" has the repetition pattern "x - - - - x" and the sequence "ABBCAC" has the repetition pattern "122313." The presence of repetitions of the same elements across a sequence has been shown to explain so-called *transfer effects*, where successful classification is achieved, although the test phase is implemented on a different set of elements, for example from a different modality (Gómez, Gerken, & Schvaneveldt, 2000; Tunney & Altmann, 1999). If repetition structure is controlled for when designing the stimulus material (e.g., simply by not letting any element repeat in any sequence), it is a sign of quality. A final pattern similarity that can be controlled is the similarity of the whole test strings compared to whole acquisition strings, for example as tested with the so-called "edit distance." Similarity-based accounts of AGL can be contrasted with rule-based accounts (Hauser, Hofmann, & Opitz, 2012), and these forms of learning are then thought to operate in parallel during a standard AGL experiment (Opitz & Hofmann, 2015). To conclude, we consider ACS to be the most important pattern to control for. More generally, any pattern that is salient to an observer of the complete stimulus set should be removed or controlled for. While pattern learning is a real issue, it is perhaps too much to expect all patterns to be controlled for in the same experiment. Thus, one good approach is, for example, to minimize the effect of terminal positions, manipulate ACS, and to get some kind of handle on the amount of pattern/similarity-based learning and how it might interact with the experimental manipulations in focus.

33.1.1.4 Which violations?

The most common way of probing grammatical knowledge is to create sequences that violate the grammar. The participant's task is then to segregate grammatical sequences from the ungrammatical sequences that include violations. Depending on how violations are constructed, different aspects of the grammar can be probed. Different violations can lead to large differences in the learning outcome (de Vries, Monaghan, Knecht, & Zwitserlood, 2008). The underlying neurobiology might also change (Opitz & Friederici, 2007). A related issue is the inclusion of proper tests for generalization, not only to new grammatical sequences that look similar, but also to new kinds of sequences (e.g., longer sequences). Although such tests help clarify which aspects of the grammar participants actually acquired, they have rarely been applied.

These aspects are important to consider when comparing AGL to other statistical learning (SL) tasks. At least for the SL studies we review in this chapter (note that this might not apply to SL tasks more generally), the main differences between AGL and SL experiments are that (1) SL regularities are not necessarily explicitly stated as following a grammar (although a formal analysis would probably often lead to the answer that they do). High transition probability is, for example, a more common way of expressing the form of regularities in SL experiments. It is more often the case that there is no generalization test at all, not even to new examples with the same transition probabilities. (2) AGL experiments often use two basic conditions: correct versus violation sequences (in all the violation sequences, large parts still follow the grammar), where SL tasks, in the context of this chapter, use correct versus random sequences (random sequences have no regularities whatsoever). In the wider SL literature, it is common to contrast higher transition probabilities with lower transition probabilities. Generally, as well as for this chapter, AGL paradigms are more homogenous than SL paradigms, and AGL can also be considered a part of a wider range of statistical learning (SL) tasks. Statistical learning is a term that can refer to the learning processes that take place during AGL paradigms, but others use this in a narrower, or wider sense. Due to this situation, it is crucial that the intended meaning of *statistical learning* is specified in the local context where it is used.

33.1.1.5 Which learning (implicit/explicit)?

When Reber (1967) introduced the AGL paradigm, the focus was the use of the paradigm for research on implicit learning. Today, there is more variation in the purpose of using the paradigm, and thus there are also varied methods that might ensure the grammar is implicitly learned, or not. Generally, it is important to keep the distinction between implicit versus explicit learning processes in mind because the processes are potentially segregated, for instance on a neurobiological level (Yang & Li, 2012, see discussion next), and this distinction also accounts for some differences in how infants acquire their L1 (implicitly) and how adults *study* languages (explicit learning). Note, however, that explicit learning is the exception and implicit learning the rule; hence, implicit learning processes will form the bulk of what is learned also during adult language learning. One of the clearer definitions of implicit learning is that by Seger (1994), reviewed in Uddén et al. (2010). In her view, implicit learning has four characteristics: (1) no or limited explicit access to the knowledge acquired and how it is put to use; (2) the acquired knowledge does not consist of simple association, but is more complex; (3) it is an incidental consequence of information processing and not explicit hypothesis testing; and (4) it does not rely on declarative memory mechanisms for learning—far from all AGL studies which describe learning processes that have all of these characteristics. This results in a literature with mixed learning styles (i.e., different proportions of implicit and explicit learning). The present situation for AGL (and SL) is that the same stimuli can be learned implicitly, explicitly, or with a mixture of these learning styles. This is a rare situation for cognitive neuroscience, and there is now an empirical literature focusing on this aspect in particular (Gheysen, Van Opstal, Roggeman, Van Waelvelde, & Fias, 2010; Wierzchon, Asanowicz, Paulewicz, & Cleeremans, 2012).

Studies emphasizing fully implicit learning processes are rare, and most study designs allow for explicit processes to influence results. Ways of assessing subjective conscious access are evolving fast, and with updated paradigms it has become clear that there is a fair amount of conscious access during standard AGL experiments (Wierzchon et al., 2012). In this study (as in the standard case), participants were engaged in a short-term memory task using an acquisition sample of sequences generated from a formal grammar. Subjects were later informed that the sequences were generated according to a complex system of rules and asked to classify novel items as grammatical or not. Subsequent ratings on five different scales, including confidence ratings, "feeling of warmth," and a rule awareness scale, suggest that increased conscious access is related to increased performance under these standard conditions. Similar findings are present with a common SL task (Batterink, Reber, Neville, & Paller, 2015). In future studies, where learning style (implicit or explicit) is of crucial importance for the interpretation of the results, a combination of rating scales should be used to assess conscious access during AGL paradigms.

There are several methods of minimizing explicit processes during the acquisition phase. As already mentioned, participants are typically engaged in a short-term memory task using an acquisition sample of sequences generated from the grammar. This means that acquisition is relatively masked, for example compared to acquisition with an explicit instruction to figure out rules behind the sequences. Another way is to use a more complex grammar, acquired during a longer learning period. Avoiding explicit recognition of patterns by minimizing them in the stimulus set (see section on controlling for patterns) is another way. In the test phase, a critical measure for showing successful implicit learning is the participants' relative *preference* for grammatical and relative aversion of non-grammatical sequences. In this supposedly more implicit version of testing for sensitivity to the grammar, participants only need to indicate whether they like or dislike a sequence and therefore there is no need to inform them about the presence of a complex generative rule system before classification. Moreover, from the participants' point of view, there are no correct or incorrect responses, and the motivation to use explicit (problem-solving) strategies is thus minimized. The fact that preferences develop as an effect of exposure has been investigated as the so-called "structural mere-exposure effect" (Manza & Bornstein, 1995; Zajonc, 1968). Using so-called *indirect measures*, for example, reaction times may also be a more sensitive method of tapping into implicit structural knowledge, when compared to the accuracy in judgment tasks (Batterink et al., 2015). Through the acquisition and testing phases, naturally the use of explicit feedback on performance should also be avoided if the goal is to minimize explicit learning.

We think it is crucial to put the discussion on the influence of learning style into proportion. It cannot be excluded that learning style has an influence on the underlying recruited neurobiology. At the same time, sensory neuroscience (i.e., neuroscience of visual perception, and so on) shows that the brain organizes according to features of stimuli. For instance, consider encountering a new creature for the first time. This will affect sensory pathways in a complex manner. Crucially however, we expect that the corresponding sensory regions will process the stimuli irrespective of whether the participant is explicitly informed about the existence of this creature (or even its parts or distinguishing features), or just encounters exemplars with familiarization as an incidental consequence (i.e., implicit learning). There might be slight variations, but the basic theme of brain organization is, in this case, according to stimulus features. While sequential structure might be considered an abstract stimulus feature, this remains to be demonstrated. We are not aware of any neuroimaging data in AGL literature that directly test this issue, for processing of structured sequences in AGL.

What about the distinction between declarative/explicit and non-declarative/procedural learning (Squire & Zola, 1996), which is clearly thought to segregate into the medial temporal lobe and the striatum, respectively? This distinction largely builds on reasoning from data across studies that use stimuli from different perceptual modalities, or alternatively, motor sequence learning. Although related proposals, linking hippocampal activation to spatial stimulus features, have appeared (O'Keefe, 1999), it is still too often overlooked that it is stimulus features that drive the distribution of activity across the medial temporal lobe and striatum. Experiments testing the same kind of regularities across perceptual and motor sequence learning modalities are needed. One study has yielded a more complicated pattern of activation across these regions for perceptual versus motor sequence learning (Gheysen et al., 2010), which cannot be accounted for by the more simple classical theory (Squire & Zola, 1996). In any case, current literature on neuroimaging studies of AGL, under fairly explicit learning conditions, may still contribute to answering a range of questions.

33.1.2 AGL performance as a trait

Traits do not vary from measurement to measurement and day to day in a participant, although some traits can change across the lifespan. If learning ability in AGL is a stable trait, it is possible that there is a link between this trait and some natural language processing trait. There have been several suggestions on which aspect of natural language performance would be most closely related to implicit learning abilities (Wells, Christiansen, Race, Acheson, & MacDonald, 2009). Among the suggestions are: discovery of phonological and distributional cues to lexical categories; acquisition of gender-like morphological systems; segmentation into syntactic phrases; relative clause comprehension; and processing of long-distance relationships between words. None of these have been sufficiently tested to draw conclusions. It has been shown that individual differences in the processing of non-adjacent dependencies in natural language are correlated with individual differences in an implicit learning task on sequences generated from an artificial grammar (Misyak, Christiansen, & Tomblin, 2009). Conway et al. (2010) found correlations in individual differences between two different implicit learning tasks (a visual implicit learning task and an auditory AGL task), and a sentence processing task where the task was to predict the final word. This effect was not mediated by individual differences in working memory (as measured with the digit span task), cognitive control (as measured with the Stroop task), or non-verbal intelligence. Individual differences in the location of regional functional activity during a natural language task, which varied from the anterior to the posterior portion of the left inferior frontal gyrus, overlapped with individual differences in the location of functional activity during sequence processing (Petersson, Folia, & Hagoort, 2012). From these correlations, it is clear that some relationships between individual differences in implicit learning and natural language processing do exist and that they, to some extent, may represent the same trait (i.e., overlapping traits). We are not aware of any studies on whether individual differences in phonological processing and AGL are correlated. This is an area for future research. For a wider discussion on SL as a trait, see Siegelman and Frost (2015).

We have already started the discussion on the relation between (adult) AGL and natural language processing, but how is this relevant to language learning? One point of view is that learning (particularly implicit learning), is a consequence of processing (e.g., through priming, see Chang, Dell, Bock, & Griffin, 2000), so in that sense, adult AGL might at least be relevant to understanding adult language learning (both implicit aspects of L2 learning and L1 adaptations). Implicit AGL paradigms are generally of higher relevance for L1 language acquisition. However, the underlying neurobiology develops/matures remarkably and changes in AGL performance are expected as a consequence of growing up. This limits the relevance of adult AGL experiments for L1 language learning.

33.2 META-ANALYZING NEUROIMAGING OF AGL

While AGL studies are used to answer a wide range of questions in adult psycholinguistic literature, it is important to understand their contribution to the literature on neuroimaging. This chapter will mostly cover studies using functional magnetic resonance imaging (FMRI), although event-related brain potential (ERP) studies and functional near-infrared spectroscopy (fNIRS) studies on infants will be covered in section 33.4 (there are yet no magnetoencephalography [MEG] studies that we are aware of).

Currently, FMRI literature on AGL spans at least 15 original studies on distinct samples (Bahlmann, Schubotz, & Friederici, 2008; Fletcher, Buchel, Josephs, Friston, & Dolan, 1999; Folia, Forkstam, Ingvar, Hagoort, & Petersson, 2011; Forkstam, Hagoort, Fernández, Ingvar, & Petersson, 2006; Friederici, Bahlmann, Heim, Schubotz, & Anwander, 2006; Hauser et al., 2012; Kepinska, de Rover, Caspers, & Schiller, 2016; Lieberman, Chang, Chiao, Bookheimer, & Knowlton, 2004; Opitz & Friederici, 2003, 2004, 2007; Petersson, Forkstam, & Ingvar, 2004; Seger, Prabhakaran, Poldrack, & Gabrieli, 2000; Skosnik et al., 2002; Strange, Henson, Friston, & Dolan, 2001; Wilson et al., 2015). A qualitative survey of this literature reveals that the left inferior frontal gyrus (LIFG), and left frontal operculum (FOP, sometimes with right homologue areas), sensory regions, striatum, the inferior frontal sulcus (IFS), the parietal cortex, and sometimes left posterior superior temporal cortex are often reported as active in AGL studies. Previous reviews have focused on LIFG contributions (Uddén & Bahlmann, 2012), and further on we will discuss contributions from other regions of noticeable interest from a natural language perspective. We will, however, start to describe the involved neural circuitry in AGL from a relatively unbiased position: by means of meta-analysis.

The above-mentioned literature is beginning to approach the volume where a systematic quantitative meta-analysis is possible. The strength of this approach is that it gives a summary of a few regions that are robustly activated by a task or *contrast* while avoiding selective biases (due to previous knowledge) that can arise during the process of interpreting, summarizing, and reviewing results. In an FMRI-context, the term *contrast* is used to refer to probing of the data of one condition relative to another condition (i.e., a comparison between two conditions). We will use the contrast comparing activity for non-grammatical sequences, over and above activity for grammatical sequences. For readers unfamiliar with terms like peaks, clusters, contrast, and multiple comparison correction in an FMRI-context, we refer to textbooks covering the basics of the method (e.g., Huettel, Song, & McCarthy, 2004).

We have used the GingerALE method in a first attempt. In order to simplify the description of this method, let us first consider its two main steps: (1) activity brain maps from different studies are overlaid on top of each other to determine coactivation, and (2) the joint activity is statistically tested (with permutation methods). In other words, by forming the union across statistical landscapes from each study, centered at the reported peak coordinates (spread determined by the number of subjects), the activation likelihood estimation (ALE) method determines the overall likelihood of activation of clusters in a union map by a permutation test (Eickhoff et al., 2009). The ingoing FMRI coordinates are, however, crucially dependent not only on the variations of paradigms (as described in the AGL key) but also on the contrasts used when probing activity. Thus, we included peak activations from one contrast (with corresponding limits on variations in the paradigm) in the meta-analysis. This is the contrast comparing activity for non-grammatical > grammatical sequences (NG > G) during the classification phase of grammaticality judgments. We considered AGL studies and studies where the task was framed as SL, but where stimuli involved a learning phase with exposure to structured sequences, as in AGL. Many studies (in particular SL studies) were excluded due to a lack of the NG > G contrast (Karuza et al., 2013; Opitz & Friederici, 2003, 2004; Weber, Christiansen, Petersson, Indefrey, & Hagoort, 2016; Yang & Li, 2012). To streamline the parameters of the ingoing studies further, we excluded peaks reported with behavioral performance included in the model (Kepinska et al., 2016) and the peaks reported when including measures from a receiver operating characteristic (ROC) analysis in the model (Hauser et al., 2012). Seven studies remained (Bahlmann, Schubotz, & Friederici, 2008; Folia, Forkstam, Ingvar, Hagoort, & Petersson, 2011; Forkstam, Hagoort, Fernández, Ingvar, & Petersson, 2006; Friederici, Bahlmann, Heim, Schubotz, & Anwander, 2006; Opitz & Friederici, 2007; Petersson, Forkstam, & Ingvar, 2004; Wilson et al., 2015). If a study used a 2×2 design and two levels of NG > G were reported, we inserted peaks from both levels. In multiday learning studies, we entered the last reported measurement (or alternatively the last day with subtracted NG > G contrasts at baseline, if not, the "last day only" was reported). In the case of one entered study, the overlap of session with grammaticality and preference instructions was used (Folia et al., 2011).

When thresholding the meta-analysis of the NG > G contrast at an FDR-corrected level of 0.05 (assumed correlations in data: independence or positive dependence) or alternatively correcting at the cluster level (using a cluster-forming threshold of $p > 0.001$) with permutation testing, six clusters were significant: the left and right frontal operculum, the left and right IFG, and the left and right middle frontal gyrus (MFG). When correcting for multiple comparisons with FDR, without any assumptions on the correlations in the data, only the bilateral frontal operculum (extending into the inferior frontal gyrus on the left), were significant. These results emphasize the relatively larger contributions from the right hemisphere seen in AGL, compared for example to complex syntax in natural language experiments, which are largely left-lateralized (Hagoort & Indefrey, 2014). These results also emphasize the contributions from the frontal operculum. A majority of adult AGL studies use visual presentation, and the literature thus has to be carefully taken into consideration as being biased toward finding the activations related to visual processing. Only one study that went into the meta-analysis of NG > G contrast was an auditory study

(Wilson et al., 2015). Interestingly, however, both the human and macaque data from this study point to the conclusion that the most robust region is the same region as in our meta-analysis: the frontal operculum (bilaterally). Right hemisphere contributions were also generally highlighted both by the meta-analysis, in right FOP, right IFG, and right MFG, as well as in the human data in Wilson et al. (2015), in right FOP, the right posterior parietal cortex (BA39), the right middle temporal gyrus, the right frontal pole, and the right lateral occipital gyrus. The bilateral FOP (often together with the neighboring anterior insula) has been implicated in cognitive (e.g., control, attention, awareness, decision-making) and perceptual (e.g., taste) processes. The FOP in particular has been established as a causal node affecting cognitive control processes (Higo, Mars, Boorman, Buch, & Rushworth, 2011). These authors assign a *"dual role [. . .] in using arbitrary rules to guide response selection [. . .] and in retrieving information from posterior regions to do so."* Under this view of the FOP, activity seen in this region in the NG > G contrast of AGL studies could be interpreted as a consequence of domain-general cognitive control processes involving the application of rules (although rules should not be thought of as in opposition to, e.g., pattern learning, in this context, see section 33.1.1.3). The anterior insula, the ventro-medial prefrontal cortex, and the FOP together form the so-called *salience network* (Craig, 2009). This network is activated, possibly linking with the sympathetic part of the autonomous nerve system, when a stimulus is particularly relevant for the participant, whether in a cognitive or emotional task, or when threatened, for example by uncertainty or pain (Seeley et al., 2007). A possible interpretation of the current FOP results in the NG > G contrast is that the non-grammatical sequences are more salient, perhaps even mildly threatening to participants (remember that they are also dispreferred in preference tests).

In summary, a relatively unbiased review of the neural circuitry involved in detecting violations (compared to correct sequences) in AGL experiments reveals a network markedly different from the regions most robustly involved in processing related aspects of natural language processing, for example natural language syntax (e.g., LIFG and left posterior superior/middle temporal gyrus). LIFG remains a region of overlap of artificial and natural syntactic processing. The robust activation of the nearby FOP region (bilaterally) is notable as a homologue pair of structures that are less often implicated in natural syntactic processing. However, the adjacent anterior insula, clearly left-lateralized, has repeatedly been implicated as one of the most reoccurring sites to display lesions in aphasia patients with both production and comprehension deficits (Bates et al., 2003; Dronkers, 1996). We will return to the left posterior superior/middle temporal gyrus in section 33.3.

33.3 AGL IN RELATION TO NATURAL LANGUAGE

We have written on the properties of grammars of AGL and natural languages. Although artificial grammars are much smaller toy models of the grammars of natural languages, artificial grammars with the same formal properties as natural grammars can be studied to mitigate other methodological issues of natural language research (such as the influence of semantic processing).

33.3.1 Syntax and phonology

We have already mentioned that syntax and phonology (more precisely phonotactics) are the two aspects of natural languages that have been studied with AGL. Recently, it has been noted that hierarchy, a hallmark of syntactic structure, is not present in phonotactic patterns (Berwick & Chomsky, 2016; Heinz & Idsardi, 2011). Finite state grammars (see section on formal grammar theory and AGL) suffice to describe phonotactically legal sequences of speech sounds. If this holds, it will be crucial to select the right kind of grammar when using AGL for studying natural language syntax and/or phonology. Whether (or how) these grammar aspects map onto differences in neurobiology would become an important future question.

Berwick and Chomsky (2016) review a way of defining more precisely what hierarchy in natural language syntax corresponds to in terms of formal grammar theory. They take the starting point of the internal merge operation as the core of human syntax. The internal merge operation corresponds to formal grammars of a class called multiple context-free grammars, which augments context-free grammars in one respect. Non-terminals (on both the left and the right hand side) can now include an extra *internal* variable (the same variable, e.g., x on the left and right). This variable can take on different words or word sequences. Application of this rule, when including the internal variable, corresponds to copying performed by internal merge (this is somewhat informally stated in Berwick & Chomsky, 2016). We also refer the interested reader to two of the more accessible, precise sources of the formal treatment of hierarchy in the context of multiple context-free grammars, that we are aware of (Clark, 2014; Stabler, 2011). Other less subtle, but laudably clearly stated definitions of hierarchical structure appear in Fitch (2014), where any structure whose graph takes the form of a rooted tree is hierarchical (where a rooted tree is an acyclic, fully connected graph with a designated root node). It is beyond the context of this AGL chapter to determine the most useful approach to hierarchical structure (when describing natural languages in formal language theory or more generally). Nonetheless, we note that this is a fundamental theoretical issue, where integration across disciplines would be fruitful.

33.3.2 AGL, hierarchically structured sequences, and the left dorsal language system

An alternative approach when reviewing neuroimaging literature on AGL is to consider the left dorsal language pathway. Not only is this particularly relevant for considering the relevance of AGL for models of natural language processing (Bornkessel-Schlesewsky & Schlesewsky, 2013; Bornkessel-Schlesewsky, Schlesewsky, Small, & Rauschecker, 2015), but it is also important for understanding the AGL literature. In the view of Bornkessel-Schlesewsky and coauthors, the dorsal pathway subserves sequence processing in general. It has previously been noted (Friederici & Singer, 2015) that one needs to be careful when discussing the function of a pathway, in particular when there is a lack of research on connectivity. There are no connectivity studies that we are aware of that would give direct support for the involvement of the dorsal pathway as such in AGL (or other sequence processing paradigms without semantics). Another point to make when discussing the model by Bornkessel-Schlesewsky and coauthors (also pointed out by Berwick & Chomsky,

2016) is that hierarchical sequence structure is not treated separately in this model. Whether the dorsal pathway (as a whole) is involved in sequence processing without discrimination of different structures or whether it is more involved in hierarchical compared to non-hierarchical sequences (Friederici, 2012) has still not been directly tested. The developmental perspective might become particularly important, as exemplified by one study on natural language syntax performance that explained behavioral variation as a function of development of the dorsal (white matter) pathway as a whole (Skeide, Brauer, & Friederici, 2016). It is beyond the scope of the chapter to fully review this line of research, but we nevertheless would like to point it out as promising.

33.3.3 Temporal lobe contributions to AGL versus complex syntax

The LIFG, together with the left posterior superior/middle temporal gyri, are the two most robustly activated regions across different contrasts of syntactic complexity, and their role has been clarified in recent models of the neurobiology of language (Friederici, 2012; Hagoort & Indefrey, 2014). For a more general introductory text on the involvement of these regions in language processing, see Kemmerer (2014). As these regions are also the "end stations" of the dorsal language pathway, we will now discuss evidence on the involvement of the left superior/middle posterior temporal lobe in AGL. We will use the abbreviation LPUTG (left posterior superior/middle, i.e., upper, temporal gyri) to refer to this anatomical location, which also includes the posterior part of the intervening left superior temporal sulcus. When reviewing the literature that include contrasts where non-grammatical items are compared with grammatical items, a notable difference, probably related to grammar type, emerges. In our meta-analysis, as well as in many studies using finite state grammars, not a single peak is located in LPUTG (Folia et al., 2011; Forkstam et al., 2006; Petersson et al., 2004). One possibility is that this is related to the absence of semantics in AGL. A related observation is the absence of temporal lobe contributions in the inflectional morphology only condition, in Goucha and Friederici (2015). However, in one study using PSG (Friederici et al., 2006) and in a final study where PSG and FSG were studied together in the NG > G contrast (Bahlmann et al., 2008), this region was more active for NG than G, suggesting that semantics should not be the determining factor for what causes posterior temporal lobe activation in the context of (complex) syntax. In two studies using versions of the BROCANTO grammar (Kepinska, de Rover, Caspers, & Schiller, 2016; Opitz & Friederici, 2007), which includes semantics, there were peaks in LPUTG for NG > G, consistent with this interpretation. Another study using BROCANTO reported null results in the NG > G contrast (Hauser et al., 2012). We are not aware of any other studies on BROCANTO, PSG, or FSG grammars that report the standard NG > G contrast. In two other studies using non-modified BROCANTO (Opitz & Friederici, 2003, 2004), there were, however, *learning-related* (i.e., this did not come from the NG > G contrast but might reflect the same underlying process) effects along the left anterior and posterior temporal lobe (including LPUTG).

In an auditory study using finite state grammars, LPUTG was also activated in human participants in the NG > G contrast (Wilson et al., 2015). In an auditory SL study, there was activation in the LPUTG in a contrast of *randomized* syllable sequence > *regular* auditory syllable sequence (McNealy, Mazziotta, & Dapretto, 2006). In this study, during the course of exposure, there was an increase in the regular condition in the LSTG. This finding was independently replicated (Cunillera et al., 2009), as an interaction in LSTG, between the first and second blocks in the random versus rest contrast. These results of AGL and SL tasks might be a consequence of the brain processing auditory features of the elements in auditory cortex near LPUTG. For instance, the activation might be a "downstream" effect, during the absence of successful prediction (in the case of NG and random sequences), observed as increased BOLD in corresponding sensory regions. Alternatively, without reference to predictive processes, computation of sequence regularities as such might be partly subserved by sensory cortices. These suggested interpretations warrant a follow-up review of visual AGL and SL studies. Is it the case that NG > G and random > structured contrasts (or other "structure-contrasts") do not engage LPUTG in visual experiments with simple regularities? Are visual areas instead active in corresponding contrasts? Indeed, two visual AGL and SL studies show bilateral or left visual ventral stream (VVS) activation, extending into the inferior temporal lobe, in structure-contrasts (Petersson et al., 2012; Turk-Browne, Scholl, Chun, & Johnson, 2009) without showing activation in LPUTG. One additional visual study did not report LPUTG, but is ambiguous with respect to a left VVS activation (Forkstam et al., 2006). There was no activity in VVS for an NG > G contrast, while a region in left VVS is reported as significant in results reporting the same contrast (shown in Figure 4B in the study). An additional visual study showed activity restricted to LIFG in an NG > G contrast (Petersson, Forkstam, & Ingvar, 2004). Are visual areas active in structure-contrasts of the auditory studies we have reviewed? Of the three studies we've just considered here, two do not show any VVS activity (Cunillera et al., 2009; McNealy et al., 2006), and one study showed right lateralized VVS activity in an NG > G contrast.

Note that this observation of modality dependence would be trivial if the contrast we discussed was grammaticality judgment versus rest. Crucially, we observe this division into auditory and visual areas when contrasting two conditions of the same (visual or auditory) elements. In these contrasts, it is only the amount of structure (i.e., regularity in the sequences) which is different across conditions and it is thus not expected that these structure-contrasts would activate visual versus auditory areas in visual versus auditory experiments, respectively, under the assumption of domain-general structure sequence operations. In this context, it is also relevant to note that there is limited so-called transfer (from some acquisition elements to a new set of elements in the test phase) in AGL (Tunney & Altmann, 1999), as recently reviewed (Frost, Armstrong, Siegelman, & Christiansen, 2015)[2]. Taken together, these findings point to non-shared neural substrates across modalities. This is in contrast to complex syntactic processing in natural language, which seems to be largely supramodal (Constable et al., 2004). Three possible factors explaining these differences are: (1) differences in what kind of regularities govern sequences (e.g., hierarchical); (2) semantics; and/or (3) the time needed for stabilizing neural representation of regularities, and during which maturational period they are acquired. In summary, the use of an auditory grammar might be a parallel reason (alongside the grammatical type described here)

---

[2] However, we do not agree with how one of the included studies (Bischoff-Grethe, Proper, Mao, Daniels, & Berns, 2000) in this review was summarized (in our view this is the only visual study in which a structure-contrast supports domain-general structured sequence processing in LPUTG).

why peaks in LPUTG are observed in an AGL paradigm. See also Figure 33.3, the Chomsky hierarchy.

Altogether, this suggest that parts of the LPUTG are sometimes activated in AGL tasks and may thus play a role in processing, perhaps particularly complex syntax, also in the absence of semantic content. However, too few studies exist to draw conclusions on exactly which conditions lead to activation in the left posterior middle/superior temporal lobe (LPUTG) in AGL experiments. One interesting possibility is that the LPUTG, and LIFG (as end-stations of the left dorsal pathway), together form a network subserving sequence processing of hierarchically structured (in the sense we have attempted to formally describe already) sequences. This overall processing network might consist of distinguishable spatio-temporal processing aspects related to, for example, online memory versus syntactic operations such as internal merge. AGL paradigms will continue to shed light on these and related issues. A concrete suggestion for a tractable hypothesis to test in future research is that the degree of activation may interact with modality (possibly more likely to be active for auditory than visual AGL) and grammar type (so far, more for nested hierarchical grammars as well as the BROCANTO grammar, compared to studies on regular grammars). We also note that a review of the (inferior) parietal cortex in AGL studies would be valuable, as this region is also an end-station of the indirect segments of the dorsal pathway and often recruited during sentence processing.

33.4 AGL RESEARCH IN INFANCY

In aiming to unravel first language acquisition, AGL studies have addressed how infants extract structural units and sequence regularities from speech input, and how they form generalizations and syntactic category knowledge (see Gómez & Gerken, 2000). Comprehensive behavioral research has revealed infants' impressive decoding of adjacent and non-adjacent relations of speech input elements as well as their realization in abstract speech patterns, so-called algebraic rules. We will briefly sketch the two associated lines of behavioral research and illustrate how neuroimaging research substantially contributes to delineating the developmental timeline of infants' structure processing abilities.

A first line of behavioral AGL research emerged from the landmark study by Saffran et al. (1996), showing that eight-month-old infants utilize transitional probabilities of syllables for defining word boundaries in continuous speech. Follow-up studies demonstrated that infants employ statistical speech properties in word segmentation (Marchetto & Bonatti, 2015; Saffran, 2001; Shukla et al., 2011), discovering non-adjacent structure regularities (Gómez & Maye, 2005; Marchetto & Bonatti, 2015), acquiring lexical-semantic categories (Lany, 2014; Lany & Saffran, 2010), and establishing grammatical categories (Höhle et al., 2004; Shi et al., 2006). A second line of behavioral AGL research is based on the seminal study by Marcus et al. (1999), reporting seven-month-old infants' ability to detect abstract speech patterns, as defined by repetitions and alternations of speech elements (see also Gómez & Gerken, 1999). This structure sensitivity might initially be perceptually driven by the detection of immediate repetitions (see Endress, Nespor, & Mehler, 2009). However, successful generalization of theses patterns attests infants' abstract representations (Marcus et al., 1999). Follow-up studies showed that six- to seven-month-olds learn these so-called algebraic rules preferably from speech input, compared to other auditory and visual input, suggesting infants' pattern sensitivity to be speech-specific at this age (Marcus et al., 2007; Rabagliati et al., 2012).

During the last decade, a growing number of neuroimaging studies have significantly complemented the insights on language acquisition gained from behavioral AGL studies. Importantly, behavior-independent neuroimaging methods can capture the earliest instances of infants' structure sensitivity and, moreover, specify the underlying brain mechanisms. In the following, we will present ERP and fNIRS evidence sketching infants' advancing processing abilities, from adjacent dependencies, to repetition-based abstract speech patterns (algebraic rules), to computationally more demanding non-adjacent dependencies.

33.4.1 Processing of adjacent dependencies

Behavioral research has shown that statistical computations of adjacent input elements are among infants' earliest speech decoding abilities, functional during the second half of infants' first year (Saffran, 2001; Saffran et al., 1996). Extending this evidence, ERP studies indicate the presence of statistical mechanisms for neighboring input elements already at birth (Kudo et al., 2011; Teinonen et al., 2009). For example, Teinonen et al. (2009) presented newborns with a stream of syllable triplets (e.g., *ea-ke-sa*) that had high within-triplet, but low between-triplet transitional probabilities. Infants' ERPs revealed more negative responses to the first than to the other triplet syllables, suggesting that infants processed the statistically defined word onset syllable differently to the other syllables. The authors concluded that newborns readily segment words from the input by computing transitional probabilities of adjacent elements. In a recent fNIRS study, Ferry et al. (2016) demonstrated that newborns process adjacent dependencies in even longer stimulus sequences, but only in the presence of supporting perceptual cues. Specifically, results showed that after being familiarized with six-syllable sequences (e.g., *si-me-bu-ta-le-fo*) infants detected a sequence-internal switch of syllables (e.g., *si-me-ta-bu-le-fo*) if the two middle syllables were separated by a short pause and thus acoustically marked. Together, these findings highlight newborns' impressive decoding abilities for directly neighboring input elements and the crucial role of facilitating statistical and acoustic input cues (see Endress, Nespor, & Mehler, 2009).

33.4.2 Sensitivity to algebraic rules

In analyzing speech input, infants are not only challenged to process adjacent dependencies of elements, but also to recognize their underlying patterns. Behaviorally, it has been shown that seven-month-olds derive generalizations from stimuli containing the same repetition-based adjacent relations (Marcus et al., 1999). Using fNIRS, Gervain et al. (2008) followed up on this evidence and tested newborns with syllable triplets of repetition-based ABB structures (e.g., *mu-ba-ba*) or random ABC structures (e.g., *mu-ba-ge*). The authors found enhanced hemodynamic responses in temporal and left frontal regions for ABB versus ABC sequences, with increasing responses over time. These results suggest that newborns readily differentiate repetition-based and random structures, preferentially processing immediate repetitions in cortical areas specific to speech processing (see also Gervain et al., 2012). The fact that infants showed this differentiation across different syllable sequences indicates that even newborns are able to form some pattern abstraction. Interestingly, the enhancement for repetition-based patterns was only observed for adjacent ABB repetitions, but not non-adjacent ABA repetitions. This difference points to newborns' processing limitations, such that they successfully extract adjacent dependencies, but not yet computationally more demanding non-adjacent dependencies.

A process highly related to the detection of repetition-based abstract patterns is the detection of sequence changes; when expectations built from stimulus repetitions are violated by the occurrence of new stimuli. Basirat et al. (2014) evaluated three-month-olds' ERP mismatch responses to local sequence changes (e.g., rare vowel *a* after frequent vowel *i*) and global sequence changes (e.g., rare sequence *a-a-a-a* after frequent sequence *a-a-a-i*). Interestingly, infants showed a mismatch response to local stimulus changes that was modulated by global sequence changes. Specifically, changes in global context resulted in enhanced mismatch responses and were, in addition, followed by a late negative slow wave, most likely indicating stimulus integration. These results imply that infants at three months are not only sensitive to immediate changes in auditory sequences, but also to more global sequence patterns.

Following the findings of repetition-based pattern processing in newborns (Gervain et al., 2008), Wagner et al. (2011) examined the developmental trajectory of this ability. Interestingly, fNIRS results of seven-month-olds resembled the outcome in newborns, such that their hemodynamic responses were stronger for repetition-based ABB structures than random ABC structures. In contrast, nine-month-old infants showed the reverse pattern with enhanced responses to ABC over ABB structures. Based on these findings, the authors discuss a potential developmental change in the processing of abstract patterns, such that infants initially favor stimulus salience (i.e., repetition), but are later drawn to novelty (i.e., stimulus variability).

33.4.3 Processing of non-adjacent dependencies

In contrast to infants' early processing of adjacent relations and their generalization, the considerably more complex processing of non-adjacent relations has been suggested to arise between children's first and second year of life (Gómez & Maye, 2005; Marchetto & Bonatti, 2015). Neuroimaging studies extend this behavioral evidence, showing that infants master non-adjacent computations before reaching their first year. Mueller et al. (2012) observed that even at three months of age infants were able to detect non-adjacent rule violations in syllable triplets, as evidenced by infant mismatch responses in the ERP. In this oddball paradigm, two frequent syllable frames (i.e., *le . . . bu* and *fi . . . to*) served as standards that established the non-adjacent dependency rule. Infrequent deviants either violated the acoustic stimulus features of the third syllable (i.e., pitch deviants) or the rule features (i.e., rule deviants). Interestingly, infants' ability to process non-adjacent dependencies was associated with their auditory processing capacities, such that only those infants who showed a more mature mismatch ERP response to pitch violations also detected the rule violations. This association suggests that infants only begin to master non-adjacent dependency processing once their processing and memory capacities can sufficiently capture distant relations. Kabdebon et al. (2015) examined non-adjacent dependency processing in infants at an older age, in full-term and preterm eight-month-olds. The authors evaluated infants' ERP responses and EEG-phase-locking to three-syllabic test words that were consistent (e.g., *ku-na-bi*) with a non-adjacent rule introduced in a familiarization speech stream (i.e., *ku . . . bi*) as compared to test words that were inconsistent with this rule (e.g., *fi-bi-na*). Regarding ERPs, consistent test words evoked larger responses than inconsistent words during the second and third syllables, interpreted as a familiarity effect driven by rule prediction. In a later time window, however, inconsistent words evoked larger ERP responses than consistent words, interpreted as an attention allocation to unexpected events. Moreover, EEG-phase-locking results during test revealed higher beta band values during the first syllable of all words and higher alpha band values after the offset of inconsistent than consistent words. In the language domain, power changes in the beta band have been consistently found to reflect the degree of a word's contextual predictability (see Lewis et al., 2016) and here likely reflect infants' expectation of the putative word onset. In contrast, increased alpha power has been observed for increased working memory loads, specifically during adults' processing of long-distance dependencies in sentences (Meyer, Obleser, & Friederici, 2013), and may imply infants' prolonged attention orientation to the unexpected, inconsistent words with an attempt to correct. Importantly, there were no processing differences between full-term and preterm-infants, thus confirming the previous finding of non-adjacent dependency processing being functional early during infants' first months of life (Mueller et al., 2012).

Complementing this AGL research, Friederici et al. (2011) demonstrated infants' early processing of non-adjacent relations for natural language learning by utilizing a non-native language. In this ERP study, German four-month-olds were familiarized with Italian sentences containing two grammatical non-adjacent dependencies between a respective auxiliary and a verb's inflection, with 32 different verb stems being the variable middle element (e.g., ***sta cant-ando;*** is singing; *puo cant-are;* can sing). Following the familiarization, infants were presented with new sentences that were either grammatical or contained a violation of the non-adjacent dependency, resulting in ungrammatical structures (e.g., ***sta arriv-are***, is arrive; *puo arriv-ando;* can singing). ERP responses in the first test phase revealed no processing differences between grammatical and ungrammatical structures, whereas in the last test phase there was a pronounced positivity in the ERP response to the dependency violations as compared to the grammatical structures. These results indicate that at four months of age, infants can acquire non-adjacent dependency rules in a natural language online, after only brief structure exposure.

Together, these studies demonstrate infants' impressive ways of extracting structural input features by means of statistical computations, abstract pattern recognition, and their generalization. To date, there is increasing evidence on the developmental timeline of these abilities, such that the ability to process adjacent structures is present at birth and advances toward non-adjacent structure processing during infants' first year of life. Thus, highly sensitive neuroimaging techniques have uncovered much earlier instances of structural learning than have been observed with behavioral techniques (Gómez & Maye, 2005; Marchetto & Bonatti, 2015). Differences in reported acquisition age, however, might not only reflect methodological differences, but also result from capturing different knowledge representations (for discussion, see Gómez, 2016). While current neuroimaging studies mostly focus on infants' fast encoding of structural patterns, future studies will have to evaluate the retention of learned patterns over time.

Despite current advances in studying infants' structural learning capacities, there is still a lack of developmental AGL studies on more complex grammatical relations typical for human language. Natural language involves not only adjacent and single non-adjacent dependencies, as described here, but also, for example, multiple embedded non-adjacent dependencies (Bever, 1974; Gibson, 1998). A first step into studying more complex structure processing is the behavioral study by Kovacs and Endress (2014), showing that seven-month-olds process embeddings in repetitive structures. The authors tested whether infants detect how word-level repetition patterns define higher-level sentence patterns. During familiarization, infants listened to three-syllable ABB words (e.g., *du-ba-ba*) or ABA words (e.g., *du-ba-du*), thus containing adjacent or non-adjacent repetitions. These words were organized in three-word ABB sentence structures, such that the two last words had the same repetitive structure (e.g., *du-ba-du lo-mo-mo za-vu-vu*). When tested with new instances of the known ABB sentence structure (e.g., *ti-pe-ti re-je-je fe-si-si*) and novel AAB sequences (e.g., *ti-pe-pe re-je-je fe-si-fe*), infants looked at the new sentence structure type longer. The fact that infants only detected the higher-level change in sentence structure, if words contained adjacent ABB repetitions, but not non-adjacent ABA repetitions, again points to infants' early processing advantage of adjacent over non-adjacent dependency relations. Nevertheless, these data reveal first evidence of infants' ability to process word-level structures embedded in higher-level structures during the first year of life. Following this work, there are now first ERP studies indicating that infants are not only able to process one level of embedding, but even multiple levels of embedding (Winkler et al., 2015, 2016). In these studies five-month-old infants were tested with seven-tone sequences that contained three non-adjacent dependencies, nested around a center marker tone. In an auditory oddball paradigm, frequent standard sequences established the multiple center-embedded structure, while infrequent deviant sequences contained violations of the two outer dependencies. Importantly, mismatch responses to these violations indicated infants' detection of the underlying structural rules. Thus, infants at this young age show impressive abilities in processing multiple nested dependencies, which even for adults are challenging to accomplish (de Vries et al., 2011; Karlsson, 2007).

Future neuroimaging research will have to specify the potentially different neural mechanisms underlying these complex processing abilities across development. Parallel to the literature showing infant learning of non-adjacent dependencies (even multiple non-adjacent dependencies), there is an ongoing line of work on adult learning of multiple non-adjacent dependencies (Ottl, Jager, & Kaup, 2015; Uddén et al., 2012). Follow-up experiments (e.g., using passive listening paradigms) in infants and adults exposed to nested, crossed, and other theoretically interesting structures would be a promising way forward for future integration of adult and developmental AGL literature.

33.5 CONCLUSION

We have created an AGL key that exposes the most relevant variations in the AGL paradigm, in the light of current open questions, for example with regard to its relevance for natural language processing and language learning. Currently, an outstanding tractable question in

AGL research is whether it can be demonstrated that domain-general sequence processing mechanisms explain at least part of the performance observed in AGL studies. We speculate that complex grammars might trigger relatively more domain-general processes than less complex ones, but this remains to be validated in both psycholinguistic and neuroimaging experiments. The lack of conclusive evidence of such domain-general processes is salient, as the lesson from sensory neuroscience is that brain organization can largely be understood as based on stimulus features. The issue of domain-generality of sequence processing is of importance for understanding the limitations of generalizability of AGL results to research on natural syntax, since there is a literature showing that syntactic processing in natural language should be understood as largely supramodal. The issue of whether implicit versus explicit sequence learning might be subserved by different neurobiological mechanisms is also still open, and studies addressing this question in the future should take novel, more sensitive ways of probing for (conscious) access into account. This is important for clarifying the relevance of the AGL paradigm for language learning. Implicit AGL paradigms are generally of higher relevance for L1 language learning, but still, the underlying neurobiology develops/matures remarkably and changes in AGL performance are expected as a consequence of growing up. This naturally limits the relevance of adult AGL experiments for L1 language learning and comparative developmental studies are warranted. Our meta-analysis of FMRI-studies including the NG > G contrast highlights *similarities and differences* between robustly activated regions in AGL and natural language processing (in particular for complex syntax). While a lot has already been said about the LIFG in this context, we now extend this discussion to also include, for instance, the FOP and LPUTG. We have also identified a problem at the interface of AGL and natural language research, which is that the central term *hierarchy* is often used without references to which out of several existing definitions it refers to. Particularly in the context of a well-defined notion of hierarchy, AGL experiments on relative learning difficulties and neural implementation of hierarchical versus non-hierarchical grammars is of continuing importance. Given methodological advancements, these open questions are now also increasingly tractable in the developmental AGL literature.

33.6 Acknowledgments

Parts of the text appeared previously in the unpublished PhD thesis by the first author. We thank Toru Hitomi, who initiated the use of the GingerALE method when reviewing the AGL literature, and Ajay Loura for discussions on the formal language theory. We also thank Angela D. Friederici for her very helpful comments on an earlier version of this chapter. The present chapter was supported by the the Max Planck Society (C. M., J. U.), the Swedish Brain Foundation (Hjärnfonden, J. U.), and the German Research Foundation (project FR 519/20-1, C.M.).

References

Altmann, G. T. M., Dienes, Z., & Goode, A. (1995). Modality independence of implicitly learned grammatical knowledge. *Journal of Experimental Psychology: Learning, Memory, and Cognition*, 21, 899–912.

Bahlmann, J., Schubotz, R. I., & Friederici, A. D. (2008). Hierarchical artificial grammar processing engages Broca's area. *NeuroImage, 42*, 525–34.

Basirat, A., Dehaene, S., & Dehaene-Lambertz, G. (2014). A hierarchy of cortical responses to sequence violations in three-month-old infants. *Cognition, 132*(2), 137–50.

Bates, E., Wilson, S. M., Saygin, A. P., Dick, F., Sereno, M. I., Knight, R. T., & Dronkers, N. F. (2003). Voxel-based lesion-symptom mapping. *Nature Neuroscience, 6*, 448–50.

Batterink, L. J., Reber, P. J., Neville, H. J., & Paller, K. A. (2015). Implicit and explicit contributions to statistical learning. *Journal of Memory and Language, 83*, 62–78.

Berwick, R. C., & Chomsky, N. (2016). *Why Only Us: Language and Evolution.* The MIT Press, Cambridge, MA.

Bever, T. G. (1974). The ascent of the specious or there's a lot we don't know about mirrors. In: Cohen, D. (Ed.), *Explaining Linguistic Phenomena.* Hemisphere Publishing Corporation, New York, NY, pp. 173-200.

Bischoff-Grethe, A., Proper, S. M., Mao, H., Daniels, K. A., & Berns, G. S. (2000). Conscious and unconscious processing of nonverbal predictability in Wernicke's area. *The Journal of Neuroscience, 20*, 1975–81.

Bornkessel-Schlesewsky, I., & Schlesewsky, M. (2013). Reconciling time, space and function: A new dorsal-ventral stream model of sentence comprehension. *Brain and Language, 125*, 60–76.

Bornkessel-Schlesewsky, I., Schlesewsky, M., Small, S. L., & Rauschecker, J. P. (2015). Neurobiological roots of language in primate audition: common computational properties. *Trends in Cognitive Sciences, 19*, 142–50.

Brooks, L. R., & Vokey, J. R. (1991). Abstract analogies and abstracted grammars—Comments on Reber (1989) and Mathews Et-Al (1989). *Journal of Experimental Psychology: General, 120*, 316–23.

Chang, F., Dell, G. S., Bock, K., & Griffin, Z. M. (2000). Structural priming as implicit learning: A comparison of models of sentence production. *Journal of Psycholinguistic Research, 29*, 217–29.

Clark, A. (2014). Learnability and Language Acquisition, "An introduction to multiple context free grammars for linguists." Available at: http://www.cs.rhul.ac.uk/home/alexc/lot2012/

Constable, R. T., Pugh, K. R., Berroya, E., Mencl, W. E., Westerveld, M., Ni, W. J., & Shankweiler, D. (2004). Sentence complexity and input modality effects in sentence comprehension: An fMRI study. *NeuroImage, 22*, 11–21.

Conway, C. M., & Christiansen, M. H. (2005). Modality-constrained statistical learning of tactile, visual, and auditory sequences. *Journal of Experimental Psychology, 31*, 24–39.

Conway, C. M., Bauernschmidt, A., Huang, S. S., & Pisoni, D. B. (2010). Implicit statistical learning in language processing: Word predictability is the key. *Cognition, 114*, 356–71.

Craig, A. D. (2009). How do you feel—now? The anterior insula and human awareness. *Nature Reviews Neuroscience, 10*, 59–70.

Cunillera, T., Camara, E., Toro, J. M., Marco-Pallares, J., Sebastián-Gallés, N., Ortiz, H., . . . & Rodriguez-Fornells, A. (2009). Time course and functional neuroanatomy of speech segmentation in adults. *NeuroImage, 48*, 541–53.

de Vries, M. H., Monaghan, P., Knecht, S., & Zwitserlood, P. (2008). Syntactic structure and artificial grammar learning: The learnability of embedded hierarchical structures. *Cognition, 107*, 763–74.

de Vries, M., Christiansen, M. H., Petersson, K. M. (2011). Learning recursion: Multiple nested and crossed dependencies. *Biolinguistics, 5*, 10–35.

Davis, M., Sigal, R., & Weyuker, E. J. (1994). *Computability, Complexity, and Languages: Fundamentals of Theoretical Computer Science*. Newnes, Oxford/Boston.

Dronkers, N. F. (1996). A new brain region for coordinating speech articulation. *Nature, 384*, 159–61.

Eickhoff, S. B., Laird, A. R., Grefkes, C., Wang, L. E., Zilles, K., & Fox, P. T. (2009). Coordinate-based activation likelihood estimation meta-analysis of neuroimaging data: A random-effects approach based on empirical estimates of spatial uncertainty. *Human Brain Mapping, 30*(9), 2907–26.

Endress, A. D., Nespor, M., & Mehler, J. (2009). Perceptual and memory constraints on language acquisition. *Trends in Cognitive Science, 13*, 348–53.

Ferry, A. L., Fló, A., Brusini, P., Cattarossi, L., Macagno, F., Nespor, M., & Mehler, J. (2016). On the edge of language acquisition: Inherent constraints on encoding multisyllabic sequences in the neonate brain. *Developmental Science, 19*, 488–503.

Fiser, J., & Aslin, R. N. (2002). Statistical learning of higher-order temporal structure from visual shape sequences. *Journal of Experimental Psychology, 28*, 458–467

Fitch, W. T. (2014). Toward a computational framework for cognitive biology: unifying approaches from cognitive neuroscience and comparative cognition. *Physics of Life Reviews, 11*, 329–64.

Fletcher, P., Buchel, C., Josephs, O., Friston, K., & Dolan, R. (1999). Learning-related neuronal responses in prefrontal cortex studied with functional neuroimaging. *Cerebral Cortex, 9*, 168–78.

Folia, V., Forkstam, C., Ingvar, M., Hagoort, P., & Petersson, K. M. (2011). Implicit artificial syntax processing: Genes, preference, and bounded recursion. *Biolinguistics, 5*, 105–32.

Forkstam, C., Elwér, Å., Ingvar, M., & Petersson, K. M. (2008). Instruction effects in implicit artificial grammar learning: A preference for grammaticality. *Brain Research, 1221*, 80–92.

Forkstam, C., Hagoort, P., Fernández, G., Ingvar, M., & Petersson, K. M. (2006). Neural correlates of artificial syntactic structure classification. *NeuroImage, 32*, 956–67.

Friederici, A. D. (2012). The cortical language circuit: From auditory perception to sentence comprehension. *Trends in Cognitive Sciences, 16*, 262–8.

Friederici, A. D., Bahlmann, J., Heim, S., Schubotz, R. I., & Anwander, A. (2006). The brain differentiates human and non-human grammars: Functional localization and structural connectivity. *Proceedings of the National Academy of Sciences of the United States of America, 103*, 2458–63.

Friederici, A. D., Mueller, J. L., & Oberecker, R. (2011). Precursors to natural grammar learning: Preliminary evidence from 4-month-old infants. *PLoS One, 6*, e17920.

Friederici, A. D., & Singer, W. (2015). Grounding language processing on basic neurophysiological principles. *Trends in Cognitive Sciences, 19*(6), 329–38.

Frost, R., Armstrong, B. C., Siegelman, N., & Christiansen, M. H. (2015). Domain generality versus modality specificity: the paradox of statistical learning. *Trends in Cognitive Sciences, 19*, 117–25.

Gervain, J., Berent, I., & Werker, J. F. (2012). Binding at birth: The newborn brain detects identity relations and sequential position in speech. *Journal of Cognitive Neuroscience, 24*, 564–74.

Gervain, J., Macagno, F., Cogoi, S., Pena, M., & Mehler, J. (2008). The neonate brain detects speech structure. *Proceedings of the National Academy of Sciences of the United States of America, 105*, 14222–7.

Gheysen, F., Van Opstal, F., Roggeman, C., Van Waelvelde, H., & Fias, W. (2010). Hippocampal contribution to early and later stages of implicit motor sequence learning. *Experimental Brain Research, 202,* 795–807.

Gibson, E. (1998). Linguistic complexity: Locality of syntactic dependencies. *Cognition, 68,* 1–76.

Gómez, R. L. (2016). Do infants retain the statistics of a statistical learning experience? Insights from a developmental cognitive neuroscience perspective. *Philosophical Transactions of the Royal Society B, Biological Sciences, 372,* 1711.

Gómez, R. L., & Gerken, L. (1999). Artificial grammar learning by 1-year-olds leads to specific and abstract knowledge. *Cognition, 70*(2), 109–35.

Gómez, R. L., & Gerken, L. (2000). Infant artificial language learning and language acquisition. *Trends in Cognitive Sciences, 4,* 178–86.

Gómez, R. L., & Maye, J. (2005). The developmental trajectory of nonadjacent dependency learning. *Infancy, 7,* 183–206.

Gómez, R. L., Gerken, L., & Schvaneveldt, R. W. (2000). The basis of transfer in artificial grammar learning. *Memory & Cognition, 28,* 253–63.

Goucha, T., & Friederici, A. D. (2015). The language skeleton after dissecting meaning: A functional segregation within Broca's Area. *NeuroImage, 114,* 294–302.

Hagoort, P., & Indefrey, P. (2014). The neurobiology of language beyond single words. *Annual Review of Neuroscience, 37,* 347–62.

Hauser, M. F., Hofmann, J., & Opitz, B. (2012). Rule and similarity in grammar: their interplay and individual differences in the brain. *NeuroImage, 60,* 2019–26.

Heinz, J., & Idsardi, W. (2011). Sentence and word complexity. *Science, 333,* 295–7.

Higo, T., Mars, R. B., Boorman, E. D., Buch, E. R., & Rushworth, M. F. (2011). Distributed and causal influence of frontal operculum in task control. *Proceedings of the National Academy of Sciences of the United States of America, 108,* 4230–5.

Höhle, B. J., Weissenborn, J., Kiefer, D., Schulz, A., & Schmitz, M. (2004). Functional elements in infants' speech processing: The role of determiners in the syntactic categorization of lexical elements. *Infancy, 5,* 341–53.

Huettel, S. A., Song, A. W., & McCarthy, G. (2004). *Functional Magnetic Resonance Imaging.* Sinauer Associates, Sunderland, MA.

Kabdebon, C., Pena, M., Buiatti, M., & Dehaene-Lambertz, G. (2015). Electrophysiological evidence of statistical learning of long-distance dependencies in 8-month-old preterm and full-term infants. *Brain and Language, 148,* 25–36.

Karlsson, F. (2007). Constraints on multiple center-embedding of clauses. *Journal of Linguistics, 43,* 365–92.

Karuza, E. A., Newport, E. L., Aslin, R. N., Starling, S. J., Tivarus, M. E., & Bavelier, D. (2013). The neural correlates of statistical learning in a word segmentation task: An fMRI study. *Brain and Language, 127,* 46–54.

Kemmerer, D. L. (2014). *Cognitive Neuroscience of Language.* Psychology Press, New York, NY.

Kepinska, O., de Rover, M., Caspers, J., & Schiller, N. O. (2016). On neural correlates of individual differences in novel grammar learning: An fMRI study. *Neuropsychologia, 98,* 156–68.

Kinder, A., & Lotz, A. (2009). Connectionist models of artificial grammar learning: what type of knowledge is acquired? *Psychological Research, 73,* 659–73.

Kovacs, A. M., & Endress, A. D. (2014). Hierarchical processing in seven-month-old infants. *Infancy, 19,* 409–25.

Kudo, N., Nonaka, Y., Mizuno, N., Mizuno, K., & Okanoya, K. (2011). On-line statistical segmentation of a non-speech auditory stream in neonates as demonstrated by event-related brain potentials. *Developmental Science, 14,* 1100–6.

Lany, J. (2014). Judging words by their covers and the company they keep: Probabilistic cues support word learning. *Child Development, 85,* 1727–39.

Lany, J., & Saffran, J. R. (2010). From statistics to meaning: infants' acquisition of lexical categories. *Psychological Science, 21,* 284–91.

Lewis, A. G., Schoffelen, J.-M., Schriefers, H., & Bastiaansen, M. (2016). A predictive coding perspective on beta oscillations during sentence-level language comprehension. *Frontiers in Human Neuroscience, 10,* 85.

Lieberman, M. D., Chang, G. Y., Chiao, J., Bookheimer, S. Y., & Knowlton, B. J. (2004). An event-related fMRI study of artificial grammar learning in a balanced chunk strength design. *Journal of Cognitive Neuroscience, 16,* 427–38.

Manza, L., & Bornstein, R. F. (1995). Affective discrimination and the implicit learning process. *Consciousness and Cognition, 4,* 399–409.

Marchetto, E., & Bonatti, L. L. (2015). Finding words and word structure in artificial speech: the development of infants' sensitivity to morphosyntactic regularities. *Journal of Child Language, 42,* 873–902.

Marcus, G. F., Fernandes, K. J., & Johnson, S. P. (2007). Infant rule learning facilitated by speech. *Psychological Science, 18,* 387–91.

Marcus, G. F., Vijayan, S., Bandi Rao, S., & Vishton, P. M. (1999). Rule learning by seven-month-old infants. *Science, 283,* 77–80.

McNealy, K., Mazziotta, J. C., & Dapretto, M. (2006). Cracking the language code: neural mechanisms underlying speech parsing. *The Journal of Neuroscience, 26,* 7629–39.

Mei, L., Xue, G., Lu, Z. L., He, Q., Zhang, M., Wei, M., ... & Dong, Q. (2014). Artificial language training reveals the neural substrates underlying addressed and assembled phonologies. *PloS One, 9,* e93548.

Meulemans, T., & Van der Linden, M. (1997). Associative chunk strength in artificial grammar learning. *Journal of Experimental Psychology, 23,* 1007–28.

Meyer, L., Obleser, J., & Friederici, A. D. (2013). Left parietal alpha enhancement during working memory-intensive sentence processing. *Cortex, 49,* 711–21.

Misyak, J. B., Christiansen, M. H., & Tomblin, J. B. (2009). Statistical learning of nonadjacencies predicts on-line processing of long-distance dependencies in natural language. *Proceedings of the Cognitive Science Society, 2009,* 177–82.

Mueller, J. L., Friederici, A. D., & Männel, C. (2012). Auditory perception at the root of language learning. *Proceedings of the National Academy of Sciences of the United States of America, 109,* 15953–8.

O'Keefe, J. (1999). Do hippocampal pyramidal cells signal non-spatial as well as spatial information? *Hippocampus, 9,* 352–64.

Opitz, B., & Friederici, A. D. (2003). Interactions of the hippocampal system and the prefrontal cortex in learning language-like rules. *NeuroImage, 19,* 1730–7.

Opitz, B., & Friederici, A. D. (2004). Brain correlates of language learning: The neuronal dissociation of rule-based versus similarity-based learning. *Journal of Neuroscience, 24,* 8436–40.

Opitz, B., & Friederici, A. D. (2007). Neural basis of processing sequential and hierarchical syntactic structures. *Human Brain Mapping, 28*, 585–92.

Opitz, B., & Hofmann, J. (2015). Concurrence of rule- and similarity-based mechanisms in artificial grammar learning. *Cognitive Psychology, 77*, 77–99.

Ottl, B., Jager, G., & Kaup, B. (2015). Does formal complexity reflect cognitive complexity? Investigating aspects of the Chomsky Hierarchy in an artificial language learning study. *PloS One, 10*, e0123059.

Petersson, K. M., Folia, V., & Hagoort, P. (2012). What artificial grammar learning reveals about the neurobiology of syntax. *Brain and Language, 120*, 83–95.

Petersson, K. M., Forkstam, C., & Ingvar, M. (2004). Artificial syntactic violations activate Broca's region. *Cognitive Science, 28*, 383–407.

Rabagliati, H., Senghas, A., Johnson, S. P., & Marcus, G. F. (2012). Infant rule learning: Advantage language or advantage speech? *Plos One, 7*, e40517.

Reber, A. S. (1967). Implicit learning of artificial grammars. *Journal of Verbal Learning & Verbal Behavior, 6*, 855–63.

Saffran, J. R. (2001). Words in a sea of sounds: the output of statistical learning. *Cognition, 81*, 149–69.

Saffran, J. R., Aslin, R. N., & Newport, E. L. (1996). Statistical learning by eight-month-old infants. *Science, 274*, 1926–8.

Seeley, W. W., Menon, V., Schatzberg, A. F., Keller, J., Glover, G. H., Kenna, H., . . . & Greicius, M. D. (2007). Dissociable intrinsic connectivity networks for salience processing and executive control. *The Journal of Neuroscience, 27*, 2349–2356

Seger, C. A. (1994). Implicit learning. *Psychological Bulletin, 115*, 163–96.

Seger, C. A., Prabhakaran, V., Poldrack, R. A., & Gabrieli, J. D. E. (2000). Neural activity differs between explicit and implicit learning of artificial grammar strings: An fMRI study. *Psychobiology, 28*, 283–92.

Shi, R., Cutler, A., Werker, J., & Cruickshank, M. (2006). Frequency and form as determinants of functor sensitivity in English-acquiring infants. *The Journal of the Acoustical Society of America, 119*, EL61–7.

Shukla, M., White, K. S., & Aslin, R. N. (2011). Prosody guides the rapid mapping of auditory word forms onto visual objects in 6-mo-old infants. *Proceedings of the National Academy of Sciences, 108*(15), 6038–43.

Siegelman, N., & Frost, R. (2015). Statistical learning as an individual ability: Theoretical perspectives and empirical evidence. *Journal of Memory and Language, 81*, 105–20.

Skeide, M. A., Brauer, J., & Friederici, A. D. (2016). Brain functional and structural predictors of language performance. *Cerebral Cortex, 26*, 2127–39.

Skosnik, P. D., Mirza, F., Gitelman, D. R., Parrish, T. B., Mesulam, M.-M., & Reber, P. J. (2002). Neural correlates of artificial grammar learning. *NeuroImage, 17*, 1306–14.

Squire, L. R., & Zola, S. M. (1996). Structure and function of declarative and nondeclarative memory systems. *Proceedings of the National Academy of Sciences of the United States of America, 93*, 13515–22.

Stabler, E. P. (2011). *Top-down recognizers for MCFGs and MGs*. Paper presented at the Proceedings of the 2nd workshop on cognitive modeling and computational linguistics. Available at: http://linguistics.ucla.edu/people/stabler/Stabler11-CMCL.pdf

Stobbe, N., Westphal-Fitch, G., Aust, U., & Fitch, W. T. (2012). Visual artificial grammar learning: comparative research on humans, kea (Nestor notabilis) and pigeons (Columba livia). *Philosophical Transactions of the Royal Society of London. Series B, Biological Sciences, 367*, 1995–2006.

Strange, B. A., Henson, R. N., Friston, K. J., & Dolan, R. J. (2001). Anterior prefrontal cortex mediates rule learning in humans. *Cerebral Cortex, 11*, 1040–6.

Sturm, J. (2011). Domain-specificity in the Acquisition of Non-adjacent Dependencies. Doctoral thesis, Northumbri.

Teinonen, T., Fellman, V., Näätänen, R., Alku, P., & Huotilainen, M. (2009). Statistical language learning in neonates revealed by event-related brain potentials. *BMC Neuroscience, 10*, 21–8.

Tessier, A.-M. (2007). *Biases and Stages in Phonological Acquisition*. (PhD Dissertation), UMass Amherst, Amherst, MA.

Tunney, R. J., & Altmann, G. T. M. (1999). The transfer effect in artificial grammar learning: Reappraising the evidence on the transfer of sequential dependencies. *Journal of Experimental Psychology: Learning, Memory, and Cognition, 25*, 1322–33.

Turk-Browne, N. B., Scholl, B. J., Chun, M. M., & Johnson, M. K. (2009). Neural evidence of statistical learning: efficient detection of visual regularities without awareness. *Journal of Cognitive Neuroscience, 21*, 1934–45.

Uddén, J. (2012). Language as structured sequences: a causal role for Broca's region in sequence processing (PhD thesis), Karolinska Institute, Stockholm. Available at: http://hdl.handle.net/10616/40842

Uddén, J., & Bahlmann, J. (2012). A rostro-caudal gradient of structured sequence processing in the left inferior frontal gyrus. *Philosophical Transactions of the Royal Society of London. Series B, Biological Sciences, 367*, 2023–2032.

Uddén, J., Folia, V., & Petersson, K. M. (2010). Neuropharmacology of implicit learning. *Current Neuropharmacology, 8*, 367–81.

Uddén, J., Ingvar, M., Hagoort, P., & Petersson, K. M. (2012). Implicit acquisition of grammars with crossed and nested non-adjacent dependencies: investigating the push-down stack model. *Cognitive Science, 36*, 1078–1101.

Wagner, J. B., Fox, S. E., Tager-Flusberg, H., & Nelson, C. A. (2011). Neural processing of repetition and non-repetition grammars in 7- and 9-month-old infants. *Frontiers in Psychology, 2*, 168.

Weber, K., Christiansen, M. H., Petersson, K. M., Indefrey, P., & Hagoort, P. (2016). fMRI syntactic and lexical repetition effects reveal the initial stages of learning a new language. *The Journal of Neuroscience: The Official Journal of the Society for Neuroscience, 36*, 6872–80.

Wells, J. B., Christiansen, M. H., Race, D. S., Acheson, D. J., & MacDonald, M. C. (2009). Experience and sentence processing: Statistical learning and relative clause comprehension. *Cognitive Psychology, 58*, 250–71.

Wierzchon, M., Asanowicz, D., Paulewicz, B., & Cleeremans, A. (2012). Subjective measures of consciousness in artificial grammar learning task. *Consciousness and Cognition, 21*, 1141–53.

Wilson, B., Kikuchi, Y., Sun, L., Hunter, D., Dick, F., Smith, K., . . . & Petkov, C. I. (2015). Auditory sequence processing reveals evolutionarily conserved regions of frontal cortex in macaques and humans. *Nature Communications, 6*, 8901.

Winkler, M., Männel, C., Friederici, A. D., & Mueller, J. L. (2015). Little grammar experts: 5-month-old infants' mismatch responses reveal the ability to process a triple center-embedding. In: Error Signals from the Brain: 7th Mismatch Negativity Conference (p. 58). Leipzig: University of Leipzig. http://event.uni-leipzig.de/mmn2015/frontend/mmn2015_abstract_book_a4_double.pdf

Winkler, M., Mueller, J. L., Friederici, A. D., & Männel, C. (2016). Ontogenetic perspective on grammar learning: Infant's ability to process nested dependencies. In: MPI CBS, Research Report 2014–2016 (p. 81). Leipzig: MPI CBS. http://www.cbs.mpg.de/174887/01-MPI-CBS-2014-2016.pdf

Yang, J., & Li, P. (2012). Brain networks of explicit and implicit learning. *PloS One, 7*, e42993.

Zajonc, R. B. (1968). Attitudinal effects of mere exposure. *Journal of Personality and Social Psychology, 9*, 1–27.

CHAPTER 34

DEVELOPMENTAL DYSLEXIA

MARIANNA E. HAYIOU-THOMAS, JULIA M. CARROLL, AND MARGARET J. SNOWLING

34.1 INTRODUCTION

IN spite of the complexities of written language systems, the majority of children learn to read successfully. However, a substantial minority have difficulty in acquiring the skills that allow print to be decoded and this, in turn, can affect the ability to read for meaning. Such children are sometimes described as dyslexic. According to the *Diagnostic and Statistical Manual for Mental Disorders* (DSM-5), "dyslexia" is a specific learning disorder, not better explained by developmental, neurological, sensory (vision or hearing), or motor disorders. Specifically, it interferes with the development of decoding, fluent reading, and spelling (American Psychiatric Association, 2013) but other skills may be in the normal range.

Most existing research focuses on dyslexia in childhood. However, dyslexia is a lifelong issue. Maughan et al. (2009) found a correlation of 0.91 between reading skill measured in adolescence and in middle age, indicating a very high degree of stability. Eighty percent of their poor reader sample left school with no qualifications, compared to 36% of the typical readers. Again, around 80% of the poor readers said they still had difficulties writing letters and 73% had difficulties filling in forms in their mid-forties. On the other hand, not all studies of dyslexia in adulthood paint such a bleak picture. Many individuals with dyslexia go on to further and higher education, and there is evidence that these individuals may overcome earlier difficulties in reading accuracy, though there may be remaining difficulties in timed tasks and spelling (Hatcher, Snowling, & Griffiths, 2002; Tops et al., 2012).

This chapter presents our current scientific understanding of dyslexia. We begin by considering the definition of dyslexia in behavioral terms and, with the typical development of literacy as a framework, discuss how its manifestation differs according to the language in which the child is learning to read. We proceed to consider causal explanations of dyslexia and evidence concerning sensory (auditory and visual), cognitive, biological, and environmental factors in its etiology. We close by discussing how theoretical advances in the field of dyslexia provide the rationale for effective interventions.

34.2 What is dyslexia?

Dyslexia (or congenital word blindness as it was then called) was first described in 1896 by a general practitioner, Pringle-Morgan (Pringle-Morgan, 1896) and during the early part of the twentieth century it was the domain of eye doctors. The scientific study of dyslexia first came to prominence in the 1960s (Rutter & Maughan, 2005, for a review), when one of the main issues was whether dyslexia was different from "plain poor reading." While there was never doubt that intelligent individuals with severe reading and spelling problems exist, the use of the term dyslexia to describe these "unexpected" problems was, and remains, debated (Elliott & Grigorenko, 2014; Rutter & Yule, 1975). As we shall see, dyslexia is not a clear-cut category—rather it is a dimensional disorder, ranging from mild to severe, and there is no clear cut-off from normal reading; similarly, there are no cognitive, genetic, or neural factors that definitively set those with dyslexia apart from "poor readers" (e.g., Stanovich, 1988), and there is nothing special about the treatments that are effective in treating dyslexia, though clearly these need to be modified according to the age and stage of the student (Hatcher, 2000; Suggate, 2010).

Notwithstanding the fact that reading skills fall on a continuum, much has been learned about the risk factors associated with dyslexia—those at the lower end of the normal distribution—and how these risks can accumulate to a threshold which demands diagnosis because it interferes with academic achievement and can lead to a downward spiral of poor education, poor career prospects, and lowered mental capital.

It is now recognized that dyslexia can occur across different levels of IQ (Shaywitz, Fletcher, Holahan, & Shaywitz, 1992; Stanovich, 1986). However, important for current conceptions is the fact that dyslexia frequently co-occurs with other disorders including Learning Disability. Research suggests that up to 50% of children with dyslexia have oral language difficulties (developmental language disorder[1]; McArthur et al., 2000); they also show an increased risk of internalizing and externalizing difficulties (Carroll, Maughan, Goodman, & Meltzer, 2005), most commonly attention deficit/hyperactivity disorder (ADHD; McGee, Prior, Williams, Smart, & Sanson, 2002; Gooch et al., 2014), and comorbid motor impairments are also observed (Rochelle & Talcott, 2006).

In short, the classic view of dyslexia as a specific or selective disorder has been overstated—comorbidity is the norm, rather than the exception (e.g., Landerl & Moll, 2010). Nonetheless, it is crucial to understand which features of dyslexia are *specific to the condition* and which are shared with these other disorders.

34.3 Manifestations of dyslexia

Although the manifestations of dyslexia vary considerably, the defining features are difficulties in reading and writing, particularly at the word level (that is, decoding or

---

[1] "Developmental language disorder" is the term now used to describe children's spoken language difficulties and is intended to replace the wide range of terms previously used in the research literature and related professions (Bishop et al., 2017; see also Chapter 35 in the present volume).

recognizing individual words or spelling). Most commonly, individuals with dyslexia show difficulties in phonological processing, that is in the domain of language which requires the use of speech-based codes (Vellutino, Fletcher, Snowling, & Scanlon, 2004) and it is well established that such difficulties persist into adulthood (Bekebrede et al., 2010; Gottardo, Siegel, & Stanovich, 1997).

In order to understand why a deficit in speech processing should cause a problem for the acquisition of written language, it is important to consider what is known about the typical development of reading and spelling (Seidenberg, 2007). According to a classic theory by Byrne (1998), learning to read in an alphabetic system depends on two critical skills: knowledge of letter sounds and of phoneme awareness. At the basic level, with these skills in place, a child can establish mappings between the letters or letter strings of printed words and the speech sounds (phonemes) of spoken words. The mappings between orthography and phonology allow novel words to be decoded and provide a foundation for the acquisition of later and more automatic reading skills.

Research in the past decade has revealed that these two basic abilities, phoneme awareness and letter knowledge, underpin learning to read not only in English but also across alphabetic orthographies. Indeed, along with a third factor, "rapid automatized naming" (RAN, the speed with which a series of digits or letters can be named), they predict individual differences in the development of reading and spelling abilities (Caravolas et al. 2012; Ziegler et al., 2010). Moreover, this so-called *triple foundation* for reading may be universal (McBride-Chang, 2016; Nag & Snowling, 2011); thus, in alphasyllabaries such as the Southern Indian language, Kannada, and in Chinese, knowledge of the symbol system, awareness of sound components of words, and RAN also predict variations in reading skills, though in these languages which arguably are more difficult to learn, other skills also assume importance.

It follows that the proximal "cause" of dyslexia is likely to be poor phonological skills, as measured by phonological awareness—this well-established idea is usually referred to as the phonological deficit hypothesis. However, as discussed next, there continues to be debate about the distal causes of dyslexia.

Perhaps reflecting the insecure phonological foundation, the most common pattern of reading deficit in dyslexia is poor non-word reading in the face of better developed word reading skills (Harm, McCandliss, & Seidenberg, 2003; Rack, Snowling, & Olson, 1992). However, this profile of phonological reading impairment is not found in all poor readers. It is possible to find children who are worse at reading so-called "exception" or irregular words than non-words and who resemble adults with surface dyslexia (Castles & Coltheart, 1993). However, several authors have reported difficulty in isolating this surface subtype and recent research indicates that the phonological subtype shows much greater longitudinal stability than the surface subtype (Peterson, Pennington, Olson, & Wadsworth, 2014). An alternative view is that reading behavior varies on a continuum, with relative strengths and weaknesses in regular vs. irregular word reading, rather than falling into sharply delimited categories of "phonological" vs. "surface" deficits. To explain this variation, Snowling and colleagues have suggested that a child's reading profile is predicted by the severity of his or her phonological deficit, in interaction with the child's other cognitive skills (Snowling, 2000).

Finally, spelling poses a significant challenge to children with dyslexia and spelling difficulties tend to be serious and pervasive (Bruck, 1990; Snowling, Goulandris, & Defty, 1996). Treiman and her colleagues (e.g., Treiman & Kessler, 2014) have demonstrated that, from a very early stage, children's writing reveals their efforts to encode phonological information. In similar vein, Caravolas, Hulme, and Snowling (2001) proposed that young spellers rely on a "scaffold" of phonological information about words in order to learn the orthographic rules required for spelling. The enduring problems with spelling can, at least in part, be explained in this light (Bruck & Treiman, 1990; Moats, 1983).

34.4 Dyslexia in alphabetic orthographies

Thus far, we have focused on the manifestations of dyslexia in English. However, writing systems vary in transparency and "granularity" (Ziegler & Goswami, 2005); since English has a high degree of inconsistency in the mappings between spellings (which can involve single or multiple letter strings) and sounds, there are in fact good reasons to consider English an "outlier" orthography (Share, 2008). Indeed, children learning English take longer to develop accurate and fluent reading skills than those learning to read in other European orthographies (Caravolas et al., 2013). An important question therefore is whether dyslexia has the same behavioral signature across orthographies.

In transparent orthographies such as German or Finnish, children with dyslexia typically show accurate but slow word reading. Their reading accuracy in languages such as French (Sprenger-Charolles, Siegel, Béchennec, & Serniclaes, 2003), German (Landerl, Wimmer, & Frith, 1997), Dutch (de Jong & van der Leij, 2003), and Greek (Georgiou, Parrila, & Papadopoulos, 2008) is typically much higher than that shown in English children with dyslexia.

Turning to phonological awareness, there is evidence for phoneme awareness difficulties in dyslexia across European languages (e.g., Czech: Caravolas et al., 2005; German: Landerl et al., 1997; Dutch: de Jong & van der Leij, 2003). However, in order to directly compare the predictors of reading in different languages, cross-linguistic studies are required. In recent years there have been some high-quality studies of this type published. Moll et al. (2014) found that phoneme awareness and RAN were independent predictors of reading in English, French, German, Hungarian, and Finnish. Ziegler et al. (2010) had similar findings with their comparison of Finnish, Hungarian, Dutch, Portuguese, and French, though they also suggested that phoneme awareness may play a less important role in reading when the correspondences between letters and phonemes are more straightforward and consistent.

A recent study compares the predictors of dyslexia across European orthographies. Landerl et al. (2013) examined dyslexia in languages with varying orthographic consistency (again English, French, Dutch, German, Hungarian, and Finnish). A standardized procedure was used to select dyslexic participants across countries. Phoneme awareness and rapid naming predicted dyslexia more strongly in languages with high orthographic complexity (English and French), and dyslexics in these countries were more highly impaired in reading compared to their typical peers. In contrast, Caravolas et al. (2012) examined phoneme awareness, letter knowledge, and RAN as predictors of reading (and dyslexia) from age five to seven years in English, Spanish, Czech, and Slovak using a multigroup model and found evidence for the importance of this "triple foundation" across languages with no significant difference in the strength of the predictors.

34.4.1 Dyslexia in Chinese

The Chinese orthography provides an interesting contrast to alphabetic orthographies we have discussed up to this point, as it differs in multiple key ways (McBride-Chang, 2015). Chinese is often considered to be a logographic script in which each character represents a morpheme. Because morphemes contain only one syllable, and words that contain two morphemes are written as two characters, there is a sense in which a character also represents a syllable, though the same phonological syllable will be written in different ways when it has a different meaning. Most Chinese characters comprise a radical and a phonetic component. There are approximately 200 different radicals, which may provide a clue to word meaning, and 1,000 different phonetics, providing a clue to word sound. Chinese characters can contain up to 12 different strokes and are therefore visually complex. The Chinese orthography is used in different Chinese languages (e.g., Mandarin and Cantonese); while readers in both languages decode the same written text when reading, the oral pronunciation may be very different. In the following discussion, we do not distinguish between the different oral languages, as the focus is on the written language.

Given the properties of the orthography, it might be predicted that phonological processing is relatively unimportant in Chinese, while visual processing and morphological awareness is more important. There is some evidence that this is the case. Shu, McBride-Chang, and Wu (2006) assessed dyslexic and typical readers on a large battery of tests that included phonological awareness, morphological awareness, and rapid naming measures. Although phonological awareness was found to account for unique variance in character reading, character writing, and reading comprehension, morphological awareness accounted for the largest amounts of unique variance in these skills. Moreover, whereas differences in morphological awareness and rapid naming performance discriminated between the groups, differences in phonological awareness did not reach statistical significance. Similarly, following a study in which Chinese children were taught either the meanings or the pronunciations of new words, Zhou, Duff, and Hulme (2015) concluded that learning to read words in Chinese entails greater reliance on mappings from orthography to semantics than learning to read words in alphabetic orthographies.

Interestingly, in a longitudinal study of bilingual children learning to read in Chinese and English, McBride-Chang et al. (2013) found that many poor readers of Chinese did not show poor reading in English, suggesting that the demands of the two languages may be different. Poor readers in Chinese only showed weaknesses in morphological awareness, those impaired in English only showed a weakness in RAN, and children who had difficulties learning English as well as Chinese had poor phonological awareness, RAN, and morphological awareness.

In summary, studies to date suggest that reading difficulties in Chinese are associated with a range of underlying difficulties. Deficits in visuo-spatial memory and morphological awareness may be the most important factors associated with dyslexia in Chinese, but there is also evidence for the role of rapid naming and phonological awareness, as in alphabetic languages (Chung & Ho, 2010).

34.5 Cognitive causes of dyslexia

The search for a causal explanation for dyslexia at the cognitive level has highlighted several possible mechanisms. For a long time, the field was focused on identifying a single causal mechanism; more recently, as discussed at the beginning of this chapter, the perspective has shifted to a multiple-deficit account. The challenge, therefore, is to identify the set of core deficits that can best account for the behavioral manifestation of dyslexia.

34.5.1 The phonological deficit account

As just discussed, the predominant theoretical account of dyslexia has viewed its primary cognitive cause as a phonological processing impairment (Ramus et al., 2003; Vellutino, Fletcher, Snowling, & Scanlon, 2004). According to one version of this hypothesis, children with dyslexia have poorly specified phonological representations (Snowling, 2000). That is, the part of their language system that maps between word meanings to speech sounds is impaired and it is assumed that for many lexical items that have a semantic representation, the phonological specification is global and not segmental in form (Metsala, 1997).

Deficits in phonological representation may explain why people with dyslexia typically have difficulties with a wide range of cognitive tasks that engage phonological processes. The most consistently reported difficulties are limitations of verbal short-term memory (Brady, Shankweiler, & Mann, 1983) and problems with phoneme awareness (Swan & Goswami, 1997). There is also evidence that individuals with dyslexia show a range of additional weaknesses in skills which tap the manipulation or use of phonological codes, such as non-word repetition (Snowling, Goulandris, Bowlby, & Howell, 1986) visual-verbal paired associate learning (Litt & Nation, 2014), phonological learning (Messbauer & de Jong, 2003), and in integrating letter and sound information (van Atteveldt, Formisano, Goebel, & Blomert, 2004).

However, the hypothesis that such deficits can be traced to the level of phonological representation has not stood the test of time and rather problems of phonological retrieval (Ramus & Szenkovits, 2008) or output phonology (Snowling & Hulme, 1994) may be key. In an important recent study, Ramus, Marshall, Rosen, and van der Lely (2013) compared children with dyslexia with children with developmental language disorder on a range of phonological tasks. The children with dyslexia did not show impairments in phonological representations—rather their problems appeared to lie in the processing demands inherent in standard phonological tasks, that is, short-term memory and meta-linguistic skills. Similarly, Mundy and Carroll (2012) found no deficits for dyslexic students in suprasegmental phonology using a prosodic priming task, despite clear deficits in a prosodic awareness task in the same group.

34.5.2 Double deficit theory

An important variant of the phonological deficit hypothesis is the "double deficit theory" proposed by Wolf and Bowers (1999). According to this hypothesis, among children with reading disabilities, there are those with single deficits in either phonological awareness or naming speed, and a further subgroup who have the most severe problems and show double deficits. Critics of this theory might argue that dissociations are to be expected when two skills—here phoneme awareness and RAN—are not perfectly correlated and hence the proposal of subtypes is not justified. Nonetheless, an important issue for this theory is how the relationship between rapid naming and reading is to be explained. Wolf and Bowers (1999) suggest that rapid naming speed is an index of the integrity of an orthography-phonology timing mechanism that is independent from the phonological system, and according to these authors, this may be indicative of a specific deficit in the ability to create orthographic representations; these may be particularly important for spelling in regular orthographies (Wimmer et al., 2000). Evidence for the theory comes from studies that show a stronger relationship between rapid naming skills and exception word reading than between phoneme awareness and exception word reading (Manis, Doi, & Bhadha, 2000). An alternative view is that RAN taps the efficiency of activation of phonological representation (Wagner & Torgesen, 1987). Vaessen, Gerretsen, and Blomert (2009) argue that naming speed measures a combination of an individual's phonological processing with fast cross-modal matching of auditory and visual information. Relatedly, Lervåg and Hulme (2009) proposed that RAN is specifically associated with growth of reading fluency because both skills tap the same neural circuitry required for automatic naming.

In line with these hypotheses, there is some preliminary evidence that individuals with dyslexia have difficulties in mapping sounds onto the appropriate letter, as a consequence of a basic phonological impairment. Indeed, there is some evidence of reduced integration of sounds and letters from fMRI data: while typical adult readers show a suppression of activation in the STG (superior temporal gyrus) when they are presented with incongruent letter-sound pairs (as compared to congruent pairs), adults with dyslexia do not show this suppressed activation (Blau et al., 2009). However, studies of letter-sound integration in young children with dyslexia have produced mixed results (Bakos et al., 2017; Nash et al., 2017) and further research is needed.

The strongest test of the causal link between RAN and reading difficulties would be a demonstration that training in RAN can improve reading skills. However, this link has not been definitively shown. Although broad-based training in reading fluency can be effective (Wolf et al., 2009), there is little evidence that RAN skills can be improved by training and that any improvements would be transferred to reading (Kirby, Georgiou, Martinussen, & Parrila, 2010; also see Wolff, 2014).

34.5.3 Speech perception

If it is accepted that a phonological deficit is indeed a core proximal deficit in dyslexia, there is still the important question of the origin of the phonological problem itself. A substantial body of work has examined the possibility that there are deficits in speech perception in individuals with dyslexia, that give rise to the phonological deficit. Further, poor speech perception may itself be secondary to more general auditory processing difficulties.

Much work in this area has focused on whether children and adults with dyslexia have atypical categorical perception; that is, whether the boundaries between phonemes are less distinct than in individuals without dyslexia. Categorical perception is typically measured using a sequence of stimuli along an acoustic continuum that varies incrementally on a single phonetic feature (e.g., /ba/-/da/, or /goat/-/coat/, which differ only in the voice onset time of the initial consonant). In an identification task, the participant has to label each stimulus as either /coat/ or /goat/; a potential problem with this paradigm is that individuals with dyslexia may have difficulties with verbal labeling per se (Marshall et al., 2001), which could compromise performance on this task. Discrimination tasks, on the other hand, do not require labeling, but rather require people to judge whether the two stimuli in a pair are the same or different.

Several studies using these paradigms have shown subtle deficits in categorical perception in children and adults with dyslexia (e.g., Adlard & Hazan, 1998; Bogliotti et al., 2008; Reed, 1989; Rosen & Manganari, 2001), but other studies have failed to show this effect (e.g., Adlard & Hazan, 1998; Blomert & Mitterer, 2004; Joanisse, Manis, Keating, & Seidenberg, 2000; Robertson, Joanisse, Desroches, & Ng, 2009). A recent meta-analysis based on 36 studies which between them assessed 756 individuals with dyslexia, in relation to chronological-age (and for a minority of studies, reading-age) controls, found a significant and moderate mean effect size for identification (Cohen's d = 0.66), and a large effect for discrimination tasks (d = 0.86) (Noordenbos & Serniclaes, 2015). Arguably, the larger effect for discrimination reflects the fact that good performance on this task requires the listener not only to discriminate between stimuli that lie across a phoneme boundary, but to ignore equivalent acoustic differences that lie within phoneme boundaries. This is consistent with the allophonic theory, which suggests that the categorical perception deficit in dyslexia reflects both poor cross-boundary discrimination, and enhanced within-category sensitivity (Serniclaes et al., 2004).

There is a large amount of variability in the literature however, which is worth considering. One possible factor is that most studies of speech perception are carried out under optimal listening conditions, in which the listener can take advantage of the redundant cues in the speech signal to compensate for subtle deficits in perceiving any single cue. If this is correct, a subtle speech deficit should become apparent in more challenging (and ecologically valid) situations, such as listening in noise. In line with this prediction, work by Ziegler and colleagues has demonstrated poor speech perception in noise in children with dyslexia, even when compared to younger reading-age matched controls (Ziegler et al., 2009); however, this effect was not replicated in a similar study by Messaoud-Galusi et al., (2011). The discrepant findings may be partly attributable to methodological differences, for example, in the type of noise masker used, or the phonetic feature targeted by the stimuli. Messaoud-Galusi et al., used stimuli on the "bea-pea" continuum, which vary in voice onset time (VOT); Ziegler et al. reported that they found deficits in stimulus sets which varied in place-of-articulation, but not in VOT. Another factor that should be taken into account is variability in the types of tasks used, and the extent to which different tasks which purport to measure the same underlying construct really do—that is, their construct validity. A small number of recent studies have attempted to examine this issue directly by using different types of tasks (e.g., adaptive vs. fixed-interval procedures) to measure speech perception in children and adults with dyslexia (Hazan et al., 2009; Messaoud-Galusi et al., 2011; Robertson et al., 2009). The results suggested significant, if small, group differences in some tasks but not others. Most interestingly, at the individual level, there was no evidence that some individuals were consistently worse across tasks. Rather, people tended to do badly on one or two tasks, and within the normal range on others; conversely, no single task was consistently more problematic than the others (Hazan et al., 2009; Messaoud-Galusi et al., 2011).

Finally, and perhaps most importantly, is the need to consider variability across people. It is well established that there are many features which frequently co-occur with dyslexia, such as poor attention or executive skills. Many psychophysical tasks—including those used to measure speech perception—are repetitive and fatiguing, and poor performance may well be due to inattention rather than genuine perceptual deficits, particularly in children (Messaoud-Galusi et al., 2011; Moore, Ferguson, Halliday, & Riley, 2008; Sutcliffe, Bishop, Houghton, & Taylor, 2006). On the other hand, Breier et al. (2001) found equivalent deficits in categorical perception in children who had both dyslexia and ADHD, and children with dyslexia alone, suggesting that the speech perception deficits were unlikely to be fully explained by inattention. It may also be the case that speech perception deficits are particularly evident in children with broader language difficulties rather than those with dyslexia per se (Joanisse et al., 2000; Robertson et al., 2009).

In summary, it has become increasingly clear over the last decade that speech perception deficits are apparent in some individuals with dyslexia, and not others. Studies which report individual data illustrate this point, with estimates for the proportion of speech perception deficits ranging from 16% to 70% of their samples (Adlard & Hazan, 1998; Manis et al., 1997; McArthur, Ellis, Atkinson, & Coltheart, 2008; Hazan et al., 2009; Messaoud-Galusi et al., 2011). This issue is common across studies of deficits in dyslexia and is discussed in more detail in the multiple risks framework later in this chapter.

34.5.4 Auditory processing impairments

Auditory theories of dyslexia argue that phonological and speech perception deficits are the downstream consequence of a deficit in low-level auditory perception. An early and highly influential auditory account was the rapid auditory processing (RAP) deficit hypothesis, first developed by Tallal and colleagues in the 1970s. The RAP account posits that difficulties in processing rapidly changing auditory information should impact disproportionately on speech perception, because much of the speech signal is composed of exactly this type of information: for example, the rapid formant transitions that are the acoustic signature of consonants. The focus of the RAP hypothesis is on a fine-grained level of temporal resolution, in the tens of milliseconds time-frame, and work in this area has mainly focused on changes in the frequency domain, rather than amplitude. The classic task is known as the Auditory Repetition Task (ART; Tallal & Piercy, 1973), in which children listen to two complex tones that differ in pitch and are trained to associate the different tones with different responses; they then hear a sequence of two or more tones and have to copy the order of the tones in the order of their responses.

In the original study, Tallal (1980) reported poor ART performance in 8 out of 20 children with reading impairment, relative to chronological-age-matched controls. Subsequent results regarding an ART deficit in dyslexia have been mixed. On the one hand, there have been several reported failures to replicate the basic behavioral finding: Nittrouer (1999) found that good and poor readers did not differ in performance on an ART-like task, nor did the poor readers show impairments in the use of brief transition to cue specific contrasts. Marshall, Snowling, and Bailey (2001) observed poor ART performance in only a quarter of the children with dyslexia in their study, and importantly, the children who were impaired on the ART task also took longer to reach criterion in a pre-test involving tone identification and response mapping. Furthermore, individual differences in performance on ART-like tasks may be related to language skills, with low scores reported only for poor readers with concomitant weak language skills (Heath, Hogben, & Clark, 1999).

Subsequent investigations using different methodologies continue to report evidence of atypical RAP in at least subgroups of individuals with dyslexia. For example, fMRI studies have reported hypoactivation of left frontal cortical areas in response to rapid non-speech frequency transitions in children and adults with dyslexia (Gaab et al., 2007; Temple et al., 2000). Most relevant for testing a causal role for the RAP, similar frontal hypoactivation was recently reported in pre-reading children at family risk of dyslexia, and individual differences in activation were associated with performance on phonological tasks (Raschle, Stering, Meissner, & Gaab, 2014): since it cannot be the consequence of atypical reading experience in this group, this pattern of performance is consistent with a causal role for RAP in dyslexia.

The rapid auditory processing theory focuses on rapid modulations in the frequency domain. However, low-level auditory impairments of different kinds including frequency discrimination, frequency modulation, intensity discrimination, and amplitude modulation have also been proposed as causal risk factors for poor reading (see Goswami, 2015; Hämäläinen, Salminen, & Leppänen, 2013; Schulte-Körne & Bruder, 2010, for reviews). A particular focus has been the slow modulations in the speech envelope which are relevant for the perception of syllables as described in the influential temporal sampling framework for developmental dyslexia (Goswami, 2011). This theory takes as its starting point current work in auditory cognitive neuroscience which describes speech perception in terms of the integration of neural oscillations across populations of neurons in auditory cortex, which are tuned to different frequency bands. Slower amplitude modulations (AM) reflect larger phonological units: the slowest modulations, below 2.5 Hz (delta band) convey prosodic information at the level of words and phrases; modulations between 2.5 to 12 Hz (theta band) are at the syllabic level, and faster modulations between 12 to 40 Hz (gamma band) capture phonemic information.

According to the temporal sampling theory, the core sensory deficit in dyslexia is inaccurate phase-locking by the neural oscillators to incoming sensory information in the slow delta and theta bands. This deficit should be reflected in poor sensitivity to syllabic "rise-time" ("the time required to reach a syllabic peak"; Goswami, 2011) and more generally in the processing of syllabic and prosodic information. The temporal sampling framework further argues that poor neural entrainment at higher levels of the "oscillatory hierarchy" will also have downstream effects on smaller phonological units (i.e., phonemes). Early work motivated by this theoretical perspective has reported poorer performance by children with dyslexia in tasks tapping slow rise-time sensitivity, using both speech and non-speech stimuli (e.g., musical rhythm judgment) and performance on these tasks was also associated with phonological awareness and reading measures (Goswami et al., 2013; Thompson & Goswami, 2008).

In summary, investigation of auditory deficits in dyslexia has extended to a very broad range of tasks examining the frequency, amplitude, and temporal characteristics of non-speech stimuli, using both behavioral and electrophysiological methods. Following their review, Hämäläinen, Salminen, and Leppänen (2013) concluded that the most consistent differences between dyslexic and control groups were related to dynamic sound features: frequency modulation (slow rates), amplitude modulation (fast rates), rise time, and duration, with at least moderate mean effect sizes across studies (Cohen's d 0.5–0.9). In addition, discrimination of small frequency differences (10% or smaller) also appeared to be compromised. By contrast, sensitivity to intensity and gap perception was generally not found to characterize the dyslexic groups. More generally, the reliability of auditory processing tasks has been questioned (Protopapas, 2014).

34.5.5 Visual processing deficits

Vision is clearly important for reading, and various theories have implicated deficits in visual processing in dyslexia. An influential causal hypothesis of dyslexia proposed by Lovegrove, Martin, and Slaghuis (1986) suggested a basic impairment in processing transient visual stimuli. A large body of research followed on the "magnocellular theory" of dyslexia, centered on the idea of a deficit in the subcortical M-pathway and/or cortical dorsal stream of the visual system (see Boden & Giaschi, 2007 for a review).

Direct evidence of magnocellular impairments in dyslexia has been sought in tasks such as contrast sensitivity (e.g., Edwards et al., 2004), oculomotor control, and smooth pursuit (e.g., Eden, Stein, Wood, & Wood, 1994; Stein & Walsh, 1997), and sensitivity to coherent motion (e.g., Witton et al, 1998). Poor performance in this type of task has been reported in children and adults with dyslexia, as well as in pre-reading children at family risk of dyslexia (Kevan & Pammer, 2008). However, findings are mixed, and some studies have found no evidence of abnormal sensitivity on tasks specifically tapping magnocellular function (e.g., Amitay, Ben-Yehudah, Banai, & Ahissar, 2002; Williams et al. 2003). The inconsistent findings in the literature may partly reflect the broad range of tasks used, some of which tap low-level sensory processing at the level of subcortical M-cells (e.g., contrast sensitivity), while others, such as coherent motion, are subserved by high-level cortical areas (MT/V5), which receive input from both the magnocellular and parvocellular paths. Skottun (2015) has argued that it is critical to make this distinction clear, and that the weight of the evidence to date supports a high-level deficit in the dorsal pathway, but not low-level magnocellular-specific deficits. As is the case for the findings on auditory processing, it needs to be borne in mind that the primary methodology used in this field is attention demanding and that performance on psychophysical tasks may reflect individual differences in executive control. The mixed findings may also be a consequence of the relatively small group differences, reflecting either genuinely small effects, heterogeneity within the dyslexic population, or a large overlap in performance between groups with and without dyslexia. In fact, the incidence of magnocellular deficits may be higher among normal readers than among readers with dyslexia (e.g., Skoyles & Skottun, 2004), a finding that cannot be accommodated by a causal theory of dyslexia.

In a related body of research, a number of groups have suggested that visual attention problems, possibly resulting from dysfunction of the posterior parietal cortex, may be a root cause of reading impairments, including difficulties with covert shifts of attention (Buchholtz & Davies, 2005), and visual-spatial orienting (Facoetti, Turatto, & Mascetti, 2001). In one such study, Roach and Hogben (2004) asked adults with dyslexia and controls to detect the orientation of a line that could appear anywhere in a circular array of points either with or without a cue. Whereas normal readers derived significant benefit from the attentional cue, the participants with dyslexia did not.

Another claim is that individuals with dyslexia respond less well to stimuli presented to their left than their right visual field (Facoetti & Molteni, 2001; Sireteanu et al., 2005), which again may reflect a right parietal impairment. In an interesting development of the theory, Bosse, Tainturier, and Valdois (2007) suggest that the visual attention deficit reduces the "attentional window" through which information is extracted from the orthographic sequence. However, as in studies of the magnocellular deficit, experimental findings have been mixed. Bosse et al. (2007) propose that phonological processing and visual attention skills are dissociable causes of dyslexia that may co-occur, although the attentional impairment may be less prevalent than the phonological. The best test of a causal theory is whether intervention focused on the putative deficit improves reading behavior: a recent intervention study in Italian targeting visual attention by training children with dyslexia on action-video games yielded positive results (Franceschini et al., 2013). Although it provides an interesting new direction, this initial study was small in scale, and it will be necessary not only to replicate the finding, but to isolate which aspects of visuomotor attention and control contributed to any improvements in reading. Although visual deficits are unlikely to be a universal cause of dyslexia, they may be part of the etiology of specific subtypes, or may represent co-occurring problems that could aggravate the condition.

34.5.6 Procedural learning deficits in dyslexia

There are also theories of dyslexia that, rather than focusing on underlying deficits, suggest weaknesses in how dyslexic children learn. For example, Lum, Ullman, and Conti-Ramsden (2013) argue that children with dyslexia show difficulties in procedural learning. Procedural learning concerns the learning of motor skills and habits—for example learning how to ride a bike or tie your shoelaces. Procedural learning is implicit and often involves learning complex sequences or probabilistic patterns. Ullman (2004) argues that this type of learning is also crucial for language learning, particularly with respect to syntactic and phonological structures. In their meta-analysis, Lum et al. (2013) find that individuals with dyslexia have significant impairments in serial reaction time tasks; a type of task that measures implicit learning of a motor sequence. However, the same caveats that apply to the studies of sensory impairments also apply here. These difficulties may well occur in some, but not all, dyslexic children and may be epiphenomenal. Nonetheless, there is supportive evidence for the role of automaticity in reading fluency (e.g., Lovett, Ransby, & Barron, 1988).

34.5.7 Multiple risk framework

We have seen that there is evidence in support of a range of deficits across domains and levels of explanation (phonological, auditory, visual, motoric). While some theories have proposed an overarching brain-based hypothesis (e.g., Stein, 2017), there is no compelling evidence that a single deficit can fully account for dyslexia. A key part of the argument that the field must consider a multiple-deficit account instead, is that individuals with dyslexia may present with weaknesses in several domains; and that not all individuals present with the same set of weaknesses. Ramus et al. (2003) showed that in a sample of 16 students with dyslexia, 10 showed an auditory deficit, four showed difficulties in motor control and two showed visual magnocellular deficits, while all 16 showed phonological deficits. They argued that the phonological deficit was core, while the other deficits were epiphenomenal, though it is important to remember this is a small sample of well-compensated dyslexics. White et al. (2006) went on to report a similar assessment of 8-12-year-old dyslexic readers, finding that just over half of them showed difficulties in phonological awareness and 14 of the 23 showed some kind of sensorimotor impairment. More recently, Carroll, Solity, and Shapiro (2016) showed in a longitudinal study following 267 children from school entry to Year 3, that around a third of the 42 children who went on to have reading difficulties showed phonological impairments at school entry, but that the sample also showed a wide range of different patterns of impairment on cognitive and sensori-motor tasks. Interestingly, all but two of this sample of future poor readers showed deficits in at least one of the areas tested, and children with more than one deficit were more likely to go on to show later literacy difficulties. Similarly, many Chinese children with dyslexia appear to have multiple cognitive deficits, though the relative importance of these different deficits may differ from those in alphabetic orthographies (Ho, Chan, Tsang, & Lee, 2002; Ho et al., 2004).

Together, such findings fit well with the multiple-deficit theory of dyslexia proposed by Pennington (2006). According to this perspective, developmental disorders occur when deficits in underlying processing occur in combination. For example, dyslexia may be caused by a combination of difficulties in phonological processing and processing speed. Deficits in phonological processing may also be part of the combination of difficulties seen in speech sound disorder (Hayiou-Thomas et al., 2016), while difficulties in processing speed may be associated with ADHD. This theory allows for the idea that somewhat different combinations of difficulty may result in dyslexia, and that those difficulties overlap with those seen in other disorders.

34.6 Etiology of dyslexia

34.6.1 Studies of children at family risk of dyslexia

The interaction of different skills in determining the literacy outcomes of children at risk of reading failure can be seen in studies of children at family risk of dyslexia followed from the preschool years. This approach is important; since children are recruited before they enter formal reading instruction, it is free of clinical bias and it allows the separation of possible causes of dyslexia from the consequences of reading problems. For example, studying children at family risk of dyslexia with and without reading problems, Moll, Loff, and Snowling (2013) found that a deficit in phonological memory was shared between the two groups, suggesting that it was a risk factor for dyslexia, but phoneme awareness was only associated with a dyslexic outcome, suggesting it was likely to be a consequence of poor reading. More generally, family-risk studies can allow the identification of protective factors which mitigate the risk of dyslexia by comparing the outcomes of children at family risk who succumb to dyslexia with those who do not (Snowling & Melby-Lervåg, 2016, for a review).

Together the findings from studies of children at family risk of dyslexia report a heightened prevalence of dyslexia in children at family risk, with estimates ranging from 29 to 66%. Perhaps not unexpectedly, given that the underlying deficits in dyslexia do not differ across alphabetic orthographies (Caravolas et al., 2012), there is no evidence that the prevalence depends upon the language of instruction; rather it depends on the arbitrary criteria used to classify a child as dyslexic on what is a continuous distribution of reading skills. Furthermore, two studies reporting findings for Chinese children at family risk reported similar deficits to those experienced by European children with dyslexia: poor knowledge of Chinese characters, deficits in phonological awareness of tones (paralleling letter knowledge and phoneme awareness in alphabetic languages), and slow rapid naming performance (RAN) (Ho, Leung, & Cheung, 2011; McBride-Chang et al., 2011).

A key finding from studies of children at family risk of dyslexia confirms that dyslexia is not a specific disorder associated with a unitary phonological deficit (Pennington, 2006). Rather, children with dyslexia experience a broad range of preschool speech and language difficulties which have been underestimated in case-control studies of poor readers defined as dyslexic in the school years. Moreover, children at family risk who do not develop reading problems also show delayed language and phonological development. While broader (non-phonological) language deficits are mostly resolved by the time of formal schooling, children with dyslexia have persisting vocabulary deficits as well as impairments of verbal memory. It seems therefore that dyslexia should be considered a deficit on the language continuum. Furthermore, children at family risk who do not fulfill criteria for dyslexia have poorer word-level literacy skills (decoding and spelling) but not poorer reading comprehension than controls, confirming that dyslexia is a dimensional disorder.

Within the broad class of family studies, an approach which has gained ground in recent years is the study of "endophenotypes": these are "markers" associated with the disorder in the population and expressed at a higher rate in unaffected relatives of probands than in the general population. Thus, in relation to dyslexia, an endophenotype is a process or impairment (such as the phonological deficit) associated with familial risk status, the impact of which can be modified by other processes including perhaps higher IQ. This approach can also elucidate the causes of comorbidities: when two or more disorders co-occur, it is probable that they have endophenotypes in common (e.g., dyslexia, speech sound disorder, and language impairment, e.g., Pennington & Bishop, 2009).

Turning to this issue, preschool deficits in phonological memory (non-word repetition) and verbal short-term memory are reported in children at family risk of dyslexia, regardless of outcome. Similarly, in the school years, children at family risk classified as normal readers as well as those with dyslexia show deficits in phonological awareness, albeit less severe. There is a different pattern of results for rapid naming; while this is impaired in children with dyslexia it is unimpaired in children at family risk without reading problems. These findings lead to a causal hypothesis: the genetic liability to dyslexia is expressed in terms of an early impairment of the phonological language system; for children who have additional problems integrating letters and sounds (e.g., Blomert, 2011), dyslexia is a more likely outcome. However, this is not the only possible scenario. Multiple risk theories of dyslexia (see previous discussion) suggest that an isolated risk factor (e.g., a phonological deficit) is less likely to lead a child to reach the diagnostic threshold for dyslexia than if the single phonological deficit coexists with another disorder, is aggravated by a sensory impairment, or is present in adverse environmental circumstances.

34.6.2 Genetic factors

34.6.2.1 Twin studies

It has been known for over a century that dyslexia runs in families, suggesting a genetic contribution to reading difficulties. However, families share both genes and experiences, making it difficult to tease their roles apart. Twin studies are a useful method of disentangling the contribution of genetic and environmental factors: identical (or monozygotic; MZ) twins share 100% of their DNA, while fraternal (dizygotic; DZ) twins share 50% of the DNA that varies from person to person. Because members of MZ and DZ twin pairs are assumed to share their environments to the same extent (the "equal environments assumption"), if MZ twins are more similar to each other on a given trait—such as reading—than DZ twins, we can infer that their greater *behavioral* similarity is due to their greater *genetic* similarity.

Twin studies have shown convincingly that there is a strong genetic contribution to dyslexia as well as to individual variation in reading across the whole range of ability, in several different countries and languages, including the UK, USA, Australia, Sweden, Norway, and China. Heritability estimates for word-level reading skills are in the range of 50–70%, regardless of whether the focus is on poor performance/dyslexia, or typical variation (Harlaar et al., 2005; Peterson & Pennington, 2012; Olson et al., 2014). The remaining variance is largely accounted for by experiences that are unique to each child, while the environmental factors shared by children in a family do not seem to play a key role. Interestingly, the role of genetic factors is strongest after formal literacy instruction begins: early reading in Scandinavian twin samples appears to be largely influenced by environmental factors (Samuelsson et al., 2008).

Twin studies have also shed light on the etiology of the core predictors of reading, such as phoneme awareness, RAN, and letter-sound knowledge. Phoneme awareness and RAN appear to be under substantial genetic influence, while letter-sound-knowledge is subject to stronger environmental effects, perhaps reflecting wide variation in families' literacy practices with preschool children. The genetic effects on phoneme awareness and RAN overlap, but there are also independent genetic factors influencing each of them, supporting the idea that these two core skills may reflect somewhat different processes. Furthermore, the genetic effects on these core predictors in preschool are largely (but not entirely) shared with early reading skills one year later, showing etiological continuity between the precursors of reading, and reading itself (Byrne et al., 2006).

34.6.2.2 Molecular genetics

Establishing the heritability of reading and dyslexia has paved the way for an explosion in molecular genetic research in the last decade or so, aiming to identify the specific genetic factors involved. Linkage studies have used the cosegregation of dyslexia with shared chromosomal regions within families to identify nine regions (DYX1-DYX9) on chromosomes 1, 2, 3, 6, 11, 15, 18, and X. Fine mapping studies within these regions have narrowed down the search to several specific candidate genes, which have had varying levels of support and replication (Newbury et al., 2011). Two of the most studied and robustly replicated of these candidate genes are *KIAA0319* and *DCDC2* on chromosome 6. These were originally identified in samples of individuals with dyslexia; subsequent work has shown that *KIAA0319* is also associated with variation in reading skills in the typical population, while *DCDC2* appears to have a more specific role in reading difficulties (Paracchini et al., 2008; Scerri et al., 2011).

Identifying genetic variations associated with dyslexia provides a window into the biological pathways by which a risk variant may exert its effects on brain structure and function. Converging evidence suggests that variants within genes associated with dyslexia, such as *KIAA0319* and *DCDC2*, have an important role to play in fetal brain development, and particularly in neuronal migration (Meng et al., 2005; Paracchini et al., 2006). Recent work in imaging genetics further shows associations between *KIAA0319* and *DCDC2* and alterations in white matter tracts and cortical thickness (Eicher et al., 2016; Marino et al., 2014). Work in this exciting area is progressing apace, but the field is still a long way from fully specifying the genetic substrate of dyslexia. Several themes do emerge from the literature however: it is almost certainly the case that complex and relatively common disorders such as dyslexia are caused by large numbers of different genetic variants (polygenicity), which also play a role in other disorders (pleiotropy); many or most of these genetic variants on their own will exert only small effects and are likely to be associated with normal variation in reading across the population. These genetic variations will interact not only with each other, but also with the environments that individuals experience in utero and throughout development. Finally, there is recognition within the field that large-scale, international collaborations will be necessary to generate the power needed to reliably characterize the genetic contribution to dyslexia.

34.6.3 Neural basis of dyslexia

One of the earliest observations about atypical brain structure in dyslexia was that of microstructural anomalies and unusual symmetry in the planum temporale, which is an associative auditory area on the surface of the posterior STG, and which has been implicated in phonological processing and language comprehension. In a postmortem study of seven brains of individuals with dyslexia, Galaburda et al. (1985) recorded symmetrical plana temporale in the left and right hemispheres, whereas these structures typically show a leftward asymmetry in the general population. Many subsequent studies tried to replicate these findings *in vivo*, with inconsistent results. However, a recent large-scale study (Altarelli et al., 2014) revisited this issue, using multiple measurements of structural MRI images for 81 children (35 with dyslexia, and 46 controls), which allowed for direct comparison with previous studies, including the original postmortem results. The authors also controlled for the effects of gender, age, and global brain measures. They found an increased proportion of rightward asymmetry in the dyslexic group, as well as more duplications of Heschl's gyrus. Interestingly, these differences were only apparent in the boys with dyslexia, compared to the typically developing boys, adding to recent evidence suggesting that there may be gender differences in the brain morphology associated with dyslexia (Evans et al., 2014).

The reading network: There is a clearly specified left hemisphere network associated with reading in adults, which has been shown to be disrupted in dyslexia, both anatomically and functionally (Richlan, Kronbichler, & Wimmer, 2009; Shaywitz & Shaywitz, 2005). The three core systems in this network are: (a) the posterior regions of the inferior frontal gyrus (IFG), which are thought to be critical for speech-motor coding and access to phonological output; (b) the temporoparietal cortex (TP), which is thought to be involved in phonological processing, and the mapping of phonology to orthographic and semantic features; and (c) the occipitotemporal cortex (OT), which includes what is known as the Visual Word Form Area, and which is involved in visual word form recognition.

Developmentally, beginning readers appear to rely on the IFG and temporal polar cortex (TP) areas, presumably reflecting the use of phonological decoding for word identification at the early stages of learning to read, while involvement of the occipitotemporal (OT) cortex appears to be the neural signature of the skilled, fluent reading of familiar material (Shaywitz et al., 2007). Both temporoparietal and occipitotemporal areas have consistently been reported to be underactivated in readers with dyslexia, while overactivation in left IFG, as well as right hemisphere areas, is thought to reflect effortful compensatory processes. Although much of the early work in this area was carried out in English, and it was possible that the results reflected the unusually opaque nature of English orthography, the structural differences and the pattern of atypical activation in the reading network appear to be similar across both deep and shallow orthographies (Martin et al., 2016; Paulesu et al., 2001; Silani et al., 2005).

A key question in this field is whether atypical function of these areas is a cause or a consequence of reading difficulties. One approach has been to make use of reading-age matched designs, to control for reading levels; a second approach has been to study children who are at family risk of dyslexia, before they start to read. The consensus emerging from these studies is that the atypical activation in temporoparietal regions precedes the onset of reading difficulties and is therefore likely to be causal. The findings with respect to occipitotemporal areas are less clear-cut, and it may be that this region tunes itself differently as a consequence of reading experience (for a recent review and quantitative meta-analysis, see Vandermosten, Hoeft, & Norton, 2016).

Most recently, attention has turned to structural and functional connectivity within the reading network, and a well-replicated finding is of reduced integrity of the arcuate fasciculus, which is one of the key white matter tracts connecting the posterior occipitotemporal regions with more frontal areas. Reduced fractional anisotropy in the arcuate fasciculus has been recorded in infants who are at family risk of dyslexia as early as 6–18 months of age, indicating that at least part of the atypical neural signature of dyslexia is present and measurable by 18 months, at the early stages of language acquisition (Langer et al., 2017). Disrupted connectivity between these regions is also reflected in functional studies, which show reduced correlations in activation between left posterior temporal areas and left IFG, not only during reading-related tasks, but also during the resting-state (Schurz et al., 2015) This further supports the idea that the atypical function of this network is not directly contingent on reading itself.

34.6.4 Environmental factors in dyslexia

In addition to these biological influences, school and home environmental factors—either alone, or in combination with individual vulnerabilities—also contribute to a child's risk of developing reading problems. At the broadest level, reading disorders show social class differences that are not entirely attributable to differences in phonological skills, and poor readers often come from large families, where later-born children may face delays in language development. Literacy-related activities in the home are also important (Stevenson &

Fredman, 1990; Whitehurst & Lonigan, 1998); these can include both direct literacy activities (e.g., tuition in letter sounds), and informal activities, such as shared storybook reading (Sénéchal & LeFevre, 2002, 2014). However, it is important to note that there are strong correlations between the home literacy environments parents provide and their own literacy skills (van Bergen, van Zuijen, Bishop, & de Jong, 2017). Thus, in families where parents themselves have literacy problems, reading-related experiences in the home may be less than optimal (Petrill, Deater-Deckard, Schatsneider, & Davis, 2005; Hamilton et al., 2016). Outside of the home, comparisons of children from the same area attending different schools have emphasized that schooling can make a substantial difference to reading achievement (Rutter & Maughan, 2002).

Importantly, genes and the environment are not independent of each other. One form of gene-environment interaction is in differing levels of heritability in different environmental contexts: Friend, DeFries, and Olson (2008) showed that the genetic effects on dyslexia were greater, and environmental effects smaller, in families in which the parents were more highly educated compared to families with lower levels of parental education. It is likely that highly educated parents provide a rich literacy environment in the home, which may mediate this effect. In addition to the environment provided for the child by his/her parents, the child's active participation in their own literacy development is likely to be important, and to be influenced by their own intrinsic, genetic predisposition (gene-environment correlation). From very early in development, children differ in their interest in books, and children at risk for dyslexia may be among those who are more difficult to interest and engage. Over time, the cumulative impact of such processes leads to massive variations in children's exposure to print—a factor shown to have an independent effect on reading progress (Harlaar, Dale, & Plomin, 2007).

In summary, as might be expected for a complex trait, the etiology of reading disorders is varied and depends on both genetic and environmental factors (Peterson & Pennington, 2012). A reasonable conclusion is that some children carry a heritable risk of reading impairment but whether or not they are classified as dyslexic depends upon the language and school context in which they learn, and on the other skills or deficits they bring to the task of reading. This is in keeping with the current move away from single-deficit models toward multifactorial models that explain the nature and causes of dyslexia.

34.7 INTERVENTIONS FOR DYSLEXIA

As just shown, the environment has an important role to play in the development of literacy. An important aspect of the environment is the type of instruction that a child receives, and there is good evidence that optimizing instruction based on theoretically motivated principles can significantly ameliorate the reading difficulties experienced by children with dyslexia. Most prominently, the relationship between phonological skills and learning to read has led to the development of effective intervention programs that promote phonological skills in the context of reading (Hulme & Melby-Lervåg, 2015; National Reading Panel, 2000, for reviews). In general terms, interventions to promote decoding (and hence remediate dyslexia) comprise training in phoneme awareness linked to letter knowledge, together with systematic phonic instruction in the context of book reading. In contrast, interventions to promote reading comprehension (which children who have dyslexia in the context of a language disorder may need) involve training to improve oral language skills, including work on vocabulary and narrative skills, and emphasize the use of inferences and metacognitive strategies to ensure coherent understanding of text (Snowling & Hulme, 2012).

An important issue, however, is the problem of children who, despite high-quality intervention, do not respond to teaching and continue to have reading impairments. These difficult-to-remediate children appear to have the most severe phonological deficits (Vellutino et al., 1996), are often socially disadvantaged, and may experience emotional and behavioral difficulties. Current evidence suggests that early interventions to strengthen the language foundations for reading will be important for helping these children. For example, Fricke et al. (2013) evaluated an oral language program to promote vocabulary, narrative, and listening skills supplemented by training in letter sounds and phoneme awareness. Children receiving the intervention made significant gains in oral language skills compared to a control group, and their phoneme awareness and letter knowledge also improved. Although the program contained no activities directed toward reading (except some work on letters and phoneme awareness), and no gains were made in decoding skills (relative to controls), an important outcome was that the intervention group showed significant gains in reading comprehension six months after the intervention had ended. Moreover, these gains were fully mediated by gains in oral language. These findings dovetail well with what we have learned from studies of children at high-risk of dyslexia; many of these children enter school without a strong foundation in oral language; without intervention they are likely to fail.

Neural effects of intervention: Recent research has examined whether and how effective reading intervention changes underlying brain processes. Phonologically-based interventions appear to "normalize" the function of the left hemisphere reading network in children (Aylward et al., 2003; Shaywitz et al., 2004; Simos et al., 2002). It is claimed that these effects are visible after as little as two months of intensive intervention (Simos et al., 2002), and are sustained for at least a year following the end of the intervention (Shaywitz et al., 2004). In adults with developmental dyslexia, improvements in reading following intervention were associated with increased activation in temporoparietal areas, as in children, but also with activation of right hemisphere sites which have previously been found to be recruited in recovering stroke patients. This suggests that the adult brain makes use of two neural systems in reading recovery, one of which is to "normalize" the reading network itself, and the other drawing on compensatory processes (Eden at al., 2004).

34.8 Conclusions

There has been rapid progress in the field of dyslexia in recent years and there is much scientific evidence concerning its nature, causes, and consequences. Dyslexia research has been a successful enterprise because it has built on cognitive models of how literacy skills develop in the normal population. Within this framework, we have argued that there is strong evidence that dyslexia is associated with a deficit in phonological processing, perhaps supplemented by deficits in a range of other areas that compromise the development of reading and spelling. This seems to occur similarly across quite different orthographies.

Modern conceptions of developmental disorder view such difficulties as dimensional rather than categorical. Thus, from an educational perspective, it may no longer be relevant to ask, "Who is dyslexic and who is not?" Rather, the heritable skills underlying the acquisition of reading are continuously distributed in the population, such that some people find learning to read and write easy whereas others have extreme difficulty. We have reviewed evidence regarding both the biological bases of dyslexia and environmental factors which might affect its outcome. Within this context we would argue that whether or not a child is diagnosed with dyslexia depends on their age and stage of development, the language in which they are learning, how they are being taught, and the criteria adopted by the educational system in which they are schooled. We anticipate that future research will be directed toward understanding how genetic variation among individuals growing up in different environments predicts their reading outcomes and will be framed within multiple risk frameworks. In parallel is the need for further research examining individual differences in responsiveness to theoretically motivated interventions that prevent or ameliorate dyslexia, and the brain bases of such variation.

References

Adlard, A., & Hazan, V. (1998). Speech perception in children with specific reading difficulties (dyslexia). *Quarterly Journal of Experimental Psychology*, 51, 153–77.

Altarelli, I., Leroy, F., Monzalvo, K., Fluss, J., Billard, C., Dehaene-Lambertz, G., ... & Ramus, F. (2014). Planum temporale asymmetry in developmental dyslexia: Revisiting an old question. *Human Brain Mapping*, 35(12), 5717–35.

American Psychiatric Association (2013). *Diagnostic and Statistical Manual of Mental Disorders* (DSM-5®). American Psychiatric Publishing, Washington, DC.

Amitay, S., Ben-Yehudah, G., Banai, K., & Ahissar, M. (2002). Disabled readers suffer from visual and auditory impairments but not from a specific magnocellular deficit. *Brain*, 125(10), 2272–85.

Aylward, E. H., Richards, T. L., Berninger, V. W., Nagy, W. E., Field, K. M., Grimme, A. C., ... & Cramer, S. C. (2003). Instructional treatment associated with changes in brain activation in children with dyslexia. *Neurology*, 61(2), 212–19.

Bakos, S., Landerl, K., Bartling, J., Schulte-Körne, G., & Moll, K. (2017). Deficits in letter-speech sound associations but intact visual conflict processing in dyslexia: Results from a novel ERP-paradigm. *Frontiers in Human Neuroscience*, 11, 116.

Bekebrede, J., van der Leij, A., Plakas, A., Share, D., & Morfidi, E. (2010). Dutch dyslexia in adulthood: Core features and variety. *Scientific Studies of Reading*, 14(2), 183–210.

Bishop, D. V. M., Snowling, M. J., Thompson, P. A., Greenhalgh, T., & and the CATALISE-2 consortium (2017). Phase 2 of CATALISE: A multinational and multidisciplinary Delphi consensus study of problems with language development: Terminology. *Journal of Child Psychology and Psychiatry, and Allied Disciplines*, 58(10), 1068–80.

Blau, V., van Atteveldt, N., Ekkebus, M., Goebel, R., & Blomert, L. (2009). Reduced neural integration of letters and speech sounds links phonological and reading deficits in adult dyslexia. *Current Biology*, 19(6), 503–8.

Blomert, L. (2011). The neural signature of orthographic–phonological binding in successful and failing reading development. *NeuroImage*, 57(3), 695–703.

Blomert, L., & Mitterer, H. (2004). The fragile nature of the speech-perception deficit in dyslexia: Natural vs. synthetic speech. *Brain and Language*, 89(1), 21–6.

Boden, C., & Giaschi, D. (2007). M-stream deficits and reading-related visual processes in developmental dyslexia. *Psychological Bulletin*, 133(2), 346.

Bogliotti, C., Serniclaes, W., Messaoud-Galusi, S., & Sprenger-Charolles, L. (2008). Discrimination of speech sounds by children with dyslexia: Comparisons with chronological age and reading level controls. *Journal of Experimental Child Psychology*, 101(2), 137–55.

Bosse, M. L., Tainturier, M. J., & Valdois, S. (2007). Developmental dyslexia: The visual attention span deficit hypothesis. *Cognition*, 104(2), 198–230.

Brady, S., Shankweiler, D., & Mann, V. (1983). Speech perception and memory coding in relation to reading ability. *Journal of Experimental Child Psychology*, 35, 345–367.

Breier, J. I., Gray, L., Fletcher, J. M., Diehl, R. L., Klaas, P., Foorman, B. R., & Molis, M. R. (2001). Perception of voice and tone onset time continua in children with dyslexia with and without attention deficit/hyperactivity disorder. *Journal of Experimental Child Psychology*, 80(3), 245–70.

Bruck, M. (1990). Word recognition skills of adults with childhood diagnoses of dyslexia. *Developmental Psychology*, 26, 439–54.

Bruck, M., & Treiman, R. (1990). Phonological awareness and spelling in normal children and dyslexics: The case of initial consonant clusters. *Journal of Experimental Child Psychology*, 50, 156–78.

Buchholz, J., & Davies, A. A. (2005). Adults with dyslexia demonstrate space-based and object-based covert attention deficits: Shifting attention to the periphery and shifting attention between objects in the left visual field. *Brain and Cognition*, 57, 30–4.

Byrne, B. (1998). *The Foundation of Literacy: The Child's Acquisition of the Alphabetic Principle*. Psychology Press, Hove.

Byrne, B., Olson, R. K., Samuelsson, S., Wadsworth, S., Corley, R., DeFries, J. C., & Willcutt, E. (2006). Genetic and environmental influences on early literacy. *Journal of Research in Reading*, 29(1), 33–49.

Caravolas, M., Hulme, C., & Snowling, M. J. (2001). The foundations of spelling ability: Evidence from a 3-year longitudinal study. *Journal of Memory and Language*, 45(4), 751–74.

Caravolas, M., Lervåg, A., Defior, S., Seidlová Málková, G., & Hulme, C. (2013). Different patterns, but equivalent predictors, of growth in reading in consistent and inconsistent orthographies. *Psychological Science*, 24(8), 1398–407.

Caravolas, M., Lervåg, A., Mousikou, P., Efrim, C., Litavsky, M., Onochie-Quintanilla, E., ... & Hulme, C. (2012). Common patterns of prediction of literacy development in different alphabetic orthographies. *Psychological Science*, 23(6), 678–86.

Caravolas, M., Volín, J., & Hulme, C. (2005). Phoneme awareness is a key component of alphabetic literacy skills in consistent and inconsistent orthographies: Evidence from Czech and English children. *Journal of Experimental Child Psychology*, 92, 107–39.

Carroll, J. M., Maughan, B., Goodman, R., & Meltzer, H. (2005). Literacy difficulties and psychiatric disorders: Evidence for comorbidity. *Journal of Child Psychology and Psychiatry*, 46(5), 524–32.

Carroll, J. M., Solity, J., & Shapiro, L. R. (2016). Predicting dyslexia using prereading skills: The role of sensorimotor and cognitive abilities. *Journal of Child Psychology and Psychiatry*, 57(6), 750–8.

Castles, A., & Coltheart, M. (1993). Varieties of developmental dyslexia. *Cognition*, 47(2), 149–80.

Chung, K. K. H., & Ho, C. S. H. (2010). Dyslexia in Chinese language: An overview of research and practice. *Australian Journal of Learning Difficulties*, 15(2), 213–24.

de Jong, P., & van der Leij, A. (2003). Developmental changes in the manifestation of a phonological deficit in dyslexic children learning to read a regular orthography. *Journal of Educational Psychology*, 95, 22–40.

Eden, G. F., Jones, K. M., Cappell, K., Gareau, L., Wood, F. B., Zeffiro, T. A., . . . Flowers, D. L. (2004). Neural changes following remediation in adult developmental dyslexia. *Neuron*, 44(3), 411–22.

Eden, G., Stein, J., Wood, H., & Wood, F. (1994). Differences in eye movements and reading problems in dyslexic and normal children. *Vision Research*, 34, 1345–58.

Edwards, V. T., Giaschi, D. E., Dougherty, R. F., Edgell, D., Bjornson, B. H., Lyons, C., & Douglas, R. M. (2004). Psychophysical indexes of temporal processing abnormalities in children with developmental dyslexia. *Developmental Neuropsychology*, 25(3), 321–54.

Eicher, J. D., Montgomery, A. M., Akshoomoff, N., Amaral, D. G., Bloss, C. S., Libiger, O., . . . & Pediatric Imaging Neurocognition Genetics study. (2016). Dyslexia and language impairment associated genetic markers influence cortical thickness and white matter in typically developing children. *Brain Imaging and Behavior*, 10(1), 272–82.

Elliott, J. G., & Grigorenko, E. L. (2014). *The Dyslexia Debate* (No. 14). Cambridge University Press, Cambridge.

Evans, T. M., Flowers, D. L., Napoliello, E. M., & Eden, G. F. (2014). Sex-specific gray matter volume differences in females with developmental dyslexia. *Brain Structure & Function*, 219(3), 1041–54.

Facoetti, A., & Molteni, M. (2001). The gradient of visual attention in developmental dyslexia. *Neuropsychologia*, 39, 352–7.

Facoetti, A., Turatto, M. L., & Mascetti, G. G. (2001). Orienting of visual attention in dyslexia: Evidence for asymmetric hemispheric control of attention. *Experimental Brain Research*, 138, 46–53.

Franceschini, S., Gori, S., Ruffino, M., Viola, S., Molteni, M., & Facoetti, A. (2013). Action video games make dyslexic children read better. *Current Biology*, 23(6), 462–6.

Fricke, S., Bowyer-Crane, C., Haley, A., Hulme, C., & Snowling, M. J. (2013). Building a secure foundation for literacy: An evaluation of a preschool language intervention. *Journal of Child Psychology and Psychiatry*, 54, 280–90.

Friend, A., DeFries, J. C., & Olson, R. K. (2008). Parental education moderates genetic influences on reading disability. *Psychological Science*, 19(11), 1124–30.

Gaab, N., Gabrieli, J. D. E., Deutsch, G. K., Tallal, P., & Temple, E. (2007). Neural correlates of rapid auditory processing are disrupted in children with developmental dyslexia and ameliorated with training: An fMRI study. *Restorative Neurology and Neuroscience*, 25(3–4), 295–310.

Galaburda, A. M., Sherman, G. F., Rosen, G. D., Aboitiz, F., & Geschwind, N. (1985). Developmental dyslexia: Four consecutive patients with cortical anomalies. *Annals of Neurology*, 18(2), 222–33.

Georgiou, G. K., Parrila, R., & Papadopoulos, T. C. (2008). Predictors of word decoding and reading fluency across languages varying in orthographic consistency. *Journal of Educational Psychology*, 100(3), 566.

Gooch, D., Hulme, C., Nash, H. M., & Snowling, M. J. (2014). Comorbidities in preschool children at family risk of dyslexia. *Journal of Child Psychology and Psychiatry*, 55(3), 237–46.

Goswami, U. (2011). A temporal sampling framework for developmental dyslexia. *Trends in Cognitive Sciences*, 15(1), 3–10.

Goswami, U. (2015). Sensory theories of developmental dyslexia: Three challenges for research. *Nature Reviews Neuroscience*, 16(1), 43–54.

Goswami, U., Huss, M., Mead, N., Fosker, T., & Verney, J. P. (2013). Perception of patterns of musical beat distribution in phonological developmental dyslexia: Significant longitudinal relations with word reading and reading comprehension. *Cortex*, 49(5), 1363–76.

Gottardo, A., Siegel, L. S., & Stanovich, K. E. (1997). The assessment of adults with reading disabilities: What can we learn from experimental tasks? *Journal of Research in Reading*, 20(1), 42–54.

Hämäläinen, J. A., Salminen, H. K., & Leppänen, P. H. (2013). Basic auditory processing deficits in dyslexia: systematic review of the behavioral and event-related potential/field evidence. *Journal of Learning Disabilities*, 46(5), 413–27.

Hamilton, L. G., Hayiou-Thomas, M. E., Hulme, C., & Snowling, M. J. (2016). The home literacy environment as a predictor of the early literacy development of children at family-risk of dyslexia. *Scientific Studies of Reading*, 20(5), 401–19.

Harlaar, N., Dale, P. S., & Plomin, R. (2007). Reading exposure: A (largely) environmental risk factor with environmentally-mediated effects on reading performance in the primary school years. *Journal of Child Psychology and Psychiatry, and Allied Disciplines*, 48(12), 1192–9.

Harlaar, N., Spinath, F. M., Dale, P. S., & Plomin, R. (2005). Genetic influences on early word recognition abilities and disabilities: A study of 7-year-old twins. *Journal of Child Psychology and Psychiatry, and Allied Disciplines*, 46(4), 373–84.

Harm, M. W., McCandliss, B. D., & Seidenberg, M. (2003). Modeling the successes and failures of interventions for disabled readers. *Scientific Studies of Reading*, 7(2), 155–83.

Hatcher, P. J. (2000). Sound links in reading and spelling with discrepancy-defined dyslexics and children with moderate learning difficulties. *Reading and Writing*, 13(3), 257–72.

Hatcher, J., Snowling, M. J., & Griffiths, Y. M. (2002). Cognitive assessment of dyslexic students in higher education. *British Journal of Educational Psychology*, 72(1), 119–33.

Hayiou-Thomas, M. E., Carroll, J. M., Leavett, R., Hulme, C., & Snowling, M. J. (2016). When does speech sound disorder matter for literacy? The role of disordered speech errors, co-occurring language impairment and family risk of dyslexia. *Journal of Child Psychology and Psychiatry, and Allied Disciplines*, 58(2), 197–205.

Hazan, V., Messaoud-Galusi, S., Rosen, S., Nouwens, S., & Shakespeare, B. (2009). Speech perception abilities of adults with dyslexia: Is there any evidence for a true deficit? *Journal of Speech, Language, and Hearing Research*, 52(6), 1510–29.

Heath, S. M., Hogben, J. H., Clark, C. D. (1999). Auditory temporal processing in disabled readers with and without oral language delay. *Journal of Child Psychology and Psychiatry*, 40, 637–47.

Ho, C. S. H., Chan, D. W. O., Tsang, S. M., & Lee, S. H. (2002). The cognitive profile and multiple-deficit hypothesis in Chinese developmental dyslexia. *Developmental Psychology*, 38(4), 543.

Ho, C. S.-H., Chan, D., Tsang, S.-M., Lee, S.-H., & Luan, V. H. (2004). Cognitive profiling and preliminary subtyping in Chinese developmental dyslexia. *Cognition*, 91, 43–75.

Ho, S. C., Leung, M., & Cheung, H. (2011). Early difficulties of Chinese preschoolers at familial risk for dyslexia: Deficits in oral language, phonological processing skills, and print-related skills. *Dyslexia, 17*(2), 143–64.

Hulme, C., & Melby-Lervåg, M. (2015). Educational interventions for children's learning difficulties. In: Thapar, A., Pine, D., Taylor, E., Leckman, J., Scott, S., & Snowling, M. (Eds.), *Rutter's Textbook of Child and Adolescent Psychiatry*, 6th Edition (pp. 533–44). Wiley-Blackwell, Hoboken, NJ.

Joanisse, M. F., Manis, F. R., Keating, P., & Seidenberg, M. S. (2000). Language deficits in dyslexic children: Speech perception, phonology, and morphology. *Journal of Experimental Child Psychology, 77*, 30–60.

Kevan, A., & Pammer, K. (2008). Visual deficits in pre-readers at familial risk for dyslexia. *Vision Research, 48*(28), 2835–9.

Kirby, J. R., Georgiou, G. K., Martinussen, R., & Parrila, R. (2010). Naming speed and reading: From prediction to instruction. *Reading Research Quarterly, 45*(3), 341–62.

Landerl, K, & Moll, K. (2010). Comorbidity of learning disorders: Prevalence and familial transmission. *Journal of Child Psychology and Psychiatry, 51*(3), 287–94.

Landerl, K., Ramus, F., Moll, K., Lyytinen, H., Leppänen, P. H., Lohvansuu, K., . . . & Kunze, S. (2013). Predictors of developmental dyslexia in European orthographies with varying complexity. *Journal of Child Psychology and Psychiatry, 54*(6), 686–94.

Landerl, K., Wimmer, H., & Frith, U. (1997). The impact of orthographic consistency on dyslexia: A German-English comparison. *Cognition, 63*, 315–34.

Langer, N., Peysakhovich, B., Zuk, J., Drottar, M., Sliva, D. D., Smith, S., . . . & Gaab, N. (2017). White matter alterations in infants at risk for developmental dyslexia. *Cerebral Cortex, 27*(2), 1027–36.

Lervåg, A., & Hulme, C. (2009). Rapid automatized naming (RAN) taps a mechanism that places constraints on the development of early reading fluency. *Psychological Science, 20*(8), 1040–8.

Litt, R. A., & Nation, K. (2014). The nature and specificity of paired associate learning deficits in children with dyslexia. *Journal of Memory and Language, 71*(1), 71–88.

Lovegrove, W., Martin, F., & Slaghuis, W. (1986). The theoretical and experimental case for a visual deficit in specific reading disability. *Cognitive Neuropsychology, 3*, 225–67.

Lovett, M. W., Ransby, M. J., & Barron, R. W. (1988). Treatment, subtype and word-type effects in dyslexic children's response to remediation. *Brain and Language, 34*, 328–49.

Lum, J. A., Ullman, M. T., & Conti-Ramsden, G. (2013). Procedural learning is impaired in dyslexia: Evidence from a meta-analysis of serial reaction time studies. *Research in Developmental Disabilities, 34*(10), 3460–76.

Manis, F. R., Doi, L. M., & Bhadha, B. (2000). Naming speed, phonological awareness, and orthographic knowledge in second graders. *Journal of Learning Disabilities, 3*, 325–33.

Manis, F. R., McBride-Chang, C., Seidenberg, M. S., Keating, P., Doi, L. M., Munson, B., & Petersen, A. (1997). Are speech perception deficits associated with developmental dyslexia? *Journal of Experimental Child Psychology, 66*, 211–35.

Marino, C., Scifo, P., Della Rosa, P. A., Mascheretti, S., Facoetti, A., Lorusso, M. L., . . . & Perani, D. (2014). The DCDC2/intron 2 deletion and white matter disorganization: Focus on developmental dyslexia. *Cortex, 57*, 227–43.

Marshall, C. M., Snowling, M. J., & Bailey, P. J. (2001). Rapid auditory processing and phonological processing in normal readers and readers with dyslexia. *Journal of Speech, Hearing, and Language Research, 44*, 925–40.

Martin, A., Kronbichler, M., & Richlan, F. (2016). Dyslexic brain activation abnormalities in deep and shallow orthographies: A meta-analysis of 28 functional neuroimaging studies. *Human Brain Mapping, 37*(7), 2676–99.

Maughan, B., Messer, J., Collishaw, S., Pickles, A., Snowling, M., Yule, W., & Rutter, M. (2009). Persistence of literacy problems: Spelling in adolescence and at mid-life. *Journal of Child Psychology and Psychiatry, 50*(8), 893–901.

McArthur, G. M., Ellis, D., Atkinson, C. M., & Coltheart, M. (2008). Auditory processing deficits in children with reading and language impairments: Can they (and should they) be treated? *Cognition, 107*(3), 946–77.

McArthur, G. M., Hogben, J. H., Edwards, V. T., Heath, S. M., & Mengler, E. D. (2000). On the "Specifics" of specific reading disability and specific language impairment. *Journal of Child Psychology and Psychiatry, and Allied Disciplines, 41*(7), 869–74.

McBride-Chang, C. A. (2016). Is Chinese special? Four aspects of Chinese literacy acquisition that might distinguish learning Chinese from learning alphabetic orthographies. *Educational Psychology Review, 28*(3), 523–49.

McBride-Chang, C. A., Shu, H., Chan, W., Wong, T., Wong, A. M. Y., Zhang, Y., . . . & Chan, P. (2013). Poor readers of Chinese and English: Overlap, stability, and longitudinal correlates. *Scientific Studies of Reading, 17*(1), 57–70.

McBride-Chang, C., Lam, F., Lam, C., Chan, B., Fong, C. Y. C., Wong, T. T. Y., & Wong, S. W.-L. (2011). Early predictors of dyslexia in Chinese children: Familial history of dyslexia, language delay, and cognitive profiles. *Journal of Child Psychology and Psychiatry, 52*(2), 204–11.

McGee, R., Prior, M., Williams, S., Smart, D., & Sanson, A. (2002). The long-term significance of teacher-rated hyperactivity and reading ability in childhood: Findings from two longitudinal studies. *Journal of Child Psychology and Psychiatry, 43*(8), 1004–17.

Meng, H., Smith, S. D., Hager, K., Held, M., Liu, J., Olson, R. K., . . . & Gruen, J. R. (2005). DCDC2 is associated with reading disability and modulates neuronal development in the brain. *Proceedings of the National Academy of Sciences of the United States of America, 102*, 17053–8.

Messbauer, V. C. S., & de Jong, P. F. (2003). Word, nonword, and visual paired associate learning in Dutch dyslexic children. *Journal of Experimental Child Psychology, 84*, 77–96.

Messaoud-Galusi, S., Hazan, V., & Rosen, S. (2011). Investigating speech perception in children with dyslexia: Is there evidence of a consistent deficit in individuals? *Journal of Speech, Language, and Hearing Research, 54*(6), 1682–701.

Metsala, J. L. (1997). Spoken word recognition in reading disabled children. *Journal of Educational Psychology, 89*, 159–69.

Moats, L. C. (1983). A comparison of the spelling errors of older dyslexic and normal second grade children. *Annals of Dyslexia, 33*, 121–40.

Moll, K., Loff, A., & Snowling, M. J. (2013). Cognitive endophenotypes of dyslexia. *Scientific Studies of Reading, 17*(6), 385–97.

Moll, K., Ramus, F., Bartling, J., Bruder, J., Kunze, S., Neuhoff, N., . . . & Tóth, D. (2014). Cognitive mechanisms underlying reading and spelling development in five European orthographies. *Learning and Instruction, 29*, 65–77.

Moore, D. R., Ferguson, M. A., Halliday, L. F., & Riley, A. (2008). Frequency discrimination in children: Perception, learning and attention. *Hearing Research, 238*(1), 147–54.

Mundy, I. R., & Carroll, J. M. (2012). Speech prosody and developmental dyslexia: Reduced phonological awareness in the context of intact phonological representations. *Journal of Cognitive Psychology, 24*(5), 560–81.

Nag, S., & Snowling, M. J. (2011). Cognitive profiles of poor readers of Kannada. *Reading and Writing*, 24(6), 657–76.

Nash, H. M., Gooch, D., Hulme, C., Mahajan, Y., McArthur, G., Steinmetzger, K., & Snowling, M. J. (2017). Are the literacy difficulties that characterize developmental dyslexia associated with a failure to integrate letters and speech sounds? *Developmental Science*, 20(4), e12423.

National Reading Panel (2000). *Report of the National Reading Panel: Reports of the subgroups*. National Institute of Child Health and Human Development Clearing House, Washington, DC.

Newbury, D. F., Paracchini, S., Scerri, T. S., Winchester, L., Addis, L., Richardson, A. J., . . . & Monaco, A. P. (2011). Investigation of dyslexia and SLI risk variants in reading- and language-impaired subjects. *Behavior Genetics*, 41(1), 90–104.

Nittrouer, S. (1999). Do temporal processing deficits cause phonological processing problems? *Journal of Speech, Language, and Hearing Research*, 42(4), 925–42.

Noordenbos, M. W., & Serniclaes, W. (2015). The categorical perception deficit in dyslexia: A meta-analysis. *Scientific Studies of Reading*, 19(5), 340–59.

Olson, R. K., Keenan, J. M., Byrne, B., & Samuelsson, S. (2014). Why do children differ in their development of reading and related skills? *Scientific Studies of Reading*, 18(1), 38–54.

Paracchini, S., Thomas, A., Castro, S., Lai, C., Paramasivam, M., Wang, Y., . . . & Monaco, A. P. (2006). The chromosome 6p22 haplotype associated with dyslexia reduces the expression of KIAA0319, a novel gene involved in neuronal migration. *Human Molecular Genetics*, 15, 1659–66.

Paracchini, S., Steer, C. D., Buckingham, L.-L., Morris, A. P., Ring, S., Scerri, T., . . . & Monaco, A. P. (2008). Association of the KIAA0319 dyslexia susceptibility gene with reading skills in the general population. *The American Journal of Psychiatry*, 165(12), 1576–84.

Paulesu, E., Démonet, J. F., Fazio, F., McCrory, E., Chanoine, V., Brunswick, N., . . . & Frith, U. (2001). Dyslexia: Cultural diversity and biological unity. *Science*, 291(5511), 2165–7.

Pennington, B. F. (2006). From single to multiple deficit models of developmental disorders. *Cognition*, 101(2), 385–413.

Pennington, B. F., & Bishop, D. V. M. (2009). Relations among speech, language, and reading disorders. *Annual Review of Psychology*, 60, 282–306.

Peterson, R. L., & Pennington, B. F. (2012). Developmental dyslexia. *The Lancet*, 379(9830), 1997–2007.

Peterson, R. L., Pennington, B. F., Olson, R. K., & Wadsworth, S. J. (2014). Longitudinal stability of phonological and surface subtypes of dyslexia. *Scientific Studies of Reading*, 18, 347–62.

Petrill, S. A., Deater-Deckard, K., Schatsneider, C., & Davis, C. (2005). Measured environmental influences on early reading: Evidence from an adoption study. *Scientific Studies of Reading*, 9, 237–60.

Pringle-Morgan, W. (1896). A case of congenital word blindness. *British Medical Journal*, 2, 1378.

Protopapas, A. (2014). From temporal processing to developmental language disorders: Mind the gap. *Philosophical Transactions of the Royal Society of London. Series B, Biological Sciences*, 369(1634), 20130090.

Rack, J. P., Snowling, M. J., & Olson, R. K. (1992). The nonword reading deficit in developmental dyslexia: A review. *Reading Research Quarterly*, 27(1), 29–53.

Ramus, F., Rosen, S., Dakin, S. C., Day, B. L., Castellote, J. M., White, S., & Frith, U. (2003). Theories of developmental dyslexia: Insights from a multiple case study of dyslexic adults. *Brain*, 126, 1–25.

Ramus, F., & Szenkovits, G. (2008). What phonological deficit? *The Quarterly Journal of Experimental Psychology*, 61(1), 129–41.

Ramus, F., Marshall, C. R., Rosen, S., & van der Lely, H. K. (2013). Phonological deficits in specific language impairment and developmental dyslexia: Towards a multidimensional model. *Brain*, 136(2), 630–45.

Raschle, N. M., Stering, P. L., Meissner, S. N., & Gaab, N. (2014). Altered neuronal response during rapid auditory processing and its relation to phonological processing in prereading children at familial risk for dyslexia. *Cerebral Cortex*, 24(9), 2489–501.

Reed, C. (1989). Speech perception and the discrimination of brief auditory cues in reading disabled children. *Journal of Experimental Child Psychology*, 48, 270–92.

Richlan, F., Kronbichler, M., & Wimmer, H. (2009). Functional abnormalities in the dyslexic brain: A quantitative meta-analysis of neuroimaging studies. *Human Brain Mapping*, 30(10), 3299–308.

Roach, N. W., & Hogben, J. H. (2004). Attentional modulation of visual processing in adult dyslexia: A spatial cuing deficit. *Psychological Science*, 15, 650–4.

Robertson, E. K., Joanisse, M. F., Desroches, A. S., & Ng, S. (2009). Categorical speech perception deficits distinguish language and reading impairments in children. *Developmental Science*, 12(5), 753–67.

Rochelle, K. S., & Talcott, J. B. (2006). Impaired balance in developmental dyslexia? A meta-analysis of the contending evidence. *Journal of Child Psychology and Psychiatry*, 47(11), 1159–66.

Rosen, S., & Manganari, E. (2001). Is there a relationship between speech and nonspeech auditory processing in children with dyslexia? *Journal of Speech, Language, and Hearing Research*, 44(4), 720–36.

Rutter, M., & Maughan, B. (2002). School effectiveness findings 1979–2002. *Journal of School Psychology*, 40, 451–75.

Rutter, M, & Maughan, B. (2005). Dyslexia: 1965–2005. *Behavioural and Cognitive Psychotherapy*, 33, 389–402.

Rutter, M., & Yule, W. (1975). The concept of specific reading retardation. *Journal of Child Psychology and Psychiatry*, 16, 181–97.

Samuelsson, S., Byrne, B., Olson, R. K., Hulslander, J., Wadsworth, S., Corley, R., . . . & DeFries, J. C. (2008). Response to early literacy instruction in the United States, Australia, and Scandinavia: A behavioral-genetic analysis. *Learning and Individual Differences*, 18(3), 289–95.

Scerri, T. S., Morris, A. P., Buckingham, L.-L., Newbury, D. F., Miller, L. L., Monaco, A. P., . . . & Paracchini, S. (2011). DCDC2, KIAA0319 and CMIP are associated with reading-related traits. *Biological Psychiatry*, 70(3), 237–45.

Schulte-Körne, G., & Bruder, J. (2010). Clinical neurophysiology of visual and auditory processing in dyslexia: A review. *Clinical Neurophysiology*, 121(11), 1794–809.

Schurz, M., Wimmer, H., Richlan, F., Ludersdorfer, P., Klackl, J., & Kronbichler, M. (2015). Resting-state and task-based functional brain connectivity in developmental dyslexia. *Cerebral Cortex*, 25(10), 3502–14.

Seidenberg, M.S. (2007). Connectionist Models of Reading. In M.G. Gaskell (Ed.), *The Oxford Handbook of Psycholinguistics*, pp. 235–250. Oxford University Press, New York, NY.

Sénéchal, M., & LeFevre, J.-A. (2014). Continuity and change in the home literacy environment as predictors of growth in vocabulary and reading. *Child Development*, 85(4), 1552–68.

Sénéchal, M., & LeFevre, J.-A. (2002). Parental involvement in the development of children's reading skill: A five-year longitudinal study. *Child Development*, 73(2), 445–60.

Serniclaes, W., Van Heghe, S., Mousty, P., Carré, R., & Sprenger-Charolles, L. (2004). Allophonic mode of speech perception in dyslexia. *Journal of Experimental Child Psychology, 87,* 336–61.

Share, D. L. (2008). On the Anglocentricities of current reading research and practice: The perils of overreliance on an "outlier" orthography. *Psychological Bulletin, 134,* 584–615.

Shaywitz, B. A., Fletcher, J. M., Holahan, J. M., & Shaywitz, S. E. (1992). Discrepancy compared to low achievement definitions of reading disability: Results from the Connecticut longitudinal study. *Journal of Learning Disabilities, 25*(10), 639–48.

Shaywitz, B. A., Shaywitz, S. E., Blachman, B. A., Pugh, K. R., Fulbright, R. K., Skudlarski, P., . . . & Gore, J. C. (2004). Development of left occipitotemporal systems for skilled reading in children after a phonologically based intervention. *Biological Psychiatry, 55*(9), 926–33.

Shaywitz, S. E., & Shaywitz, B. A. (2005). Dyslexia (specific reading disability). *Biological Psychiatry, 57*(11), 1301–9.

Shaywitz, B. A., Skudlarski, P., Holahan, J. M., Marchione, K. E., Constable, R. T., Fulbright, R. K., . . . & Shaywitz, S. E. (2007). Age-related changes in reading systems of dyslexic children. *Annals of Neurology, 61*(4), 363–70.

Shu, H., McBride-Chang, C., & Wu, S. (2006). Understanding Chinese developmental dyslexia: Morphological awareness as a core cognitive construct. *Journal of Educational Psychology, 98,* 122–33.

Silani, G., Frith, U., Demonet, J.-F., Fazio, F., Perani, D., Price, C., . . . & Paulesu, E. (2005). Brain abnormalities underlying altered activation in dyslexia: A voxel-based morphometry study. *Brain, 128*(Pt 10), 2453–61.

Simos, P. G., Fletcher, J. M., Bergman, E., Breier, J. I., Foorman, B. R., Castillo, E. M., . . . & Papanicolaou, A. C. (2002). Dyslexia-specific brain activation profile becomes normal following successful remedial training. *Neurology, 58*(8), 1203–13.

Sireteanu, R., Goertz, R., Bachert, I., & Wandert, T. (2005). Children with developmental dyslexia show a left visual "minineglect". *Vision Research, 45*(25), 3075–82.

Skottun, B. C. (2015). The need to differentiate the magnocellular system from the dorsal stream in connection with dyslexia. *Brain and Cognition, 95,* 62–6.

Skoyles, J., & Skottun, B. (2004). On the prevalence of magnocellular deficits in the visual system of non-dyslexic individuals. *Brain and Language, 88,* 79–82.

Snowling, M. J. (2000). *Dyslexia,* 2nd Edition. Blackwell, Oxford.

Snowling, M., Goulandris, N., Bowlby, M., & Howell, P. (1986). Segmentation and speech perception in relation to reading skill: A developmental analysis. *Journal of Experimental Child Psychology, 41*(3), 489–507.

Snowling, M. J., Goulandris, N., & Defty, N. (1996). A longitudinal study of reading development in dyslexic children. *Journal of Educational Psychology, 88*(4), 653–69.

Snowling, M., & Hulme, C. (1994). The development of phonological skills. *Philosophical Transactions of the Royal Society B: Biological Sciences, 346*(1315), 21–7.

Snowling, M. J., & Hulme, C (2012). Interventions for children's language and literacy difficulties. *International Journal of Disorders of Language & Communication, 47*(1), 27–34.

Snowling, M. J., & Melby-Lervåg, M. (2016). Oral language deficits in familial dyslexia: A meta-analysis and review. *Psychological Bulletin, 142*(5), 498–545.

Sprenger-Charolles, L., Siegel, L., Béchennec, D., & Serniclaes, W. (2003). Development of phonological and orthographic processing in reading aloud, in silent reading, and in spelling: A four-year longitudinal study. *Journal of Experimental Child Psychology, 84,* 194–217.

Stanovich, K. E. (1986). Matthew effects in reading: Some consequences of individual differences in the acquisition of literacy. *Reading Research Quarterly*, 21, 360–4.

Stanovich, K. E. (1988). Explaining the differences between the dyslexic and the garden-variety poor reader: The phonological-core variable-difference model. *Journal of Learning Disabilities*, 21(10), 590–604.

Stein, J. (2017). Does dyslexia exist? *Language, Cognition and Neuroscience*, 1–8. doi: 10.1080/23273798.2017.1325509

Stein, J., & Walsh, V. (1997). To see but not to read: The magnocellular theory of dyslexia. *Trends in Neurosciences*, 20(4), 147–52.

Stevenson, J., & Fredman, G. (1990). The social environmental correlates of reading ability. *The Journal of Child Psychology and Psychiatry, and Allied Disciplines*, 31, 681–98.

Suggate, S. P. (2010). Why what we teach depends on when: Grade and reading intervention modality moderate effect size. *Developmental Psychology*, 46, 1556–79.

Sutcliffe, P. A., Bishop, D. V., Houghton, S., & Taylor, M. (2006). Effect of attentional state on frequency discrimination: A comparison of children with ADHD on and off medication. *Journal of Speech, Language, and Hearing Research*, 49(5), 1072–84.

Swan, D., & Goswami, U. (1997). Phonological awareness deficits in developmental dyslexia and the phonological representations hypothesis. *Journal of Experimental Child Psychology*, 60, 334–53.

Tallal, P. (1980). Auditory-temporal perception, phonics and reading disabilities in children. *Brain and Language*, 9, 182–98.

Tallal, P., & Piercy, M. (1973). Developmental aphasia: Impaired rate of non-verbal processing as a function of sensory modality. *Neuropsychologia*, 11, 389–98.

Temple, E., Poldrack, R. A., Protopapas, A., Nagarajan, S., Salz, T., Tallal, P., . . . & Gabrieli, J. D. (2000). Disruption of the neural response to rapid acoustic stimuli in dyslexia: Evidence from functional MRI. *Proceedings of the National Academy of Sciences of the United States of America*, 97(25), 13907–12.

Thompson, J. M., & Goswami, U. (2008). Rhythmic processing in children with developmental dyslexia: Auditory and motor rhythms link to reading and spelling. *Journal of Physiology, Paris*, 102(1–3), 120–9.

Tops, W., Callens, M., Lammertyn, J., Van Hees, V., & Brysbaert, M. (2012). Identifying students with dyslexia in higher education. *Annals of Dyslexia*, 62(3), 186–203.

Treiman, R., & Kessler B. (2014). *How Children Learn to Spell Words*. Oxford University Press, New York, NY.

Ullman, M. T. (2004). Contributions of memory circuits to language: The declarative/procedural model. *Cognition*, 92(1), 231–70.

Vaessen, A., Gerretsen, P., & Blomert, L. (2009). Naming problems do not reflect a second independent core deficit in dyslexia: Double deficits explored. *Journal of Experimental Child Psychology*, 103(2), 202–21.

van Atteveldt, N., Formisano, E., Goebel, R., & Blomert, L. (2004). Integration of letters and speech sounds in the human brain. *Neuron*, 43(2), 271–82.

van Bergen, E., van Zuijen, T. L., Bishop, D. V. M., & de Jong, P. F. (2017). Why are home-literacy environment and children's reading skills associated? What parental skills reveal. *Reading Research Quarterly*, 52(2), 147–60.

Vandermosten, M., Hoeft, F., & Norton, E. S. (2016). Integrating MRI brain imaging studies of pre-reading children with current theories of developmental dyslexia: A review and quantitative meta-analysis. *Current Opinion in Behavioral Sciences*, 10, 155–61.

Vellutino, F. R., Scanlon, D. M., Sipay, E., Small, S., Pratt, A., Chen, R., ... & Denckla, M. B. (1996). Cognitive profiles of difficult-to-remediate and readily-remediated poor readers: Early intervention as a vehicle for distinguishing between cognitive and experiential deficits as basic causes of specific reading disability. *Journal of Educational Psychology, 88*, 601–38.

Vellutino, F. R., Fletcher, J. M., Snowling, M. J., & Scanlon, D. M. (2004). Specific reading disability (dyslexia): what have we learned in the past four decades? *Journal of Child Psychology and Psychiatry, 45*, 2–40.

Wagner, R. K., & Torgesen, J. K. (1987). The nature of phonological processing and its causal role in the acquisition of reading skills. *Psychological Bulletin, 101*, 192–212.

White, S., Milne, E., Rosen, S., Hansen, P., Swettenham, J., Frith, U., & Ramus, F. (2006). The role of sensorimotor impairments in dyslexia: A multiple case study of dyslexic children. *Developmental Science, 9*(3), 237–55.

Whitehurst, G. J., & Lonigan, C. J. (1998). Child development and emergent literacy. *Child Development, 69*, 848–72.

Williams, M. J., Stuart, G. W., Castles, A., & McAnally, K. I. (2003). Contrast sensitivity in subgroups of developmental dyslexia. *Vision Research, 43*, 467–77.

Wimmer, H., Mayringer, H., & Landerl, K. (2000). The double-deficit hypothesis and difficulties in learning to read a regular orthography. *Journal of Educational Psychology, 92*, 668–80.

Witton, C., Talcott, J. B., Hansen, P. C., Richardson, A. J., Griffiths, T. D., Rees, A., ... & Green G. G. (1998). Sensitivity to dynamic auditory and visual stimuli predicts nonword reading ability in both dyslexic and normal readers. *Current Biology, 8*, 791–7.

Wolf, M., & Bowers, P. G. (1999). The double-deficit hypothesis for the developmental dyslexias. *Journal of Educational Psychology, 91*(3), 415–38.

Wolf, M., Barzillai, M., Gottwald, S., Miller, L., Spencer, K., Norton, E., ... & Morris, R. (2009). The RAVE-O Intervention: Connecting neuroscience to the classroom. *Mind, Brain, and Education, 3*(2), 84–93.

Wolff, U. (2014). RAN as a predictor of reading skills, and vice versa: results from a randomised reading intervention. *Annals of Dyslexia, 64*(2), 151–65.

Zhou, L., Duff, F. J, & Hulme, C. (2015). Phonological and semantic knowledge are causal influences on learning to read words in Chinese. *Scientific Studies of Reading, 19*(6), 409–18.

Ziegler, J. C., & Goswami, U. (2005). Reading acquisition, developmental dyslexia, and skilled reading across languages: A psycholinguistic grain size theory. *Psychological Bulletin, 131*(1), 3.

Ziegler, J. C., Pech-Georgel, C., George, F., & Lorenzi, C. (2009). Speech-perception-in-noise deficits in dyslexia. *Developmental Science, 12*(5), 732–45.

Ziegler, J. C., Bertrand, D., Tóth, D., Csépe, V., Reis, A., Faísca, L., ... & Blomert, L. (2010). Orthographic depth and its impact on universal predictors of reading: A cross-language investigation. *Psychological Science, 21*, 551–9.

CHAPTER 35

DEVELOPMENTAL LANGUAGE DISORDER

CRISTINA MCKEAN, JAMES LAW,
ANGELA MORGAN, AND SHEENA REILLY

35.1 Introduction

In this chapter we turn to the topic of Language Disorder in children, an umbrella term used to describe the difficulties some children have learning language (Bishop et al., 2016, 2017). The chapter starts by looking at the historical context associated with the concept of language learning difficulty and the way that the terminology has changed over time in line with changes in methodological approach. We then focus on three approaches to studying child language where there has been significant recent development: population methods, the characterization of longitudinal change, and the neurobiology of child language (Schwartz, 2017)[1]. We conclude by posing a series of research questions about language disorder emerging from these and other recent discoveries—a research agenda for the next decade.

35.2 The History of Labels in Developmental Language Disorder

Labels are important, and the history of developmental language disorder has been framed by the use of a wide range of diagnostic terms since it was first described nearly two centuries ago (see Fig. 35.1). While some have been used for short periods before being hastily discarded, others have had more traction. Recently, Bishop (2014) showed that most child language terms comprised the use of a prefix (e.g., specific), descriptor (language), and a noun (impairment). She went on to identify 138/160 possible combinations in a Google Scholar search demonstrating that the term Specific Language Impairment (SLI) has become in recent years the most commonly used label. However, Reilly and colleagues (2014) found limited

---

[1] We refer readers interested in a review of explanatory theories of language disorders to the excellent comprehensive summary presented in Schwartz (2017).

empirical evidence to support the use of the term SLI and the exclusionary criteria used in its diagnosis and went on to argue that the term was a convenient label for researchers, but that the current classification was unacceptably arbitrary. To understand why these arguments have arisen it is important to present the historical context.

One of the earliest mentions of children having a significant difficulty acquiring oral language skills in the absence of obvious learning difficulties was in the second quarter of the nineteenth century (Gall, 1835) and the terms "congenital aphasia" (Vaisse, 1866) and "hearing mutism" (Coen, 1886) were coined later in the century. The 1900s saw the introduction of terms such as "delayed speech development" (Froschels, 1918), "congenital word deafness" (McCall, 1911), "congenital auditory imperceptions" (Worster-Drought & Allen, 1929), and "congenital verbal auditory agnosia" (Karlin, 1954). The term aphasia was reintroduced in combinations such as "developmental aphasia" (Kerr, 1917) and "infantile aphasia" and differentiation between expressive and receptive skills became evident ("expressive developmental aphasia"; see Fig. 35.1). Aphasia and dysphasia had originally been terms used to describe adults with acquired brain injury, for example following stroke and they have tended to drop out of the diagnostic lexicon as distinctions were drawn between acquired conditions and the types of development difficulties experienced by children. The earliest descriptions came from the clinical observations of physicians, with an interest in child development in general and language in particular. The development of standardized "performance" or IQ tests (such as the Stanford Binet) developed in the field of psychology, led to more formal and replicable measurement of child performance. Initially these combined a wide range of different skills but gradually these became more differentiated with IQ tests comprising verbal and non-verbal scales and specific language tests being developed in their own right (such as the Illinois Test of Psycholinguistic Abilities). Such tests heralded the widespread identification and study of language impaired children.

In the 1970s a range of terms such as "deviant language" (Leonard, 1972), "language disorder" (Rees, 1973), "delayed language" (Weiner, 1974), and "developmental language disorder" (Aram & Nation, 1975) were all introduced. In the early 1980s, the word "specific" was introduced in terms such as "specific language deficit" (Stark & Tallal, 1981) and "specific language impairment" (SLI) (Fey & Leonard, 1983; Leonard, 1981). More recently the use of the word "specific" has been debated and its validity and clinical utility challenged (Bishop, 2014; Reilly et al., 2014). In fact diagnostic approaches used for clinical services, such as the most recent versions of the *Diagnostic and Statistical Manual of Mental Disorders* (DSM 5) (American Psychiatric Association, 2013) and the UK Education System have largely moved away from the term "SLI." In preference, these have moved toward broader umbrella terms ("Language Disorder" and "Speech Language and Communication needs," respectively) within which practitioners then describe individual children's strengths and weaknesses. Most recently Bishop et al. conducted a Delphi process to arrive at expert consensus regarding the thorny issues of diagnosis and labeling (Bishop et al., 2016, 2017). From this work the term Language Disorder emerged as the preferred umbrella term for all children with difficulties learning their native language and Developmental Language Disorder for those without any associated biomedical condition. In this definition children are not diagnosed according to any threshold in language ability but rather if they have low language, a poor prognosis, and experience functional limitations in their everyday communication and/or broader functioning. As Bishop acknowledges there are still gaps in the evidence in respect to this new definition and its operationalization for services and researchers (Bishop et al., 2017).

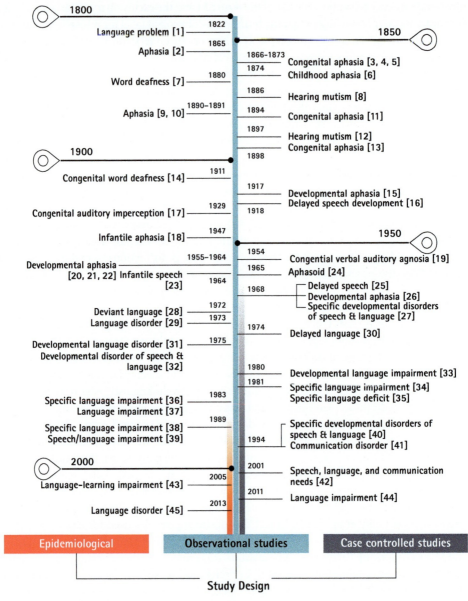

FIG. 35.1 History of terminology used to describe children with language disorder and overview of the predominant study designs (indicated by the red, blue and grey bars) since the 1800s.

35.2.1 Approaches to studying child language

Just as the descriptions and diagnoses changed so the research methods used to draw inferences about language disorder changed too. Single case descriptions, gave way to group studies, and then case control studies and, most recently epidemiological studies,

1. Gall FJ. On the functions of the brain and each of its parts: Boston: Marsh, Capen & Lyon; 1835.
2. Benedikt M. Ueber Aphaise, Agraphic und verwandte pathologische Zustande: Wiener Medizinische Presse; 1865.
3. Vaisse L. Des sourds-muets et de certains cas d'aphasie congenitale: Bulletin de la Societe d'Anthropologie de Paris; 1866.
4. Broadbent WH. On the cerebral mechanism of speech and thought. 15: Med.-Chi. Trans; 1872. p. 145-94.
5. Waldenburg L. Ein fall von angeborener Aphasie: Berliner Klinische Wochenschrift; 1873.
6. Clarus A. Ueber aphasie bei kindern: Jahrbuch fur kinderheilkunde und physische erziehung; 1874.
7. Bastian H. The brain as an organ of mind. New York: Appleton; 1880.
8. Coen R. Pathologie und therapie der sprachanomalien. Vienna: Urban & Schwarzenberg; 1886.
9. Uchermann V. Drei falle von stummheit (aphasie): Zeitschrift fur ohrenheilkunde; 1891.
10. Treitel L. Uber aphasie im kindesalter: Sammlung klinischer vortrage; 1893.
11. Wyllie J. The disorders of speech. Edinburgh: Oliver & Boyd; 1894.
12. Lavrand M. Mutite chez des entendants. Revue Internationale de Rhinologie. 1897;3:95-7.
13. Moyer H. Dumbness or congenital aphasia of a family type without deafness or obvious mental defect. Chicago Medical Recorder. 1898;15:305-9.
14. McCall E. Two Cases of Congenital Aphasia in Children. British Medical Journal. 1911;1(2628):1105.
15. Kerr J. Congenital or developmental aphasia. Journal of Delinquency. 1917:2-6.
16. Froschels E. Kindersprache und aphasie. Berlin: Karger; 1918.
17. Worster-Drought C, Allen I. Congenital auditory imperceptions (congenital word deafness): With report of a case. Journal of Neurology and Psychopathology. 1929;9:193-208.
18. Gessel A, Amatruda C. Developmental diagnosis. 2 ed. New York: Hoeber; 1947.
19. Karlin IW. Aphasias in Children. AMA American Journal of Diseases of Children. 1954;87(6):752-67.
20. Morley M, Court D, Miller H. Delayed Speech and Developmental Aphasia. British Medical Journal. 1955;2(Aug20):463-7.
21. Ingram TTS, Reid JF. Developmental Aphasia Observed in a Department of Child Psychiatry. Archives of disease in Childhood. 1956;31(157):161-72.
22. Benton A. Developmental aphasia and brain damage. Cortex. 1964;1:40-52.
23. Menyuk P. Comparison of Grammar of Children with Functionally Deviant and Normal Speech. Journal of Speech and Hearing Research. 1964;7(2):109-21.
24. Lowe AD, Campbell RA. Temporal Discrimination in Aphasoid and Normal-Children. Journal of Speech and Hearing Research. 1965;8(3):313-4.
25. Lovell K, Hoyle HW, Siddall MQ. A Study of Some Aspects of Play and Language of Young Children with Delayed Speech. Journal of Child Psychology and Psychiatry. 1968;9(1):41-&.
26. Eisenson J. Developmental Aphasia - Speculative View with Therapeutic Implications. Journal of Speech and Hearing Disorders. 1968;33(1):3-13.
27. **ICD-8**
28. Leonard LB. What Is Deviant Language? Journal of Speech and Hearing Disorders. 1972;37(4):427-46.
29. Rees NS. Noncommunicative Functions of Language in Children. Journal of Speech and Hearing Research. 1973;38(1):98-110.
30. Weiner PS. Language-Delayed Child at Adolescence. Journal of Speech and Hearing Disorders. 1974;39(2):202-12.
31. Aram DM, Nation JE. Patterns of Language Behavior in Children with Developmental Language Disorders. Journal of Speech and Hearing Research. 1975;18(2):229-41.
32. **ICD-9**
33. Wolfus B, Moscovitch M, Kinsbourne M. Subgroups of Developmental Language Impairment. Brain and Language. 1980;10(1):152-71.
34. Leonard LB. An Invited Article Facilitating Linguistic Skills in Children with Specific Language Impairment. Applied Psycholinguistics. 1981;2(2):89-118.
35. Stark RE, Tallal P. Selection of Children with Specific Language Deficits. Journal of Speech and Hearing Disorders. 1981;46(2):114-22.
36. Fey M, Leonard L. Pragmatic skills of children with specific language impairment. Gallaher TM, Prutting CA, editors. San Diego: College-Hill Press; 1983.
37. Johnston JR, Ramstad V. Cognitive-Development in Pre-Adolescent Language Impaired Children. British Journal of Disorders of Communication. 1983;18(1):49-55.
38. Tallal P, Ross R, Curtiss S. Familial Aggregation in Specific Language Impairment. Journal of Speech and Hearing Disorders. 1989;54(2):167-73.
39. Beitchman JH, Hood J, Rochon J, Peterson M, Mantini T, Majumdar S. Empirical Classification of Speech Language Impairment in Children .1. Identification of Speech Language Categories. Journal of the American Academy of Child Psychiatry. 1989;28(1):112-7.
40. **ICD-10**
41. **DSM-IV-TR**
42. **DfES**
43. Marler JA, Champlin CA. Sensory processing of backward-masking signals in children with language-learning impairment as assessed with the auditory brainstem response. Journal of Speech, Language, and Hearing Research. 2005;48(1):189-203.
44. Justice LM, Skibbe LE, McGinty AS, Piasta SB, Petrill S. Feasibility, Efficacy, and Social Validity of Home-Based Storybook Reading Intervention for Children With Language Impairment. Journal of Speech, Language, and Hearing Research. 2011;54(2):523-38.
45. **DSM-5**

FIG. 35.1 Continued.

as highlighted by the colored bars indicating the time-lines of each study design in Figure 35.1. Similarly, when assessing the value of intervention simple "before and after" descriptions gave way to quasi-experimental groups studies and single subject experimental designs, and, by the 1950s, we see the earliest examples of randomized controlled trials. Although study designs became more sophisticated the criteria for participant inclusion varied considerably and, while superficially the children appeared similar by virtue of a diagnosis of Language Disorder or SLI, groups were not always comparable across studies due to variation in the thresholds adopted for verbal and non-verbal scores.

35.3 Evidence from population/epidemiological methods

Basing conclusions on highly selected samples is perfectly reasonable in the sense that it makes it possible to explore a specific condition in detail, but it does depend on that condition being readily identifiable with an agreed set of parameters as to who should and should not be included in a given group. The problem as far as language disorder is concerned is that there is no such consensus and criteria differ from one study to another. This makes it difficult to both avoid selection bias and to compare across studies. An arguably more valid alternative to the "clinical" sample is the adoption of epidemiological approaches and representative population samples. Although the threshold issue remains a concern for some forms of analyses within these samples it is, at least, possible to say that ALL children meeting criteria were included in the study and that it is therefore possible to generalize to the population as a whole. Furthermore analyses, which move away from the use of cut-points to explore the nature and drivers of individual differences across a population, become possible.

35.3.1 The social gradient

One obvious example necessitating epidemiological method is the study of the relationship between language and social disadvantage. In a "clinical" sample we have no way of knowing to what extent the children are representative of the population. Indeed, in some earlier iterations of SLI, "low SES" was considered to be an explicit exclusion criterion. Thus, it is quite possible to construct a sample of children in which SES is not a determinant of language outcomes, as is the case in the early Manchester cohort of children attending "language units" in the United Kingdom (Botting et al., 2001). However, the figures tell a rather different story (Fig. 35.2). They represent population data from three different birth cohorts in three different countries (England: the Millennium Cohort Study (MCS), Scotland: Growing Up in Scotland Study (GUS), Australia: the Early Language in Victoria Study (ELVS)) in which we see a consistent social gradient. But to avoid overinterpretation it is important to note that a wide range of abilities is present at each quintile.

35.3.2 The prevalence of language disorder in different social quintiles

The clear social gradient in these different population studies raises the question of the prevalence of language disorder at the different social quintiles. The nature and scale of these studies mean that the children have not received comprehensive evaluation by speech and language therapists or psychologists. Instead we rely on their performance on a standardized assessment of language and consider the proportion of children with language scores outside the putative psychometric norm (i.e., one standard deviation (SD) below the mean for the population concerned). Our knowledge of the standardized distribution of these tests indicates that 16.6% of the population should be scoring below this threshold across the population. In Table 35.1 we report the proportion of children scoring below our threshold for each quintile. In the most disadvantaged quintile the proportion of children having scores >1 SD below the mean in the three cohorts is 18%, 23%, and 21% respectively. We note, with one anomaly (quintile 4 in the ELVS study), the predicted pattern of reducing prevalence holds across the studies.

One would expect the prevalence rate to increase as the level of social disadvantage increases and indeed this is exactly what we find from two other UK studies. Using the same criterion as that used in Table 35.1 (i.e., >1 SD below the mean), Locke and colleagues reported a prevalence of 50% in four-year-old children in nursery in very disadvantaged areas of Sheffield whom were in the lowest Index of Multiple Deprivation (IMD) quintile (Locke et al., 2002). Law and colleagues reported similarly high figures for a population in a school in Edinburgh where all the children's postcodes fell within the lowest quintile (Law et al., 2011). Why such associations are present and what they then mean for interventions for language impairment (LI) should be a priority for future research.

35.3.3 Comorbidity and co-occurring difficulties

Another advantage of population approaches to the study of language disorder is the capacity to increase the understanding of the prevalence and nature of co-occurring difficulties in other developmental domains: issues often precluded, by research methods focused on highly selective groups or significantly biased in "clinically" referred samples, the

Table 35.1 Prevalence of language delay (%) at five years with a threshold of −1 standard deviations below the mean

Cohort	Quintile 1	Quintile 2	Quintile 3	Quintile 4	Quintile 5
Millennium Cohort study	18	10	7	5	3
Growing up in Scotland	23	18	15	11	10
Early Language in Victoria Study	21	16	7	12	6

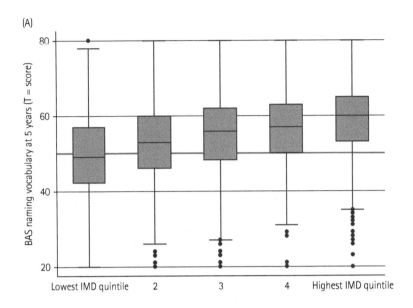
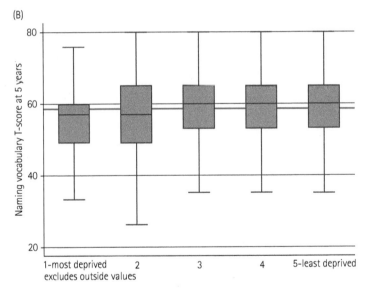

FIG. 35.2 Data from three population studies illustrating the social gradient in language outcomes among five-year-old children: (A) naming vocabulary of five-year-old children in the Millennium Cohort Study (MCS). Children are grouped in quintiles according to the Index of Multiple Deprivation (IMD); (B) naming vocabulary of five-year-old children in the Growing Up in Scotland (GUS) study. Children are grouped in quintiles according to the IMD; and (C) core language standard scores for five-year-old children in the Early Language in Victoria Study (ELVS). Children are grouped in quintiles according to the Socio-Economic Indexes for Areas (SEIFA). For all graphs, the reference line is the standardization mean for the assessment.

Reproduced from Sheena Reilly, Bruce Tomblin, James Law, Cristina McKean, Fiona K. Mensah, Angela Morgan, Sharon Goldfeld, Jan M. Nicholson and Melissa Wake, Specific language impairment: a convenient label for whom?, *International Journal of Language and Communication Disorders*, 49 (4), pp. 416–51, Figure 4, doi: 10.1111/1460-6984.12102 ©2014 published by John Wiley and Sons Ltd on behalf of The Royal College of Speech and Language Therapists. This work is licensed under the Creative Commons Attribution License (CC BY-NC-ND). It is attributed to the authors.

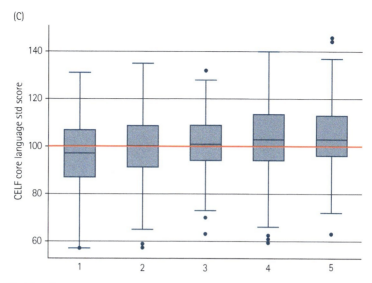

FIG. 35.2 Continued

latter having the potential to both under and overestimate co-occurrence depending on the approach taken. In a recent evaluation of community ascertained sample of seven-year-old children, those with low language abilities were more likely than their typically developing peers to have associated difficulties with literacy, socioemotional, and behavioral adjustment, hyperactivity, and inattention, lower non-verbal IQ, and diagnoses of autistic spectrum condition (McKean et al., 2017). A key area of debate with respect to the diagnosis of specific language disorder is the role played by non-verbal IQ. Do children with better non-verbal IQ but poorer language skills fare differently from those whose language and other skills are within the typical range or those whose verbal and non-verbal skills are both low? Cross-sectionally, Norbury and colleagues found no differences between four to five-year-old children with Language Disorder with average and low-average non-verbal scores with respect to the severity of language impairment, social, emotional, and behavioral problems, or educational attainment (Norbury et al., 2016). Tomblin reported similar findings longitudinally comparing educational and social-emotional outcomes in late adolescence of children with a history of specific Language Disorder or non-specific Language Disorder (that is in the context of low non-verbal scores) at five to six years (Tomblin, 2008). Furthermore, a recent meta-analysis of response to intervention effects for children suggested that the effects of IQ were minimal (Stuebing et al., 2015), and the authors of several language interventions have suggested that IQ does not affect children's response to intervention (Boyle et al., 2009; Wake et al., 2014). However, questions remain regarding the *developmental relationships* between non-verbal skills and language over time

Socioemotional difficulties and poor language abilities (Yew & O'Kearney, 2013) co-occur at rates much higher than chance. Although there remains a question as to whether these developmental domains are correlated across the full range of abilities, in representative populations it is clear that the difficulties overlap considerably in clinical populations. A variety of views have been expressed about whether they are causally related, for example, do children frustrated from poor communication skills, act out and respond in a negative manner, or is there a third factor such as neurodevelopmental immaturity or marked social disadvantage which effectively accounts for both domains? A number of other mechanisms have been proposed. For example, that it is the relationship between language and literacy that is the key to understanding behavior (Tomblin et al., 2000), that it is pragmatics rather than structural language which is key (Law et al., 2015), and, most recently, that because language can vary so much across childhood that it is the language trajectory rather than ability at any one time point which is critical (Westrupp et al., submitted). Ultimately longitudinal analyses in population samples are likely to be the key to understanding these relationships.

35.4 Evidence from methods characterizing longitudinal change

Understanding the process and drivers of developmental change has been a central aim of language acquisition research. However, it is only recently that explanatory models of language disorder have *explicitly* placed the process of developmental change at the center of our understanding of the nature of the impairment. Next, we outline the case for and potential application of work which considers the processes of change in language and its predictors to our understanding of Language Disorder and go on to summarize the current evidence in this regard.

35.4.1 Why characterize developmental change in language abilities and its predictors?

Language development is the result of complex interactions, played out over time, between the child's biological make-up, their family, wider community, and the social and cultural context in which they live and grow (Asbury et al., 2005). Several theories of language disorder place the process of development at the core of our understanding (Bishop, 1997; Chiat, 2001; Leonard, 2007; Thomas, 2005). They differ as to whether Language Disorder is conceptualized as the extreme end of normal variation in the "language endowment spectrum" (Ellis Weismer, 2007; Kovas & Plomin, 2006) or as an atypical and qualitatively different developmental pathway (Leonard, 2007). Whichever perspective is taken, understanding the ontogeny of language disorder, that is describing the nature and drivers of individual differences in the *process of development*, is essential if we are to test and elaborate these theories. As highlighted in Table 35.2 key questions remain about timing, interactivity, compensation, and heterogeneity for fully elaborated developmental explanations of Language Disorder to be described (Thomas et al., 2009).

Despite their centrality to our understanding to date there have been few attempts to address these questions in longitudinal studies. Efforts to understand the biological, genetic, and environmental mechanisms underpinning Language Disorder, have been hampered by diagnostic approaches, typically determined by a range of behavioral measures taken at a single time point and using arbitrary cut-points. This approach is particularly problematic when searching for phenotype-genotype associations as static, cross-sectional descriptions

Table 35.2 Key research questions relating to developmental change in language development and language impairment

Knowledge domain	Questions
Timing	Is there an "optimal language developmental window" such that a particular threshold of competence within that time-frame needs to be reached for a child to have a good outcome?
Interactivity	How do interactions (i) between the child and the environment and (ii) between processing domains (e.g., linguistic, cognitive) play out over developmental time?
Compensation	Do subgroups of children exist with the same poor early language skills but different long-term outcomes?
Heterogeneity	What is the nature and degree of heterogeneity in developmental language pathways and comorbidities?

may mask phenotypic differences between children in their pattern of impairment over time or may overestimate phenotypic differences which simply reflect the differing developmental stage of the child who may be following the same developmental pathway as their peers but at a differing rate.

Different outcomes emerge regarding heritability estimates for Language Disorder depending on the diagnostic criteria applied (Bishop & Hayiou-Thomas, 2008; Hayiou-Thomas, Oliver, & Plomin, 2005) and the age of the child (Hayiou-Thomas et al., 2012). It is possible that if *trajectories* were used in place of single time-point data to determine behavioral phenotypes of Language Disorder that new genotype-phenotype associations may be uncovered.

35.4.2 The nature of change in child language development

As featured throughout this chapter, study design inevitably influences study findings and thence the characterization and theories of language disorder. Most of the growing body of longitudinal research in the field of Language Disorder falls into three groups. Those that aim to:

1) identify earlier predictors of later language outcomes (Reilly et al., 2007, 2010; Rice et al., 2008);
2) compare long-term outcomes of children with and without a history of poor language (Durkin & Conti-Ramsden, 2010; Johnson et al., 1999, 2010; Roulstone et al., 2011; Schoon et al., 2010; Stothard et al., 1998; Tomblin, 2008); and
3) examine the stability of language status (Language Disorder or Typically Developing (TD)) or language profile over time (Beitchman et al., 1996; Bishop & Edmundson, 1987; Conti-Ramsden & Botting, 1999; Henrichs et al., 2011; Law et al., 2012; Snowling et al., 2016; Tambyraja et al., 2015; Tomblin et al., 2003; Zambrana et al., 2014; Zubrick et al., 2015).

Studies of stability have tended to apply a categorical approach, assigning children to either impaired or unimpaired groups at specific cut-points in language scores at two or more time points. In this way children are categorized as stable TD, or stable, resolving, or late emerging Language Disorder. Although this approach, has delivered many useful insights, it may overestimate the degree of instability observed. That is, measurement error will inevitably lead to instability in group membership for children whose scores fall near a cut-point. Furthermore, regression to the mean can suggest changes in children's profile that are, in fact, artifacts of repeated measurement.

Recently two other approaches (four and five, below) have emerged which aim to explore *individual differences in the nature of developmental change* and which also tackle the effects of measurement error and regression to the mean. These are:

4) longitudinal latent class analyses (Conti-Ramsden et al., 2012; Määttä et al., 2012; Ukoumunne et al., 2012); and
5) the multilevel model for change, often also described as "growth curve analysis" or "growth trajectories" (Law et al., 2008; McKean et al., 2015; Rice et al., 1998; Taylor et al., 2013).

In the following we describe findings from studies which seek to understand the *nature of change* in child language development and adopt approaches 3, 4, and 5. While we acknowledge that the third "categorical" approach has the inherent methodological weaknesses identified earlier, the vast majority of previous work has utilized this approach, and so we include these studies here with the caveat that they are interpreted with caution. Finally, we summarize what these studies can tell us about predictors of change.

35.4.2.1 *Stability of language status*

Longitudinal population approaches to the study of Language Disorder have challenged previous long held beliefs about the stability or otherwise of Language Disorder status over development. While it was once thought that all children with a language disorder had a history of late language emergence, population studies have demonstrated that there is a late emerging Language Disorder group, where children appear to make a positive start in their language acquisition process but fall behind their TD peers later in development (Reilly et al., 2015). The progress of children with a diagnosis of Language Disorder or of "late talkers" have been followed in longitudinal studies but often without an original matched control group measured concurrently (Conti-Ramsden et al., 2001) or with a control group of matched TD children recruited at a later time(s) (Bishop & Edmundson, 1987; Stothard et al., 1998). Where a control group is also followed longitudinally many studies have very small samples making the identification of a range of trajectories unlikely (Ellis Weismer et al., 1994; Rescorla, 2002).

Current evidence suggests that there is substantial diversity in language trajectory under the age of five to six years followed by a more uniform pattern of progress after that age (Beitchman et al., 2008; Bishop & Edmundson, 1987; Conti-Ramsden et al., 2012; Henrichs et al., 2011; Johnson et al., 1999; Law et al., 2012; Stothard et al., 1998; Zambrana et al., 2014; Zubrick et al., 2007). However, knowledge about language stability derives largely from longitudinal studies of clinically referred populations (Bishop & Edmundson, 1987; Conti-Ramsden et al., 2012; Law et al., 2008) and these represent only a subgroup of the population of children with language disorder. Clinically referred groups tend to have higher levels of comorbidity, more severe language difficulties, and are more likely to have persisting difficulties. Such studies may therefore overestimate the homogeneity in the trajectory of children with language disorder after five years. Notable exceptions are where children with language disorder are identified in wider populations (Beitchman et al., 1996; Beitchman et al., 2008; Henrichs et al., 2011; Law et al., 2012; Reilly et al., 2010, 2015; Tomblin et al., 2003; Zubrick et al., 2015). Again, when taken together, their findings concur that pre-school language trajectories are more volatile than those of school-age children. However, these cohorts tend to focus only on "fragments" of the developmental trajectory: *either* on pre-school (up to four years) *or* school-aged children (five years and over), with few bridging that gap. The ELVS community cohort does span this age range and findings suggest that Language Disorder status continues to fluctuate between four and seven (Reilly et al., 2014). Of the children in this sample at seven years experiencing low language, 46% had typical language abilities at four, and of the children at four years with low language, 39% had recovered by seven years. Further longitudinal population studies with repeated language measures are therefore needed to determine the level of stability or otherwise of language disorder status over development.

35.4.2.2 *Longitudinal latent class analyses*

More recently sophisticated longitudinal latent class analyses have been applied as illustrated in Table 35.3 (Conti-Ramsden et al., 2012; Määttä et al., 2012; Ukoumunne et al., 2012).

On the whole, findings from these analyses align with those applying a categorical approach (pre-school instability–school-age stability) however the issues of clinical samples and the examination of only fragments of the developmental window are also present here. We therefore urge researchers to apply longitudinal latent class analyses to data spanning the pre-school to school-age period in population samples in order to validate these patterns.

35.4.2.3 *Individual differences in growth trajectory*

The advent of growth trajectory or growth curve modeling has allowed researchers to characterize language trajectories in terms of their starting point (intercept), rate (slope), and, on some occasions, shape, of language progress, and to explore the predictors of differences in those features of the trajectories (Beitchman et al., 2008; Conti-Ramsden et al., 2012; Farkas & Beron, 2004; Fergusson & Horwood, 1993; Law et al., 2008; Luyten & ten Bruggencate, 2011; Peisner-Feinberg et al., 2001; Rice et al., 2004; Taylor et al., 2013). Two recent studies characterized the degree of individual differences which exist in language growth trajectories in *population samples*: Taylor et al. (2013) considered vocabulary from four to eight years and McKean et al. (2015) explored language abilities using an omnibus language test from four to seven years. Both found a substantial degree of variability between individuals in both their intercept and their slope across this age range suggesting the stability found in previous studies (Law et al., 2008) may reflect more limited variability in clinical samples or may be a characteristic of trajectories for later age ranges. Again, these findings underline the need for further longitudinal work in population samples and the application of appropriate analytical methods.

Table 35.3 Summary of findings from studies adopting longitudinal latent class analyses

Author	Sample	Finding
Määttä et al., 2012	Community ascertained sample	No clear continuity between subgroups from 12 to 21 months and their language abilities at five years.
Ukoumunne et al., 2012	Community ascertained sample	Unstable communication and language profiles from eight months to four years in 25% of children in the ELVS cohort.
Conti-Ramsden et al., 2012	Clinically ascertained sample	Defined seven relatively stable subgroups from 7 to 17 years defined only by the children's starting point.

35.4.3 Predictors of change

Studies of change profiles, either categorical or latent, have found differing profiles (persisting, recovering, late-emerging) may be associated with different predictors, suggesting the possibility of diverse underlying etiological mechanisms, interactivity over time between developmental domains and between the child and their environment. Furthermore, growth trajectories suggest a number of factors are associated with differences in *rate* of language development. Next, we discuss factors that have emerged as important in this regard.

The social gradient: Social background is key to understanding both risk and resilience. Thus, social *advantage* has been found to be associated with resolving language profiles in young children (up to four years) (Ukoumunne et al., 2012), and social *disadvantage* associated with persistent language disorder profiles in older children (from 3–8 and 3–5 years) (Snowling et al., 2016; Zambrana et al., 2014).

The importance of social disadvantage as a risk of persisting difficulties is underlined by the findings of studies considering the *rate* of children's language progress from four to seven or eight years (McKean et al., 2015; Taylor et al., 2013). That is children living with disadvantage and limited family resources (e.g., low SES, low income, low maternal education), had poorer language at four years and did not "catch up" with their more advantaged peers between four and eight years, underlining the importance of the early years in setting up child inequalities which may last a lifetime (Marmot et al., 2010). Indeed, for vocabulary knowledge low socioeconomic status (SES) was associated with slower progress suggesting a widening gap over time (Taylor et al., 2013). Importantly, a large proportion of the variability in the *rate* of children's language progress between four and seven years was explained by factors in the child's home learning environment over and above their level of social disadvantage (e.g., TV viewing, number of children's books in the home, frequency of being read to in the early years) (McKean et al., 2015) suggesting potential levers for language interventions in socially disadvantaged families.

How social disadvantage is defined varies among studies as does the developmental window and these factors impact on the findings; for example, low paternal education is associated with a persisting profile (Zambrana et al., 2014) and low maternal education with an improving profile (Henrichs et al., 2011; Zambrana et al., 2014).

In the Australian ELVS cohort SES was not predictive of language ability at two years but was at age four (Reilly et al., 2007, 2010) These findings suggest that while biological mechanisms are more critical drivers for very early language development in infancy, SES influences may take time to exert their effects. Letts et al. (2013) also found a changing association with language scores of maternal education in a large representative sample reporting an association from two to five years, but not from five to seven years. While these findings may be influenced by measurement issues and sampling they might indicate that differing drivers of language development emerge over time, and there may be cumulative effects of risks or possible compensatory effects of factors, for example the universal effect of schooling. A further possibility is that the predictors themselves change.

In statistical models of child development, it is often assumed that risk factors measured typically at baseline, such as a child's SES or family income, are fixed. However, parental income, address, and profession may all change over the course of their child's life. Recently King and colleagues (2017) explored the effect of *change* in maternal education on children's word reading abilities at age seven years: a skill heavily predicated on a child's language development. Increasing maternal education over time, in a model adjusted for income, parity, maternal age, poverty, and child gender, was associated with improved child literacy outcomes. Such analyses speak to issues of shared genetic versus environmental mechanisms for the intergenerational transmission of poor literacy development and, while not definitive, are suggestive of a role of environmental factors over and above shared genetic risks.

Non-verbal skills: Children with low expressive vocabulary at three years in a large nationally representative sample were more likely to be in a resolving than persisting or late emerging language disorder group if they had good rather than poor non-verbal skills (Law et al., 2012). Furthermore, change in non-verbal skills over time may also be important for language pathway profiles with *declining non-verbal skills* shown to be associated with poorer language overall in children with language disorder between 7 and 17 years (Conti-Ramsden et al., 2012) and with late emerging or persisting language disorder in an "at risk" sample of children between three and eight years (Snowling et al., 2016). The nature and degree of reciprocity and interactivity between the language and non-verbal domains over time would appear to be an important area for future research, particularly in community ascertained samples.

Receptive language: Early receptive language difficulties have been proposed as an important risk factor for persisting language difficulties (Marchman & Fernald, 2013) although population studies have demonstrated that these, and other "risks," have limited explanatory power when predicting later language outcomes (Dale et al., 2014; Henrichs et al., 2011). However, receptive language may play an important role in language pathways between three and eight years given that poorer receptive language was a feature of persisting rather than resolving language disorder pathways (Snowling et al., 2016; Zambrana et al., 2014).

Family history: A family history of language and/or literacy difficulties has been associated with persistence of low language in children who are "late talkers," although, as with receptive language difficulties, with limited predictive power. Recently Zambrana et al. (2014) and Snowling et al. (2016) also found an association of family history with *late emerging* profiles from three to five and three to eight years. Snowling et al. (2016) suggest that this may be indicative of differing language disorder phenotypes such that this group may be experiencing the downstream effects of early phonological deficits on progress in broader oral language skills.

35.5 Evidence from neuroimaging studies of DLD

Many of the developmental relationships that we have described are likely to have neurobiological correlates. For this reason, it is important in any discussion of Language Disorder to draw upon the most recent developments in this field. Here we focus on the structure and functions of the brain regions and networks that control language, specifically, as revealed by magnetic resonance imaging (MRI) approaches. We posit that furthering our understanding of neurobiology will inform brain–behavior relationships in the field to refine theoretical models, and arguably has the potential to also inform diagnosis, prognosis, and, potentially, treatment of Language Disorders.

As regards diagnosis, until recently there has been little opportunity for an informed appreciation of the neurobiology of language development and Language Disorder. In the past, we were unable to non-invasively or accurately quantify changes in healthy brain development over time, nor were we able to detect the subtle changes or anomalies associated with neurodevelopmental communication disorders. Thus, we had little insight into the neurological contributions of developmental language and its disorders. To make matters worse in some earlier conceptualizations of Specific Language Impairment, neurological anomalies, had they been identified would have effectively precluded such a diagnosis at all. With the advent of quantitative MRI however, and using matched cohort experimental designs, it is clear that neurodevelopmental communication disorders such as stuttering, childhood apraxia of speech, and language disorder are associated with arguably subtle neural anomalies or differences compared to the brains of TD children. Into the future, there may be the potential to rely more heavily on an individual's neurobiological profile when forming a diagnosis in developmental conditions including Language Disorder, just as we do now in acquired populations (e.g., for differential diagnosis of Language Disorders following stroke).

Greater knowledge of neurobiology may also help inform prognosis. At present, based on our study of "surface" language symptoms alone, we have a limited understanding of which children will have Language Disorders that resolve, which children will have persistent problems and which children will be best placed to compensate for their difficulties. Much MRI work has been conducted on aphasia prognosis following stroke for example, examining an individual's propensity for *absolute* recovery (return to pre-injury levels) versus *relative* recovery (e.g., improvement but not full recovery from the acute injury) (Saur & Hartwigsen, 2012). Further, MRI studies in adults (see Turkeltaub et al., 2011 for a review) and pediatric fields (Liégeois et al., 2014) have indicated that maintaining left hemisphere dominant language function (intrahemispheric reorganization) typically results in better outcomes than becoming right hemisphere dominant for language (interhemispheric reorganization). The general conclusion remains that the left hemisphere appears highly specialized for subserving language and that prognosis will be optimized in cases where left hemisphere function is sufficiently spared or reorganized. In the future, it is plausible that the provision of similar MRI brain data on individuals with developmental language difficulties may assist with predicting outcome.

Greater understanding of neurobiology may also inform development of more targeted therapies based on both brain and symptomatology profiles (Turkeltaub et al., 2011), in better understanding how our treatments work to alter brain function or structure, and in predicting treatment response. Researchers in dyslexia for example have reported that differences in activation in a particular region of the brain (i.e., left inferior parietal lobe) are able to differentiate treatment responders and non-responders (Odegard et al., 2008). In combination with other critical variables, such as environmental factors, into the future we may be able to predict whether individuals with a particular neural profile will be good candidates for particular types of treatments.

35.5.1 The neural correlates of language and language difficulties

A growing body of neuroimaging evidence suggests that differences in language behaviors in children with Language Disorder and TD controls are associated with differences in neural structure and/or function of the brain. Specifically, that children with Language Disorder have anomalies in traditionally recognized language areas including the inferior frontal gyrus (IFG), posterior superior temporal sulcus (pSTG), caudate nucleus, and putamen (see Liégeois et al., 2014; Mayes et al., 2015; Morgan et al., 2016; for reviews). A key hypothesis is that children with Developmental Language Disorder do not show the same left-dominant structural or functional lateralization in core *language brain regions* as observed in children with typical language trajectories (Badcock et al., 2012; de Guibert et al., 2011). This deficit hypothesis has held for almost three decades (Plante et al., 1989) yet empirical brain-based work in this area has been relatively limited until recently, because of a lack of appropriate imaging acquisition and analysis techniques.

While some key findings are relatively consistent across studies, it is important to highlight limitations of existing literature (Liégeois et al., 2014; Mayes et al., 2015; Morgan et al., 2016). Firstly, the inclusion criteria employed for defining Language Disorders across studies, despite the fact that the authors characterize the participants as having "specific" language disorder, varies markedly. As in other aspects of Language Disorder discussed here, this can make drawing comparisons and robust conclusions challenging (Liégeois et al., 2014; Mayes et al., 2015; Morgan et al., 2016). Not only are inclusion criteria for defining Language Disorders disparate, but studies are also variable in the reported cut-points for non-verbal or performance IQ. Studies have also used widely variable methods as regards MRI data acquisition and analysis approaches. Finally, participant samples in existing studies are relatively small and often drawn from clinical samples, limiting generalization of findings to the broader population of individuals with language disorder.

In summary, the field of magnetic resonance neuroimaging has advanced our knowledge of the neurobiological bases of Language Disorders over recent decades. Studies have confirmed that key brain regions thought by our forefathers of postmortem lesion studies to subserve communication hold true for adults and are seen in children. The development of whole brain analysis has advanced historical knowledge that was focused on particular isolated regions of the brain (e.g., Wernicke's and Broca's areas), with a new emphasis on the importance of brain networks (multiple brain regions and their connections) in subserving communication. We have modern theoretical brain-behavior models informed by quantitative structural and functional MRI studies (Skeide et al., 2014). These models not only serve to advance our current understanding of the field but also provide valuable platforms for future hypothesis generation and testing.

There is a long way to go however, before knowledge of the neurobiology of communication can directly impact on education or management for the vast majority of individuals with language disorder. MRI scans remain prohibitively expensive. Further and most critically, subtle anomalies in key brain regions to date can only be detected at a group level. We are still some way from MRI revealed neurobiological data guiding monitoring of typical communication acquisition, learning, and trajectories for individual children.

35.6 Conclusions

We are still a long way from fully describing and understanding the ontogeny of language disorder. Epidemiological, longitudinal, and neurobiological studies have begun to uncover the nature of individual differences between children in their language trajectories, the neural correlates of these differences, their social antecedents, and associated risk and protective factors. On balance, the data relating to social risks and developmental change have shown considerable potential although there remain many issues to address, not least issues of causality. By contrast imaging studies aimed at understanding the neurobiology underpinning Language Disorder have promised much but, to date, have delivered relatively little.

The role of genes in the observed individual differences is also undeniable (see Chapter 37 in this volume). How environmental, genetic, epigenetic, biological, and neurobiological effects interact and unfold over developmental time and what this means for our conceptualization of and interventions for children with language disorder are clearly the next priorities for research.

The science has progressed considerably in the past decade and there is every reason to think that it will continue to do so. It is clear that language disorder is an area which has attracted considerable research interest, albeit not necessarily the corresponding research funding. Researchers commonly cry "more research is needed" but rather than following this tradition we suggest several specific research questions for the next decade which we feel could help us advance the field considerably in the light of the discussion here.

1. How do we integrate what we understand about the temporal characteristics of language change into a meaningful description and diagnostic system that meets the needs of researcher, practitioner, and child? Can we develop time sensitive behavioral phenotypes?
2. Moving beyond categorical toward a dimensional view of language, to what extent do within child characteristics (such as non-verbal performance, memory, executive function) interact across time?

3. To what extent does language mediate the relationship between social risk factors and mental health and/or well-being and does targeted intervention affect such outcomes?
4. What can new technologies (MRI, and so on) tell us about the changing nature of brain structure in childhood and what implications will these have for our understanding of language and language disorder?
5. What evidence is there for genetic and epigenetic effects determining language, language profiles, and indeed language change over time?
6. If change is central to the notion of language disorder what implications does this have for the notion of intervention to ameliorate low language skills or to reduce their impact?

Such an agenda will require interdisciplinarity, collaboration, and the continued adoption of new and rigorous methodologies that has characterized and shaped the history of language disorder.

References

American Psychiatric Association (2013). *Diagnostic and Statistical Manual of Mental Disorders: DSM-5*. American Psychiatric Association, Washington, DC.
Aram, D. M., & Nation, J. E. (1975). Patterns of language behavior in children with developmental language disorders. *Journal of Speech and Hearing Research, 18*, 229–41.
Asbury, K., Wachs, T. D., & Plomin, R. (2005). Environmental moderators of genetic influence on verbal and nonverbal abilities in early childhood. *Intelligence, 33*, 643–61.
Badcock, N. A., Bishop, D. V. M., Hardiman, M. J., Barry, J. G., & Watkins, K. E. (2012). Co-localisation of abnormal brain structure and function in specific language impairment. *Brain and Language, 120*, 310–20.
Beitchman, J. H., Jiang, H., Koyama, E., Johnson, C. J., Escobar, M., Atkinson, L., . . . & Vida, R. (2008). Models and determinants of vocabulary growth from kindergarten to adulthood. *Journal of Child Psychology and Psychiatry, 49*, 626–34.
Beitchman, J. H., Wilson, B., Brownlie, E. B., Walters, H., Inglis, A., & Lancee, W. (1996). Long-term consistency in speech/language profiles: II. Behavioral, emotional, and social outcomes. *Journal of the American Academy of Child and Adolescent Psychiatry, 35*, 815–25.
Bishop, D. V. M. (1997). Cognitive neuropsychology and developmental disorders: uncomfortable bedfellows. *The Quarterly Journal of Experimental Psychology, 50A*, 899–923.
Bishop, D. V. M. (2014). Ten questions about terminology for children with unexplained language problems. *International Journal of Language and Communication Disorders, 49*, 381–415.
Bishop, D. V. M., & Edmundson, A. (1987). Language-impaired 4-year-olds: Distinguishing transient from persistent impairment. *Journal of Speech and Hearing Disorders, 52*, 156–73.
Bishop, D. V. M., & Hayiou-Thomas, M. E. (2008). Heritability of specific language impairment depends on diagnostic criteria. *Genes, Brain and Behavior, 7*(3), 365–72.
Bishop, D. V. M., Snowling, M., Thompson, P. A., Greenhalgh, T., & Catalise Consortium (2016). Catalise: A Multinational and Multidisciplinary Delphi Consensus Study. Identifying Language Impairments in Children. *PLoS One, 11*(7), e0158753.

Bishop, D. V. M., Snowling, M. J., Thompson, P. A., Greenhalgh, T., & Catalise Consortium (2017). Phase 2 of CATALISE: a multinational and multidisciplinary Delphi consensus study of problems with language development: Terminology. *Journal of Child Psychology and Psychiatry*, 58, 1068–80.

Botting, N., Faragher, B., Simkin, Z., Knox, E., & Conti-Ramsden, G. (2001). Predicting pathways of specific language impairment: What differentiates good and poor outcome? *Journal of Child Psychology and Psychiatry*, 42, 1013–20.

Boyle, J. M., McCartney, E., O'Hare, A., & Forbes, J. (2009). Direct versus indirect and individual versus group modes of language therapy for children with primary language impairment: principal outcomes from a randomized controlled trial and economic evaluation. *International Journal of Language and Communication Disorders*, 44, 826–46.

Chiat, S. (2001). Mapping theories of developmental language impairment: Premises, predictions, and evidence. *Language and Cognitive Processes*, 16, 113–42.

Coen, R. (1886). *Pathologie und therapie der sprachanomalien*. Urban & Schwarzenberg, Vienna.

Conti-Ramsden, G., & Botting, N. (1999). Classification of children with specific language impairment: Longitudinal considerations. *Journal of Speech, Language, and Hearing Research*, 42, 1195–204.

Conti-Ramsden, G., Botting, N., Simkin, Z., & Knox, E. (2001). Follow-up of children attending infant language units: outcomes at 11 years of age. *International Journal of Language and Communication Disorders*, 36, 207–19.

Conti-Ramsden, G., St Clair, M. C., Pickles, A., & Durkin, K. (2012). Developmental trajectories of verbal and nonverbals skills in individuals with a history of specific language impairment: from childhood to adolescence. *Journal of Speech, Language, and Hearing Research*, 55, 1716–35.

Dale, P. S., McMillan, A. J., Hayiou-Thomas, M. E., & Plomin, R. (2014). Illusory recovery: Are recovered children with early language delay at continuing elevated risk? *American Journal of Speech-Language Pathology*, 23, 437–47.

de Guibert, C., Maumet, C., Jannin, P., Ferre, J. C., Treguier, C., Barillot, C., & Biraben, A. (2011). Abnormal functional lateralization and activity of language brain areas in typical specific language impairment (developmental dysphasia). *Brain*, 134, 3044–58.

Durkin, K., & Conti-Ramsden, G. (2010). Young people with specific language impairment: A review of social and emotional functioning in adolescence. *Child Language Teaching and Therapy*, 26, 105–21.

Ellis Weismer, S. (2007). Typical talkers, late talkers and children with specific language impairment: A language endowment spectrum? In: Paul, R. (Ed.), *Language Disorders from a Developmental Perspective*. Lawrence Erlbaum, New York, NY.

Ellis Weismer, S., Murray-Branch, J., & Miller, J. F. (1994). A prospective longitudinal study of language development in late talkers. *Journal of Speech, Language, and Hearing Research*, 37, 852–67.

Farkas, G., & Beron, K. (2004). The detailed age trajectory of oral vocabulary knowledge: Differences by class and race. *Social Science Research*, 33, 464–97.

Fergusson, D. M., & Horwood, L. J. (1993). The effect of lead levels on the growth of word recognition in middle childhood. *International Journal of Epidemiology*, 22, 891–7.

Fey, M. E., & Leonard, L. B. (1983). Pragmatic skills of children with specific language impairment. In: Gallagher, T. M., & Prutting, C. (Eds.), *Pragmatic Assessment and Intervention Issues in Language*. College-Hill Press, San Diego, CA.

Froschels, E. (1918). *Kindersprache und aphasie*. Karger, Berlin.
Gall, F. J. (1835). *On the Functions of the Brain and Each of its Parts*, Boston, Marsh, Capen & Lyon.
Hayiou-Thomas, M. E., Dale, P. S., & Plomin, R. (2012). The etiology of variation in language skills changes with development: A longitudinal twin study of language from 2 to 12 years. *Developmental Science, 15*, 233–49.
Hayiou-Thomas, M. E., Oliver, B., & Plomin, R. (2005). Genetic influences on specific versus nonspecific language impairment in 4-year-old twins. *Journal of Learning Disabilities, 38*(3), 222–32.
Henrichs, J., Rescorla, L., Schenk, J. J., Schmidt, H. G., Jaddoe, V. W. V., Hofman, A., . . . & Tiemeier, H. (2011). Examining continuity of early expressive vocabulary development: The generation R study. *Journal of Speech, Language, and Hearing Research, 54*, 854–69.
Johnson, C. J., Beitchman, J. H., & Brownlie, E. B. (2010). Twenty-year follow-up of children with and without speech-language impairments: Family, educational, occupational, and quality of life outcomes. *American Journal of Speech-Language Pathology, 9*, 51–65.
Johnson, C. J., Beitchman, J. H., Young, A., Escobar, M., Atkinson, L., . . . & Wang, M. (1999). Fourteen-year follow-up of children with and without speech/language impairments: Speech/language stability and outcomes. *Journal of Speech, Language, and Hearing Research, 42*, 744–60.
Karlin, I. W. (1954). Aphasias in children. *A.M.A American Journal of Diseases of Children, 87*, 752–67.
Kerr, J. (1917). Congenital or developmental aphasia. *Journal of Delinquency, 2*, 6.
King, T., McKean, C., Rush, R., Westrupp, E., Mensah, F., Reilly, S., & Law, J. (2017). Acquisition of maternal education and its relation to single word reading in middle childhood: An analysis of the Millennium Cohort Study. *Merrill-Palmer Quarterly, 63*(2), 181–209.
Kovas, Y., & Plomin, R. (2006). Generalist genes: Implications for cognitive sciences. *Trends in Cognitive Sciences, 10*, 198–203.
Law, J., McBean, K., & Rush, R. (2011). Communication skills in a population of primary school-aged children raised in an area of pronounced social disadvantage. *International Journal of Language and Communication Disorders, 46*, 657–64.
Law, J., Rush, R., Anandan, C., Cox, M., & Wood, R. (2012). Predicting language change between 3 and 5 years and its implications for early identification. *Pediatrics, 130*, 132–7.
Law, J., Rush, R., Clegg, J., Peters, T., & Roulstone, S. (2015). The role of pragmatics in mediating the relationship between social disadvantage and adolescent behavior. *Journal of Developmental and Behavioral Pediatrics, 36*, 389–98.
Law, J., Tomblin, J. B., & Zhang, X. (2008). Characterizing the growth trajectories of language-impaired children between 7 and 11 years of age. *Journal of Speech, Language, and Hearing Research, 51*, 739–49.
Leonard, L. B. (1972). What is deviant language? *Journal of Speech and Hearing Disorders, 37*, 427–46.
Leonard, L. B. (1981). Facilitating linguistic skills in children with specific language impairment. *Applied Psycholinguistics, 2*, 89–118.
Leonard, L. B. (2007). Processing limitations and the grammatical profile of children with specific language impairment. In: Kail, R. V. (Ed.), *Advances in Child Development and Behaviour*. Elsevier Inc, New York, NY.
Letts, C., Edwards, S., Sinka, I., Schaefer, B., & Gibbons, W. (2013). Socio-economic status and language acquisition: children's performance on the new Reynell Developmental Language Scales. *International Journal of Language and Communication Disorders, 48*(2), 131–43.

Liégeois, F. J., Mayes, A., & Morgan, A. T. (2014). Neural correlates of developmental speech and language disorders: Evidence from neuroimaging. *Current Developmental Disorders Reports*, *1*, 215–27.

Locke, A., Ginsborg, J., & Peers, I. (2002). Development and disadvantage: Implications for the early years and beyond. *International Journal of Language and Communication Disorders*, *37*, 3–15.

Luyten, H., & ten Bruggencate, G. (2011). The presence of Matthew effects in Dutch primary education, development of language skills over a six-year period. *Journal of Learning Disabilities*, *44*, 444–58.

Määttä, S., Laakso, M. L., Tolvanen, A., Ahonen, T., & Aro, T. (2012). Developmental trajectories of early communication skills. *Journal of Speech and Language, and Hearing Research*, *55*, 1083–96.

Marchman, V. A., & Fernald, A. (2013). Variability in real-time spoken language processing in typically developing and late-talking toddlers. In: Rescorla, L. A., & Dale, P. S. (Eds.), *Late Talkers: Language Development, Interventions, and Outcomes* (pp. 145–66). Brookes, Baltimore MD.

Marmot, M., Atkinson, A., Bell, J., Black, C., Broadfoot, P., Cumberlege, J., . . . & Mulgan, G. (2010). *Strategic Review of Health Inequalities in England post-2010: Fair Society, Healthy Lives: The Marmot Review*. UCL, London.

Mayes, A., Reilly, S., & Morgan, A. (2015). Neural correlates of childhood language disorder: A systematic review. *Developmental Medicine and Child Neurology*, *57*, 706–17.

McCall, E. (1911). Two cases of congenital aphasia in children. *British Medical Journal*, *1*, 1105.

McKean, C., Mensah, F. K., Eadie, P., Bavin, E. L., Bretherton, L., Cini, E., & Reilly, S. (2015). Levers for language growth: Characteristics and predictors of language trajectories between 4 and 7 years. *PLoS One*, *10*, e0134251.

McKean, C., Reilly, S., Bavin, E. L., Bretherton, L., Cini, E., Conway, L., . . . & Mensah, F. (2017). Language outcomes at 7 years: Early predictors and co-occurring difficulties. *Pediatrics*, *139*(3), pii: e20161684.

Morgan, A., Bonthrone, A., & Liegeois, F. (2016). Brain basis of childhood speech and language disorders: Are we closer to clinically meaningful MRI markers? *Current Opinion in Pediatrics*, *28*, 725–30.

Norbury, C. F., Gooch, D., Wray, C., Baird, G., Charman, T., Simonoff, E., . . . & Pickles, A. (2016). The impact of nonverbal ability on prevalence and clinical presentation of language disorder: evidence from a population study. *Journal of Child Psychology and Psychiatry*, *57*(11), 1247–57.

Odegard, T. N., Ring, J., Smith, S., Biggan, J., & Black, J. (2008). Differentiating the neural response to intervention in children with developmental dyslexia. *Annals of Dyslexia*, *58*, 1–14.

Peisner-Feinberg, E. S., Burchinal, M. R., Clifford, R. M., Culkin, M. L., Howes, C., Kagan, S. L., & Yazejian, N. (2001). The relation of preschool child-care quality to children's cognitive and social developmental trajectories through second grade. *Child Development*, *72*, 1534–53.

Plante, E., Swisher, L., & Vance, R. (1989). Anatomical correlates of normal and impaired language in a set of dizygotic twins. *Brain and Language*, *37*, 643–55.

Rees, N. S. (1973). Noncommunicative functions of language in children. *Journal of Speech and Hearing Research*, *38*, 98–110.

Reilly, S., McKean, C., Morgan, A., & Wake, M. (2015). Identifying and managing common childhood language and speech impairments. *British Medical Journal (Clinical research ed.), 350*, h2318.

Reilly, S., Tomblin, B., Law, J., McKean, C., Mensah, F. K., Morgan, A., . . . & Wake, M. (2014). Specific language impairment: A convenient label for whom? *International Journal of Language and Communication Disorders, 49*, 416–51.

Reilly, S., Wake, M., Bavin, E. L., Prior, M., Williams, J., Bretherton, L., . . . & Ukoumunne, O. C. (2007). Predicting language at 2 years of age: A prospective community study. *Pediatrics, 120*, e1441–e1449.

Reilly, S., Wake, M., Ukoumunne, O. C., Bavin, E., Prior, M., Cini, E., . . . & Bretherton, L. (2010). Predicting language outcomes at 4 years of age: Findings from the Early Language in Victoria Study. *Pediatrics, 126*, e1530–7.

Rescorla, L. (2002). Language and reading outcomes to age 9 in late-talking toddlers. *Journal of Speech, Language, and Hearing Research, 45*, 360–71.

Rice, M. L., Taylor, C. L., & Zubrick, S. R. (2008). Language outcomes of 7-year-old children with or without a history of late language emergence at 24 months. *Journal of Speech, Language, and Hearing Research, 51*, 394–407.

Rice, M. L., Tomblin, J. B., Hoffman, L., Richman, W. A., & Marquis, J. (2004). Grammatical tense deficits in children with SLI and nonspecific language impairment: Relationships with nonverbal IQ over time. *Journal of Speech, Language, and Hearing Research, 47*, 816–34.

Rice, M. L., Wexler, K., & Hershberger, S. (1998). Tense over time: the longitudinal course of tense acquisition in children with Specific Language Impairment. *Journal of Speech, Language, and Hearing Research, 41*, 1412–31.

Roulstone, S., Law, J., Rush, R., Clegg, J., & Peters, T. (2011). *Investigating the role of language in children's early educational outcomes*: An analysis of data from the Avon Longitudinal Study of Parents and Children (ALSPAC). Nottingham, Department of Education.

Saur, D., & Hartwigsen, G. (2012). Neurobiology of language recovery after stroke: Lessons from neuroimaging studies. *Archives of Physical Medicine and Rehabilitation, 93*, S15–S25.

Schoon, I., Parsons, S., Rush, R., & Law, J. (2010). Children's language ability and psychosocial development: A 29-year follow-up study. *Pediatrics, 126*, e73–80.

Schwartz, R. G. (2017). Specific language impairment. In: Schwartz, R. G. (Ed.), *Handbook of Child Language Disorders*, 2nd Edition (pp. 3–43). Psychology Press, Hove.

Skeide, M. A., Brauer, J., & Friederici, A. D. (2014). Syntax gradually segregates from semantics in the developing brain. *NeuroImage, 100*, 106–11.

Snowling, M. J., Duff, F. J., Nash, H. M., & Hulme, C. (2016). Language profiles and literacy outcomes of children with resolving, emerging, or persisting language impairments. *Journal of Child Psychology and Psychiatry, 57*(12), 1360–9.

Stark, R. E., & Tallal, P. (1981). Selection of children with specific language deficits. *Journal of Speech and Hearing Disorders, 46*, 114–22.

Stothard, S. E., Snowling, M. J., Bishop, D. V. M., Chipchase, B. B., & Kaplan, C. A. (1998). Language-impaired preschoolers: A follow-up into adolescence. *Journal of Speech, Language, and Hearing Research, 41*, 407–18.

Stuebing, K. K., Barth, A. E., Trahan, L. H., Radhika, R., Reddy, R. R., Miciak, J., & Fletcher, J. M. (2015). Are child cognitive characteristics strong predictors of responses to intervention? A meta-analysis. *Review of Educational Research, 85*, 395–429.

Tambyraja, S. R., Schmitt, M. B., Farquharson, K., & Justice, L. M. (2015). Stability of language and literacy profiles of children with language impairment in the public schools. *Journal of Speech, Language, and Hearing Research, 58*, 1167–81.

Taylor, C. L., Christensen, D., Lawrence, D., Mitrou, F., & Zubrick, S. R. (2013). Risk factors for children's receptive vocabulary development from four to eight years in the Longitudinal Study of Australian Children. *PLoS One, 8*, e73046.

Thomas, M. S. C. (2005). Constraints on language development: Insights from developmental disorders. In: Fletcher, P., & Miller, J. F. (Eds.), *Developmental Theory and Language Disorders*, 4th Edition. John Benjamins Publishing Company, Amsterdam.

Thomas, M. S., Annaz, D., Ansari, D., Scerif, G., Jarrold, C., Karmiloff-Smith, A. (2009). Using developmental trajectories to understand developmental disorders. *Journal of Speech, Language, and Hearing Research, 52*(2), 336–58.

Tomblin, B. (2008). Validating diagnostic standards for specific language impairment using adolescent outcomes. In: Norbury, C. F., Tomblin, B., & Bishop, D. V. M. (Eds.), *Understanding Developmental Language Disorders: From Theory to Practice* (pp. 93–114). Psychology Press, Hove.

Tomblin, J. B., Zhang, X., Buckwalter, P., & Catts, H. (2000). The association of reading disability, behavioral disorders, and language impairment among second-grade children. *Journal of Child Psychology and Psychiatry, 41*, 473–82.

Tomblin, J. B., Zhang, X., Buckwalter, P., & O'Brien, M. (2003). The stability of primary language disorder: Four years after kindergarten diagnosis. *Journal of Speech, Language, and Hearing Research, 46*, 1283–96.

Turkeltaub, P. E., Messing, S., Norise, C., & Hamilton, R. H. (2011). Are networks for residual language function and recovery consistent across aphasic patients? *Neurology, 76*, 1726–34.

Ukoumunne, O. C., Wake, M., Carlin, J., Bavin, E. L., Lum, J., Skeat, J., . . . & Reilly, S. (2012). Profiles of language development in pre-school children: A longitudinal latent class analysis of data from the Early Language in Victoria Study. *Child: Care, Health and Development, 38*, 341–9.

Vaisse, L. (1866). Des sourds-muets et de certains cas d'aphasie congenitale. *Bulletin de la Societe d'Anthropologie de Paris*.

Wake, M., Tobin, S., Levickis, P., Gold, L., Zens, N., Goldfeld, S., . . . & Reilly, S. (2014). Five-year old outcomes of population-based intervention for preschoolers with language delay: The Language for Learning randomised trial. *Pediatrics, 132*, e895–904.

Weiner, P. S. (1974). Language-delayed child at adolescence. *Journal of Speech and Hearing Disorders, 39*, 202–12.

Westrupp, E., Reilly, S., McKean, C., Law, J., Mensah, F., & Nicholson, J. (submitted). Language growth and trajectories of hyperactivity-inattention and emotional symptoms from childhood to adolescence: The role of literacy and peer problems.

Worster-Drought, C., & Allen, I. (1929). Congenital auditory imperceptions (congenital word deafness): With report of a case. *Journal of Neurology and Psychopathology, 9*, 193–208.

Yew, S. G. K., & O'Kearney, R. (2013). Emotional and behavioural outcomes later in childhood and adolescence for children with specific language impairments: Meta-analyses of controlled prospective studies. *Journal of Child Psychology and Psychiatry, 54*, 516–24.

Zambrana, I. M., Pons, F., Eadie, P., & Ystrom, E. (2014). Trajectories of language delay from age 3 to 5: persistence, recovery and late onset. *International Journal of Language and Communication Disorders, 49*, 304–16.

Zubrick, S. R., Taylor, C. L., & Christensen, D. (2015). Patterns and predictors of language and literacy abilities 4–10 years in the longitudinal study of Australian children. *PLoS One, 10*, e0135612.

Zubrick, S. R., Taylor, C. L., Rice, M. L., & Slegers, D. W. (2007). Late language emergence at 24 months: An epidemiological study of prevalence, predictors, and covariates. *Journal of Speech, Language, and Hearing Research, 50*, 1562–92.

SECTION II
Phylogenetic development

CHAPTER 36

EVOLUTION OF SPEECH

BART DE BOER AND TESSA VERHOEF

36.1 Introduction

SPEECH is the physical signal used to convey language. This article focuses on the evolution of modern humans' anatomical and cognitive abilities to deal with these physical signals. The focus of the article will be on spoken language (i.e., the vocal-auditory modality), but many of the cognitive abilities needed for dealing with speech are also essential for dealing with sign language. Therefore, the article will also refer to the visual-gestural modality when necessary.

Because speech is a physical signal, it is easier to find precursors in closely related species such as apes and monkeys and analogues in more distantly related species, such as songbirds and parrots. Thus, it is possible to establish what has evolved since the (presumably non-linguistic) last common ancestor with apes and what ecological circumstances may have influenced the evolution of speech and language. Moreover, there may be physical/anatomical adaptations to speech that can be traced in the fossil record, thus making it possible to establish some limits on when complex vocal behavior (and presumably language) may have started to evolve. Therefore, the first section of this article will discuss speech-related behaviors and anatomical adaptations in other species, while fossil evidence that may be pertinent to speech will be discussed in the second part.

In addition to being physical signals, speech (and sign) are pre-symbolic in the sense that they do not consist of clearly distinguishable discrete building blocks. Indeed, it turns out to be extremely hard to build computer systems that can cut up a continuous and noisy stream of speech (or sign) into words, syllables, or phonemes (Versteegh et al., 2015 present a benchmark and a list of example computational approaches to this problem). This indicates that the human ability to learn the building blocks of speech and the rules with which they are combined involves complex and potentially specialized cognitive mechanisms. It has been proposed that the cognitive mechanisms for dealing with this phonological structure are the precursors for dealing with syntactic structure (Carstairs-McCarthy, 1999). Cognitive mechanisms for dealing with speech have of course been the subject of study in linguistics for a long time, and the subject is too vast for this article. Therefore, we focus on studies that take an explicit evolutionary point of view.

Taking evolution into account does complicate the study of cognitive adaptations for speech somewhat. First of all, it means that we are not just interested in how language works in the brain, but also in which of the cognitive mechanisms have undergone selective pressure related to speech and language. Secondly, language is not just the result of biological evolution; it is also the result of cultural evolution. It has been shown that cultural evolution tends to complicate the relation between cognitive biases and observed properties of language. Cultural evolution may instigate certain properties of language without there being cognitive specializations (i.e., universals of vowel systems can be explained as the effect of cultural evolution under pressure for effective communication, de Boer, 2000). Furthermore, for certain types of cognitive biases related to discrete traits of language (e.g., a preference for a certain word order) it has been shown that only small biases can evolve (Thompson, Kirby, & Smith, 2016).

Such biases will be difficult to detect experimentally. On the other hand, it has also been shown that for continuously variable traits the co-evolution of biology and culture can result in arbitrarily strong adaptation (de Boer, 2016). When experimentally investigating cognitive adaptations related to speech, sign, and language, one therefore needs to tease apart the effects of culture and cognition and in addition one needs to figure out which aspects of the cognitive machinery may have undergone changes (with respect to the last common ancestor) that were selected for through evolution because of speech and language. Experimental work along these lines will therefore be discussed in the third part of this article.

36.2 Comparative evidence

Comparing human abilities for speech with those of other apes makes it possible to establish the abilities of the last common ancestor (the one with chimpanzees lived about five to eight million years ago, Jensen-Seaman & Hooper-Boyd, 2013) and therefore which abilities must have emerged since. Comparing other groups (such as monkeys or mammals) with humans makes it possible to establish when characteristics that are shared with apes may have evolved. Here we will focus mostly on comparison with other primates (apes and monkeys) because the changes that occurred since the last common ancestor (and therefore recently) may have happened under selective pressure related to language and speech and can thus be candidates for genuine adaptations[1] to language.

36.2.1 Comparison with apes—evolutionary homologies

One important difference between humans and all other apes is in the anatomy of the vocal tract (see Fig. 36.1). Humans are unique in that they have a rounded tongue, a lower

---

[1] We are of course aware that adaptation is not the only process that happens in evolution; especially random drift is a very important process in small populations. However, the properties of human (linguistic) cognition that are interesting for linguists are the ones that have undergone selective pressures related to speech and language, hence our focus on adaptation.

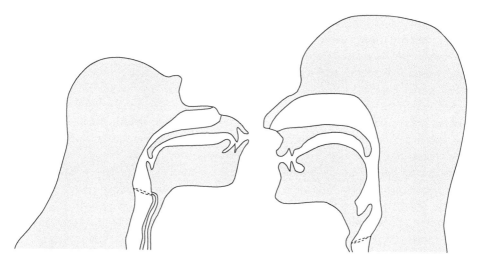

FIG. 36.1 Comparison of mid-sagittal outlines of the chimpanzee (left) and modern human vocal tract. White areas indicate air spaces. Dashed lines indicate the vocal folds.

larynx, and a velum that cannot connect with the epiglottis. Moreover, humans lack air sacs (Fitch, 2000).

The most important difference in vocal tract anatomy between humans and other apes is that the human tongue is rounder. In all other apes (and indeed all other primates) the horizontal (oral) part of the tongue is much longer than the vertical (pharyngeal) part. This anatomy is related to the position of the larynx, which is lower in humans than in other apes, and the anatomy of the velum (the soft palate), which in apes reaches down to the epiglottis—the cartilaginous structure that closes the trachea (windpipe) when food is swallowed. Because of the lower larynx and the higher velum, adult humans cannot make a seal between the nasal passage and the trachea and therefore have a somewhat higher risk of choking on their food (Heimlich, 1975). According to a long tradition of research (de Boer, 2010; Lieberman, Crelin, & Klatt, 1972; Negus, 1938) this unusual anatomical configuration is advantageous for producing a larger number of speech sounds, and the selective advantage this provides offsets the selective disadvantage of the higher risk of choking.

According to this point of view, the configuration of the human vocal tract with an approximately equally long horizontal and vertical part makes it easier to control two acoustic cavities independently: one in the pharyngeal part of the vocal tract and one in the oral part. The typical primate vocal tract with a flat tongue can easily control one cavity that spans the whole vocal tract, but has more difficulties controlling two independent cavities (e.g., de Boer & Fitch, 2010). The two-cavity vocal tract (often somewhat misleadingly referred to as a two-tube vocal tract) makes it easier to make distinctions in the second formant. Phonetically this corresponds to more distinctions along the continuum from [i] to [u] and to more extreme front and back vowels such as [i] and [u] whereas an ape would typically be limited to [ɨ] and [ʉ]. As for distinctions in the first formant (roughly corresponding to vowel height), the modern human vocal tract does not have an advantage over the typical ape vocal tract.

Although much has been made of this difference in older work (Lieberman et al., 1972) more recent work downplays its importance somewhat. One reason is that there are modern human languages with limited vowel systems (for an overview of vowel system diversity, see J.-L. Schwartz, Boë, Vallée, & Abry, 1997) indicating that a full vowel space is not required for complex language. Another reason is that it has been found that descent of the larynx already occurs in chimpanzees (Nishimura, 2003) thus indicating that larynx descent may have started under selective pressures unrelated to speech. Finally, it turns out that chewing, swallowing, and sucking involve tongue motion and control that can be as extreme (or more extreme) as in speech (Hiiemae & Palmer, 2003), thus undermining the argument that speech requires modifications of the control of the tongue. Nevertheless, if it can be established that the human vocal tract is in some way optimal for producing as large a range of speech sounds as possible, and is less optimal for other functions (such as chewing or swallowing) than the ancestral vocal tract, this is an indication that it has undergone selective pressure related to speech, even though such anatomical adaptations may not be a necessary condition for intelligible speech. Debate about this question is not settled however (Badin, Boë, Sawallis, & Schwartz, 2014; de Boer, 2010).

Another important difference between (great) apes and humans is that all great apes except humans (as well as some gibbon and monkey species) have air sacs (Hewitt, MacLarnon, & Jones, 2002). Air sacs in great apes are large volumes that are connected to the vocal tract just above the vocal folds. They tend to be located on the chest in chimpanzees, gorillas, and orangutans. Their function is hypothesized to be related to vocalization and it turns out that air sacs help to amplify low-pitched sounds (de Boer, 2009; Riede, Tokuda, Munger, & Thomson, 2008). This would make them useful to either exaggerate size or to signal over long distance through dense foliage. At the same time, the presence of an air sac reduces the ability of a vocal tract to make distinctive sounds (de Boer, 2012b) and would potentially also interfere with the ability of the vocal folds to vibrate regularly (de Boer, 2012a). It therefore seems highly likely that air sacs were lost in the human lineage and at least plausible that this was related to vocal behavior. Moreover, there is fossil evidence related to the loss of air sacs (see the next section).

In addition to anatomical differences, there are also important behavioral differences between humans and other (great) apes with respect to vocalization. First of all, apes tend to have less voluntary control over vocalization in the sense that their vocalizations tend to be more directly triggered by external events (Tomasello & Zuberbühler, 2002). Such vocalizations are comparable to human laughter and cries of pain, pleasure, or exertion. Secondly, they are very bad at imitating sounds: humans are much better at imitating sounds than any other ape, and probably than any other mammal.

Both humans' better ability for voluntary control over vocalization and for vocal imitation may be related to humans having more direct connections between the cortex and the motor neurons controlling the larynx (Fitch, 2010, section 9.4 and references therein contains a discussion of these matters). Nevertheless, other apes do have some rudimentary abilities for vocal control and vocal learning. From the wild there is evidence of vocal learning in chimpanzees (Crockford, Herbinger, Vigilant, & Boesch, 2004), and a case has also been made for a cultural variation in orangutan calls (Lameira et al., 2013). In captivity chimpanzees have learned to produce at least some very simple speech-like sounds (Hayes & Hayes, 1951) while groups of chimpanzees in zoos can adapt their vocalizations to those of other groups (Watson et al., 2015). Orangutans in captivity have learned to whistle and blow raspberries (Wich et al., 2009) and the captive gorilla Koko has learned to produce several oral behaviors: coughing on command (i.e., making and releasing a glottal stop), blowing into a harmonica, huffing on (and polishing) glasses, and grunting into a toy telephone (de Boer & Perlman, 2014; Perlman, Patterson, & Cohn, 2012). In addition, it has been observed that chimpanzees appear to use alarm calls in an intentional way (Schel et al., 2013) and adapt their vocalization to whether there is an audience present or not, indicating at least some degree of control over these supposedly involuntary vocalizations. All in all, it appears that although vocal control and the ability for vocal imitation in humans is much better than that of other apes, nevertheless the beginnings of these behaviors were already present in the last common ancestor with other apes. Interestingly, it appears that apes are better at imitating and voluntarily using gestures (Pika, Liebal, Call, & Tomasello, 2005).

Summarizing, it appears that since the last common ancestor with other apes, some important modifications have taken place to the human vocal tract, and it is likely that these modifications were under selective pressure related to language and speech. On the other hand, it is unlikely that these modifications were essential in the sense that language would have been impossible without them. In this respect, the cognitive adaptations to speech that happened since the last common ancestor—the ability for precise vocal and articulatory control and the ability to learn and imitate speech sounds—appear to be more fundamental.

36.2.2 Comparison with other species— functional "universals"

A rather different way of using comparative data is trying to establish how evolutionary pressures determine a behavior by looking at the evolution of comparable behaviors in species that do not inherit that behavior from a common ancestor. The process by which similar traits evolve independently in similar circumstances is called evolutionary analogy or parallel evolution. In the case of human language, candidate parallel behaviors would be, for instance, learned vocalizations of different orders of birds, learned vocalizations in whales and dolphins, and learned vocalizations in several other species, such as bats, elephants, and seals.

One thing that can be learned from such comparisons is whether there are universal mechanisms and phenomena that re-occur in independently evolved vocal communication systems. Examples of such universal phenomena could be the use of some kind of combinatorial structure in systems with many utterances (e. g. Zuidema & de Boer, 2009) the existence of a critical period in learned systems (e. g. Doupe & Kuhl, 1999) and the interaction of biological constraints and cultural transmission to drive learned systems of signals toward certain preferred sets of signals (de Boer, 2000; Feher et al., 2009).

Combinatorial structure is the reuse of a (small) number of building blocks to build a larger set of utterances or to build more extended utterances. It is a property of many signaling systems that are often described as song: whale song (Payne & McVay, 1971), birdsong (Bolhuis, Okanoya, & Scharff, 2010; Doupe & Kuhl, 1999), or gibbon song (Geissmann, 2002; Mitani & Marler, 1989). It is also a property of human speech. It turns out that sequentially combining a limited set of building blocks is in fact an optimal way of creating a large set of signals that is robust to noise (Zuidema & de Boer, 2009). It seems that in most if not all larger primate call systems, some form of recombination is used (see the references in Table 1 of McComb & Semple, 2005).

A critical period is a limited period in early life in which a behavior can be acquired. After this period, it becomes impossible or much more difficult to acquire the behavior. Language and especially speech provide prime examples of a critical period: although language is acquired effortlessly early in life, after a certain age (which may be different for different aspects of language, but which is usually considered to be before puberty, Hurford, 1991) learning it becomes much more difficult. The critical period is especially relevant for speech, as accent-less pronunciation is very hard to acquire for most adults learning a new language. Critical periods are also an important element of song learning in many songbird species (Doupe & Kuhl, 1999). However, it seems that critical periods may have very different reasons in different species. In human language, critical periods have been explained as a side effect of either first language learning (Kuhl, Williams, Lacerda, Stevens, & Lindblom, 1992) or of the evolutionary trade-off between the cost and the benefits of language learning (Hurford, 1991; Komarova & Nowak, 2001). Arguments have also been made about a critical period being evolutionary advantageous because it can cause language to be an honest signal of group membership (e. g. Cohen, 2012). Different arguments have been proposed for a critical period in songbirds: in songbirds, the critical period has been proposed as an essential element to make the complexity of the learned song an honest signal of the individual's fitness (Catchpole & Slater, 2008, section 7.8). In addition, there are species that learn complex vocalizations but that do not appear to have a critical period: some songbirds as well as parrots (Toft & Wright, 2015, pp. 104–7) continue to be able to learn new signals during their lives, and humpback whales change their songs regularly (Mercado, Herman, & Pack, 2005). Even in humans the critical period effect is much less strong for vocabulary learning than for learning of speech sounds or morphology.

The interaction between cultural transmission and biological constraints plays a role in all learned systems of behaviors. This interaction can sometimes lead to somewhat surprising results. For instance, an experiment with zebra finches has shown that although zebra finches that are raised in isolation will learn to sing atypical songs, the songs of subsequent generations that first learn from this isolated individual and then subsequently from each other, will after only a few (two or three) generations revert to a song that is indistinguishable from normal song (Feher et al., 2009). Apparently, there are slight biases in zebra finch song learning that nudge them toward a species-typical song, without completely constraining the song. Similar mechanisms operate in human speech: although human infants learn to imitate their parents and peers very closely (much closer in fact than necessary to produce the basic phonological distinctions in a language, as is evident from the subtle differences in pronunciation between closely related dialects) when learning is repeated over many generations, the resulting sound systems show clear universal tendencies (de Boer, 2000; Maddieson, 1984). It has been proposed that this interaction between small biases and cultural evolution plays an important role in explaining many properties of human language (Kirby, Griffiths, & Smith, 2014). The field of language evolution has only recently started coming to terms with the implications of this interaction (see also section 36.4 and Chapter 38, this volume, for empirical investigation of some of these issues).

36.2.3 Comparison with other species—evolutionary analogy

Another way that comparisons of human speech with independently evolved vocal behaviors can shed light on the evolution of speech is by elucidating what the evolutionary pressures were that led to the observed behaviors. By analogy, these pressures may also have played a role in the evolution of human speech and language. In this case, it is essential that one can compare multiple species that show different levels of complexity of the trait under investigation, and that one identifies the selective pressures that led to (for instance) complex vocal learning in one case and innately specified vocalizations in another.

Songbirds are perhaps the best-investigated group of species that have evolved parallel vocal behaviors. There are indeed striking parallels between bird song and human speech (Bolhuis et al., 2010; Doupe & Kuhl, 1999). Both have a critical period for learning, both combine discrete building blocks into larger utterances and both show similar organization in the brain. Even some of the genetic and molecular underpinnings may be shared in song birds and humans (Bolhuis et al., 2010, Box 5)[2]. Moreover, there is a very large number of song bird species with widely differing vocal learning abilities, ranging from species that do not learn at all (e.g., song sparrows) through species that adapt their songs a little (e.g., chaffinches) and species that learn their songs, but rely on a species-specific repertoire of building blocks (e.g., zebra finches) up to highly accomplished imitators (e.g., reed warblers and lyre birds). Even within closely related groups of species (e.g., the warblers) imitation abilities vary enormously.

A lot of the research in this area focuses on single species, with a bias toward those species that are easy to keep in captivity such as zebra finches. Through experiments and fieldwork about mating preferences, it has been shown that in songbirds most of the selective pressure appears to be due to sexual selection (Catchpole & Slater, 2008, Ch. 7) Apparently vocal learning ability is an honest signal for overall fitness. This may have to do with the fact that parasite load influences the ability to learn song, and therefore individuals with a lower parasite load have better (more diverse, more complex) songs (Catchpole & Slater, 2008, section 7.8). As parasite load correlates inversely with an individual's ability to raise young, it makes sense that females prefer mates with a lower parasite load.

Although research on individual species therefore allows us to understand what the selective advantage of vocal learning is in *that* species, the results do not necessarily generalize to other birds, let alone to humans.

There is however research that tackles the question of different selective pressures in closely related species directly. The work by Honda and Okanoya (1999) investigates (domesticated) Bengalese finches and their wild ancestors, white-rumped munias. They find that the relaxation of selective pressure due to domestication leads to more complex songs. Interestingly, domestication (or rather self-domestication) has been proposed as one of the factors leading to complex human language (Deacon, 2010).

Bird song may in fact not be the best analogy to human speech when studying its evolution. Bird song tends to be produced almost exclusively by males, and for very limited

---

[2] Shared molecular underpinnings do not necessarily mean that traits are inherited from a shared common ancestor. They can also indicate that evolution has recruited similar structures for similar functions, comparable to the way front limbs have turned into wings in bats, birds, and pterosaurs.

purposes: territorial defense and attracting mates. Although these differences may be less important when studying the neurology and the genetics of bird song and language, they are extremely important when studying the selective pressures that led to more complex speech. A better parallel in birds is to be found in parrots. Parrots are proverbial vocal learners, and their learned vocalizations tend to be contact calls, which signify individual identity and group membership (Toft & Wright, 2015, pp. 104–7). Moreover, in parrots both males and females are vocal learners, although males do seem to do a bit more learning as adults. In the parrots and their allies (order Psittaciformes) there is also a wide variety of species with different abilities for vocal learning, although they are less studied in this respect.

Research with the African Grey parrot Alex has shown evidence for phonological awareness (Pepperberg, 2007) in the sense that he could identify phonological building blocks of the words he learned, and could recombine these into novel utterances. Although songbirds also combine song elements into new songs and may even incorporate elements from other species' songs (or even environmental sounds) this ability is generally considered more comparable to human syntactic ability, where words are combined into sentences. It is not clear whether parrot abilities and songbird abilities are different in this respect. However, in comparative research of zebra finch (song bird) and budgerigar (parrot) learning, it has been shown that budgerigars can learn somewhat more complex patterns (Spierings & Ten Cate, 2016). Finally, cockatoos have been shown to be able to entrain to a beat (Patel, Iversen, Bregman, & Schulz, 2009), an ability that the authors propose as related to vocal learning.

Although these are behaviors from three different species, it appears as if parrots are at least as interesting as vocal learners as songbirds are. This makes them more attractive targets for research into evolutionary analogy, because the role of their vocalizations is more similar to that of language which has been proposed by Dunbar (1996) to have evolved from vocal grooming, a function that is closely related to that of contact calls. Unfortunately, parrots are much more difficult to investigate in captivity in an ethically appropriate manner than small songbirds while in the wild many of the larger-brained parrot species are highly endangered.

There are several other groups of species that have been proposed as promising candidates for examples of evolutionary analogy to human speech. Bats form a very large group of mammals, and some are vocal learners (Boughman, 1998). The advantage of bats is that they are relatively easy to study in a laboratory setting in principle, that they tend to be social species (such that the use of their vocalizations is more closely related to the way primates use their vocalizations than birdsong is) and that they are mammals (i.e., more closely related to humans than any bird species). A disadvantage is that they appear to use vocal learning in much more limited ways than songbirds or parrots. Their vocal learning is perhaps more comparable to that of certain humming bird species. Another group of mammals that has been proposed is that of seals, sea lions, and walruses—the pinnipeds (Ravignani et al., 2016, for a review). This is a group of animals that is relatively easy to study in captivity and to train for experiments, that is social and intelligent, and that shows different levels of vocal behaviors in different species. A possible disadvantage is that their vocal learning appears to be related mostly to sexual display analogous to birdsong. Finally, elephants (Poole, Tyack, Stoeger-Horwath, & Watwood, 2005) and cetaceans are also vocal learners, but it is obviously very difficult to study these animals experimentally, while in the case of elephants there are only three species so ecological comparison is hardly possible.

36.3 Fossil evidence

Because speech is the most physical aspect of language, it is the aspect of language for which there may be the most direct physical evidence. However, speech itself is ephemeral, and leaves no fossil traces. Moreover, the vocal tract consists almost exclusively of soft tissue, and this does not fossilize well. Although there are some examples of prehistoric *Homo sapiens* individuals that have been mummified (Ötzi the iceman probably being the most famous example) no such remains exist of other members of the genus *Homo*. Fortunately, there are several other fossil indicators that may be informative.

The most discussed (if not the most notorious) proposed fossil indicator of the presence of speech is the position of the larynx (see also the discussion in section 36.2.1 about comparison with apes). The problem with the position of the larynx is not only that it may be less important than once thought, but also that fossils do not provide good evidence of its position. Some indication can be obtained by looking at a number of bony landmarks, such as the position of the skull, vertebrae, and the lower jaw, and by looking at the shape of the hyoid bone (Fig. 36.2), but even then, there is considerable leeway in reconstructing the vocal tract. However, there does appear to be an emerging consensus toward a more modern human-like vocal tract for Neanderthals (Barney, Martelli, Serrurier, & Steele, 2012, for review).

The hyoid bone however, which is the only bony part of the vocal tract, provides other more concrete indications. Several fossil hyoid bones and fragments have been found for Neanderthals (Arensburg et al., 1989) *Homo heidelbergensis* of 400,000 years ago (Martínez et al., 2008) and another approximately equally old European *Homo* species (Capasso, Michetti, & D'Anastasio, 2008) as well as an *Australopithecus afarensis* hyoid fragment of approximately 3.15 million years old (Alemseged et al., 2006). Comparison of the shape of

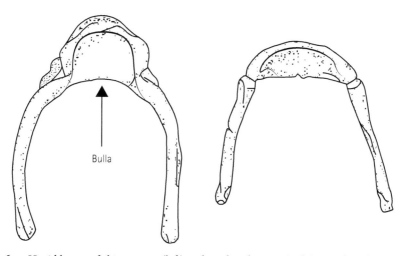

FIG. 36.2 Hyoid bones of chimpanzee (left) and modern human (right) seen from below with the front to the top. The bulla is indicated with an arrow. Note that it is absent in the modern human hyoid.

© Bart de Boer, 2017.

the fossil hyoid bones (and more specifically its bulla) indicate that by 400,000 years ago the hyoid bone was essentially the same as that of modern *Homo sapiens*, while the earlier *Australopithecus* hyoid bone was essentially chimpanzee-like. This has been interpreted to indicate that Australopithecines still had air sacs, while *Homo heidelbergenis* (and by implication Neanderthals) had lost them. As has been pointed out here, the loss of air sacs may have been an adaptation to complex vocal communication. Moreover, a study of the detailed structure of a Neanderthal hyoid bone (D'Anastasio et al., 2013) has shown that the way muscles attached to it was essentially the same as in modern humans. This indicates that tongue musculature was very similar for Neanderthals and modern humans.

A very different fossil indicator of the presence of speech has to do with the fine control over breathing that is necessary for speech. MacLarnon and Hewitt (2004) have proposed that for such fine control a better innervation of the intercostal muscles (the muscles between the ribs that control breathing during speaking) is necessary, and that this is reflected in a relatively larger thoracic vertebral canal (the hole in the spinal column through which the relevant nerves pass). Measuring the thoracic vertebral canal in different extinct and living species, MacLarnon and Hewitt draw the conclusion that the thoracic vertebral canal is enlarged in modern humans and Neanderthals compared to chimpanzees, but of chimpanzee-like size in *Homo ergaster*. This indicates comparable breathing control in modern humans and Neanderthals, but not in hominins that lived about 1.5 million years ago.

A similar study was attempted for the hypoglossal canal, the hole (or rather two holes because of bilateral symmetry) in the occipital bone through which the hypoglossal nerves that innervate the tongue pass (Kay, Cartmill, & Balow, 1998) and concluded that Neanderthals and *Homo sapiens* had similarly enlarged hypoglossal nerves, while earlier hominins and other apes did not. It turned out however, that the study was underpowered and using a more appropriate analysis, it was shown that a statistically significant difference between the different groups could not be shown (DeGusta, Gilbert, & Turner, 1999).

All the aforementioned studies have looked at the production of complex vocalizations. One study has looked at the perception of speech. Martínez et al. (2004) have reconstructed the sensitivity of hearing of different living and fossil species by modeling the acoustic properties of the middle ear on the basis of the dimensions of the different bones and holes involved. They find that *Homo heidelbergensis* and modern humans have increased sensitivity in the range from 2 to 4 KHz compared to chimpanzees and interpret this as an indication of evolution related to speech. However, the frequency range that is generally assumed to be most important for speech is between 0.25 to 3 KHz and in addition, the sensitivity curves that Martínez et al. calculate are expected to be very sensitive to small changes in parameter values, but they do not present any measure of variation, and therefore this result must be considered somewhat tentative.

There are undoubtedly more potential fossil indications of speech that have not been investigated yet. One potential property is the modern human chin: humans are the only ape that has a protruding chin, and even Neanderthals did not have a protruding chin (J. H. Schwartz & Tattersall, 2000). It has been argued that the chin has undergone selection (Pampush, 2015) and there has been at least a century of speculation that it may have something to do with speech (Ichim, Kieser, & Swain, 2007; Weidenreich, 1904). However, there is as yet not widely accepted theory that links the modern human chin to speech rather than to other possible functions in an evolutionary scenario.

36.4 Experimental Work

In the field of language evolution as well as in studies of the evolution of speech specifically (e.g., de Boer, 2000, 2000; de Boer & Zuidema, 2010) computer simulations have been used effectively to investigate the effects of evolutionary processes and mechanisms in a controlled way. These models made it possible to fast-forward developments in populations of interacting individuals over many generations in a short time. They were used for instance to show that self-organizing principles could explain the emergence of basic features of language and speech without the need to assume language-specific innate structures in the human brain. Such models planted the seeds for important new insights in how language may have evolved, but to achieve the necessary levels of abstraction in the creation of these models, they are often quite far removed from the full complexity of human communication. In response to this, researchers started to recreate the controlled, simulated set-up of computational models in the laboratory with human participants.

Most human participants, however, already have life-long experience with a spoken language. So, how can we investigate the evolution of speech in the laboratory with modern humans? In language evolution experiments participants typically do not communicate with an existing spoken language, but they develop or learn a fictional miniature language. These artificial languages are usually produced with a special device or involve restrictions so that the influence of previous experience with speech can be reduced.

One of the first studies that explicitly modeled the emergence of a communication system with human participants was conducted by Galantucci (2005). In this experiment, pairs of participants were asked to play a multiplayer video game in which communication was limited to the use of a special graphical device. This device was designed to be different from real spoken language, but it resembled features of the speech signal. The graphical signals faded over time and the mapping between the drawing and what the other person perceived was not transparent. This prevented the use of symbols or pictures. The success of solving the game depended on cooperation between the participants, and communication systems emerged quickly. Interestingly, the sign systems that emerged all were approximately equally effective as communication systems, but there was a wide variation in the types of signals and what these signals encoded.

Experiments like these reveal what kind of aspects of speech signals might emerge as the result of cultural processes, and what kind of constraints emerging signals might adapt to. Various processes drive the cultural evolution of languages. One example is *social coordination*. As people repeatedly interact with each other, they have to find alignment and agree on shared signals to communicate expressively (Fusaroli & Tylén, 2012; Garrod & Doherty, 1994; Garrod, Fay, Lee, Oberlander, & MacLeod, 2007; Steels, 2006). Mappings between signal and meaning and conventions emerge on the basis of shared communication history. This process has been studied experimentally with the use of methods such as those in the study by Galantucci (2005) just described, but also through more direct *communication game tasks*, in which participants communicate in dyads or small groups about certain concepts, often using a communication medium that is linguistically novel to them (Fay, Arbib, & Garrod, 2013; Garrod et al., 2007; Healey, Swoboda, Umata, & King, 2007; Theisen, Oberlander, & Kirby, 2010).

Another important process is *transmission*. Languages are passed on from generation to generation as new individuals learn by observing others. This transmission process also influences how linguistic systems are shaped (Christiansen & Chater, 2008; Kirby, Cornish, & Smith, 2008; Kirby & Hurford, 2002; Smith, Kirby, & Brighton, 2003). When a system is transmitted from generation to generation it is filtered through the cognitive constraints of learners. Only structures that are easily learned and remembered will be reproduced. This process is simulated in experiments within the framework of iterated learning. Iterated learning is defined as "The process by which an individual learns a behavior by exposure to another individual's behavior, who acquired that behavior in the same way" (Kirby, Griffiths, & Smith, 2014) and it is discussed in more detail in Chapter 38, but see also Kirby et al. (2014) for a recent overview of this framework.

In iterated learning experiments, participants are asked to learn and reproduce an artificial language. The signals they are exposed to come from the reproductions of a previous participant in the same experiment and the participants' own output is used as input for the next participant. In this way *chains of transmission* are created. The development of the set of signals that is being transmitted can be closely investigated and it reveals how individual (cognitive) biases and learning gradually influence emerging signaling systems. In a seminal study, Kirby et al. (2008) demonstrated the emergence of compositional syntactic structure using this experimental method.

Most of the experiments discussed in this chapter use one of these methods or a combination of both. Here, we focus on experiments that were designed to answer questions related to the evolution of speech.

36.4.1 Emergence of combinatorial structure

One of the basic ways in which speech sounds are organized is through their *combinatorial structure*: a small set of meaningless building blocks (e.g., phonemes) is combined into an unlimited set of words. This type of structure is part of the regularity Hockett (1960) called "duality of patterning" and he identified it as one of the basic design features of human language. Since this property is so central to speech, it has received considerable attention in studies of the evolution of speech.

Perhaps surprisingly, for some of the first experimental studies in this area, the main inspiration for how to model the emergence of combinatorial structure in the laboratory did not come from data on spoken languages, but was directly inspired by findings in an emerging sign language.

Established sign languages have phonological structure that uses discreteness and recombination just as spoken languages do (Corina & Sandler, 1993). Signs can be decomposed into basic elements such as movements, locations, handshape, and hand orientations. Changing one of these properties may change the meaning of the sign. Al-Sayyid Bedouin Sign Language (ABSL) is a sign language that is only a few generations old and this case has provided researchers with a unique opportunity to observe the emergence of linguistic structure as it happens (Wendy Sandler, Meir, Padden, & Aronoff, 2005). Interestingly, discreteness and recombination at the sublexical level was found to be still in the process of emerging in this young language (Israel & Sandler, 2011; Sandler, Aronoff, Meir, & Padden, 2011). Even though it is a fully functional and expressive sign language, its combinatorial structure is less discrete than those of established sign languages (Sandler et al., 2011). This example suggests that it might take a few generations of language transmission for combinatorial structure to emerge. The emergence of this type of regularity therefore seemed to be a perfect case for an iterated learning experiment.

A first attempt at modeling this in an experimental setting was done by del Giudice, Kirby, and Padden (2010); del Giudice (2012). In this iterated learning experiment participants were invited to learn and reproduce a set of graphical signals. These signals were produced with the use of a graphical device that was built following the design by Galantucci (2005) mentioned here. An initial set of random squiggles developed into a set that exhibited reuse of basic elements over generations in which the output of one participant was used as the input for the next. Combinatorial structure appeared to increase as a result of repeated transmission. This study provided a novel approach for modeling the evolution of signals over generations. Although the results were promising, the small number and unequal lengths of chains in this work made it difficult to quantify the emergence of combinatorial structure.

Galantucci, Kroos, and Rhodes (2010) and Roberts and Galantucci (2012) also used Galantucci's (2005) device to study combinatorial structure in the laboratory but in communicative game settings, with no transmission over generations. Galantucci et al. (2010) showed that rapidity of fading influences the emergence of combinatorial structure. When signals fade faster (i.e., stay visible for a shorter time), more reuse of basic graphical elements was observed. In the study conducted by Roberts and Galantucci (2012), participants play naming games and communicate about animal silhouettes using the graphical device. The influence of both conventionalization and set size (vocabulary size) was studied and the results indicated that an increase in combinatorial structure could happen due to the process of conventionalization, while the influence of vocabulary size seemed less clear.

Another iterated learning study, inspired by del Giudice's (2012) work, was conducted by Verhoef et al. (2011), with the goal to move away from the graphical modality into something more speech-like. Participants in this case created signals using a device to manipulate vowel sounds. Signals were produced by making mouse gestures in a two-dimensional visual space on the screen. Each position in this space converted to a signal with acoustic energy concentrated around two frequencies, resulting in a vowel-like sound. Signals were continuous trajectories through this vowel space, resulting in complex multivowel progressions. Figure 36.3 shows a visual representation of the sound production device. Even though some interesting cases of emerging structure could be observed in the data, a persistent and measurable increase of combinatorial structure was lacking. One important factor causing this result was that the mapping between the mouse gesture and sound was too complicated for most people to grasp. Many participants therefore failed to pick up on any potential structure and were unable to transmit it. However, there were a few participants who had less difficulty with the task and in these cases some introduction of structure did happen. These participants were often familiar with the vowel chart (for instance due to classes they took in phonetics/phonology), which provided them with a mental map that made the task cognitively easier.

A more intuitive auditory signal production device seemed to be the logical next step, and this is what Verhoef (2012) and Verhoef, Kirby, and de Boer (2014) implemented next. In their study, slide whistles were used for signal production. Slide whistles are suitable because participants can easily use them to produce a rich repertoire of acoustic signals in an intuitive way, while only very little interference from pre-existing linguistic knowledge is expected. Participants were asked to memorize and reproduce a set of different whistle sounds, initially containing as little structure as possible. The reproductions of the first participant were used to train the next. This process of transmission was continued in this manner until there

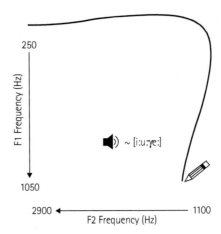

FIG. 36.3 Representation of the sound production device in Verhoef et al. (2011). The participants did not see the axes or transcriptions, the scribble area on the screen was empty.

Adapted from Tessa Verhoef, Bart de Boer, Alex del Giudice, Carol Padden, and Simon Kirby, Cultural evolution of combinatorial structure in ongoing artificial speech learning experiments, *Center for Research in Language: Technical Report*, 23 (1), p. 5, Figure 1 ©2011 Center for Research in Language.

were ten participants in each chain and four parallel chains were completed. The whistle languages became increasingly easier to learn, that is, when comparing for each participant the signals they produced with the set of signals they were exposed to, participants in later generations made significantly fewer errors and produced signals that were more similar to their input. Combinatorial structure was measured through the information-theoretic measure of entropy (Shannon, 1948), assessing whether the whistle sets in later generations were composed of a smaller set of basic building blocks that were increasingly reused and combined. A significant decrease of entropy showed that combinatorial structure gradually emerged as signals were transmitted down the chains. Figure 36.4 shows some of the sounds in one such

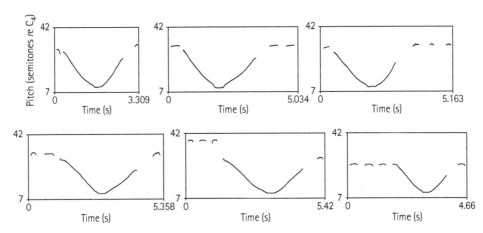

FIG. 36.4 Whistle sounds plotted as pitch tracks in the last set of a transmission chain. Basic elements can be identified that are systematically recombined.

emerged system, where the pitch is plotted against time. Basic elements are clearly visible. This work demonstrated quantitatively that cultural transmission can cause a system of auditory signals to become organized in a speech-like way.

36.4.2 The influence of iconicity

The experiments discussed so far mostly studied the emergence of phonological structure as an independent system with organized signals. In natural human languages, however, signals are tightly linked to their meaning and this is expected to have an impact on the evolution of linguistic structure.

A powerful way to construct meaning in language is to use *iconicity*, where there is a relation of resemblance between signal and meaning (Dingemanse, 2012; Perniss, Thompson, & Vigliocco, 2010). The source on which resemblance is based can be many different things: shared cultural practices or experience with the physics of the world, structural analogy or the looks and sounds of the actual meaning (e.g., the "purr" of a cat, or the sign for "tree" in American Sign Language, shown in Figure 36.5). Iconicity is a great way to leverage common ground and might therefore be especially important in the early emergence of a new language (Fay et al., 2013).

How the emergence of combinatorial structure in signals interacts with the potential existence of iconic form-meaning mappings in language has been studied with experiments as well.

Roberts, Lewandowski, and Galantucci (2015) investigated whether the emergence of combinatorial structure is hindered by the availability of iconicity as a means to map signal to meaning. Pairs of participants played guessing games and communicated with the Galantucci (2005) graphical interface. The meanings to be communicated were manipulated in such a way that there was one condition in which signals could straightforwardly resemble their meaning, providing an opportunity for iconic mappings, while this was not the case for

FIG. 36.5 The ASL sign for "tree".

Reproduced from Tennant, R. A. and Brown, M. G., *The American Sign Language Handshape Dictionary*, 2nd Ed. © Gallaudet University Press, 2010.

the other condition. The results showed that combinatorial structure emerged to a greater extent when iconicity was not possible.

In Roberts et al.'s (2015) condition with iconic mappings, the resemblance between signal and meaning was actually more than just iconic. Signals were often nearly exactly the same as the meaning, since signals and meanings were line drawings referring to line drawings, or colors referring to colors. In speech however, most words do not refer to sounds, so in the development of iconic mappings, the nature of the resemblance is often more abstract. In a related study, Verhoef, Kirby, and de Boer (2015) model signals and meanings that do not exist in the same modality, but they investigate mappings in which the signals are acoustic (whistles produced with a slide whistle) and meanings are visual. In this experiment language evolution is modeled through iterated learning chains in which participants learn and reproduce whistle-meaning mappings. To control for the potential use of iconicity, this experiment manipulates the way the signal-meaning pairs are transmitted to the next person in the chain. In the "intact" condition, the signals of the previous participant were used to train the next person exactly as they were produced. The mapping from signals to meanings was kept intact. In the "scrambled" condition, the output of the previous participant is altered before it is given to the next person. The set of meanings was entirely replaced, and the produced whistled signals were randomly paired with these new meanings between consecutive generations. In this way, potential iconicity would only be helpful for the participants in the intact condition. For the scrambled condition, any semantics-related structure was broken down in between the transmission steps and only the signal sets stayed intact. As in the previously discussed similar experiment without meanings (Verhoef, 2012; Verhoef et al., 2014), combinatorial structure emerged in the artificial languages as they were transmitted. In line with Roberts et al.'s (2015) finding, structure did seem to emerge with a slight delay in the condition where iconicity was possible.

These two findings suggest that there may be a tension between iconicity and structure, in which the emergence of structure may come with a loss of iconicity. This has also been described as a process happening over time in sign languages (Frishberg, 1975). However, findings from both spoken (Dingemanse, 2012) and signed (Emmorey, 2014; Meir, Padden, Aronoff, & Sandler, 2013; Padden et al., 2014; Padden, Hwang, Lepic, & Seegers, 2015) languages also show that iconicity often occurs in a patterned, systematic way and is not necessarily in competition with structure (Emmorey, 2014; Meir et al., 2013). How iconic building blocks may get organized into a systematic pattern has been studied with laboratory experiments as well. Verhoef, Roberts, and Dingemanse (2015) for instance had pairs of participants interact about meanings that differed in how easily they could be mapped onto the signaling medium. Signals were produced using a virtual slide whistle (controlled by sliding a finger over a touch screen). This work showed how affordances of the signaling space, which constrained the mappability of signal-meaning pairs, drove the emergence of structure. Iconic signals formed the building blocks for wider patterns that emerged.

Iconic patterns do not necessarily require a relationship that is intrinsically resembling between form and meaning. Sometimes, patterns we might call iconic can simply be based on a suitable, and consistently used mapping between the topologies of signal and meaning spaces in a domain (de Boer & Verhoef, 2012). For instance, in bee dance, larger distance to the food source is expressed iconically by the duration of the waggle phase. An initial investigation into the effect of matching versus mismatching dimensionalities between the signal space and meaning space was conducted by Little, Eryılmaz, and de Boer (2015) and found that participants make use of iconic mappings to express complex meanings in the theoretically expected way.

Another study that looked at the influence of affordances of the communication medium was designed by Janssen, Winter, Dediu, Moisik and Roberts (2016). They took into account the fact that the relationship between changes in movement and acoustic properties of the sound produced in the human vocal tract is in many ways non-linear. These articulatory constraints are expected to play a role in the emergence of phonological patterns. In their iterated learning experiment a virtual whistle interface was used for sound production, but it differed from earlier work in that the whistle was manipulated to have non-linearities, creating some more stable and unstable regions in the signaling space. As expected, the artificial languages changed toward increased use of the more stable regions, demonstrating constraints on the kinds of building blocks that emerged.

36.4.3 The effects of modality

It looks like iconicity and affordances may have an influence on the emergence of phonology-like regularities, but it has also been argued that iconicity might not actually play a very prevalent role in the spoken modality, as compared to for instance in gesture (Fay et al., 2013; Fay, Lister, Ellison, & Goldin-Meadow, 2014; Goldin-Meadow & McNeill, 1999). The iconic potential of gesture is one of the reasons why some researchers argue that gestural communication may have preceded vocal communication. There have been studies that explored this experimentally. Fay et al. (2013, 2014) invited pairs of participants in a communication game task, comparing modalities. Some pairs were allowed to use only gesture, others used only non-linguistic vocalizations, and a third group could use both. Pairs in the condition with gesture only communicated more successfully and more efficiently, suggesting that gesture was a more suitable modality for grounding initial communication systems in their task.

However, it has also been shown experimentally that the iconic potential of vocalizations might be higher than we think. Perlman, Dale, and Lupyan (2015) also asked participants to play communication games in pairs using only non-linguistic vocalizations and found that there was a rapid increase in communicative success and convergence on a shared set of vocalizations. Moreover, the emerged vocalizations were tested for interpretability with new participants who were not part of the interaction, and they could guess the right meanings at a rate much higher than chance. Evidence for iconicity was also found by looking at the acoustic properties in relation to the meanings and links were found between, for instance, the use of signal duration to contrast the meanings "long" and "short," pitch for "small" versus "big," and noise for "rough" versus "smooth."

Most of the earlier work on comparisons with gesture in laboratory experiments did not analyze the form-related properties of gestures directly. Comparisons were made mostly on the basis of communicative success and temporal efficiency (Fay et al., 2013, 2014). In the context of the evolution of speech we are mostly interested in properties of the signal, and how these change and adapt to become more like language. Although we have many different ways of quantifying properties of sounds, there is very little we can currently map out quantitatively from gesture data, other than measures based on hand coding. Recently, researchers have started to develop methods that will make it possible to do more quantitative analyses with gestures in laboratory experiments. Namboodiripad, Lenzen, Lepic, and Verhoef (2016) were able to measure formal changes in gestures as these signals evolved over several rounds of communication games between pairs of participants. They used Microsoft Kinect to record the movements of participants in 3D. Similar to what had been described impressionistically as historical changes in sign languages, a reduction in gesture space could be observed and measured quantitatively.

In sum, there is a wide variety of questions relevant to the evolution of speech that can be addressed by running experiments in the laboratory with human participants. These studies shed light on the role of cultural evolution processes in the emergence of speech sounds.

36.5 Conclusion

There is a lot of evidence that can be brought to bear on the evolution of speech. Comparative evidence shows what needs to have evolved: the ability to control vocalizations consciously and to learn to imitate vocally, as well as an ability to learn combinatorial repertoires of signals and to use these productively. In addition, some physical modifications—the disappearance of air sacs, better breathing control, and some modifications of the vocal tract, perhaps some modifications of hearing and potentially other modifications—have helped humans to produce and perceive a larger repertoire of signals. Analogous behaviors in other animals—songbirds, parrots, pinnipeds, and bats—may help to elucidate what the ecological pressures were that caused speech to evolve and what the universal constraints on socially transmitted complex signaling systems are. Experiments may help to elucidate what elements of speech are due to functional constraints, what elements are due to cognitive biases and what elements are due to cultural processes. In any case, it is clear that the interaction between culture and biology is complex and crucial to understand the evolution of speech.

Fossil evidence is still rather equivocal, but it is interesting to note that Neanderthals appear to be the same as modern humans in all aspects that have been investigated in the fossil record, with the possible exception of the chin. Although each individual element of evidence is not very strong, this convergent evidence appears to indicate that Neanderthals had the same physical abilities to produce complex vocalizations as modern humans do. If this is due to common descent (which is likely) it follows that hominins living about 400,000 years ago (*Homo heidelbergensis*) already had adaptations for complex vocalization. *Australopithecus afarensis* and *Homo ergaster* on the other hand do not share all these adaptations. This indicates that speech may have started to evolve somewhere between 1.5 and 0.5 million years ago. The cultural processes that are studied by some of the experiments described here probably already started shaping the systems of vocalizations that were used. It should be noted that this does not mean that those systems had a complexity comparable to that of modern language. Still, as it seems plausible that physical adaptations for complex vocalization were driven by cognitive innovations, it can be concluded that some precursor of language had started to evolve by this time.

References

Alemseged, Z., Spoor, F., Kimbel, W. H., Bobe, R., Geraads, D., Reed, D., & Wynn, J. G. (2006). A juvenile early hominin skeleton from Dikika, Ethiopia. *Nature, 443*(7109), 296–301.

Arensburg, B., Tillier, A. M., Vandermeersch, B., Duday, H., Schepartz, L. A., & Rak, Y. (1989). A Middle Palaeolithic human hyoid bone. *Nature*, *338*(6218), 758–60.

Badin, P., Boë, L.-J., Sawallis, T. R., & Schwartz, J.-L. (2014). Keep the lips to free the larynx: Comments on de Boer's articulatory model (2010). *Journal of Phonetics*, *46*, 161–7.

Barney, A., Martelli, S., Serrurier, A., & Steele, J. (2012). Articulatory capacity of Neanderthals, a very recent and human-like fossil hominin. *Philosophical Transactions of the Royal Society of London B*, *367*(1), 88–102.

Bolhuis, J. J., Okanoya, K., & Scharff, C. (2010). Twitter evolution: Converging mechanisms in birdsong and human speech. *Nature Reviews Neuroscience*, *11*(11), 747–59.

Boughman, J. W. (1998). Vocal learning by greater spear-nosed bats. *Proceedings of the Royal Society of London B: Biological Sciences*, *265*(1392), 227–33.

Capasso, L., Michetti, E., & D'Anastasio, R. (2008). A Homo Erectus hyoid bone: Possible implications for the origin of the human capability for speech. *Collegium Antropologicum*, *32*(4), 1007–11.

Carstairs-McCarthy, A. (1999). *The Origins of Complex Language: An Inquiry into the Evolutionary Beginnings of Sentences, Syllables, and Truth*. Oxford University Press, Oxford.

Catchpole, C. K., & Slater, P. J. B. (2008). *Bird Song: Biological Themes and Variations*, 2nd Edition. Cambridge University Press, Cambridge.

Christiansen, M. H., & Chater, N. (2008). Language as shaped by the brain. *Behavioral and Brain Sciences*, *31*(5), 489–509.

Cohen, E. (2012). The evolution of tag-based cooperation in humans. *Current Anthropology*, *53*(5), 588–616.

Corina, D. P., & Sandler, W. (1993). On the nature of phonological structure in sign language. *Phonology*, *10*(2), 165–207.

Crockford, C., Herbinger, I., Vigilant, L., & Boesch, C. (2004). Wild chimpanzees produce group-specific calls: A case for vocal learning? *Ethology*, *110*, 221–43.

D'Anastasio, R., Wroe, S., Tuniz, C., Mancini, L., Cesana, D. T., Dreossi, D., . . . & Capasso, L. (2013). Micro-biomechanics of the Kebara 2 hyoid and its implications for speech in Neanderthals. *PLoS One*, *8*(12), 1–7.

Deacon, T. W. (2010). A role for relaxed selection in the evolution of the language capacity. *Proceedings of the National Academy of Sciences*, *107*(Suppl 2), 9000–6.

de Boer, B. (2000). Self-organization in vowel systems. *Journal of Phonetics*, *28*(4), 441–65.

de Boer, B. (2009). Acoustic analysis of primate air sacs and their effect on vocalization. *Journal of the Acoustical Society of America*, *126*(6), 3329–43.

de Boer, B. (2010). Investigating the acoustic effect of the descended larynx with articulatory models. *Journal of Phonetics*, *38*(4), 679–86.

de Boer, B. (2012a). Air sacs and vocal fold vibration: Implications for evolution of speech. *Theoria et Historia Scientiarum*, *IX*, 13–28.

de Boer, B. (2012b). Loss of air sacs improved hominin speech abilities. *Journal of Human Evolution*, *62*(1), 1–6.

de Boer, B. (2016). Modeling co-evolution of speech and biology. *Topics in Cognitive Science*, *8*, 459–68.

de Boer, B., & Fitch, W. T. (2010). Computer models of vocal tract evolution: An overview and critique. *Adaptive Behavior*, *18*(1), 36–47.

de Boer, B., & Perlman, M. (2014). Physical mechanisms may be as important as brain mechanisms in evolution of speech. *Behavioral and Brain Sciences*, *37*(5).

de Boer, B., & Verhoef, T. (2012). Language dynamics in structured form and meaning spaces. *Advances in Complex Systems*, 15(3&4), 1150021.

de Boer, B., & Zuidema, W. (2010). Multi-agent simulations of the evolution of combinatorial phonology. *Adaptive Behavior*, 18(2), 141–54.

DeGusta, D., Gilbert, W. H., & Turner, S. P. (1999). Hypoglossal canal size and hominid speech. *Proceedings of the National Academy of Sciences*, 96(4), 1800–4.

del Giudice, A. (2012). The emergence of duality of patterning through iterated learning: Precursors to phonology in a visual lexicon. *Language and Cognition*, 4(4), 381–418.

del Giudice, A., Kirby, S., & Padden, C. (2010). Recreating duality of patterning in the laboratory: A new experimental paradigm for studying emergence of sublexical structure. In: Smith, A. D. M., Schouwstra, M., de Boer, B., & Smith, K. (Eds.), *The Evolution of Language: Proceedings of the 8th International Conference* (pp. 399–400). World Scientific Press, London.

Dingemanse, M. (2012). Advances in the Cross-Linguistic Study of Ideophones. *Language and Linguistics Compass*, 6(10), 654–72.

Doupe, A. J., & Kuhl, P. K. (1999). Birdsong and human speech: Common themes and mechanisms. *Annual Review of Neuroscience*, 22, 567–631.

Dunbar, R. I. M. (1996). *Grooming, Gossip and the Evolution of Language*. Faber and Faber, London.

Emmorey, K. (2014). Iconicity as structure mapping. *Philosophical Transactions of the Royal Society B*, 369(1651), 20130301.

Fay, N., Arbib, M., & Garrod, S. (2013). How to bootstrap a human communication system. *Cognitive Science*, 37(7), 1356–67.

Fay, N., Lister, C. J., Ellison, T. M., & Goldin-Meadow, S. (2014). Creating a communication system from scratch: Gesture beats vocalization hands down. *Frontiers in Psychology*, 5, 1–12.

Feher, O., Wang, H., Saar, S., Mitra, P. P., & Tchernichovski, O. (2009). De novo establishment of wild-type song culture in the zebra finch. *Nature*, 459(7246), 564–8.

Fitch, W. T. (2000). The evolution of speech: A comparative review. *Trends in Cognitive Sciences*, 4(7), 258–67.

Fitch, W. T. (2010). *The Evolution of Language*. Cambridge University Press, Cambridge.

Frishberg, N. (1975). Arbitrariness and iconicity: Historical change in American Sign Language. *Language*, 51(3), 696–719.

Fusaroli, R., & Tylén, K. (2012). Carving language for social coordination: A dynamical approach. *Interaction Studies*, 13(1), 103–24.

Galantucci, B. (2005). An experimental study of the emergence of human communication. *Cognitive Science*, 29, 737–67.

Galantucci, B., Kroos, C., & Rhodes, T. (2010). The effects of rapidity of fading on communication systems. *Interaction Studies*, 11(1), 100–11.

Garrod, S., & Doherty, G. (1994). Conversation, co-ordination and convention: An empirical investigation of how groups establish linguistic conventions. *Cognition*, 53(3), 181–215.

Garrod, S., Fay, N., Lee, J., Oberlander, J., & MacLeod, T. (2007). Foundations of representation: Where might graphical symbol systems come from? *Cognitive Science*, 31(6), 961–87.

Geissmann, T. (2002). Duet-splitting and the evolution of gibbon songs. *Biological Reviews of the Cambridge Philosophical Society*, 77, 57–76.

Goldin-Meadow, S., & McNeill, D. (1999). The role of gesture and mimetic representation in making language the province of speech. In: Corballis, M. C., & Lea, S. E. G. (Eds.), *The

Descent of Mind: Psychological Perspectives on Hominid Evolution (pp. 155–72). Oxford University Press, New York, NY.

Hayes, K. J., & Hayes, C. (1951). The intellectual development of a home-raised chimpanzee. *Proceedings of the American Philosophical Society*, 95(2), 105–9.

Healey, P. G. T., Swoboda, N., Umata, I., & King, J. (2007). Graphical language games: Interactional constraints on representational form. *Cognitive Science*, 31(2), 285–309.

Heimlich, H. J. (1975). A life-saving maneuver to prevent food-choking. *Journal of the American Medical Association*, 234(4), 398–401.

Hewitt, G. P., MacLarnon, A., & Jones, K. E. (2002). The functions of laryngeal air sacs in primates: A new hypothesis. *Folia Primatologica*, 73, 70–94.

Hiiemae, K. M., & Palmer, J. B. (2003). Tongue movements in feeding and speech. *Critical Reviews in Oral Biology & Medicine*, 14(6), 413–29.

Hockett, C. F. (1960). The origin of speech. *Scientific American*, 203, 88–96.

Honda, E., & Okanoya, K. (1999). Acoustical and syntactical comparisons between songs of the white-backed munia (Lonchura striata) and its domesticated strain, the Bengalese finch (Lonchura striata var. domestica). *Zoological Science*, 16, 319–26.

Hurford, J. R. (1991). The evolution of the critical period for language acquisition. *Cognition*, 40(3), 159–201.

Ichim, I., Kieser, J., & Swain, M. (2007). Tongue contractions during speech may have led to the development of the bony geometry of the chin following the evolution of human language: A mechanobiological hypothesis for the development of the human chin. *Medical Hypotheses*, 69(1), 20–4.

Israel, A., & Sandler, W. (2011). Phonological category resolution in a new sign language: A comparative study of handshapes. In: Channon, R., & van der Hulst, H. (Eds.), *Formational Units in Sign Languages* (pp. 177–202). Ishara Press, Nijmegen.

Janssen, R., Winter, B., Dediu, D., Moisik, S. R., & Roberts, S. G. (2016). Nonlinear biases in articulation constrain the design space of language. In: Roberts, S. G., Cuskley, C., McCrohon, L., Barceló-Coblijn, L., Feher, O., & Verhoef, T. (Eds.), *The Evolution of Language: Proceedings of the 11th International Conference (EVOLANG11)*.

Jensen-Seaman, M. I., & Hooper-Boyd, K. A. (2013). Molecular Clocks: Determining the age of the human–chimpanzee divergence. In *eLS*. John Wiley & Sons, Ltd. Available at: http://dx.doi.org/10.1002/9780470015902.a0020813.pub2

Kay, R. F., Cartmill, M., & Balow, M. (1998). The hypoglossal canal and the origin of human vocal behavior. *Proceedings of the National Academy of Sciences*, 95, 5417–19.

Kirby, S., Cornish, H., & Smith, K. (2008). Cumulative cultural evolution in the laboratory: An experimental approach to the origins of structure in human language. *Proceedings of the National Academy of Sciences*, 105(31), 10681–6.

Kirby, S., Griffiths, T. L., & Smith, K. (2014). Iterated learning and the evolution of language. *Current Opinion in Neurobiology*, 28(1), 108–14.

Kirby, S., & Hurford, J. R. (2002). The emergence of linguistic structure: An overview of the iterated learning model. In: Cangelosi, A., & Parisi, D. (Eds.), *Simulating the Evolution of Language* (pp. 121–47). Springer, London.

Komarova, N. L., & Nowak, M. A. (2001). Natural selection of the critical period for language acquisition. *Proceedings of the Royal Society of London B: Biological Sciences*, 268(1472), 1189–96.

Kuhl, P. K., Williams, K. A., Lacerda, F., Stevens, K. N., & Lindblom, B. (1992). Linguistic experience alters phonetic perception in infants by 6 months of age. *Science*, 255, 606–8.

Lameira, A. R., Hardus, M. E., Nouwen, K., Topelberg, E., Delgado, R. A., Spruijt, B. M., ... & Wich, S. A. (2013). Population-specific use of the same tool-assisted alarm call between two wild orangutan populations (Pongo pygmaeus wurmbii) indicates functional arbitrariness. *PLoS One*, 8(7), e69749.

Lieberman, P. H., Crelin, E. S., & Klatt, D. H. (1972). Phonetic ability and related anatomy of the newborn and adult human, neanderthal man, and the chimpanzee. *American Anthropologist*, 74, 287–307.

Little, H., Eryılmaz, K., & de Boer, B. (2015). Linguistic modality affects the creation of structure and iconicity in signals. In: Noelle, D. C., Dale, R., Warlaumont, A. S., Yoshimi, J., Matlock, T., Jennings, C. D., & Maglio, P. P. (Eds.), *The Proceedings of the 37th Annual Cognitive Science Society Meeting*. Cognitive Science Society, Austin, TX. Available at: https://www.semanticscholar.org/paper/Linguistic-Modality-Affects-the-Creation-of-Little-Eryilmaz/166c6a18ae2044843495506632ec74c161bfd7fc

MacLarnon, A., & Hewitt, G. P. (2004). Increased breathing control: Another factor in the evolution of human language. *Evolutionary Anthropology*, 13, 181–97.

Maddieson, I. (1984). *Patterns of Sounds*. Cambridge University Press, Cambridge.

Martínez, I., Arsuaga, J.-L., Quam, R., Carretero, J.-M., Gracia, A., & Rodríguez, L. (2008). Human hyoid bones from the middle Pleistocene site of the Sima de los Huesos (Sierra de Atapuerca, Spain). *Journal of Human Evolution*, 54, 118–24.

Martínez, I., Rosa, M., Arsuaga, J.-L., Jarabo, P., Quam, R., Lorenzo, C., ... & Carbonell, E. (2004). Auditory capacities in Middle Pleistocene humans from the Sierra de Atapuerca in Spain. *Proceedings of the National Academy of Sciences*, 101(27), 9976–81.

McComb, K., & Semple, S. (2005). Coevolution of vocal communication and sociality in primates. *Biology Letters*, 1(4), 381–5.

Meir, I., Padden, C., Aronoff, M., & Sandler, W. (2013). Competing iconicities in the structure of languages. *Cognitive Linguistics*, 24(2), 10.1515/cog-2013-0010.

Mercado, E., Herman, L. M., & Pack, A. A. (2005). Song copying by humpback whales: themes and variations. *Animal Cognition*, 8(2), 93–102.

Mitani, J. C., & Marler, P. (1989). A phonological analysis of male gibbon singing behavior. *Behaviour*, 109, 20–45.

Namboodiripad, S., Lenzen, D., Lepic, R., & Verhoef, T. (2016). Measuring conventionalization in the manual modality. *Journal of Language Evolution*, 1(2), 109–18.

Negus, V. E. (1938). Evolution of the speech organs of man. *Archives of Otolaryngology*, 28, 313–28.

Nishimura, T. (2003). Comparative morphology of the hyo-laryngeal complex in anthropoids: Two steps in the evolution of the descent of the larynx. *Primates*, 44(1), 41–9.

Padden, C., Hwang, S.-O., Lepic, R., & Seegers, S. (2015). Tools for language: Patterned iconicity in sign language nouns and verbs. *Topics in Cognitive Science*, 7(1), 81–94.

Padden, C., Meir, I., Hwang, S.-O., Lepic, R., Seegers, S., & Sampson, T. (2014). Patterned iconicity in sign language lexicons. *Gesture*, 13(3), 287–308.

Pampush, J. D. (2015). Selection played a role in the evolution of the human chin. *Journal of Human Evolution*, 82, 127–36.

Patel, A. D., Iversen, J. R., Bregman, M. R., & Schulz, I. (2009). Experimental evidence for synchronization to a musical beat in a nonhuman animal. *Current Biology*, 19(10), 827–30.

Payne, R. S., & McVay, S. (1971). Songs of humpback whales. *Science*, 173, 585–97.

Pepperberg, I. M. (2007). Grey parrots do not always "parrot": the roles of imitation and phonological awareness in the creation of new labels from existing vocalizations. *Language Sciences*, 29(1), 1–13.

Perlman, M., Dale, R., & Lupyan, G. (2015). Iconicity can ground the creation of vocal symbols. *Royal Society Open Science, 2*(8), 150152.

Perlman, M., Patterson, F. G., & Cohn, R. H. (2012). The human-fostered gorilla koko shows breath control in play with wind instruments. *Biolinguistics, 6*(3–4), 433–44.

Perniss, P., Thompson, R., & Vigliocco, G. (2010). Iconicity as a general property of language: evidence from spoken and signed languages. *Frontiers in Psychology, 1*, 227.

Pika, S., Liebal, K., Call, J., & Tomasello, M. (2005). The gestural communication of apes. *Gesture, 5*(1/2), 41–56.

Poole, J. H., Tyack, P. L., Stoeger-Horwath, A. S., & Watwood, S. (2005). Animal behaviour: Elephants are capable of vocal learning. *Nature, 434*(7032), 455–6.

Ravignani, A., Fitch, W. T., Hanke, F. D., Heinrich, T., Hurgitsch, B., Kotz, S. A., . . . & de Boer, B. (2016). What pinnipeds have to say about human speech, music, and the evolution of rhythm. *Frontiers in Neuroscience, 10*, 274.

Riede, T., Tokuda, I. T., Munger, J. B., & Thomson, S. L. (2008). Mammalian laryngseal air sacs add variability to the vocal tract impedance: Physical and computational modeling. *Journal of the Acoustical Society of America, 124*(1), 634–47.

Roberts, G., & Galantucci, B. (2012). The emergence of duality of patterning: Insights from the laboratory. *Language and Cognition, 4*(4), 297–318.

Roberts, G., Lewandowski, J., & Galantucci, B. (2015). How communication changes when we cannot mime the world: Experimental evidence for the effect of iconicity on combinatoriality. *Cognition, 141*, 52–66.

Sandler, W., Aronoff, M., Meir, I., & Padden, C. (2011). The gradual emergence of phonological form in a new language. *Natural Language & Linguistic Theory, 29*(2), 503–43.

Sandler, W., Meir, I., Padden, C., & Aronoff, M. (2005). The emergence of grammar: Systematic structure in a new language. *Proceedings of the National Academy of Sciences of the United States of America, 102*(7), 2661–5.

Schel, A. M., Townsend, S. W., Machanda, Z., Zuberbühler, K., & Slocombe, K. E. (2013). Chimpanzee alarm call production meets key criteria for intentionality. *PLoS One, 8*(10), e76674.

Schwartz, J. H., & Tattersall, I. (2000). The human chin revisited: What is it and who has it? *Journal of Human Evolution, 38*(3), 367–409.

Schwartz, J.-L., Boë, L.-J., Vallée, N., & Abry, C. (1997). Major trends in vowel system inventories. *Journal of Phonetics, 25*, 233–5.

Shannon, C. E. (1948). A mathematical theory of communication. *The Bell System Technical Journal, 27*, 379–423, 623–656.

Smith, K., Kirby, S., & Brighton, H. (2003). Iterated learning: A framework for the emergence of language. *Artificial Life, 9*(4), 371–86.

Spierings, M., & Ten Cate, C. (2016). Budgerigars and zebra finches differ in how they generalize in an artificial grammar learning experiment. *Proceedings of the National Academy of Sciences, 113*(27), E3977–84.

Steels, L. (2006). Experiments on the emergence of human communication. *Trends in Cognitive Sciences, 10*(8), 347–9.

Tennant, R. A., Gluszak Brown, M., & Nelson-Metlay, V. (2010). *The American Sign Language Handshape Dictionary*. Gallaudet University Press, Washington, DC.

Theisen, C. A., Oberlander, J., & Kirby, S. (2010). Systematicity and arbitrariness in novel communication systems. *Interaction Studies, 11*(1), 14–32.

Thompson, B., Kirby, S., & Smith, K. (2016). Culture shapes the evolution of cognition. *Proceedings of the National Academy of Sciences, 113*(16), 4530–5.

Toft, C. A., & Wright, T. F. (2015). *Parrots of the Wild: A Natural History of the World's Most Captivating Birds*. University of California Press, Oakland, CA.

Tomasello, M., & Zuberbühler, K. (2002). Primate vocal and gestural communication. In: Bekoff, M., Allen, C., & Burghardt, G. M. (Eds.), *The Cognitive Animal: Empirical and Theoretical Perspectives on Animal Cognition* (pp. 293–29). MIT Press, Cambridge MA.

Verhoef, T. (2012). The origins of duality of patterning in artificial whistled languages. *Language and Cognition*, 4(4), 357–80.

Verhoef, T., de Boer, B., del Guidice, A., Padden, C., & Kirby, S. (2011). Cultural evolution of combinatorial structure in ongoing artificial speech learning experiments. *CRL Technical Report*, 23(1), 3–11.

Verhoef, T., Kirby, S., & de Boer, B. (2014). Emergence of combinatorial structure and economy through iterated learning with continuous acoustic signals. *Journal of Phonetics*, 43, 57–68.

Verhoef, T., Kirby, S., & de Boer, B. (2015). Iconicity and the emergence of combinatorial structure in language. *Cognitive Science*, 40(8), 1969–94.

Verhoef, T., Roberts, S. G., & Dingemanse, M. (2015). Emergence of systematic iconicity: transmission, interaction and analogy. In: Noelle, D. C., Dale, R., Warlaumont, A. S., Yoshimi, J., Matlock, T., Jennings, C. D., & Maglio, P. P. (Eds.), *Proceedings of the 37th Annual Meeting of the Cognitive Science Society*. Cognitive Science Society.

Versteegh, M., Thiolliere, R., Schatz, T., Cao, X. N., Anguera, X., Jansen, A., & Dupoux, E. (2015). The zero-resource speech challenge 2015. Presented at the Proc. of INTERSPEECH.

Watson, S. K., Townsend, S. W., Schel, A. M., Wilke, C., Wallace, E. K., Cheng, L., . . . & Slocombe, K. E. (2015). Vocal learning in the functionally referential food grunts of chimpanzees. *Current Biology*, 25(4), 495–9.

Weidenreich, F. (1904). Die Bildung des Kinnes und seine angebliche Beziehung zur Sprache. *Anatomischer Anzeiger*, 24(21), 545–55.

Wich, S. A., Swartz, K. B., Hardus, M. E., Lameira, A. R., Stromberg, E., & Shumaker, R. W. (2009). A case of spontaneous acquisition of a human sound by an orangutan. *Primates*, 50(1), 56–64.

Zuidema, W., & de Boer, B. (2009). The evolution of combinatorial phonology. *Journal of Phonetics*, 37(2), 125–44.

CHAPTER 37

THE GENETICS OF LANGUAGE

From complex genes to complex communication

PAOLO DEVANNA, DAN DEDIU, AND SONJA C. VERNES

37.1 INTRODUCTION

THIS chapter discusses the genetic foundations of language and speech, a topic of particular interest for anybody aiming to understand the fascinating phenomenon that is human language. Indubitably there is a genetic basis for language as shown by several salient facts including that we are the only living species capable of it, that human children effortlessly acquire the language(s) of their community, and that there are pathologies affecting language with a clear genetic component. However, its actual genetic foundations, the mechanisms through which pieces of DNA ultimately affect aspects of language and speech, the manner in which DNA interacts with the environment (culture[1] included) to produce linguistic beings and how this all has evolved, turn out to be exceptionally complex, fascinating, and sometimes even counterintuitive.

We report here on an ongoing, massively multidisciplinary research effort to understand language genetics that has been advancing our understanding for more than half a century, but which has been accelerating during the last two decades due to advances in molecular genetics, statistics, evolutionary biology, and the language sciences. As such, this chapter aims to be both an introduction to the conceptual and methodological bases of genetics relevant

---

[1] Throughout this chapter we use "culture" in its technical sense of socially learned information shaped by evolutionary processes and various types of biases (e.g., Dediu et al., 2013; Richerson & Boyd, 2005); language then is a type of culture, and applying concepts and methods from, among others, Cultural Evolution, Gene-Culture Co-evolution, Cultural Niche Construction, and Iterated Transmission, helps understand how language emerged, changes and diversifies, as well as its multiple interactions with non-linguistic factors (Dediu et al., 2013; Dediu, Janssen, & Moisik, 2017).

for language as well as a snapshot of the most recent findings and most promising avenues of research in the next decade, supplemented by numerous references to the primary literature. The main message of our chapter is that the genetic foundations of language are truly complex, but not indecipherable, and that only an interdisciplinary, empirical approach will be successful in providing the full picture.

Language is an extremely complex phenomenon (as clearly shown by the other chapters in this book) and, while we need to have a relatively well-formed concept of language when embarking on studying its genetic foundations, we feel it is beyond our remit to try to give a detailed definition here. Suffices to say that for our purposes it is not useful to use very constraining definitions that identify a so-called FLN (faculty of language in the narrow sense) as opposed to FLB (in a broad sense) and that propose that fundamentally language is characterized by recursion (Hauser, Chomsky, & Fitch, 2002) or Merge (Hauser et al., 2014). Instead we take the view that language is a complex multicomponent system that has both biological and sociocultural components (Dediu et al., 2013). This broader view naturally allows the integration of multiple lines of research from several scientific fields, using a multitude of methods and even model organisms, into a coherent complex story about language. We can, for example, not only inquire about syntactic structures in modern English but also about patterns of cross-linguistic diversity, we can adduce evidence from historical language change and even the fossil record. Importantly for this chapter, we can understand which genes affect language and speech in humans by looking at natural genetic variation in the population and linking this to the normal range of abilities observed for language or conversely search out rare, deleterious mutations that cause severe disorders of speech and language in humans. We can also actively investigate the functional mechanisms associated with these genes in model organisms such as mice, songbirds, bats, or even in isolated cells in a dish.

But what relevance do mice, bats, or birds have for language and speech (and more so, an isolated cell), you might rightfully ask? If we view language as a broad, complex phenomenon with a biological basis that has evolved naturally (just like anything else) then there are likely to be features of language and speech that we share—in one form or another—with other animals. For example, children need to learn their spoken language[2] through what is generally known as the capacity for *vocal learning*; but some songbirds, dolphins, and bats (among others) also show vocal learning (Janik & Slater, 1997; Knornschild, 2014; Petkov & Jarvis, 2012) and it is much more feasible to study the neurobiology and genetics of this capacity in non-human models (Vernes, 2017). Thus, much of what we understand about the genetic components of human language and speech can in fact come from such non-human models. Moreover, our language and speech certainly rest on the structure and properties of our brains, larynges, lungs, lips, tongues, ears, and so on, complex organs composed of cells that interact in complex ways during development and functioning. Isolated cells or small populations of cells in a dish, together with comparative animal studies offer some of the best ways to understand these individual processes and the genetic mechanisms involved.

However, no matter how fascinating and complicated the story presented in this chapter might seem, no matter how advanced the methods, how large the datasets, and the sample

---

[2] Sign languages are another fascinating case that we will only briefly touch upon here, but see for example Dediu (2015) for a discussion of the genetics of hearing loss and emergent sign languages.

sizes required, no matter how much computer power is needed, we must again acknowledge that we are truly at the beginning of the road toward a full understanding of the genetic bases of language and speech. We tried to focus on those aspects most likely to withstand the passage of time but unavoidably—this is science!—some of what we write here will be expanded upon, modulated, or simply proven wrong by future advances. Likewise, we currently only understand small pieces of this enormous puzzle, so many aspects of language cannot be addressed here. Nevertheless, we think there are some take-home messages and principles that will survive time: first, there is no single language gene (and even the concept does not make much sense), but rather complex networks of many interacting genes underlie the human capacity for language. Second, we must approach this problem from many perspectives and incorporate information from multiple models and approaches, even if it comes from zebra finches, cell lines, dyslexia, autism, neuroimaging, or massive association studies of speech rate in the normal population. Third, no matter how much we will know about the genetic bases of language and speech we must never forget the cultural side of this evolutionary spiral.

With those thoughts in mind, we will now lay out the fundamental architecture of the genome, how this drives neural development, what we can learn from animal models and how all of this informs our understanding of the genetic mechanisms underlying human speech and language.

37.2 THE GENOME

That the human specific ability to acquire and use language depends on some genetic factors transmitted across generations is now well established by a myriad of genetic, familial, and heritability studies (Bishop, 2009; Graham, Deriziotis, & Fisher, 2015; Stromswold, 2001). It then follows that the human genome must encode these factors, providing dynamic information directing the development of our bodies and shaping form and function to allow humans to employ speech and language.

To unravel the genetic underpinnings of language and be able to use this to give insight into how human language arose and functions, it is essential to understand the human genome and how its information is encoded and enacted. Our understanding of the genome has rapidly increased over recent years, revealing how genetic factors operate and interact in order to build integrated biological systems that determine complex traits. Although perhaps counterintuitive at first, many of these general features of the genome are relevant for understanding a specialized ability like language. This is because subtle changes in timing, dosage, and location of action for a molecular pathway that may seem on the surface to be general, can have highly specific effects, influencing particular cells, brain circuits, or behaviors.

In discussing the human genome, herein we refer to the DNA and its physical packaging, which constitutes the entire complement of information needed for the development of a human individual. At its most fundamental level, the information in the genome is encoded by DNA which consists of four nucleotides (which can be represented as the letters; A, G, C, and T). Despite there being only four possible letters in DNA it can direct the assembly of all molecules and proteins that make up cells of the body, how those cells assemble into tissues and organs (e.g., the brain) and how those organs function (e.g., the activity of the brain to produce certain behaviors). This staggeringly complex task is made possible because of many levels of control that allow the genome to produce a variety of outcomes at different times during development and in different places in the body. Thus, despite the fact that every cell in the body starts off with the same genome, an almost unimaginable level of diversity can be produced. This is highlighted by the example of a neuron vs. a muscle cell. Both cell types start with the same basic genetic code, however each displays a vastly different reading of that code. In a neuron, the necessary genes are switched on (i.e., the letters are "read") that drive neuronal morphology, the formation of synapses, and the presence of ion channels facilitating the transmission of electrical signals (among other things). By contrast, a muscle cell will express genes that allow it to form a tubular morphology, receive input signals from nerves, and translate these into mechanical force.

It is important to note that the genome of a cell is not just used once during development to direct cellular identity and then forgotten. For a cell to continue to perform its normal function and to be able to react to environmental influences or behavioral changes, dynamic and continuous access to the genomic information is required. Thus, the genetic code may be essentially read in a particular way in a neuronal cell[3], but this may change frequently throughout the lifetime of that neuron, allowing it to respond to the different signals it receives over time. An example of this is that during learning, we may strengthen or weaken synapses in our brain to change our behavioral response to a stimulus. This "synaptic plasticity" is well characterized at a molecular level and is facilitated by the switching on or off of specific genes and proteins that influence synapse strength (Shen & Cowan, 2010; Sweatt, 2016).

In the remainder of this section, we will detail how this temporal and spatial complexity and control is embedded in the genome and how genomic factors involved in these processes have been shown to influence language-relevant phenotypes. (e.g., the observable property, characteristics, or traits of a system (Churchill, 1974)).

37.2.1 Genes and proteins

DNA in the genome can be broadly classified into two categories, "coding" and "non-coding" DNA. Coding DNA refers to the part of the genome that encodes genes and, perhaps surprisingly, this DNA accounts for only a small fraction of the genome (~2%). The vast majority of the genome (~98%) is non-coding DNA—it does not code for genes. Historically this was called "junk" DNA as it was thought to not have a purpose, however this idea has now been roundly dismissed as it has been discovered that much of this DNA has a crucial role in regulating when, where, and how genes are read (Doolittle, 2013; Ecker, 2012; Pennisi, 2012) (as will be discussed in later sections).

In order to read the genomic code of a cell, the relevant portion of DNA (the gene) is copied into another, very similar nucleotide code (known as RNA) in a process known as transcription (Alberts et al., 2014; Lewin, Krebs, Kilpatrick, Goldstein, & Lewin, 2011;

---

[3] Importantly this is also a generalization. There are many different types of neurons and each of these employs its own unique "reading" of the genetic code.

Strachan, Read, & Strachan, 2011). This RNA "message" (messenger RNA or mRNA) is then "translated" by the machinery of the cell, resulting in the production of proteins (Chapeville et al., 1962; Crick, 1958). For this reason, genes were traditionally defined as "DNA that encodes the sequence of a protein" (Lewin, 1990). Broader definitions of a "gene" are now regularly used since it was discovered that certain RNA molecules produced by transcription do not undergo translation into protein, but rather act to influence cellular functions in their RNA form (Bartel, 2004; Phizicky & Hopper, 2010; Rinn & Chang, 2012) (see section 37.2.4). Thus, a more up-to-date definition of a gene is: "a union of genomic sequences encoding a coherent set of potentially overlapping functional products" (Gerstein et al., 2007).

Proteins represent the bulk of the functional machinery within cells that allows the genetic code to direct phenotypic outcomes. For this reason, we will predominantly discuss protein coding genes, although the role of some RNA encoding genes will be addressed in section 37.2.4. Proteins can fulfill an array of different functions in a cell. They may contribute to the shape and morphology of the cell (structural proteins), act as catalysts of chemical reactions (enzymes), form molecular connections between cells allowing them to exchange molecules or signals (channels), and much more.

Because the DNA code dictates the protein code and the protein code dictates protein function, changes at the level of DNA sequence can have severe effects on protein function. This is particularly striking when detrimental mutations are present. Even a single letter change in the DNA can result in severe effects on the concomitant protein product, sometimes even resulting in a complete loss of protein function. Depending on how reliant a particular cell is on the activity of that protein, this can have a range of consequences (from mild to severe) for how the cell functions or even on its survival. This is a major driver of phenotypic diversity in the human population; small changes at the DNA level might result in a change in a protein that affects something benign like eye color, or highly detrimental (or even lethal) like microcephaly (development of an extremely small size brain) (Faheem et al., 2015; F. Liu, Wen, & Kayser, 2013). Genetic variation that alters or destroys protein function has been linked to language ability in humans—the most well-known example of which is the *FOXP2*[4] gene (see section 37.2.3).

37.2.2 Chromatin structure controls access to genes

We have talked about the genetic code being read, and in this context it is easy to imagine the DNA as a long string of letters awaiting transcription. However, this could not be further from reality. The "string of letters" in the genome is in fact stored as a heavily folded, highly condensed three-dimensional molecule. One reason this occurs is physical; it allows the enormous human genome (composed of three billion "letters") to be packaged into a microscopic cell (Strick, Allemand, Bensimon, & Croquette, 1998). The three-dimensional structure is also thought to control which parts of the genome are available for transcription

---

[4] Following the guidelines on gene nomenclature, in this chapter human and primate gene symbols are italicized and in upper-case (*FOXP2*), rodent gene symbols are italicized with only the first letter in upper-case (*Foxp2*), and other species in upper and lower (*FoxP2*). Protein names are not italicized (FOXP2/Foxp2/FoxP2) (Kaestner, Knochel, & Martinez, 2000; Maltais et al., 2002; Wain et al., 2002).

at a given time or place, making it an important factor dictating the complexity generated from the genome.

In a cell, DNA is tightly wrapped around small proteins called histones and then groups of DNA and histones are further condensed into clusters called nucleosomes (Luger, Mader, Richmond, Sargent, & Richmond, 1997). Together this highly condensed structure is called chromatin, which is itself wound many times into increasingly compressed structures, ultimately forming a *chromosome*[5] (see Fig. 37.1). DNA in tightly packed chromatin cannot be read, and must be unwound before this process can occur[6] (Boeger et al., 2005). A major mechanism by which chromatin structure is relaxed and DNA is made accessible for reading is by the activity of proteins encoded in the genome (known as *chromatin remodelers*) which interact with histones to either (i) add a chemical tag to the histone and change its shape, or (ii) move/remove histones in localized DNA regions (Cutter & Hayes, 2015; Kouzarides, 2007). Such *histone modifications* and the resulting chromatin remodeling are known as *epigenetic mechanisms*. These changes can be prompted by developmental, intra/extracellular, or environmental cues and do not directly change the DNA code, but affect how and when the code can be read.

Epigenetic mechanisms are important for the activity of brain circuits (Amador-Arjona et al., 2015; Brami-Cherrier et al., 2014) and are likely to influence, and in turn be influenced by language acquisition and use. However, it is important to note that the epigenetic modifications that occur within neurons over the lifetime of an individual are not passed to the next generation. Only the genetic material contained in the gametes (sex cells) of an organism are inherited and thus the vast array of different chromatin landscapes that are found in different cells of the body are not passed to the offspring (Jobling, Hurles, & Tyler-Smith, 2004). However, this does not mean that there is no heritability of epigenetic factors. An important distinction must be made between the architecture itself (the specific chromatin marks) and the "architects" (the chromatin remodelers). Chromatin remodeling genes are encoded in the genome and as such their activity can be inherited. For example, if there is a variant within a chromatin remodeling gene that makes it less efficient at responding to environmental cues, this will affect how the epigenetic changes occur in the brain of that individual. The offspring of this individual may then inherit the less efficient chromatin remodeler and for this reason may have a similar epigenetic response to environmental cues as their parent did (Mathies et al., 2015).

In any given cell, many chromatin remodelers are expressed simultaneously, working in a coordinated and combinatorial fashion to mold the architecture of the chromatin structure across the genome. The combination of remodelers and resulting chromatin structure are specific to individual cells, making genes that encode chromatin remodeling highly important for the processes that generate complexity from the genome. Mutations in chromatin remodeling genes can cause complex disorders involving impaired language and thus point to genetic factors that influence the normal development of language-related neural

---

[5] Each human cell contains 23 pairs of chromosomes, one of each pair is transmitted from each of the parents.

[6] This view is an approximation of what is postulated to happen at molecular level. Other factors should be taken into account contributing to accessibility and chemical interaction between proteins and DNA (Bulut-Karslioglu et al., 2012; Lawrence, Daujat, & Schneider, 2016; Saksouk, Simboeck, & Dejardin, 2015).

circuitry in the brain. Here we will discuss the example of *MECP2*, mutations of which are the major cause of Rett syndrome—a neurological disorder related to ASD (autism spectrum disorder) (Hagberg, Aicardi, Dias, & Ramos, 1983; Zappella, Meloni, Longo, Hayek, & Renieri, 2001) that involves repetitive movements, apraxia, intellectual disability, and communication impairments (Lyst & Bird, 2015; Pohodich & Zoghbi, 2015). The MECP2 protein modifies chromatin structure to influence how genes are expressed, and this regulation is important for neuron function and neuronal connectivity (Na & Monteggia, 2011; Na, Nelson, Kavalali, & Monteggia, 2013). Loss of *Mecp2* in animal models has shown its importance for the development and function of specific brain regions (Armstrong, 2005; Kishi & Macklis, 2004). Mecp2 activity is crucial during postnatal stages in the striatum, a region controlling executive function and motor output (including vocal-motor control) (Zhao, Goffin, Johnson, & Zhou, 2013). These data suggest that the function of *Mecp2* is still required after embryonic development is completed, and for normal functioning of the circuits controlling motor/cognitive tasks and their response to environmental cues. This fits well with human phenotypes, where children with Rett syndrome (and loss of MECP2 function) often develop normally for a period postnatally, before showing severe regression with symptoms affecting motor outputs, cognitive functions, and language (Lyst & Bird, 2015; Pohodich & Zoghbi, 2015).

37.2.3 Non-coding DNA is a gate-keeper for gene expression

Although chromatin remodeling is crucial, simply unwinding DNA is not enough to ensure the code will be read. Further levels of control then ensure that the right genes are read in the appropriate cell types and time points for normal development and tissue function.

Surrounding each gene in the genome are non-coding DNA sequences that determine how genes are regulated (i.e., when/where they are expressed). Directly before a gene are "promoter" sequences and spaced, often at very large distances from genes, are "enhancer" sequences (see Fig. 37.1). Both of these regions of DNA interact with proteins in the cell known as transcription factors ("TFs") to facilitate or block the machinery responsible for copying DNA into the RNA message. Thus, by binding to the promoter of a gene, a transcription factor can ensure it is read in that cell type, or prevent its expression.

TFs interact with specific strings of letters in the DNA sequence of promoters and enhancers. These letter strings (motifs) can be as short as six letters and the motif for a given transcription factor may be found in regulatory sequences for thousands of genes (Bulyk, 2003; Hannenhalli, 2008). For this reason, the product of a single TF gene (which can produce many copies of its protein) could bind thousands of regions of the genome simultaneously allowing complex regulation of hundreds or thousands of genes. A single TF often regulates the expression of multiple genes that have similar functions or participate in a shared molecular pathway (Vernes et al., 2011). TFs are often called master regulators—they control the expression of large numbers of genes, some of which will also be TFs and in this way, they can initiate regulatory "cascades" and have substantial effects on cell development and function (Thiel, 2006). For this reason, mutation of a transcription factor can lead to large imbalances in the combinations of proteins expressed by a cell. Such disruptions can severely compromise the morphology, function, or survival of many different cell types, making them strong candidates for causes of cognitive disorders (Thiel, 2006).

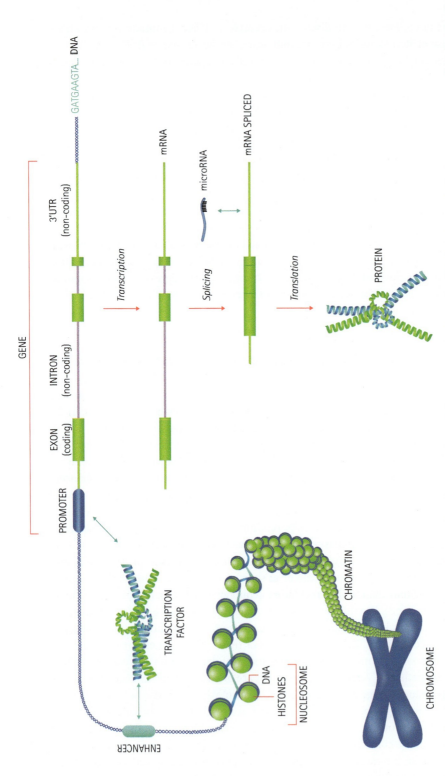

FIG. 37.1. Schematic representation of the complexity of the genome. On the left, the structure of genomic DNA is depicted. DNA is wrapped around histones to form nucleosomes and chromatin that is further condensed to form chromosomes. The top part of the figure represents the linear structure of a gene and its regulatory elements (e.g., enhancers and promoters). A gene comprises coding elements (the exons) and non-coding elements (introns and 3'UTR). Red arrows represent the cellular processes involved in the production of proteins from DNA. Transcription factors bind to enhancers and promoters to control transcription of genes into messenger RNA (mRNA). Splicing removes non-coding introns from the mRNA and microRNAs dynamically bind to 3'UTRs to regulate translation into protein.

Increasing the complexity of this regulation, many TFs rely on interaction with other proteins that regulate transcription (including other TFs) and thus regulation might only occur when the two (or more) required TFs are both expressed at the same time and place. Layer this onto the regulation of the chromatin structure of each gene, and the fact that there are about 20,000 genes in the human genome (Ezkurdia et al., 2014; Ota et al., 2004) and you can start to see the huge diversity and dynamicity that can be generated from this system. Hypothetically, at a single time point, the chromatin surrounding thousands of genes may be unwound, but the cell may only express the TFs needed to drive the expression of a subset of these sites. However, with a change in external signals to the cell, a new transcription factor could be switched on that then drives a whole other subset of these unwound genes or specifically represses some of them blocking an entire genetic pathway.

Several TFs have been implicated in normal speech and language via the identification of mutations in patients with disorders involving speech and/or language deficits. A mutation in the *FOXP2* TF gene was the first case of a monogenic cause of speech/language disorder (Lai et al., 2001). Several unrelated families and individuals have now been identified that have a severe disorder of speech articulation (orofacial dyspraxia) with expressive and receptive language deficits caused by mutation of the *FOXP2* gene (Feuk et al., 2006; Fisher & Scharff, 2009; MacDermot et al., 2005; Rice et al., 2012; Shriberg et al., 2006; Turner et al., 2013). Patient mutations that altered the protein sequence were shown to severely disrupt the function of the FOXP2 protein which normally acts as a transcription factor in the brain (and some other tissues) (Vernes et al., 2006). FOXP2 has been shown to regulate the expression of hundreds of target genes involved in neuronal differentiation, migration, neurite outgrowth, and connectivity (Konopka et al., 2009; Spiteri et al., 2007; Vernes et al., 2011; Vernes et al., 2007), and it is likely that many of these genes are dysregulated in the brains of affected individuals (although we cannot directly measure gene expression in the brains of living people).

Several other TFs have been linked to disorders involving speech and language deficits, and many of these are known to interact with FOXP2, forming a "mini-network." This includes *FOXP1*, a TF gene that is very closely related to *FOXP2* (having similar structure and function) and *TBR1*, a TF involved in brain development and function (Han et al., 2011; Huang et al., 2014). Mutations in both *FOXP1* and *TBR1* cause ASD and people with *FOXP1* mutations also display intellectual disability and speech disorders (Deriziotis et al., 2014; Hamdan et al., 2010; Huang & Hsueh, 2015; O'Roak et al., 2011). It is interesting that with increased patient screening and deeper investigations into the molecular function of mutated genes we are finding that many of the genes mutated in disorders involving language impairment act in overlapping molecular networks. To understand the genetic components of language, it will thus be necessary to understand these networks and how they relate to one another, a topic we will return to in section 37.3.

37.2.4 Who controls the message?

Thus far we have seen that in order to be read, a gene must have the right code, the gene region must be unwound by epigenetic mechanisms at the appropriate time, the right transcription factor (or combination thereof) must be present in the cell, and these must interact with the appropriate motifs in the promoter and/or enhancer of the gene. This complicated cascade of steps all leads to the production of the messenger RNA that is ultimately going to result in production of functional protein. But even at this stage, there is yet another layer of control exerted on the messenger RNA to determine when, where, and how much protein is produced. Two examples of "controlling the message" (also known as post-transcriptional regulation) that we will discuss here are "alternative splicing," and "microRNA-based control of expression."

The mRNA produced from a gene includes not only the coding region of that gene (exons), but also sequences that are not converted into protein. These regions can be at the start or end of the gene sequence (known as the untranslated regions), or within the gene between the blocks of sequence that code for protein (introns). Introns are removed from the messenger RNA before translation into protein in a process called splicing (see Fig. 37.1). To envisage how splicing works, imagine the editing of a movie. From an initial linear recording, only specific clips are retained, and these are stitched together to produce the final film. A similar process turns a long messenger RNA into a shorter, edited molecule that is translated into protein (Berget, Moore, & Sharp, 1977; Chow, Gelinas, Broker, & Roberts, 1977). In the same way that film can be edited to focus on different parts of a story, messenger RNAs undergo "alternative splicing" that removes different parts of the original transcript to result in slightly different proteins (Zheng & Black, 2013). Alternative splicing occurs more frequently in the brain compared to other tissues (Blencowe, 2006; Yeo, Holste, Kreiman, & Burge, 2004), underscoring its importance in generating diversity by increasing the number of different proteins that can be produced by each gene (up to thousands per gene in extreme cases) (Missler, Fernández-Chacon, & Sudhof, 1998).

A family of proteins known as RBFOXs are known to regulate splicing in the brain. All three family members (RBFOX1-3) are strongly expressed in partially overlapping regions of the brain where they regulate splicing of transcripts involved in neuronal development. Mutation of both *RBFOX1* and *RBFOX2* in mice leads to motor and motor learning impairments (Gehman et al., 2012; Underwood, Boutz, Dougherty, Stoilov, & Black, 2005; Zhang et al., 2008). Because they regulate the splicing of many brain expressed messenger RNAs, variations in *RBFOXs* (common variants or rare mutations) have the potential to affect whole networks contributing to brain development and function. Accordingly, these genes have been implicated in neurodevelopmental disorders including ASD, ID (Intellectual Disability), epilepsy, ADHD (Attention Deficit Hyperactivity Disorder), bipolar disorder, and schizophrenia (Bhalla et al., 2004; Elia et al., 2010; Gehman et al., 2011; Hamshere et al., 2009; Le-Niculescu et al., 2009; J. A. Lee et al., 2016; Martin et al., 2007; Xu et al., 2008). Interestingly, *RBFOX1*, a transcriptional target of FOXP2, underwent evolutionary selection in modern humans (Ayub et al., 2013). This may point to selective pressure on *RBFOX1* related to evolutionary changes in human cognitive functions and possibly language abilities. In a study of people with reading or language disorders, common variation in the *RBFOX2* gene was associated with multiple measures of language and reading (Gialluisi et al., 2014). The variety of phenotypes associated with *RBFOX* genes and their links to FOXP2 reinforce the idea that shared molecular networks underlie language pathways in the brain.

Another mechanism for controlling the message is mediated by a part of messenger RNA known as the 3'UTR (3' Un-Translated Region) which is found at the end of each gene. The 3'UTR exerts fine grained control over how much of the messenger RNA can be translated into protein (Schwerk & Savan, 2015). A well-established function of the 3'UTR is to interact with small molecules called microRNAs (Bartel, 2004; R. C. Lee, Feinbaum, & Ambros, 1993). MicroRNAs are encoded in the genome and are transcribed into RNA, but do not get translated into protein. Instead they are active RNA molecules that interact with the 3'UTR of messenger RNAs (see Fig. 37.1) (Bartel, 2004; Seok, Ham, Jang, & Chi, 2016). This interaction prevents the messenger RNA from being translated into protein by physically blocking this process or degrading the messenger RNA (Bartel, 2004). Genetic variation in either the microRNA or the 3'UTR can interfere with this interaction, affecting gene expression and resulting in disorders (Sun & Shi, 2015; Xu, Karayiorgou, & Gogos, 2010). We recently identified such a variant in a cohort of specific language impairment (SLI)—a disorder characterized by language impairment in the absence of other explanatory factors. The variant was in the 3'UTR of the *ARHGEF39* gene and it interfered with the microRNA regulation of the messenger RNA, resulting in altered expression (Devanna et al., 2017). This variant was found more commonly in affected than unaffected children and was significantly associated with performance on non-word repetition tasks—a common measure for language impairment[7] (Devanna et al., 2017). In future, it is likely that exploring such non-coding variation in the genome will lead to a better understanding of the genetic causes of such disorders and as a result a better understanding of the genetic mechanisms underlying normal language development.

37.3 FROM GENES TO SYSTEMS

We have discussed how the genome is non-linear, complex, and dynamic, but how do these concepts translate to the systems level and language? To understand this, we must consider that genes do not act alone, but rather in coordinated molecular networks, and furthermore understand how these factors influence phenotypes during the development and function of the brain.

37.3.1 Genome-wide variation and coordinated molecular networks

The human genome is estimated to code for about 20,000 genes (Ezkurdia et al., 2014; Ota et al., 2004) and each cell expresses a unique combination of thousands of these genes which are dynamically regulated by the mechanisms we have outlined here. The resulting proteins do not act in isolation; rather the thousands of proteins that are simultaneously present in a given cell interact with each other in overlapping molecular networks to produce specific phenotypes relevant for a cell type, time point or response to an external stimulus (Lassek, Weingarten, & Volknandt, 2015).

---

[7] Although it is debated what non-word repetition tasks measure (e.g., phonological memory, motor programming, and so on), deficits in this task are a core feature of a range of language impairments and often used in diagnostic criteria.

Recent advances have elevated the study of complex traits from single gene-phenotype connections to the contributions of complex gene networks (Khatri, Sirota, & Butte, 2012). It is now possible to survey across the genome of an individual simultaneously, rather than surveying individual genes and proteins. Genome-wide association studies (GWAS), whole exome sequencing (WES), and whole genome sequencing (WGS) technology sample large numbers of genetic variants spread throughout the DNA of an individual. This makes it possible to consider the phenotype of an individual as the result of the collection of much (or in the case of WGS, all) of the variants in their genome, rather than looking at isolated genes and variants (Burton et al., 2007; Fu et al., 2013; Moorthie, Mattocks, & Wright, 2011; Shendure & Ji, 2008; Visscher, Brown, McCarthy, & Yang, 2012). This presents a formidable challenge given the size of the genome and the estimated three million variants each of us possess in our DNA (Altshuler et al., 2015). However, analysis methods are rapidly advancing, making it possible, under the right experimental conditions and hypothesis, to identify genetic variants associated with phenotypic variation using the normal population as a natural "test-tube" (Narasimhan et al., 2016). These methods have already linked common genetic variants to variation in phenotypic traits like brain volume or activity (Becker et al., 2016; Hibar et al., 2015; Udden, Snijders, Fisher, & Hagoort, 2016), and in the future it is likely that these approaches will also give insight into the wider genetic mechanisms underlying language phenotypes.

At a functional level, ChIP-Sequencing methodology surveys every position in the genome where a transcription factor binds to a promoter/enhancer region (Robertson et al., 2007), making it possible to get a cellular "snapshot" of the hundreds or thousands of genes that are simultaneously being regulated by a protein like FOXP2. Conversely RNA-Sequencing surveys the expression levels of every gene in the genome making it possible to see how mutations or changes in behavior or environmental conditions affect the output of the genome (Hitzemann et al., 2013; Z. Wang, Gerstein, & Snyder, 2009). Coupling these techniques with genome-wide sampling of DNA variation in populations can help to bridge the molecular gap, demonstrating how the genetic variation we identify in individuals can cause functional changes in gene expression and lead to the resulting phenotypes.

This paradigm shift, from a reductionist to a holistic approach (i.e., considering all the genes expressed in the cell and how they interact) (Fang & Casadevall, 2011) underscores the idea that a single "gene for language" does not exist (Fisher & Marcus, 2006; Graham & Fisher, 2013). Rather, we should appreciate that dynamic, interacting gene networks produce a complex biological system and influence cellular functions that ultimately result in structures (neurological and peripheral) that contribute to language.

37.3.2 From genes to phenotypes—migration and neurite outgrowth

Brain development is a complex process that requires many overlapping processes to occur in a precisely timed fashion, directed by the genome. Here we discuss two processes, migration and neurite outgrowth, that are fundamental to brain development, contribute to language-related circuitry, and start to bridge the gap between genes and language phenotypes.

The human cortex is a massive, complex structure crucial for our use and understanding of speech and language (Friederici, 2011; Hagoort, 2013; Hickok & Poeppel, 2007). The cortex can be subdivided into many regions, but always maintains a laminar structure, the majority of which is composed of neurons arranged in specific patterns across six layers (Fernández, Llinares-Benadero, & Borrell, 2016; X. Tan & Shi, 2013). To form this structure, neurons must migrate—often across large distances—to reach their final destination in the appropriate layer of the developing cortex (Fernández et al., 2016; Gao, Sultan, Zhang, & Shi, 2013; Marin, Valiente, Ge, & Tsai, 2010; X. Tan & Shi, 2013). During this process both the final position reached and the timing of the neurons' arrival are crucial for the normal development of the brain. If either position or timing is altered, the brain may display both structural and functional abnormalities as this mistiming can result in incorrect wiring of the neural circuitry underlying brain function (Sarnat, Philippart, Flores-Sarnat, & Wei, 2015). The migration of neurons during development is influenced by the genes that they and the surrounding cells express: different genes promote or inhibit cellular migration; thus, the specific balance of gene expression determines the neuronal migration pattern (Kwan, Sestan, & Anton, 2012; Luhmann, Fukuda, & Kilb, 2015). In both mouse and animal models, FOXP2 was shown to slow or prevent cellular migration (Clovis, Enard, Marinaro, Huttner, & De Pietri Tonelli, 2012; Devanna, Middelbeek, & Vernes, 2014), suggesting that some of the speech and language phenotypes caused by *FOXP2* mutation could in part be related to subtle neuronal migration defects. Aberrant migration has become a key theme in another language-related disorder, dyslexia. Developmental dyslexia involves deficits in reading and spelling ability in the absence of explanatory factors such as low IQ or reduced opportunity (Paracchini, Scerri, & Monaco, 2007). Large scale searches for the genetic causes of dyslexia have converged on genes involved in migration. *DCDC2*, *KIAA0319*, *DYX1C1*, and *ROBO1*—the first and strongest dyslexia candidate genes—all play a role in directing neuronal migration (Hannula-Jouppi et al., 2005; Meng et al., 2005; Paracchini et al., 2008; Scerri & Schulte-Korne, 2010; Taipale et al., 2003). Aberrant neuronal migration was also identified in the postmortem brains of individuals with dyslexia (Galaburda & Kemper, 1979; Galaburda et al., 1985), supporting this link between migration, dyslexia, and use of written language.

Once neurons have found their appropriate place in the brain they start to "wire up" the neural circuits that underlie behavior. To do this, they must grow long and complex networks of cellular protrusions known as neurites, of which there are two types; axons and dendrites (Chedotal & Richards, 2010). The axon of one neuron extends to connect to the dendrite of another neuron. At this junction a structure known as a synapse is formed which allows information to pass from the axon of one neuron to the dendrite of the next, ultimately resulting in connected neural circuits (Chia, Li, & Shen, 2013). Like migration, the growth of axons and dendrites is influenced by genetic mechanisms (Kolodkin & Tessier-Lavigne, 2011; A. E. West & Greenberg, 2011). At the appropriate time, genes are switched on that drive the growth of these protrusions, but also that control the distance and route the protrusions take, thus controlling which other neurons in the brain they can connect to (Jongbloets & Pasterkamp, 2014). The *FOXP2* gene also has a role to play in this important neurodevelopmental phenotype. Using mouse and human model systems it has been shown that *FOXP2* promotes the outgrowth of neurites and in this way is likely to affect connectivity of neural networks (Devanna et al., 2014; Vernes et al., 2011). The involvement of *FOXP2* in both neuronal migration and neurite outgrowth may contribute to the subtle structural and functional differences that have been observed in speech/language disorder patients carrying mutations in this gene (Liegeois et al., 2003; Watkins, 2011).

37.3.3 From genes to phenotypes—synapses and neural circuits

Formation and maintenance of synapses, the physical connections between axons and dendrites, is fundamental to the development and activity of functional neural circuitry (Chia et al., 2013; Krueger, Tuffy, Papadopoulos, & Brose, 2012; Shen & Cowan, 2010). Synaptogenesis—the formation of synapses—begins during late gestational periods and continues at a high rate into adolescence, but at lower rates throughout the lifespan of an individual (Waites, Craig, & Garner, 2005). Once created, synapses can be maintained, strengthened, or pruned depending on the neural signaling that passes through the circuit (Ebert & Greenberg, 2013; Holtmaat & Svoboda, 2009; Shen & Cowan, 2010). Synapses in active circuits will be maintained, but inactive synapses will be pruned. This process (known as synaptic plasticity) is facilitated by the genes and proteins expressed in the cell/synapse and if these genes are mutated, synapses may not be maintained or may not respond appropriately when a neural circuit is activated (Ebert & Greenberg, 2013; Holtmaat & Svoboda, 2009). In addition to regulating cell migration and neurite outgrowth, the *FOXP2* transcription factor also affects synaptic activity and signaling through circuits. In mouse models, loss of *Foxp2* results in altered synaptic plasticity (Groszer et al., 2008) and neuronal firing (French et al., 2012). Given that its function is to regulate the expression of other genes, we can begin to bridge the gap between genes and language phenotypes by understanding how *FOXP2* "target" genes can influence neural circuits.

FOXP2 was found to regulate the expression of a synaptic gene known as *CNTNAP2* which has been implicated in a range of neurodevelopmental disorders. In particular people with rare mutations in *CNTNAP2* often display language-related disorders including speech apraxia, ASD, language regression, as well as more widespread deficits such as intellectual disability and epilepsy (Rodenas-Cuadrado, Ho, & Vernes, 2014; Rodenas-Cuadrado et al., 2016). Common variation in the *CNTNAP2* gene that can be found spread throughout the population is associated with specific language impairment, ASD, dyslexia, and early communicative behavior (Rodenas-Cuadrado et al., 2014). Such common variation in *CNTNAP2* has also been implicated in the structure and function of brain circuits relevant for language. These subtle changes have been associated with differences in gray matter volume (G. C. Tan, Doke, Ashburner, Wood, & Frackowiak, 2010; Udden et al., 2016), brain responses to syntax violations (Kos et al., 2012) and brain activation during sentence or artificial syntax processing (Folia, Forkstam, Ingvar, Hagoort, & Petersson, 2011; Whalley et al., 2011). Thus, both rare and common variation in *CNTNAP2* provides compelling evidence for a link between this gene and language-related phenotypes.

The importance of *CNTNAP2* in language-related circuitry may be related to its synaptic function. The protein produced from the *CNTNAP2* gene (called CASPR2) travels to the synapses of neurons[8] (Bakkaloglu et al., 2008) where it mediates dendritic arborization,

---

[8] The CNTNAP2 protein is also found in other places including parts of myelinated nerves (Poliak et al., 1999, 2001).

spine development, and synaptic activity (Anderson et al., 2012; Varea et al., 2015). When modeled in mice, loss of mouse *CNTNAP2* resulted in reduced neurite outgrowth, reduced activity of individual synapses, and reduced overall neural network activity (Anderson et al., 2012; Varea et al., 2015). *CNTNAP2* is not ubiquitously expressed throughout the brain, rather it is dynamically expressed (increasing in the postnatal brain) and is enriched in regions known to mediate higher order cortical functions such as cortico-striatal-thalamic circuits and perisylvian cortical regions (Abrahams et al., 2007; Alarcon et al., 2008; Gordon et al., 2016). Taken together, these data suggest that CNTNAP2 acts downstream of *FOXP2* and is required for the normal function of a subset of synapses and neural circuits which may act as part of language networks in the brain.

37.3.4 From genes to phenotypes—peripheral mechanisms

While the brain clearly plays the central role in language, we should not forget the means through which we perceive and produce it—hearing, seeing, speaking, and gesturing—all of which also have a genetic component. We will briefly review here aspects of the genetics of hearing loss and of the development of vocal tract structures, leaving aside vision, facial expressions, and manual gestures.

Hearing is a complex process (Stover & Diensthuber, 2011) and there are multiple causes of hearing loss, including trauma, powerful noises, infections, and normal aging, but the most interesting from a genetic (and linguistic) point of view are the various types of congenital (i.e., present at birth) non-syndromic (i.e., no other phenotypes present) hearing loss, most of them with an identifiable genetic cause (see, for example, https://ghr.nlm.nih.gov/condition/nonsyndromic-hearing-loss). Interestingly, the genetic mechanisms behind congenital non-syndromic hearing loss are multiple and sometimes surprising, highlighting the complexity of the genetic architecture of even such "external" aspects of language and speech. For example, one broad type of congenital non-syndromic hearing loss (Kokotas, Petersen, & Willems, 2007) is due to mutations in a mitochondrial gene, *MTRNR1*, that encodes a specific subunit (actually not a protein but an RNA molecule) of the mitochondrial ribosome. Certain antibiotics (such as gentamycin and streptomycin) are known to affect hearing at high doses or after prolonged exposure, but in people carrying mutations in *MTRNR1* even small doses might result in hearing loss (Bindu & Reddy, 2008; Kokotas et al., 2007) because these particular mutations make the mitochondrial ribosomes susceptible to damage from these antibiotics (Ballana et al., 2006). This example highlights several fascinating issues, including the importance of the interaction between genotype (the *MTRNR1* mutation), the individual's wider genomic background (other genes modulate the mutation's effects) and the environment (the presence of the antibiotics), and the phenotypic specificity of a mutation that affects all mitochondria (essential for energy production) throughout the body. Other interesting examples concerns recessive hearing loss (i.e., an individual needs two copies of the mutation to develop deafness). One cause of which (mutation of the *MYO15A* gene) plays a role in the structure of the stereocilia of the hearing cells (Manor et al., 2011) and resulted in the development of the emergent sign language *Kata Kolok* in the village of Bengkala, on the island of Bali, Indonesia (de Vos, 2013; A. Wang et al., 1998; Winata et al., 1995). Another cause (mutation of the DFNB1 locus involving the *GJB2* and *GJB6* genes) is implicated in the emergence of *ABSL* (Al-Sayyid Bedouin Sign Language) in the Negev desert, Israel (Sandler, Aronoff, Meir, & Padden, 2011). Such emergent sign languages are a very hot topic, as they may shed light on the feedback between biology and culture in language evolution and change. In brief, when recessive mutations involved in congenital hearing loss occur in communities with high rates of inbreeding or assortative mating and a good social integration of deaf members, the usual negative selective pressure against such mutations is relaxed, resulting, across generations, in the emergence and co-evolution of, on the one hand, a sign language used by both deaf and hearing members of the community and, on the other, the increase in the frequency of the mutation (Levinson & Dediu, 2013).

Moving to the production end of speech, the development of the vocal tract is a very complex embryological process (Greene & Pisano, 2010) and we know a lot about the genetics of various pathologies such as cleft lip and palate (Dixon, Marazita, Beaty, & Murray, 2011; Leslie & Marazita, 2013), but much less is known about the genetic architecture of normal variation and its effects on speech production. Understanding the genetics and development of the vocal tract and its impact on phonetics and phonology is currently an active field of investigation bringing together phonetics (Zhou et al., 2008), computer modeling (Janssen, Dediu, & Moisik, 2015; Moisik & Dediu, 2015), various imaging techniques (Dediu & Moisik, 2016) and genetics.

37.4 Animal models

Several genes have now been associated with disorders that affect some aspects of speech and language via patient studies, genetic associations, and population studies. However, identifying these genes is not the end goal for language genetics. Rather, gene identification presents important new avenues for understanding the biological pathways that can bridge the gap between what is encoded in the genome and the biological readout—be it normal language or language disorder. Animal models are an invaluable way to bridge this gap since in these systems genes can be manipulated, switched on and off, or patient variants introduced to the genome and read-outs can be measured at multiple levels; molecular, cellular, neurological, and behavioral. In this way we can use cutting edge techniques to essentially survey the gene "in action," allowing us to understand its normal function and the consequences for the organism when the gene is mutated or lost.

The complex, multicomponent system that is language is unique to humans and thus can obviously not be studied directly in animal model systems. However, it is exactly by considering language as a multicomponent system that gives us the possibility to make meaningful investigations in animal systems. If we consider some specific aspects that are shared with animals, it is not hard to start thinking of valuable ways to study shared traits and evolutionary differences. Apart from the shared genetics and neurobiology, we can consider behavioral aspects that contribute to speech and/or language such as voluntary vocal control, syntax, rhythm, vocal learning, auditory perception, speech perception, turn taking, social interactions, social communication, gesture, and so on (Fitch, 2000; Fitch, Huber, & Bugnyar, 2010; Hoeschele et al., 2015; Jurgens, 1998; Konopka & Roberts, 2016; Nottebohm et al., 1990; Taglialatela et al., 2015; ten Cate, 2014; M. J. West & King, 1988). So, while no animal encompasses all these traits, by investigating these individual traits across different animal models we can start to build models of key aspects that are part of language or its evolutionary precursors. Furthermore, by using animal models we can trace the biological underpinnings of these traits from the behavioral, back to the molecules and genes that are essential for their execution. In this section, we outline two examples of animal studies that illustrate this approach; the investigation of vocal learning in songbirds and stuttering in mouse models.

37.4.1 The genetics of vocal learning—songbirds

Vocal learning is a key component of spoken language as it is the ability to modify vocalizations by learning from others of the same species (Janik & Slater, 2000). Songbirds are one of the few species other than humans that are vocal learners and as such have been extensively studied, epitomizing the power and potential of animal models (Brainard & Doupe, 2013; Condro & White, 2014; Doupe, Solis, Kimpo, & Boettiger, 2004; Mello, 2014; Mooney, 2014; Nottebohm et al., 1990). In songbirds it has been possible to perform in depth documentation of the behavioral contexts of vocal learning and how factors such as social interaction influence this trait (Chen, Matheson, & Sakata, 2016; Kriengwatana, Spierings, & ten Cate, 2016; W. C. Liu & Nottebohm, 2007; Tchernichovski & Marcus, 2014; ten Cate, 2014; M. J. West & King, 1988). Using the zebra finch songbird, it has also been possible to map in exquisite detail the neural circuitry that underlies this behavior and differentiate the overlapping circuits and brain regions that contribute to vocal learning (anterior forebrain pathway; AFP) vs. vocal production (vocal-motor circuit) (Bertram, Daou, Hyson, Johnson, & Wu, 2014; Doupe et al., 2004; Garst-Orozco, Babadi, & Olveczky, 2014; Kubikova et al., 2014; Nottebohm, 2005). Having this neuro-behavioral framework has also made it possible to gain unprecedented insight into how genes underlie this trait in birds (Abe, Matsui, & Watanabe, 2015; Feenders et al., 2008; Heston & White, 2015; Hilliard, Miller, Fraley, Horvath, & White, 2012; Hilliard, Miller, Horvath, & White, 2012; Mori & Wada, 2015; Pfenning et al., 2014; Wada et al., 2006; Whitney et al., 2014; Whitney et al., 2015). By surveying expression changes of virtually every gene in the genome in a part of the vocal learning circuitry in behaving birds, it has been possible to build a picture of functional molecular networks that underlie singing (Hilliard, Miller, Fraley, et al., 2012; Hilliard, Miller, Horvath, et al., 2012). This revealed networks of genes that were being switched on or off in response to singing and highlighted functional pathways (such as synaptic activity) and specific genes (such as *FoxP2*) that are likely to be involved (Hilliard, Miller, Fraley, et al., 2012; Hilliard, Miller, Horvath, et al., 2012). Because it is possible to manipulate the genomes of animal models, investigations need not stop at identification, but rather can show direct involvement of genes and pathways in vocal learning. *FoxP2* is highly expressed in parts of the vocal learning circuitry in birds and it changes its expression during undirected singing (the variable "practice" phase of singing) (Teramitsu, Poopatanapong, Torrisi, & White, 2010; Teramitsu & White, 2006). It was hypothesized that *FoxP2* may be important for vocal learning in birds, as it is in humans. This proved to be the case, as when the songbird version of *FoxP2* was switched off in a key region of the vocal learning circuitry in living animals, these birds could no longer learn their song correctly (Haesler et al., 2007). This showed a direct causative link between *FoxP2* and vocal learning in birds. Further, it has been possible to bridge the gap for why *FoxP2* has this effect by investigating its role in the formation and activity of specific neural circuits in the songbird brain. Knockdown (reduction of expression of a gene via genetic engineering techniques) of *FoxP2* in juvenile animals leads to alteration of dendritic synapse formation (Schulz, Haesler, Scharff, & Rochefort, 2010), and in adults *FoxP2* knockdown changes the speed of signal propagation through the vocal learning circuit by disrupting dopamine modulation of signals (Murugan, Harward, Scharff, & Mooney, 2013). Taken together, this body of work demonstrates causal links between genetic factors, neurobiology, and behavior in a way that would not be possible in the human system and shows how valuable animal models can be for understanding the biology of language-relevant traits.

37.4.2 The genetics of stuttering—mice

Studies of the genetics of stuttering, although still in their infancy, already tell a remarkable story of how the molecular approach can lead to a better understanding of a speech disorder and the potential for animal models to increase our understanding beyond what would be possible in human systems.

Stuttering is a speech disorder characterized by features that disrupt the smooth flow of speech including blocks (hesitations or pauses) and frequent repetition or prolongation of syllables—most often at the beginning of words or sentences (Seery, Watkins, Mangelsdorf, & Shigeto, 2007; E. Yairi, 2007; Ehud Yairi, Watkins, Ambrose, & Paden, 2001). Although many twin, family, and adoption studies clearly indicated that stuttering has genetic causes, for a long time these causes were obfuscated by unclear modes of inheritance and the lack of any strong candidate genes (Dworzynski, Remington, Rijsdijk, Howell, & Plomin, 2007; Felsenfeld et al., 2000; Kraft & Yairi, 2012; Newbury & Monaco, 2010; Viswanath, Lee, & Chakraborty, 2004). However, in 2010, mutations in a gene known as *GNPTAB* were identified in a large inbred family with recurrent stuttering (Fisher, 2010; Kang et al., 2010). Mutations in this same gene were then identified in unrelated stutterers, but rarely in the general (non-stuttering) population, suggesting that mutation of this gene was a cause of stuttering (Drayna & Kang, 2011). However, mutations in this gene could not account for most known cases of stuttering, and so in a move that perfectly illustrates the power of the molecular approach, the researchers turned to a molecular understanding of this gene to find further causes of stuttering. It was already known that *GNPTAB* encoded a protein that functioned in the lysosomal enzyme targeting pathway (involved in the degradation of cellular products) and this pathway was well characterized (Drayna & Kang, 2011; Reitman & Kornfeld, 1981). Thus, it was possible to identify other members of this pathway and ask if they are also candidates for stuttering. Strikingly, these predictions proved correct and mutations in two closely related genes that act in this pathway, *GNPTG* and *NAGPA*, were found in stutterers, but not in the general population (Drayna & Kang, 2011). Highly destructive mutations in these genes (e.g., that completely destroy the protein product) cause a group of severe metabolic disorders that are lethal in early life with widespread pathology affecting cognition, bone development, connective tissue, eyesight, organ function, and so on (Kudo, Brem, & Canfield, 2006; Raas-Rothschild et al., 2000). Despite carrying mutations in these same genes, people who stutter generally display no other impairments in cognitive, motor, or language tasks (Drayna & Kang, 2011; Kang et al., 2010; Raza et al., 2016). This discrepancy is thought to be due to the type of mutation found in stutterers, which unlike the destructive mutations found in metabolic disorders, represent subtle, often single letter changes to the protein sequence (Drayna & Kang, 2011; Kang et al., 2010; Raza et al., 2016). In total, mutations in these three genes now account for up to 16% of all cases of stuttering (Drayna & Kang, 2011; Kang et al., 2010; Raza et al., 2016), providing convincing evidence that this pathway contributes to speech and its disruption leads to the stuttering speech disorder.

The clear link between the lysosome targeting pathway and speech/disorder presented a conundrum because these genes are expressed, and this pathway is active, in every cell in the body. So how do mutations in a very general process result in a highly specific phenotype-like stuttering? Investigating why lysosomal targeting pathways affect specific neural circuitry affecting speech represents a major challenge in humans, making animal models an attractive alternative. Although mice do not speak, they do exhibit high homology with the genetics and neurobiology of humans and use vocalizations to communicate (Arriaga, Zhou, & Jarvis, 2012; Fischer & Hammerschmidt, 2011; Holy & Guo, 2005). Thus, studying links between the lysosomal targeting pathway and vocal production becomes a tractable neuromolecular question when asked in mice. Just like in humans, complete loss of these genes causes widespread pathology and lethality in mouse models, but when one of the patient-identified mutations in *GNPTAB* was introduced in mice, much more subtle vocal related effects were observed (Barnes et al., 2016; Idol et al., 2014; Paton et al., 2014). Mice carrying the patient mutation in *GNPTAB* produced significantly fewer vocalizations than normal mice due to significantly longer pause lengths between bouts of vocalizing (Barnes et al., 2016). Furthermore, these mice displayed reduced diversity in sequencing of syllables and more stereotyped vocalizations (Barnes et al., 2016). Although this doesn't exactly recapitulate human stuttering, it does show similarities with the human phenotype as human stutterers show speech characterized by frequent repetitions of syllables, fewer vocalizations, and longer pauses between vocalizations (Barnes et al., 2016; Seery et al., 2007; E. Yairi, 2007). The phenotypic similarity observed between humans and mice carrying the same mutation now presents a superb opportunity to understand how this genetic mechanism leads to normal and disrupted neurobiology underlying vocal production. It will be of great interest to see what we learn from this animal model in the future that can be applied to our understanding of the molecular and neurobiological underpinnings of both stuttering and normal speech in humans.

37.4.3 Animal models—concluding remarks

An important consideration with animal models is to choose the right animal system for the question under study. For example, mice are strong genetic models with sequenced genomes and relatively easy methods for switching off genes in whole organisms, tissues, or even specific brain circuits—however they are not vocal learners (Hammerschmidt et al., 2012; Kikusui et al., 2011; Mahrt, Perkel, Tong, Rubel, & Portfors, 2013). By contrast songbirds are extremely good vocal learners and while they do have a sequenced genome it is still extremely difficult to produce genetic manipulations, limiting the volume and speed by which genetic mechanisms can be studied (Velho & Lois, 2014). To understand the full range of language-relevant traits we must use a range of animal systems considering the strengths of each. In summary, multidisciplinary investigations into complementary animal models at genetic, neurological, and behavioral levels are essential if we are to understand how genetic factors functionally program the biological components relevant to language and translate this knowledge back to the human system.

37.5 Discussion and conclusions

This chapter has now covered the basic principles of the genome, how complex molecular mechanisms control genes to produce language-relevant neuronal and behavioral phenotypes and how we can study models from the basic cell in a dish to complex animal systems to bridge the gap between genes and language. But before ending, we must return to the third principle highlighted in the introduction, namely that "no matter how much we will know about the genetic bases of language and speech we must never forget the cultural side of this evolutionary spiral." Language is intrinsically a chimera with both a biological component (rooted in genetics) and a sociocultural component, locked in a complex dynamics of co-evolution. It is unquestionable that language is a full cultural evolutionary system in its own (Dediu et al., 2013; Pagel, 2009) and that we must understand language evolution and change, and the resulting patterns of diversity and cross-linguistically shared properties in this framework. However, we must not lose sight of the fact that language is not a purely cultural phenomenon, evolving somehow detached from the biology of its users and the environment they inhabit, but that these extralinguistic factors (genetics being a major—even if indirect—one) generate forces (strong or weak) that shape the constraints and affordances to which language adapts (Bickel et al., 2015; Christiansen & Chater, 2008; Dediu, 2011; Everett, Blasí, & Roberts, 2016; Levinson & Dediu, 2013). In turn, language must have generated strong enough pressures on our genome that explain the various adaptations we seem to possess for producing, perceiving, processing, and acquiring language, but, more importantly, language is a major component of our uniquely impressive capacity for cumulative cultural evolution (Richerson & Boyd, 2005) and cultural niche construction (Kendal, Tehrani, & Odling-Smee, 2011; Odling-Smee, Laland, & Feldman, 2003) that, in turn, shaped and still shapes our genome (Dediu et al., 2013; Fisher & Ridley, 2013; Gerbault et al., 2011).

We hope that this brief review has managed to kindle interest in this fascinating, dynamic, and complex scientific endeavor that aims at unraveling the genetic foundations of language, and that the pointers to the literature we have provided will offer an accessible entry point in this dense, technical, and multidisciplinary literature. We hope to see the readers of this chapter contributing to the future breakthroughs that will better bridge the "lower-level" approaches using molecular techniques, cell lines grown in dishes, and various animal models, with the "higher-level" aspects of human language better captured by the language sciences and the cognitive neurosciences.

References

Abe, K., Matsui, S., & Watanabe, D. (2015). Transgenic songbirds with suppressed or enhanced activity of CREB transcription factor. *Proceedings of the National Academy of Sciences of the United States of America*, 112(24), 7599–604.

Abrahams, B. S., Tentler, D., Perederiy, J. V., Oldham, M. C., Coppola, G., & Geschwind, D. H. (2007). Genome-wide analyses of human perisylvian cerebral cortical patterning. *Proceedings of the National Academy of Sciences of the United States of America, 104*(45), 17849–54.

Alarcon, M., Abrahams, B. S., Stone, J. L., Duvall, J. A., Perederiy, J. V., Bomar, J. M., . . . & Geschwind, D. H. (2008). Linkage, association, and gene-expression analyses identify CNTNAP2 as an autism-susceptibility gene. *American Journal of Human Genetics, 82*(1), 150–9.

Alberts, B., Johnson, A., Lewis, J., Morgan, D., Raff, M. C., Roberts, K., . . . & Hunt, T. (2014). *Molecular Biology of the Cell*, 6th Edition. Garland Science, New York, NY.

Altshuler, D. M., Durbin, R. M., Abecasis, G. R., Bentley, D. R., Chakravarti, A., Clark, A. G., . . . & Consortium, G. P. (2015). A global reference for human genetic variation. *Nature, 526*(7571), 68–74.

Amador-Arjona, A., Cimadamore, F., Huang, C. T., Wright, R., Lewis, S., Gage, F. H., & Terskikh, A. V. (2015). SOX2 primes the epigenetic landscape in neural precursors enabling proper gene activation during hippocampal neurogenesis. *Proceedings of the National Academy of Sciences of the United States of America, 112*(15), E1936–45.

Anderson, G. R., Galfin, T., Xu, W., Aoto, J., Malenka, R. C., & Sudhof, T. C. (2012). Candidate autism gene screen identifies critical role for cell-adhesion molecule CASPR2 in dendritic arborization and spine development. *Proceedings of the National Academy of Sciences of the United States of America, 109*(44), 18120–5.

Armstrong, D. D. (2005). Neuropathology of Rett syndrome. *Journal of Child Neurology, 20*(9), 747–53.

Arriaga, G., Zhou, E. P., & Jarvis, E. D. (2012). Of mice, birds, and men: The mouse ultrasonic song system has some features similar to humans and song-learning birds. *PLoS One, 7*(10), e46610.

Ayub, Q., Yngvadottir, B., Chen, Y., Xue, Y. L., Hu, M., Vernes, S. C., . . . & Tyler-Smith, C. (2013). FOXP2 targets show evidence of positive selection in European populations. *American Journal of Human Genetics, 92*(5), 696–706.

Bakkaloglu, B., O'Roak, B. J., Louvi, A., Gupta, A. R., Abelson, J. F., Morgan, T. M., . . . & State, M. W. (2008). Molecular cytogenetic analysis and resequencing of contact in associated protein-like 2 in autism spectrum disorders. *American Journal of Human Genetics, 82*(1), 165–73.

Ballana, E., Morales, E., Rabionet, R., Montserrat, B., Ventayol, M., Bravo, O., . . . & Estivill, X. (2006). Mitochondrial 12S rRNA gene mutations affect RNA secondary structure and lead to variable penetrance in hearing impairment. *Biochemical and Biophysical Research Communications, 341*(4), 950–7.

Barnes, T. D., Wozniak, D. F., Gutierrez, J., Han, T. U., Drayna, D., & Holy, T. E. (2016). A mutation associated with stuttering alters mouse pup ultrasonic vocalizations. *Current Biology*, pii: S0960-9822(16)30179-8.

Bartel, D. P. (2004). MicroRNAs: Genomics, biogenesis, mechanism, and function. *Cell, 116*(2), 281–97.

Becker, M., Guadalupe, T., Franke, B., Hibar, D. P., Renteria, M. E., Stein, J. L., . . . & Fisher, S. E. (2016). Early developmental gene enhancers affect subcortical volumes in the adult human brain. *Human Brain Mapping, 37*(5), 1788–800.

Berget, S. M., Moore, C., & Sharp, P. A. (1977). Spliced segments at the 5' terminus of adenovirus 2 late mRNA. *Proceedings of the National Academy of Sciences of the United States of America, 74*(8), 3171–5.

Bertram, R., Daou, A., Hyson, R. L., Johnson, F., & Wu, W. (2014). Two neural streams, one voice: Pathways for theme and variation in the songbird brain. *Neuroscience, 277*, 806–17.

Bhalla, K., Phillips, H. A., Crawford, J., McKenzie, O. L., Mulley, J. C., Eyre, H., . . . & Callen, D. F. (2004). The de novo chromosome 16 translocations of two patients with abnormal phenotypes (mental retardation and epilepsy) disrupt the A2BP1 gene. *Journal of Human Genetics, 49*(6), 308–311.

Bickel, B., Witzlack-Makarevich, A., Choudhary, K. K., Schlesewsky, M., & Bornkessel-Schlesewsky, I. (2015). The neurophysiology of language processing shapes the evolution of grammar: Evidence from case marking. *PLoS One, 10*(8), e0132819.

Bindu, L. H., & Reddy, P. P. (2008). Genetics of aminoglycoside-induced and prelingual non-syndromic mitochondrial hearing impairment: a review. *International Journal of Audiology, 47*(11), 702–7.

Bishop, D. V. (2009). Genes, cognition, and communication: insights from neurodevelopmental disorders. *Annals of the New York Academy of Sciences, 1156*, 1–18.

Blencowe, B. J. (2006). Alternative splicing: new insights from global analyses. *Cell, 126*(1), 37–47.

Boeger, H., Bushnell, D. A., Davis, R., Griesenbeck, J., Lorch, Y., Strattan, J. S., . . . & Kornberg, R. D. (2005). Structural basis of eukaryotic gene transcription. *FEBS Letters, 579*(4), 899–903.

Brainard, M. S., & Doupe, A. J. (2013). Translating birdsong: songbirds as a model for basic and applied medical research. *Annual Review of Neuroscience, 36*, 489–517.

Brami-Cherrier, K., Anzalone, A., Ramos, M., Forne, I., Macciardi, F., Imhof, A., & Borrelli, E. (2014). Epigenetic reprogramming of cortical neurons through alteration of dopaminergic circuits. *Molecular Psychiatry, 19*(11), 1193–200.

Bulut-Karslioglu, A., Perrera, V., Scaranaro, M., de la Rosa-Velazquez, I. A., van de Nobelen, S., Shukeir, N., . . . & Jenuwein, T. (2012). A transcription factor-based mechanism for mouse heterochromatin formation. *Nature Structural & Molecular Biology, 19*(10), 1023–78.

Bulyk, M. L. (2003). Computational prediction of transcription-factor binding site locations. *Genome Biology, 5*(1), 201.

Burton, P. R., Clayton, D. G., Cardon, L. R., Craddock, N., Deloukas, P., Duncanson, A., . . . & Collaborat, B. C. S. (2007). Genome-wide association study of 14,000 cases of seven common diseases and 3,000 shared controls. *Nature, 447*(7145), 661–78.

Chapeville, F., Lipmann, F., Von Ehrenstein, G., Weisblum, B., Ray, W. J., Jr., & Benzer, S. (1962). On the role of soluble ribonucleic acid in coding for amino acids. *Proceedings of the National Academy of Sciences of the United States of America, 48*, 1086–92.

Chedotal, A., & Richards, L. J. (2010). Wiring the brain: the biology of neuronal guidance. *Cold Spring Harbor Perspectives in Biology, 2*(6), a001917.

Chen, Y., Matheson, L. E., & Sakata, J. T. (2016). Mechanisms underlying the social enhancement of vocal learning in songbirds. *Proceedings of the National Academy of Sciences of the United States of America, 113*(24), 6641–6.

Chia, P. H., Li, P., & Shen, K. (2013). Cell biology in neuroscience: Cellular and molecular mechanisms underlying presynapse formation. *Journal of Cell Biology, 203*(1), 11–22.

Chow, L. T., Gelinas, R. E., Broker, T. R., & Roberts, R. J. (1977). An amazing sequence arrangement at the 5' ends of adenovirus 2 messenger RNA. *Cell, 12*(1), 1–8.

Christiansen, M. H., & Chater, N. (2008). Language as shaped by the brain. *Behavioral and Brain Sciences, 31*(5), 489–508.

Churchill, F. B. (1974). William Johannsen and the genotype concept. *Journal of the History of Biology*, 7(1), 5–30.

Clovis, Y. M., Enard, W., Marinaro, F., Huttner, W. B., & De Pietri Tonelli, D. (2012). Convergent repression of Foxp2 3'UTR by miR-9 and miR-132 in embryonic mouse neocortex: implications for radial migration of neurons. *Development*, 139(18), 3332–42.

Condro, M. C., & White, S. A. (2014). Recent advances in the genetics of vocal learning. *Comparative Cognition & Behavior Reviews*, 9, 75–98.

Crick, F. H. (1958). On protein synthesis. *Symposia of the Society for Experimental Biology*, 12, 138–63.

Cutter, A. R., & Hayes, J. J. (2015). A brief review of nucleosome structure. *FEBS Letters*, 589(20 Pt A), 2914–22.

de Vos, C. (2013). Sign-spatiality in Kata Kolok: How a village sign language of Bali inscribes its signing space. *Sign Language & Linguistics*, 16(2), 277–84.

Dediu, D. (2011). Are languages really independent from genes? If not, what would a genetic bias affecting language diversity look like? *Human Biology*, 83(2), 279–96.

Dediu, D. (2015). *An Introduction to Genetics for Language Scientists: Current Concepts, Methods and Findings*. Cambridge University Press, Cambridge.

Dediu, D., Cysouw, M., Levinson, S. C., Baronchelli, A., Christiansen, M. H., Croft, W., . . . & Lieven, E. (2013). *Cultural Evolution of Language*. In: Richerson, P. J., & Christiansen, M. H. (Eds.), *Cultural Evolution: Society, Technology, Language, and Religion, Vol. 12* (pp. 303–32). MIT Press, Cambridge, MA.

Dediu, D., Janssen, R., & Moisik, S. R. (2017). Language is not isolated from its wider environment: Vocal tract influences on the evolution of speech and language. *Language & Communication*, 54, 9–20.

Dediu, D., & Moisik, S. (2016). Anatomical biasing of click learning and production: An MRI and 3D palate imaging study. In: Roberts, S. G., Cuskley, C., McCrohon, L., Barceló-Coblijn, L., Fehér, O., & Verhoef, T. (Eds.), *The Evolution of Language: Proceedings of the 11th International Conference (EVOLANGX11)*. Available at: http://evolang.org/neworleans/papers/57.html

Deriziotis, P., O'Roak, B. J., Graham, S. A., Estruch, S. B., Dimitropoulou, D., Bernier, R. A., . . . & Fisher, S. E. (2014). De novo TBR1 mutations in sporadic autism disrupt protein functions. *Nature Communications*, 5, 4954.

Devanna, P., Chen, X. S., Ho, J., Gajewski, D., Smith, S. D., Gialluisi, A., . . . & Vernes, S. C. (2017). Next-gen sequencing identifies non-coding variation disrupting miRNA-binding sites in neurological disorders. *Molecular Psychiatry*. doi: 10.1038/mp.2017.30

Devanna, P., Middelbeek, J., & Vernes, S. C. (2014). FOXP2 drives neuronal differentiation by interacting with retinoic acid signaling pathways. *Frontiers in Cellular Neuroscience*, 8, 305.

Dixon, M. J., Marazita, M. L., Beaty, T. H., & Murray, J. C. (2011). Cleft lip and palate: Understanding genetic and environmental influences. *Nature Reviews Genetics*, 12(3), 167–78.

Doolittle, W. F. (2013). Is junk DNA bunk? A critique of ENCODE. *Proceedings of the National Academy of Sciences of the United States of America*, 110(14), 5294–300.

Doupe, A. J., Solis, M. M., Kimpo, R., & Boettiger, C. A. (2004). Cellular, circuit, and synaptic mechanisms in song learning. *Annals of the New York Academy of Sciences*, 1016, 495–523.

Drayna, D., & Kang, C. (2011). Genetic approaches to understanding the causes of stuttering. *Journal of Neurodevelopmental Disorders*, 3(4), 374–80.

Dworzynski, K., Remington, A., Rijsdijk, F., Howell, P., & Plomin, R. (2007). Genetic etiology in cases of recovered and persistent stuttering in an unselected, longitudinal sample of young twins. *American Journal of Speech-Language Pathology*, 16(2), 169–78.

Ebert, D. H., & Greenberg, M. E. (2013). Activity-dependent neuronal signalling and autism spectrum disorder. *Nature*, 493(7432), 327–37.

Ecker, J. R. (2012). FORUM: Genomics ENCODE explained. *Nature*, 489(7414), 52–3.

Elia, J., Gai, X., Xie, H. M., Perin, J. C., Geiger, E., Glessner, J. T., . . . & White, P. S. (2010). Rare structural variants found in attention-deficit hyperactivity disorder are preferentially associated with neurodevelopmental genes. *Molecular Psychiatry*, 15(6), 637–46.

Everett, C., Blasí, D. E., & Roberts, S. G. (2016). Language evolution and climate: The case of desiccation and tone. *Journal of Language Evolution*, 1(1), 33–46.

Ezkurdia, I., Juan, D., Rodriguez, J. M., Frankish, A., Diekhans, M., Harrow, J., . . . & Tress, M. L. (2014). Multiple evidence strands suggest that there may be as few as 19,000 human protein-coding genes. *Human Molecular Genetics*, 23(22), 5866–78.

Faheem, M., Naseer, M. I., Rasool, M., Chaudhary, A. G., Kumosani, T. A., Ilyas, A. M., . . . & Jamal, H. S. (2015). Molecular genetics of human primary microcephaly: an overview. *BMC Medical Genomics*, 8.

Fang, F. C., & Casadevall, A. (2011). Reductionistic and holistic science. *Infection and Immunity*, 79(4), 1401–4.

Feenders, G., Liedvogel, M., Rivas, M., Zapka, M., Horita, H., Hara, E., . . . & Jarvis, E. D. (2008). Molecular mapping of movement-associated areas in the avian brain: a motor theory for vocal learning origin. *PLoS One*, 3(3), e1768.

Felsenfeld, S., Kirk, K. M., Zhu, G., Statham, D. J., Neale, M. C., & Martin, N. G. (2000). A study of the genetic and environmental etiology of stuttering in a selected twin sample. *Behavior Genetics*, 30(5), 359–66.

Fernández, V., Llinares-Benadero, C., & Borrell, V. (2016). Cerebral cortex expansion and folding: What have we learned? *EMBO Journal*, 35(10), 1021–44.

Feuk, L., Kalervo, A., Lipsanen-Nyman, M., Skaug, J., Nakabayashi, K., Finucane, B., . . . & Hannula-Jouppi, K. (2006). Absence of a paternally inherited FOXP2 gene in developmental verbal dyspraxia. *American Journal of Human Genetics*, 79(5), 965–72.

Fischer, J., & Hammerschmidt, K. (2011). Ultrasonic vocalizations in mouse models for speech and socio-cognitive disorders: insights into the evolution of vocal communication. *Genes, Brain and Behavior*, 10(1), 17–27.

Fisher, S. E. (2010). Genetic susceptibility to stuttering. *New England Journal of Medicine*, 362(8), 750–52.

Fisher, S. E., & Marcus, G. F. (2006). The eloquent ape: Genes, brains and the evolution of language. *Nature Reviews Genetics*, 7(1), 9–20.

Fisher, S. E., & Ridley, M. (2013). Culture, genes, and the human revolution. *Science*, 340(6135), 929–30.

Fisher, S. E., & Scharff, C. (2009). FOXP2 as a molecular window into speech and language. *Trends in Genetics*, 25(4), 166–77.

Fitch, W. T. (2000). The evolution of speech: A comparative review. *Trends in Cognitive Sciences*, 4(7), 258–67.

Fitch, W. T., Huber, L., & Bugnyar, T. (2010). Social cognition and the evolution of language: Constructing cognitive phylogenies. *Neuron*, 65(6), 795–814.

Folia, V., Forkstam, C., Ingvar, M., Hagoort, P., & Petersson, K. M. (2011). Implicit artificial syntax processing: Genes, preference, and bounded recursion. *Biolinguistics*, 5, 105–32.

French, C. A., Jin, X., Campbell, T. G., Gerfen, E., Groszer, M., Fisher, S. E., & Costa, R. M. (2012). An aetiological Foxp2 mutation causes aberrant striatal activity and alters plasticity during skill learning. *Molecular Psychiatry, 17*(11), 1077–85.

Friederici, A. D. (2011). The brain basis of language processing: from structure to function. *Physiological Reviews, 91*(4), 1357–92.

Fu, W. Q., O'Connor, T. D., Jun, G., Kang, H. M., Abecasis, G., Leal, S. M., . . . & Project, N. E. S. (2013). Analysis of 6,515 exomes reveals the recent origin of most human protein-coding variants. *Nature, 493*(7431), 216–20.

Galaburda, A. M., & Kemper, T. L. (1979). Cytoarchitectonic abnormalities in developmental dyslexia: A case study. *Annals of Neurology, 6*(2), 94–100.

Galaburda, A. M., Sherman, G. F., Rosen, G. D., Aboitiz, F., & Geschwind, N. (1985). Developmental dyslexia: four consecutive patients with cortical anomalies. *Annals of Neurology, 18*(2), 222–33.

Gao, P., Sultan, K. T., Zhang, X. J., & Shi, S. H. (2013). Lineage-dependent circuit assembly in the neocortex. *Development, 140*(13), 2645–55.

Garst-Orozco, J., Babadi, B., & Olveczky, B. P. (2014). A neural circuit mechanism for regulating vocal variability during song learning in zebra finches. *Elife, 3*, e03697.

Gehman, L. T., Meera, P., Stoilov, P., Shiue, L., O'Brien, J. E., Meisler, M. H., . . . & Black, D. L. (2012). The splicing regulator Rbfox2 is required for both cerebellar development and mature motor function. *Genes & Development, 26*(5), 445–60.

Gehman, L. T., Stoilov, P., Maguire, J., Damianov, A., Lin, C. H., Shiue, L., . . . & Black, D. L. (2011). The splicing regulator Rbfox1 (A2BP1) controls neuronal excitation in the mammalian brain. *Nature Genetics, 43*(7), 706–11.

Gerbault, P., Liebert, A., Itan, Y., Powell, A., Currat, M., Burger, J., . . . & Thomas, M. G. (2011). Evolution of lactase persistence: an example of human niche construction. *Philosophical Transactions of the Royal Society B, Biological Sciences, 366*(1566), 863–77.

Gerstein, M. B., Bruce, C., Rozowsky, J. S., Zheng, D., Du, J., Korbel, J. O., . . . & Snyder, M. (2007). What is a gene, post-ENCODE? History and updated definition. *Genome Research, 17*(6), 669–81.

Gialluisi, A., Newbury, D. F., Wilcutt, E. G., Olson, R. K., DeFries, J. C., Brandler, W. M., . . . & Fisher, S. E. (2014). Genome-wide screening for DNA variants associated with reading and language traits. *Genes, Brain and Behavior, 13*(7), 686–701.

Gordon, A., Salomon, D., Barak, N., Pen, Y., Tsoory, M., Kimchi, T., & Peles, E. (2016). Expression of Cntnap2 (Caspr2) in multiple levels of sensory systems. *Molecular and Cellular Neuroscience, 70*, 42–53.

Graham, S. A., Deriziotis, P., & Fisher, S. E. (2015). Insights into the genetic foundations of human communication. *Neuropsychology Review, 25*(1), 3–26.

Graham, S. A., & Fisher, S. E. (2013). Decoding the genetics of speech and language. *Current Opinion in Neurobiology, 23*(1), 43–51.

Greene, R. M., & Pisano, M. M. (2010). Palate morphogenesis: current understanding and future directions. *Birth Defects Research Part C: Embryo Today, 90*(2), 133–54.

Groszer, M., Keays, D. A., Deacon, R. M., de Bono, J. P., Prasad-Mulcare, S., Gaub, S., . . . & Fisher, S. E. (2008). Impaired synaptic plasticity and motor learning in mice with a point mutation implicated in human speech deficits. *Current Biology, 18*(5), 354–62.

Haesler, S., Rochefort, C., Georgi, B., Licznerski, P., Osten, P., & Scharff, C. (2007). Incomplete and inaccurate vocal imitation after knockdown of FoxP2 in songbird basal ganglia nucleus Area X. *PLoS Biol, 5*(12), e321.

Hagberg, B., Aicardi, J., Dias, K., & Ramos, O. (1983). A progressive syndrome of autism, dementia, ataxia, and loss of purposeful hand use in girls—Rett's syndrome—report of 35 cases. *Annals of Neurology*, 14(4), 471–9.

Hagoort, P. (2013). MUC (Memory, Unification, Control) and beyond. *Frontiers in Psychology*, 4, 416.

Hamdan, F. F., Daoud, H., Rochefort, D., Piton, A., Gauthier, J., Langlois, M., . . . & Michaud, J. L. (2010). De novo mutations in FOXP1 in cases with intellectual disability, autism, and language impairment. *American Journal of Human Genetics*, 87(5), 671–8.

Hammerschmidt, K., Reisinger, E., Westekemper, K., Ehrenreich, L., Strenzke, N., & Fischer, J. (2012). Mice do not require auditory input for the normal development of their ultrasonic vocalizations. *BMC Neuroscience*, 13, 40.

Hamshere, M. L., Green, E. K., Jones, I. R., Jones, L., Moskvina, V., Kirov, G., . . . & Craddock, N. (2009). Genetic utility of broadly defined bipolar schizoaffective disorder as a diagnostic concept. *British Journal of Psychiatry*, 195(1), 23–9.

Han, W. Q., Kwan, K. Y., Shim, S., Lam, M. M. S., Shin, Y., Xu, X. M., . . . & Sestan, N. (2011). TBR1 directly represses Fezf2 to control the laminar origin and development of the corticospinal tract. *Proceedings of the National Academy of Sciences of the United States of America*, 108(7), 3041–6.

Hannenhalli, S. (2008). Eukaryotic transcription factor binding sites—modeling and integrative search methods. *Bioinformatics*, 24(11), 1325–31.

Hannula-Jouppi, K., Kaminen-Ahola, N., Taipale, M., Eklund, R., Nopola-Hemmi, J., Kaariainen, H., & Kere, J. (2005). The axon guidance receptor gene ROBO1 is a candidate gene for developmental dyslexia. *PLoS Genetics*, 1(4), e50.

Hauser, M. D., Chomsky, N., & Fitch, W. T. (2002). The faculty of language: what is it, who has it, and how did it evolve? *Science*, 298(5598), 1569–79.

Hauser, M. D., Yang, C., Berwick, R. C., Tattersall, I., Ryan, M. J., Watumull, J., . . . & Lewontin, R. C. (2014). The mystery of language evolution. *Frontiers in Psychology*, 5, 401.

Heston, J. B., & White, S. A. (2015). Behavior-linked FoxP2 regulation enables zebra finch vocal learning. *Journal of Neuroscience*, 35(7), 2885–94.

Hibar, D. P., Stein, J. L., Renteria, M. E., Arias-Vasquez, A., Desrivieres, S., Jahanshad, N., . . . & Medland, S. E. (2015). Common genetic variants influence human subcortical brain structures. *Nature*, 520(7546), 224–9.

Hickok, G., & Poeppel, D. (2007). The cortical organization of speech processing. *Nature Reviews Neuroscience*, 8(5), 393–402.

Hilliard, A. T., Miller, J. E., Fraley, E. R., Horvath, S., & White, S. A. (2012). Molecular microcircuitry underlies functional specification in a basal ganglia circuit dedicated to vocal learning. *Neuron*, 73(3), 537–52.

Hilliard, A. T., Miller, J. E., Horvath, S., & White, S. A. (2012). Distinct neurogenomic states in basal ganglia subregions relate differently to singing behavior in songbirds. *PLoS Computational Biology*, 8(11), e1002773.

Hitzemann, R., Bottomly, D., Darakjian, P., Walter, N., Iancu, O., Searles, R., . . . & McWeeney, S. (2013). Genes, behavior and next-generation RNA sequencing. *Genes, Brain and Behavior*, 12(1), 1–12.

Hoeschele, M., Merchant, H., Kikuchi, Y., Hattori, Y., & ten Cate, C. (2015). Searching for the origins of musicality across species. *Philosophical Transactions of the Royal Society B, Biological Sciences*, 370(1664), 39–47.

Holtmaat, A., & Svoboda, K. (2009). Experience-dependent structural synaptic plasticity in the mammalian brain. *Nature Reviews Neuroscience*, 10(9), 647–58.

Holy, T. E., & Guo, Z. S. (2005). Ultrasonic songs of male mice. *PLoS Biology*, 3(12), 2177–86.

Huang, T. N., Chuang, H. C., Chou, W. H., Chen, C. Y., Wang, H. F., Chou, S. J., & Hsueh, Y. P. (2014). Tbr1 haploinsufficiency impairs amygdalar axonal projections and results in cognitive abnormality. *Nature Neuroscience, 17*(2), 240–7.

Huang, T. N., & Hsueh, Y. P. (2015). Brain-specific transcriptional regulator T-brain-1 controls brain wiring and neuronal activity in autism spectrum disorders. *Frontiers of Neuroscience, 9*, 406.

Idol, R. A., Wozniak, D. F., Fujiwara, H., Yuede, C. M., Ory, D. S., Kornfeld, S., & Vogel, P. (2014). Neurologic abnormalities in mouse models of the lysosomal storage disorders mucolipidosis II and mucolipidosis III gamma. *PLoS One, 9*(10), e109768.

Janik, V. M., & Slater, P. J. (2000). The different roles of social learning in vocal communication. *Animal Behavior, 60*(1), 1–11.

Janik, V. M., & Slater, P. J. B. (1997). Vocal learning in mammals. *Advances in the Study of Behavior, 26*, 59–99.

Janssen, R., Dediu, D., & Moisik, S. R. (2015). Bezier modelling and high accuracy curve fitting to capture hard palate variation. In: The Scottish Consortium for ICPhS 2015 (Ed.), *Proceedings of the 18th International Congress of Phonetic Sciences*. University of Glasgow, Glasgow.

Jobling, M., Hurles, M., & Tyler-Smith, C. (2004). *Human Evolutionary Genetics: Origins, Peoples & Disease* (p. 23). Garland Science, New York, NY.

Jongbloets, B. C., & Pasterkamp, R. J. (2014). Semaphorin signalling during development. *Development, 141*(17), 3292–7.

Jurgens, U. (1998). Neuronal control of mammalian vocalization, with special reference to the squirrel monkey. *Naturwissenschaften, 85*(8), 376–88.

Kaestner, K. H., Knochel, W., & Martinez, D. E. (2000). Unified nomenclature for the winged helix/forkhead transcription factors. *Genes & Development, 14*(2), 142–6.

Kang, C., Riazuddin, S., Mundorff, J., Krasnewich, D., Friedman, P., Mullikin, J. C., & Drayna, D. (2010). Mutations in the lysosomal enzyme-targeting pathway and persistent stuttering. *New England Journal of Medicine, 362*(8), 677–85.

Kendal, J., Tehrani, J. J., & Odling-Smee, J. (2011). Human niche construction in interdisciplinary focus: Introduction. *Philosophical Transactions of the Royal Society B, Biological Sciences, 366*(1566), 785–92.

Khatri, P., Sirota, M., & Butte, A. J. (2012). Ten years of pathway analysis: current approaches and outstanding challenges. *PLoS Computational Biology, 8*(2), e1002375.

Kikusui, T., Nakanishi, K., Nakagawa, R., Nagasawa, M., Mogi, K., & Okanoya, K. (2011). Cross fostering experiments suggest that mice songs are innate. *PLoS One, 6*(3), e17721.

Kishi, N., & Macklis, J. D. (2004). MECP2 is progressively expressed in post-migratory neurons and is involved in neuronal maturation rather than cell fate decisions. *Molecular and Cellular Neuroscience, 27*(3), 306–21.

Knornschild, M. (2014). Vocal production learning in bats. *Current Opinion in Neurobiology, 28*, 80–5.

Kokotas, H., Petersen, M. B., & Willems, P. J. (2007). Mitochondrial deafness. *Clinical Genetics, 71*(5), 379–91.

Kolodkin, A. L., & Tessier-Lavigne, M. (2011). Mechanisms and molecules of neuronal wiring: A primer. *Cold Spring Harbor Perspectives in Biology, 3*(6), a001727.

Konopka, G., Bomar, J. M., Winden, K., Coppola, G., Jonsson, Z. O., Gao, F., . . . & Geschwind, D. H. (2009). Human-specific transcriptional regulation of CNS development genes by FOXP2. *Nature, 462*(7270), 213–17.

Konopka, G., & Roberts, T. F. (2016). Animal models of speech and vocal communication deficits associated with psychiatric disorders. *Biological Psychiatry, 79*(1), 53–61.

Kos, M., van den Brink, D., Snijders, T. M., Rijpkema, M., Franke, B., Fernández, G., & Hagoort, P. (2012). CNTNAP2 and language processing in healthy individuals as measured with ERPs. *PLoS One, 7*(10), e46995.

Kouzarides, T. (2007). Chromatin modifications and their function. *Cell, 128*(4), 693–705.

Kraft, S. J., & Yairi, E. (2012). Genetic bases of stuttering: The state of the art, 2011. *Folia Phoniatrica Et Logopaedica, 64*(1), 34–47.

Kriengwatana, B., Spierings, M. J., & ten Cate, C. (2016). Auditory discrimination learning in zebra finches: effects of sex, early life conditions and stimulus characteristics. *Animal Behaviour, 116*, 99–112.

Krueger, D. D., Tuffy, L. P., Papadopoulos, T., & Brose, N. (2012). The role of neurexins and neuroligins in the formation, maturation, and function of vertebrate synapses. *Current Opinion in Neurobiology, 22*(3), 412–22.

Kubikova, L., Bosikova, E., Cvikova, M., Lukacova, K., Scharff, C., & Jarvis, E. D. (2014). Basal ganglia function, stuttering, sequencing, and repair in adult songbirds. *Scientific Reports, 4*, 6590.

Kudo, M., Brem, M. S., & Canfield, W. M. (2006). Mucolipidosis II (I-cell disease) and mucolipidosis IIIA (classical pseudo-hurler polydystrophy) are caused by mutations in the GlcNAc-phosphotransferase alpha/beta-subunits precursor gene. *American Journal of Human Genetics, 78*(3), 451–63.

Kwan, K. Y., Sestan, N., & Anton, E. S. (2012). Transcriptional co-regulation of neuronal migration and laminar identity in the neocortex. *Development, 139*(9), 1535–46.

Lai, C. S., Fisher, S. E., Hurst, J. A., Vargha-Khadem, F., & Monaco, A. P. (2001). A forkhead-domain gene is mutated in a severe speech and language disorder. *Nature, 413*(6855), 519–23.

Lassek, M., Weingarten, J., & Volknandt, W. (2015). The synaptic proteome. *Cell Tissue Research, 359*(1), 255–65.

Lawrence, M., Daujat, S., & Schneider, R. (2016). Lateral thinking: How histone modifications regulate gene expression. *Trends in Genetics, 32*(1), 42–56.

Le-Niculescu, H., Patel, S. D., Bhat, M., Kuczenski, R., Faraone, S. V., Tsuang, M. T., ... & Niculescu, A. B., 3rd. (2009). Convergent functional genomics of genome-wide association data for bipolar disorder: comprehensive identification of candidate genes, pathways and mechanisms. *American Journal of Medical Genetics Part B: Neuropsychiatric Genetics, 150B*(2), 155–81.

Lee, J. A., Damianov, A., Lin, C. H., Fontes, M., Parikshak, N. N., Anderson, E. S., ... & Martin, K. C. (2016). Cytoplasmic Rbfox1 regulates the expression of synaptic and autism-related genes. *Neuron, 89*(1), 113–28.

Lee, R. C., Feinbaum, R. L., & Ambros, V. (1993). The C-Elegans heterochronic gene Lin-4 encodes small Rnas with antisense complementarity to Lin-14. *Cell, 75*(5), 843–54.

Leslie, E. J., & Marazita, M. L. (2013). Genetics of cleft lip and cleft palate. *American Journal of Medical Genetics Part C: Seminars in Medical Genetics, 163C*(4), 246–58.

Levinson, S. C., & Dediu, D. (2013). The interplay of genetic and cultural factors in ongoing language evolution. In: Richerson, P. J., & Christiansen, M. H. (Eds.), *Cultural Evolution: Society, Technology, Language, and Religion*, Vol. 12 (pp. 219–32). MIT Press, Cambridge, MA.

Lewin, B. (1990). *Gene IV*. Oxford Cell Press, Oxford.

Lewin, B., Krebs, J. E., Kilpatrick, S. T., Goldstein, E. S., & Lewin, B. (2011). *Lewin's Genes X*. Jones and Bartlett, Sudbury, MA.

Liegeois, F., Baldeweg, T., Connelly, A., Gadian, D. G., Mishkin, M., & Vargha-Khadem, F. (2003). Language fMRI abnormalities associated with FOXP2 gene mutation. *Nature Neuroscience, 6*(11), 1230–7.

Liu, F., Wen, B., & Kayser, M. (2013). Colorful DNA polymorphisms in humans. *Seminars in Cell & Developmental Biology*, 24(6–7), 562–75.

Liu, W. C., & Nottebohm, F. (2007). A learning program that ensures prompt and versatile vocal imitation. *Proceedings of the National Academy of Sciences of the United States of America*, 104(51), 20398–403.

Luger, K., Mader, A. W., Richmond, R. K., Sargent, D. F., & Richmond, T. J. (1997). Crystal structure of the nucleosome core particle at 2.8 angstrom resolution. *Nature*, 389(6648), 251–60.

Luhmann, H. J., Fukuda, A., & Kilb, W. (2015). Control of cortical neuronal migration by glutamate and GABA. *Frontiers in Cellular Neuroscience*, 9, 4.

Lyst, M. J., & Bird, A. (2015). Rett syndrome: A complex disorder with simple roots. *Nature Reviews Genetics*, 16(5), 261–75.

MacDermot, K. D., Bonora, E., Sykes, N., Coupe, A. M., Lai, C. S., Vernes, S. C., . . . & Fisher, S. E. (2005). Identification of FOXP2 truncation as a novel cause of developmental speech and language deficits. *American Journal of Human Genetics*, 76(6), 1074–80.

Mahrt, E. J., Perkel, D. J., Tong, L., Rubel, E. W., & Portfors, C. V. (2013). Engineered deafness reveals that mouse courtship vocalizations do not require auditory experience. *Journal of Neuroscience*, 33(13), 5573–83.

Maltais, L. J., Blake, J. A., Chu, T., Lutz, C. M., Eppig, J. T., & Jackson, I. (2002). Rules and guidelines for mouse gene, allele, and mutation nomenclature: A condensed version. *Genomics*, 79(4), 471–4.

Manor, U., Disanza, A., Grati, M., Andrade, L., Lin, H., Di Fiore, P. P., . . . & Kachar, B. (2011). Regulation of stereocilia length by myosin XVa and whirlin depends on the actin-regulatory protein Eps8. *Current Biology*, 21(2), 167–72.

Marin, O., Valiente, M., Ge, X. C., & Tsai, L. H. (2010). Guiding neuronal cell migrations. *Cold Spring Harbor Perspectives in Biology*, 2(2), a001834.

Martin, C. L., Duvall, J. A., Ilkin, Y., Simon, J. S., Arreaza, M. G., Wilkes, K., . . . & Geschwind, D. H. (2007). Cytogenetic and molecular characterization of A2BP1/FOX1 as a candidate gene for autism. *American Journal of Medical Genetics Part B: Neuropsychiatric Genetics*, 144B(7), 869–76.

Mathies, L. D., Blackwell, G. G., Austin, M. K., Edwards, A. C., Riley, B. P., Davies, A. G., & Bettinger, J. C. (2015). SWI/SNF chromatin remodeling regulates alcohol response behaviors in Caenorhabditis elegans and is associated with alcohol dependence in humans. *Proceedings of the National Academy of Sciences of the United States of America*, 112(10), 3032–7.

Mello, C. V. (2014). The zebra finch, Taeniopygia guttata: an avian model for investigating the neurobiological basis of vocal learning. *Cold Spring Harb Protocols*, 2014(12), 1237–42.

Meng, H., Smith, S. D., Hager, K., Held, M., Liu, J., Olson, R. K., . . . & Gruen, J. R. (2005). DCDC2 is associated with reading disability and modulates neuronal development in the brain. *Proceedings of the National Academy of Sciences of the United States of America*, 102(47), 17053–8.

Missler, M., Fernández-Chacon, R., & Sudhof, T. C. (1998). The making of neurexins. *Journal of Neurochemistry*, 71(4), 1339–47.

Moisik, S., & Dediu, D. (2015). Anatomical biasing and clicks: Preliminary biomechanical modelling. In: Hannah, L. (Ed.), *The Evolution of Phonetic Capabilities: Causes, Constraints, Consequences* (pp. 8–13). Glasgow, UK. Available at: https://ai.vub.ac.be/sites/default/files/proceedingsfinal.pdf

Mooney, R. (2014). Auditory-vocal mirroring in songbirds. *Philosophical Transactions of the Royal Society of London. Series B, Biological Sciences, 369*(1644), 20130179.

Moorthie, S., Mattocks, C. J., & Wright, C. F. (2011). Review of massively parallel DNA sequencing technologies. *HUGO Journal, 5*(1–4), 1–12.

Mori, C., & Wada, K. (2015). Audition-independent vocal crystallization associated with intrinsic developmental gene expression dynamics. *Journal of Neuroscience, 35*(3), 878–89.

Murugan, M., Harward, S., Scharff, C., & Mooney, R. (2013). Diminished FoxP2 levels affect dopaminergic modulation of corticostriatal signaling important to song variability. *Neuron, 80*(6), 1464–76.

Na, E. S., & Monteggia, L. M. (2011). The role of MeCP2 in CNS development and function. *Hormones and Behavior, 59*(3), 364–8.

Na, E. S., Nelson, E. D., Kavalali, E. T., & Monteggia, L. M. (2013). The impact of MeCP2 loss- or gain-of-function on synaptic plasticity. *Neuropsychopharmacology, 38*(1), 212–19.

Narasimhan, V. M., Hunt, K. A., Mason, D., Baker, C. L., Karczewski, K. J., Barnes, M. R., . . . & van Heel, D. A. (2016). Health and population effects of rare gene knockouts in adult humans with related parents. *Science, 352*(6284), 474–7.

Newbury, D. F., & Monaco, A. P. (2010). Genetic advances in the study of speech and language disorders. *Neuron, 68*(2), 309–20.

Nottebohm, F. (2005). The neural basis of birdsong. *PLoS Biol, 3*(5), e164.

Nottebohm, F., Alvarezbuylla, A., Cynx, J., Kirn, J., Ling, C. Y., Nottebohm, M., . . . & Williams, H. (1990). Song learning in birds—the relation between perception and production. *Philosophical Transactions of the Royal Society of London Series B, Biological Sciences, 329*(1253), 115–24.

O'Roak, B. J., Deriziotis, P., Lee, C., Vives, L., Schwartz, J. J., Girirajan, S., . . . & Eichler, E. E. (2011). Exome sequencing in sporadic autism spectrum disorders identifies severe de novo mutations. *Nature Genetics, 43*(6), 585–9.

Odling-Smee, F. J., Laland, K. N., & Feldman, M. W. (2003). *Niche Construction: The Neglected Process in Evolution*. Princeton University Press, Princeton, NJ.

Ota, T., Suzuki, Y., Nishikawa, T., Otsuki, T., Sugiyama, T., Irie, R., . . . & Sugano, S. (2004). Complete sequencing and characterization of 21,243 full-length human cDNAs. *Nature Genetics, 36*(1), 40–5.

Pagel, M. (2009). Human language as a culturally transmitted replicator. *Nature Reviews Genetics, 10*(6), 405–15.

Paracchini, S., Scerri, T., & Monaco, A. P. (2007). The genetic lexicon of dyslexia. *Annual Review of Genomics and Human Genetics, 8*, 57–79.

Paracchini, S., Steer, C. D., Buckingham, L. L., Morris, A. P., Ring, S., Scerri, T., . . . & Monaco, A. P. (2008). Association of the KIAA0319 dyslexia susceptibility gene with reading skills in the general population. *American Journal of Psychiatry, 165*(12), 1576–84.

Paton, L., Bitoun, E., Kenyon, J., Priestman, D. A., Oliver, P. L., Edwards, B., . . . & Davies, K. E. (2014). A novel mouse model of a patient mucolipidosis II mutation recapitulates disease pathology. *Journal of Biological Chemistry, 289*(39), 26709–21.

Pennisi, E. (2012). GENOMICS ENCODE project writes eulogy for junk DNA. *Science, 337*(6099), 1159–61.

Petkov, C. I., & Jarvis, E. D. (2012). Birds, primates, and spoken language origins: Behavioral phenotypes and neurobiological substrates. *Frontiers in Evolutionary Neuroscience, 4*, 12.

Pfenning, A. R., Hara, E., Whitney, O., Rivas, M. V., Wang, R., Roulhac, P. L., . . . & Jarvis, E. D. (2014). Convergent transcriptional specializations in the brains of humans and song-learning birds. *Science, 346*(6215), 1256846.

Phizicky, E. M., & Hopper, A. K. (2010). tRNA biology charges to the front. *Genes & Development*, 24(17), 1832–60.

Pohodich, A. E., & Zoghbi, H. Y. (2015). Rett syndrome: disruption of epigenetic control of postnatal neurological functions. *Human Molecular Genetics*, 24(R1), R10–R16.

Poliak, S., Gollan, L., Martinez, R., Custer, A., Einheber, S., Salzer, J. L., ... & Peles, E. (1999). Caspr2, a new member of the neurexin superfamily, is localized at the juxtaparanodes of myelinated axons and associates with K+ channels. *Neuron*, 24(4), 1037–47.

Poliak, S., Gollan, L., Salomon, D., Berglund, E. O., Ohara, R., Ranscht, B., & Peles, E. (2001). Localization of Caspr2 in myelinated nerves depends on axon-glia interactions and the generation of barriers along the axon. *Journal of Neuroscience*, 21(19), 7568–75.

Raas-Rothschild, A., Cormier-Daire, V., Bao, M., Genin, E., Salomon, R., Brewer, K., ... & Canfield, W. M. (2000). Molecular basis of variant pseudo-Hurler polydystrophy (mucolipidosis IIIC). *Journal of Clinical Investigation*, 105(5), 673–81.

Raza, M. H., Domingues, C. E., Webster, R., Sainz, E., Paris, E., Rahn, R., ... & Drayna, D. (2016). Mucolipidosis types II and III and non-syndromic stuttering are associated with different variants in the same genes. *European Journal of Human Genetics*, 24(4), 529–34.

Reitman, M. L., & Kornfeld, S. (1981). Lysosomal enzyme targeting. N-Acetylglucosaminylphosphotransferase selectively phosphorylates native lysosomal enzymes. *Journal of Biological Chemistry*, 256(23), 11977–80.

Rice, G. M., Raca, G., Jakielski, K. J., Laffin, J. J., Iyama-Kurtycz, C. M., Hartley, S. L., ... & Shriberg, L. D. (2012). Phenotype of FOXP2 haploinsufficiency in a mother and son. *American Journal of Medical Genetics Part A*, 158A(1), 174–81.

Richerson, P. J., & Boyd, R. (2005). *Not by Genes Alone: How Culture Transformed Human Evolution*. University of Chicago Press, Chicago, IL.

Rinn, J. L., & Chang, H. Y. (2012). Genome regulation by long noncoding RNAs. *Annual Review of Biochemistry*, 81, 145–66.

Robertson, G., Hirst, M., Bainbridge, M., Bilenky, M., Zhao, Y. J., Zeng, T., ... & Jones, S. (2007). Genome-wide profiles of STAT1 DNA association using chromatin immunoprecipitation and massively parallel sequencing. *Nature Methods*, 4(8), 651–7.

Rodenas-Cuadrado, P., Ho, J., & Vernes, S. C. (2014). Shining a light on CNTNAP2: Complex functions to complex disorders. *European Journal of Human Genetics*, 22(2), 171–8.

Rodenas-Cuadrado, P., Pietrafusa, N., Francavilla, T., La Neve, A., Striano, P., & Vernes, S. C. (2016). Characterisation of CASPR2 deficiency disorder—a syndrome involving autism, epilepsy and language impairment. *BMC Medical Genetics*, 17, 8.

Saksouk, N., Simboeck, E., & Dejardin, J. (2015). Constitutive heterochromatin formation and transcription in mammals. *Epigenetics & Chromatin*, 8, 3.

Sandler, W., Aronoff, M., Meir, I., & Padden, C. (2011). The gradual emergence of phonological form in a new language. *Natural Language & Linguistic Theory*, 29(2), 503–43.

Sarnat, H. B., Philippart, M., Flores-Sarnat, L., & Wei, X. C. (2015). Timing in neural maturation: arrest, delay, precociousness, and temporal determination of malformations. *Pediatric Neurology*, 52(5), 473–86.

Scerri, T. S., & Schulte-Korne, G. (2010). Genetics of developmental dyslexia. *European Child and Adolescent Psychiatry*, 19(3), 179–97.

Schulz, S. B., Haesler, S., Scharff, C., & Rochefort, C. (2010). Knockdown of FoxP2 alters spine density in Area X of the zebra finch. *Genes, Brain and Behavior*, 9(7), 732–40.

Schwerk, J., & Savan, R. (2015). Translating the untranslated region. *Journal of Immunology*, 195(7), 2963–71.

Seery, C. H., Watkins, R. V., Mangelsdorf, S. C., & Shigeto, A. (2007). Subtyping stuttering II: Contributions from language and temperament. *Journal of Fluency Disorders, 32*(3), 197–217.

Seok, H., Ham, J., Jang, E. S., & Chi, S. W. (2016). MicroRNA target recognition: Insights from transcriptome-wide non-canonical interactions. *Molecules and Cells, 39*(5), 375–81.

Shen, K., & Cowan, C. W. (2010). Guidance molecules in synapse formation and plasticity. *Cold Spring Harbor Perspectives in Biology, 2*(4), a001842.

Shendure, J., & Ji, H. (2008). Next-generation DNA sequencing. *Nature Biotechnology, 26*(10), 1135–45.

Shriberg, L. D., Ballard, K. J., Tomblin, J. B., Duffy, J. R., Odell, K. H., & Williams, C. A. (2006). Speech, prosody, and voice characteristics of a mother and daughter with a 7;13 translocation affecting FOXP2. *Journal of Speech, Language, and Hearing Research, 49*(3), 500–25.

Spiteri, E., Konopka, G., Coppola, G., Bomar, J., Oldham, M., Ou, J., . . . & Geschwind, D. H. (2007). Identification of the transcriptional targets of FOXP2, a gene linked to speech and language, in developing human brain. *American Journal of Human Genetics, 81*(6), 1144–57.

Stover, T., & Diensthuber, M. (2011). Molecular biology of hearing. *GMS Current Topics in Otorhinolaryngology—Head and Neck Surgery, 10*, Doc06.

Strachan, T., Read, A. P., & Strachan, T. (2011). *Human Molecular Genetics*, 4th Edition. Garland Science, New York, NY.

Strick, T. R., Allemand, J. F., Bensimon, D., & Croquette, V. (1998). Behavior of supercoiled DNA. *Biophysical Journal, 74*(4), 2016–28.

Stromswold, K. (2001). The heritability of language: A review and metaanalysis of twin, adoption, and linkage studies. *Language, 77*(4), 647–723.

Sun, E., & Shi, Y. H. (2015). MicroRNAs: Small molecules with big roles in neurodevelopment and diseases. *Experimental Neurology, 268*, 46–53.

Sweatt, J. D. (2016). Neural plasticity & behavior—sixty years of conceptual advances. *Journal of Neurochemistry, 139* Suppl 2, 179–99.

Taglialatela, J. P., Russell, J. L., Pope, S. M., Morton, T., Bogart, S., Reamer, L. A., . . . & Hopkins, W. D. (2015). Multimodal communication in chimpanzees. *American Journal of Primatology, 77*(11), 1143–8.

Taipale, M., Kaminen, N., Nopola-Hemmi, J., Haltia, T., Myllyluoma, B., Lyytinen, H., . . . & Kere, J. (2003). A candidate gene for developmental dyslexia encodes a nuclear tetratricopeptide repeat domain protein dynamically regulated in brain. *Proceedings of the National Academy of Sciences of the United States of America, 100*(20), 11553–8.

Tan, G. C., Doke, T. F., Ashburner, J., Wood, N. W., & Frackowiak, R. S. (2010). Normal variation in fronto-occipital circuitry and cerebellar structure with an autism-associated polymorphism of CNTNAP2. *NeuroImage, 53*(3), 1030–42.

Tan, X., & Shi, S. H. (2013). Neocortical neurogenesis and neuronal migration. *Wiley Interdisciplinary Reviews: Developmental Biology, 2*(4), 443–59.

Tchernichovski, O., & Marcus, G. (2014). Vocal learning beyond imitation: mechanisms of adaptive vocal development in songbirds and human infants. *Current Opinion in Neurobiology, 28*, 42–7.

ten Cate, C. (2014). On the phonetic and syntactic processing abilities of birds: from songs to speech and artificial grammars. *Current Opinion in Neurobiology, 28*, 157–64.

Teramitsu, I., Poopatanapong, A., Torrisi, S., & White, S. A. (2010). Striatal FoxP2 is actively regulated during songbird sensorimotor learning. *PLoS One, 5*(1), e8548.

Teramitsu, I., & White, S. A. (2006). FoxP2 regulation during undirected singing in adult songbirds. *Journal of Neuroscience, 26*(28), 7390–4.

Thiel, G. (2006). *Transcription Factors in the Nervous System: Development, Brain Function and Diseases*. Wiley-VCH, Weinheim.

Turner, S. J., Hildebrand, M. S., Block, S., Damiano, J., Fahey, M., Reilly, S., ... & Morgan, A. T. (2013). Small intragenic deletion in FOXP2 associated with childhood apraxia of speech and dysarthria. *American Journal of Medical Genetics Part A*, 161A(9), 2321–6.

Udden, J., Snijders, T. M., Fisher, S. E., & Hagoort, P. (2016). A common variant of the CNTNAP2 gene is associated with structural variation in the left superior occipital gyrus. *Brain and Language*, 172, 16–21.

Underwood, J. G., Boutz, P. L., Dougherty, J. D., Stoilov, P., & Black, D. L. (2005). Homologues of the Caenorhabditis elegans Fox-1 protein are neuronal splicing regulators in mammals. *Molecular and Cellular Biology*, 25(22), 10005–16.

Varea, O., Martin-de-Saavedra, M. D., Kopeikina, K. J., Schurmann, B., Fleming, H. J., Fawcett-Patel, J. M., ... & Penzes, P. (2015). Synaptic abnormalities and cytoplasmic glutamate receptor aggregates in contact in associated protein-like 2/Caspr2 knockout neurons. *Proceedings of the National Academy of Sciences of the United States of America*, 112(19), 6176–81.

Velho, T. A., & Lois, C. (2014). Generation of transgenic zebra finches with replication-deficient lentiviruses. *Cold Spring Harbor Protocols*, 2014(12), 1284–89.

Vernes, S. C. (2017). What bats have to say about speech and language. *Psychonomic Bulletin & Review*, 24(1), 111–17.

Vernes, S. C., Nicod, J., Elahi, F. M., Coventry, J. A., Kenny, N., Coupe, A. M., ... & Fisher, S. E. (2006). Functional genetic analysis of mutations implicated in a human speech and language disorder. *Human Molecular Genetics*, 15(21), 3154–67.

Vernes, S. C., Oliver, P. L., Spiteri, E., Lockstone, H. E., Puliyadi, R., Taylor, J. M., ... & Fisher, S. E. (2011). Foxp2 regulates gene networks implicated in neurite outgrowth in the developing brain. *PLoS Genetics*, 7(7), e1002145.

Vernes, S. C., Spiteri, E., Nicod, J., Groszer, M., Taylor, J. M., Davies, K. E., ... & Fisher, S. E. (2007). High-throughput analysis of promoter occupancy reveals direct neural targets of FOXP2, a gene mutated in speech and language disorders. *American Journal of Human Genetics*, 81(6), 1232–50.

Visscher, P. M., Brown, M. A., McCarthy, M. I., & Yang, J. (2012). Five years of GWAS discovery. *American Journal of Human Genetics*, 90(1), 7–24.

Viswanath, N., Lee, H. S., & Chakraborty, R. (2004). Evidence for a major gene influence on persistent developmental stuttering. *Human Biology*, 76(3), 401–12.

Wada, K., Howard, J. T., McConnell, P., Whitney, O., Lints, T., Rivas, M. V., ... & Jarvis, E. D. (2006). A molecular neuroethological approach for identifying and characterizing a cascade of behaviorally regulated genes. *Proceedings of the National Academy of Sciences of the United States of America*, 103(41), 15212–17.

Wain, H. M., Bruford, E. A., Lovering, R. C., Lush, M. J., Wright, M. W., & Povey, S. (2002). Guidelines for human gene nomenclature. *Genomics*, 79(4), 464–70.

Waites, C. L., Craig, A. M., & Garner, C. C. (2005). Mechanisms of vertebrate synaptogenesis. *Annual Review of Neuroscience*, 28, 251–74.

Wang, A., Liang, Y., Fridell, R. A., Probst, F. J., Wilcox, E. R., Touchman, J. W., ... & Friedman, T. B. (1998). Association of unconventional myosin MYO15 mutations with human nonsyndromic deafness DFNB3. *Science*, 280(5368), 1447–51.

Wang, Z., Gerstein, M., & Snyder, M. (2009). RNA-Seq: a revolutionary tool for transcriptomics. *Nature Reviews Genetics*, 10(1), 57–63.

Watkins, K. (2011). Developmental disorders of speech and language: From genes to brain structure and function. *Progress in Brain Research*, 189, 225–38.
West, A. E., & Greenberg, M. E. (2011). Neuronal activity-regulated gene transcription in synapse development and cognitive function. *Cold Spring Harbor Perspectives in Biology*, 3(6), pii: a005744.
West, M. J., & King, A. P. (1988). Female visual displays affect the development of male song in the cowbird. *Nature*, 334(6179), 244–6.
Whalley, H. C., O'Connell, G., Sussmann, J. E., Peel, A., Stanfield, A. C., Hayiou-Thomas, M. E., . . . & Hall, J. (2011). Genetic variation in CNTNAP2 alters brain function during linguistic processing in healthy individuals. *American Journal of Medical Genetics Part B: Neuropsychiatric Genetics*, 156B(8), 941–8.
Whitney, O., Pfenning, A. R., Howard, J. T., Blatti, C. A., Liu, F., Ward, J. M., . . . & Jarvis, E. D. (2014). Core and region-enriched networks of behaviorally regulated genes and the singing genome. *Science*, 346(6215), 1256780.
Whitney, O., Voyles, T., Hara, E., Chen, Q., White, S. A., & Wright, T. F. (2015). Differential FoxP2 and FoxP1 expression in a vocal learning nucleus of the developing budgerigar. *Developmental Neurobiology*, 75(7), 778–90.
Winata, S., Arhya, I. N., Moeljopawiro, S., Hinnant, J. T., Liang, Y., Friedman, T. B., & Asher, J. H., Jr. (1995). Congenital non-syndromal autosomal recessive deafness in Bengkala, an isolated Balinese village. *Journal of Medical Genetics*, 32(5), 336–43.
Xu, B., Karayiorgou, M., & Gogos, J. A. (2010). MicroRNAs in psychiatric and neurodevelopmental disorders. *Brain Research*, 1338, 78–88.
Xu, B., Roos, J. L., Levy, S., van Rensburg, E. J., Gogos, J. A., & Karayiorgou, M. (2008). Strong association of de novo copy number mutations with sporadic schizophrenia. *Nature Genetics*, 40(7), 880–5.
Yairi, E. (2007). Subtyping stuttering I: A review. *Journal of Fluency Disorders*, 32(3), 165–96.
Yairi, E., Watkins, R., Ambrose, N., & Paden, E. (2001). What is stuttering? *Journal of Speech, Language, and Hearing Research*, 44(3), 585.
Yeo, G., Holste, D., Kreiman, G., & Burge, C. B. (2004). Variation in alternative splicing across human tissues. *Genome Biology*, 5(10), R74.
Zappella, M., Meloni, I., Longo, I., Hayek, G., & Renieri, A. (2001). Preserved speech variants of the Rett syndrome: Molecular and clinical analysis. *American Journal of Medical Genetics*, 104(1), 14–22.
Zhang, C. L., Zhang, Z., Castle, J., Sun, S. Y., Johnson, J., Krainer, A. R., & Zhang, M. Q. (2008). Defining the regulatory network of the tissue-specific splicing factors Fox-1 and Fox-2. *Genes & Development*, 22(18), 2550–63.
Zhao, Y. T., Goffin, D., Johnson, B. S., & Zhou, Z. (2013). Loss of MeCP2 function is associated with distinct gene expression changes in the striatum. *Neurobiology of Disease*, 59, 257–66.
Zheng, S., & Black, D. L. (2013). Alternative pre-mRNA splicing in neurons: growing up and extending its reach. *Trends in Genetics*, 29(8), 442–8.
Zhou, X., Espy-Wilson, C. Y., Boyce, S., Tiede, M., Holland, C., & Choe, A. (2008). A magnetic resonance imaging-based articulatory and acoustic study of "retroflex" and "bunched" American English /r/. *Journal of the Acoustical Society of America*, 123(6), 4466–81.

CHAPTER 38

MODELS OF LANGUAGE EVOLUTION

CATHLEEN O'GRADY AND KENNY SMITH

38.1 Introduction

LANGUAGE is startling in its complexity and expressive power. Unlike any other animal communication system, language provides a system for building complex signals from subcomponents in a way that yields an endless set of possible combinations, capable of conveying an infinite array of possible meanings.

This open-ended expressivity arises through duality of patterning (Hockett, 1960), which is the capacity of language to combine simpler structures to create more complex structures, at two distinct levels. At the first level, language combines meaningless units (that is, phonemes) into meaningful words and morphemes. For example, consider the English phonemes /d/, /b/, and /a/. None of these units have meaning on their own, but they can be combined into different meaningful combinations, such as "bad" and "dad." This is combinatoriality, and it gives us a highly efficient and expressive system. For example, most varieties of English have 40–45 phonemes (e.g., Ladefoged (2006) lists 44 phonemes in the inventory of Received Pronunciation), which can be recombined to form the 291,500 entries in the second edition of the Oxford English Dictionary (Dictionary Facts, Oxford English Dictionary, 2016).

At the second level of combination, meaningful words and morphemes are combined into larger, more complex meaningful units at the level of the phrase and sentence. For instance, the morpheme "bed" can be combined with the plural morpheme to create the word "beds," which in turn can be combined with other morphemes in a sentence like "The hotel room had two beds." This compositionality makes it easy for people to generalize rules they have already learned to new items they encounter. For instance, young children might learn the word "bed" and its plural "beds," the word "dog" and its plural "dogs," and so on. Then, when presented with a nonsense word "wug," they generalize what they have learned about the plural morpheme to create the word "wugs" (Berko, 1958). The same processes of generalization apply at the level of multiword utterances—compositional structure allows us to routinely produce and understand sentences that we have never seen (or that have never been uttered) before.

A major challenge for evolutionary linguists is to establish how a system like this can evolve, and why only humans have a communication system that works in this way. One potential explanation is that language is the result of *cultural evolution* (Christiansen & Chater, 2008; Kirby, 2001). Language, in common with many other human behaviors, is culturally transmitted: we are exposed to language by listening to those around us, and based on this linguistic input, we learn that language. Then, in turn, we produce linguistic output which forms the basis for language learning in others, who pass the language on themselves, and so on. This chapter will review a growing body of evidence suggesting that this type of multigenerational transmission process (sometimes known as iterated learning: Kirby & Hurford, 2002) forces languages to adapt to constraints that affect how humans learn and transmit languages. Both computer models and experimental work on human learning suggest that this process of cultural evolution can result in the emergence of linguistic structure.

38.2 Computational Models of Language Evolution

Early work investigating language evolution used computational modeling to simulate evolutionary processes acting on communication systems (Hurford, 1989; Steels, 1999). In a seminal paper, Kirby (2000) used computer simulations of iterated learning to demonstrate that compositionality could emerge in a model where each generation of computational agents learned a communication system from linguistic data produced by a previous generation that had learned in the same way. Kirby initialized his simulations with holistic systems (where meanings are communicated by signals that have no internal structure); as this "language" was passed from generation to generation, with each generation of learners searching for generalizations in the data they were presented with, compositional structure gradually developed, until after many hundreds of generations an elegant, compositional language had formed, where signals are composed through the rule-governed recombination of meaningful subcomponents.

An important finding of this modeling work is the role played by learning bottlenecks in iterated learning systems (Brighton, Smith, & Kirby, 2005; Kirby, 2000, 2002; Zuidema, 2003). These bottlenecks appear between generations, as one generation of language users presents the next generation of users with only a limited set of linguistic data, on the basis of which they are required to learn an open-ended expressive system. As languages are repeatedly transmitted through a series of bottlenecks, compositional structure develops.

The role of the bottleneck in driving the emergence of structure can be best illustrated through an example. Imagine a virtual world with moving shapes of various colors: there are squares, circles, and triangles, which can be red, blue, or green, and move in spirals, bounces, or straight lines. If each possible referent in this world is expressed with a holistic signal (that is, one signal for a blue square that bounces, another completely distinct signal for a blue square that spirals, yet another unrelated signal for a red square that spirals, and so on), 27 signals would be required in order to express the full range of referents. If a learner is only exposed to some of the 27 words (perhaps half of them), they have no way to accurately reconstruct the "correct" signals for referents they haven't seen labeled, because there is no pattern underlying how labels are associated with referents.

However, if the communication system is compositional, 27 meanings can be expressed using only nine signals (three signals expressing color, three shapes, and three expressing motion) and one rule for combining them (for example, combine them in the order color-motion-shape). In this case, a learner does not need exposure to all 27 labels in order to learn the full language, but instead can infer the underlying system from a smaller number of observations (for an optimal generalizer, simply encountering each of the nine component parts once is sufficient), and subsequently exploit the compositional structure to produce labels which they didn't encounter while learning.

Whenever there is a learning bottleneck, language learners are forced to generalize, because the input they receive does not provide labels for all the meanings they might like to convey. This forces learners to hunt for commonalities across holistic labels (for instance observing that the syllable "ka" appears on two bouncing shapes, and then using it for all future bouncing shapes). Over time, these generalizations accumulate, and holistic languages gradually change to become compositional.

This seminal modeling work has been built on in two important directions. A related body of work focuses on phonological systems, showing that interaction and cultural transmission can explain how the phonemes found in the world's languages are organized in acoustic and articulatory space, and how combinatorial sound systems emerge (de Boer, 2000, 2001; Oudeyer, 2005, 2006; Wedel, 2006, 2012; Zuidema & de Boer, 2009). Another recent body of computational and mathematical modeling work has built on the earlier simulation-based results to extract general principles for how iterated learning and transmission bottlenecks shape linguistic systems (Griffiths & Kalish, 2007; Kirby, Dowman, & Griffiths, 2007; Perfors & Navarro, 2014), and to explore how cultural and biological evolution interact to shape languages and language learners (Smith & Kirby, 2008; Thompson, Kirby, & Smith, 2016).

38.3 Language Evolution in the Lab

Computational and mathematical models continue to play a vital role in the emerging study of cultural evolution as it applies to language. However, skepticism regarding the applicability of these models to human language learners necessitates supplementing computational work with experiments using human participants. Experiments on cultural evolution are based on the same principle as the models described here: they explore how data transmitted across generations of individuals is shaped by the process of transmission. In an experimental setting, this method of creating "transmission chains" of participants has been highly successful in understanding cultural evolutionary processes more generally (Whiten, Caldwell, & Mesoudi, 2016). In a standard transmission chain experiment, the first participant in a chain is presented with some material (e.g., a drawing to copy, or a miniature language to learn) and then required to reproduce it. This reproduction is then used as the training material for the next participant in the chain of transmission, and so on.

Importantly, each participant in a chain of transmission is not simply reproducing the material they are given, but rather forming a mental representation of it, and then using this mental representation to reproduce the material they were earlier presented with (Mesoudi & Whiten, 2008). Because of this process of internalization and recall, if participants have any pre-existing cognitive biases or expectations about the material, those biases will be imposed on their representation and subsequent recreation of the material, allowing for a transformation of the material as it is passed from person to person (Griffiths, Christian, & Kalish, 2008; Kalish, Griffiths, & Lewandowsky, 2007).

The earliest study done using transmission chains, called "serial reproduction" (Bartlett, 1932), found that the contents of certain genres of stories were transmitted more fully than others, and that story contents became distorted over time to match participants' pre-existing knowledge. More recent studies have used the method to study cultural change, finding that social information such as gossip is transmitted more accurately than non-social information (Mesoudi, Whiten, & Dunbar, 2006).

Cultural transmission therefore entails two vital steps: first learning the information, and then reproducing it. An important question, then, is which of these two processes is responsible for the changes that occur to systems that are transmitted through iterated learning. Tamariz and Kirby (2015) manipulated these pressures in a simple drawing task: participants in transmission chains were asked to look at a drawing created by the previous participant in the chain and reproduce it. In one set of chains, each participant was given time to memorize the drawing, and then reproduced it from memory; in the other set, participants were able to reproduce the drawing directly, while looking at it and without having to memorize it first. In the chains where participants had to memorize the drawing before reproducing it, the drawings became smaller and less complex over successive generations, and began to tend toward conventional cultural symbols such as numbers. In the chains that simply copied the drawing directly, there was no decrease in size or complexity, and no tendency toward symbolism. This suggests that learning, rather than reproducing, is what creates the bias toward compressibility.

These transmission chain methods therefore allow researchers to establish what kinds of information are best retained and transmitted, and infer what systemic biases might be at play during transmission (Mesoudi & Whiten, 2008). Taken together, the growing list of biases can help to explain current cultural phenomena, such as religion, music—and language (Chater & Christiansen, 2010).

38.3.1 Learnability and linguistic structure

Applying these techniques to artificial languages or communicative games allows us to investigate how communication systems evolve through cultural transmission, providing a close experimental analogue to the computational models reviewed in section 38.2. In an early paper directly inspired by this modeling work, Kirby et al. (2008) taught participants a series of randomly generated holistic labels for the set of 27 shapes described in section 38.2 (27 shapes generated by combining three colors, three shapes, and three kinds of motion). After the training phase, participants were required to provide labels for these shapes, with their output used as the training input for the next participant in the chain. The transmission chain entailed a learning bottleneck between each generation: each participant was trained only on labels for a subset of the total set of shapes (14 of the 27), but was required to produce labels for the full set. This forced participants to provide labels for shapes they had never seen the label for, introducing a strong pressure for generalization (although many did not realize that many of the test stimuli were previously unseen).

Although the labels provided to the first generation in each chain were random, the artificial languages evolved over the transmission chains to become regular and generalizable. In an initial experiment, the labels became highly simplified (e.g., "poi" for anything moving in a spiral pattern, regardless of shapes or color). Languages like this are highly learnable—there simply isn't much to learn—but not very useful for communicating, because each label would drastically underspecify its intended referent (e.g., "poi" would fail to distinguish between a spiraling black triangle and a spiraling red circle). In a second experiment, Kirby et al. (2008) manipulated each participant's output before passing it on to the subsequent learner in the chain, removing duplicate labels from each participant's test answers. This experimental manipulation was intended to mimic the natural pressure, acting on real languages, to be useful for communication[1]. In this second experiment, the languages evolved over repeated episodes of transmission and developed compositional structure: subcomponents of each label specified subcomponents of the stimulus. For example, the first syllable might specify the color, the second the shape, and the third syllable the kind of movement. This compositional structure makes the language simple enough for experimental participants to learn fairly accurately, while by-passing the ambiguity filter by providing every object with a unique label.

Subsequent work shows that a similar result is obtained if this artificial prohibition is replaced by actual communicative interaction. Kirby et al. (2015) ran an iterated learning experiment where pairs of participants were trained on an artificial language and then used it to communicate, taking turns to label pictures for each other—ambiguous labels would be problematic during this communicative task, but were not prohibited. The language produced during communication was then passed on to a fresh pair of participants, who in turn learned the language and used it to communicate, and so on. As expected, this repeated process of learning and use resulted in the gradual emergence of compositional structure. Kirby et al. (2015) also showed that the development of structure is dependent on transmission: when a single pair of participants play the same communication game over and over, compositional structure does not develop, showing that both learning and use play crucial roles.

Similar techniques have been used to explore the emergence of combinatoriality. As discussed in the introduction, combinatoriality allows us to use a few 10s of speech sounds to generate tens of thousands of meaningful words. Hockett (1960) suggested that combinatoriality might therefore be a consequence of a pressure to create many distinct meaningful signals—that is, as the potential number of meanings in a communication system grows, and it becomes more difficult to create new holistic signals, the communication system might begin to reuse components of the holistic signals in a combinatorial fashion. However, at least one human language doesn't use combinatoriality to solve this problem. Al-Sayyid Bedouin Sign Language (ABSL), an emerging sign language, is still in the process of developing structure at the phonological level (which in the case of sign

---

[1] Similar pressures were included in the computational models outlined in section 38.2 (e.g., in the form of a prohibition on pairing multiple referents with a single ambiguous label), again as a proxy for pressures presumably arising from communication in the real-world case.

languages is achieved by handshapes that are meaningless on their own but combined into meaningful units) (Israel & Sandler, 2011; Sandler, Aronoff, Meir, & Padden, 2011). Despite lacking phonemes, ABSL is nonetheless capable of expressing a wide array of meanings, and is used for all the functions that other human languages are used for. This suggests that a fully functional language can develop a large meaning space without combinatoriality, implying that a growing meaning space alone is not sufficient pressure for combinatoriality to emerge.

Verhoef et al. (2011) used an iterated language learning experiment to show instead that the pressure of learning holistic signals can, through cultural transmission, explain the emergence of combinatoriality. In an experiment in which participants are required to learn and then reproduce a sequence of 12 slide whistle sounds—which are holistic in the first generation of the chain (i.e., with no internal structure), simply random, and continuous slide whistle movements/sounds—they show that the whistle sounds begin to show structure, with internal components of the holistic signals beginning to be reused within and between different sounds in the sequence. As a result, the sequence becomes more easily learnable and more accurately transmitted. This suggests that combinatorial structure can emerge independently of pressures arising from the number of meanings which need to be conveyed.

This finding is corroborated by Roberts and Galantucci (2012), who used a communication game to compare the effects of conventionalization and number of meanings on the emergence of combinatoriality. Participant pairs, separated from each other at separate computers, were presented with a grid with simple animal drawings, and had to communicate to each other which drawing to select. Communication was possible using a stylus that distorted their drawings to prevent participants from simply sketching the animal to be communicated. Conventionalization over the course of this repeated drawing game resulted in the emergence of drawings which exhibited combinatorial structure (subelements of drawings that were repeated across drawings), but the number of meanings was only weakly correlated with combinatoriality, which the authors suggest may be due to the limitations on the number of meanings that could be used in the experiment (in this case, only 20).

Properties of the communication medium may also contribute to the emergence of combinatoriality, namely *rapid fade*. Signals in spoken and signed language (and in Verhoef et al.'s slide whistle experiment) are transient: signals linger for only a short period of time (Hockett, 1960). Galantucci, Kroos, and Rhodes (2010), using a graphical communication task similar to that employed by Roberts and Galantucci (2012), manipulated the rapidity of fade of signals by changing the speed with which communicative drawings faded from the screen. They found that more rapid fading led to a higher degree of combinatoriality. The number of meanings to be communicated was again not related to the degree of combinatoriality, providing further evidence against the hypothesis that larger meaning spaces drive the emergence of combinatoriality.

38.3.2 Communication and the emergence of iconicity

Transmission chain experiments such as these are therefore capable of explaining how linguistic structure arises. Perhaps surprisingly, similar methods have also provided insights into the very nature of linguistic signals, namely the fact that they are composed of *arbitrary symbols* for conveying concepts.

Garrod, Fay, Lee, Oberlander, and Macleod (2007) use a Pictionary™-like task involving a list of easily confused concepts—such as "art gallery," "museum," "parliament," and "theater"—presented to a pair of participants. The Drawer in each turn must draw a randomly selected word from the list, while the Matcher must attempt to guess which of the words on the list the Drawer is attempting to draw. As each pair of participants repeatedly plays this game, drawing the same concept multiple times, their drawings gradually become simpler and more abstract, and partners playing together converge, producing more similar drawings for a given concept. For instance, "cartoon" in one pair was initially drawn as a cartoon bunny and a bird, and over six rounds, simplified to become just a pair of stylized bunny ears. These results illustrate how iconic representations—representations that depict the content being communicated through resemblance—become abstract and symbolic through repeated use (Garrod et al., 2007), linked to their meaning only by convention.

Interaction appears to be an essential component of this process: transmission alone does not result in either convergence on shared representations or simplification (Garrod, Fay, Rogers, Walker, & Swoboda, 2010). However, in an experiment that combined the community-based game with a transmission chain, by periodically removing the most experienced member of the group and replacing them with a naïve participant, drawings became symbolic to the extent that newcomers were required to learn their community's conventionalized symbols for the list of concepts (Caldwell & Smith, 2012). A similar effect is found when a drawing task occurs in a community-like setting that has eight participants interacting in a closed circle of shuffled pairs (Fay, Garrod, Roberts, & Swoboda, 2010).

These graphical communication paradigms show how symbolic, arbitrary systems arise through repeated interaction (whether in a pair or community), while the iterated learning paradigm shows how arbitrary systems become systematic through repeated learning. Theisen, Oberlander, and Kirby (2009) and Theisen-White, Kirby, and Oberlander (2011) combine the two paradigms to demonstrate how the arbitrary symbols come to be used systematically, as they are in language. These studies use a graphical communication task with the potential for compositionality, by creating a list of items with shared semantic features: for example, five different kinds of entity (like people or buildings) through ten different themes (like education). Thus, the person in the education theme would be a teacher (Theisen et al., 2009).

As in previous experiments in the graphical communication paradigm, Theisen et al. (2009) found that drawings become increasingly arbitrary over time, while the arbitrary elements came to be used systematically: over repeated interactions, pairs of participants began to use increasingly symbolic elements to indicate components of the meanings they were communicating. For instance, if the first instance of "teacher" in a pair resulted in a drawing of a blackboard, subsequent school-related drawings ("teacher," but also "school" and "school bus") for that pair might include a simplified chalkboard element, plus a second simple component specifying which school-related concept was being conveyed. When a transmission chain was added, by using the first generation's drawings as training material for a second generation of interlocutors, the level of systematicity increased (Theisen-White et al., 2011). This suggests that both horizontal interaction and vertical transmission play a role in creating arbitrary and compositional systems, and that both communicative utility and learnability (by new players in the game) play an essential role in the emergence of structure, mirroring the results just discussed from Kirby et al. (2015).

38.3.3 Regularity and systematicity

The studies just reviewed focus on how languages and other communication systems are shaped by pressures inherent in their transmission—the requirements of learners to produce utterances for new meanings, or to learn and reproduce sets of rapidly fading signals. A related strand of work (underpinned by a series of mathematical and computational models, e.g., Griffiths & Kalish, 2007) explores how biases of learners, rather than external features of the transmission process, might also contribute to shaping language evolution. In particular, an intriguing body of work shows that even very weak biases in learning can have large effects on how languages are structured, because those weak biases accumulate over generations to create a substantial effect.

Some of the experimental work showing that this is the case has been concerned with the evolution of linguistic variation. Languages provide language users with multiple roughly equivalent possibilities for particular forms, e.g., allophones (such as dark or light /l/), allomorphs (e.g., the past tense "-ed" is pronounced differently on the words "jumped" and "dragged"), or synonyms. The variant that is deployed in any given situation tends to be fairly predictable, being conditioned on sociolinguistic, phonological, semantic, or other criteria (Givon, 1985).

Naively, we might therefore expect that the conditioned, predictable nature of variation in language therefore reflects a strong bias in language learning, strongly predisposing learners to condition or eliminate unpredictable variation wherever it occurs. Counterintuitively, adults appear to show no such tendency: if trained on unpredictable language data, they instead tend to *probability match*. For instance, if a particular variant appears 70% of the time in their training data, they tend toward using it at roughly the same rate and in a similarly unconditioned fashion (Hudson Kam & Newport, 2005; Wonnacott & Newport, 2005). This means that, in individual language learners, variant forms are preserved and remain unpredictable.

However, Reali and Griffiths (2009) show that this picture changes when unpredictably variable linguistic systems are passed along transmission chains. Using an approximation of synonymy in natural language, participants in their experiment were presented objects paired with labels. Each participant saw two labels for each object, with the two labels appearing with varying probability (e.g., for one object the two labels might appear in a 50:50 ratio, for another object the ratio of the labels might be 80:20). After training, when participants were asked to repeatedly label each object, single learners showed only a weak tendency toward regularization, essentially matching the probability distribution of the input. However, across transmission chains, where these systems of object labeling were passed from person to person, there was a strong tendency toward regularization, resulting in the loss of one of the variants.

One explanation for this result is that transmission chains automatically bring about the elimination of variation. However, Smith and Wonnacott (2010) find that variation can be maintained in a transmission chain, if that variation can become conditioned. In their experiment, adult learners learned and attempted to reproduce a variable system of plural markers; they learned a language in which the plural could be marked in one of two ways, with both forms occurring completely unpredictably. In line with the results from Reali and Griffiths (2009), individual learners did not exhibit a detectable tendency toward eliminating or conditioning this variation. However, after these miniature languages had been transmitted down chains, the variation was preserved (both plural markers lived on), but became predictable—each plural marker gradually became associated with a subset of the nouns, such that some nouns always took one plural marker and other nouns took the other. In their experiment, conditioning on the noun was the only possible way for the variation to become conditioned; in real languages, multiple such contexts exist, allowing for potentially complex but ultimately predictable systems of conditioned variation.

Collectively, these results provide reason for caution in extrapolating from individual-level experiments to assumptions about the emergence of linguistic features: finding no, or limited, evidence of a bias in a single generation of learners does not imply that the bias would not emerge as a factor on a population level.

38.3.4 Typological universals

Some features of linguistic structure are common to all (in the case of compositionality and systematicity), or virtually all (in the case of combinatoriality) of the world's languages. There are also many other features in which languages vary, for instance in the order in which words are typically combined. However, even here there are significant tendencies toward particular features, with multiple languages appearing to converge on the same structural solutions.

For instance, basic word order rules governing the sequence of subjects (S), objects (O), and verbs (V) in sentences could logically result in six different combinations (SOV, SVO, VSO, VOS, OSV, OVS). However, most of the world's languages use either SVO or SOV order. Although historical relationships between languages are likely to explain a number of these statistical tendencies (e.g., Dunn, Greenhill, Levinson, & Gray, 2011), a new and growing body of experimental work suggests that biases in learning are also likely to play a role in explaining such tendencies, in word order (Culbertson, Smolensky, & Legendre, 2012), morphological encoding of information (Fedzechkina, Jaeger, & Newport, 2012), and phonological patterning (Wilson, 2003).

Experiments using *silent gesture* paradigms are ideal for investigating questions like these, by allowing us to see which ordering strategies participants use when communicating in a novel medium. In these experiments, participants with no experience in any sign language are required to use silent gesture to express propositions, often as part of a communicative game, a little like the parlor game Charades. In these experiments, silent gesturers show a preference for SOV word order—for instance, when presented with a picture of a pirate throwing a guitar, a participant would gesture "pirate," "guitar," and "throw," in that order. This preference appears regardless of the dominant word order in participants' native languages (Goldin-Meadow, So, Ozyurek, & Mylander, 2008).

However, although this might explain the prevalence of SOV in the world's languages, it cannot explain the prevalence of SVO. Schouwstra and de Swart (2014) show that the semantic content of a message results in different word orders in silent gesture. Specifically, *extensional* verbs that describe the relationship between specific and existent entities, such as "throw" or "kick," are expressed with a preference for SOV word order. *Intensional* verbs like "imagine," which take objects that may be non-existent or non-specific, are expressed with a preference for SVO word order. Both preferences hold true regardless of whether a participant's native language uses SVO or SOV.

While these results go some way toward explaining why both SOV and SVO are common word orders in the world's languages, they are unable to explain why individual languages are usually consistent in their use of *either* SOV *or* SVO, rather than conditioning word order on the semantics of the verb. This tendency for consistency can be explained by cultural transmission. Schouwstra et al. (2016) combined the silent gesture task with a transmission chain approach, where groups of participants played a Charades-like communicative game while new group members gradually replaced more experienced individuals. While at the early stages each group's system of gestures showed a mix of SOV and SVO, conditioned on verb semantics, over time, word order became conventionalized to either all-SOV or all-SVO, as in earlier transmission chain experiments with artificial languages that found a tendency toward regularization (Reali & Griffiths, 2009; Smith & Wonnacott, 2010).

More fine-grained typological patterns also appear to be mirrored in the biases of language learners. For instance, most languages exhibit harmonic patterns governing the ordering of adjectives and numerals that modify nouns (Greenberg, 1963): most of the world's languages have both post-nominal adjectives and numerals, or prenominal adjective and numerals (as in English: "blue cup," "three cups"), rather than a mix of pre- and post-nominal modifiers.

Culbertson et al. (2012) presented adult participants with an artificial language that had either mainly harmonic (adjectives and numerals both appeared pre- or post-nominally) or non-harmonic (adjectives appeared prenominally, numerals post-nominally, or the reverse) ordering, with a scattering of other word orders. Participants trained on languages which were mainly harmonic tended to make the language more harmonic, reducing the proportion of "noisy" other orders. However, participants trained on mainly non-harmonic patterns behaved differently, either simply maintaining a mix of orderings, or failing to reproduce the dominant non-harmonic patterns entirely. This suggests that the cross-linguistic preference for harmonic orders, as well as the scarcity of certain non-harmonic orders in the world's languages, may arise from learning biases on the part of language learners. Subsequent work has shown the presence of similar but stronger biases in child learners (Culbertson & Newport, 2015), and other typological patterns (Culbertson & Adger, 2014).

38.4 Cross-cultural comparisons and biological evolution

Computational and experimental models of language evolution have shown how iterated learning can generate compositionality, combinatoriality, and regularity in language; how communication interacts with cultural transmission to create an expressivity pressure that contributes to the emergence of structure; and how artificial language learning paradigms can illuminate the biases that are related to typological universals.

However, there are still several open questions in the field. Most notably, cultural transmission is not a process unique to humans: many species have culturally transmitted repertoires of behavior, and there are even other species who exhibit communicative behaviors that are culturally transmitted. Bird song, for example, is culturally transmitted in many species—birds learn their song early in development through exposure to species-typical song input. These systems have striking parallels with language: they have combinatorial (albeit not compositional or semantic) structure (Berwick, Okanoya, Beckers, & Bolhuis, 2011); and although isolated songbirds do not acquire a fully fledged system, but rather a degenerate and simplified one, this degenerate isolate song can revert to wild-type "natural" song when passed through a transmission chain of songbirds (Fehér et al., 2009). This suggests the existence of learning biases that shape the evolution of song (in zebra finches, and presumably in other species), much in the same way that human learning biases and cultural evolution shape the evolution of language (Claidière, Smith, Kirby, & Fagot, 2014; Kirby, Griffiths, & Smith, 2014).

These findings cohere with the models presented in this chapter, which predict the emergence of structure in an expressive system that is culturally transmitted (Kirby et al., 2015; Verhoef et al., 2011). Crucially, the nature of the expressivity pressure in birds is substantially different from that found in humans: whereas humans use signals to differentiate between possible referents in a communicative context, songbirds express mate quality through the size of their signal repertoire (Collins, 2004). Similarly, many species have small repertoires of unlearned, holistic referential signals (e.g., vervet monkeys have a small set of alarm calls signaling different kinds of predators) (Seyfarth, Cheney, & Marler, 1980), which is consistent with the prediction that communication systems emerging without a pressure for learnability will be holistic, with no compositional or combinatorial structure. Comparative studies investigating the similarities and differences between human communication and cultural transmission, and similar systems found in other species, are likely to continue be a fruitful area of investigation for better understanding of our own cognition.

Finally, some accounts of the evolution of human language have argued that language is underpinned by language-specific cognitive apparatus, which has evolved through evolution by natural selection because the ability to communicate in this open-ended way is adaptive (e.g., Pinker & Bloom, 1990). This suggests that linguistic structure is the result of biological adaptation, a reflection of a human-unique capacity and predisposition to acquire communication systems with these properties. The evidence reviewed in this chapter suggests that cultural evolution is capable of explaining linguistic structure without appealing to additional, biological mechanisms: the processes involved in language learning and use are sufficient to result in the evolution of structure. But this is not to say that biological evolution should be ignored: a comprehensive account of language evolution will also need to explain the biological adaptations that led to our particular cultural environment, cognitive biases, and ability to learn complex signaling systems.

References

Bartlett, F. C. (1932). *Remembering*. Cambridge University Press, Cambridge.
Berko, J. (1958). The child's learning of English morphology. *Word*, 14(2–3), 150–77.
Berwick, R. C., Okanoya, K., Beckers, G. J. L., & Bolhuis, J. J. (2011). Songs to syntax: The linguistics of birdsong. *Trends in Cognitive Sciences*, 15(3), 113–21.
Brighton, H., Smith, K., & Kirby, S. (2005). Language as an evolutionary system. *Physics of Life Reviews*, 2(3), 177–226.

Caldwell, C. A., & Smith, K. (2012). Cultural evolution and perpetuation of arbitrary communicative conventions in experimental microsocieties. *PLoS One*, 7(8), e43807.

Chater, N., & Christiansen, M. H. (2010). Language acquisition meets language evolution. *Cognitive Science*, 34(7), 1131–57.

Christiansen, M. H., & Chater, N. (2008). Language as shaped by the brain. *The Behavioral and Brain Sciences*, 31(5), 489–508; discussion 509–58.

Claidière, N., Smith, K., Kirby, S., & Fagot, J. (2014). Cultural evolution of systematically structured behaviour in a non-human primate. *Proceedings. Biological Sciences/The Royal Society*, 281(1797), 20141541.

Collins, S. (2004). Vocal fighting and flirting: The functions of birdsong. In: Marler, P., & Slabbekoorn, H. (Eds.), *Nature's Music: The Science of Birdsong* (pp. 39–79). Academic Press, Cambridge, MA.

Culbertson, J., & Adger, D. (2014). Language learners privilege structured meaning over surface frequency. *Proceedings of the National Academy of Sciences of the United States of America*, 111(16), 5842–7.

Culbertson, J., & Newport, E. L. (2015). Harmonic biases in child learners: In support of language universals. *Cognition*, 139, 71–82.

Culbertson, J., Smolensky, P., & Legendre, G. (2012). Learning biases predict a word order universal. *Cognition*, 122(3), 306–29.

de Boer, B. (2000). Self-organization in vowel systems. *Journal of Phonetics*, 28(4), 441–65.

de Boer, B. (2001). *The Origins of Vowel Systems*. Oxford University Press, Oxford.

Dictionary Facts—Oxford English Dictionary. (2016). Available at: http://public.oed.com/history-of-the-oed/dictionary-facts/

Dunn, M., Greenhill, S. J., Levinson, S. C., & Gray, R. D. (2011). Evolved structure of language shows lineage-specific trends in word-order universals. *Nature*, 473(7345), 79–82.

Fay, N., Garrod, S., Roberts, L., & Swoboda, N. (2010). The interactive evolution of human communication systems. *Cognitive Science*, 34(3), 351–86.

Fedzechkina, M., Jaeger, T. F., & Newport, E. L. (2012). Language learners restructure their input to facilitate efficient communication. *Proceedings of the National Academy of Sciences of the United States of America*, 109(44), 17897–902.

Fehér, O., Wang, H., Saar, S., Mitra, P. P., & Tchernichovski, O. (2009). De novo establishment of wild-type song culture in the zebra finch. *Nature*, 459(7246), 564–8.

Galantucci, B., Kroos, C., & Rhodes, T. (2010). The effects of rapidity of fading on communication systems. *Interaction Studies*, 11, 100–11.

Garrod, S., Fay, N., Lee, J., Oberlander, J., & Macleod, T. (2007). Foundations of representation: where might graphical symbol systems come from? *Cognitive Science*, 31(6), 961–87.

Garrod, S., Fay, N., Rogers, S., Walker, B., & Swoboda, N. (2010). Can iterated learning explain the emergence of graphical symbols? *Interaction Studies*, 11(1), 33–50.

Givon, T. (1985). Function, structure, and language acquisition. In: Slobin, D. (Ed.), *The Crosslinguistic Study of Language Acquisition*, Vol. 2 (pp. 1005–28). Lawrence Erlbaum, Hillsdale, NJ.

Goldin-Meadow, S., So, W. C., Ozyurek, A., & Mylander, C. (2008). The natural order of events: How speakers of different languages represent events nonverbally. *Proceedings of the National Academy of Sciences of the United States of America*, 105(27), 9163–8.

Greenberg, J. H. (1963). Some universals of grammar with particular reference to the order of meaningful elements. In: Greenberg, J. H. (Ed.), *Universals of Language* (pp. 73–113). MIT Press, Cambridge, MA.

Griffiths, T. L., Christian, B. R., & Kalish, M. L. (2008). Using category structures to test iterated learning as a method for identifying inductive biases. *Cognitive Science*, 32(1), 68–107.

Griffiths, T. L., & Kalish, M. L. (2007). Language evolution by iterated learning with bayesian agents. *Cognitive Science*, 31(3), 441–80.

Hockett, C. F. (1960). The origin of speech. *Scientific American*, 203, 88–111.

Hudson Kam, C. L., & Newport, E. (2005). Regularizing unpredictable variation: The roles of adult and child learners in language formation and change. *Language Learning and Development*, 1(2), 151–95.

Hurford, J. R. (1989). Biological evolution of the Saussurean sign as a component of the language acquisition device. *Lingua*, 77(2), 187–222.

Israel, A., & Sandler, W. (2011). Phonological category resolution: A study of handshapes in younger and older sign languages. In: Channon, R., & van der Hulst, H. (Eds.), *Formational Units in Sign Language* (pp. 177–202). Mouton de Gruyter, Berlin/Boston/Nijmegen.

Kalish, M. L., Griffiths, T. L., & Lewandowsky, S. (2007). Iterated learning: Intergenerational knowledge transmission reveals inductive biases. *Psychonomic Bulletin & Review*, 14(2), 288–94.

Kirby, S. (2000). Syntax without natural selection: How compositionality emerges from vocabulary in a population of learners. In: Knight, C., Studdert-Kennedy, M., & Hurford, J. (Eds.), *The Evolutionary Emergence of Language: Social Function and the Origins of Linguistics Form*, (pp. 303–23). Cambridge University Press, Cambridge.

Kirby, S. (2001). Spontaneous evolution of linguistic structure—an iterated learning model of the emergence of regularity and irregularity. *IEEE Transactions on Evolutionary Computation*, 5(2), 102–10.

Kirby, S. (2002). Learning, bottlenecks and the evolution of recursive syntax. In: Briscoe, T. (Ed.), *Linguistic Evolution through Language Acquisition: Formal and Computational Models* (pp. 173–204). Cambridge University Press, Cambridge.

Kirby, S., Cornish, H., & Smith, K. (2008). Cumulative cultural evolution in the laboratory: An experimental approach to the origins of structure in human language. *PNAS*, 105(31), 10681–6.

Kirby, S., Dowman, M., & Griffiths, T. L. (2007). Innateness and culture in the evolution of language. *Proceedings of the National Academy of Sciences*, 104(12), 5241–5.

Kirby, S., Griffiths, T., & Smith, K. (2014). Iterated learning and the evolution of language. *Current Opinion in Neurobiology*, 28, 108–14.

Kirby S., & Hurford J.R. (2002) The emergence of linguistic structure: An overview of the iterated learning model. In: Cangelosi A., & Parisi D. (Eds.), *Simulating the Evolution of Language* (Chapter 6). Springer, London.

Kirby, S., Tamariz, M., Cornish, H., & Smith, K. (2015). Compression and communication in the cultural evolution of linguistic structure. *Cognition*, 141, 87–102.

Ladefoged, P. (2006). *A Course in Phonetics*, 5th Edition. Thomson Wadsworth, Belmont, CA.

Mesoudi, A., & Whiten, A. (2008). The multiple roles of cultural transmission experiments in understanding human cultural evolution. *Philosophical Transactions of the Royal Society of London. Series B, Biological Sciences*, 363(1509), 3489–501.

Mesoudi, A., Whiten, A., & Dunbar, R. I. M. (2006). A bias for social information in human cultural transmission. *British Journal of Psychology*, 97(3), 405–23.

Oudeyer, P.-Y. (2005). The self-organization of speech sounds. *Journal of Theoretical Biology*, 233(3), 435–49

Oudeyer, P.-Y. (2006). *Self-organization in the Evolution of Speech*. Oxford University Press, Oxford.

Perfors, A., & Navarro, D. J. (2014). Language evolution can be shaped by the structure of the world. *Cognitive Science, 38*(4), 775–93.

Pinker, S., & Bloom, P. (1990). Natural language and natural selection. *Behavioral and Brain Sciences, 13*, 707–84.

Reali, F., & Griffiths, T. L. (2009). The evolution of frequency distributions: Relating regularization to inductive biases through iterated learning. *Cognition, 111*(3), 317–28.

Roberts, G., & Galantucci, B. (2012). The emergence of duality of patterning: Insights from the laboratory. *Language and Cognition, 4*(4), 297–318.

Sandler, W., Aronoff, M., Meir, I., & Padden, C. (2011). The gradual emergence of phonological form in a new language. *Natural Language and Linguistic Theory, 29*(2), 503–43.

Schouwstra, M., & de Swart, H. (2014). The semantic origins of word order. *Cognition, 131*(3), 431–36.

Seyfarth, R. M., Cheney, D. L., & Marler, P. (1980). Monkey responses to three different alarm calls: evidence of predator classification and semantic communication. *Science (New York, N.Y.), 210*(4471), 801–3.

Schouwstra, M., Smith, K., & Kirby, S. (2016). From natural order to convention in silent gesture. In: Roberts, O. F. & T. V. S. G., Cuskley, C., McCrohon, L., & Barceló-Coblijn, L. (Eds.), *The Evolution of Language: Proceedings of the 11th International Conference (EVOLANG11)*. EVOLANG XI, New Orleans, United States, March 20-24, 2016.

Smith, K., & Kirby, S. (2008). Cultural evolution: implications for understanding the human language faculty and its evolution. *Philosophical Transactions of the Royal Society B: Biological Sciences, 363*(1509), 3591–603.

Smith, K., & Wonnacott, E. (2010). Eliminating unpredictable variation through iterated learning. *Cognition, 116*(3), 444–9.

Steels, L. (1999). *The Talking Heads Experiment*. Laboratorium, Antwerp.

Tamariz, M., & Kirby, S. (2015). Culture: Copying, compression, and conventionality. *Cognitive Science, 39*(1), 171–83.

Theisen-White, C., Kirby, S., & Oberlander, J. (2011). Integrating the horizontal and vertical cultural transmission of novel communication systems. *Expanding the Space of Cognitive Science: Proceedings of the 33rd Annual Meeting of the Cognitive Science Society*, (2010), 956–61.

Theisen, C. A., Oberlander, J., & Kirby, S. (2009). Systematicity and arbitrariness in novel communication systems. In: Taatgen, N., & van Rijn, H. (Eds.), *CogSci 2009 Proceedings* (pp. 1971–6). Cognitive Science Society.

Thompson, B., Kirby, S., & Smith, K. (2016). Culture shapes the evolution of cognition. *Proceedings of the National Academy of Sciences, 113*(16), 4530–5.

Verhoef, T., Kirby, S., & Padden, C. (2011). Cultural emergence of combinatorial structure in an artificial whistled language. In: Carlson, T., Hölscher, L., & Shipley, C. (Eds.), *Proceedings of the 33rd Annual Conference of the Cognitive Science Society* (pp. 483–8). Cognitive Science Society, Austin, TX.

Wedel, A. (2006). Exemplar models, evolution and language change. *The Linguistic Review, 23*, 247–74.

Wedel, A. (2012). Lexical contrast maintenance and the organization of sublexical contrast systems. *Language and Cognition, 4*(4), 319–55.

Whiten, A., Caldwell, C. A., & Mesoudi, A. (2016). Cultural diffusion in humans and other animals. *Current Opinion in Psychology, 8*, 15–21.

Wilson, C. (2003). Experimental investigation of phonological naturalness. *West Coast Conference on Formal Linguistics 22 (WCCFL22)*, 101–14.

Wonnacott, E., & Newport, E. L. (2005). Novelty and regularization: The effect of novel instances on rule formation. In: Brugos, A., Clark-Cotton, M. R., & Ha, S., (Eds.), *BUCLD 29: Proceedings of the 29th Annual Boston University Conference on Language Development*. Cascadilla Press, Somerville, MA (pp. 1–11).

Zuidema, W. (2003). How the poverty of the stimulus solves the poverty of the stimulus. In: Becker, O. K., & Thrun, S. (Eds.), *Advances in Neural Information Processing Systems 15 (Proceedings of NIPS'02), Vol. 1* (pp. 43–50). MIT Press, Cambridge, MA.

Zuidema, W., & de Boer, B. (2009). The evolution of combinatorial phonology. *Journal of Phonetics, 37*, 125–44.

PART V
METHODOLOGICAL ADVANCES IN PSYCHOLINGUISTIC RESEARCH

CHAPTER 39

GENERALIZING OVER ENCOUNTERS
Statistical and theoretical considerations

DALE J. BARR

39.1 INTRODUCTION

How do we evaluate evidence for the generality of phenomena in psycholinguistics and related fields? For decades, researchers have recognized the importance of treating not only participants, but also stimuli, as sampled rather than fixed (Clark, 1973). It is only by taking both subject and stimulus populations into account during analysis—and critically, doing so *simultaneously*—that claims about psycholinguistic phenomena are supported in their full generality. In this chapter, I argue that simultaneous by-subject and by-item analysis is a special (albeit common) case of a more general problem of generalizing over particular *types of encounters*, defined in terms of the sampled units involved in the situation and the connections between them. This approach is more general inasmuch as it encompasses the traditional two-party encounters between subjects and stimulus materials but also handles two-party dyadic communicative encounters, or even three-party encounters involving participants making judgments about stimuli that were produced by participants in response to other stimuli. I argue that the goal of analysis is to make claims that are maximally likely to generalize to new encounters of the same type, and propose that the relevant encounter types involved in an experiment can be identified by thinking about the boundaries of what would constitute a legitimate "replication" of that experiment. These ideas have important implications far beyond psycholinguistics; indeed, nearly all areas of psychology and neuroscience make claims that are intended to generalize to new encounters, although it is only psycholinguistics that consistently uses the statistical apparatus required to support such claims.

This chapter is organized as follows. In the first part, I review the historical development of these issues within the field of psycholinguistics. Next, in what is the main contribution of this chapter, I propose a more general perspective on the issue of simultaneous generalization by developing the notion of *encounter types* and argue that simultaneous generalization over subjects and items is a special case of this more general problem. In the third and final section, I discuss the consequences of neglecting this perspective, address some common misconceptions, and consider the technical challenges involved in statistical generalization over encounters.

39.2 Background: The "language-as-fixed-effect" fallacy

Since Coleman (1964) and Clark (1973), psycholinguists have typically analyzed data treating both participants and stimuli as random factors. Clark, like Coleman before him, pointed out that researchers who use language materials (such as words or sentences) as stimuli obviously do not sample exhaustively from the population of possible stimuli, but use only a subset of materials that they present repeatedly to different participants. Because people's responses to particular stimuli will vary systematically (e.g., some words will be more memorable or easier to recognize than others), the various responses to a given stimulus are not independent. If this variation is not accounted for in the inferential analysis, it will tend to inflate the false positive rate. Clark (1973) proposed an analysis of variance (ANOVA)-based inferential approach which took by-subject and by-item variation into account through statistics such as F' or min-F'. Although there was initially some controversy about the need for by-item analysis (see Cohen, 1976; Smith, 1976; Wike & Church, 1976), psycholinguists quickly adopted Clark's proposals, and statistics such as min-F' became a regular feature of psycholinguistics papers.

Clark's advice was heeded in spirit, but within a decade, researchers were more often doing a kind of analysis that he had advised against—separately conducted by-subject and by-item analyses, with by-subject analyses reported as F_1 (or t_1) and by-item analyses reported as F_2 (or t_2)—and not the *simultaneous* analyses embodied in the single statistic min-F'. It is unclear why this happened, although researchers probably abandoned min-F' upon realizing that it is overly conservative in certain cases (Forster & Dickinson, 1976). In the separate analysis version (henceforth $F_1 \times F_2$), researchers would conclude that an effect was significant only if *both* F_1 and F_2 were significant. At least that was the idea; in practice, more weight was given to the by-subject analysis, and authors, editors, and reviewers would sometimes let a non-significant F statistic slide if it was from the by-item analysis. But, as Clark pointed out, the $F_1 \times F_2$ analysis is invalid, because the test for each sampling unit is influenced by variation from the sampling unit neglected in that analysis. Because of this, both F_1 and F_2 can be significant individually even when the null hypothesis is true, with the significance of F_1 driven by neglected by-item variation and that of F_2 driven by neglected by-subject variation. And despite additional attempts to call attention to the invalidity of $F_1 \times F_2$ in the late 1990s (Raaijmakers, Schrijnemakers, & Gremmen, 1999) as well as more recently (Barr, Levy, Scheepers, & Tily, 2013), to this day, $F_1 \times F_2$ remains the most common approach among ANOVA users in psycholinguistics.

Use of ANOVA, however, rapidly diminished in psycholinguistics once linear mixed-effects models (LMEMs) appeared on the scene, especially after an influential paper by Baayen, Davidson, and Bates (2008) introduced psycholinguists to the lme4 package for R

(Bates, Mächler, Bolker, & Walker, 2015) and showed how it could be used to support simultaneous generalization. The idea of using LMEMs in this way had been suggested before (Locker, Hoffman, & Bovaird, 2007; Quené & van den Bergh, 2004), but it was the wide availability of the lme4 package and tutorial examples in Baayen et al. (2008) that accelerated its uptake. LMEMs were attractive not only because they solved the problem of simultaneous generalization, but also because they made it easier to model effects of continuous covariates (e.g., time, age, word frequency) while simultaneously offering greater flexibility to adjust distributional assumptions to the type of data being analyzed (e.g., using binomial distributions for dichotomous data or Poisson distributions for count data). Psycholinguists took up LMEMs with enthusiasm, but many of the early papers did not heed warnings about the need to carefully consider how sampling unit variation should be structured in the model (Barr et al., 2013).

Sampling units such as subjects or items introduce variation that can be associated with different components of a linear model, and this variation is typically divided into *random intercept* and *random slope* variance. Many researchers who were new to LMEMs were fitting models that accounted for random intercept variation, but did not worry about random slope variation. Random intercept variance is the variance associated with the intercept term of a linear model. Much like a political poll by a particular organization can have a "house effect"—a consistent bias toward a particular party or candidate—a given sampling unit can also push a response variable in a consistent direction by a consistent amount. Certain subjects will be systematically less accurate or slower in their responses than others across trials. Likewise, certain stimuli will occasion greater delay or higher rates of errors than others. But sampling units can vary not just in this kind of "house effect" but can also vary in their sensitivity to experimental manipulations, introducing random slope variation. Some participants will be more sensitive than others to the difference between concrete and abstract words, or more impaired by a cognitive load manipulation. The variance associated with both these types of "house effects" should be considered when estimating a mixed-effects model.

Of the early psycholinguistics papers using mixed-effects modeling, many—perhaps even most—estimated random intercept variation but ignored random slope variation, with potentially dire inferential consequences. Use of random intercept-only models was also rampant among early adopters of mixed-effects models in fields outside of psychology (Schielzeth & Forstmeier, 2009). Monte Carlo simulations suggested that applying random intercept-only models to the very common experimental design in which a factor was manipulated within subjects and within items produced higher false positive rates than ANOVA performed on subjects alone. Barr et al. (2013) therefore encouraged researchers to "keep it maximal": identify those potential sources of sampling unit variation that are identifiable (i.e., that can be distinguished from residual error), and ensure they are accounted for in the model. Their simulations demonstrated that under a wide range of scenarios, a model with maximal random effects structure showed the best performance in terms of both Type I error and power. Indeed, the power of maximal models was much greater than min-F' and comparable to that obtained using the (invalid but widely used) ANOVA-based $F_1 \times F_2$ approach. While Barr et al. (2013) argued that judgments about random effects should be driven by the experimental design, others have suggested letting the data determine the random effects structure (Matuschek, Kliegl, Vasishth, Baayen, & Bates, 2017). Both approaches recognize that considering both random intercept and random slope variance is essential for sound inference.

39.3 A BROADER PERSPECTIVE: GENERALIZING OVER ENCOUNTERS

Although Clark's points about the conditions necessary for full generalization are applicable to many research areas, his framing of the problem in terms of language stimuli may have limited the uptake of these ideas outside of psycholinguistics. Also, discussion of the problem in terms of separate subject and stimulus populations may have contributed to the misconception that the problem is solved by separate by-subject and by-item analyses. In this section, I argue that the proper unit of analysis is the *encounter*: we seek to say something general about what happens when a particular type of sampling unit (e.g., subject) interacts with another type of sampling unit (e.g., stimulus). This perspective locates the traditional case of simultaneous generalization to subjects and items as one point in a larger space of theoretical possibilities. I suggest that thinking about statistical generalization in this way makes it easier to translate a study's design into an appropriate analysis plan.

Many claims in psycholinguistics are inherently claims about *encounters*—neither claims about people nor claims about language considered separately—but claims about particular types of people producing or understanding particular types of language in particular types of contexts. For instance, a claim that speakers are primed more by low- than high-frequency syntactic structures is a claim about what happens when a particular type of sampling unit (speaker) encounters another particular type of sampling unit (sentence); we say they are sampled because the claim is intended to apply to the effect of any arbitrary sentence structure on any arbitrary speaker, not just the sentences and speakers used in the experiment. Similarly, the claim that certain hormones modulate the level of attraction female participants feel toward dominant male faces is a claim about an encounter between an arbitrarily chosen female participant and an arbitrarily chosen male face. In short, in experiments involving samples of subjects and stimuli, it is not so much that we wish to generalize "simultaneously" to multiple target populations, but that we wish to say something about the single population of possible encounters between the two types of units.

I believe there are certain benefits to this way of viewing the problem of statistical generalization. First, by emphasizing generalization to events rather than generalization to things, it becomes clearer that the type of entity involved in the event—people, pictures, words, voices, birds—is not important; what is important is the fact that they are sampled as well as the manner in which they relate to one other in the study. There is no good reason why psycholinguists routinely treat their stimuli as random while face perception researchers routinely treat their stimuli as fixed; it is merely different analytical conventions for different fields. It doesn't matter what is being measured (behavior or brain responses) or even whether the study involves human populations at all. A researcher who studies birds' reactions to bird songs would aim to say something general about how a certain type of bird responds to a certain type of song, and unless her sampling procedure exhausts the possible combinations of these types of birds and types of songs, she would need to treat both birds and songs as random in her analysis. Other fields need to learn the lessons of psycholinguistics, and are more likely to learn these lessons if they are framed in terms of the general properties of events, not of things.

Second, the notion of an *encounter* provides a single target population for inferential claims: a population of events of a given type involving certain sampling units organized in a certain way. It is easier to think about scientific claims in terms of a single target population rather than in terms of multiple target populations simultaneously. For instance, claims about the procedures involved in lexical access are about people perceiving and reacting to words, not claims about people, or claims about words. Viewed thus, it becomes much clearer why separate by-subject and by-item analyses are inappropriate. To say something general about a type of event, one must be able to separate out general characteristics of the encounter from the idiosyncratic properties of the units (subjects or items) involved. Inference at the subject (or item) level alone, in which trials are aggregated together to calculate a set of participant (or item) means, inevitably confounds these sources of variation, and because they cannot be pulled apart, inference becomes bound to the specific units that are neglected in the analysis.

Thinking about generalization in terms of encounters may also aid interpretation of fixed effects in a mixed-effects model. An encounter is essentially an idealized typical trial in an experiment. Thinking about what units are involved in a given trial and whether they should be treated as sampled or fixed is key to identifying the appropriate analysis. And the fixed effects estimates from a linear mixed-effects model with crossed random effects are directly interpretable in terms of the basic encounter being studied: they can be viewed as the model's best guess at how a typical participant responds to a typical item on a typical trial. Thus, inferences that models provide about these parameter estimates are, in fact, inferences about a target population of encounters.

Finally, thinking about generalization to new events may aid in appreciating the limits on the generality of a study's claims. For instance, many studies of dialogue often involve a listener who interprets expressions from a speaker, while some aspect of the listener's behavior (e.g., eye gaze) is measured. The fundamental event in such studies involves three units: a speaker, a listener, and a linguistic expression. In principle, the researcher would like to make general claims about events involving an arbitrary listener interpreting a particular type of expression produced by an arbitrary speaker. However, for reasons of convenience, such studies often will use a fixed speaker for all participants in the experiment while at the same time sampling listeners and expressions. There will be idiosyncratic characteristics of this fixed unit (e.g., the speaker is male or female, enthusiastic or disengaged, has a dialect reflecting a particular socioeconomic status) that can impact how listeners respond to his or her expressions, and that may even impact different kinds of listeners in different ways. At one extreme, the experiment could even be considered as a case study of this particular speaker. Making fully general claims would require sampling not just listeners and expressions but also speakers. If this is impractical, the researcher would need to provide arguments as to why this speaker should be treated as representative. But one seldom sees discussion of such limitations in papers on dialogue, possibly because of the focus on generalizing things (subjects and stimuli) rather to event types.

39.3.1 Types of encounters

The problem of generalizing over participants and stimuli is just a special case (albeit, an extremely common one) of the more general problem of generalizing over encounters. In this section, we consider how this perspective can be extended to different kinds of encounters, involving different types of units, different numbers of these types (e.g., three-party encounters instead of two-party encounters), and different organizations of the units in the encounter.

Most obviously, encounters can involve stimuli of a non-linguistic nature. To choose but one example, studies of face perception investigate how particular classes of people judge certain classes of faces. It may be of interest, for example, to examine how dominance characteristics in male faces interact with a female respondent's hormonal profile to influence attractiveness judgments. In such a study, both female participants and male faces should be considered sampled; however, most face perception studies ignore the sampled nature of materials, but without circumscribing their claims to the particular sample of stimuli. Consequently, claims may generalize to new female respondents encountering the same male faces, but not to new samples of male faces. The same goes for studies in social psychology, where stimuli are often chosen to represent people or objects of social relevance (Judd, Westfall, & Kenny, 2012). For instance, studies looking at the detection of vocal signals of competence or trustworthiness must account for the sampled nature of the voices used in the experiment.

It should also be fairly obvious that the problem of generalizing over encounters is completely independent of the type of dependent measure involved in a study. Given this, it is perplexing that neuroimaging studies—even neuroimaging studies carried out by psycholinguists—rarely take stimulus variation into account, despite calls to do so (Bedny, Aguirre, & Thompson-Schill, 2007). But even the few studies that implement item analyses often do so inappropriately, pursuing separate rather than simultaneous generalization. One barrier might be the complexity of estimating many mixed-effects models over many variables (EEG sensors or voxels), but recent work by Westfall, Nichols, and Yarkoni (2016) shows that this is technically feasible, and improves the quality of inference.

Sometimes the encounters one wishes to generalize over involve people reacting to particular types of people rather than particular types of stimuli. A recent study that received much media attention reported gender bias in students' evaluations of instructors, with male instructors rated as better than female instructors (MacNell, Driscoll, & Hunt, 2015). Students interacted online with either a male or female instructor and later rated aspects of the instructor's performance. The online nature of the interaction made it possible for experimenters to manipulate students' perceptions of the gender of the instructor independently of the instructor's actual gender. This was accomplished by having one male and one female instructor lead a discussion group either under their own identity or while pretending to be the instructor of the opposite gender. The study found that students gave lower ratings when they perceived the instructor to be female than when they perceived the instructor as male. While this finding is interesting, the study's use of only two instructors makes it essentially a case study of the performances of these particular instructors. It would require multiple instructors of each gender to have any confidence in its generality.

Certain types of studies involve three-party encounters, such as when pairs of participants communicate about pictorial stimuli (Garrod, Fay, Lee, Oberlander, & MacLeod, 2007). Or, a three-party encounter might involve a single participant responding to stimuli from two different populations, such as in a priming study where a picture is flashed on the screen prior to the presentation of a probe word. In the latter case, whether the stimuli should be treated in the analysis as separate random factors or as a single random factor representing each pair would depend upon whether each individual stimulus is ever used outside of a single pairing. If each stimulus is only used within a pair, it wouldn't be possible to statistically distinguish effects of the pairing from the individual effects of each picture and word, and so the pairs of stimuli should be treated as a single factor.

A final, interesting case is offered by studies that use human subjects as "measuring devices" to assess perceptual constructs whose physical characteristics are not well-established or are subjective and therefore difficult to measure. For example, in a study on face perception, a set of participants might provide attractiveness ratings for a set of faces that are then presented to another set of participants. In psycholinguistics, this kind of situation arises in the AXB discrimination task, in which participants rate whether a spoken word token X is more similar to token A or token B. For instance, Pardo (2006) used an AXB task to examine phonetic convergence between pairs of interacting speakers. Encounters in this study involved multiple sampling units: the pairs of participants whose interaction gave rise to individual speech tokens, and the raters who later assessed the similarities of these tokens. What is interesting about this type of study is that it involves subjects from one sample making judgments about the behaviors produced by another set of subjects. Indeed, there is also a fourth potential sampling unit involved: the particular word the speaker uttered (a landmark on a map). Although the real target of generalization is the conversational encounter between the interacting participants, the measurements of this encounter will also be influenced by characteristics of the particular set of raters that were sampled. Unfortunately, we currently know little about the inferential consequences of treating raters as fixed in these types of studies.

In sum, human subjects responding to stimuli is but one of a large variety of encounter types that can arise in different areas of psychology and neuroscience. Given this variety, how does one recognize the target population of encounters to which findings should be generalized? Characterizing the encounter type is not difficult because it usually follows directly from the main claim the study is seeking to support, which in turn is often realized in the structure of a typical trial within the experiment. But what can be more difficult to identify is which aspects of an encounter should be treated as fixed and which should be treated as random.

This latter judgment can be aided by thinking in terms of replication: which aspects of the encounter are essential and should be preserved in a direct replication, and which should be allowed to vary? Usually the essential part involves the *structure* of the encounter and the *types* of entities it involves, and the arbitrary part involves the identities of these types as they are realized through the set of sampled subjects and/or stimuli. For instance, when considering a replication of the study on instructor gender bias already mentioned (MacNell et al., 2015), it becomes clear that the particular identities of the instructors are nonessential to the study's claims, as the claims are intended to apply generally to any male or female instructors. Thus, a more robustly generalizable test of this hypothesis would have required a sample of male and female instructors in addition to the obtained sample of students, and without this additional sampling claims about generality should be tempered.

We would not be inclined to count a study as a "replication" if it was conducted on the exact same participants as the original, and not just because there is no magic way to wipe away subjects' memories of their experience in the original before participating in the replication. A good replication should sample new "levels" of the subject factor to help minimize the possibility that the original result is due to sampling error. In contrast, researchers regularly view it as *desirable* and even *essential* to use the exact same set of stimulus materials in a replication as in an original study, often counting the use of the same stimuli as a criterion for being a "direct" replication. However, this sacrifices generalizability for the sake of fidelity; if the claims are about the class of stimuli involved in the encounter, and not the particular stimuli involved, then a direct replication should involve new stimuli as well as new participants (Westfall, Judd, & Kenny, 2015). More precisely, it should involve new encounters among new sampling units from the constituent populations.

39.4 Statistical issues in generalizing over encounters

In this section, I consider the issue of how to specify a statistical model so that claims based on the model will best generalize to a new sample from a target population of encounters. The section begins by presenting the general problem that is created by crossing sampling units in a series of encounters: namely, each repeated observation on sampled units erroneously treated as fixed amplifies the impact of sampling error on interference. Along the way, I discuss how to determine which random effects to include in a model, and the consequences of treating units as fixed rather than random. I close by discussing a few cases that are commonly misconceived as requiring only by-subject analysis.

39.4.1 Repetition amplifies the impact of sampling error

A sample from a population, being a subset of that population, is unlikely to be completely representative of the population as a whole. The extent to which it is representative depends on the size of the sample relative to the population, along with the magnitude of variation in the population. Proportionally small samples will tend to be less representative on average than larger samples. Even fixing the sample size, departures from the target population will differ from sample to sample.

This issue of sampling error is well-known, and its implications are fairly obvious. However, what is often underappreciated is that when treating sampled units (subjects, stimuli) as fixed in the analysis, each repeated measurement on these same sampled units amplifies the distorting influence of sampling error. In a design with crossed random factors of subjects and stimuli, each new subject typically implies a new repetition of measurements across the same set of stimuli. Likewise, each additional stimulus implies a repetition of measurement across the same set of subjects. In an analysis where subjects are considered as random but stimuli are neglected, increasing the by-subject sample size will tend to increase the distorting influence of the sampling error associated with stimuli. So long as a sampling unit in the encounter is neglected, increasing the sample size of any other considered unit may actually *increase* the false positive rate and thus *decrease* the generality of any claims with regard to the target population of encounters.

Researchers who conduct large scale replication studies involving many subjects at many different sites should take heed of this. While the ever-increasing ease of data collection

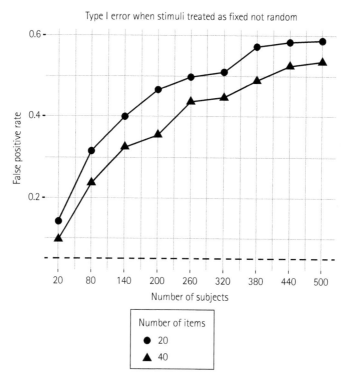

FIG. 39.1 False positive rates for analyses neglecting stimulus variation as a function of subject sample size (20–500 in steps of 60) and stimulus sample size (20 or 40).

through online methods would, at first blush, seem a boon for generalizability and replicability, large samples with the wrong analysis can paradoxically lead to greater rates of false positive findings.

A simple Monte Carlo simulation demonstrates this phenomenon. The simulation assumes there is variation in sensitivity to a manipulation over subjects and items, but no consistent overall effect. Thus, any significant result is a false positive. We kept the magnitude of this variation fixed while varying the size of the stimulus sample (20 vs. 40) and the size of the subject sample (from 20 to 500 in steps of 60)[1]. Figure 39.1 presents the results where each analysis treated subjects as random but ignored stimulus variation. The false positive rate was clearly unacceptably large at all sample sizes, but increased dramatically as the subject sample size increased, approaching 0.6 for the largest samples, nearly four times the rate observed for the smallest samples.

This phenomenon also has implications for studies where stimuli or subjects are matched across conditions. In some psycholinguistic studies, for example, researchers take care to match the properties of words (e.g., frequency, imageability, word length) used in different experimental conditions. Upon observing no significant differences between the two sets of stimuli along these dimensions, they will argue that the matching procedure succeeded

---

[1] The code for the simulation can be found at https://gist.github.com/dalejbarr/8f6adabdbf2ab9b3458cf51c7bfee484

in creating equivalent sets. But the sets are of course never *exactly* equivalent, and the significance test that is supposed to demonstrate this is performed on a single instance of each stimulus. However, because each new subject involves a full repetition of the sets of items, any small differences become amplified as new subjects are added, and this noise will be increasingly likely to be mistaken for signal so long as the stimuli are not accounted for in the analysis.

A related case concerns studies in which the same stimuli are used in different conditions, having been also appropriately counterbalanced across conditions. It is a misconception that this exempts the analyst from having to consider items in the analysis. Although a paper by Raaijmakers et al. (1999) seems to suggest this, this misses a critical detail of that paper: their analysis for the within-item design actually *did* take item effects into account[2]. All that repeating items across conditions control for is the *random intercept* variation associated with items, ensuring that this variation is not confounded with the factor of interest. However, it ignores the likelihood of *treatment variation* across items (i.e., that items will vary in the extent to which they show an effect across conditions). For instance, in studies on perspective taking in language comprehension, it is common to manipulate the identity of privileged objects: objects that listeners can see but know that speakers can't see and don't know about. A speaker might, for example, ask the listener to *move the tape one space right*, and listeners might see, in addition to a "target" tape that is shared with the speaker, a hidden object that is also called *tape* ("competitor" condition) or is called something else such as an *apple* ("non-competitor" condition). Listeners are more likely to look at the privileged object when it matches the target, but whatever effect the competitor manipulation produces for this particular set of stimuli, it would differ from the competitor effect for another set (e.g., *move the small cup one space right*, when there is a large and smaller "target" cup, and the privileged competitor is either an even smaller cup or a toy monkey). Each stimulus has a unique "house effect." If every participant encounters all of the stimuli, then each participant also replicates the house effect for each one, and these idiosyncrasies accumulate.

As Clark (1973) noted, there is one situation in which it is legitimate to neglect sampled units in an analysis, and that is when each sampled unit appears only once in the entire sample (i.e., when a sampled unit does not participate in more than one encounter). This approach works because variation associated with the sampled units is fully absorbed in the residual variance (in technical terms, the variation is not *identifiable* by any statistical model). For instance, if each subject in the sample responds to a unique set of words, then the variance associated with each word is fully accounted for by the model residual, and only a by-subjects analysis is needed.

39.4.2 How to account for sampling variation in a statistical model?

It is important not only *whether* a particular source of variation is taken into account in an analysis, but also *how* this variation is captured by the model. As we've already noted, following the landmark Baayen et al. (2008) paper on linear mixed-effects models, many

---

[2] Albeit indirectly, through the proxy of a "list" effect included in the model.

researchers mistakenly assumed that incorporating sampling units as random intercepts was sufficient for generalization. However, as Barr et al. (2013) pointed out, such random-intercepts-only models are only appropriate when sampling units are nested within levels of experimental factors, and such designs are unusual in psycholinguistics. When sampling units participate in multiple encounters at each level of an experimental factor, this introduces variation that must be accounted for by estimating random slope variation associated with those units. Failure to do so can increase false positive rates dramatically; indeed, Barr et al. (2013) found that for certain designs where a factor was administered within subjects as well as within items, random-intercepts-only models showed *worse* generalization than a by-subjects analysis alone.

Barr et al. (2013) provide some guidelines for determining what the *maximal* random effects structure should be for a particular design, and encourage researchers to try to estimate models with maximal random effects. The general idea is that each sampling unit gets a random intercept, and random slopes for any factor for which two conditions are satisfied: (1) the levels of the factor are administered within-unit, and (2) there are multiple observations for each unit at each level of the factor. The researcher should consider whether or not to include random slopes from the point of view of each sampling unit in the study. For instance, a by-subject random slope for factor X may be needed if both criteria are satisfied from the point of view of individual subjects, but a by-item random slope may not be needed if they are not satisfied from the point of view of individual items (e.g., the factor is administered between items). One should also consider whether observations are replicated over individual encounters; it is possible that each participant encounters the same stimulus multiple times during the experiment, and if this is the case, then by-encounter random intercepts and random slopes should also be considered, following the same logic[3]. For guidance on specifying interaction terms in factorial designs, see Barr (2013).

39.5 Conclusion

The basic claim of this paper is that the target of generalization in psychology and neuroscience has been misidentified as a particular population of subjects, or in some cases, separate populations of subjects and items. I have argued that the proper target of generalization is a population of events involving encounters between sampling units: language users encountering particular types of sentences, female raters encountering particular types of male faces, students encountering particular types of instructors, brains encountering particular types of scenes, potential employers encountering different types of potential employees, birds encountering particular types of songs. The inferential target in such cases is clearly the populations of events of which the sampling units are but constituent elements. This broader perspective clarifies that the need to consider stimuli in one's analysis has very much to do with the fact they are sampled and very little to do with whether the stimuli are words, faces, images, or something else. It also provides a non-technical motivation for

---

[3] Note that for studies involving person-stimulus encounters, the "encounter" is what Barr et al. (2013) refer to as the "subject-by-stimulus interaction."

why separate analyses for each of the populations involved in the encounter fail to justify claims about the target population of events. Finally, this broader perspective might help researchers appreciate limits on the generality of a study as well as what aspects of a study should be targeted in a replication effort.

Generalizing over encounters presents several practical challenges that are beyond the scope of this chapter (for discussion, see Barr et al., 2013; Matuschek et al., 2017; Westfall et al., 2016). While the advent of mixed-effects modeling has made it possible to flexibly model all sources of sampling error within a single framework, in practice, the estimation algorithm is not guaranteed to arrive at a solution, often requiring a reduction in the random effects structure. Although there are conflicting ideas about whether it is prudent to perform significance tests on random slope variance when specifying a model, all experts agree that it is essential to consider associated random slope variance when performing significance tests on fixed effects.

Mixed-effects models are powerful, but they have the critical weakness of requiring explicit estimation of variation even in situations in which such variation is best considered as "nuisance" variation that is not of theoretical interest. McNeish, Stapleton, and Silverman (2017) criticized the "unnecessary ubiquity" of mixed-effects models in psychology, pointing out that other "population-average models" (PAMs) exist, such as Generalized Estimation Equations (Liang & Zeger, 1986). Such models do not require explicit estimation of such variation and thus analyses are less likely to suffer convergence problems. However, there are currently no PAM approaches that allow for crossed random factors. Until such approaches are developed, linear mixed-effects models remain the best available option.

Psycholinguistics has had much to contribute to the improvement of statistical methods across psychology and neuroscience, as it is currently only the field of psycholinguistics that gets statistical generalization consistently right, although it is only very recently in its historical development that it can claim to do so. It is hoped that by viewing generalization from a more general perspective based on encounters, more researchers will appreciate the critical role that statistical modeling plays in supporting valid, replicable claims about phenomena in psychology and neuroscience.

Author's note

Thanks to M. Gareth Gaskell and Lisa Debruine for comments on an earlier draft of this paper.

References

Baayen, R. H., Davidson, D. J., & Bates, D. M. (2008). Mixed-effects modeling with crossed random effects for subjects and items. *Journal of Memory and Language, 59,* 390–412.

Barr, D. J. (2013). Random effects structure for testing interactions in linear mixed-effects models. *Frontiers in Psychology, 4,* 328.

Barr, D. J., Levy, R., Scheepers, C., & Tily, H. J. (2013). Random effects structure for confirmatory hypothesis testing: Keep it maximal. *Journal of Memory and Language, 68*, 255–78.

Bates, D., Mächler, M., Bolker, B. M., & Walker, S. C. (2015). Fitting linear mixed-effects models using lme4. *Journal of Statistical Software, 67*, 1–48.

Bedny, M., Aguirre, G. K., & Thompson-Schill, S. L. (2007). Item analysis in functional magnetic resonance imaging. *NeuroImage, 35*, 1093–102.

Clark, H. H. (1973). The language-as-fixed-effect fallacy: A critique of language statistics in psychological research. *Journal of Verbal Learning and Verbal Behavior, 12*, 335–59.

Cohen, J. (1976). Random means random. *Journal of Verbal Learning and Verbal Behavior, 15*, 261–2.

Coleman, E. B. (1964). Generalizing to a language population. *Psychological Reports, 14*, 219–26.

Forster, K., & Dickinson, R. (1976). More on the language-as-fixed-effect fallacy: Monte Carlo estimates of error rates for F1, F2, F', and min F'. *Journal of Verbal Learning and Verbal Behavior, 15*, 135–42.

Garrod, S., Fay, N., Lee, J., Oberlander, J., & MacLeod, T. (2007). Foundations of representation: Where might graphical symbol systems come from? *Cognitive Science, 31*, 961–87.

Judd, C. M., Westfall, J., & Kenny, D. A. (2012). Treating stimuli as a random factor in social psychology: a new and comprehensive solution to a pervasive but largely ignored problem. *Journal of Personality and Social Psychology, 103*, 54–69.

Liang, K.-Y., & Zeger, S. (1986). Longitudinal data analysis using generalized linear models. *Biometrika, 73*, 13–22.

Locker, L., Hoffman, L., & Bovaird, J. (2007). On the use of multilevel modeling as an alternative to items analysis in psycholinguistic research. *Behavior Research Methods, 39*, 723–30.

MacNell, L., Driscoll, A., & Hunt, A. N. (2015). What's in a name? Exposing gender bias in student ratings of teaching. *Innovative Higher Education, 40*, 291–303.

Matuschek, H., Kliegl, R., Vasishth, S., Baayen, H., & Bates, D. (2017). Balancing Type I error and power in linear mixed models. *Journal of Memory and Language, 94*, 305–15.

McNeish, D., Stapleton, L. M., & Silverman, R. D. (2017). On the unnecessary ubiquity of hierarchical linear modeling. *Psychological Methods, 22*, 114–40.

Pardo, J. S. (2006). On phonetic convergence during conversational interaction. *Journal of the Acoustical Society of America, 119*, 2382–93.

Quené, H., & van den Bergh, H. (2004). On multi-level modeling of data from repeated measures designs: a tutorial. *Speech Communication, 43*, 103–21.

Raaijmakers, J. G. W., Schrijnemakers, J. M. C., & Gremmen, F. (1999). How to deal with "the language-as-fixed-effect fallacy": Common Misconceptions and alternative solutions. *Journal of Memory and Language, 41*, 416–26.

Schielzeth, H., & Forstmeier, W. (2009). Conclusions beyond support: overconfident estimates in mixed models. *Behavioral Ecology, 20*, 416–20.

Smith, J. E. K. (1976). The assuming-will-make-it-so fallacy. *Journal of Verbal Learning and Verbal Behavior, 15*, 262–3.

Westfall, J., Judd, C. M., & Kenny, D. A. (2015). Replicating studies in which samples of participants respond to samples of stimuli. *Perspectives on Psychological Science, 10*, 390–9.

Westfall, J., Nichols, T. E., & Yarkoni, T. (2016). Fixing the stimulus-as-fixed-effect fallacy in task fMRI. *Wellcome Open Research, 1*, 23.

Wike, E., & Church, J. (1976). Comments on Clark's "The language-as-fixed-effect fallacy." *Journal of Verbal Learning and Verbal Behavior, 15*, 249–55.

CHAPTER 40

COGNITIVE ELECTROPHYSIOLOGY OF LANGUAGE

THOMAS P. URBACH AND MARTA KUTAS

"It is possible to give EEG studies a more nearly experimental character by providing a controlled sensory stimulus and recording its effect upon both the EEG and other variables."—V. J. Walter and W. Grey Walter, 1949*

LANGUAGE researchers are increasingly likely to encounter if not undertake event-related brain potential (ERP) studies in their areas of specialization. Several recent reviews focus on language-related ERPs in well-studied psycholinguistic designs (e.g., Hoeks & Brouwer, 2014; Kuperberg, 2013; Kutas & Federmeier, 2011; Steinhauer & Connolly, 2008; Swaab et al., 2011). Rather than reiterate these reviews, we situate contemporary psycholinguistic ERP studies in the historical landscape of electroencephalography (EEG) and cognitive electrophysiology more generally. Although the human brain is adept at processing language, it never *just* processes language. This remarkable ability is scaffolded by many other concurrent processes in the perception-action arc that are also implemented by ongoing neural activity. This general point holds for the investigation of real-time brain activity during language processing regardless of how this activity is measured, for example, via microelectrodes implanted within the brain (Halgren et al., 2015) or at its surface (electrocorticogram, ECoG; Martin et al., 2016) or via recordings of brain-generated magnetic fields (magnetoencephalogram, MEG, alone or in combination with EEG; Wöstmann et al., 2017; also see Chapter 41 by Hauk, this volume). In this chapter, we focus on measures of electrical brain activity derived from potentials (voltages) measured at the scalp—the human EEG. Decades of research show that scalp potentials are modulated in frequency, amplitude, timing, and spatial distribution by a variety of stimulus, task, and contextual variables (Luck & Kappenman, 2012; Regan, 1989). This sensitivity makes ERPs

---

* Reprinted from Electroencephalography and Clinical Neurophysiology, 1 (1), V. J. Walter and W. Grey Walter, The central effects of rhythmic sensory stimulation, pp. 57–86, Copyright © 1949, Elsevier Ireland Ltd. with permission from Elsevier.

a versatile experimental measure for tracking covert processes, including but not limited to language processing. Inattention to these sensitivities leads to poor design choices and/or misinterpretation of ERP language experiments, as does the absence of a clear answerable question.

Since the previous edition of this handbook, the pace of brainwave research has accelerated such that the number of important studies and research programs we omit far exceeds those that could possibly be included. In what remains, we offer the general lay of the land and some things to think about as we share our cautious optimism about the prospects for using scalp recorded potentials to learn more about how the brain understands and produces language.

40.1 EEG: THE HUMAN ELECTROENCEPHALOGRAM

After multiple failures, Berger in 1929 observed human electrical brain activity recorded at the scalp, primarily alpha waves, oscillations of ~10 Hz visible to the naked eye, that systematically varied in amplitude with changes in visual sensation and mentation (Berger, 1930). Adrian and Matthews reported replicating the findings (Fig. 40.1 Panel A; see also Gibbs et al., 1935), but they knew that EEG did not reflect action potentials and that the skull attenuates potentials generated by current flow in the brain; they were still deeply skeptical: "What evidence is there to show that these potentials are developed in the brain?" (Adrian & Matthews, 1934, p. 357). Evidence marshaled from numerous control experiments implicated brain sources, and ruled out non-cortical sources, e.g., in muscles of the face, neck, eyes (e.g., by mechanically actuated eyeball movements, op. cit, p. 360). Since light levels modulated alpha amplitude, the visual system was clearly involved so Adrian and Matthews flickered light at different frequencies to stimulate the visual system and found the frequency of EEG oscillation could track the flicker frequency up to about 25 c/sec (Fig. 40.1, Panel B).

These two types of stimulus manipulations, i.e., a punctate change in stimulation (turning lights on or off) vs. repetitive stimulation (visual flicker) broadly divide stimulus-evoked brain responses into *transient* and *steady state* potentials, depending on the timing and regularity of the stimulation (see Regan, 1989). The original reports of alpha waves map the fluctuation of voltage magnitudes over time (i.e., as a function in the time domain, at around 10 cycles per second). The amplitude and phase of periodic oscillations in scalp potentials also can be represented in the frequency domain via Fourier analysis as a sum of sine and cosine waves of given amplitude and phase. Time-domain representations are useful for quantifying brief transient potentials; frequency domain representations are of value where experimental interest is in sustained activity. Transient responses to punctate stimulation may also be observed as changes in frequency-band characteristics (amplitude, phase) over time. The potential value of real-time-frequency analyses motivated Walter and Shipton to construct the "toposcope," a 24 channel electroenecephalograph with cathode ray tube displays for visualizing interchannel phase relations (Walter & Shipton, 1951). Since then, time-frequency analysis of EEG has become more routine as advances in digital computing hardware and scientific computing software have made time-frequency analysis more readily accessible

(A) Transient event-related brain potentials (ERPs)

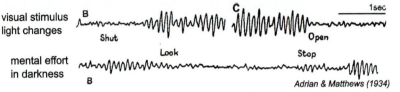

(B) Steady state flicker-evoked brain potentials

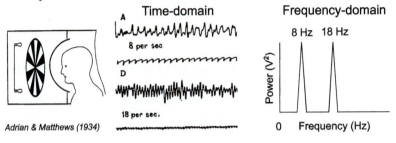

(C) Transient time-domain average ERPs

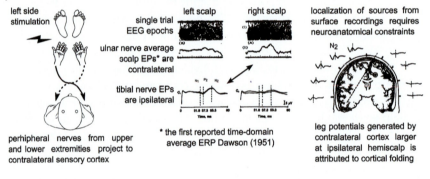

(D) EEG data acquisition, visualization, and analysis

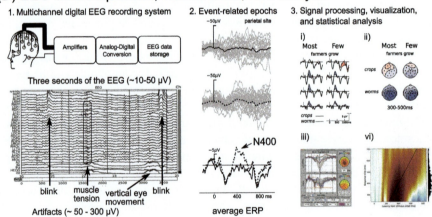

FIG. 40.1 Electroencephalographic recordings and analyses. (A) Adrian and Matthew's replication of Berger's alpha potentials responding to external stimuli (eyes open vs. shut in an illuminated room) and mental acts (trying to see in a darkened box), hence "event-related brain potentials" in the general sense. (B) Periodic brain responses evoked by periodic visual stimulation at frequencies other than

to researchers without the need for specialized instrumentation (for overviews of time-frequency methods, see Hauk, Chapter 41, this volume and, e.g., Gross, 2014; Herrmann et al., 2014; Wacker & Witte, 2013; for widely used open-source software implementations see Brainstorm, Tadel et al., 2011; Fieldtrip, Oostenveld et al., 2011; MNE, Gramfort et al., 2014; EEGLAB, Delorme et al., 2011). In clinical application, transient and steady state evoked responses are used to investigate sensory systems and their functional integrity (Martin et al., 2008; Musiek et al., 2015; Dimitrijevic & Cone, 2015). Regan (1989) points out the distinction between the transient and steady state potentials blurs as the interval between periodic stimuli decreases. Language research is an interesting case for the dichotomy since typical speaking and reading rates (natural and experimental) involve quasi-periodic stimulation by foveated visual words and syllables between about 1 and 10 per second. To date, transient time-domain evoked potential analyses still comprise the clear majority of language ERP experiments, but there is growing interest in the relation between language processes and oscillatory brain activity that may be better characterized in the frequency domain (see Hauk, Chapter 41 this volume).

FIG. 40.1 Continued

the "intrinsic" alpha oscillation at rest. (C) The first reported time-domain averaged evoked potentials (Dawson, 1954). Arm and leg sensory evoked cortical potentials are larger over opposite sides of the head even though the peripheral nerves both project to the same contralateral cerebral hemisphere. The "paradoxical" ipsilateral leg EP is attributed to cortical folding and consistent with generators in contralateral primary cortex. (D) 1. Schematic multichannel EEG data acquisition and analysis pipeline for ERPs illustrating the continuous digital EEG record, contamination of the EEG by non-cerebral artifacts; 2. EEG epochs (50 μV scale) and time-domain averages (5 μV scale), time-locked to visually presented words at 0 ms; 3. signal processing and visualization, for example: (i) grand mean waveforms; (ii) contour maps of scalp potential distributions; (iii) hypothesis testing via error-rate controlled mass univariate tests (Groppe et al., 2011a, 2011b); (iv) predictions from a linear regression model (slope rERPs, Smith & Kutas, 2015a, 2015b) computed at each time point with response time as a continuous predictor variable; black line indicates time of button-press response. Not illustrated are conventional parametric statistical tests, (e.g., ANOVA, MANOVA). Figures reproduced by permission.

Figure 40.1A) Adapted from E.D. Adrian and B.H.C. Matthews, The Berger Rhythm: Potential Changes from the Occipital Lobes in Man, *Brain*, 4 (57), p. 358, Figure 10, https://doi.org/10.1093/brain/57.4.355 Copyright © 1934, Oxford University Press. Figure 40.1B) Adapted from E.D. Adrian and B.H.C. Matthews, The Berger Rhythm: Potential Changes from the Occipital Lobes in Man, *Brain*, 4(57), p. 358, Figures 9 and 19a and d, https://doi.org/10.1093/brain/57.4.355 Copyright © 1934, Oxford University Press. Figure 40.1C) middle column (top). Adapted with permission from G.D. Dawson, Proceedings of the Physiological Society: A summation technique for detecting small signals in a large irregular background, *The Journal of Physiology*, 115 (Supplement), p. 2, Figure 1c, DOI: 10.1113/jphysiol.1951.sp004684 ©1951 The Physiological Society. Figure 40.1C) middle column (bottom) and right column. Adapted with permission from Robert Cruse, George Klem, Ronald P. Lesser, and Hans Lueders, Paradoxical Lateralization of Cortical Potentials Evoked by Stimulation of Posterior Tibial Nerve, *JAMA Neurology*, 39 (4), pp. 222–5, Figures 8 and 4, doi:10.1001/archneur.1982.00510160028005, Copyright © 1982, American Medical Association. All rights reserved. Figure 40.1Di). Reprinted from *Journal of Memory and Language*, 63 (2), Thomas P. Urbach and Marta Kutas, Quantifiers more or less quantify on-line: ERP evidence for partial incremental interpretation, pp. 158–79, Experiment 2, Part d, doi.org/10.1016/j.jml.2010.03.008, Copyright © 2010 Elsevier Inc., with permission from Elsevier. Figure 40.1Dii). Reprinted from *Journal of Memory and Language*, 63 (2), Thomas P. Urbach and Marta Kutas, Quantifiers more or less quantify on-line: ERP evidence for partial incremental interpretation, pp. 158–79, Experiment 2, Part b, doi.org/10.1016/j.jml.2010.03.008 © 2010 Elsevier Inc., with permission from Elsevier. Figure 40.1Diii) Reproduced from David M. Groppe, Thomas P. Urbach, and Marta Kutas, Mass univariate analysis of event-related brain potentials/fields I: A critical tutorial review, *Psychophysiology*, 48 (12), pp. 1711–25, DOI: 10.1111/j.1469-8986.2011.01273.x, Copyright © 2011 Society for Psychophysiological Research. Figure 40.1Div) Reproduced from Nathaniel J. Smith and Marta Kutas, Regression-based estimation of ERP waveforms: II. Nonlinear effects, overlap correction, and practical considerations, *Psychophysiology*, 52 (2), pp. 169–81, Figure 3c, DOI: 10.1111/psyp.12320, Copyright © 2014 Society for Psychophysiological Research.

40.2 Time-domain averaging

"It was suggested by Dr. J. N. Hunt that the discrimination against irregular deflections, in favour of those waves regularly evoked by the stimuli, would be greatly increased if the records could in some way be added . . . it illustrates a principle long known and well tried in other fields."—G. D. Dawson (1954) p. 65

Interest in recruiting EEG for basic science and clinical language application was recognized from the outset; for example, with studies of alpha during speech production in stutterers and non-stutterers (Travis & Knott, 1936), and while reading silently and aloud (Knott, 1938). Knott (1938) notes that task instructions (e.g., *"React to this light"*) can alter the cortical response to light. In outline, this inference that sentence comprehension can impact the electrical brain activity presumed to mediate mental function and behavior is an archetype for the inferences drawn in contemporary EEG language research. Progress was stymied, however, because the signs of healthy and disordered language function in the continuous scalp recorded EEG are not readily visible. The watershed occurred in 1951, when Dawson demonstrated that stimulus-evoked potentials too small to detect by unaided observation could be revealed by temporally aligning short EEG epochs relative to stimulus occurrence and summing or averaging across them at each time point so random epoch-to-epoch variation tends to cancel out and reveal the much smaller signal of interest (Fig. 40.1, Panel C, ulnar nerve evoked potential).

This simple method of averaging reveals systematic cortical responses to sensory stimulation in all the modalities. Among the striking subsequent discoveries was the auditory brain stem response (ABR). By aligning a few thousand epochs to a brief auditory click or tone burst, the afferent volley through the auditory nerve and brain stem is visible in potentials recorded at the top of the head as a series of peaks and troughs, fractions of one millionth of a volt in amplitude, lasting ~12 ms (Jewett et al., 1970). While attempting to replicate the ABR, Moushegian accidentally presented tones instead of clicks and discovered in the time-domain average, a small auditory evoked potential (AEP) that aligned with the frequency of the stimulus, a much smaller auditory analog of the flicker following response (frequency-following response, FFR, Moushegian et al., 1973).

Averaging also opened the door to the discovery of "cognitive" needles in the EEG haystack. While investigating the habituation of evoked potentials to repeated stimuli, Walter and colleagues observed a slowly increasing negative potential between a warning stimulus and a subsequent imperative stimulus to respond (Walter et al., 1964). This so-called *contingent negative variation (CNV)* did not depend on any specific physical stimulus property or the execution of a motor response, but rather on appreciation of an association between the eliciting stimuli. The CNV was linked to "expectancy" for the upcoming stimulus, a covert mental process (Cohen & Walter, 1966). Expectancy, a theoretical precursor of "prediction" (c.f., Bruner & Postman, 1949) inevitably brings along CNV during language processing whether or not this contribution to the electrical brain activity is of theoretical interest to psycholinguists. Kornhuber and Deecke (1965) reported slow cortical potentials leading up to a voluntary movement, the *Bereitschaftspotential* or *readiness potential* time-locked to the movement. The asymmetry of the latter half of this pre-movement activity serves as the basis of the derived lateralized readiness potential (LRP, Dejong et al., 1988; Gratton et al.,

1988; Smid et al., 1987; reviewed in Smulders & Miller, 2012)—an index of differential motor activation—used in studies of language production to avoid speech-related artifacts (Schmitt et al., 2000; van Turennout et al., 1997). Sutton et al. (1965) reported a large (8–10 μV) positive deflection around 300 ms (P300) regardless of stimulus modality to unpredictable stimuli in a guessing paradigm (explicit prediction). A similar potential was elicited in "oddball" paradigms where task-relevant stimuli or even omissions thereof ("deviants" or "oddballs") occurred infrequently and unpredictably among other stimuli ("standards"; Sutton et al., 1967). Like the mental acts that modulated the seminal reports of alpha oscillations, these systematic responses were not strictly stimulus-evoked but rather were defined in relation to the timing of an "event" in a sense broad enough to include both the occurrence and non-occurrence of stimulation. These are time-domain average event-related brain potentials—ERPs—as this term is generally used today. Numerous investigations of the stimulus, response, and task conditions modulating P300 parameters implicated multiple likely neural sources responding systematically, albeit differently, to different experimental manipulations; this led to a fractionation of "the P300" into P3b, P3a, and still further downstream late positivities comprising a late positive complex (LPC) and subsequent slow waves (SW). This research prompted vigorous debate about functional significances (Donchin & Coles, 1988; Polich & Kok, 1995; Sutton & Ruchkin, 1984); whatever process it reflects, some P3 activity invariably accompanies every decision. There is good reason to believe that the frontal and parietal P600s identified in language studies are members of the P3 family, sensitive to the same variables (e.g., subjective probability, attention, and so on; Coulson et al., 1998, but also see Frisch et al., 2003; Osterhout et al., 1996).

40.3 LANGUAGE

The possibilities for probing the function of the nervous system with auditory and visual modality stimuli are limitless. The auditory system responds measurably to simple clicks, tones, and noise bursts, as well as shorter and longer complex stimuli with time-varying power spectra, among them speech sounds, and the sequences of them comprising syllables, words, and connected speech. Similarly, the visual system responds to simple monochromatic flashes of varying luminance as well as more complex patterns (e.g., checkerboards, sine gratings, and the orthographic letters and sequences of them comprising individual words, phrases, sentences, and discourse). Investigation into what might be learned about and from electrical brain responses to complex visual and auditory stimuli that were, in addition, meaningful took off in the sixties (Regan, 1989, may be relied on for an insightful and thorough review of work during this period; see also Pratt, 2012). Cohen and Walter (1966) claim priority for ERP studies of meaning, using pictures. John et al. (1967) observed similar ERPs to similar geometric shapes regardless of size, and different ERPs to different shapes (squares, triangles) and different words ("*square*," "*triangle*") compared to flashes. Brown et al. (1973) observed different ERPs to ambiguous words preceded by a disambiguating context, "*sit by the fire*" vs. "*ready, aim, fire*" but not when context followed (e.g., "*fire is hot*" vs. "*fire the gun*"). Since the physical stimulus is the same, the difference in ERPs is plausibly attributable to the impact of the different upstream verbal contexts. Context effects on language processing from measures of, e.g., response speed, accuracy, detection threshold, were well-known (e.g., Miller et al., 1951; Tulving & Gold, 1963); those derived from ERP measures in the absence of overt behavior were not.

The Fourth International Congress on Event-related Slow Potentials of the Brain (EPIC IV) in 1976 was a poignant milestone, dedicated to Grey Walter in memoriam, as cognitive electrophysiologists began to tackle language in greater numbers. While psychologists elsewhere were pitching explanations of language processes in terms of implementation-independent representations and algorithms, the language panel sought to frame theories in terms of the nervous system transforming sensory stimulation at the periphery into internal representations that mediate behavior. And as psychophysiologists, their attention was not just on the brain, but the eyes, ears, somatic, and chemical senses, as well as circulatory, respiratory, and motor systems—an approach now more widely embraced under the aegis of cognitive neuroscience and embodied cognition. A growing body of ERPs had already been experimentally linked to neural activity implementing sensation, perception, attention, decision-making, memory, and movement. Language doesn't happen without them.

While the EPIC IV Language panelists were mulling the prospects for rapprochement between cognitive electrophysiology and linguistic theory, over in the Information Processing and Cognition panel, Kutas and Donchin reported a series of experiments showing that P300 latency tracks (accurate) categorization time even for categorization based on word meaning, not just physical features (Kutas & Donchin, 1978). Soon thereafter, a variant of the semantic P300 design manipulated whether the last word in a sentence was a good semantic fit in context (75%) or not (25%). It yielded unexpected results: a large, parietal negative deflection around 400 ms (N400) instead of a canonical P300, although both posterior and frontal positivities (P600) have since been observed at times in some participants in similar task conditions (Kos et al., 2012). Negative deflections evoked by surprising stimuli were known (e.g., N200 co-occurring with P300), though elicited under different conditions and with different timing and scalp distributions. Only when Kutas and Hillyard were reasonably confident—via a series of replications and extensions—that the large negativity was not an artifact, was observed in most people, and varied systematically under experimental manipulation were the findings submitted for publication and defended in review, eventually appearing as the seminal reports of the "language" N400 (Kutas & Hillyard, 1980a, 1980b, 1980c). Although the N400 is seen most clearly in the grand average ERPs to sentence final words (Fig. 40.2), this analysis and visual representation obscures both individual variation and whatever might be happening prior. So, these reports also included single subject ERPs as well as average potentials spanning the sentence; important information to have when drawing inferences about processing in light of what is or is not observed in a grand average.

40.4 ERPs and Language

Researchers investigating the language system in every modality and on every timescale have since expanded the experimental repertoire, adapting familiar electrophysiological paradigms to study language and familiar psychobehavioral paradigms for use with EEG/ERPs to provide continuous measures of electrical brain activity as visual and spoken words, sentences, and speech are comprehended and produced. In suitable designs, the near-continuous recording of scalp potentials can afford language researchers the opportunity to track sensory, motoric, and cognitive processes evolving on different time scales, from tens of milliseconds to seconds, with or without an explicit task that draws the participants' attention to particular stimulus properties and with or without an explicit response. The following is a sampler of ERP research that notes some canonical ERPs and illustrates a variety of language-related topics they have been used to investigate.

Auditory evoked potentials (AEPs). In adults, AEPs include transient and steady state potentials on different temporal scales (see, e.g., Burkard & Don, 2015; Picton, 2013). Transient AEPs evoked by a brief stimulus (e.g., tone pip or noise burst) are divided into fast (ABR, ~ 0—15 ms), middle ~20–60 ms (Na, Pa, Nb), and slow potentials ~60–300 + ms (P_1, N_1, P_2, N_2). The earliest AEPs likely generated by auditory cortex are P_1 and N_1, peaking ~ 60–80 ms. Steady state frequency-following AEPs elicited by sustained pitch stimuli include the cochlear microphonic (CM) generated by hair cells on the basilar membrane at frequencies in the audible range (~ 20 kHz) and FFRs up to about 2,000 Hz thought to be generated in the mid-brain (Eggermont, 2006).

ABR and FFR are responses to different types of stimuli and opinions diverge on whether their neural mechanisms are distinct or whether the FFR is overlapping ABR (see Bidelman, 2015, for a review). This debate is instructive. Even where the likely neural generators are relatively small and localized, the neuroanatomy is relatively well-understood, depth recordings have been made in humans, and there are animal models where experimentally lesioning pathways and structures to selectively spare or abolish surface potentials provide critical hypothesis tests, it *still* remains extremely difficult to definitively identify the mechanisms and location of neural generators of the surface-recorded potentials. This is a sobering lesson in the travails of identifying mechanisms and networks generating the scalp recorded potentials. However, language processing is fundamentally a temporally dynamic process that evolves on multiple scales (milliseconds to seconds plus) and the temporal resolution of EEG neuroimaging (and its magnetic and optical counterparts) provides numerous useful applications even without exact knowledge of the responsible neural generators.

Because they track auditory information as it arrives at cortex, AEPs make a useful proving ground for investigating the relative contributions of "bottom-up" stimulus information and "top down" influences on auditory perception generally (Starr & Golob, 2006), and speech perception, in particular. Language experience and contextual variables (e.g., immediate and distant past, the current allocation of attention), clearly impact speech perception, and ERPs can reveal if and when these "higher" factors influence neural activity. AEPs in particular, can indicate whether "higher" cortical systems (can) modulate processing in the mid-brain. Although the earliest reliable effects of attention in canonical selective attention paradigms are on the mid-latency P_{20-50}, Ikeda et al. (2008) report attentional modulation of ABRs (waves II–VI), when discriminating monaural tone pips with high intensity contralateral masking noise. The FFR has also been reported to be enhanced by attention (Galbraith et al., 1998; Lehmann & Schonwiesner, 2014), suggesting that attention, which impacts language comprehension at multiple levels, can have a "top-down" influence even on the earliest sensory processing of speech-relevant information.

Several lines of research investigate language using speech sounds to elicit transient AEPs and FFRs. Kraus and colleagues have used these potentials to implicate subcortical auditory

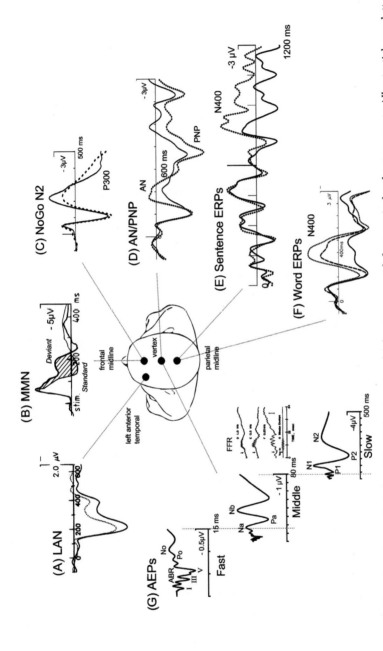

FIG. 40.2 A selection of transient evoked potentials widely encountered in language research from seminal and recent reports. All potentials are plotted negative up, except the FFR. (A) LAN: ERPs recorded at left anterior scalp elicited by the word "you" in subject position of a wh-interrogative ("Who have you ... ") are more relatively negative (dotted line) vs. a Yes-No interrogative ("Have you ... "). (B) MMN: Mismatch Negativity. More negative going ERPs evoked by rare 1,032 Hz tones (thick line) among standards (1,000 Hz) recorded while individuals were reading; the difference between them is the MMN, indicated by cross hatching. (C) No-go Nz: ERPs

at an anterior mid-line electrode by individual words, judged for graspability. Trials on which a response was correctly withheld elicit a more negative going N2 followed by a more positive going P300. (D) AN/PNP: The dotted line indicates a greater anterior negativity (AN) followed by a post-N400 positivity (PNP) elicited by syntactic violations relative to controls (solid line) at the vertex electrode. (E) Sentence ERPs: Event-knowledge violations elicit a large N400 (dotted line) relative to controls (solid line) in sentences describing agents and actions read word by word. Ticks indicate word onsets every 300 ms. (F) Word ERPs: Following the introduction of an event scenario, N400 elicited by expected words (solid line) is reduced relative to N400 elicited by unexpected words that are unrelated to the scenario (dotted line). Words comparably unexpected yet related to the scenario elicit an intermediate N400 (dashed line). (G) AEPs typical of click evoked stimuli recorded at the vertex electrode. FFR: Evoked potential responses at the indicated frequencies to sounds 70 dB above individual pure tone threshold, bottom trace is the stimulus artifact for the 500 c/sec sound. Calibration bar 0.5 uV, vertex positive up; 64 ms sweeps at intervals of 62.5 μsec.

Figure 40.2A) Adapted from Robert Kluender and Marta Kutas, Bridging the Gap: Evidence from ERPs on the Processing of Unbounded Dependencies, *Journal of Cognitive Neuroscience*, 5 (2), pp. 196–214, Figure 1, doi: 10.1162/jocn.1993.5.2.196 © 1993, Massachusetts Institute of Technology. Reprinted by permission of MIT Press Journals. Figure 40.2B) Adapted from *Electroencephalography and Clinical Neurophysiology*, 62 (6), M Sams, P Paavilainen, K Alho, and R Näätänen. Auditory frequency discrimination and event-related potentials, pp. 437–48. Figure 1, doi.org/10.1016/0168-5597(85)90054-1 © 1985, Elsevier Ireland Ltd. Figure 40.2C) Adapted from *NeuroImage*, 77 (1), Ben D. Amsel, Thomas P. Urbach, and Marta Kutas, Alive and grasping: Stable and rapid semantic access to an object category but not object graspability, pp. 1–13, doi.org/10.1016/j.neuroimage.2013.03.058, © 2013 Elsevier Inc., with permission from Elsevier. Figure 40.2E) Data from Klinton Bicknell, Jeffrey L. Elman, Mary Hare, Ken McRae, Marta Kutas, Effects of event knowledge in processing verbal arguments, *Journal of Memory and Language*, 63 (4), pp. 489–505, doi.org/10.1016/j.jml.2010.08.004, 2010. Figure 40.2F) Data from Ross Metusalem, Marta Kutas, Thomas P. Urbach, Mary Hare, Ken McRae, Jeffrey L. Elman, Generalized event knowledge activation during online sentence comprehension, *Journal of Memory and Language*, 66 (4), pp. 545–67, Figure 1, doi.org/10.1016/j.jml.2012.01.001, 2012. Figure 40.2Gi) Adapted from Terence Picton, Hearing in Time: Evoked Potential Studies of Temporal Processing, *Ear and Hearing*, 34 (4), pp. 385–401, Figure 1, doi: 10.1097/AUD.0b013e31827ada02 © 2013, Lippincott Williams. Figure 40.2Gii) Adapted from *Electroencephalography and Clinical Neurophysiology*, 35 (6), George Moushegian, Allen L Rupert, and Robert D Stillman, Scalp recorded early responses in man to frequencies in the speech range, pp. 665–7, Figure 1, doi.org/10.1016/0013-4694(73)90223-X © 1973, Elsevier Ireland Ltd., with permission.

pathways as a locus of plasticity associated with musical experience and auditory "brain training" regimens. Across many series of studies in children with learning disabilities, older adults, and in difficult listening conditions, they observed pre- vs. post-training changes in these potentials, consistent with, and in some cases correlated with, the degree of change in behavioral performance (Anderson et al., 2013; Kraus, 2012; but see also McFarland & Cacace, 2012). Of note, after brief auditory perceptual training, learning impaired children produced more robust cortical (N1/P2) responses in noise, with no changes in the ABR (Hayes et al., 2003).

Besides following the fundamental frequency of vowel sounds (~200 Hz for adult female, ~120 Hz adult male), FFRs also follow the slower energy amplitude envelope of the speech signal as the vocal tract opens and closes. These speech rhythms occur at ~3–40 Hz for phonemes and ~2–10 Hz for syllables, with frequencies in the range 4–16 Hz contributing most to the intelligibility of speech (Shannon et al., 1995; Picton, 2013). By correlating the speech envelope with scalp recorded potentials, Aiken and Picton (2008) were able to extract a speech envelope following response generated by auditory cortex. This EEG response has been reported to track the attended talker in competing speech streams (e.g., Horton et al., 2014; O'Sullivan et al., 2015; Power et al., 2012). Research on rhythmic brain-sound synchronization in auditory perception generally and speech perception in particular is accelerating, albeit not without controversy (e.g., Ng et al., 2012 vs. van Rullen & McLelland, 2013; and Giraud & Poeppel, 2012 vs. Obleser et al., 2012).

Mismatch negativity (MMN). The MMN is a stimulus-locked response to deviations in physical stimulus properties (e.g., frequency, intensity, duration) as well as in abstract rules (e.g., the higher the tone frequency, the lower its intensity sequence), which unlike for the P300 (P3b), need not be attended. MMN is canonically an auditory ERP, though there may be a visual analog (vMMN, e.g, Czigler, 2014). In a seminal application to language, Näätänen et al. (1997) found that deviant speech sounds in one's native language elicit larger MMNs and interpreted the effect as evidence for language-specific phonemic memory traces. Acoustic deviant MMN-like effects (phonological MMN) have also been observed around 200 ms in attended connected speech (e.g., Connolly et al., 1992). The MMN is well-suited and widely used to study the impact of acoustic signal properties on auditory and speech perception (e.g., Bartha-Doering et al., 2015; Guannan & Froud, 2015; Hisagi et al., 2015). Although speech sound MMNs may dissociate from other acoustic deviant MMNs in some respects, e.g., the length of the sequences required to establish complex contingencies (Bendixen et al., 2015), if the criterial properties of the MMN are observed, the presumptive interpretation is pre-attentive acoustic deviance detection. MMNs have been recruited to investigate topics as varied as hemispheric asymmetry for speech and non-speech sound processing (Asano et al., 2015), underspecification theories of phonemic representation (e.g., Hestvik & Durvasula, 2016), morphemic representation (Boudelaa et al., 2010), the interplay of emotion and speech perception (Pakarinen et al., 2014), automaticity of syntactic processing (Pulvermuler et al., 2008), and prediction in auditory processing (reviewed in Bendixen et al., 2012).

N400s. Negative going potentials recorded between scalp and a mastoid reference and measured relative to mean amplitude in a pre-stimulus interval of a few tens to hundreds of milliseconds may be observed between about 200 and 500 ms after any potentially meaningful item in any modality, such as written or spoken words, pseudowords, pictures, gestures, signs, acronyms, environmental sounds, even odors. These spatiotemporal patterns of scalp potentials—these N400s—vary with many factors and defy simple explanation, but in the context of reading and listening to words and sentences are generally linked to lexicosemantic activation in the comprehension network as well as contextual integration (Kutas & Federmeier, 2011). However, N400s are not language-specific or modality specific, they do not solely track semantic violation detection, nor are they a direct index of congruity, prediction, or plausibility.

N400s are not language-specific because they are also elicited by images and arithmetic problems. They are not modality specific because they are elicited by visual, auditory, and olfactory stimuli, although they are modality sensitive, exhibiting different durations, and scalp distributions. They do not track semantic violation detection, because they can be elicited when there is no semantic violation, and are not always elicited when there is a semantic violation. They are not a direct index of (in)congruity, because although a large N400 is elicited by a contextually incongruous word the first time a sentence is read, no N400 to that word is seen by the third time that sentence is read. They are not a direct index of prediction, though the amplitude often correlates with predictability; inferring prediction requires the appropriate design. They are not a direct index of plausibility, because, for instance, in the absence of quantifier-licensing discourse, N400 to *worms* in *Most farmers grow worms*... vs. *Few farmers grow worms* is driven by the typicality of what farmers grow not the plausibility of the quantified proposition, which does, however, drive N400 amplitude modulation when there is a quantifier-licensing discourse (Urbach et al., 2015; Urbach & Kutas, 2010; for a similar relation between N400s and plausibility involving negated propositions in and out of supporting discourse contexts, see Fischler et al., 1983; Holcomb & Kounios, 1990; Nieuwland & Kuperberg, 2008; Staab, 2007).

N400 amplitude is correlated with the probability of a word in context (Kutas & Hillyard, 1984), for example, *Most farmers grow* ___, as determined by relative frequency of response in normative fill-in-the-blank testing (c.f., "cloze" procedures, Taylor, 1953; Taylor, 1957). N400 amplitude also varies with the relation between the item and its context (e.g., a single word, a sound, a sentence, a discourse, or a scene). N400 amplitude also seems to be sensitive to the ease of accessing information from long-term memory, varying with recency, frequency of usage, repetition, and orthographic neighborhood size. N400s have been used for the past three decades to answer questions, for example, about the incrementality of language processing; nature and time course of lexicosentential-pragmatic interactions; prediction during routine language comprehension; the role of co-speech gesture; the role of perceptuo-lexical-semantic-event knowledge in comprehension; the role of quantifiers and negation (e.g., Kutas & Federmeier, 2011; Swaab et al., 2011).

P600s. An early striking discovery was not only that N400 was a default response but also that not all types of anomalous words in sentences elicited N400s. Words ungrammatical in context (e.g., phrase structure violations), elicited a late positivity peaking ~600 ms (Neville et al., 1991), as did words incompatible with the preferred/initial structural interpretation of locally ambiguous (i.e., "garden path") contexts (P600, Hagoort et al., 1993; Osterhout & Holcomb, 1992; for an extensive review of N400 and P600 literatures see Swaab et al., 2011). Although the sensitivity of N400s to manipulation of meaning-related expectancy and P600s to manipulation of grammatical structures may seem to accord with a theoretical distinction between semantics and syntax, there are numerous observations that thematically related semantic violations can also elicit late positivities, so-called semantic P600s (*For breakfast the boys/eggs would only eat toast*..., Kuperberg et al., 2003, see also Hoeks et al., 2004; Kim & Osterhout, 2005; Kolk et al., 2003; Kuperberg et al., 2006; van Herten et al., 2005; for review and synthesis see Brouwer et al., 2012). Positive deflections occurring after N400 (post-N400 positivity, PNP; LPC) vary between individuals (e.g., Kos et al., 2012) and between experiments (on average across individuals), and may be larger over posterior or anterior scalp, reviewed in van Petten and Luka (2012). PNPs and late positivities more generally in language are widely attested and recently have been used to address questions as diverse as, for example, the interplay between morphological complexity and syntax (Mehravari et al., 2015), lexical vs. discourse processes (Huang et al., 2014), code-switching (e.g., Ng et al., 2014), temporal-order sequences of events (Drummer et al., 2016), and structure in visual narrative (Cohn et al., 2014). Emotion and emotional valence also tend to enhance LPCs and an extensive literature investigates their impact on language processing (for reviews, see Citron, 2012; Kissler et al., 2006). Van Petten and Luka argue that posterior and anterior PNPs may reflect different functional processes. Late positivities have been widely interpreted in terms of prediction violation and/or revision processes (e.g., Brothers et al., 2015; Federmeier et al., 2007; Thornhill & van Petten, 2012; though for alternatives see, e.g., Davenport & Coulson, 2013; Droge et al., 2016; Kuperberg & Jaeger, 2016).

Anterior negativities: LAN, eLAN, nRef. In addition to N400s and P600s, several ERP studies of sentence processing observe negative deflections over anterior scalp, often larger over the left than right (LAN) when not bilateral. Anterior negativities (AN) starting around 300–400 ms have been observed for morphosyntactic agreement violations in reading (e.g., Kutas and Hillyard, 1983) often concomitant with P600 (e.g., Munte et al., 1993; see Molinaro et al., 2011 for an extensive review). LAN and P600 have also been investigated in connected speech with the negativity emerging earlier, ~180 ms, for phrase structure (eLAN) than for morphosyntactic violations (e.g., Friederici et al., 1993). However, grammatical violations are not necessary for eliciting ANs which have also been observed in well-formed sentences at a critical word where interpretation requires resolving a long-distance dependency. Examples include linking a verb back to one of its thematic arguments, for example *saw* and *bird* in "*The bird that the children saw chirped twice and flew away*" (c.f., Kluender and Kutas, 1993), and establishing anaphoric reference back to previously introduced discourse entities, for example, via a definite NP description (Anderson & Holcomb, 2005). Establishing reference back to existing discourse entities via anaphoric pronouns is also associated with a more sustained anterior negativity (nRef) emerging ~300–400 ms. Nor does language comprehension seem necessary for ANs which have also been observed to systematically increase with the number of items maintained in short-term memory during the retention interval of S1–S2 match-to-sample paradigms (e.g., Ruchkin et al., 1990); remember the CNV.

ANs have been observed under a variety of eliciting conditions with varying morphology (phasic, sustained) and timing (early onset ~100–200 ms, later onset 300–400 ms). They have been linked variously to more vs. less specific language comprehension processes, for example, stage of syntactic process (e.g., Friederici & Weissenborn, 2007; see also Steinhauer & Drury, 2012, for a critical review), sensitivity to linguistic features, for example, person, number, gender (Molinaro et al., 2011) or general, non-specific memory-related processes (e.g., Barkley et al., 2015; see also van Berkum et al., 2007). As of yet, there is no clear consensus on their functional significance(s).

40.4.1 Vignettes

By this point it should be clear that there are many different potentials linked to a variety of covert processes from sensation to cognition to motor responses that can serve in appropriate designs to answer clear questions about language acquisition, processing, learning, production, and loss. Since a comprehensive review is not possible here, instead we have elected to outline three quite different types of studies (of the many possible) to hint at the breadth of questions that might be put to the test.

40.4.1.1 Perceptually grounded vs. amodal knowledge representation.

ERPs have played an increasingly important role in adjudicating theories that make distinct, mutually-exclusive predictions. A case in point is the "grounded" or "embodied" versus amodal view of cognition; grounded views hold that sensory systems continue to play a functional role in object and event representations, whereas "amodal" views posit they do not, relying instead on symbolic semantic knowledge representations abstracted away from the specifics of the sensory, perceptual, and motor modalities that deliver them (Barsalou, 2008). Remarkably, it has proven difficult to experimentally distinguish these views since findings consistent with one may also be compatible with the other (see e.g., Chatterjee, 2010; Hauk & Tschentscher, 2013; Mahon & Caramazza, 2008). Amsel et al. (2014) propose that evidence against strongly amodal views would be to show that the relevant perceptual system (e.g., vision), is specifically recruited in accessing conceptual knowledge. They used the time course of the no-go N200 effect to clock the timing of access to color versus location information to that end.

When a speeded go response is contingent on a decision about a stimulus, N2 amplitude in the no-go condition is markedly larger over anterior scalp and the earliest latency at which the go and no-go ERPs reliably diverge can reasonably be taken as an upper bound on the latency of the decision; this follows whether the N200 (likely generated in anterior cingulate cortex) reflects response inhibition or conflict (Pritchard et al., 1991; Folstein & van Petten, 2008). Comparison of onset latencies of go/no-go N200 effects based on different types of information provides evidence about the relative timing of the decisions which, in turn, supports inferences about the relative timing of access to the information used to make the decision (Schmitt et al., 2000; van Turennout et al., 1997).

Amsel et al. compared the go/no-go effects to the second of a pair of written words (e.g., *lime*) based on the validity of color (*green, purple*) or location (*kitchen, pond*) information. These decisions were crossed with visual contrast (high vs. low) to modulate general visual processing because only on the embodied view should the visual system be engaged in representing and accessing knowledge of color in ways it is not for attributes that are not exclusively visual (e.g., location).

In line with the literature, low-visual contrast delayed the peak latency of the transient visual evoked P2 potential prominent over visual cortex within the first 200 ms following a visual stimulus onset for both location and color decisions by ~50 ms, consistent with both grounded and amodal views. The no-go N200 results—150 ms later for color than location decisions under low contrast—however, unequivocally showed that differential processing in the visual system which varies in high vs. low contrast modulated the time course of accessing specifically visual feature information (color) in semantic memory. Strict amodal views have no principled explanation for why differential activity in the visual sensory processing should impact visual vs. other knowledge access in the abstract amodal store.

40.4.1.2 Multisensory integration

ERP paradigms are likewise especially well-suited to analyze multisensory processing as in the McGurk effect and co-speech gesture integration, among others. Indeed, several labs have adapted a violation or lexical disambiguation paradigm to demonstrate via N400 modulations that paralinguistic gestures contribute to the semantic analysis of verbal language (e.g., Biau & Soto-Faraco, 2013; Cornejo et al., 2009; Wu & Coulson, 2010).

In a series of elegant studies Obermeier and Gunter delimited the time window of co-speech gesture integration via systematic manipulation of gesture-speech synchrony during sentence meaning construction (Obermeier & Gunter, 2015). Their participants watched videos of an actress uttering sentences like "*She was impressed by the BALL because of the GAME/DANCE*" accompanied by an iconic gesture that disambiguated the homonym to its dominant or subordinate meaning. These studies are noteworthy for surmounting methodological obstacles (reducing temporal variability during ERP averaging). Specifically, they used gating procedures to determine the identification point (IP) of the homonym as well as the earliest point at which the meaning of each gesture in each video clip could be consistently identified in the context of the corresponding homonym (the disambiguation point), but not otherwise. Truncated video clips also were tested to ensure they were *not* identifiable without the context word. The gesture-ambiguous word asynchrony was varied more precisely in this way with the disambiguation point of the gesture appearing at lags of -600 ms, -200 ms, 0 ms, and + 120 ms relative to the IP of the ambiguous word (homonym). There was a significant ERP difference to homonyms related to the subordinate vs. dominant gesture fragment between -200 to 120 ms (greater N400 to subordinate) and significant gesture disambiguation (N400 modulation) on the subordinate but not dominant target word at all lags, revealing multiple sites of gesture-speech integration.

40.4.1.3 Pinpointing whether, and if so when, commitments (e.g., scalar implicatures) are made

ERPs—all ERPs, language-related or not—are instantaneous reflections of ion flow across (mostly neocortical pyramidal cell) membranes leading to post-synaptic potentials; they have millisecond temporal resolution and thus offer exquisite measures of neural/mental timing. This is especially relevant to psycholinguists because many of their questions if not theoretical debates hinge on timing and/or time course. ERPs, for example, have been used to probe the time course of scalar implicatures in connected speech (with MMN) and written sentences (with N400). It is pragmatically odd though not untrue to continue *Some X are Y* with *In fact they all are*, indicating that an assertion of *Some X are Y* brings along an unstated, defeasible commitment to *And Some X are not Y*, i.e., a scalar implicature. The psycholinguistic question is whether comprehenders routinely incorporate such commitments into their real-time interpretations and if so, when. Nieuwland et al. (2010) tested this by recording ERPs to written sentences like, for example, *Some people have pets/lungs ...* , interpreting the smaller N400 to *pets* vs. *lungs* as evidence of incremental pragmatic interpretation. Extending this approach to spoken Chinese, *Some tigers/animals have tails*, Zhao et al. (2015) observed an MMN when *tails* occurs as a pragmatic deviant in the context of *tigers* vs. *animals*. In both studies, the ERP effects were restricted to a high pragmatic ability group, defined by an Autism Quotient subscore test. Increasingly, ERP studies of language are forced by the data to highlight individual differences.

40.4.1.4 Language proficiency

ERPs have shown sensitivity to factors such as fluency, working memory capacity, and language proficiency, among others. Pakulak and Neville (2010) for instance, analyzed ERPs to insertion phrase structure violations in spoken English sentences in adult monolinguals and found different patterns as a function of language proficiency (based on standardized language proficiency tests): ERPs to violations in high proficiency (compared to low proficiency) participants were characterized by a more temporally and spatially focal LAN and a larger and more widespread P600. Adult linguistic proficiency also was significantly correlated with self-reported childhood social economic status.

Despite the unstated assumption that monolingual native speakers of a language (L1) will exhibit the same ERP signatures of language processing, the actual data seem to reveal significant systematic variability not only quantitatively but also qualitatively. For example, the same linguistic violation has been shown to elicit an N400, a P600, or a biphasic N400–P600 in individual participants in L1 as well as within individual participants as they learn a second language (L2) (e.g., Tanner et al., 2014). As a consequence, Tanner and colleagues have argued that grand average ERPs may be even less representative than caution would allow, and that cross-subject variability as seen in L2 grammar processing should be treated as a "source of evidence rather than a source of noise" (Tanner et al., 2013, p. 368).

40.5 CONCLUSION

There are many more such examples we have no room to share. We do hope, however, that we have whetted the reader's appetite for the invaluable role of EEG/ERPs in language research. In our view, the prospects for advancing scientific understanding of the human language system with measurements of electrical brain activity in the hands of imaginative experimentalists seem bright. At the same time, the sensitivity of scalp potential measurements to real-time brain activity that makes them appealing for studying fleeting real-time language processes is a double-edged sword. These measures are just as sensitive to processes not specific to language and we also hope the glances back at earlier work make it clear why, for success in the psycholinguistic endeavor, imagination must be coupled with a broad understanding of electrophysiological research, methods, and analyses—past and present (e.g., Fig. 40.1, Panel D and see especially Keil et al., 2014). Though much has certainly changed since the early days in the cognitive electrophysiology of language, some things have not:

> "... all the problems of other areas of EP research must be considered, along with the linguistic ones. Distinguishing language effects per se from both lower-order effects, such as sensory, motor, and artifactual, and higher-order effects, such as general states and cognitive processes, is difficult. Thus, key issues often revolve around the question of the specificity of EP differences that might be related to language."
>
> —Robert Chapman, 1976. Chair, Language Section, Fourth International Congress on Event-related Slow Potentials of the Brain (EPIC IV)

Acknowledgment

This work was supported by NICHD Grant R01HD22614 to MK.

References

Adrian, E. D., & Matthews, B. H. C. (1934). The Berger rhythm potential changes from the occipital lobes in man. *Brain, 57*, 355–85.

Aiken, S. J., & Picton, T. W. (2008). Human cortical responses to the speech envelope. *Ear and Hearing, 29*, 139–57.

Amsel, B. D., Urbach, T. P., & Kutas, M. (2014). Empirically grounding grounded cognition: The case of color. *NeuroImage, 99*, 149–57.

Anderson, J. E., & Holcomb, P. J. (2005). An electrophysiological investigation of the effects of coreference on word repetition and synonymy. *Brain and Language, 94*, 200–16.

Anderson, S., White-Schwoch, T., Parbery-Clark, A., & Kraus, N. (2013). Reversal of age-related neural timing delays with training. *Proceedings of the National Academy of Sciences of the United States of America, 110*, 4357–62.

Asano, S., Shiga, T., Itagaki, S., & Yabe, H. (2015). Temporal integration of segmented-speech sounds probed with mismatch negativity. *NeuroReport, 26*, 1061–4.

Barkley, C., Kluender, R., & Kutas, M. (2015). Referential processing in the human brain: An event-related potential (ERP) study. *Brain Research, 1629*, 143–59.

Barsalou, L. W. (2008). Grounded cognition. *Annual Review of Psychology, 59*, 617–45.

Bartha-Doering, L., Deuster, D., Giordano, V., Zehnhoff-Dinnesen, A. A., & Dobel, C. (2015). A systematic review of the mismatch negativity as an index for auditory sensory memory: From basic research to clinical and developmental perspectives. *Psychophysiology, 52*, 1115–30.

Bendixen, A., Sanmiguel, I., & Schroger, E. (2012). Early electrophysiological indicators for predictive processing in audition: A review. *International Journal of Psychophysiology, 83*, 120–31.

Bendixen, A., Schwartze, M., & Kotz, S. A. (2015). Temporal dynamics of contingency extraction from tonal and verbal auditory sequences. *Brain and Language, 148*, 64–73.

Berger, H. (1930). Electroencephalogram of man. In: Gloor, P. (Ed.), *Hans Berger on the Electroencephalogram of Man: The Fourteen Original Reports on the Human Electroencephalogram* (1969). *Electroencephalography and Clinical Neurophysiology*, supplement 28. Elsevier, New York, NY.

Biau, E., & Soto-Faraco, S. (2013). Beat gestures modulate auditory integration in speech perception. *Brain and Language, 124*, 143–52.

Bidelman, G. M. (2015). Multichannel recordings of the human brainstem frequency-following response: Scalp topography, source generators, and distinctions from the transient ABR. *Hearing Research, 323,* 68–80.

Boudelaa, S., Pulvermuller, F., Hauk, O., Shtyrov, Y., & Marslen-Wilson, W. (2010). Arabic morphology in the neural language system. *Journal of Cognitive Neuroscience, 22,* 998–1010.

Brothers, T., Swaab, T. Y., & Traxler, M. J. (2015). Effects of prediction and contextual support on lexical processing: Prediction takes precedence. *Cognition, 136,* 135–49.

Brouwer, H., Fitz, H., & Hoeks, J. C. J. (2012). Getting real about Semantic Illusions: Rethinking the functional role of the P600 in language comprehension. *Brain Research, 1446,* 127–43.

Brown, W. S., Marsh, J. T., & Smith, J. C. (1973). Contextual meaning effects on speech-evoked potentials. *Behavioral Biology, 9,* 755–61.

Bruner, J. S., & Postman, L. (1949). On the perception of incongruity: A paradigm. *Journal of Personality, 18,* 206–23.

Burkard, R., & Don, M. (2015). Introduction to auditory evoked potentials. In: Katz, J., Chasin, M., English, K., Hood, L., & Tillery, K., L. (Eds.) *Handboodk of Clinical Audiology.* Wolters Kluwer, Philadelphia, PA.

Chapman, R. M. (1976). Langauge and evoked potentials: A summary of issues. In: Otto, D. A. (Ed.), *Multidisciplinary Perspectives in Event-Related Brain Potential Research: Proceedings of the Fourth International Congress on Event-related Slow Potentials of the Brain (EPIC IV).* U.S. Environmental Protection Agency, Hendersonville, NC.

Chatterjee, A. (2010). Disembodying cognition. *Language and Cognition, 2,* 79–116.

Citron, F. M. M. (2012). Neural correlates of written emotion word processing: A review of recent electrophysiological and hemodynamic neuroimaging studies. *Brain and Language, 122,* 211–26.

Cohen, J., & Walter, W. G. (1966). The interaction of responses in the brain to semantic stimuli. *Psychophysiology, 2,* 187–96.

Cohn, N., Jackendoff, R., Holcomb, P. J., & Kuperberg, G. R. (2014). The grammar of visual narrative: Neural evidence for constituent structure in sequential image comprehension. *Neuropsychologia, 64,* 63–70.

Connolly, J. F., Phillips, N. A., Stewart, S. H., & Brake, W. G. (1992). Event-related potential sensitivity to acoustic and semantic properties of terminal words in sentences. *Brain and Language, 43,* 1–18.

Cornejo, C., Simonetti, F., Ibanez, A., Aldunate, N., Ceric, F., Lopez, V., & Nunez, R. E. (2009). Gesture and metaphor comprehension: Electrophysiological evidence of cross-modal coordination by audiovisual stimulation. *Brain and Cognition, 70,* 42–52.

Coulson, S., King, J. W., & Kutas, M. (1998). ERPs and domain specificity: Beating a straw horse. *Language and Cognitive Processes, 13,* 653–72.

Czigler, I. (2014). Visual mismatch negativity and categorization. *Brain Topography, 27,* 590–8.

Davenport, T., & Coulson, S. (2013). Hemispheric asymmetry in interpreting novel literal language: An event-related potential study. *Neuropsychologia, 51,* 907–21.

Dawson, G. D. (1954). A summation technique for the detection of small evoked potentials. *Electroencephalography and Clinical Neurophysiology, 6,* 65–84.

Dejong, R., Wierda, M., Mulder, G., & Mulder, L. J. M. (1988). Use of partial stimulus information in response processing. *Journal of Experimental Psychology: Human Perception and Performance, 14,* 682–92.

Delorme, A., Mullen, T., Kothe, C., Acar, Z. A., Bigdely-Shamlo, N., Vankov, A., & Makeig, S. (2011). EEGLAB, SIFT, NFT, BCILAB, and ERICA: New Tools for Advanced EEG Processing. *Computational Intelligence and Neuroscience, 2011,* 130714.

Dimitrijevic, A., & Cone, B. (2015). Auditory steady-state response. In: Katz, J., Chasin, M., English, K., Hood, L. J., & Tillery, K., L. (Eds.), *Handbook of Clinical Audiology* (pp. 11–35). Lippincott Williams & Wilkins, Philadelphia, PA.

Donchin, E., & Coles, M. G. H. (1988). Is the P300 component a manifestation of context updating? *Behavioral and Brain Sciences*, 11, 357–74.

Droge, A., Fleischer, J., Schlesewsky, M., & Bornkessel-Schlesewsky, I. (2016). Neural mechanisms of sentence comprehension based on predictive processes and decision certainty: Electrophysiological evidence from non-canonical linearizations in a flexible word order language. *Brain Research*, 1633, 149–66.

Drummer, J., Van Der Meer, E., & Schaadt, G. (2016). Event-related potentials in response to violations of content and temporal event knowledge. *Neuropsychologia*, 80, 47–55.

Eggermont, J. J. (2006). Electric and magnetic fields of synchronous neural activity: Peripheral and central origins of auditory-evoked potentials. In: Burkard, R. F., Don, M., & Eggermont, J. J. (Eds.), *Auditory Evoked Potentials: Basic Principles and Clinical Applications* (pp. 482–507). Lippincott Williams & Wilkins, Philadelphia, PA.

Federmeier, K. D., Wlotko, E. W., De Ochoa-Dewald, E., & Kutas, M. (2007). Multiple effects of sentential constraint on word processing. *Brain Research*, 1146, 75–84.

Fischler, I., Bloom, P. A., Childers, D. G., Roucos, S. E., & Perry, N. W. (1983). Brain potentials related to stages of sentence verification. *Psychophysiology*, 20, 400–9.

Folstein, J. R., & Van Petten, C. (2008). Influence of cognitive control and mismatch on the N2 component of the ERP: A review. *Psychophysiology*, 45, 152–70.

Friederici, A. D., Pfeifer, E., & Hahne, A. (1993). Event-related brain potentials during natural speech processing—effects of semantic, morphological and syntactic violations. *Cognitive Brain Research*, 1, 183–92.

Friederici, A. D., & Weissenborn, J. (2007). Mapping sentence form onto meaning: The syntax-semantic interface. *Brain Research*, 1146, 50–8.

Frisch, S., Kotz, S. A., Von Cramon, D. Y., & Friederici, A. D. (2003). Why the P600 is not just a P300: The role of the basal ganglia. *Clinical Neurophysiology*, 114, 336–40.

Galbraith, G. C., Bhuta, S. M., Choate, A. K., Kitahara, J. M., & Mullen, T. A. (1998). Brain stem frequency-following response to dichotic vowels during attention. *NeuroReport*, 9, 1889–93.

Gibbs, F. A., Davis, H., & Lennox, W. G. (1935). The electro-encephalogram in epilepsy and in conditions of impaired consciousness. *Archives of Neurology and Psychiatry*, 34, 1133–48.

Giraud, A. L., & Poeppel, D. (2012). Cortical oscillations and speech processing: emerging computational principles and operations. *Nature Neuroscience*, 15, 511–17.

Gramfort, A., Luessi, M., Larson, E., Engemann, D. A., Strohmeier, D., Brodbeck, C., … & Hamalainen, M. S. (2014). MNE software for processing MEG and EEG data. *NeuroImage*, 86, 446–60.

Gratton, G., Coles, M. G. H., Sirevaag, E. J., Eriksen, C. W., & Donchin, E. (1988). Prestimulus and poststimulus activation of response channels—a psychophysiological analysis. *Journal of Experimental Psychology: Human Perception and Performance*, 14, 331–44.

Groppe, D. M., Urbach, T. P., & Kutas, M. (2011a). Mass univariate analysis of event-related brain potentials/fields I: A critical tutorial review. *Psychophysiology*, 48, 1711–25.

Groppe, D. M., Urbach, T. P., & Kutas, M. (2011b). Mass univariate analysis of event-related brain potentials/fields II: Simulation studies. *Psychophysiology*, 48, 1726–37.

Gross, J. (2014). Analytical methods and experimental approaches for electrophysiological studies of brain oscillations. *Journal of Neuroscience Methods*, 228, 57–66.

Guannan, S., & Froud, K. (2015). Neurophysiological correlates of perceptual learning of Mandarin Chinese lexical tone categories: An event-related potential study. *Journal of the Acoustical Society of America, 137*, 2384.

Hagoort, P., Brown, C., & Groothusen, J. (1993). The syntactic positive shift (SPS) as an ERP measure of syntactic processing. *Language and Cognitive Processes, 8*, 439–83.

Halgren, E., Kaestner, E., Marinkovic, K., Cash, S. S., Wang, C., Schomer, D. L., Madsen, J. R., & Ulbert, I. (2015). Laminar profile of spontaneous and evoked theta: Rhythmic modulation of cortical processing during word integration. *Neuropsychologia, 76*, 108–24.

Hauk, O., & Tschentscher, N. (2013). The body of evidence: What can neuroscience tell us about embodied semantics? *Frontiers in Psychology, 4*, 50.

Hayes, E. A., Warrier, C. M., Nicol, T. G., Zecker, S. G., & Kraus, N. (2003). Neural plasticity following auditory training in children with learning problems. *Clinical Neurophysiology, 114*, 673–84.

Herrmann, C. S., Rach, S., Vosskuhl, J., & Struber, D. (2014). Time-frequency analysis of event-related potentials: A brief tutorial. *Brain Topography, 27*, 438–50.

Hestvik, A., & Durvasula, K. (2016). Neurobiological evidence for voicing underspecification in English. *Brain and Language, 152*, 28–43.

Hisagi, M., Shafer, V. L., Strange, W., & Sussman, E. S. (2015). Neural measures of a Japanese consonant length discrimination by Japanese and American English listeners: Effects of attention. *Brain Research, 1626*, 218–31.

Hoeks, J. C. J., & Brouwer, H. (2014). Electrophysiological research on conversation and discourse. In: Holtgraves, T. M. (Ed.), *The Oxford Handbook of Language and Social Psychology*, (pp. 365–86). Oxford University Press, New York, NY.

Hoeks, J. C. J., Stowe, L. A., & Doedens, G. (2004). Seeing words in context: the interaction of lexical and sentence level information during reading. *Cognitive Brain Research, 19*, 59–73.

Holcomb, P. J., & Kounios, J. (1990). The electrophysiology of semantic memory. *Bulletin of the Psychonomic Society, 28*, 502.

Horton, C., Srinivasan, R., & D'zmura, M. (2014). Envelope responses in single-trial EEG indicate attended speaker in a "cocktail party." *Journal of Neural Engineering, 11*, 4.

Huang, Y. T., Hopfinger, J., & Gordon, P. C. (2014). Distinguishing lexical- versus discourse-level processing using event-related potentials. *Memory & Cognition, 42*, 275–91.

Ikeda, K., Sekiguchi, T., & Hayashi, A. (2008). Attention-related modulation of auditory brainstem responses during contralateral noise exposure. *NeuroReport, 19*, 1593–9.

Jewett, D. L., Romano, M. N., & Williston, J. S. (1970). Human auditory evoked potentials—possible brain stem components detected on scalp. *Science, 167*, 1517–8.

John, E. R., Herrington, J. D., & Sutton, S. (1967). Effects of visual form on evoked response. *Science, 155*, 1439–442.

Keil, A., Debener, S., Gratton, G., Junghofer, M., Kappenman, E. S., Luck, S. J., ... & Yee, C. M. (2014). Committee report: Publication guidelines and recommendations for studies using electroencephalography and magnetoencephalography. *Psychophysiology, 51*, 1–21.

Kim, A., & Osterhout, L. (2005). The independence of combinatory semantic processing: Evidence from event-related potentials. *Journal of Memory and Language, 52*, 205–25.

Kissler, J., Assadollahi, R., & Herbert, C. (2006). Emotional and semantic networks in visual word processing: Insights from ERP studies. In: Anders, S., Ende, G., Junghoffer, M., Kissler, J., & Wildgruber, D. (Eds.), *Understanding Emotions* (pp. 31–51). Elsevier Science, Amsterdam.

Kluender, R., & Kutas, M. (1993). Bridging the gap—evidence from ERPs on the processing of unbounded dependencies. *Journal of Cognitive Neuroscience, 5*, 196–214.

Knott, J. R. (1938). Brain potentials during silent and oral reading. *Journal of General Psychology*, 18, 57–62.

Kolk, H. H. J., Chwilla, D. J., van Herten, M., & Oor, P. J. W. (2003). Structure and limited capacity in verbal working memory: A study with event-related potentials. *Brain and Language*, 85, 1–36.

Kornhuber, H. H., & Deecke, L. (1965). Hirnpotentialanderungen bei willkurbewegungen und passiven bewegungen des menschen—bereitschaftspotential und reafferente potentiale. *Pflugers Archiv Fur Die Gesamte Physiologie Des Menschen Und Der Tiere*, 284, 1–17.

Kos, M., Van Den Brink, D., & Hagoort, P. (2012). Individual variation in the late positive complex to semantic anomalies. *Frontiers in Psychology*, 3, 1–10.

Kraus, N. (2012). Biological impact of music and software-based auditory training. *Journal of Communication Disorders*, 45, 403–10.

Kuperberg, G. R. (2013). The proactive comprehender: What event-related potentials tell us about the dynamics of reading comprehension. In: Miller, B., Cutting, L., & McCardle, P. (Eds.), *Unraveling the Behavioral, Neurobiological, and Genetic Components of Reading Comprehension* (pp. 176–92). Paul Brookes Publishing, Baltimore, MD.

Kuperberg, G. R., Caplan, D., Sitnikova, T., Eddy, M., & Holcomb, P. J. (2006). Neural correlates of processing syntactic, semantic, and thematic relationships in sentences. *Language and Cognitive Processes*, 21, 489–530.

Kuperberg, G. R., & Jaeger, T. F. (2016). What do we mean by prediction in language comprehension? *Language Cognition and Neuroscience*, 31, 32–59.

Kuperberg, G. R., Sitnikova, T., Caplan, D., & Holcomb, P. J. (2003). Electrophysiological distinctions in processing conceptual relationships within simple sentences. *Cognitive Brain Research*, 17, 117–29.

Kutas, M., & Donchin, E. (1978). Variations in the latency of P300 as a function of variations in semantic categorization. In: Otto, D. A. (Ed.), *Multidisciplinary Perspectives in Event-Related Brain Potential Research: Proceedings of the Fourth International Congress on Event-Related Slow Potentials of the Brain (EPIC IV)*. U.S. Enviromental Protection Agency. Hendersonville, North Carolina, April 4–10.

Kutas, M., & Federmeier, K. D. (2011). Thirty years and counting: finding meaning in the N400 component of the event-related brain potential (ERP). *Annual Review of Psychology*, 62, 621–47.

Kutas, M., & Hillyard, S. A. (1980a). Event-related brain potentials to semantically inappropriate and surprisingly large words. *Biological Psychology*, 11, 99–116.

Kutas, M., & Hillyard, S. A. (1980b). Reading between the lines—event-related brain potentials during natural sentence processing. *Brain and Language*, 11, 354–73.

Kutas, M., & Hillyard, S. A. (1980c). Reading sensless sentences: Brain potentials reflect semantic incongruity. *Science*, 207, 203–5.

Kutas, M., & Hillyard, S. A. (1983). Event-related brain potentials to grammatical errors and semantic anomalies. *Memory & Cognition*, 11, 539–50.

Kutas, M., & Hillyard, S. A. (1984). Brain potentials during reading reflect word expectancy and semantic association. *Nature*, 307, 161–3.

Lehmann, A., & Schonwiesner, M. (2014). Selective attention modulates human auditory brainstem responses: Relative contributions of frequency and spatial cues. *PLoS One*, 9(1), e85442.

Luck, S. J., & Kappenman, E. S. (Eds.) (2012). *The Oxford Handbook of Event-Related Potential Components*. Oxford University Press, New York, NY.

Mahon, B. Z., & Caramazza, A. (2008). A critical look at the embodied cognition hypothesis and a new proposal for grounding conceptual content. *Journal of Physiology-Paris, 102*, 59–70.

Martin, B. A., Tremblay, K. L., & Korczak, P. (2008). Speech evoked potentials: From the laboratory to the clinic. *Ear and Hearing, 29*, 285–313.

Martin, S., Millán, J. D. R., Knight, R. T., & Pasley, B. N. (2016). The use of intracranial recordings to decode human language: Challenges and opportunities. *Brain and Language*. Available at: http://europepmc.org/abstract/med/27377299

McFarland, D. J., & Cacace, A. T. (2012). Questionable reliability of the speech-evoked auditory brainstem response (sABR) in typically-developing children. *Hearing Research, 287*, 1–2.

Mehravari, A. S., Tanner, D., Wampler, E. K., Valentine, G. D., & Osterhout, L. (2015). Effects of grammaticality and morphological complexity on the p600 event-related potential component. *PloS One, 10*(1), e0140850.

Miller, G. A., Heise, G. A., & Lichten, W. (1951). The intelligibility of speech as a function of the context of the test materials. *Journal of Experimental Psychology, 41*, 329–35.

Molinaro, N., Barber, H. A., & Carreiras, M. (2011). Grammatical agreement processing in reading: ERP findings and future directions. *Cortex, 47*, 908–30.

Moushegian, G., Rupert, A. L., & Stillman, R. D. (1973). Scalp-recorded early responses in man to frequencies in speech range. *Electroencephalography and Clinical Neurophysiology, 35*, 665–7.

Munte, T. F., Heinze, H. J., & Mangun, G. R. (1993). Dissociation of brain activity related to syntactic and semantic aspects of language. *Journal of Cognitive Neuroscience, 5*, 335–44.

Musiek, F., Gonzalez, J. E., & Baran, J. A. (2015). Auditory brainstem response: Differential diagnosis. In: Katz, J., Chasin, M., English, K., Hood, L. J., & Tillery, K., L. (Eds.), *Handbook of Clinical Audiology* (pp. 231–48). Lippincott Williams & Wilkins, Philadelphia, PA.

Näätänen, R., Lehtokoski, A., Lennes, M., Cheour, M., Huotilainen, M., Iivonen, A., ... & Alho, K. (1997). Language-specific phoneme representations revealed by electric and magnetic brain responses. *Nature, 385*, 432–4.

Neville, H., Nicol, J. L., Barss, A., Forster, K. I., & Garrett, M. F. (1991). Syntactically based sentence processing classes—evidence from event-related brain potentials. *Journal of Cognitive Neuroscience, 3*, 151–65.

Ng, B. S. W., Schroeder, T., & Kayser, C. (2012). A precluding but not ensuring role of entrained low-frequency oscillations for auditory perception. *Journal of Neuroscience, 32*, 12268–76.

Ng, S., Gonzalez, C., & Wicha, N. Y. Y. (2014). The fox and the cabra: An ERP analysis of reading code switched nouns and verbs in bilingual short stories. *Brain Research, 1557*, 127–40.

Nieuwland, M. S., Ditman, T., & Kuperberg, G. R. (2010). On the incrementality of pragmatic processing: An ERP investigation of informativeness and pragmatic abilities. *Journal of Memory and Language, 63*, 324–46.

Nieuwland, M. S., & Kuperberg, G. R. (2008). When the truth is not too hard to handle: An event-related potential study on the pragmatics of negation. *Psychological Science, 19*, 1213–18.

O'Sullivan, J. A., Power, A. J., Mesgarani, N., Rajaram, S., Foxe, J. J., Shinn-Cunningham, B. G., ... & Lalor, E. C. (2015). Attentional selection in a cocktail party environment can be decoded from single-trial EEG. *Cerebral Cortex, 25*, 1697–706.

Obermeier, C., & Gunter, T. C. (2015). Multisensory integration: The case of a time window of gesture-speech integration. *Journal of Cognitive Neuroscience, 27*, 292–307.

Obleser, J., Herrmann, B., & Henry, M. J. (2012). Neural oscillations in speech: don't be enslaved by the envelope. *Frontiers in Human Neuroscience, 6*, 4.

Oostenveld, R., Fries, P., Maris, E., & Schoffelen, J. M. (2011). FieldTrip: Open source software for advanced analysis of MEG, EEG, and invasive electrophysiological data. *Computational Intelligence and Neuroscience, 2011*, 156869.

Osterhout, L., & Holcomb, P. J. (1992). Event-related brain potentials elicited by syntactic anomaly. *Journal of Memory and Language, 31*, 785–806.

Osterhout, L., Mckinnon, M. C., Bersick, M., & Corey, V. (1996). On the language specificity of the brain response to syntactic anomalies: Is the syntactic positive shift a member of the p300 family? *Journal of Cognitive Neuroscience, 8*, 507–26.

Pakarinen, S., Sokka, L., Leinikka, M., Henelius, A., Korpela, J., & Huotilainen, M. (2014). Fast determination of MMN and P3a responses to linguistically and emotionally relevant changes in pseudoword stimuli. *Neuroscience Letters, 577*, 28–33.

Pakulak, E., & Neville, H. J. (2010). Proficiency differences in syntactic processing of monolingual native speakers indexed by event-related potentials. *Journal of Cognitive Neuroscience, 22*, 2728–44.

Picton, T. (2013). Hearing in time: Evoked potential studies of temporal processing. *Ear and Hearing, 34*, 385–401.

Polich, J., & Kok, A. (1995). Cognitive and biological determinants of p300—an integrative review. *Biological Psychology, 41*, 103–46.

Power, A. J., Foxe, J. J., Forde, E. J., Reilly, R. B., & Lalor, E. C. (2012). At what time is the cocktail party? A late locus of selective attention to natural speech. *European Journal of Neuroscience, 35*, 1497–503.

Pratt, H. (2012). Sensory ERP components. In: Luck, S. J., & Kappenman, E. (Eds.), *The Oxford Handbook of Event-related Potential Components* (pp. 89–114). Oxford University Press, New York, NY.

Pritchard, W. S., Shappell, S. A., & Brandt, M. E. (1991). Psychophysiology of N200/N400: A review and classification scheme. *Advances in Psychophysiology, 4*, 43–106.

Pulvermuler, F., Shtyrov, Y., Hasting, A. S., & Carlyon, R. P. (2008). Syntax as a reflex: Neurophysiological evidence for early automaticity of grammatical processing. *Brain and Language, 104*, 244–53.

Regan, D. (1989). *Human Brain Electrophysiology: Evoked Potentials and Evoked Magnetic Fields in Science and Medicine*. Elsevier, New York, NY.

Ruchkin, D. S., Johnson, R., Canoune, H., & Ritter, W. (1990). Short-term-memory storage and retention—an event-related brain potential study. *Electroencephalography and Clinical Neurophysiology, 76*, 419–39.

Schmitt, B. M., Munte, T. F., & Kutas, M. (2000). Electrophysiological estimates of the time course of semantic and phonological encoding during implicit picture naming. *Psychophysiology, 37*, 473–84.

Shannon, R. V., Zeng, F. G., Kamath, V., Wygonski, J., & Ekelid, M. (1995). Speech recognition with primarily temporal cues. *Science, 270*, 303–4.

Smid, H., Mulder, G., & Mulder, L. (1987). The continuous flow model revisited: perceptual and central motor aspects. *Electroencephalography and Clinical Neurophysiology. Supplement, 40*, 270.

Smith, N. J., & Kutas, M. (2015a). Regression-based estimation of ERP waveforms: I. The rERP framework. *Psychophysiology, 52*(2), 157–68.

Smith, N. J., & Kutas, M. (2015b). Regression-based estimation of ERP waveforms: II. Nonlinear effects, overlap correction, and practical considerations. *Psychophysiology, 52*(2), 169–81.

Smulders, F. T., & Miller, J. O. (2012). The lateralized readiness potential. In: Kappenman, E., & Luck, S. J. (Eds.), *The Oxford Handbook of Event-Related Potential Components* (pp. 209–29). Oxford University Press, Oxford.

Staab, J. (2007). *Negation in Context: Electrophysiological and Behavioral Investigations of Negation Effects in Discourse Processing* [Ph.D. disertation]. University of California, San Diego, CA.

Starr, A., & Golob, E. J. (2006). Cognitive factors modulating auditory cortical potentials. In: Burkard, R. F., Don, M., & Eggermont, J. J. (Eds.), *Auditory Evoked Potentials: Basic Principles and Clinical Applications* (p. 510). Lippincott Williams & Wilkins, Philadelphia, PA.

Steinhauer, K., & Connolly, J. F. (2008). Event-related potentials in the study of language. In: Stemmer, B., & Whitaker, H. (Eds.), *Handbook of the Cognitive Neuroscience of Language* (pp. 91–104). Elsevier, New York, NY.

Steinhauer, K., & Drury, J. E. (2012). On the early left-anterior negativity (ELAN) in syntax studies. *Brain and Language*, 120, 135–62.

Sutton, S., Braren, M., Zubin, J., & John, E. R. (1965). Evoked-potential correlates of stimulus uncertainty. *Science*, 150, 1187–8.

Sutton, S., & Ruchkin, D. S. (1984). The late positive complex—advances and new problems. *Annals of the New York Academy of Sciences*, 425, 1–23.

Sutton, S., Tueting, P., Zubin, J., & John, E. R. (1967). Information delivery and sensory evoked potential. *Science*, 155, 1436–9.

Swaab, T. Y., Ledoux, K., Camblin, C. C., & Boudewyn, M. A. (2011). Language-related ERP components. In: Luck, S. J., & Kappenman, E. S. (Eds.), *The Oxford Handbook of Event-Related Potential Components* (pp. 397–440). Oxford University Press, New York, NY.

Tadel, F., Baillet, S., Mosher, J. C., Pantazis, D., & Leahy, R. M. (2011). Brainstorm: A user-friendly application for MEG/EEG analysis. *Computational Intelligence and Neuroscience*, 2011, 13.

Tanner, D., Inoue, K., & Osterhout, L. (2014). Brain-based individual differences in online L2 grammatical comprehension. *Bilingualism-Language and Cognition*, 17, 277–93.

Tanner, D., Mclaughlin, J., Herschensohn, J., & Osterhout, L. (2013). Individual differences reveal stages of L2 grammatical acquisition: ERP evidence. *Bilingualism-Language and Cognition*, 16, 367–82.

Taylor, W. L. (1953). "Cloze Procedure": A new tool for measuring readability. *Journalism Quarterly*, 30, 415–33.

Taylor, W. L. (1957). Cloze readability scores as indexes of individual differences in comprehension and aptitude. *Journal of Applied Psychology*, 41, 19–26.

Thornhill, D. E., & van Petten, C. (2012). Lexical versus conceptual anticipation during sentence processing: Frontal positivity and N400 ERP components. *International Journal of Psychophysiology*, 83, 382–92.

Travis, L. E., & Knott, J. R. (1936). Brain potentials from normal speakers and stutterers. *Journal of Psychology*, 2, 137–50.

Tulving, E., & Gold, C. (1963). Stimulus information and contextual information as determinants of tachistoscopic recognition of words. *Journal of Experimental Psychology*, 66, 319–27.

Urbach, T. P., Delong, K. A., & Kutas, M. (2015). Quantifiers are incrementally interpreted in context, more than less. *Journal of Memory and Language*, 83, 79–96.

Urbach, T. P., & Kutas, M. (2010). Quantifiers more or less quantify online: ERP evidence for partial incremental interpretation. *Journal of Memory and Language*, 63, 158–79.

van Berkum, J. J. A., Koornneef, A. W., Otten, M., & Neuwland, M. S. (2007). Establishing reference in language comprehension: An electrophysiological perspective. *Brain Research, 1146*, 158–71.

van Herten, M., Kolk, H. H. J., & Chwilla, D. J. (2005). An ERP study of P600 effects elicited by semantic anomalies. *Cognitive Brain Research, 22*, 241–55.

van Petten, C., & Luka, B. J. (2012). Prediction during language comprehension: Benefits, costs, and ERP components. *International Journal of Psychophysiology, 83*, 176–90.

van Rullen, R., & McLelland, D. (2013). What goes up must come down: EEG phase modulates auditory perception in both directions. *Frontiers in Psychology, 4*, 3.

van Turennout, M., Hagoort, P., & Brown, C. M. (1997). Electrophysiological evidence on the time course of semantic and phonological processes in speech production. *Journal of Experimental Psychology: Learning, Memory, and Cognition, 23*, 787–806.

Wacker, M., & Witte, H. (2013). Time-frequency techniques in biomedical signal analysis: A tutorial review of similarities and differences. *Methods of Information in Medicine, 52*, 279–96.

Walter, V. J., & Walter, W. G. (1949). The central effects of rhythmic sensory stimulation. *Electroencephalography and Clinical Neurophysiology, 1*, 57–86.

Walter, W. G., & Shipton, H. W. (1951). A new toposcopic display system. *Electroencephalography and Clinical Neurophysiology, 3*, 281–92.

Walter, W. G., Winter, A. L., Cooper, R., Mccallum, W. C., & Aldridge, V. J. (1964). Contingent negative variation—electric sign of sensorimotor association and expectancy in human brain. *Nature, 203*, 380–4.

Wöstmann, M., Fiedler, L., & Obleser, J. (2017). Tracking the signal, cracking the code: Speech and speech comprehension in non-invasive human electrophysiology. *Language, Cognition and Neuroscience, 32*, 855–69.

Wu, Y. C., & Coulson, S. (2010). Gestures modulate speech processing early in utterances. *NeuroReport, 21*, 522–6.

Zhao, M., Liu, T., Chen, G., & Chen, F. Y. (2015). Are scalar implicatures automatically processed and different for each individual? A mismatch negativity (MMN) study. *Brain Research, 1599*, 137–49.

CHAPTER 41

SOURCE ESTIMATION, CONNECTIVITY, AND PATTERN ANALYSIS OF EEG/MEG DATA IN PSYCHOLINGUISTICS

OLAF HAUK

41.1 Introduction

THE unique advantage of electro and magnetoencephalography (EEG and MEG) over other non-invasive neuroimaging methods is their temporal resolution in the millisecond range, well-suited to monitor rapid perceptual, cognitive, and language processes in real time. The high temporal resolution offers the possibility to study brain responses in different frequency ranges that have previously been associated with different cognitive functions or states. It also allows characterizing brain connectivity on the basis of temporal activation sequences and frequency characteristics. EEG and MEG provide information in up to five dimensions (three in space, plus time and frequency), making them attractive for machine learning applications. Unfortunately, the interpretation of EEG and MEG results is complicated by their limited spatial resolution. Source estimation methods can provide estimates of cortical activity, which make use of different modeling assumptions that need to be justified by the experimenter. Thus, the application of sophisticated analysis methods to EEG/MEG data requires a good understanding of the principles of the recording techniques and signal analysis methods.

General guidelines for the analysis of EEG and MEG data have been published previously (Cohen, 2014; Gross et al., 2013; Hansen, Kringelbach, & Salmelin, 2010; Picton et al., 2000). Here, I will provide a brief primer on emerging analysis methods for EEG/MEG data (i.e., source estimation, connectivity, and MVPA). I will then illustrate the potential of these methods for the neuroscience of language on the basis of recent studies in two research areas: the role of phonology in visual word recognition, and the brain networks underlying semantic word processing. I will also briefly present some recent developments in EEG/MEG research on speech processing and in multimodal neuroimaging of language functions.

41.2 A PRIMER ON SOURCE ESTIMATION, CONNECTIVITY, AND PATTERN ANALYSIS

41.2.1 Source estimation and the inverse problem

EEG and MEG measure the electric potentials on the scalp and the magnetic fields surrounding the head, respectively, that result from electrical currents generated by the firing of neurons in the brain (Hämäläinen et al., 1993). The main generators of these neural signals are the apical dendrites of pyramidal neurons in the cortical gray matter, not the action potentials along axons. Even though EEG and MEG measure different physical phenomena, the underlying generators of these signals are the same (i.e., EEG and MEG are differentially sensitive to the same neurophysiological processes). Source estimation can be applied to both EEG and MEG. MEG is often credited with having better spatial resolution than EEG, not only because whole-head MEG systems usually contain more sensors than typical EEG systems, but also because the MEG signal is less affected by the geometry of the head. However, MEG is less sensitive to radial, deep, or spatially extended sources (Ahlfors, Han, Belliveau, & Hämäläinen, 2010; Ahlfors, Han, Lin, et al., 2010; Goldenholz et al., 2009), and therefore a combination of EEG and MEG will provide the most complete information about neural activity.

In some experiments (e.g., when we are only looking at early sensory-evoked brain responses), we expect very focal activation with a spatial extent of several square millimeters or a few centimeters (e.g., in primary auditory cortex, or visual area V1). Such a small patch of electrically active cortex can be modeled as a current "dipole," that is, a point source of electric current at a certain location and with a certain orientation that represents a small patch of active cortex (Scherg & Berg, 1991). When cortical activity must be assumed to be more spatially distributed, e.g., in experiments of higher cognitive function or for very noisy data, brain activity can be approximated by a large number of dipoles (100s or 1,000s) distributed across the cortical surface or brain volume (Dale & Sereno, 1993).

Ideally, we would like to reconstruct the exact distribution of brain activity in the brain that has given rise to our measured signals. Unfortunately, with many more possible dipole sources (infinitely many in the continuous case) but only several dozen or hundred sensors, the best we can hope for is an approximation of the real source distribution. This "inverse problem" is called a problem because every distribution of measured EEG and MEG signals, no matter how accurate, can in principle be generated by infinitely many source distributions inside the brain. In order to obtain an interpretable solution, we either have to introduce meaningful a priori constraints (e.g., about where we expect likely sources to be, and how many dipoles there are), or use minimal a priori assumptions and accept the limited spatial resolution of our result, that is, interpret it as a "blurred version" of the true brain activity (Fig. 41.1A). Methods of the former type are often called "dipole models" (Scherg & Berg, 1991), and of the latter type "distributed source solutions" (Dale & Sereno, 1993).

Brain activity in psycholinguistic experiments can be expected to be complex and noisy, and therefore distributed source solutions appear most appropriate. Examples of these are "minimum norm"-type methods (Dale & Sereno, 1993; Hauk, Wakeman, & Henson, 2011), "beamformers" (Hillebrand et al., 2005; Sekihara & Nagarajan, 2008) and multiple sparse priors (Friston et al., 2008; Henson, Wakeman, Litvak, & Friston, 2011). The combination of EEG and MEG generally improves the spatial resolution of these methods (Henson, Mouchlianitis, & Friston, 2009; Molins, Stufflebeam, Brown, & Hämäläinen, 2008; Sharon et al., 2007).

A detailed overview of the substantial number of source estimation methods is not within the scope of this chapter, but several overviews are available (e.g., Baillet, Mosher, & Leahy, 2001; Hansen et al., 2010; Michel et al., 2004; Sekihara & Nagarajan, 2015). As a general rule, the methods should follow your assumptions, and not vice versa. A good understanding of the basic principles of these methods, and in particular their limitations, is essential for any analysis that is based on source estimation.

41.2.2 Oscillations and connectivity

One of the first discoveries in EEG research was that changes in mental states (e.g., from alert to drowsy) can change the frequency characteristics of brain responses. Certain conspicuous frequency ranges received labels such as alpha (typically ~10 Hz), beta (~20 Hz), gamma (~40 Hz), theta (~7 Hz), and so on (Buzsaki, 2011). Activity in these frequency ranges is often referred to as "rhythms" or "waves." The exact upper and lower borders of frequency ranges vary a lot across studies, especially when frequency ranges are further subdivided (e.g., into "high and low gamma"). It is not yet established how brain rhythms measured at the macroscopic scale using EEG/MEG relate to cognition and language and specific neuronal mechanisms, and it is unlikely that we will find a one-to-one mapping between frequency ranges and cognitive functions.

Several authors have suggested that neuronal oscillations support brain connectivity, that is, brain areas recruited for particular tasks synchronize and exchange information by means of neuronal oscillations in certain frequency ranges (Engel & Fries, 2010; Lachaux, Rodriguez, Martinerie, & Varela, 1999; Siegel, Donner, & Engel, 2012) (Fig. 41.1B). Specifically, activity in the beta band has been found to reflect attentional top-down processes, while the gamma band has been linked to bottom-up processing (Engel & Fries, 2010; Siegel et al., 2012). These frequency bands have been associated with specific mechanisms in the framework of predictive coding. In this framework, cognitive processes are modeled as a chain of interacting levels of a processing hierarchy, with higher levels generating predictions about activity at lower levels (Rao & Ballard, 1999). It has been suggested that gamma band activity reflects the "prediction error" between the predictions from higher levels and the actual activity at lower levels, while beta band activity is associated with the generation of predictions (Bastos et al., 2012). This framework has recently been applied to aspects of language processing (Gagnepain, Henson, & Davis, 2012; Lewis & Bastiaansen, 2015).

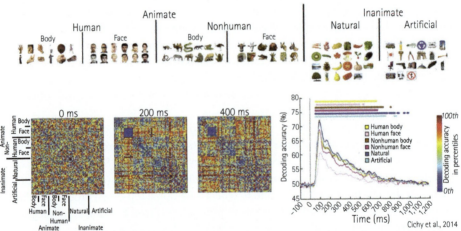

FIG. 41.1 Illustration of EEG/MEG source estimation, connectivity, and pattern analysis.

(A) Illustration of the spatial resolution of distributed source estimation in different brain areas. Each column presents the magnetic field distribution across magnetometers (top) and the minimum norm estimate (bottom) for a point source of electrical activity ("dipole," indicated by small black circles). Point sources were placed in the occipital cortex, central sulcus, and insular cortex, respectively. Topographies and MNE distributions were scaled with respect to their individual maxima, but while the maximum value on the scale bar is normalized with respect to the occipital source (left). A decline in amplitude, that is, decreasing sensitivity of the sensor configuration to the source, is reflected in more widespread source distribution (i.e., a loss in spatial resolution). For the deep source in insular cortex, activity is completely mislocalized.

A detailed description of the various methods for the characterization of brain connectivity from EEG/MEG data is not possible here (see e.g., Bastos & Schoffelen, 2015; Greenblatt, Pflieger, & Ossadtchi, 2012; Valdes-Sosa, Roebroeck, Daunizeau, & Friston, 2011, for reviews). Some of the most common connectivity methods test for stable phase and/or amplitude relationships across trials in specific frequency ranges, e.g., using coherence or phase-locking measures (Bastos & Schoffelen, 2015; Lachaux et al., 1999; Palva & Palva, 2012) (Fig. 41.1B). These functional connectivity methods can establish whether different brain areas show systematic covariation, and because they are relatively easy to compute they can provide connectivity estimates for many locations in the brain. However, they cannot reveal the direction of activity flow among brain regions. Some methods estimate the directionality of connections on the basis of temporal precedence. For example, Granger Causality (a type of auto-regressive modeling) tests whether knowing the past of a signal in one region reduces the uncertainty about the future of a signal in another region (e.g., Seth, Barrett, & Barnett, 2015, and aforementioned reviews). The phase-slope index estimates whether there is a consistent phase difference between signals across frequencies (Ewald, Avarvand, & Nolte, 2013). Ideally, causal brain connections should be determined on the basis of a biophysical dynamic model of the generated signals, e.g., taking into account frequency characteristics and decay rates of different neuron populations (Valdes-Sosa et al., 2011). This is the motivation for dynamic causal modeling (DCM) (Friston, Moran, & Seth, 2013; Kiebel, Garrido, Moran, Chen, & Friston, 2009). While in principle this method allows strong conclusions about effective connectivity among brain regions, it also relies on strong assumptions with respect to biophysics, neurophysiology, and the selection of ROIs (Lohmann, Erfurth, Muller, & Turner, 2012).

FIG. 41.1 Continued

Adapted from Olaf Hauk, Daniel G. Wakeman, and Richard Henson, Comparison of noise-normalized minimum norm estimates for MEG analysis using multiple resolution metrics, *NeuroImage*, 54 (3), pp. 1966–74, Figure 3, https://doi.org/10.1016/j.neuroimage.2010.09.053 ©2009 Olaf Hauk, Daniel G. Wakeman, and Richard Henson. This work is licensed under the Creative Commons Attribution License (CC BY 3.0). It is attributed to the authors Olaf Hauk, Daniel G. Wakeman, and Richard Henson.

(B) Left: Spectral connectivity is commonly measured as the degree of phase synchronization between two brain areas in a particular frequency band. For example, a consistent phase difference between signals from two regions across trials may indicate functional connectivity between those regions. This approach is common in studies using event-related experimental designs. It is also possible to compute the amplitude correlation over time between two regions, after computing the amplitude envelope for band-pass filtered data. This is a common procedure for resting state analyses. Spectral connectivity measures can also be applied between signals in different frequency bands (cross-frequency coupling).

Right: Spectral connectivity measures can be used to test hypotheses that assume that cognitive processes within a particular experimental setting can be decomposed into distinct computations, which are reflected in coherent oscillations within specific frequency bands.

Adapted from Markus Siegel, Tobias H. Donner and Andreas K. Engel, Spectral fingerprints of large-scale neuronal interactions, *Nature Reviews Neuroscience*, 13 (2), pp. 121–34, doi:10.1038/nrn3137, Copyright © 2012, Rights Managed by Nature Publishing Group.

(C) Many experimental stimuli, such as pictures of objects, can be categorized along several dimensions (top). If the brain is sensitive to a particular type of categorization at a particular latency, the corresponding patterns of brain activation should be more similar within a category than across categories. This can be tested by comparing the predicted similarity structure with that observed in the data (bottom left). Note the "blue rectangle" for human faces at 200 and 400 ms, suggesting that the brain response clearly distinguishes members of this category from other stimuli. The decoding accuracy of brain responses for different stimulus categories can be tracked across time (bottom right).

Adapted from Radoslaw Martin Cichy, Dimitrios Pantazis, and Aude Oliva, Resolving human object recognition in space and time, *Nature Neuroscience*, 17 (3), pp. 455–62, doi:10.1038/nn.3635 Copyright © 2014, Nature Publishing Group.

The interpretation of results from connectivity analyses strongly depends on the type of data that were subjected to it. Some problems associated with preprocessing are for example discussed in Bastos and Schoffelen (2015). Connectivity results in sensor space are difficult to interpret, since even a single dipole (not connected to anything) will produce coherent activity in many measurement channels, which may erroneously be interpreted as connected (this is the problem of "signal leakage"). This problem is also present for source estimates, as the inherently limited spatial resolution of EEG/MEG measurements will result in a spatially blurred version of the true sources. Furthermore, some connectivity methods may produce biased results depending on the number of trials (e.g., some phase-locking measures) or may produce spurious connectivity results when the signal-to-noise ratio differs between regions (e.g., Granger causality) (Bastos & Schoffelen, 2015; Friston et al., 2014; Haufe, Nikulin, Muller, & Nolte, 2013; Nolte et al., 2008).

41.2.3 Pattern analysis

When we are asking "Is there a difference in activation between conditions A and B in this region," we would traditionally test whether one condition produces more average activation than the other. However, activity in regions such as Broca's or Wernicke's has a spatial distribution, that is, it may vary from voxel to voxel in a volume (or from vertex to vertex on a surface). It is well possible that two very different distributions produce the same average activation. Imagine, for example, a region with only two vertices. Condition A may produce the pattern [-1 1], while condition B shows the pattern [1 -1]. The average activation is not only the same for A and B, it even looks like there is nothing going on in this region at all, since average activation is zero in both cases. The patterns of activation across vertices carry information that gets lost during averaging, and this information could be used to discriminate between A and B. This is the main idea behind multivoxel pattern analysis (MVPA), which has extensively been applied to fMRI data (Haxby, 2012; Kriegeskorte, 2011), and has recently gained momentum in EEG/MEG research (Stokes, Wolff, & Spaak, 2015).

One way of applying MVPA is to "decode" stimulus properties or categories from brain activation patterns. In the example just mentioned, if we project the patterns—or "feature vectors"—for A and B onto the classification vector [-1 1], then we will obtain a positive value for A: $(-1)*(-1) + 1*1 = 2$, and a negative value for B: $1*(-1) + (-1)*1 = -2$. If the patterns for A and B here represent average patterns for two stimulus categories, respectively, then we can compute this projection for individual trials for every stimulus and test the accuracy with which positive and negative values correctly classify the category of the stimulus. Machine learning algorithms such as support vector machines or linear discriminant analysis can be used to find optimal projection vectors to distinguish between stimulus categories. These methods can be used to test whether patterns of activation at a particular latency and/or in a particular brain region can distinguish between stimulus categories, and if so, compare the accuracies across regions and latencies (Cichy, Pantazis, & Oliva, 2014; Sudre et al., 2012) (Fig. 41.1C).

Furthermore, these patterns can be used to describe the similarity of brain responses among a set of stimuli and compare the resulting similarity structure to those predicted by different models. Imagine we have three stimuli that produce the patterns [1 2 3], [2 3 4] and [3 2 1], respectively. The correlation between the first two patterns is 1, and the correlations between the first two patterns and the third one are -1, respectively. Now assume the first two stimuli are nouns and the third one a verb. The results show that this region produces very similar patterns across nouns, but very different patterns between nouns and verbs. This would be evidence that this brain region categorically distinguishes between word classes. This is the principle of representational similarity analysis (RSA; Laakso & Cottrell, 2000), which—as for MVPA—was originally developed for fMRI analysis but has recently also been applied to EEG/MEG data (Kriegeskorte, 2011; Tyler, Cheung, Devereux, & Clarke, 2013). One very useful property of pattern similarity measures is that they can be compared across time ranges, brain regions, and even neuroimaging modalities. For example, during object viewing, is the similarity structure among patterns in inferior temporal cortex similar to those of MEG topographies at 100 ms after picture onset? This is the RSA approach taken by Kriegeskorte et al. (2008) and Cichy et al. (2014) (see also Fig. 41.1C).

In principle, these methods can be applied in signal space (i.e., without source estimation, since similar patterns of activation in the brain will usually result in similar patterns across the sensors). However, this does not allow inferences about the brain sources of these effects. It is possible to apply RSA to regions of interest, or "search lights," across the whole brain or cortical surface (Su et al., 2014). In this case, it is important to take into account that the spatial resolution of EEG/MEG data is much lower than for comparable fMRI data, and it may vary considerably across brain regions (e.g., with source depth) (Fig. 41.1A).

41.3 Applications to Questions in Psycholinguistics

41.3.1 Early effects of phonology in visual word recognition

To what degree we activate and use the phonological representations of words during reading has been a long-standing issue in psycholinguistics. Masked phonological priming effects and effects of phonology on eye-movements during natural reading have been taken as evidence for an early activation of phonology during visual word recognition (Jared, Levy, & Rayner, 1999; Rastle & Brysbaert, 2006). EEG and MEG offer the unique opportunity to track the corresponding processes in real time, and the anatomical localization of phonological effects may provide further clues as to their functional locus.

Cornelissen et al. (2009) presented words, consonant strings, and unfamiliar faces to healthy participants in an MEG experiment. They found differential brain responses among stimulus categories in the beta frequency band around 20 Hz, which were larger for word stimuli compared to the two other categories. Importantly, in beamformer source estimates this effect peaked around 130 ms after stimulus onset in left inferior frontal gyrus (LIFG), shortly after visual processing areas (115 ms), but simultaneously with areas in the temporal lobes. The authors interpreted the enhanced activation to words in LIFG as evidence for an involvement of speech motor codes in early visual word recognition.

However, there are several differences between real words and consonant strings that may have confounded an interpretation in terms of speech codes. For example, words are

(A) Early effects of phonology in left inferior frontal cortex

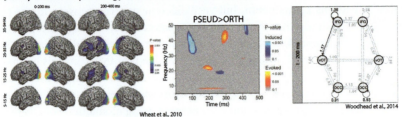

Wheat et al., 2010   Woodhead et al., 2014

(B) Semantic brain regions and networks

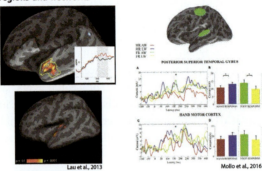

Lau et al., 2013   Mollo et al., 2016

(C) Decoding semantic information from brain responses

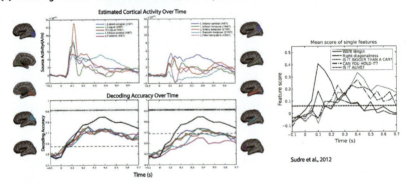

Sudre et al., 2012

FIG. 41.2 Examples of EEG/MEG studies that employed source estimation, connectivity, and pattern analyses, respectively.

(A) Several MEG studies have found activation in left inferior frontal brain regions during visual word recognition. In this example, this activity occurred already in a time window 0–200 ms, and was most pronounced in the beta frequency band (15–35 Hz) (Left). Importantly, activity in this region depended on the type of priming (Middle): stronger brain responses were observed for pseudohomophone priming ("brain" primed by "brein") compared to orthographic priming ("brain" primed by "broin"). In a different study, a change of directed connection strength between inferior frontal cortex and ventral occipito-temporal cortex for word and false font stimuli within 200 ms was found using dynamic causal modeling (DCM). These results suggest that phonological information is involved in early visual word recognition processes.

Figs. 41.2Ai and 41.2Aii) Reproduced from Katherine L. Wheat, Piers L. Cornelissen, Stephen J. Frost, and Peter C. Hansen, During Visual Word Recognition, Phonology Is Accessed within 100 ms and May Be Mediated by a Speech Production Code: Evidence from Magnetoencephalography, *The Journal of Neuroscience*, 30 (15), pp. 5229–33, Figures 1a and 1c, doi: 10.1523/JNEUROSCI.4448-09.2010 Copyright © 2010, The Society for Neuroscience.

Fig. 41.2Aiii) Reproduced from Z.V.J. Woodhead, G.R. Barnes, W. Penny, R. Moran, S. Teki, C.J. Price, and A.P. Leff, Reading Front to Back: MEG Evidence for Early Feedback Effects During Word Recognition, *Cerebral Cortex*, 24 (3), p. 822, Figure 4, doi: 10.1093/cercor/bhs365 Copyright © 2012, The Authors. This work is licensed under the Creative more familiar and carry semantic information. In another MEG study, Wheat et al. (2010) scrutinized early brain responses in LIFG in more detail, presenting words in a masked priming paradigm. Target words (e.g., "train") could be preceded by three possible types of masked prime stimuli, which were all non-words: pseudohomophones that shared most letters with the target words and had the same pronunciation ("brein"); orthographic controls that shared most letters but would be pronounced differently ("broin"); and orthographically and phonologically unrelated pseudowords ("lopus"). Using an analysis strategy similar to that of the previous study, the authors reported stronger priming effects for pseudohomophones compared to orthographic primes around LIFG already around 100 ms (Fig. 41.2A). Based on this specific effect, the authors concluded that phonological information, and possibly speech codes that are shared with production, are activated simultaneously with orthographic information at the early stages of visual word recognition.

This interpretation was further supported by a recent MEG study that reported a masked onset priming effect (MOPE) on activity in LIFG around 100 ms (Klein et al., 2015). Pseudoword primes that shared an initial phoneme with the target word produced a stronger priming effect in LIFG than unrelated primes. Interestingly, this effect was found in an overt naming task, but not in a lexical decision task. Similarly, a combined EEG/MEG study found larger activity in left precentral gyrus for silent word reading compared to lexical and semantic decision, respectively (Chen, Davis, Pulvermüller, & Hauk, 2013). Thus, word processing even at such an early stage may already be susceptible to top-down control.

FIG. 41.2 Continued

Commons Attribution License (CC BY NC). It is attributed to the authors Z.V.J. Woodhead, G.R. Barnes, W. Penny, R. Moran, S. Teki, C.J. Price, and A.P. Leff.

(B) EEG/MEG have been employed to reveal brain areas involved in general semantic processing, as well as to characterize differences between semantic word categories. In an MEG study, masked semantic priming effects were found in the left anterior temporal lobe (ATL), starting around 300 ms after word onset (top left). The ATL activation time course for primed versus unprimed words is shown in the inlet. The corresponding priming effects in fMRI data (next) are also localized in temporal lobe, but more superiorly and posteriorly. The MEG data suggest a central role of left ATL in the rapid processing of semantic associations. Discrepancies between imaging modalities may arise from differences in the physiological basis of the generated signals, or due to their sensitivity to different stages of word processing. Another EEG/MEG study used movement priming to investigate the involvement of motor cortex in semantic action-word processing. Subjects pre-activated their hand- and foot-motor cortex by pressing a button with their finger or foot, respectively. They were then presented with a word that could be related to either a hand or a foot action. A congruency effect between the effector-type of the movement and of the action-word category was found already around 150 ms, in hand-motor cortex as well as posterior superior temporal gyrus. This suggests a connection from motor areas to general semantic processing areas at early stages of semantic processing. HR/FR: Hand-/Foot-Response; AW/LW: Arm-/Leg-Word.

Fig. 41.2Bi) Reproduced from Ellen F. Lau, Alexandre Gramfort, Matti S. Hämäläinen and Gina R. Kuperberg, Automatic Semantic Facilitation in Anterior Temporal Cortex Revealed through Multimodal Neuroimaging, *The Journal of Neuroscience*, 33 (43), pp. 17174–81, Figures 3 and 5, doi: 10.1523/JNEUROSCI.1018-13.2013 Copyright © 2013, The Society for Neuroscience.

Fig. 41.2Bii) Reproduced from Giovanna Mollo, Friedemann Pulvermüller, and Olaf Hauk, Movement priming of EEG/MEG brain responses for action-words characterizes the link between language and action, *Cortex*, 74 (1), pp. 262–76, Figure 4, doi: 10.1016/j.cortex.2015.10.021 ©2016 Giovanna Mollo, Friedemann Pulvermüller, and Olaf Hauk. This work is licensed under the Creative Commons Attribution License (CC BY). It is attributed to the authors.

(C) EEG/MEG can be used to decode perceptual and semantic features of words from brain responses in different brain regions. The time courses for source activation (Top) and decoding accuracies (Bottom) are shown for different regions of interest. Chance accuracy is 50%, and the light dashed line indicates the significance level. Source activations and accuracies show very different time courses. Several regions significantly decoded perceptual and semantic features as early as 100 ms. A more fine-grained analysis (right) revealed that semantic features, such as animacy and manipulability, were encoded after 250 ms, while perceptual features, such as word length, were already encoded at 100 ms. The combination of regions for decoding markedly improved decoding accuracy (black curve).

Reprinted from *NeuroImage*, 62 (1), Gustavo Sudre, Dean Pomerleau, Mark Palatucci, Leila Wehbe, Alona Fyshe, Riitta Salmelin, and Tom Mitchell, Tracking neural coding of perceptual and semantic features of concrete nouns, pp. 451–63, doi: 10.1016/j.neuroimage.2012.04.048 Copyright © 2012 Elsevier Inc., with permission from Elsevier.

These studies suggest that several brain areas, including LIFG, are sensitive to phonological variables simultaneously at early latency, but they do not characterize the connectivity among these areas. Woodhead et al. (2014) used a combination of DCM connectivity analysis and dipole modeling of MEG data to determine the connectivity among bilateral IFG, occipital cortex (OCC), and ventral occipitotemporal cortex (vOT). They presented their subjects with real words and false font stimuli. In a time window between 0 to 200 ms, they found a directed top-down effect from LIFG on left vOT, with larger connectivity for words compared to false fonts (Fig. 41.2A). While differences between words and false fonts cannot unambiguously be interpreted in terms of phonology, this study provides evidence for an early modulation of left vOT activity by LIFG, and together with previous MEG studies this suggests an early interaction of orthographic and phonological processes.

41.3.2 Evaluation

This section demonstrates how the combination of temporal and spatial information can be used to address long-standing questions in psycholinguistics. Several MEG studies have interpreted effects between 100–200 ms in LIFG during visual word recognition as evidence for an early activation of phonological representations or speech codes during reading. In comparison with the behavioral literature, the number of EEG/MEG studies addressing a specific question is usually low. This presumably reflects the effort it takes to access an MEG scanner and run analyses on the data. A single MEG study usually employs only a few, or even only one, experimental manipulation, which means the interpretation of results from a single study is often limited. Comparison and synthesis of results across studies is complicated by the fact that different studies can use very different analysis methods (in addition to experimental paradigms, stimuli, and subjects). For example, the studies reviewed here used beamforming and dipole modeling for source estimation, analyzed evoked and time-frequency data, and the one study that employed connectivity analysis used an experimental contrast that is functionally rather unspecific (words versus false fonts). Thus, there is still a lot of work to be done to establish the brain networks that mediate orthographic and phonological processes in visual word recognition.

41.4 Semantic brain networks

When we read a word, we usually do so to retrieve its meaning. There are two major on-going debates about the neural basis of semantic word processing, which originated in the neuroimaging, behavioral, and neuropsychological literature, but have recently been addressed by EEG and MEG studies. The first one concerns the role of "non-classical" language areas in semantics (i.e., brain areas not within the perisylvian language areas such as Broca's and Wernicke's areas). More specifically, the debate focuses on the question as to whether sensorimotor systems are required to understand the meaning of certain words (Hauk & Tschentscher, 2013; Mahon, 2014; Pulvermüller, 2013). For example, do we recruit our motor cortex to make sense of the word "kick"? The second debate concerns the question as to which brain regions are central to general semantic processing, independent of word category. Is there one central semantic hub region that is the gateway between input word forms and distributed brain areas involved in semantics, argued to be necessary for basic semantic processes such as word categorization and generalization (Patterson, Nestor, & Rogers, 2007; Rogers et al., 2004)? Or are amodal semantic processes themselves distributed across multiple "convergence zones," that may be recruited depending on task and context (Binder & Desai, 2011; Meyer & Damasio, 2009)?

41.4.1 Amodal semantic brain areas: The role of the anterior temporal lobe

The N400 event-related potential (ERP) component has traditionally been associated with semantic processing, as it is sensitive to a broad range of lexical, semantic, and context variables (Kutas & Federmeier, 2011). Based on neuroimaging, MEG, and intracranial electrophysiological recordings related to the N400, a model for the brain networks underlying semantics was proposed (Lau, Phillips, & Poeppel, 2008). The middle temporal gyrus (MTG) was implicated in the retrieval of lexical information, anterior temporal lobe (ATL) and angular gyrus (AG) in context integration, and IFG in the top-down control of lexicosemantic information retrieval. However, a recent EEG and MEG study using a semantic masked priming paradigm found prominent priming effects only in the left ATL (Lau, Gramfort, Hämäläinen, & Kuperberg, 2013), indicating a central role for anterior temporal regions in the retrieval of semantic information (Fig. 41.2B).

Behavioral and ERP studies have indicated that semantic information for single words becomes available already before 200 ms, that is, before the traditional N400 latency window (Amsel, Urbach, & Kutas, 2013; Hauk, Coutout, Holden, & Chen, 2012). In line with this, Hauk et al. (2012) found more activation for words compared to pseudowords in the left anterior middle temporal lobe. In an MEG study on object naming, Clarke et al. (2011) found phase-locking effects between left ATL and left fusiform gyrus in the gamma band starting at 120 ms. Connectivity was stronger when objects had to be named at the basic level (e.g., "cow," "hammer") rather than at the domain level ("living," "man-made"). These results suggest that the retrieval of more specific semantic information relies more strongly on recurrent activation from anterior temporal to visual processing areas. However, phase-locking analysis does not provide unambiguous information about the directionality of connectivity. Yvert et al. (2012) analyzed EEG data using DCM and found stronger forward connectivity from posterior inferior temporal areas to ATL in a semantic decision task compared to pseudowords in a phonological task between 240 to 300 ms, accompanied by larger ATL activation to words than pseudowords.

Evidence from studies on combinatorial semantics and semantic integration also points to a special role of ATL in semantic processing. Van Ackeren et al (2014) recorded MEG while subjects verified two perceptual features (e.g., "red" and "big") on a target word ("bus"). They found differences in left ATL between cases where the two perceptual features were from the same modality (e.g., both visual or auditory) versus when they were from different modalities (e.g., one visual and one auditory). Interestingly, effects in the same-modality condition were reflected in enhanced power in the high gamma band (80–120 Hz) between 150 to 350 ms after target word onset, while in the different-modality condition effects occurred at low frequencies (2–8 Hz) between 580 to 1,000 ms. In a similar EEG study, low frequency activity in the theta range (4–6 Hz) was also localized to left ATL in a late time window (750–850 ms) (van Ackeren & Rueschemeyer, 2014). In addition, a functional connectivity analysis revealed long-range interactions between left ATL and a widespread cortical network, supporting ATL's central role for semantic processing.

Several studies have implicated left ATL in combinatorial semantics during language production. Pylkkänen et al. (2014) found larger activation in both left ATL and ventromedial prefrontal cortex (vmPFC) for the production of phrases ("red star") than for non-compositional word lists ("green, brown"), starting already at 180 ms after the onset of the colored shape to be named. A comparison of these results with those of previous studies on combinatorial semantics in language comprehension (Bemis & Pylkkänen, 2013) led the authors to conclude that combinatorial processes in comprehension and production involve the same processes, but in different temporal order.

41.4.2 Distributed semantic brain areas: The role of sensorimotor systems

Several studies have reported differential activation in sensorimotor systems for different semantic word categories as early as 200 ms or even earlier. For example, Hauk and Pulvermüller (2004) reported differences among hand-, leg- and face-related actions words in fronto-central areas using EEG-based source estimation around 220 ms of word onset. In a combined EEG/MEG study, Moseley et al. (2013) found a dissociation among action, object, and abstract words between frontocentral and temporo-occipital regions of interest already around 150 ms. Similar effects have been reported for objects with acoustic perceptual features (Kiefer et al., 2008).

In the frequency domain, an EEG study found differences between words with visual and auditory semantic properties in the theta band, but did not report source estimation results (Bastiaansen, Oostenveld, Jensen, & Hagoort, 2008). Other authors have proposed a role for beta oscillations in semantics, especially action-semantics (Weiss & Mueller, 2012), as well as for sentence-level processing (Lewis, Schoffelen, Schriefers, & Bastiaansen, 2016). In line with this, an MEG study found that imageability of hand- and foot-related action verbs differentially modulated beta band power suppression (Klepp et al., 2015).

A recent EEG/MEG study probed the connectivity between motor areas and core language areas using a movement priming paradigm (Mollo, Pulvermüller, & Hauk, 2016). Subjects initiated a trial by pressing a button either with their finger or foot. They kept the button pressed, thus pre-activating the corresponding effector-specific part of motor cortex, and released it in response to a particular stimulus category (e.g., words in a lexical decision task), or at the end of the trial (for the alternative category). The stimuli contained hand- and foot-related action words. The authors reported an effect of congruency between response-effector type and word category not just in hand-motor cortex, but also in posterior superior temporal lobe (Fig. 41.2B). This suggests that activity in motor areas affects semantic word processing in a modality-specific manner. However, no congruency effects were found in behavioral data.

41.4.3 Evaluation

There is growing evidence for the role of left ATL in semantic object and word processing. However, the latencies of ATL effects vary considerably across studies. This may be due to differences in experimental paradigm, subject groups, or analysis methods, and requires further investigation and replication. Evidence for connectivity within language networks from source-estimated EEG/MEG data is still scarce. In particular, there is no direct evidence for functional or effective connectivity between sensorimotor systems and amodal language areas, and the directionality of connectivity within semantic networks is largely unexplored.

This will be an exciting research area for the application of sophisticated EEG/MEG analysis methods.

41.5 Decoding conceptual and semantic information from EEG/MEG data

Over the last decade or so, machine learning algorithms have become increasingly popular for the analysis of EEG/MEG data. Gonzalez Andino (2007) used a support vector machine to classify stimulus categories (including words and non-words) at the single-trial level from source-estimated time-frequency EEG data. They reported that decoding accuracies from EEG data even exceeded the subjects' behavioral response accuracy. Cichy et al. (2014) used multivariate pattern analysis (MVPA) with MEG data to decode object categories already from about 100 ms after picture onset. Interestingly, using RSA they compared pattern similarities between MEG and fMRI data from a primary visual brain area (V1) and an inferior temporal (IT) area. For V1, a significant correlation emerged around 100 ms, while for IT it started at 250 ms. A similar correlation with electrophysiological data from monkey IT reached significance already at 54 ms. Similar methods have been used in other recent studies on visual object processing (Carlson, Tovar, Alink, & Kriegeskorte, 2013) and auditory sentence processing (Tyler et al., 2013).

Sudre et al. (2012) used brain activity estimated from MEG recordings to distinguish between different individual nouns. In a first step, they used regression analysis to characterize the sensitivity of different brain regions at different latencies to a number of semantic features (e.g., "Is it alive?," "Is it round?"). This resulted in a linear transformation that mapped neural patterns onto semantic features (and vice versa). Applying this transformation to activity patterns produced by novel nouns yields an estimate of their semantic features, which can be used to identify or classify individual words. Best decoding accuracy for semantic features was achieved in a latency window 250–450 ms, following earlier effects of perceptual features. Most informative brain areas were located in the left temporal, parietal, and occipital lobes, as well as LIFG.

41.6 EEG/MEG and fMRI—comparing or combining?

The limited spatial resolution of EEG/MEG raises the question as to how one can complement the temporal resolution of EEG/MEG with the high localization accuracy of fMRI. While sophisticated methods for constraining EEG/MEG source estimates using fMRI results exist (Ahlfors & Simpson, 2004; Dale et al., 2000; Henson, 2010), the fundamentally different physiology between the two measurement modalities (Logothetis, 2002) makes the interpretation of those results in the case of complex source distributions difficult.

Several empirical studies have therefore compared rather than combined fMRI and EEG/MEG results in the same word or object recognition paradigms. They found some overlap, but also significant differences between measurement modalities (Chen et al., 2013; Kujala et al., 2014; Liljestrom, Stevenson, Kujala, & Salmelin, 2015).

41.7 Speech

EEG and MEG offer unique opportunities for EEG/MEG research on speech, which is itself a rapidly time-varying signal. For example, it has been suggested that activity in different frequency bands, especially gamma and theta bands, reflects specific mechanisms that extract information from speech signals at different temporal scales, such as the phonemic and syllabic level (Luo & Poeppel, 2012). In line with this idea, a recent MEG study investigated phase-locking between the acoustic envelope of the speech signal and source time courses (Peelle, Gross, & Davis, 2013). The authors reported enhanced phase-locking for intelligible compared to unintelligible speech in left temporal cortex in the theta frequency range, where the speech envelopes carried the most power.

EEG and MEG can track the rapid brain processes associated with inflectional spoken word processing, e.g., contrasting words that contain an inflectional suffix (e.g., "play-ed") with words that do not ("claim"). Combined EEG and MEG revealed enhanced functional connectivity for morphologically complex words even before the onset of a suffix, between temporal and inferior frontal brain regions in the left hemisphere in the gamma band (Fonteneau, Bozic, & Marslen-Wilson, 2015). The occurrence of this effect before suffix onset points toward predictive processing in speech perception and underlines the importance of high temporal resolution for the functional interpretation of such effects. Other MEG studies have provided evidence for predictive processes at the word and sentence level (Gagnepain et al., 2012; Lewis & Bastiaansen, 2015). Granger connectivity analysis of EEG/MEG data has been used to characterize the role of several perisylvian language areas in speech processing, and in particular interactive processes involving posterior superior temporal gyrus (Gow & Caplan, 2012).

41.8 Conclusion

The five dimensions of EEG/MEG data (i.e., space, time, and frequency) provide the basis for exciting new methods development and experimental research into perceptual and cognitive brain processes. However, this wealth of information is a blessing as well as a curse: there are numerous methods to choose from, and each method requires the choice of multiple parameters. Many of these methods are still under development and evaluation, and there is often no consensus about the optimal choice of analysis method or parameter settings. The most elegant hypothesis is not worth much if the methods to test it either do not exist or are applied inappropriately—as Churchill once said: "No matter how enmeshed a commander becomes in the elaboration of his own thoughts, it is sometimes necessary to take the enemy into account." If the commander is a cognitive neuroscientist, the enemy is often the limitations of the methods. A more detailed description of emerging EEG/MEG analysis methods was beyond the scope of this chapter, and I could only provide a brief methods primer with a few selected examples of recent applications that involved these methods.

These examples already highlight that empirical evidence on a specific topic is often scarce and scattered across several studies that may differ significantly with respect to experimental paradigm, stimuli, and analysis methods. For neuroimaging studies, it takes a lot of effort to perform a systematic series of studies, in order to evaluate methodology and to rule out confounding variables, as is more common in the behavioral literature. Hopefully, more automated analysis pipelines and larger computing power will make this easier in the future. This should also lead to the creation of openly available large-scale datasets, which can be used by researchers without direct access to neuroimaging facilities. As in most areas of empirical science, EEG/MEG research is prone to publication and confirmation bias. Recent developments with respect to the standardized reporting of analysis parameters and pre-registering analysis strategies may significantly increase the effectiveness of neuroscientific research into language and cognition.

REFERENCES

Ahlfors, S. P., Han, J., Belliveau, J. W., & Hamalainen, M. S. (2010). Sensitivity of MEG and EEG to source orientation. *Brain Topography*, 23(3), 227–32.

Ahlfors, S. P., Han, J., Lin, F. H., Witzel, T., Belliveau, J. W., Hamalainen, M. S., & Halgren, E. (2010). Cancellation of EEG and MEG signals generated by extended and distributed sources. *Human Brain Mapping*, 31(1), 140–9.

Ahlfors, S. P., & Simpson, G. V. (2004). Geometrical interpretation of fMRI-guided MEG/EEG inverse estimates. *NeuroImage*, 22(1), 323–32.

Amsel, B. D., Urbach, T. P., & Kutas, M. (2013). Alive and grasping: Stable and rapid semantic access to an object category but not object graspability. *NeuroImage*, 77, 1–13.

Baillet, S., Mosher, J. C., & Leahy, R. M. (2001). Electromagnetic brain mapping. *IEEE Signal Processing Magazine*, 18(6), 14–30.

Bastiaansen, M. C., Oostenveld, R., Jensen, O., & Hagoort, P. (2008). I see what you mean: Theta power increases are involved in the retrieval of lexical semantic information. *Brain and Language*, 106(1), 15–28.

Bastos, A. M., & Schoffelen, J. M. (2015). A tutorial review of functional connectivity analysis methods and their interpretational pitfalls. *Frontiers in Systems Neuroscience*, 9, 175.

Bastos, A. M., Usrey, W. M., Adams, R. A., Mangun, G. R., Fries, P., & Friston, K. J. (2012). Canonical microcircuits for predictive coding. *Neuron*, 76(4), 695–711.

Bemis, D. K., & Pylkkänen, L. (2013). Basic linguistic composition recruits the left anterior temporal lobe and left angular gyrus during both listening and reading. *Cerebral Cortex*, 23(8), 1859–73.

Binder, J. R., & Desai, R. H. (2011). The neurobiology of semantic memory. *Trends in Cognitive Science*, 15(11), 527–36.

Buzsaki, G. (2011). *Rhythms of the Brain*. Oxford University Press, New York, NY.

Carlson, T., Tovar, D. A., Alink, A., & Kriegeskorte, N. (2013). Representational dynamics of object vision: The first 1,000 ms. *Journal of Visualized Experiments*, 13(10), pii: 1.

Chen, Y., Davis, M. H., Pulvermüller, F., & Hauk, O. (2013). Task modulation of brain responses in visual word recognition as studied using EEG/MEG and fMRI. *Frontiers of Human Neuroscience*, 7, 376.

Cichy, R. M., Pantazis, D., & Oliva, A. (2014). Resolving human object recognition in space and time. *Nature Neuroscience*, 17(3), 455–62.

Clarke, A., Taylor, K. I., & Tyler, L. K. (2011). The evolution of meaning: Spatio-temporal dynamics of visual object recognition. *Journal of Cognitve Neuroscience*, 23(8), 1887–99.

Cohen, M. X. (2014). *Analyzing Neural Time Series Data—Theory and Practice*. MIT Press, Cambridge, MA.

Cornelissen, P. L., Kringelbach, M. L., Ellis, A. W., Whitney, C., Holliday, I. E., & Hansen, P. C. (2009). Activation of the left inferior frontal gyrus in the first 200 ms of reading: Evidence from magnetoencephalography (MEG). *PLoS One*, 4(4), e5359.

Dale, A. M., Liu, A. K., Fischl, B. R., Buckner, R. L., Belliveau, J. W., Lewine, J. D., & Halgren, E. (2000). Dynamic statistical parametric mapping: Combining fMRI and MEG for high-resolution imaging of cortical activity. *Neuron*, 26(1), 55–67.

Dale, A. M., & Sereno, M. I. (1993). Improved localization of cortical activity by combining EEG and MEG with MRI cortical surface reconstruction: A linear approach. *Journal of Cognitive Neuroscience*, 5(2), 162–76.

Engel, A. K., & Fries, P. (2010). Beta-band oscillations—signalling the status quo? *Current Opinion in Neurobiology*, 20(2), 156–65.

Ewald, A., Avarvand, F. S., & Nolte, G. (2013). Identifying causal networks of neuronal sources from EEG/MEG data with the phase slope index: A simulation study. *Biomedical Technology (Berlin)*, 58(2), 165–78.

Fonteneau, E., Bozic, M., & Marslen-Wilson, W. D. (2015). Brain network connectivity during language comprehension: Interacting linguistic and perceptual subsystems. *Cerebral Cortex*, 25(10), 3962–76.

Friston, K. J., Bastos, A. M., Oswal, A., van Wijk, B., Richter, C., & Litvak, V. (2014). Granger causality revisited. *NeuroImage*, 101, 796–808.

Friston, K., Harrison, L., Daunizeau, J., Kiebel, S., Phillips, C., Trujillo-Barreto, N., ... & Mattout, J. (2008). Multiple sparse priors for the M/EEG inverse problem. *NeuroImage*, 39(3), 1104–20.

Friston, K., Moran, R., & Seth, A. K. (2013). Analysing connectivity with Granger causality and dynamic causal modelling. *Current Opinion in Neurobiology*, 23(2), 172–8.

Gagnepain, P., Henson, R. N., & Davis, M. H. (2012). Temporal predictive codes for spoken words in auditory cortex. *Current Biology*, 22(7), 615–21.

Goldenholz, D. M., Ahlfors, S. P., Hamalainen, M. S., Sharon, D., Ishitobi, M., Vaina, L. M., & Stufflebeam, S. M. (2009). Mapping the signal-to-noise-ratios of cortical sources in magnetoencephalography and electroencephalography. *Human Brain Mapping*, 30(4), 1077–86.

Gonzalez Andino, S. L., Grave de Peralta, R., Khateb, A., Pegna, A. J., Thut, G., & Landis, T. (2007). A glimpse into your vision. *Human Brain Mapping*, 28(7), 614–24.

Gow, D. W., Jr., & Caplan, D. N. (2012). New levels of language processing complexity and organization revealed by Granger causation. *Frontiers in Psychology*, 3, 506.

Greenblatt, R. E., Pflieger, M. E., & Ossadtchi, A. E. (2012). Connectivity measures applied to human brain electrophysiological data. *Journal of Neuroscience Methods*, 207(1), 1–16.

Gross, J., Baillet, S., Barnes, G. R., Henson, R. N., Hillebrand, A., Jensen, O., ... & Schoffelen, J. M. (2013). Good practice for conducting and reporting MEG research. *NeuroImage*, *65*, 349–63.

Hämäläinen, M. S., Hari, R., Ilmoniemi, R. J., Knuutila, J., & Lounasmaa, O. V. (1993). Magnetoencephalography—theory, instrumentation, and applications to noninvasive studies of the working human brain. *Reviews of Modern Physics*, *65*, 413–97.

Hansen, P., Kringelbach, M. L., & Salmelin, R. (Eds.) (2010). *MEG—An Introduction to Methods*. Open University Press, Maidenhead.

Haufe, S., Nikulin, V. V., Muller, K. R., & Nolte, G. (2013). A critical assessment of connectivity measures for EEG data: A simulation study. *NeuroImage*, *64*, 120–33.

Hauk, O., Coutout, C., Holden, A., & Chen, Y. (2012). The time-course of single-word reading: Evidence from fast behavioral and brain responses. *NeuroImage*, *60*(2), 1462–77.

Hauk, O., & Pulvermüller, F. (2004). Neurophysiological distinction of action words in the fronto-central cortex. *Human Brain Mapping*, *21*(3), 191–201.

Hauk, O., & Tschentscher, N. (2013). The body of evidence: What can neuroscience tell us about embodied semantics? *Frontiers in Psychology*, *4*, 50.

Hauk, O., Wakeman, D. G., & Henson, R. (2011). Comparison of noise-normalized minimum norm estimates for MEG analysis using multiple resolution metrics. *NeuroImage*, *54*(3), 1966–74.

Haxby, J. V. (2012). Multivariate pattern analysis of fMRI: The early beginnings. *NeuroImage*, *62*(2), 852–5.

Henson, R. N., Mouchlianitis, E., & Friston, K. J. (2009). MEG and EEG data fusion: Simultaneous localisation of face-evoked responses. *NeuroImage*, *47*(2), 581–9.

Henson, R. N. A. (2010). Multimodal integration: Constraining MEG localization with EEG and fMRI. *17th International Conference on Biomagnetism Advances in Biomagnetism—Biomag 2010*, *28*, 97–100.

Henson, R. N., Wakeman, D. G., Litvak, V., & Friston, K. J. (2011). A parametric empirical Bayesian framework for the EEG/MEG inverse problem: Generative models for multi-subject and multi-modal integration. *Frontiers in Human Neuroscience*, *5*(76), 1–16.

Hillebrand, A., Singh, K. D., Holliday, I. E., Furlong, P. L., & Barnes, G. R. (2005). A new approach to neuroimaging with magnetoencephalography. *Human Brain Mapping*, *25*(2), 199–211.

Jared, D., Levy, B. A., & Rayner, K. (1999). The role of phonology in the activation of word meanings during reading: Evidence from proofreading and eye movements. *Journal of Experimental Psychology*, *128*(3), 219–64.

Kiebel, S. J., Garrido, M. I., Moran, R., Chen, C. C., & Friston, K. J. (2009). Dynamic causal modeling for EEG and MEG. *Human Brain Mapping*, *30*(6), 1866–76.

Kiefer, M., Sim, E. J., Herrnberger, B., Grothe, J., & Hoenig, K. (2008). The sound of concepts: Four markers for a link between auditory and conceptual brain systems. *Journal of Neuroscience*, *28*(47), 12224–30.

Klein, M., Grainger, J., Wheat, K. L., Millman, R. E., Simpson, M. I., Hansen, P. C., & Cornelissen, P. L. (2015). Early activity in broca's area during reading reflects fast access to articulatory codes from print. *Cerebral Cortex*, *25*(7), 1715–23.

Klepp, A., Niccolai, V., Buccino, G., Schnitzler, A., & Biermann-Ruben, K. (2015). Language-motor interference reflected in MEG beta oscillations. *NeuroImage*, *109*, 438–48.

Kriegeskorte, N. (2011). Pattern-information analysis: From stimulus decoding to computational-model testing. *NeuroImage*, *56*(2), 411–21.

Kriegeskorte, N., Mur, M., Ruff, D. A., Kiani, R., Bodurka, J., Esteky, H., . . . & Bandettini, P. A. (2008). Matching categorical object representations in inferior temporal cortex of man and monkey. *Neuron, 60*(6), 1126–41.

Kujala, J., Sudre, G., Vartiainen, J., Liljestrom, M., Mitchell, T., & Salmelin, R. (2014). Multivariate analysis of correlation between electrophysiological and hemodynamic responses during cognitive processing. *NeuroImage, 92*, 207–16.

Kutas, M., & Federmeier, K. D. (2011). Thirty years and counting: Finding meaning in the N400 component of the event-related brain potential (ERP). *Annual Review of Psychology, 62*, 621–47.

Laakso, A., & Cottrell, G. (2000). Content and cluster analysis: assessing representational similarity in neural systems. *Philosophical Psychology, 13*(1), 47–76.

Lachaux, J. P., Rodriguez, E., Martinerie, J., & Varela, F. J. (1999). Measuring phase synchrony in brain signals. *Human Brain Mapping, 8*(4), 194–208.

Lau, E. F., Gramfort, A., Hamalainen, M. S., & Kuperberg, G. R. (2013). Automatic semantic facilitation in anterior temporal cortex revealed through multimodal neuroimaging. *Journal of Neuroscience, 33*(43), 17174–81.

Lau, E. F., Phillips, C., & Poeppel, D. (2008). A cortical network for semantics: (De)constructing the N400. *Nature Reviews Neuroscience, 9*(12), 920–33.

Lewis, A. G., & Bastiaansen, M. (2015). A predictive coding framework for rapid neural dynamics during sentence-level language comprehension. *Cortex, 68*, 155–68.

Lewis, A. G., Schoffelen, J. M., Schriefers, H., & Bastiaansen, M. (2016). A predictive coding perspective on beta oscillations during sentence-level language comprehension. *Frontiers of Human Neuroscience, 10*, 85.

Liljestrom, M., Stevenson, C., Kujala, J., & Salmelin, R. (2015). Task- and stimulus-related cortical networks in language production: Exploring similarity of MEG- and fMRI-derived functional connectivity. *NeuroImage, 120*, 75–87.

Logothetis, N. K. (2002). The neural basis of the blood-oxygen-level-dependent functional magnetic resonance imaging signal. *Philosophical Transactions of the Royal Society of London: B Biological Sciences, 357*(1424), 1003–37.

Lohmann, G., Erfurth, K., Muller, K., & Turner, R. (2012). Critical comments on dynamic causal modelling. *NeuroImage, 59*(3), 2322–9.

Luo, H., & Poeppel, D. (2012). Cortical oscillations in auditory perception and speech: Evidence for two temporal windows in human auditory cortex. *Frontiers in Psychology, 3*, 170.

Mahon, B. Z. (2014). What is embodied about cognition? *Language, Cognition and Neuroscience, 30*(4), 420–9.

Meyer, K., & Damasio, A. (2009). Convergence and divergence in a neural architecture for recognition and memory. *Trends in Neuroscience, 32*(7), 376–82.

Michel, C. M., Murray, M. M., Lantz, G., Gonzalez, S., Spinelli, L., & Grave De Peralta, R. (2004). EEG source imaging. *Clinical Neurophysiology, 115*(10), 2195–222.

Molins, A., Stufflebeam, S. M., Brown, E. N., & Hamalainen, M. S. (2008). Quantification of the benefit from integrating MEG and EEG data in minimum l(2)-norm estimation. *NeuroImage, 42*(3), 1069–77.

Mollo, G., Pulvermüller, F., & Hauk, O. (2016). Movement priming of EEG/MEG brain responses for action-words characterizes the link between language and action. *Cortex, 74*, 262–76.

Moseley, R. L., Pulvermüller, F., & Shtyrov, Y. (2013). Sensorimotor semantics on the spot: Brain activity dissociates between conceptual categories within 150 ms. *Scientific Reports, 3*, 1928.

Nolte, G., Ziehe, A., Nikulin, V. V., Schlogl, A., Kramer, N., Brismar, T., & Muller, K. R. (2008). Robustly estimating the flow direction of information in complex physical systems. *Physical Review Letters, 100*(23), 234101.

Palva, S., & Palva, J. M. (2012). Discovering oscillatory interaction networks with M/EEG: Challenges and breakthroughs. *Trends in Cognitive Science, 16*(4), 219–30.

Patterson, K., Nestor, P. J., & Rogers, T. T. (2007). Where do you know what you know? The representation of semantic knowledge in the human brain. *Nature Reviews Neuroscience, 8*(12), 976–87.

Peelle, J. E., Gross, J., & Davis, M. H. (2013). Phase-locked responses to speech in human auditory cortex are enhanced during comprehension. *Cerebral Cortex, 23*(6), 1378–87.

Picton, T. W., Bentin, S., Berg, P., Donchin, E., Hillyard, S. A., Johnson, R., Jr., ... & Taylor, M. J. (2000). Guidelines for using human event-related potentials to study cognition: Recording standards and publication criteria. *Psychophysiology, 37*(2), 127–52.

Pulvermüller, F. (2013). How neurons make meaning: Brain mechanisms for embodied and abstract-symbolic semantics. *Trends in Cognitive Science, 17*(9), 458–70.

Pylkkänen, L., Bemis, D. K., & Blanco Elorrieta, E. (2014). Building phrases in language production: An MEG study of simple composition. *Cognition, 133*(2), 371–84.

Rao, R. P., & Ballard, D. H. (1999). Predictive coding in the visual cortex: A functional interpretation of some extra-classical receptive-field effects. *Nature Neuroscience, 2*(1), 79–87.

Rastle, K., & Brysbaert, M. (2006). Masked phonological priming effects in English: Are they real? Do they matter? *Cognitive Psychology, 53*(2), 97–145.

Rogers, T. T., Lambon Ralph, M. A., Garrard, P., Bozeat, S., McClelland, J. L., Hodges, J. R., & Patterson, K. (2004). Structure and deterioration of semantic memory: A neuropsychological and computational investigation. *Psychological Review, 111*(1), 205–35.

Scherg, M., & Berg, P. (1991). Use of prior knowledge in brain electromagnetic source analysis. *Brain Topography, 4*(2), 143–50.

Sekihara, K., & Nagarajan, S. S. (2008). *Adaptive Spatial Filters for Electromagnetic Brain Imaging*. Springer, Berlin Heidelberg.

Sekihara, K., & Nagarajan, S. S. (2015). *Electromagnetic Brain Imaging—A Bayesian Perspective*. Springer, Berlin Heidelberg.

Seth, A. K., Barrett, A. B., & Barnett, L. (2015). Granger causality analysis in neuroscience and neuroimaging. *Journal of Neuroscience, 35*(8), 3293–7.

Sharon, D., Hamalainen, M. S., Tootell, R. B., Halgren, E., & Belliveau, J. W. (2007). The advantage of combining MEG and EEG: Comparison to fMRI in focally stimulated visual cortex. *NeuroImage, 36*(4), 1225–35.

Siegel, M., Donner, T. H., & Engel, A. K. (2012). Spectral fingerprints of large-scale neuronal interactions. *Nature Reviews Neuroscience, 13*(2), 121–34.

Stokes, M. G., Wolff, M. J., & Spaak, E. (2015). Decoding rich spatial information with high temporal resolution. *Trends in Cognitive Sciences, 19*(11), 636–8.

Su, L., Zulfiqar, I., Jamshed, F., Fonteneau, E., & Marslen-Wilson, W. (2014). Mapping tonotopic organization in human temporal cortex: Representational similarity analysis in EMEG source space. *Frontiers in Neuroscience, 8*, 368.

Sudre, G., Pomerleau, D., Palatucci, M., Wehbe, L., Fyshe, A., Salmelin, R., & Mitchell, T. (2012). Tracking neural coding of perceptual and semantic features of concrete nouns. *NeuroImage, 62*(1), 451–63.

Tyler, L. K., Cheung, T. P., Devereux, B. J., & Clarke, A. (2013). Syntactic computations in the language network: Characterizing dynamic network properties using representational similarity analysis. *Frontiers in Psychology, 4*, 271.

Valdes-Sosa, P. A., Roebroeck, A., Daunizeau, J., & Friston, K. (2011). Effective connectivity: Influence, causality and biophysical modeling. *NeuroImage*, 58(2), 339–61.

van Ackeren, M. J., & Rueschemeyer, S. A. (2014). Cross-modal integration of lexical-semantic features during word processing: Evidence from oscillatory dynamics during EEG. *PLoS One*, 9(7), e101042.

van Ackeren, M. J., Schneider, T. R., Musch, K., & Rueschemeyer, S. A. (2014). Oscillatory neuronal activity reflects lexical-semantic feature integration within and across sensory modalities in distributed cortical networks. *Journal of Neuroscience*, 34(43), 14318–23.

Weiss, S., & Mueller, H. M. (2012). "Too many betas do not spoil the broth": The role of beta brain oscillations in language processing. *Frontiers in Psychology*, 3, 201.

Wheat, K. L., Cornelissen, P. L., Frost, S. J., & Hansen, P. C. (2010). During visual word recognition, phonology is accessed within 100 ms and may be mediated by a speech production code: Evidence from magnetoencephalography. *Journal of Neuroscience*, 30(15), 5229–33.

Woodhead, Z. V., Barnes, G. R., Penny, W., Moran, R., Teki, S., Price, C. J., & Leff, A. P. (2014). Reading front to back: MEG evidence for early feedback effects during word recognition. *Cerebral Cortex*, 24(3), 817–25.

Yvert, G., Perrone-Bertolotti, M., Baciu, M., & David, O. (2012). Dynamic causal modeling of spatiotemporal integration of phonological and semantic processes: An electroencephalographic study. *Journal of Neuroscience*, 32(12), 4297–306.

CHAPTER 42

NEW FMRI METHODS FOR THE STUDY OF LANGUAGE

ROEL M. WILLEMS AND MARCEL A. J. VAN GERVEN

42.1 INTRODUCTION

FUNCTIONAL magnetic resonance imaging (fMRI) has become a standard part of the toolkit of psycholinguists. Ever since Ogawa and colleagues described how to measure a signal from the human brain which is a correlate of local brain activation (the Blood Oxygenation Level Dependent, or BOLD signal) (Ogawa et al., 1990), the first fMRI studies on language comprehension were performed[1]. A PubMed search with keywords Language AND fMRI shows that the number of publications has increased about threefold since the turn of the century (from on average 250 publications per year between 1998 and 2002, to around 750 publications per year in the 2011–2015 period). With its increased popularity, knowledge about the possibilities and impossibilities of research using fMRI has also grown. Some of the "what you cannot do with fMRI"-knowledge is outdated, and the first part of this chapter is devoted to challenging a few popular beliefs about the limits of using fMRI in language research. Most of these issues were valid in the early days of fMRI research, but new developments in hardware and analysis techniques render that they can be overcome. An important advance is that novel fMRI data analysis techniques allow for the use of more naturalistic language stimuli (e.g., the presentation of continuous language recordings or movies). The second part of the chapter builds on this by introducing and discussing several analysis techniques which promise to provide a better insight into the neurocognitive underpinnings of language. These are advanced and relatively novel techniques and here we aim to illustrate their potential for the use of more naturalistic stimuli in fMRI studies of language.

---

[1] Note that earlier neuroimaging studies of language comprehension were done using positron emission tomography (PET) (e.g. Mazoyer et al., 1993; Petersen et al., 1990; Price et al., 1994). The focus of this chapter is on fMRI and we will not discuss PET and its applications, except for noting that the popularity of PET has decreased given its invasive nature (a contrast agent has to be inserted), and refinement of fMRI techniques.

42.2 Part 1: Common beliefs about fMRI in language research

Here are three common beliefs about fMRI that researchers consider when designing a psycholinguistic fMRI experiment:

- Stimuli should be separated by relatively long intertrial intervals or ITIs (in the order of five to six seconds), so presentation of continuous language stimuli is not possible (section 42.2.1)
- Stimuli cannot be presented auditorily because of the loud noise produced by the magnetic resonance (MR) scanner (section 42.2.2)
- Participants cannot speak in the MR environment so studying speech production is impossible (section 42.2.3)

In the remainder of part 1, we will show that these common beliefs are outdated. They can be relatively easily overcome.

42.2.1 fMRI can be used with continuous stimuli

Presenting continuous stimuli (e.g., spoken narratives, movies, recordings of conversations) is typically avoided in fMRI research. The reason has to do with the slowness of the BOLD response. Figure 42.1 shows an idealized BOLD response. A stimulus is presented at time point 0, and as can be seen in the figure the BOLD response only peaks about six seconds later (one time point in the figure is one time to repetition (TR) which is two seconds in this case). This poses a problem for rapid presentation of stimuli. If we present stimuli in rapid succession, the hemodynamic responses (BOLD curves) to each stimulus will start to overlap, and it will be impossible to assess which stimulus generated which response. Even worse, when we present stimuli very rapidly after one another the estimated BOLD response will start to plateau (i.e., it will have no variance left). Figure 42.2A illustrates this. What we see here is the *estimated* BOLD response (so not an actually measured BOLD response) in a hypothetical experiment in which a word was presented every two seconds, for a duration of 500 ms per word (intertrial interval = 1.5 seconds). What we see in the figure is that the estimated BOLD response rises quickly at the start of the experiment, and then plateaus to become a flat line. The standard way of doing fMRI data analysis is to fit for each and every voxel the *estimated* BOLD response to the *actual* BOLD response and see how good the fit is. This is linear regression and trying to regress an (almost) flat line onto a signal will not give a good fit. It becomes impossible to assess whether a given voxel was sensitive to presentation of the words.

One way to solve this issue of overlapping (plateauing) BOLD curves is to present a stimulus, and then wait for the BOLD response to go back to baseline before presenting the next stimulus. This is called slow event-related fMRI. With intertrial intervals of around 16–20 seconds it is very inefficient in that it takes a long time to collect data for a reasonable amount of trials. A better solution is rapid event-related fMRI in which stimuli are presented

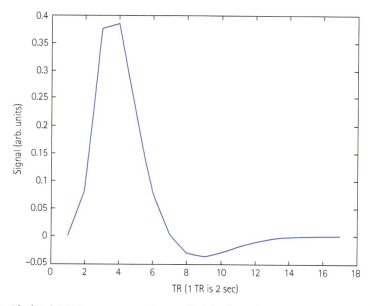

FIG. 42.1 Idealized BOLD curve, sometimes called the hemodynamic response function (HRF). The curve peaks around 6–8 seconds after stimulus onset (stimulus onset is point 0). The shape of the idealized BOLD curve is based on measurement of the actual BOLD curve in the human cortex. The time axis (x-axis) is in TRs, with one TR being two seconds. The y-axis expresses signal intensity in arbitrary units.

relatively fast after one another (~4 seconds ITI), but with *variable* intertrial intervals. That is, sometimes the ITI is 4 seconds, sometimes it is 2.5 seconds, sometimes it is 6.5 seconds, and so on. In this way we create variance in the estimated BOLD signal, as is illustrated in Figure 42.2B. In the figure we see the estimated BOLD curve (in blue) for stimuli presented with an average ITI of five seconds, but this ITI varies from trial to trial (the stimulus onsets are represented in red). We see that there is variance in the estimated BOLD signal, and linear regression of the estimated onto the actual BOLD signal can be used. The introduction of rapid event-related fMRI was a breakthrough for the field (see Miezin et al., 2000 for an excellent explanation), but it still places a limit on the speed with which we can present stimuli. The ITI cannot be too short (how short it can be is a matter of debate). An extra handicap is the slow sampling rate in a typical fMRI experiment. The brain is usually sampled every two seconds, and hence we measure the BOLD curve only very sparsely.

Intertrial intervals of five seconds or more are still too slow when using continuous stimuli such as speech spoken at a normal rate. Yarkoni and colleagues introduced a clever trick which allows stimuli to be presented much more rapidly (Yarkoni et al., 2008). They had participants read short narratives one word at a time. Each word was on the screen for 200 ms, with an intertrial interval (interword interval) of 150 ms. Estimating the BOLD response to the single words leads to a plateaued response (this is the situation as in Fig. 42.2A). Instead of estimating the BOLD curve to the words, Yarkoni and colleagues estimated the BOLD curves to several word *characteristics*. For instance, they asked which brain regions were sensitive to differences in lexical frequency between words. The lexical frequencies

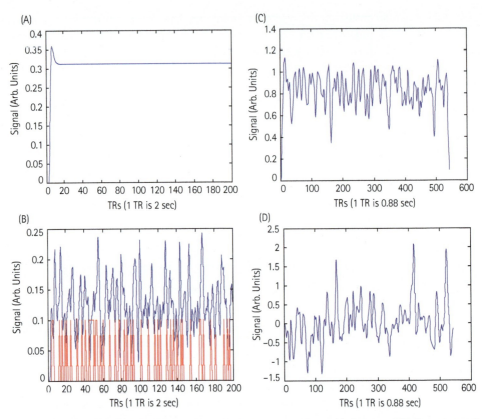

FIG. 42.2 Estimated BOLD time courses for different experimental designs. (A) The estimated BOLD time course for an experiment in which a stimulus is presented every two seconds. Each stimulus takes 500 milliseconds. Because of the slowness of the BOLD response, the BOLD curves to the stimuli quickly start to overlap and the overall response plateaus. This makes it impossible to regress the estimated time course onto the actually measured time courses (the data). (B) In this scenario the stimuli are presented with an average intertrial interval of five seconds (stimulus duration again is 500 ms). Importantly, the ITI is variable: it is sometimes longer or shorter than five seconds. This leads to the necessary variation in the estimated BOLD time course (blue). The red line illustrates presentation of the stimuli. (C) Estimated BOLD time course from an experiment in which participants listened to a continuous spoken narrative. Every word in the narrative was modeled as a separate trial. Due to the inherent variation in onsets and durations of the words, the response does not plateau as in (A). (D) Estimated BOLD time course for surprisal values of the words presented in the experiment (same experiment as in (C)). Because words had considerable variation in surprisal values (see text), the estimated BOLD curve has enough variance to be useful in the analysis.

This is the approach described by Yarkoni et al. (2008). Examples 42.2C and 42.2D are based on the experimental design in Willems et al. (2016).

naturally differed considerably between the words, and this creates the necessary variance in the estimated BOLD curve for lexical frequency. The approach is illustrated in Figures 42.2C and 42.2D, which show estimated BOLD responses from an experiment in which we applied this approach (Willems et al., 2016). In the experiment participants listened to short narratives spoken at a natural rate. The sampling rate (TR) of the experiment was higher than usual. Brain activity was measured every 880 ms (TR = 0.88 sec). Since words have different durations (in the spoken modality), and the pauses between words are not constant, there is a naturally occurring jitter between words. First note that this means that the estimated BOLD response to *words* does not plateau (Fig. 42.2C), but shows some variance. This means that we can fit brain responses to words with very high efficiency: in this example 1,291 words were presented and only eight minutes of data collection per subject was sufficient to collect all data for the experiment (note that the information in Fig. 42.2C was only a subset of the design of the original experiment). Second, and the main point of the technique pioneered by Yarkoni and colleagues, we asked which brain regions were sensitive to differences in surprisal value between the words. Surprisal value is a measure derived from information theory and is related to the expectancy of a given word. The estimated BOLD response to surprisal value is shown in Figure 42.2D and as we can see, the variance in the estimated signal is considerable, despite the rapid presentation of words. Note that this approach also works for natural reading, if eye movements are recorded during the scanning session (eye-tracking combined with fMRI) (Choi et al., 2014; Schuster et al., 2015).

Here we end the more technical exposition (there is a large literature on design efficiency and estimability in fMRI; see Liu, 2004; Liu & Frank, 2004), and formulate the take home message of this section. The take home message is that one can present stimuli very rapidly ("continuously") in an fMRI experiment, if there is enough variance in the stimuli with respect to the characteristic of interest. This will ensure that the estimated BOLD response does not plateau but has enough variance in it to be regressed onto the actual measured BOLD response. One advantage of this approach is that stimuli can be presented at a more natural pace than with standard fast event-related fMRI. Another advantage is a dramatic increase in efficiency: many trials can be presented within a short amount of scanning time. Finally, an advantage is that the approach allows for post-hoc characterization of the stimuli. If a researcher wants to investigate a different characteristic than the main reason of performing the study, this is possible (with sufficient variance in the characteristic of interest in the stimulus). This opens up the possibility of reusing existing data sets, further increasing experimental efficiency (e.g., Hanke et al., 2014).

In the remainder of this section we briefly mention a few other ways of analyzing fMRI data that are acquired while participants were presented with continuous language stimuli. The first is a straightforward variant on the Yarkoni et al. (2008) approach. Instead of creating an estimated BOLD response including all stimuli presented in rapid succession, one can also focus on only few time points within a continuous stream of information. Zacks and colleagues for instance showed brief movie clips to participants and created an estimated BOLD response to the points in time in which an event change occurred in the movie clip (Zacks et al., 2001). In this way the BOLD events were separated far enough from each other in non-regular intervals to lead to an estimated BOLD response which does not plateau (see also Speer et al., 2009). In a similar vein we modeled the BOLD response to action and mentalizing events occurring within a narrative presented at a normal speech rate (Nijhof & Willems, 2015).

Another way of analyzing fMRI data that are acquired while participants engage in viewing or listening to continuous stimuli was applied by Lerner and colleagues (Lerner et al., 2011). They presented a short narrative which was scrambled in time at different time scales. Participants would listen to the original narrative (no scrambling), to a version in which paragraphs were scrambled (breaking continuity at that particular time scale), to a version in which sentence order was scrambled, or to a version in which words were scrambled. They used intersubject correlation analysis to assess which brain regions show a similar time course across participants for the original story. They then compared this to brain areas which show the same time course across participants for the versions in which paragraphs, sentences, or words were scrambled. Other analysis techniques exist for analyzing data from continuous language stimuli. Some of these are introduced in part 2, next. For an excellent overview, the interested reader is referred to Andric and Small (2015).

42.2.2 fMRI can be used with auditory stimuli

While collecting images the MR machine produces very loud noises. These are caused by switching of the magnetic gradients and by the very large force applied to, for instance, cables in the MRI machine. For this reason, participants need to wear ear protection to avoid hearing damage. There are, however, dedicated inner ear phones that allow for presenting auditory stimuli and at the same time minimizing disturbance from the scanner noise. Next to this, modern MRI machines tend to be equipped with hardware which reduces scanner noise. Together this means that auditory presentation works well for single-word presentation and up (i.e., single sentences or extended pieces of discourse). For presentation of, for instance, phonemes, the interference of the scanner noise is sometimes considered too disturbing and sparse scanning sequences can be used (see Peelle, 2014, for overview). These are scanning sequences in which the machine is not collecting images *during* presentation of the stimuli (and hence no loud noise is emitted), but only *after* presentation of the stimuli. This approach takes advantage of the slowness of the BOLD response. The reasoning is that since the BOLD response lags behind neural activation anyway, it is not necessary to sample BOLD at the time of presentation of the stimulus. After all, the signal that we measure will only peak several seconds after presentation of the stimulus. By sampling only when activation is expected to be measurable, a silent stimulus presentation can be combined with measurement of the neural response to the stimulus. The price that is paid with this approach is that the brain activation is not sampled continuously, and that it relies on having a reliable estimate of the time course of the BOLD curve. These are relatively minor shortcomings, and the approach has shown its merits in assorted studies. A technique which tries to optimize silence and coverage is called interleaved silent steady state imaging (ISSS), and the interested reader is referred to Peelle (2014); Schwarzbauer, Davis, Rodd, and Johnsrude (2006).

As we have already mentioned, from our experience, recent advances in scanner hardware as well as presentation equipment (e.g., headphones) render silent scanning not necessary for the bulk of auditory language experiments.

42.2.3 Studying speech production with fMRI works

Movements of the participant can be detrimental to fMRI data. Movements of the head are most problematic, but it should be noted that large movements of for instance the arms can hardly be performed without moving the head, albeit even slightly. Precautions are taken to avoid head movements: participants are asked to lie as still as possible, and the head is fixated to further reduce head motion. Cushions can be placed in the empty spaces between the head and the head coil to constrain movement of the head. Other options to stabilize the head are head casts and bite bars. One reason why head motion is bad for fMRI is that it makes voxels "move" artificially. In the data analysis we assume that a voxel which is at a given location at the beginning of the experiment, will still be in that location at the end of the experiment. If there is a displacement of the head, let's say halfway through the experiment, the time course of that voxel will be contaminated: it will have the time course of voxel X for the first half of the experiment and the time course of voxel Y for the second half of the experiment. While this is very bad in the case of large displacements, in typical group analyses the data are spatially smoothed (or "blurred"), rendering the effect of small head movements manageable (except for cases in which spatial smoothing is unwanted, see part 2). Motion can also lead to *edge artifacts*. These can occur at the edges of the brain, where neural tissue borders other kinds of tissue or fluids. Examples are the ventricles which are filled with cerebrospinal fluid (CSF), or the tissue and CSF which surrounds the cortex at the outer part of the brain, just beneath the skull. These parts of the brain are most likely not involved in cognitive processes, and the BOLD response of CSF will be low and (most likely) be unrelated to language comprehension. Now suppose there is an area for which BOLD response is very sensitive to language comprehension, and there is a displacement of the head around halfway the experiment, just when the participant heard a stimulus of condition A. Due to the displacement, voxels which were silent in the first part of the experiment (voxels in the CSF) are replaced by cortical voxels which are sensitive to the stimulus. In our statistical analysis, there will be a very large artificial "response" to condition A at the time point of the displacement, which will not be present for condition B. Proper stimulus randomization will take care of such influences to a large degree when the motion is not systematically correlated with the stimulus. When studying speech production, there is a more severe problem with head motion. In speech production, the event of interest is by definition when participants move their head (i.e., when they speak). Now if for some reason the movement is slightly more during one condition compared to the other, the contrast between the two conditions will show a lot of edge artifacts. The statistical map will show bright colors (high statistical values) at the edges of the cortex and the skull, and around the ventricles. If motion is strongly correlated with the events of interest (the trials), it potentially becomes impossible to separate artificial "activations" (edge artifacts) from real activations, related to speaking. Because of the harmful effect of stimulus-correlated motion speech production studies were traditionally avoided in fMRI (instead, positron emission tomography (PET) was used as a preferred method). Interestingly, speech production studies show that it is possible to have a reliable signal while participants speak in the scanner (e.g., Segaert et al., 2012). So, while it is important to consider the points raised here, experience shows that in practice it is possible to study neural activity related to speech production with fMRI.

As a final note we would like to point out that verbal responses can be recorded in a scanner environment. Although these recordings can be noisy (due to the scanner noises), online and offline filtering will make them eligible and suited for scoring, both during as well as after the experiment (de Boer et al., 2013; Willems et al., 2010). A way of using fMRI which deserves mention here is so-called *hyperscanning*. In hyperscanning the brains of two individuals are scanned simultaneously using—unsurprisingly—one scanner per brain. An obvious but still somewhat underrepresented way of using this technique is for the study of conversation. The study of typical "conversation" issues such as turn taking is possible with hyperscanning, as is the question of how brain areas "align" or "couple" their activations in conversational partners. We refer the interested reader to some recent overviews and empirical papers (e.g., Bögels, Barr, Garrod, & Kessler, 2015; Bögels & Levinson, 2017; Konvalinka & Roepstorff, 2012; Kuhlen, Allefeld, Anders, & Haynes, 2015; Kuhlen, Bogler, Brennan, & Haynes, 2017; Schoot, Hagoort, & Segaert, 2016; Stolk et al., 2013).

42.3 Part 2: New approaches for fMRI analysis

Next to the use of experimental designs that approach increasingly realistic conditions of speech perception and production, new analysis approaches are paving the way toward a more fine-grained understanding of how the human brain processes linguistic stimuli. We here discuss several approaches that have gained prominence in recent years. These approaches provide increased sensitivity compared to the contrast-based general linear model (GLM) approach that is conventionally used in cognitive neuroscience. Furthermore, they allow for a more detailed modeling of how human brain activity is perturbed by high-dimensional and semantically rich sensory input. Due to space limitations, we will not address Bayesian or meta-analytic approaches, instead referring to Leff et al. (2008) and Yarkoni et al. (2010) for an entry point.

42.3.1 Multivariate pattern analysis

Multivariate pattern analysis (MVPA) refers to the decoding of task regressors from *multivariate patterns* of brain activity (Cox & Savoy, 2003; Haynes & Rees, 2006; Heinzle et al., 2012; Norman, Polyn, Detra, & Haxby, 2006; Tong & Pratte, 2012). This can be contrasted with the conventional GLM approach, where task and nuisance regressors are used to predict *univariate* single-voxel responses. A main advantage of MVPA over the GLM approach is that it uses multivariate response patterns rather than responses in individual voxels, thereby increasing sensitivity (but see Allefeld & Haynes, 2014, for a multivariate extension of the GLM). We refer to Görgen and colleagues (2017) for a discussion of some of the pitfalls associated with MVPA.

Prediction of task regressors from patterns of brain activity is achieved by estimating a predictive model on training data and evaluating its predictive performance on test data which has not been used for model estimation, see Bzdok (2016) for a review of such models. Model evaluation is typically repeated in multiple regions of interest (ROI) or using a searchlight approach (Kriegeskorte, Goebel, & Bandettini, 2006) which uses small spherical ROIs centered at each voxel in the brain to obtain a measure of predictive performance across the brain proper.

As a case in point, consider the study by Abrams et al. (2013) which showed that using MVPA a more extensive brain network was identified which discriminates between intelligible and unintelligible speech compared to the use of a univariate GLM. In the same vein, Staeren et al. (2009) showed that information related to presented sound categories could be detected from fMRI responses using MVPA but remained undetectable using conventional contrast-based approaches.

MVPA has not only been used to isolate regions involved in low-level linguistic processing but also to isolate regions pertaining to more abstract semantic processing. For example, Simanova et al. (2014) have used MVPA to show that conceptual information independent from input modality is represented in frontal areas as well as left inferior temporal cortex. This was achieved by training a classifier on one input modality and testing it on another input modality (cf. Fig. 42.3A). In related work, an MVPA searchlight approach was used to show that fMRI-based decoding of spoken words in bilinguals revealed language-independent semantic representations in anterior temporal lobe (Correia et al., 2014). As another example of the decoding of high-level semantic information, Frankland and Greene (2015) have used MVPA to demonstrate the involvement of left mid-superior temporal cortex in the encoding of sentence meaning.

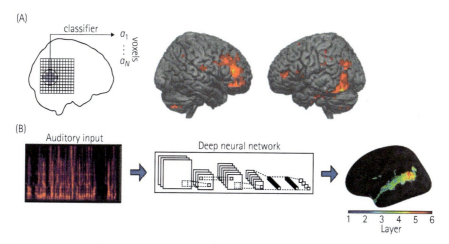

FIG. 42.3 Examples of computational approaches in cognitive neuroscience. (A) A classifier is used to predict from a sphere of voxels whether subjects are viewing animal or tool stimuli. By consecutively repositioning the sphere an accuracy value a_i is obtained for each voxel i across the brain volume. By training the classifier on one modality (pictures, spoken words, written words, natural sounds) and testing it on another modality, accuracy maps are obtained that inform about those brain regions that respond to conceptual information in an amodal manner.
(B) A deep neural network trained for tagging of music fragments is used to transform raw sensory input into auditory features that become more complex in deeper layers of the neural network. Using a representational similarity analysis (RSA), it is shown that activity patterns in different brain regions correspond to different deep neural network layers, revealing a representational gradient.

Fig. 42.3A Reproduced from Irina Simanova, Peter Hagoort, Robert Oostenveld, and Marcel A. J. van Gerven, Modality-Independent Decoding of Semantic Information from the Human Brain, *Cerebral Cortex*, 24 (2), pp. 426–34, Figures 1a and 3a, doi: 10.1093/cercor/bhs324 Copyright © 2012, Oxford University Press.

42.3.2 Encoding models

Encoding models (Naselaris, Kay, Nishimoto, & Gallant, 2011; van Gerven, 2017) are a family of models that, similar to the GLM, predict voxel-specific responses from a set of regressors. However, in case of encoding models, the objective is not to define a small set of task regressors that are hypothesized to modulate brain activity, but rather to come up with a computational model that explains as much of the variance in the data as possible. In other words, an important difference between the conventional GLM approach and the present one is that a predictive model is generated on the basis of the *data*. In the conventional GLM approach, a predictive model is generated by the *researcher*, who tests the hypothesis that voxels will respond to the stimuli in a particular way by introducing suitable task regressors. By comparing different encoding models in terms of explanatory power, we may select among competing hypotheses about brain function.

Encoding models consist of a feature model and a forward model. The feature model maps input (e.g., visual images or presented words) to a feature space whose features are thought to modulate brain activity. The forward model is used to predict brain measurements from feature values. Encoding models can, for example, be used to elucidate how primary auditory cortex responds to naturalistic input in terms of low-level sensory features (Santoro et al., 2014). Results show that neuronal populations in posterior auditory regions prefer coarse spectral information at high temporal precision whereas neuronal populations in anterior auditory regions prefer fine-grained spectral information at low temporal precision. In the language domain, the use of encoding models was pioneered by Mitchell et al. (2008), who have shown that fMRI activation patterns induced by nouns that have not been seen before by the encoding model can be predicted by mapping nouns to their associated verbs using Wordnet (Miller, 1995) and subsequently mapping verbs to fMRI voxel responses using a linear regression model. In a more recent variant of this approach, Huth et al. (2016) constructed a stimulus representation based on word co-occurrences which was used to map semantic selectivity across cortex using fMRI data collected while subjects listened to hours of narrative stories. Results showed that selectivity was relatively symmetric between hemispheres and largely reproducible across subjects. Encoding models can be used to transform complex naturalistic stimuli into more meaningful representations that can be shown to drive neural responses. The task of the computational modeler is to isolate which stimulus representation most accurately drives the responses. These representations are becoming increasingly intricate. For example, Wehbe et al. (2014) have used low-level, syntactic, semantic, and discourse features to examine which brain regions are involved in story reading subprocesses, whereas de Heer et al. (2017) have examined how spectral, articulation, and semantic features are represented across cortex by fitting encoding models to BOLD responses elicited by natural narrative stories.

Finally, it should be mentioned that within the domain of vision it has been shown that an encoding model trained on one subject can be applied to predict the brain responses of other subjects (Güçlü & van Gerven, 2017). Crucially, this approach depends on *hyperalignment*, which transforms data of individual subjects into a common space via a Procrustean transform (Haxby et al., 2011).

Another closely related approach is representational similarity analysis (RSA) (Kriegeskorte, Mur, & Bandettini, 2008). As in encoding models, a feature model is used to transform input stimuli to feature values. However, rather than mapping these feature values to observed brain measurements using a forward model, RSA bypasses the construction of a forward model and uses the feature values to evaluate whether the representational structure of the employed feature model matches that of the response patterns in a particular brain region. This is realized by evaluating the (dis)similarities between trials according to the feature model as well as according to the brain region at hand. If the (dis)similarity patterns match, the feature model and the brain region are considered to reflect similar computational properties. In the language domain, RSA has been used, for instance, to reveal commonalities and differences in the semantic processing of words and objects (Devereux, Clarke, Marouchos, & Tyler, 2013) as well as to reveal a hierarchical organization of auditory and motor representations in speech perception (Evans & Davis, 2015).

Recently, researchers have started to explore the use of artificial neural networks (ANNs) as models of human brain function both in the context of the encoding and the RSA approach (Kriegeskorte, 2015; van Gerven, 2017; Yamins & Dicarlo, 2016). ANNs consist of coupled elements called artificial neurons that are able to learn complex non-linear mappings from input vectors to output vectors. They are particularly attractive as computational models in cognitive neuroscience. First, due to new advances in deep and recurrent neural network learning (Cox & Dean, 2014; LeCun, Bengio, & Hinton, 2015), their performance is starting to approach that of humans in cognitively challenging tasks. Second, as ANNs are loosely modeled after their biological counterparts, they provide an opportunity to gain new insights into the nature of representation learning in biological neural networks (Chung, Lee, & Sompolinsky, 2016; Saxe, McClelland, & Ganguli, 2013).

In the past, neural networks have been used to learn representations of semantic information that can account for behavioral data (Joanisse & McClelland, 2015; McClelland, 2003). For example, Hinton and Shallice (1991) showed that a recurrent neural network which was trained to output semantic feature vectors when presented with letter strings exhibited characteristics that are associated with dyslexia when the network was lesioned. More recently, ANNs have started to become used to predict neural response patterns induced by subjects' processing of sensory input. As an example, ANNs can learn representations of distributional semantics by mapping single words to dense output vectors that capture the semantic content of individual words (Mikolov, Yih, & Zweig, 2013). These distributed codes have been used in the context of encoding models to indirectly map single-word representations of visual images to BOLD activation patterns (Güçlü & van Gerven, 2015b; Nishida et al., 2015). Expanding on this work, by using recurrent neural networks that capture temporal dynamics, researchers have demonstrated improved predictions of fMRI responses to conceptual information (Güçlü & van Gerven, 2016) and have produced natural language descriptions of experienced stimuli from fMRI activation patterns (Matsuo et al., 2016).

New advances in deep learning (LeCun et al., 2015), in which ANNs are employed that consist of many layers of increasingly complex representations of a stimulus are also starting to have an impact in the language domain. It has, for example, transformed research in computational linguistics (Manning, 2015). In cognitive neuroscience, deep neural networks have been shown to provide state-of-the-art predictions of neural responses to naturalistic stimuli, with deep layers projecting to increasingly downstream areas of the ventral and dorsal visual pathways (Güçlü & van Gerven, 2015a; Güçlü & van Gerven, 2017). Deep neural networks that have been trained to represent speech (Kell, Yamins, Norman-Haignere, & McDermott, 2016) or music (Güçlü, Thielen, Hanke, & van Gerven, 2016) stimuli are now starting to shed light on the functional organization of auditory cortex, showing that areas distal from primary auditory cortex capture increasingly complex stimulus features (Güçlü et al., 2016). See Figure 42.3B for an example.

One may ask to what extent neural networks can be considered accurate models of human brain function. Our response to this question is that, as Box famously quipped, *all models are wrong but some are useful* (Box, 1979). We may add to this that usefulness should always be evaluated relative to our objectives. If the goal is to identify which brain regions are modulated by a particular task regressor then the GLM can be the model of choice. If, on the other hand, the goal is to come up with a model which best explains the behavioral and neural data obtained as subjects engage in cognitively challenging tasks, an artificial neural network would be the preferred model. In the language domain, such an ANN would have to account for all the intricacies associated with processing of linguistic information. This includes explaining how raw sensory signals (e.g., speech or written words) are transformed by neural computations to yield highly abstract and semantically meaningful representations as well as how predictive and attentional processes shape the processing of linguistic information (Clark, 2016).

Concluding, we consider the use of advanced computational models such as contemporary neural networks to be an exciting and important development, as it shifts the research focus from human brain *mapping* to human brain *modeling*. That is, rather than demonstrating the involvement of a particular brain region in a certain restricted task, we are in the business of developing models that aim to predict as accurately as possible how the whole brain responds to naturalistic and ecologically valid input (Einhäuser & König, 2010) as measured using increasingly sophisticated experimental and acquisition protocols. We expect the endeavor to build explicit models of human brain function that can solve cognitively challenging tasks to become increasingly important in the neuroscience of language.

42.4 Summary and Concluding Remarks

In this chapter, we described recent developments in fMRI research which extend the possibilities of using fMRI for language research beyond what was typically considered possible. We illustrated that with relatively straightforward adaptations, continuous stimuli can be used in fMRI research. Examples are narratives or other discourse spoken at a natural rate or read with a natural reading pace. We additionally described that fMRI can be used to study auditory stimuli (despite the loud noise from the scanner), and that speech production can be studied despite head motion inherent to speaking. We then illustrated new possibilities for fMRI research that employs novel analysis techniques. Examples are approaches that generate a model of relevant features of stimuli using one part of the data and test the fit of this model on another part of the data, and approaches in which the fit of predictions from—for instance—competing cognitive models onto neural data is assessed. These approaches are computationally demanding and require expertise which is not typically part of the skill set of psycholinguists. Close collaboration will therefore be required between those who know which are the relevant exciting new questions that need to be asked, and those who are capable of designing the sophisticated analysis techniques that allow these questions to be addressed.

REFERENCES

Abrams, D. A., Ryali, S., Chen, T., Balaban, E., Levitin, D. J., & Menon, V. (2013). Multivariate activation and connectivity patterns discriminate speech intelligibility in Wernicke's, Broca's, and Geschwind's areas. *Cerebral Cortex, 23*(7), 1703–14.

Allefeld, C., & Haynes, J. D. (2014). Searchlight-based multi-voxel pattern analysis of fMRI by cross-validated MANOVA. *NeuroImage, 89*, 345–57.

Andric, M., & Small, S. L. (2015). fMRI methods for studying the neurobiology of language under naturalistic conditions. In: Willems, R. M. (Ed.), *Cognitive Neuroscience of Natural Language Use*. Cambridge University Press, Cambridge.

Bögels, S., Barr, D. J., Garrod, S., & Kessler, K. (2015). Conversational interaction in the scanner: Mentalizing during language processing as revealed by MEG. *Cerebral Cortex (New York, N.Y.: 1991), 25*(9), 3219–34.

Bögels, S., & Levinson, S. C. (2017). The brain behind the response: Insights into turn-taking in conversation from neuroimaging. *Research on Language and Social Interaction, 50*(1), 71–89.

Box, G. E. P. (1979). Robustness in the strategy of scientific model building. In: Launer, R. L. & Wilkinson, G. N. (Eds.), *Robustness in Statistics* (pp. 201–36). Academic Press, Cambridge, MA.

Bzdok, D. (2016). Classical statistics and statistical learning in imaging neuroscience. *Frontiers in Neuroscience, 11*, 543.

Choi, W., Desai, R. H., & Henderson, J. M. (2014). The neural substrates of natural reading: A comparison of normal and nonword text using eyetracking and fMRI. *Frontiers in Human Neuroscience, 8*, 1024.

Chung, S., Lee, D. D., & Sompolinsky, H. (2016). Linear readout of object manifolds. *Physical Review E, 93*(6), 60301.

Clark, A. (2016). *Surfing Uncertainty: Prediction, Action, and the Embodied Mind*. Oxford University Press, Oxford.

Correia, J., Formisano, E., Valente, G., Hausfeld, L., Jansma, B., & Bonte, M. (2014). Brain-based translation: fMRI decoding of spoken words in bilinguals reveals language-independent semantic representations in anterior temporal lobe. *The Journal of Neuroscience, 34*(1), 332–8.

Cox, D. D., & Dean, T. (2014). Neural networks and neuroscience-inspired computer vision. *Current Biology, 24*(18), R921–9.

Cox, D. D., & Savoy, R. L. (2003). Functional magnetic resonance imaging (fMRI) "brain reading": Detecting and classifying distributed patterns of fMRI activity in human visual cortex. *NeuroImage, 19*, 261–70.

de Boer, M., Toni, I., & Willems, R. M. (2013). What drives successful verbal communication? *Frontiers in Human Neuroscience, 7*, 622.

de Heer, W. A., Huth, A. G., Griffiths, T. L., Gallant, J. L., Theunissen, F. E. (2017). The hierarchical cortical organization of human speech processing. *Journal of Neuroscience, 37*(27), 6539–57.

Devereux, B. J., Clarke, A., Marouchos, A., & Tyler, L. K. (2013). Representational similarity analysis reveals commonalities and differences in the semantic processing of words and objects. *The Journal of Neuroscience, 33*(48), 18906–16.

Matsuo, E., Kobayashi, I., Nishimoto, S., Nishida, S., & Asoh, H. (2016). Generating natural language descriptions for semantic representations of human brain activity. In: *Proceedings of the 54th Annual Meeting of the Association for Computational Linguistics* (pp. 22–27). Berlin, Germany.

Einhäuser, W., & König, P. (2010). Getting real—Sensory processing of natural stimuli. *Current Opinion in Neurobiology, 20*(3), 389–95.

Evans, S., & Davis, M. H. (2015). Hierarchical organization of auditory and motor representations in speech perception: Evidence from searchlight similarity analysis. *Cerebral Cortex, 25*(12), 4772–88.

Frankland, S. M., & Greene, J. D. (2015). An architecture for encoding sentence meaning in left mid-superior temporal cortex. *Proceedings of the National Academy of Sciences of the United States of America, 112*(37), 11732–7.

Görgen, K., Hebart, M. N., Allefeld, C., & Haynes, J. (2017). The same analysis approach: Practical protection against the pitfalls of novel neuroimaging analysis methods. *NeuroImage*, doi: 10.1016/j.neuroimage.2017.12.083.

Güçlü, U., Thielen, J., Hanke, M., & van Gerven, M. A. J. (2016). Brains on Beats. In: *Neural Information Processing Systems* (pp. 1–12) arXiv:1606.02627 [q-bio.NC].

Güçlü, U., & van Gerven, M. A. J. (2015a). Deep neural networks reveal a gradient in the complexity of neural representations across the ventral stream. *Journal of Neuroscience, 35*(27), 10005–14.

Güçlü, U., & van Gerven, M. A. J. (2015b). Semantic vector space models predict neural responses to complex visual stimuli. *arXiv Preprint, 1510.04738*, 1–7.

Güçlü, U., & van Gerven, M. A. J. (2016). Modeling the dynamics of human brain activity with recurrent neural networks. *Frontiers in Systems Neuroscience*, 1–19.

Güçlü, U., & van Gerven, M. (2017). Increasingly complex representations of natural movies across the dorsal stream are shared between subjects. *NeuroImage, 145*(Pt B), 329–36.

Hanke, M., Baumgartner, F. J., Ibe, P., Kaule, F. R., Pollmann, S., Speck, O., ... & Stadler, J. (2014). A high-resolution 7-Tesla fMRI dataset from complex natural stimulation with an audio movie. *Scientific Data, 1*, 1–18.

Haxby, J., Guntupalli, J., Connolly, A., Halchenko, Y., Conroy, B., Gobbini, M., ... & Ramadge, P. (2011). A common, high-dimensional model of the representational space in human ventral temporal cortex. *Neuron, 72*(2), 404–16.

Haynes, J.-D., & Rees, G. (2006). Decoding mental states from brain activity in humans. *Nature Reviews Neuroscience, 7*, 523–34.

Heinzle, J., Anders, S., Bode, S., Bogler, C., Chen, Y., Cichy, R. M., ... & Haynes, J.-D. (2012). Multivariate decoding of fMRI data. *E-Neuroforum, 3*(1), 1–16.

Hinton, G. E., & Shallice, T. (1991). Lesioning an attractor network: Investigations of acquired dyslexia. *Psychological Review, 98*(1), 74–95.

Huth, A. G., Heer, W. A. De, Griffiths, T. L., Theunissen, F. E., & Jack, L. (2016). Natural speech reveals the semantic maps that tile human cerebral cortex. *Nature, 532*(7600), 453–8.

Joanisse, M. F., & McClelland, J. L. (2015). Connectionist perspectives on language learning, representation and processing. *Wiley Interdisciplinary Reviews: Cognitive Science, 6*(3), 235–47.

Kell, A., Yamins, D., Norman-Haignere, S., & McDermott, J. (2016). Speech-trained neural networks behave like human listeners and reveal a hierarchy in auditory cortex. In: *CoSyne 2016* (pp. 109–110).

Konvalinka, I., & Roepstorff, A. (2012). The two-brain approach: How can mutually interacting brains teach us something about social interaction? *Frontiers in Human Neuroscience, 6*, 215.

Kriegeskorte, N. (2015). Deep neural networks: A new framework for modeling biological vision and brain information processing. *Annual Review of Vision Science, 1*(1), 417–46.

Kriegeskorte, N., Goebel, R., & Bandettini, P. (2006). Information-based functional brain mapping. *Proceedings of the National Academy of Sciences of the United States of America*, *103*(10), 3863–8.

Kriegeskorte, N., Mur, M., & Bandettini, P. (2008). Representational similarity analysis—connecting the branches of systems neuroscience. *Frontiers in Systems Neuroscience*, *2*, 4.

Kuhlen, A. K., Allefeld, C., Anders, S., & Haynes, J. D. (2015). Towards a multi-brain perspective on communication in dialogue. In: Willems, R. M. (Ed.), *Cognitive Neuroscience of Natural Language Use* (pp. 182–200). Cambridge University Press, Cambridge.

Kuhlen, A. K., Bogler, C., Brennan, S. E., & Haynes, J.-D. (2017). Brains in dialogue: Decoding neural preparation of speaking to a conversational partner. *Social, Cognitive and Affective Neuroscience*, *12*(6), 871–80.

LeCun, Y., Bengio, Y., & Hinton, G. (2015). Deep learning. *Nature*, *521*(7553), 436–44.

Leff, A. P., Schofield, T. M., Stephan, K. E., Crinion, J. T., Friston, K. J., & Price, C. J. (2008). The cortical dynamics of intelligible speech. *Journal of Neuroscience*, *28*, 13209–15.

Lerner, Y., Honey, C. J., Silbert, L. J., & Hasson, U. (2011). Topographic mapping of a hierarchy of temporal receptive windows using a narrated story. *Journal of Neuroscience*, *31*(8), 2906–15.

Liu, T. T. (2004). Efficiency, power, and entropy in event-related fMRI with multiple trial types. Part II: Design of experiments. *NeuroImage*, *21*(1), 401–13.

Liu, T. T., & Frank, L. R. (2004). Efficiency, power, and entropy in event-related FMRI with multiple trial types. Part I: Theory. *NeuroImage*, *21*(1), 387–400.

Manning, C. D. (2015). Computational linguistics and deep learning. *Computational Linguistics*, *41*(4), 701–7.

Mazoyer, B. M., Tzourio, N., Frak, V., Syrota, A., Murayama, N., Levrier, O., ... & Mehler, J. (1993). The cortical representation of speech. *Journal of Cognitive Neuroscience*, *5*(4), 467–79.

McClelland, J. L. (2003). The parallel distributed processing approach to semantic cognition. *Nature Reviews Neuroscience*, *4*, 310–22.

Miezin, F. M., Maccotta, L., Ollinger, J. M., Petersen, S. E., & Buckner, R. L. (2000). Characterizing the hemodynamic response: Effects of presentation rate, sampling procedure, and the possibility of ordering brain activity based on relative timing. *NeuroImage*, *11*(6 Pt 1), 735–59.

Mikolov, T., Yih, W., & Zweig, G. (2013). Linguistic regularities in continuous space word representations. *Proceedings of NAACL-HLT* (June) (pp. 746–51).

Miller, G. A. (1995). WordNet: A lexical database for English. *Communications of the ACM*, *38*(11), 39–41.

Mitchell, T. M., Shinkareva, S. V, Carlson, A., Chang, K.-M., Malave, V. L., Mason, R. A., & Just, M. A. (2008). Predicting human brain activity associated with the meanings of nouns. *Science*, *320*(5880), 1191–5.

Naselaris, T., Kay, K. N., Nishimoto, S., & Gallant, J. L. (2011). Encoding and decoding in fMRI. *NeuroImage*, *56*(2), 400–10.

Nijhof, A. D., & Willems, R. M. (2015). Simulating fiction: Individual differences in literature comprehension revealed with fMRI. *PLoS One*, *10*(2), e0116492.

Norman, K. A., Polyn, S. M. M., Detra, G. J., & Haxby, J. V. (2006). Beyond mind-reading: Multi-voxel pattern analysis of fMRI data. *Trends in Cognitive Sciences*, *10*(9), 424–30.

Ogawa, S., Lee, T. M., Kay, A. R., & Tank, D. W. (1990). Brain magnetic resonance imaging with contrast dependent on blood oxygenation. *Proceedings of the National Academy of Sciences of the United States of America*, *87*(24), 9868–72.

Peelle, J. E. (2014). Methodological challenges and solutions in auditory functional magnetic resonance imaging. *Frontiers in Neuroscience, 8*, 253.

Petersen, S. E., Fox, P. T., Snyder, A. Z., & Raichle, M. E. (1990). Activation of extrastriate and frontal cortical areas by visual words and word-like stimuli. *Science, 249*(4972), 1041–4.

Price, C. J., Wise, R. J., Watson, J. D., Patterson, K., Howard, D., & Frackowiak, R. S. (1994). Brain activity during reading. The effects of exposure duration and task. *Brain: A Journal of Neurology, 117 (Pt 6)*, 1255–69.

Nishida S., Huth, A. G., Gallant, J. L., Nishimoto, S. (2015). Word statistics in large-scale texts explain the human cortical semantic representation of objects, actions, and impressions. Society for Neuroscience, Annual Meeting 2015, 333.13.

Santoro, R., Moerel, M., de Martino, F., Goebel, R., Ugurbil, K., Yacoub, E., & Formisano, E. (2014). Encoding of natural sounds at multiple spectral and temporal resolutions in the human auditory cortex. *PLoS Computational Biology, 10*(1), e1003412.

Saxe, A., McClelland, J., & Ganguli, S. (2013). Dynamics of learning in deep linear neural networks. *Advances in Neural Information Processing Systems*, 1–9.

Schoot, L., Hagoort, P., & Segaert, K. (2016). What can we learn from a two-brain approach to verbal interaction? *Neuroscience & Biobehavioral Reviews, 68*, 454–9.

Schuster, S., Hawelka, S., Richlan, F., Ludersdorfer, P., & Hutzler, F. (2015). Eyes on words: A fixation-related fMRI study of the left occipito-temporal cortex during self-paced silent reading of words and pseudowords. *Scientific Reports, 5*, 12686.

Schwarzbauer, C., Davis, M. H., Rodd, J. M., & Johnsrude, I. (2006). Interleaved silent steady state (ISSS) imaging: A new sparse imaging method applied to auditory fMRI. *NeuroImage, 29*(3), 774–82.

Segaert, K., Menenti, L., Weber, K., Petersson, K. M., & Hagoort, P. (2012). Shared syntax in language production and language comprehension—an FMRI study. *Cerebral Cortex 22*(7), 1662–70.

Simanova, I., Hagoort, P., Oostenveld, R., & van Gerven, M. (2014). Modality-independent decoding of semantic information from the human brain. *Cerebral Cortex, 24* (2), 426–34.

Speer, N. K., Reynolds, J. R., Swallow, K. M., & Zacks, J. M. (2009). Reading stories activates neural representations of visual and motor experiences. *Psychological Science, 20*(8), 989–99.

Staeren, N., Renvall, H., De Martino, F., Goebel, R., & Formisano, E. (2009). Sound categories are represented as distributed patterns in the human auditory cortex. *Current Biology: CB, 19*(6), 498–502.

Stolk, A., Verhagen, L., Schoffelen, J.-M., Oostenveld, R., Blokpoel, M., Hagoort, P., ... & Toni, I. (2013). Neural mechanisms of communicative innovation. *Proceedings of the National Academy of Sciences of the United States of America, 110*(36), 14574–9.

Tong, F., & Pratte, M. M. S. (2012). Decoding patterns of human brain activity. *Annual Review of Psychology, 63*, 483–509.

van Gerven, M. A. J. (2017). A primer on encoding models in sensory neuroscience. *Journal of Mathematical Psychology, 76*(Part B), 172–83.

Wehbe, L., Murphy, B., Talukdar, P., & Fyshe, A. (2014). Simultaneously uncovering the patterns of brain regions involved in different story reading subprocesses. *PLoS One, 9*(11), e112575.

Willems, R. M., de Boer, M., de Ruiter, J. P., Noordzij, M. L., Hagoort, P., & Toni, I. (2010). A cerebral dissociation between linguistic and communicative abilities in humans. *Psychological Science, 21*(1), 8–14.

Willems, R. M., Frank, S. L., Nijhof, A. D., Hagoort, P., & van den Bosch, A. (2016). Prediction during natural language comprehension. *Cerebral Cortex, 26*(6), 2506–16.

Yamins, D. L. K., & Dicarlo, J. J. (2016). Using goal-driven deep learning models to understand sensory cortex. *Nature Neuroscience, 19*(3), 356–65.

Yarkoni, T., Poldrack, R. A., Van Essen, D. C., & Wager, T. D. (2010). Cognitive neuroscience 2.0: Building a cumulative science of human brain function. *Trends in Cognitive Science, 14,* 489–96.

Yarkoni, T., Speer, N. K., Balota, D. A., McAvoy, M. P., & Zacks, J. M. (2008). Pictures of a thousand words: Investigating the neural mechanisms of reading with extremely rapid event-related fMRI. *NeuroImage, 42*(2), 973–87.

Zacks, J. M., Braver, T. S., Sheridan, M. A., Donaldson, D. I., Snyder, A. Z., Ollinger, J. M., ... & Raichle, M. E. (2001). Human brain activity time-locked to perceptual event boundaries. *Nature Neuroscience, 4*(6), 651–5.

CHAPTER 43

INTRACRANIAL ELECTROPHYSIOLOGY IN LANGUAGE RESEARCH

ADEEN FLINKER, VITÓRIA PIAI, AND ROBERT T. KNIGHT

43.1 INTRODUCTION

INTRACRANIAL electrophysiological recording in humans has been a long-standing technique in neurosurgical treatment for epilepsy and have served as an important window in to how the human brain processes language. This chapter is aimed to introduce the reader to the technique, how it historically contributed to language mapping, its advantages and disadvantages as a research tool, and analysis techniques that have provided novel findings and approaches in the area of language processing.

43.2 HISTORY OF EPILEPSY SURGERY

The pioneering work of Paul Broca and Carl Wernicke localizing speech deficits to the inferior frontal gyrus (IFG) (Broca, 1861) and posterior temporal lobe (Wernicke, 1874) sparked a new era in the neurobiology of language, as well as greatly influencing subsequent approaches to neurosurgical treatment of epilepsy. Broca's observation together with the finding that electrical stimulation of cortex can produce specific motor responses (Hitzig, 1900) paved the road to consider epilepsy a form of irritated tissue and treatable by resection of the disruptive tissue (Feindel et al., 2009). Cortical resection became a safe and effective treatment for focal epilepsy based on stimulation mapping of motor function as well as epileptic foci (Horsley, 1909; Krause & Thorek, 1912). These stimulation techniques were augmented after the discovery of Electroencephalography (EEG) by Hans Berger (Berger, 1929, 1931) and its acceptance by the international community (Adrian & Matthews, 1934; Feindel et al., 2009). EEG proved to be a powerful tool in the classification and diagnosis of epileptic activity (Gibbs et al., 1936; Jasper & Kershman, 1941) and was first recorded intraoperatively in humans under local anesthesia while subjects were awake and stimulation mapping was performed (Feindel et al., 2009; Foerster & Altenburger, 1935). Electrocorticography (ECoG) or intracranial EEG (iEEG) soon became a routine technique in aiding neurosurgeons during cortical mapping (Jasper et al., 1951; Penfield & Erickson, 1941).

During these early surgeries stimulation mapping provided great insight into the topographic organization of motor and somatosensory cortices culminating in the famous cortical homunculus diagram (Penfield & Boldrey, 1937). While mapping of motor cortex was prevalent since the turn of the twentieth century (Cushing, 1909), Penfield and colleagues in the Montreal Neurological Institute (MNI) were the first to systematically extend stimulation mapping to language and devised protocols that remain largely unchanged to this day (Penfield & Roberts, 1959). During a typical electrical stimulation mapping (ESM) procedure, the patient is awakened from anesthesia while cortex is still exposed and is asked to perform the same tasks Penfield first employed over 80 years ago: counting and picture naming. While the patient engages in counting or picture naming, different cortical sites are repeatedly stimulated. If the applied electrical current reliably disrupts the patient's speech output, or causes naming errors with intact speech output, the cortical site is deemed to be critical for language and is spared from resection. ESM has been invaluable in sparing neocortical sites critical for language, but these sites have been found over distributed regions of frontal, temporal, and parietal cortex and with a high degree of intersubject variability (Ojemann et al., 1989; Sanai et al., 2008). Even though counting and picture-naming tasks tap into a relatively small subset of language functions, sparing of sites identified by cortical stimulation dramatically reduces postoperative deficits and the procedure remains the gold standard in the field (Chang et al., 2014; Sanai et al., 2008).

43.3 Intracranial EEG monitoring

ESM and definition of the epileptogenic zone are mostly performed in the operating room, as pioneered by Penfield and colleagues. However, this constrains the time available for testing and monitoring the patients. In cases where the epileptic zone is unclear, patients are implanted with an array of electrodes for a period spanning several days to weeks (Ojemann, 1987; Wieser & Elger, 2012). During this time, intracranial EEG is recorded from the electrodes to more clearly define epileptic zones as well as map function via electrical stimulation. After clinical assessment has completed, the electrodes are removed, and epileptic tissue is resected. In addition to providing a more refined mapping of cognitive function for clinical purposes, the extended time these patients spend in the monitoring unit provides ample opportunity to engage with patients in research studies (Crone, 2000). During lulls in clinical treatment, patients may consent to different cognitive and language tasks at their convenience in a bedside setting. The acquisition of electrical signals directly from cortex provides a valuable opportunity to explore language function and while electrode locations are solely guided by the clinical necessity of the patient, they often sample peri-sylvian regions.

During the late 1990s there was a surge of research performed in the chronic bedside setting. The most common procedure in North America is the implantation of subdural grids and strips, referred to as electrocorticography (ECoG), which provide a wide spatial coverage on the surface of cortex but are typically limited to one hemisphere and the surface of cortex surrounding the area of the craniotomy (Gonzalez Martinez et al., 2013; Risinger & Gumnit, 1995; Widdess-Walsh et al., 2007). In cases where deeper structures, such as the hippocampus, amygdala, orbitofrontal cortex, or insula, need to be monitored for epileptic activity depth electrodes with several contacts are implanted as well (Ojemann, 1987). An alternative approach was developed in the Paris school of Talairach and colleagues whereby depth electrodes are implanted stereotactically, stereotactic EEG or sEEG, enabling the monitoring of epileptic activity across the depth of cortical structures in both hemispheres and is more widely adapted in Europe (Crandall & Babb, 1993; Lüders, 2008; Talairach et al., 1958). Both have clinical advantages and disadvantages (Wellmer et al., 2012) and can be complementary approaches depending on the hypothesized epileptogenic zone (Mullin et al., 2016).

43.4 Methodological Considerations

Due to the nature of epilepsy, that often involves temporal lobe structures, as well as the clinical necessity to map critical language sites prior to resection of tissue, electrode coverage often involves peri-sylvian cortices. This cortical sampling as well as the combined temporal and spatial resolution provided by intracranial recordings offer a unique opportunity to address language processing. Compared with non-invasive electrophysiology (EEG, MEG), intracranial recordings do not suffer from volume conduction outside of cortex providing a much higher signal to noise ratio, a spatial resolution limited only by the electrode spacing (typically 1 cm; Lachaux et al., 2003) as well as a lower susceptibility to muscle and eye movement artifacts (Crone, 2000). Both sEEG and ECoG are largely immune to muscle artifacts from eye, jaw, lip, and tongue making them ideal for speech production studies (Llorens et al., 2011) as well as research on reading. Nevertheless, contamination from eye movements has been reported especially in the vicinity of the temporal pole and orbitofrontal cortex (Ball et al., 2009; Jerbi et al., 2009; Kovach et al., 2011), requiring some care classifying electrodes that may be prone to the effect.

While intracranial recordings provide an excellent combined temporal and spatial resolution which cannot be established by noninvasive electrophysiology (EEG, MEG) or neuroimaging (fMRI, PET) alone, they do hold several drawbacks. Typical ECoG coverage involves a grid of electrodes (typically 8 × 8 with 1 cm spacing) as well as depth electrodes and supplementary strips depending on the clinical necessity (Fig. 43.1, right). The insertion of these electrodes requires a craniotomy and is limited to one hemisphere (although some limited sampling of the other hemisphere may be provided by insertion of depth or strip electrode via burr holes). This limits the spatial sampling to mainly one hemisphere and constrains within-subject approaches for hypotheses concerning function of both hemispheres, such as hemispheric asymmetry. Conversely, in sEEG the typical coverage involves depth electrodes bilaterally (burr holes bilaterally without a craniotomy) but the sampling is sparse and limited to the number of depth probes inserted (Fig. 43.1, left). Lastly,

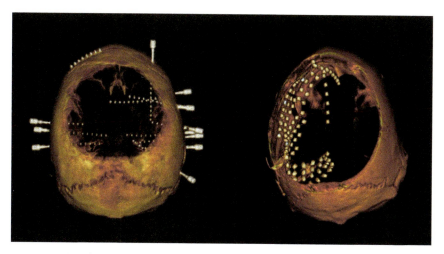

FIG. 43.1 sEEG and ECoG typical coverage. Superior view of 3D reconstructions of computed tomography (CT) scans in a sEEG (left) and ECoG (right) implantation of intracranial electrodes.

intracranial research is most commonly recorded from patients with epilepsy that may have had some degree of cortical reorganization during development to compensate for epileptic tissue. To address this issue, it is important to remove all epileptic electrodes from research analysis and include multiple subjects with varying epileptic sources.

Signals acquired directly from cortex in animal models allow for varying degrees of invasiveness as well as insertion of electrode probes on multiple scales. In human intracranial research the most common electrodes provide a sampling of several millimeters of cortex. The typical clinical electrode is 4.0 mm in diameter and has 2.3 mm exposed to cortex with 1 cm interelectrode spacing (smaller and higher density pediatric grids are also used with 0.4–0.5 mm interelectrode spacing). These electrodes record activity from large neuronal populations beneath the area of cortex exposed to the electrode (Wieser & Elger, 2012). In some cases, small microwire electrodes (20–50 μm diameter) are used which produce a signal typically referred to as a Local Field Potential (LFP)—although the nomenclature is freely used to reflect various recording techniques from cortex (Buzsáki et al., 2012) and the extent to which LFP is spatially limited is still debated (Kajikawa & Schroeder, 2011). The LFP signal is extremely rich with both broadband information (i.e., delta, theta, alpha, beta, gamma rhythms, and high-gamma activity >70 Hz and up to 250 Hz) as well as activity in the kHz range which can be used to extract multiunit activity and in some instances individual neurons (single-unit activity). The use of microwire recordings is rare in language research although there have been several reports from anterior temporal cortex, including neuronal responses in the superior and middle temporal gyri to specific phonetic cues in auditory sentences (Creutzfeldt et al., 1989), spatially organized tonotopic responses in Heschel's gyrus (Howard et al., 1996a), robust tracking of compressed speech (Nourski et al., 2009), as well as visual word recognition in the ventral temporal lobe (Halgren et al., 2006, 2015). Microwire electrodes are typically part of a larger clinical depth electrode with microcontacts at the tip using a hybrid approach (Howard et al., 1996b).

43.5 Intracranial Event-Related Potentials

Early intracranial recordings and analysis were limited to evoked potentials. Fried et al. recorded intraoperative event-related potentials (ERP) during presentation of pictures. They found that premotor sites (likely IFG) showed a sustained negativity that was specific to a rhyming task compared with a visual angle discrimination task (Fried et al., 1981). In contrast to ECoG surface and depth recordings, sEEG provides routine coverage of both hemispheres. Liégeois-Chauvel et al. localized early auditory evoked responses to specific regions of Heschel's gyrus (Liégeois-Chauvel et al., 1991). Additionally, the authors provided direct electrophysiological evidence for a left hemisphere specificity to voice onset time (Liégeois-Chauvel et al., 1999) and for a hemispheric difference in processing temporal modulations (Liégeois-Chauvel et al., 2004). Similarly, deep brain regions such as the medial temporal lobe, and the hippocampus in particular, can only be reached with depth electrodes. Previous studies have focused on different research questions regarding the involvement of medial temporal lobe regions in language. McCarthy et al. tested patients reading correct sentences and sentences ending with a semantic violation (e.g., "I ordered a ham and cheese scissors.") (McCarthy et al., 1995). A negative deflection was observed in the ERPs for the semantic violations relative to the correct sentences, peaking around 400–500 ms post-target word onset. This effect was focal, found in contacts in the anterior medial temporal lobe bilaterally. In another study (Nobre & McCarthy, 1995), participants saw word(-like) stimuli presented individually on a screen. Their task was to press a button when a word was of a particular category (e.g., a body part). In one experiment, the stimuli presented consisted of different types of words: orthographically illegal non-words (e.g., gtprlm), pseudowords (e.g., glubbalt), function words (e.g., hence), and content words (e.g., truck). In another experiment, all stimuli were content words that were paired as prime-target words. Primes could either be semantically related or unrelated to the target words. Content words (including the primes) elicited a negative deflection in the ERPs peaking around 400 ms post-stimulus onset in the anterior medial temporal lobe. The amplitude of this negative deflection decreased for pseudowords, and further decreased for function words and non-words. An attenuation of this negative deflection was also observed for semantically primed target words. In both studies, the N400-like potentials measured in contacts in the anterior medial temporal lobe likely reflects activity from the anterior fusiform and parahippocampal gyri, but not from the hippocampus proper. Meyer et al. had their participants read three types of sentences: correct sentences (e.g., "The door was being closed"), sentences containing semantic violations (e.g., "The ocean was being closed"), and sentences containing syntactic violations (i.e., a phrase structure violation, e.g., "The shop was being on closed") (Meyer et al., 2005). Recordings from the rhinal cortex revealed a negative deflection in the ERPs between 200 and 500 ms post-target word onset for the correct and semantically incorrect sentences that was absent in the sentences with syntactic violations. By contrast, hippocampal recordings revealed a negative deflection between 500 and 800 ms for the syntactic violations that was absent in the other two types of sentences.

43.6 Intracranial time-frequency signatures

In a series of ECoG papers Crone et al., investigated how different frequency bands can index and track cognitive function across a range of language (Crone et al., 1994, 2001a) and motor tasks (Crone et al., 1998a, 1998b). Alpha power decreases were found in three language production tasks, namely picture naming, word reading, and word repetition. These effects were found in electrodes over sensorimotor regions, superior temporal gyrus, and basal temporal-occipital cortex.

The early studies of Crone and colleagues focused on the alpha and beta frequency bands given their well-known relation to the sensorimotor cortex. In the memory domain, however, the theta band has been consistently linked to mnemonic processes in medial temporal lobe regions (Buzsáki & Moser, 2013; Lega et al., 2012; Rutishauser et al., 2010). Based on this evidence, Piai and colleagues focused on the theta frequency band in the medial temporal lobe during a language task. They employed a sentence-completion task in which participants named pictures that completed semantically constrained (e.g., "She swept the floor with a," [picture: BROOM]) or neutral sentences (Piai et al., 2016). Piai et al. observed increases in theta power for semantically constrained relative to neutral sentences during sentence processing, preceding picture presentation. Figure 43.2 shows this effect for 10 different patients. This effect was found not only in the hippocampus proper, but also in the parahippocampal gyrus and entorhinal cortex. These results provided evidence that medial temporal lobe structures contribute to language processing online, relating words in the sentence to stored semantic knowledge. Moreover, this process seems to be supported by the same neuronal computations performed by these structures for memory function, as reflected in theta oscillations.

43.7 Discovery of high-gamma activity

One of the key findings in the studies of Crone and colleagues was the existence of high-gamma activity (70–150 Hz) that tracked cortical processing and provided a more robust and localized within-subject index compared with low frequency desynchronization and ERPs (Crone, 2000; Crone et al., 2001b, 2006). While the extent to which high-gamma power reflects band-limited oscillations or broadband activity has been debated, it has been successfully employed across cognitive domains to track cortical activity (Jacobs et al., 2010; Crone et al., 2011; Miller, 2010). High-gamma activity has been shown to be correlated with the spiking rate of underlying neurons as well as coupled to the hemodynamic BOLD response in both animal (Allen et al., 2007; Belitski et al., 2008; Ray et al., 2008) and human cortex (Mukamel et al., 2005; Nir et al., 2007). These findings have been followed by a growth of intracranial research elucidating cognitive function while leveraging this high frequency band (HFB) signal which is hard to detect outside the skull. The high frequency signal (referred to as high-gamma, HFB and sometimes broadband signal) has become one of the most common cortical indices used to map cognitive function as well as track the perception and production of language.

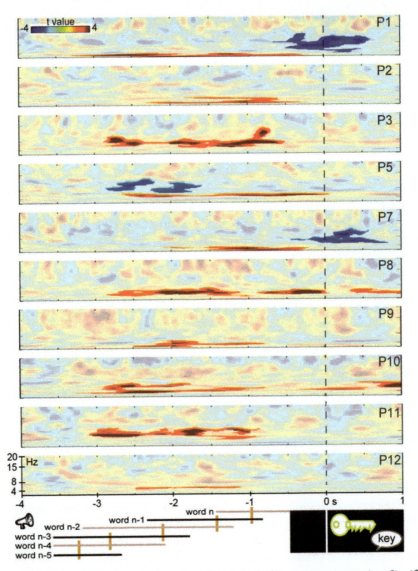

FIG. 43.2 Context effect (constrained vs. neutral) time locked to picture presentation. Significant theta effect is shown in stronger colors (multiple comparisons corrected). Trial events are shown at the bottom. The timing of each word position is indicated by the continuous lines. The left end of each line indicates the earliest possible word onset. The right end indicates the latest possible word offset (and next word onset). Median word onset (and previous word offset) is indicated by the orange vertical bars.

Adapted from Vitória Piai, Kristopher L. Anderson, Jack J. Lin, Callum Dewar, Josef Parvizi, Nina F. Dronkers, and Robert T. Knight, Direct brain recordings reveal hippocampal rhythm underpinnings of language processing, *Proceedings of the National Academy of Sciences of the United States of America*, 113 (40), pp. 11366–71, Figure 3, doi: 10.1073/pnas.1603312113 ©2016 Vitória Piai, Kristopher L. Anderson, Jack J. Lin, Callum Dewar, Josef Parvizi, Nina F. Dronkers, and Robert T. Knight. This work is licensed under the Creative Commons Attribution License (CC BY-NC-ND). It is attributed to the authors.

The high-gamma signal allows for a unique window into language function as it provides a signature for neural activity that is robust on the level of single trials with high temporal resolution as well as activation signatures similar to fMRI. In non-invasive electrophysiology, the high-gamma signal is virtually inaccessible due to volume conductance effects and a sharp drop in power in higher frequencies when passing the skull. Furthermore, unlike neuroimaging and non-invasive electrophysiology, the position of electrodes directly on (or in) the brain renders intracranial signals minimally contaminated by motor artifacts from speech production or movement.

Using a picture-naming task and sEEG recordings from the medial temporal lobe, Hamamé et al. observed increases in high-gamma power between picture presentation and initial articulation in the hippocampus (Hamamé et al., 2014). The peak latency of the high-gamma activity correlated with the participants' picture-naming latencies. Finally, tip-of-the-tongue states (i.e., when a speaker recognizes an object but cannot retrieve its name) were associated with no increases in hippocampal high-gamma activity relative to a pre-stimulus baseline.

Recordings from the surface of the temporal cortex have been mostly focused on acoustic, phonetic, and lexical levels of processing. Studies have established strong high-gamma responses to auditory stimulation in the superior temporal gyrus (STG) when presented with non-speech stimuli (Crone et al., 2001a; Brugge et al., 2009; Edwards, 2005), phonemes (Chang et al., 2011; Crone et al., 2001a; Flinker et al., 2010; Fukuda et al., 2010), and words (Brown et al., 2008; Canolty et al., 2007; Crone et al., 2001b; Edwards et al., 2010; Flinker et al., 2011; Pei et al., 2011). Sites on the lateral surface of the STG respond more robustly as the hierarchy of linguistic input is increased, that is, phonemes > tones (Crone et al., 2001a), words > phonemes (Flinker et al., 2011), and words > non-words (Canolty et al., 2007). One of the striking aspects of high-gamma responses is the ability to track activity within a subject, both temporally and spatially on the level of single trials. Cortical activity while listening to words (contrasted with an acoustic control) has been shown to propagate across the STG to the superior temporal sulcus (STS) (Canolty et al., 2007) and when production is required follows to the IFG motor cortices (Brown et al., 2008; Edwards et al., 2010; Flinker et al., 2015; Fukuda et al., 2010; Pei et al., 2011; Towle et al., 2008). Flinker et al. investigated auditory word repetition and found that Broca's area was active as early as 200 ms poststimulus onset and activity was absent by the time the word was articulated (Fig. 43.3). This early pattern of activity in Broca's area, commencing prior to articulation, and fading by the time of articulation, was evident across a range of tasks including repetition of auditory monosyllabic words, repetition of auditory multisyllabic words and overt word reading (Flinker et al., 2015).

Early activity in Broca's area has also been reported during lexical and inflectional processing of words without overt articulation (Sahin et al., 2009). The monosyllabic words employed by Flinker et al. were comprised of both real words (e.g., hope) as well as pronounceable pseudowords matched for phonotactic probabilities (e.g., yode). Articulation of a novel sequence of phonemes elicited more activity in Broca's area compared with real words but this was not the case in motor cortex. These findings taken together with the early window of activity implicate Broca's area in the formation of an articulatory plan rather than coordination of the articulators themselves. The authors also leveraged the high-gamma signals together with Granger-causal connectivity analyses to show the directional flow of cortical activity during word repetition. During perception of the auditory word there was

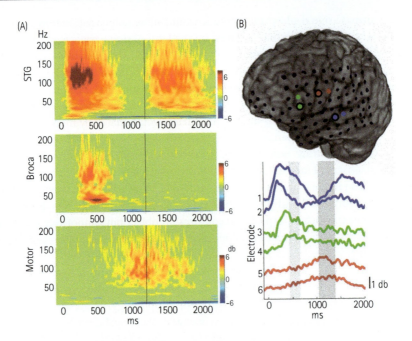

FIG. 43.3 Repetition of monosyllabic words in a representative subject. (A) Event-related spectral perturbations (ERSPs), averaged across trials, and locked to the onset of auditory word stimulus. Cortical activation indexed by power increases in high frequencies is first apparent in STG during word perception, subsequently in Broca's area, and finally extends to motor cortex during word production (vertical lines mark mean articulation onset). (B) High-frequency power (γ_{high}, 70–150 Hz) traces, averaged across trials, and locked to word stimulus onset are shown for STG (blue), Broca (green), and motor (red) electrodes. The first electrode in every pair is marked by a black circle and corresponds to the ERSP plotted on the left. The shaded gray area marks the distribution of word offset (light gray) and articulation onset (dark gray) for this subject (1 SD in each direction).

Adapted from Adeen Flinker, Anna Korzeniewska, Avgusta Y. Shestyuk, Piotr J. Franaszczuk, Nina F. Dronkers, Robert T. Knight, and Nathan E. Crone, Redefining the role of Broca's area in speech, *Proceedings of the National Academy of Sciences of the United States of America*, 11 (9), pp. 2871–5, Figure 1, doi: 10.1073/pnas.1414491112 ©2015 Adeen Flinker, Anna Korzeniewska, Avgusta Y. Shestyuk, Piotr J. Franaszczuk, Nina F. Dronkers, Robert T. Knight, and Nathan E. Crone. This work is licensed under the Creative Commons Attribution License (CC BY-NC-ND). It is attributed to the authors.

a peak of Granger-causal flow from STG to Broca's area followed by reciprocal feedback from Broca's area to STG. This feedback influence from Broca's area onto STG was evident until 200 ms prior to articulation onset and in parallel there was Granger-causal flow from Broca's area to motor cortices lasting up to articulation onset as well as feedback from motor cortices onto Broca's area. These temporal dynamics reveal a key role Broca's area plays in manipulating and forwarding cortical representations as a heard word is processed and transformed into an articulatory code.

Individual electrodes over the posterior STG (pSTG) have often shown responses to a linguistic unit regardless of input modality when multiple tasks were employed, such as word reading and auditory repetition (Crone et al., 2001b; Flinker et al., 2010) as well as picture naming (Crone et al., 2001b). Similarly, this invariability has been reported across languages in multilingual patients performing a picture-naming task where a majority of STG responses were common to both L1 and L2 speech (albeit some sites with L2 specificity) (Cervenka et al., 2011). An interesting finding arising from intracranial research has been the rich spatial variability of responses in STG whether exhibiting modality invariance or selectivity to linguistic hierarchy. Flinker et al. found neighboring sites 4 mm apart with distinct functional responses: one site responding to both syllables and words and its neighbor selective to words (Flinker et al., 2011). Figure 43.4 shows the distribution of responses over STG in one subject listening to words or phonemes (CV syllables). Similarly, some sites in STG showed a typical suppression during production of speech while neighboring sites showed a selectivity for speech output (Flinker et al., 2010, 2011). While STG reduced activity during speech production has been consistently reported (Crone et al., 2001b; Edwards et al., 2010; Flinker et al., 2010; Fukuda et al., 2010; Pei et al., 2011; Towle et al., 2008), the topography of suppression can vary across the STG during auditory feedback as well as pitch perturbation (Chang et al., 2013; Flinker et al., 2010; Greenlee et al., 2011). This rich topography of responses is sometimes only visible when employing higher density electrode arrays. Chang et al. showed that the spatial topography of pSTG responses encoded the phonetic category

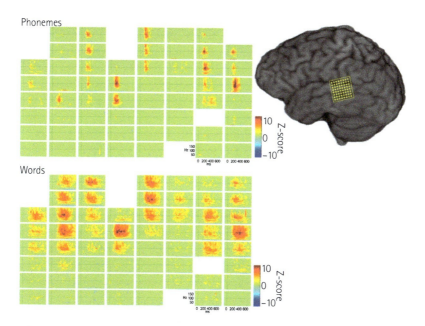

FIG. 43.4 Spatiotemporal responses in a subject listening to phonemes (top) and words (bottoms) during two consecutive recordings across a 64 contact 8 × 8 high-density electrode grid. ERSPs are shown for each electrode locked to the onset of stimuli. Color scale represents statistically significant changes in power with most activity in the high frequency range (horizontal line in each electrode marks 100 Hz). Electrodes with no contact or abnormal signal are not shown.

Adapted from *Brain and Language*, 117 (3), A. Flinker, E.F. Chang, N.M. Barbaro, M.S. Berger, and R.T. Knight, Sub-centimeter language organization in the human temporal lobe, pp. 103–9, doi: 10.1016/j.bandl.2010.09.009, Copyright © 2010 Elsevier Inc., with permission from Elsevier.

of CV syllables rather than the acoustic continuum used to synthesize them (Chang et al., 2010). Similarly, Mesgarani et al. used high-density ECoG arrays to decode responses during auditory sentences that spanned the English phonetic lexicon. They show that individual electrodes are highly selective to different phonemes and encode acoustic-phonetic features. Similarly, high-density recordings from Rolandic cortex (pre and postcentral gyri) have shown a somatotopical organization of speech articulators which are phonetically grouped (Bouchard et al., 2013) as well as a surprising acoustic receptive field representation within motor cortex (Cheung et al., 2016).

The discovery of the high-gamma signal together with leveraging computational approaches has sparked avenues of research that were previously mostly limited to animal research. For example, the spectro-temporal receptive field (STRF) has been traditionally limited to modeling the relationship between acoustic input and neuronal firing rates. Pasley et al. were the first to use high-gamma activity in STRF modeling providing evidence for a robust acoustic representation in STG which consistently reconstructs neural responses based on the acoustic input (Pasley et al., 2012). Similar techniques have been used to elucidate the acoustic-phonetic organization in STG (Mesgarani et al., 2014) and how auditory cortex enhances speech intelligibility by rapid tuning of the underlying receptive fields (Holdgraf et al., 2016). In addition to these encoding models (predicting neural activity based on stimulus features) there has been great interest in decoding activity from cortex (predicting a stimulus class based on the neural activity). Pasley et al. provided a reconstruction of the auditory sentences played to the patients based solely on the neural activity in STG (Pasley et al., 2012). Similar approaches are being used to decode imagined speech (Martin et al., 2016a, 2016b) and try to drive a speech prosthesis (Leuthardt et al., 2011). Decoding techniques have also been employed in decoding sensory-motor transformations providing evidence that speech transformations occur bilaterally (Cogan et al., 2014).

43.8 Future directions

Intracranial electrophysiology provides an exciting opportunity to explore language processing in the human cortex with high temporal and spatial resolution. While much progress has been made, there still remain many unresolved questions and unaddressed areas in language processing. High gamma has provided an unprecedented index of cortical activity, but its relationship to low frequency and ERP findings in the non-invasive language literature remains understudied. Moreover, a great number of intracranial studies focus on sublexical and lexical processing and there is a lack of research studying higher-order linguistic operations. Recent studies have leveraged the high-gamma signal in advanced machine learning techniques to reconstruct signals based on sets of features. Such approaches are valuable and illuminating but very often are limited to acoustic or sublexical features. For example, acoustic STRF modeling (also known as a type of an encoding model) predicts the neural signal based on the auditory input (e.g., speech) the patient heard. When the model is robust then one can reliably reconstruct the neural signal given a new set of speech stimuli, but such models are limited to the time-frequency acoustics of the signal and do not necessarily account for phonetic, sublexical, lexical, semantic, and grammatical structure. That said, such modeling techniques could easily incorporate higher-order linguistic structures. Similarly, machine learning decoding techniques that try to predict a target class or variable (e.g., acoustic spectrogram, phoneme, and so on) given a set of neural signals could be augmented to classify lexical, semantic, and syntactic representations. Critically these models have to be driven by and interpreted within current (or novel) theoretical frameworks of language processing.

There has been increasing interest in the role of the medial temporal lobe in language (Covington & Duff, 2016; Duff & Brown-Schmidt, 2017), partly fueled by recent findings from sEEG research (Hamamé et al., 2014; Jafarpour et al., 2017; Llorens et al., 2016; Piai et al., 2016). The combination of excellent temporal and spatial resolution of iEEG recordings is particularly important for understanding the role of these deeper regions, as they cannot be easily recorded with scalp-based techniques and fMRI approaches are limited in temporal resolution necessary to track the dynamics of speech and language. Future evidence from iEEG recordings will likely greatly expand our understanding of the relations between the language and memory systems.

The finding that Broca's area is not involved during articulation per se but rather coordinating articulatory planning is a striking example of the unique advantage intracranial studies provide. Previous non-invasive electrophysiological studies were limited by both the spatial specificity of neural generators as well as motor artifacts during speech production. In contrast, neuroimaging studies of speech production could resolve activity within Broca's area but could not elucidate the exact timing and stage of recruitment. The combined temporal and spatial resolution provided by intracranial recordings, together with minimal contamination from motor artifacts, ideally situates it to elucidate the role of Broca's area during speech production. Nevertheless, such an endeavor requires more than simple speech production tasks such as word repetition and overt reading. Ideally, spontaneous speech and longer, more complex utterances should be investigated. Such an endeavor is not trivial, as it requires novel speech production paradigms that prompt continuous segments of spontaneous speech that are experimentally controlled and are optimally recorded in tandem with neural recordings. One approach that is likely to benefit both speech production research as well as impact patient care is employing decoding and machine learning techniques on large corpora of speech together with the intracranial signals in Broca's area and motor cortices. Such an approach could reveal receptive field properties in frontal cortices while providing a stepping-stone toward a neural speech production prosthesis. While the ability to reliably reproduce speech based on intracranial signals is still far in the future, it could provide invaluable insight into the speech production network and its temporal dynamics.

References

Adrian, E. D., & Matthews, B. H. C. (1934). The Berger rhythm: potential changes from the occipital lobes in man. Brain 57:355–385.

Allen, E. A., Pasley, B. N., Duong, T., & Freeman, R. D. (2007). Transcranial magnetic stimulation elicits coupled neural and hemodynamic consequences. *Science*, 317, 1918–21.

Ball, T., Kern, M., Mutschler, I., Aertsen, A., & Schulze-Bonhage, A. (2009). Signal quality of simultaneously recorded invasive and non-invasive EEG. *NeuroImage*, 46, 708–16.

Belitski, A., Gretton, A., Magri, C., Murayama, Y., Montemurro, M. A., Logothetis, N. K., & Panzeri, S. (2008). Low-frequency local field potentials and spikes in primary visual cortex convey independent visual information. *Journal of Neuroscience, 28*, 5696–709.

Berger, H. (1929). Über das Elektrenkephalogramm des Menschen. *Archiv f Psychiatrie, 87*, 527–70.

Berger, H. (1931). Über das Elektrenkephalogramm des Menschen. *Archiv f Psychiatrie, 94*, 16–60.

Bouchard, K. E., Mesgarani, N., Johnson, K., & Chang, E. F. (2013). Functional organization of human sensorimotor cortex for speech articulation. *Nature, 495*, 327–32.

Broca, P. (1861). Remarques sur le siege de la faculté du langage articulé, suivies d'une observation d'aphémie (perte de la parole). *Bulletins et mémoires de la Société Anatomique de Paris, 36*, 330–56.

Brown, E. C., Rothermel, R., Nishida, M., Juhász, C., Muzik, O., Hoechstetter, K., ... & Asano, E. (2008). In vivo animation of auditory-language-induced gamma-oscillations in children with intractable focal epilepsy. *NeuroImage, 41*, 1120–31.

Brugge, J. F., Nourski, K. V., Oya, H., Reale, R. A., Kawasaki, H., Steinschneider, M., & Howard, M. A. (2009). Coding of repetitive transients by auditory cortex on Heschl's gyrus. *Journal of Neurophysiology, 102*, 2358–74.

Buzsáki, G., Anastassiou, C. A., & Koch, C. (2012). The origin of extracellular fields and currents—EEG, ECoG, LFP and spikes. *Nature Reviews Neuroscience, 13*, 407–20.

Buzsáki, G., & Moser, E. I. (2013). Memory, navigation and theta rhythm in the hippocampal-entorhinal system. *Nature Neuroscience, 16*, 130–8.

Canolty, R. T., Soltani, M., Dalal, S. S., Edwards, E., Dronkers, N. F., Nagarajan, S. S., ... & Knight, R. T. (2007). Spatiotemporal dynamics of word processing in the human brain. *Frontiers in Neuroscience, 1*, 185–96.

Cervenka, M. C., Boatman-Reich, D., Ward, J., Franaszczuk, P. J., & Crone, N. (2011). Language mapping in multilingual patients: Electrocorticography and cortical stimulation during naming. *Frontiers in Human Neuroscience, 5*, 13.

Chang, E. F., Edwards, E., Nagarajan, S. S., Fogelson, N., Dalal, S. S., Canolty, R. T., ... & Knight, R. T. (2011). Cortical spatio-temporal dynamics underlying phonological target detection in humans. *Journal of Cognitive Neuroscience, 23*, 1437–46.

Chang, E. F., Niziolek, C. A., Knight, R. T., Nagarajan, S. S., & Houde, J. F. (2013). Human cortical sensorimotor network underlying feedback control of vocal pitch. *Proceedings of the National Academy of Sciences of the United States of America, 110*, 2653–2658.

Chang, E. F., Raygor, K. P., & Berger, M. S. (2014). Contemporary model of language organization: An overview for neurosurgeons. *Journal of Neurosurgery, 122*, 250–61.

Chang, E. F., Rieger, J. W., Johnson, K., Berger, M. S., Barbaro, N. M., & Knight, R. T. (2010). Categorical speech representation in human superior temporal gyrus. *Nature Neuroscience, 13*, 1428–32.

Cheung, C., Hamilton, L. S., Johnson, K., & Chang, E. F. (2016). The auditory representation of speech sounds in human motor cortex. *eLife Sciences, 5*, e12577.

Cogan, G. B., Thesen, T., Carlson, C., Doyle, W., Devinsky, O., & Pesaran, B. (2014). Sensory-motor transformations for speech occur bilaterally. *Nature, 507*, 94–8.

Covington, N. V., & Duff, M. C. (2016). Expanding the language network: Direct contributions from the hippocampus. *Trends in Cognitive Sciences, 20*, 869–70.

Crandall, P. H., & Babb, T. L. (1993). The UCLA Epilepsy Program: historical review 1960–1992. *Journal of Clinical Neurophysiology, 10*, 226–38.

Creutzfeldt, O., Ojemann, G., & Lettich, E. (1989). Neuronal activity in the human lateral temporal lobe. *Experimental Brain Research, 77*, 451–75.

Crone, N. E. (2000). Functional mapping with ECoG spectral analysis. *Advances in Neurology, 84*, 343–51.

Crone, N. E., Boatman, D., Gordon, B., & Hao, L. (2001a). Induced electrocorticographic gamma activity during auditory perception. *Clinical Neurophysiology, 112*, 565–82.

Crone, N. E., Hao, L., Hart, J., Boatman, D., Lesser, R. P., Irizarry, R., & Gordon, B. (2001b). Electrocorticographic gamma activity during word production in spoken and sign language. *Neurology, 57*, 2045–53.

Crone, N. E., Hart, J., Boatman, D., Lesser, R. P., & Gordon, B. (1994). Regional cortical activation during language and related tasks identified by direct cortical electrical recording. *Brain and Language, 47*, 466–8.

Crone, N. E., Korzeniewska, A., & Franaszczuk, P. J. (2011). Cortical γ responses: Searching high and low. *International Journal of Psychophysiology, 79*, 9–15.

Crone, N. E., Miglioretti, D. L., Gordon, B., Lesser, R. P. (1998a). Functional mapping of human sensorimotor cortex with electrocorticographic spectral analysis. II. Event-related synchronization in the gamma band. *Brain, 121*(Pt 12), 2301–15.

Crone, N. E., Miglioretti, D. L., Gordon, B., Sieracki, J. M., Wilson, M. T., Uematsu, S., & Lesser, R. P. (1998b). Functional mapping of human sensorimotor cortex with electrocorticographic spectral analysis. I. Alpha and beta event-related desynchronization. *Brain, 121*, 2271–99.

Crone, N. E., Sinai, A., & Korzeniewska, A. (2006). High-frequency gamma oscillations and human brain mapping with electrocorticography. *Progress in Brain Research, 159*, 275–95.

Cushing, H. (1909). A note upon the faradic stimulation of the postcentral gyrus in conscious patients.1. *Brain, 32*, 44–53.

Duff, M. C., & Brown-Schmidt, S. (2017). Hippocampal contributions to language use and processing. In: Hannula, D. E., & Duff, M. C. (Eds.), *The Hippocampus from Cells to Systems: Structure, Connectivity, and Functional Contributions to Memory and Flexible Cognition* (pp. 503–36). Springer International Publishing, Cham.

Edwards, E. (2005). High gamma activity in response to deviant auditory stimuli recorded directly from human cortex. *Journal of Neurophysiology, 94*, 4269–80.

Edwards, E., Nagarajan, S. S., Dalal, S. S., Canolty, R. T., Kirsch, H. E., Barbaro, N. M., & Knight, R. T. (2010). Spatiotemporal imaging of cortical activation during verb generation and picture naming. *NeuroImage, 50*, 291–301.

Feindel, W., Leblanc, R., de Almeida, A. N. (2009). Epilepsy surgery: Historical highlights 1909–2009. *Epilepsia, 50*, 131–51.

Flinker, A., Chang, E. F., Barbaro, N. M., Berger, M. S., & Knight, R. T. (2011). Sub-centimeter language organization in the human temporal lobe. *Brain and Language, 117*, 103–9.

Flinker, A., Chang, E. F., Kirsch, H. E., Barbaro, N. M., Crone, N. E., & Knight, R. T. (2010). Single-trial speech suppression of auditory cortex activity in humans. *Journal of Neuroscience, 30*, 16643–50.

Flinker, A., Korzeniewska, A., Shestyuk, A. Y., Franaszczuk, P. J., Dronkers, N. F., Knight, R. T., & Crone, N. E. (2015). Redefining the role of Broca's area in speech. *Proceedings of the National Academy of Sciences of the United States of America, 112*, 2871–5.

Foerster, O., & Altenburger, H. (1935). Elektrobiologische Vorgänge an der menschlichen Hirnrinde. *Deutsche Zeitschrift f Nervenheilkunde, 135*, 277–88.

Fried, I., Ojemann, G. A., & Fetz, E. E. (1981). Language-related potentials specific to human language cortex. *Science, 212*, 353–6.

Fukuda, M., Rothermel, R., Juhász, C., Nishida, M., Sood, S., & Asano, E. (2010). Cortical gamma-oscillations modulated by listening and overt repetition of phonemes. *NeuroImage, 49*, 2735–45.

Gibbs, F. A., Lennox, W. G., Gibbs, E. L. (1936). The electro-encephalogram in diagnosis and in localization of epileptic seizures. *Archives of Neurology & Psychiatry, 36*, 1225–35.

Gonzalez Martinez, J., Bulacio, J., Alexopoulos, A., Jehi, L., Bingaman, W., & Najm, I. (2013). Stereoelectroencephalography in the "difficult to localize" refractory focal epilepsy: Early experience from a North American epilepsy center. *Epilepsia, 54*, 323–30.

Greenlee, J. D. W., Jackson, A. W., Chen, F., Larson, C. R., Oya, H., Kawasaki, H., ... & Howard, M. A. III (2011). Human auditory cortical activation during self-vocalization. *PLoS One, 6*, e14744.

Halgren, E., Kaestner, E., Marinkovic, K., Cash, S. S., Wang, C., Schomer, D. L., ... & Ulbert, I. (2015). Laminar profile of spontaneous and evoked theta: Rhythmic modulation of cortical processing during word integration. *Neuropsychologia, 76*, 108–24.

Halgren, E., Wang, C., Schomer, D. L., Knake, S., Marinkovic, K., Wu, J., & Ulbert, I. (2006). Processing stages underlying word recognition in the anteroventral temporal lobe. *NeuroImage, 30*, 1401–13.

Hamamé, C. M., Alario, F. X., Llorens, A., Liégeois-Chauvel, C., Trébuchon-Da Fonseca, A. (2014). High frequency gamma activity in the left hippocampus predicts visual object naming performance. *Brain and Language, 135*, 104–14.

Hitzig, E. (1900). Hughlings Jackson and the cortical motor centres in the light of physiological research. *Brain, 23*, 545–81.

Holdgraf, C. R., de Heer, W., Pasley, B., Rieger, J., Crone, N., Lin, J. J., ... & Theunissen, F. E. (2016). Rapid tuning shifts in human auditory cortex enhance speech intelligibility. *Nature Communications, 7*, 13654.

Horsley, V. (1909). The Linacre Lecture on the function of the so-called motor area of the brain: Delivered to the Master and Fellows of St. John's College, Cambridge, May 6, 1909. *British Medical Journal, 2*, 121–32.

Howard, M. A. III, Volkov, I. O., Abbas, P. J., Damasio, H., Ollendieck, M. C., & Granner, M. A. (1996a). A chronic microelectrode investigation of the tonotopic organization of human auditory cortex. *Brain Research, 724*, 260–4.

Howard, M. A., Volkov, I. O., Granner, M. A., Damasio, H. M., Ollendieck, M. C., & Bakken, H. E. (1996b). A hybrid clinical-research depth electrode for acute and chronic in vivo microelectrode recording of human brain neurons. Technical note. *Journal of Neurosurgery, 84*, 129–32.

Jacobs, J., Manning, J. R., & Kahana, M. J. (2010). Response to Miller: "Broadband" vs. "high gamma" electrocorticographic signals. *Journal of Neuroscience, 30*(19).

Jafarpour, A., Piai, V., Lin, J. J., & Knight, R. T. (2017). Human hippocampal pre-activation predicts behavior. *Scientific Reports, 7*, 5959.

Jasper, H., & Kershman, J. (1941). Electroencephalographic classification of the epilepsies. *Archives of Neurology and Psychiatry, 45*, 903–43.

Jasper, H., Pertuisset, B., & Flanigin, H. (1951). EEG and cortical electrograms in patients with temporal lobe seizures. *AMA Archives of Neurology and Psychiatry, 65*, 272–90.

Jerbi, K., Freyermuth, S., Dalal, S., Kahane, P., Bertrand, O., Berthoz, A., & Lachaux, J. P. (2009). Saccade related gamma-band activity in intracerebral EEG: Dissociating neural from ocular muscle activity. *Brain Topography, 22*, 18–23.

Kajikawa, Y., & Schroeder, C. E. (2011). How local is the local field potential? *Neuron, 72*, 847–58.

Kovach, C. K., Tsuchiya, N., Kawasaki, H., Oya, H., Howard, M. A. III, & Adolphs, R. (2011). Manifestation of ocular-muscle EMG contamination in human intracranial recordings. *NeuroImage*, 54, 213–33.

Krause, F., & Thorek, M. (1912). *Surgery of the brain and spinal cord: based on personal experiences*. (Haubold, A. and Thorek, M., Trans). Rebman, New York, NY.

Lachaux, J. P., Rudrauf, D., & Kahane, P. (2003). Intracranial EEG and human brain mapping. *Journal of Physiology-Paris*, 97, 613–28.

Lega, B. C., Jacobs, J., & Kahana, M. (2012). Human hippocampal theta oscillations and the formation of episodic memories. *Hippocampus*, 22, 748–61.

Leuthardt, E. C., Gaona, C., Sharma, M., Szrama, N., Roland, J., Freudenberg, Z., ... & Schalk, G. (2011). Using the electrocorticographic speech network to control a brain-computer interface in humans. *Journal of Neural Engineering*, 8, 036004.

Liégeois-Chauvel, C., de Graaf, J. B., Laguitton, V., & Chauvel, P. (1999). Specialization of left auditory cortex for speech perception in man depends on temporal coding. *Cerebral Cortex*, 9, 484–96.

Liégeois-Chauvel, C., Lorenzi, C., Trébuchon, A., Régis, J., & Chauvel, P. (2004). Temporal envelope processing in the human left and right auditory cortices. *Cerebral Cortex*, 14, 731–40.

Liégeois-Chauvel, C., Musolino, A., & Chauvel, P. (1991). Localization of the primary auditory area in man. *Brain*, 114(Pt 1A), 139–51.

Llorens, A., Dubarry, A.-S., Trébuchon, A., Chauvel, P., Alario, F.-X., & Liégeois-Chauvel, C. (2016). Contextual modulation of hippocampal activity during picture naming. *Brain and Language*, 159, 92–101.

Llorens, A., Trébuchon, A., Liégeois-Chauvel, C., & Alario, F. X. (2011). Intra-cranial recordings of brain activity during language production. *Frontiers in Psychology*, 2, 375.

Lüders, H. O. (2008). *Textbook of Epilepsy Surgery*. Informa, London.

Martin, S., Brunner, P., Iturrate, I., del R. Millán, J., Schalk, G., Knight, R. T., & Pasley, B. N. (2016a). Word pair classification during imagined speech using direct brain recordings. *Scientific Reports*, 6, 25803.

Martin, S., Millán, J. D. R., Knight, R. T., & Pasley, B. N. (2016b). The use of intracranial recordings to decode human language: Challenges and opportunities. *Brain and Language*. doi: 10.1016/j.bandl.2016.06.003

McCarthy, G., Nobre, A. C., Bentin, S., & Spencer, D. D. (1995). Language-related field potentials in the anterior-medial temporal lobe: I. Intracranial distribution and neural generators. *Journal of Neuroscience*, 15, 1080–9.

Mesgarani, N., Cheung, C., Johnson, K., & Chang, E. F. (2014). Phonetic feature encoding in human superior temporal gyrus. *Science (New York, NY)*, 343, 1006–10.

Meyer, P., Mecklinger, A., Grunwald, T., Fell, J., Elger, C. E., & Friederici, A. D. (2005). Language processing within the human medial temporal lobe. *Hippocampus*, 15, 451–9.

Miller, K. J. (2010). Broadband spectral change: Evidence for a macroscale correlate of population firing rate? *Journal of Neuroscience*, 30, 6477–9.

Mukamel, R., Gelbard, H., Arieli, A., Hasson, U., Fried, I., & Malach, R. (2005). Coupling between neuronal firing, field potentials, and fMRI in human auditory cortex. *Science*, 309, 951–4.

Mullin, J. P., Sexton, D., Al-Omar, S., Bingaman, W., & Gonzalez Martinez, J. (2016). Outcomes of subdural grid electrode monitoring in the stereoelectroencephalography era. *World Neurosurgery*, 89, 255–8.

Nir, Y., Fisch, L., Mukamel, R., Gelbard-Sagiv, H., Arieli, A., Fried, I., & Malach, R. (2007). Coupling between neuronal firing rate, gamma LFP, and BOLD fMRI is related to interneuronal correlations. *Current Biology*, 17, 1275–85.

Nobre, A. C., & McCarthy, G. (1995). Language-related field potentials in the anterior-medial temporal lobe: II. Effects of word type and semantic priming. *Journal of Neuroscience, 15,* 1090–8.

Nourski, K. V., Reale, R. A., Oya, H., Kawasaki, H., Kovach, C. K., Chen, H., ... & Brugge, J. F. (2009). Temporal envelope of time-compressed speech represented in the human auditory cortex. *Journal of Neuroscience, 29,* 15564–74.

Ojemann, G., Ojemann, J., Lettich, E., & Berger, M. (1989). Cortical language localization in left, dominant hemisphere: an electrical stimulation mapping investigation in 117 patients. *Journal of Neurosurgery, 71,* 316–26.

Ojemann, G. A. (1987). Surgical therapy for medically intractable epilepsy. *Journal of Neuoscience, 66,* 489–99.

Pasley, B. N., David, S. V., Mesgarani, N., Flinker, A., Shamma, S. A., Crone, N. E., ... & Chang, E. F. (2012). Reconstructing speech from human auditory cortex. *PloS Biol, 10,* e1001251.

Pei, X., Leuthardt, E. C., Gaona, C. M., Brunner, P., Wolpaw, J. R., Schalk, G. (2011). Spatiotemporal dynamics of electrocorticographic high gamma activity during overt and covert word repetition. *NeuroImage, 54,* 2960–72.

Penfield, W., & Boldrey, E. (1937). Somatic motor and sensory representation in the cerebral cortex of man as studied by electrical stimulation. *Brain, 60,* 389–443.

Penfield, W., & Erickson, T. C. (1941). *Epilepsy and Cerebral Localization*. Charles C. Thomas, Oxford.

Penfield, W., & Roberts, L. (1959). *Speech and Brain Mechanisms*. Princeton University Press, Princeton, NJ.

Piai, V., Anderson, K. L., Lin, J. J., Dewar, C., Parvizi, J., Dronkers, N. F., & Knight, R. T. (2016). Direct brain recordings reveal hippocampal rhythm underpinnings of language processing. *Proceedings of the National Academy of Sciences of the United States of America, 113,* 11366–71.

Ray, S., Hsiao, S. S., Crone, N. E., Franaszczuk, P. J., & Niebur, E. (2008). Effect of stimulus intensity on the spike-local field potential relationship in the secondary somatosensory cortex. *Journal of Neuroscience, 28,* 7334–43.

Risinger, M. W., & Gumnit, R. J. (1995). Intracranial electrophysiologic studies. *Neuroimaging Clinics of North America, 5,* 559–73.

Rutishauser, U., Ross, I. B., Mamelak, A. N., & Schuman, E. M. (2010). Human memory strength is predicted by theta-frequency phase-locking of single neurons. *Nature, 464,* 903–7.

Sahin, N. T., Pinker, S., Cash, S. S., Schomer, D., & Halgren, E. (2009). Sequential processing of lexical, grammatical, and phonological information within Broca's area. *Science, 326,* 445–9.

Sanai, N., Mirzadeh, Z., & Berger, M. S. (2008). Functional outcome after language mapping for glioma resection. *New England Journal of Medicine, 358,* 18–27.

Talairach, J., David, M., & Tournoux, P. (1958). *L'exploration chirurgicale stéréotaxique du lobe temporal dans l'épilepsie temporale: Repérage anatomique stéréotaxique et technique chirurgicale*. Masson, Paris.

Towle, V. L., Yoon, H. A., Castelle, M., Edgar, J. C., Biassou, N. M., Frim, D. M., ... & Kohrman, M. H. (2008). ECoG gamma activity during a language task: differentiating expressive and receptive speech areas. *Brain, 131,* 2013–27.

Wellmer, J., Groeben, von der F., Klarmann, U., Weber, C., Elger, C. E., Urbach, H., ... & Lehe, von M. (2012). Risks and benefits of invasive epilepsy surgery workup with implanted subdural and depth electrodes. *Epilepsia, 53,* 1322–32.

Wernicke, C. (1874). *Symptomenkomplex: Eine psychologische Studie auf anatomischer Basis.* Cohn und Weigert, Breslau.

Widdess-Walsh, P., Jeha, L., Nair, D., Kotagal, P., Bingaman, W., Najm, I. (2007). Subdural electrode analysis in focal cortical dysplasia: predictors of surgical outcome. *Neurology*, 69, 660–7.

Wieser, H. G., & Elger, C. E. (2012). *Presurgical Evaluation of Epileptics: Basics, Techniques, Implications.* Springer-Verlag, Berlin.

Name Index

A

Abrams, D.A. 983
Abutalebi, J. 135
Adams, D.R. 447
Adelman, J.S. 51
Adolphs, R. 648
Adrian, E.D. 931–2
Aiken, S.J. 940
Akar, D. 739
Akhtar, N. 720
Alario, F.X. 351
Allen, J. 185
Altarriba, J. 218, 219–20
Altmann, G.T.M. 185
Amsel, B.D. 943
Anderson, A. 577
Anderson, A.J. 75
Andrews, M. 74
Andrews, S. 55
Anthony, J.L. 272
Argyropoulos, G.P. 499
Aslin, R.N. 705, 715
Austerweil, J.L. 186–7
Austin, J.L. 610

B

Baayen, R.H. 41, 918–19, 926–7
Bahrami, B. 77, 580
Bailey, P.J. 792
Bajo, T. 126
Bak, T.H. 77
Bargh, J.A. 583
Bar-Hillel, Y. 609
Baron-Cohen, S. 639
Baroni, M. 74
Barr, D.J. 634–5, 919, 927
Barry, C. 415
Barsalou, L.W. 86
Bartlett, F.C. 203, 616
Basirat, A. 773
Bastiaanse, R. 248
Bastos, A.M. 960
Bates, D.M. 918
Bates, E. 222, 723
Bates, T.C. 420
Battison, R. 261

Baus, C. 407
Beattie, G. 599
Becker, C.A. 83
Bekkering, H. 83, 84
Bélanger, N.N. 271, 273, 274
Bellugi, U. 259, 267, 275
Benjamin, A.S. 555
Benzing, L. 403
Bergelson, E. 719
Berger, H. 931, 992
Berndt, R.S. 248
Berwick, R.C. 768
Bever, T.G. 175
Bien, H. 348
Bierce, A. 614
Bine, H. 348
Bishop, D.V.M. 814, 815
Blasko, D.G. 33
Blomert, L. 790
Bloom, P. 720
Blumstein, S. 244
Bock, J.K. 484
Bock, K. 230, 242, 352, 386–7
Bollt, A. 708–9
Bölte, J. 347
Bonin, P. 403, 406, 407, 415
Bonnefon, J.F. 628
Booth, A. 720
Bootzin, R.R. 707
Borca, P. 992
Borning, L. 219
Bornkessel-Schlesewsky, I. 768
Bortfeld, H. 16, 20
Bosse, M.L. 795
Bosworth, R.G. 267
Bott, L. 627
Bowers, J.S. 339
Bowers, P.G. 789–90
Box, G.E.P. 986
Bradley, L. 417–18
Bradlow, A.R. 576
Branigan, H.P. 442, 448, 484, 576–7, 578
Bransford, J.D. 611–13, 614, 615, 618
Breheny, R. 628
Breier, J.I. 792
Breining, B. 352

Brennan, J. 202
Brennan, S.E. 632, 634
Brent, M.R. 715, 717, 724
Briscoe, T. 11
Broca, P. 109
Brothers, T. 131
Brown, A.S. 513
Brown, G.D.A. 51, 388–9
Brown-Schmidt, S. 443, 555, 561
Brown, W.S. 935
Bruni, E. 74
Bryant, G.A. 581–2
Bryant, P.E. 205, 417–18
Brysbaert, M. 51
Buchwald, A. 400–1, 413, 415–16
Burt, J.S. 408
Butterfield, S. 17
Butterworth, B. 248–9
Byrne, B. 786

C

Caarston, R. 624
Cai, Z.G. 106, 577
Cain, K. 205
Campos, J.J. 722
Canell, L. 415
Capek, C.M. 268
Caplan, D. 243, 245, 250–1, 699
Caramazza, A. 240, 246, 337, 354, 378n, 383, 402–3, 412, 413, 414
Carando, A. 230
Caravolas, M. 787
Carpenter, M. 720
Carreiras, M. 131, 263–4
Carroll, J.M. 789, 796
Carruthers, J. 408
Carter, D.M. 17
Casaponsa, A. 131, 132
Castles, A. 420
Cates, M.D. 272
Chan, A.H.D. 226
Chan, K.Y. 39
Chang, E.F. 1001–2
Chang, F. 186, 386–7, 388, 441, 447, 539
Chapman, R.M. 946
Chartrand, T.L. 583
Chater, N. 343
Chatterjee, M. 23
Chemla, E. 630
Chen, J.Y. 417
Chen, Q. 56, 351
Chen, T. 313
Cherng, R.J. 417
Chierchia, G. 629–30
Chomsky, N. 177, 242, 247, 768
Christiansen, M.H. 343, 697, 699–700, 701
Chu, K. 391

Chu, M. 595
Churchill, W. 969
Cichy, R.M. 961, 967
Cimiano, P. 577
Clark, A. 760
Clark, H.H. 552, 559, 612, 614, 632, 634, 637, 918, 920, 926
Clarke, A. 965
Cleland, A.A. 448, 576, 578–9
Cohen Priva, U. 186–7
Coleman, E.B. 918
Collina, S. 81
Coltheart, M. 55, 419
Connell, L. 83
Connine, C. 33
Content, A. 9
Conti-Ramsden, G. 795
Conway, C.M. 764
Cook, A.E. 617, 618
Cook, S.W. 595
Cop, U. 124, 130
Corbett, F. 152
Corbetta, M. 532
Corina, D.P. 261, 263, 267, 272–3
Cornelissen, P.L. 961
Costa, A. 351, 354, 378n, 407, 464–6, 469, 473
Coulson, S. 600
Cowles, H.W. 445
Cox, F. 678
Coyle, J.M. 585
Crone, N.E. 997
Csibra, G. 741
Culbertson, J. 908
Cunillera, T. 12, 704
Cutler, A. 6, 7, 8–9, 10, 11, 17, 18, 22, 31, 42

D

Dale, R. 857
Damasio, A.R. 648–9
Damian, M.F. 339, 405, 406–7, 415
Davidson, D.J. 918
Davis, C. 56, 57, 251
Davis, M.H. 318
Dawson, C. 708
Dawson, G.D. 934
Deblinger-Tangi, R. 743
de Boer, B. 853, 856–7
De Bree, E. 701
Declercq, M. 230
Dediu, D. 857
Deecke, L. 934
DeFries, J.C. 801
de Gelder, B. 12, 18
de Groot, A.M.B. 218
de Heer, W.A. 984
DeJesus, J. 747
De Klerk, M. 701

Delery, D.B. 724
del Giudice, A.A. 272, 853
Dell, G.S. 186, 341, 344, 346, 349, 352, 375, 382, 383, 385, 388, 439, 447, 510, 513, 518, 519
Demberg, V. 182–3
Demuth, K. 677, 678, 679, 681, 683
de Neys, W. 628
DePaolis, R.A. 718–19
De Simone, F. 81
Desmet, T. 230
de Souza, R.A. 230
de Swart, H. 907
Dick, A.S. 601
Dickens, C. 183
Dickey, M.W. 244
Diermeier, D. 582
Diesendruck, G. 739, 743
Dijksterhuis, A. 583
Dijkstra, T. 98–9, 122, 125, 126, 127, 128, 131, 221
Ding, N. 23
Dingemanse, M. 856
Dirix, N. 124
Dohmes, P. 347
Dommergues, J.Y. 7
Donchin, E. 936
Drieghe, D. 124, 128, 129
Du Bois, J.W. 583
Duff, F.J. 788
Dufor, O. 409, 412
Dumay, N. 9
Duñabeitia, J.A. 131
Dunbar, R.I.M. 848
Dunlop Fisher, R. 717
Dupoux, E. 9
Durlik, J. 126
Dussias, P.E. 229
Duyck, W. 124, 128, 129, 221

E
Edwards, R. 726
Eimas, P.D. 720
Ellis, A.W. 415
Elman, J.L. 35–6, 37, 87, 173
Elston-Güttler, K.E. 220
Elston-Güttler, K.E. 129
Embrick, D. 43
Emmorey, K. 261, 262, 263, 267
Endress, A.D. 775
Erickson, L.C. 695
Eryilmaz, K. 856–7
Everett, D.L. 739

F
Fadiga, L. 312–13
Falconer, C. 415–16
Fang, X. 103
Farkas, I. 135

Fay, N. 857, 904–5
Fayol, M. 403, 406
Fazio, P. 323
Fedorenko, E. 739
Fernald, A. 726
Fernandes, T. 694, 695
Fernández, E.M. 227, 229, 230
Ferreira, F. 175, 441, 443, 618
Ferreira, V.S. 445, 580
Ferry, A.L. 721, 772
Ferstl, E.C. 207, 208
Fikkert, P. 680–1
Finkbeiner, M. 470
Firato, C.E. 445
Fischer-Baum, S. 412, 414
Fischler, I. 120
Fisher, C. 20
Fitch, W.T. 768
Flinker, A. 999, 1001
Floccia, C. 21
Fodor, J.A. 449, 646
Fodor, J.D. 184
Foltz, A. 577
Forrest, L.B. 534
Forster, K.I. 32, 35, 57
Fowler, C.A. 313
Foygel, D. 510
Francis, D.J. 272
Frank, M.C. 707, 739–40
Frank, S.L. 183
Frankland, S.M. 983
Frauenfelder, U.H. 9, 77
Fraundorf, S.H. 561
Frazier, L. 17
Frege, G. 610
Frenck-Mestre, C. 132, 228–9
Fricke, S. 802
Friederici, A.D. 531, 725, 774
Friedman, N. 246
Friedrich, M. 725
Friel, B.M. 122
Friend, A. 801
Frijda, N.H. 648, 650
Frost, R. 50, 700, 707
Fusaroli, R. 580

G
Galaburda, A.M. 799
Galantucci, B. 313, 314, 851, 853, 855, 904
Ganger, J. 715, 724
Garbin, G. 470
Garnham, A. 199, 614, 617
Garrett, M.F. 443, 483–4
Garrod, S. 186, 313, 448, 484–5, 538, 558, 573, 577, 614, 904–5
Gaskell, M.G. 101–2
Gaspers, J. 577

Gelman, S.A. 721, 743
Gentner, D. 267, 745
Gergely, G. 741
Gerken, L. 682, 683–4, 698, 699, 702, 708–9
Gernsbacher, M.A. 619
Gerretsen, P. 790
Gerrig, R.J. 443, 558–9, 637
Gervain, J. 772–3
Gervais, M.M. 581–2
Geurts, B. 630
Gibbons, R. 583
Gibbs, R.W. 636–7, 638
Gibson, E. 177, 707, 739
Gillard, A. 16
Giora, R. 636–7
Gleitman, L.R. 534, 535–6, 537
Glenberg, A.M. 617
Gogate, L.J. 720, 721, 724
Goldfield, B.A. 724
Goldinger, S.D. 576
Goldrick, M. 352, 374, 383, 391
Goldsmith, H.H. 619
Gómez, R.L. 696, 698, 699, 700, 701, 707, 708
Gonzales, A.L. 583
Gonzales, K. 699, 708
Gonzalez Andino, S.L. 967
Gonzalez, C. 220
Goodglass, H. 245
Gordon, J.K. 388
Gordon, P.C. 177
Goulandris, N.K. 421
Graesser, A.C. 200, 202, 614, 617, 619
Graf Estes, K. 692–3, 695
Grainger, J. 55, 127, 221
Grande, M. 499
Green, D.W. 135
Greenberg, J.H. 738
Greene, J.D. 983
Gregory, S.W. 584
Grice, P.H. 610, 612–13, 623–4, 625–6, 629, 636–7, 640
Griffin, Z.M. 242, 386–7, 443
Griffiths, T.L. 73, 906
Grodzinsky, Y. 242, 246, 249
Grootjen, F. 98–9, 122
Grosjean, F. 217
Grossi, G. 124
Grosvald, M. 261, 262
Guajardo, J.J. 722
Gunter, T.C. 129, 600, 944
Guo, T. 472
Gupta, P. 388
Gutiérrez, E. 261, 264

H

Habets, B. 602–3
Hagoort, P. 110, 125, 208, 486, 494–6, 500, 501

Hahne, A. 531
Hale, J. 182
Hämäläinen, J.A. 793
Hamamé, C.M. 999
Hancock, J.T. 583
Hanulíková, A. 17
Harnishfeger, K.K. 86
Harrington, J. 16
Harris, L. 702
Harris, M. 724
Hartsuiker, R.J. 128, 129, 230, 518
Hauk, O. 965, 966
Haviland, S.E. 612, 614
Hayne, H. 725, 728
Helder, A. 208
Heller, D. 554, 555, 560
Herbert, J.S. 725, 728
Heredia, R. 218
Hernández, A.E. 219, 224, 225
Hespos, S.J. 721
Hewitt, G.P. 850
Heyman, G.D. 743
Hickok, G. 312, 320
Hillis, A. 246, 401, 412
Hillyard, S.A. 936
Hinton, G.E. 985
Hockett, C. 175, 852, 903
Hoenig, K. 84
Hoffman, P. 152
Hogben, J.H. 794
Holle, H. 600
Holler, J. 602
Holmes, V.M. 408
Honda, E. 847
Horn, L. 626
Horton, W.S. 555, 558–9, 576
Hoshino, D. 126
Hoversten, L.J. 131
Howard, D. 249, 513–14
Hsu, H.J. 701–2
Hsu, N.S. 80
Huang, Y.T. 628
Huettig, F. 185
Hulme, C. 388–9, 787, 788, 790
Hung, Y.-C. 202
Hunt, J.N. 934
Huth, A.G. 87, 984
Hwang, H. 537

I

Iacoboni, M. 315
Ida, K. 219
Ikeda, K. 937
Imai, M. 745
Indefrey, P. 402, 486, 494–6, 497, 499, 500
Ireland, M.E. 581
Isaacs, E.A. 559

J

Jabès, A. 725–6
Jackendoff, R. 531–2, 655
Jackson, G.M. 468, 470
Jacovina, M.E. 443
Jaeger, T.F. 185, 342, 447
Jakobson, R. 677, 718
Janssen, N. 348
Janssen, R. 857
Janyan, A. 535
Jastrzembski, J.E. 100
Jeschenniak, J.D. 338, 354–5
John, E.R. 935
Johns, B.T. 74
Johnson, E.K. 693, 694
Johnson, M. 679
Johnson-Laird, P.N. 617
Johnsrude, I.S. 318
Jones, M. 74, 78
Juhola, M. 375
Junge, C. 717
Jusczyk, P.W. 719
Just, M.A. 208

K

Kabdebon, C. 774
Kaiser, E. 537
Kamhi, A. 724
Kamp, H. 609
Kandel, S. 413, 418
Kaplan, D. 609
Karuza, E.A. 703
Kaschak, M.P. 585
Kawamoto, A.H. 184
Kean, M.L. 245
Kearns, R.K. 9
Keller, F. 182–3
Kelly, S.D. 599–600, 602–3
Kelter, S. 576
Kemmerer, D. 83
Kempen, G. 485
Kennison, S.M. 122
Keren-Portnoy, T. 717, 718–19
Kerkhoff, A. 701
Kerkhofs, R. 126
Keysar, B. 555, 633–4
Kilborn, K. 224
Kim, D. 12–13
Kim, M. 576
King, T. 827
Kintsch, E. 204
Kintsch, W. 199, 201, 202, 203, 204, 615, 616
Kinzler, K.D. 747
Kirby, S. 852, 853, 856, 900, 902, 903, 905
Kita, S. 595, 598
Kittleson, M.M. 692
Kittredge, A.K. 338, 344, 388

Klein, G. 623, 625
Kleinman, D. 580
Klima, E. 259, 275
Kline, M.A. 581–2
Knapp, H.P. 261
Knott, J.R. 934
Kohler, E. 309
Kolinsky, R. 694
Kolk, H.H.J. 518
Konopka, A.E. 443
Kopp, S. 599
Kornhuber, H.H. 934
Kostov, K. 535
Kotz, S.A. 129
Kousta, S.T. 78
Kovacs, A.M. 775
Kraljic, T. 580
Kraus, N. 937
Krauss, R.M. 583
Krieger-Redwood, K. 323
Kriegeskorte, N. 961
Kroll, J.F. 129, 218, 219
Kronmüller, E. 634–5
Kroos, C. 853, 904
Kubus, O. 270
Kuperberg, G.R. 185
Kutas, M. 206, 936

L

Laganaro, M. 402, 407
La Heij, W. 463
Lahiri, A. 350, 356
Laine, M. 12, 375
Lakin, J.L. 583
Lakusta, L. 698, 699
Landau, B. 531–2
Landerl, K. 787
Langston, M.C. 617
Lany, J. 698, 700–1
Lapointe, S. 245
Lashley, K.S. 414
Lauro, J. 130
Lavric, A. 59
Law, F. II 726
Law, J. 821
Lazarus, R.S. 648
Lebois, L.A. 83
Lee, J. 904–5
Lee, M. 247
Lemhöfer, K. 122
Lenzen, D. 857
Lepic, R. 857
Leppänen, P.H. 793
Lerner, Y. 980
Lervåg, A. 790
Letts, C. 827
Lev-Ari, S. 584

NAME INDEX

Levelt, W.J.M.   43, 185, 335–6, 338, 353–4, 375, 378, 442, 482–4, 513, 528, 576
Levinson, S.C.   609, 613, 626, 627
Levy, B.J.   473
Lewandowski, J.   855
Lewis, D.   550
Lewis, S.S.   58
Lew-Williams, C.   692–3
Li, P.   135, 226
Libben, M.R.   221
Liberman, A.M.   272, 307
Liégeois-Chauvel, C.   996
Lindblom, B.   19
Lindemann, O.   83
Lipka, K.   409
Litman, D.   580
Little, H.   856–7
Liu, D.   740
Liu, H.   224
Locke, A.   821
Loebell, H.   230
Loff, A.   796
Lorch, R.F. Jr.   618
Love, T.   244
Lovegrove, W.   794
Luce, P.A.   34, 263
Luciano, M.   420
Luka, B.J.   942
Lum, J.A.   795
Lupker, S.J.   219
Lupyan, G.   857
Lynott, D.   83

M

MacDonald, M.C.   176, 445, 450
Macizo, P.   126
MacLarnon, A.   850
MacLeod, C.   81
Macleod, T.   904–5
MacWhinney, B.   222, 225, 226, 231, 529
Maddux, W.W.   582
Magliano, J.P.   200
Magnusdottir, S.   251
Maia, J.M.   229
Majorano, M.   718
Mak, W.M.   202
Malisz, Z.   599
Mandler, J.M.   531
Manson, J.H.   581–2
Marcus, G.F.   771–2
Markow, D.B.   742
Marr, D.   182, 617
Marshall, C.M.   792
Marshall, C.R.   552, 789
Marslen-Wilson, W.D.   33, 37, 101–2
Martin, C.D.   351
Martin, F.   794
Martín, M.C.   126
Martin, N.   382
Martínez, I.   850
Martinez-Beck, I.   739
Mason, R.A.   208
Massaro, D.   313
Mathews, A.   81
Matthews, B.H.C.   931–2
Mattys, S.L.   11, 12, 14, 16, 18–19
Maughan, B.   784
Mayberry, R.I.   272
Maye, J.   696, 700, 708
Mazzarella, D.   629
McBride-Chang, C.   788
McCarthy, G.   996
McCarthy, R.   248
McClelland, J.L.   35–6, 37, 385
McCullough, E.   683
McCune, L.   718, 723, 724
McDonald, J.L.   224
McGillion, M.M.   718
McIntosh, B.   682
McKean, C.   826
McKoon, G.   613–14, 616
McNamara, D.   202, 204
McNealy, K.   704
McNeill, D.   593
McNeish, D.   928
McQueen, J.M.   10, 11, 12, 16, 17, 38, 42
Mehler, J.   8–9
Meister, I.G.   317
Melhorn, J.F.   12
Menenti, L.   501, 579
Menyuk, P.   723
Mesgarani, N.   1002
Messaoud-Galusi, S.   791
Meteyard, L.   77
Metzing, C.   634
Meunier, C.   9
Meyer, A.S.   185, 375, 378, 443, 447
Meyer, P.   996
Miceli, G.   247, 248, 413, 414
Middleton, E.L.   518
Midgley, K.J.   124
Miles, K.   678
Miller, G.A.   177, 179
Mintz, T.H.   696, 697
Miozzo, M.   378n, 412, 415
Mirković, J.   185
Mirman, D.   56, 351
Misra, M.   472
Misyak, J.B.   697, 699–700
Mitchell, D.C.   176, 181
Mitchell, T.M.   984
Mitterer, H.   17
Moisik, S.R.   857
Moll, K.   787, 796
Momma, S.   443

Monaghan, P. 697, 707
Monsell, S. 408, 409, 513
Montague, R. 609, 613
Morbury, C. 78
Moreno, E.M. 220
Morford, J.P. 270
Morris, C.W. 609
Morsella, E. 415
Moscoso Del Prado Martin, F. 583
Moseley, R.L. 966
Moushegian, G. 934
Mueller, J.L. 773
Mundy, I.R. 789
Muszyński, M. 126
Myachykov, A. 534–5, 536–7, 538

N
Näätänen, R. 940
Nadel, L. 707
Nadig, A.S. 555
Nakayama, M. 219
Namboodiripad, S. 857
Nelson, C.A. 725–6
Nespoulous, J.L. 246
Neville, H.J. 231, 945
Nevins, A. 16
Newman, R.S. 12, 16, 17, 19
Newport, E.L. 705, 715
Ng, S. 220
Nichols, T.E. 922
Nicoladis, E. 720
Nieuwland, M.S. 944
Nittrouer, S. 792
Noles, N.S. 721
Norbury, C.F. 108, 821
Norman, D.A. 414
Norris, D. 6, 8–9, 10, 11, 18, 37, 38, 42
Noveck, I.A. 627, 636
Novick, J.M. 111
Nozari, N. 352, 512–13

O
Oakhill, J.V. 205
Oberlander, J. 904–5
Obermeier, C. 944
O'Brien, E.J. 617, 618
Ogawa, S. 975
Okanoya, K. 847
Olson, R.K. 801
Oppenheim, G.M. 341, 344, 388, 513–14
Oppermann, F. 355
O'Seaghdha, P.G. 439
Osterhout, L. 232
Ostrin, R. 246
Otake, T. 22
Özçalişkan, S. 598
Özdemir, R. 43
Özyürek, A. 598, 600

P
Padden, C. 853
Pakulak, E. 945
Pandit, R. 224
Panksepp, J. 648
Papafragou, A. 746
Papagno, C. 383
Paradis, M. 217
Pardo, J.S. 583, 923
Parisien, C. 555
Pasley, B.N. 1002
Paulmann, S. 129
Pearlmutter, N.J. 450
Pecher, D. 83
Peelle, J.E. 321
Peereman, R. 403, 406
Peeters, D. 221
Pelucchi, B. 692
Penfield, W. 993
Pennebaker, J.W. 581, 583
Pennington, B.E. 796
Perfetti, C. 103, 202
Perlman, M. 857
Perret, C. 402, 407, 418
Peterson, C.C. 740
Philipp, A.M. 471
Piaget, J. 725, 741
Piai, V. 997
Pickering, M.J. 186, 313, 442, 448, 484–5, 558, 573, 576, 577, 578–9
Picton, T.W. 940
Piñar, P. 274, 275
Pinto, J.P. 726
Pisoni, D.B. 34, 263
Plante, E. 702–3
Poeppel, D. 43
Pokhoday, M. 534–5
Ponari, M. 78
Potts, C. 630–1
Pouscoulous, N. 630
Preece, T. 388–9
Prentice, J.L. 532–3
Pringle-Morgan, W. 785
Prior, A.N. 609
Pulvermüller, F. 312–13, 314, 966
Purcell, J.J. 401, 409
Pylkkanen, L. 208, 966
Pynte, J. 228

Q
Qu, Q.Q. 405, 406–7, 415
Quinn, P.C. 720

R
Raaijmakers, J.G.W. 83, 926
Rabagliati, H. 108, 738
Race, D.S. 251
Ramachandran, V.S. 308

Ramscar, M. 41
Ramus, F. 789, 796
Ransdell, S.E. 120
Rapp, B. 352, 374, 383, 400–1, 402, 403, 409, 412, 413, 414, 415
Ratcliff, R. 613–14
Rayner, K. 274
Reali, F. 906
Reber, A.S. 755–6, 762
Recchia, G. 78
Reed, K.D. 447
Regan, D. 933
Reichenbach, H. 609
Reilly, S. 815
Reyes, I. 225
Reznick, J.S. 724
Rhodes, T. 853, 904
Richardson, J. 702
Riffel, B. 352
Rizzolatti, G. 308, 309
Roach, N.W. 794
Roberts, G. 853, 855, 856, 857, 904
Robertson, R.R.W. 619
Robinson, C.W. 721
Rodd, J.M. 59, 81, 82, 98, 101–2, 110
Rodríguez-Fornells, A. 12, 704
Roelofs, A. 43, 375
Rohde, D.L.T. 388
Rohrer, C. 609
Romani, C. 349, 421
Rommetveit, R. 533
Rosen, S. 16, 789
Rosenkrantz, S.L. 720
Roug-Hellichius, L. 724
Roux, S. 415, 416
Rovee-Collier, C. 724
Rubenstein, H. 58
Rubenstein, M.A. 58
Rueschemeyer, S.A. 83, 84
Rumelhart, D.E. 198, 385, 414
Rumiati, R.I. 83
Ruml, W. 383
Runnqvist, E. 473–4
Russell, B. 610
Ryskin, R.A. 555

S
Sadat, J. 351
Saffran, E.M. 247, 382
Saffran, J.R. 692, 698, 700–1, 705, 709, 715, 771
Sagarra, N. 229
Sage, K. 415
Sagi, E. 582
St.Clair, M.C. 697
Salminen, H.K. 793
Sanders, L.D. 704
Sanders, T.J.M. 202

Sanford, A.J. 614
Sanford, T. 618
Santesteban, M. 469
Schaeken, W. 628
Scheepers, C. 538
Schepens, J. 98–9, 122
Scherer, K.R. 648
Schnur, T.T. 354
Schoffelen, J.M. 960
Schoot, L. 501
Schouwstra, M. 907–8
Schriefers, H. 125, 355, 378
Schuchard, J. 518
Schumacher, P.B. 202
Schwanenflugel, P.J. 86
Schwartz, A.I. 129, 130
Schwartz, M.F. 153, 246, 320, 341, 382, 383, 385, 388, 510–11, 513, 515–16, 518, 519, 521
Scott, D. 609
Scott, S.K. 312, 313, 319
Searle, J. 610
Sebastián-Gallés, N. 9, 704
Sedivy, J.C. 555
Segaert, K. 501, 579
Seger, C.A. 762
Segui, J. 7, 9
Seidenberg, M.S. 106, 185
Seidl, A. 693, 694
Selimis, S. 746
Sevald, C.A. 352
Shallice, T. 985
Shannon, C.E. 182
Shaoul, C. 41
Shapiro, L.R. 796
Shatz, M. 739
Shipton, H. 931
Sholl, A. 218
Shovelton, H. 599
Shtyrov, Y. 534–5
Shu, H. 788
Shutts, K. 747
Siegleman, N. 700
Siew, C.S.Q. 39–40
Silbert, L.J. 579
Silverman, R.D. 928
Simanova, I. 983
Simon, H.A. 182
Simon, J.Z. 23
Simon, K.N. 707
Sinaceur, M. 582
Siskind, J.M. 717
Siu, Y. 580
Skipper, J. 87, 601, 603
Skoruppa, K. 16
Skottun, B.C. 794
Slaghuis, W. 794
Slobin, D.I. 449, 739

Sloutsky, V.M. 720, 721
Smith, K. 906
Smith, L.B. 720, 722, 741
Smith, M. 443
Snedeker, J. 104, 628
Snider, N.E. 447
Snoeren, N.D. 131
Snowling, M.J. 421, 786, 787, 792, 796, 828
Sohail, J. 694
Solity, J. 796
Song, J.Y. 678
Songer, N.B. 204
Spector, B. 630
Speer, N.K. 207
Spelke, E.S. 740, 747
Spence, C. 535
Sperber, D. 610, 637
Spinelli, E. 22, 413
Spotorno, N. 636, 638
Srinivasan, M. 104, 738
Staeren, N. 983
Stafura, J. 103, 202
Stalnaker, R.C. 550, 632
Stapleton, L.M. 928
Steinhauer, K. 232
Stenneken, P. 577
Stevenson, S. 555
Stokoe, W. 261
Storkel, H.L. 103
Stowe, R.W. 86
Straube, B. 601, 603
Strawson, P.F. 610
Strijkers, K. 407, 439–40
Sudre, G. 967
Sullivan, M.P. 352
Suppes, A. 583
Sutton, S. 935
Swaab, R. 582
Swaab, T.Y. 131
Swets, B. 443
Swingley, D. 719, 726
Swinney, D. 244
Szewczyk, J. 126

T
Tabossi, P. 81
Tainturier, M.J. 795
Talairach, J. 486
Tallal, P. 792
Talmy, L. 596
Tamariz, M. 902
Tanenhaus, M.K. 173, 244
Tanenhaus, M.K. 595
Tanner, D. 232, 945
Tate, H. 408
Taylor, C.L. 826
Teinonen, T. 772

Ten Brinke, S. 125
Tenenbaum, J.B. 707
Theisen, C.A. 905
Theisen-White, C. 905
Thiele, K. 577
Thierry, G. 126, 270
Thiessen, E.D. 694, 695
Thompson, C.L. 247
Thompson, H.E. 153
Thompson, R.L. 266, 267
Thompson-Schill, S.L. 81
Thornton, R. 176
Thorsen, J. 716
Thothathiri, W. 250–1
Tikkala, A. 375
Tincoff, R. 719
Tisdale, J. 388
Titone, D.A. 33, 221
Tokowicz, N. 226, 231
Tokura, H. 20
Tomasello, M. 450, 655–6, 720
Tomasino, B. 83
Tomblin, J.B. 701, 821
Tomlin, R.S. 534, 536–7
Torgesen, J.K. 272
Torkildsen, J.V.K. 726
Toro, J.M. 704
Tournoux, P. 486
Trabasso, T. 617
Tran, N.K. 74
Traxler, C.B. 274
Traxler, M.J. 131
Treiman, R. 418, 786–7
Tremblay, A. 22, 413
Tullis, J. 555
Turner, E.A. 533
Turvey, M.T. 313
Tyler, L.K. 250–1
Tyler, M.D. 693

U
Uddén, J. 762
Ullman, M.T. 795

V
Vaessen, A. 790
Vaid, J. 132, 224
Valdois, S. 418, 795
van Ackeren, M.J. 965
van Assche, E.V. 128, 129, 130
van Dam, W.O. 83, 84
van den Bos, E. 697
van den Broek, P. 617
van der Lely, H.K. 789
van der Schoot, M. 108
van Dijk, M. 84
van Dijk, T.A. 199, 201, 203, 615

van Galen, G.P. 402
van Hell, J.G. 122, 127
van Heuven, W.J.B. 123, 124, 125, 127
Van Jaarsveld, H. 125
van Kesteren, R. 132
van Petten, C. 942
van Zonneveld, R. 248
Ventura, P. 694
Verhoef, K. 470, 853, 856
Verhoef, T. 857, 904
Vigliocco, G. 76, 77, 78, 266
Vihman, M.M. 718–19, 723, 724
Vihman, M.V. 717
Vinson, D.P. 76, 266
Visser, M.E.J. 148
Vitevitch, M.S. 39–40, 352
von Cramon, D. 207
Vousden, J.I. 388, 389
Vroomen, J. 18
Vygotsky, L.S. 741

W

Wagner, J.B. 773
Wagner, P. 599
Wagner, R.K. 272
Walter, V.J. 930
Walter, W.G. 930, 931, 934, 936
Wang, C. 405–6
Wang, Y. 468
Warburg, O. 623–4, 625
Ward, A. 580
Warker, J.A. 388
Warrington, E.K. 153
Warrington, E.M. 248
Wartenburger, I. 231
Waters, G.S. 245, 699
Waxman, S.R. 719–20, 721, 725, 742
Weatherholtz, K. 584
Weber, A. 22
Weber-Fox, C. 231
Webster, S. 584
Wehbe, L. 984
Weiss, D.J. 708
Wellman, H.M. 740
Welsh, A. 33
Welvaert, M. 128
Wernicke, C. 992
Westbury, C. 720
Westfall, J. 922
Wheat, K.L. 963

Wheeldon, L.R. 352, 443, 513
White, L. 12, 16
White, S. 796
Wicha, N.Y. 220
Wijnen, F. 701
Wild, C.J. 319
Williams, J.M.G. 81
Willits, J. 41
Wilson, B. 767
Wilson, D. 610, 637
Wilson, S.M. 314, 315
Winter, B. 857
Wittgenstein, J. 84
Wodniecka, Z. 126
Wolf, M. 789–90
Woll, B. 266
Wong, P.C. 321
Wonnacott, E. 906
Woodhead, Z.V. 964
Woodward, A.L. 722
Wu, S. 788
Wu, Y. 600
Wu, Y.J. 270

X

Xiang, H.D. 496
Xu, J. 601

Y

Yap, D.F. 600
Yarkoni, T. 56, 922, 977, 979
Yee, E. 81
Yu, C. 722
Yuen, I. 678
Yvert, G. 965

Z

Zacks, J.M. 207, 979
Zajonc, R.B. 651
Zambrana, I.M. 828
Zeelenberg, R. 83
Zhang, Q. 404, 405–7
Zhao, M. 945
Zhao, X. 135
Zhou, L. 788
Zhu, X.B. 405
Ziegler, J.C. 791
Zurif, E.B. 240, 244
Zwaan, R.A. 85, 200, 201, 617
Zwitserlood, P. 347

Subject Index

A

aberrant neuronal migration 877
absence of belief 550
abstraction effect in statistical learning 707
abstract letter identity hypothesis 49, 411–12
abstract meanings 78
abstract syntactic learning 181
abstract words 73, 88
accent 747
   phrasal 8
   pitch 18
accessibility effects in grammatical encoding 444–5
acoustic cues 12–13, 19
acoustic-phonetic information in spoken word recognition 33, 34, 36
acquired distinctiveness 716
acquisition
   bilingualism 218
   of novel phonotactic constraints 388
   see also age of acquisition
action-compatibility effect (ACE) 202
action comprehension task 323
Action Generation Hypothesis 595
Action Naming Test 247
action words 136
activation 18, 294
activation likelihood estimation (ALE) method 766
activation patterns 373
activation-verification model 54
active/passive voice alternation 230–1
additive factors logic 415
adjacent dependencies
   artificial grammar learning (AGL) 771, 772, 773
   statistical learning 699–701, 705–6
advance organizers 205
adverb modification 175–6
affective language comprehension (ALC) model 652–65
   communicative intention 657
   inferring bonus meaning 657
   inferring speaker's referential intention 655
   inferring speaker's social intention 656
   inferring speaker's stance 655–6
   rude verbal insult, comprehension of 653–5
      input: multimodal, composite signs 653
      interpreting speaker's communicative move 655
      recognizing/parsing signs presented by speaker 653, 655
affective stance 656, 659
affordances 595, 857
Africa 675
African Gray parrot 848
age of acquisition
   bilingualism 218, 231–2
   first word learning 716
   orthographic representations 50–2
   sign languages and deaf populations 266
   spelling/writing 401
   spoken word production 338
   visual word recognition 61
   writing and speaking 406–7
age-related decline in speech perception and production 320–1
age-related differences in statistical learning 702, 706–8
agrammatism 245–9, 292
   expressive 249
AI systems 210
algebraic rules in artificial grammar learning (AGL) 771, 772–3
alignment during interaction 573–86
   at different levels 575–8
   channels of alignment 573–4
   and communicative success 580–2
   compensatory proactive link 585
   integration between levels 578–80
   interactive 557–8
   linguistic alignment 581–2
   linguistic mechanisms 575–85
   modulatory routes 582–4
   non-linguistic alignment 582
   semantics 577–8
   situation-model alignment 581
   social accounts 582–5
   sound 575–6
   strategic routes 584–5
   syntactic alignment 574, 576–7, 579
allophones 906
allophonic cues 21, 22
allophonic theory 791
allophony 17, 23
alpha band 957, 995, 997

SUBJECT INDEX

Al-Sayyid Bedouin Sign Language (ABSL) 852–3, 879, 903–4
alternative splicing 874
Alzheimer's disease 77, 243
ambiguity 6, 19
   advantage 99–102
   disadvantage 102
   grammatical encoding 445–6
   lexico-semantic 79, 88, 486, 494
   localist approach 99–101
   pragmatics and inference 616
   quantifier scope 184
   reordered access model of ambiguity resolution 106
   resolution, innate mechanism vs. experience-driven accounts of 175–6
   resolution, reordered access model of 106
   sentence comprehension 175–6, 178–9, 181, 184
   syntactic 171, 173–5, 483–4, 496
   word-class 486
   see also lexical ambiguity
American English
   ambiguity 106–7
   first word learning 715, 716, 718, 724
   segmentation of speech 20, 21
American Sign Language (ASL) 259–62, 264, 266–8, 270, 272–3, 275, 444, 855
amodal approach to lexico-semantics 72, 75, 76, 77–9
amodal areas: anterior temporal lobe (ATL) 965–6
analysis-by-synthesis 308
analysis of variance (ANOVA) 918
anaphora 550
anaphoric expressions 611–12
animacy 224
animal models
   apes 842–5
   bats 845, 848, 858, 866
   cetaceans 848
   dolphins 845, 866
   elephants 845, 848
   genetics 880–3
      mice: stuttering 882–3
      songbirds: vocal learning 881–2
   gibbon song 845
   mice 866, 882–4
   pinnipeds 848
   sea lions 848
   seals 845, 848
   vervet monkeys 909
   walruses 848
   whales 845, 846
   see also birds
anterior negativities (AN) 938, 942
anterior temporal lobe (ATL) 153, 155–6, 966
   as graded hub 147–8
   heteromodal semantic hub 146–7
   input processing deficits 149–50
   semantic deficit 145–9

anti-Gricean turn 629–31
apes 842–5
aphasia 205–6, 264, 815
   artificial grammar learning 767
   Broca's aphasia 241–2, 244, 245, 320
   conduction aphasia 241, 296–7, 301
   connectionist principles and speech production 382
   mixed transcortical or global aphasia 151
   semantic aphasia 144–5, 151–3, 154, 156
   speech errors 338, 344, 347, 349, 380
   speech perception and production 299, 312, 323
   transcortical sensory aphasia 151, 154
   Wernicke's aphasia (WA) 144, 150, 153, 156, 244, 320
   word production and related processes 350, 352, 506–22
      conflict model of monitoring 512–13
      dark side model 513–14
      interactive two-step model of naming 507–8
      learning and monitoring 514–18
      models 508–11
   see also sentence level aphasia
apparent diffusion coefficient (ADC) 251
applied educational research 204–5
apraxia of speech in childhood 828
Arabic 42
arbitrary relations 722
arbitrary symbols 904–5
argumentation 208
arousal states 136
articulator 528
articulatory imprecision 19
articulatory/motoric processes 372
artificial grammar learning (AGL) 755–76
   abstract visual shapes 757
   auditory paradigms 757
   BROCANTO grammar 758, 760, 769, 771
   consonant-vowel (CV) syllables 757
   context-sensitive grammars 760
   elements of 757
   explicit learning 762–4, 765
   finite state grammars (FSGs) 758, 760, 769
   formal grammars 759
   hybrid languages 760
   implicit learning 762–4, 765
   indirect measures 763
   infancy 771–5
      adjacent dependencies 771, 772, 773
      algebraic rules 771, 772–3
      non-adjacent dependencies 771, 773–5
   multiple context-free grammars 760
   and natural language comparison 760, 764–5, 766, 767–71, 775, 776
      hierarchically structured sequences and left dorsal language system 768–9
      syntax and phonology 768
      temporal lobe contributions vs. complex syntax 769–71
   nested hierarchical grammars 771
   neuroimaging meta-analysis 765–7

non-adjacent dependencies 764, 771, 773–5
  in infancy 771, 773–5
 performance as a trait 764–5
 pseudowords 757
 REBER grammar 757–8
 regular grammars 759
 simpler features 760–1
 and statistical learning 762–3, 765, 766, 769–70
 symbols 757
 tactile paradigms 757
 violations 761–2
 visual stimulus presentation 757
 visual tiles 757
 written consonants 757
artificial grammar learning task, auditory 764
artificial language
 evolution of speech 852, 856
 models of language evolution 902–3, 908
 segmentation of speech 12, 14, 15, 17, 18, 21
 statistical learning 692–8, 703, 706–7, 709
artificial neural networks (ANNs) 294, 985–6
Asia 675
associative chunk strength (ACS) 761
associative priming 575
attention deficit hyperactivity disorder (ADHD) 419, 785, 792, 796, 874
attention and structural choice in sentence production 527–41
 linguistic stages 528, 530
 perceptual priming 533–5, 536–7, 538–40, 541
  interactive properties 538–40
 positional vs. grammatical-role hypothesis 535–8
 referential priming 532–3
attributional theories 72–3, 74, 76
audience design factors 445, 448, 549
auditory artificial grammar learning task 764
auditory brain response (ABR) 934, 937, 940
auditory deficit 796
auditory evoked potentials (AEPs) 937, 938, 940
auditory-motor weight 300
auditory naming task 34
auditory paradigms 757, 767
auditory processing impairments 792–4
Auditory Repetition Task (ART) 792–3
auditory stimuli 980, 986
auditory and visual compounds in first word learning 721
auditory-visual discrimination task 320
auditory word-picture matching task 320
Australia 798
 Early Language in Victoria Study (ELVS) 818–21, 825, 827
Australopithecus afarensis 849–50, 858
autism quotient (AQ) 639, 945
autism spectrum disorder (ASD) 738–9, 871, 873, 874, 878
autosegmental phonology 348–9
AXB discrimination/matching task 575, 923

B
babbling 714, 718
backpropagation of error 294, 385, 387
backward analysis 515, 517
backward transfer 224–5
'bags of words' models 74
Bantu language 678
baselines signs 262
base model 506, 507–8
bats 845, 848, 858, 866
Bayesian models 38, 40, 42
Bayes' rule 181–2
behavioral priming paradigms 60
behavioral reaction time paradigms 270
behavioral semantic relatedness paradigm 126
behavioral studies/approach
 ambiguity 111
 attention and structural choice in sentence production 530
 bilingualism 221
 grammatical encoding 449
 lexico-semantics 72
 segmentation of speech 21
 visual word recognition 49
  in multilinguals 119, 123, 129
Bengalese finches 847
best guess 106–7
beta band 957, 961, 966, 995, 997
bidirectional connections 53
Bilingual Interactive Activation (BIA) 134, 135
bilingualism
 ambiguity 98
 conceptual development 742
 connectionist principles of speech production 391
 deaf populations 260–1, 269–71
 domains 218
 dominance 218, 219
 first word learning 726
 fixation durations 219
 functional magnetic resonance imaging (fMRI) 983
 perspective-taking 552
 proficiency 219, 231–2
 spoken word production 344
 spoken word recognition 42
 statistical learning 707
 see also bilingual language production; bilingual sentence processing; first and second language acquisition
bilingual language production 461–75
 'hard problem', origin of 461–2
 language switching 467–72
  blocked language switching task 472
  trial-by-trial language switching task 467–72
 mechanisms 462–5
  language-non-specific selection models: inhibitory control model 464–5
  language-specific selection models 463–4
 picture-word interference (PWI) paradigm 465–7

bilingual sentence processing 217–33
  age of acquisition and proficiency 231–2
  emergent properties 225–7
  parsing 227–31
  semantic processing 217–22
  syntactic processing and competition model 222–5
binding problem 437
biological components 866
biological constraints 846
biological factors in developmental language disorder 823, 830
biological homeostasis 650
bipolar disorder 874
birds 845, 866
  Bengalese finches 847
  bird-song 845–6, 847–8, 908–9
  budgerigars 848
  chaffinches 847
  cockatoos 848
  humming birds 848
  lyre birds 847
  parrots 846, 848, 858
  reed warblers 847
  songbirds 846, 847–8, 858, 866, 881–2, 883, 908–9
  song sparrows 847
  white-rumped munias 847
  zebra finches 846, 847, 848, 881, 909
bi- and trigrams 760–1
blank spaces 32
blindness and gesture 598
blocked language switching task 472, 474
blocked naming 340–1
BOLD see functional magnetic resonance imaging (fMRI)
bonus meanings 658, 660, 662, 664
bootstrapping language acquisition 19
Boston Naming Test 247, 462
boundaries see segmentation of speech
boundary-straddling sequences 20
bounded rationality 182, 561
brain damage 413
Brazilian Portugese 739
breathing control 850
British Lexicon Project 135
British Sign Language (BSL) 266
BROCANTO grammar 758, 760, 769, 771
Broca's aphasia 241–2, 244, 245, 320
Broca's area 309, 830, 960, 999–1000, 1003
  ambiguity 109
  speech perception and production 312
  syntactic production and comprehension 499
budgerigars 848

C

Canadian-English 21
Canadian-French 20–1, 716
Cantonese 42, 788
cascading 339–40, 354
  connectionist principles and speech production 380, 381, 383
  emotion and sociality 649
  grammatical encoding 439
  spelling/writing 418
  written language production 414–16
Catalan 9
categorical perception 790–1
categorization 736, 737, 742–4, 745
  first word learning 720–1, 722, 725
  pragmatics 628
category-specific deficits 72
CDP+ model 49
center-embedded or object relative clauses 177
chaffinches 847
CHILDES database 683
childhood apraxia of speech 828
children see first word learning
chin 850
China 798
Chinese 945
  bilingualism 223
  developmental dyslexia 788, 796, 797
  dyslexia 786, 788
  sign languages and deaf populations 273
  spelling/writing 403, 404–5, 406–7, 415, 416–17
  spoken word production 349
  visual word recognition in multilinguals 122
  see also Cantonese; Chinese-English; Mandarin
Chinese-English 224, 226, 468
  sign languages and deaf populations 270, 272
  visual word recognition in multilinguals 127, 135
ChIP-Sequencing methodology 876
choice rule 34
Chomsky hierarchy 759, 771
chromatin 873
  marks 870
  remodelers 870
  structure 869–71
chromosomes 870
chunking 179, 530, 760–1
clarity of domain 75
classifiers 265–6
coarticulation 41, 307
cockatoos 848
code overlap 127
code-switching 220, 391
cognates
  ambiguity 98–9
  bilingualism 221, 222
  facilitation effect 126–7, 221, 461
  grammatical encoding 439
  identical 127–8, 129–30
  non-identical 127–8, 129–30
  visual word recognition in multilinguals 120, 122–3, 125–30, 133–6

cognitive communication impairments 206
cognitive constraints on planning 343
cognitive context in lexico-semantics 71
cognitive differences in perspective-taking 557
cognitive electrophysiology 930–46
   language 935–6
   time-domain averaging 934–5
   see also electroencephalography (EEG); event-related potential (ERP)
cognitive embodiment 306
cognitive functions in text comprehension 203–4
cognitive models 43
cognitive neuropsychological research 399
cognitive neuroscience 23
   of motor theories of speech perception 314–19
      perceptual representations of speech in cortical motor system 314–17
      task-dependency, environmental factors and turn-taking 317–19
   of speech perception 308–14
      motor cortex and speech 313–14
      new Motor Theory: support and criticisms 312–13
cognitive psychology 31, 35
coherence 199, 204, 959–60
cohesion 199, 204–5
   text 201
Coh-Metrix 204
cohort size 18
cohort theory/model 33, 34, 35, 37, 40, 261
Coltheart's N 55
combinatoriality
   conceptual development 740
   evolution of speech 845, 852–5, 856
   grammatical encoding 442
   models of language evolution 899, 901, 903–4, 907, 908
   semantics 965–6
common ground
   emotion and sociality 657
   evolution of speech 855
   gesture 595
   perspective-taking 550, 551–2, 553, 555–6, 559, 561, 563
   pragmatics 632–3
   strong 633–4
communication game tasks 851, 857, 858
Communicative Accommodation Theory (CAT) 584
communicative grunts 724
communicative intention 657, 722
communicative project 660
communicative signals 741
communicative success and alignment during interaction 580–2
community detection analysis 39–40
community membership 552, 559
comorbidity and developmental language disorder 818–19, 821–2, 825

compensatory proactive link 585
competence theories 646
competing constraints 681
competition 18
   and syntactic processing 222–5
   visual word recognition 54
competitor words 121
complex grammars 776
compositionality and models of language evolution 899, 900–1, 903, 905, 907, 908
comprehension *see* emotion, comprehension and sociality; syntactic production and comprehension; text comprehension
comprehensive production models 335
computational adequacy 35–6
computational linguistics 73
computational models 37, 646
   perspective-taking 560
   sentence comprehension 173, 179, 180–2, 186
   speech production 294
   text comprehension 210
concepts
   lexico-semantics 76
   pre-existing 738
   visual word recognition in multilinguals 120–1
concept selection account 462
conceptual development 736–48
   combinatoriality 740
   language builds on and reveals conceptual structure 736, 737–9
   language invites categorization 736, 737, 742–4
   language is a social marker 736, 737, 746–8
   language is a tool for action and attention 736, 737, 741–2
   language is a tool for thinking 736, 737, 739–40
   specific languages have specific influences 736, 737, 744–6
conceptual information and decoding 967
conceptualization process 434
conceptualizer component 513, 527
conceptual knowledge and lexico-semantics 76
conceptual learning in first word learning 722
conceptual links 133
conceptual message in syntactic production and comprehension 482–3
conceptual pacts 558, 632
conceptual plan in attention and structural choice in sentence production 527–8
conceptual processing
   bilingualism 218
   connectionist principles and speech production 376
conceptual tasks in lexico-semantics 75
concreteness
   bilingualism 218
   lexico-semantics 74, 78
conditional probability 38
conditioned variation 907

conduction aphasia 241, 296–7, 301
conflict model of monitoring 506, 512 13
conflict resolution account in ambiguity 111
congruent completion 220
conjoined noun phrase (CNP) 536
connectionist approach 372–92
   ambiguity 102
   connection weight parameter 382
   distributed representations: learning and
      processing 384–91
      connectionist principles outside localist
         framework 384–5
      Gradient Symbolic Computation (GSC) 390–1
      learning and syntactic priming 385–8
      oscillator models 388–90
      selection 388–91
   grammatical encoding 449
   inhibitory 10, 35–6, 53, 134
   learning 372, 392
   PARSYN connectionist model 37
   pragmatics and inference 616
   segmentation of speech 10
   sentence comprehension 184, 185
   speech production 372–3, 380, 382–3, 384
      phonological errors 379–80, 383
      semantic errors 379–80, 382, 383
   spoken word recognition 35–7
   spreading activation between localist
      representations 373–84
      generic localist connectionist framework 374–6
      impairments of speech production 377, 382–4
      localist connectionist principles and empirical
         data 373–4, 377–84
      mixed error effect 377, 379–81
      semantic interference vs. phonological facilitation
         in picture naming 377, 378–9
   visual word recognition 51
   word production 506
   see also distributed connectionist approach
connections, excitatory 35–6, 53
connectivity
   and oscillations 957–60
   speech perception and production 318
   see also source estimation, connectivity and pattern
      analysis of EEG/MEG data
consensus model
   grammatical encoding 432–8, 440, 441, 448, 451
      content subprocesses 435
      division and unity 437–8
      message encoding 434
      structure subprocesses 435–7
consonants
   ambisyllabic 8, 17
   artificial grammar learning (AGL) 757
   consonant-vowel-consonant (CVC)
      sequence 292, 680
   consonant-vowel (CV) babbling 677

consonant-vowel (CV) syllables 757
   lengthening 15
   onset 14
   segmentation of speech 15–16
   word-initial 14
constituent structures 435–6
constraint-based models 174–5, 181, 553
constraint effect in bilingualism 219
construction-integration model 201, 616
constructivist processes 318
   pragmatics and inference 612–15, 616, 618
content processing in grammatical
      encoding 438–40, 441–2
content of representations in lexico-semantics 77–9
content subprocesses and consensus model 435
context
   bilingualism 220
   -dependency 624
   -flexible words 723
   -limited words 723
   -sensitive grammars 760
   -sensitive lexical access hypothesis 119
   spoken word production 342
   visual word recognition in multilinguals 128–31
   see also under lexico-semantics
contextual diversity in visual word recognition 51
contextual factors in segmentation of speech 12
contextual information in pragmatics and
      inference 609, 611
contextual reinstatement 561
continual learning 41
continuity thesis 510
control signal theory 388, 390
control words in bilingualism 221
conventionalization 904
conventions-constrained-by-concepts 738
convergence zones 76, 77, 78–9, 147, 965
Conversational Maxims 657
conversational pressure 343–4
conversation structure 610
cooperative behavior 581
Cooperative Principle 625–6, 635
co-ordination problem 437
cortical motor system and perceptual representations
      of speech 314–17
co-speech gesture integration 944
cost-free processing in spoken word recognition 34
covert shift 532
critical period in evolution of speech 846–7
cross-boundary decoarticulation 14
cross-boundary glottalization 15
cross-linguistic language production *see* bilingual
      language production
cross-modal lexical decision tasks 198
cross-modal priming 18, 33
   fragment priming 11
   identity-priming 12–13, 16

lexical priming (CMLP) 244
long-lasting repetition priming 405–6
semantic priming 105–6
cross-script similarities and differences in written language production 416–17
cueing paradigm 532
cues
　auditory 535
　in combination 18–19
　cost 222
　cultural 552
　distributional 698, 700
　endogenous 532
　environmental 870
　exogenous 532
　explicit 6, 532, 534
　implicit 532, 534, 537
　infant-directed 741
　lexical 13
　linguistic 552
　pedagogical 741–2
　perceptual 536
　phonological 697–8, 700
　phonotactic 15–17, 694–6
　prosodic 13, 21
　semantic 13
　strength 223
　subject-verb agreement 225–6
　unimodal and bimodal sensory 535
　validity 222–3
　visual 533–4, 537, 539, 552
　word-initial pitch 18
　see also language-specific cues under segmentation of speech
cultural evolution/transmission 846, 900, 901–2, 904, 907–8, 909
cumulative frequency in orthographic representations 50–2
cumulative semantic interference (CSI) 340–1, 473–4, 513
cyclic blocked picture naming task 352
Czech 787

D

dark side model of cumulative semantic interference and incremental learning 507, 513–14, 521
dative alternation 230–1
declarative/explicit learning 764
declarative memory 726, 728
decoarticulation 18, 21
　cross-boundary 14
decompositional models in spoken word production 336
deep dyslexia 246
deep learning 985
deficit hypothesis 829
delta band 23, 995
dependency distance 178

description schemes 577
descriptions theory 610
determiner-noun agreement 226–7
developmental deficits 419–21
developmental dysgraphia 419–21
developmental dyslexia 419, 784–803
　in alphabetic orthographies 787–8
　behavioral difficulties 802
　Chinese 788, 796, 797
　cognitive causes 789–95
　　auditory processing impairments 792–4
　　double deficit theory 789–90
　　phonological deficit account 789
　　speech perception 790–2
　　visual processing deficits 794–5
　definition 785
　emotional difficulties 802
　environmental factors 800–1, 803
　gene-environment interaction 801
　genetic factors 798–800, 801
　　$DCDC_2$ 798–9
　　$KIAA_{0319}$ 798–9
　　molecular genetics 798–9
　　neural basis 799–800
　　reading network 799–800
　　twin studies 798
　interventions 828–32
　　neural effects 802
　large families 800
　literacy-related activities in the home 800–1
　magnocellular theory of dyslexia 794
　manifestations 785–7
　multiple-deficit theory 795–6
　oral language program 802
　procedural learning deficits 795–801
　　etiology 796–7
　　family-risk studies 796–7
　　multiple risk framework 795–6, 797
　proximal cause 786
　schooling 801
　social disadvantage 800, 802
　speech envelope modulations 793
　spelling 786–7
　surface dyslexia 786
developmental language disorder 785, 789, 814–31
　age of child 823
　approaches to studying child language 816, 818
　autistic spectrum condition 821
　behavioral adjustment 821
　biological factors 823, 830
　comorbidity 818–19, 821–2, 825
　compensation 823
　educational attainment 821
　environmental factors 823, 827, 830
　epigenetics 830
　evidence from methods characterizing longitudinal change 822–8

developmental language disorder (Cont.)
   individual differences in growth trajectory 825–6
   longitudinal latent class analyses 825
   nature of change in child language development 823–6
   non-verbal skills 827
   predictors of change 826–8
   reasons for characterizing change in abilities 822–3
   receptive language 827–8
   social gradient 826–7
   stability of language status 824–5
  evidence from population/epidemiological methods 818–22
   comorbidity and co-occurring difficulties 821–2
   prevalence in different social quintiles 819–21
   social gradient 818–19
  genetics 823, 827, 828, 830
  growth curve analysis/growth trajectories 824, 825–6
  heterogeneity 823
  history of terminology 816–17
  inattention 821
  interactivity 823
  labels 814–18
  language impairment severity 821
  late talkers 828
  longitudinal latent class analyses 824, 826
  low non-verbal IQ 821
  neurobiological effects 830
  neurodevelopmental immaturity 822
  neuroimaging studies 828–30
   neural correlates 829–30
  paternal/maternal education 827
  population samples 826
  process of development 822
  social gradient 818–19, 826–7
  social risks 830
  socioemotional difficulties 821, 822
  specific language disorder 828, 829
  specific language impairment (SLI) 814–15, 818
  timing 823
developmental pathway 822
developmental phonological dysgraphia 420
developmental surface dysgraphia 420
DevLex-II 135
diagraphs 412–13
dialect 707, 747
dialogue contexts 448–9
diffusion weighted imaging (DWI) 251
digit span task 764
dipole modeling 956–7, 964
Direct Access view 636–7
Directions into Velocities of Articulators (DIVA) model of speech production 309
direct realist account 318
disambiguation 105, 110, 175, 944

discourse contexts in bilingualism 221
discreteness-versus-interactivity debate 440
discrimination task 791
discriminative learning 40–1
distance modification in sentence comprehension 175–6
distributed activation patterns 384
distributed areas: sensorimotor systems 966
distributed connectionist approach
  ambiguity 111
  visual word recognition 49
   in multilinguals 135
distributed models
  ambiguity 100–2
  spoken word recognition 37
  visual word recognition in multilinguals 135
distributed-plus-hub theory of semantic memory and semantic dementia 518
distributed representations 77
  see also under connectionist approach
distributed semantic control network: convergent evidence 154–5
distributional cues 19, 698, 700
distributional information 74–5
distributional knowledge in statistical learning 705
distributional learning 715–16, 717
distributional theories in lexico-semantics 72, 73–4
dolphins 845, 866
domain-general executive control tasks 136, 468–9
domain-general task switching 467, 471
Doppler ultrasound imaging 315
double deficit theory (developmental dyslexia) 789–90
double indexing 609
doubling 391, 414
drawing task 902, 905
DRC model 49
duality of patterning 852, 899
dual-path mapping 539
dual-path structure 58
dual-path system 540
dual-task paradigm 107, 628
dumb attentional mechanism 720
Dutch 597
  alignment during interaction 576
  ambiguity 98, 99, 106
  bilingualism 223
  dyslexia 787
  emotion and sociality 663
  first word learning 715, 716, 717
  grammatical encoding 444
  lexico-semantics 76
  prosodic phonology 677, 680–1
  segmentation of speech 9, 15, 16, 18
  sign languages and deaf populations 270, 273
  spoken word production 348, 352
  visual word recognition in multilinguals 123, 127, 131

Dutch-English 98, 221, 230
  visual word recognition in multilinguals 120, 121, 122, 124–5, 128, 129–30
Dutch-English-French 127
Dutch Lexicon Project 135
dynamic causal modeling (DCM) 318, 959–60, 964, 965
dynamic systems theory 722
dysgraphia 412, 417, 420
dyslexia 419, 420, 829
  comorbid motor impairments 785
  deep 246
  functional magnetic resonance imaging (fMRI) 985
  genetics 877
  letter knowledge 786–7
  phoneme awareness 786–7, 789–90, 796, 798, 802
  phonological awareness 786, 787–8, 790, 797
  speech production 292
  statistical learning 701
  see also developmental dyslexia
dysphasia 815
dyspraxia, orofocial 873

E
Early Language in Victoria Study (ELVS) (Australia) 818–21, 825, 827
early selections strategy in ambiguity 107
echoic mention account 637
edge artifacts 981
edit distance 761
egocentricity 551, 555, 633–4, 741
eLAN 942
electrical stimulation mapping (ESM) 993
electrocorticography (ECoG) 314, 316, 930, 993, 994, 995, 997, 1002
electroencephalography (EEG) 930, 931–3, 936, 937, 945
  alpha waves 931–2, 934
  artificial grammar learning 774
  auditory brain stem response (ABR) 934
  auditory evoked potential (AEP) 934
  Bereitschafspotential (readiness potential) 934
  contingent negative variation (CNV) 934
  data acquisition, visualization and analysis 932
  emotion and sociality 660
  epilepsy 992–3
  expectancy 934
  frequency-following response (FFR) 934
  gesture 600
  lateralized readiness potential (LRP) 934–5
  lexico-semantics 87
  pragmatics 638
  prosodic phonology 684
  segmentation of speech 23
  semantic deficit 147
  speech perception and production 314, 319
  spelling/writing 402, 407
  steady state flicker-evoked brain potentials 932–3
  steady state potentials 931, 933
  stimulus-evoked potentials 934
  text comprehension 206
  time-domain averaging 934–5
  time-frequency analysis 931
  transient event-related brain potentials (ERPs) 932–3
  transient potentials 931, 933
  transient time-domain average event-related potentials (ERPs) 932–3
  visual word recognition in multilinguals 124, 126, 136
  word production in aphasia 512
  see also source estimation, connectivity and pattern analysis of EEG/MEG data
electropalatography 315, 406
electrophysiological data
  bilingualism 221, 468, 470
  grammatical encoding 439
  segmentation of speech 21
  sign languages and deaf populations 262, 264, 270
  spoken word recognition 43
  text comprehension 206
  visual word recognition 58, 60
  see also cognitive electrophysiology
elephants 845, 848
embedded words 10–11
embodied cognition 147
embodied theories of language 322–3
  lexico-semantics 72–3, 76, 77–9, 83, 85
embodied variables in lexico-semantics 75
embodiment and inference 617–18
emotional Stroop task 81
emotion, comprehension and sociality 644–65
  action tendencies 650
  affective evaluation is low-intensity emotion 651
  behavioral changes 650
  code-cracking focus 646
  code model position 647–8
  cognitive changes 650
  emotional conditioning 651
  emotionally competent stimulus (ECS) 649, 654, 658–62
    scope of model 661–2
  emotions are not necessarily conscious 650
  emotions are triggered by appraisal of something as relevant to our concerns 648–9
  emotions briefly take control 650
  emotions have ancient triggers but can hook up to new ones via learning 650–1
  emotions involve a package of automatic, short-lived, synchronized changes in multiple systems 649–50
  historical factors 645–7
  inference 618–19
  informing 656

emotion, comprehension and sociality (Cont.)
   modularity focus 646-7
   mood 652
   motivational changes 650
   negative emotion 658
   physiological changes 650
   requesting or manipulating 656
   sharing 656
   technological systems focus 645-6
   uniqueness focus 647
   word valence 662-4
   see also affective language comprehension (ALC) model
emotion grounding 78
emotion-laden words 136
empathy 659
encoding models 984-6
endophenotypes 797
English
   ambiguity 96, 97, 98, 106
   attention and structural choice in sentence production 529, 533, 536-7, 538, 540-1
   bilingualism 222, 223-4, 226, 464
   conceptual development 739, 740, 745, 746
   connectionist principles and speech production 382, 391
   dyslexia 786, 787, 788, 800
   emotion, comprehension and sociality 663
   first word learning 715, 716, 718, 723
   gesture 594, 597-8
   grammatical encoding 443-4, 447-8
   lexico-semantics 76, 82
   prosodic phonology 675, 676, 677-8, 680-2, 684-5
   segmentation of speech 7, 11, 13, 14, 15, 16, 17, 18, 19, 21, 22
   sentence comprehension 171, 176, 177, 178, 183
   sentence level aphasia 247
   sign languages and deaf populations 270, 273, 274-5
   speech perception and production 315
   spelling/writing 403, 404, 406, 416, 420
   spoken word production 348
   spoken word recognition 42
   statistical learning 692, 693, 696, 698, 709
   text comprehension 203
   visual word recognition 52, 56
      in multilinguals 118, 123, 131
   see also American English; Canadian-English
English-French 22, 224, 228
English-Portugese 229
English-Spanish 219, 226, 231
English-Welsh 124
enhancers 873
   sequences 871
entropy 854
   reduction 182-3
environmental factors 84-6
   developmental dyslexia 800-1, 803

developmental language disorder 823, 827, 830
   perception and production in speech 317-19
epigenetic mechanisms 830, 870, 873
epilepsy 878
   see also intracranial electrophysiology and epilepsy
epistemic stance 656
equal environment assumption 798
error-based learning 388
error-based learning rule (delta rule) 514, 517
error-driven learning algorithm 41
errors
   backpropagation of 294, 385, 387
   formal 508
   fragment 516-17
   mixed error effect 377, 379-81, 508
   morphological substitution 292
   non-word 382, 508
   phonological 379-80, 383, 516-18, 520
   prediction 957
   root mean square (RMSE) 299
   sampling 924-6, 928
   segmental 349, 354
   semantic 379-80, 382-3, 508, 516-19, 520
   semantic-phonological 513
   severity/error type interaction 508, 510
   speech 349, 350, 354, 389, 391, 450
   unrelated 382
   word substitution 292
essentialism 743-5
Estonian 716, 723
European Union 118
evaluative stance 656
event indexing model 202, 617
event-related potential (ERP) 930-1, 933, 935-45
   anterior negativities (AN) 938, 942
   artificial grammar learning 765, 772, 773, 774, 775
   attention and structural choice in sentence production 530, 531
   auditory brain response (ABR) 934, 937, 940
   auditory evoked potentials (AEPs) 937, 938, 940
   bilingualism 220, 221, 226, 227, 231-2, 468, 472
   CNV 942
   eLAN 938, 942
   FFR 937, 940
   first word learning 717, 725, 726
   gesture 600, 602
   intracranial electrophysiology and epilepsy 1002
   language proficiency 945
   late positive complex (LPC) 935, 942
   left anterior negativity (LAN) 938, 942, 945
   mismatch negativity (MMN) 938, 940, 944-5
   multisensory integration 944
   N100 23, 704
   N200 129, 468, 470, 472, 936
   N250 132
   N400 129, 936, 940-1, 944-5, 965, 996
   no-go N200 effect 938, 943

nRef 938, 942
P300 935, 936
P600 936, 941–2, 945
perceptually grounded vs. amodal knowledge representation 943–4
PNP 938, 942
pragmatics 638
scalar implicatures 944–5
segmentation of speech 12, 14, 16, 23
sentence comprehension 172, 173, 938
sign languages and deaf populations 262, 264, 268
slow waves (SW) 935
statistical learning 702, 704, 706
text comprehension 200, 206, 209, 210
transient 932–3, 938–9
visual word recognition 57, 59
  in multilinguals 119, 123, 124, 127, 129, 131, 132, 136
word 938
see also event-related potential (ERP): N400
event-related spectral perturbations (ERSPs) 1000–1
event semantics 386, 531
evolution of speech 841–58
  air sacs 844
  anatomical differences 843–4
  artificial languages 852, 856
  behavioral differences 844
  breathing control 850
  combinatoriality 845, 852–5, 856
  comparative evidence 842–8
    apes: evolutionary homologies 842–5
    comparison with other species: evolutionary analogy 847–8, 858
    comparison with other species: functional universals 845–6
  critical period 846–7
  domestication of species 847
  experimental work 851–8
    combinatorial structure 845, 852–5, 856
    iconicity 855–7
    modality 857–8
  fossil evidence 849–50, 858
  gestures 845, 857–8
  hyoid bone 849–50
  imitation 845
  iterated learning 852–3, 856–7
  larynx 849
  modality 857–8
  sign languages 852, 855–6
  vocalizations 844–5
  see also models of language evolution
excitatory connections in visual word recognition in multilinguals 134
executive control impairments 153
executive control tasks, domain-general 136, 468–9
executive functions 210, 557
exemplars 42
exhaustive access model 105

expectations 719–20
experience-based accounts
  sentence comprehension 175, 176, 177–80, 181, 182
  statistical learning 708
experience-driven modification of connection weights 387
experimental pragmatics 623–40
  informativeness and inference: scalar implicature 625–31
    anti-Gricean turn 629–31
    experimental turn 627–9
  irony 635–9
    intention 637–9
  reference 631–5
    egocentric approach 633–4
    naming objects 632–3
    ongoing debate and meta-analysis 634–5
explicit learning 762–4, 765
expressions of motion events 596–7
extended language network (ELN) 206–8
eye gaze 581, 741
eye-tracking
  bilingualism 221, 227–8
  first word learning 726
  lexico-semantics 82
  pragmatics 634
  sentence comprehension 172–3, 186–7
  sentence level aphasia 244
  sign languages and deaf populations 271, 274–5
  text comprehension 209–10
  visual word recognition in multilinguals 119, 129–30

F
facilitation effects 466
  visual word recognition 55–7
    in multilinguals 125, 129–30
faculty of language in the broad sense (FLB) 866
faculty of language in the narrow sense (FLN) 866
false belief 550, 557, 739–40
  task 550
false friends 98, 220
  visual word recognition in multilinguals 120, 121–2, 124–6, 127, 129–30, 133–4, 136
false positive rates 924–5, 927
familiarity effect 716, 721
Farsi 738
feature layer 36
feature model 984–5
feedback
  connectionist principles and speech production 380–1
  grammatical encoding 439
feed-forward models 37, 350
FFR 937, 940
figurative language 610–11
filler stories (decoys) 638
filler syllables 681–2

filtering of information 532
finite state automata 759
finite state grammars (FSGs) 758, 760, 769
Finnish
   attention and structural choice in sentence
       production 536–7, 541
   dyslexia 787
   segmentation of speech 13, 17, 18
   spelling/writing 416
first and second language acquisition 19–23
   infant-directed speech 19–20
   infant sensitivity to segmentation cues 20–2
   non-native segmentation 22–3
   segmentation of speech 23
first word learning 714–28
   babbling 714
   referential function of language 722–7
   word forms 715–19
   word meanings 719–22
FishFilm paradigm 534, 536–7
fixed effects 921
fixed word order languages 436
fluent aphasia see Wernicke's aphasia
fluorodeoxyglucose (FDG)-positron emission
       tomography (PET) 251
formal error 508
formal grammar 759, 768
formal pragmatics of indexicals 613
format of representations in lexico-semantics 75, 77–9
format-specific hypothesis 411
form priming 352, 354
formulation processes 372
forward models 313, 984
forward transfer 224–5, 228–9
fragment error 516–17
frame-and-slot models 292
frame-based view 441–2
frame-filling theories of phonological encoding 349
free recall 218
free word order languages 436
French
   alignment during interaction 576
   bilingualism 222, 223
   dyslexia 787
   first word learning 716
   gesture 597
   prosodic phonology 678, 679, 680, 683
   segmentation of speech 7–8, 9, 21
   spelling/writing 415, 416, 418
   visual word recognition in multilinguals 122
   see also Canadian-French
French-English 124, 132, 221, 229
frequency
   ambiguity 108, 110
   bilingualism 218
   cumulative 50–2
   lexico-semantics 82, 88
   orthographic representations 50–2

sentence comprehension 178–9
sequential 22
spoken word recognition 32, 35
visual word recognition, in multilinguals 126, 134
word 36, 38, 338
writing and speaking 406–7
functional magnetic resonance imaging
       (fMRI) 975–86
   adaptation paradigm 500–2
   alignment during interaction 579
   ambiguity 107, 109
   artificial grammar learning 765–6, 776
   artificial neural networks (ANNs) 985–6
   attention and structural choice in sentence
       production 530
   auditory stimuli 980, 986
   bilingualism 226, 468, 472
   blood-oxygen-level-dependent (BOLD) 84, 322,
       770, 978
      activation patterns 985
      curve (hemodynamic response
          function) 976–7, 979
      response 87, 315, 318–19, 324, 410, 601, 976–7, 979,
         980, 981, 984, 997
      signal 321, 975, 977
      time course 978
   continuous stimuli 976–80
   developmental language disorder 830
   dyslexia 790, 793
   edge artifacts 981
   encoding models 984–6
   feature model 984–5
   forward model 984
   general linear model approach (GLM) 982–3,
       984, 986
   gesture 600–1, 602
   head movements and stabilization methods 981, 986
   hyperalignment 984
   hyperscanning 982
   interleaved silent steady state imaging (ISSS) 980
   intersubject correlation analysis 980
   intertrial interval 977–8
   multivariate pattern analysis (MVPA) 960, 982–3
   Procrustean transform 984
   rapid event-related 976–7
   regions of interest (ROIs) 959, 982–3
   representational similarity analysis
       (RSA) 983, 984–5
   search-light approach 982
   semantic deficit 146–8, 154
   slow event-related 976
   speech perception and production 307, 310, 312, 314,
       315–17, 321, 323, 325, 981–2
   spelling/writing 408, 412
   statistical learning 702–4
   surprisal value 979
   syntactic production and comprehension 485, 497
   take home message 979

text comprehension 206, 209
time to repetition (TR) 976, 979
visual word recognition in multilinguals 119, 125, 136
functional near infrared spectroscopy (fNIRS) 16, 765, 772, 773
functional phrases 343
functional processing 435
function assignment 436
function words 435
Fuzzy Logical model 313

G
gabbling foreigner effect 22
gamma band 957, 965, 968, 995
  high-gamma activity 997–1002
Garden Path model 174–5, 183, 227–8, 483, 941
gating activation 263, 264, 375
gaze-contingent boundary paradigm 273
generalization
  models of language evolution 899, 901–2
  statistical learning 700, 707, 709
Generalized Estimation Equations 928
generalized word use 727
generalizing over encounters 917–28
  analysis of variance (ANOVA) 918
  by-item and by-subject analysis 918, 920–1, 927
  false positive rates 924–5, 927
  fixed effects 921
  $F_1 \times F_2$ 918, 919
  house effect 919
  language-as-fixed-effect fallacy 918–19
  linear mixed-effects models (LMEMs) 918
  lme$_4$ package for R 918–19
  maximal random effects structure 927
  min-F' 918, 919
  mixed-effects models 919, 921, 922, 926–7, 928
  Monte Carlo simulations 919, 925
  random intercept variance 919, 926–7
  random slope variance 919, 927, 928
  replication 923–5
  sample size 924
  sampling error 928
  statistical issues 924–7
    repetition amplifies impact of sampling error 924–6
    sampling variation 926–7
  structure of encounter 923
  subject-by-stimulus interaction 927n
  three-party encounters 922–3
  treatment variation 926
  types of encounters 921–4
  types of entities 923
general linear model approach (GLM) 982–3, 984, 986
general theory of signs 609
generation effect 561
generic statements 743–4
genetics 865–84
  animal models 866, 880–3

mice: stuttering 882–3
songbirds: vocal learning 881–2
$ARHGEF_{39}$ 875
axons 877
$CASPR_2$ 878
$CNTNAP_2$ 878–9
$DCDC_2$ 877
dendrites 877
developmental deficits 420
developmental dyslexia 798–800, 801
  molecular genetics 798–9
  neural basis 799–800
  twin studies 798
developmental language disorder 823, 827, 828, 830
DNA 865, 867–70
DYX_1C_1 877
$FOXP_2$ 869n, 873, 874, 876, 877, 878–9, 881
$FOXP_1$ 873
genome 867–75
  chromatin structure 869–71
  genes and proteins 868–9
  non-coding DNA as gate-keeper for gene expression 871–3
  post-transcriptional regulation (controlling the message) 873–5
genome-wide association studies (GWAS) 876
$GNPTAB$ 882–3
$GNPTG$ 882
$KIAA_{0319}$ 877
$MECP_2$ 871
$MTRNR_1$ 879
$MYO_{15}A$ 879
$NAGPA$ 882
neurites 877
nucleotides 867
RBFOXs 874
$ROBO_1$ 877
synapse 877
systems 875–80
  genome-wide variation and coordinated molecular networks 875–6
  migration and neurite outgrowth 876–7
  peripheral mechanisms 879–80
  synapses and neural circuits 878–9
TBR_1 873
3'UTR (3' Un-Translated Region) 874–5
genome see genetics
German
  ambiguity 99
  artificial grammar learning 774
  bilingualism 222, 223–4
  dyslexia 787
  grammatical encoding 444
  segmentation of speech 16
  sign languages and deaf populations 270
  spelling/writing 416, 420
  text comprehension 202
  visual word recognition in multilinguals 122, 127

German-English 22, 129, 220, 230
gesture 6, 592–604
  beats 592
  communicative 601, 602–3
  complementary 601
  conceptual development 737
  co-speech gesture integration 944
  evolution of speech 845, 857–8
  first word learning 724, 727
  Gesture as Simulated Action (GSA) 595, 597
  grooming (self-adaptors) 601
  hand 581
  iconic 592, 593–4, 596–7, 600–1, 602
  incongruent 602
  integration of 603
  interactive, pragmatic 592
  models 593–8
  pointing 592, 595–6
  preparation 593
  redundant 601
  retraction (hold) 593
  sign languages and deaf populations 262
  silent 907–8
  stroke 593, 602
  unified account 603–4
gibbon song 845
Gibson's Dependency Locality Theory 177
GingerALE method 766
global damage mechanisms 382–4
global discourse context 129
glottalization, cross-boundary 15
goal-oriented action observation in speech perception and production 322
Good Enough approach 175, 617–18
goodness of fit 10
graded activation account 355
graded effects 11
graded hub hypothesis 149, 156
Graded Salience hypothesis 636–7
gradient representations in perspective-taking 561
Gradient Symbolic Computation (GSC) 388, 390–1, 392
grammar
  BROCANTO 758, 760, 769, 771
  complex 760, 768, 776
  context-sensitive 760
  finite state 758, 760, 769
  formal 759, 768
  lexicalized tree-adjoining 441
  natural 760
  nested hierarchical 771
  REBER 757–8
  regular 759
  story 198, 200
  universal
  see also artificial grammar learning (AGL)
grammatical encoding 291–2, 432–51
  accessibility 442
  combinatoriality 442
  consensus model 432–8, 440, 441, 448, 451
    content subprocesses 435
    division and unity 437–8
    message encoding 434
    structure subprocesses 435–7
  content 432, 437–40, 441–2
  dialogue contexts 448–9
  emerging debates 446–9
  fundamental debates 438–42
  fundamental insights 449–51
  grammatical category labels 437
  grammatical functions 435
  incrementality 432, 442–4
  linguistic knowledge and non-linguistic knowledge distinction 449–50
  ongoing debates 442–6
  ongoing learning effects 447–8
  rational models of sentence production 446–7
  retrieval 432, 437
  scope 432, 442–4
  selection 432, 437
  selection-then-retrieval 432, 439–40
  stages 438–41
  structure 432, 437–8, 440–2
  syntax 432, 444–6, 450–1
grammaticality judgment test 697
grammatical role assignment 529–30, 537–8, 540–1
grammatical structure (functional level representation) 483
Granger Causality 959–60, 999–1000
Granger connectivity analysis 968
graphical communication task 904, 905
Greek 746, 787
Greek-French 127
grounding 556
  emotion 78
  perspective-taking 552, 561
  pragmatics and inference 617
Growing Up in Scotland (GUS)(UK) study 818–21
growth curve analysis/growth trajectories 824

H

handwritten production model 402
Hanoi problem 595
head-turn preference procedure 701, 716
hearing sensitivity 850
Hebbian learning phase 135
Hebrew 50, 223, 245, 420
Hebrew-English 127
herpes simplex encephalitis 149
heteromodal semantic hub in anterior temporal lobes 146–7
heteromodal semantic impairment 151
heuristics 227, 552, 560, 564
hierarchical state feedback control (HSFC) theory 295
hierarchical structure
  artificial grammar learning (AGL) 776
  and natural language comparison 768–9

Chomsky 759, 771
  sentence level aphasia 239–40
high frequency band (HFB) 997
Hindi 223, 738
Hindi-English 224
histone modifications 870
holistics
  approach 876
  labels 901–2
  learnability 901, 904, 909
  mapping mechanism 529
  representations of word meanings 336
  signals 900, 903–4, 909
  specifications in sign language 265
Homo ergaster 850, 858
homographs 97, 104, 120, 221
  interlingual 124–6, 127, 128, 129, 131, 220
  intralingual 121–3
Homo heidelbergensis 849–50, 858
homonyms 98, 101
homophones 58, 97, 120, 127
  interlingual 125
  intralingual 121–2
Homo sapiens 850
HSVE 156
hub-and-spokes model 145, 147–8, 149, 155–6
humming birds 848
Hungarian 223, 787
Hungarian-English 22
hybrid and combined models 74–5, 78
hybrid languages 760
hyoid bone 849–50
hyperarticulation/hypoarticulation 8, 19
hyperscanning 982
hypertext systems (World Wide Web) 204
hypoglossal canal 850

I
iambic words 20–1
iconicity
  evolution of speech 855–7
  models of language evolution 904–5
  sign languages and deaf populations 265–7
ideational apraxia following stroke 149
identification task 791
identification point (IP) 944
ignition stage 440
Illinois Test of Psycholinguistic Abilities 815
imageability 74, 75, 78
imitation 573, 845
Immersed Experiencer 201–2
implemented models 49
implicatures 550, 610–13, 635–6
  conventional 625
  conversational 625, 635
  generalized 625, 626
  local 631

particularized 625, 626
  see also scalar implicature
implicit causality 614
implicit learning 762–4, 765
implicit priming 347, 349–52, 405
inconsistency paradigm 200
incrementality 183, 348, 432, 442–4
independent components analysis 325
indeterminacy hypothesis 624
indexicals 609
indirect speech act 610–11
individual difference studies 243, 272
individual (role of experience and current cognitive context) 80–2
individual words 337–8
Indo-European languages 50, 61
inductive inferences 742, 744
infancy
  artificial grammar learning (AGL) 771–5
    adjacent dependencies 771, 772, 773
    algebraic rules 771, 772–3
    non-adjacent dependencies 771, 773–5
infant-directed cues 741
infant-directed intonation 741
infant-directed speech
  first and second language acquisition 19–20
  first word learning 716
  segmentation of speech 6, 13
  statistical learning 693–4
infant sensitivity to segmentation cues 20–2
inference 611–18
  and bonus meaning 657
  Bransford's three ideas 611–13
  causal 617
  coherence-creating 613–14
  elaborative 613
  embodiment and good-enough representations 617–18
  and emotions 618–19
  inductive 742, 744
  and intentions 658
  mental models and situation models 615–16
  necessary 613
  perspective-taking 560
  referential 617
  and referential intention 655
  scalar-like 629–30
  and social intention 656
  and stance 655–6
  text comprehension 199–200, 202, 207, 208, 210
  see also experimental pragmatics
inferior frontal gyrus (IFG)
  gesture 600–1
  semantic deficit 154
  speech perception and production 309, 312
  statistical learning 703
  syntactic production and comprehension 495–6, 497, 499, 501, 502

inferior temporal gyrus (ITG) 148, 496
information questions 562-3
information structure 436, 482-3, 610-11
Information Theory 182-3
information transmission model 6
informativeness *see under* experimental pragmatics
inhibition
    spoken word production 341
    visual word recognition 55-7
        in multilinguals 125-6
inhibitory connections 10, 35-6, 53, 134
inhibitory control model (ICM) 464-5, 468-71
innate mechanism vs. experience-driven accounts of ambiguity resolution 175-6
innovative approaches in spoken word recognition 37-41
input coding: letters and letter positions 49-50
input layer in spoken word recognition 41
input processing deficits in anterior temporal lobe (ATL) 149-50
Integrated Systems hypothesis 603
integration 612-13
    during production of full sentences 341-5
        controlling lexical access 344-5
        planning scope 342-4
        producing words in sentences 341-2
    pragmatics and inference 613-14, 618
    speech production 295-7
    statistical learning 706-7
intellectual disability (ID) 874, 878
intelligence quotient (IQ) 785, 797, 815, 821, 830
intensifiers 657
intention 623
    communicative 657, 722
    inferred 658
    and irony 637-9
    referential 655, 661
    social 656, 658-9, 662, 663
interaction 510
    gesture 596
    see also alignment during interaction
interactive-activation 36-7, 53-4, 55-7, 134, 346
interactive alignment 557-8
interactive hypothesis 538
interactive two-step model of naming 507-8, 519
Interface Hypothesis 595-6
interfacing representations 433
interference
    bilingualism 466
    paradigmatic 344
    phonological form repetition 352
    position-dependent interference effects of form overlap 352
    semantic 103, 377, 378-9, 445, 513
    sentence level aphasia 243, 244
    see also picture-word interference (PWI) paradigm
interjections 657

interleaved silent steady state imaging (ISSS) 980
internalizing and externalizing difficulties 785
internal merge operation 768
interpersonal relationships 747
interpreting the present 183-4
interpreting speaker's communicative move 655
intersensory redundancy 720
intersubject correlation analysis 980
intonation 6, 676
    boundaries 15
    infant-directed 741
intracranial electrophysiology and epilepsy 992-1003
    BOLD response 997
    electrical stimulation mapping (ESM) 993
    electrocorticography (ECoG) 993, 994, 995, 997, 1002
    electroencephalography (EEG) 992-3
    event-related potentials (ERP) 1002
    event-related spectral perturbations (ERSPs) 1000-1
    high frequency band (HFB) 997
    high-gamma activity 997-1002
    history of epilepsy surgery 992-3
    intracranial electroencephalography (iEEG) 993, 1003
    intracranial event-related potentials (iERPs) 996
    Local Field Potential (LFP) 995
    methodological considerations 994-5
    monitoring 993-4
    spectro-temporal receptive field (STRF) 1002-3
    stereotactic electroencephalograpy (sEEG) 994, 995, 996, 999, 1003
    time-frequency signatures, intracranial 997
irony 624, 635-9
    and intention 637-9
Italian
    artificial grammar learning 774
    bilingualism 222, 223
    first word learning 715, 717, 718
    prosodic phonology 681, 683-4
    segmentation of speech 9, 11, 16, 20
    sentence level aphasia 245
    spelling/writing 403, 413-14, 416-17, 420
    statistical learning 692, 704
    visual word recognition in multilinguals 122
iterated learning
    evolution of speech 852-3, 856-7
    models of language evolution 900-3, 905, 908

J

Japanese
    ambiguity 98
    bilingualism 223, 738
    conceptual development 745
    first word learning 716, 717
    gesture 594, 597
    grammatical encoding 443

lexico-semantics 76
segmentation of speech 20
sentence comprehension 178
spelling/writing 416
spoken word production 349–50
visual word recognition in multilinguals 122
Japanese-English 22, 127
jTRACE 39

K

Kannada (Southern Indian language) 786
Kata Kolok sign language (Indonesia) 879
Korean 178, 536–7, 745, 746
Korean-English 127

L

labeling 721, 725
lack of invariance problem 307
Landscape Model 201, 617
language acquisition device 719
language-as-fixed-effect fallacy 918–19
language decision 131
language disorders 738–9, 828
  see also aphasia; developmental language disorder
language endowment spectrum 822
language-general cues 13–15
  cross-boundary decoarticulation 14
  cross-boundary glottalization 15
  intonational boundaries 15
  pauses 13–14
  prosodic lengthening 14–15
language impairment 108–9, 797
  see also specific language impairment (SLI)
language membership
  lexical level 131–2
  sentence level 132–3
  sublexical level 132
  visual word recognition in multilinguals 119, 130–3
language non-specific activation process 136
language non-specific lexical access hypothesis 119, 121
language-non-specific models 469, 473–4
language-non-specific selection models: inhibitory control model 464–5
language-or structure-driven hypothesis 538
language production see bilingual language production
language production theory 353, 482–3
language proficiency 945
language regression 878
language-specific cues 15–18
  allophony 17, 21, 22
  lexical stress 17–18
  phonotactics 15–17, 694–6
  vowel harmony 17
language specific lexical access hypothesis 119
language-specific models 462, 463–4, 465, 469, 473–4
language-specific sublexical information 136

language style matching (LSM) 581–2
language switching 467–72, 474
  blocked language switching task 472
  trial-by-trial task 467–72
large-fiber sensory neuropathy 293
larynx 849
late anterior negativity (LAN) 220
Late Closure principle 176, 227–9
latent semantic analysis (LSA) 73, 210, 582
late positive component (LPC) 126, 220, 935, 942
late talkers 824, 828
Latin America 675
Latvia 118
learning bottlenecks 900–2
learning-centred PDP approach 385
learning difficulties and disabilities (LDD) 705, 785
learning effect 515
left anterior negativity (LAN) 531, 938, 942, 945
left dorsal language system 768–9
left inferior frontal gyrus (LIFG) 109–11, 961, 963–4
  artificial grammar learning 771, 776
  syntactic production and comprehension 495–6
left posterior superior/middle temporal gyri (LPUTG) 769–71, 776
lemma dilemma 403
lemma nodes 442
lemmas 291, 336–7, 339–40
  attention and structural choice in sentence production 528, 539
  bilingualism 464
  connectionist principles and speech production 376
  grammatical encoding 435, 438–9, 443–4
  spelling/writing 402–3, 407, 414
  spoken word production 346, 354, 355
  syntactic production and comprehension 482
lesionable parameters 510
letter position coding 50
letter-sound knowledge 798
letter-string hypothesis 409
Levenshtein distance 56, 121–2, 134
lexemes 291, 336–7
  connectionist principles and speech production 376
  grammatical encoding 435, 438
  spelling/writing 403, 415
  spoken word production 355
lexical access 336–7, 338–9
  competitive/non-competitive 339
  connectionist principles of speech production 391
  perspective-taking 553
lexical activation 344
lexical ambiguity 96–112
  brain mechanisms of ambiguity resolution 108–11
  learning 102–4
  representation 99–102
  syntactic production and comprehension 484, 500
  understanding ambiguous words in sentences 104–8

lexical-auditory weight (LA) 299–300
lexical boost 578, 579
lexical category acquisition 697–9
lexical cohort 336
lexical competition 10, 11, 18
lexical components in attention and structural choice in sentence production 538–9
lexical concepts 336
lexical cues 13
lexical decision task 11
   ambiguity 100
   bilingualism 226
   cross-modal 198
   lexico-semantics 74
   spoken word recognition 34
   visual word recognition 51
lexical entry 435
lexical form 133
lexical information in segmentation of speech 18–19
lexical integration 335
lexical islands 39
lexical items in bilingualism 462
lexicality in word recognition and segmentation of speech 11–13
lexicalized tree-adjoining grammar 441
lexical level
   bilingualism 226
   connectionist principles and speech production 375–6
   language membership 131–2
lexically-based models 441
lexically based theories of syntax 438
lexical match in attention and structural choice in sentence production 539
lexical-motor weight (LM) 299–300
lexical onsets 9
lexical processing 218, 343
   see also spoken word production
lexical recognition 18
lexical representations 335
   alignment during interaction 574
   spoken word recognition 40–1, 42
lexical retrieval 435, 439
   serial/interactive 339–40
lexical richness 78
lexical selection 335, 383, 435, 439
lexical stress 6, 8, 17–18, 22, 226
lexical switch 220
lexical system 41
lexical units in connectionist principles and speech production 374–5
lexicon-external task-schemas 464
lexicon structure 122–3
lexico-semantics 71–89, 386, 714–15, 719–22
   ambiguities 486, 494
   content of representations 77–9
   context 80–8

availability hypothesis 86
definition 80–1
dependency 71, 78, 79–80
environment (role of physical context) 84–6
goal-driven short-term 80
individual (role of experience and current cognitive context) 80–2
-invariance 71, 79–80, 88
physical 71, 80, 89
task 71, 80, 88, 89
task (role of goal-driven, short-term context) 82–4
theories of context-dependent lexico-semantics 86–8
embodied theories of language 72–3, 76, 77–9, 83, 85
format of representations 75, 77–9
interference 103
key issues 75–80
   concepts 76
   context-invariance vs. context-dependency 79–80
   format and content of representations: embodied/ amodal approaches 77–9
networks 73
theoretical approaches 72–5
   attributional theories 72–3
   distributional theories 73–4
   hybrid, multilevel and combined models 74–5
lexomes 41
LI group 824
linear mixed-effects models (LMEMs) 918
linguistic context in lexico-semantics 73
linguistic co-presence 552
Linguistic Inquiry and Word Count (LIWC) 210
linguistic knowledge and non-linguistic knowledge distinction 449–50
linking hypothesis 173, 187
links (edges) 38–40
lip protrusion 308
Lithuania 118
local damage mechanisms 383–4
Local Field Potential (LFP) 995
localist connectionist approach 73, 75, 76, 77, 134, 385, 388, 389–90
   connectionist principles and speech production 372, 378–9, 383, 384, 392
   lexico-semantics 73, 75, 76, 77
   see also under connectionist approach
local sentence context 129
logogen models 53
logographeme (stroke pattern) 417
long-term learning 388
long-term memory
   emotion and sociality 653–4, 659
   first word learning 715
   pragmatics and inference 616
   sentence comprehension 179–80

spoken word recognition 32
statistical learning 706-7
text comprehension 203
see also orthographic long-term memory (O-LTM)
low attachment 175
Luxembourg 118
lyre birds 847
lysosome targeting pathway 883

M
MacArthur Communicative Development Inventories (CDI) 700
McGurk effect 944
machine learning decoding techniques 1003
machine learning techniques in speech perception and production 315
magnetic resonance imaging (MRI)
developmental language disorder 828-9, 830
dyslexia 799
speech perception and production 318, 321
see also functional magnetic resonance imaging (fMRI)
magnetoencephalography (MEG) 209, 930
semantic deficit 147
sentence comprehension 172
speech perception and production 314, 318
see also source estimation, connectivity and pattern analysis of EEG/MEG data
Malagasy 537-8
Malta 118
Mandarin
dyslexia 788
sentence comprehension 178
spelling/writing 406
spoken word production 348
spoken word recognition 42
manipulation affordances 535
map task 575
masked onset priming effect (MOPE) 963
masked priming 56-7
semantic 59, 965
spelling/writing 405-6
visual word recognition in multilinguals 131, 132
meaning dominance 106
memory
declarative 726, 728
first word learning 720
ordinary 558-9
perspective-taking 559
phonological 797
recognition 725
relational 725-6
semantic 336
sentence comprehension 177-80
tests for pragmatics and inference 613
visual 420-1

see also long-term memory; short-term memory; working memory
memory-based text processing 616
mental lexicon 31-2
ambiguity 99-100
spoken word production 336, 338, 341, 342, 346
spoken word recognition 39, 41
syntactic production and comprehension 482
visual word recognition 48-9
in multilinguals 120-1, 123, 128
mental models in pragmatics and inference 612, 615-16, 617, 618
message-driven hypothesis 538
messenger RNA (mRNA) 871, 874, 875
metalinguistic syllabification tasks 9
metaphor/metaphoric meaning 31-2, 493
metrical information 10
mice 866, 883-4
microelectrodes 930
micro RNA-based control of expression 874-5
middle frontal gyrus (MFG) 497, 501
middle temporal gyrus (MTG)
gesture 601, 602
statistical learning 703-4
syntactic production and comprehension 495-6, 501
migration and neurite outgrowth 876-7
Millennium Cohort Study (MCS)(UK) 818-21
mimicry 582
mind wandering 204
Minimal Attachment 227
Minimalist Hypothesis 614
minimal words 677-8
mirror neurons 306, 308, 312-13, 322, 448
mismatch negativity (MMN) 938, 940, 944-5
mispronunciations and lexical access 38
mixed effects modeling 209-10
mixed error effect 377, 379-81, 508
mixed transcortical or global aphasia 151
mixing costs 475
modality specificity 376
models of language evolution 899-909
arbitrary symbols 904-5
artificial languages 902-3, 908
combinatoriality 899, 901, 903-4, 907, 908
compositionality 899, 900-1, 903, 905, 907, 908
conditioned variation 907
conventionalization 904
cross-cultural comparisons and biological evolution 908-9
cultural evolution/transmission 900, 901-2, 904, 907-8, 909
emerging sign languages 903-4
generalizations 899, 901-2
holistic learnability 901, 904, 909
iconicity 904-5
interaction 905
iterated learning 900-3, 905, 908

models of language evolution (*Cont.*)
    learnability and linguistic structure 902–4
    learning bottlenecks 900–2
    linguistic variation 906
    regularity 905–7, 908
    systematicity 905–7
    transmission chains 901–6, 908–9
    typological universals 907–8
modular conceptualization of the mind 553
modularity debate 439
monitoring and adjustment model 555
Monte Carlo simulations 919, 925
moral reasoning 208
More than One Mechanism (MOM) hypothesis 706–7
morphemes 291
    bilingualism 222
    dyslexia 788
    grammatical 685
    inflectional 684
    language evolution models 899
    spelling/writing 412–13
    spoken word production 346–8, 349, 351
    visual word recognition 52
morphological awareness in dyslexia 788
morphological family size effects 123
morphological markedness patterns 738
morphological structure in visual word recognition 57
morphological substitution errors 292
morphology
    bilingualism 223, 231
    grammatical encoding 438
    orthographic representations 52
    spoken word production 335
    spoken word recognition 42
    visual word recognition 60–1
        in multilinguals 120, 136
morpho-orthography hypothesis 412
motor control approach 293–6, 796
motor cortex 234–5, 313–14
motor-evoked potentials (MEPs) 311, 319
motor imagery in speech perception and production 322
motor invariants 308
motor learning impairments 874
motor neuron disease 77, 322
motor planning for articulation 291
Motor Theory of Speech Perception (MTSP) 306–8, 311, 314, 315, 322–3, 408
movement priming paradigm 966
MROM model 49
multidimensional hypothesis 409
multilevel models in lexico-semantics 74–5
multilingualism 356, 1001
    see also visual word recognition in multilinguals
Multilink 16, 135
multimodal communication 556
multimodal, composite signs 653
multimodal representations in lexico-semantics 77

multiparty conversation 556
multiple context-free grammars 760, 768
multiple risk framework in developmental dyslexia 795–6
multiple-word forms, activation of 33–5
multisensory integration 944
multivoxel/multivariate pattern analysis (MVPA) 955, 960, 967, 982–3
    speech perception and production 315–16
    visual word recognition 60
mutual knowledge 552

N
n-1 shift cost 467, 471
n-2 repetition cost 471
naming latencies in bilingualism 219
naming objects 632–3
naming response distribution 301
nativist (rationalist) position 719
natural grammar 760
natural language
    and artificial grammar learning (AGL) comparison 760, 764–5, 766, 767–71, 775, 776
    hierarchically structured sequences and left dorsal language system 768–9
    syntax and phonology 768
    temporal lobe contributions vs. complex syntax 769–71
    and statistical learning 692, 694–5, 697, 702, 704–5, 708
naturally redundant relations 722
Neanderthals 849, 850, 858
neighbors/neighborhood 121
    activation model 34–5, 37, 40, 261
    addition 121
    attention and structural choice in sentence production 539
    deletion 121
    density 34, 268, 351
    frequency 34
    probability rule 34
    semantic 380–1
    sign languages and deaf populations 263–4
    spoken word recognition 39–40
    visual word recognition 54–6
        in multilinguals 120, 121, 123–4, 134, 136
Neo-Griceans 626, 627
nested hierarchical grammars 771
Netherlands 118
network science 38–40, 41, 43
neural adaptation approach 409
neural correlates in developmental language disorder 829–30
neural models 43
neural priming effects in visual word recognition 60
neuroanatomical reasons for attention and structural choice in sentence production 530
neurobiological effects in developmental language disorder 830

neurobiological processing principles 382
neuroimaging
    ambiguity 108
    artificial grammar learning (AGL) 765-7
    bilingualism 468, 470
    developmental language disorder 828-30
    lexico-semantics 84
    semantic deficit 146
    sign language processing, deaf populations 269-71
    spoken word recognition 43
    text comprehension 197, 198, 200, 206
    visual word recognition in multilinguals 119, 134, 136
    see also specific imaging techniques
neurophysiological maturation 725-6
neurophysiological studies 49, 76, 77, 136
neuroscience
    lexico-semantics 76
    segmentation of speech 23
    text comprehension 200, 205-9
    visual word recognition 49, 60
    see also cognitive neuroscience
new Motor Theory: support and criticisms 312-13
nodes 38-40, 53-4, 56-7
    ambiguity 99
    combinatorial 442
    segmentation of speech 10
    speech production 294
    visual word recognition 59
no-go N200 effect 938, 943
noise 14, 184
    ambiguity 100
    connectionist principles and speech production 383
    environmental 19
    sentence level aphasia 243
    speech perception and production 317-18, 319
NOLB model 601
nominal event 725
non-adjacent dependencies 696-7
    artificial grammar learning (AGL) 764, 771, 773-5
    statistical learning 699-702, 704-9
non-canonical word order 495
non-coding DNA as gate-keeper for gene expression 871-3
non-cognates 439
non-declarative/procedural learning 764
non-decompositional models 336
non-fluent aphasia see Broca's aphasia
non-homophonic words 58
non-language-specific models in bilingualism 462, 465
non-lexical cues 10, 13-18, 19, 20, 21, 22
non-linguistic processing in attention and structural choice in sentence production 528, 530
non-linguistic task switching in bilingualism 469
non-pseudohomophonic non-words 58
non-shared information 559
non-specific language disorder 821
non-syntactic expressions in first word learning 723
non-verbal signs, emotion and sociality 653

non-verbal skills in developmental language disorder 827
non-word errors 382, 508
non-word primes 56-7
non-words in spoken word recognition 33
Norway 798
Norwegian 692, 702
Norwegian-English 132
noun phrase (NP) 223, 239-40
noun-verb agreement 226-7
novel phonological sequences 388
novelty effect 721, 773
now-or-never proposal 343
nRef 938, 942
numerical reasoning 739-40

O

object manipulation task 251
object naming 407, 965
object relative clauses 177, 178, 486
obligatory phonological mediation hypothesis 403
oddball paradigm 773, 775, 935
offline metalinguistic judgment task 12
offsets 9
one unit per meaning approach 101
ongoing learning effects 447-8
onsets 9, 11, 14, 16
OPC/POC systems 420
open bigram model 50
optic ataxia 296
Optimality Theory 679
ORCs 274-5
order encoding/learning deficits 420
ordinary memory processes 558-9
orofacial dyspraxia 873
orthographic autonomy hypothesis 403-4
Orthographic Levenshtein Distance 20 (OLD20) 56
orthographic long-term memory (O-LTM) 399-402, 408-9, 411, 416-18, 420
orthographic working memory (O-WM) 399-402, 411-14, 420
orthography
    alphabetic, in developmental dyslexia 787-8
    ambiguity 98, 101
    bilingualism 221, 226
    cumulative semantic interference 50-2
    dyslexia 786, 788
    sign languages and deaf populations 269, 273
    spelling/writing 398, 406-7, 415-18, 421
    spoken word production 342
    spoken word recognition 32, 39
    visual word recognition 48-52, 60-1
        in multilinguals 120-2, 123-5, 126, 127-8, 130, 132, 134-5, 136
    written language production 409-14
orthotactic properties in visual word recognition in multilinguals 132

oscillator models 388–90
    and connectivity 957–60
    non-repeating 389
    time-varying 389–90
output-input coordination 577
overlap 11, 50, 231–2
    bilingualism 226–7
    code 127
    sign languages and deaf populations 270
    somatotopic 314
    spoken word production 348, 351–3
overt attentional shift 532

P
paradigmatic interference 344
paragrammatism 245–6, 248–9
parallel-distributed processing framework 449
paraphrasing task 485
Parkinson's disease 77, 322
parrots 846, 848, 858
parsing 227–31, 243, 714
    syntactic 483–5, 553
PARSYN connectionist model 37
passive listening paradigm 775
passivization 537
pattern analysis see source estimation, connectivity and pattern analysis of EEG/MEG data
pattern-based accounts 761
pauses 6, 13–14, 32
perception and production in speech 36, 291–301, 306–25
    age-related decline 320–1
    cognitive neuroscience of motor theories of speech perception 314–19
        perceptual representations of speech in cortical motor system 314–17
        task-dependency, environmental factors and turn-taking 317–19
    cognitive neuroscience of speech perception 308–14
        motor cortex and speech 313–14
        new Motor Theory: support and criticisms 312–13
    embodied theories of language 322–3
    environmental factors 317–19
    motor cortex role 234–5
    Motor Theory of Speech Perception (MTSP) 306–8, 311, 314, 315, 322–3, 408
    patient evidence and healthy aging 320–2
    perceptual representations of speech in cortical motor system 314–17
    sensorimotor transformations in posterior cortical fields 323–4
perceptual identification 34, 51
Perceptual Loop Theory 380, 513, 518
perceptually grounded vs. amodal knowledge representation 943–4
perceptual priming 533–5, 536–7, 538–40, 541
perceptual span in deaf populations 271
perceptual task in lexico-semantics 80

performance as a trait 764–5
performatives 610
perfusion weighted imaging (PWI) 251, 469
perisylvian association cortex 250
persistence, syntactic 440–2, 444, 447–8, 449–50
perspective meaning 434, 436–7, 445
perspective-taking 549–64
    common ground 550, 551–2, 553, 555–6, 559, 561, 563
    future 560–3
    heuristics 552, 560, 564
    language processing 550
    language production 555
    past 551–6
    present 556–9
    referential communication task 551–2
PGD 411, 420–1
phase-locking 959–60, 965, 968
phase-slope index 959
Philadelphia Naming Test (PNT) 508, 512
phoneme-grapheme conversion (PGC) 399, 401, 407, 416–18
phonemes 292
    alignment during interaction 578
    awareness in dyslexia 786–7, 789–90, 796, 798, 802
    boundary in dyslexia 791
    connectionist principles and speech production 374–5, 378–9
    language evolution models 899
    semantic deficit 150
    sequences in spoken word recognition 39–40
    speech perception and production 294, 307–8, 310–11, 319
    spoken word recognition 33, 36–7, 39–40
phonetic accommodation 558
phonetic properties in spoken word production 351
phonological awareness deficits 420
phonological awareness in dyslexia 786, 787–8, 790, 797
phonological deficit 786, 789, 796, 802
phonological encoding 291
phonological errors 379–80, 383, 516–18, 520
phonological facilitation vs. semantic interference in picture naming 377, 378–9
phonological influences on visual word recognition 58–9
phonological learning 716
phonological memory 797
phonological neighborhood density (PND) 350–1, 352, 354
phonological neighbors in spoken word recognition 35
phonological paraphasias and neologisms 150
phonological processing 208
    deficits 420
    see also spoken word production
phonological recoding 403
phonological representations in connectionist principles and speech production 374–6
phonological retrieval 789

phonological structures in connectionist principles of speech production 389
phonological theory, strong 58-9
phonology
    alignment during interaction 574
    ambiguity 98, 101
    artificial grammar learning (AGL) and natural language comparison 768
    autosegmental 348-9
    bilingualism 222, 226
    connectionist principles of speech production 372, 390, 392
    dyslexia 801
    fast 58
    grammatical encoding 433, 436, 438, 439
    language evolution models 901
    output 789
    sentence comprehension 177
    sentence level aphasia 243
    sign languages and deaf populations 259, 265, 266, 269, 273
    speech perception and production 292, 317-18
    spelling/writing 414-15, 418
    spoken word production 335, 338, 340, 341
    spoken word recognition 32, 39, 42
    visual word recognition 48, 961-4
        in multilinguals 120-1, 122, 125, 126, 127, 128, 134, 135, 136
    writing and speaking 404-6
    see also prosodic phonology
phonotactics 15-17, 447
    segmentation of speech 18, 21, 23
    statistical learning 705
    visual word recognition in multilinguals 132
phrasal accent 8
physical context 71, 80, 89
physical co-presence 552
physiological measures of difficulty 172
picture-based rhyming task 273
picture description tasks 355
picture naming task 999
    sentence level aphasia 247
    sign languages and deaf populations 266
    speech production 298
    spelling/writing 405
    spoken word production 352
picture-picture priming 405
picture-word interference (PWI) paradigm
    bilingual language production 465-7
    connectionist principles and speech production 378
    lexico-semantics 81
    spelling/writing 306, 404, 405
    spoken word production 338-9, 347, 351, 354
picture-word matching task 321
Pirahã (Brazil) 739-40
pitch accent 18
planning frames 246
planning scope 342-4

plan reuse 450
plausibility judgment task 245
PNP 938, 942
Polish-English 126
polysemy 97-8, 101-2, 738
polysyllabic shortening 14
population-average models (PAMs) 928
Portuguese
    bilingualism 228
    Brazilian 739
    dyslexia 787
    grammatical encoding 447
    prosodic phonology 685
Portuguese-English 229
positional assignment mechanism 540-1
positional processing/structures 435
positional timing effects 17
positional view in attention and structural choice in sentence production 528-9
positional vs. grammatical-role hypothesis 535-8
position-dependent interference effects of form overlap 352
position uncertainty in visual word recognition 50
positron emission tomography (PET) 975n, 981
    semantic deficit 146-7
    syntactic production and comprehension 497
    text comprehension 206
Possible Word Constraint (PWC) 10, 16-17
posterior cortical fields 323-4
posterior middle temporal gyrus (pMTG) 148
posterior probabilities 38
posterior superior temporal gyrus (STG) 148
post-transcriptional regulation (controlling the message) 873-5
posture 581
pragmatics 609-11
    bilingualism 223
    and inference
        constructivist processes 612-15, 616, 618
        mental models 612, 615-16, 617, 618
    segmentation of speech 12
    visual word recognition in multilinguals 120
    see also experimental pragmatics
prediction 185, 186
    error 957
prediction-by-association 314
prediction-by-simulation 314
prelexical representations 40, 42
prepositional phrase 228
    modification 175
presbycusis 321
presupposition 550, 610-12
pre-verbal messages 433-4
priming
    behavioral 60
    bilingualism 219, 466, 472
    form 352, 354
    gesture 599-600

priming (*Cont.*)
   implicit 347, 349–52, 405
   lexicality in visual word recognition 56
   lexico-semantics 82–3
   neural 60
   non-word 56–7
   perceptual 533–5, 536–7, 538–40, 541
   picture-picture 405
   referential 532–3
   repetition 408, 513
   sequential form 352
   sign languages and deaf populations 264
   spoken word production 347
   syntactic production and comprehension 501
   visual word recognition 58
      in multilinguals 126, 133–4, 135
   word 57
   word-meaning 106
   see also cross-modal priming; masked priming; semantic priming; syntactic priming
private speech 741
privileged ground 551, 556, 562–3
proactive control 475
probabilistic models 180–2, 184
   Bayesian 560
probability 38
   conditional 38
   match 906
   transitional 22, 691–6, 704–6
procedural learning deficits *see* developmental dyslexia
processing cascade in emotion and sociality 649
process issue in visual word recognition in multilinguals 123
process-oriented question in visual word recognition in multilinguals 119
Procrustean transform 984
pro-drop languages 222–3
production of agreement 450
Production, Distribution Comprehension (PDC) account 186
production effect 561
production tasks in spelling/writing 406
projection problem 610
promoters 871, 873
pronunciation 32, 43
proofreading task 485
propositional content in sentence level aphasia 239
propositionalization 208
prosodic constituents in segmentation of speech 19
prosodic cues 13, 21
prosodic information in segmentation of speech 18
prosodic lengthening 14–15
prosodic phonology 348–9, 675–85
   feet and unmarked Prosodic Word (PW) structures 680–1
   higher levels of prosodic structure 681–5
   Intonational Phrase (IP) 676, 682–3, 684–5
   minimal words 677–8
   Phonological Phrase (PP) 676, 682, 684–5
   Phonological Utterance (Utt.) 676
   Prosodic Hierarchy 676
   Prosodic Licensing Hypothesis 682–3, 685
   Prosodic Words (PW) 676, 677, 678, 679, 682, 684
   subminimal words 679–80
prosodic phrasing in segmentation of speech 20
prosodification 349
prosody 5, 20
protein 874, 875
Providence Corpus 683
pseudohomophones 58
pseudosigns 262
pseudowords 757
   superiority effect 53–4
PSG 769
psychological adequacy 36
psychophysical tasks in dyslexia 792
Puerto Rican Spanish 739
puns 96
pure word deafness (PWD) 150, 156
p-weight parameters 511–12, 521

Q

qualitative and quantitative predictions 560
quantifier scope ambiguities 184
quantization constraint 390–1
Quechua (language) 746

R

random intercept variance 919, 926–7
random slope variance 919, 927, 928
rapid auditory processing (RAP) deficit hypothesis 792–3
rapid automatized naming (RAN) 390, 786–7, 788, 797, 798
rapid fade 904
rapid serial visual presentation (RSVP) paradigm 129
Rasch models of accuracy 242, 243
rationalist view in first word learning 720
rational models of sentence production 446–7
reaction times (RTs) 72, 227
   behavioral 270
   visual word recognition in multilinguals 125, 126, 129, 131
reactive control 475
readability measures in text comprehension 204
reading network in developmental dyslexia 799–800
reading span test 203
Reading Systems Framework 201
reading system visual word recognition 57–9
real-time language comprehension/processing 550, 553
REBER grammar 757–8
receiver operating characteristic (ROC) analysis 766

receptive language in developmental language
    disorder 827-8
receptive vocabulary 727
reciprocal alternation 230-1
recognition memory 725
recognition task in statistical learning 699
recognizing/parsing signs presented by
    speaker 653, 655
recovery-from preemption 634
recurrent network architecture 386
recursion 866
reed warblers 847
reference 631-5, 639, 662
    diaries model 552
    egocentric approach 633-4
    naming objects 632-3
reference-making 624
referential arena processes 434
referential communication task 551-2
referential function of language 722-7
referential intention 655, 661
referential meaning 663
referential phenomena in perspective-taking 562
referential priming in attention and structural choice
    in sentence production 532-3
referential situation in emotion and sociality 659
referential word use 727
referring expressions 552
regular grammars 759
regularity in models of language evolution
    905-7, 908
Reicher-Wheeler experiments 53
relational meaning 434, 436
relational memory 725-6
relational/perspective meaning 437
relational points 722
relative clauses 228-9, 230
    sentence comprehension 176, 178-9, 186
    sentence level aphasia 244, 245
    syntactic production and comprehension 495
Relevance Theory 610, 626-7
reordered access model of ambiguity resolution 106
repeat-READ condition 409
repeat trials in bilingualism 467-8
repetition 6, 340
repetition cost, n-2 471
repetition priming 408, 513
repetition structure account 761
replication in generalizing over encounters 923-5
representation 23, 345-50
    see also written language production
representational dis-similarity matrix (RDM) 315
representational parity 573, 575
Representational Similarity Analysis (RSA) 60, 315,
    961, 967, 983, 984-5
re-revised Hierarchical Model 218
Rescorla-Wagner equation 41

resource reduction models 243, 246
response exclusion hypothesis 339
response monitoring in connectionist principles and
    speech production 380
restricted search hypothesis 553
retrieval
    in grammatical encoding 432, 437
    -induced forgetting (RIF) effect 473-4
    of other words in spoken word production 351-3
    words and their neighbours
        individual words 337-8
        words in networks 338-40
Rett syndrome 871
reverberation stage 440
Revised Hierarchical Model (RHM) 133-4, 218-19
rewrite rules 759
rhyming task 996
rhythm class 20-1
RI-Val model 201, 617
RNA 868, 875
    micro RNA-based control of expression 874-5
    Sequencing 876
    see also messenger RNA (mRNA)
root mean square error (RMSE) 299
routines in bilingualism 227
rude verbal insult, comprehension of 653-5
    input: multimodal, composite signs 653
    interpreting speaker's communicative move 655
    recognizing/parsing signs presented by
        speaker 653, 655
    see also swear words
rule-based accounts 761
Russian 222, 702, 738
    attention and structural choice in sentence
        production 529, 536-7, 540-1

S
salience
    artificial grammar learning 767, 773
    attention and structural choice in sentence
        production 527-30, 538, 539-40
    Graded Salience Hypothesis 636-7
sample size in generalizing over encounters 924
sampling error in generalizing over
    encounters 924-6, 928
Sapir-Whorf hypothesis 745
satellite-framed languages (S-languages) 596
scalar enrichments 630-1
scalar implicature
    event-related brain potentials (ERPs) 944-5
    pragmatics 625-31, 639
        anti-Gricean turn 629-31
        experimental turn 627-9
    see also experimental pragmatics
scalar utterances 627-9
schematic theory of text comprehension 613
schizophrenia 874

scope of activation and planning
   grammatical encoding 442–4
   spoken word production 354–6
sea lions 848
seals 845, 848
search models 54, 57
search space 7
second-noun strategy for interpreting NNV and VNN sentences 225
segmental errors 349, 354
segmentation of speech 5–24
   ambisyllabic consonants 8
   boundaries 5–6, 9–10
   boundary cues 14, 20
   boundary perception 12
   boundary-straddling words 11
   and classification, contrast between 6–7
   continuity 6–7
   cues in combination 18–19
   explicit non-lexical cues 6
   first and second language acquisition 19–23
      infant-directed speech 19–20
      infant sensitivity to segmentation cues 20–2
      non-native segmentation 22–3
   first word learning 716–17
   full vowel/reduced vowel 8
   hyperarticulation/hypoarticulation 8, 19
   implicit segmentation 6, 11
   language-specific cues 15–18
      allophony 17, 21, 22
      lexical stress 17–18
      phonotactics 15–17
      vowel harmony 17
   lexically driven segmentation 20
   lexical stress 8, 17–18
   metrical segmentation 20, 21
   non-lexical cues 6, 10, 11, 13–18, 19, 20, 21, 22, 23
      cross-boundary decoarticulation 14
      cross-boundary glottalization 15
      intonational boundaries 15
      language-general cues 13–15
      pauses 13–14
      prosodic lengthening 14–15
   non-native 22–3
   phonotactic segmentation 22
   phrasal accent 8
   prosodic segmentation cues 221
   segmental segmentation cues 20–2, 221
   segmentation algorithm based on trigram occurrence 16
   segmentation boost 10
   segmentation-by-lexical subtraction 11–12, 22
   segmentation heuristics 16
   segmentation of words from fluent speech 38
   spoken word recognition 32
   strong syllable/weak syllable 8, 9, 10, 13, 17–18, 22
   suprasegmental cues 20

syllable boundaries 7
syllable effect 7, 9
Syllable Onset Segmentation Heuristic (SOSH) 9–10
syllables in prelexical classification 7–10
   variation 6–7
   vowel-harmony segmentation 13
   word recognition and implicit segmentation 10–13
      lexicality 11–13
      models 10–11
      semantics 11–13
      syntax 11–13
      word recognition models 10–11
   words 691–5
selection
   connectionist principles 388–91
   individual words 337–8
   spoken word production 350–1
   by threshold mechanism 462
   words in networks 338–40
self-directed speech 741
self-monitoring 294
self-paced listening 244–5
self-paced moving window reading 172
self-paced reading 271, 628
semantically incongruent signs 262
semantic aphasia (SA) 144–5, 151–3, 154, 156
semantic boost 578, 579
semantic brain networks 964–7
   amodal areas: anterior temporal lobe (ATL) 965–6
   distributed areas: sensorimotor systems 966
   evaluation 966–7
semantic complexity in syntactic production and comprehension 495–6
semantic cues 13
semantic decisions in lexico-semantics 74
semantic deficit 144–56
   access deficits: controlled retrieval and selection impairments 150–3
   anterior temporal lobe (ATL) 145–9
      as graded hub 147–8
      heteromodal semantic hub 146–7
      input processing deficits 149–50
   semantic control across modalities 154–5
      distributed semantic control network 154–5
   semantic dementia (SD) 145–6
   spokes: category-specific deficits 148–9
semantic demands in syntactic production and comprehension 496
semantic dementia (SD) 144, 148–9, 151–3, 155–6, 521
   distributed-plus-hub theory 518
semantic distractors 339
semantic errors 508, 516–19, 520
   connectionist principles and speech production 379–80, 382, 383
semantic influences 59, 271–5
semantic information 60, 499, 967

semantic integration 965
semantic interference 445, 513
  vs. phonological facilitation in picture
    naming 377, 378-9
  see also cumulative semantic interference (CSI)
semantic-lexical-auditory-motor (SLAM)
  model 298-301
semantic-lexical weight 300
semantic mapping in signed languages 265-7
semantic masked priming paradigm 59, 965
semantic meaning 434, 437
semantic memory 336
semantic neighbors 380-1
semantic-phonological error-detection 513
Semantic-Phonological (SP) model 297-8, 299, 301,
  506, 510-13
semantic priming
  bilingualism 218-19
  lexico-semantics 72, 73
  sign languages and deaf populations 268
  visual word recognition 59
    in multilinguals 129
  word production in aphasia 513
semantic processing 217-22, 231, 495-6
  see also spoken word production
semantic relatedness 270, 347
semantic representations 374-6, 386
semantics
  alignment during interaction 577-8
  ambiguity 101
  bilingualism 223, 227, 232
  event 386, 531
  evolution of speech 855
  lexical 386
  segmentation of speech 12
  speech perception and production 318
  spoken word production 335, 338, 341
  spoken word recognition 32, 39
  visual word recognition 48, 58
    in multilinguals 120-1, 128, 134-5
  word recognition and implicit segmentation 11-13
  see also lexico-semantics
semantic transparency 347
semantic violations 486, 495
sensorimotor transformations in posterior cortical
  fields 323-4
sensory feedback 294, 295
sensory information in motor control 293
sentence
  event-related brain potentials (ERPs) 938
  language evolution models 899
  language membership 132-3
sentence completion task 997
sentence comprehension 171-87
  computational models 173, 179, 180-2, 186
  constraint-based models 174-5, 181
  experience-based accounts 175, 176, 177-80, 181, 182

interpreting the present 183-4
learning mechanisms 180-2
local modification 175-6
measurement of sentence processing 172-3
modular approaches 174-5
predicting the future 185
and production 185-6
sentence processing models 171, 173-83, 764
  information theoretic approaches 182-3
  innate mechanism vs. experience-driven accounts
    of ambiguity resolution 175-6
  learning mechanisms, probabilistic models and
    computational models 180-2
  syntactic complexity, memory and
    experience 177-80
  see also bilingual sentence processing
syntactic complexity 173-4, 177-80
updating the past 184
sentence interpretation paradigm 222, 224-5
sentence level aphasia 239-52
  the dog that scratched the cat killed the
    mouse 239-40
  functional neuroanatomy of syntactic
    processing 250-1
  global parsing or interpretive failure 241
  increased interference 241
  late delayed operations 241
  production deficits and comprehension deficits,
    relation of 249-50
  resource reduction 241
  selecting parsing or interpretive failure 241
  slowed processing 241
  syntactic comprehension disorders 240-51
  syntactic production disorders 245-9
sentence-picture matching (SPM) 242, 244-5, 248
sentence-picture verification task 202
sentence processing see bilingual sentence processing;
  sentence comprehension
sentence production 446-7, 497
  see also attention and structural choice in sentence
    production
sentential context 353-4
sequences of words 340-1, 351-3
sequential encoding 347
sequential form priming 352
sequential frequencies 22
Serbo-Croatian 223
serial order general theory 388
serial order information 74
serial reproduction 902
Sesotho (Bantu language) 678-9, 682-3
severity/error type interaction 508, 510
shadowing studies 33
shared experiences 556, 559
shared knowledge 595
shared space 595
shift cost, n-1 467, 471

Shortlist model 10, 37, 38, 40
short-term learning 388
short-term memory 942
    artificial grammar learning 763
    dyslexia 789, 797
    sentence level aphasia 243
    sign languages and deaf populations 272
    statistical learning 699–700, 705
    text comprehension 203
signal degradation 6, 19
signal leakage 960
sign languages and deaf populations 259–75, 866n
    Al-Sayyid Bedouin Sign Language (ABSL) 852–3, 879, 903–4
    American Sign Language (ASL) 259–62, 264, 266–8, 270, 272–3, 275, 444, 855
    British Sign Language (BSL) 266
    conceptual development 737, 740
    emerging sign languages 266, 852–3, 879–80, 903–4
    evolution of speech 852, 855–6
    genetics 879–80
    handshape 261, 263–6, 268, 270
    'home' 737
    Kata Kolok sign language (Indonesia) 879
    lexical recognition of signs 261–5
        sublexical properties of lexicon 263–5
    linguistic structure of signs 261
    location 261, 263–5, 268, 270
    movement 261, 265, 270
    neuroimaging studies of sign language processing 269–71
        bilingualism 269–71
        perceptual span 271
        reading 269
    orientation 261, 265
    semantic mapping in signed languages 265–7
    space 266
    Spanish Sign Language (LSE) 264
    spatial location in sign grammar 267–9
    spoken language phonology 271–5
        syntactic and semantic influences 273–5
sign-picture matching 266
silences 10, 32
similarity-based accounts 761
similarity metric 121
simple recurrent networks (SRNs) 173, 183
simultaneous reading and speaking paradigm 485
single abstract letter identity 49
single word lexical decision experiments 270–1
single word naming 248
situated conversation 556
situated language processing 85
situation models 201–2, 204
    alignment 581
    emotion and sociality 655
    grammatical encoding 448
    pragmatics and inference 612, 615–16, 617, 618

text comprehension 200, 202, 207, 210
sleep processes 180
slips of the ear 35, 43
slips of the tongue 35
slot-based coding 49–50
Slovak 17, 787
Slovenia 118
social context in first word learning 722
social coordination 851
social factors and alignment during interaction 582–6
social gradient in developmental language disorder 818–19, 826–7
social intention 658–9, 662, 663
    and inference 656
social interaction 881
sociality *see* emotion, comprehension and sociality
social marker, language as 736, 737, 746–8
social skill score 639
sociocultural components 866
SOLAR model 49
somatotopic involvement/overlap in speech perception and production 310–11, 314
SOMBIP Model (Self-Organizing Model of Bilingual Processing) 135
song 845–6
songbirds 846, 847–8, 858, 866, 881–2, 883, 908–9
song sparrows 847
source estimation, connectivity and pattern analysis of EEG/MEG data 955–69
    beamformers 957
    decoding conceptual and semantic information 967
    dipole modeling 956–7, 964
    distributed source solutions 957
    dynamic causal modeling (DCM) 959–60, 964, 965
    evaluation 964
    functional magnetic resonance imaging (fMRI) comparison/combination 967–8
    inverse problem and source estimation 956–7
    minimum norm-type methods 957
    multiple sparse priors 957
    multivariate/multivoxel pattern analysis (MVPA) 955, 960–1, 967
    oscillations and connectivity 957–60
    phonology and visual word recognition 961–4
    regions of interest (ROIs) 959
    representational similarity analysis (RSA) 961, 967
    semantic brain networks 964–7
        amodal areas: anterior temporal lobe (ATL) 965–6
        distributed areas: sensorimotor systems 966
        evaluation 966–7
southern Africa 678
Spanish
    ambiguity 99
    bilingualism 220, 222, 223, 224, 228, 464–5
    conceptual development 738
    dyslexia 787

grammatical encoding 443
prosodic phonology 677, 681, 683-4
segmentation of speech 9
sign languages and deaf populations 273
spelling/writing 416-17
spoken word recognition 42
visual word recognition in multilinguals 122
Spanish-Basque 132
Spanish-English 22, 126, 129, 218, 225, 229-30, 466
Spanish Sign Language (LSE) 264
spatial coding model 50
spatial language and spatial cognition 556
spatial location in sign grammar 267-9
speaker-specificity 633
specialized speech module 308
specific concept-to-word mapping 341
specific deficit models 241
specific language impairment (SLI) 821
  genetics 875
  lexico-semantics 78
  prosodic phonology 684-5
  speech production 292
  statistical learning 701-2
spectro-temporal receptive field (STRF) 1002-3
speech act 434
speech act theory 610
speech apraxia 878
speech-error observations in grammatical
  encoding 450
speech errors 349, 350, 354, 389, 391, 450
speech production
  brain circuits 294-5
  computational models 294
  functional magnetic resonance imaging
    (fMRI) 981-2
  impairments 77, 377, 382-4
  integration 295-7
  processes 294
  psycholinguistic and motor control approaches,
    overlap of 294-5
  representations 294
  semantic-lexical-auditory-motor model
    (SLAM) 298-301
  semantic-phonological model (SP) 297-8
  spoken word recognition 43
  see also perception and production in speech
speech signals 42-3, 851
speech sound disorder 796, 797
speech-specific processes 308
speech style 21
speech-to-song illusion (auditory) 43
speed-accuracy tradeoff measures 172
speeded syllable repetition task 352
spelling
  developmental dyslexia 786-7
  and reading, relationship between 408-9
  spoken word recognition 32, 43

spelling-to-dictation 405
splicing 874
spoken language difficulties 419
spoken language phonology in deaf populations 271-5
spoken object naming 407
spoken production task 415
spoken word production 335-56
  future directions 356
  implicit priming 347, 349-50, 351-2
  morphological and phonological processing 345-56
    integration and context 353-6
    morphological structure 346-8
    phonological structure 348-50
    representation 345-50
    scope of activation and planning 354-6
    selection 350-1
    sentential context 353-4
    sequences of words and retrieval of other
      words 351-3
  semantic and lexical processing 336-45
    integration during production of full
      sentences 341-5
    representation: words in networks 336-7
    selection and retrieval 337-40
    sequences of words 340-1
spoken word recognition 31-43
  challenges 41-3
  connectionist approaches 35-7
  innovative approaches 37-41
    Bayesian models 38
    discriminative learning 40-1
    network science 38-40
  letters 32
  multiple-word forms, activation of 33-5
  searching the lexicon 31-3
spoken and written picture naming 402
spokes: category-specific deficits 148-9
spreading activation 349-50
  pragmatics and inference 615-17
  speech production 294, 297
  visual word recognition 59
  see also under connectionist approach
SQ3R technique 205
stability studies 824
stage theories 418
stance 655-8, 662
  affective 656, 659
  epistemic 656
  evaluative 656
Standard Pragmatic Model (SPM) 251, 635-6
Stanford Binet test 815
state feedback control (SFC) theory 294, 295-6, 299
statistical learning 690-709, 715-16
  adjacent dependencies 699-701, 705-6
  age-related differences 702, 706-8
  artificial grammar learning 762-3, 765, 766, 769-70
  bilingualism and dialects 708

statistical learning (Cont.)
  extraction 706–7
  generalization 700, 707, 709
  imaging 702–4, 705
    event-related potential (ERP) 702, 704, 706
    functional magnetic resonance imaging (fMRI) 702–4
  individual differences 699–702
    atypical populations 701–2
    specific language impairment and language learning delay 701–2
    variation within typical populations 699–701
  and natural language 692, 694–5, 697, 702, 704–5, 708
  non-adjacent dependencies 699–702, 704–9
  retention 707
  syntax 696–9
    lexical category acquisition 697–9
    non-adjacent dependencies 696–7
  theories 706–7
  trajectory of learning 708–9
  transitional probabilities (TPs) 691–6, 704–6
  utterance boundaries (UBs) 693–5, 705
  word learning/lexicalization 695–6
  word segmentation 691–5
statistical methods in text comprehension 209
statistical regularities 21–2
stereotactic electroencephalogram (sEEG) 994, 995, 996, 999, 1003
stereotypical beliefs 557
stimulus-onset asynchrony (SOA) 406, 602
stimulus-preceding negativity (SPN) 12
stimulus variation 922
story grammar 198, 200
strength hypothesis 515
stress
  lexical 6, 8, 17–18, 22–3, 226
  shift 675–6
string sets 759
stroke 154, 802
  acute 251
  aphasia 146, 149–50
  chronic 250, 251
  and language disorders 828
  and speech perception and production 320
Stroop effect 80–1
Stroop task 405–6, 764
  emotional 81
structural assembly in attention and structural choice in sentence production 528
structural choice see attention and structural choice in sentence production
structural mere-exposure effect 763
structural priming see syntactic priming
structural storage 348
structure
  grammatical encoding 440–2
  segmentation of speech 20
  visual word recognition in multilinguals 123

structure mapping theory in sign languages and deaf populations 267
structure-oriented question 118–19
structure subprocesses in consensus model 435–7
stuttering 828, 882–3, 934
subject-object-verb (SOV) structure 391, 907–8
subject relative clauses 177, 178, 486
subject-verb agreement 222
  cues 225–6
subject-verb-object (SVO) structure 223, 391, 535–7, 907–8
sublexical classification 7
sublexical level in language membership 132
sublexical properties of lexicon 263–5
sublexical speech perception tasks 321
subminimal words 679–80
subordinate meanings 82, 88
substitution 441
superior frontal gyrus (SFG) 497, 501
superior temporal gyrus (STG) 495–6, 601, 703–4
surprisal 182–3, 979
suspense 208
sustained attention 343
swear words 657, 659–60, 663, 664
Sweden 118, 798
Swedish 717
s-weights 511–12, 514, 521
switch code 220, 391
switch cost 467, 475
  asymmetrical 468, 470–1
  symmetrical 470
switch, lexical 220
switch task 467–8, 469, 726
Syllable Onset Segmentation Heuristic (SOSH) 9–10
syllable-position constraint 447
syllables
  filler 681–2
  metalinguistic syllabification tasks 9
  polysyllabic shortening 14
  in prelexical classification 7–10
  speeded syllable repetition task 352
  stressed 14, 17, 20
  strong/weak 8
  structure 355
  unstressed 14, 677
  see also segmentation of speech
symbolic theories in lexico-semantics 77
synapses and neural circuits 878–9, 881
synaptic plasticity 868, 878
synonyms 906
syntactic, violations 486
syntactic alignment 574, 576–7, 579
syntactic ambiguity 171, 173–5, 483–4, 495, 496
syntactic choice in grammatical encoding 432, 444–6
syntactic complexity in sentence comprehension 173–4, 177–80, 495–6
syntactic components in attention and structural choice in sentence production 538–9

syntactic comprehension disorders see sentence level aphasia
syntactic frame constraints 388
syntactic functions in bilingualism 231–2
syntactic influences in spoken language phonology 271–5
syntactic parsing 483–5, 553
syntactic persistence 440–2, 444, 447–8, 449–50
syntactic phrasing in segmentation of speech 20
syntactic planning in connectionist principles of speech production 391
syntactic priming 292
    alignment during interaction 578
    attention and structural choice in sentence production 539
    connectionist principles 385–8
    perspective-taking 557–8
    sentence comprehension 181
    sign languages and deaf populations 268
    syntactic production and comprehension 484
syntactic processing
    bilingualism 230
    and competition model 222–5
    text comprehension 208
syntactic production and comprehension 482–502
    adaptation paradigm 497
    ambiguities 483–4, 495, 496
    brain area involvement in sentence comprehension 486–96
        sentences compared with control conditions below sentence level 494
        sentences with higher demands on syntactic or semantic processing 495–6
        types of contrasts used in hemodynamic studies 487–93
    brain area involvement in sentence production 488, 497–500
        sentence comprehension and production activation patterns comparisons 499–500
        sentence production compared with word production 497–8
        syntactically more vs. less demanding sentences 498–9
    complexity 495–6
    demands 496
    violations 486, 495, 496, 499, 502
    within- and between-modality repetition effects 501
syntactic properties in spoken word production 336
syntactic representations in bilingualism 217
syntactic structure
    alignment during interaction 580
    attention and structural choice in sentence production 529
    perspective-taking 558
    segmentation of speech 12
    sentence comprehension 171–3, 176
    sentence level aphasia 239–40, 243, 247, 249
syntactic structures in sentence comprehension 171–3
syntactic 'traffic cop' 344, 388

syntactic-versus-phonological distinction 438
syntactic violations 486, 495, 496, 499, 502
syntagmatic interference 344
syntax 696–9
    alignment during interaction 574, 576–7, 579
    artificial grammar learning (AGL) and natural language comparison 768, 769–71
    attention and structural choice in sentence production 531
    bilingualism 227
    connectionist principles of speech production 392
    grammatical encoding 444–6, 450–1
    lexical category acquisition 697–9
    lexically based theories 438
    non-adjacent dependencies 696–7
    pragmatics and inference 611
    spoken word production 344
    spoken word recognition 32
    statistical learning 696–9
        lexical category acquisition 697–9
        non-adjacent dependencies 696–7
    word recognition and implicit segmentation 11–13
systematicity and models of language evolution 905–7

T
taboo words 136
tactile paradigms 757
take home message 979
Tamil 391
target words 11
task context 71, 80, 88, 89
task dependency in perception and production in speech 317–19
task (role of goal-driven, short-term context) 82–4
task switching
    domain-general 467, 471
    non-linguistic 469
TD peers 824, 828, 829
telegraphese 675
temporal sampling theory 793
tense marking 226
textbase 201
text cohesion 201
text comprehension 197–210
    concepts and theoretical background 197–202
        coherence 199
        cohesion 199
        inferences 199–200
        models 201–2
        situation model 200
        text structure 198–9
    methodological developments 209–10
    reading times 210
    research topics and recent developments 202–10
        applied educational research 204–5
        cognitive functions 203–4
        methodological developments 209–10
        neuroscience 205–9

text representation 201
texts 198
　argumentative 198
　expository 198
　hypertext systems (World Wide Web) 204
　literary 198
　multiple 204
　narrative 198, 200
　procedural 198
thematic structure in attention and structural choice in sentence production 529
Theory-of-Mind 207, 208, 210
　conceptual development 739–40
　first word learning 720
　perspective-taking 550, 553, 563
　　pragmatics 638n
　　and inference 618
theta band 23, 965, 966, 968, 995, 997, 998
thinking-for-speaking approach 449, 739–40
thoracic vertebral canal 850
time-domain averaging 934–5
timed verbal fluency tasks 462
time frequency analysis (TFA) 638
time frequency signatures, intracranial 997
timestep 294
tip-of-the-tongue states 291, 350, 462, 999
TLE patients 146
tone 42, 676, 708, 797
tongue elevation 308
tongue kinematics 319
tongue twister style tasks 292, 352
topicalization 535n, 536–7, 540–1
topic models 73–4
trace deletion hypothesis 241–2, 249
TRACE model 10, 35–7, 40, 261
trajectory of learning 708–9
transcortical sensory aphasia 151, 154
transcranial magnetic stimulation (TMS) 148, 149, 209
　speech perception and production 311, 312, 314, 317–18, 319, 320, 323
transcription 868
transcription factors (TFs)(master regulators) 871, 873, 876
transfer effects 761
transient-evoked potentials 938–9
transitional probabilities (TPs) 22, 691–6, 704–6
transmission chains 852, 901–6, 908–9
transmission control protocol/internet protocol (TCP-IP) 647–8, 664
transmission process 852
transposed letter effects 50
tree pruning hypothesis 246–7, 249
trial-by-trial language switching task 467–72
triphones 41
triple foundation for reading 786–7
trisyllabic target 11
trochaic words 20–1

Turkish 223
　conceptual development 738, 739
　gesture 594, 597–8
　sign languages and deaf populations 273
　spelling/writing 416–17
turn-taking 317–19
two-alternative forced-choice task 694, 699
two-step assumption 510
typicality in lexico-semantics 79
typological universals 907–8

U

underinformative statements 627–8
underspecification hypothesis 746
unification 208
Unified Model of Language Learning (UMLL) 225–6
uniform density account 342
Uniform Information Density 446–7
uniqueness points 33–4
unitary and language-independent sentence processing routines 223
unitary semantic concept nodes 376
United Kingdom 798, 818
　Growing Up in Scotland (GUS)(UK) study 818–21
　Millennium Cohort Study (MCS) 818–21
United States 615, 747, 798
universal grammar (UG) 719
unrelated error 508
unrestricted search hypothesis 553
updating the past 184
utterance boundaries (UBs) 693–5, 705
utterance formulator 528

V

valence in emotion and sociality 662–4
variation
　segmentation of speech 6–7
　in spoken word recognition 43
Verbal Inhibitory Control model 135
verbal working memory (vWM) 699–701, 705–6
verb-framed languages (V-languages) 596
verb-match effect 539
verb phrase (VP) in sentence level aphasia 239
verbs
　agreement 224
　　violations 268
　bilingualism 226
　extensional 907
　intensional 907
　sentence level aphasia 247–8
　structure 292
vervet monkeys 909
Vietnamese 42, 447
visual angle discrimination task 996
visual attentional deficits 419
visual implicit learning task 764
visual lexical decision task 99, 101

visual magnocellular deficits 796
visual materials in text comprehension 198
visual memory deficits 420–1
visual processing deficits in developmental dyslexia 794–5
visual processing in dyslexia 788
visual search paradigm 628
visual stimulus presentation 757
Visual Word Form Area (VWFA) 409–10, 800
visual word recognition 32, 43, 48–61
  further directions 59–61
  no effect 55
  orthographic representations 48–52
    frequency, cumulative frequency and age of acquisition 50–2
    input coding: letters and letter positions 49–50
    morphology 52
  and phonology 961–4
  processing dynamics and mechanisms for selection 52–7
    interactive-activation model 53–4
    masked form priming effects 56–7
    neighborhood (N) effects 54–6
  reading system 57–9
    phonological influences 58–9
    semantic influences 59
  see also visual word recognition in multilinguals
visual word recognition in multilinguals 118–37
  cognates 122, 126–8, 129–30
  context effects 128–31
    cognates 129–30
    false friends 129–30
  false friends 120, 121–2, 124–6, 127, 129–30, 133–4, 136
  language membership 130–3
    lexical level 131–2
    sentence level 132–3
    sublexical level 132
  limitations and future research 136–7
  models 133–5
  neighbors 121, 123–4
  process of recognition 123–8
    cognates 126–8
    false friends 124–6
    neighbors 123–4
  prominent word types 120–2
    cognates 122
    false friends 121–2
    neighbors 121
  storage of words 122–3
visual world paradigm
  perspective-taking 551
  pragmatics 635
  sentence level aphasia 244
  text comprehension 209
visual world studies 172
vocabulary size 726

vocabulary spurt 715, 724, 727
vocal learning 866, 881
vocal motor schemes (VMS) 718–19
vocal production 881
voice-onset time (VOT) to initial consonants 351
VOS language 537–8
vowels 15
  front and back 13
  full/reduced 8
  harmony 6, 17, 18
  preboundary lengthening of 14
  space 20
Voxel-based Lesion Symptom Mapping (VLSM) 323, 401, 511

W

walruses 848
Warlpiri 223
WEAVER++ model 336, 346, 349, 350, 355–6, 392, 462
weight-decay models 510–11
Welsh 403, 583, 717, 718
Welsh-English 715
Wernicke's aphasia (WA) 144, 150, 153, 156, 244, 320
Wernicke's area 830, 960
whales 845, 846
white-rumped munias (bird) 847
whole exome sequencing (WES) 876
whole genome sequencing (WGS) 876
Whorf-Sapir hypothesis 449
Williams Syndrome 738
winner-take-all selection algorithm 389
word-by-word encoding strategy 343
word class ambiguities 486
word edges 10
word errors 382
word form encoding 348
word forms 714, 715–19
word frequency 338
  effect 36, 38
word informativity 342
word initial pitch cues 18
word layer 36–7
word learning
  constraints 720
  statistical learning 695–6
  see also first word learning
word meaning
  priming 106
  see also lexico-semantics
word monitoring latencies 7
word naming latencies 462
word onset-association N100 22
word order rules 907
word picture matching task, auditory 320
word prevalence 51, 338
word primes 57

word production 718, 723
  detection 516–18, 520
  syntactic production and comprehension 497–8
  see also under aphasia; spoken word production
word recognition see segmentation of speech; spoken word recognition; visual word recognition
word segmentation 691–5
word spotting 16
word storage in visual word recognition in multilinguals 122–3
word substitution errors 292
word superiority effect 53
word use 723
word valence 662–4
working memory 945
  artificial grammar learning 764, 774
  perspective-taking 557
  sentence comprehension 179, 185
  sentence level aphasia 243
  sign languages and deaf populations 274
  speech perception and production 312, 324
  spoken word production 343
  statistical learning 700, 703, 705, 706
  text comprehension 203, 206
  verbal 699–701, 706
  see also orthographic working memory (O-WM)
written language production 398–421
  cognitive processes of spelling and neural substrates 399–402
  developmental deficits 419–21
  normal trajectory 417–18
  representation levels and interactions 409–17
    cascadedness 414–16
    cross-script similarities and differences 416–17
    orthographic representations 409–14
  and speaking, relationship between 402–7
    frequency and age of onset 406–7
    orthographic autonomy 403–4
    phonology 404–6
  spelling/writing 398, 408–9
written object naming 407
written picture naming: copying of written words 405
Wundt's principle 442

Z

zebra finches 846, 847, 848, 881, 909